BOOKS FOR COLLEGE LIBRARIES

A CORE COLLECTION OF 40,000 TITLES

Second edition

A project of the Association of College and Research Libraries

Volume III
History

American Library Association
Chicago 1975

Library of Congress Cataloging in Publication Data
Main entry under title:

Books for college libraries; a core collection of 40,000 titles.

CONTENTS: v. 1. Humanities.—v. 2. Language and literature.—v. 3. History. [etc.]
1. Bibliography—Best books. 2. Libraries, University and college. I. Association of College and Research Libraries.

Z1035.B72 1974   011   74-13743

ISBN 0-8389-0178-6

Copyright © 1975 by the American Library Association
All rights reserved. No part of this publication may be reproduced in any form without permission in writing from the publisher, except by a reviewer who may quote brief passages in a review.
Printed in the United States of America

BOOKS FOR COLLEGE LIBRARIES

Vol. I–VI Contents

Vol. I	**HUMANITIES**	GN	Anthropology. Prehistoric Archaeology
A	General Works	GR–GT	Folklore. Customs. Costume
B–BD, BH–BJ	Philosophy	GV	Recreation. Sports. Dance
BL–BX	Religion. Mythology. Rationalism	H–HA	Social Sciences: General. Statistics
M–MT	Music	HB–HJ	Economics. Population
N–NX	Fine Arts	HM–HV	Sociology. Social History. Social Pathology
Vol. II	**LANGUAGE AND LITERATURE**	HX	Socialism. Communism. Anarchism. Utopias
P	Language and Literature: General	J	Political Science
PA	Classical Languages and Literatures	K	Law
PB–PH	Modern European Languages	L	Education
PJ–PL	Oriental Languages and Literatures		
PN	Literature: General and Comparative	**Vol. V**	**PSYCHOLOGY. SCIENCE. TECHNOLOGY. BIBLIOGRAPHY**
PN1560–3299	Performing Arts		
PN4700–5650	Journalism. The Press		
PQ	Romance Literatures: French, Italian, Spanish, Portuguese	BF	Psychology
		Q–QA	Science. Mathematics. Computer Science
PR–PS	English and American Literatures	QB–QE	Physical Sciences: Astronomy, Physics, Meteorology, Chemistry, Geology
PT	Germanic and Scandinavian Literatures		
		QH–QR	Natural Sciences: Biology, Botany, Zoology, Anatomy, Physiology, Bacteriology
Vol. III	**HISTORY**		
C	Auxiliary Sciences of History		
CB	History of Civilization and Culture	R	Medicine. Psychiatry. Nursing
CC–CN	Archaeology. Minor Historical Sciences	S	Agriculture. Conservation. Veterinary Medicine
CR–CT	Heraldry. Genealogy. General Biography	T	Technology. Engineering
		TR	Photography
D	History: General. Historiography	TS–TX	Manufactures. Crafts. Home Economics
DA–DR	Europe		
DS	Asia		
DT	Africa	U–V	Military Science. Naval Science
DU	Australia. New Zealand. Oceania	Z	Book Industries. Bibliography. Library Science.
E–F	The Americas		
Vol. IV	**SOCIAL SCIENCES**	**Vol. VI**	**INDEXES**
G–GF	Geography. Oceanography. Human Ecology		

Vol. III   Contents

	Introduction	vii
	Acknowledgments	xi

	C	**AUXILIARY SCIENCES OF HISTORY**	**1**
CB		History of Civilization and Culture	1
CC–CN		Archaeology. Minor Historical Sciences	8
CR–CT		Heraldry. Genealogy. Biography: General	10

	D	**HISTORY: GENERAL. HISTORIOGRAPHY**	**13**
D51–95		Ancient History	18
D111–203		Medieval History	19
D204–847		Modern History	22
D220–297		16th–18th Centuries	22
D351–400		19th Century	24
D410–847		20th Century	26
D501–838		World War I. World War II	27

D901–DR		**EUROPE**	**42**
	DA	Great Britain	44
DA900–995		Ireland. Northern Ireland	67
	DB	Austria. Hungary. Czechoslovakia	69
	DC	France	73
	DD	Germany	85
	DE–DG	Greece. Italy	96
	DH–DJ	Netherlands. Belgium	112
DK1–276		Russia	114
DK400–443		Poland	124
DK450–465		Finland. Special Regions of Russia	125
	DL	Scandinavia	127
	DP	Spain. Portugal	130
	DQ	Switzerland	134
	DR	Eastern Europe. Balkan Peninsula	135

	DS	**ASIA**	**140**
DS35–326		Near East	141
DS335–498		South Asia	152
DS501–689		East Asia: General. Southeast Asia	160
DS701–798		China	166
DS801–897		Japan	174
DS901–925		Korea	179

	DT	**AFRICA**	**182**
DT43–346		Egypt. North Africa	185
DT351–364		Central and Sub-Saharan Africa	188
DT365–469		East Africa	189
DT471–720		West Africa	192
DT730–995		Southern Africa	196

	DU	**AUSTRALIA. NEW ZEALAND. OCEANIA**	**201**

E1–143	**AMERICA: GENERAL**	**208**
E51–99	Pre-Columbian America. Indians of North America	208
E101–135	Discovery of America. Early Exploration	215

E151–F970	**UNITED STATES**	**217**
E162–169	Description. Travel. Civilization	217
E171–856	History. Historiography	224
E183.7–.8	Diplomatic History	232
E184–185	Elements in the Population: Ethnic Groups. Negroes	238
E186–856	American History, by Period	246
E186–298	Colonial and Revolutionary Periods	246
E301–738	19th Century. Civil War	250
E740–856	20th Century	274
F1–970	U.S. Local History	289

F1001–1140	**CANADA**	**319**

F1201–3799	**LATIN AMERICA**	**326**
F1201–1392	Mexico	326
F1401–1419	Latin America: General	330
F1421–2175	Central America. West Indies. Caribbean Sea	335
F2201–3799	South America	339

Introduction

This second edition of BOOKS FOR COLLEGE LIBRARIES (BCL II) is both a revision of the first edition (BCL I) and the outcome of a separate bibliographic project. As revision, it has been compiled for the same audience of undergraduate libraries and is based on BCL I through the use of that work as the major checklist of titles considered for this edition. New aspects include the sharp reduction in number of titles to a minimal "core collection"; the expansion of individual entries to provide more complete cataloging and classification information; and the use of automated techniques for the production of the list itself. This third aspect was accomplished by using machine-readable catalog records comprised of regular MARC records issued by the Library of Congress, MARC records released by the Library of Congress especially for use in producing this publication, and records converted expressly for this collection from older Library of Congress catalog records. The conversion was done by contract and according to MARC standards. This printed list thus represents only one dimension of the potential availability of the data base which has been constructed.

HISTORY

The 1963 closing date for titles for the University of California New Campuses Program, published in 1967 as the first *Books for College Libraries,* was timed to coincide with the March 1964 birth of *Choice*. This current monthly reviewing service, aimed specifically at the undergraduate library, was foreseen as the automatic and sufficient supplementary selection tool. Since that time, book publishing and book reviewing journals (including *Choice*) have enjoyed a seemingly relentless expansion. Higher education budgets have not kept pace, although many new campuses have opened. The book collections of many college libraries have continued to range below the minimum recommended by the 1959 American Library Association *Standards for College Libraries*.[1] Book selection has remained a problem, particularly for new libraries: there is not much staff or money, there are so many books. Book-trade figures for new titles and new editions issued in the United States between 1931 (Charles B. Shaw's list of 14,000 titles) and 1963 (BCL I, with 53,400 titles) total over 204,000. Between 1964 and 1972 (the closing date for new titles in this edition), that same figure exceeds 290,000.[2] *Choice* reviewed 3,388 titles its first year; 6,561, during 1972/73.

In 1969/70, a pair of proposals changed hands. The first, a staff study from the Council on Library Resources, suggested to the American Library Association that one aid for the combined staffing and budget problems of book selection, acquisition, and processing might be the formation of a package library, complete with catalog. The second, from ALA to the Council, demurred at entering the book distribution business, but asked for funds to undertake the selection and cataloging aspects of the project. For the production of the catalog, both plans assumed the use—and extension to older books—of the new machine-readable cataloging program, MARC, which had recently been developed at the Library of Congress. The Council accepted and approved a final proposal dated July 1970. An advisory committee and a computer contractor were named and editorial staff were hired to create a highly selective retrospective tool as a counterpart to the current services of *Choice*.

SIZE AND SCOPE

The proposal called for a collection of approximately 40,000 titles, four-fifths the minimum recommended by 1959 ALA standards for even the smallest four-year academic library. Books recommended were to constitute "the bare minimum of titles needed to support an average college instructional program of good quality." Further qualifications assumed independence: "without the support of large academic libraries or special collections" and comprehensiveness: "containing some information on all fields of knowledge of interest to the academic community." Libraries were to choose the fifth portion to strengthen those subjects emphasized in the curricula of their particular institutions, the whole serving "as a base upon which a richer and more varied collection can later be built."[3] The bias of the four-fifths presented here is inevitably toward the liberal arts. Even undergraduates in the sciences and technology rely heavily on periodicals and special reports for the current information in these rapidly changing fields. No collection limited, as this bibliography is, to books only can present as satisfactory subject coverage in science and technology as in the arts and the social sciences. Perhaps only those works already sufficiently out-dated to be ranked as history may safely be included in a "basic" collection. The science and technology sections have been kept deliberately brief so, at best, to encourage local book selection or, at worst, merely to disappoint rather than to mislead.

The number of titles actually listed in this edition is 38,651. Volume-to-title ratio is high because of the presence of single entries for many basic reference sets and for monographic series. The apportionment of titles among the various subject fields is: volume I, General Works and Humanities (Philosophy, Religion, Art, Music)—5,823; volume II, Language and Literature—

11,627; volume III, History—7,600; volume IV, Social Sciences—8,201; volume V, Psychology, Science, Technology, and Bibliography—5,400.

The level emphasized is not only the undergraduate library, but primarily the undergraduate user of that library, although the necessary provision for independent study by the exceptional student requires the listing of some advanced and specialized works in each field. Some of the reference works and bibliographies listed will be used chiefly by library staff in their service to undergraduates. Language is almost wholly English except in the more commonly taught European literatures. Here works are listed both in the foreign language and in English.

This collection is limited to books, including some monographic series, annual reviews, etc. Contributors were asked not to recommend classroom texts except those acknowledged to set the standards for their fields or those with exceptionally fine bibliographies. They were also requested to exclude books of "readings" unless these comprise hard-to-find items whose sources are unlikely to be available in a college library. There was no special attempt to recommend a model selection of government publications, as such, although many are included. Excellent annotated sources are the new annual *Government Reference Books,* edited by Sally Wynkoop (Libraries Unlimited, 1970-   ), and the second edition of an old standard by Laurence F. Schmeckebier and Roy B. Eastin, *Government Publications and Their Use* (Brookings, 1969). Evan Farber's *Classified List of Periodicals for the College Library* (5th ed., Faxon, 1972) and William Katz's *Magazines for Libraries* (2d ed., Bowker, 1972) offer comparable selections of journals. Current availability was not an absolute determinant. The latest new titles listed are 1972 publications. Some 1973 revisions and reprints of older works have been included.

Titles listed are highly recommended. They are not dictated as the only possible choice of every scholar for every library. They are not guaranteed against obsolescence.

COMPILATION AND PRODUCTION

Authority. Teaching scholars, specialist librarians, and staff members of several professional associations were invited to check or compile lists of books for their specialized subject fields. Many of these subject experts are *Choice* consultants; some worked on sections of BCL I. They represent a wide range of institutions. All are named—and thanked—individually in the volume which contains their contribution. Most of the final lists represent a consensus of contributor opinion, occasionally augmented by the editor's recourse to bookshelves or bibliographies. Editorial intervention was largely limited to holding the lists to size.

Selection and Review. There were two distinct stages of compilation. During 1971, the project was under the direction of editor Richard Tetreau and occupied an office near *Choice* in Middletown, Connecticut. The editor recruited contributors and compiled working lists which included pages from BCL I, titles favorably reviewed in *Choice* between 1964 and 1970, and sections from recent basic bibliographies. Contributors were asked to check those titles judged essential for undergraduates and to eliminate those obviously expendable, with no regard for numerical quotas. In a few subject areas the returned lists showed a clear pattern of consensus and also seemed to offer comprehensive coverage. Most areas, however, required further review.

The year 1972/73 saw changes in location and editor. Philip J. McNiff, director of the Boston Public Library and chairman of the BCL II advisory committee, offered the project an office in the Boston Public Library. This gift of space bought time, for arrangements for the MARC-tagging of older titles now forced an extension of the original deadline within the same budget limits. The new editor, Virginia Clark, recruited additional contributors, some highly specialized to fill particular gaps and some more generalized to survey for overall balance the suggestions of previous specialists.

Titles and Editions. The BCL II editorial staff checked those titles finally chosen to see whether any editions were in print. Textual considerations seeming equal, the in-print, hardcover, U.S. edition at the lowest price was generally preferred. The fact that a particular edition had already been cataloged in the MARC data base was often a decisive factor. In the case of competing reprints of the same title, considerations included the addition of significant scholarly introductions, updated bibliographies, indexes, etc.; publisher reputation for availability and quality; and price. If the Library of Congress had not cataloged an edition which the editor judged to be simply a reissue or a reprint, an edition with LC cataloging was preferred. This policy was dictated by the nature of the establishment and staffing of the editorial office: it had been set up to serve only as a clearinghouse, to turn lists of recommended titles into catalog entries without handling the books themselves. This limitation obviously meant maximum use of existing Library of Congress cataloging. In addition, all planning of the project had stressed reliance on the authority of the Library of Congress.

Arrangement and Entry Content. Within the call-number blocks included in each volume, entries follow strict LC classified order. Two sections of the LC classification have been moved out of order to provide relatively homogenous subject groupings and volumes of approximately equal size. "BF" (Psychology) precedes "Q" at the beginning of volume V, Psychology, Science, Technology, and Bibliography. The "C–L" group (History–Social Sciences) has been shifted to volumes III and IV, thus allowing "B," "M," "N," and "P" to form a Humanities–Literature sequence as volumes I and II.

Subheadings outline the classification and indicate the method of arrangement of special sequences. Each work appears only once in this classified list, but is accessible

Introduction

through several approaches in the indexes. Books are listed almost always under the call number and always under the main entry assigned by the Library of Congress. The titles or editions which had to be cataloged especially for this publication can be identified by the absence of an LC card number in the entry. All call numbers assigned by BCL II staff or completed from LC bracketed class numbers have an identifying "x" at the first point of potential shelflist conflict. If the Library of Congress assigned two call numbers, one as a separate, the other within a series, the separate call number was always preferred as the main one. The printed entries do not reveal the cases in which this involved a switch of LC priority unless the number preferred was incomplete and hence received an "x." All fiction classed by LC in "PZ 3" or "PZ 4" has been classed in the appropriate national literature sequence, with the "PZ" number shown as an alternate. All LC-assigned numbers except obvious typographical errors and numbers eliminated by revisions in LC classification have been retained as alternates. The BCL II staff did not verify or proofread Dewey Decimal class numbers.

In preparation for the MARC-tagging of older entries and in consultation with staff at the MARC office, the editor set standards for minor editing of cards. This was limited to reexpression (in terms of the 1967 *Anglo-American Cataloging Rules*) of data already on cards and was in no sense complete recataloging. Editing included removal of dots of elision at the heads of titles, simplification of imprint and paging statements, raising of half-centimeter sizes, and changes in capitalization, particularly of corporate names and of German substantives.

All MARC data elements present on a card were tagged. This printed version omits certain categories of notes, among them bibliography and contents notes. All elements are in the data base, however, and can be retrieved.

Computerized Storage and Retrieval. As titles were selected, they were checked against the MARC data base held by the computer contractor. For those not already on file, BCL II staff ordered, edited, and sent to the contractor a Library of Congress card. The contractor's staff MARC-tagged the entries, which were added to the data base after proofreading by both BCL II staff and the contractor. When title selection was complete, the file was separated for computer sorting, indexing, and conversion into typeset printers' negatives, ready for the offset press.

Indexing. The computer generated the author and title indexes. The author index includes all main entries (except title) and all joint authors, editors, translators, and institutions associated with the authorship of the work—in short, all tracings (except title and series) numbered with roman numerals on LC printed cards. The title index lists main-entry titles, all title-page titles whether traced or not, and variant titles if traced. The present subject index is a limited selection of LC subject headings. There is a note of explanation at the head of that index.

LACUNAE, ERRORS, AND REVISIONS

The original proposal contemplated presentation of the list in four segments, by recommended priority of purchase. The first segment, containing 10 percent of the titles, was to include "reference and very basic works," with successive annual segments of 25, 30, and 35 percent to complete the collection. This priority ranking has not been carried out, largely because of the existence of the frequently revised *Choice* "Opening Day Collection" and of James W. Pirie's *Books for Junior College Libraries* (ALA, 1969), which fill the need for a very short list or for a list for lower-division undergraduates. The seemingly duplicate listings, particularly in the literature sections, of both "complete" and "selected" works for the same author are also designed to serve small collections or collections in progress. Indeed, some of the "complete" works are themselves in progress and their authors must be represented by selections and individual titles until the definitive edition is complete or until the smaller library's budget can afford the complete set.

Another omission is the full subject analysis which could be provided by a computer print-out of all subject headings, with references to the item numbers of all entries with each heading. Such an index would require a separate volume and would be only as useful as the subject heading assignment in the original cataloging. Time and budget limits reinforced an editorial decision that the product might not be worth the effort, paper, or extra cost to users without a thorough check of older headings and cross-references to incorporate the many additions and changes made by the Library of Congress.

Any compilation such as this will have errors despite proofreading. Reports of errors found and any other suggestions for improvements should be sent to: Editor, Books for College Libraries, c/o *Choice,* 100 Riverview Center, Middletown, Connecticut, 06457.

This edition has been produced as inexpensively as possible in a format chosen to allow a process of continuous revision, one volume at a time. The five-volume set, with separate index volume, was also designed for the easier handling of smaller volumes and for the possibility of consultation by several users at once.

Any basic working undergraduate collection needs constant weeding and addition. Through the cooperation of *Choice* and the corps of BCL II contributors and through the use of computer technology, the organization, the subject and bibliographic skills, and the machinery exist to maintain a continuing and useful service to the undergraduate library.

HOW TO READ THE ENTRIES

Entries are simply Library of Congress cards printed in run-on style. Consecutive entry numbers have been added. (The few numbers with an added letter and the few gaps in the numbering reveal last-minute corrections.) All information on older printed cards used as the basis for encoding and all elements in entries printed from MARC tapes are included except contents notes, bibliography notes, prices, and foreign bibliography numbers. These are omitted from the printed version but are in the data base. The compact form used for printing may raise some queries from non-librarian users, especially about open entries or entries with dashed-on supplements. These entries lack the conventional blank spaces which in themselves convey information to users of printed cards in more usual format. The possible elements of an entry are analyzed in an example shown in figure 1.

NOTES

1. In 1970/71, at the beginning of the project, 70 percent of all colleges with enrollments under 500 had fewer than 50,000 volumes.
2. *Bowker Annual of Library and Book Trade Information* (Bowker, various years).
3. All quotations in this paragraph are from an unpublished document: "A project statement for the selection, preparation, and publication of a book catalog for core collections for college libraries, presented by the American Library Association to the Council on Library Resources, Inc., June 1970."

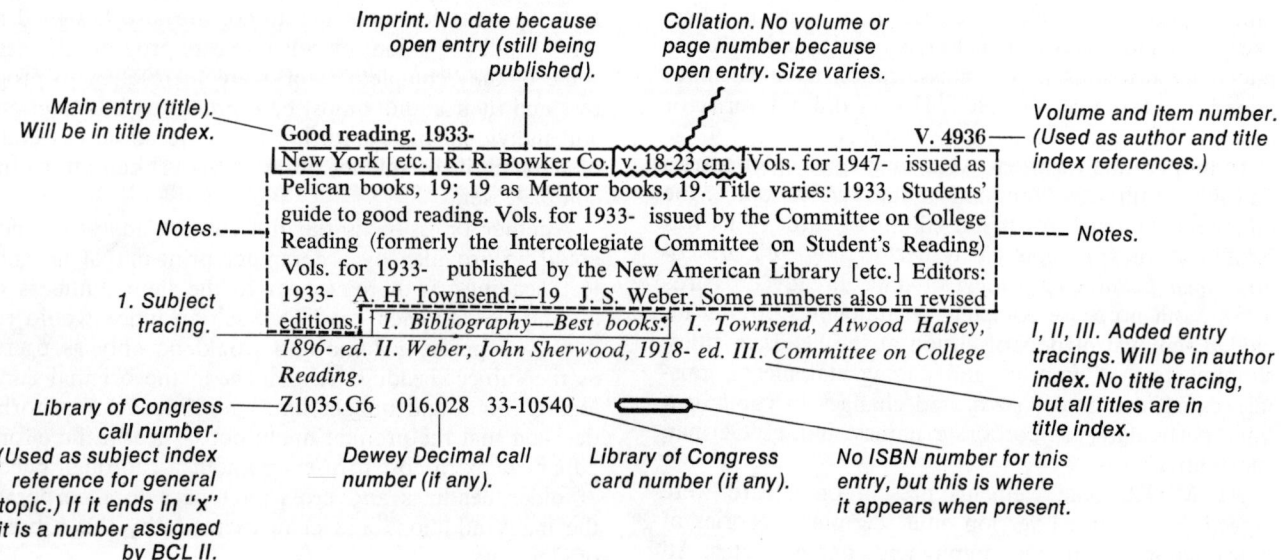

Fig. 1. Analysis of a sample entry

Acknowledgments

Both the editorial staff and the users of this bibliography owe special thanks not only to the contributors of subject lists, who are named in each volume, but also to several organizations to whom this publication owes its actual existence.

The Council on Library Resources supported the project with both funds and advice. Foster E. Mohrhardt served as liaison to the advisory committee, and Melville J. Ruggles helped in the initial planning.

The Library of Congress was generous with staff time and information and made special arrangements for the purchase and use of materials. Thanks are particularly due William J. Welsh, Director, Processing Department; Henriette D. Avram, Chief, MARC Development Office; Kay Guiles, MARC Development Office; and Ernest C. Hedges, Jr., Card Division.

At *Choice,* two successive editors, Peter M. Doiron and Richard K. Gardner, played major roles in suggesting and recruiting contributors to BOOKS FOR COLLEGE LIBRARIES, second edition, from among *Choice* reviewers. The editors also served on the BCL II advisory committee. Associate editor Louise F. Lockwood and the assistant editors responsible for subject sections of the magazine also helped with recruitment and in some cases worked on the subject lists. BCL II staff are deeply grateful to Kenneth McLintock, Marie V. Patrucco, Kenneth I. Werner, and the late Nancy L. Garbutt.

The Association of College and Research Libraries, a division of the American Library Association, coordinated the project and provided staff help. Beverly P. Lynch, Executive Secretary of ACRL, served as Project Manager. Chairman of the BCL II advisory committee was Philip J. McNiff, Director of the Boston Public Library. Permanent voting members of that committee were: Stephen Ford, Grand Valley State College; Sarah D. Jones, Goucher College; and Warren B. Kuhn, Iowa State University and Chairman of the ALA Editorial Committee. Others serving ex officio for shorter terms were: as Chairman of the *Choice* Editorial Board, George S. Bobinski, State University of New York at Buffalo, and Joseph H. Treyz, University of Wisconsin–Madison; as President of ACRL, Anne C. Edmonds, Mount Holyoke College, Joseph H. Reason, Howard University, emeritus, and Russell Shank, Smithsonian Institution; as Chairman of the ALA Editorial Committee, Donald E. Wright, Evanston Public Library; as Executive Secretary of ACRL, J. Donald Thomas, University of Maryland; and as Project Manager, Robert Gillespie, ALA Publishing Services.

As Director of the Boston Public Library, Philip J. McNiff offered the project office space during its last two years. The staff of the Boston Public Library continued to welcome a guest who stayed twice as long as planned and who asked for—and received—help from almost every department.

The Ohio College Library Center allowed bibliographic searching on the computer terminals of two of its members. BCL II staff are grateful to William Dameron, Librarian of Kenyon College, and John D. Slinn, Librarian of Newton College, for this access to OCLC files through their installations.

Every problem in the editorial and bibliographic processes which brought the list to completion called forth only greater skill, enthusiasm, and determination from the BCL II staff: Mary J. Cronin, Assistant to the Editor, Susan E. McGannon, and Linda Demmers.

The production of the list, including tagging of non-MARC entries, was handled by Inforonics, Inc.

CONTRIBUTORS

The original title selection in some subjects was reviewed during the second stage of the project. Some contributors who worked only during the first stage are so indicated in case they may not wish to be identified with the final selection. Subjects are listed in approximately the order in which they appear in the volume.

GENERAL HISTORY. HISTORY OF CIVILIZATION. GENERAL EUROPEAN HISTORY: *Ancient and Archaeology:* Stephen L. Dyson, Wesleyan University. (Stage I: Emanuel Levine, Rider College; William A. Longacre, University of Arizona.) *Medieval:* Robert L. Baker, Kenyon College; Norton Downs, Trinity College (Conn.) *Early Modern:* John C. Rule, Ohio State University. *Modern:* Keith Eubank, Queens College, CUNY; Marion S. Miller, University of Illinois at Chicago Circle.

PARTICULAR EUROPEAN COUNTRIES: *Great Britain:* Reed Browning, Kenyon College. (Stage I: Robert Irrmann, Beloit College.) *Scotland:* J. Wilson Ferguson, Russell Sage College. *Ireland:* J. V. Kelleher, Harvard University. *British Commonwealth:* Robin W. Winks, Yale University. *France:* Nathanael Greene, Wesleyan University; John C. Rule, Ohio State University. (Stage I: John J. Baughman, DePauw University; Lynn Osen, Beloit College.) *Germany:* Richard S. Levy, University of Illinois at Chicago Circle. (Stage I: Frederick B. M. Hollyday, Duke University.) *Austria, Hungary, Czechoslovakia, Poland, Switzerland:* Paul P. Bernard, University of Illinois. *Greece:* Stephen L. Dyson, Wesleyan University; A. L. Macrakis, Regis College. *Italy:* Stephen L. Dyson, Wesleyan University; Marion S. Miller, University of Illinois at Chicago Circle. (Stage I: John J. Baughman, DePauw University.) *Netherlands and Belgium:* John C. Rule, Ohio State University. *Russia:* Leonard Bushkoff, Boston State College. (Stage I: G. Douglas Nicoll, Beloit College; Justus Rosenberg, Bard College.) *Scandinavia and Finland:* Barry D. Jacobs, Montclair State College; Filippa Rolf, Boston University. *Spain and Portugal:* Edward Malefakis, University of Michigan. *Turkey and Balkans:* Leonard Bushkoff, Boston State College. (Stage I: Sherman D. Spector, Russell Sage College.)

ASIA: *Middle East and Arab North Africa:* Miroslav Krek, Brandeis University; Jacob Neusner, Brown University; Howard Sachar, George Washington University. *South Asia:* Louis A. Jacob, Library of Congress. *Southeast Asia:* Paul Bixler, Antioch College, emeritus. (Stage I: Giok Po Oey, Cornell University.) *China:* E. M. Frederick, Kenyon College. *Japan:* Jackson H. Bailey, Earlham College; Mikiso Hane, Knox College.

AFRICA: Marion E. Doro, Connecticut College; Peter Duignan, Hoover Institution, Stanford University.

For Asia and Africa, additional selections were drawn from the set of fine interdisciplinary area bibliographies issued by the Foreign Area Materials Study Center of the State University of New York: *Africa South of the Sahara,* edited by Peter Duignan; *East Asia,* edited by Donald Gillin; *Middle East and North Africa,* edited by Harry N. Howards; *South Asia,* edited by Louis A. Jacob; *Southeast Asia,* edited by Donald Clay Johnson.

OCEANIA: *Australia and New Zealand:* Robin W. Winks, Yale University. *Hawaii and Pacific Oceania:* Robert H. Horwitz, Kenyon College; David Kittelson, University of Hawaii; Norman Mellor, University of Hawaii.

THE AMERICAS: *Pre-Columbian America:* Gordon R. Willey, Peabody Museum, Harvard University. *United States:* John Braeman, University of Nebraska, Lincoln. (Stage I: Harry L. Coles, Ohio State University; Nelson Van Valen, Beloit College.) *Afro-American Studes:* Ann Allen Shockley, Fisk University; Kenneth S. Wilson, Howard University. *Canada:* Robin W. Winks, Yale University. *Latin America:* Joseph T. Criscenti, Boston College. (Stage I: John F. McCamant, University of Denver; Fred Gillette Sturm, Western College.)

SPECIAL FORMS: *Biography:* Roland H. Moody, Northeastern University. *Genealogy and Heraldry:* Social Sciences Reference Staff, Boston Public Library. *Military and Naval History:* See contributors listed in volume V, Military Science and Naval Science. *Politics and Government.* See note in contributors list in volume IV, Political Science. *Social and Economic History:* See note in contributors list in volume IV, Economic History and Social History.

C Auxiliary Sciences of History

CB HISTORY OF CIVILIZATION AND CULTURE

Columbia University. Columbia College. III. 1
Introduction to contemporary civilization in the West; a source book prepared by the Contemporary civilization staff of Columbia College, Columbia University. 3d ed. New York, Columbia University Press, 1960-61. v. 24 cm. First published in 1941 under title: Contemporary civilization source book. *1. Civilization — History — Sources. I. T:Contemporary civilization in the West.*
CB5.C575   914   60-16650

Lee, Dorothy D. III. 2
Freedom and culture; [essays] [Englewood Cliffs, N.J.] Prentice-Hall [1959] 179 p. 21 cm. (A Spectrum book, S-6) *1. Culture. I. T.*
CB7.L4   301.2   59-15584

Mumford, Lewis, 1895- III. 3
The human prospect. Edited by Harry T. Moore and Karl W. Deutsch. Boston, Beacon Press [1955] 319 p. 21 cm. (Beacon paperbacks, 13) "Essays and other writings ... from ... [the author's] books and previously uncollected magazine articles." *1. Civilization, Modern — Addresses, essays, lectures. I. T.*
CB7.M8   901   55-10921

CB19   Philosophy. Theory

Abell, Walter. III. 4
The collective dream in art; a psycho-historical theory of culture based on relations between the arts, psychology, and the social sciences. Cambridge, Harvard University Press, 1957. xv, 378 p. 39 plates. 25 cm. *1. Civilization — Philosophy. 2. Civilization — History. 3. Art — Psychology. I. T.*
CB19.A25   901   57-9067

Eliot, Thomas Stearns, 1888- III. 5
Notes towards the definition of culture. [1st American ed.] New York, Harcourt, Brace [1949] 128 p. 22 cm. *1. Culture. I. T.*
CB19.E48 1949   901   49-1605

Kroeber, Alfred Louis, 1876-1960. III. 6
An anthropologist looks at history. With a foreword by Milton Singer. Edited by Theodora Kroeber. Berkeley, University of California Press, 1963. xix, 213 p. 20 cm. *1. Civilization — History — Addresses, essays, lectures. I. T.*
CB19.K686 1963   901.9   63-16250

Kroeber, Alfred Louis, 1876- III. 7
Style and civilizations. Ithaca, N.Y., Cornell University Press [1957] 191 p. 23 cm. *1. Civilization — Philosophy. I. T.*
CB19.K687   901   57-4434

Kroeber, Alfred Louis, 1876- III. 8
Culture; a critical review of concepts and definitions, by A. L. Kroeber and Clyde Kluckhohn, with the assistance of Wayne Untereiner and appendices by Alfred G. Meyer. Cambridge, Mass., the Museum, 1952. viii, 223 p. 27 cm. (Papers of the Peabody Museum of American Archaeology and Ethnology, Harvard University, v.47, no. 1) *1. Culture. 2. Civilization. I. Kluckhohn, Clyde, 1905- joint author. (S:Harvard University. Peabody Museum of American Archaeology and Ethnology. Papers, v.47, no. 1)*
CB19.K7x (E51.H337 vol. 47, no. 1)   901   A53-9890

Nef, John Ulric, 1899- III. 9
A search for civilization. Chicago, H. Regnery Co., 1962. 210 p. 21 cm. *1. Civilization — Philosophy. I. T.*
CB19.N42   901.9   62-10716

Northrop, Filmer Stuart Cuckow, 1893- ed. III. 10
Ideological differences and world order; studies in the philosophy and science of the world's cultures. Edited by F. S. C. Northrop. Westport, Conn., Greenwood Press [1971, c1949] xi, 486 p. 23 cm. *1. Civilization — Philosophy. I. T.*
CB19.N59 1971   901.9/4   74-136078   ISBN:0837152283

Northrop, Filmer Stuart Cuckow, 1893- III. 11
The meeting of East and West, an inquiry concerning world understanding, by F. S. C. Northrop ... New York, Macmillan, 1946. xxii, 531 p. col. front., xvi pl. (incl. plan) on 8 l., diagrs. 22 cm. *1. Civilization — Philosophy. I. T.*
CB19.N6   901   46-4813

Rougemont, Denis de, 1906- III. 12
Man's Western quest; the principles of civilization. Translated from the French by Montgomery Belgion. [1st ed.] New York, Harper [1957] 197 p. 20 cm. (World perspectives, v.13) Translation of L'aventure occidentale de l'homme. *1. Civilization — Philosophy. 2. Civilization, Occidental. I. T.*
CB19.R653   901   57-6127

Schweitzer, Albert, 1875-1965. III. 13
The philosophy of civilization. Tr. by C. T. Campion. 1st American ed. New York, Macmillan, 1951. xvii, 347 p. 22 cm. Contains the author's The decay and the restoration of civilization and his Civilization and ethics, each originally published separately. *1. Civilization — Philosophy. I. T.*
CB19.S423   901   49-6468

Spengler, Oswald, 1880-1936. III. 14
Man and technics; a contribution to a philosophy of life; translated from the German by Charles Francis Atkinson. [1st ed.] New York, Knopf, 1932. 104 p. 21 cm. *1. Man. 2. Civilization — History. 3. Technology. I. Atkinson, Charles Francis, 1880- tr. II. T.*
CB19.S63   901   32-5140

Toynbee, Arnold Joseph, 1889- III. 15
Comparing notes: a dialogue across a generation [by] Arnold and Philip Toynbee. London, Weidenfeld and Nicolson [1963] 155 p. 23 cm. "Conversations between Arnold Toynbee and his son, Philip ... as they were recorded on tape." *I. Toynbee, Philip. II. T.*
CB19.T62   192   64-5454

White, Leslie A., 1900- III. 16
The science of culture; a study of man and civilization, by Leslie A. White. [2d ed.] New York, Farrar, Straus and Giroux [1969] xl, 444 p. 21 cm. *1. Culture. 2. Civilization. I. T.*
CB19.W48 1969   301.2   75-7130

Wilson, Colin, 1931- III. 17
The outsider. Boston, Houghton Mifflin, 1956. 288 p. 22 cm. *1. Civilization — Philosophy. I. T.*
CB19.W53 1956a   901   56-11983

Wilson, Colin, 1931- III. 18
Religion and the rebel. Boston, Houghton Mifflin, 1957. x, 338 p. 21 cm. *1. Civilization — Philosophy. 2. Religious thought — 20th cent. I. T.*
CB19.W533   901   57-14602

CB51 – 113 General Works, 1801 –   , by Nationality

CB51 – 59 American

Barnes, Harry Elmer, 1889- III. 19
An intellectual and cultural history of the Western World, by Harry Elmer Barnes [and others] 3d rev. ed. New York, Dover Publications [1965] 3 v. (xii, 1381 p.) illus. 22 cm. *1. Civilization — History. 2. Civilization, Occidental. I. T.*
CB53.B36 1965   914   63-21675

Kroeber, Alfred Louis, 1876- III. 20
Configurations of culture growth, by A. L. Kroeber. Berkeley, University of

California Press, 1944. x, 882 p. illus. (map) diagrs. 24 cm. *1. Civilization — History. 2. Culture. 3. Sociology. I. T.*
CB53.K7   901   A45-694

Lovejoy, Arthur Oncken, 1873-1962. III. 21
Primitivism and related ideas in antiquity, by Arthur O. Lovejoy [and] George Boas. With supplementary essays by W. F. Albright and P.-E. Dumont. New York, Octagon Books, 1965 [c1935] xv, 482 p. 25 cm. (Contributions to the history of primitivism) First published in 1935 as v.1 of A documentary history of primitivism and related ideas, edtited by A. O. Lovejoy. *1. Primitivism. 2. Progress. 3. Civilization. I. Boas, George, 1891- joint author. II. T. (S)*
CB53.L58 1965   901.901   65-25872

Mumford, Lewis, 1895- III. 22
The condition of man [by] Lewis Mumford. New York, Harcourt, Brace [1944] x, 467 p. plates. 24 1/2 cm. "First edition." *1. Civilization — History. I. T.*
CB53.M8   901   44-5038

Mumford, Lewis, 1895- III. 23
The transformations of man. [1st ed.] New York, Harper [1956] 249 p. 20 cm. (World perspectives, v.7) *1. Civilization — History. 2. Man. I. T.*
CB53.M82   901   56-6030

Whitehead, Alfred North, 1861-1947. III. 24
Adventure of ideas, by Alfred North Whitehead. New York, Macmillan, 1933. xii, 392 p. 22 cm. *1. Civilization — History. 2. Sociology — History. 3. Cosmology — History. 4. Philosophy — History. 5. History — Philosophy. 6. Ideology. I. T.*
CB53.W5   901   33-5611

Muller, Herbert Joseph, 1905- III. 25
The uses of the past; profiles of former societies. New York, Oxford University Press, 1952. xi, 394 p. 22 cm. *1. Civilization — History. I. T.*
CB57.M9   901   52-6168

Bowle, John. III. 26
Man through the ages, from the origins to the eighteenth century. [1st ed.] Boston, Little, Brown [1963, c1962- v. illus. 24 cm. "Published in Great Britain under the title A new outline of world history." *1. Civilization — History. I. T.*
CB59.B63   901.9   62-17032

Honigmann, John Joseph. III. 27
Understanding culture. New York, Harper & Row [1963] 468 p. illus. 25 cm. *1. Culture. I. T.*
CB59.H6   301.2   63-7293

Kroeber, Alfred Louis, 1876-1960. III. 28
A roster of civilizations and culture. Chicago, Aldine Pub. Co. [1962] 96 p. 26 cm. (Viking Fund publications in anthropology, no. 33) *1. Civilization — History — Outlines, syllabi, etc. I. T.*
CB59.K7   901.902   62-14933

McNeill, William Hardy, 1917- III. 29
The rise of the West; a history of the human community. Drawings by Béla Petheö. Chicago, University of Chicago Press [1963] 829 p. illus. 25 cm. *1. Civilization — History. 2. Civilization, Occidental. I. T.*
CB59.M3   901.9   63-13067

Parkinson, Cyril Northcote, 1909- III. 30
East and West. Boston, Houghton Mifflin, 1963. xxii, 330 p. maps. 22 cm. *1. Civilization — History. I. T.*
CB59.P28   901.9   63-17631

CB61 – 68   English

Buckle, Henry Thomas, 1821-1862. III. 31
History of civilization in England. Summarized and abridged by Clement Wood. Introd. by Hans Kohn. New York, Ungar [1964] xvi, 137 p. 21 cm. (Milestones of thought in the history of ideas) *1. Civilization — History. I. T. (S)*
CB63.B8 1964   914   64-15688

Toynbee, Arnold Joseph, 1889- III. 32
A study of history, by Arnold J. Toynbee. London, Oxford University Press, H. Milford, 1934-   v. tables (1 fold.) 23 cm. "Issued under the auspices of the Royal institute of international affairs." Index to v.1-3 at end of v.3; to v.4-6 at end of v.6. *1. Civilization. 2. History — Philosophy. I. Royal institute of international affairs.*
CB63.T6   901   34-20998

Gargan, Edward T., 1922- ed. III. 33
The intent of Toynbee's History; a cooperative appraisal. Pref. by Arnold J. Toynbee. Chicago, Loyola University Press, 1961. viii, 224 p. 24 cm. *1. Toynbee, Arnold Joseph, 1889- A study of history. I. T.*
CB63.T68G3   901.9   61-10704

Barker, Ernest, Sir, 1874-1960. III. 34
Traditions of civility; eight essays. [Hamden, Conn.] Archon Books, 1967. viii, 369 p. front. 22 cm. Reprint of the 1948 ed. *1. Civilization — Addresses, essays, lectures. I. T.*
CB67.B3 1967   901.9   67-28551

Bury, John Bagnell, 1861-1927. III. 35
The idea of progress: an inquiry into its origin and growth, by J. B. Bury. Introduction by Charles A. Beard. New York, Macmillan, 1932. xl, 357 p. 23 cm. *1. Progress. 2. History — Philosophy. I. Beard, Charles Austin, 1874- II. T.*
CB67.B8 1932   901   32-11686

Clark, Kenneth McKenzie, Baron Clark, 1903- III. 36
Civilisation: a personal view [by] Kenneth Clark. [1st U.S. ed.] New York, Harper & Row [1970, c1969] xviii, 359 p. illus. (part col.) 26 cm. *1. Civilization — History. 2. Art — History. I. T.*
CB68.C55 1970   901.9   75-97174

CB71 – 113   Other

Grousset, René, 1885- III. 37
The sum of history. English version by A. and H. Temple Patterson. [Hadleigh, Essex] Tower Bridge Publications [1951] 254 p. 22 cm. *1. Civilization — History. I. T.*
CB77.G713   901   52-1840

Chamberlain, Houston Stewart, 1855-1927. III. 38
The foundations of the nineteenth century; a translation from the German by John Lees, with an introd. by Lord Redesdale. London, New York, J. Lane, 1911. 2 v. illus., maps. 22 cm. *1. Nineteenth century. 2. History — Philosophy. 3. Civilization — History. I. T.*
CB83.C45 1911   901   A11-252

Spengler, Oswald, 1880-1936. III. 39
The decline of the West. Special ed. Authorised translation by Charles Francis Atkinson. New York, Knopf [1939] 2 v. in 1. tables (3 fold.) 24 cm. Each volume has special t.-p. *1. Civilization — History. I. Atkinson, Charles Francis, 1880- ed. and tr. II. T.*
CB83.S63 1939   A41-431

Weber, Alfred, 1868- III. 40
Farewell to European history; or, The conquest of nihilism. Tr. from the German by R. F. C. Hull. New Haven, Yale Univ. Press, 1948. xx, 204 p. 23 cm. "Published on the Louis Stern Memorial Fund." Translation of Abschied von der bisherigen Geschichte. *1. Civilization — History. 2. Philosophy — History. 3. Nihilism. I. Hull, Richard Francis Carrington, tr. II. The conquest of nihilism. III. T.*
CB83.W384 1948   901   48-6494

Ortega y Gasset, José, 1883-1955. III. 41
Man and crisis. Translated from the Spanish by Mildred Adams. [1st ed.] New York, Norton [1958] 217 p. 22 cm. Translation of En torno a Galileo. *1. Civilization — History. I. T.*
CB103.O683   901   58-9282

Ortega y Gasset, José, 1883-1955. III. 42
The revolt of the masses. Authorized translation from the Spanish. [25th anniversary ed.] New York, Norton [1957, c1932] 190 p. 22 cm. Translation of La rebelión de las masas. *1. Civilization. 2. Europe — Civilization. 3. Proletariat. I. T.*
CB103.O72 1957   901.9   61-3774

Birket-Smith, Kaj, 1893- III. 43
The paths of culture; a general ethnology. Translated from the Danish by Karin Fennow. Madison, University of Wisconsin Press, 1965. xi, 535 p. plates. 25 cm. *1. Civilization — History. 2. Ethnology. I. T.*
CB113.D3B513   301.2   64-8488

Polak, Frederik Lodewijk. III. 44
The image of the future; enlightening the past, orientating the present, forecasting the future. Leyden, A. W. Sythoff; New York, Oceana Publications, 1961. 2 v. 24 cm. (European aspects; a collection of studies relating to European integration. Series A: Culture, no. 1) L.C. copy imperfect: Index of names wanting. Translation of De toekomst is verleden tijd. *1. Culture. 2. Civilization — History. 3. Utopias. I. T. (S)*
CB113.D8P713   301.23   61-8137

CB151 – 155   Special Aspects

Barzun, Jacques, 1907- III. 45
Of human freedom, by Jacques Barzun. [1st ed.] Boston, Little, Brown, 1939.

334 p. 21 cm. "An Atlantic monthly press book." *1. Culture. 2. Democracy. I. T.*
CB151.B3   901   39-27843

Bernal, John Desmond, 1901-   III. 46
Science in history [by] J. D. Bernal. [3d ed.] New York, Hawthorn Books [1965] xxviii, 1039 p. illus., maps. 23 cm. *1. Science and civilization. 2. Civilization — History. I. T.*
CB151.B4 1965   901.9   65-22660

Caillois, Roger, 1913-   III. 47
Man, play, and games. Translated from the French by Meyer Barash. [New York] Free Press of Glencoe [1961] 208 p. 22 cm. Translation of Les jeux et les hommes. *1. Play. 2. Civilization — Philosophy. I. T.*
CB151.C273   790.13   61-14109

Huizinga, Johan, 1872-1945.   III. 48
Homo ludens; a study of the play-element in culture. Boston, Beacon Press [1955, c1950] 220 p. 21 cm. (Humanitas, Beacon reprints in humanities. Beacon paperbacks, 15.) *1. Play. 2. Civilization — Philosophy. I. T.*
CB151.H815x   901   55-13793

Jacob, Heinrich Eduard, 1889-1967.   III. 49
Six thousand years of bread; its holy and unholy history. Translated by Richard and Clara Winston. Westport, Conn., Greenwood Press [1970, c1944] xiv, 399 p. illus. 24 cm. *1. Bread. 2. Civilization — History. I. T.*
CB151.J34 1970   901.9   75-110043   ISBN:0837144310

Laski, Harold Joseph, 1893-1950.   III. 50
Faith, reason, and civilization; an essay in historical analysis. Freeport, N.Y., Books for Libraries Press [1972, c1944] 187 p. 23 cm. (Essay index reprint series) *1. Civilization. 2. Christianity. 3. Socialism. 4. Communism — Russia. I. T.*
CB151.L36 1972   901.9   74-167375   ISBN:0836926625

Lindsay, Robert Bruce, 1900-   III. 51
The role of science in civilization. [1st ed.] New York, Harper & Row [1963] 318 p. illus. 22 cm. *1. Science and civilization. I. T.*
CB151.L5   901.9   63-10752

Redfield, Robert, 1897-   III. 52
The primitive world and its transformations. Ithaca, N.Y., Cornell University Press [1953] 185 p. 23 cm. *1. Social change. 2. Cities and towns. I. T.*
CB151.R38   901   53-8239

Taylor, Henry Osborn, 1856-1941.   III. 53
Freedom of the mind in history. Westport, Conn., Greenwood Press [1970] xii, 297 p. 23 cm. Reprint of the 1923 ed. *1. Civilization. 2. Progress. 3. Learning and scholarship. I. T.*
CB151.T3 1970   901.9   74-109861   ISBN:837143527

Becker, Carl Lotus, 1873-1945.   III. 54
Progress and power; introd. by Leo Gershoy. [1st Borzoi ed.] New York, Knopf, 1949. xli, 116 p. 20 cm. "Lectures delivered at Stanford University, on the Raymond Fred West Memorial Foundation, in April 1935." *1. Progress. 2. Inventions. 3. Civilization — Philosophy. I. T.*
CB155.B4 1949   901   49-10663

Edelstein, Ludwig, 1902-1965.   III. 55
The idea of progress in classical antiquity. Baltimore, Johns Hopkins Press [1967] xxxiii, 211 p. 24 cm. *1. Progress. 2. Philosophy, Ancient. I. T.*
CB155.E26   901   67-16483   Augusta

Murray, Gilbert, 1866-   III. 56
Hellenism and the modern world. Boston, Beacon Press [1954] 60 p. 19 cm. *1. Hellenism. 2. Civilization, Modern.*
CB155.M78 1954   913.38   54-1637

CB160 – 161 Prophecies

Darwin, Charles Galton, Sir, 1887-   III. 57
The next million years. [1st American ed.] Garden City, N.Y., Doubleday, 1953 [c1952] 210 p. 21 cm. *1. Prophecies. I. T.*
CB160.D3 1953   504   52-13372

Kahn, Herman, 1922-   III. 58
The year 2000; a framework for speculation on the next thirty-three years, by Herman Kahn and Anthony J. Wiener, with contributions from other staff members of the Hudson Institute. Introd. by Daniel Bell. New York, Macmillan [1967] xxviii, 431 p. illus. 24 cm. *1. Twentieth century — Forecasts. I. Wiener, Anthony J., joint author. II. Hudson Institute. III. T.*
CB160.K3 1967   301.2   67-29488

Beckwith, Burnham Putnam.   III. 59
The next 500 years; scientific predictions of major social trends. With a foreword by Daniel Bell. [1st ed.] New York, Exposition Press [1967] xvi, 341 p. 22 cm. (An Exposition-university book) *1. Twenty-fifth century — Forecasts. I. T.*
CB161.B4   901.9   67-26389

McHale, John.   III. 60
The future of the future. New York, G. Braziller [1969] ix, 322 p. illus. 22 cm. *1. Technology and civilization. 2. Twenty-first century — Forecasts. I. T.*
CB161.M3   301.3   69-15827

Toward the year 2018: the challenge to United States foreign policy.   III. 61
[New York? 1968?] 12 pieces in 1 v. 28-36 cm. Cover title. Program, papers, and abstracts of papers of a convocation organized by the Foreign Policy Association and held May 27-29, 1968, in New York. "Culminates the celebration of the fiftieth year of the Foreign Policy Association." *1. Twenty-first century — Forecasts — Congresses. I. Foreign Policy Association.*
CB161.T62   327.73   71-298863

CB195 – 281 Nationalities. Regions

Taylor, Harold, 1914-   III. 62
The world as teacher. [1st ed.] Garden City, N.Y., Doubleday, 1969. x, 322 p. 22 cm. "Research sponsored by the American Association of Colleges for Teacher Education under U.S. Office of Education contract OE-6-10-116." *1. Intercultural education. I. American Association of Colleges for Teacher Education. II. T.*
CB199.T3   370.19/6   69-14969

CB203 – 245 WESTERN CIVILIZATION

Barker, Ernest, Sir, 1874-   III. 63
National character and the factors in its formation. [4th and rev. ed.] London, Methuen [1948] xix, 268 p. 23 cm. *1. National characteristics. 2. National characteristics, English. I. T.*
CB203.B3 1948   901   49-14737

Barker, Ernest, Sir, 1874- ed.   III. 64
The European inheritance, edited by Sir Ernest Barker, Sir George Clark [and] P. Vaucher. Oxford, Clarendon Press, 1954. 3 v. illus., maps (part fold.) 23 cm. Erratum slip inserted. *1. Europe — Civilization. I. T.*
CB245.B35   901   54-9923

Baumer, Franklin Le Van, ed.   III. 65
Main currents of Western thought; readings in Western European intellectual history from the Middle Ages to the present. 2d ed., rev. [and enl.] New York, Knopf, 1964. xviii, 746 p. 25 cm. *1. Civilization, Occidental — History — Sources. I. T.*
CB245.B37 1964   914   64-14416   901, B 327a

Bolgar, R. R.   III. 66
The classical heritage and its beneficiaries. Cambridge [Eng.] University Press, 1954. vii, 591 p. 24 cm. *1. Civilization, Occidental — History. I. T.*
CB245.B63   901   54-13284

Brinton, Clarence Crane, 1898-1968.   III. 67
Ideas and men; the story of Western thought. 2d ed. Englewood Cliffs, N.J., Prentice-Hall [1963] 484 p. 24 cm. *1. Civilization — History. 2. Civilization, Occidental. I. T.*
CB245.B73 1963   901   63-13270

Columbia University. Columbia College.   III. 68
Chapters in Western civilization, edited by the Contemporary civilization staff of Columbia College, Columbia University. 3d ed. New York, Columbia University Press, 1961- v. 24 cm. Vol. 2: Prelim. 3d ed., issued without chapters 2 and 4; chapters 2 and 4 in a separate pamphlet, inserted. *1. Civilization, Occidental. 2. Civilization — History. I. T.*
CB245.C632   914   61-13862

Dawson, Christopher Henry, 1889-   III. 69
Understanding Europe. New York, Sheed and Ward, 1952. 261 p. 22 cm. *1. Europe — Civilization. 2. Civilization, Occidental. I. T.*
CB245.D37   901   52-10609

Hayes, Carlton Joseph Huntley, 1882-   III. 70
Christianity and Western civilization. Stanford, Stanford University Press [1954] 63 p. 23 cm. (The Raymond Fred West memorial lectures at Stanford University, 1954) *1. Civilization, Occidental. 2. Civilization, Christian. I. T.*
CB245.H35   901   54-11786

Lopez, Robert Sabatino, 1910-   III. 71
The birth of Europe [by] Robert S. Lopez. New York, M. Evans; distributed in association with Lippincott, Philadelphia [1967] xxiii, 442 p. illus. (part col.) maps (part col.), plans. 27 cm. Translation of Naissance de l'Europe. *1. Civilization, Occidental. I. T.*
CB245.L613 1967b   910.09/18/21   66-23414

Muller, Herbert Joseph, 1905-   III. 72
Freedom in the Western World, from the Dark Ages to the rise of democracy. [1st ed.] New York, Harper & Row [1963] 428 p. illus. 25 cm. *1. Civilization, Occidental. 2. Liberty. I. T.*
CB245.M8   914   63-8427

Webb, Walter Prescott, 1888-1963.   III. 73
The Great Frontier. Introd. by Arnold J. Toynbee. Austin, University of Texas Press [1964] xviii, 434 p. illus., maps. 24 cm. *1. Civilization, Occidental. 2. Social history. I. T.*
CB245.W4 1964   914   64-10321

Weber, Eugen Joseph, 1925- comp.   III. 74
The Western tradition. [Compiled by] Eugen Weber. 3d ed. Lexington, Mass., Heath [1972] 2 v. (xxxii, 1019 p.) 24 cm. *1. Civilization, Occidental. I. T.*
CB245.W44 1972   910/.03/1812   72-172911
ISBN:0669811661 (v. 1) 0669811580 (v. 2)

CB251   EAST AND WEST

Baudet, Henri.   III. 75
Paradise on earth; some thoughts on European images of non-European man. Translated by Elizabeth Wentholt. New Haven, Yale University Press, 1965. xii, 87 p. 23 cm. *1. East and West. I. T.*
CB251.B3813   301.154   65-11174

Grousset, René, 1885-1952.   III. 76
The civilizations of the East. Translated from the French by Catherine Alison Phillips. [New York] Cooper Square Publishers [1967, c1931-34] 4 v. illus. 24 cm. Translation of Les civilisations de l'Orient. *1. Civilization, Oriental. 2. Art, Oriental. I. T.*
CB251.G72 1967   915/.03   66-30807

Hudson, Geoffrey Francis, 1903-   III. 77
Europe & China; a survey of their relations from the earliest times to 1800. Boston, Beacon Press [1961, c1931] 336 p. illus. 22 cm. *1. Europe — Civilization. 2. China — Civilization. 3. Europe — Relations (general) with China. 4. China — Relations (general) with Europe. I. T.*
CB251.H78x   327.4051   A63-5056

Jackson, Barbara (Ward) 1914-   III. 78
The interplay of East and West, points of conflict and cooperation. [1st ed.] New York, Norton [1957] 152 p. 22 cm. (The Sir Edward Beatty memorial lectures, ser. 2) *1. East and West. I. T. (S)*
CB251.J3   901   57-8337

Malraux, André, 1901-   III. 79
The temptation of the West. Translated and with an introd. by Robert Hollander. New York, Vintage Books [1961] 122 p. 19 cm. (A Vintage original, V-193) *1. China — Civilization. 2. Europe — Civilization. I. T.*
CB251.M313   901.9   60-12160

Toynbee, Arnold Joseph, 1889-   III. 81
Civilization on trial, and The world and the West. New York, Meridian Books [1960] 348 p. 18 cm. (Meridian books, M52) "The argument of A study of history, by D. C. Somervell": p. [299]-348. *1. Civilization — Addresses, essays, lectures. 2. History — Philosophy. 3. East and West. I. Somervell, David Churchill, 1885- II. T. III. T:The world and the West.*
CB251.T69 1960   901.9   58-8525

United Nations Educational, Scientific and Cultural Organization.   III. 82
Interrelations of cultures, their contribution to international understanding. Westport, Conn., Greenwood Press [1971, c1953] 387 p. 23 cm. (Its Collection of intercultural studies) *1. Acculturation. I. T. (S)*
CB251.U53 1971   301.2/41   72-88956   ISBN:0837131537

Zinkin, Maurice.   III. 83
Asia and the West. [New and rev. ed.] New York, International Secretariat, Institute of Pacific Relations, 1953. xii, 304 p. maps. 21 cm. *1. East and West. I. T.*
CB251.Z5x   A54-8866

CB253   ORIENTAL CIVILIZATION

Conference on Oriental Civilization in General Education, Columbia University, 1961.   III. 84
Approaches to Asian civilizations. [Proceedings] Edited by Wm. Theodore de Bary and Ainslie T. Embree. New York, Columbia University Press, 1964. xxv, 293 p. 22 cm. *1. Civilization, Oriental — Congresses. I. De Bary, William Theodore, 1918- ed. II. Embree, Ainslie Thomas, ed. III. Columbia University. IV. T.*
CB253.C6 1961   63-20226

Dean, Vera (Micheles) 1903-   III. 85
The nature of the non-Western World. [New York] New American Library [1957] 284 p. illus. 18 cm. (A Mentor book, MD190) *1. Civilization, Oriental. 2. Africa — Civilization. 3. Latin America — Civilization. I. T.*
CB253.D4   901   57-8030

Nakamura, Hajime, 1912-   III. 86
Ways of thinking of Eastern peoples: India, China, Tibet, Japan. Rev. English translation, edited by Philip P. Wiener. Honolulu, East-West Center Press [c1964] xx, 712 p. 24 cm. *1. National characteristics, Oriental. I. T.*
CB253.N313 1964   915   64-63438

Reischauer, Edwin Oldfather, 1910-   III. 87
A history of East Asian civilization [by] Edwin O. Reischauer [and] John K. Fairbank. Boston, Houghton Mifflin [1960-1965] 2 v. illus., maps (part fold.) 25 cm. Includes bibliographical references. *1. Civilization, Oriental — History. I. Fairbank, John K. II. T. III. T:East Asian civilization.*
CB253.R4   915   60-4269

CB301 – 428   Periods of Civilization
CB301 – 303   ORIGINS

Braidwood, Robert John, 1907-   III. 88
The Near East and the foundations for civilization; an essay in appraisal of the general evidence. Eugene, Oregon State System of Higher Education, 1952. 45 p. illus., maps. 26 cm. (Condon lectures) *1. Civilization, Ancient. 2. Man, Prehistoric. 3. Near East — History. I. T. (S)*
CB301.B63   913.3   53-62030

Clark, John Grahame Douglas.   III. 89
Aspects of prehistory [by] Grahame Clark. Berkeley, University of California Press, 1970. xiii, 161 p. illus., maps. 23 cm. *1. Man, Prehistoric. 2. Evolution. I. T.*
CB301.C57   913.03/1   73-94989   ISBN:520015843

Hawkes, Charles Francis Christopher, 1905-   III. 90
The prehistoric foundations of Europe to the Mycenean age, by C. F. C. Hawkes. With 12 plates, 6 maps and tables and many text illustrations. London, Methuen [1940] xv, 414 p. illus., XII pl., VI maps (part fold.) 23 cm. "First published in 1940." *1. Man, Prehistoric — Europe. 2. Europe — Civilization — History. 3. Europe — History. I. T.*
CB301.H3   901   41-17904

Mellaart, James.   III. 91
Earliest civilizations of the Near East. New York, McGraw-Hill [1965] 143 p. illus. (part col.) maps. 22 cm. (The Library of early civilizations) *1. Stone age — Near East. 2. Civilization, Ancient. I. T.*
CB301.M38   913.35031   65-19415

Piggott, Stuart, ed.   III. 92
The dawn of civilization; the first world survey of human cultures in early times. Texts by Grahame Clark [and others] New York, McGraw-Hill [1961] 403 p. illus. (part col.) maps (part col.) diagrs. 36 cm. *1. Civilization, Ancient. I. Clark, John Grahame Douglas. II. T.*
CB301.P5 1961   901.91   61-11703

CB311 – 325 ANCIENT

Aymard, André. III. 93
L'Orient et la Grèce antique. (4. éd. rev. et corr.) par André Aymard et Jeannine Auboyer. Préf. générale par Maurice Crouzet. Paris, Presses universitaires de France, 1961. xii, 701 p. illus., maps. 24 cm. (Histoire générale des civilisations, t.1) *1. Civilization, Ancient. I. Auboyer, Jeannine, joint author. II. T. (S)*
CB311.A9 1961   A62-1252

Bibby, Geoffrey. III. 94
Four thousand years ago; a world panorama of life in the second millennium B.C. [1st ed.] New York, Knopf, 1961. 398 p. illus. 25 cm. *1. Civilization, Ancient. I. T.*
CB311.B5   901.91   61-14367

Childe, Vere Gordon, 1892- III. 95
Man makes himself, by V. Gordon Childe. London, Watts [1936] xii, 275 p. front., illus. (incl. map) diagrs. 21 cm. (The library of science and culture.) *1. Civilization, Ancient. 2. Archaeology. 3. Man, Prehistoric. 4. Progress. I. T.*
CB311.C5   901.91   37-2189

Childe, Vere Gordon, 1892-1957. III. 96
Progress and archaeology. Westport, Conn., Greenwood Press [1971] 119 p. 23 cm. Reprint of the 1944 ed. *1. Progress. 2. Civilization, Ancient. 3. Archaeology. I. T.*
CB311.C52 1971   913.03/1   70-114499   ISBN:0837147794

Childe, Vere Gordon, 1892-1957. III. 97
What happened in history [by] Gordon Childe. London, M. Parrish [1960, c1942] 250 p. maps. 23 cm. *1. Civilization, Ancient. 2. History, Ancient. 3. Man, Prehistoric. I. T.*
CB311.C54x   901.91   64-57366

Green, Peter, 1924- III. 98
Essays in antiquity. [1st ed.] Cleveland, World Pub. Co. [1960] 224 p. 23 cm. *1. Civilization, Ancient — Addresses, essays, lectures. I. T.*
CB311.G69 1960   901.91   60-13359

Horizon (New York, 1958-) III. 99
The Horizon book of lost worlds, by the editors of Horizon magazine. Editor in charge: Marshall B. Davidson. Narrative by Leonard Cottrell. New York, American Heritage Pub. Co.; book trade distribution by Doubleday [1962] 431 p. illus. (part col.) maps (part col.) 32 cm. *1. Civilization, Ancient. I. Davidson, Marshall B., ed. II. Cottrell, Leonard. III. T. IV. T:Lost worlds.*
CB311.H65   901.91   62-19438

Rostovtsev, Mikhail Ivanovich, 1870- III. 100
Out of the past of Greece & Rome. New York, Biblo and Tannen, 1963. xvii, 129 p. illus. 24 cm. (Biblo and Tannen's Graeco life and times series, v.6) *1. Civilization, Ancient. 2. Civilization, Greek. 3. Cities and towns, Ancient. I. T.*
CB311.R6 1963   913.3   63-18047

Symposium on Urbanization and Cultural Development in the Ancient Near East, University of Chicago, 1958. III. 101
City invincible; a Symposium on Urbanization and Cultural Development in the Ancient Near East held at the Oriental Institute of the University of Chicago, December 4-7, 1958. Edited for the Planning Committee by Carl H. Kraeling and Robert M. Adams. Chicago, University of Chicago Press [1960] xiv, 447 p. illus., maps (1 fold.) 25 cm. ([Chicago. University] Oriental Institute. Special publication) *1. Cities and towns, Ancient. 2. Civilization, Ancient. I. Kraeling, Carl Hermann, 1897- ed. II. Adams, Robert M., 1926- ed. III. T. (S)*
CB311.S9 1958   901.91   60-13791

CB351 – 355 MEDIEVAL

Artz, Frederick Binkerd, 1894- III. 102
The mind of the Middle Ages, A.D. 200-1500; an historical survey. 3d ed., rev. New York, Knopf, 1958 [c1954] 566 p. illus. 24 cm. *1. Civilization, Medieval. 2. Middle Ages — Intellectual life. I. T.*
CB351.A56 1958   901   58-11857

Bark, William Carroll, 1908- III. 103
Origins of the medieval world. Stanford, Stanford University Press, 1958. ix, 162 p. 24 cm. (Stanford studies in history, economics, and political science, 14) *1. Middle Ages. I. T. (S:Stanford University. Stanford studies in history, economics, and political science, 14)*
CB351.B38 (AS36.L54 vol. 14)   940.1   58-6706

Evans, Joan, 1893- ed. III. 104
The flowering of the Middle Ages. Texts by Christopher Brooke [and others] New York, McGraw-Hill [1966] 360 p. illus., facsims. (part col.), maps, plans, plates (part col.), ports. (part col.) 36 cm. *1. Middle Ages. I. Brooke, Christopher Nugent Lawrence. II. T.*
CB351.E9 1966a   914.031708   66-18208

Herlihy, David, comp. III. 105
Medieval culture and society. New York, Harper & Row [1968] xv, 410 p. 21 cm. (Documentary history of Western civilization. Harper torchblocks, TB1340.) *1. Civilization, Medieval. I. T.*
CB351.H4   914.03/1   68-13326

Hoyt, Robert Stuart. III. 106
Europe in the Middle Ages [by] Robert S. Hoyt. 2d ed. New York, Harcourt, Brace & World [1966] xiv, 684 p. illus., maps (part col.) 24 cm. *1. Civilization, Medieval. 2. Europe — History — 476-1492. I. T.*
CB351.H6 1966   940.1   66-16060

Jarrett, Bede, 1881-1934. III. 107
Social theories of the Middle Ages 1200-1500. 1st ed., new impression. London, Cass, 1968. ix, 280 p. 22 cm. First ed. originally published, London, Benn, 1926. *1. Civilization, Medieval. 2. Social history — Medieval. I. T.*
CB351.J3 1968   300/.9/02   68-100853

Laistner, Max Ludwig Wolfram, 1890- III. 108
Thought and letters in western Europe, A.D. 500 to 900. [New ed., rev. and re-set] Ithaca, N.Y., Cornell University Press [1957] 416 p. 22 cm. *1. Civilization, Medieval. 2. Literature, Medieval — History and criticism. 3. Learning and scholarship. I. T.*
CB351.L27x   A57-5744

Painter, Sidney, 1902- III. 109
Mediaeval society. Ithaca, Cornell University Press [1951] 109 p. 22 cm. (The Development of Western civilization) *1. Civilization, Medieval. I. T.*
CB351.P3   901   51-7082

Rand, Edward Kennard, 1871-1945. III. 110
Founders of the Middle Ages. New York, Dover Publications [1957, c1928] 365 p. 21 cm. *1. Civilization, Medieval. 2. Literature, Medieval — History and criticism. 3. Middle Ages. I. T.*
CB351.R3 1957   901   57-59148

Southern, Richard William. III. 111
The making of the middle Ages. New Haven, Yale University Press, 1953. 280 p. illus., map. 24 cm. *1. Middle Ages. I. T.*
CB351.S6 1953a   940.1   A53-5280

Stephenson, Carl, 1886- III. 112
Mediaeval institutions; selected essays. Edited by Bryce D. Lyon. Ithaca, N.Y., Cornell University Press [1954] xiv, 289 p. illus. 24 cm. *1. Middle Ages. 2. Civilization, Medieval. I. T.*
CB351.S75   940.1   54-4979

Taylor, Henry Osborn, 1856-1941. III. 113
The mediaeval mind; a history of the development of thought and emotion in the Middle Ages. 4th ed. Cambridge, Harvard University Press, 1949. 2 v. 22 cm. *1. Middle Ages. 2. Civilization, Medieval. 3. Philosophy, Medieval. I. T.*
CB351.T3x   901   A49-9872

Wolff, Philippe, 1913- III. 114
The cultural awakening. Translated from the French by Anne Carter. [1st American ed.] New York, Pantheon Books, [c1968] 314 p. maps. 22 cm. *1. Civilization, Medieval. I. T.*
CB351.W613 1968   914/.03/1   68-13014

CB353   Special Aspects

Boas, George, 1891- III. 115
Essays on primitivism and related ideas in the Middle Ages. New York, Octagon Books, 1966 [c1948] xii, 227 p. 26 cm. (Contributions to the history of primitivism) *1. Primitivism. 2. Civilization, Medieval. I. T. (S)*
CB353.B6 1966   901.903   66-17502

Dawson, Christopher Henry, 1889- III. 116
The making of Europe; an introduction to the history of European unity. New York, Meridian Books, 1956. 274 p. illus. 18 cm. (Meridian books, M35) *1. Europe — Civilization — History. 2. Church history — Middle Ages. 3. Civilization, Medieval. I. T.*
CB353.D3x   901   56-10016

Holmes, Urban Tigner, 1900- III. 117
Daily living in the twelfth century, based on the observations of Alexander Neckam in London and Paris. Madison, University of Wisconsin Press, 1952. 337 p. illus. 22 cm. *1. Twelfth century. 2. Civilization, Medieval. 3. London — Social life and customs. 4. Paris — Social life and customs. 5. France — Social life and customs. I. Neckam, Alexander, 1157-1217. II. T.*
CB353.H65   901   52-62000

Powicke, Frederick Maurice, Sir, 1879-1963. III. 118
The Christian life in the middle ages and other essays, by F. M. Powicke. Oxford, Clarendon Press, 1935. vi, 176 p. fold. geneal. tab. 23 cm. *1. Civilization, Medieval. 2. Christianity — Middle ages. I. T.*
CB353.P6   901   36-6971

White, Lynn Townsend, 1907- III. 119
Medieval technology and social change. Oxford, Clarendon Press, 1962. 194 p. illus. 22 cm. *1. Civilization, Mediaeval. 2. Technology and civilization. I. T.*
CB353.W5   901.92   62-2973

Wisconsin. University. Division of Humanities. III. 120
Twelfth-century Europe and the foundations of modern society; proceedings of a symposium sponsored by the Division of Humanities of the University of Wisconsin and the Wisconsin Institute for Medieval and Renaissance Studies, November 12-14, 1957. Edited by Marshall Clagett, Gaines Post and Robert Reynolds. Madison, University of Wisconsin Press, 1961. xvi, 219 p. illus. 25 cm. *1. Twelfth century. I. Clagett, Marshall, 1916- ed. II. Wisconsin. University. Wisconsin Institute for Medieval and Renaissance Studies.*
CB353.W65 1957   940.14   60-5663

CB357 – 427   MODERN

Friedell, Egon, 1878-1938. III. 121
A cultural history of the modern age; the crisis of the European soul from the black death to the world war, by Egon Friedell; translated from the German by Charles Francis Atkinson. New York, Knopf, 1930-32. 3 v. 27 cm. *1. Europe — Civilization — History. I. Atkinson, Charles Francis, 1880- tr. II. T.*
CB357.F73   30-1796

Smith, Preserved, 1880-1941. III. 122
A history of modern culture. New introd. by Crane Brinton. New York, Collier Books [1962] 2 v. 18 cm. *1. Civilization — History. I. T.*
CB357.S6 1962   901.9   62-20297

Barzun, Jacques, 1907- III. 123
Science: the glorious entertainment. [1st ed.] New York, Harper & Row [1964] x, 322 p. 22 cm. *1. Science and civilization. I. T.*
CB358.B3   901.94   62-14520

Plaine, Henry L., ed. III. 124
Darwin, Marx, and Wagner; a symposium. [Columbus] Ohio State University Press [1962] viii, 165 p. 22 cm. "A group of faculty members at Ohio State planned ... [the] conference for October 1959." *1. Darwin, Charles Robert, 1809-1882. 2. Marx, Karl, 1818-1883. 3. Wagner, Richard, 1813-1883. 4. Ohio. State University, Columbus. 5. Civilization, Modern — Addresses, essays, lectures.*
CB358.P53 1962   901   61-12066

CB361 – 369   Renaissance

The Civilization of the Renaissance, III. 125
by James Westfall Thompson [and others] New York, Ungar [1959] 136 p. illus. 19 cm. *1. Renaissance. 2. Art, Renaissance. I. Thompson, James Westfall, 1869-1941.*
CB361.C5 1959   901.93   58-59873

Ferguson, Wallace Klippert, 1902- III. 126
The renaissance, by Wallace K. Ferguson. New York, Holt [c1940] viii, 148 p. 20 cm. (Half-title: The Berkshire studies in European history) *1. Renaissance.*
CB361.F37   940.21   40-5856

Ferguson, Wallace Klippert, 1902- III. 127
The Renaissance in historical thought; five centuries of interpretation. Boston, Houghton Mifflin [1948] xiii, 429 p. 22 cm. *1. Renaissance. 2. Historiography. I. T.*
CB361.F373   940.21   48-9685

F 381r

Kristeller, Paul Oskar, 1905- III. 128
Studies in Renaissance thought and letters. Roma, Edizioni di storia e letteratura, 1956. xvi, 680 p. facsims. 26 cm. (Storia e letteratura, v.54) Italian or English. Errata slip inserted. *1. Ficino, Marsilio, 1433-1499. 2. Renaissance — Addresses, essays, lectures. I. T.*
CB361.K7   901   A58-2341

Kristeller, Paul Oskar, 1905- III. 129
The classics and Renaissance thought. Cambridge, Published for Oberlin College by Harvard University Press, 1955. 106 p. 22 cm. (Martin classical lectures, v.15) *1. Renaissance. 2. Humanism. I. T.*
CB361.K7x (PA25.M3 vol. 15)   940.21   55-9440

Mazzeo, Joseph Anthony, 1923- III. 130
Renaissance and revolution; the remaking of European thought. New York, Pantheon Books [1966, c1965] xi, 349 p. 22 cm. *1. Renaissance. 2. Humanism. I. T.*
CB361.M39   914.0321   65-25080

New York. Metropolitan Museum of Art. III. 131
The Renaissance; six essays by Wallace K. Ferguson [and others] New York, Harper & Row [1962] 184 p. illus. 21 cm. (Harper torchbooks. The Academy library) "Originally published by the Metropolitan Museum of art in 1953 under the title: The Renaissance, a symposium." *1. Renaissance — Addresses, essays, lectures.*
CB361.N412   940.21082   63-1056

Symposium on the Renaissance, University of Wisconsin, III. 132
Milwaukee, 1959.
The Renaissance: a reconsideration of the theories and interpretations of the age. Edited by Tinsley Helton. Contributors: Garrett Mattingly [and others] Madison, University of Wisconsin Press, 1961. xiii, 160 p. 22 cm. *1. Renaissance — Congresses. I. Helton, Tinsley, ed. II. T.*
CB361.S93 1959   901.93   61-5903

Utley, Francis Lee, 1907- ed. III. 133
The foreward movement of the fourteenth century. Columbus, Ohio State University Press [1961] 166 p. plates. 24 cm. *1. Fourteenth century. I. T.*
CB365.U8   901.903   60-14642

Allen, Percy Stafford, 1869-1933. III. 134
The age of Erasmus; lectures delivered in the universities of Oxford and London. New York, Russell & Russell, 1963. 303 p. 23 cm. *1. Erasmus, Desiderius, d. 1536. 2. Renaissance. I. T.*
CB367.A5 1963   922.2492   63-11026

Haydn, Hiram Collins, 1907- III. 135
The counter-Renaissance. New York, Scribner, 1950. xvii, 705 p. 24 cm. Issued also as thesis, Columbia University. *1. Renaissance. I. T.*
CB369.H35   901   50-7225

Taylor, Henry Osborn, 1856-1941. III. 136
Thought and expression in the sixteenth century. 2d rev. ed. New York, Ungar [1959] 2 v. 22 cm. *1. Europe — Intellectual life. 2. Humanism. 3. Sixteenth century. I. T.*
CB369.T3 1959   940.22   59-11670

CB401 – 411   16th, 17th, 18th Centuries

Clark, George Norman, Sir, 1890- III. 137
The seventeenth century. 2d ed. Oxford, Clarendon Press, 1947. xix, 378 p. fold. maps. 23 cm. *1. Europe — Civilization. I. T.*
CB401.C6x   A48-3857   940.22 547a

Clark, George Norman, Sir, 1890- III. 138
War and society in the seventeenth century. Cambridge [Eng.] University Press, 1958. 156 p. 22 cm. (The Wiles lectures, 1956) *1. War and society. 2. Seventeenth century.*
CB401.C62   172.4   58-1704

Elliott, John Huxtable. III. 139
The old world and the new 1492-1650, by J. H. Elliott. Cambridge [Eng.] University Press, 1970. x, 118 p. front. 22 cm. (The Wiles lectures, 1969. Cambridge studies in early modern history.) *1. Europe — Civilization — History — Addresses, essays, lectures. 2. America — Discovery and exploration — Addresses, essays, lectures. I. T. (S)*
CB401.E43   914/.03   73-121362   ISBN:521079373

Friedrich, Carl Joachim, 1901- III. 140
The age of power [by]Carl J. Friedrich and Charles Blitzer. Ithaca, N.Y., Cornell University Press [1957] 200 p. illus. 22 cm. (The Development of Western civilization) *1. Seventeenth century. I. Blitzer, Charles, joint author. II. T.*
CB401.F7   901   57-4449

Hatton, Ragnhild Marie. III. 141
Europe in the age of Louis XIV [by] Ragnhild Hatton. [New York] Harcourt, Brace & World [1969] 263 p. illus. (part col.), geneal. table, maps, ports. 21 cm. (History of European civilization library) *1. Europe — Civilization. I. T.*
CB401.H3 1969b   914/.03/25   70-78869

Chaunu, Pierre.   **III. 142**
La civilisation de l'Europe classique. [Paris] Arthaud, 1966. 705 p. illus., facsims., maps (part fold. col.) plates (part col.) ports. 23 cm. (Collection Les Grandes civilisations, 5) *1. Civilization, Modern. I. T. (S)*
CB411.C45   66-99945

Cobban, Alfred.   **III. 143**
The eighteenth century: Europe in the age of enlightenment. Texts by Alfred Cobban [and others] Edited by Alfred Cobban. New York, McGraw-Hill [1969] 360 p. illus. (part col.), maps, ports. 36 cm. *1. Eighteenth century. I. T.*
CB411.C6 1969   914/.03/25   78-75160

Hampson, Norman.   **III. 144**
A cultural history of the Enlightenment. [1st American ed.] New York, Pantheon Books [c1968] 304 p. 22 cm. *1. Enlightenment — History. I. T.*
CB411.H38 1968   914/.03/253   68-26043

Kraus, Michael, 1901-   **III. 145**
The Atlantic civilization: eighteenth-century origins. New York, Russell & Russell, 1961 [c1949] 334 p. 22 cm. *1. Civilization, Modern — 18th cent. 2. U.S. — Relations (general) with Europe. 3. Europe — Relations (general) with the U.S. I. T.*
CB411.K7 1961   901.93   61-12131

Mazzeo, Joseph Anthony, 1923- ed.   **III. 146**
Reason and the imagination; studies in the history of ideas, 1600-1800. New York, Columbia University Press, 1962. viii, 321 p. plates. 23 cm. The studies are in honor of Marjorie Hope Nicolson. *1. Nicolson, Marjorie Hope, 1894- 2. Seventeenth century — Addresses, essays, lectures. 3. Eighteenth century — Addresses, essays, lectures. I. T.*
CB411.M3   901.93   62-7773

CB415 – 428   19th – 20th Centuries

Masur, Gerhard, 1901-   **III. 147**
Prophets of yesterday; studies in European culture, 1890-1914. New York, Macmillan, 1961. 481 p. 22 cm. *1. Civilization, Modern — 19th cent. 2. Europe — Intellectual life. I. T.*
CB417.M36   914   61-9729

Regin, Deric.   **III. 148**
Culture and the crowd; a cultural history of the proletarian era. [1st ed.] Philadelphia, Chilton Book Co. [1968] xii, 512 p. 24 cm. *1. Civilization, Modern — 19th century. 2. Civilization, Modern — 20th century. I. T.*
CB417.R4   901.9/4   68-19178

Berdiaev, Nikolaĭ Aleksandrovich, 1874-1948.   **III. 149**
The fate of man in the modern world. [Translated by Donald A. Lowrie. Ann Arbor] University of Michigan Press [1961, c1935] 131 p. 21 cm. (Ann Arbor paperbacks, AA59) *1. Civilization — Philosophy. 2. Collectivism. 3. Nationalism. 4. Sociology, Christian. I. T.*
CB425.B37 1961   901.94   61-65396

Boulding, Kenneth Ewart, 1910-   **III. 150**
The meaning of the twentieth century; the great transition by Kenneth E. Boulding. [1st ed.] New York, Harper & Row [1964] xvi, 199 p. 20cm. (World perspectives, v.34) *1. Civilization, Modern — 1950- I. The great transition. II. T. (S)*
CB425.B668   301.24   64-20540

Crouzet, Maurice.   **III. 151**
L'Époque contemporaine, à la recherche d'une civilisation nouvelle ... 5e édition revue et augmentée. Paris, Presses universitaires de France, 1969. 944 p. illus., maps, plates. 24 cm. (Histoire générale des civilisations, t.7) *1. Twentieth century. I. T. (S)*
CB425.C77 1969   70-410869

Harrington, Michael.   **III. 152**
The accidental century. New York, Macmillan [1965] 322 p. 22 cm. *1. Civilization, Modern — 20th cent. I. T.*
CB425.H24   901.94   65-16935

Huxley, Julian Sorell, Sir, 1887- ed.   **III. 153**
The humanist frame. [1st ed.] New York, Harper [1962, c1961] 432 p. 25 cm. Essays. *1. Civilization — Philosophy. I. T.*
CB425.H86 1962   144   62-7898

The Impact of America on European culture   **III. 154**
[by] Bertrand Russell [and others] Boston, Beacon Press, 1951. 100 p. 22 cm. *1. Europe — Civilization — American influences. 2. U.S. — Civilization. I. Russell, Bertrand Russell, 3d earl, 1872-*
CB425.I43   901   51-9998

Jaspers, Karl, 1883-   **III. 155**
Man in the modern age, by K. Jaspers. Translated by Eden and Cedar Paul. London, Routledge, 1933. vii, 243 p. 23 cm. "First published in England 1933." "The fifth edition ... of the German original, entitled 'Die geistige Situation der Gegenwart,' was published in 1932." First German edition, 1931, entitled: Die Geistige Situation der Zeit. *1. Civilization, Modern. I. Paul, Eden, 1865- tr. II. Paul, Cedar, joint tr. III. T.*
CB425.J342   901   33-30267

Kohn, Hans, 1891-   **III. 156**
The twentieth century; the challenge to the West and its response. New and enl. ed. New York, Macmillan, 1957. 300 p. 21 cm. *1. Twentieth century.*
CB425.K65 1957   901   57-10778

Krutch, Joseph Wood, 1893-   **III. 157**
Human nature and the human condition. New York, Random House [1959] 211 p. 22 cm. *1. Civilization, Modern — 1950- I. T.*
CB425.K75   901.94   59-10808

Public opinion, 1935-1946.   **III. 158**
Under the editorial direction of Hadley Cantril. Prepared by Mildred Strunk. Princeton, Princeton University Press, 1951. lix, 1191 p. 30 cm. "Opinion poll results ... collected from 23 organizations in 16 countries." *1. Public opinion. 2. Twentieth century. I. Cantril, Hadley, 1906- ed. II. Strunk, Mildred.*
CB425.P79   301.154   51-272

Romains, Jules, 1885-   **III. 159**
As it is on earth. Translated from the French by Richard Howard. New York, Macmillan, 1962. 111 p. 22 cm. Translation of Situation de la terre. *1. Civilization, Modern — 20th cent. I. T.*
CB425.R7233   901.94   62-10647

Chase, Stuart, 1888-   **III. 160**
The most probable world. [1st ed.] New York, Harper & Row [c1968] xii, 239 p. 22 cm. *1. Civilization, Modern — 20th century — Addresses, essays, lectures. I. T.*
CB427.C48   901.9/4   67-28803

Fabun, Don.   **III. 161**
The dynamics of change, by Don Fabun, assisted by Niels Sundermeyer. Art director: Bob Conover, Englewood Cliffs, N.J., Prentice-Hall [1967] 1 v. (various pagings) illus. (part col.) 29 cm. "Material ... originated in commemoration of the twentieth anniversary of Kaiser Aluminum & Chemical Corporation. It first appeared in a special series of six issues of Kaiser aluminum news." *1. Civilization, Modern — 1950- I. Sundermeyer, Niels. II. T.*
CB427.F25   901.94   67-25569

Sakharov, Andrei Dmitrievich, 1921-   **III. 162**
Progress, coexistence, and intellectual freedom, by Andrei D. Sakharov. Translated by the New York Times. With introd., afterword, and notes, by Harrison E. Salisbury. [1st ed.] New York, Norton [1968] 158 p. 22 cm. Originally published in the New York Times, July 22, 1968. *1. Civilization, Modern — 1950- — Addresses, essays, lectures. I. Salisbury, Harrison Evans, 1908- ed. II. T.*
CB427.S2313 1968   901.94/5   68-57368

Toynbee, Arnold Joseph, 1889-   **III. 163**
Surviving the future [by] Arnold Toynbee. London, New York, Oxford University Press, 1971. xii, 164 p. 23 cm. Revision of a dialogue between Kei Wakaizumi and Arnold Toynbee, originally published, in Japanese, in installments, in the Mainichi Shimbun. *1. Civilization, Modern — 1950- — Addresses, essays, lectures. 2. Civilization — Philosophy. I. Wakaizumi, Kei, 1930- II. T.*
CB428.T69 1971   901.9   77-167854   ISBN:0192152521

CB440 – 481   Special Topics

Clough, Shepard Bancroft, 1901-   **III. 164**
The rise and fall of civilization; an inquiry into the relationship between economic development and civilization. New York, McGraw-Hill [1951] xiii, 291 p. maps. 21 cm. *1. Civilization — History. 2. Economic conditions. I. T.*
CB448.C57   901   51-12730

Foster, George McClelland, 1913-   **III. 165**
Traditional cultures, and the impact of technological change. New York, Harper [1962] 292 p. 22 cm. *1. Technology and civilization. I. T.*
CB478.F6   301.24   62-10483

Mumford, Lewis, 1895-   **III. 166**
The myth of the machine. [1st ed.] New York, Harcourt, Brace & World [1969-70] 2 v. illus. 25 cm. Vol. 2 has imprint: New York, Harcourt Brace Jovanovich. *1. Technology and civilization. I. T.*
CB478.M78   67-16088

Nef, John Ulric, 1899- III. 167
Cultural foundations of industrial civilization. Cambridge [Eng.] University Press, 1958. xiv, 163 p. 22 cm. (The Wiles lectures, 1956) Erratum slip inserted. *1. Technology and civilization. 2. Civilization — History. I. T. (S)*
CB478.N4   A59-642

Peccei, Aurelio. III. 168
The chasm ahead. [New York] Macmillan [1969] xvi, 297 p. illus. 22 cm. *1. Technology and civilization. I. T.*
CB478.P4   901.9   69-11395

Taylor, Gordon Rattray. III. 169
The doomsday book; can the world survive? New York, World Pub. Co. [1970] 335 p. 22 cm. *1. Technology and civilization. 2. Human ecology. I. T.*
CB478.T38 1970b   301.31   75-124280

Nef, John Ulric, 1899- III. 170
War and human progress; an essay on the rise of industrial civilization, by John U. Nef. New York, Russell & Russell [1968, c1950] ix, 464 p. 24 cm. *1. War and civilization. I. T.*
CB481.N4 1968   901.9   68-10934

CC ARCHAEOLOGY

Binford, Sally R. III. 171
New perspectives in archeology. Edited by Sally R. Binford and Lewis R. Binford. Chicago, Aldine Pub. Co. [1968] x, 373 p. illus., maps, plans. 25 cm. Includes 11 papers, (substantially rev.), presented at a symposium held during the 64th annual meeting of the American Anthropological Association, Denver, Nov. 1965. *1. Archaeology — Addresses, essays, lectures. I. Binford, Lewis Roberts, 1930- joint author. II. American Anthropological Association. III. T.*
CC65.B5   913.03/1   67-27386

Heizer, Robert Fleming, 1915- ed. III. 172
The archaeologist at work; a source book in archaeological method and interpretation. New York, Harper [1959] xiv, 520 p. illus., maps, diagrs., profiles, tables. 25 cm. *1. Archaeology — Collections. 2. Archaeology — Methodology. I. T.*
CC65.H4   913   58-59878

Science. III. 173
New roads to yesterday; essays in archaeology. Articles from Science, edited by Joseph R. Caldwell. New York, Basic Books [1966] viii, 546 p. illus., maps. 24 cm. *1. Archaeology — Addresses, essays, lectures. I. Caldwell, Joseph Ralston, 1916- ed. II. T.*
CC65.S2   913.03108   65-25225

The Concise encyclopedia of archaeology. III. 174
Edited by Leonard Cottrell. The contributors: P. J. Adams [and others. 1st ed.] New York, Hawthorn Books [1960] 512 p. illus. (part col.) ports., maps. 26 cm. *1. Archaeology — Dictionaries. I. Cottrell, Leonard, ed.*
CC70.C6   913.03   60-10337

CC73 – 77 Methodology

Noël Hume, Ivor. III. 175
Historical archaeology. [1st ed.] New York, Knopf, 1969. xiii, 355, v p. illus. 24 cm. *1. Archaeology — Methodology. I. T.*
CC73.N6 1969   913.03/1028   68-12662

Atkinson, Richard John Copland, 1920- III. 176
Field archaeology. [2d ed., rev.] London, Methuen [1953] 233 p. illus. 19 cm. *1. Archaeology — Methodology. 2. Excavations (Archaeology) I. T.*
CC75.A8 1953   913   54-36205

Brothwell, Don R., ed. III. 177
Science in archaeology; a survey of progress and research. Edited by Don Brothwell and Eric Higgs. With a foreword by Grahame Clark. Rev. and enl. ed. New York, Praeger [1970] 720 p. illus., maps, plates. 26 cm. *1. Archaeology — Methodology. I. Higgs, Eric S., joint ed. II. T.*
CC75.B73 1970   913.03/1/018   76-92580

Childe, Vere Gordon, 1892- III. 178
Piecing together the past; the interpretation of archæological data. New York, Praeger [1956] 176 p. illus. 23 cm. *1. Archaeology — Methodology. I. T.*
CC75.C45   913   55-11524

Clark, John Grahame Douglas. III. 179
Archaeology and society; reconstructing the prehistoric past. [3d ed. rev. and reset] London, Methuen; New York, Barnes & Noble [1960] 272 p. illus. 21 cm. (University paperbacks, UP-10) *1. Archaeology. I. T.*
CC75.C5 1960   913   61-3382

Clarke, David L. III. 180
Analytical archaeology [by] David L. Clarke. London, Methuen, 1968. iii-xx, 684 p. 2 plates, illus., forms, maps. 24 cm. "Distributed in the U.S.A. by Barnes & Noble, Inc." *1. Archaeology — Methodology. I. T.*
CC75.C535   913.03/1/018   68-143156

Coon, Carleton Stevens, 1904- III. 181
The seven caves; archaeological explorations in the Middle East. [1st ed.] New York, Knopf, 1957 [c1956] 338 p. illus. 22 cm. *1. Caves. 2. Excavations (Archaeology) I. T.*
CC75.C6   913.56 (956)   56-8918

Dating techniques for the archaeologist. III. 182
Coedited by Henry N. Michael and Elizabeth K. Ralph. Cambridge, MIT Press [1971] xi, 226 p. illus. 24 cm. *1. Archaeology — Methodology. I. Michael, Henry N., ed. II. Ralph, Elizabeth K., ed.*
CC75.D36   913.03/10285   79-153296   ISBN:0262130742

Heizer, Robert Fleming, 1915- ed. III. 183
The application of quantitative methods in archaeology, edited by Robert F. Heizer and Sherburne F. Cook. Chicago, Quadrangle Books, 1960. x, 358 p. illus., tables. 26 cm. (Viking Fund publications in anthropology, no.28) Papers presented at an international symposium on the application of quantitative methods in archaeology, held at the Wenner-Gren Foundation for Anthropological Research, Burg Wartenstein, Austria, July 1-9, 1959. *1. Archaeology — Methodology. I. Cook, Sherburne Friend, 1896- joint ed. II. T. (S)*
CC75.H44   913.018   61-987

Heizer, Robert Fleming, 1915- III. 184
A guide to field methods in archaeology; approaches to the anthropology of the dead, by Robert F. Heizer and John A. Graham. With a chapter by Sonia Ragir. [New rev. ed.] Palo Alto, Calif., National Press [1967] ix, 274 p. illus. 27 cm. First published in 1949 under title: A manual of archaeological field methods. *1. Archaeology — Methodology. I. Graham, John Allen, joint author. II. T.*
CC75.H45 1967   913   67-20072

Laet, Siegfried J. de. III. 185
Archaeology and its problems; translated by Ruth Daniel. With a foreword by Glyn E. Daniel. New York, Macmillan [1957] 136 p. illus., plates. 22 cm. *1. Archaeology. I. T.*
CC75.Lx   A57-7365

Oakley, Kenneth Page, 1911- III. 186
Frameworks for dating fossil man [by] Kenneth P. Oakley. Chicago, Aldine Pub. Co. [c1964] x, 355 p. illus.,maps. 23 cm. Errata slip inserted. *1. Archaeology — Methodology. I. T.*
CC75.O15   571.018   64-8452

Piggott, Stuart. III. 187
Approach to archaeology. Cambridge, Harvard University Press, 1959. 134 p. illus. 23 cm. *1. Archaeology. I. T.*
CC75.P5   571   59-16950

Symposium on Archaeological Chemistry, 4th, Atlantic City, 1968. III. 188
Science and archaeology; [papers] Robert H. Brill, editor. Cambridge, Mass., MIT Press [1971] xi, 288 p. illus. (part col.), maps. 29 cm. *1. Archaeology — Methodology — Congresses. 2. Archaeological chemistry — Congresses. I. Brill, Robert H., ed. II. T.*
CC75.S95 1968   913.03/10285   70-113731   ISBN:0262020610

Wheeler, Robert Eric Mortimer, Sir, 1890- III. 189
Archaeology from the earth. Oxford, Clarendon Press, 1954. xi, 221 p. illus., maps (1 fold.) 23 cm. *1. Archaeology — Methodology. I. T.*
CC75.W46   A54-4655

Woolley, Charles Leonard, Sir, 1880- III. 190
Digging up the past. [2d ed.] London, Benn [1954] 125 p. illus. 19 cm. *1. Excavations (Archaeology) I. T.*
CC75.W6 1954   913   54-36891

Deuel, Leo. III. 191
Flights into yesterday; the story of aerial archaeology. Pref. by Glyn Daniel. New York, St. Martin's Press, 1969. xx, 332 p. illus., maps, ports. 22 cm. *1. Aerial photography in archaeology. I. T.*
CC76.A3D4   913/.031/028   73-86386

Bass, George Fletcher. III. 192
Archaeology under water [by] George F. Bass. New York, Praeger [1966] 224 p. illus., maps (1 fold.), ports. 21 cm. (Ancient peoples and places, v. 48) *1. Underwater archaeology. I. T.*
CC77.B3   913.031028   66-12992

Chang, Kwang-chih. III. 193
Rethinking archaeology [by] K. C. Chang. New York, Random House [1967] xiv, 172 p. illus. 19 cm. (Studies in anthropology, AS6) Lectures delivered at an anthropology seminar at Yale University in 1966. *1. Archaeology — Methodology. I. T. (S:Studies in anthropology (New York) AS6)*
CC77.C48   913/.001/8   67-10916

CC100 – 115   History. Biography

Marek, Kurt W. III. 194
Gods, graves, and scholars; the story of archaeology, by C. W. Ceram. Translated from the German by E. B. Garside and Sophie Wilkins. 2d, rev. and substantially enl. ed. New York, Knopf, 1967. xvi, 441 p. illus., maps, 32 plates, ports. 22 cm. Translation of Götter, Gräber, und Gelehrte. *1. Archaeology — History. I. T.*
CC100.M313 1967   913.03/1   67-1119

Mongaĭt, Aleksandr L'vovich. III. 195
Archaeology in the U.S.S.R. [Translated from the Russian by David Skbirsky, Moscow, Foreign Languages Pub. House, 1959. 428 p. illus. (part col.) maps (part fold.) 27 cm. At head of title: Academy of Sciences of the U.S.S.R. Institute of the History of Material Culture. Errata slip inserted. *1. Archaeology — History. 2. Russia — Antiquities. I. T.*
CC105.R9M613   913.47   60-37241

Wheeler, Robert Eric Mortimer, Sir, 1890- III. 196
Still digging; interleaves from an antiquary's notebook. London, M. Joseph [1955] 236 p. illus. 23 cm. *1. Archaeologists — Correspondence, reminiscences, etc. I. T.*
CC115.W58A3 1955   925.71   55-22546

CC160 – 165   General Works

Childe, Vere Gordon, 1892- III. 197
A short introduction to archaeology. London, F. Muller [1956] 142 p. illus. 20 cm. (Man and society series) *1. Archaeology. I. T.*
CC165.C5   913   57-212

Woolley, Charles Leonard, Sir, 1880- III. 198
History unearthed; a survey of eighteen archaeological sites throughout the world. London, E. Benn, 1958. 183 p. illus. 28 cm. *1. Excavations (Archaeology) I. T.*
CC165.W6   913   59-29205

CD – CE   DIPLOMATICS. ARCHIVES. CHRONOLOGY

Stenton, Frank Merry, 1880- III. 199
The Latin charters of the Anglo-Saxon period. Oxford, Clarendon Press, 1955. 103 p. 20 cm. *1. Gt. Brit. — Charters, grants, privileges. 2. Land grants — Gt. Brit. I. T.*
CD79.G7S8   942.01   55-2614

Harmer, Florence Elizabeth, ed. and tr. III. 200
Anglo-Saxon writs. [Manchester, Eng.] Manchester University Press [1952] xxii, 604 p. illus. 22 cm. (The Ward bequest, v.10) *1. Writs — Gt. Brit. I. T. (S:Victoria University of Manchester. Ward Bequest. Publications, v.10)*
CD105.H3   942.01   52-10196

Schellenberg, Theodore R., 1903- III. 201
The management of archives [by] T. R. Schellenberg. New York, Columbia University Press, 1965. xvi, 383 p. 24 cm. (Columbia University studies in library service, no. 14) *1. Archives. I. T. (S)*
CD950.S29   025.171   65-14409

U. S. National Historical Publications Commission. III. 202
A guide to archives and manuscripts in the United States. Philip M. Hamer, ed. New Haven, Yale University Press, 1961. xxiii, 775 p. 27 cm. *1. Archives — U. S. 2. Manuscripts — U. S. I. Hamer, Philip May, 1891-   , ed. II. T.*
CD3022.A45   025.171   61-6878

Posner, Ernst. III. 203
American state archives. Chicago, London, University of Chicago Press [1964] xiv, 397 p. 25 cm. "Basic bibliography of writings on public archives administration in the United States": p. 377-386. *1. Archives — U.S. I. T.*
CD3024.P6   64-23425

Michels, Agnes Kirsopp. III. 204
The calendar of the Roman Republic. Princeton, N.J., Princeton University Press, 1967. xvi, 227 p. illus. 23 cm. *1. Calendar, Roman. I. T.*
CE46.M5   529/.32/207   67-12349

CJ   NUMISMATICS

Kraay, Colin M. III. 205
Greek coins, by Colin M. Kraay. Photos. by Max Hirmer. New York, H. N. Abrams [1966] 396 p. maps, plates (part mounted col.) 31 cm. *I. Hirmer, Max. II. T.*
CJ335.K7   737.49495   66-13272

Seltman, Charles Theodore, 1886- III. 206
Greek coins; a history of metallic currency and coinage down to the fall of the Hellenistic kingdoms. [2d ed.] London, Methuen [1955] xxvi, 311 p. illus., maps. 23 cm. (Methuen's handbooks of archaeology) *1. Coinage — Greece — History. 2. Coins, Greek. I. T.*
CJ335.S4 1955   737.4   55-2059

Grant, Michael, 1914- III. 207
Roman history from coins; some uses of the imperial coinage to the historian. Cambridge [Eng.] University Press, 1958. 95 p. plates. 20 cm. *1. Numismatics, Roman. 2. Rome — History. I. T.*
CJ833.Gx   A58-5633

Mattingly, Harold, 1884-1964. III. 208
Roman coins from the earliest times to the fall of the Western Empire. Reprinted with further corrections and additional notes. London, Methuen, 1967. xiv, 305 p. 64 plates. 22 cm. Distributed in the U.S.A. by Barnes & Noble. *1. Numismatics, Roman. 2. Coinage — Rome — History. I. T.*
CJ833.M3 1967   737.493   67-98240

CN   INSCRIPTIONS

Cleator, Philip Ellaby, 1908- III. 209
Lost languages. [1st American ed.] New York, John Day Co. [1961] 192 p. illus. 22 cm. *1. Inscriptions. I. T.*
CN120.C55 1961   419.25   61-8278

Woodhead, Arthur Geoffrey. III. 210
The study of Greek inscriptions. Cambridge [Eng.] University Press, 1959. 138 p. illus. 22 cm. *1. Inscriptions, Greek.*
CN350.W65   481.7   59-16150

Meiggs, Russell. III. 211
A selection of Greek historical inscriptions to the end of the fifth century B.C.; edited by Russell Meiggs and David Lewis. Oxford, Clarendon P., 1969. xix, 308 p. 23 cm. English and Greek. *1. Inscriptions, Greek. I. Lewis, David Malcolm, joint author. II. T.*
CN360.M4   70-418962   ISBN:198142668

Ventris, Michael. III. 212
Documents in Mycenaean Greek; three hundred selected tablets from Knossos, Pylos, and Mycenae with commentary and vocabulary by Michael

Ventris and John Chadwick. With a foreword by Alan J. B. Wace. Cambridge [Eng.] University Press, 1956. xxx, 452 p. illus., plans. 26 cm. *1. Inscriptions, Linear B. I. Chadwick, John, 1920- joint author. II. T.*
CN362.V4   481.7   57-404

CR HERALDRY

Franklyn, Julian. III. 213
An encyclopaedic dictionary of heraldry, by Julian Franklyn and John Tanner. Illustrated by Violetta Keeble. [1st ed.] Oxford, New York, Pergamon Press [1970] xiii, 367 p. illus. (part col.) 26 cm. *1. Heraldry — Dictionaries. I. Tanner, John, 1927- joint author. II. T.*
CR13.F7 1970   929.6/03   79-15403   ISBN:080132979

Boutell, Charles, 1812-1877. III. 214
Boutell's Heraldry. Revised by J. P. Brooke-Little. [Rev. ed.] London, New York, F. Warne [1970] xii, 343 p. illus., coats of arms, col. plates. 24 cm. *1. Heraldry. 2. Heraldry — Great Britain. I. Brooke-Little, John Phillip, ed.*
CR21.B7 1970   929.6   72-477199   ISBN:0723211205

Franklyn, Julian. III. 215
Shield and crest: an account of the art and science of heraldry; with a foreword by A. C. T. White, illustrated by Norman Manwaring with shields and crests current in the XXth century. 3rd ed. London, MacGibbon & Kee, 1967. xvii, 521 p. col. front., illus., 16 plates. 22 1/2 cm. *1. Heraldry. I. T.*
CR21.F76 1967   929.6   67-94354

Allcock, Hubert. III. 216
Heraldic design, its origins, ancient forms and modern usage. New York, Tudor Pub. Co. [1962] 96 p. illus. 28 cm. *1. Heraldry. I. T.*
CR27.A5   929.6   62-19117

Child, Heather. III. 217
Heraldic design; a handbook for students. With a foreword by A. Colin Cole. London, G. Bell [1965] 180 p. illus., coats of arms, facsims. 26 cm. On label mounted on t.p.: Distributed by Heraldic Book Co., Baltimore. *1. Heraldry. 2. Heraldry, Ornamental. I. T.*
CR31.C5   745.66   66-21223

Fairbairn, James, comp. III. 218
Fairbairn's Book of crests of the families of Great Britain and Ireland. Reprint of the 4th ed., rev. and enl. Baltimore, Heraldic Book Co., 1968. 2 v. in 1. illus. 25 cm. Vol. 1, text; v. 2, plates. *1. Heraldry — Great Britain. 2. Heraldry — Ireland. 3. Crests. I. Book of crests of the families of Great Britain and Ireland. II. T.*
CR57.G7F2 1968   929.8   68-18941

Elvin, Charles Norton. III. 219
A hand-book of mottoes borne by the nobility, gentry, cities, public companies, &c. With an added index and a suppl. Translated and illustrated with notes and quotations by C. N. Elvin. Baltimore, Genealogical Pub. Co., 1971. xi, 294 p. 20 cm. "Originally published 1860." *1. Mottoes. I. T.*
CR75.G7E5 1971   929.6   70-151294   ISBN:0806304812

Flags of the world; with 370 flags in full colour and over 375 text drawings. III. 220
Edited by E. M. Barraclough. London, New York, F. Warne [c1969] ix, 284 p. illus., 40 col. plates. 24 cm. Based on The flags of the world: their history, blazonry, and associations, by F. Edward Hulme, published in 1897. *1. Flags. I. Barraclough, E. M. C., ed. II. Hulme, Frederick Edward, 1841-1909. The flags of the world: their history, blazonry and associations.*
CR101.F55 1969   929.9   68-22445

Pedersen, Christian Fogd. III. 221
The international flag book in color. Color plates: Wilhelm Petersen. Editor of the English language edition: John Bedells. [Translated by Frederick and Christine Crowley] New York, Morrow [1971] 237 p. illus. (part col.), coats of arms (part col.) 19 cm. Translation of Alverdens flag i farver. *1. Flags. I. T.*
CR109.P413 1971   929.9   73-136268

Eggenberger, David. III. 222
Flags of the U.S.A. Enl. ed. New York, Crowell [1964] 222 p. illus. (part col.) 21 cm. *1. Flags — United States.*
CR113.E35 1964   929.90973   64-12115

Pine, Leslie Gilbert. III. 223
International heraldry, by L. G. Pine. [1st ed.] Rutland, Vt., C. E. Tuttle Co. [1970] 244 p. illus., coats of arms. 23 cm. *1. Heraldry. I. T.*
CR191.P55 1970b   929.6   72-109405   ISBN:0804809003

Rietstap, Johannes Baptist, 1828-1891. III. 224
Armorial général. Baltimore, Genealogical Pub. Co., 1965. 2 v. illus., coats of arms. 24 cm. "Reprinted from the edition of 1950." *1. Heraldry — Dictionaries. I. T.*
CR1179.R52 1965a   929.603   65-21472

Rolland, Victor, 1843-1912. III. 225
V. & H. V. Rolland's illustrations to the Armorial général by J. B. Riestap. Baltimore, Heraldic Book Co., 1967. 6 v. in 3. illus. 29 cm. Originally published in 1903-1926. Translation of Armoiries des familles contenues dans l'Armorial général de J. B. Rietstap. *1. Heraldry. I. Rolland, Henri, 1887- II. Rietstap, Johannes Baptist, 1828-1891. Armorial général.*
CR1179.R653   66-29998

Burke, John Bernard, Sir, 1814-1892. III. 226
The general armory of England, Scotland, Ireland, and Wales; comprising a registry of armorial bearings from the earliest to the present time. With a supplement. Baltimore, Genealogical Pub. Co., 1969. cxxx, 1185 p. illus., coats of arms. 27 cm. Reprint of the 1884 ed. First ed., by J. Burke and Sir J. B. Burke, published in 1842 under title: A general armory of England, Scotland, and Ireland. Cf. BM. *1. Heraldry — Great Britain. I. Burke, John, 1787-1842. A general armory of England, Scotland, and Ireland. II. T.*
CR1619.B73 1969   929.8   73-11215

Measures, Howard, 1894- III. 227
Styles of address; a manual of usage in writing and in speech. 3d ed. New York, St. Martin's Press [1970, c1969] vii, 161 p. 23 cm. *1. Forms of address. I. T.*
CR3515.M4 1970   395   72-85142

[Armiger] pseud. III. 228
Titles and forms of address; a guide to their correct use. 10th ed. London, A. & C. Black [1958] 164 p. 19 cm. First ed. published in 1918 under title: Titles, being a guide to the right use of British titles and honours, by Armiger. *1. Great Britain — Peerage. 2. Titles of honor and nobility — Great Britain. 3. Forms of address. I. T.*
CR3891.A7 1958   929.7   59-575

CR4501 – 4595   Chivalry

Painter, Sidney, 1902- III. 229
French chivalry; chivalric ideas and practices in mediaeval France, by Sidney Painter. Baltimore, The Johns Hopkins Press, 1940. ix, 179 p. 22 cm. *1. Chivalry. 2. France — Civilization — History. 3. Civilization, Medieval. I. T. II. T:Chivalric ideas and practices in mediaeval France.*
CR4529.F8P3   914.4   40-8951

CS GENEALOGY. FAMILY HISTORIES

Doane, Gilbert Harry, 1897- III. 230
Searching for your ancestors; the how and why of genealogy. 3d ed. Minneapolis, University of Minnesota Press [1960] 198 p. illus. 23 cm. *1. Genealogy. 2. Genealogy — Bibliography. 3. U.S. — History — Revolution — Registers, lists, etc. — Bibliography. I. T.*
CS16.D6 1960   929.1   60-12200

Whittemore, Henry, b. 1833. III. 231
Genealogical guide to the early settlers of America, with a brief history of those of the first generation and references to the various local histories, and other sources of information where additional data may be found. Baltimore, Genealogical Pub. Co., 1967. 438 p. coats of arms. 26 cm. "Excerpted and reprinted from the Spirit of '76, volumes 5-12, September, 1898-June, 1906." *1. U.S. — Genealogy. I. Spirit of '76 (New York) II. T.*
CS61.W5   929.2/0973   67-23072

Bowen, Catherine (Drinker) 1897- III. 232
Family portrait. [1st ed.] Boston, Little, Brown [1970] xvi, 301 p. illus., ports. 25 cm. "An Atlantic Monthly Press book." *1. Drinker family. I. T.*
CS71.D77 1970   917.3/03/90922   75-105569

Waters, John J., 1935-   III. 233
The Otis family, in Provincial and Revolutionary Massachusetts [by] John J. Waters, Jr. Chapel Hill, Published for the Institute of Early American History and Culture at Williamsburg, Va., by the University of North Carolina Press [1968] xi, 221 p. illus., maps, ports. 24 cm. *1. Otis family. I. Institute of Early American History and Culture, Williamsburg, Va. II. T.*
CS71.O88 1968   929.2/09744   68-54951

Wagner, Anthony Richard, Sir, 1908-   III. 234
English genealogy. 2d ed., enl. Oxford, Clarendon Press, 1972. xii, 461 p. geneal. tables. 22 cm. *1. Great Britain — Genealogy. I. T.*
CS414.W3 1972   929/.1/0942   72-187811   ISBN:019822334X

Rye, Walter, 1843-1927.   III. 235
Records and record searching; a guide to the genealogist and topographer. 2d ed. London, G. Allen, 1897. Detroit, Gale Research Co., 1969. viii, 253 p. illus. 22 cm. *1. Genealogy. 2. Archives — Great Britain. I. T.*
CS415.R8 1969   929.1/072/042   68-30663

Burke's genealogical and heraldic history of the peerage, baronetage and knightage.   III. 236
London, Burke's Peerage Ltd. [etc.] v. illus., ports., coats of arms (part col.) 20-28 cm. Frequency varies. Began publication in 1826. Title varies: 18 A General and heraldic dictionary of the peerage and baronetage of the British Empire. — 18 -1906, A Genealogical and heraldic dictionary of the peerage and baronetage of the British Empire (varies slightly) — 1907-37, A Genealogical and heraldic history of the peerage and baronetage. Founded by J. Burke; for many years edited by J. B. Burke. Supplement accompanies vol. for 1953. *1. Gt. Brit. — Peerage. 2. Heraldry — Gt. Brit. I. Burke, John, 1787-1848, ed. II. Burke, John Bernard, Sir, 1814-1892.*
CS420.B85   35-32046

Burke, John Bernard, Sir, 1814-1892.   III. 237
A genealogical and heraldic history of the colonial gentry. Baltimore, Genealogical Pub. Co., 1970. 2 v. in 1 (862, xi p.) coats of arms. 23 cm. Cover title: Burke's colonial gentry. Vol. 2 edited by Ashworth P. Burke. Reprint of the 1891-95 ed. *1. Great Britain — Colonies — Genealogy. 2. Heraldry — Great Britain — Colonies. 3. Great Britain — Colonies — Gentry. I. Burke's colonial gentry. II. T.*
CS425.B72   929.7/2   78-119335   ISBN:0806304154

Burke, John Bernard, Sir, 1814-1892.   III. 238
Burke's genealogical and heraldic history of the landed gentry. Edited by Peter Townend. 18th ed. London, Burke's Peerage, 1965-   v. illus. 28 cm. *1. Gt. Brit. — Gentry. 2. Heraldry — Gt. Brit. I. Townend, Peter, ed. II. Genealogical and heraldic history of the landed gentry.*
CS425.B82   929.7205   66-5918

Arthur, William, 1796-1875.   III. 239
An etymological dictionary of family and Christian names; with an essay on their derivation and import. New York, Sheldon, Blakeman, 1857. Detroit, Gale Research Co., 1969. iv, 300 p. 22 cm. *1. Names, Personal. 2. Names — Etymology. I. T.*
CS2309.A7 1969   929.4   68-17911

Withycombe, Elizabeth Gidley, 1902-   III. 240
The Oxford dictionary of English Christian names. 2d ed. Oxford, Clarendon Press, 1950. xlvii, 294 p. 19 cm. *1. Names, Personal — English. I. T.*
CS2375.G7W5 1950   929.4   51-5089

Reaney, Percy Hide.   III. 241
A dictionary of British surnames. London, Routledge and Paul [1958] lix, 366 p. 26 cm. *1. Names, Personal — English. I. T.*
CS2385.R4   929.4   58-3233

Smith, Elsdon Coles, 1903-   III. 242
Dictionary of American family names. [1st ed.] New York, Harper [1956] xxxiv, 244 p. 22 cm. Published in 1972 under title: New dictionary of American family names. *1. Names, Personal — United States. I. American family names.*
CS2481.S55   929.4   56-8766

Smith, Elsdon Coles, 1903-   III. 243
American surnames [by] Elsdon C. Smith. [1st ed.] Philadelphia, Chilton Book Co. [1969] xx, 370 p. 24 cm. *1. Names, Personal — United States. I. T.*
CS2485.S63   929.4   71-85245

Bardsley, Charles Wareing Endell, 1843-1898.   III. 244
English surnames; their sources and significations. Rutland, Vt., C. E. Tuttle Co. [1968] xxix, 612 p. 20 cm. Reprint of the 1889 ed. First ed. published in 1873 under title: Our English surnames. *1. Names, Personal — English. I. T.*
CS2505.B33 1968   929.4   68-18605

Cottle, Basil.   III. 245
The Penguin dictionary of surnames. Harmondsworth, Penguin, 1967. 334 p. 18 1/2 cm. (Penguin reference books, R32) *1. Names, Personal — Gt. Brit. I. T.*
CS2505.C67   929.4   67-112240

Dolan, J. R.   III. 246
English ancestral names; the evolution of the surname from medieval occupations [by] J. R. Dolan. [1st ed.] New York, C. N. Potter; distributed by Crown Publishers [1972] xvi, 381 p. 24 cm. *1. Names, Personal — English. 2. English language — Etymology — Names. I. T.*
CS2505.D65 1972   929.4   73-139349

CT   BIOGRAPHY

Bowen, Catherine (Drinker) 1897-   III. 247
Biography: the craft and the calling. [1st ed.] Boston, Little, Brown [1969] xvi, 174 p. 21 cm. "An Atlantic Monthly Press book." *1. Biography (as a literary form) I. T.*
CT21.B564   808.06/6/92   69-11259

Altick, Richard Daniel, 1915-   III. 248
Lives and letters; a history of literary biography in England and America, by Richard D. Altick. [1st ed.] New York, Knopf, 1965. xvii, 438 p. 25 cm. *1. Biography (as a literary form) I. T.*
CT31.A4   828.08   64-17699

Bayle, Pierre, 1647-1706.   III. 249
Historical and critical dictionary; selections. Translated, with an introd. and notes, by Richard H. Popkins, with the assistance of Craig Brush. Indianapolis, Bobbs-Merrill [1965] xliv, 456 p. 21 cm. (The Library of liberal arts) *1. Biography — Dictionaries. I. T.*
CT95.B333 1965   920.02   64-16703

Current biography yearbook.   III. 250
New York, H. W. Wilson, 1940-   v. ports. 26 cm. Annual. Cumulated from monthly numbers. Title varies: 1940-54, Current biography; who's news and why. Editors: 1940-43, M. Block. — 1944-52, A. Rothe. — 1953- M. D. Candee. Vols. for 1941-50 include indexes cumulative from 1940. Vols. for 1951- include indexes cumulative from 1951. *1. Biography — 20th cent. I. Block, Maxine, ed. II. Rothe, Anna Hertha, ed. III. Candee, Marjorie Dent, 1904- ed. IV. Wilson, H. W., firm, publishers.*
CT100.C8   40-27432

Webster's biographical dictionary; a dictionary of names of noteworthy persons with pronunciations and concise biographies.   III. 251
1st ed. Springfield, Mass., G. & C. Merriam Co. [1971] xxxvi, 1697 p. 26 cm. "A Merriam-Webster." *1. Biography — Dictionaries.*
CT103.W4 1971   920.02   77-23207   ISBN:0877790434

Who's Who in the world.   III. 252
1st- ed.; 1971/72-   Chicago, Marquis Who's Who, Inc. v. 31 cm. *1. Biography — 20th century — Dictionaries.*
CT120.W5   79-139215

The New York times obituaries index, 1858-1968.   III. 253
New York, New York times, 1970. 1136 p. 29 cm. *1. Obituaries — Indexes. I. New York times.*
CT213.N47   929.3   72-113422

Semonche, John E.   III. 254
Ray Stannard Baker; a quest for democracy in modern America, 1870-1918, by John E. Semonche. Chapel Hill, University of North Carolina Press [1969] ix, 350 p. port. 24 cm. *1. Baker, Ray Stannard, 1870-1946.*
CT275.B313S4   070.9/24 (B)   69-16215

Harris, Leon A., 1926-   III. 255
Only to God; the extraordinary life of Godfrey Lowell Cabot [by] Leon Harris. [1st ed.] New York, Atheneum, 1967. xiv, 361 p. ports. 25 cm. *1. Cabot, Godfrey Lowell, 1861-1962. I. T.*
CT275.C13H3   917.3/03/90924 (B)   67-25482

Wall, Joseph Frazier.   III. 256
Andrew Carnegie. New York, Oxford University Press [1970] xii, 1137 p. illus., ports. 24 cm. *1. Carnegie, Andrew, 1835-1919.*
CT275.C3W33   917.3/03/80924 (B)   74-83056

Darrow, Clarence Seward, 1857-1938.   III. 257
The story of my life. New York, Grosset & Dunlap [1957, c1932] 465 p. 21 cm. (Grosset's universal library, UL-27) *1. Lawyers — U.S. — Correspondence, reminiscences, etc. I. T.*
CT275.D2374A3x   923.473   57-3510

Matthiessen, Francis Otto, 1902-   III. 258
The James family, including selections from the writings of Henry James, Senior, William, Henry & Alice James. [1st ed.] New York, A. A. Knopf, 1947. xvi, 706, viii p. ports. 25 cm. *1. James family (William James,*

1771-1832) 2. *James, Henry, 1811-1882.* 3. *James, William, 1842-1910.* 4. *James, Henry, 1843-1916.* 5. *James, Alice, 1848-1892.*
CT275.J28M3   47-11259

James, Alice, 1848-1892.   III. 259
The diary of Alice James. Edited with an introd. by Leon Edel. New York, Dodd, Mead [1964] x, 241 p. facsim., ports. 22 cm. First published in 1934 under title: Alice James, her brothers — her journal. *1. James family.* 2. *James, William, 1842-1910.* 3. *James, Henry, 1843-1916.* 4. *James, Garth Wilkinson, 1845-1883.* 5. *James, Robertson, 1846-1910. I. Edel, Leon, 1907- ed. II. T.*
CT275.J29A3 1964   920.7   64-18879

Mungo, Raymond, 1946-   III. 260
Famous long ago; my life and hard times with Liberation News Service. Boston, Beacon Press [1970] 202 p. illus. 22 cm. *1. Liberation News Service. I. T.*
CT275.M755A3 1970   070/.924 (B)   77-103937   ISBN:807061824

Who's who in Latin America; a biographical dictionary of notable   III. 261
living men and women of Latin America.
Edited by Ronald Hilton. 3d ed. Stanford, Calif., Stanford University Press. Detroit, B. Ethridge, 1971 [c1945] 2 v. 24 cm. *1. Latin America — Biography — Dictionaries. I. Hilton, Ronald, 1911- ed.*
CT506.W48 1971   920.08   76-165656   ISBN:0879170212

Marshall, George N.   III. 262
Schweitzer; a biography, by George Marshall and David Poling. [1st ed.] Garden City, N.Y., Doubleday [1971] xviii, 342 p. illus., ports. 24 cm. *1. Schweitzer, Albert, 1875-1965. I. Poling, David, 1928- joint author.*
CT1098.S45M34   266/.025/0924 (B)   71-130888

Grieder, Jerome B.   III. 263
Hu Shih and the Chinese renaissance; liberalism in the Chinese revolution, 1917-1937 [by] Jerome B. Grieder. Cambridge, Harvard University Press, 1970. xiii, 420 p. illus., ports. 25 cm. (Harvard East Asian series, 46) *1. Hu, Shih, 1891-1962. I. T. (S)*
CT1828.H8G75   181/.11 (B)   78-106958   ISBN:674412508

Mphahlele, Ezekiel.   III. 264
Down Second Avenue. [1st ed.] Garden City, N.Y., Anchor Books, 1971 [c1959] xxvi, 210 p. 19 cm. *I. T.*
CT1929.M66A3 1971   916.8/06/96 (B)   75-139080

CT3200 – 3830   Women

Bradford, Gamaliel, 1863-1932.   III. 265
Portraits of American women. Freeport, N.Y., Books for Libraries Press [1969, c1919] x, 276 p. ports. 23 cm. (Essay index reprint series) *1. Women in New England — Biography. I. T.*
CT3260.B74 1969   917.4/0922 (B)   69-17564   ISBN:0836900049

Bradford, Gamaliel, 1863-1932.   III. 266
Wives. New York, Arno Press, 1972 [c1925] xiii, 298 p. ports. 23 cm. (American women: images and realities) *1. Women in the United States — Biography. I. T. (S)*
CT3260.B743 1972   920.7/2   72-2591   ISBN:0405044488

Notable American women, 1607-1950; a biographical dictionary.   III. 267
Edward T. James, editor. Janet Wilson James, associate editor. Paul S. Boyer, assistant editor. Cambridge, Mass., Belknap Press of Harvard University Press, 1971. 3 v. 27 cm. "Prepared under the auspices of Radcliffe College." *1. Women in the United States — Biography. I. James, Edward T., ed. II. James, Janet Wilson, 1918- ed. III. Boyer, Paul S., ed. IV. Radcliffe College.*
CT3260.N57   920.72/0973   76-152274   ISBN:0674627318

Who's who of American women; a biographical dictionary of   III. 268
notable living American women.
v.1-   ; 1958/59-   . Chicago, Marquis Who's who. v. 28 cm. biennial. *1. Women in the United States — Biography.*
CT3260.W5   920.7   58-13264

D1 – 847 History: General

D1 – 24 GENERAL WORKS. COLLECTIONS

The Annual register of world events; a review of the year. 1758-   **III. 269**
London, New York, Longmans, Green [etc.] v. in maps. 21-23 cm. Vols. for 1784-85 issued in combined form; 1820, in 2 pts. Vols. for 1863-1946 called new ser. Vols. for 1920- called v.162- Some vols. in rev. editions. Title varies, 1758-1953, The Annual register. Subtitle varies. Originated with Robert Dodsley, at the suggestion of Edmund Burke, who was for some years editor and principal contributor. Some time after 1791, the copyright and stock were purchased by Otridge and other booksellers. Messrs. Rivington published a rival continuation, which lasted from 1791 to 1812, and again from 1820 to 1824, when the two were merged into one. Cf. Lowndes. Bibliographer's manual, v.1. INDEXES: 1758-80. 1 v. 1758-1819. 1 v. 1781-92. 1 v. *1. History — Yearbooks. I. Burke, Edmund, 1729?-1797, ed.*
D2.A7   04-17979

Cheyney, Edward Potts, 1861-1947.   **III. 270**
The dawn of a new era, 1250-1453, by Edward P. Cheyney. [1st ed.] New York, Harper, 1936. x, 389 p. illus., maps, plates, ports. 23 cm. (The rise of modern Europe. [I]) Maps on lining-papers. *1. Europe — History — 476-1492. I. T.*
D6.R5 vol. 1   940.18   36-3968

Gilmore, Myron Piper, 1910-   **III. 271**
The world of humanism, 1453-1517. [1st ed.] New York, Harper [1952] xv, 326 p. illus., ports., maps. 23 cm. (The Rise of modern Europe [2]) *1. Renaissance. 2. Humanism. I. T. (S)*
D6.R5 vol. 2   940.2   52-11685

Friedrich, Carl Joachim, 1901-   **III. 272**
The age of the baroque, 1610-1660. [1st ed.] New York, Harper [1952] xv, 367 p. illus., ports., maps (on lining paper) 22 cm. (The Rise of modern Europe [v.5]) *1. Europe — History — 17th cent. I. T. (S)*
D6.R5 vol. 5   940.22   52-5435

Nussbaum, Frederick Louis, 1885-   **III. 273**
The triumph of science and reason, 1660-1685. [1st ed.] New York, Harper [1953] xiv, 304 p. illus., ports., map (on lining papers) 22 cm. (The Rise of modern Europe [6]) *1. Europe — History — 1648-1715. 2. Seventeenth century. I. T. (S)*
D6.R5 vol. 6   940.22   52-7295

Wolf, John Baptist, 1907-   **III. 274**
The emergence of the great powers, 1685-1715. [1st ed.] New York, Harper [1951] xv, 336 p. illus., ports., map (on lining papers) 22 cm. (The Rise of modern Europe [7]) *1. Europe — Politics — 1648-1715. 2. Europe — Intellectual life. I. T. (S)*
D6.R5 vol. 7   940.2   51-12900

Roberts, Penfield, 1892-1944.   **III. 275**
The quest for security, 1715-1740, by Penfield Roberts. New York, Harper, 1947. x, 300 p. front. (facsim.) plates, ports. 22 cm. (The Rise of modern Europe, ed. by W. L. Langer. [Vol.VIII]) The plates, which precede t.-p., have half-title: Fifty-four illustrations drawn from unusual sources and specially chosen by the author. Map on lining-papers. "First edition." *1. Europe — History — 18th cent. I. T.*
D6.R5 vol. 8   940.22   47-3219

Gershoy, Leo, 1897-   **III. 276**
From despotism to revolution, 1763-1789, by Leo Gershoy. [1st ed.] New York, Harper, 1944. xvi, 355 p. fronts. (incl. ports.) 23 cm. (The Rise of modern Europe, ed. by W. L. Langer. [x]) Maps on lining-papers. *1. Europe — History — 1648-1789. I. T.*
D6.R5 vol. 10 (D289.G4)   940.22   44-5542

Brinton, Clarence Crane, 1898-   **III. 277**
A decade of revolution, 1789-1799, by Crane Brinton. [1st ed.] New York and London, Harper & brothers, 1934. x, 330 p. plates, ports., maps. 23 cm. (The Rise of modern Europe, [vol.XI]) Maps on lining-papers. *1. France — History — Revolution, 1789-1799. 2. Europe — History — 1789-1815. I. T.*
D6.R5 vol. 11   944.04   34-33841

Bruun, Geoffrey, 1898-   **III. 278**
Europe and the French imperium, 1799-1814, by Geoffrey Bruun. New York and London, Harper, 1938. xiv p., 280 p. illus. (maps) plates, ports. 23 cm. (The Rise of modern Europe [vol. XII]) Maps on lining-papers. The plates, which precede t.-p., have half-title. Sixty-two illustrations drawn from unusual sources and specially chosen by the author. "First edition." *1. Napoléon I, emperor of the French, 1769-1821. 2. Europe — History — 1789-1815. 3. France — History — Consulate and empire, 1799-1815. I. T.*
D6.R5 vol.12   940.27   38-12852

Langer, William Leonard, 1896-   **III. 279**
Political and social upheaval, 1832-1852, by William L. Langer. [1st ed.] New York, Harper & Row [1969] xviii, 674 p. illus., maps, ports. 22 cm. (The Rise of modern Europe [14]) *1. Europe — Politics — 1815-1848. 2. Europe — Social conditions. 3. Europe — Economic conditions. I. T. (S)*
D6.R5 vol. 14   940.2/83   69-17284

Binkley, Robert Cedric, 1897-1940.   **III. 280**
Realism and nationalism, 1852-1871, by Robert C. Binkley. 1st ed. New York and London, Harper, 1935. xx, 337 p. plates, ports., maps. 23 cm. (The Rise of modern Europe, [vol.XV]) Maps on lining-papers. *1. Europe — History — 1848-1871. I. T.*
D6.R5 vol. 15   940.28   36-11

Hayes, Carlton Joseph Huntley, 1882-   **III. 281**
A generation of materialism, 1871-1900, by Carlton J. H. Hayes. 1st ed. New York and London, Harper, 1941. xii p., 390 p. illus. (maps) plates, ports. 23 cm. (The Rise of modern Europe. [Vol.XVI]) Maps on lining-papers. *1. Europe — History — 1871-1918. 2. Europe — History — Philosophy. I. T.*
D6.R5 vol. 16   940.28   41-22911

Hale, Oron James.   **III. 282**
The great illusion, 1900-1914, by Oron J. Hale. [1st ed.] New York, Harper & Row [c1971] xv, 361 p. illus., maps, ports. 22 cm. (The Rise of modern Europe [17] *1. Europe — History — 1871-1918. I. T. (S)*
D6.R5 vol. 17   914/.03/288   76-123933

Sontag, Raymond James, 1897-   **III. 283**
A broken world, 1919-1939, by Raymond J. Sontag. [1st ed.] New York, Harper & Row [1971] xviii, 415 p. illus., maps (on lining papers), ports. 23 cm. (The Rise of modern Europe, 19) *1. Europe — History — 1918-1945. I. T. (S)*
D6.R5 vol. 19 (D720)   940.5   77-156572   ISBN:0060139544

Wright, Gordon, 1912-   **III. 284**
The ordeal of total war, 1939-1945. [1st ed.] New York, Harper & Row [1968] xv, 315 p. illus., maps, ports. 22 cm. (The Rise of modern Europe, 20) *1. World War, 1939-1945. 2. Europe — History — 1918-1945. I. T. (S)*
D6.R5 vol. 20   940.53   68-28221

Braudel, Fernand.   **III. 285**
Écrits sur l'histoire. [Paris] Flammarion [1969] 314 p. 18 cm. (Science de l'histoire) *1. History — Addresses, essays, lectures. I. T.*
D7.B75   72-448385

Huizinga, Johan, 1872-1945.   **III. 286**
Men and ideas: history, the Middle Ages, the Renaissance; essays. Translated by James S. Holmes and Hans van Marle. New York, Meridian Books [1959] 378 p. 19 cm. (Meridian books, M61) "Translated from texts in 'Verzamelde werken' (1948-53)" *1. History — Collected works. I. T.*
D7.H823   940.1   59-7177

Kohn, Hans, 1891-   **III. 287**
Reflections on modern history; the historian and human responsibility. Princeton, N.J., D. Van Nostrand [1963] xvi, 360 p. 24 cm. *1. History, Modern — Addresses, essays, lectures. I. T.*
D7.K73   908   63-6466

Mommsen, Theodor Ernst, 1905-1958.   **III. 288**
Medieval and Renaissance studies. Edited by Eugene F. Rice, Jr. Ithaca, N.Y., Cornell University Press [1959] xiii, 353 p. group port. 24 cm. *1.*

III. 289　　　　　　　　　　　　　History: General　　　　　　　　　　　　　　D7

Petrarca, Francesco, 1304-1374 — Addresses, essays, lectures. 2. Italy — History — Addresses, essays, lectures. 3. Christian literature, Early — Addresses, essays, lectures. I. T.
D7.M77　　908.1　　60-125

Schmitt, Bernadotte Everly, 1886-　　　　　　　　　　　　III. 289
The fashion and future of history; historical studies and addresses. Cleveland, Press of Western Reserve University, 1960. 205 p. 24 cm. *1. History, Modern — Addresses, essays, lectures. I. T.*
D7.S323　　909.8　　60-15088

Trevor-Roper, Hugh Redwald.　　　　　　　　　　　　III. 290
Men and events; historical essays. New York, Harper [1957] 324 p. 22 cm. London ed. (Macmillan) has title: Historical essays. *1. History — Addresses, essays, lectures. I. T.*
D7.T79 1957a　　904　　58-6157

Wedgwood, Cicely Veronica, 1910-　　　　　　　　　　　　III. 291
The sense of the past. [London] Cambridge University Press, 1957. 26 p. 19 cm. (The Leslie Stephen lecture, 1957) *1. James, Henry, 1843-1916. The sense of the past. 2. History — Addresses, essays, lectures. I. T.*
D8.W4　　58-1771

D11　Chronology

Delorme, Jean.　　　　　　　　　　　　III. 292
Chronologie des civilisations. [2. ed.] Paris, Presses Universitaires de France, 1956. xiv, 453 p. 24 cm. (Clio; introduction aux études historiques) *1. Chronology, Historical.*
D11.D38x　　A57-2985

Mayer, Alfred, 1888- comp.　　　　　　　　　　　　III. 293
Annals of European civilization, 1501-1900. Foreword by G. P. Gooch. London, Cassell [1949] xxii, 457 p. 23 cm. "Annals" (p. [43]-305) gives in chronological order the principal events of European cultural history. "Summaries" (p. [307]-457) presents them in their special contexts according to subjects. *1. Chronology, Historical — Tables. 2. Europe — Civilization — History.*
D11.M3x　　A50-6559

Putnam, George Palmer, 1814-1872, comp.　　　　　　　　　　　　III. 294
Dictionary of events, a handbook of universal history; a series of chronological tables presenting, in parallel columns, a record of the noteworthy events of history from the earliest times to the present day, together with an index of subjects and genealogical tables, compiled by George Palmer Putnam, and George Haven Putnam, and associates. New York, Grosset & Dunlap [c1936] vi, 565, [71] p. geneal. tables. 21 cm. Previously published under titles: Tabular views of universal history; Putnam's handbook of universal history; Putnam's dictionary of events. *1. Chronology, Historical — Tables. I. Putnam, George Haven, 1844-1930, joint comp.*
D11.P97 1936　　902　　36-11557

Steinberg, Sigfrid Henry, 1899-　　　　　　　　　　　　III. 295
Historical tables: 58 B.C.-A.D. 1965, by S. H. Steinberg; with a foreword by G. P. Gooch. 8th ed. London, Melbourne [etc.] Macmillan; New York, St. Martin's P., 1966. x, 261 p. 22 cm. (Papermac, 156) *1. Chronology, Historical — Tables. I. T.*
D11.S83 1966　　902/.02　　67-77988

Collison, Robert Lewis.　　　　　　　　　　　　III. 296
Dictionary of dates, compiled by Robert Collison. New York, Greenwood Press [1969, c1961] 428 p. 23 cm. Title on spine: Newnes dictionary of dates. London editions published 1962- under title: Newnes dictionary of dates. *1. Calendars. 2. Anniversaries — Dictionaries. I. Newnes dictionary of dates. II. T.*
D11.5.C6 1969　　902/.02　　77-95116　　ISBN:837124956

D13 – 15　Historiography

Barnes, Harry Elmer, 1889-　　　　　　　　　　　　III. 297
A history of historical writing. 2d rev. ed. New York, Dover Publications [1962] 440 p. illus. 22 cm. *1. Historiography. I. T.*
D13.B32 1962　　907.2　　62-53030

Barraclough, Geoffrey, 1908-　　　　　　　　　　　　III. 298
History in a changing world. Oxford, Blackwell, 1955. viii, 246 p. 22 cm. *1. Historiography. I. T.*
D13.B33　　907　　A56-2540

Barzun, Jacques, 1907-　　　　　　　　　　　　III. 299
The modern researcher [by] Jacques Barzun & Henry F. Graff. Rev. ed. New York, Harcourt, Brace & World [1970] xvii, 430 p. 22 cm. *1. Historiography. 2. Technical writing. I. Graff, Henry Franklin, 1921- joint author. II. T.*
D13.B334 1970　　907.2　　72-115861　　ISBN:151614822

Becker, Carl Lotus, 1873-1945.　　　　　　　　　　　　III. 300
Detachment and the writing of history: essays and letters of Carl L. Becker. Edited by Phil L. Snyder. Westport, Conn., Greenwood Press [1972, c1958] xvi, 240 p. 22 cm. *1. Historiography — Addresses, essays, lectures. I. T.*
D13.B38 1972　　907/.2　　70-152590　　ISBN:0837160235

Bloch, Marc Léopold Benjamin, 1886-1944.　　　　　　　　　　　　III. 301
The historian's craft; introd. by Joseph R. Strayer. Translated from the French by Peter Putnam. [1st American ed.] New York, Knopf, 1953. 197 p. 20 cm. Translation of Apologie pour l'histoire. *1. Historiography. I. T.*
D13.B5613　　907　　52-12182

Butterfield, Herbert, 1900-　　　　　　　　　　　　III. 302
Man on his past; the study of the history of historical scholarship. Cambridge [Eng.] University Press, 1955. xvi, 237 p. 22 cm. (The Wiles lectures, 1954) *1. Historiography. I. T. (S)*
D13.B79　　907　　55-13806

Butterfield, Herbert, 1900-　　　　　　　　　　　　III. 303
The whig interpretation of history, by H. Butterfield. London, G. Bell, 1931. vi, 132 p. 20 cm. *1. History — Historiography. I. T.*
D13.B8　　31-35009

Collingwood, Robin George, 1889-1943.　　　　　　　　　　　　III. 304
The idea of history, by R. G. Collingwood. Oxford, Clarendon Press, 1946. xxvi, 339 p. 23 cm. Based on lectures written in 1936 on the philosophy of history. cf. Editor's preface signed: T. M. Knox. *1. Historiography. 2. History — Philosophy. I. Knox, Thomas Malcolm, 1900- ed. II. T.*
D13.C6　　907　　47-113

Croce, Benedetto, 1866-1952.　　　　　　　　　　　　III. 305
History as the story of liberty. [Translated by Sylvia Sprigge] Chicago, Regnery [1970] 320 p. 21 cm. "A Gateway edition." Translation of La storia come pensiero e come azione. *1. Historiography. 2. History — Philosophy. I. T.*
D13.C682 1970　　907/.2　　71-105123

Croce, Benedetto, 1866-1952.　　　　　　　　　　　　III. 306
History: its theory and practice. Authorized translation by Douglas Ainslie. New York, Russell & Russell, 1960. 317 p. 22 cm. Translation of Teoria e storia della storiografia. *1. Historiography.*
D13.C7 1960　　907.2　　60-14177

Fueter, Eduard, 1876-1928.　　　　　　　　　　　　III. 307
Geschichte der neueren Historiographie. 3., um einen Nachtrag verm. Aufl., besorgt von Dietrich Gerhard und Paul Sattler. New York, Johnson Reprint Corp. [1968, c1911] xxii, 670 p. 25 cm. Reprint of the edition published in Munich by R. Oldenbourg in 1936. *1. Historiography. 2. History, Modern — Bibliography. 3. Historians. I. Gerhard, Dietrich, 1896- ed. II. Sattler, Paul, 1901- ed. III. T.*
D13.F77 1968　　74-4546

Gooch, George Peabody, 1873-　　　　　　　　　　　　III. 308
History and historians in the nineteenth century. With a new introd. by the author. Boston, Beacon Press [1959] 547 p. 21 cm. (Beacon paperback no. 76) *1. Historiography. 2. Historians.*
D13.G7 1959　　907.2　　59-6390

Gottschalk, Louis Reichenthal, 1899-　　　　　　　　　　　　III. 309
Understanding history; a primer of historical method [by] Louis Gottschalk. 2d ed. New York, Knopf [1969] xix, 310, vi p. 21 cm. *1. Historiography. I. T.*
D13.G75 1969　　907.2　　69-10669

Hexter, Jack H., 1910-　　　　　　　　　　　　III. 310
Reappraisals in history. [Evanston, Ill.] Northwestern University Press, 1961. 214 p. 23 cm. *1. Historiography. 2. Great Britain — History — Addresses, essays, lectures. I. T.*
D13.H42 1961a　　907.2　　61-17740

Higham, John.　　　　　　　　　　　　III. 311
History [by] John Higham, with Leonard Krieger and Felix Gilbert. Englewood Cliffs, N.J., Prentice-Hall [1965] xiv, 402 p. 22 cm. (The Princeton studies: humanistic scholarship in America) *1. Historiography. I. Krieger, Leonard. II. Gilbert, Felix, 1905- (S)*
D13.H43　　907.2　　64-23563

Jaspers, Karl, 1883-　　　　　　　　　　　　III. 312
The origin and goal of history. [Translated from the German by Michael

Bullock] New Haven, Yale University Press, 1953. 294 p. 23 cm. *1. Historiography. I. T.*
D13.J314 1953a   907   53-11595

Lefebvre, Georges, 1874-1959.   III. 313
La naissance de l'historiographie moderne. Préf. de Guy P. Palmade. Paris, Flammarion [1971] 348 p. 21 cm. (Nouvelle bibliothèque scientifique) Previously published under title: Notions d'historiographie moderne. *1. Historiography — History. I. T.*
D13.L45 1971   78-854244

Momigliano, Arnaldo.   III. 314
Studies in historiography. New York, Harper & Row [1966] viii, 263 p. 21 cm. (Harper torchbooks. The Academy library, TB1288) *1. Historians. 2. Historiography — Addresses, essays, lectures. I. T.*
D13.M64 1966a   907.2   66-27622

Neff, Emery Edward, 1892-   III. 315
The poetry of history; the contribution of literature and literary scholarship to the writing of history since Voltaire. New York, Columbia University Press, 1947. viii, 258 p. 22 cm. *1. Literature and history. 2. Historiography. I. T.*
D13.N35   907   47-30933

Salvemini, Gaetano, 1873-   III. 316
Historian and scientist; an essay on the nature of history and the social sciences, by Gaetano Salvemini. Cambridge, Mass., Harvard University Press, 1939. viii, 203 p. 20 cm. "Four lectures delivered in December 1938 at the University of Chicago ... [with] the addition of a section on the sources of historical knowledge, and the lecture 'What is culture?' which has been added as an appendix." — Pref. *1. History — Historiography. 2. Social sciences — Addresses, essays, lectures. I. T.*
D13.S35   907   39-25859

Thompson, James Westfall, 1869-1941.   III. 317
A history of historical writing, by James Westfall Thompson with the collaboration of Bernard J. Holm. Gloucester, Mass., P. Smith, 1967 [c1942] 2 v. illus. 24 cm. *1. Historiography. I. Holm, Bernard J., joint author. II. T.*
D13.T5 1967   907/.2/01821   67-8627

Geyl, Pieter, 1887-   III. 318
Encounters in history. Cleveland, Meridian Books [1962, c1961] 405 p. 19 cm. (Meridian books, M114) *1. Historiography — Addresses, essays, lectures. I. T.*
D13.2.G42   907.2   61-11475

Angus-Butterworth, Lionel Milner.   III. 319
Ten master historians. Freeport, N.Y., Books for Libraries Press [1969, c1961] x, 184 p. ports. 23 cm. (Essay index reprint series) *1. Historians, British. I. T.*
D14.A6 1969   942/.0072/022   69-18919   ISBN:836900006

Schmitt, Bernadotte Everly, 1886- ed.   III. 320
Some historians of modern Europe; essays in historiography, edited by Bernadotte E. Schmitt. Port Washington, N.Y., Kennikat Press [1966, c1942] ix, 533 p. 22 cm. *1. Historians. I. T.*
D14.S35 1966   940.0922   66-25941

Beringause, Arthur F., 1919-   III. 321
Brooks Adams; a biography. [1st ed.] New York, Knopf, 1955. xiii, 404, x p. port. 25 cm. *1. Adams, Brooks, 1848-1927.*
D15.A3B4   928.1   55-8357

Wilkins, Burleigh Taylor.   III. 322
Carl Becker; a biographical study in American intellectual history. Cambridge, M.I.T. Press, 1961. 246 p. illus. 24 cm. *1. Becker, Carl Lotus, 1873-1945. I. T.*
D15.B33W5   928.1   61-7870

Namier, Julia, Lady.   III. 323
Lewis Namier: a biography by Julia Namier. London, New York, Oxford University Press, 1971. xvii, 347 p., 12 plates; illus., 2 maps, ports. 23 cm. *1. Namier, Lewis Bernstein, Sir, 1888-1960.*
D15.N3N35 1971   907/.2/024 (B)   76-852488   ISBN:0192117068

Von Laue, Theodore Hermann.   III. 324
Leopold Ranke, the formative years. Princeton, Princeton University Press, 1950. ix, 230 p. port. 23 cm. (Princeton studies in history, v.4) *1. Ranke, Leopold von, 1795-1886. (S:Princeton University. Princeton studies in history, v.4)*
D15.R3V6   928.3   50-3230

Brumfitt, J. H.   III. 325
Voltaire, historian. [London] Oxford University Press, 1958. 178 p. 22 cm. (Oxford modern languages and literature monographs) "A shortened version of a doctoral thesis presented in the University of Oxford." *1. Voltaire, François Marie Arouet de, 1694-1778.*
D15.V6B7   907   58-923

D16   Methodology

Bodin, Jean, 1530-1596.   III. 326
Method for the easy comprehension of history. Translated by Beatrice Reynolds. New York, Octagon Books, 1966 [c1945] xxix, 402 p. 24 cm. (Records of civilization: sources and studies, no. 37) *1. History — Study and teaching. 2. History — Methodology. I. Reynolds, Beatrice, 1891- ed. and tr. II. T. (S)*
D16.B642 1966   901.8   66-16000

The Dimensions of quantitative research in history.   III. 327
Edited by William O. Aydelotte, Allan G. Bogue [and] Robert William Fogel. Contributors: William O. Aydelotte [and others. Princeton, N.J.] Princeton University Press [1972] ix, 435 p. illus. 25 cm. (Quantitative studies in history) *1. History — Statistical methods — Addresses, essays, lectures. 2. Social sciences — Statistical methods — Addresses, essays, lectures. I. Aydelotte, William Osgood, ed. II. Bogue, Allan G., ed. III. Fogel, Robert William, ed. (S)*
D16.D47   907/.2   75-166370   ISBN:0691075441

The Dimensions of the past; materials, problems, and opportunities for quantitative work in history.   III. 328
Edited by Val R. Lorwin and Jacob M. Price. New Haven, Yale University Press, 1972. vi, 568 p. 24 cm. "Essays presented to the American Historical Association's Committee on Quantitative Data." *1. History — Statistical methods — Addresses, essays, lectures. I. Lorwin, Val Rogin, 1907- ed. II. Price, Jacob M., ed. III. American Historical Association. Committee on Quantitative Data.*
D16.D48   907/.2073   78-151587

Fischer, David Hackett, 1935-   III. 329
Historians' fallacies; toward a logic of historical thought. [1st ed.] New York, Harper & Row [1970] xxii, 338 p. 24 cm. *1. History — Methodology. I. T.*
D16.F53   901/.8   69-15583

Garraghan, Gilbert Joseph, 1871-1942.   III. 330
A guide to historical method, by Gilbert J. Garraghan; edited by Jean Delanglez. New York, Fordham University Press, 1946. xv, 482 p. diagrs. 24 cm. With this is bound, as issued: Appel, L. Bibliographical citation in the social sciences ... Madison, 1946. *1. History — Methodology. I. Delanglez, Jean, 1896- ed.*
D16.G37   901.8   46-8087

Hughes, Henry Stuart, 1916-   III. 331
History as art and as science; twin vistas on the past. [1st ed.] New York, Harper & Row [1964] xix, 107 p. 20 cm. (World perspectives, v.32) *1. History — Methodology. I. T. (S)*
D16.H775   901.8   63-20291

The Psychoanalytic interpretation of history,   III. 332
edited by Benjamin B. Wolman. Foreword by William L. Langer. New York, Basic Books [1971] x, 240 p. 25 cm. *1. Psychoanalysis in historiography — Addresses, essays, lectures. 2. Stalin, Iosif, 1879-1953. 3. Herzl, Theodor, 1860-1904. 4. Hitler, Adolf, 1889-1945. I. Wolman, Benjamin B., ed.*
D16.P8   907.2/2   71-135561   ISBN:0465065937

Renier, Gustaaf Johannes, 1892-   III. 333
History, its purpose and method. Boston, Beacon Press, 1950. 272 p. 23 cm. *1. History — Philosophy. 2. History — Methodology.*
D16.Rx   A52-9828

Teggart, Frederick John, 1870-1946.   III. 334
Theory and processes of history. Berkeley, University of California Press, 1960. 323 p. 19 cm. A reprint of the edition published by the University of California Press in 1941, containing the author's Theory of history and The processes of history. *1. History — Methodology. 2. Historiography. I. T.*
D16.T32 1960   907   60-16196

White, Morton Gabriel, 1917-   III. 335
Foundations of historical knowledge, by Morton White. [1st ed.] New York, Harper & Row [1965] 299 p. 22 cm. *1. History — Methodology. 2. History — Philosophy. I. T.*
D16.W59   901   64-25124

Seton-Watson, Robert William, 1879-   III. 336
The historian as a political force in central Europe. An inaugural lecture delivered on 2 November 1922 by R. W. Seton-Watson. [London] School of Slavonic Studies in the University of London, King's College [1922] 36 p. 22 cm. *1. Europe — History — Study and teaching. 2. History — Historiography. I. T.*
D16.2.S3   26-1663

Historical study in the west: France, Great Britain, Western Germany, the United States — III. 337
[by] Michel François [and others] With an introd. by Boyd C. Shafer. New York, Appleton-Century-Crofts [1968] viii, 239 p. 22 cm. On cover and spine Shafer's name appears first. *1. History — Study and teaching. I. François, Michel. II. Shafer, Boyd C.*
D16.25.H46   907/.2   68-19485

Steward, Julian Haynes, 1902- — III. 338
Area research, theory and practice. New York, Social Science Research Council, 1950. xix, 164 p. 23 cm. ([Social Science Research Council] Bulletin 63) *1. Area studies. (S)*
D16.25.S8   307   50-14624

Perkins, Dexter, 1889- — III. 339
The education of historians in the United States [by] Dexter Perkins, John L. Snell and Committee on Graduate Education of the American Historical Association. New York, McGraw-Hill, 1962. xiii, 244 p. 22 cm. (The Carnegie series in American education) This study was sponsored by the American Historical Association through its Committee on Graduate Education. *1. History — Study and teaching — U.S. I. American Historical Association. Committee on Graduate Education. II. T. (S)*
D16.3.P4   907   61-16529

Fussner, F. Smith. — III. 340
The historical revolution; English historical writing and thought, 1580-1640. New York, Columbia University Press, 1962. 343 p. 23 cm. *1. Historiography. 2. Historians, English. I. T.*
D16.4.G7F8 1962a   907   62-10147

Shteppa, Konstantin Feodos'evich, 1896-1958. — III. 341
Russian historians and the Soviet State. New Brunswick, N.J., Rutgers University Press [1962] 437 p. 25 cm. *1. History — Study and teaching — Russia. 2. Historians, Russian. I. T.*
D16.4.R9S45   907   61-10266

D16.7 – 16.9 Philosophy of History

D16.7 To 1800

Ibn Khaldūn, 1332-1406. — III. 342
The Muqaddimah, an introduction to history. Translated from the Arabic by Franz Rosenthal. Abridged and edited by N. J. Dawood. [Princeton, N.J.] Princeton University Press [1969] xiv, 465 p. 21 cm. (Bollingen series, 160) Translation of the author's introduction to his Kitāb al-'ibar (romanized form) *1. History — Philosophy. 2. Civilization. I. Rosenthal, Franz, 1914- ed. II. Dawood, N. J., ed. III. T. (S)*
D16.7.I2333 1969   901.9   72-8164

D16.8 1801 –

A – B

Adams, Henry, 1838-1918. — III. 343
The degradation of the democratic dogma. With an introd. by Brooks Adams. New York, P. Smith, 1949. 317 p. 21 cm. *1. Adams, John Quincy, Pres. U.S., 1767-1848. 2. History — Philosophy. 3. Science. I. Democratic dogma. II. T.*
D16.8.A2x   A50-9750

Arendt, Hannah. — III. 344
Between past and future, six exercises in political thought. New York, Viking Press, 1961. 246 p. 22 cm. *1. History — Philosophy. I. T.*
D16.8.A65   901   61-7281

Ariès, Philippe. — III. 345
Le temps de l'histoire. Monaco, Éditions du Rocher [1954] 325 p. 19 cm. *1. History — Philosophy. I. T.*
D16.8.A67   54-29857

Aron, Raymond, 1905- — III. 346
The dawn of universal history; translated from the French by Dorothy Pickles. New York, Praeger [1961] 70 p. 21 cm. (Praeger paperbacks, PPS-40. Books that matter.) "Based on the fourth Herbert Samuel lecture delivered on 18th February, 1960, under the auspices of the British Friends of the Hebrew University of Jerusalem." *1. History — Philosophy. I. T.*
D16.8.A693   901   61-7815

Aron, Raymond, 1905- — III. 347
Introduction to the philosophy of history; an essay on the limits of historical objectivity. Translated by George J. Irwin. Boston, Beacon Press [1961] 351 p. 21 cm. *1. History — Philosophy.*
D16.8.A723   901   61-5882

Bagby, Philip. — III. 348
Culture and history; prolegomena to the comparative study of civilizations. Berkeley, University of California Press, 1959. 244 p. illus. 23 cm. *1. History — Philosophy. 2. Civilization. 3. Culture.*
D16.8.B27 1959   901   60-871

Becker, Carl Lotus, 1873-1945. — III. 349
Everyman his own historian; essays on history and politics, by Carl L. Becker. Chicago, Quadrangle Books [1966] 325 p. 21 cm. (Quadrangle paperbacks, 33) *1. History — Philosophy. I. T.*
D16.8.B318 1966   907   67-1041

Berdiaev, Nikolaĭ Aleksandrovich, 1874-1948. — III. 350
The meaning of history. Translated from the Russian by George Reavey. Cleveland, Meridian Books [1962, c1936] 191 p. 19 cm. (Living age books, LA36) *1. History — Philosophy. 2. Christianity — Philosophy. I. T.*
D16.8.B326 1962   901   Cd62-287

Burckhardt, Jakob Christoph, 1818-1897. — III. 351
Force and freedom; reflections on history [by] Jacob Burckhardt. Edited by James Hastings Nichols. [New ed.] New York, Pantheon Books [1964, c1943] vi, 382 p. 22 cm. Translation of Weltgeschichtliche Betrachtungen. *1. History — Philosophy. I. T.*
D16.8.B812 1964   901   64-5204

Burke, Kenneth, 1897- — III. 352
Attitudes toward history. [2d ed., rev.] Los Altos, Calif., Hermes Publications, 1959. 375 p. 22 cm. *1. History — Philosophy. I. T.*
D16.8.B83 1959   901   58-12006

D16.8 C – G

Carr, Edward Hallett, 1892- — III. 353
What is history? [1st American ed.] New York, Knopf, 1962 [c1961] 209 p. 20 cm. (The George Macaulay Trevelyan lectures, 1961) *1. History — Philosophy. I. T.*
D16.8.C33 1962   901   61-17812

Danto, Arthur Coleman, 1924- — III. 354
Analytical philosophy of history, by Arthur C. Danto. Cambridge [Eng.] University Press, 1965. xi, 318 p. 24 cm. *1. History — Philosophy. I. T.*
D16.8.D23   901   65-11205

D'Arcy, Martin Cyril, 1888- — III. 355
The sense of history: secular and sacred. London, Faber and Faber [1959] 309 p. 23 cm. *1. History — Philosophy. I. T.*
D16.8.D25   901   59-2975

Denton, Robert Claude, 1901- ed. — III. 356
The idea of history in the ancient Near East, by Roland H. Bainton [and others] New Haven, Yale University Press, 1955. ix, 376 p. 25 cm. (American Oriental series, v.38) "Lectures of the Department of Near Eastern Languages and Literatures at Yale University." *1. History — Philosophy. I. Bainton, Roland Herbert, 1894- II. T. (S)*
D16.8.D37   901   55-6144

Dilthey, Wilhelm, 1833-1911. — III. 357
Pattern & meaning in history; thoughts on history & society. Edited & introduced by H. P. Rickman. New York, Harper [1962, c1961] 170 p. 21 cm. (Harper torchbooks, TB1075. The Academy library) Translation of "the texts ... taken from volume VII of Dilthey's works, published by the Teubner Verlag, Stuttgart." *1. History — Philosophy. I. T.*
D16.8.D49 1962   901   62-5023

Dray, William H. — III. 358
Philosophy of history. Englewood Cliffs, N.J., Prentice-Hall [1964] ix, 116 p. 22 cm. (Foundations of philosophy series) *1. History — Philosophy. I. T.*
D16.8.D7   901   64-16442

Dray, William H., ed. — III. 359
Philosophical analysis and history, edited by William H. Dray. [New York, Harper & Row, 1966] 390 p. 21 cm. (Sources in contemporary philosophy) *1. History — Philosophy — Collections. I. T.*
D16.8.D72   901   66-12554

Gallie, W. B., 1912- — III. 360
Philosophy and the historical understanding [by] W. B. Gallie. 2d ed. New York, Schocken Books [1968] xii, 236 p. 21 cm. *1. History — Philosophy. I. T.*
D16.8.G27 1968   901   68-16656

Gardiner, Patrick L., 1922- ed. — III. 361
Theories of history; readings from classical and contemporary sources, by

Patrick Gardiner. Glencoe, Ill., Free Press [1959] 549 p. 25 cm. (The Free Press textbooks in philosophy) *1. History — Philosophy. I. T.*
D16.8.G33   901   58-6481

Geyl, Pieter, 1887- III. 362
Debates with historians. New York, Meridian Books [1958] 287 p. 18 cm. (Meridian books, M57) *1. History — Philosophy. I. T.*
D16.8.G435 1958   907   58-11924

Geyl, Pieter, 1887-1966. III. 363
Use and abuse of history. [Hamden, Conn.] Archon Books, 1970 [c1955] vi, 97 p. 19 cm. *1. History — Philosophy. I. T.*
D16.8.G44 1970   901   77-113016

D16.8   H – S

Hegel, Georg Wilhelm Friedrich, 1770-1831. III. 364
The philosophy of history. With prefaces by Charles Hegel and the translator, J. Sibree, and a new introd. by C. J. Friedrich. New York, Dover Publications [1956] xvi, 457 p. 21 cm. "An unabridged and unaltered republication of the last revision of the Sibree translation. [1944?]" Translation of Vorlesungen über die Philosophie der Geschichte. *1. History — Philosophy.*
D16.8.H46 1956   901   57-401

Klibansky, Raymond, 1905- ed. III. 365
Philosophy & history; essays presented to Ernst Cassirer. Edited by Raymond Klibansky and H. J. Paton. New York, Harper & Row [1963] xii, 363 p. illus., port. 21 cm. (Harper torchbooks. The Academy library) "TB1115." This book has been edited with the support of the Warburg Institute, London. *1. History — Philosophy. 2. Philosophy — Addresses, essays, lectures. I. Paton, Herbert James, 1887- joint ed. II. Cassirer, Ernst, 1874-1945. III. London. University. Warburg Institute. IV. T.*
D16.8.K52 1963   901   64-2913

Mandelbaum, Maurice H., 1908- III. 366
The problem of historical knowledge; an answer to relativism, by Maurice Mandelbaum. Pref. by the author. New York, Harper & Row [1967] x, 338, 4 p. 21 cm. (Harper torchbooks, TB1338) Reissue of the 1938 ed. *1. History — Philosophy. 2. History — Methodology. I. Historical knowledge. II. T.*
D16.8.M26 1967   901   68-172

Federn, Karl, 1868-1942. III. 367
The materialist conception of history; a critical analysis. Westport, Conn., Greenwood Press [1971] xiv, 262 p. 23 cm. Reprint of the 1939 ed. *1. Marx, Karl, 1818-1883. 2. History — Philosophy. I. T.*
D16.8.M294F4 1971   901   75-114523   ISBN:0837147891

Mazlish, Bruce, 1923- III. 368
The riddle of history; the great speculators from Vico to Freud. New York, Harper & Row [1966] viii, 484 p. 22 cm. *1. History — Philosophy. I. T.*
D16.8.M37   901   66-12559

Meiland, Jack W. III. 369
Scepticism and historical knowledge [by] Jack W. Meiland. New York, Random House [1965] vii, 209 p. 19 cm. (Random House studies in philosophy, SPH 5) *1. History — Philosophy. I. T.*
D16.8.M43   901   65-17445

Meinecke, Friedrich, 1862-1954. III. 370
Historism; the rise of a new historical outlook. [Translated by J. E. Anderson. New York] Herder and Herder [1972] lxi, 524 p. 22 cm. Translation of Die Entstehung des Historismus. *1. History — Philosophy. 2. Historiography — History. I. T.*
D16.8.M4613 1972b   907/.2   73-186993

New York University Institute of Philosophy. 5th, 1962. III. 371
Philosophy and history, a symposium. Edited by Sidney Hook. [New York] New York University Press, 1963. x, 403 p. 21 cm. *1. History — Philosophy — Congresses. I. Hook, Sidney, 1902- ed. II. T.*
D16.8.N43 1962   901   63-11298

Ortega y Gasset, José, 1883-1955. III. 372
History as a system, and other essays toward a philosophy of history. With an afterword by John William Miller New York, Norton [1961] 269 p. 22 cm. These essays were originally published under the title: Toward a philosophy of history. *1. History — Philosophy. I. T.*
D16.8.O72 1961   901   61-5613

Popper, Karl Raimund, 1902- III. 373
The poverty of historicism, by Karl R. Popper. New York, Harper & Row [1964, c1961] x, 166 p. 21 cm. (Harper torchbooks. The Academy library) "TB 1126." *1. History — Philosophy. I. T.*
D16.8.P57 1964   901   64-3717

Russell, Bertrand Russell, 3d earl, 1872- III. 374
History as an art. Aldington, Kent, Hand and Flower Press [1954] 23 p. 22 cm. (Hermon Ould memorial lecture, 2) *1. History — Philosophy. I. T. (S)*
D16.8.R95   901   55-21195

Sée, Henri Eugène, 1864-1936. III. 375
The economic interpretation of history. Translation and introd. by Melvin M. Knight. New York, A. M. Kelley, 1968. viii, 154 p. 21 cm. (Reprints of economic classics) Translation of Matérialisme historique et interprétation économique de l'histoire. Reprint of the 1929 ed. *1. Marx, Karl, 1818-1883. 2. History — Philosophy. 3. Economics. I. T.*
D16.8.S4 1968   901   67-30863

Strayer, Joseph Reese, 1904- ed. III. 376
The interpretation of history, by Jacques Barzun, Hajo Holborn, Herbert Heaton, Dumas Malone [and] George La Piana; edited with an introduction by Joseph A. Strayer. Princeton, Princeton University Press, 1943. 186 p. 23 cm. (Princeton books in the humanities) The Spencer Trask lectures for 1941-1942. *1. History — Philosophy. I. Barzun, Jacques, 1907- II. Holborn, Hajo, 1902- III. Heaton, Herbert, 1890- IV. Malone, Dumas, 1892- V. La Piana, George, 1879- VI. T.*
D16.8.S87   901   A43-1106

D16.8   T – Z

Taylor, Henry Osborn, 1856-1941. III. 377
A historian's creed. Port Washington, N.Y., Kennikat Press [1969, c1939] 137 p. 21 cm. (Essay and general literature index reprint series) *1. History — Philosophy. 2. Man. 3. Continuity. I. T.*
D16.8.T28 1969   901   70-86065   ISBN:804605904

Taylor, Henry Osborn, 1856- III. 378
A layman's view of history, by Henry Osborn Taylor. New York, Macmillan, 1935. vii, 133 p. 21 cm. *1. History — Philosophy. 2. European war, 1914-1918 — Addresses, essays, lectures. I. T.*
D16.8.T3   35-3699

Walsh, William Henry. III. 379
An introduction to philosophy of history. London, New York, Hutchinson's University Library, 1951. 173 p. 19 cm. (Hutchinson's university library: philosophy) *1. History — Philosophy.*
D16.8.W28   901   51-13553

Weiss, Paul, 1901- III. 380
History: written and lived. Carbondale, Southern Illinois University Press [1962] 245 p. 23 cm. *1. History — Philosophy.*
D16.8.W39   901   62-15006

D16.9   Special Topics

Adams, Brooks, 1848-1927. III. 381
The law of civilization and decay; an essay on history. With an introd. by Charles A. Beard. New York, Books for Libraries Press [1971, c1943] 349, xi p. 23 cm. (Essay index reprint series) *1. History — Philosophy. 2. Civilization — History. 3. Degeneration. I. T.*
D16.9.A2 1971   901.9   71-37125   ISBN:0836924789

Berlin, Isaiah. III. 382
Historical inevitability. London, New York, Oxford University Press [1955] 79 p. 23 cm. (Auguste Comte memorial trust lecture, no. 1) "Delivered on 12 May 1953 at the London School of Economics and Political Science." *1. History — Philosophy. I. T. (S)*
D16.9.B4   901   55-14152

Dray, William H. III. 383
Laws and explanation in history, by William Dray. [London] Oxford University Press, 1957. 174 p. 22 cm. (Oxford classical & philosophical monographs) *1. History — Philosophy. I. T.*
D16.9.D7   901   57-59125

Ferrero, Guglielmo, 1871-1942. III. 384
The principles of power; the great political crises of history, by Guglielmo Ferrero; translated by Theodore R. Jaeckel. New York, Putnam [1942] ix, 333 p. 23 cm. Translation of Potere. "The third volume of a trilogy. The first two volumes — The gamble and The reconstruction of Europe — were originally published in Paris. The principles of power is appearing in New York because it could not be published in Europe on account of the greatly increased censorship." — Pref. *1. Europe — History — Philosophy. 2. Revolutions. I. Jaeckel, Theodore R., tr. II. T.*
D16.9.F452   940   42-19725

Gardiner, Patrick L., 1922- III. 385
The nature of historical explanation, by Patrick Gardiner. London, Oxford University Press, 1952. xii, 142 p. 23 cm. (Oxford classical & philosophical monographs) *1. History — Philosophy. I. T:Historical explanation.*
D16.9.G34   901   52-4279

Hook, Sidney, 1902- III. 386
The hero in history, a study in limitation and possibility. New York,

History: General

Humanities Press [1950, c1943] xiv, 273 p. 21 cm. *1. History — Philosophy. 2. Heroes. I. T.*
D16.9.H6x   A52-5214

Kann, Robert A., 1906-   **III. 387**
The problem of restoration; a study in comparative political history, by Robert A. Kann. Berkeley, University of California Press, 1968 [c1967] xi, 441 p. 24 cm. *1. Restorations, Political. I. T.*
D16.9.K354   320.3   68-10380

Löwith, Karl, 1897-   **III. 388**
Meaning in history. [Chicago] University of Chicago Press [1957, c1949] 257 p. 21 cm. (Phoenix books, P16) *1. History — Philosophy. I. T.*
D16.9.Lx   901   57-7900

Niebuhr, Reinhold, 1892-   **III. 389**
Faith and history; a comparison of Christian and modern views of history. New York, C. Scribner's Sons, 1949. viii, 257 p. 22 cm. *1. History — Philosophy. 2. Christianity — Philosophy. 3. Apologetics — 20th cent. I. T.*
D16.9.N5   901   49-8484

D17 – 21 World Histories. Outlines

International Commission for a History of the Scientific and Cultural Development of Mankind.   **III. 390**
History of mankind: [cultural and scientific development. 1st ed.] New York, Harper & Row [1963-   v. illus., plates, maps. 25 cm. Errata slip inserted in v.1. *1. World history. I. T.*
D20.I66   909   62-15718

Peuples et civilisations; histoire générale. [t.]1-   **III. 391**
Paris, F. Alcan [etc.] 1926-   v. fold. maps. 23 cm. "Publiée sous la direction de Louis Halphen et Philippe Sagnac." Some volumes also in revised editions. *1. World history. I. Halphen, Louis, 1880-1950, ed. II. Sagnac, Philippe, 1868- ed.*
D20.P37   909   52-25504

Pirenne, Jacques, 1891-   **III. 392**
The tides of history. Translated from the French by Lovett Edwards. [1st ed.] New York, Dutton, 1962-   v. maps (part fold.) 23 cm. "Translated from Les grands courants de l'histoire universelle." *1. World history. I. T.*
D20.P513   909   62-7800

Propyläen Weltgeschichte;   **III. 393**
eine Universalgeschichte. Hrsg. von Golo Mann und Alfred Heuss. Berlin, Propyläen-Verlag [1960-   v.1, 1961] v. illus. (part col.) ports. (part col.) maps (part fold., part col.) facsims. (part in pocket) 27 cm. Vol.5-7 edited by G. Mann and A. Nitschke; v.8-10 edited by G. Mann. *1. World history. 2. Civilization — History. 3. History — Bibliography. I. Mann, Golo, 1909- ed. II. Heuss, Alfred, 1909- ed. III. Nitschke, August, 1926- ed.*
D20.P946   60-35516

Burckhardt, Jakob Christoph, 1818-1897.   **III. 394**
Judgments on history and historians. Translated by Harry Zohn, with an introd. by H. R. Trevor-Roper. Boston, Beacon Press [1958] xxiv, 280 p. 21 cm. Translation of Historische Fragmente. *1. World history. I. T.*
D21.B973   909   58-6250

Langer, William Leonard, 1896-   **III. 395**
An encyclopedia of world history; ancient, medieval, and modern, chronologically arranged. Compiled and edited by William L. Langer. 5th ed., rev. and enl. with maps and geneal. tables. Boston, Houghton Mifflin, 1972. xxxix, 1569 p. illus. 25 cm. *1. History — Outlines, syllabi, etc. I. T.*
D21.L27 1972   902/.02   72-186219   ISBN:0395135923

Halecki, Oskar, 1891-   **III. 396**
The limits and divisions of European history. London, New York, Sheed & Ward, 1950. xiii, 242 p. 21 cm. *1. Europe — History — Outlines, syllabi, etc. I. T.*
D21.3.H3 1950   940   50-2807

D21.5 Historical Geography

Cornish, Gaughan, 1862-   **III. 397**
The great capitals; an historical geography, by Vaughan Cornish, D.SC. With two maps. London, Methuen; New York, Doran [1923] xii, 296 p. 2 fold. maps. 23 cm. *1. Geography, Historical. 2. Capitals (Cities) I. T.*
D21.5.C6 1923a   23-13496

East, William Gordon.   **III. 398**
An historical geography of Europe, by Gordon East. London, Methuen, 1966. xx, 492 p. 64 maps, tables. 21 cm. (University paperbacks, UP169) Label mounted on t.p.: Distributed in the United States by Barnes & Noble. *1. Europe — Historical geography. 2. Geography, Historical. I. T.*
D21.5.E3 1966a   911.4   67-93050

Raynal, Guillaume Thomas François, 1713-1796.   **III. 399**
Philosophical and political history of the settlements and trade of the Europeans in the East and West Indies. Newly translated from the French by J. O. Justamond, with a new set of maps. 2d ed. New York, Negro Universities Press [1969] 6 v. illus. 22 cm. Translation of Histoire philosophique et politique des établissemens et du commerce des Européens and dans les deux Indes. Reprint of the 1798 ed. *1. East Indies. 2. Colonization — History. 3. America — Discovery and exploration. 4. Commerce — History. I. T.*
D22.R334   973.1   69-18996

D25 – 27 MILITARY AND NAVAL HISTORY

Dupuy, Richard Ernest, 1887-   **III. 400**
The encyclopedia of military history; from 3500 B.C. to the present [by] R. Ernest Dupuy and Trevor N. Dupuy. [1st ed.] New York, Harper & Row [1970] xiii, 1406 p. illus., maps. 24 cm. *1. Military history. I. Dupuy, Trevor Nevitt, 1916- joint author. II. T.*
D25.A2D8   355/.0009   74-81871

Eggenberger, David.   **III. 401**
A dictionary of battles. New York, Crowell [1967] x, 526 p. plans (part col.) 26 cm. "Covers ... the first battle of Megiddo in 1479 B.C. to the fighting in Vietnam during the 1960's." *1. Battles — Dictionaries. I. T.*
D25.E35   904/.7   67-12400

Liddell Hart, Basil Henry, 1895-   **III. 402**
Strategy [by] B. H. Liddell Hart. 2d rev. ed. New York, Praeger [1967] 430 p. maps. 21 cm. First published in 1929 under title: The decisive wars of history. *1. Military history. 2. Strategy.*
D25.L45 1967   355.4/3   67-23638

Mahan, Alfred Thayer, 1840-1914.   **III. 403**
The influence of sea power upon history, 1660-1783; by Captain A. T. Mahan ... 15th ed. Boston, Little, Brown, and company, 1898. xxiv, 557 p. 4 maps (1 fold.) plans. 23 1/2 cm. *1. Naval history. I. T.*
D27.M215   01-11051

Potter, Elmer Belmont, 1908- ed.   **III. 404**
Sea power; a naval history. Associate editor: Chester W. Nimitz; assistant editors: J. R. Fredland [and] Henry H. Adams. Authors: Henry H. Adams [and others] Englewood Cliffs, N.J., Prentice-Hall, 1960. xii, 932 p. illus., maps. 26 cm. *1. Naval history. I. Nimitz, Chester William, 1885- ed. II. T.*
D27.P65   359.09   60-15619

D51 – 95 ANCIENT HISTORY

Godolphin, Francis Richard Borroum, ed.   **III. 405**
The Greek historians. The complete and unabridged historical works of

Herodotus, translated by George Rawlinson; Thucydides, translated by Benjamin Jowett; Xenophon, translated by Henry G. Dakyns [and] Arrian, translated by Edward J. Chinnock. Edited, with an introduction, revisions and additional notes, by Francis R. B. Godolphin. [1st ed.] New York, Random House [1942] 2 v. fold. map. 24 cm. *1. History, Ancient — Collections. 2. Greek historians. I. Herodotus. II. Thucydides. III. Xenophon. IV. Arrianus, Flavius. V. Rawlinson, George, 1812-1902, tr. VI. Jowett, Benjamin, 1817-1893, tr. VII. Dakyns, Henry Graham, tr. VIII. Chinnock, Edward James, tr. IX. T.*
D52.G6 938.0082 42-11883

Ehrich, Robert W., ed. **III. 406**
Chronologies in Old World archaeology, edited by Robert W. Ehrich. Chicago, University of Chicago Press [1965] xii, 557 p. illus., maps. 23 cm. "Supersedes the earlier Relative chronologies in Old World archaeology, published ... in 1954." *1. History, Ancient — Chronology. I. T.*
D54.5.E4 1965 930.02 65-17296

Teggart, Frederick John, 1870- **III. 407**
Rome and China; a study of correlations in historical events [by] Frederick J. Teggart. Berkeley, University of California Press, 1939. xvii, 283 p. maps (1 fold.) 24 cm. *1. History — Methodology. 2. Rome — History — Republic, B.C. 265-30. 3. Rome — History — Empire, B.C. 30-A.D. 284. 4. China — History — Early to 1643. I. Correlations in historical events II. T.*
D56.T4 930 40-86

The Cambridge ancient history. **III. 408**
3rd ed. London, Cambridge University Press, 1970- v. illus., maps (some col.). 24 cm. Individual chapters have already appeared as fascicles, 1961-1968. *1. History, Ancient.*
D57.C252 913 75-85719 ISBN:0521070511 (v. 1, pt. 1)

Rostovtsev, Mikhail Ivanovich, 1870-1952. **III. 409**
A history of the ancient world, by M. Rostovtzeff. Westport, Conn., Greenwood Press [1971] 2 v. illus., maps, plans, ports. 24 cm. Translation of Ocherk istorii drevniago mira. *1. History, Ancient. I. T.*
D57.R8 1971 930 73-109834 ISBN:0837144167(v.1)

Breasted, James Henry, 1865-1935. **III. 410**
The conquest of civilization, by James Henry Breasted including new text, the author's own revisions and notes; edited by Edith Williams Ware. New York, Harper, 1938. xii, 669 p. front., illus., plates. 22 cm. At head of title: New edition, fully revised and reset. Illustrated lining-papers. The plates, which precede t.-p., have half-title: Sixteen pages of photographs specially selected by Charles Breasted, many of them through the courtesy of the Oriental institute, for The conquest of civilization. *1. Civilization — History. 2. History, Ancient. I. Ware, Edith Williams, ed. II. T.*
D59.B78 1938 930 38-27362

Starr, Chester G., 1914- **III. 411**
A history of the ancient world [by] Chester G. Starr. New York, Oxford University Press, 1965. xvii, 742 p. illus., maps. 24 cm. *1. History, Ancient. I. T.*
D59.S75 930 64-22365

Ehrenberg, Victor, 1891- **III. 412**
Aspects of the ancient world; essays and reviews. New York, W. Salloch, 1946. ix, 256 p. plates. 23 cm. *1. History, Ancient — Addresses, essays, lectures. I. T.*
D60.Ex 930.04 A49-2397

Childe, Vere Gordon, 1892-1957. **III. 413**
The dawn of European civilization. 6th ed., rev. New York, Knopf, 1958 [c1957] xii, 367 p. illus., maps. 24 cm. (The History of civilization. [Pre-history and antiquity]) *1. Europe — Civilization — History. 2. Archaeology. 3. Man, Prehistoric. I. T. (S:The History of civilization. Pre-history and antiquity (New York))*
D65.C5 1958 901 58-5914

Piggott, Stuart. **III. 414**
Ancient Europe, from the beginnings of agriculture to classical antiquity; a survey. Chicago, Aldine Pub. Co. [1966, c1965] xxiii, 340 p. illus., maps, plans. 26 cm. *1. Europe — Antiquities. 2. Europe — History — To 476. I. T.*
D65.P65 1966 913/.36/03 64-21369

Chadwick, Nora (Kershaw) 1891- **III. 415**
The Celts [by] Nora Chadwick. With an introductory chapter by J. X. W. P. Corcoran. [Harmondsworth, Eng.] Penguin Books [1970] 301 p. illus. 18 cm. (Pelican books A1211) *1. Celts.*
D70.C47 909.04/916 70-25718

Dillon, Myles, 1900- **III. 416**
The Celtic realms [by] Myles Dillon and Nora K. Chadwick. New York] New American Library [1967] 355 p. illus., maps. 25 cm. *1. Celts. I. Chadwick, Nora (Kershaw) 1891- joint author. II. T.*
D70.D48 1967b 910.03/174/916 67-15326

Powell, Thomas George Eyre, 1916- **III. 417**
The Celts. New York, Praeger [1958] 282 p. illus., plates, maps. 21 cm. (Ancient peoples and places, v.6) *1. Celts.*
D70.P6 936.4 58-8173

Casson, Lionel, 1914- **III. 418**
The ancient mariners: seafarers and sea fighters of the Mediterranean in ancient times. New York, Macmillan, 1959. 286 p. illus. 22 cm. *1. Naval history, Ancient. I. T.*
D95.C35 930 58-12437

D101 – 847 MEDIEVAL AND MODERN HISTORY

Previté-Orton, Charles William, 1877-1947. **III. 419**
A history of Europe from 1198 to 1378. [3d ed., rev.] New York, Barnes & Noble [1951] 464 p. illus. 23 cm. (History of medieval and modern Europe, v.3) *1. Europe — History — 476-1492.*
D102.M42 vol. 3 1951 940.1 52-9644

Waugh, William Templeton, 1884-1932. **III. 420**
A history of Europe from 1378 to 1494. 3d ed. London, Methuen, 1949. xiii, 545 p. maps (part fold.) 22 cm. (Methuen's history of medieval and modern Europe) *1. Europe — History — 476-1492. (S)*
D102.W39x A53-9913

Blum, Jerome, 1913- **III. 421**
The European world; a history [by] Jerome Blum, Rondo Cameron [and] Thomas G. Barnes. Boston, Little, Brown [1966] xx, 1120 p. illus., maps (part fold.), ports. 23 cm. Published also, without general title, in two separate vols. under the following titles: The emergence of the European world. The European world since 1815. *1. Europe — History. 2. Europe — Civilization — History. I. Cameron, Rondo E., joint author. II. Barnes, Thomas Garden, joint author. III. T.*
D103.B55 940 66-13544

Hay, Denys. **III. 422**
Europe: the emergence of an idea. Revised ed. Edinburgh, Edinburgh U.P., 1968. xxiv, 151 p. 9 plates, illus., facsims., geneal. table, maps. 21 cm. (Edinburgh University publications; history, philosophy and economics, no. 7) *1. Europe (The word) 2. Europe — Historical geography. I. T. (S:Edinburgh. University. Edinburgh University publications; history, philosophy, and economics, no. 7)*
D104.H27 1968 911.4 68-19886 ISBN:0852240112

Hill, David Jayne, 1850-1932. **III. 423**
A history of diplomacy in the international development of Europe. New York, H. Fertig, 1967. 3 v. map. 24 cm. Reprint of the 1905 ed. *1. Europe — Politics. I. T.*
D105.H62 940 67-14185

Schuman, Frederick Lewis, 1904- **III. 424**
International politics; anarchy and order in the world society [by] Frederick L. Schuman. Maps by George Brodsky. 7th ed. New York, McGraw-Hill [1968, c1969] xx, 751 p. maps. 23 cm. (McGraw-Hill series in political science) *1. World politics. 2. International relations — History. 3. State, The. 4. Nationalism. 5. Imperialism. I. T.*
D105.S35 1969 327 68-27512

Gooch, George Peabody, 1873- **III. 425**
Courts and cabinets, by G. P. Gooch. London, New York [etc.] Longmans, Green [1944] 323 p. 23 cm. "First published 1944." Studies of the memoirs of thirteen English, French and German writers with quotations from their works. Seven of the studies are reprinted from Contemporary review. cf. Pref. *1. Courts and courtiers. 2. Europe — Kings and rulers. I. T.*
D107.G6 940.204 44-9069

D111 – 203 Medieval History

Froissart, Jean, 1338?-1410? **III. 426**
Chronicles. In Lord Berners' translation. Selected, edited, and introduced by Gillian and William Anderson. Carbondale, Southern Illinois University Press [1963] xiv, 224 p. 26 cm. (Centaur classics) *1. Hundred Years' War,*

III. 427 History: General D113

1339-1453. 2. France — History — House of Valois, 1328-1589. 3. Gt. Brit. — History — 14th cent. 4. Flanders — History. 5. Burgundy — History. 6. Europe — History — 476-1492.
D113.F77 1963   944.025   63-14937

Froissart, Jean, 1338?-1410?   III. 427
Chronicles. Translated and edited by John Jolliffe. New York, Modern Library [1968, c1967] xxiii, 448 p. geneal. tables, maps. 19 cm. (The Modern library of the world's best books [ML387]) *1. Hundred Years' War, 1339-1453. 2. France — History — House of Valois, 1328-1589. 3. Gt. Brit. — History — 14th cent. 4. Flanders — History. 5. Burgundy — History. 6. Europe — History — 476-1492. I. Jolliffe, John Edward Austin, 1891- ed.*
D113.F77 1968   944/.025   66-21508

Crump, Charles George, 1862-1935, ed.   III. 428
The legacy of the middle ages, edited by C. G. Crump & E. F. Jacob. Oxford, The Clarendon press [1948] xii, 549, [1] p. front., 41 pl. (incl. facsims.) 19 cm. "First published 1926." *1. Middle ages. 2. Civilization, Medieval. 3. Art, Medieval. 4. Paleography. I. Jacob, Ernest Fraser, 1894- joint ed. II. T.*
D113.5.C7 1948   901   44-7247

Mahdi, Muhsin.   III. 429
Ibn Khaldūn's philosophy of history: a study in the philosophic foundation of the science of culture. [Chicago] University of Chicago Press [1964] 325 p. 21 cm. (Phoenix books) *1. Ibn Khaldūn, 1332-1406. I. T.*
D116.7.I3M3 1964   901   64-23414

Brooke, Zachary Nugent, 1883-1946.   III. 430
A history of Europe from 911 to 1198 [by] Z. N. Brooke. [3rd ed.] London, Methuen, 1969. xx, 553 p. 22 cm. (University paperbacks, 298) "Distributed in the USA by Barnes & Noble Inc." *1. Europe — History — 476-1492. I. T.*
D117.B7x 1969   940.1   76-402132   ISBN:416296408 (pbk)

The Cambridge medieval history.   III. 431
[2d ed.] Cambridge [Eng.] University Press, 1966- v. fold. col., maps. 24 cm. Planned by J. B. Bury. *1. Middle Ages — History. I. Bury, John Bagnell, 1861-1927. II. Hussey, Joan Mervyn, ed.*
D117.C32   909.07   66-4537

Painter, Sidney, 1902-   III. 432
A history of the Middle Ages: 284-1500. [1st ed.] New York, Knopf, 1953. 497 p. illus. 25 cm. *1. Middle Ages.*
D117.P3   940.1   52-12411

Pirenne, Henri, 1862-1935.   III. 433
A history of Europe: from the invasions to the XVI century. With a new introd. to the American ed. by Jan-Albert Goris. [Translated by Bernard Miall from the French of the 8th ed.] New York, University Books [c1956] xxii, 625 p. 22 cm. *1. Europe — History — 476-1492. 2. Europe — History — 1432-1648.*
D117.P52 1956   940.1   56-7831

Hoyt, Robert Stuart.   III. 434
Life and thought in the early Middle Ages, edited by Robert S. Hoyt. Minneapolis, University of Minnesota Press [1967] 165 p. 23 cm. "Originated as public lectures given by the authors in the annual spring lecture series, 1963, sponsored by the General Extension Division of the University of Minnesota." *1. Middle Ages. I. Life and thought in the Middle Ages. II. T.*
D118.H65   940.1   67-15065

Morrall, John B.   III. 435
The medieval imprint: the founding of the Western European tradition [by] John B. Morrall. New York, Basic Books [1968, c1967] xi, 156 p. illus. 22 cm. *1. Middle Ages — History — Addresses, essays, lectures. I. T.*
D119.M68 1968   914/.03/1   68-9591

Studies in medieval and Renaissance history.   III. 436
v.1- Lincoln, University of Nebraska Press, 1964- v. 24 cm. Annual. Editor: v.1- W. M. Bowsky. *1. Middle Ages — History — Addresses, essays, lectures. I. Bowsky, William M., ed.*
D119.S8   901.92082   63-22098

Dopsch, Alfons, 1896-1953.   III. 437
The economic and social foundations of European civilization. With an introd. by Robert Latouche. New York, H. Fertig, 1969. xvii, 404 p. 23 cm. Translation of Wirtschaftliche und soziale Grundlagen der europäishchen Kulturentwicklung. *1. Europe — History — 392-814. 2. Civilization, Medieval. 3. Germanic tribes. I. T.*
D121.D62 1969   901.92/1   68-9591

Moss, Henry St. Lawrence Beaufort.   III. 438
The birth of the Middle Ages, 395-814. [London] Oxford University Press [1963] xvi, 291 p. illus., maps (1 col.) 20 cm. (Oxford paperbacks, no. 60) *1. Europe — History — 392-814. 2. Civilization, Medieval. I. T.*
D121.M6 1963   940.1   63-24170

Pirenne, Henri, 1862-1935.   III. 439
Mohammed and Charlemagne; [translated from the French by Bernard Miall]. 1st ed., 5th impression. London, Allen & Unwin, 1968. 3-293 p. 22 cm. (Unwin university books, 61) Translation of Mohomet et Charlemagne. *1. Europe — History — 392-814. 2. Islamic empire — History. I. T.*
D121.P52 1968   940.1/1   72-363566

Wallace-Hadrill, John Michael.   III. 440
The barbarian West, 400-1000 [by] J. M. Wallace-Hadrill. 3rd (revised) ed. London, Hutchinson, 1967. 176 p. maps. 22 cm. (Hutchinson university library: History) *1. Middle Ages — History. 2. Migration of nations. I. T.*
D121.W3 1967   940.1   67-74988

Power, Eileen Edna, 1889-1940.   III. 441
Medieval people. [10th ed.] London, Methuen; New York, Barnes & Noble [1963] xii, 210 p. illus., fold. map. 22 cm. *1. Civilization, Medieval. I. T.*
D127.P6 1963   901.92   63-24493

Strayer, Joseph Reese, 1904-   III. 442
Western Europe in the Middle Ages, a short history. New York, Appleton-Century-Crofts [1955] 245 p. illus. 22 cm. *1. Middle Ages — History. I. T.*
D127.S68   940.1   54-10683

Lewis, Archibald Ross, 1914-   III. 443
Naval power and trade in the Mediterranean, A.D. 500-1100. Princeton, Princeton University Press, 1951. xii, 271 p. maps. 25 cm. (Princeton studies in history, 5) *1. Mediterranean region — Commerce. 2. Naval history. I. T. (S:Princeton University. Princeton studies in history, 5)*
D128.L4   940   51-706

Bloch, Marc Léopold Benjamin, 1886-1944.   III. 444
Feudal society. Translated from the French by L. A. Manyon. Foreword by M. M. Postan. [Chicago] University of Chicago Press [1961] xxi, 498 p. plates. 24 cm. *1. Feudalism. 2. Europe — History — 476-1492. I. T.*
D131.B513 1961   940.14   61-4322

Stephenson, Carl, 1886-   III. 445
Mediaeval feudalism, by Carl Stephenson ... Ithaca, N.Y., Cornell university press, 1942. ix, 116 p. incl. front., illus. 20 1/2 cm. *1. Feudalism. I. T.*
D131.S8   940.14   42-8382

Falco, Giorgio, 1888-1966.   III. 446
The Holy Roman Republic; a historic profile of the Middle Ages. Translated by K. V. Kent. New York, A. S. Barnes [1965, c1964] 336 p. 24 cm. Translation of La Santa romana repubblica. *1. Middle Ages — History. 2. Holy Roman Empire — History. 3. Church history — Middle Ages. I. T.*
D133.F313 1965   940.1   65-24847

D135 – 148 MIGRATIONS

Bury, John Bagnell, 1861-1927.   III. 447
The invasion of Europe by the barbarians. New York, Russell & Russell, 1963. 296 p. 23 cm. *1. Barbarian invasions of Rome. 2. Migrations of nations. I. T.*
D135.B8 1963   937.09   63-8359

Thompson, E. A.   III. 448
A history of Attila and the Huns. Oxford, Clarendon Press, 1948. xii, 228 p. 23 cm. *1. Attila, d. 453. 2. Huns.*
D141.T5   937.09   48-9260

Dvornik, Francis, 1893-   III. 449
The Slavs in European history and civilization. New Brunswick, N.J., Rutgers University Press [1962] xxviii, 688 p. maps. 25 cm. *1. Slavs — History. I. T.*
D147.D84   947   61-10259

Dvornik, Francis, 1893-   III. 450
The Slavs: their early history and civilization. Boston, American Academy of Arts and Sciences, 1956. 394 p. maps. 25 cm. (Survey of Slavic civilization, v.2) *1. Slavs — History. (S)*
D147.D85   936.7   56-58178

Haskins, Charles Homer, 1870-1937.   III. 451
The Normans in European history. New York, Ungar [1959] 258 p. 22 cm. *1. Europe — History. 2. Great Britain — History — Medieval period, 1066-1485. 3. Normans.*
D148.H3 1959   940.1   59-9150

D151 – 173 CRUSADES

Shaw, Margaret Renée Bryers, ed. and tr.   **III. 452**
Chronicles of the Crusades. Baltimore, Penguin Books [1963] 362 p. maps. 18 cm. (The Penguin classics, L124) *1. Crusades. I. Villehardouin, Geoffroi de, d. ca. 1212. The conquest of Constantinople. II. Joinville, Jean, sire de, 1224?-1317? The life of Saint Louis. III. T.*
D151.S5   940.18   63-5725

Dubois, Pierre, fl. 1300.   **III. 453**
The recovery of the Holy Land. Translated with an introd. and notes by Walther I. Brandt. New York, Columbia University Press, 1956. xvi, 251 p. 24 cm. (Records of civilization: sources and studies, no. 51) *1. Crusades. I. Brandt, Walther Immanuel, 1893- tr. II. T. (S)*
D152.D813   940.18   53-10013

Guilelmus, abp. of Tyre, ca. 1130-ca. 1190.   **III. 454**
A history of deeds done beyond the sea, by William, archbishop of Tyre. Translated and annotated by Emily Atwater Babcock and A. C. Krey. New York, Columbia University Press, 1943. 2 v. maps (1 fold.) 23 1/2 cm. (Records of civilization: sources and studies. No. XXXV) Translation of Historia rerum in partibus transmarinis gestarum. "The edition of William's history used as the basis of this translation is that prepared by A. Beugnot and A. Le Prevost for the French academy ... The present translation has been done by Mrs. Babcock." — Introd., v.1, p. 44. *1. Crusades. 2. Jerusalem — History — Latin kingdom, 1099-1244. I. Babcock, Emily Atwater, ed. and tr. II. Krey, August Charles, 1887- ed. III. T.*
D152.G78   940.18   A44-583

Runciman, Steven, Sir, 1903-   **III. 455**
A history of the Crusades. [1st ed.] Cambridge [Eng.] University Press, 1951-54. 3 v. illus., ports., maps, fold. geneal. table. 22 cm. *1. Crusades.*
D157.R8   940.18   51-10801

Setton, Kenneth Meyer, 1914-   **III. 456**
A history of the Crusades. Kenneth M. Setton, general editor. [2d ed.] Madison, University of Wisconsin Press, 1969-   v. illus., col. maps, plates. 26 cm. *1. Crusades. I. T.*
D157.S482   940.1/8   68-9837

Newhall, Richard Ager.   **III. 457**
The Crusades. Rev. ed. New York, Holt, Rinehart and Winston [1963] 136 p. 19 cm. (Berkshire studies in European history) *1. Crusades.*
D158.N4 1963   940.18   63-11881

Atiya, Aziz Suryal, 1898-   **III. 458**
Crusade, commerce, and culture [by] Aziz S. Atiya. Gloucester, Mass., P. Smith, 1969 [c1962] 280 p. maps (2 fold.) 21 cm. "Companion volume to [the author's] The crusade: historiography and bibliography." *1. Crusades. I. T.*
D160.A8 1969   940.1/8   70-10643

Smail, R. C.   **III. 459**
Crusading warfare, 1097-1193. Cambridge [Eng.] University Press, 1956. xi, 272 p. illus., maps, plans. 23 cm. (Cambridge studies in medieval life and thought, new ser., v.3) *1. Crusades. 2. Military art and science — History. I. T.*
D160.S55   940.18   56-58455

Krey, August Charles, 1887- ed. and tr.   **III. 460**
The first Crusade; the accounts of eye-witnesses and participants. Gloucester, Mass., P. Smith, 1958. viii, 299 p. maps (part. fold.) 21 cm. *1. Crusades — First, 1096-1099. I. T.*
D161.1.A3K7x

Odo de Deuil, Abbot of Saint Denis, d. ca. 1162.   **III. 461**
De profectione Ludovici VII in orientem. The journey of Louis VII to the East [by] Odo de Deuil. Edited, with an English translation, by Virginia Gingerick Berry. New York, Norton [1965, c1948] xliv, 154 p. facsim., maps. 21 cm. (Records of civilization: sources and studies) Originally written as the editor's doctoral dissertation, University of Chicago. *1. Louis VII, le Jeune, King of France, 1119-1180. 2. Crusades — Second, 1147-1149. I. Berry, Virginia (Gingerick) 1915- ed. and tr. II. T. III. T:The journey of Louis VII to the East. (S)*
D162.1.O3 1965   909.07   65-21620

Villehardouin, Geoffroi de, d. ca. 1212.   **III. 462**
Memoirs of the crusades, by Villehardouin & De Joinville. Tr. by Sir Frank Marzials. London, J. M. Dent; New York, E. P. Dutton [1908] xli, 340 p. 18 cm. (Everyman's library. History. [No. 333]) *1. Louis IX, Saint, king of France, 1214-1270. 2. Crusades — Fourth, 1202-1204. 3. Crusades — Seventh, 1248-1250. 4. Constantinople — History. 5. Latin empire, 1204-1261. I. Joinville, Jean, sire de, 1224?-1317? II. Marzials, Frank Thomas, Sir, 1840-1912, tr.*
D164.A3Vx   A10-2386

Atiya, Aziz Suryal, 1898-   **III. 463**
The crusade in the later Middle Ages, by Aziz S. Atiya. 2d ed. New York, Kraus Reprint Co., 1970. xvi, 604 p. illus., maps. 24 cm. Reprint of the 1965 ed. *1. Crusades — Later, 13th, 14th and 15th centuries. I. T.*
D171.A88 1970   909.07   78-126642

D175 – 195 LATIN KINGDOM OF JERUSALEM

Philippe, of Novara, 13th cent.   **III. 464**
The wars of Frederick II against the Ibelins in Syria and Cyprus, by Philip de Novare. Translated, with notes and introduction, by John L. La Monte, with verse translation of the poems by Merton Jerome Hubert. New York, Columbia University Press, 1936. ix, 230 p. illus. geneal. tab. maps, plates. 24 cm. (Records of civilization: sources and studies; edited under the auspices of the Department of history, Columbia university. 25) "The text followed is that established by Charles Kohler in his Mémoires de Philippe de Novare, published in 'Les classiques français du moyen âge,' Paris, 1913." — Pref. *1. Jerusalem — History — Latin kingdom, 1099-1244. 2. Cyprus — History. I. La Monte, John Life, 1902- ed. and tr. II. Hubert, Merton Jerome. III. T.*
D181.P5A32 1936   940.187   36-21032

D198 – 199 ISLAMIC EMPIRE

Rosenthal, Franz, 1914-   **III. 465**
A history of Muslim historiography. 2d rev. ed. Leiden, E. J. Brill, 1968. xvi, 656 p. 25 cm. *1. Historians, Arab. 2. Near East — Historiography. 3. Islam — Historiography. I. Muslim historiography. II. T.*
D198.2.R67 1968   68-113306

Who's who in the Arab world.   **III. 466**
1st- ed.; 1965/66-   Beirut, Publitec Editions. v. 21 cm. Companion vol. to Who's who in Lebanon. *1. Arab countries — Biography — Dictionaries.*
D198.3.W5   920.05   Ne67-1244

Arnold, Thomas Walker, Sir, 1864-1930, ed.   **III. 467**
The legacy of Islam, edited by the late Sir Thomas Arnold and Alfred Guillaume. Oxford, Clarendon Press, 1931. xvi, 416 p. front., illus., plates. 19 cm. *1. Civilization, Islamic. 2. Islam. I. Guillaume, Alfred, 1888- joint ed. II. T.*
D199.3.A7   297   31-34509

Gibb, Hamilton Alexander Rosskeen, Sir, 1895-   **III. 468**
Studies on the civilization of Islam. Edited by Stanford J. Shaw and William R. Polk. Boston, Beacon Press [1962] 369 p. 22 cm. (Beacon books on world affairs) "Articles ... drawn from a wide variety of publications over a span of nearly four decades." *1. Civilization, Mohammedan.*
D199.3.G5   915.6   62-7195

Goitein, Solomon Dob Fritz, 1900-   **III. 469**
A Mediterranean society; the Jewish communities of the Arab world as portrayed in the documents of the Cairo Geniza [by] S. D. Goitein. Berkeley, University of California Press, 1967-   v. illus., facsims., maps. 24 cm. "Published under the auspices of the Near Eastern Center, University of California, Los Angeles." *1. Cairo Genizah. 2. Jews in the Islamic Empire — Civilization. 3. Islamic Empire — Civilization. I. California. University. University at Los Angeles. Near Eastern Center. II. T.*
D199.3.G58   915.6/09/74924   67-22430

The Islamic city: a colloquium [held at All Souls College, June 28-July 2, 1965] published under the auspices of the Near Eastern History Group, Oxford, and the Near East Centre, University of Pennsylvania;   **III. 470**
edited by A. H. Hourani and S. M. Stern. Oxford, Cassirer; [Philadelphia] University of Pennsylvania Press, 1970. 222 p. 11 plates, illus., maps, plans. 25 cm. (Papers on Islamic history, no. 1) Papers delivered at a meeting organized by the Near Eastern History Group, Oxford. English or French. *1. Cities and towns, Islamic — Addresses, essays, lectures. I. Hourani, Albert Habib, ed. II. Stern, S. M., ed. III. Near Eastern History Group. (S)*
D199.3.I789   301.3/64/091767   75-105944   ISBN:0571090850

Watt, William Montgomery.   **III. 471**
Islamic political thought: the basic concepts [by] W. Montgomery Watt. Edinburgh, Edinburgh U.P., 1968. xi, 186 p. 21 cm. (Islamic surveys, 6) *1. Islamic Empire — Politics. 2. Political science — History — Islamic Empire. I. T.*
D199.3.I8 no. 6   320/.09176/7   68-22846   ISBN:0852240325

Watt, William Montgomery.   **III. 472**
Islamic philosophy and theology. Edinburgh, University Press [1962] xxiii, 196 p. 21 cm. (Islamic surveys, 1) *1. Philosophy, Islamic. 2. Islamic theology. I. T. (S)*
D199.3.I8 no.1   181.947   62-51017

III.473   History: General   D199.3

Cragg, Kenneth.   **III. 473**
Counsels in contemporary Islam. Edinburgh, University Press [1965] xiv, 255 p. 22 cm. (Islamic surveys, 3) *1. Islam — 20th century. 2. Islam — Essence, genius, nature. I. T. (S)*
D199.3.I8 no.3   65-4825

Watt, William Montgomery.   **III. 474**
A history of Islamic Spain [by] W. Montgomery Watt, with additional sections on literature by Pierre Cachia. Edinburgh, Edinburgh U.P., [1965] xi, 210 p. 16 plates, 2 maps. 21 cm. (Islamic surveys, 4) *1. Spain — History — Arab period, 711-1492. I. T. (S)*
D199.3.I8 no.4   946.02   66-2646

Bosworth, Clifford Edmund.   **III. 475**
The Islamic dynasties; a chronological and genealogical handbook. Edinburgh, University P., 1967. xviii, 245 p. 21 cm. (Islamic surveys, 5) *1. Islamic countries — Kings and rulers. 2. Islamic countries — History — Outlines, syllabi, etc. I. T. (S)*
D199.3.I8 no.5   909.091767   67-17613

Mez, Adam, 1869-1917.   **III. 476**
The renaissance of Islam, by Adam Mez; translated into English by Salahuddin Khuda Bukhsh and D. S. Margoliouth. 1st ed. London, Luzac, 1937. iii, 538 p. 26 cm. *1. Islamic empire. 2. Civilization, Arabic. I. Khuda Bakhsh, Salahuddin, 1877-1931, tr. II. Margoliouth, David Samuel, 1858- tr. III. T.*
D199.3.M42   950   38-22662

Nöldeke, Theodor, 1836-1930.   **III. 477**
Sketches from Eastern history [by] Theodore Nöldeke. Translated by John Sutherland Black and rev. by the author. Beirut, Khayats, 1963. 288 p. 23 cm. (Khayats oriental reprints, no. 2) "Reprinted from the edition of 1892." *1. Bar Hebraeus, 1226-1286. 2. Theodore II, negus of Ethiopia, d. 1868. 3. Semites. 4. Islam. 5. Saints — Syric. I. Black, John Sutherland, 1846-1923, tr. II. T.*
D199.3.N66 1963   65-3972

Von Grunebaum, Gustave Edmund, 1909-   **III. 478**
Islam: essays in the nature and growth of a cultural tradition. New York, Barnes & Noble [1961] 266 p. 22 cm. *1. Civilization, Mohammedan. I. T.*
D199.3.V62 1961a   915.6   61-66666

Von Grunebaum, Gustave Edmund, 1909-   **III. 479**
Medieval Islam; a study in cultural orientation. 2d ed. Chicago, University of Chicago Press [1953] vii, 378 p. (on lining papers) 24 cm. (An Oriental Institute essay) *1. Islam. 2. Civilization, Islamic. I. T. (S:Chicago. University. Oriental Institute. Oriental Institute essay)*
D199.3.V64 1953   950   53-9941

D200 – 203   LATER MIDDLE AGES (14TH – 15TH CENTURIES)

Heer, Friedrich, 1916-   **III. 480**
The medieval world: Europe, 1100-1350. Translated from the German by Janet Sondheimer. [1st ed.] Cleveland, World Pub. Co. [1962] 365 p. illus. 25 cm. Translation of Mittelalter. *1. Civilization, Medieval. I. T.*
D200.H413 1962   940.17   61-12020

Brooke, Christopher Nugent Lawrence.   **III. 481**
Europe in the central Middle Ages, 962-1154 [by] Christopher Brooke. New York, Holt, Rinehart and Winston [1964?] xvi, 403 p. geneal. tables, maps. 22 cm. (A General history of Europe) *1. Europe — History — 476-1492. I. T.*
D201.B7   901.92   64-12616

Hay, Denys.   **III. 482**
Europe in the fourteenth and fifteenth centuries. New York, Holt, Rinehart and Winston [c1966] x, 420 p. geneal. tables, maps. 22 cm. (A General history of Europe) *1. Fourteenth century. 2. Fifteenth century. I. T.*
D202.8.H3   914/.03/17   66-23561

Aston, Margaret.   **III. 483**
The fifteenth century; the prospect of Europe. [1st American ed. New York] Harcourt, Brace & World [1968] 216 p. illus. (part col.), facsims., maps (part col.), ports. 22 cm. ([History of European civilization library]) *1. Fifteenth century.*
D203.A8 1968b   940.2   67-27968

D204 – 847   Modern History

Harper encyclopedia of the modern world; a concise reference   **III. 484**
history from 1760 to the present.
Edited by Richard B. Morris and Graham W. Irwin. [1st ed.] New York, Harper & Row [1970] xxxii, 1271 p. maps. 24 cm. *1. History, Modern — Dictionaries. I. Morris, Richard Brandon, 1904- ed. II. Irwin, Graham W., ed.*
D205.H35 1970   903   73-81879

The Making of the modern world;   **III. 485**
general editor Douglas Johnson. London, Benn; New York, Barnes & Noble, 1971-   v.   illus., facsims., maps, ports. 23 cm. *1. History, Modern. I. Johnson, Douglas W. J., ed.*
D208.M33   901.9/3   70-26009
ISBN:0389041289 (Barnes & Noble) (v. 1)

The New Cambridge modern history.   **III. 486**
Cambridge [Eng.] University Press, 1957-1970. 14 v. 24 cm. Includes also the 2d ed. of v.12 with title: The shifting balance of world forces, 1898-1945, edited by C. L. Mowat. *1. History, Modern.*
D208.N4   940.2   57-14935

Palmer, Robert Roswell, 1909-   **III. 487**
A history of the modern world, by R. R. Palmer and Joel Colton. 3d ed. New York, Knopf, 1965. xiv, 996, xxxv p. illus., maps. 24 cm. *1. History, Modern. I. Colton, Joel G., 1918- joint author. II. T.*
D209.P26 1965   909   65-11962

Acton, John Emerich Edward Dalberg Acton, baron, 1834-1902.   **III. 488**
Lectures on modern history. With an introd. by Hugh Trevor-Roper. New York, Meridian Books [1961, c1960] 319 p. 18 cm. (Meridian books, M109) *1. History, Modern — Addresses, essays, lectures.*
D210.A2 1961   940.2   60-15294

Namier, Lewis Bernstein, Sir, 1888-   **III. 489**
Personalities and powers. London, Hamilton [1955] 157 p. 23 cm. *1. History, Modern — Addresses, essays, lectures. I. T.*
D210.N32   55-3092

Pollard, Albert Frederick, 1869-1948.   **III. 490**
Factors in modern history. Boston, Beacon Press [1960] 338 p. 21 cm. (Beacon paperbacks, BP96) *1. Gt. Brit. — History — Philosophy. 2. Gt. Brit. — History — Tudors, 1485-1603. 3. Gt. Brit. — History — Stuarts, 1603-1714.*
D210.P7 1960   942   60-16085

The Responsibility of power; historical essays in honor of Hajo   **III. 491**
Holborn.
Edited by Leonard Krieger and Fritz Stern. London, Melbourne, Macmillan, 1968. [1], xiv, 464 p. 23 cm. *1. History, Modern — Addresses, essays, lectures. 2. Power (Philosophy) — Addresses, essays, lectures. I. Holborn, Hajo, 1902- II. Krieger, Leonard, ed. III. Stern, Fritz Richard, 1926-1969, ed.*
D210.R43 1968   320/.01   74-363904

Taylor, Alan John Percivale, 1906-   **III. 492**
Englishmen and others. London, H. Hamilton [1956] vii, 192 p. 23 cm. *1. History, Modern — Addresses, essays, lectures. I. T.*
D210.T3   A57-2855

Petrie, Charles Alexander, Sir, bart., 1895-   **III. 493**
Diplomatic history, 1713-1933, by Sir Charles Petrie, bt. London, Hollis and Carter, 1946. xii, 384 p. front., maps. 23 cm. "First published 1946." *1. World politics. I. T.*
D217.P4   327   46-6073

Petrie, Charles Alexander, Sir, bart., 1895-   **III. 494**
Earlier diplomatic history, 1492-1713. New York, Macmillan, 1949. xii, 251 p. col. maps. 23 cm. A companion volume to the author's Diplomatic history, 1713-1933. *1. World politics. I. T.*
D217.P42 1949a   327   49-50377

D220 – 234   16TH CENTURY (1453 – 1648)

Matthews, George Tennyson, 1917- ed.   **III. 495**
News and rumor in Renaissance Europe; the Fugger newsletters. New York,

Capricorn Books [1959] 253 p. 19 cm. (A Putnam Capricorn book CAP9) *1. Fugger family. 2. Europe — History — 1517-1648. 3. Sixteenth century. 4. Manners and customs. I. T. II. T:The Fugger newsletters.*
D220.F82M3   940.23   59-9113

Koenigsberger, Helmut Georg.   III. 496
Europe in the sixteenth century [by] H. G. Koenigsberger and George L. Mosse. New York, Holt, Rinehart and Winston [1968] xiii, 399 p. illus., geneal. tables, maps. 21 cm. (A General history of Europe) *1. Europe — History — 1492-1648. I. Mosse, George Lachmann, joint author. II. T.*
D220.K6 1968b   914/.03/23   68-17107   ISBN:030836344

Davis, James Cushman, comp.   III. 497
Pursuit of power; Venetian ambassadors' reports on Spain, Turkey, and France in the age of Philip II, 1560-1600. Edited and translated by James C. Davis. New York, Harper & Row [1970] xi, 283 p. illus., maps, ports. 22 cm. (A Torchbook Library edition) *1. Europe — History — 1517-1648 — Sources. I. T.*
D221.V4D3 1970   940.2/32   70-134281

Chudoba, Bohdan.   III. 498
Spain and the Empire, 1519-1643. New York, Octagon Books, 1969. xi, 299 p. geneal. tables, maps (on lining papers) 24 cm. Reprint of the 1952 ed., with a new pref. by the author. *1. Europe — History — 1517-1648. 2. Spain — History — House of Austria, 1516-1700. 3. Holy Roman Empire — History — 1517-1648. I. T.*
D228.C48 1969   946/.04   71-84177

Clark, George Norman, Sir, 1890-   III. 499
Early modern Europe from about 1450 to about 1720. London, New York, Oxford University Press, 1957. 261 p. illus. 17 cm. (The Home university library of modern knowledge, 232) *1. Europe — History — 1492-1648. 2. Europe — History — 1648-1715. I. T.*
D228.C52   940.2   57-59170

Elliott, John Huxtable.   III. 500
Europe divided, 1559-1598 [by] J. H. Elliott. New York, Harper & Row [1969, c1968] 432 p. illus., geneal. tables, maps. 21 cm. (The Fontana history of Europe. Harper Torchbooks TB1414.) *1. Europe — History — 1517-1648. I. T.*
D228.E38 1969   940.2/32   69-15491

Green, Vivian Hubert Howard.   III. 501
Renaissance and Reformation; a survey of European history between 1450 and 1660, by V. H. H. Green. [2d ed.] New York, St Martin's Press 1964. 462 p. geneal. tables, maps. 24 cm. *1. Europe — History — 1492-1648. I. T.*
D228.G74 1964   940.21   64-20945

Koenigsberger, Helmut Georg.   III. 502
The Habsburgs and Europe, 1516-1660, by H. G. Koenigsberger. Ithaca [N.Y.] Cornell University Press [1971] xv, 304 p. illus., geneal. table, maps (1 fold.) ports. 22 cm. *1. Habsburg, House of. 2. Europe — History — 1517-1648. I. T.*
D228.K6 1971   940.2/3   73-145868   ISBN:0-8014-0624-2

Mousnier, Roland.   III. 503
Les XVIe [i.e. Seizième] et XVIIe siècles; la grande mutation intellectuelle de l'humanité, l'avènement de la science moderne et l'expansion de l'Europe. 4. ed., rev., corr. et augm. Paris, Presses universitaires de France, 1965 [c1953] 686 p. illus., maps, plates. 24 cm. (Histoire générale des civilisations, t.4) First ed. published in 1954 under title: Les XVIe et XVIIe siècles; les progrès de la civilisation européenne et le déclin de l'orient (1492-1715) *1. Sixteenth century. 2. Seventeenth century. I. T. (S)*
D228.M6 1965   67-59240

Thomson, Samuel Harrison, 1895-   III. 504
Europe in Renaissance and Reformation. New York, Harcourt, Brace & World [1963] 854 p. illus. 24 cm. *1. Europe — History — 476-1492. 2. Europe — History — 1492-1648.*
D228.T46   940   63-14421

D242 – 283 17TH CENTURY
(1601 – 1715)

Pennington, Donald H.   III. 505
Seventeenth-century Europe [by] D. H. Pennington. New York, Holt, Rinehart and Winston [1970] x, 486 p. geneal. tables, maps. 22 cm. (A General history of Europe) *1. Europe — History — 17th century. I. T.*
D246.P45 1970b   914/.03/22   71-115980   ISBN:003084883X

Merriman, Roger Bigelow, 1876-1945.   III. 506
Six contemporaneous revolutions. Hamden, Conn., Archon Books, 1963. viii, 230 p. 23 cm. An expansion of the David Murray lecture, University of Glasgow, 1937. *1. Revolutions — Europe. 2. Europe — History — 17th cent. I. T.*
D247.M42 1963   940.22   64-10706

Mousnier, Roland.   III. 507
Peasant uprisings in seventeenth-century France, Russia, and China. Translated from the French by Brian Pearce. [1st U.S. ed.] New York, Harper & Row [1970] xx, 358 p. illus., maps. 22 cm. (Great revolutions) Translation of Fureurs paysannes, les paysans dans les révoltes du XVIIe siècle (France, Russie, Chine). *1. Peasant uprisings. I. T.*
D247.M6813 1970   322/.42   72-95975

Pagès, Georges, 1867-1939.   III. 508
The Thirty Years War, 1618-1648. Translated by David Maland and John Hooper. Foreword by Theodore K. Rabb. New York, Harper [1970] 269 p. map. 23 cm. (A Torchbook library edition) Translated from La guerre de trente ans, 1618-1648. *1. Thirty Years' War, 1618-1648. I. T.*
D258.P313   940.2/4   77-148426   ISBN:0061360341

Wedgwood, Cicely Veronica, 1910-   III. 509
The thirty years war, by C. V. Wedgwood ... New Haven, Yale University Press, 1939. 544 p. illus. (incl. plans) plates, ports. fold. map, fold. geneal. tab. 23 cm. "Published on the Foundation established in memory of William McKean Brown. [Publication no. 11]" *1. Habsburg, House of. 2. Thirty years' war, 1618-1648.*
D258.W4 1939   A40-3275

Stoye, John Walter.   III. 510
Europe unfolding, 1648-1688 [by] John Stoye. New York, Harper & Row [1970, c1969] 416 p. geneal. tables, maps. 21 cm. (History of Europe. Harper torchbooks, TB1501] *1. Europe — History — 1648-1715. I. T.*
D273.S78 1970   940.2/52   77-95987

Hazard, Paul, 1878-1944.   III. 511
The European mind, the critical years, 1680-1715. New Haven, Yale University Press, 1953. 454 p. 23 cm. "This translation from the original French, La crise de la conscience européenne ... was made by J. Lewis May." *1. Europe — Intellectual life. 2. Eighteenth century. 3. Seventeenth century. 4. Philosophy, Modern — History. 5. Literature, Modern — 18th cent. — History and criticism. I. T.*
D273.5.H32 1953a   914   53-12258

Williams, E. Neville.   III. 512
The ancien régime in Europe; government and society in the major states, 1648-1789 [by] E. N. Williams. [1st U.S. ed.] New York, Harper & Row [1970] xv, 599 p. 22 cm. *1. Europe — Politics — 1648-1789. 2. Europe — Economic conditions. I. T.*
D273.5.W54 1970   914/.03/25   70-122614

James II, King of Great Britain, 1633-1701.   III. 513
The memoirs of James II: his campaigns as Duke of York, 1652-1660. Translated by A. Lytton Sells from the Bouillon manuscript, edited and collated with the Clarke edition. With an introd. by Arthur Bryant. Bloomington, Indiana University Press, 1962. 301 p. illus., ports., facsims., plans. 25 cm. *1. Europe — History — 1648-1715 — Sources. I. Sells, Arthur Lytton, 1895- ed. and tr.*
D274.J3A3   940.25   62-8916

Kamen, Henry Arthur Francis.   III. 514
The War of Succession in Spain, 1700-15 [by] Henry Kamen. Bloomington, Indiana University Press [1969] xii, 436 p. 23 cm. *1. Spanish Succession, War of, 1701-1714. I. T.*
D281.5.K3 1969   946/.055   75-85088   ISBN:253190258

Geikie, Roderick, 1874-1910.   III. 515
The Dutch Barrier, 1705-1719, by Roderick Geikie and Isabel A. Montgomery. With a memoir of Roderick Geikie by G. M. Trevelyan and a general introd. by P. Geyl. New York, Greenwood Press, 1968. xxi, 418 p. map. 23 cm. Reprint of the 1930 ed. Appendix B contains the text of the Barrier Treaties in French. *1. Barrier Treaties, 1709, 1713, 1715. 2. Great Britain — Politics and government — 1702-1714. 3. Spanish Succession, War of, 1701-1714. I. Montgomery, Isabel Annie (Morison) II. T.*
D282.G5 1968   940.2/526   69-10096

D284 – 297 18TH CENTURY
(1715 – 1789)

Anderson, Matthew Smith.   III. 516
Europe in the eighteenth century, 1713-1783. New York, Holt, Rinehart and Winston [1961] 364 p. illus. 22 cm. (A General history of Europe) *1. Europe — History — 18th cent. I. T.*
D286.A5   940.25   61-12769

Devèze, Michel.   **III. 517**
L'Europe et le monde à la fin du XVIII siècle. [Paris] A. Michel [1971] 703 p. maps. 18 cm. (L'Évolution de l'humanité, 27) Previously appeared as v.71 of the Bibliothèque de synthèse historique "L'Évolution de l'humanité." *1. Europe — History — 18th century. 2. Colonization — History. I. T.*
D288.D46   70-23737

Dorn, Walter Louis.   **III. 518**
Competition for empire, 1740-1763. New York, Harper & Row [1963] xii, 424 p. illus., ports., maps. 21 cm. (The Rise of modern Europe [v.9]) Harper torchbooks. The University library. *1. Europe — History — 1648-1789. I. T.* (S)
D289.D6 1963   940.25   63-24039

Postgate, Raymond William, 1896-   **III. 519**
Story of a year: 1798 [by] Raymond Postgate. [1st ed.] New York, Harcourt, Brace & World [1969] viii, 248 p. illus., col. maps (on lining papers), ports. 22 cm. *1. History — Yearbooks — 1798. I. T.*
D289.P53   909.7   69-14839

Gagliardo, John G.   **III. 520**
Enlightened despotism [by] John G. Gagliardo. New York, Crowell [1967] ix, 118 p. 21 cm. (Europe since 1500; a paperbound series) *1. Europe — History — 18th cent. — Addresses, essays, lectures. I. T.*
D290.G3   321.6   67-14301

Palmer, Robert Roswell, 1909-   **III. 521**
The age of the democratic revolution; a political history of Europe and America, 1760-1800. Princeton, N.J., Princeton University Press, 1959-64. 2 v. 25 cm. *1. Europe — Politics — 18th cent. 2. Constitutional history. I. T: The democratic revolution.*
D295.P3   940.25   59-10068

D299   1789 –

Historical Association, London.   **III. 522**
From Metternich to Hitler; aspects of British and foreign history, 1814-1939, Historical Association essays. Edited by W. N. Medlicott. New York, Barnes & Noble [1963] viii, 267 p. 23 cm. *1. History, Modern — Addresses, essays, lectures. I. Medlicott, William Norton, 1900- ed. II. T.*
D299.H53x   909.8   63-24055

Hobsbawm, Eric J.   **III. 523**
The age of revolution: Europe 1789-1848 [by] E. J. Hobsbawm. New York, Praeger Publishers [1969, c1962] xvi, 356 p. illus., maps, ports. 25 cm. (History of civilization) *1. Europe — History — 1789-1900. 2. Industry — History. I. T.*
D299.H6 1969   914/.03/28   75-99597

Palmer, Alan Warwick.   **III. 524**
A dictionary of modern history, 1789-1945, by A. W. Palmer. Philadelphia, Dufour Editions, 1964. vii, 314 p. 22 cm. *1. History, Modern — Dictionaries. I. T.*
D299.P32 1964   909.03   64-18500

Thomson, David, 1912-   **III. 525**
Europe since Napoleon. Newly revised ed. Harmondsworth, Penguin, 1966. 1004 p. 27 maps, 6 diagrs. 20 cm. (Pelican book, A724) *1. Europe — History — 1789-1900. 2. Europe — History — 20th century. I. T.*
D299.T53 1966   940.28   66-70236

D301 – 309   FRENCH REVOLUTION (1789 – 1815)

(see also: DC119 – 249)

Ford, Franklin Lewis, 1920-   **III. 526**
Europe, 1780-1830 [by] Franklin L. Ford. New York, Holt, Rinehart and Winston [c1970] xvii, 423 p. maps. 21 cm. (A General history of Europe) *1. Europe — History — 1789-1815. 2. Europe — History — 1815-1848. I. T.*
D308.F65 1970   914/.03/27   76-110097   ISBN:0030861470

Hampson, Norman.   **III. 527**
The first European revolution, 1776-1815. [New York] Harcourt, Brace & World [1969] 215 p. illus. (part col.), maps, ports. (part col.) 21 cm. (History of European civilization library) *1. Europe — History — 1789-1815. 2. France — History — Revolution. 3. Europe — Intellectual life. I. T.*
D308.H3 1969b   940.2/7   77-78868

Palmer, Robert Roswell, 1909-   **III. 528**
The world of the French Revolution [by] R. R. Palmer. [1st U.S. ed.] New York, Harper & Row [1971] vi, 282 p. 22 cm. (Great revolutions) *1. Europe — History — 1789-1815. 2. France — History — Revolution — Influence. I. T.*
D308.P26 1971   940.2/7   78-81880

Rudé, George F. E.   **III. 529**
Revolutionary Europe, 1783-1815 [by] George Rudé. Cleveland, Meridian Books [1964] 350 p. maps. 21 cm. (Meridian histories of modern Europe) *1. Europe — History — 1789-1815. 2. France — History — 1789-1815. I. T.*
D308.R8   940.27   64-23497

D351 – 400   19TH CENTURY

Postgate, Raymond William, 1896- ed.   **III. 530**
Revolution from 1789 to 1906; documents selected and edited with notes and introductions by Raymond Postgate. Gloucester, Mass., P. Smith, 1969. xvi, 398 p. 21 cm. Reprint of the 1962 ed. *1. Europe — History — 1789-1900 — Sources. 2. Revolutions — Europe — History — Sources. I. T.*
D351.P86 1969   940.2/7   70-10678

Woodward, Ernest Llewellyn, Sir, 1890-   **III. 531**
Three studies in European conservatism: Metternich, Guizot, the Catholic Church in the nineteenth century. [Hamden, Conn.] Archon Books, 1963. viii, 350 p. 23 cm. *1. Metternich-Winneburg, Clemens Lothar Wenzel, Fürst von, 1773-1859. 2. Guizot, François Pierre Guillaume, — 1787-1874. 3. Catholic Church — History. 4. Europe — Politics — 1789-1900. I. T.*
D355.W6 1963   940.28   63-15493

Namier, Lewis Bernstein, Sir, 1888-   **III. 532**
Vanished supremacies; essays on European history, 1812-1918. London, H. Hamilton [1958] vi, 179 p. 23 cm. (His Collected essays, v.1) *1. Europe — History — 1789-1900. 2. Europe — History — 1871-1918. I. T.*
D359.Nx   A59-4778

Taylor, Alan John Percivale, 1906-   **III. 533**
From Napoleon to Stalin; comments on European history. London, Hamilton [1950] 224 p. 23 cm. *1. Europe — History — 1789-1900. 2. Europe — History — 20th cent. I. T.*
D359.T3   940.27   51-446

Taylor, Alan John Percivale, 1906-   **III. 534**
The struggle for mastery in Europe, 1848-1918. Oxford, Clarendon Press, 1954. xxxvi, 638 p. maps (3 fold.) 23 cm. (Oxford history of modern Europe) *1. Europe — History — 1848-1871. 2. Europe — History — 1871-1918. I. T.* (S)
D359.T33   54-13436

Woodward, Ernest Llewellyn, Sir, 1890-   **III. 535**
War and peace in Europe, 1815-1870, and other essays. [Hamden, Conn.] Archon Books, 1963. vii, 291 p. 23 cm. *1. Europe — Politics — 1815-1871. 2. Historiography. 3. History, Modern — Sources. 4. France — History — 1789-1900. I. T.*
D359.W6 1963   940.28   63-25313

Baumont, Maurice.   **III. 536**
L'essor industriel et l'impérialisme colonial (1878-1904) par Maurice Baumont. Paris, F. Alcan, 1937. 610 p. 23 cm. (Peuples et civilisations; histoire générale. [XVIII]) *1. Imperialism. 2. Competition, International. 3. Europe — Politics. 4. Europe — Civilization. I. T.*
D359.7.Bx   37-23599

Anderson, Eugene Newton, ed.   **III. 537**
Europe in the nineteenth century; a documentary analysis of change and conflict, by Eugene N. Anderson, Stanley J. Pincetl, Jr. [and] Donald J. Ziegler. [1st ed. Indianapolis, Bobbs-Merrill, 1961] 2 v. 21 cm. *1. Europe — History — 1815-1871. 2. Europe — History — 1871-1918. 3. Europe — Social conditions — Collections. I. T.*
D360.A5   940.2082   61-13154

Howard, Michael Eliot, 1922-   **III. 538**
Studies in war and peace [by] Michael Howard. New York, Viking Press [1971, c1970] 262 p. 23 cm. *1. Military history, Modern — 19th century — Addresses, essays, lectures. 2. Military history, Modern — 20th century — Addresses, essays, lectures. 3. Disarmament — Addresses, essays, lectures. I. T.*
D361.H75   341.3   70-134325   ISBN:670679747

Albrecht-Carrié, René, 1904-   **III. 539**
A diplomatic history of Europe since the Congress of Vienna. New York, Harper [1958] 736 p. illus. 25 cm. *1. Europe — History — 1789-1900. 2. Europe — History — 20th century. I. T.*
D363.A58   940.28   58-6131

D371 – 378 Eastern Question
(see also: D461 – 472)

Anderson, Matthew Smith.   **III. 540**
The Eastern question, 1774-1923: a study in international relations [by] M. S. Anderson. London, Melbourne [etc.] Macmillan; New York, St. Martin's P., 1966. xxi, 436 p. 10 maps. 23 cm. *1. Eastern question. 2. Eastern question (Balkan) 3. Turkey — Foreign relations. I. T.*
D371.A43 1966   949.6   66-13896

Marriott, John Arthur Ransome, Sir, 1859-1945.   **III. 541**
The Eastern question; an historical study in European diplomacy, by J. A. R. Marriott. 4th ed. Oxford, Clarendon Press, 1940. xii, 602 p. maps (2 fold., incl. front.) 20 cm. *1. Eastern question (Balkan) 2. Eastern question.*
D371.M32 1940   949.6   A40-3618

Sorel, Albert, 1842-1906.   **III. 542**
The Eastern question in the eighteenth century; the partition of Poland and the Treaty of Kainardji. New York, H. Fertig, 1969. xxii, 270 p. map. 21 cm. Reprint of the 1898 ed. Translation of La question d'Orient au XVIII[superscript e] siècle. *1. Poland — History — Partition period, 1763-1796. 2. Eastern question (Balkan) 3. Kuchuk Kainarji, Treaty of, 1774. I. T.*
D373.S72 1969   943.8/02   68-9661

Stojanović, Mihailo D.   **III. 543**
The great powers and the Balkans, 1875-1878, by Mihailo D. Stojanović. Cambridge [Eng.] The University Press, 1939. x, 296 p. 22 cm. "Originally written as a thesis for the PH.D. degree ... approved by the University of London in 1930 under the title: 'Serbia in international politics, 1875-1878'. It has been revised and completed since, so that in its present form it differs considerably from the earlier manuscript." — Pref. *1. Eastern question (Balkan) 2. Balkan peninsula — History. 3. Europe — Politics — 1871- I. T.*
D374.S7 1939   949.6   39-17334

Medlicott, William Norton, 1900-   **III. 544**
The Congress of Berlin and after; a diplomatic history of the Near Eastern settlement 1878-1880. 2d ed. [Hamden, Conn.] Archon Books, 1963. 442 p. illus. 22 cm. *1. Berlin. Congress, 1878. 2. Eastern question (Balkan) 3. Balkan Peninsula — Politics. 4. Berlin, Treaty of 1878. 5. Europe — Politics — 1871-1918.*
D375.3.M4 1963   909.81   63-3197

Seton-Watson, Robert William, 1879-1951.   **III. 545**
Disraeli, Gladstone, and the Eastern question; a study in diplomacy and party politics. London, Cass [1962] xiii, 590 p. 23 cm. Imprint covered by label: New York, Barnes & Noble. *1. Eastern question. 2. Gt. Brit. — Foreign relations — 1837-1901. 3. Gt. Brit. — Politics and government — 1837-1901. 4. Europe — Politics — 1871-1918. I. T.*
D376.G7S4 1962   940.28   63-2605

Temperley, Harold William Vazeille, 1879-1939.   **III. 546**
England and the Near East: The Crimea. By Harold Temperley. [Hamden, Conn.] Archon Books, 1964. xxx, 548 p. 3 fold. maps, port. 22 cm. Vol. 1 of a planned 3 vol. work. No more published. "Unaltered and unabridged edition." *1. Eastern question. 2. Gt. Brit. — Foreign relations — 1837-1901. 3. Europe — Politics — 1848-1871. 4. Crimean War, 1853-1856. 5. Turkey — History — 1829-1878. I. T.*
D376.G7T4 1964   949.6   64-15911

Sumner, Benedict Humphrey, 1893-1951.   **III. 547**
Russia and the Balkans 1870-1880. Hamden [Conn.] Archon Books, 1962. 724 p. illus. 22 cm. *1. Eastern question (Balkan) 2. Russia — Foreign relations — 1855-1881. 3. Balkan Peninsula — History. 4. Europe — Politics — 1871-1918. 5. Panslavism. I. T.*
D376.R7S8 1962   949.6   62-51020

Kohn, Hans, 1891-   **III. 548**
Pan-Slavism: its history and ideology. 2d ed., rev. New York, Vintage Books, 1960. 468 p. 19 cm. (Vintage Russian library, V-710) *1. Panslavism.*
D377.3.K57 1960   327.47   60-51957

D383 Holy Alliance. Quadruple Alliance (1815 – 1830)

Artz, Frederick Binkerd, 1894-   **III. 549**
Reaction and revolution, 1814-1832, by Frederick B. Artz. [1st ed.] New York, and London, Harper, 1934. viii, 317 p. plates, ports. 23 cm. (The Rise of modern Europe, ed. by W. L. Langer. [vol. XIII]) Maps on lining-papers. *1. Europe — History — 1815-1848. I. T.*
D383.Ax (D6.R5 vol. 13)   940.28   34-33840

Droz, Jacques, 1909-   **III. 550**
Europe between revolutions, 1815-1848. Translated by Robert Baldick. [1st U.S. ed.] New York, Harper & Row [1967] 286 p. maps. 22 cm. (History of Europe) *1. Europe — History — 1815-1848. I. T.*
D383.D7   914/.03/282   67-22496

Kissinger, Henry Alfred.   **III. 551**
A world restored; Metternich, Castlereagh and the problems of peace. 1812-22. Boston, Houghton Mifflin, 1957. 354 p. illus. 23 cm. *1. Metternich-Winneburg, Clemens Lothar Wenzel, Fürst von, 1773-1859. 2. Londonderry, Robert Stewart, 2d marquis of, 1769-1822. 3. Europe — Politics — 1815-1848. I. T.*
D383.K5 1957a   940.27   57-10969

May, Arthur James, 1899-   **III. 552**
The age of Metternich, 1814-1848. Rev. ed. New York, Holt, Rinehart and Winston [c1963] viii, 152 p. 19 cm. (Berkshire studies in European history) *1. Metternich-Winneburg, Clemens Lothar Wenzel, Fürst von, 1773-1859. 2. Europe — History — 1815-1848. 3. Europe — Politics — 1815-1848. I. T. (S)*
D383.M3 1963   940.28   63-22477

Temperley, Harold William Vazeille, 1879-1939.   **III. 553**
The foreign policy of Canning, 1822-1827; England, the neo-holy alliance, and the New World. With a new introd. by Herbert Butterfield. [2d ed.] Hamden, Conn.] Archon Books, 1966. xlvi, 636 p. facsim., ports. 23 cm. *1. Canning, George, 1770-1827. 2. Gt. Brit. — History — George IV, 1820-1830. 3. Europe — History — 1815-1848. I. T.*
D383.T4 1966a   327.42   66-4116

Walker, Mack, comp.   **III. 554**
Metternich's Europe. New York, Walker [1968] vi, 352 p. 24 cm. (The Documentary history of Western civilization) *1. Europe — History — 1815-1848 — Sources.*
D383.W27 1968   940.2/82/08   68-27383

Webster, Charles Kingsley, 1886-   **III. 555**
The foreign policy of Castlereagh, 1812-1815, Britain and the reconstruction of Europe, by C. K. Webster. London, G. Bell, 1931. xv, 589 p. plates, 2 port. (incl. front.) 23 cm. "Notes on the system of references": p. xiv-xv. *1. Londonderry, Robert Stewart, 2d marquis of, 1769-1822. 2. Gt. Brit. — Foreign relations — 1800-1837. 3. Europe — Politics — 1789-1815. I. T.*
D383.W38   327.42   31-23150

D387 – 393   1848 – 1870

Fejtö, François, 1909- ed.   **III. 556**
The opening of an era: 1848; an historical symposium. With an introd. by A. J. P. Taylor. New York, Grosset & Dunlap [1973, c1948] xxvii, 444 p. 21 cm. (The Universal library [267]) "The essays, with the exception of those on Great Britain and the U.S.A., were translated by Hugh Shelley." Translation of Le printemps des peuples, 1848 dans le monde. *1. Europe — History — 1848-1849. I. T.*
D387.F4213 1973   940.2/84   73-158929   ISBN:0448002671

Hertzen, Aleksandr Ivanovich, 1812-1870.   **III. 557**
From the other shore, and The Russian people and socialism, an open letter to Jules Michelet. Introd. by Isaiah Berlin. [1st American ed.] New York, G. Braziller, 1956. 208 p. 19 cm. (Library of ideas) *1. Europe — History — 1848-1849. I. Hertzen, Aleksandr Ivanovich, 1812-1870. The Russian people and socialism. II. T. III. T:The Russian people and socialism.*
D387.H413   940.28   56-41455

Namier, Lewis Bernstein, Sir, 1888-1960.   **III. 558**
1848: the revolution of the intellectuals. Garden City, N.Y., Anchor Books [1964] 153 p. 19 cm. "A385." *1. Europe — History — 1848-1849. I. The revolution of the intellectuals. II. T.*
D387.N3 1964   940.28   64-3105

Robertson, Priscilla (Smith)   **III. 559**
Revolutions of 1848, a social history. Princeton, Princeton University Press, 1952. xi, 464 p. maps. 25 cm. *1. Europe — History — 1848-1849. 2. Revolutions — Europe. I. T.*
D387.R6   940.28   52-5838

Taylor, Alan John Percivale, 1906-   **III. 560**
The Italian problem in European diplomacy, 1847-1849, by A. J. P. Taylor. [Manchester, Eng.] Manchester University Press; New York, Barnes & Noble [1970] viii, 252 p. 22 cm. "First published 1934." *1. Europe — Politics — 1848-1871. 2. Italy — History — Revolution of 1848. 3. Italian question, 1848-1870. 4. Italy — Foreign relations — 1849-1870. I. T.*
D387.T3 1970   327.4/045   73-21516   ISBN:0719003997

Whitridge, Arnold, 1891-   **III. 561**
Men in crisis; the revolutions of 1848. [Hamden, Conn.] Archon Books, 1967 [c1949] 364 p. illus., port. 23 cm. *1. Europe — History — 1848-1849. 2. U.S. — Foreign relations — 1845-1849. I. T.*
D387.W5 1967   940.2/84   67-26662

Albrecht-Carrié, René, 1904- comp. III. 562
The Concert of Europe. New York, Walker [1968] 384 p. 24 cm. (Documentary history of Western civilization) *1. Concert of Europe.*
D388.A55   341.184   68-13327

Case, Lynn Marshall, 1903- III. 563
French opinion on war and diplomacy during the Second Empire. Philadelphia, University of Pennsylvania Press, 1954. xii, 339 p. 24 cm. *1. Public opinion — France. 2. Europe — History — 1848-1871. I. T.*
D389.C3   940.28   54-5009

Pouthas, Charles Hippolyte, 1886- III. 564
Démocraties et capitalisme (1848-1860) par Charles-H. Pouthas. Paris, Presses Universitaires de France, 1941. 639 p. 22 cm. (Peuples et civilisations; histoire générale. [XVI]) *1. Europe — History — 1848-1871. 2. World politics. I. T.*
D389.Px   909   A44-890

Hauser, Henri, 1866- III. 565
Du libéralisme à l'impérialisme (1860-1878) par Henri Hauser, Jean Maurain, [et] Pierre Benaerts. Paris, F. Alcan, 1939. 555 p. 23 cm. (Peuples et civilisations; histoire générale, pub. sous la direction de Louis Halphen et Philippe Sagnac. [XVII]) *1. History, Modern — 19th cent. 2. Liberalism. 3. Imperialism. 4. Europe — Politics — 1848-1871. 5. Europe — Politics — 1871-1918. I. Maurain, Jean, d. 1939. II. Benaerts, Pierre. III. T.*
D392.Hx (D20.P37 vol. 17)   940.28   39-25470

D394 – 400   1870 –

Falls, Cyril Bentham, 1888- III. 566
A hundred years of war. With 20 maps by B. G. Lewis. [2d ed.] London, Duckworth [1961] 421 p. plans. 23 cm. ([The Hundred years series]) *1. Military history, Modern — 19th cent. 2. Military history, Modern — 20th cent. I. T.* (S)
D396.F3 1961   66-35731

Gooch, George Peabody, 1873-1968. III. 567
Studies in diplomacy and statecraft. New York, Russell & Russell [1969] vii, 373 p. 22 cm. Essays. Reprint of the 1942 ed. *1. Europe — History — 1871-1918 — Addresses, essays, lectures. I. T.*
D397.G58 1969   327.2   77-75464

Langer, William Leonard, 1896- III. 568
European alliances and alignments, 1871-1890 [by] William L. Langer. 1st ed. New York, Knopf, 1931. xiii p., 509, xiv p. maps, diagrs. 25 cm. *1. Europe — Politics — 1871-1918. I. T.*
D397.L28   940.28   31-23943

Langer, William Leonard, 1896- III. 569
The diplomacy of imperialism, 1890-1902. 2d ed., with supplementary bibliographies. New York, Knopf, 1951 [c1950] xxii, 797, xxii p. maps, diagr. 25 cm. Half title: Bureau of International Research, Harvard University and Radcliffe College. *1. World politics. 2. History, Modern — 19th cent. 3. Colonies. 4. Imperialism. I. T.*
D397.L282 1951   940.28   51-343

Langer, William Leonard, 1896- III. 570
The Franco-Russian Alliance, 1890-1894. New York, Octagon Books, 1967 [c1929] ix, 455 p. 24 cm. (Harvard historical studies, v.30) *1. Franco-Russian Alliance. 2. Europe — Politics — 1871-1918.* (S)
D397.L3 1967   940.2/87   67-18772

Medlicott, William Norton, 1900- III. 571
Bismarck, Gladstone, and the Concert of Europe, by W. N. Medlicott. New York, Greenwood Press [1969] xiv, 353 p. maps. 23 cm. *1. Europe — Politics — 1871-1918. 2. Concert of Europe. 3. Bismarck, Otto, Fürst von, 1815-1898. 4. Gladstone, William Ewart, 1809-1898. I. T.*
D397.M4 1969   320.9/4   69-13994

Schmitt, Bernadotte Everly, 1886-1969. III. 572
Triple alliance and triple entente. New York, H. Fertig, 1971 [c1961] viii, 131 p. illus. 21 cm. *1. Triple Alliance, 1882. 2. Triple Entente, 1907. 3. Europe — Politics — 1871-1918. 4. European War, 1914-1918 — Causes.*
D397.S26 1971   940.2/8   70-80590

D410 – 847   20TH CENTURY

Facts on file yearbook. v.1- 1941- III. 573
New York. v. 28 cm. A compilation of the 52 weekly issues of Facts on file, v.1- (no. 10- Vols.6-10, 1946-50. 1 v. Vols.11-15, 1951-55. 1 v. *1. History — Yearbooks.*
D410.F3   42-24704

Cameron, James, 1911- III. 574
1914. London, Cassell [1959] vi, 209 p. 23 cm. *1. History — Yearbooks — 1914. 2. European War, 1914-1918. I. T.*
D410.5 1914.Cx   942.083   64-57367

Acheson, Dean Gooderham, 1893- III. 575
Sketches from life of men I have known. [1st ed.] New York, Harper [1961] 206 p. illus. 22 cm. *1. Statesmen. I. T.*
D412.6.A2   923.2   61-9701

Joll, James. III. 576
Three intellectuals in politics. [New York] Pantheon Books [1961, c1960] xiv, 203 p. 23 cm. Published in 1960 under title: Intellectuals in politics. *1. Blum, Léon, 1872-1950. 2. Rathenau, Walther, 1867-1922. 3. Marinetti, Filippo Tommaso, 1876-1944. I. T.*
D412.6.J64 1961   923.24   61-10030

Taylor, Edmond, 1908- III. 577
The fall of the dynasties; the collapse of the old order, 1905-1922. [1st ed.] Garden City, N.Y., Doubleday, 1963. 421 p. illus. 25 cm. (Mainstream of the modern world series) *1. Europe — History — 1871-1918. 2. Europe — Kings and rulers. I. T.*
D412.7.T3   940.28   63-10518

Fischer, Louis, 1896-1970. III. 578
Men and politics: an autobiography. With an appendix of letters from Eleanor Roosevelt added to the reprint ed. Westport, Conn., Greenwood Press [1970, c1946] ix, 672 p. 24 cm. *1. Europe — Politics — 1918-1945. 2. Journalists — Correspondence, reminiscences, etc. I. T.*
D413.F5A3 1970   940.5/0924   73-111498   ISBN:0837146410

Lyons, Eugene, 1898- III. 579
Assignment in Utopia. Westport, Conn., Greenwood Press [1971, c1937] xiii, 658 p. 23 cm. Autobiography. *1. Journalists — Correspondence, reminiscences, etc. 2. Communism — Russia. 3. Russia — Description and travel — 1917-. I. T.*
D413.L9A3 1971   914.7/03/842   76-110271   ISBN:0837149973

Beloff, Max, 1913- III. 580
The great powers; essays in twentieth century politics. London, Allen & Unwin [1959] 240 p. 23 cm. *1. World politics — Addresses, essays, lectures. I. T.*
D415.B4   909.82   62-53403

Hancock, William Keith, 1898- III. 581
Four studies of war and peace in this century. Cambridge [Eng.] University Press, 1961. 129 p. 22 cm. (The Wiles lectures, 1960) *1. Military history, Modern — 20th cent. 2. Passive resistance to government. 3. International cooperation. I. T.*
D415.H3   341.1   61-16234

Renouvin, Pierre, 1893- III. 582
World War II and its origins; international relations, 1929-1945. Translated by Rémy Inglis Hall. [1st ed.] New York, Harper & Row [1968, c1969] x, 402 p. 22 cm. Translation of Les crises du XXe siècle. 2. De 1929 à 1945. *1. History, Modern — 20th century. I. T.*
D421.R413 1969   940.53   72-1076

Holborn, Hajo, 1902- III. 583
The political collapse of Europe. [1st ed.] New York, Knopf, 1951. xi, 207 p. 20 cm. *1. Europe — Politics — 20th cent. I. T.*
D424.H6   940.5   51-10940

Hughes, Henry Stuart, 1916- III. 584
Contemporary Europe; a history [by] H. Stuart Hughes. 2d ed. Englewood Cliffs, N.J., Prentice-Hall [1966] xiv, 582 p. illus., maps, ports. 25 cm. *1. Europe — History — 20th century. I. T.*
D424.H83 1966   940.5   66-10610

Aron, Raymond, 1905- III. 585
The century of total war. [1st ed.] Garden City, N.Y., Doubleday, 1954. 379 p. 22 cm. *1. Military history, Modern — 20th cent. 2. World politics. I. T.*
D431.A7   940.5 (909.82)   54-5714

D440 – 472   Political and Diplomatic History

Survey of international affairs. 1920-23-- III. 586
London, New York, Oxford University Press [etc.] v.in maps (part fold., part col.) 25 cm. *1. World politics — Yearbooks. I. Toynbee, Arnold Joseph, 1889- II. Macartney, Carlile Aylmer, 1895- III. Toynbee, Veronica Marjorie (Boulter) IV. Laffan, Robert George Dalrymple, 1887- V. Calvocoressi, Peter. VI. Kirk, George Eden, 1911- VII. McNeill, William Hardy, 1917- VIII. Jones, Francis Clifford. IX. Balfour, Michael Leonard Graham, 1908-*
D442.S8   909.82   25-22280

Documents on international affairs. 1928-   **III. 587**
London, New York [etc.] Oxford University Press, 1929 v. in 25 cm. "Prepared ... to accompany and supplement the annual Survey of international affairs produced by Proffessor Arnold J. Toynbee." 1932- issued, under the auspices of the Royal institute of international affairs. "Norway and the war, September 1939-December 1940, edited by Monica Curtis" was published in advance of the regular 1940 volume. *1. International relations — Sources. 2. World politics. I. Royal institute of international affairs.*
D442.S82   341.08   30-10914

Bowman, Isaiah, 1878-   **III. 588**
The new world; problems in political geography, by Isaiah Bowman. 4th ed., with 257 maps. Yonkers-on-Hudson, N.Y., World Book Company [c1928] v, 803 p. illus., maps (2 fold.) 25 cm. *1. World politics. 2. European war, 1914-1918 — Territorial questions. 3. Boundaries. I. T.*
D443.B6 1928   28-29089

Royal institute of international affairs. Information Dept.   **III. 589**
South-eastern Europe; a political and economic survey, prepared by the Information department of the Royal institute of international affairs in collaboration with the London and Cambridge economic service. London, The Royal Institute of International Affairs; New York, Toronto [etc.] Oxford University Press [1939] xvi, 203 p. illus. (maps) diagrs. 23 cm. *1. Europe — Politics — 1918-1945. 2. Europe — Economic conditions — 1918-1945. 3. Balkan peninsula. I. London and Cambridge economic service. II. T.*
D443.R69   940.5   39-17709

Stillman, Edmund O.   **III. 590**
The politics of hysteria; the sources of twentieth-century conflict [by] Edmund Stillman and William Pfaff. [1st ed.] New York, Harper & Row [c1964] x, 273 p. 22 cm. *1. World politics. I. Pfaff, William, 1928- joint author. II. T.*
D443.S77   909.82   62-20118

Wolfers, Arnold, 1892-   **III. 591**
Britain and France between two wars; conflicting strategies of peace since Versailles. Hamden, Conn., Archon Books, 1963 [c1940] 467 p. 22 cm. *1. Peace. 2. Gt. Brit. — Foreign relations — 20th cent. 3. France — Foreign relations — 1914-1940. 4. Europe — Politics — 1918-1945. I. T.*
D443.W63 1963   940.51   63-16552

Yost, Charles Woodruff.   **III. 592**
The insecurity of nations; international relations in the twentieth century, by Charles Yost. New York, Published for the Council on Foreign Relations [by] Praeger [1968] x, 276 p. 22 cm. *1. History, Modern — 20th century. I. Council on Foreign Relations. II. T.*
D443.Y63   909.82   68-11324

Clarke, Ignatius Frederick.   **III. 593**
Voices prophesying war, 1763-1984 [by] I. F. Clarke. London, New York [etc.] Oxford U.P., 1966. x, 254 p. illus., facsims. 22 1/2 cm. *1. Imaginary wars and battles. I. T.*
D445.C6   355.48   66-77284

Fitzgerald, Walter, 1898-   **III. 594**
The new Europe, an introduction to its political geography, by Walter Fitzgerald. New York, Harper [1946] xiii, 298 p. illus. (maps) 22 cm. *1. Europe — Politics. 2. Geopolitics. 3. Boundaries. I. T.*
D445.F5 1946   940   46-4243

Kohn, Hans, 1891-   **III. 595**
The age of nationalism; the first era of global history. [1st ed.] New York, Harper [1962] 172 p. 20 cm. (World perspectives, v.28) *1. History, Modern — 20th cent. 2. Nationalism. I. T.*
D445.K58   909.82   62-11474

Snyder, Louis Leo, 1907-   **III. 596**
The new nationalism, by Louis L. Snyder. Ithaca, N.Y., Cornell University Press [1968] xiv, 387 p. 24 cm. *1. Nationalism. 2. History, Modern — 20th century. I. T.*
D445.S66   320.1/58   68-16391

Meyer, Henry Cord, 1913-   **III. 597**
Mitteleuropa in German thought and action, 1815-1945. The Hague, Nijhoff, 1955. xv, 378 p. 25 cm. (International scholars forum: a series of books by American scholars, 4) *1. Central Europe — Politics. 2. Pangermanism. 3. Germany — History — Historiography. I. T. (S)*
D447.M4   A56-2311

Namier, Lewis Bernstein, 1888-   **III. 598**
Facing East. New York, Harper, 1948. 159 p. 19 cm. *1. Europe — Politics — 20th cent. 2. Pangermanism. I. T.*
D447.N3 1948   940.2   48-4739

D461 – 472 EASTERN QUESTION
(see also: D371 – 378)

Earle, Edward Mead, 1894-   **III. 599**
Turkey, the great powers, and the Bagdad railway; a study in imperialism, by Edward Mead Earle. New York, Macmillan, 1923. xiii, 364 p. maps. 20 cm. Author's doctoral dissertation, Columbia university, 1923, but not issued as a thesis. *1. Bagdad railroad. 2. Turkey — Economic conditions — 1918- 3. Eastern question. I. T.*
D463.E2   23-11389

Kerner, Robert Joseph, 1887-1956.   **III. 600**
The Balkan conferences and the Balkan entente, 1930-1935; a study in the recent history of the Balkan and Near Eastern peoples, by Robert Joseph Kerner and Harry Nicholas Howard. Westport, Conn., Greenwood Press [1970] x, 271 p. maps, ports. 23 cm. Reprint of the 1936 ed. *1. Eastern question (Balkan) 2. Balkan conference. 3. Balkan Entente, 1934- 4. Balkan Peninsula — Politics. I. Howard, Harry Nicholas, 1902- joint author. II. T.*
D463.K4 1970   341/.242   77-110850   ISBN:0837145171

Kohn, Hans, 1891-   **III. 601**
Nationalism and imperialism in the hither East. New York, Harcourt, Brace, 1932. viii, 339 p. illus. (maps) 24 cm. "Translated by Margaret M. Green." — p. [iv] *1. Eastern question. 2. Nationalism and nationality. 3. Imperialism. 4. Mohammedans. I. Green, Margaret Minna, 1886- tr. II. T.*
D463.K6x   956 (950)   A32-2285

Stavrianos, Leften Stavros.   **III. 602**
Balkan federation; a history of the movement toward Balkan unity in modern times [by] L. S. Stavrianos. Hamden, Conn., Archon Books, 1964. x, 338 p. 24 cm. "Originally published, 1942, Smith College studies in history, vol. 27, nos. 1-4. Reprinted, 1964, unaltered and unabridged." *1. Balkan Peninsula — Politics. 2. Balkan Peninsula — History. 3. Eastern question (Balkan) I. T.*
D463.S7 1964   949.6   64-19945

Schmitt, Bernadotte Everly, 1886-1969.   **III. 603**
The annexation of Bosnia, 1908-1909. New York, H. Fertig, 1970. viii, 264 p. 21 cm. Reprint of the 1937 ed. *1. Bosnia and Herzegovina — Annexation to Austria. 2. Eastern question (Balkan) 3. Europe — Politics — 1871-1918. I. T.*
D465.S33 1970   949.7/42   71-80588

D501 – 680 World War I (1914 – 1918)

Geiss, Imanuel, ed.   **III. 604**
July 1914; the outbreak of the First World War; selected documents. New York, Scribner [1968, c1967] 400 p. 24 cm. Translation of Juli 1914, an abridged ed. of the compiler's 2 vol. work, Julikrise und Kriegsausbruch 1914. *1. European War, 1914-1918 — Diplomatic history. I. T.*
D505.G2713 1968   940.3/112/08   68-11752

Snyder, Louis Leo, 1907- ed.   **III. 605**
Historic documents of World War I. Princeton, N.J., Van Nostrand [1958] 192 p. 18 cm. (An Anvil original, no. 33) *1. European War, 1914-1918 — Documents, etc., sources. I. T.*
D505.S7   940.3082   58-14438

D511 – 520 CAUSES. AIMS

Albertini, Luigi, 1871-1941.   **III. 606**
The origins of the war of 1914. Translated and edited by Isabella M. Massey. London, New York, Oxford University Press, 1952-57. 3 v. fold. maps. 26 cm. *1. European War, 1914-1918 — Causes. 2. Europe — Politics — 1871-1918. 3. European War, 1914-1918 — Diplomatic history. I. T.*
D511.A574   940.311   52-12126

Barnes, Harry Elmer, 1889-1968.   **III. 607**
The genesis of the World War; an introduction to the problem of war guilt. New York, Knopf, 1929. Grosse Pointe, Mich., Scholarly Press, 1968. xxvii, 754 p. port. 23 cm. *1. European War, 1914-1918 — Causes. I. T.*
D511.B28 1968   940.3/11   70-416

Fay, Sidney Bradshaw, 1876-   **III. 608**
The origins of the World War. 2d ed., rev. New York, Free Press [1966] 2 v. facsim., maps. 21 cm. (A Free Press paperback) *1. European War, 1914-1918 — Causes. 2. Europe — Politics — 1871-1918. I. T.*
D511.F23 1966   940.3/11   68-2275

Lafore, Laurence Davis.   **III. 609**
The long fuse, an interpretation of the origins of World War I [by] Laurence

Lafore. [1st ed.] Philadelphia, Lippincott [1965] 282 p. maps. 21 cm. (Critical periods of history) *1. European War, 1914-1918 — Causes. I. T.*
D511.L19   940.3112   65-15251

Montgelas, Maximilian Maria Karl Desiderius, graf von, 1860-   III. 610
The case for the Central powers, an impeachment of the Versailles verdict, by Count Max Montgelas, translated by Constance Vesey. New York, A. A. Knopf, 1925. 255 p. 23 cm. Translation of Leitfaden zur Kriegsschuldfrage. *1. European war, 1914-1918 — Causes. 2. European war, 1914-1918 — Germany. I. Vesey, Constance, tr. II. T.*
D511.M5543 1925a   25-12058

Schmitt, Bernadotte Everly, 1886-   III. 611
The coming of the war, 1914, by Bernadotte E. Schmitt. New York, H. Fertig, 1966 [c1958] 2 v. 24 cm. *1. European War, 1914-1918 — Causes. 2. Europe — Politics — 1871-1918. I. T.*
D511.S275 1966   940.3112   66-24353

Schmitt, Bernadotte Everly, 1886-   III. 612
England and Germany, 1740-1914. New York, H. Fertig, 1967. 524 p. maps. 24 cm. Reprint of the 1916 ed. *1. European War, 1914-1918 — Causes. 2. Gt. Brit. — Foreign relations — Germany. 3. Germany — Foreign relations — Gt. Brit. I. T.*
D511.S28 1967   940.3/11   67-24596

Tuchman, Barbara (Wertheim)   III. 613
The Zimmermann telegram [by] Barbara W. Tuchman. [New ed.] New York, Macmillan [1966] xii, 244 p. facsim., ports. 22 cm. *1. European War, 1914-1918 — Causes. 2. Zimmermann, Arthur, 1864-1940. I. T.*
D511.T77 1966   940.3112   66-26604

Bethmann-Hollweg, Theobald von, 1856-1921.   III. 614
Reflections on the world war, by Th. von Bethmann Hollweg; translated by George Young. London, T. Butterworth [1920]- v. front. (port.) 23 cm. *1. European war, 1914-1918. 2. Europe — Politics — 1871- I. Young, George, Sir, bart., 1872- tr.*
D515.B4665   21-831

Fischer, Fritz, 1908-   III. 615
Germany's aims in the First World War. With introd. by Hajo Holborn and James Joll. New York, W. W. Norton [1967] xxviii, 652 p. illus., maps, ports. 25 cm. Translation of Griff nach der Weltmacht. *1. European War, 1914-1918 — Causes. 2. European War, 1914-1918 — Germany. 3. Germany — Foreign relations — 1888-1918. I. T.*
D515.F2713 1967b   940.3/11   64-23876

D521 – 523 GENERAL WORKS

Churchill, Winston Leonard Spencer, Sir, 1874-1965.   III. 616
The world crisis. London, T. Butterworth [1923-31] 6 v. illus., facsims., maps (part fold., part col.) ports. 25 cm. *1. European War, 1914-1918. 2. European War, 1914-1918 — Gt. Brit. 3. Reconstruction (1914-1939) 4. World politics. I. T.*
D521.C513   65-59059

Cruttwell, Charles Robert Mowbray Fraser, 1887-1941.   III. 617
A history of the great war, 1914-1918, by C. R. M. F. Cruttwell. 2d ed. Oxford, The Clarendon Press, 1936. xii, 655 p. illus., fold. map. 23 cm. *1. European war 1914-1918.*
D521.C7 1936   940.3   38-2895

Edmonds, James Edward, Sir, 1861-1956, comp.   III. 618
A short history of World War I. New York, Greenwood Press, 1968. xxxiv, 454 p. maps (part fold. col.) 22 cm. Reprint of the 1951 ed. *1. European War, 1914-1918. I. T.*
D521.E457 1968   940.3   68-54989

Falls, Cyril Bentham, 1888-   III. 619
The Great War. New York, Putnam [1959] 447 p. 22 cm. *1. European War, 1914-1918. I. T.*
D521.F25   940.3   59-7851

Liddell Hart, Basil Henry, 1895-   III. 620
The real war, 1914-1918. Boston, Little, Brown [1963, c1930] xii, 508 p. maps (part fold.) 20 cm. "31." *1. European War, 1914-1918. I. T.*
D521.L48 1963   940.4   63-24492

Masăryk, Tomáš Garrigue, Pres. Czechoslovak Republic, 1850-1937.   III. 621
The making of a state; memories and observations, 1914-1918. An English version, arr. and prepared with an introd. by Henry Wickham Steed. New York, H. Fertig, 1969. 461 p. port. 23 cm. Reprint of the 1927 ed. Translation of Světová revoluce za války a ve válce, 1914-1918. *1. European War, 1914-1918. 2. European War, 1914-1918 — Bohemia. 3. Czechoslovak Republic — Politics and government. I. Steed, Henry Wickham, 1871-1956. II. T.*
D521.M423 1969   320/.08   68-57829

Taylor, Alan John Percivale, 1906-   III. 622
The First World War, an illustrated history. London, H. Hamilton [1963] 224 p. illus., ports., maps. 24 cm. *1. European War, 1914-1918 — Pictorial works. I. T.*
D522.T3 1963   64-39475

Albrecht-Carrié, René, 1904-   III. 623
The meaning of the First World War. Englewood Cliffs, N.J., Prentice-Hall [1965] x, 181 p. maps. 21 cm. (A Spectrum book) *1. European War, 1914-1918 — Influence and results. I. T.*
D523.A546   940.3   65-13180

Mackinder, Halford John, Sir, 1861-1947.   III. 624
Democratic ideals and reality. With additional papers. Edited and with an introd. by Anthony J. Pearce. New York, Norton [1962] 278 p. illus. 20 cm. *1. League of Nations. 2. Sociology. 3. World politics. 4. Geography. 5. European War, 1914-1918 — Peace. I. T.*
D523.M1535 1962   327   63-3605

D530 – 578 MILITARY OPERATIONS
D530 – 549 Western Europe

Barnett, Correlli.   III. 625
The swordbearers; supreme command in the First World War. New York, Morrow, 1964 [c1963] xv, 392 p. illus., ports., maps, diagrs. 25 cm. *1. European War, 1914-1918 — Campaigns. 2. European War, 1914-1918 — Biography. I. T.*
D530.B26 1964   940.414   64-16445

Pitt, Barrie.   III. 626
1918, the last act. [1st American ed.] New York, W. W. Norton [1963, c1962] 318 p. illus. 22 cm. *1. European War, 1914-1918. I. T.*
D530.P5 1963   940.43   62-10104

Tuchman, Barbara (Wertheim)   III. 627
The guns of August. New York, Macmillan, 1962. 511 p. illus. 24 cm. London ed. (Constable) has title: August 1914. *1. European War, 1914-1918 — Campaigns. I. T.*
D530.T8   940.421   62-7515

Hubatsch, Walther, 1915-   III. 628
Germany and the Central Powers in the World War, 1914-1918. Edited by Oswald P. Backus. Introd. by Henry Cord Meyer. Lawrence [University of Kansas] 1963. 133 p. 23 cm. (University of Kansas publications. Social science studies) *1. European War, 1914-1918 — Germany. I. T.*
D531.H8   940.343   62-63208

Ludendorff, Erich, 1865-1937.   III. 629
Ludendorff's own story, August 1914-November 1918; the Great War from the siege of Liège to the signing of the armistice as viewed from the grand headquarters of the German Army. Freeport, N.Y., Books for Libraries Press [1971, c1920] 2 v. illus., maps (part fold., mounted on lining papers) 23 cm. Translation of Meine Kriegserinnerungen, 1914-1918. *1. European War, 1914-1918 — Germany. I. T.*
D531.L7713 1971   940.4/09/43   72-165647   ISBN:0836959566

Wolff, Leon.   III. 630
In Flanders fields; the 1917 campaign. New York, Viking Press, 1958. 308 p. illus. 22 cm. *1. European War, 1914-1918 — Belgium. I. T.*
D541.W7   940.4313   58-10607

Asprey, Robert B.   III. 631
The first Battle of the Marne. [1st ed.] Philadelphia, Lippincott [1962] 212 p. illus. 21 cm. (Great battles series) *1. Marne, Battle of the, 1914.*
D545.M3A8   940.421   62-7177

Hankey, Maurice Pascal Alers Hankey, baron, 1877-   III. 632
The Supreme Command, 1914-1918. London, Allen and Unwin [1961] 2 v. illus. 24 cm. *1. Gt. Brit. Committee of Imperial Defense. 2. Gt. Brit. War Cabinet. 3. European War, 1914-1918 — Gt. Brit. I. T.*
D546.H43   940.40942   61-3901

Lloyd George, David Lloyd George, 1st earl, 1863-1945.   III. 633
War memoirs of David Lloyd George. London, I. Nicholson & Watson [1933-36] 6 v. plates, ports., maps, facsims. (1 fold.) 23 cm. Paged continuously. *1. European war, 1914-1918. I. T.*
D546.L5 1933   940.342   33-28755

Woodward, Ernest Llewellyn, Sir, 1890-   III. 634
Great Britain and the War of 1914-1918 [by] Llewellyn Woodward. Boston, Beacon Press [1970] xxxix, 610 p. maps. 21 cm. (Europe in the twentieth century, BP 372) *1. European War, 1914-1918 — Great Britain. I. T.*
D546.W6 1970   940.3/42   71-125402   ISBN:080705657X

Watt, Richard M., 1930-   III. 635
Dare call it treason. Introd. by Colonel John Elting. New York, Simon and Schuster, 1963. 344 p. illus. 24 cm. *1. France. Armée — History. 2. European*

War, 1914-1918 — Campaigns — France. 3. Mutiny — France. I. T.
D548.W3   940.457   62-17979

D550 – 569 Eastern Campaigns

Churchill, Winston Leonard Spencer, Sir, 1874-1965.   III. 636
The unknown war; the eastern front, by the Rt. Hon. Winston S. Churchill. New York, Scribner, 1931. xv, 396 p. geneal. table. ports., maps (1 fold.) 23 cm. *1. European war, 1914-1918. 2. European war, 1914-1918 — Campaigns — Eastern. I. The eastern front. II. T.*
D550.C4   940.4147   31-32920

Graves, William Sidney, 1865-1940.   III. 637
America's Siberian adventure, 1918-1920 [by] William S. Graves. New York, P. Smith, 1941. xxiii, 363 p. illus. (map) plates, ports. 23 cm. "Reprinted 1941." *1. Russia — History — Allied intervention, 1918-1920. I. T.*
D558.G7 1941   940.4385   44-36193

Morley, James William, 1921-   III. 638
The Japanese thrust into Siberia, 1918. New York, Columbia University Press, 1957 [c1954] xiii, 395 p. map. 24 cm. (Studies of the Russian Institute, Columbia University) Issued in microfilm form in 1954 as thesis, Columbia University, under title: Samurai in Siberia. *1. Japanese in Siberia. 2. Japan — Foreign relations. 3. Russia — History — Allied intervention, 1918-1920. I. T. (S:Columbia University. Russian Institute. Studies)*
D558.M6 1957   940.4385   57-5805

Higgins, Trumbull.   III. 639
Winston Churchill and the Dardanelles, a dialogue in ends and means. New York, Macmillan [1963] 308 p. illus. 22 cm. *1. Churchill, Winston Leonard Spencer, Sir, 1874-1965. 2. European War, 1914-1918 — Campaigns — Turkey and the Near East — Gallipoli.*
D568.3.H5   940.425   63-14536

James, Robert Rhodes, 1933-   III. 640
Gallipoli. New York, Macmillan, 1965. xi, 384 p. illus., maps, plans, ports. 24 cm. *1. European War, 1914-1918 — Campaigns — Turkey and the Near East — Gallipoli. I. T.*
D568.3.J3 1965a   940.425   65-12661

Lawrence, Thomas Edward, 1888-1935.   III. 641
Seven pillars of wisdom; a triumph. Garden City, N.Y., Doubleday, 1966 [c1935] xiv, 622 p. maps. 22 cm. *1. European War, 1914-1918 — Campaigns — Turkey and the Near East. 2. Arabs. 3. Bedouins. 4. Wahhabis. 5. Arabia — Social life and customs. I. T.*
D568.4.L4 1966   940.415   65-29663

Lawrence, Thomas Edward, 1888-1935.   III. 642
The mint; notes made in the R.A.F. Depot between August and December, 1922, and at Cadet College in 1925, by T. E. Lawrence (352087 A/c Ross) Regrouped and copied in 1927 and 1928 at Aircraft Depot, Karachi. Garden City, N.Y., Doubleday, 1955. 250 p. 24 cm. "The present edition follows the [author's] revised text." *1. Gt. Brit. Royal Air Force. I. T.*
D568.4.L45A33 1955   358.4 (358)   55-6066

Lawrence, Thomas Edward, 1888-1935.   III. 643
Selected letters. Edited by David Garnett. London, Cape [1952] 384 p. 20 cm.
D568.4.L45A4 1952   923.542   53-24128

Lawrence, Thomas Edward, 1888-1935.   III. 644
T. E. Lawrence to his biographers, Robert Graves and Liddell Hart. Garden City, N.Y., Doubleday, 1963. viii, 187, iv, 260 p. 22 cm. Published in 1938 as two separate works under titles: T. E. Lawrence to his biographer, Robert Graves, and T. E. Lawrence to his biographer, Liddell Hart. *I. Graves, Robert, 1895- II. Liddell, Hart, Basil Henry, 1895-*
D568.4.L45A43   63-11220

Aldington, Richard, 1892-   III. 645
Lawrence of Arabia, a biographical enquiry. London, Collins, 1955. 448 p. illus. 22 cm. *1. Lawrence, Thomas Edward, 1888-1935.*
D568.4.L45A6   923.542   55-1583

Liddell Hart, Basil Henry, 1895-   III. 646
'T. E. Lawrence' in Arabia and after, by Liddell Hart. London, J. Cape [1936] 491 p. plates, ports., maps (part fold.) 23 cm. (Academy books, no. 20) "First published March 1934 ... third impression March 1934; reissued in Academy books, May 1935; reprinted ... September 1935; new and enlarged edition, December 1935; reprinted March 1936." American edition (New York, Dodd, Mead & company) has title: Colonel Lawrence, the man behind the legend. *1. Lawrence, Thomas Edward, 1888-1935. 2. European war, 1914-1918 — Campaigns — Turkey and the Near East. 3. European war, 1914-1918 — Arabia.*
D568.4.L45L52 1936   940.4153 (923.542)   36-31721

Barker, A. J.   III. 647
The bastard war; the Mesopotamian campaign of 1914-1918 [by] A. J. Barker. New York, Dial Press, 1967. xiv, 449 p. illus., maps, ports. 24 cm.

London ed. (Faber) has title: The neglected war. *1. European War, 1914-1918 — Campaigns — Turkey and the Near East — Mesopotamia. I. T.*
D568.5.B33 1967b   940.4/15   66-27391

D570 United States

Coffman, Edward M.   III. 648
The war to end all wars; the American military experience in World War I [by] Edward M. Coffman. New York, Oxford University Press, 1968. xvi, 412 p. illus., plans, ports. 24 cm. *1. European War, 1914-1918 — United States. I. T.*
D570.C6   940.4/12/73   68-29715

Palmer, Frederick, 1873-   III. 649
Newton D. Baker; America at war, based on the personal papers of the secretary of war in the world war; his correspondence with the President and important leaders at home and abroad; the confidential cablegrams between the War department and headquarters in France; the minutes of the War industries board, and other first-hand material, by Frederick Palmer ... New York, Dodd, Meade & Company, 1931. 2 v. fronts., plates, ports., maps, facsims. 23 1/2 cm. *1. Baker, Newton Diehl, 1871-1937. 2. European war, 1914-1918 — U.S.*
D570.P32   940.373   31-28311

Pershing, John Joseph, 1860-1948.   III. 650
My experiences in the world war, by John J. Pershing with sixty-nine reproductions from photographs and numerous maps. [1st ed.] New York, Frederick A. Stokes company, 1931. 2 v. plates, ports., maps (part fold.) diagr. 25 cm. *1. European war, 1914-1918 — U.S. I. T.*
D570.P44 1931   940.41273   31-10662

Cummings, Edward Estlin, 1894-1962.   III. 651
The enormous room. [Introd. by Robert Graves] New York, Liveright [1970, c1922] xix, 9-271 p. 21 cm. (Liveright paperbound edition) "Liveright L-1." *1. European War, 1914-1918 — Personal narratives, American. I. T.*
D570.9.C82 1970   940.4/81/73   77-114387

D580 – 595 NAVAL OPERATIONS

Frothingham, Thomas Goddard, 1865-   III. 652
The naval history of the world war by Thomas G. Frothingham. Cambridge, Harvard university press, 1924-26. 3 v. fold. maps, plans (part fold.) diagrs. 22 cm. "This work has been compiled from data provided by the historical section, United States Navy." *1. European war, 1914-1918 — Naval operations.*
D580.F75   24-14384

Hoehling, Adolph A.   III. 653
The Great War at sea; a history of naval action, 1914-18, by A. A. Hoehling. New York, Crowell [1965] x, 336 p. illus., facsims., maps, plans, ports. 22 cm. *1. European War, 1914-1918 — Naval operations. I. T.*
D580.H6   940.45   65-12508

Scheer, Reinhard, 1863-1928.   III. 654
Germany's high sea fleet in the world war, by Admiral Scheer, with a portrait and twenty-eight plans. New York, P. Smith, 1934. xiv, 375 p. port., maps (1 fold.), plans (1 fold.) 23 cm. *1. Germany. Kriegsmarine. 2. European war, 1914-1918 — Naval operations. I. T.*
D581.S25 1934   940.45943   34-23784

Sims, William Sowden, 1858-1936.   III. 655
The victory at sea, by William Sowden Sims in collaboration with Burton J. Hendrick. Garden City, New York, Doubleday, Page, 1920. xiii, 410 p. port., maps. 24 cm. *1. European war, 1914-1918 — Naval operations — Submarine. 2. European war, 1914-1918 — U.S. I. Hendrick, Burton Jesse, 1870- joint author. II. T.*
D589.U6S6   20-18578

D600 – 607 AERIAL OPERATIONS

Reynolds, Quentin James, 1902-1965.   III. 656
They fought for the sky; the dramatic story of the first war in the air. New York, Rinehart [1957] 304 p. illus. 22 cm. *1. European War, 1914-1918 — Aerial operations. I. T.*
D600.R48   940.44   57-7503

Mitchell, William, 1879-1936.   III. 657
Memoirs of World War I: "from start to finish of our greatest war." New York, Random House [1960] 312 p. illus. 24 cm. *1. European War, 1914-1918 — Aerial operations, American. I. From start to finish of our greatest war. II. T.*
D606.M5   940.44973   60-5548

D610 – 621 DIPLOMATIC HISTORY

Gottlieb, Wolfram Wilhelm.   III. 658
Studies in secret diplomacy during the First World War. London, Allen & Unwin [1957] 430 p. map. 23 cm. *1. European War, 1914-1918 — Diplomatic history. I. T.*
D610.G62   940.32   57-4503

Mayer, Arno J.   III. 659
Political origins of the new diplomacy, 1917-1918 [by] Arno J. Mayer. New York, H. Fertig, 1969. xiv, 435 p. 23 cm. (Yale historical publications. [Studies, 18]) Reprint of the 1959 ed. *1. European War, 1914-1918 — Diplomatic history. I. New diplomacy. II. T. (S)*
D610.M33 1969   940.3/2   68-9616

Martin, Laurence W.   III. 660
Peace without victory; Woodrow Wilson and the British liberals [by] Laurence W. Martin. Port Washington, N.Y., Kennikat Press [1973, c1958] xiv, 230 p. 22 cm. Original ed. issued in series: Yale historical publications. Miscellany 70. *1. European War, 1914-1918 — Diplomatic history. 2. European War, 1914-1918 — Great Britain. 3. European War, 1914-1918 — United States. 4. Wilson, Woodrow, Pres. U.S., 1856-1924. I. T.*
D611.M37 1973   940.3/22/73   72-85282   ISBN:0804617015

Wheeler-Bennett, John Wheeler, 1902-   III. 661
The forgotten peace, Brest-Litovsk, March 1918, by John W. Wheeler-Bennett. New York, W. Morrow, 1939. xx, 478 p. pl., ports., fold. map. 23 cm. (Studies in modern history. General editor: L. B. Namier ...) Printed in Great Britain. *1. Brest-Litovsk, Treaty of, Mar. 3, 1918 (Russia) I. T.*
D614.B6W45 1939   940.3141   39-3075

Bailey, Thomas Andrew, 1902-   III. 662
The policy of the United States toward the neutrals, 1917-1918, by Thomas A. Bailey. Baltimore, The Johns Hopkins Press, 1942. xvii, 520 p. illus. (maps) 20 cm. (The Albert Shaw lectures on diplomatic history, 1941. The Walter Hines Page school of international relations) *1. European war, 1914-1918 — U.S. 2. U.S. — Foreign relations — 1913-1921. 3. Neutrality. I. T.*
D619.B25   940.32273   42-25074

Cooper, John Milton, comp.   III. 663
Causes and consequences of World War I. Edited with an introd. by John Milton Cooper, Jr. [New York] Quadrangle Books [1972] 360 p. 22 cm. *1. European War, 1914-1918 — United States — Addresses, essays, lectures. 2. European War, 1914-1918 — Causes — Addresses, essays, lectures. 3. European War, 1914-1918 — Peace — Addresses, essays, lectures. I. T.*
D619.C69   940.3/14   74-190134   ISBN:0812902521 0812961943 (pbk)

Gregory, Ross.   III. 664
The origins of American intervention in the First World War. [1st ed.] New York, Norton [1971] xi, 162 p. 21 cm. (The Norton essays in American history) *1. European War, 1914-1918 — United States. I. T.*
D619.G73 1971   940.531/2   70-141588
    ISBN:0393054381 0393099806 (pbk)

Lansing, Robert, 1864-1928.   III. 665
War memoirs of Robert Lansing, Secretary of State. Westport, Conn., Greenwood Press [1970] 383 p. port. 24 cm. Reprint of the 1935 ed. *1. European War, 1914-1918 — United States. 2. United States — Foreign relations — 1913-1921. 3. United States — Neutrality. I. T.*
D619.L347 1970   940.3/22/73   78-110853   ISBN:0837145201

Mamatey, Victor S.   III. 666
The United States and East Central Europe, 1914-1918; a study in Wilsonian diplomacy and propaganda, by Victor S. Mamatey. Port Washington, N.Y., Kennikat Press [1972, c1957] xi, 431 p. 23 cm. *1. United States — Foreign relations — 1913-1921. 2. European War, 1914-1918 — Diplomatic history. 3. Europe, Eastern — Foreign relations. I. T.*
D619.M33 1972   940.3/22/73   73-159092   ISBN:0804616353

May, Ernest R.   III. 667
The World War and American isolation, 1914-1917. Cambridge, Harvard University Press, 1959. viii, 482 p. 22 cm. (Harvard historical studies, v.71) *1. European War, 1914-1918 — Diplomatic history. 2. U.S. — For. rel., 1913-1921. I. T. (S)*
D619.M383   940.32   58-12971

Millis, Walter, 1899-1968.   III. 668
Road to war; America, 1914-1917. New York, H. Fertig, 1970 [c1935] ix, 466 p. illus., ports. 23 cm. *1. United States — Foreign relations — 1913-1921. 2. European War, 1914-1918 — United States. 3. America, 1914-1917. II. T.*
D619.M47 1970   940.3/2273   68-9614

Seymour, Charles, 1885-1963.   III. 669
American neutrality, 1914-1917; essays on the causes of American intervention in the World War. [Hamden, Conn.] Archon Books, 1967 [c1935] vii, 187 p. 22 cm. *1. U.S. — Neutrality. 2. U.S. — Foreign relations — 1913-1921. 3. European War, — 1914-1918 — U.S. I. T.*
D619.S435 1967   940.3/2   67-17250

La Fargue, Thomas Edward, 1900-   III. 670
China and the world war. Stanford, Stanford University Press; London, H. Milford, Oxford University Press, 1937. x, 278 p. map 23 cm. (Hoover War Library Publications, no. 12) *1. European war, 1914-1918 — China. I. T.*
D621.C6L3   940.32251 (940.345102)   37-39237

D622 – 640 SPECIAL TOPICS.
PERSONAL NARRATIVES

Mock, James Robert.   III. 671
Words that won the war; the story of the Committee on Public Information, 1917-1919, by James R. Mock and Cedric Larson. New York, Russell & Russell [1968] xvi, 372 p. illus., facsims., ports. 25 cm. Reprint of the 1939 ed. *1. United States. Committee on Public Information. 2. Creel, George, 1876-1953. 3. Propaganda, American. 4. European War, 1914-1918 — Public opinion. 5. European War, 1914-1918 — United States. I. Larson, Cedric, 1908- joint author. II. T.*
D632.M64 1968   940.4/886/73   68-25073

Hoover, Herbert Clark, Pres. U.S., 1874-1964.   III. 672
An American epic. Chicago, H. Regnery Co., 1959- v. illus. 25 cm. *1. International relief. 2. European War, 1914-1918 — Civilian relief. 3. Commission for Relief in Belgium. I. T.*
D637.H6   361.53   59-13696

Horn, Daniel.   III. 673
The German naval mutinies of World War I. New Brunswick, N.J., Rutgers University Press [1969] xiii, 346 p. 22 cm. *1. Germany. Kriegsmarine. 2. Mutiny — Germany. 3. European War, 1914-1918 — Naval operations, German. I. T.*
D639.M82G45   940.4/59/43   71-75677   ISBN:813505984

Hanssen, Hans Peter, 1862-1936.   III. 674
Diary of a dying Empire. Translated by Oscar Osburn Winther. Edited by Ralph H. Lutz, Mary Schofield, and O. O. Winther. Introd. by Ralph H. Lutz. Bloomington, Indiana University Press [1955] liii, 409 p. maps (on lining papers) 24 cm. (Indiana University publications. Social science series, no. 14) Translation of Fra krigstiden. *1. European War, 1914-1918 — Personal narratives. 2. European War, 1914-1918 — Germany. I. T. (S:Indiana. University. Indiana University publications. Social science series, no. 14)*
D640.H35336   940.343   55-13698

Sassoon, Siegfried Lorraine, 1886-   III. 675
Memoirs of an infantry officer. New York, Coward, McCann, 1930. 322 p. 20 cm. Sequel: Sherston's progress. *1. European war, 1914-1918 — Personal narratives, English. I. T.*
D640.S3415   940.48142   30-25630

D641 – 651 ARMISTICE. PEACE

Keynes, John Maynard, 1883-1946.   III. 676
Two memoirs: Dr. Melchior, a defeated enemy, and My early beliefs. Introduced by David Garnett. New York, A. M. Kelley, 1949. 106 p. front. 21 cm. *1. Melchoir, Carl, 1871- 2. European War, 1914-1918 — Armistices. 3. European War, 1914-1918 — Food question — Germany. I. T.*
D641.K4   940.3141   51-51

Rudin, Harry Rudolph, 1898-   III. 677
Armistice, 1918, by Harry R. Rudin. [Hamden, Conn.] Archon Books, 1967 [c1944] vii, 442 p. fold. map. 23 cm. *1. European War, 1914-1918 — Armistices. 2. Germany — History — 1918-1933. I. T.*
D641.R8 1967   940.4/39   67-15927

Bailey, Thomas Andrew, 1902-   III. 678
Wilson and the peacemakers; combining Woodrow Wilson and the lost peace and Woodrow Wilson and the great betrayal. New York, Macmillan Co., 1947. 2 v. in 1. illus., maps. 22 cm. Each vol. has also special t.p. *1. Wilson, Woodrow, Pres. U.S., 1856-1924. 2. Paris. Peace Conference, 1919. 3. Versailles, Treaty of, June 28, 1919 (Germany) 4. European War, 1914-1918 — U.S. 5. U.S. — Politics and government — 1913-1921. I. T:Woodrow Wilson and the great betrayal. II. T. III. T:Woodrow Wilson and the lost peace.*
D643.A7B32   940.3141   48-5001

Birdsall, Paul.   III. 679
Versailles twenty years after. Hamden, Conn., Archon Books, 1962 [c1941] xiii, 350 p. 22 cm. *1. Paris. Peace Conference, 1919. 2. Versailles, Treaty of, June 28, 1919 (Germany) I. T.*
D643.A7B5 1962   940.3141   62-1863

United States. Dept. of State.   III. 680
The Treaty of Versailles and after; annotations of the text of the treaty. New

York, Greenwood Press [1968] xiv, 1018 p. maps. 24 cm. Reprint of the 1944 ed. "Annotations were prepared by Mr. Denys P. Myers." *1. Versailles, Treaty of, June 28, 1919 (Germany) 2. European War, 1914-1918 — Influence and results. I. Myers, Denys Peter, 1884- II. T.*
D643.A7U5 1968   940.3/141   68-55121

Baker, Ray Stannard, 1870-1946.   III. 681
Woodrow Wilson and world settlement; written from his unpublished and personal material. Gloucester, Mass., P. Smith, 1960 [c1922] 3 v. illus., ports., maps, diagr., facsims. 21 cm. "The first two volumes contain the narratives of what happened at Paris: the third is devoted wholly to the text of letters, memoranda, minutes, and other crucial documents referred to or quoted from in the narrative." *1. Wilson, Woodrow, Pres. U.S., 1856-1924. 2. Paris. Peace Conference, 1919.*
D644.B27 1960   940.3141   60-52263

Gelfand, Lawrence Emerson, 1926-   III. 682
The Inquiry; American preparations for peace, 1917-1919. New Haven, Yale University Press, 1963. xiv, 387 p. 24 cm. *1. Paris. Peace Conference, 1919 U.S. Territorial Section. 2. European War, 1914-1918 — Peace.*
D644.G4 1963   940.312   63-7933

Hankey, Maurice Pascal Alers Hankey, baron, 1877-   III. 683
The supreme control at the Paris Peace Conference 1919; a commentary. London, Allen and Unwin [1963] 206 p. 25 cm. *1. Paris, Peace Conference, 1919. I. T.*
D644.H2   940.3141   64-2860

House, Edward Mandell, 1858-1938, ed.   III. 684
What really happened at Paris; the story of the Peace conference, 1918-1919, by American delegates, ed. by Edward Mandell House and Charles Seymour. New York, Scribner, 1921. xiii, 528 p. illus. (maps) 22 cm. A series of talks given at the Academy of music in Philadelphia, 1920-21. *1. Paris. Peace conference, 1919. 2. Versailles, Treaty of, June 28,1919 (Germany) I. Seymour, Charles, 1885- joint ed. II. T.*
D644.H7   21-8042

Lansing, Robert, 1864-1928.   III. 685
The peace negotiations; a personal narrative. Westport, Conn., Greenwood Press [1971] vi, 328 p. illus., facsims., ports. 23 cm. Reprint of the 1921 ed. *1. Paris. Peace Conference, 1919. 2. Wilson, Woodrow, Pres. U.S., 1856-1924. 3. League of Nations. I. T.*
D644.L3 1971   940.3/142   74-110852   ISBN:0837145198

Lloyd George, David Lloyd George, 1st Earl, 1863-1945.   III. 686
Memoirs of the Peace Conference. New York, H. Fertig, 1972. 2 v. (xix, 964 p.) illus. 24 cm. Reprint of the 1939 ed. of the work first published in 1938 under title: The truth about the peace treaties. *1. European War, 1914-1918 — Peace. 2. Paris. Peace Conference, 1919. I. T.*
D644.L55 1972   940.3/141   70-80566

Nicolson, Harold George, Sir, 1886-   III. 687
Peacemaking, 1919, by Harold Nicolson. New York, Grossett & Dunlap [1965] vii, 378 p. front. 21 cm. (The Universal library. UL-178) First published in 1933. *1. Paris. Peace conference. 1919. 2. European War, 1914-1918 — Peace. I. T.*
D644.N36 1965   940.3141   65-13213

Seymour, Charles, 1885-   III. 688
Geography, justice, and politics at the Paris Conference of 1919. New York, American Geographical Society, 1951. iv, 24 p. 23 cm. (Bowman memorial lectures, ser. 1) *1. Paris. Peace Conference, 1919. 2. European War, 1914-1918 — Territorial questions. I. T. (S)*
D644.S46   940.31412   51-8380

Temperley, Harold William Vazeille, 1879-1939, ed.   III. 689
A history of the Peace Conference of Paris, edited by H. W. V. Temperley. London, New York, Oxford University Press [1969] 6 v. maps (part fold.) 25 cm. First published 1920-24. "Issued under the auspices of the Royal Institute of International Affairs." *1. Paris. Peace Conference, 1919. 2. European War, 1914-1918. I. Royal Institute of International Affairs. II. T.*
D644.T42   940.3/141   76-432641

Bonsal, Stephen, 1865-1951.   III. 690
Suitors and suppliants; the little nations at Versailles. Introd. by Arthur Krock. Port Washington, N.Y., Kennikat Press [1969, c1946] xiii, 301 p. 22 cm. (Essay and general literature index reprint series) *1. Paris. Peace Conference, 1919. 2. European War, 1914-1918 — Peace. 3. European War, 1914-1918 — Territorial questions. I. T.*
D645.B6 1969   940.3/141   68-26226

Marston, Frank Swain.   III. 691
The Peace conference of 1919, organization and procedure, by F. S. Marston. Issued under the auspices of the Royal institute of international affairs. London, New York [etc.] Oxford University Press, 1944. xi, [1], 276 p. diagr. 22 cm. *1. Paris, Peace conference, 1919. I. Royal institute of international affairs.*
D645.M387   940.31412   45-6755

Tillman, Seth P.   III. 692
Anglo-American relations at the Paris Peace Conference of 1919. Princeton, N.J., Princeton University Press, 1961. xiv, 442 p. 25 cm. Based on the author's doctoral dissertation. *1. Paris. Peace Conference, 1919. 2. U.S. — Foreign relations — Gt. Brit. 3. Gt. Brit. — Foreign relations — U.S. I. T.*
D645.T5   940.3141   61-7426

Bennett, Edward W.   III. 693
Germany and the diplomacy of the financial crisis, 1931. Cambridge, Harvard University Press, 1962. viii, 342 p. 21 cm. (Harvard historical monographs, 50) "Developed from a doctoral dissertation." *1. European War, 1914-1918 — Reparations. 2. Germany — Politics and government — 1918-1933. I. T. (S)*
D649.G3B38   940.31422   62-13261

D650 – 651   Individual Countries

King, Jere Clemens.   III. 694
Foch versus Clemenceau; France and German dismemberment, 1918-1919. Cambridge, Harvard University Press, 1960. vi, 137 p. 21 cm. (Harvard historical monographs, 44) *1. Foch, Ferdinand, 1851-1929. 2. Clemenceau, Georges Eugène Benjamin, 1841-1929. 3. European War, 1914-1918 — Territorial questions — Rhine River and Valley. (S)*
D650.M5K5   944.08   60-11557

Deák, Francis, 1898-1972.   III. 695
Hungary at the Paris Peace Conference; the diplomatic history of the Treaty of Trianon. New York, H. Fertig, 1972 [c1942] xxii, 594 p. 23 cm. *1. Paris. Peace Conference, 1919. Hungary. 2. Trianon, Treaty of, June 4, 1920 (Hungary) 3. European War, 1914-1918 — Territorial questions — Hungary. 4. European War, 1914-1918 — Sources. I. T. (S:Carnegie Endowment for International Peace. The Paris Peace Conference, history and documents.)*
D651.H7D4 1972   940.3/142   77-80541

Albrecht-Carrié, René, 1904-   III. 696
Italy at the Paris Peace Conference. Hamden, Conn., Archon Books, 1966 [c1938] xiv, 575 p. maps. 23 cm. "First published ... for the Carnegie Endowment for International Peace in the series The Paris Peace Conference, history and documents." *1. Paris. Peace Conference, 1919. Italy. I. T.*
D651.I7A8 1966   940.3141   66-13339

Spector, Sherman David, 1927-   III. 697
Rumania at the Paris Peace Conference; a study of the diplomacy of Ioan I. C. Brătianu. New York, Bookman Associates [1962] 368 p. illus. 23 cm. *1. Brătianu, Ioan I. C., 1864-1927. 2. Paris. Peace Conference, 1919. Rumania. 3. European War, 1914-1918 — Rumania. I. T.*
D651.R6S7   62-15528

Thompson, John M.   III. 698
Russia, Bolshevism, and the Versailles peace [by] John M. Thompson. Princeton, N.J., Princeton University Press, 1966 [i.e. 1967] vii, 429 p. maps. 24 cm. (Studies of the Russian Institute, Columbia University) *1. European War, 1914-1918 — Russia. 2. European War, 1914-1918 — Peace. 3. Communism — Russia. I. T. (S:Columbia University. Russian Institute. Studies)*
D651.R8T5   940.3/141   66-17712

Lederer, Ivo J.   III. 699
Yugoslavia at the Paris Peace Conference; a study in frontiermaking. New Haven, Yale University Press, 1963. xiv, 351 p. ports., maps (1 fold.) 24 cm. *1. Paris, Peace Conference, 1919, Yugoslavia. I. T.*
D651.Y8L4   940.31425   63-13966

D652 – 728   1919 – 1939

Toynbee, Arnold Joseph, 1889-   III. 700
The world after the Peace conference, being an epilogue to the 'History of the Peace conference of Paris' and a prologue to the 'Survey of international affairs, 1920-1923,' by Arnold J. Toynbee. London, New York [etc.] H. Milford, Oxford University Press, 1925. 91 p. fold. map. 25 cm. "Issued under the auspices of the British institute of international affairs." Originally written as an introduction to the author's Survey of international affairs in 1920-23 and intended for publication as part of the same volume. cf. Pref. *1. European war, 1914-1918 — Influence and results. 2. World politics. I. Royal Institute of international affairs. II. T.*
D653.T6   25-19520

Angell, James Waterhouse, 1898-   III. 701
The recovery of Germany, by James W. Angell. Enl. and rev. ed. Westport, Conn., Greenwood Press [1972, c1932] xix, 442 p. 22 cm. Original ed. issued in series: Publications of the Council on Foreign Relations. *1. Reconstruction (1914-1939) — Germany. 2. Germany — Economic conditions — 1918-1945. I. T.*
D659.G3A7 1972   330.943/08   75-138197   ISBN:0837155509

Kohn, Hans, 1891- III. 702
Revolutions and dictatorships; essays in contemporary history. Freeport, N.Y., Books for Libraries Press [1969, c1939] xii, 437 p. 23 cm. (Essay index reprint series) *1. Revolutions. 2. Dictators. 3. Nationalism. 4. History, Modern — 20th century. 5. World politics — 20th century. I. T.*
D720.K6 1969   909.82   75-80388   ISBN:836911458

Namier, Lewis Bernstein, Sir, 1888-1960. III. 703
Europe in decay; a study in disintegration, 1936-1940. Gloucester, Mass., P. Smith, 1963. 329 p. 21 cm. *1. Europe — History — 1918-1945. 2. World War, 1939-1945 — Causes. I. T.*
D720.N3 1963   940.52   63-4320

Nolte, Ernst, 1923- III. 704
Three faces of fascism; Action Française, Italian fascism, National Socialism. Translated from the German by Leila Vennewitz. [1st ed.] New York, Holt, Rinehart and Winston [1966, c1965] xi, 561 p. 24 cm. Translation of Der Faschismus in seiner Epoche. *1. Fascism — History. I. T.*
D726.5.N613   320.533   66-10262

Chamberlain, Neville, 1869-1940. III. 705
In search of peace. Freeport, N.Y., Books for Libraries Press [1971] viii, 309 p. port. 24 cm. (Essay index reprint series) Reprint of the 1939 ed. *1. Europe — Politics — 1918-1945 — Addresses, essays, lectures. 2. Great Britain — Foreign relations — 1936-1945 — Addresses, essays, lectures. 3. Peace — Addresses, essays, lectures. I. T.*
D727.C5 1971   942.084   77-156627   ISBN:0836922743

Churchill, Winston Leonard Spencer, Sir, 1874-1965. III. 706
Step by step, 1936-1939. Freeport, N.Y., Books for Libraries Press [1971, c1939] xii, 323 p. port. 24 cm. (Essay index reprint series) *1. Europe — Politics — 1918-1945 — Addresses, essays, lectures. 2. Great Britain — Foreign relations — 1936-1945 — Addresses, essays, lectures. I. T.*
D727.C54 1971   940.5/2   72-156631   ISBN:0836923103

Craig, Gordon Alexander, 1913- ed. III. 707
The diplomats: 1919-1939. Edited by Gordon A. Craig and Felix Gilbert. Princeton, Princeton University Press, 1953. x, 700 p. ports. 25 cm. *1. World politics. I. Gilbert, Felix, 1905- joint ed. II. T.*
D727.C7   940.51   53-6378

Eubank, Keith. III. 708
Munich. [1st ed.] Norman, University of Oklahoma Press [1963] xiv, 322 p. illus., ports., maps. 24 cm. *1. Munich four-power agreement, 1938. 2. World War, 1939-1945 — Causes.*
D727.E9   940.5312   63-8987

Gafencu, Grigore, 1892- III. 709
Last days of Europe; a diplomatic journey in 1939. Translated by E. Fletcher-Allen. [Hamden, Conn.] Archon Books, 1970 [c1948] viii, 239 p. ports. 22 cm. Translation of Derniers jours de l'Europe. *1. Europe — Politics — 1918-1945. I. T.*
D727.G313 1970   320.94   73-120373   ISBN:208009558

Robbins, Keith. III. 710
Munich 1938. London, Cassell, 1968. [10], 398 p. 16 plates, illus., 2 maps, ports. 22 cm. *1. Munich four-power agreement, 1938. 2. Czechoslovak Republic — History — 1918-1938. 3. Germany — Foreign relations — 1933-1945. 4. Europe — Politics — 1918-1945. I. T.*
D727.R6   940.531/2   68-108772   ISBN:0304931292

Salvemini, Gaetano, 1873- III. 711
Prelude to World War II. London, Gollancz, 1953 [c1951] 519 p. 22 cm. Errata slip mounted on p. 15. *1. World politics. 2. World War, 1939-1945 — Causes. I. T.*
D727.Sx   A54-1895

D731 – 838 World War II (1939 – 1945)

Hutton, Oram C. III. 712
The story of the Stars and Stripes, by Bud Hutton and Andy Rooney. Westport, Conn., Greenwood Press [1970, c1946] ix, 240 p. 23 cm. *1. Stars and Stripes. I. Rooney, Andrew A., joint author. II. T.*
D731.S73H8 1970   940.53/05   70-112324   ISBN:0837147123

U.S. Dept. of State. III. 713
The Conferences at Malta and Yalta, 1945. Washington, U.S. Govt. Print. Off., 1955. lxxviii, 1032 p. group ports., fold. maps (part col.) facsims. 24 cm. (Its Foreign relations of the United States: diplomatic papers. [U.S.] Dept. of State. Publication 6199.) "The compiling and professional editing of this volume were done by a special staff in the Historical Division of the Department of State, under the direction of the chief of the division. The technical editing was done by the Division of Publishing Services." *1. Malta, Conference, 1945. 2. Crimea Conference, Yalta, Russia, 1945. 3. World War, 1939-1945 — Documents, etc., sources. I. T. (S) (S:U.S. Dept. of State. Publication 6199)*
D734.A1U555   940.531   56-60328

Wilson, Theodore A., 1940- III. 714
The first summit; Roosevelt and Churchill at Placentia Bay 1941 [by] Theodore A. Wilson. Boston, Houghton Mifflin, 1969. xvi, 344 p. illus., facsims., ports. 22 cm. *1. Atlantic declaration, August 14, 1941. I. T.*
D734.A8W5   940.531/4   69-15032

Feis, Herbert, 1893- III. 715
Between war and peace; the Potsdam Conference. Princeton, N.J., Princeton University Press, 1960. viii, 367 p. maps. 24 cm "A continuation of the narrative in [the author's] Churchill-Roosevelt-Stalin." *1. Berlin, Conference, 1945. I. T.*
D734.B4 1945ad   940.5314   60-12230

Snell, John L., ed. III. 716
The meaning of Yalta; Big Three diplomacy and the new balance of power. With a foreword by Paul H. Clyde. Baton Rouge, Louisiana State University Press [1956] xiii, 239 p. illus., maps. 23 cm. *1. Crimea Conference, Yalta, Russia, 1945. 2. World War, 1939-1945 — Territorial questions. 3. World politics — 1945- I. T.*
D734.C7 1945j   940.531   56-7960

Stettinius, Edward Reilly, 1900-1949. III. 717
Roosevelt and the Russians; the Yalta Conference. Edited by Walter Johnson. Westport, Conn., Greenwood Press [1970, c1949] xvi, 367 p. illus., facsims., group ports. 23 cm. *1. Crimea Conference, Yalta, 1945. 2. Roosevelt, Franklin Delano, Pres. U.S., 1882-1945. I. T.*
D734.C7 1970   940.531   75-100179   ISBN:837129761

Eisenhower, Dwight David, Pres. U.S., 1890-1969. III. 718
The papers of Dwight David Eisenhower; the war years. Alfred D. Chandler, Jr., editor. Stephen E. Ambrose, associate editor [and others] Baltimore, Johns Hopkins Press [1970] 5 v. facsims., maps, ports. 24 cm. *1. World War, 1939-1945 — Sources. I. Chandler, Alfred Dupont, ed.*
D735.E37   940.54/012   65-27672   ISBN:801810787

Germany. Auswärtiges Amt. III. 719
Documents and materials relating to the eve of the Second World War. New York, International Publishers [1948] 2 v. facsims. 20 cm. "Secret documents from the archives of the German Ministry of Foreign Affairs captured by the Soviet army in Berlin." *1. Germany — Foreign relations — 1933-1945. 2. World War, 1939-1945 — Diplomatic history. I. Dirksen, Herbert von, 1882-*
D735.G366 1948a   940.53243   49-7210

Langsam, Walter Consuelo, 1906- ed. III. 720
Historic documents of World War II. Princeton, N.J., Van Nostrand [1958] 192 p. 18 cm. (An Anvil original, no. 34) *1. World War, 1939-1945 — Documents, etc., sources. I. T.*
D735.L3   940.53082   58-14435

Russia (1923- U.S.S.R.) Komissiia po izdaniiu diplomaticheskikh dokumentov. III. 721
Stalin's correspondence with Churchill, Attlee, Roosevelt, and Truman: 1941-45. New York, Dutton, 1958. 400, 301 p. 23 cm. Contains the 2 vols. as published in 1957 by the Foreign Languages Pub. House in Moscow under title: Correspondence between the Chairman of the Council of Ministers of the U.S.S.R. and the Presidents of the U.S.A. and the Prime Ministers of Great Britain during the Great Patriotic War of 1941-1945. Translation of (romanized form) Perepiska Predsedatelia Soveta Ministrov SSSR *1. World War, 1939-1945 — Sources. I. Stalin, Iosif, 1879-1953. II. T.*
D735.R853x   940.532247   63-1395

D741 – 742 CAUSES

Lafore, Laurence Davis. III. 722
The end of glory; an interpretation of the origins of World War II [by] Laurence Lafore. [1st ed.] Philadelphia, J. B. Lippincott Co. [1970] 280 p. 21 cm. (Critical periods of history) *1. World War, 1939-1945 — Causes. I. T.*
D741.L26   940.531/12   72-88739

Mosley, Leonard, 1913- III. 723
On borrowed time; how World War II began. New York, Random House [1969] xvi, 509 p. illus., maps (on lining papers), ports. 25 cm. *1. World War, 1939-1945 — Causes. 2. Europe — Politics — 1918-1945. I. T.*
D741.M65   940.531/12   69-16427

Nikonov, A. D. III. 724
Proiskoozhdenie Vtoroi Mirovoi voiny I Evropeiskii politicheskii predvoennyi krizis. Moskva, Izd-vo. Akademii Nauk SSSR, 1955. 96 p. 20 cm. Russian and English. Added t.p.: The origin of World War II and the prewar European political crisis of 1939. On cover: Doklady sovetskoi delegatsii na X Mezhdunarodnom Kongresse Istorikov V Rime. (Document of Soviet delegates at the Tenth International Congress of Historians in

Rome.) *1. World War, 1939-1945 — Causes. I. The origin of World War II. II. T.*
D741.N5   56-31098

Taylor, Alan John Percivale, 1906- III. 725
The origins of the Second World War. [1st American ed.] New York, Atheneum, 1962 [c1961] 296 p. illus. 22 cm. *1. World War, 1939-1945 — Causes. I. T.*
D741.T34 1962   940.5311   62-7543

Jaspers, Karl, 1883- III. 726
The question of German guilt, tr. by E. B. Ashton [pseud.] New York, Dial Press, 1947 [i.e. 1948] 123 p. 21 cm. Translation of Die Schuldfrage, ein Beitrage zur deutschen Frage. *1. World War, 1939-1945 — Causes. I. Basch, Ernst, 1909- tr. II. T.*
D742.G4J23   940.5314443   48-5014

Churchill, Winston Leonard Spencer, Sir, 1874- III. 727
War speeches. Compiled by Charles Eade. Boston, Houghton, Mifflin, 1953. 3 v. 25 cm. *1. World War, 1939-1945 — Addresses, sermons, etc. 2. World War, 1939-1945 — Gt. Brit. I. T.*
D742.G7C55943   940.5304   52-9584

Schroeder, Paul W. III. 728
The Axis alliance and Japanese-American relations, 1941. Ithaca, N.Y., Published for the American Historical Association [by] Cornell University Press [1958] ix, 246 p. 24 cm. *1. Anti-comintern pact. 2. World War, 1939-1945 — Causes. 3. U.S. — Foreign relations — Japan. 4. Japan — Foreign relations — U.S. I. T.*
D742.J3S38   940.5324   58-2112

Trefousse, Hans Louis. III. 729
Germany and American neutrality, 1939-1941 [by] H. L. Trefousse. New York, Octagon Books, 1969 [c1951] 247 p. ports. 24 cm. *1. World War, 1939-1945 — Causes. 2. Germany — Foreign relations — United States. 3. United States — Foreign relations — Germany. I. T.*
D742.U5T66 1969   327.43/073   71-76012

D743 – 744   GENERAL WORKS

Alexander, Harold Rupert Leofric George Alexander, 1st earl, 1891- III. 730
The Alexander memoirs, 1940-1945. Edited by John North. New York, McGraw-Hill [c1962] xiii, 209 p. illus., group ports., maps (part fold.) 22 cm. *1. World War, 1939-1945 — Campaigns. I. T.*
D743.A57 1962a   940.542   63-12437

Bryant, Arthur, Sir, 1899- III. 731
Triumph in the west; a history of the war years based on the diaries of Field-Marshal Lord Alanbrooke, chief of the Imperial General Staff. [1st ed.] Garden City, N.Y., Doubleday, 1959. xviii, 438 p. maps. 24 cm. *1. World War, 1939-1945. I. Alanbrooke, Alan Francis Brooke, 1st viscount, 1883- II. T.*
D743.B73   940.53   59-13960

Churchill, Winston Leonard Spencer, Sir, 1874-1965. III. 732
The Second World War. Boston, Published in association with the Cooperation Pub. Co. [by] Houghton Mifflin, 1948-53. 6 v. illus., maps. 22 cm. Vols. 3-6 published by Houghton Mifflin. *1. World War, 1939-1945. 2. World War, 1939-1945 — Gt. Brit. I. T.*
D743.C47   940.53   48-2880

Eisenhower, Dwight David, Pres. U.S., 1890- III. 733
Crusade in Europe. Garden City, N.Y., Garden City Books [1952, c1948] 573 p. illus. 19 cm. *1. World War, 1939-1945 — Campaigns. I. T.*
D743.E35 1952   940.542   52-2207

Fuller, John Frederick Charles, 1878- III. 734
The Second World War, 1939-45: a strategical and tactical history, by J. F. C. Fuller. New York, Meredith Press [1968] 431 p. illus., maps, plans. 22 cm. First published 1948; 3d impression (with revisions) 1954; 3d printing, 1968. *1. World War, 1939-1945 — Campaigns. I. T.*
D743.F85 1968   940.541   70-2043

Greenfield, Kent Roberts, 1893- III. 735
American strategy in World War II: a reconsideration. Baltimore, John Hopkins Press, 1963. viii, 145 p. 22 cm. "Based on the tenth series of J. P. Young lectures in American history ... at Memphis State University on October 28-30, 1962." *1. World War, 1939-1945. 2. Strategy. I. T.*
D743.G666   940.54012   63-19554

Jacobsen, Hans Adolf, ed. III. 736
Decisive battles of World War II; the German view. Edited by H. A. Jacobsen and J. Rohwer. Introd. by Cyril Falls. Translated from the German by Edward Fitzgerald. [1st American ed.] New York, Putnam [1965] 509 p. illus., maps, group ports. 24 cm. *1. World War, 1939-1945. I. Rohwer, Jürgen, joint ed. II. T.*
D743.J313 1965   940.54   64-13541

Liddell Hart, Basil Henry, Sir, 1895-1970. III. 737
History of the Second World War. [1st American ed.] New York, Putnam [1971, c1970] xvi, 768 p. maps. 25 cm. *1. World War, 1939-1945. I. T.*
D743.L514 1971   940.53   79-136796

Morison, Samuel Eliot, 1887- III. 738
Strategy and compromise. [1st ed.] Boston, Little, Brown [1958] 120 p. 20 cm. *1. World War, 1939-1945 — Campaigns. I. T.*
D743.M74   940.542   58-6030

Patton, George Smith, 1885-1945. III. 739
War as I knew it. Annotated by Colonel Paul D. Harkins. Boston, Houghton Mifflin, 1947. xix, 425 p. port., maps. 22 cm. Edited by Beatrice Ayer Patton. *1. World War, 1939-1945 — Campaigns — Africa, North. 2. World War, 1939-1945 — Campaigns — Western. 3. World War, 1939-1945 — Personal narratives, American. I. Harkins, Paul Donal, 1904- II. Patton, Beatrice (Ayer) 1886- ed. III. T.*
D743.P3   940.542   47-6664

U.S. War dept. III. 740
Prelude to invasion, an account based upon official reports by Henry L. Stimson, secretary of war. [Washington] Public Affairs Press [1944] iii, 332 p. illus. 23 cm. Preface signed: M. B. Schnapper, editor. "Published with the cooperation of the American council on public affairs." *1. World war, 1939-1945 — Chronology. 2. World war, 1939-1945 — U.S. I. Stimson, Henry Lewis, 1867- II. Schnapper, Morris Bartel, 1912- ed. III. American council on public affairs. IV. T.*
D743.U5 1944   940.542   44-9701

Wedemeyer, Albert Coady, 1896- III. 741
Wedemeyer reports! [1st ed.] New York, Holt [1958] 497 p. illus. 22 cm. *1. World War, 1939-1945. I. T.*
D743.W4   940.53   58-14458

Higgins, Trumbull. III. 742
Winston Churchill and the second front, 1940-1943. New York, Oxford University Press, 1957. 281 p. 22 cm. *1. Churchill, Winston Leonard Spencer, Sir, 1874-1965. 2. World War, 1939-1945 — Campaigns. 3. Strategy. I. Second front.*
D744.H5   940.54012   57-10388

Snyder, Louis Leo, 1907- ed. III. 743
Masterpieces of war reporting: the great moments of World War II. New York, J. Messner [1962] 555 p. 24 cm. *1. World War, 1939-1945 — Anecdotes. I. T.*
D744.S59   940.53082   62-16675

D745   WAR POETRY. SATIRE

Brée, Germaine comp. III. 744
Defeat and beyond; an anthology of French wartime writing, 1940-1945. Germaine Brée and George Bernauer, editors. New York, Pantheon Books [1970] x, 381 p. 22 cm. *1. World War, 1939-1945 — France — Literary collections. 2. French literature — Translations into English. 3. English literature — Translations from French. I. Bernauer, George, joint comp. II. T.*
D745.2.B647   914.4/03/816   69-15472

Mauldin, William Henry, 1921- III. 745
Up front. Text and pictures by Bill Mauldin. Foreword by David Halberstam. New York, Norton [1968] x, 228 p. illus. 25 cm. Reprint of the 1945 ed. with a new introduction. *1. World War, 1939-1945 — Humor, caricatures, etc. I. T.*
D745.2.M34 1968   741.5973   68-24264

D748 – 754   DIPLOMATIC HISTORY

Feis, Herbert, 1893- III. 746
Churchill, Roosevelt, Stalin; the war they waged and the peace they sought. Princeton, N.J., Princeton University Press, 1957. xi, 692 p. maps. 24 cm. *1. World War, 1939-1945 — Diplomatic history. I. T.*
D748.F4   940.5322   57-5470

McNeill, William Hardy, 1917- III. 747
America, Britain, & Russia: their co-operation and conflict, 1941-1946. New York, Johnson Reprint Corp., 1970. xviii, 819 p. maps. 23 cm. Reprint of the 1953 ed., which was issued as part of Survey of international affairs. *1. World War, 1939-1945 — Diplomatic history. I. T.*
D748.M23 1970   940.53/22   71-129286

Namier, Lewis Bernstein, 1888- III. 748
Diplomatic prelude, 1938-1939. London, Macmillan, 1948. xviii, 502 p. 21 cm. *1. World War, 1939-1945 — Diplomatic history. 2. World War, 1939-1945 — Causes. I. T.*
D748.N3   940.532   48-18171

Henderson, Nevile, Sir, 1882-1942. III. 749
Failure of a mission; Berlin 1937-1939, by the Right Honorable Sir Nevile

Henderson. New York, G. P. Putnam [c1940] xi, 334 p. port. 22 cm. *1. World war, 1939-1945 — Diplomatic history. 2. World war, 1939 — 1945 — Gt. Brit. 3. Europe — Politics — 1918-1945. 4. Gt. Brit. — Foreign relations — Germany. 5. Germany — Foreign relations — Gt. Brit. I. T.*
D750.H4   940.531   40-27393

Spears, Edward Louis, Sir, bart., 1886-   **III. 750**
Assignment to catastrophe. New York, Wyn [1954-55] 2 v. illus. 22 cm. *1. World War, 1939-1945 — Diplomatic history. 2. Gt. Brit. — Foreign relations — France. 3. France — Foreign relations — Gt. Brit. I. T.*
D750.S62   940.542   54-11363

Woodward, Ernest Llewellyn, Sir, 1890-   **III. 751**
British foreign policy in the Second World War, by Sir Llewellyn Woodward. London, H.M.S.O., 1970-   v.   26 cm. (History of the Second World War) *1. World War, 1939-1945 — Diplomatic history. 2. Gt. Brit. — Foreign relations — 1936-1945. I. T. (S)*
D750.W62   940.532/2/42   70-143172   ISBN:116300523 (v. 1)

Divine, Robert A., comp.   **III. 752**
Causes and consequences of World War II. Edited with an introd. by Robert A. Divine. Chicago, Quadrangle Books, 1969. 375 p. 22 cm. *1. World War, 1939-1945 — Diplomatic history — Addresses, essays, lectures. 2. World War, 1939-1945 — United States — Addresses, essays, lectures. I. T.*
D753.D56   940.532/2/73   71-78305

Divine, Robert A.   **III. 753**
The reluctant belligerent; American entry into World War II [by] Robert A. Divine. New York, Wiley [1965] xi, 172 p. maps. 22 cm. (America in crisis) *1. World War, 1939-1945 — Causes. 2. World War, 1939-1945 — United States. 3. United States — Foreign relations — 1933-1945. I. T. (S)*
D753.D57   940.5373   65-14618

Feis, Herbert, 1893-   **III. 754**
The road to Pearl Harbor; the coming of the war between the United States and Japan. Princeton, Princeton University Press, 1950. xii, 356 p. fold. map. 25 cm. *1. World War, 1939-1945 — U.S. 2. World War, 1939-1945 — Japan. 3. U.S. — Foreign relations — Japan. 4. Japan — Foreign relations — U.S. I. T.*
D753.F4   940.532273   50-9585

Kimball, Warren F.   **III. 755**
The most unsordid act; lend-lease, 1939-1941 [by] Warren F. Kimball. Baltimore, Johns Hopkins Press [1969] ix, 281 p. 24 cm. *1. Lend-lease operations (1941-1945) 2. United States — Politics and government — 1933-1945. I. T.*
D753.K5   320.9/73   69-14712   ISBN:0801810175

Langer, William Leonard, 1896-   **III. 756**
Our Vichy gamble, by William L. Langer. Hamden, Conn., Archon Books, 1965 [c1947] ix, 412, xi p. 22 cm. "The Murphy-Weygand accord": p. 399-401. "Text of the protocols signed at Paris May 27-28, 1941": p. 402-412. *1. U.S. — Foreign relations — France. 2. France — Foreign relations — U.S. 3. World War, 1939-1945 — Diplomatic history. 4. World War, 1939-1945 — U.S. I. T.*
D753.L25 1965   940.532273   65-15013

Smith, Gaddis.   **III. 757**
American diplomacy during the second World War, 1941-1945. New York, Wiley [1965] ix, 194 p. maps. 22 cm. (America in crisis) *1. World War, 1939-1945 — Diplomatic history. 2. U.S. — Foreign relations — 1933-1945. I. T. (S)*
D753.S54   940.5322   64-8713

Ike, Nobutaka, ed.   **III. 758**
Japan's decision for war; records of the 1941 policy conferences. Translated, edited, and with an introd. by Nobutaka Ike. Stanford, Calif., Stanford University Press, 1967. xxx, 306 p. map. 24 cm. *1. World War, 1939-1945 — Japan. 2. Japan — History — Showa period — 1926- — Sources. I. T.*
D754.J3I4   940.5352   67-13659

Rozek, Edward J.   **III. 759**
Allied wartime diplomacy; a pattern in Poland. New York, Wiley [1958] xvii, 481 p. maps. 24 cm. *1. World War, 1939-1945 — Diplomatic history. 2. Poland — Politics and government — 1918-1945. I. T.*
D754.P7R6   940.5332   57-13449

Weinberg, Gerhard L.   **III. 760**
Germany and the Soviet Union 1939-1941, by Gerhard L. Weinberg. Leiden, E. J. Brill, 1972. vii, 218 p. 25 cm. (Studies in east European history, 1) (U.S.) Imprint covered by label: Distributed in the U.S.A. by Humanities Press, New York. Reprint of the 1954 edition. *1. World War, 1939-1945 — Diplomatic history. 2. Russia — Foreign relations — Germany. 3. Germany — Foreign relations — Russia. I. T. (S)*
D754.R9W4 1972   940.53/2   72-196908

Beaufre, André.   **III. 761**
1940; the fall of France. Translated from the French by Desmond Flower. With a pref. by Sir Basil Liddell Hart. [1st American ed.] New York, Knopf, 1968 [c1967] xxi, 215, xii p. maps. 22 cm. Translation of Le drame de 1940. *1. World War, 1939-1945 — Personal narratives, French. 2. World War, 1939-1945 — France. I. T.*
D755.B3813 1968   944.081/0924   67-18628

Ball, Adrian.   **III. 762**
The last day of the Old World. [1st ed. in the U.S.A.] Garden City, N.Y., Doubleday, 1963. 278 p. illus. 22 cm. *1. World War, 1939-1945. I. T.*
D755.1.B3 1963a   940.5342   63-12984

D756 – 769 MILITARY OPERATIONS
D756 – 763 Western Europe

Benoist-Méchin, Jacques Gabriel Paul Michel, baron, 1901-   **III. 763**
Sixty days that shook the West; the fall of France, 1940. Edited with a pref. by Cyril Falls. Translated from the French by Peter Wiles. [1st American ed.] New York, Putnam [1963] 559 p. illus. 25 cm. *1. World War, 1939-1945 — Campaigns — Western. I. T.*
D756.B453   940.5421   63-9652

Bradley, Omar Nelson, 1893-   **III. 764**
A soldier's story. [1st ed.] New York, Holt [1951] xix, 618 p. illus., ports., maps. 22 cm. *1. World War, 1939-1945 — Campaigns — Western. 2. World War, 1939-1945 — Personal narratives, American. I. T.*
D756.B7   940.542   51-11294

Ellis, Lionel Frederic, 1885-   **III. 765**
Victory in the West, by L. F. Ellis with G. R. G. Allen, A. E. Warhurst [and] Sir James Robb. London, H. M. Stationery Off., 1962-68. 2 v. illus., ports., maps (part fold., part col.) plans (part fold., part col.) 26 cm. (History of the Second World War; United Kingdom military series) Vol.2 by L. F. Ellis with A. E. Warhurst. Stamped on t.p.: Agents in America, British Information Services, New York. *1. World War, 1939-1945 — Campaigns — Western. 2. World War, 1939-1945 — Campaigns — Normandy. I. T. (S)*
D756.E39   940.5421   63-1156

Goutard, Adolphe.   **III. 766**
The Battle of France, 1940. Translated by A. R. P. Burgess. Foreword by B. H. Liddell Hart. New York, I. Washburn, 1959. 280 p. illus. 22 cm. Translation of 1940; la guerre des occasions perdues. *1. World War, 1939-1945 — Campaigns — Western. I. T.*
D756.G613 1959   940.5421   59-12251

MacDonald, Charles Brown, 1922-   **III. 767**
The mighty endeavor; American armed forces in the European theater in World War II [by] Charles B. MacDonald. New York, Oxford University Press, 1969. 564 p. illus., maps, ports. 24 cm. *1. World War, 1939-1945 — Campaigns — Western. 2. World War, 1939-1945 — United States. I. T.*
D756.M27   940.542/1   70-83047

Rowe, Vivian.   **III. 768**
The great wall of France; the triumph of the Maginot Line. [1st American ed.] New York, Putnam [1961, c1959] 328 p. illus. 22 cm. *1. World War, 1939-1945 — Campaigns — France. 2. Maginot Line. I. T.*
D756.R6 1961   940.5421   60-8481

Taylor, Telford.   **III. 769**
The march of conquest; the German victories in Western Europe, 1940. New York, Simon and Schuster, 1958. xiv, 460 p. illus., ports., maps. 24 cm. *1. World War, 1939-1945 — Campaigns — Western. I. T.*
D756.T3   940.542   58-7507

Wilmot, Chester.   **III. 770**
The struggle for Europe. Westport, Conn., Greenwood Press [1972, c1952] 766 p. maps. 23 cm. *1. World War, 1939-1945 — Campaigns — Western. I. T.*
D756.W53 1972   940.53   75-138138   ISBN:0837157110

Eisenhower, John S. D., 1922-   **III. 771**
The bitter woods; the dramatic story, told at all echelons, from supreme command to squad leader, of the crisis that shook the Western coalition: Hitler's surprise Ardennes offensives, by John S. D. Eisenhower. New York, Putnam [1969] 506 p. illus., plans, ports. 25 cm. *1. Ardennes, Battle of the, 1944-1945. I. T.*
D756.5.A7E4   940.542/1   68-15504

Taylor, Telford,   **III. 772**
The breaking wave; the Second World War in the summer of 1940. New York, Simon and Schuster [1967] ix, 378 p. illus. (incl. ports.) maps (part fold.) 24 cm. *1. Germany. Wehrmacht. 2. Britain, Battle of, 1940. I. T.*
D756.5.B7T3   940.542/1   66-20249

Harrison, Gordon A.   **III. 773**
Cross-channel attack. Washington, Office of the Chief of Military History, Dept. of the Army, 1951. xvii, 519 p. illus., ports., maps (part fold., col., 1 in pocket) 26 cm. (United States Army in World War II: The European theater of operations) *1. World War, 1939-1945 — Campaigns — Normandy. 2.*

D764.3   *History: General*   III. 797

World War, 1939-1945 — Amphibious operations. I. T. (S:U.S. Dept. of the Army. Office of Military History. United States in World War II)
D756.5.N6Hx (D769.A533 vol. 3, pt.2)   940.542   51-61669

Ryan, Cornelius.   III. 774
The longest day: June 6, 1944. New York, Simon and Schuster, 1959. 350 p. illus., ports., col. maps (on lining papers) 24 cm. *1. World War, 1939-1945 — Campaigns — Normandy. I. T.*
D756.5.N6R9   940.5421   59-9499

D757   Germany

Germany. Wehrmacht. Oberkommando.   III. 775
Hitler directs his war; the secret records of his daily military conferences, selected and annotated by Felix Gilbert, from the manuscript in the University of Pennsylvania Library. New York, Oxford University Press, 1950. xxxiii, 187 p. maps. 21 cm. *1. World War, 1939-1945 — Germany. I. Hitler, Adolf, 1889-1945. II. Gilbert, Felix, 1905- ed. III. T.*
D757.A5 1950   940.5401343   50-10858

Guderian, Heinz, 1888-1954.   III. 776
Panzer leader. Foreword by B. H. Liddell Hart. Translated from the German by Constantine Fitzgibbon. New York, Dutton, 1952. 528 p. illus. 24 cm. Translation of Erinnerungen eines Soldaten. *1. World War, 1939-1945 — Germany. 2. World War, 1939-1945 — Personal narratives, German. I. T.*
D757.G813 1952a   940.5343 (943.086)   52-7787

Liddell Hart, Basil Henry, 1895-   III. 777
The German generals talk. New York, W. Morrow, 1948. xi, 308 p. maps. 22 cm. London ed. (Cassell) pub. under title: The other side of the hill. *1. World War, 1939-1945 — Campaigns. 2. World War, 1939-1945 — Germany. 3. Generals — Germany. I. T.*
D757.L5 1948a   940.5343   48-4499

Speidel, Hans, 1897-   III. 778
Invasion 1944; Rommel and the Normandy campaign. Introd. by Truman Smith. Westport, Conn., Greenwood Press [1971, c1950] xiii, 176 p. illus. 23 cm. *1. World War, 1939-1945 — Germany. 2. World War, 1939-1945 — Campaigns — Normandy. 3. Rommel, Erwin, 1891-1944. I. T.*
D757.S7713 1971   940.542/1   79-147223   ISBN:0837159881

Stein, George H., 1934-   III. 779
The Waffen SS; Hitler's elite guard at war, 1939-1945, by George H. Stein. Ithaca, N.Y., Cornell University Press [1966] xxxiv, 330 p. illus., fold. maps, ports. 24 cm. *1. Nationalsozialistische Deutsche Arbeiter-Partei. Waffenschutzstaffel. 2. World War, 1939-1945 — Germany. I. T.*
D757.85.S8   940.541343   66-11049

D759 – 761   Britain. France

Bryant, Arthur, Sir, 1899-   III. 780
The turn of the tide; a history of the war years based on the diaries of Field-Marshal Lord Alanbrooke, chief of the Imperial General Staff. [1st ed.] Garden City, N.Y., Doubleday, 1957. 624 p. illus. 25 cm. *1. World War, 1939-1945 — Gt. Brit. I. Alanbrooke, Alan Francis Brooke, 1st viscount, 1883- II. T.*
D759.B78 1957a   940.5342   57-6705

Bloch, Marc Léopold Benjamin, 1886-1944.   III. 781
Strange defeat; a statement of evidence written in 1940. With an introd. by Sir Maurice Powicke and a foreword by Georges Altman. Translated from the French by Gerard Hopkins. New York, Octagon Books, 1968. xxii, 178 p. 21 cm. Reprint of the 1949 ed. *1. World War, 1939-1945 — France. 2. World War, 1939-1945 — Personal narratives, French. I. T.*
D761.B562 1968   940.5344   68-15797

Gaulle, Charles de, Pres. France, 1890-   III. 782
War memoirs. New York, Simon and Schuster, 1955-60. 5 v. illus. 22 cm. *1. World War, 1939-1945 — France. I. T.*
D761.G3733   940.5344   55-8440

Géraud, André, 1882-   III. 783
The gravediggers of France: Gamelin, Daladier, Reynaud, Pétain, and Laval; military defeat, armistice, counterrevolution, by Pertinax. New York, H. Fertig, 1968 [c1944] xi, 612 p. maps. 24 cm. Translation of Les fossoyeurs. *1. Gamelin, Maurice Gustave, 1872- 2. Daladier, Édouard, 1884- 3. Reynaud, Paul, 1878- 4. Petain, Henri Philippe Benoni Omer, 1856-1951. 5. Laval, Pierre, 1883-1945. 6. World War, 1939-1945 — France. I. T.*
D761.G462 1968   940.534/4   67-13637

D763   Italy. Netherlands

Badoglio, Pietro, 1871-   III. 784
Italy in the Second World War; memories and documents. Tr. by Muriel Currey. London, New York, Oxford Univ. Press, 1948. x, 234 p. 19 cm. *1. World War, 1939-1945 — Italy. 2. Italy — History — Allied occupation, 1943-1947. 3. World War, 1939-1945 — Personal narratives. Italian.*
D763.18B27   940.5345   48-4978

Maass, Walter B.   III. 785
The Netherlands at war: 1940-1945, by Walter B. Maass. London, New York Abelard-Schuman [1970] 264 p. illus., map (on lining paper), ports. 22 cm. *1. World War, 1939-1945 — Netherlands. I. T.*
D763.N4M3 1970   940.53492   68-14569   ISBN:200715526

D764 – 766   Russia. Eastern Europe. Near East. Africa

Bialer, Seweryn, comp.   III. 786
Stalin and his generals; Soviet military memoirs of World War II. New York, Pegasus [1969] x, 644 p. maps. 24 cm. *1. Stalin, Iosif, 1879-1953. 2. World War, 1939-1945 — Russia. 3. World War, 1939-1945 — Personal narratives, Russian. 4. Generals — Russia. I. T.*
D764.B47   940.54/0947   67-25506

Chuĭkov, Vasiliĭ Ivanovich, 1900-   III. 787
The battle for Stalingrad. Introd. by Hanson W. Baldwin. Translated from the Russian by Harold Silver. New York, Holt, Rinehart and Winston [1964] 364 p. illus., ports., maps. 22 cm. Translation of Nachalo puti (romanized form) *1. Stalingrad, Battle of, 1942-1943. I. T.*
D764.C48513   940.5421   64-11015

Chuĭkov, Vasiliĭ Ivanovich, 1900-   III. 788
The beginning of the road. Translated from the Russian by Harold Silver. London, Macgibbon & Kee, 1963. 388 p. illus., ports., maps (1 fold.) 22 cm. *1. Stalingrad, Battle of, 1942-1943. I. T.*
D764.C48513 1963   64-36008

Ehrenburg, Il'ia Grigor'evich, 1891-   III. 789
The war, 1941-45 [by] Ilya Ehrenburg. Translated by Tatiana Shebunina, in collaboration with Yvonne Kapp. London, MacGibbon & Kee, 1964. 198 p. ports. 23 cm. Vol.5 of the author's Men, years — life. *1. World War, 1939-1945 — Russia. I. T.*
D764.E352 1964   65-87534

Fischer, George, 1923-   III. 790
Soviet opposition to Stalin, a case study in World War II. Westport, Conn., Greenwood Press [1970, c1952] viii, 230 p. 23 cm. *1. Vlasov, Andreĭ Andreevich, 1900-1946. 2. Komitet osvobozhdeniia narodov Rosii. 3. Russkaia osvoboditel'naia armiia. 4. World War, 1939-1945 — Russia. I. T.*
D764.F555 1970   940.5347   70-97344   ISBN:837130980

Gouré, Leon.   III. 791
The siege of Leningrad. Stanford, Calif., Stanford University Press, 1962. xii, 363 p. illus., maps. 24 cm. "An earlier version of this study was submitted to Georgetown University in February 1961 ... for the degree of Doctor of Philosophy." *1. Leningrad — Seige, 1941-1944.*
D764.G66 1962   940.5421   62-8662

Schmidt, Paul Karl.   III. 792
Hitler's war on Russia [by] Paul Carell; translated from the German by Ewald Osers. London, Transworld, 1966. x, 691 p. plates (some col.), maps. 18 cm. (A Corgi book) Translation of Unternehmen Barbarossa. *1. World War, 1939-1945 — Campaigns — Eastern. I. T.*
D764.S3613 1966   940.542/1   68-95227

Schröter, Heinz.   III. 793
Stalingrad. Translated from the German by Constantine Fitzgibbon. [1st American ed.] New York, Dutton, 1958. 263 p. illus. 21 cm. Translation of Stalingrad " ... bis zur letzten Patrone." *1. Stalingrad, Battle of, 1942-1943.*
D764.S372 1958a   940.5421   58-7821

Stalin, Iosif, 1879-1953.   III. 794
The great patriotic war of the Soviet Union. New York, Greenwood Press [1969, c1945] 167 p. 23 cm. *1. World War, 1939-1945 — Addresses, sermons, etc. 2. World War, 1939-1945 — Russia. I. T.*
D764.S825 1969   940.5347   70-97320   ISBN:837125596

Werth, Alexander, 1901-   III. 795
Russia at war, 1941-1945. New York, Dutton, 1964. xxv, 1100 p. maps (part fold.) 23 cm. *1. World War, 1939-1945 — Russia. I. T.*
D764.W48   940.5347   64-19533

Salisbury, Harrison Evans, 1908-   III. 796
The 900 days; the siege of Leningrad [by] Harrison E. Salisbury. [1st ed.] New York, Harper & Row [1969] xi, 635 p. illus., maps (1 col.) 25 cm. *1. Leningrad — Siege, 1941-1944. I. T.*
D764.3.L4S2   940.542/1   68-28215

Howard, Michael Eliot, 1922-   III. 797
The Mediterranean strategy in the Second World War [by] Michael Howard. New York, Praeger [1968] xii, 82 p. 23 cm. "This book comprises the

Lee-Knowles lectures, delivered by Michael Howard at the University of Cambridge, England, in 1966." *1. World War, 1939-1945 — Mediterranean Sea. I. T.*
D766.H6 1968   940.542/1   68-19851

Heckstall-Smith, Anthony, 1904-   III. 798
Greek tragedy, 1941 [by] Anthony Heckstall-Smith and H. T. Baillie-Grohman. [1st ed.] New York, W. W. Norton [1961] 238 p. illus. 22 cm. (Norton books on modern warfare) *1. World War, 1939-1945 — Campaigns — Greece. I. Baillie-Grohman, Harold Tom, 1888- joint author. II. T.*
D766.3.H37   940.5421   61-11348

Rommel, Erwin, 1891-1944.   III. 799
The Rommel papers, edited by B. H. Liddell Hart, with the assistance of Lucie-Maria Rommel, Manfred Rommel, and Fritz Bayerlein. Translated by Paul Findlay. [1st American ed.] New York, Harcourt, Brace, 1953. xxx, 545 p. illus., ports., maps (2 fold.) 22 cm. *1. World War, 1939-1945 — Campaigns — Africa, North. 2. World War, 1939-1945 — Campaigns — Italy. I. Liddell Hart, Basil Henry, 1895- ed.*
D766.82.R57 1953   940.542   53-5656

D767   Far East

Eichelberger, Robert L.   III. 800
Dear Miss Em: General Eichelberger's war in the Pacific, 1942-1945. Jay Luvaas, editor. Westport, Conn., Greenwood Press [1972] xvi, 322 p. illus. 24 cm. (Contributions in military history, 2) *1. World War, 1939-1945 — Pacific Ocean. 2. World War, 1939-1945 — Personal narratives, American. I. Eichelberger, Emma Gudger. II. Luvaas, Jay, ed. III. T. (S)*
D767.E37   940.54/26/0924 (B)   71-176429   ISBN:0837162785

United States. Strategic Bombing Survey.   III. 801
The campaigns of the Pacific war. [Washington] U.S. Strategic Bombing Survey (Pacific), Naval Analysis Division. New York, Greenwood Press [1969] xv, 389 p. illus. (part fold.), maps (part fold.) 29 cm. Reprint of the 1946 ed. *1. World War, 1939-1945 — Pacific Ocean. 2. World War, 1939-1945 — Naval operations, Japanese. 3. World War, 1939-1945 — Naval operations, American. 4. World War, 1939-1945 — Aerial operations. I. T.*
D767.U55 1969   940.542/6   77-90739   ISBN:0837123135

Feis, Herbert, 1893-   III. 802
The atomic bomb and the end of World War II. [Rev. ed.] Princeton, N.J., Princeton University Press, 1966. vi, 213 p. 24 cm. "Originally published in 1961 under the title: Japan subdued." *1. World War, 1939-1945 — Japan. 2. United States. Army. Manhattan Engineer District. I. T.*
D767.2.F4 1966   940.5425   66-13312

Hachiya, Michihiko, 1903-   III. 803
Hiroshima diary; the journal of a Japanese physician, August 6-September 30, 1945. Translated and edited by Warner Wells. Chapel Hill, University of North Carolina Press [1955] 238 p. illus. 21 cm. *1. World War, 1939-1945 — Japan — Hiroshima. 2. Atomic bomb — Physiological effect. 3. Hygiene, Public — Hiroshima. I. T.*
D767.25.H6H3   940.544   55-14686

Hersey, John Richard, 1914-   III. 804
Hiroshima [by] John Hersey. 1st ed. New York, Knopf, 1946. 117 p. 20 cm. At head of title: John Hersey. "Originally appeared in the New Yorker." *1. World war, 1939-1945 — Japan — Hiroshima. 2. Atomic bomb. I. T.*
D767.25.H6H4 1946   940.544   46-11953

Knebel, Fletcher.   III. 805
No high ground, by Fletcher Knebel and Charles W. Bailey II. [1st ed.] New York, Harper [1960] 272 p. illus. 22 cm. *1. Atomic bomb. 2. Hiroshima. I. Bailey, Charles W., joint author. II. T.*
D767.25.H6K55   940.5442   60-7531

Lifton, Robert Jay, 1926-   III. 806
Death in life; survivors of Hiroshima. New York, Random House [1968, c1967] viii, 594 p. 24 cm. *1. Hiroshima — Bombardment, 1945. 2. Atomic warfare — Psychological aspects. I. T.*
D767.25.H6L4   155.9/35   67-22658

Nu, U.   III. 807
Burma under the Japanese, pictures and portraits, by Thakin Nu. Edited and translated, with introd. by J. S. Furnivall. London, Macmillan; New York, St Martin's Press, 1954. 132 p. illus. 23 cm. *1. World War, 1939-1945 — Burma. I. T.*
D767.6.N8   940.53591 (959.1)   54-2221

Lord, Walter, 1917-   III. 808
Day of infamy. Illustrated with photos. [1st ed.] New York, Holt [1957] 243 p. illus. 22 cm. *1. Pearl Harbor, Attack on, 1941. I. T.*
D767.92.L6   940.542   57-6189

Wohlstetter, Roberta.   III. 809
Pearl Harbor; warning and decision. Stanford, Calif., Stanford University Press, 1962. 426 p. illus. 25 cm. *1. Intelligence service — U.S. 2. Pearl Harbor, Attack on, 1941. I. T.*
D767.92.W6   940.5426   62-15966

Hersey, John Richard, 1914-   III. 810
Into the valley; a skirmish of the marines [by] John Hersey. Illustrations by Major Donald L. Dickson. 1st ed. New York, A. A. Knopf, 1943. 138 p. plates. 20 cm. *1. World war, 1939-1945 — Solomon islands. 2. World war, 1939-1945 — Personal narratives, American. I. T.*
D767.98.H4   940.542   43-1318

Tregaskis, Richard William, 1916-   III. 811
Guadalcanal diary. New York, Random House [1955] 180 p. illus. 22 cm. (Landmark books, 55) "This edition ... was taken from the longer, original edition ... Extra chapters [have been added]" *1. U.S. Marine Corps. 2. World War, 1939-1945 — Campaigns — Solomon Islands. 3. World War, 1939-1945 — Personal narratives, American. I. T.*
D767.98.T7 1955   940.542   55-5820

D769   United States

U.S. Dept. of the Army. Office of Military History.   III. 812
United States Army in World War II. Washington, 1947-   v. illus., ports., maps (part fold., col.) 26 cm. Master index; reader's guide. Compiled by the Chief Historian. Washington, 1955-   v. 26 cm. D769.A533 Index *1. U.S. Army — History — World War, 1939-1945. 2. World War, 1939-1945 — U.S.*
D769.A533   940.541273   47-46404

Buchanan, Albert Russell, 1906-   III. 813
The United States and World War II. [1st ed.] New York, Harper & Row [1964] 2 v. (xvii, 635 p.) illus., ports., maps. 22 cm. (New American Nation series) *1. World War, 1939-1945 — U.S. I. T.*
D769.B8   63-20287

Pratt, Fletcher, 1897-1956.   III. 814
War for the world; a chronicle of our fighting forces in World War II. New Haven, Yale University Press, 1950. xi, 364 p. illus., maps. 21 cm. (The Chronicles of America series, v.54) *1. World War, 1939-1945 — U.S. I. T. (S)*
D769.P73 (E173.C55 vol. 54)   940.5373   50-8830

United States. Marine Corps.   III. 815
History of U.S. Marine Corps operations in World War II. [Washington] Historical Branch, G-3 Division, Headquarters, U.S. Marine Corps [1958-71; v.5; 1968] 5 v. illus., maps (part fold. col.) 26 cm. Vol. 4 issued by Historical Division, Headquarters, U.S. Marine Corps. *1. United States Marine Corps — History — World War, 1939-1945. 2. World War, 1939-1945 — Regimental histories — United States Marine Corps. I. T.*
D769.369.U53   940.54/12/73   58-60002

Broom, Leonard.   III. 816
The managed casualty; the Japanese-American family in World War II, by Leonard Broom and John I. Kitsuse. Berkeley, University of California Press, 1956. iv, 226 p. maps, diagrs. 24 cm. (University of California publications in culture and society, v.6) *1. Concentration camps — U.S. 2. Japanese in the U.S. 3. Family — U.S. 4. World War, 1939-1945 — Evacuation of civilians. I. Kitsuse, John I., joint author. II. T. (S:California. University. University of California publications in culture and society, v.6)*
D769.8.A6B7x (H31.C17 vol. 6)   940.547273   A57-9006

Daniels, Roger.   III. 817
Concentration camps USA: Japanese Americans and World War II. New York, Holt, Rinehart and Winston [1971] xiv, 188 p. illus. 23 cm. (Berkshire studies in history. Berkshire studies in minority history) *1. Japanese in the United States. 2. Concentration camps — United States. 3. World War, 1939-1945 — Evacuation of civilians. I. T.*
D769.8.A6D35   940.547/2/73   72-143320
ISBN:0030818699 (College) 0030884748 (trade)

Grodzins, Morton.   III. 818
Americans betrayed: politics and the Japanese evacuation. Chicago, Univ. of Chicago Press [1949] xvii, 444 p. diagrs. 24 cm. *1. Japanese in the U.S. 2. World War, 1939-1945 — Evacuation of civilians. I. T.*
D769.8.A6G7   940.547273   49-9724

D770 – 784   NAVAL OPERATIONS

Puleston, William Dilworth, 1881-   III. 819
The influence of sea power in World War II, by W. D. Puleston. Westport, Conn., Greenwood Press [1970, c1947] x, 310 p. maps. 23 cm. *1. World War, 1939-1945 — Naval operations. I. T.*
D770.P8 1970   940.545   71-104248   ISBN:083713997X

Ruge, Friedrich.   III. 820
Der Seekrieg; the German Navy's story, 1939-1945. Translated by M. G. Saunders. Annapolis, U.S. Naval Institute [1957] 440 p. illus. 24 cm. *1. World War, 1939-1945 — Naval operations. I. The German Navy's story. II. T.*
D770.R833   940.545   57-14768

Roskill, Stephen Wentworth.   **III. 821**
The war at sea, 1939-1945. London, H. M. Stationery Off., 1954-61. 3 v. in 4. illus., ports., maps (part fold., part col.) 25 cm. (History of the Second World War: United Kingdom military series) *1. World War, 1939-1945 — Naval operations, British. I. T. (S)*
D771.R68   940.545   54-3972

Roskill, Stephen Wentworth.   **III. 822**
White ensign; the British navy at war, 1939-1945. Annapolis, Md., U.S. Naval Institute [1960] 480 p. illus. 24 cm. *1. World War, 1939-1945 — Naval operations, British. I. T.*
D771.R69 1960   940.545942   60-15791

Wheatley, Ronald.   **III. 823**
Operation Sea Lion; German plans for the invasion of England, 1939-1942. Oxford, Clarendon Press, 1958. viii, 201 p. illus., ports., fold. maps. 22 cm. Thesis (B. LITT.) — Oxford. Without thesis statement. *1. Operation Sea Lion.*
D771.W38 1958   940.542   58-2322

Morison, Samuel Eliot, 1887-   **III. 824**
History of United States naval operations in World War II. [1st ed.] Boston, Little, Brown, 1947-62. 15 v. illus., ports., maps (part fold., part col.) 23 cm. Includes rev. ed. of v. 2 and latest printings of other volumes. *1. World War, 1939-1945 — Naval operations, American.*
D773.M6   940.545973   47-1571

Morison, Samuel Eliot, 1887-   **III. 825**
The two-ocean war, a short history of the United States Navy in the Second World War. [1st ed.] Boston, Little, Brown [1963] 611 p. illus. 24 cm. *1. World War, 1939-1945 — Naval operations, American. I. T.*
D773.M62   940.545973   63-8307

Willoughby, Malcolm Francis.   **III. 826**
The U.S. Coast Guard in World War II. Annapolis, United States Naval Institute [1957] xvii, 347 p. illus., ports., maps. 28 cm. *1. U.S. Coast Guard. 2. World War, 1939-1945 — Naval operations.*
D773.W48   940.545973   57-9314

Bragadin, Marc'Antonio, 1906-   **III. 827**
The Italian Navy in World War II. Giuseppe Fioravanzo, editorial supervisor. Translated by Gale Hoffman. Annapolis, Md., U.S. Naval Institute [1957] 380 p. illus. 26 cm. *1. World War, 1939-1945 — Naval operations, Italian. I. T.*
D775.B683   940.545945   57-6515

Itō, Masanori, 1889-1962.   **III. 828**
The end of the Imperial Japanese Navy, by Masanori Ito with Roger Pineau. Translated by Andrew Y. Kuroda and Roger Pineau. [1st ed.] New York, Norton [1962] 240 p. illus. 22 cm. Translation of Rengō kantai no saigo (romanized form) *1. Japan. Kaigun — History. 2. World War, 1939-1945 — Naval operations, Japanese. I. T.*
D777.I813   940.545952   60-7577

The Japanese Navy in World War II; an anthology of articles by former officers of the Imperial Japanese Navy, and Air Defense Force, originally published in the U.S. Naval Institute Proceedings.   **III. 829**
Introd. and commentary by Raymond O'Connor. Annapolis, Md., U.S. Naval Institute [c1969] ix, 147 p. illus. maps, ports. 25 cm. *1. World War, 1939-1945 — Naval operations, Japanese. 2. World War, 1939-1945 — Aerial operations, Japanese. 3. Japan. Kaigun. I. O'Connor, Raymond Gish. II. United States Naval Institute. Proceedings.*
D777.J3   940.545/9/52   79-101501

Auphan, Gabriel Adrien Joseph Paul, 1894-   **III. 830**
The French Navy in World War II, by Paul Auphan and Jacques Mordal. Translated by A. C. J. Sabalot. Annapolis, United States Naval Institute [1959] xvi, 413 p. illus., maps (2 fold. on lining-papers) 25 cm. *1. France. Marine — History. 2. World War, 1939-1945 — Naval operations, French. I. Mordal, Jacques, joint author. II. T.*
D779.F7A823   940.545944   59-8595

Dönitz, Karl, 1891-   **III. 831**
Memoirs: ten years and twenty days. Translated by R. H. Stevens, in collaboration with David Woodward. [1st ed.] Cleveland, World Pub. Co. [1959] 500 p. maps., ports. 23 cm. Translation of Zehn Jahre und zwanzig Tage. *1. World War, 1939-1945 — Naval operations — Submarine. 2. World War, 1939-1945 — Naval operations, German. 3. World War, 1939-1945 — Germany. I. Ten years and twenty days.*
D781.D613   940.545943   59-11370

D785 – 792   AERIAL OPERATIONS

Tedder, Arthur William Tedder, baron, 1890-   **III. 832**
Air power in war. London, Hodder and Stoughton [1948] 124 p. maps (on lining-papers) diagrs. 23 cm. (The Lees Knowles lectures, 1947) *1. Air warfare. 2. World War, 1939-1945 — Aerial operations. I. T. (S)*
D785.T4x   A49-2621

U.S. Strategic bombing survey.   **III. 833**
The United States Strategic bombing survey: summary report (European war) September 30, 1945. [Washington, U.S. Govt. Print. Off., 1945] ii, 18 p. 26 cm. (Its Reports. European war. 1) *1. World war, 1939-1945 — Aerial operations. 2. World war, 1939-1945 — Europe.*
D785.U6 no. 1   940.544   46-27646

United States. Strategic Bombing Survey.   **III. 834**
The effects of the atomic bomb on Hiroshima, Japan [by] the U.S. Strategic Bombing Survey, Physical Damage Division. Dates of survey: 14 Oct.-26 Nov. 1945. [Washington] 1947. 3 v. illus., maps (part fold., part col.) 27 cm. (Its Reports, Pacific war, 92) *1. Atomic bomb. 2. Hiroshima — Bombardment, 1945. I. T. (S)*
D785.U63 no. 92   55-57769

United States. Strategic Bombing Survey.   **III. 835**
Effects of the atomic bomb on Nagasaki, Japan [by] the U.S. Strategic Bombing Survey, Physical Damage Division. Dates of survey: 13 Oct.-20 Nov. 1945. [Washington] 1947. 3 v. illus., maps (part fold., part col.) 27 cm. (Its Reports, Pacific war, 93) One fold. col. map in pocket of each vol. *1. Atomic bomb. Nagasaki — Bombardment, 1945. I. T. (S)*
D785.U63 no. 93   55-57770

Verrier, Anthony.   **III. 836**
The bomber offensive. [1st American ed. New York] Macmillan [1969, c1968] x, 373 p. illus., maps, ports. 24 cm. *1. World War, 1939-1945 — Aerial operations. 2. Bombardment. I. T.*
D785.V47 1968b   940.544/2   76-75410

Webster, Charles Kingsley, Sir, 1886-   **III. 837**
The strategic air offensive against Germany, 1939-1945, by Charles Webster and Noble Frankland. London, H. M. Stationery Off., 1961. 4 v. illus., ports., maps (part fold., part col.) 25 cm. (History of the Second World War; United Kingdom military series) Stamped on t.p.: Agents in America: British Information Services, New York. *1. World War, 1939-1945 — Aerial operations. I. Frankland, Noble, 1922- joint author. II. T. (S)*
D785.W38   940.544   61-65443

Wood, Derek, 1930-   **III. 838**
The narrow margin; the Battle of Britain and the rise of air power 1930-40 [by] Derek Wood & Derek Dempster. [1st ed.] New York, McGraw-Hill [1961] 536 p. illus. 22 cm. *1. Britain, Battle of, 1940. 2. World War, 1939-1945 — Aerial operations. I. Dempster, Derek D., joint author. II. T.*
D785.W6 1961   940.5442   61-15451

Lyall, Gavin.   **III. 839**
The war in the air: the Royal Air Force in World War II edited by Gavin Lyall. New York, Morrow [1969, c1968] xv, 422 p. illus., ports. 24 cm. Published in 1968 under title: The war in the air 1939-1945: an anthology of personal experience. *1. World War, 1939-1945 — Aerial operations, British. I. T.*
D786.L93 1969   940.544/9/42   69-12310

Bartz, Karl, 1900-1956.   **III. 840**
Swastika in the air; the struggle and defeat of the German Air Force 1939-1945. [2d ed. Translated from the German by Edward Fitzgerald] London, W. Kimber [1956] 204 p. plates, ports. 22 cm. Translation of Als der Himmel brannte. *1. Germany. Luftwaffe — History. 2. World War, 1939-1945 — Aerial operations, German. I. T.*
D787.B25x   A56-7008

Middleton, Drew, 1913-   **III. 841**
The sky suspended; the Battle of Britain. London, Secker & Warburg [1960] 255 p. illus. 21 cm. *1. Britain, Battle of, 1940. I. T.*
D787.M5 1960a   940.5421   61-2011

United States. Air Force. USAF Historical Division.   **III. 842**
The Army Air Forces in World War II. Prepared under the editorship of Wesley Frank Craven [and] James Lea Cate. [Chicago] University of Chicago Press [1948-58] 7 v. illus., ports., maps (part fold.) 25 cm. Vols. 1-2 prepared by the division under its earlier names: v. 1 by the Office of Air Force History and v. 2 by the Air Historical Group. *1. United States. Army Air Forces. 2. World War, 1939-1945 — Aerial operations, American. I. Craven, Wesley Frank, 1905- ed. II. Cate, James Lea, 1899- ed. III. T.*
D790.A47   940.544973   48-3657

Inoguchi, Rikihei.   **III. 843**
The divine wind; Japan's Kamikaze Force in World War II, by Rikihei Inoguchi and Tadashi Nakajima with Roger Pineau. Foreword by C. R. Brown. Annapolis, United States Naval Institute [1958] 240 p. illus. 24 cm. Translation of Kamikaze Tokubetsu Kōgekitai *1. Japan. Kaigun. Kamikaze Tokubetsu Kōgekitai. 2. World War, 1939-1945 — Aerial operations, Japanese. I. Nakajima, Tadashi, joint author. II. T.*
D792.J3I513   940.544952   58-13974

D802 OCCUPIED TERRITORY

Holborn, Hajo, 1902-   III. 844
American military government, its organization and policies, by Hajo Holborn. 1st ed. Washington, Infantry Journal Press [1947] xiii, 243 p. illus. (maps) 24 cm. *1. Allied military government. 2. U.S. — Foreign relations — 1933- 3. World war, 1939-1945 — Occupied territories. I. T.*
D802.A2H6   940.5338   47-3001

Rennell, Francis James Rennell Rodd, Baron, 1895-   III. 845
British military administration of occupied territories in Africa during the years 1941-1947, by Lord Rennell of Rodd. Westport, Conn., Greenwood Press [1970] viii, 637 p. maps (part fold.) 23 cm. Reprint of the 1948 ed. *1. World War, 1939-1945 — Africa. 2. Italy — Colonies — Africa. I. T.*
D802.A33R4 1970   355.49   70-109828   ISBN:837143195

Marshall, Bruce, 1899-   III. 846
The White Rabbit, by Bruce Marshall from the story told to him by F. F. E. Yeo-Thomas. London, Evans Bros. [1952] 262 p. illus. 22 cm. *1. Yeo-Thomas, Forest Frederick Edward. 2. World War, 1939-1945 — Underground movements — France. I. Yeo-Thomas, Forest Frederick Edward. II. T.*
D802.F8M27 1952   940.5344 (944.081)   52-2259

Novick, Peter, 1934-   III. 847
The Resistance versus Vichy; the purge of collaborators in liberated France. New York, Columbia University Press, 1968. xv, 245 p. 23 cm. *1. World War, 1939-1945 — Collaborationists — France. 2. Criminal justice, Administration of — France. I. T.*
D802.F8Nx   320.9/44   68-14772

Vomécourt, Philippe de.   III. 848
An army of amateurs. [1st ed. in the U.S.A.] Garden City, N.Y., Doubleday, 1961. 307 p. 22 cm. London ed. (Hutchinson) has title: Who lived to see the day. *1. World War, 1939-1945 — Underground movements — France. I. T.*
D802.F8V65 1961a   940.5344   61-14326

Zink, Harold, 1901-   III. 849
American military government in Germany, by Harold Zink. New York, Macmillan, 1947. 272 p. illus., maps, diagrs. 22 cm. "First printing." *1. Germany — History — Allied occupation, 1945- I. T.*
D802.G3Z5   940.5343   47-3558

Blakeslee, George Hubbard, 1871-1954.   III. 850
The Far Eastern Commission; a study in international cooperation: 1945 to 1952. [Washington] Dept. of State [1953] v, 239 p. 24 cm. (Department of State publication 5138. Far Eastern series, 60) *1. Far Eastern Commission. 2. Japan — History — Allied occupation, 1945-1952. (S:U.S. Dept. of State. Publication 5138.) (S:U.S. Dept. of State. Far Eastern series, 60)*
D802.J3B5   940.5352   53-63288

Steinberg, David Joel.   III. 851
Philippine collaboration in World War II. Ann Arbor, University of Michigan Press [1967] viii, 235 p. 24 cm. *1. World War, 1939-1945 — Collaborationists — Philippine Islands. 2. National characteristics, Philippine. I. T.*
D802.P5S7   991.4/035   66-17017

Dallin, Alexander.   III. 852
German rule in Russia, 1941-1945; a study of occupation policies. London, Macmillan; New York, St Martin's Press, 1957. xx, 695 p. illus., maps. 23 cm. *1. Russia — History — German occupation, 1941-1944. I. T.*
D802.R8D3   940.5347   57-13949

Reitlinger, Gerald, 1900-   III. 853
The house built on sand; the conflicts of German policy in Russia, 1939-1945. New York, Viking Press, 1960. 459 p. fold. maps. 23 cm. *1. Russia — History — German occupation, 1941-1944. I. T.*
D802.R8R4 1960a   940.532443   60-9628

Deakin, Frederick William, 1913-   III. 854
The embattled mountain [by] F. W. Deakin. New York, Oxford University Press, 1971. xiii, 284 p. illus., maps, ports. 22 cm. *1. World War, 1939-1945 — Underground movements — Yugoslavia. 2. World War, 1939-1945 — Personal narratives, English. I. T.*
D802.Y8D4   940.5342/0924   74-169160

D804 WAR CRIMES

(see also: JX6731)

Göring, Hermann, 1893-1946, defendant.   III. 855
Trial of the major war criminals before the International Military Tribunal, Nuremberg, 14 November 1945-1 October 1946. Nuremberg, Ger., 1947-49. 42 v. 24 cm. Trial of Hermann Göring and 23 others. *1. Nuremberg Trial of Major German War Criminals, 1945-1966. I. International Military Tribunal.*
D804.G42I55   341.4   47-31575

Jackson, Robert Houghwout, 1892-   III. 856
The Nürnberg case, as presented by Robert H. Jackson, chief of counsel for the United States, together with other documents. 1st ed. New York, A. A. Knopf, 1947. xviii, 268 p. plates, ports. 22 cm. "A Borzoi book." *1. War crimes — Trials — Nuremberg, 1945-1946. I. International military tribunal.*
D804.G42J32   341.3   47-1412

Russell, Edward Frederick Langley Russell, baron, 1895-   III. 857
The Knights of Bushido; the shocking history of Japanese war atrocities, by Lord Russell. [1st ed.] New York, Dutton, 1958. 334 p. illus. 21 cm. Companion vol. to the author's The scourge of the Swastika. *1. World War, 1939-1945 — Atrocities. 2. World War, 1939-1945 — Japan. I. T.*
D804.J3R8 1958   940.54056   58-9587

Zawodny, Janusz Kazimierz.   III. 858
Death in the forest; the story of the Katyn Forest Massacre. [Notre Dame, Ind.] University of Notre Dame Press, 1962. 235 p. illus. 23 cm. (International studies of the Committee on International Relations, University of Notre Dame) *1. Katyn Forest Massacre, 1940. I. T.*
D804.R9Z3   940.5405   62-16639

D805 PRISONERS. PRISONS.

Nansen, Odd, 1901-   III. 859
From day to day; tr. by Katherine John. New York, G. P. Putnam's Sons [1949] xiii, 485 p. illus., ports. 23 cm. "This diary ... has ... been much reduced in the English version." *1. World War, 1939-1945 — Prisoners and prisons, German. 2. World War, 1939-1945 — Personal narratives, Norwegian. I. John, Katherine (Gower) tr. II. T.*
D805.G3N352   940.547243   49-7431

Poller, Walter.   III. 860
Medical block, Buchenwald; the personal testimony of inmate 996, block 36. New York, L. Stuart, 1961 [c1960] 277 p. illus. 21 cm. Translation of Arztschreiber in Buchenwald. *1. Buchenwald (Concentration camp) I. T.*
D805.G3P6463 1961   940.547243   61-17324

Reid, Patrick R., 1910-   III. 861
The Colditz story. Philadelphia, Lippincott, 1953 [c1952] 288 p. illus. 22 cm. Sequel: Men of Colditz. *1. Colditz, Ger. Castle. 2. World War, 1939-1945 — Prisoners and prisons, German. I. T.*
D805.G3R35 1953   940.547243   52-13728

Gordon, Ernest.   III. 862
Through the valley of the Kwai. [1st ed.] New York, Harper [1962] 257 p. illus. 22 cm. *1. Burma-Siam Railroad. 2. World War, 1939-1945 — Prisoners and prisons, Japanese. I. T.*
D805.J3G65   940.547252   62-11127

Gollwitzer, Helmut.   III. 863
Unwilling journey; a diary from Russia [Translated by E. M. Delacour with help from Robert Fenn] London, SCM Press [1956] 316 p. 23 cm. Translation of ... und führen, wohin du nicht willst. *1. World War, 1939-1945 — Prisoners and prisons, Russian. I. T.*
D805.R9G62x   65-7324

Leighton, Alexander Hamilton, 1908-   III. 864
The governing of men; general principles and recommendations based on experience at a Japanese relocation camp [by] Alexander H. Leighton. Princeton, N.J., Princeton University Press, 1945. xvi, 404 p. illus. maps, plans, plates, diagrs. 23 cm. "Published in cooperation with the American council, Institute of Pacific relations, inc." *1. Poston relocation center, Arizona. 2. World war, 1939-1945 — Evacuation of civilians. 3. Concentration camps. I. Institute of Pacific relations. American council. II. T.*
D805.U5L4   940.547273   A45-3337

D809 CIVILIAN RELIEF

Titmuss, Richard Morris, 1907-   III. 865
Problems of social policy, by Richard M. Titmuss. Westport, Conn., Greenwood Press [1971] xi, 596 p. illus. 24 cm. Reprint of the 1950 ed. *1. World War, 1939-1945 — Civilian relief. 2. World War, 1939-1945 — Evacuation of civilians. 3. World War, 1939-1945 — Great Britain. I. T.*
D809.G7T5 1971   940.53/42   79-110872   ISBN:0837145511

D810.J4 HOLOCAUST

Frank, Anne, 1929-1945.   III. 866
The diary of a young girl; translated from the Dutch by B. M. Mooyaart-Doubleday, with an introd. by Eleanor Roosevelt. [1st ed.] Garden City, N.Y., Doubleday, 1952. 285 p. illus. 20 cm. Translation of Het achterhuis. *1. World War, 1939-1945 — Jews. 2. Netherlands — History — German occupations, 1940-1945. I. T.*
D810.J4F715   940.53492 (949.2)   52-6355

Hilberg, Raul, 1926- comp. III. 867
Documents of destruction; Germany and Jewry, 1933-1945. Edited with commentary by Raul Hilberg. Chicago, Quadrangle Books, 1971. xii, 242 p. 22 cm. *1. Holocaust, Jewish (1939-1945) — History — Sources. I. T.*
D810.J4H52 940.54/05 77-152092
ISBN:0812901924 081296165X (pbk.)

Levin, Nora. III. 868
The holocaust; the destruction of European Jewry, 1933-1945. New York, T. Y. Crowell Co. [1968] xvi, 768 p. illus., facsims., maps, ports. 24 cm. *1. World War, 1939-1945 — Jews. I. T.*
D810.J4L455 940.531/5 67-23676

Poliakov, Léon, 1910- III. 869
Harvest of hate; the Nazi program for the destruction of the Jews of Europe. Foreword by Reinhold Niebuhr. Westport, Conn., Greenwood Press [1971, c1954] xiii, 338 p. map. 23 cm. Translation of Bréviaire de la haine. *1. Holocaust, Jewish (1939-1945) I. T.*
D810.J4P614813 940.531/5/03924 74-110836 ISBN:0837126335

D811 PERSONAL NARRATIVES

Stilwell, Joseph Warren, 1883-1946. III. 870
The Stilwell papers, arr. and ed. by Theodore H. White. New York, W. Sloane Associates [1948] xvi, 357 p. illus., ports., maps, facsims. 22 cm. *1. World War, 1939-1945 — Personal narratives, American. 2. World War, 1939-1945 — East (Far East) I. White, Theodore H., 1915- ed.*
D811.S83 940.54 48-6966

Yank, the army weekly. III. 871
The best from Yank, the army weekly, selected by the editors of Yank. 1st ed. New York, Dutton, 1945. xv, 304 p. illus., plates. 28 cm. *1. World war, 1939-1945 — Personal narratives, American. 2. World war, 1939-1945 — Humor, caricatures, etc. 3. World war, 1939-1945 — Pictorial works. 4. World war, 1939-1945 — Fiction. 5. World war, 1939-1945 — Poetry. I. T.*
D811.Y3 940.549 45-3686

Alfieri, Dino, 1886- III. 872
Dictators face to face. Translated by David Moore. New York, New York University Press, 1955 [c1954] x, 307 p. illus., ports. 23 cm. Translation of Due dittatori di fronte. Errata slip inserted. *1. World War, 1939-1945 — Personal narratives, Italian. 2. Italy — Foreign relations — Germany. 3. Germany — Foreign relations — Italy. I. T.*
D811.5.A533x 940.548245 56-5399

Dos Passos, John, 1896- III. 873
Tour of duty. Decorations by Howard Baer. Boston, Houghton Mifflin, 1946. 336 p. illus. 22 cm. *1. World war, 1939-1945 — Personal narratives, American. 2. World war, 1939-1945 — Pacific ocean. 3. Germany — History — Allied occupation, 1945- I. T.*
D811.5.D64 940.548173 46-5929

Pyle, Ernest Taylor, 1900-1945. III. 874
Brave men [by] Ernie Pyle. New York, H. Holt [1944] 474 p. 22 cm. "First printing." *1. World war, 1939-1945 — Personal narratives, American. 2. World war, 1939-1945 — Campaigns — Italy. 3. World war, 1939-1945 — Campaigns — France. I. T.*
D811.5.P88 940.542 44-8735

Pyle, Ernest Taylor, 1900-1945. III. 875
Here is your war. Drawings by Carol Johnson. New York, H. Holt [1943] 304 p. illus. 22 cm. At head of title: Ernie Pyle. *1. World war, 1939-1945 — Personal narratives, American. 2. World war, 1939-1945 — Campaigns — Tunisia. I. T.*
D811.5.P92 940.542 43-15418

Shirer, William Lawrence, 1904- III. 876
Berlin diary; the journal of a foreign correspondent, 1934-1941 [by] William L. Shirer. 1st ed. New York, A. A. Knopf, 1941. vi, 605 p. 22 cm. Sequel: End of a Berlin diary. *1. World war, 1939-1945 — Personal narratives, American. 2. World war, 1939-1945 — Germany. 3. Europe — Politics — 1918-1945. 4. Germany — Politics and government — 1933-1945. I. T.*
D811.5.S5 1941 940.5343 41-9746

D812 – 829 PEACE. RECONSTRUCTION

Dunn, Frederick Sherwood, 1893-1962. III. 877
Peace-making and the settlement with Japan. Principal collaborators: Annemarie Shimony, Percy E. Corbett [and] Bernard C. Cohen. Princeton, N.J., Princeton University Press, 1963. 210 p. 23 cm. *1. World War, 1939-1945 — Peace. 2. World War, 1939-1945 — Japan. 3. U.S. — Foreign relations — Administration. I. T.*
D814.8.D84 940.5314 63-7155

Armstrong, Anne. III. 878
Unconditional surrender; the impact of the Casablanca policy upon World War II. New Brunswick, N.J., Rutgers University Press [1961] 304 p. 22 cm. *1. World War, 1939-1945 — Peace. 2. Anti-Nazi movement. 3. Capitulations, Military. I. T.*
D815.A7 940.54012 61-10253

Byrnes, James Francis, 1879- III. 879
Speaking frankly. [1st ed.] New York, Harper [1947] xii, 324 p. illus., ports., map (on lining-papers) 22 cm. *1. World War, 1939-1945 — Peace. 2. World politics — 1945- 3. World War, 1939-1945 — Diplomatic history. I. T.*
D815.B9 940.531 47-11175

Kecskemeti, Paul. III. 880
Strategic surrender; the politics of victory and defeat. Stanford, Calif., Stanford University Press, 1958. 287 p. 23 cm. "Prepared as part of the research program undertaken for the United States Air Force by the Rand Corporation." *1. Capitulations, Military. 2. World War, 1939-1945 — Peace. I. T.*
D816.K38 940.5314 58-7840

O'Connor, Raymond Gish. III. 881
Diplomacy for victory; FDR and unconditional surrender [by] Raymond G. O'Connor. [1st ed.] New York, Norton [1971] xiii, 143 p. maps. 21 cm. (The Norton essays in American history) *1. World War, 1939-1945 — Peace. 2. World War, 1939-1945 — Diplomatic history. 3. United States — Foreign relations — 1933-1945. I. T.*
D816.O24 1971 940.532/2/73 70-155986
ISBN:0393054411 039309765X (pbk.)

Kuklick, Bruce, 1941- III. 882
American policy and the division of Germany; the clash with Russia over reparations. Ithaca [N.Y.] Cornell University Press [1972] viii, 286 p. 22 cm. *1. World War, 1939-1945 — Germany. 2. World War, 1939-1945 — Peace. 3. World War, 1939-1945 — Reparations. I. T.*
D821.G4K85 940.53/14 78-38121 ISBN:0801407109

Snell, John L. III. 883
Wartime origins of the East-West dilemma over Germany. New Orleans, Hauser Press [1959] 268 p. 23 cm. *1. World War, 1939-1945 — Peace. 2. World War, 1939-1945 — Territorial questions — Germany. I. T.*
D821.G4S55 940.5314 59-12404

Butow, Robert Joseph Charles, 1924- III. 884
Japan's decision to surrender. Foreword by Edwin O. Reischauer. Stanford, Stanford University Press, 1954. xi, 259 p. 25 cm. (The Hoover Library on War, Revolution, and Peace. Publication no. 24) *1. World War, 1939-1945 — Japan. I. T. (S:Stanford University. Hoover Institute and Library on War, Revolution, and Peace. Publication no.24)*
D821.J3B8 1954 940.5314 54-8145

Montgomery, John Dickey, 1920- III. 885
Forced to be free; the artificial revolution in Germany and Japan. [Chicago] University of Chicago Press [1957] 209 p. 23 cm. *1. Germany — History — Allied occupation, 1945- 2. Japan — History — Allied occupation, 1945-1952. 3. Democracy. I. T. II. T:Artificial revolution.*
D825.M6 940.5343 57-11210

D839 – 847 Post-War History

Hammarskjöld, Dag, 1905-1961. III. 886
Markings. Translated from the Swedish by Leif Sjöberg & W. H. Auden. With a foreword by W. H. Auden. [1st American ed.] New York, Knopf, 1964. xxiii, 221 p. 22 cm. Translation of Vägmärken. Verse and prose. *I. T.*
D839.7.H3A313 839.7874 64-19087

Stolpe, Sven, 1905- III. 887
Dag Hammarskjöld, a spiritual portrait. English translation by Naomi Walford. New York, Scribner [1966] 127 p. port. 22 cm. Translation of Dag Hammarskjöld's andliga väg. *1. Hammarskjöld, Dag, 1905-1961.*
D839.7.H3S753 248.2 66-12027

Horowitz, Irving Louis. III. 888
Three worlds of development; the theory and practice of international stratification. New York, Oxford University Press, 1966. xiv, 475 p. 21 cm. *1. World politics — 1945- 2. Social history — 1945- I. T.*
D840.H6 309 66-15421

Kennan, George Frost, 1904- III. 889
Russia, the atom and the West. [1st ed.] New York, Harper [1958] 116 p. 22 cm. *1. World politics — 1955- I. T.*
D840.K4 909.82 58-8078

Seton-Watson, Hugh. III. 890
Neither war nor peace; the struggle for power in the postwar world. New York, Praeger [1960] 504 p. 23 cm. (Books that matter) *1. World politics — 1945- 2. International relations. I. T.*
D840.S4 909.82 60-6992

American Universities Field Staff. III. 891
Expectant peoples; nationalism and development. Under the editorship of K. H. Silvert. With a pref. by Kenneth W. Thompson. New York, Random House [c1963] xxi, 489 p. 22 cm. *1. Nationalism. 2. History, Modern — 1945- 3. Community development. I. Silvert, Kalman H., ed. II. T.*
D842.A765   909.82   63-19716

Pearcy, George Etzel, 1905- III. 892
A handbook of new nations [by] G. Etzel Pearcy & Elvyn A. Stoneman. Cartography by Frank J. Ford & Clare Ford. New York, Crowell [1968] xx, 327 p. maps. 24 cm. *1. States, New — Handbooks, manuals, etc. I. Stoneman, Elvyn A., joint author. II. New nations. III. T.*
D842.P4   910   68-11070

D843 – 847 POLITICAL AND DIPLOMATIC HISTORY

Aron, Raymond, 1905- III. 893
On war. Translated from the French by Terence Kilmartin. New York, W. W. Norton [1968] ix, 143 p. 20 cm. (The Norton library, 107) Translation of De la guerre, an essay in a book entitled Espoir et peur du siècle originally published in 1957. *1. World politics — 1955- 2. War. I. T.*
D843.A683 1968   909.82   68-2039

Ball, George W. III. 894
The discipline of power; essentials of a modern world structure, by George W. Ball. [1st ed.] Boston, Little, Brown [1968] 363 p. 22 cm. "An Atlantic Monthly Press book." *1. World politics — 1945- — Addresses, essays, lectures. I. T.*
D843.B25   327   67-28228

Bell, Coral. III. 895
Negotiation from strength; a study in the politics of power. [1st American ed.] New York, Knopf, 1963. viii, 248, iv p. 22 cm. "First conceived as a Ph.D. thesis for the University of London." *1. U.S. — Foreign relations — 1953-1961. 2. World politics — 1945- I. T.*
D843.B4 1963   327.73   63-9119

Churchill, Winston Leonard Spencer, Sir, 1874-1965. III. 896
The sinews of peace, post-war speeches; ed. by Randolph S. Churchill. Boston, Houghton Mifflin Co., 1949. 256 p. 22 cm. "Covers the ... period from ... June, 1945, to the close of ... 1946." *1. World politics — 1945- 2. Gt. Brit. — Politics and government — 1945- I. T.*
D843.C53   940.55   49-9229
C475

Crozier, Brian. III. 897
The rebels; a study of post-war insurrections. Boston, Beacon Press [1960] 256 p. 21 cm. *1. Revolutions. 2. World politics — 1945- I. T.*
D843.C73 1960   909.82   60-11735

European-American Colloquium, Washington, D.C., 1964. III. 898
Changing East-West relations and the unity of the West; papers presented May 1 and 2, 1964, at the Washington Center of Foreign Policy Research, School of Advanced International Studies, the Johns Hopkins University. Edited by Arnold Wolfers. Baltimore, Johns Hopkins Press [1964] xiii, 242 p. 21 cm. *1. World politics — 1955- — Congresses. I. Wolfers, Arnold, 1892- ed. II. Washington Center of Foreign Policy Research. III. T.*
D843.E85 1964   327.082   64-25076

Feis, Herbert, 1893- III. 899
From trust to terror; the onset of the cold war, 1945-1950. [1st ed.] New York, Norton [1970] xx, 428 p. illus., map, ports. 25 cm. *1. World politics — 1945-1955. I. T.*
D843.F387 1970   327/.1   70-116122   ISBN:39305425X

Fischer, Louis, 1896- III. 900
Russia, America, and the world. [1st ed.] New York, Harper [1961] 244 p. 22 cm. *1. World politics — 1955- I. T.*
D843.F52   909.82   61-6193

Fischer, Louis, 1896- III. 901
This is our world. [1st ed.] New York, Harper [1956] 522 p. illus. 22 cm. *1. World politics — 1945- I. T.*
D843.F53   909.82   55-8020

Gaitskell, Hugh Todd Naylor, 1906- III. 902
The challenge of coexistence. Cambridge, Harvard University Press, 1957. 114 p. 21 cm. (The Godkin lectures at Harvard University, 1957) *1. World politics — 1955- 2. International cooperation. I. T.*
D843.G26   909.82   57-9075

Gaulle, Charles de, Pres. France, 1890-1970. III. 903
Memoirs of hope: renewal and endeavor. Translated by Terence Kilmartin. New York, Simon and Schuster [1971] 392 p. 23 cm. Translation of Mémoires d'espoir. *1. World politics — 1945- I. T.*
D843.G2813 1971b   944.083/0924   76-163103

Halle, Louis Joseph, 1910- III. 904
The cold war as history, by Louis J. Halle. [1st U.S. ed.] New York, Harper & Row [1967] xiv, 434 p. 22 cm. *1. History, Modern — 1945- I. T.*
D843.H26 1967a   909.825   67-21259

Jackson, Barbara (Ward) Lady, 1914- III. 905
Policy for the West, by Barbara Ward. Westport, Conn., Greenwood Press [1970, c1951] viii, 317 p. 23 cm. *1. World politics — 1945- 2. International organization. I. T.*
D843.J3 1970   327/.11/09044   73-100236   ISBN:837134285

Jaspers, Karl, 1883-1969. III. 906
The future of mankind. Translated by E. B. Ashton. [Chicago] University of Chicago Press [1961] 342 p. 24 cm. Translation of Die Atombombe und die Zukunft des Menschen. *1. World politics — 1955- 2. Atomic bomb. I. T.*
D843.J3714   909.82   60-7237
J512

Kaplan, Morton A. III. 907
The revolution in world politics. Morton A. Kaplan, editor. [Contributors: Vernon V. Aspaturian and others] New York, Wiley [1962] xxii, 477 p. 24 cm. *1. World politics — 1955- 2. Revolutions. I. T.*
D843.K34   909.82   62-19149

Lerner, Max, 1902- III. 908
The age of overkill; a preface to world politics. New York, Simon and Schuster, 1962. 329 p. 24 cm. *1. World politics — 1955- 2. Balance of power. I. T.*
D843.L38   909.82   62-19077

Lippmann, Walter, 1889- III. 909
Western unity and the Common Market. [1st ed.] Boston, Little, Brown [1962] 51 p. 20 cm. *1. World politics — 1955- 2. European Economic Community. I. T.*
D843.L52   909.82   62-18624

Russell, Bertrand Russell, 3d earl, 1872- III. 910
Common sense and nuclear warfare. New York, Simon and Schuster, 1959. 92 p. 20 cm. *1. World politics — 1955- 2. International relations. 3. Disarmament. I. T.*
D843.R8 1959   341.67   59-1519

Sigmund, Paul E., ed. III. 911
The ideologies of the developing nations. Edited by Paul E. Sigmund. 2d rev. ed. New York, Praeger [1972] viii, 483 p. 21 cm. *1. World politics — 1945- 2. Underdeveloped areas — Politics and government. I. T.*
D843.S52 1972   320.9/172/4   71-150706

Thant, U, 1909- III. 912
Toward world peace; addresses and public statements, 1957-1963. Selected by Jacob Baal-Teshuva. Foreword by Adlai E. Stevenson. New York, T. Yoseloff [1964] 404 p. illus., ports. (part col.) 22 cm. *1. World politics — Addresses, essays lectures. I. T.*
D843.T417 1964   341.13081   64-21343

Tugwell, Rexford Guy, 1891- III. 913
A chronicle of jeopardy, 1945-55. [Chicago] University of Chicago Press [1955] 488 p. 24 cm. *1. World politics — 1945- I. T.*
D843.T8   909.82   55-8360

Wadsworth, James Jeremiah, 1905- III. 914
The price of peace. New York, Praeger [1962] 127 p. 21 cm. (Books that matter) *1. World politics — 1965- I. T.*
D843.W25   341.67   62-13748

Zacharias, Ellis M., 1890- III. 915
Behind closed doors; the secret history of the cold war, by Ellis M. Zacharias in collaboration with Ladislas Farago. New York, Putnam [1950] viii, 367 p. 22 cm. *1. World politics — 1945- 2. Russia — Foreign relations — 1945- I. T.*
D843.Z2 1950   940.55   50-8878

Russell, Bertrand Russell, 3d earl, 1872-1953. III. 916
Unarmed victory. New York, Simon and Schuster, 1963. 155 p. 21 cm. *1. World politics — 1955- 2. Military bases, Russian — Cuba. 3. Sino-Indian Border Dispute, 1957- I. T.*
D844.R89   327   63-16994

Shulman, Marshall Darrow. III. 917
Beyond the cold war, by Marshall D. Shulman. New Haven, Yale University Press, 1966. vi, 111 p. 21 cm. (A Yale paperbound, Y-166) Rev. and enl. version of a series of lectures presented before the Council on Foreign Relations in New York City during April, 1965. *1. World politics — 1965- 2. Russia — Foreign relations — 1953- I. T.*
D844.S47   327   65-22338

Stevenson, Adlai Ewing, 1900-1965. III. 918
Call to greatness. [1st ed.] New York, Harper [1954] 110 p. 22 cm. "Taken from the Godkin lectures delivered at Harvard University, March, 1954, under the title 'A troubled world.'" *1. World politics — 1945- 2. U.S. — Foreign relations — 1945- I. T.*
D844.S79   940.55 (909.82)   54-6028

D845   NATO

(see also: UA646.3)

Kissinger, Henry Alfred. III. 919
The troubled partnership; a re-appraisal of the Atlantic alliance, by Henry A. Kissinger. [1st ed.] New York, Published for the Council on Foreign Relations by McGraw-Hill [1965] xiv, 266 p. 22 cm. (Atlantic policy studies) Based on 3 lectures delivered at the Council on Foreign Relations in March 1964. *1. North Atlantic Treaty Organization. I. T. (S)*
D845.K5   327.4   65-17493

Furniss, Edgar Stephenson, 1918- ed. III. 920
The Western Alliance, its status and prospects, edited by Edgar S. Furniss, Jr. [Columbus] Ohio State University Press [1965] vii, 182 p. 23 cm. *1. North Atlantic Treaty Organization. I. T.*
D845.2.F85   355.031   65-25644

D847   Communist Countries.

Warsaw Pact

Brzezinski, Zbigniew K., 1928- III. 921
The Soviet bloc, unity and conflict, by Zbigniew K. Brzezinski. Rev. and enl. ed. Cambridge, Harvard University Press, 1967. xviii, 599 p. 24 cm. (Russian Research Center studies, 37) *1. Communist countries. I. T. (S:Harvard University. Russian Research Center. Studies, 37)*
D847.B7 1967   909.82   67-12531

Change in Communist systems. III. 922
Contributors: Jeremy R. Azrael [and others] Edited by Chalmers Johnson. Stanford, Stanford University Press, 1970. xiii, 368 p. 24 cm. Based on discussions of the Workshop on the Comparative Study of Communism held at the Center for Advanced Study in the Bahavioral Sciences in 1968. *1. Communist countries — Politics and government. 2. Communist countries — Economic policy. I. Azrael, Jeremy R., 1935- II. Johnson, Chalmers A., ed. III. Workshop on the Comparative Study of Communism, Center for Advanced Study in the Behavioral Sciences, 1968.*
D847.C45   320.9/171/7   77-97914   ISBN:0804707235

Remington, Robin Alison. III. 923
The Warsaw pact; case studies in Communist conflict resolution. Cambridge, Mass., MIT Press [1971] xix, 268 p. illus. 24 cm. (Studies in communism, revisionism, and revolution) *1. Warsaw pact, 1955. (S)*
D847.2.R45 1971   355.03/1   76-148971   ISBN:0262180502

D901 – 1065   Europe: General

D901 – 980 DESCRIPTION. TRAVEL

Egli, Emil. III. 924
Europe from the air, by Emil Egli and Hans Richard Müller, editor. With an introd. by Salvador de Madariaga. Translated from the German by E. Osers. New York, W. Funk [1960, c1959] 223 p. plates (part col.) 29 cm. Translation of Flugbild Europas. *1. Europe — Description and travel — Aerial. I. Müller, Hans Richard, ed. II. T.*
D907.E353 1960   914   60-1592

Gottmann, Jean. III. 925
A geography of Europe. 3d ed. New York, Holt, Rinehart and Winston [1962] 788 p. illus. 25 cm. *1. Europe — Description and travel. I. T.*
D907.G6 1962   914   62-8176

Hoffman, George Walter, 1914- ed. III. 926
A geography of Europe; including Asiatic U.S.S.R., edited by George W. Hoffman. Contributing authors: Dieter Brunnschweiler [and others] 3d ed. New York, Ronald Press Co. [1969] vi, 671 p. illus., maps. 26 cm. *1. Europe — Description and travel — 1945- I. Brunnschweiler, Dieter, 1925- II. T.*
D907.H6 1969   914   69-14670

Ogilvie, Alan Grant, 1887- III. 927
Europe and its borderlands. Edinburgh, New York, T. Nelson [1957] xii, 340 p. maps, diagrs. 25 cm. *1. Europe — Description and travel. I. T.*
D907.O34   914   57-2576

Montaigne, Michel Eyquem de, 1533-1592. III. 928
Journal de voyage en Italie, par la Suisse et l'Allemagne en 1580 et 1581. Nouv. éd. établie sur le texte de l'édition originale posthume de 1774, avec les principales variantes des autres éditions, une introduction, un appendice et des notes par Maurice Rat. Paris, Garnier Frères [1942] xxxii, 298 p. 19 cm. (Classiques Garnier) At head of title: Montaigne. *1. Italy — Description and travel. 2. Germany — Description and travel. 3. Switzerland — Description and travel. I. Rat, Maurice, ed.*
D913.M6 1942   914.5   45-34637

Karamzin, Nikolai Mikhailovich, 1766-1826. III. 929
Letters of a Russian traveler, 1789-1790; an account of a young Russian gentleman's tour through Germany, Switzerland, France, and England. Translated and abridged by Florence Jonas. Introd. by Leon Stilman. New York, Columbia University Press, 1957. 351 p. illus. 21 cm. (Columbia Slavic studies) *1. Europe — Description and travel — 17th-18th cent. I. T.*
D917.K313   914   57-11744

Cooper, James Fenimore, 1789-1851. III. 930
Gleanings in Europe by James Fenimore Cooper, edited by Robert E. Spiller. New York [etc.] Oxford University Press, 1928-   v. ports. 21 cm. *1. France — Description and travel. 2. France — Social life and customs. 3. England — Desc. and travel. 4. England — Social life and customs. I. Spiller, Robert Ernest, 1896- ed. II. T.*
D919.C8   910.8   28-18308

James, Henry, 1843-1916. III. 931
Portraits of places. With an essay on James as a traveller, by George Alvin Finch. New York, Lear Publishers [1948] 350 p. 23 cm. *1. Europe — Description and travel — 1800-1918. I. Finch, George Alvin. II. T.*
D919.J27 1948   914   48-6262

Pounds, Norman John Greville. III. 932
Europe and the Soviet Union [by] Norman J. G. Pounds. With a contribution by George J. Demko. 2d ed. New York, McGraw-Hill [1966] 528 p. illus., maps. 24 cm. (McGraw-Hill series in geography) First published in 1953 under title: Europe and the Mediterranean. *1. Europe — Description and travel. 2. Mediterranean region — Description and travel. I. T.*
D921.P6835 1966   914   65-24529

Wilson, Edmund, 1895- III. 933
Europe without Baedeker; sketches among the ruins of Italy, Greece, and England, together with notes from a European diary, 1963-1964. [2d ed.] New York, Farrar, Straus and Giroux [1966] xi, 467 p. 20 cm. *1. Europe — Description and travel — 1945- I. T.*
D921.W525 1966   914.0455   66-14040

Monkhouse, Francis John. III. 934
A regional geography of Western Europe [by] F. J. Monkhouse. 3d ed. [rev. & enl.] New York, F. A. Praeger [1967] xx, 727 p. illus., maps. 23 cm. (Praeger advanced geographies) *1. Europe — Description and travel — 1945- I. Western Europe. II. T.*
D967.M693 1967   914   67-25038

D972 – 973 Mediterranean Sea

Halliburton, Richard, 1900-1939. III. 935
The glorious adventure. New York, Triangle Books [1941] 354 p. illus. 20 cm. "Triangle books edition published April 1941." *1. Mediterranean sea — Description and travel. I. T.*
D972.H2 1941   910.4   41-12940

Braudel, Fernand. III. 935a
The Mediterranean and the mediterranean world in the age of Philip II. Translated from French by Siân Reynolds. [1st U.S. ed.] New York, Harper & Row [1972-   v. illus. 24 cm. Translation of La Méditerranée et le monde méditerranéen à l'époque de Philippe II. *1. Mediterranean region — History. 2. Physical geography — Mediterranean region. I. T.*
D973.A2B7x   (DE80.B7713)   910/.09/1822   72-138708
ISBN:006010452X (v. 1)

Rose, John Holland, 1855-1942. III. 936
The Mediterranean in the ancient world, by J. Holland Rose. 2d ed. Cambridge [Eng.] The University Press, 1934. xi, 184 p. illus. (maps) 20 cm. Map on lining-paper. "First edition, 1933. Second edition, 1934." *1. Mediterranean sea — History. 2. History, Ancient. I. T.*
D973.A2R6 1934   930 (910.4)   36-10977

Birot, Pierre. III. 937
La Méditerranée et le Moyen-Orient, par Pierre Birot et Jean Dresch. [1. ed.] Paris, Presses universitaires de France, 1953-56 [c1955] 2 v. illus., plates, maps. 24 cm. ("Orbis"; introduction aux études de géographie) *1. Mediterranean region — Description and travel. I. Dresch, Jean, joint author. II. T. (S:Orbis)*
D973.B615   A54-7204

Semple, Ellen Churchill, 1863-1932. III. 938
The geography of the Mediterranean region; its relation to ancient history, by Ellen Churchill Semple. New York, Holt [c1931] viii, 737 p. front., maps. 23 cm. *1. Mediterranean region — Historical geography. 2. Physical geography — Mediterranean region. 3. History, Ancient.*
D973.S45   910.4   31-33866

Siegfried, André, 1875-1959. III. 939
The Mediterranean. Translated from the French by Doris Hemming. London, Cape [1948] 221 p. illus., maps. 22 cm. Translation of Vue générale de la Méditerranée. *1. Mediterranean Sea.*
D973.S5x   914   A50-776

Walker, Donald Smith. III. 940
The Mediterranean lands. London, Methuen; New York, Wiley [1960] xxiii, 524 p. illus., maps. 21 cm. *1. Mediterranean region. I. T.*
D973.W18   914   61-850

D1050 – 1065   HISTORY

Brinton, Clarence Crane, 1898-1968. III. 941
The temper of Western Europe. Westport, Conn., Greenwood Press [1970, c1953] ix, 118 p. 23 cm. (The James W. Richards lectures in history, 1953) *1. Europe — History — 1945- — Addresses, essays, lectures. I. T. (S)*
D1051.B75 1970   914/.03/55   70-97339   ISBN:837127998

Lichtheim, George, 1912-   III. 942
The new Europe: today, and tomorrow. New York, Praeger [1963] 232 p. 21 cm. *1. Europe — History — 1945- I. T.*
D1051.L5 1963   940.55   63-11152

White, Theodore Harold, 1915-   III. 943
Fire in the ashes: Europe in mid-century. New York, Sloane, 1953. 405 p. 22 cm. *1. Europe — Politics — 1945- 2. U.S. — Foreign relations — 1945- I. T.*
D1051.W4   940.55   53-10166

Co-operation in Europe.   III. 944
Ed. [by] Johan Galtung with the assistance of Sverre Lodgaard. Assen, Van Gorcum; New York, Humanities Press, 1970. 379 p. 23 cm. (IPRA studies in peace research, 3) English, French, or German. *1. European cooperation. I. Galtung, Johan, ed. II. Lodgaard, Sverre, ed. (S:International Peace Research Association. IPRA studies in peace research, 3)*
D1053.C58 1970b   71-574620   ISBN:9023201310

Beloff, Max, 1913-   III. 945
Europe and the Europeans, an international discussion. With an introd. by Denis de Rougemont. A report prepared at the request of the Council of Europe. London, Chatto & Windus, 1957. xix, 288 p. 23 cm. *1. Europe — Civilization. 2. European federation. I. Council of Europe. II. T.*
D1055.B4   A58-2321

Lukacs, John A.   III. 946
Decline and rise of Europe; a study in recent history, with particular emphasis on the development of a European consciousness, by John Lukacs. [1st ed.] Garden City, N.Y., Doubleday, 1965. xii, 295 p. 22 cm. *1. Europe — Civilization. 2. European federation. I. T.*
D1055.L8   914   65-10638

Rougemont, Denis de, 1906-   III. 947
The meaning of Europe. Translated from the French by Alan Braley. New York, Stein and Day [1965, c1963] 126 p. 22 cm. *1. Europe — Civilization. I. T.*
D1055.R633 1965   914   65-22272

Hallstein, Walter, 1901-   III. 948
United Europe; challenge and opportunity. Cambridge, Harvard University Press, 1962. 109 p. 22 cm. (The William L. Clayton lectures on international economic affairs and foreign policy, 1961-1962) *1. European federation. I. T.*
D1060.H3   940.55   62-19216

Zurcher, Arnold John, 1902-   III. 949
The struggle to unite Europe, 1940-1958; an historical account of the development of the contemporary European movement from its origin in the Pan-European Union to the drafting of the treaties for Euratom and the European common market. [New York] New York University Press, 1958. 254 p. 22 cm. *1. European federation. I. T.*
D1060.Z8   940.55   58-6825

D1065.U5 Europe and the United States

Beloff, Max, 1913-   III. 950
The United States and the unity of Europe. Washington, Brookings Institution [1963] 124 p. 24 cm. *1. U.S. — Foreign relations — Europe. 2. European federation. I. T.*
D1065.U5B4   327.7304   63-15630

Servan-Schreiber, Jean Jacques.   III. 951
The American challenge [by] J. -J. Servan-Schreiber. With a foreword by Arthur Schlesinger, Jr. Translated from the French by Ronald Steel. [1st ed.] New York, Atheneum, 1968. xviii, 291 p. 22 cm. Translation of Le Défi américain. *1. United States — Relations (general) with Europe. 2. Europe — Relations (general) with the United States. I. T.*
D1065.U5S413   332.67/373/04   68-19793

DA1 – 890 Great Britain

DA1 – 3 HISTORIOGRAPHY

Butterfield, Herbert, Sir, 1900-   **III. 952**
The Englishman and his history, by H. Butterfield. With a new pref. by the author. [Hamden, Conn.] Archon Books, 1970. x, 142 p. 18 cm. Reprint of the 1944 ed. *1. Great Britain — Historiography — Addresses, essays, lectures. 2. Great Britain — Politics and government — Addresses, essays, lectures. I. T.*
DA1.B875 1970   942/.0072/042   76-121754   ISBN:0208009930

Winks, Robin W., ed.   **III. 953**
The historiography of the British Empire-Commonwealth; trends, interpretations and resources, edited by Robin W. Winks. With twenty-one essays by George Bennett [and others] Durham, N.C., Duke University Press, 1966. xiv, 596 p. 24 cm. *1. Commonwealth of Nations — History — Historiography. 2. Commonwealth of Nations — History — Bibliography. 3. Gt. Brit. — Colonies — History — Historiography. 4. Gt. Brit. — Colonies — History — Bibliography. I. T.*
DA1.W55   909.09171242   66-15555

Douglas, David Charles, 1898-   **III. 954**
English scholars, 1660-1730. [2d rev. ed.] London, Eyre & Spottiswoode [1951] 291 p. ports. 23 cm. *1. Scholars, British. 2. Learning and scholarship — England. 3. Historians, British. 4. Gt. Brit. — History — 1660-1714. I. T.*
DA3.A1D6 1951   942.007   52-1346

DA10 – 18 BRITISH EMPIRE. COMMONWEALTH OF NATIONS

Darby, Henry Clifford, 1909- ed.   **III. 955**
An historical geography of England before A.D. 1800; fourteen studies, edited by H. C. Darby. Cambridge [Eng.] University Press, 1936. xii, 566 p. illus. (maps, plans) diagrs. 24 cm. *1. Gt. Brit. — Historical geography. 2. Gt. Brit. — History. I. T.*
DA13.D3   911.42   36-18359

The Cambridge history of the British Empire.   **III. 956**
[2d ed.] Cambridge [Eng.] University Press, 1963- v. 24 cm. *1. Gt. Brit. — History. 2. Gt. Brit. — Colonies — History. I. Walker, Eric Anderson, 1886- ed.*
DA16.C252   942   63-24285

Carrington, Charles Edmund, 1897-   **III. 957**
The British overseas: exploits of a nation of shopkeepers, by C. E. Carrington. 2nd ed. London, Cambridge U.P., 1968- v. plates, illus., maps, ports. 21 cm. *1. Gr. Brit. — Colonies — History. I. T.*
DA16.C32   325.3/42   68-23176   ISBN:052109514X

Churchill, Winston Leonard Spencer, Sir, 1874-1965.   **III. 958**
A history of the English-speaking peoples. [1st ed.] New York, Dodd, Mead, 1956-58. 4 v. maps. 22 cm. *1. Gt. Brit. — History. I. T.*
DA16.C47   942   56-6868

Cross, Colin.   **III. 959**
The fall of the British Empire, 1918-1968. [1st American ed.] New York, Coward-McCann [1969, c1968] 359 p. col. maps (on lining papers), ports. 23 cm. *1. Great Britain — History — 20th century. 2. Commonwealth of Nations. I. T.*
DA16.C87 1969   909/.09/71242082   68-11877

Grierson, Edward, 1914-   **III. 960**
The imperial dream: the British Commonwealth and Empire, 1775-1969. London, Collins, 1972. 320 p. 24 cm. American ed. published under title: The death of the imperial dream. *1. Commonwealth of Nations — History. 2. Great Britain — Colonies. I. T.*
DA16.G736   909/.09/71242   72-180114   ISBN:0002114119

Hall, Hessel Duncan, 1891-   **III. 961**
Commonwealth: a history of the British Commonwealth of Nations [by] H. Duncan Hall, with an introduction by Sir Robert Menzies. London, New York, Van Nostrand Reinhold, 1971. xxxvi, 1015 p. 33 plates (7 fold.) illus., maps, ports. 26 cm. *1. Commonwealth of Nations — History. I. T.*
DA16.H19   909/.09/71242   70-83655   ISBN:0442022018

Huttenback, Robert A.   **III. 962**
The British imperial experience [by] Robert A. Huttenback. New York, Harper & Row [1966] xi, 225 p. maps. 21 cm. *1. Gt. Brit. — Colonies — History. 2. Imperialism. I. T.*
DA16.H9   909.0971242   66-15671

Knaplund, Paul, 1885-1964.   **III. 963**
The British empire, 1815-1939. New York, H. Fertig, 1969. xx, 850 p. maps. 23 cm. *1. Great Britain — Colonies — History. 2. Imperial federation. I. T.*
DA16.K65 1969   325.3/42   68-9617

Mansergh, Nicholas.   **III. 964**
The Commonwealth experience. New York, Praeger [1969] xix, 471 p. illus., maps, ports. 25 cm. (Praeger history of civilization) *1. Commonwealth of Nations — History. I. T.*
DA16.M248 1969b   909/.09/71242   69-10570

Mansergh, Nicholas, ed.   **III. 965**
Documents and speeches on British Commonwealth affairs, 1931-1952. London, New York, Oxford University Press, 1953. 2 v. (xli, 1308 p.) 24 cm. *1. Commonwealth of Nations — History — Sources. I. T:British Commonwealth affairs, 1931-1952.*
DA16.M25   942.084   53-4142

Morris, James, 1926-   **III. 966**
Pax Britannica; the climax of an empire. [1st American ed.] New York, Harcourt, Brace & World [1968] 544 p. illus., col. maps (on lining papers) ports. 22 cm. "A Helen and Kurt Wolff book." Sequel to: Heaven's command. *1. Great Britain — Colonies — History. 2. Great Britain — History — Victoria, 1837-1901. I. T.*
DA16.M598 1968b   909/.09/71242   68-24395

Seeley, John Robert, Sir, 1834-1895.   **III. 967**
The expansion of England. Edited and with an introd. by John Gross. Chicago, University of Chicago Press [1971] xxvii, 248 p. 23 cm. (Classics of British historical literature) "Consists of two sets of lectures which were originally delivered to Cambridge undergraduates in the autumn of 1881 and the spring of 1882." *1. Great Britain — Colonies — Addresses, essays, lectures. 2. Great Britain — History — 18th century — Addresses, essays, lectures. 3. India — Politics and government — 1765-1947 — Addresses, essays, lectures. I. T.*
DA16.S45 1971   909/.09/71242   73-152225
ISBN:0226744280 0226744299 (pbk)

Burt, Alfred LeRoy, 1888-   **III. 968**
The evolution of the British Empire and Commonwealth from the American Revolution. Boston, Heath [1956] 950 p. illus. 25 cm. *1. Commonwealth of Nations. 2. Gt. Brit. — Colonies — History. I. T.*
DA18.B8   942   56-6105

Carter, Gwendolen Margaret, 1906-   **III. 969**
The British commonwealth and international security; the role of the dominions, 1919-1939, by Gwendolen M. Carter. Issued under the auspices of the Canadian Institute of International Affairs. Toronto, Ryerson Press [1947] xx, 326 p. 25 cm. *1. Gt. Brit. — Foreign relations — 20th cent. 2. Gt. Brit. — Colonies. 3. Security, International. I. T.*
DA18.C36   942.083   47-2017

Hancock, William Keith, 1898-   **III. 970**
Survey of British commonwealth affairs. London, New York, Oxford University Press, 1937-42. 2 v. in 3. maps (part col.) 25 cm. "Issued under the auspices of the Royal Institute of International Affairs." *1. Gt. Brit. —*

DA30   *Great Britain*   III. 988

Foreign relations — 20th cent. 2. Gt. Brit. — Colonies. 3. Imperial federation. 4. Nationalism. I. T.
DA18.H26   354.4201   37-23223

Keith, Arthur Berriedale, 1879-1944, ed.   **III. 971**
Speeches and documents on the British dominions, 1918-1931; from self-government to national sovereignty; edited with an introduction and notes by Arthur Berriedale Keith. London, Oxford University Press [1932] xlvii, 501 p. 16 cm. (The World's classics. CDIII) *1. Gt. Brit. — Politics and government — 1910-1936. 2. Gt. Brit. — Colonies. 3. Gt. Brit. — Foreign relations — 1910-1936. 4. Imperial federation. I. T.*
DA18.K4   942   33-4173

Mansergh, Nicholas.   **III. 972**
Survey of British Commonwealth affairs. London, New York, Oxford University Press, 1952-58. 2 v. tables. 25 cm. "Issued under the auspices of the Royal Institute of International Affairs." *1. Gt. Brit. — Foreign relations — 20th cent. 2. Gt. Brit. — Colonies. 3. Imperial federation. 4. Nationalism. I. T.*
DA18.M328   327.42   52-3954

Miller, John Donald Bruce.   **III. 973**
The Commonwealth in the world, by J. D. B. Miller. 3d ed. Cambridge, Harvard University Press, 1965. 304 p. illus. 23 cm. *1. Commonwealth of Nations. I. T.*
DA18.M46 1965   320.9171242   65-8789

Winks, Robin W., comp.   **III. 974**
The age of imperialism, edited by Robin W. Winks. Englewood Cliffs, N.J., Prentice-Hall [1969] viii, 184 p. 20 cm. (Sources of civilization in the West) A Spectrum book. *1. Imperial federation — Collections. 2. Imperialism — Collections. I. T. (S)*
DA18.W52 1969   321/.03/08   75-79441   ISBN:130185493

DA20 – 690   ENGLAND

English historical documents.   **III. 975**
General editor: David C. Douglas. [New York, Oxford University Press, 195 v. illus., maps (part fold.) geneal. tables. 25 cm. Half title; each volume has special t. p. *1. Gt. Brit. — History — Sources. I. Douglas, David Charles, 1898- , ed.*
DA26.E55   942   53-1506

Maitland, Frederic William, 1850-1906.   **III. 976**
Selected historical essays. Chosen and introduced by Helen M. Cam. Cambridge, [Eng.] Published in association with the Selden Society at the University Press, 1957. xxix, 277 p. 23 cm. *1. Gt. Brit. — History — Addresses, essays, lectures. 2. Law — Gt. Brit. — History and criticism.*
DA27.M26   942.004   57-14461

DA28   Biography

The Dictionary of national biography,   **III. 977**
founded in 1882 by George Smith; edited by Sir Leslie Stephen and Sir Sidney Lee; from the earliest times to 1900 ... London, Oxford University Press [1921-22] 22 v. front. (port.) 24 cm. First published 1885-1901, in 66 volumes. Vol. 22, "Supplement." "Memoir of George Smith": v.1, p. [xxi]-lix. ... [Second] Supplement, January 1901-December 1911, edited by Sir Sidney Lee ... London, Oxford University Press [1927] 3 v. in 1. 24 cm. ... [Third supplement] 1912-1921, edited by H. W. C. Davis and J. R. H. Weaver, with an index covering the years 1901-1921 in one alphabetical series. London, Oxford University Press [1927] xxvi, 623 [1] p. 24 cm. ... [Fourth supplement] 1922-1930, edited by J. R. H. Weaver, with an index covering the years 1901-1930 in one alphabetical series. London, Oxford University Press [1937] xiv, 962 p. 24 cm. [Fifth supplement] 1931-1940, edited by L. G. Wickham Legg, with an index covering the years 1901-1940 in one alphabetical series. London, Oxford University Press, 1949. xvi, 968 p. 24 cm. [Sixth supplement] 1941-1950, edited by L. G. Wickham Legg and E. T. Williams, with an index covering the years 1901-1950 in one alphabetical series. [London] Oxford University Press, 1959. xxi, 1031 p. 24 cm. [Seventh supplement] 1951-1960, edited by E. T. Williams and H. M. Palmer, with an index covering the years 1901-1960 in one alphabetical series. [London] Oxford University Press, 1971. xxvi, 1150 p. 24 cm. *1. Smith, George, 1824-1901. 2. Gt. Brit. — Biography. 3. Gt. Brit. — Bio-bibliography. 4. Gt. Brit. — Biography — Dictionaries. I. Stephen, Leslie, Sir, 1832-1904, ed. II. Lee, Sidney, Sir, 1859-1926, ed. III. Davis, Henry William Carless, 1874-1928, ed. IV. Weaver, John Reginald Homer, 1882- ed.*
DA28.D47   920.042

Who's who; an annual biographical dictionary, with which is incorporated "Men and women of the time".   **III. 978**
London, Baily Brothers, 18 - , A. & C. Black [18 -19] v. 19 cm. Subtitle varies. Editors: 18 -64, C. H. Oakes. — 1865-   W. J. Lawson. — 1897-99, Douglas Sladen. *1. Gt. Brit. — Biography. 2. Biography — Dictionaries. I. Oakes, Charles Henry, 1810-1864, ed. II. Lawson, William John, ed. III. Sladen, Douglas Brooke Wheelton, 1856- , ed.*
DA28.W6   04-16933

Who was who, a companion to Who's who, containing the biographies of those who died.   **III. 979**
London, A. & C. Black, 1897/1915- 5 v. 22 cm. Vol.1 is 4th rev. ed., publ. 1953. *1. Gt. Brit. — Biography. 2. Biography — Dictionaries.*
DA28.W65   920.042   20-14622

DA30 – 35   History: General Works

Clark, George Norman, Sir, 1890-   **III. 980**
English history: a survey, George Clark. Oxford, Clarendon Press, 1971. xix, 567 p.; maps. 21 cm. *1. Great Britain — History. I. T.*
DA30.C6   942   70-595865   ISBN:0198223390

Williamson, James Alexander, 1886-   **III. 981**
The Tudor Age. [2d ed., with appendices] London, New York, Longmans, Green [1957] xxiii, 468 p. maps. 23 cm. (A history of England [v.4]) *1. Gt. Brit. — History — Tudors, 1485-1603. I. T. (S:Medlicott, William Norton, 1900- ed. A history of England [v.4])*
DA30.M455 vol. 4 1957   942.05   58-4372

Davis, Henry William Carless, 1874-1928.   **III. 982**
England under the Normans and Angevins, 1066-1272. 13th ed., rev. London, Methuen; New York, Barnes & Noble [1957] 591 p. illus. 23 cm. (A History of England, v.2) *1. Gt. Brit. — History — Medieval period, 1066-1485. I. T.*
DA30.O6 vol. 2, 1957   942.01   60-51002

Whitelock, Dorothy.   **III. 983**
The beginnings of English society, by D. Whitelock. Harmondsworth [Eng.] Penguin Books [1952] 256 p. 18 cm. (The Pelican history of England, v.2) Pelican books, A245. *1. Gt. Brit. — Civilization — To 1066. I. T. (S)*
DA30.P4 vol. 2   66-46212

Stenton, Doris Mary (Parsons) Lady.   **III. 984**
English society in the early middle ages, (1066-1307) [by] Doris Mary Stenton. 4th ed. Harmondsworth, Penguin, 1965. 320 p. 18 1/2 cm. (The Pelican history of England, 3) Pelican books, A252. *1. Gt. Brit. — History — Medieval period, 1066-1454. I. T. (S)*
DA30.P4 vol. 3, 1965   914.2/03/2   67-96327

Myers, Alec Reginald.   **III. 985**
England in the late Middle Ages, by A. R. Myers. Harmondsworth, Middlesex, Penguin Books [1952] xv, 263 p. maps. 18 cm. (The Pelican history of England, v.4) *1. Gt. Brit. — History — Medieval period, 1066-1485. I. T. (S)*
DA30.P4 vol. 4   67-4045

Fisher, Herbert Albert Laurens, 1865-1940.   **III. 986**
The history of England, from the accession of Henry VII to the death of Henry VIII, 1485-1547. New York, Greenwood Press [1969] xx, 518 p. maps. 23 cm. (The Political history of England, 5) Reprint of the 1906 ed. *1. Great Britain — History — Tudors, 1485-1603. I. T. (S)*
DA30.P762 vol. 5   942.05/1   69-13896

Pollard, Albert Frederick, 1869-1948.   **III. 987**
The history of England from the accession of Edward VI to the death of Elizabeth (1547-1603) New York, Greenwood Press [1969] xxv, 524 p. 3 geneal. tables, 2 maps. 23 cm. (The Political history of England, v. 6) Reprint of the 1915 ed. *1. Great Britain — History — Tudors, 1485-1603. I. T. (S)*
DA30.P762 vol. 6   942.05   69-14037

Montague, Francis Charles, 1858-1935.   **III. 988**
The history of England from the Accession of James I to the Restoration, 1603-1660. New York, Greenwood Press [1969] xix, 516 p. maps. 23 cm. (The

Political history of England, v. 7) Reprint of the 1907 ed. *1. Great Britain — History — Stuarts, 1603-1714. I. T. (S)*
DA30.P762 vol. 7   942.06   69-14000

Adams, George Burton, 1851-1925.   **III. 989**
The history of England, from the Norman Conquest to the death of John, 1066-1216. London, New York, Longmans, Green, 1905. New York, AMS Press, 1969. x, 473 p. col. maps. 23 cm. (The Political history of England, v. 2) *1. Great Britain — History — Medieval period, 1066-1485. I. T.*
DA30.P7622 vol. 2   942   79-5634

Trevelyan, George Macaulay, 1876-   **III. 990**
Illustrated English social history. Illus. selected by Ruth C. Wright. London, New York, Longmans, Green [1949-1952] 4 v. illus. (part col.) maps. 23 cm. First ed. published in 1942 under title: English social history. *1. Gt. Brit. — History. 2. Gt. Brit. — Social conditions. I. T.*
DA32.T74873   942   50-5891

Cheney, Christopher Robert, 1906- ed.   **III. 991**
Handbook of dates for students of English history, edited by C. R. Cheney. London, Office of the Royal historical society, 1945. xvii, 164 p. 22 x 18 cm. (Royal historical society guides and handbooks, no. 4) *1. Chronology, Historical. 2. Great Britain — History — Chronology. 3. Chronology, Ecclesiastical. (S:Royal historical society, London. Guides and handbooks, no. 4)*
DA34.C5   942.002   A46-270

Powicke, Frederick Maurice, Sir, 1879- , ed.   **III. 992**
Handbook of British chronology, edited by F. Maurice Powicke and E. B. Fryde. 2d ed. London, Offices of the Royal Historical Society, 1961. xxxviii, 565 p. 25 cm. (Royal Historical Society, London. Guides and handbooks, no. 2) *1. Gt. Brit. — History — Chronology. I. Fryde, E B , joint ed. II. T. (S)*
DA34.P6 1961   942.002   62-3079

Steinberg, Sigfrid Henry, 1899- ed.   **III. 993**
Steinberg's Dictionary of British history, edited by S. H. Steinberg and I. H. Evans. [Contributors] P. M. Barnes [and others] 2d ed. New York, St. Martin's Press [1971] vi, 421 p. 23 cm. 1963 and 1964 editions published under title: A new dictionary of British history. *1. Great Britain — History — Dictionaries. I. Evans, Ivor H., joint ed. II. Barnes, Patricia M. III. T.*
DA34.S7 1971   942/.003   79-140431   ISBN:0713155523

DA40 – 48   Political and Diplomatic History

Strang, William Strang, baron, 1893-   **III. 994**
Britain in world affairs; the fluctuation in power and influence from Henry VIII to Elizabeth II. New York, Praeger [1961] 426 p. 21 cm. (Books that matter) *1. Gt. Brit. — Foreign relations. I. T.*
DA42.S85 1961   327.42   61-10747

Seeley, John Robert, Sir, 1834-1895.   **III. 995**
The growth of British policy; an historical essay. Cambridge, University Press, 1903. St. Clair Shores, Mich., Scholarly Press, 1972. 2 v. 22 cm. *1. Great Britain — History. 2. Great Britain — Foreign relations. I. T.*
DA45.S45 1972   327.42   72-145289   ISBN:0403012031

Taylor, Alan John Percivale, 1906-   **III. 996**
The trouble makers; dissent over foreign policy, 1792-1939. Bloomington, Indiana University Press, 1958. 207 p. 23 cm. *1. Gt. Brit. — Foreign relations — 19th cent. 2. Gt. Brit. — Foreign relations — 20th cent. I. T.*
DA45.T3 1958   327.42   58-9370

Ward, Adolphus William, Sir, 1837-1924, ed.   **III. 997**
The Cambridge history of British foreign policy, 1783-1919. Edited by A. W. Ward and G. P. Gooch. New York, Octagon Books, 1970. 3 v. 24 cm. Reprint of the 1922-23 ed. *1. Great Britain — Foreign relations. 2. World politics. I. Gooch, George Peabody, 1873-1968, joint ed. II. T.*
DA45.W35 1970   327.42   70-119436

Horn, David Bayne, 1901-   **III. 998**
Great Britain and Europe in the eighteenth century. Oxford, Clarendon P., 1967. xi, 411 p. plate (map). 22 1/2 cm. *1. Gt. Brit. — Foreign relations — Europe. 2. Europe — Foreign relations — Gt. Brit. 3. Gt. Brit. — Foreign relations — 18th cent. I. T.*
DA47.H6   327.4/042   67-88613

Thomson, Mark Alméras.   **III. 999**
William III and Louis XIV: essays 1680-1720, by and for Mark A. Thomson. Edited by Ragnhild Hatton and J. S. Bromley. Toronto, University of Toronto Press, 1968. 332 p. port. 24 cm. *1. Great Britain — Foreign relations — France. 2. France — Foreign relations — Great Britain. 3. William III, King of Great Britain, 1650-1702. 4. Louis XIV, King of France, 1638-1715. I. Hatton, Ragnhild Marie, ed. II. Bromley, John Selwyn, ed. III. T.*
DA47.1.T48 1968   327/.42/044   68-98219

Woodward, Ernest Llewellyn, Sir, 1890-   **III. 1000**
Great Britain and the German Navy. [Hamden, Conn.] Archon Books, 1964. 524 p. 23 cm. *1. Germany. Kriegsmarine. 2. Gt. Brit. Navy. 3. Gt. Brit. — Foreign relations — Germany. 4. Germany — Foreign relations — Gt. Brit. 5. European War, 1914-1918 — Causes. 6. Europe — Politics — 20th cent. I. T.*
DA47.2.W6 1964   327.42043   64-9601

Wilson, Charles Henry.   **III. 1001**
Queen Elizabeth and the revolt of the Netherlands [by] Charles Wilson. Berkeley, University of California Press, 1970. xiv, 168 p. map, plates. 23 cm. *1. Great Britain — Foreign relations — Netherlands. 2. Netherlands — Foreign relations — Great Britain. 3. Netherlands — History — Wars of Independence, 1556-1648. I. T.*
DA47.3.W52 1970b   949/.203   76-119009   ISBN:0520017447

Austin, Dennis, 1922-   **III. 1002**
Britain and South Africa. London, issued under the auspices of the Royal Institute of International Affairs [by] Oxford U. P., 1966. x, 191 p. map, tables. 22 1/2 cm. *1. Gt. Brit. — Relations (general) with South Africa. 2. Africa, South — Relations (general) with Gt. Brit. I. Royal Institute of International Affairs. II. T.*
DA47.9.A4A9   301.2942068   66-72226

Clifford, Nicholas Rowland.   **III. 1003**
Retreat from China; British policy in the Far East, 1937-1941 [by] Nicholas R. Clifford. [Seattle] University of Washington Press [1967] ix, 222 p. maps. 23 cm. Based on the author's thesis, Harvard. *1. Gt. Brit. — Foreign relations — East (Far East) 2. East (Far East) — Foreign relations — Gt. Brit. I. T.*
DA47.9.E2C5 1967   327.42/051   67-12395

DA49 – 69   Military History

Barnett, Correlli.   **III. 1004**
Britain and her army, 1509-1970; a military, political, and social survey. New York, W. Morrow, 1970. xx, 529 p. illus., facsims., maps, ports. 25 cm. *1. Great Britain — History, Military. I. T.*
DA65.B283 1970   355/.00942   74-116805

Willcox, William Bradford, 1907-   **III. 1005**
Portrait of a general; Sir Henry Clinton in the War of Independence. [1st ed.] New York, Knopf; [distributed by Random House] 1964. xxii, 534, xiv p. illus., ports., maps. 25 cm. *1. Clinton, Henry, Sir, 1738?-1795. 2. U.S. — History — Revolution — Campaigns and battles. I. T.*
DA67.1.C55W5   973.33   64-12311

Luvaas, Jay.   **III. 1006**
The education of an army; British military thought, 1815-1940. [Chicago] University of Chicago Press [1964] xi, 454 p. 23 cm. *1. Gt. Brit. Army — Biography. 2. Gt. Brit. — History, Military — 19th cent. 3. Gt. Brit. — History, Military — 20th cent. I. T.*
DA68.1.A1L8   355.0942   64-25717

Longford, Elizabeth (Harman) Pakenham, Countess of, 1906-   **III. 1007**
Wellington [by] Elizabeth Longford. [1st U.S. ed.] New York, Harper & Row [1970-73, c1969-72] 2 v. illus., facsim., maps, ports. 25 cm. *1. Wellington, Arthur Wellesley, 1st Duke of, 1769-1852.*
DA68.12.W4L62   942.07/092/4 (B)   75-95973
    ISBN:0060126698 (v. 1)   006012671X (v. 2)

Magnus, Philip Montefiore, Sir, Bart., 1906-   **III. 1008**
Kitchener: portrait of an imperialist [by] Philip Magnus. Harmondsworth, Penguin, 1968. 485 p. 16 plates, illus., 2 maps, ports. 18 cm. *1. Kitchener, Horatio Herbert Kitchener, 1st Earl, 1850-1916.*
DA68.32.K6M3 1968   942.08/0924 (B)   72-366576

Tedder, Arthur William Tedder, baron, 1890-   **III. 1009**
With prejudice: the war memoirs of Marshal of the Royal Air Force, Lord Tedder. [1st American ed.] Boston, Little, Brown [1967, c1966] 692 p. illus., maps, ports. 22 cm. *1. World War, 1939-1945 — Aerial operations, British. I. T.*
DA69.3.T35A3 1967   940.544942   67-18108

DA70–89 Naval History

Lloyd, Christopher, 1906-   III. 1010
The nation and the navy; a history of naval life and policy. [Rev. ed.] London, Cresset Press, 1961. 314 p. illus. 23 cm. *1. Gt. Brit. Navy — History. 2. Gt. Brit. — History, Naval. I. T.*
DA85.L55 1961   942   62-4180

Andrews, Kenneth R.   III. 1011
Drake's voyages: a re-assessment of their place in Elizabethan maritime expansion [by] Kenneth R. Andrews. New York, Scribner [1968, c1967] 190 p. 7 maps. 22 cm. *1. Great Britain — History, Naval — Tudors, 1485-1603. 2. Drake, Francis, Sir, 1540?-1596. I. T.*
DA86.A7 1968   942.05/5/0924   68-12504

Corbett, Julian Stafford, Sir, 1854-1922.   III. 1012
England in the Mediterranean; a study of the rise and influence of British power within the Straits, 1603-1713; by Julian S. Corbett. London, New York and Bombay, Longmans, Green, 1904. 2 v. fronts., 2 maps (incl. front.) 23 cm. "The substance of the present work has been given ... partly in lectures before the Senior and the flag officers' war courses at Greenwich, and partly in the Ford lectures on English history for 1903 at Oxford." — Pref. *1. Gt. Brit. — History, Naval — Stuarts, 1603-1714.*
DA86.C7   04-8067

Powell, John Rowland.   III. 1013
The navy in the English Civil War. With an introd. by C. V. Wedgwood. Hamden [Conn.] Archon Books, 1962. 240 p. illus. 22 cm. *1. Gt. Brit. — History, Naval — Stuarts, 1603-1714. 2. Gt. Brit. — History — Civil War, 1642-1649. I. T.*
DA86.P6   942.062   62-20453

Richmond, Herbert William, Sir, 1871-1946.   III. 1014
The Navy as an instrument of policy, 1558-1727. Edited by E. A. Hughes. Cambridge [Eng.] University Press, 1953. 404 p. 24 cm. *1. Gt. Brit. — History, Naval — Tudors, 1485-1603. 2. Gt. Brit. — History, Naval — Stuarts, 1603-1714. I. T.*
DA86.R5   942.05   53-13130

Corbett, Julian Stafford, Sir, 1854-1922.   III. 1015
Drake and the Tudor navy, with a history of the rise of England as a maritime power. New York, B. Franklin [1965] 2 v. illus., maps, port. 25 cm. (Burt Franklin research and source works series, #88) Reprint of the "new [i.e. 2d] edition," 1899. *1. Drake, Francis, Sir, 1540?-1596. 2. Gt. Brit. — History, Naval — Tudors, 1485-1603. I. T.*
DA86.22.D7C7 1965   942.05/5/0924 (B)   65-169/1

Corbett, Julian Stafford, Sir, 1854-1922.   III. 1016
Sir Francis Drake. New York, AMS Press [1969] vi, 209 p. port. 23 cm. Reprint of the 1890 ed. *1. Drake, Francis, Sir, 1540?-1596.*
DA86.22.D7C8 1969   942.055/0924   77-105513

Williamson, James Alexander, 1886-   III. 1017
Hawkins of Plymouth; a new history of Sir John Hawkins and of the other members of his family prominent in Tudor England, by James A. Williamson. 2d ed. New York, Barnes & Noble [1969] xi, 348 p. illus., facsims., maps, ports. 23 cm. *1. Hawkins, John, Sir, 1532-1595. I. T.*
DA86.22.H3W49 1969b   942.05/5/0924 (B)   72-7944
ISBN:389012033

Magnus, Philip Montefiore, Sir, bart., 1906-   III. 1018
Sir Walter Raleigh, by Philip Magnus. Hamden, Conn., Archon Books [1968] 158 p. maps, ports. 21 cm. (Makers of history) *1. Raleigh, Walter, Sir, 1552?-1618.*
DA86.22.R2M17 1968   942.05/5/0924 (B)   68-3593

Strathmann, Ernest Albert, 1906-   III. 1019
Sir Walter Ralegh, a study in Elizabethan skepticism. New York, Columbia University Press, 1951. ix, 292 p. 23 cm. *1. Raleigh, Walter, Sir, 1552?-1618. 2. Skepticism. I. T.*
DA86.22.R2S86   923.942 (923.242)   51-10319

942.055
R138st

Bennett, Geoffrey Martin.   III. 1020
Nelson, the commander [by] Geoffrey Bennett. New York, Scribner [1972] xii, 322 p. illus. 23 cm. *1. Nelson, Horatio Nelson, Viscount, 1758-1805. I. T.*
DA87.1.N4B37 1972b   359.3/3/0924 (B)   71-38567
ISBN:0684128861

Grenfell, Russell.   III. 1021
Horatio Nelson: a short biography; with a foreword by S. W. Roskill. [New ed.]. London, Faber, 1968. xv, 247 p. 5 plates, illus., plans, port. 21 cm. First published in 1949 under title: Nelson the sailor. *1. Nelson, Horatio Nelson, Viscount, 1758-1805.*
DA87.1.N4G7 1968   942.07/3/0924 (B)   68-96403

Mahan, Alfred Thayer, 1840-1914.   III. 1022
The life of Nelson, the embodiment of the sea power of Great Britain. 2d ed., rev. New York, Haskell House, 1969. xvi, 764 p. illus., maps, plans, ports. 23 cm. This ed. was first published in 1899. *1. Nelson, Horatio Nelson, Viscount, 1758-1805. I. T.*
DA87.1.N4M3 1969   942.07/3/0924 (B)   68-26361   ISBN:838301827

Southey, Robert, 1774-1843.   III. 1023
The life of Horatio, Lord Nelson, by Robert Southey. London & Toronto, J. M. Dent; New York, E. P. Dutton [1919] viii, 271 p. 18 cm. (Everyman's library. Biography [no. 52]) Title-page and page facing it (with quotation) within ornamental border. "First issue of this edition March 1906. Reprinted ... August 1919." *1. Nelson, Horatio Nelson, viscount, 1758-1805.*
DA87.1.N4S7 1919   923.542   34-35586

Spinney, David.   III. 1024
Rodney. London, Allen & Unwin, 1969. 3-484 p. 13 plates, illus., facsims., geneal. tables, maps, plans, ports. 25 cm. *1. Rodney, George Brydges Rodney, Baron, 1719-1792. 2. Gt. Brit. — History, Naval — 18th century.*
DA87.1.R6S6   359.3/31/0924   71-455500

Graham, Gerald Sandford, 1903-   III. 1025
The politics of naval supremacy; studies in British maritime ascendancy, by Gerald S. Graham. Cambridge [Eng.] University Press, 1965. viii, 131 p. 2 fold. maps. 23 cm. (The Wiles lectures, 1964) *1. Gt. Brit. — History, Naval. 2. Sea-power. 3. Gt. Brit. — Foreign relations — 19th cent. 4. World politics. I. T. (S)*
DA88.G7   359.030942   65-21788

Jameson, William Scarlett, Sir, 1899-   III. 1026
The fleet that Jack built: nine men who made a modern navy. [1st American ed.] New York, Harcourt, Brace & World [1962] 344 p. illus. 23 cm. *1. Gt. Brit. Navy — Biography. 2. Gt. Brit. — History, Naval. I. T.*
DA88.1.A1J3 1962a   923.542   62-15423

Cunningham, Andrew Browne Cunningham, 1st viscount, 1883-   III. 1027
A sailor's odyssey; the autobiography of Admiral of the Fleet, Viscount Cunningham of Hyndhope. [1st ed.] New York, Dutton, 1951. 715 p. illus. 24 cm. *1. World War, 1939-1945 — Naval operations, British. 2. World War, 1939-1945 — Mediterranean Sea. I. T.*
DA89.1.C8A3 1951a   923.542   51-14146

Hough, Richard Alexander, 1922-   III. 1028
Admiral of the fleet; the life of John Fisher [by] Richard Hough. [1st American ed. New York] Macmillan [1970, c1969] 392 p. illus., facsim., ports. 25 cm. "First published in Great Britain in 1969 by George Allen and Unwin Ltd. under the title: First sea lord." *1. Fisher, John Arbuthnot Fisher, Baron, 1841-1920. I. T.*
DA89.1.F5H6 1970   359.3/3/10924 (B)   72-77970

DA110–125 Civilization. Intellectual Life. Ethnography

Barker, Ernest, Sir, 1874- ed.   III. 1029
The character of England. Oxford, Clarendon Press, 1947. xii, 595 p. illus., ports., facsims. 25 cm. Collection of articles describing "what is characteristically English in each field, and ... the characteristic English contribution in that field." *1. Great Britain. 2. Gt. Brit. — Civilization. 3. National characteristics, English. I. T.*
DA110.B36   914.2   A48-17

Chambers, Robert, 1802-1871.   III. 1030
The book of days; a miscellany of popular antiquities in connection with the calendar, including anecdote, biography and history, curiosities of literature, and oddities of human life and character. Detroit, Gale Research Co., 1967. 2 v. illus. 27 cm. Reprint of a work first published 1862-64; title page includes original imprint: London, W. & R. Chambers; Philadelphia, Lippincott. *1. Days. 2. Holidays. 3. Fasts and feasts. 4. Gt. Brit. — Antiquities. 5. Anecdotes — Gt. Brit. I. T.*
DA110.C52 1967   67-13009

Hoggart, Richard, 1918-   III. 1032
The uses of literacy; changing patterns in English mass culture. Fair Lawn, N.J., Essential Books, 1957. 319 p. 23 cm. *1. Labor and laboring classes — Gt. Brit. 2. Gt. Brit. — Intellectual life. 3. Recreation — Gt. Brit. I. T.*
DA115.H6 1957a   914.2   58-96

Patterson, Sheila, 1918-   III. 1033
Immigration and race relations in Britain, 1960-1967. London, New York, Published for the Institute of Race Relations [by] Oxford U.P., 1969. xviii, 460 p. 23 cm. *1. Great Britain — Race question. 2. Great Britain — Emigration and immigration. I. Institute of Race Relations. II. T.*
DA125.A1P33   301.45/0942   75-427762   ISBN:0192181742

Rose, Eliot Joseph Benn, 1909-   III. 1034
Colour and citizenship: a report on British race relations [by] E. J. B. Rose in association with Nicholas Deakin [and others] London, New York [etc.] Published for the Institute of Race Relations by Oxford U.P., 1969. xxiii, 815 p. illus., maps. 23 cm. *1. Minorities — England. 2. England — Race question. 3. Great Britain — Emigration and immigration. I. Institute of Race Relations. II. T.*
DA125.A1R6 1969   301.451/96/042   75-418974

DA130 – 592 English History, by Period
DA130 – 260 EARLY. MEDIEVAL, TO 1485

Brooke, Christopher Nugent Lawrence.   III. 1035
From Alfred to Henry III, 871-1272. Edinburgh, T. Nelson [1961] xii, 276 p. illus., maps, geneal. tables. 23 cm. (A History of England, v.2) *1. Gt. Brit. — History — Anglo-Saxon period, 449-1066. 2. Gt. Brit. — History — Medieval period, 1066-1485. (S:A History of England (Edinburgh, T. Nelson) v.2)*
DA130.B87   942.01   61-66045

Essays in medieval history presented to Thomas Frederick Tout.   III. 1036
Edited by A. G. Little and F. M. Powicke. Freeport, N.Y., Books for Libraries Press [1967] x, 432 p. 24 cm. (Essay index reprint series) Reprint of the 1925 ed. *1. Gt. Brit. — History — To 1485 — Addresses, essays, lectures. I. Little, Andrew George, 1863-1945, ed. II. Powicke, Frederick Maurice, Sir, 1879-1963, ed. III. Tout, Thomas Frederick, 1855-1929.*
DA130.E8 1967   942   67-23213

Poole, Austin Lane, 1889-1963, ed.   III. 1037
Medieval England. A new ed. rewritten and rev. Oxford, Clarendon Press, 1958. 2 v. (xxviii, 661 p.) illus., plates, maps, coats of arms. 24 cm. *1. Great Britain — Civilization — Medieval period, 1066-1485. I. T.*
DA130.P65 1958   942   58-4429

Sayles, George Osborne, 1901-   III. 1038
The medieval foundations of England. [2d ed., rev. and with new introductory chapter] London, Methuen [1950] xxv, 482 p. 23 cm. *1. Gt. Brit. — History — To 1485. I. T.*
DA130.S39 1950a   942.01   50-58227

DA135 – 162 To 1066

Blair, Peter Hunter.   III. 1039
Roman Britain and early England, 55 B.C.-A.D. 871. Edinburgh, T. Nelson [1963] xii, 292 p. plates, maps, plans. 23 cm. (A History of England, v.1) *1. Gt. Brit. — History — To 1066. I. T. (S:A History of England (Edinburgh) v.1)*
DA135.B59   942.01   63-24835

Hodgkin, Thomas, 1831-1913.   III. 1040
The history of England, from the earliest times to the Norman Conquest. New York, Greenwood Press [1969] xxi, 528 p. maps. 23 cm. (The Political history of England, 1) Reprint of the 1914 impression of the work first published in 1906. *1. Great Britain — History — To 1066. I. T. (S)*
DA135.H6x (DA30.P762 vol. 1)   942.01   69-13933

Geoffrey of Monmouth, Bp. of St. Asaph, 1100?-1154.   III. 1041
History of the Kings of Britain. Translated by Sebastian Evans. Rev. by Charles W. Dunn. Introd. by Gwyn Jones. London, Dent [1963, c1958] xxii, 281 p. 19 cm. (Everyman's library no. 577) *1. Arthur, King. 2. Merlin. 3. Gt. Brit. — History — To 449. 4. Legends, Celtic. I. Evans, Sebastian, 1830-1909, tr. II. T.*
DA140.G353   65-1872

Tatlock, John Strong Perry, 1876-1948.   III. 1042
The legendary history of Britain: Geoffrey of Monmouth's Historia Regum Britanniae and its early vernacular versions. Berkeley, University of California Press, 1950. xi, 545 p. 25 cm. *1. Geoffrey of Monmouth, Bp. of St. Asaph, 1100?-1154. Historia Britonum. I. T.*
DA140.G37T3 1950   942.01   50-7428

Hawkins, Gerald S.   III. 1043
Stonehenge decoded [by] Gerald S. Hawkins in collaboration with John B. White. [1st ed.] Garden City, N.Y., Doubleday, 1965. viii, 202 p. illus., maps, plates. 24 cm. *1. Stonehenge. 2. Astronomy, Ancient. I. T.*
DA142.H3   913.36   65-19933

DA145 – 147 ROMANS

Collingwood, Robin George, 1889-1943.   III. 1044
The archaeology of Roman Britain [by] R. G. Collingwood and Ian Richmond; with a chapter by B. R. Hartley on Samian ware. [New] ed., entirely revised. London, Methuen, 1969. xxv, 350 p. 27 plates, illus., plans. 25 cm. (Methuen's handbooks of archaeology) Distributed in the U.S.A. by Barnes & Noble, New York. *1. Great Britain — Antiquities, Roman. I. Richmond, Ian Archibald, Sir, 1902-1965. II. T.*
DA145.C57 1969   913.3/6   79-407851   ISBN:041627580X

Collingwood, Robin George, 1889-1943.   III. 1045
Roman Britain and the English settlements, by R. G. Collingwood and J. N. L. Myres. 2d ed. Oxford, Clarendon Press, 1937. xxv, 515 p. maps (part fold.) 23 cm. (The Oxford history of England.) *1. Gt. Brit. — History — Roman period, 55 B.C.-449 A.D. 2. Gt. Brit. — History — Anglo-Saxon period, 449-1066. I. Myres, John Nowell Linton. II. T.*
DA145.C583 1937   942.01   38-2347

Ward, John, 1856-1922.   III. 1046
The Roman era in Britain. Port Washington, N.Y., Kennikat Press [1971] xi, 289 p. illus., maps, plans. 22 cm. Reprint of the 1911 ed. *1. Great Britain — Antiquities, Roman. I. T.*
DA145.W2 1971   913.36/03   79-118507   ISBN:0804612552

DA150 – 155 SAXONS

Anglo-Saxon chronicle.   III. 1047
The Anglo-Saxon chronicle. Translated with an introd. by G. N. Garmonsway. London, Dent; New York, Dutton [1953] xlviii, 295 p. facsim. 19 cm. (Everyman's library, 624. History) *1. Gt. Brit. — History — Anglo-Saxon period, 449-1066 — Sources. I. Garmonsway, George Norman, ed. and tr.*
DA150.A58 1953   942.01   53-13456

Anglo-Saxon chronicle.   III. 1048
The Anglo-Saxon chronicle. A revised translation edited by Dorothy Whitelock, with David C. Douglas and Susie I. Tucker. Introd. by Dorothy Whitelock. New Brunswick, N.J., Rutgers University Press [1962, c1961] xxxii, 240 p. geneal. tables. 26 cm. *1. Gt. Brit. — History — Anglo-Saxon period, 449-1066 — Sources. I. Whitelock, Dorothy, ed.*
DA150.A6 1962   942.01   61-17284

Ethelwerd, d. 998.   III. 1049
The chronicle of Æthelweard. Edited by A. Campbell. London, New York, Nelson [1962] lxiii, 56, 56, 57-68 p. 23 cm. (Medieval texts) Added t.p.: Chronicon Æthelweardi. Latin and English on opposite pages numbered in duplicate. *1. Gt. Brit. — History — Anglo-Saxon period, 449-1066. I. Campbell, Alistair, 1907- ed. II. T. III. T:Chronicon Æthelweardi. (S:Medieval classics (London))*
DA150.E8 1962   942.01   64-5203

Blair, Peter Hunter.   III. 1050
An introduction to Anglo-Saxon England. Cambridge [Eng.] University Press, 1956. 381 p. illus. 23 cm. *1. Gt. Brit. — History — Anglo-Saxon period, 449-1066. I. T:Anglo-Saxon England.*
DA152.B55   942.01   56-13556

Hodgkin, Robert Howard, 1877-   III. 1051
A history of the Anglo-Saxons. 3d ed. London, Oxford University Press, 1952. 2 v. (xxxi, 796 p.) illus., maps (part fold. col.) facsims., geneal. tables, plans. 25 cm. *1. Anglo-Saxons. 2. Gt. Brit. — History — Anglo-Saxon period, 449-1066.*
DA152.H62   942.01   53-34534

Hollister, Charles Warren.   III. 1052
Anglo-Saxon military institutions on the eve of the Norman Conquest. Oxford, Clarendon Press, 1962. 170 p. 23 cm. *1. Anglo-Saxons. 2. Gt. Brit. — History, Military. I. T.*
DA152.H66   942.01   63-158

Stenton, Frank Merry, Sir, 1880-1967.   III. 1053
Anglo-Saxon England, by F. M. Stenton. 3d ed. Oxford [Eng.] Clarendon Press, 1971. xli, 765 p. maps (1 fold.) 22 cm. (The Oxford history of England

2) *1. Gt Brit. — History — Anglo-Saxon period, 449-1066. 2. Anglo-Saxons. I. T. (S)*
DA152.S74 1971   942.01   71-22751   ISBN:0198217161

Thomas, Charles, 1928-   **III. 1054**
Britain and Ireland in early Christian times, AD 400-800. New York, McGraw-Hill [1971] 144 p. illus. (part col.), maps. 22 cm. (Library of medieval civilization) *1. Great Britain — Civilization — To 1066. 2. Great Britain — Antiquities. I. T.*
DA152.2.T48 1971b   942.01   75-138860   ISBN:0070642389

Asser, Bp. of Sherborne, d. 909?   **III. 1055**
Life of King Alfred. Translated with introd. and notes by L. C. Jane. New York, Cooper Square Publishers, 1966. lix, 163 p. illus., facsim., geneal. table. 17 cm. (The Medieval library) Translation of De rebus gestis Aelfredi as published in 1848 in Monumenta historica Britannica. *1. Alfred the Great, King of England, 849-901. I. Jane, Lionel Cecil, 1879-1932, ed. and tr. II. T.*
DA153.A88 1966   942.01/0924   66-27658

Duckett, Eleanor Shipley.   **III. 1056**
Alfred the Great. [Chicago] University of Chicago Press [1956] 220 p. 22 cm. *1. Alfred the Great, King of England, 849-901.*
DA153.D85   923.142   56-13050

The life of King Edward, who rests at Westminster.   **III. 1057**
Attributed to a monk of St. Bertin. Edited and translated with introd. and notes by Frank Barlow. London, Nelson [1962] lxxxii, 81, 81, 85-145 p. illus., geneal. table. 23 cm. (Medieval texts) English and Latin on opposite pages numbered in duplicate. *1. Edward, the Confessor, King of England, Saint, d. 1066. I. A monk of St. Bertin. II. Barlow, Frank, ed. and tr. (S:Medieval classics (London))*
DA154.8.V5   923.142   62-6101

DA170 – 260 Medieval (1066 – 1485)

Barlow, Frank.   **III. 1058**
The feudal kingdom of England, 1042-1216. London, New York, Longmans, Green [1955] xi, 465 p. maps (part fold.) fold. geneal. tables. 23 cm. (A History of England) *1. Gt. Brit. — History — Medieval period, 1066-1485. 2. Gt. Brit. — History — Edward, the Confessor, 1042-1066. I. T. (S)*
DA175.B26   942.02   55-1881

Holmes, George Andrew.   **III. 1059**
The later Middle Ages, 1272-1485. Edinburgh, T. Nelson [1962] 276 p. illus. 23 cm. (A History of England, v.3) *1. Gt. Brit. — History — Medieval period, 1066-1485. I. T.*
DA175.H58 1962   942.035   62-53078

Oman, Charles William Chadwick, Sir, 1860-1946.   **III. 1060**
The history of England from the accession of Richard II to the death of Richard III, 1377-1485. New York, Greenwood Press [1969] xvi, 525 p. geneal. tables, maps. 23 cm. (The Political history of England, v. 4) Reprint of the 1906 ed. *1. Great Britain — History — Richard II, 1377-1399. 2. Great Britain — History — Lancaster and York, 1399-1485. I. T. (S)*
DA175.O4x (DA30.P76 vol. 4 1969)   942./038   69-14021

Poole, Austin Lane, 1889-1963.   **III. 1061**
From Domesday book to Magna Carta, 1087-1216. 2d ed. Oxford, Clarendon Press, 1955. xv, 541 p. maps. 23 cm. (The Oxford history of England [v. 3]) *1. Great Britain — History — Medieval period, 1066-1485. I. T. (S)*
DA175.P6 1955   942.02   56-13761

Studies in medieval history presented to Frederick Maurice Powicke,   **III. 1062**
ed. by R. W. Hunt, W. A. Pantin [and] R. W. Southern. Oxford, Clarendon Press, 1948. xii, 504 p. port., maps, facisms. 25 cm. *1. Powicke, Frederick Maurice, 1879- 2. Gt. Brit. — History — Medieval period, 1066-1485. 3. Middle Ages — History. I. Hunt, Richard William, 1908- ed.*
DA175.S935   942.02   49-3377

Vickers, Kenneth Hotham, 1881-   **III. 1063**
England in the later Middle Ages. [7th ed.] London, Methuen [1950] xiii, 542 p. fold. col. maps. 23 cm. (A history of England. General editor: Sir Charles Oman. v.3) *1. Gt. Brit. — History — Medieval period, 1066-1485. I. T. (S:Oman, Charles William Chadwick, Sir, 1860- ed. A history of England, v.3)*
DA175.V5 1950   942   51-24835

Barrow, G. W. S.   **III. 1064**
Feudal Britain; the completion of the medieval kingdoms, 1066-1314. London, E. Arnold [1956] 452 p. illus. 23 cm. *1. Feudalism — Gt. Brit. 2. Gt. Brit. — Politics and government — 1066-1485. I. T.*
DA176.B3 1956   942.02   57-112

Beresford, Maurice Warwick, 1920-   **III. 1065**
Deserted medieval villages: studies. Edited by Maurice Beresford and John G. Hurst. New York, St. Martin's Press [1972, c1971] xviii, 340 p. illus. 26 cm. *1. Cities and towns, Ruined, extinct, etc. — Great Britain. 2. Excavations (Archaeology) — Great Britain. I. Hurst, John G., 1927- joint author. II. T.*
DA176.B44 1972   914.2/03   75-190102

Cam, Helen Maud, 1885-   **III. 1066**
Liberties & communities in medieval England; collected studies in local administration and topography, by Helen M. Cam. New York, Barnes & Noble [1963] xiv, 267 p. geneal. tables, maps (1 fold.) 23 cm. *1. Gt. Brit. — History, Local. 2. Local government — Gt. Brit. I. T.*
DA176.C3 1963   942   64-3937

Coulton, George Gordon, 1858-1947.   **III. 1067**
Medieval panorama; the English scene from conquest to Reformation. New York [Noonday Press] 1955. 801 p. illus. 21 cm. (Meridian books, MG2) *1. Gt. Brit. — History — Medieval period, 1066-1485. 2. Gt. Brit. — Civilization — History. 3. Civilization, Medieval. 4. Catholic Church in England. I. T.*
DA185.C865x   942   55-7582

Historical Association, London.   **III. 1068**
Social life in early England; Historical Association essays. Edited by Geoffrey Barraclough. New York, Barnes & Noble [1960] xi, 264 p. illus., maps (1 fold.) plans (part fold.) 23 cm. *1. Gt. Brit. — Social life and customs. 2. Arms and armor. 3. Trade routes. I. Barraclough, Geoffrey, 1908- ed. II. T.*
DA185.H58   914.2   59-15211

Homans, George Caspar, 1910-   **III. 1069**
English villagers of the thirteenth century. New York, Russell & Russell, 1960 [c1941] 478 p. illus. 23 cm. *1. Village communities — Gt. Brit. 2. England — Social life and customs. 3. Agriculture — England. 4. Peasantry — England. I. T.*
DA185.H685 1960   942.033   60-8200

Jusserand, Jean Adrien Antoine Jules, 1855-1932.   **III. 1070**
English wayfaring life in the Middle Ages. Translated from the French by Lucy Toulmin Smith. [4th ed.] New York, Putnam [1950] 315 p. illus. 23 cm. Translation of Les Anglais au Moyen Âge. *1. England — Social life and customs. 2. Wayfaring life — Gt. Brit. 3. Travel, Medieval. 4. Pilgrims and pilgrimages — England. I. T.*
DA185.J8x   914.2   A51-4881

Powicke, Frederick Maurice, Sir, 1879-1963.   **III. 1071**
Medieval England, 1066-1485 [by] Maurice Powicke. [New. ed.]. London, New York [etc.] Oxford U.P., 1969. [3], 136 p. 21 cm. (Oxford paperbacks, no. 169) *1. Great Britain — History — Medieval period, 1066-1485. 2. Great Britain — Social conditions. I. T.*
DA185.P6 1969   914.2/03   74-423176   ISBN:019285027X

Stenton, Frank Merry, Sir, 1880-   **III. 1072**
The first century of English feudalism, 1066-1166. 2d ed. Oxford, Clarendon Press, 1961. 312 p. 22 cm. (The Ford lectures, 1929) *1. Feudalism — Gt. Brit. I. T.*
DA185.S8 1961   942.02   61-19123

DA190 – 199 NORMANS

Finn, Rex Welldon.   **III. 1073**
An introduction to Domesday book. New York, Barnes & Noble [1963] 306 p. 23 cm. *1. Domesday book. 2. Gt. Brit. — Social conditions.*
DA190.D7F5   942.021   63-1541

Galbraith, Vivian Hunter, 1889-   **III. 1074**
The making of Domesday book. Oxford, Clarendon Press, 1961. 242 p. illus. 22 cm. *1. Domesday book. I. T.*
DA190.D7G3   942.021   61-66609

Round, John Horace, 1854-1928.   **III. 1075**
Feudal England; historical studies on the eleventh and twelfth centuries, by J. H. Round. Foreword by F. M. Stenton. New York, Barnes & Noble [1964] 444 p. geneal. tables (part fold.) 23 cm. "First published 1895 ... Reset with new foreword 1964." *1. Domesday book. 2. Gt. Brit. — History — Norman period, 1066-1154. I. T.*
DA195.R86 1964a   942.02   65-1163

Gesta Stephani, Regis Anglorum.   **III. 1076**
The deeds of Stephen. Translated from the Latin with introd. and notes by K. R. Potter. London, New York, Nelson [1955] xxxii, 159, 159, 161-163 p. map. 23 cm. (Medieval texts) Latin and English on opposite pages numbered in duplicate; added t.p.: Gesta Stephani. *1. Stephen, King of England, 1097?-1154. I. Potter, Kenneth Reginald, ed. and tr. II. Gesta Stephani, Regis Anglorum. English. (S:Medieval classics (London))*
DA198.5.G42   942.024   A55-7651

William of Malmesbury, d. 1143?   **III. 1077**
The Historia novella. Translated from the Latin with introd. and notes by K. R. Potter. London, New York, Nelson [1955] xliii, 77, 77, [78]-84 p. map. 23

cm. (Medieval texts) Latin and English on opposite pages numbered in duplicate. *1. Gt. Brit. — History — Stephen, 1135-1154. I. T.*
DA198.5.W52   942.024   55-3699

Kealey, Edward J. **III. 1078**
Roger of Salisbury, viceroy of England, by Edward J. Kealey. Berkeley, University of California Press, 1972. xvi, 312 p. 25 cm. *1. Roger of Salisbury, Bp. of Salisbury, 1065?-1139. 2. Great Britain — Politics and government — 1066-1154. I. T.*
DA199.R6K4   942.02/092/4   (B)   78-92681   ISBN:0520019857

DA200 – 209 ANGEVINS (1154 – 1216)

Norgate, Kate. **III. 1079**
England under the Angevin kings. New York, Haskell House, 1969. 2 v. maps, plans. 24 cm. Reprint of the 1887 ed. *1. Great Britain — History — Angevin period, 1154-1216. I. T.*
DA205.N838 1969b   942/.03   68-25255   ISBN:0838301843

Holt, James Clarke. **III. 1080**
The northerners, a study in the reign of King John. Oxford, Clarendon Press, 1961. 272 p. illus. 23 cm. *1. Gt. Brit. — History — John, 1199-1216. I. T.*
DA208.H6   942.033   61-65767

Norgate, Kate. **III. 1081**
John Lackland. New York, AMS Press [1970] vi, 303 p. maps. 23 cm. Reprint of the 1902 ed. *1. John, King of England, 1167?-1216.*
DA208.N8 1970   942.03/3/0924   (B)   71-110740   ISBN:404006140

Painter, Sidney, 1902-1960. **III. 1082**
The reign of King John. Baltimore, John Hopkins Press, 1949. viii, 397 p. 24 cm. *1. John, King of England, 1167?-1216. 2. Great Britain — History — John, 1199-1216. I. T.*
DA208.P3   942.033   49-49221

Kelly, Amy Ruth, 1878- **III. 1083**
Eleanor of Aquitaine and the four kings. Cambridge, Harvard University Press, 1950. xii, 431 p. illus., map (on lining papers) 24 cm. *1. Eleanor, of Aquitaine, consort of Henry II, 1122?-1204. 2. Gt. Brit. — History — Plantagenets, 1154-1399.*
DA209.E6K45 1950   923.142   50-6545

Painter, Sidney, 1902- **III. 1084**
William Marshal, knight-errant, baron, and regent of England, by Sidney Painter. Baltimore, The Johns Hopkins Press, 1933. xi, 305 p. 24 cm. (The Johns Hopkins historical publications) "This biography was originally written as a dissertation for the degree of doctor of philosophy in Yale University [1930]" — Pref. *1. Pembroke, William Marshal, earl of, 1144?-1219. 2. Gt. Brit. — History — Angevin period, 1154-1216.*
DA209.P4P3   923.242   33-8958

DA220 – 237 PLANTAGENETS (1216 – 1399)

Green, Vivian Hubert Howard. **III. 1085**
The later Plantagenets; a survey of English history between 1307 and 1485. London, E. Arnold [1955] 438 p. maps, diagr., geneal. tables. 23 cm. *1. Gt. Brit. — History — 14th cent. 2. Gt. Brit. — History — Lancaster and York, 1399-1485. I. T.*
DA225.G7   942.03   55-4313

Powicke, Frederick Maurice, Sir, 1879-1963. **III. 1086**
The thirteenth century, 1216-1307. 2d ed Oxford, Clarendon Press, 1962. xiv, 829 p. 4 maps, geneal. tables (1 fold.) 23 cm. (The Oxford history of England, 4) *1. Great Britain — History — 13th century. I. T. (S)*
DA225.P65 1962   942.034   62-6745

Tout, Thomas Frederick, 1885-1929. **III. 1087**
The history of England from the accession of Henry III to the death of Edward III, 1216-1377. New York, Greenwood Press [1969] xxiv, 496 p. maps. 23 cm. (The Political history of England, v. 3) Reprint of the 1905 ed. *1. Great Britain — History — Henry III, 1216-1272. 2. Great Britain — History — Edward I-III, 1272-1377. I. T. (S)*
DA225.T65x (DA30.P762 vol. 3)   942.03   69-14120

Powicke, Frederick Maurice Sir, 1879- **III. 1088**
King Henry III and the Lord Edward; the community of the realm in the thirteenth century, by F. M. Powicke. Oxford, Clarendon Press, 1947. 2 v. maps (part fold.) 25 cm. *1. Henry III, king of England, 1207-1272. 2. Edward I, king of England, 1239-1307. 3. Gt. Brit. — History — Henry III, 1216-1272.*
DA227.P6   942.034   47-4620

Treharne, Reginald Francis, 1901- **III. 1089**
The baronial plan of reform, 1258-1263, by R. F. Treharne. Including the Raleigh lecture on history delivered to the British Academy, 1954. [Reprinted with additional material] [Manchester, Eng.] Manchester University Press; New York, Barnes & Noble [1971- v. 22 cm. (Publications of the University of Manchester, no. 221. Historical series, no. 62. The Ward bequest, v. 6) *1. Barons' War, 1263-1267. 2. Great Britain — Politics and government — 1216-1272. 3. Montfort, Simon of, earl of Leicester, 1208?-1265. I. T. (S:Victoria University of Manchester. Publications, no. 221) (S:Victoria University of Manchester. Publications. Historical series, no. 62) (S:Victoria University of Manchester. [Publications] The Ward bequest, v. 6)*
DA227.5.T72   942.03/4   72-182919
ISBN:0389041165 (Barnes & Noble) (v. 1)

Labarge, Margaret Wade. **III. 1090**
Simon de Montfort. [1st American ed.] New York, Norton [1963, c1962] 312 p. illus. 23 cm. *1. Montfort, Simon of, earl of Leicester, 1208?-1265.*
DA228.M7L3x   923.242   63-6618

The life of Edward the Second, **III. 1091**
by the so-called Monk of Malmesbury. Translated from the Latin with introd. and notes by N. Denholm-Young. London, New York, Nelson [1957] xxviii, 145, 145, [146]-150 p. 23 cm. (Medieval texts) Added t.-p.: Vita Edwardi Secundi. Latin and English on opposite pages, numbered in duplicate. "Thomas Hearne's original transcript ... survives in the Bodleian Library, Oxford ... and is the source of this new edition." *1. Edward II, King of England, 1284-1327. I. Monk of Malmesbury. II. Denholm-Young, Noël, ed. and tr. (S:Medieval classics (London))*
DA230.L5   923.142   57-4170

McKisack, May. **III. 1092**
The fourteenth century, 1307-1399. Oxford, Clarendon Press, 1959. xix, 598 p. maps, geneal. tables. 23 cm. (The Oxford history of England, 5) *1. Gt. Brit. — History — 14th cent. I. T. (S)*
DA230.M25   942.037   59-16710

Tout, Thomas Frederick, 1855-1929. **III. 1093**
The place of the reign of Edward II in English history, based upon the Ford lectures delivered in the University of Oxford in 1913, by T. F. Tout. 2d ed., revised throughout by Hilda Johnstone. Manchester, The University Press, 1936. xx, 375 p. 23 cm. (Publications of the University of Manchester ... Historical series, no. XXI) Publications of the University of Manchester, no. CCLII. "Addendum et corrigendum" slip inserted. *1. Edward II, king of England, 1284-1327. 2. Gt. Brit. — History — Edward II, 1307-1327. I. Johnstone, Hilda, 1882- ed.*
DA230.T6 1936   942.036   37-34889

Oman, Charles William Chadwick, Sir, 1860-1946. **III. 1094**
The great revolt of 1381. New York, Haskell House Publishers, 1968. viii, 219 p. maps. 24 cm. Reprint of the 1906 ed. *1. Tyler's Insurrection, 1381. I. T.*
DA235.O58 1968   942.03/8   68-25257

Steel, Anthony Bedford, 1900- **III. 1095**
Richard II, by Anthony Steel. With a foreword by G. M. Trevelyan. Cambridge [Eng.] University Press, 1941. x, 320 p. facsim. 22 cm. *1. Richard II, king of England, 1367-1400. 2. Gt. Brit. — History — Richard II, 1377-1399.*
DA235.S8   A42-750

Trevelyan, George Macaulay, 1876- **III. 1096**
England in the age of Wycliffe; by George Macaulay Trevelyan. New ed. London, New York and Bombay, Longmans, Green, 1904. xiv, 380 p. 3 fold. maps. 23 cm. "Originally composed as a dissertation sent in to compete for a fellowship at Trinity college, Cambridge." — Pref. Supplemented by "The peasants' uprising and the Lollards; a collection of unpublished documents forming an appendix to 'England in the age of Wycliffe,' edited by Edgar Powell and G. M. Trevelyan. London, 1899." *1. Wycliffe, John, d 1384. 2. Gt. Brit. — History — Richard II, 1377-1399. 3. Tyler's insurrection, 1381. 4. Gt. Brit. — Church history — Medieval period.*
DA235.T83   942.02   05-41997

DA240 – 260 LANCASTER. YORK (1399 – 1485)

Bennett, Henry Stanley, 1889- **III. 1097**
The Pastons and their England: studies in an age of transition, by H. S. Bennett. 2nd ed. reprinted. London, Cambridge U.P., 1968. xvi, 271 p. 21 cm. *1. Paston letters. 2. England — Social life and customs — Medieval period, 1066-1485. I. T.*
DA240.B4 1968   914.2/03/4   68-23175   ISBN:0521095131

Holinshed, Raphael, d. 1580? comp. **III. 1098**
Holinshed's Chronicles: Richard II, 1398-1400, and Henry V, edited by R. S. Wallace and Alma Hansen. Oxford, Clarendon Press, 1917. 79, 136 p. 19 cm. *1. Gt. Brit. — History — Richard II, 1377-1399. 2. Gt. Brit. — History — Henry V, 1413-1422. I. Wallace, Robert Strachan, 1882- ed. II. Hansen, Alma, ed.*
DA240.H6 1917   A18-675

Paston letters. **III. 1099**
Paston letters and papers of the fifteenth century; [in 3 parts], edited by Norman Davis. Oxford, Clarendon Press, 1971-   v. 15 plates. facsims.,

map. 24 cm. *1. England — Social life and customs — Medieval period, 1066-1485. I. Davis, Norman, 1913- ed.*
DA240.P294   914.2/03/408   71-27731   ISBN:0-19-812415-5 (v.1)

Paston letters. **III. 1100**
The Paston letters ... London, Dent; New York, Dutton [1935?] 2 v. double geneal. tab. 18 cm. Everyman's library. History. [no. 752-753] "Edited by John Fenn and re-edited by Mrs. Archer-Hind." "First published in this edition 1924." "List of editions of the Paston letters": v.1, p. ix. *1. Gt. Brit. — Social life and customs. I. Fenn, John, Sir, 1739-1794, ed. II. Archer-Hind, Laura, ed.*
DA240.P3x   (AC1.E8 no. 752-753)   942.04   37-30971

Paston letters. **III. 1101**
Paston letters: selected and edited with an introduction, notes and glossary by Norman Davis; critical comment by Horace Walpole, Virginia Woolf and others. Oxford, Clarendon Press, 1971. xxx, 165 p., plates. facsim., map. 19 cm. (Clarendon medieval and Tudor series) Index. *1. England — Social life and customs — Medieval period, 1066-1485. I. Davis, Norman, 1913- ed.*
DA240.P32 1971   914.2/03/408   72-181315   ISBN:0-19-871024-0

Jacob, Ernest Fraser, 1894- **III. 1102**
The fifteenth century, 1399-1485. Oxford, Clarendon Press, 1961. xvi, 775 p. maps (part fold.) 23 cm. (The Oxford history of England, v. 6) Errata slip inserted. *1. Great Britain — History — Lancaster and York, 1399-1485. (S)*
DA245.J3   942.04   61-66708

Kingsford, Charles Lethbridge, 1862-1926. **III. 1103**
Prejudice and promise in fifteenth century England. [London] F. Cass, 1962. vi, 215 p. maps (part fold. col.) 23 cm. Imprint covered by label: Barnes & Noble, New York [1963] *1. England — Social life and customs. 2. Gt. Brit. — History — Lancaster and York, 1399-1485. I. T.*
DA245.K5 1962   914.2   63-585

Jacob, Ernest Fraser, 1894- **III. 1104**
Henry V and the invasion of France. London, Published by Hodder & Stoughton for the English Universities Press [1947] xiii, 207 p. port., maps (on lining-papers) 18 cm. (Teach yourself history library) *1. Henry V, King of England, 1387-1422. 2. Gt. Brit. — History — Henry V, 1413-1422. 3. France — History — Charles VI, 1380-1422. (S)*
DA256.J3   942.042   A48-916

Scofield, Cora Louise. **III. 1105**
The life and reign of Edward the Fourth, King of England and of France and Lord of Ireland [by] Cora L. Scofield. New York, Octagon Books, 1967. 2 v. 22 cm. Reprint of the 1923 ed. *1. Edward IV, King of England, 1442-1483. 2. Gt. Brit. — History — Edward IV, 1461-1483. I. T.*
DA258.S4 1967   942.04/0924 (B)   67-14886

Gairdner, James, 1828-1912, ed. **III. 1106**
Letters and papers illustrative of the reigns of Richard III. and Henry VII. Edited by James Gairdner. London, Longman, Green, Longman, and Roberts, 1861-63. 2 v. front. (fold. facsim.) 25 cm. ([Gt. Brit. Public record office] Rerum britannicarum medii ævi scriptores. [No. 24]) *1. Gt. Brit. — History — Lancaster and York, 1399-1485. 2. Gt. Brit. — History — Tudors, 1485-1603.*
DA260.G3x   (DA25.B5 no. 24)   01-721

Kendall, Paul Murray. **III. 1107**
Richard the Third. [1st American ed.] New York, W. W. Norton [1956] 602 p. illus. 22 cm. *1. Richard III, King of England, 1452-1485.*
DA260.K4 1956   923.142   56-10090

DA300 – 592   MODERN (1485 –

Routh, Charles Richard Nairne, comp. **III. 1108**
They saw it happen; an anthology of eye-witnesses' accounts of events in British history, 1485-1688. With a foreword by R. Birley. Oxford, Blackwell, 1956. 220 p. 23 cm. *1. Gt. Brit. — History — 1500-1800 — Sources. I. T.*
DA300.R6   942.05   57-763

DA310 – 360   Tudors (1485 – 1603)

Elton, Geoffrey Rudolph. **III. 1109**
England under the Tudors. New York, Putnam [1955 or 6] xi, 504 p. maps, geneal. table. 22 cm. (A history of England, 4) *1. Gt. Brit. — History — Tudors, 1485-1603. I. T. (S:Oman, Charles William Chadwick, Sir, 1860-1946, ed. A history of England, v.4)*
DA315.E6x   942.05   56-13898

Froude, James Anthony, 1818-1894. **III. 1110**
History of England, from the fall of Wolsey to the death of Elizabeth. New York, AMS Press [1969] 12 v. port. 23 cm. "Reprinted from the edition of 1862-1870." Vols. 11-12 have title: History of England from the fall of Wolsey to the defeat of the Spanish Armada. *1. Great Britain — History — Tudors, 1485-1603. I. T.*
DA315.F78   942.05   71-91303

Read, Conyers, 1881- **III. 1111**
The Tudors; personalities and practical politics in sixteenth century England, by Conyers Read. New York, Holt [c1936] xi, 264 p. ports. 23 cm. *1. Gt. Brit. — History — Tudors, 1485-1603. I. T.*
DA315.R4   942.05   36-10687

Wernham, Richard Bruce, 1906- **III. 1112**
Before the Armada: the emergence of the English Nation, 1485-1588 [by] R. B. Wernham. [1st American ed.] New York, Harcourt, Brace & World [1966] 447 p. maps. 22 cm. *1. Great Britain — Foreign relations — 16th century. I. T.*
DA315.W4 1966a   327.42   66-23809

Pollard, Albert Frederick, 1869-1948. **III. 1113**
Thomas Cranmer and the English reformation, 1489-1556. [Unaltered and unabridged ed.] Hamden, Conn., Archon Books, 1965 [c1905] xv, 399 p. illus., ports. 19 cm. *1. Cranmer, Thomas, Abp. of Canterbury, 1489-1556. I. T.*
DA317.8.C8P8 1965   282.0924   65-24503

Ridley, Jasper. **III. 1114**
Thomas Cranmer. Oxford, Clarendon Press, 1962. 450 p. illus. 23 cm. *1. Cranmer, Thomas, Abp. of Canterbury, 1489-1556.*
DA317.8.C8R5   922.342   62-2124

Williams, Neville, 1924- **III. 1115**
Thomas Howard, fourth duke of Norfolk. New York, Dutton [1965, c1964] xiii, 289 p. facsims., ports. 23 cm. *1. Norfolk, Thomas Howard, 4th duke of, 1538-1572. I. T.*
DA317.8.N6W5 1965   923.242   64-66165

Einstein, Lewis 1877- **III. 1116**
The Italian Renaissance in England; studies. New York, B. Franklin [1962] xvii, 420 p. plates, ports., facsim. 21 cm. (Burt Franklin research and source works series, no. 26) *1. Italians in England. 2. Renaissance — England. 3. Gt. Brit. — Civilization — Italian influences. I. T.*
DA320.E3 1962   914.2   63-6418

Laslett, Peter. **III. 1117**
The world we have lost. New York, Scribner [1966, c1965] xvi, 280 p. 24 cm. "Notes to the text": p. [241]-272. *1. Great Britain — Social conditions. I. T.*
DA320.L3   914.203   66-18543

Wright, Louis Booker, 1899- ed. **III. 1118**
Life and letters in Tudor and Stuart England, edited by Louis B. Wright and Virginia A. LaMar. [1st collected ed.] Ithaca, N.Y., Published for the Folger Shakespeare Library by Cornell University Press [1962] vii, 528 p. illus., ports., maps, facsims. (incl. music) plans. 23 cm. (Folger series, 1) *1. Gt. Brit. — History — Tudors, 1485-1603. 2. Gt. Brit. — History — Stuarts, 1603-1714. 3. England — Civilization. I. LaMar, Virginia A., joint ed. II. T. (S)*
DA320.W7   942.05   62-21552

Zeeveld, William Gordon, 1902- **III. 1119**
Foundations of Tudor policy. Cambridge, Harvard University Press, 1948. vii, 291 p. ports. 22 cm. *1. Learning and scholarship — England. 2. Humanism. 3. Gt. Brit. — Politics and government — 1509-1547. I. T.*
DA320.Z4   942.05   48-7421

Mackie, John Duncan, 1887- **III. 1120**
The earlier Tudors, 1485-1558. Oxford, Clarendon Press, 1952. xxi, 699 p. maps (1 fold.) geneal. tables. 23 cm. (The Oxford history of England) *1. Great Britain — History — Tudors, 1485-1603. I. T. (S)*
DA325.M3   942.05   52-4641

Pickthorn, Kenneth William Murray, 1892- **III. 1121**
Early Tudor government; Henry VII, by Kenneth Pickthorn. New York, Octagon Books, 1967. ix, 192 p. 24 cm. Reprint of the 1934 ed. *1. Gt. Brit. — Politics and government — 1485-1603. I. T.*
DA325.P48 1967   942.05/1   67-18780

Pickthorn, Kenneth William Murray, 1892- **III. 1122**
Early Tudor government; Henry VIII, by Kenneth Pickthorn. Cambridge [Eng.] University Press, 1934. xiv, 564 p. 24 cm. *1. Gt. Brit. — Politics and government — 1509-1547. I. T.*
DA325.P5   942.052   35-10021

DA330   Henry VII, 1485 – 1509

Pollard, Albert Frederick, 1869-1948, ed. **III. 1123**
The reign of Henry VII from contemporary sources. Selected and arr. ... with an introd. by A. F. Pollard. New York, AMS Press [1967] 3 v. 23 cm. Reprint of the 1913-1914 ed., which was issued as no. 1 of the University of London historical series. *1. Great Britain — History — Henry VII, 1485-1509 —*

Sources. I. T. (S:London. University. University of London historical series, no. 1.)
DA330.A3P72   942.05/1/0924   73-181970

Gairdner, James, 1828-1912.   III. 1124
Henry the Seventh. London, Macmillan, 1926. St. Clair Shores, Mich., Scholarly Press [1969?] vi, 219 p. 23 cm. (Twelve English statesmen) 1. Henry VII, King of England, 1457-1509. 2. Great Britain — History — Henry VII, 1485-1509. (S)
DA330.G14 1969   942.05/1   79-7750   ISBN:0403000203

Storey, R. L.   III. 1125
The reign of Henry VII [by] R. L. Storey. New York, Walker [1968] xii, 243 p. illus., facsims., ports. 21 cm. ([Problems of history]) 1. Great Britain — History — Henry VII, 1485-1509. I. T.
DA330.S75 1968b   942.05/1   68-13996

DA331 – 339   Henry VIII, 1509 – 1547

Elton, Geoffrey Rudolph.   III. 1126
Policy and police; the enforcement of the Reformation in the age of Thomas Cromwell [by] G. R. Elton. Cambridge [Eng.] University Press, 1972. xi, 446 p. 24 cm. 1. Great Britain — Politics and government — 1509-1547. 2. Reformation — England. 3. Treason — England. I. T.
DA332.E496   942.05/2   79-172831   ISBN:0521083834

Pollard, Albert Frederick, 1869-1948.   III. 1127
Henry VIII. Introd. to the Torchbook ed. by A. G. Dickens. New York, Harper & Row [1966] xxx, 385 p. ports. 21 cm. (Harper torchbooks. The Academy library) "Originally published in 1902." 1. Henry VIII, King of England, 1491-1547.
DA332.P78 1966   942.0520924   (B)   66-4649

Scarisbrick, J. J.   III. 1128
Henry VIII, by J. J. Scarisbrick. Berkeley, University of California Press, 1968. xiv, 561 p. illus., ports. (1 col.) 24 cm. 1. Henry VIII, King of England, 1491-1547.
DA332.S25 1968b   942.05/2/0924   (B)   68-10995

Smith, Lacey Baldwin, 1922-   III. 1129
Henry VIII: the mask of royalty. [1st American ed.] Boston, Houghton Mifflin Co., 1971. xii, 335 p. illus. 24 cm. 1. Henry VIII, King of England, 1491-1547. I. T.
DA332.S63 1971b   942.05/2/0924   (B)   70-162004   ISBN:0395127238

Mattingly, Garrett, 1900-   III. 1130
Catherine of Aragon, by Garrett Mattingly. London, Cape [1942] 343 p. geneal. tables, front. (port.) 23 cm. 1. Catharine of Aragon, consort of Henry VIII, King of England, 1485-1536.
DA333.A6M3 1942   923.142   42-20687

Chambers, Raymond Wilson, 1874-1942.   III. 1131
Thomas More. [Ann Arbor] University of Michigan Press [1958] 416 p. 21 cm. (Ann Arbor paperbacks, AA18) 1. More, Thomas, Saint, Sir, 1478-1535.
DA334.M8C45 1958   923.242   58-927

Ferguson, Charles Wright, 1901-   III. 1132
Naked to mine enemies; the life of Cardinal Wolsey. [1st ed.] Boston, Little, Brown [1958] 543 p. illus. 22 cm. 1. Wolsey, Thomas, Cardinal, 1475?-1530. 2. Gt. Brit. — Politics and government — 1509-1547. I. T.
DA334.W8F38   923.242 (922.242)   57-9320

Pollard, Albert Frederick, 1869-1948.   III. 1133
Wolsey; church and state in sixteenth-century England. Introd. to the Torchbook ed. by A. G. Dickens. New York, Harper & Row [1966] xxxv, 393 p. ports. 21 cm. (Harper torchbooks. The Academy library) "Originally published in 1929." 1. Wolsey, Thomas, Cardinal 1475?-1530.
DA334.W8P6 1966   942.0520924   66-4726

Sylvester, Richard Standish, ed.   III. 1134
Two early Tudor lives: The life and death of Cardinal Wolsey, by George Cavendish [and] The life of Sir Thomas More, by William Roper. Edited by Richard S. Sylvester and Davis P. Harding. New Haven, Yale University Press, 1962. xxi, 260 p. 21 cm. 1. Wolsey, Thomas, Cardinal, 1475?-1530. 2. More, Thomas, Sir, Saint, 1478-1535. I. Harding, Davis Philoon, 1914- joint ed. II. Cavendish, George, 1500-1561? The life and death of Cardinal Wolsey. III. Roper, William, 1496-1578. The life of Sir Thomas More. IV. T.
DA334.W8S85   923.242   62-8232

DA345   Edward VI, 1547 – 1553

Jordan, Wilbur Kitchener, 1902-   III. 1135
Edward VI: the threshold of power; the dominance of the Duke of Northumberland, by W. K. Jordan. London, Allen & Unwin [1970] 565 p. 23 cm. 1. Gt. Brit. — History — Edward VI, 1547-1553. 2. Somerset, Edward Seymour, 1st Duke of, 1506?-1552. 3. Northumberland, John Dudley, 1st Duke of, 1502-1553.
DA345.J59   942.05/3   78-556152   ISBN:0049420836

Jordan, Wilbur Kitchener, 1902-   III. 1136
Edward VI: the young King; the protectorship of the Duke of Somerset, by W. K. Jordan. London, Allen & Unwin, 1968. 3-544 p. 23 cm. 1. Great Britain — History — Edward VI, 1547-1553. 2. Somerset, Edward Seymour, 1st Duke of, 1506?-1552.
DA345.J6   942.05/3   74-369313   ISBN:0049420720

Pollard, Albert Frederick, 1869-1948.   III. 1137
England under Protector Somerset; an essay, by A. F. Pollard. New York, Russell & Russell, 1966. xii, 362 p. 23 cm. "First published in 1900." 1. Somerset, Edward Seymour, 1st duke of, 1506?-1552. 2. Gt. Brit. — History — Edward VI, 1547-1553. I. T.
DA345.P77 1966   942.053   66-15433

DA347   Mary I, 1553 – 1558

Prescott, Hilda Frances Margaret, 1896-   III. 1138
Mary Tudor. [Rev.] New York, Macmillan, 1953. xiii, 439 p. ports. 22 cm. Published in England, 1940, under title: Spanish Tudor. 1. Mary I, Queen of England, 1516-1558. I. T.
DA347.P7 1953a   923.142   53-12739

DA350 – 360   Elizabeth I, 1558 – 1603

Prothero, George Walter, Sir, 1848-1922, comp.   III. 1139
Select statutes and other constitutional documents illustrative of the reigns of Elizabeth and James I; ed. by G. W. Prothero. 4th ed. Oxford, Clarendon Press, 1913. cxxv, 490 (i.e. 501) p. 20 cm. Includes extra numbered pages 472a-472k. 1. Gt. Brit. — Constitutional history — Sources. 2. Gt. Brit. — History — Elizabeth, 1558-1603 — Sources. 3. Gt. Brit. — History — James I, 1603-1625 — Sources. I. Gt. Brit. Laws, statutes, etc.
DA350.P967 1913   W13-75

Elizabeth, Queen of England, 1533-1603.   III. 1140
The letters of Queen Elizabeth I. Edited by G. B. Harrison. New York, Funk & Wagnalls [1968] xvi, 323 p. port. 22 cm. Reprint of the 1935 ed. I. Harrison, George Bagshawe, 1894- ed.
DA355.A18 1968b   942.05/5/0924   68-25020

Black, John Bennett, 1883-1964.   III. 1141
The reign of Elizabeth, 1558-1603. 2d ed. Oxford, Clarendon Press, 1959. xxvi, 539 p. maps, fold. geneal. tables. 23 cm. (The Oxford history of England, 8) 1. Great Britain — Civilization — 16th century. 2. Church and state in Great Britain. I. T. (S)
DA355.B65 1959   942.055   59-3629

Harrison, George Bagshawe, 1894-   III. 1142
The Elizabethan journals, being a record of those things most talked of during the years 1591-1603. Comprising An Elizabethan journal, 1591-4, A second Elizabethan journal, 1595-8, A last Elizabethan journal, 1599-1603. Ann Arbor, University of Michigan Press, 1955. xiii, 395, 379, 364 p. 22 cm. "With a few exceptions each entry in the journals was based on a contemporary source, which is recorded in the notes." Sequel: A Jacobean journal. 1. Gt. Brit. — History — Elizabeth, 1558-1603. 2. Gt. Brit. — Social life and customs. 3. Gt. Brit. — Intellectual life. I. T.
DA355.H34 1955   942.055   56-581

Jenkins, Elizabeth, 1907-   III. 1143
Elizabeth the Great. [1st American ed.] New York, Coward-McCann [1959, c1958] 336 p. illus. 22 cm. 1. Elizabeth, Queen of England, 1533-1603. I. T.
DA355.J4   923.142   59-5455

MacCaffrey, Wallace T.   III. 1144
The shaping of the Elizabethan regime, by Wallace MacCaffrey. Princeton, N.J., Princeton University Press, 1968. xiv, 501 p. ports. 23 cm. 1. Great Britain — History — Elizabeth, 1558-1603. I. T.
DA355.M27   942.05/5   68-27409

Neale, John Ernest, Sir, 1890-   III. 1145
Queen Elizabeth I. London, J. Cape [1959] 402 p. illus. 23 cm. (The Bedford historical series, 1) First published in 1934 under title: Queen Elizabeth. 1. Elizabeth, Queen of England, 1533-1603.
DA355.N4 1959   923.142   59-16032

Rowse, Alfred Leslie, 1903-   III. 1146
The expansion of Elizabethan England. London, Macmillan; New York, St Martin's Press, 1955. xiii, 449 p. illus., ports., maps, facsim. 23 cm. (His The Elizabethan age [2]) 1. Gt. Brit. — Foreign relations — 1558-1603. 2. Gt. Brit. — Politics and government — 1558-1603. I. T.
DA355.R67 1955a   942.055   56-171

Williams, Neville, 1924-   III. 1147
Elizabeth the First, Queen of England. New York, Dutton, 1968 [c1967] xii,

386 p. illus., geneal. table, ports. 25 cm. First published in 1967 under title: *Elizabeth, Queen of England*. *1. Elizabeth, Queen of England, 1533-1603. I. T.*
DA355.W482 1968   942.05/5/0924 (B)   68-12449

Williams, Neville, 1924-   III. 1148
The life and times of Elizabeth I. Introd. by Antonia Fraser. Garden City, N.Y., Doubleday, 1972. 224 p. illus. 26 cm. *1. Elizabeth, Queen of England, 1533-1603. I. T.*
DA355.W483 1972   942.05/5/0924 (B)   74-187567

Williamson, James Alexander, 1886-   III. 1149
The age of Drake. 4th ed. London, A. & C. Black [1960] viii, 399 p. maps (1 fold. col.) 23 cm. (The Pioneer histories) Imprint covered by label: New York, Barnes & Noble. *1. Drake, Francis, Sir, 1540?-1596. 2. Gt. Brit. — History — Elizabeth, 1558-1603. 3. Gt. Brit. — History, Naval — Tudors, 1485-1603. I. T. (S:The Pioneer histories (London))*
DA355.W484 1960   942.055   63-4459

Campbell, Mildred Lucile, 1897-   III. 1150
The English yeoman under Elizabeth and the early Stuarts, by Mildred Campbell. New York, A. M. Kelley, 1968. xiii, 453 p. 22 cm. (Reprints of economic classics) Reprint of the 1942 ed. *1. Great Britain — Social life and customs — 16th century. 2. Great Britain — Social life and customs — 17th century. 3. Yeomanry (Social class) 4. Country life — England. 5. Agriculture — England — History. I. T.*
DA356.C3 1968   914.2/03/55   68-4919

McGrath, Patrick.   III. 1151
Papists and Puritans under Elizabeth I. New York, Walker [1967] x, 434 p. illus., facsims., maps, ports. 21 cm. (Blandford history series) *1. Great Britain — History — Elizabeth, 1558-1603. 2. Great Britain — Church history — Modern period. I. T.*
DA356.M25 1967b   942.05/5   67-23085

Neale, John Ernest, Sir, 1890-   III. 1152
Elizabeth I and her Parliaments. New York, St Martin's Press, 1958. 2 v. illus. 23 cm. *1. Elizabeth, Queen of England, 1533-1603. 2. Gt. Brit. — Politics and government — 1558-1603. I. T.*
DA356.N42   942.055   58-319

Neale, John Ernest, Sir, 1890-   III. 1153
Essays in Elizabethan history. New York, St Martin's Press [1959, c1958] 255 p. 21 cm. *1. Gt. Brit. — History — Elizabeth, 1558-1603 — Addresses, essays, lectures. I. T. II. T:Elizabethan history.*
DA356.N43   942.055   58-13823

Rowse, Alfred Leslie, 1903-   III. 1154
The England of Elizabeth; the structure of society. New York, Macmillan, 1951 [c1950] xv, 546 p. illus., ports., maps. 25 cm. (His The Elizabethan age, v.1) *1. Gt. Brit. — History — Elizabeth, 1558-1603. I. T.*
DA356.R65 1951   942.055   51-4102

Stone, Lawrence.   III. 1155
The crisis of the aristocracy, 1558-1641. Oxford, Clarendon Press, 1965. xxiv, 841 p. illus. 24 cm. *1. Upper classes — Gt. Brit. 2. Gt. Brit. — Nobility. 3. Gt. Brit. — Civilization — 16th cent. I. T.*
DA356.S8   914.2   65-3206

DA358 Biography of Contemporaries

Beckingsale, B. W.   III. 1156
Burghley: Tudor statesman, 1520-1598 [by] B. W. Beckingsale. London, Melbourne [etc.] Macmillan; New York, St. Martin's P., 1967. x, 340 p. front., 16 plates (incl. ports., facsims.): 22 1/2 cm. *1. Burghley, William Cecil, Baron, 1520-1598. I. T.*
DA358.B9B4   942.05/0924 (B)   67-19278

Read, Conyers, 1881-1959.   III. 1157
Lord Burghley and Queen Elizabeth. New York, Knopf, 1960. 603 p. ports., facsim. 26 cm. Sequel to Mr. Secretary Cecil and Queen Elizabeth. *1. Burghley, William Cecil, 1520-1598. 2. Elizabeth, Queen of England, 1533-1603. I. T.*
DA358.B9R38   923.242   60-1682

Read, Conyers, 1881-   III. 1158
Mr. Secretary Cecil and Queen Elizabeth. New York, Knopf, 1955. 510 p. illus., ports. 26 cm. Erratum slip inserted. *1. Burghley, William Cecil, baron, 1520-1598. 2. Elizabeth, Queen of England, 1533-1603. I. T.*
DA358.B9R4x   923.242   54-7211

Bald, Robert Cecil, 1901-   III. 1159
Donne & the Drurys. Cambridge [Eng.] University Press, 1959. 175 p. illus. 23 cm. *1. Donne, John, 1573-1631. 2. Drury, Robert, Sir, 1575-1615. 3. Drury, Anne (Bacon) Lady, 1572?-1624.*
DA358.D76B3   923.242   59-2100

Lacey, Robert.   III. 1160
Robert, Earl of Essex. [1st Amer. ed.] New York, Atheneum, 1971. xiii, 338 p. illus., maps, ports. 24 cm. *1. Essex, Robert Devereux, Earl of, 1566-1601.*
DA358.E8L3   942.05/5/0924 (B)   70-139313

Osborn, James Marshall.   III. 1161
Young Philip Sidney, 1572-1577 [by] James M. Osborn. New Haven, Published for the Elizabethan Club [by] Yale University Press, 1972. xxiv, 565 p. illus. 25 cm. (The Elizabethan Club series, 5) *1. Sidney, Philip, Sir, 1554-1586. I. T. (S)*
DA358.S5O8 1972   942.05/5/0924 (B)   77-151584   ISBN:0300014430

Read, Conyers, 1881-   III. 1162
Mr. Secretary Walsingham and the policy of Queen Elizabeth, by Conyers Read. Oxford, Clarendon Press, 1925. 3 v. front., ports., 3 facsim. (2 fold.) 24 cm. *1. Walsingham, Francis, Sir, 1530?-1590. 2. Elizabeth, queen of England, 1533-1603. 3. Gt. Brit. — History — Elizabeth, 1558-1603. 4. Gt. Brit. — Politics and government — 1558-1603. I. T.*
DA358.W2R4   26-932

DA360 Armada

Mattingly, Garrett, 1900-1962.   III. 1163
The Armada. Boston, Houghton Mifflin, 1959. 443 p. illus. 22 cm. *1. Armada, 1588.*
DA360.M3   942.055   59-8861

DA375 – 462 17th Century

Aiken, William Appleton, 1907-1957, ed.   III. 1164
Conflict in Stuart England; essays in honour of Wallace Notestein. Edited by William Appleton Aiken and Basil Duke Henning. [Hamden, Conn.] Archon Books, 1970 [c1960] 271 p. port. 22 cm. *1. Great Britain — History — Stuarts, 1603-1714 — Addresses, Essays, lectures. 2. Notestein, Wallace, 1878-1969. I. Henning, Basil Duke, joint ed. II. T.*
DA375.A68 1970   942.06   75-138974   ISBN:0208010297

Clark, George Norman, Sir, 1890-   III. 1165
Three aspects of Stuart England. London, New York, Oxford University Press, 1960. 77 p. 19 cm. (The Whidden lectures, series 5) *1. Gt. Brit. — History — Stuarts, 1603-1714. I. T.*
DA375.C53   942.06   60-51527

Hill, John Edward Christopher, 1912-   III. 1166
The century of revolution, 1603-1714. Edinburgh, T. Nelson [1961] 340 p. illus. 23 cm. (A History of England, v. 5) *1. Great Britain — History — Stuarts, 1603-1714. I. T. (S:A History of England (Edinburgh, v. 5))*
DA375.H5   942.06   61-66046

Jones, James Rees.   III. 1167
Britain and Europe in the seventeenth century, by J. R. Jones. New York, Norton [c1967] vi, 119 p. 21 cm. (Foundations of modern history) *1. Gt. Brit. — History — Stuarts, 1603-1714. 2. Gt. Brit. — Relations (general) with Europe. 3. Europe — Relations (general) with Great Britain. I. T.*
DA375.J62 1967   942.06   66-28650

Kenyon, John Philipps, 1927-   III. 1168
The Stuarts; a study in English kingship. London, B. T. Batsford [1958] 240 p. ports., geneal. table. 23 cm. *1. Stuart, House of. 2. Gt. Brit. — History — Stuarts, 1603-1714.*
DA375.K4   942.06   A59-384

Ranke, Leopold von, 1795-1886.   III. 1169
A history of England principally in the seventeenth century. New York, AMS Press, 1966. 6 v. Reprint of the 1875 ed. *1. Gt. Brit. — History — Stuarts, 1603-1714. I. T.*
DA375.R198x

Roberts, Clayton.   III. 1170
The growth of responsible government in Stuart England. Cambridge, Cambridge U.P., 1966. xii, 467 p. 24 cm. *1. Gt. Brit. — Politics and government — 1603-1714. 2. Ministerial responsibility — Gt. Brit. 3. Gt. Brit. — Constitutional history. I. T.*
DA375.R6   320.942   66-11033

Trevelyan, George Macaulay, 1876-   III. 1171
England under the Stuarts. New York, Putnam, 1949. xiii, 466 p. col. maps (part fold.) 23 cm. *1. Gt. Brit. — History — Stuarts, 1603-1714. I. T.*
DA375.T7 1949   942.06   50-14448

DA377 COLLECTIVE BIOGRAPHY

Walton, Izaak, 1593-1683.   III. 1172
The lives of Dr. John Donne, Sir Henry Wotton, Mr. Richard Hooker, Mr.

George Herbert, 1670. Menston, (Yorks.) Scolar P., 1969. [431] p. 2 ports. 24 cm. "A Scolar Press facsimile." Facsimile reprint of 1st ed., London, printed by Tho. Newcomb for Richard Marriott, 1670. Wing W671. 1. Donne, John, 1573-1631. 2. Wotton, Henry, Sir, 1568-1639. 3. Hooker, Richard, 1553 or 4-1600. 4. Herbert, George, 1593-1633. I. T.
DA377.W2 1670a   914.2/03/610922   75-473305   ISBN:854171657

Novarr, David.   **III. 1173**
The making of Walton's Lives. Ithaca, N.Y., Cornell University Press [1958] xvi, 527 p. 25 cm. (Cornell studies in English, v.41) 1. Walton, Izaac, 1593-1683. The lives of Dr. John Donne, Sir Henry Wotton, Mr. Richard Hooker, Mr. George Herbert and Dr. Robert Sanderson. I. T. (S:Cornell University. Cornell studies in English, v.41)
DA377.W27N6   928.2   58-1012

DA380 CIVILIZATION

Greene, Donald Johnson.   **III. 1174**
The age of exuberance; backgrounds to eighteenth-century English literature [by] Donald Greene. New York, Random House [1970] x, 184 p. 21 cm. (Studies in language and literature) 1. Great Britain — Civilization — 17th century. 2. Great Britain — Civilization — 18th century. I. T.
DA380.G7 1970   914.2/03/7   67-22327

Hill, John Edward Christopher, 1912-   **III. 1175**
Intellectual origins of the English Revolution. Oxford, Clarendon Press, 1965. ix, 333 p. 23 cm. 1. Gt. Brit. — Intellectual life — 17th cent. 2. Gt. Brit. — History — Puritan Revolution, 1642-1660. I. T.
DA380.H48   942.06   65-3182

Hill, John Edward Christopher, 1912-   **III. 1176**
Puritanism and revolution: studies in interpretation of the English Revolution of the 17th century. New York, Schocken Books [1964, c1958] xii, 402 p. 20 cm. (Schocken paperbacks) "SB74" 1. Gt. Brit. — History — Puritan Revolution, 1642-1660. 2. Gt. Brit. — Social conditions. I. T.
DA380.H5 1964   942.062   64-15220

Hill, John Edward Christopher, 1912-   **III. 1177**
Society and Puritanism in pre-Revolutionary England. New York, Schocken Books [1964] 520 p. 23 cm. 1. Gt. Brit. — History — Civil War, 1642-1649 — Causes. 2. Puritans — Gt. Brit. 3. Gt. Brit. — Social conditions. I. T.
DA380.H52 1964   942.062   64-13350

Notestein, Wallace, 1878-   **III. 1178**
The English people on the eve of colonization, 1603-1630. [1st ed.] New York, Harper [1954] xvii, 302 p. illus., ports., maps. 22 cm. (The New American nation series) 1. Gt. Brit. — History — Early Stuarts, 1603-1649. 2. England — Civilization. I. T.
DA380.N6   942.061   54-8978

DA390 EARLY STUARTS
(1603 – 1642)

Bridenbaugh, Carl.   **III. 1179**
Vexed and troubled Englishmen, 1590-1642. New York, Oxford University Press, 1968 [c1967] xix, 487 p. 24 cm. (The Beginnings of the American people, 1) 1. Great Britain — History — Early Stuarts, 1603-1649. 2. Great Britain — Emigration and immigration. I. T.
DA390.B7   942.06   68-17604

Davies, Godfrey, 1892-1957.   **III. 1180**
The early Stuarts, 1603-1660. 2d ed. Oxford, Clarendon Press, 1959. xxiii, 458 p. maps. 23 cm. (The Oxford history of England, 9) 1. Great Britain — History — Early Stuarts,1603-1649. 2. Great Britain — History — Commonwealth and Protectorate, 1649-1660. I. T. (S)
DA390.D3 1959   942.06   59-1862

Gardiner, Samuel Rawson, 1829-1902.   **III. 1181**
History of England from the accession of James I. to the outbreak of the civil war 1603-1642, by Samuel R. Gardiner ... London, Longmans, Green, 1884-86. 10 v. fronts. (v.6, 10) maps. 20 cm. Vol. 2: 2d ed.; v.8-10 dated 1884. 1. Gt. Brit. — History — James I, 1603-1625. 2. Gt. Brit. — History — Charles I, 1625-1649.
DA390.G121 1884   16-2846

Gardiner, Samuel Rawson, 1829-1902.   **III. 1182**
History of the great civil war, 1642-1649, by Samuel R. Gardiner. London, New York, [etc.] Longmans, Green, 1898-1901. 4 v. maps (part fold.) 20 cm. 1. Gt. Brit. — History — Civil war, 1642-1649.
DA390.G122   942.062   02-21027

Gardiner, Samuel Rawson, 1829-1902.   **III. 1183**
History of the commonwealth and protectorate, 1649-1656; by Samuel Rawson Gardiner. New ed. London, New York [etc.] Longmans, Green,
1903. 4 v. maps (part fold.) 20 cm. 1. Gt. Brit. — History — Commonwealth and protectorate, 1649-1660.
DA390.G123   942.063   03-25350

DA391 – 394 James I, 1603 – 1625

Akrigg, G. P. V.   **III. 1184**
Jacobean pageant; or, The court of King James I. Cambridge, Harvard University Press, 1962. xi, 431 p. illus., ports., plan. 26 cm. 1. James I, King of Great Britain, 1566-1625. 2. Gt. Brit. — Court and courtiers. I. T.
DA391.A4   942.061   62-5508

McElwee, William Lloyd, 1907-   **III. 1185**
The wisest fool in Christendom; the reign of King James I and VI. [1st American ed.] New York, Harcourt, Brace [1958] 296 p. illus. 22 cm. 1. James I, King of Great Britain, 1566-1625. I. T.
DA391.M23   923.142   58-10894

Mitchell, Williams M.   **III. 1186**
The rise of the revolutionary party in the English House of Commons, 1603-1629. New York, Columbia University Press, 1957. xvi, 209 p. 23 cm. "Outgrowth of a dissertation for the degree of doctor of philosophy at Yale University." 1. Gt. Brit. Parliament. 2. Gt. Brit. — Politics and government — 1603-1649. I. T.
DA391.M5   942.061   57-13029

Willson, David Harris, 1901-   **III. 1187**
King James VI and I. New York, Holt [1956] 480 p. illus. 22 cm. 1. James I, King of Great Britain, 1566-1625.
DA391.W47   942.061   56-2623

DA395 – 398 Charles I, 1625 – 1649

Zagorin, Perez.   **III. 1188**
The court and the country; the beginning of the English Revolution. [1st American ed.] New York, Atheneum, 1970 [c1969] xiv, 366 p. 25 cm. 1. Great Britain — History — Charles I, 1625-1649. 2. Great Britain — Social conditions. I. T.
DA395.Z3 1970   320.9/42   72-104129

Wingfield-Stratford, Esmé Cecil, 1882-   **III. 1189**
King Charles and King Pym, 1637-1643. London, Hollis & Carter, 1949. x, 394 p. ports., maps. 23 cm. 1. Charles I, King of Great Britain, 1600-1649. 2. Pym, John, 1584-1643.
DA396.A2W495   923.142   49-4388

Wingfield-Stratford, Esmé Cecil, 1882-   **III. 1190**
King Charles the martyr, 1643-1649. London, Hollis & Carter, 1950. xi, 385 p. plates, ports., maps. 22 cm. 1. Charles I, King of Great Britain, 1600-1649. 2. Gt. Brit. — History — Civil war, 1642-1649. I. T.
DA396.A2W52   923.142   50-14449

Lenanton, Carola Mary Anima (Oman) 1897-   **III. 1191**
Henrietta Maria, by Carola Oman. London, Hodder and Stoughton, 1936. xiii, 366 p. front., ports. 23 cm. 1. Henrietta Maria, consort of Charles I, King of Great Britain, 1609-1669.
DA396.A5L4 1963a   923.142   37-4059

Hexter, Jack H., 1910-   **III. 1192**
The reign of King Pym, by J. H. Hexter. Cambridge, Harvard University Press, 1941. 245 p. 23 cm. (Harvard historical studies. vol.XLVIII) 1. Pym, John, 1584-1643. 2. Gt. Brit. — History — Early Stuarts, 1603-1649. 3. Gt. Brit. — Politics and government — 1603-1649. I. T.
DA396.P9H4   923.242   A41-4164

Wedgwood, Cicely Veronica, Dame, 1910-   **III. 1193**
Strafford, 1593-1641, by C. V. Wedgwood. Westport, Conn., Greenwood Press [1970] 366 p. ports. 23 cm. Reprint of the 1935 ed. 1. Strafford, Thomas Wentworth, 1st Earl of, 1593-1641. 2. Great Britain — History — Charles I, 1625-1649.
DA396.S8W4 1970   942.06/2/0924 (B)   76-110882
ISBN:083714566X

D'Ewes, Simonds, Sir, bart., 1602-1650.   **III. 1194**
The journal of Sir Simonds D'Ewes; from the first recess of the Long Parliament to the withdrawal of King Charles from London. Edited by Willson Havelock Coates. [Hamden, Conn.] Archon Books, 1970 [c1942] xliv, 459 p. 23 cm. 1. Great Britain. Parliament, 1640-1648. 2. Great Britain — Politics and government — 1625-1649. I. Coates, Willson Havelock, ed.
DA397.D43 1970   942.06/2/0924   71-122400   ISBN:0208009485

DA400 – 407 Civil War, 1642 – 1649

Clarendon, Edward Hyde, 1st earl of, 1609-1674.   **III. 1195**
The history of the rebellion and civil wars in England begun in the year 1641, by Edward, earl of Clarendon. Re-edited from a fresh collation of the

original ms. in the Bodleian library, with marginal dates and occasional notes, by W. Dunn Macray ... Oxford, Clarendon Press, 1888. 6 v. 20 cm. *1. Gt. Brit. — History — Stuarts, 1603-1714. I. Macray, William Dunn, 1826-1916, ed.*
DA400.C6 1888   01-3232

Gardiner, Samuel Rawson, 1829-1902, ed. III. 1196
The constitutional documents of the Puritan revolution 1625-1660, selected and edited by Samuel Rawson Gardiner. 2d ed., rev. and enl. Oxford, Clarendon Press, 1899. lxviii, 476 p. 20 cm. *1. Gt. Brit. — Constitutional history. 2. Gt. Brit. — History — Puritan revolution, 1642-1660. I. Gt. Brit. Parliament.*
DA400.G22   03-26688

Haller, William, 1885- ed. III. 1197
The Leveller tracts, 1647-1653. Edited by William Haller and Godfrey Davies. Gloucester, Mass., P. Smith, 1964 [c1944] vi, 481 p. illus. 21 cm. *1. Lilburne, John, 1614?-1657. 2. Levellers. 3. Gt. Brit. — History — Puritan Revolution, 1642-1660 — Sources. 4. Gt. Brit. — Politics and government — 1642-1660. I. Davies, Godfrey, 1892-1957, joint ed. II. T.*
DA400.H3 1964   942.063   64-4072

Hobbes, Thomas, 1588-1679. III. 1198
Behemoth: the history of the causes of the civil wars of England, and of the counsels and artifices by which they were carried on from the year 1640 to the year 1660. Edited by William Molesworth. New York, B. Franklin [1963] 256 p. 24 cm. (Burt Franklin research and source works series, no. 38) *1. Gt. Brit. — History — Puritan Revolution, 1640-1660. I. T.*
DA400.H6 1963   942.062   63-14025

Bernstein, Eduard, 1850-1932. III. 1199
Cromwell & communism; socialism and democracy in the great English revolution, by Eduard Bernstein, translated by H. J. Stenning. London, Allen & Unwin [1930] 287 p. 22 cm. Translation of Sozialismus und Demokratie in der grossen englischen Revolution, which was published as one of the volumes of Karl Kautsky's comprehensive history of socialism. cf. Foreword. *1. Communism — Gt. Brit. 2. Gt. Brit. — Politics and government — 1642-1660. 3. Levellers. 4. Utopias. I. Stenning, Henry James, 1889- tr. II. T.*
DA405.B4   942.06   31-2126

Brunton, Douglas, 1917-1952. III. 1200
Members of the Long Parliament [by] D. Brunton and D. H. Pennington. Introd. by R. H. Tawney. [Hamden, Conn.] Archon Books, 1968. xxi, 256 p. 22 cm. Reprint of the 1954 ed. *1. Great Britain. Parliament, 1640-1653. 2. Great Britain — Politics and government — 1642-1660. I. Pennington, Donald H., joint author. II. T.*
DA405.B88 1968   328.42/09   68-8014   ISBN:0208006869

Frank, Joseph, 1916- III. 1201
The Levellers; a history of the writings of three seventeenth-century social democrats: John Lilburne, Richard Overton [and] William Walwyn. New York, Russell & Russell [1969] 345 p. 22 cm. Reprint of the 1955 ed. Based on thesis, Harvard University. *1. Levellers. 2. Lilburne, John, 1614?-1657. 3. Overton, Richard, fl. 1646. 4. Walwyn, William, fl. 1649.*
DA405.F7 1969   942.06/2   68-27058

Roots, Ivan Alan. III. 1202
Commonwealth and Protectorate; the English Civil War and its aftermath [by] Ivan Roots. New York, Schocken Books [1966] x, 326 p. 23 cm. (The Fabric of British history series) London ed. (Batsford) has title: The Great Rebellion. *1. Gt. Brit. — History — Puritan Revolution, 1642-1660. I. T.*
DA405.R65 1966a   942.06   66-26727

Wedgwood, Cicely Veronica, 1910- III. 1203
The King's peace, 1637-1641. New York, Macmillan, 1955. 510 p. illus., ports. 22 cm. (Her The Great rebellion [1]) *1. Gt. Brit. — History — Charles I, 1625-1649. I. T.*
DA405.W42 vol. 1   942.062   55-3603

Wedgwood, Cicely Veronica, 1910- III. 1204
The King's war, 1641-1647. New York, Macmillan, 1959 [c1958] 702 p. ports., maps. 22 cm. (Her The great rebellion [2]) *1. Gt. Brit. — History — Civil War, 1642-1649. I. T.*
DA405.W42 vol. 2   942.062   59-7446

Ashley, Maurice Percy. III. 1205
Cromwell's generals. New York, St Martin's Press, 1955. 256 p. illus. 23 cm. *1. Cromwell, Oliver, 1599-1658. 2. Gt. Brit. — History — Commonwealth and Protectorate, 1649-1660. 3. Generals — Gt. Brit. I. T.*
DA407.A1A8x   942.063   55-9052

Gregg, Pauline. III. 1206
Free-born John; a biography of John Lilburne. London, Harrap [1961] 424 p. illus. 22 cm. *1. Lilburne, John, 1614?-1657. I. T.*
DA407.L65G7   62-5784

Haley, Kenneth Harold Dobson. III. 1207
The first Earl of Shaftesbury, by K. H. D. Haley. Oxford, Clarendon P.,

1968. xii, 767 p. plate, port. 24 cm. *1. Shaftesbury, Anthony Ashley Cooper, 1st Earl of, 1621-1683. I. T.*
DA407.S5H3   942.06/6/0924   68-111124   ISBN:0198213697

Solt, Leo Frank, 1921- III. 1208
Saints in arms; Puritanism and democracy in Cromwell's army [by] Leo F. Solt. Stanford, Calif., Stanford University Press, 1959. [New York, AMS Press, 1971] 150 p. 23 cm. (Stanford University publications. University series. History, economics, and political science, v. 18) *1. Great Britain — History — Civil War, 1642-1649. 2. Chaplains, Military — Great Britain. 3. Puritans — Great Britain. 4. Christianity and politics. I. T. (S:Stanford studies in history, economics, and political science, v. 18.)*
DA415.S65 1971   320.9/42/062   74-153355   ISBN:0404509762

DA420 – 429 Commonwealth, 1649 – 1660.
Cromwell

Brailsford, Henry Noel, 1873-1958. III. 1209
The Levellers and the English revolution. Edited and prepared for publication by Christopher Hill. [Stanford, Calif.] Stanford University Press, 1961. xvi, 715 p. 23 cm. *1. Levellers. 2. Gt. Brit. — Politics and government — 1642-1660. I. T.*
DA425.B7   942.062   61-11501

Davies, Godfrey, 1892-1957. III. 1210
The restoration of Charles II, 1658-1660. London, Oxford U.P., 1969. viii, 383 p. 24 cm. "First published in 1955." *1. Great Britain — History — Commonwealth and Protectorate 1649-1660. 2. Charles II, King of Great Britain, 1630-1685. I. T.*
DA425.D39 1969   942.06/5   73-413014

Firth, Charles Harding, Sir, 1857-1936. III. 1211
The last years of the Protectorate, 1656-1658. New York, Russell & Russell, 1964. 2 v. plans. 23 cm. "First published in 1909." "A continuation of 'History of the Commonwealth and Protectorate' "by S. R. Gardiner. *1. Gt. Brit. — History — Commonwealth and Protectorate, 1649-1660. I. Gardiner, Samuel Rawson, 1829-1902. History of the Commonwealth and Protectorate, 1649-1660. II. T.*
DA425.F5 1964   942.064   64-15029

Underdown, David. III. 1212
Royalist conspiracy in England, 1649-1660. [Hamden, Conn.] Archon Books, 1971 [c1960] xvii, 374 p. ports. 24 cm. "Chapters 4-10 represent an expansion and revision of ... [the author's] B. Litt. dissertation, presented at Oxford in 1953." *1. Great Britain — History — Commonwealth and Protectorate, 1649-1660. 2. Royalists, 1642-1660. I. T.*
DA425.U5 1971   942.06/3   74-122409   ISBN:0208009604

Cromwell, Oliver, 1599-1658. III. 1213
The writings and speeches of Oliver Cromwell. With an introd., notes and a sketch of his life by Wilbur Cortez Abbott, with the assistance of Catherine D. Crane. New York, Russell & Russell [1970, c1937-47] 4 v. illus., maps, ports. 25 cm. Vols. 3-4, with the assistance of Catherine D. Crane and Madeleine R. Gleason. *1. Great Britain — History — Commonwealth and Protectorate, 1649-1660. I. Abbott, Wilbur Cortez, 1869-1947.*
DA426.A15 1970   942.06/4   68-25071

Ashley, Maurice Percy. III. 1214
The greatness of Oliver Cromwell. New York, Macmillan, 1958 [c1957] 382 p. illus. 22 cm. *1. Cromwell, Oliver, 1599-1658.*
DA426.A74 1958   942.064   57-13140

Firth, Charles Harding, Sir, 1857-1936. III. 1215
Oliver Cromwell and the rule of Puritans in England. With an introd. by G. M. Young. London, New York, Oxford University Press [1953] xx, 488 p. 16 cm. (The World's classics, 536) *1. Cromwell, Oliver, 1599-1658. 2. Gt. Brit. — History — Commonwealth and Protectorate, 1649-1660. 3. Gt. Brit. — History — Civil War, 1642-1649.*
DA426.F52 1953   923.142   53-4098

Hill, John Edward Christopher, 1912- III. 1216
God's Englishman; Oliver Cromwell and the English Revolution [by] Christopher Hill. New York, Dial Press, 1970. 324 p. illus., ports. 22 cm. (Crosscurrents in world history) *1. Cromwell, Oliver, 1599-1658. 2. Gt. Brit. — History — Puritan Revolution, 1642-1660. I. T.*
DA426.H49 1970b   942.06/4/0924   (B)   75-111450

DA430 – 462 LATER STUARTS (1660 – 1714)

Beloff, Max, 1913- III. 1217
Public order and popular disturbances, 1660-1714. [London] F. Cass, 1963. viii, 168 p. fold. map. 22 cm. Imprint covered by label: Barnes & Noble,

New York. *1. Gt. Brit. — History — 1660-1714. 2. Gt. Brit. — Social conditions. 3. Riots — Gt. Brit. I. T.*
DA435.B4 1963   942.06   63-24321

Clark, George Norman, Sir, 1890-   **III. 1218**
The later Stuarts, 1660-1714, by Sir George Clark. 2d ed. [reprinted with corrections] Oxford, Clarendon Press [1961] xxiii, 479 p. geneal. tables, maps. 23 cm. (The Oxford history of England, 10) *1. Great Britain — History — Stuarts, 1603-1714. I. T. (S)*
DA435.C55 1961   68-105542

Holmes, Geoffrey S., 1928-   **III. 1219**
Britain after the Glorious Revolution, 1689-1714, edited by Geoffrey Holmes. London, Macmillan, New York, St. Martin's Press, 1969. ix, 245 p. 23 cm. (Problems in focus series) *1. Gt. Brit. — History — 1689-1714. I. T.*
DA435.H6 1969   942.06/8   76-83201   ISBN:333044169

Macaulay, Thomas Babington Macaulay, 1st baron, 1800-1859.   **III. 1220**
History of England from the accession of James II. Introd. by Douglas Jerrold. London, Dent; New York, Dutton [1953] 4. v. 19 cm. (Everyman's library, 34-37. History) *1. Gt. Brit. — History — James II, 1685-1688. 2. Gt. Brit. — History — William and Mary, 1689-1702.*
DA435.M14 1953   942.067   53-11664

Ogg, David, 1887-1965.   **III. 1221**
England in the reigns of James II and William III. London, Oxford U.P., 1969. xiii, 567 p. 21 cm. "A sequel to the author's 'England in the reign of Charles II,' first published in 1934." *1. Great Britain — History — 1660-1714. I. T.*
DA435.O35 1969   942.06/7   77-432120   ISBN:0198811543

Kenyon, John Philipps, 1927-   **III. 1222**
Robert Spencer, earl of Sunderland, 1641-1702. London, New York, Longmans, Green [1958] 396 p. illus. 23 cm. *1. Sunderland, Robert Spencer, 2d earl of, 1640-1702.*
DA437.S8K4 1958   923.242   58-59402

Horwitz, Henry.   **III. 1223**
Revolution politicks: the career of Daniel Finch, second Earl of Nottingham, 1647-1730. London, Cambridge U.P., 1968. xii, 306 p. plate, port. 23 cm. *1. Winchilsea and Nottingham, Daniel Finch, Earl of, 1647-1730. I. T.*
DA437.W5H6   942.07/1/0924 (B)   68-11284   ISBN:0521053404

DA445 – 448   Charles II, 1660 – 1685

Feiling, Keith Grahame, 1884-   **III. 1224**
British foreign policy, 1660-1672, by Keith Feiling. London, Macmillan, 1930. xii, 385 p. 23 cm. *1. Gt. Brit. — Foreign relations — 1660-1688. I. T.*
DA445.F4   942.066 (327.421)   31-1831

Lee, Maurice.   **III. 1225**
The Cabal. Urbana, University of Illinois Press, 1965. 275 p. ports. 24 cm. *1. Gt. Brit. — History — Restoration, 1660-1688. I. T.*
DA445.L4   942.066   65-11735

Ogg, David, 1887-   **III. 1226**
England in the reign of Charles II. 2d ed. Oxford, Clarendon Press, 1955. 2 v. 23 cm. *1. Gt. Brit. — History — Charles II, 1660-1685. I. T.*
DA445.O5x   A57-8602

DA447   Biography. Memoirs

Aubrey, John, 1626-1697.   **III. 1227**
Brief lives. Edited from the original manuscripts and with a life of John Aubrey by Oliver Lawson Dick. Foreword by Edmund Wilson. Ann Arbor, University of Michigan Press [1957] cvi, 341 p. 24 cm. *1. Gt. Brit. — Biography. I. Dick, Oliver Lawson, 1920- ed.*
DA447.A3A8 1957   920.042   57-13981

Wormald, B. H. G.   **III. 1228**
Clarendon: politics, historiography, and religion, 1640-1660, by B. H. G. Wormald. Cambridge [Eng.] University Press, 1964. x, 330 p. 23 cm. Published in 1951 under title: Clarendon: politics, history, & religion, 1640-1660. *1. Clarendon, Edward Hyde, 1st earl of, 1609-1674. I. T.*
DA447.C6W6 1964   942.06   65-1164

Evelyn, John, 1620-1706.   **III. 1229**
Diary. Now first printed in full from the MSS. belonging to John Evelyn, and edited by E. S. de Beer. Oxford, Clarendon Press, 1955. 6 v. illus., ports., fold. map, facsims., geneal. tables. 23 cm. *1. Gt. Brit. — History — Stuarts, 1603-1714. 2. Gt. Brit. — Court and courtiers.*
DA447.E9A44   928.2   56-13545

Browning, Andrew, 1889-   **III. 1230**
Thomas Osborne, earl of Danby and duke of Leeds, 1632-1712. Glasgow, Jackson, 1944-51. 3 v. port., facsims. 22 cm. *1. Leeds, Thomas Osborne, 1st duke of, 1631-1712.*
DA447.L4B82   923.242   45-8887

Pepys, Samuel, 1633-1703.   **III. 1231**
The diary of Samuel Pepys. A new and complete transcription edited by Robert Latham and William Matthews. Contributing editors: William A. Armstrong [and others] Berkeley, University of California Press [1970]- v. illus., facsims., maps, ports. 23 cm. *1. Gt. Brit. — Social life and customs — 17th century. I. Latham, Robert, 1912- ed. II. Matthews, William, 1905- ed. III. T.*
DA447.P4A4 1970   914.2/03/6   70-96950
ISBN:0520015754 (v. 1) varies

Pepys, Samuel, 1633-1703.   **III. 1232**
The diary of Samuel Pepys transcribed by Mynors Bright from the shorthand manuscript in the Pepysian Library. Magdalene College, Cambridge. Edited with additions by Henry B. Wheatley. New York, Random House [1946] 2 v. port. 24 cm. *1. Gt. Brit. — History — Stuarts, 1603-1714 — Sources. 2. Gt. Brit. — Social life and customs. I. Bright, Mynors, 1818-1883. II. Wheatley, Henry Benjamin, 1838-1917, ed.*
DA447.P4A4x   A48-18

Bryant, Arthur, Sir, 1899-   **III. 1233**
Samuel Pepys. [New ed.] London, Collins [1948- v. plates, ports., maps (on lining-papers) 23 cm. *1. Pepys, Samuel, 1633-1703.*
DA447.P4B83   928.2 (923.242)   48-23036

Heath, Helen Truesdell, ed.   **III. 1234**
The letters of Samuel Pepys and his family circle. Oxford, Clarendon Press, 1955. xi, 253 p. port., facsim., geneal. tables. 23 cm. "Previous editions of the letters": p. 246. *1. Pepys, Samuel, 1633-1703.*
DA447.P4H4   928.2   55-1764

Tanner, Joseph Robson, 1860-1931.   **III. 1235**
Mr. Pepys; an introduction to the Diary together with a sketch of his later life. Westport, Conn., Greenwood Press [1971] xv, 308 p. port. 23 cm. Reprint of the 1925 ed. *1. Pepys, Samuel, 1633-1703. I. T.*
DA447.P4T4 1971   828.4/03 (B)   71-110870   ISBN:083714549X

DA448   Special Topics

Jones, James Rees.   **III. 1236**
The first Whigs; the politics of the Exclusion Crisis, 1678-1683. London, New York, Oxford University Press, 1961. 224 p. 23 cm. (University of Durham publications) *1. Gt. Brit. — Politics and government — 1660-1688. 2. Whig Party (Gt. Brit.) I. T:Exclusion Crisis.*
DA448.J6   942.066   61-66249

Kenyon, John Philipps, 1927-   **III. 1237**
The Popish Plot [by] John Kenyon. New York, St. Martin's Press [1972] 300 p. illus. 23 cm. *1. Popish Plot, 1678.*
DA448.K45 1972   942.06/6   72-76795

Witcombe, Dennis Trevor.   **III. 1238**
Charles II and the Cavalier House of Commons, 1663-1674, by D. T. Witcombe. Manchester, Manchester U.P.; New York, Barnes & Noble [1966] xiv, 218 p. 22 1/2 cm. *1. Charles II, King of Great Britain, 1630-1685. 2. Gt. Brit. — Politics and government — 1660-1688. I. T.*
DA448.W5   942.066   66-78067

DA450 – 452   James II, 1685 – 1688

Buranelli, Vincent.   **III. 1239**
The King & the Quaker; a study of William Penn and James II. Philadelphia, University of Pennsylvania Press [1962] 241 p. 22 cm. *1. Penn, William, 1644-1718. 2. James II, King of Great Britain, 1633-1701. 3. Gt. Brit. — Politics and government — 1660-1688. I. T.*
DA452.B89 1962   942.067   61-6620

Trevelyan, George Macaulay, 1876-   **III. 1240**
The English revolution, 1688-1689, by George Macaulay Trevelyan. London, Butterworth, [1939] 255 p. geneal. tab. 17 cm. (The home university library of modern knowledge) *1. Gt. Brit. — History — Revolution of 1688. I. T.*
DA452.T7 1939a   942.067   40-6687

DA460 – 462   William and Mary, 1689 – 1702

Baxter, Stephen Bartow, 1929-   **III. 1241**
William III and the defense of European liberty, 1650-1702, by Stephen B. Baxter. 1st American ed.] New York, Harcourt, Brace & World, [1966] xi,

462 p. illus., geneal. table, 2 maps, ports. 22 cm. *1. William III, King of Great Britain, 1650-1702. I. T.*
DA460.B3 1966a   942.0680924 (B)   66-19482

Turberville, Arthur Stanley, 1888-1945. III. 1242
The House of Lords in the reign of William III. Westport, Conn., Greenwood Press [1970] vi, 264 p. 23 cm. (Oxford historical and literary studies) Continued by the author's The House of Lords on the XVIII century. Reprint of the 1913 ed. *1. Great Britain. Parliament. House of Lords — History. 2. Great Britain — Politics and government — 1689-1702. I. T. (S)*
DA460.T84 1970   328.42/07/031   77-110877   ISBN:0837145589

Churchill, Winston Leonard Spencer, Sir, 1874-1965. III. 1243
Marlborough, his life and times. London, G. G. Harrap [1947] 2 v. illus., ports., maps (part fold., part col.) 23 cm. *1. Marlborough, John Churchill, 1st duke of, 1650-1722. 2. Gt. Brit. — History — 1660-1714.*
DA462.M3C45 1947   923.542   48-19354

DA470 – 522   18th Century

Charles-Edwards, Thomas Charles, comp. III. 1244
They saw it happen; an anthology of eyewitnesses' accounts of events in British history, 1689-1897, by T. Charles-Edwards and B. Richardson. With a foreword by David Mathew. Oxford, Blackwell, 1958. xix, 311 p. coats of arms (on lining papers) 22 cm. *1. Gt. Brit. — History — Sources. I. Richardson, Brian, joint comp. II. T.*
DA470.C4x   A58-6362

Cole, George Douglas Howard, 1889- III. 1245
The common people, 1746-1946, by G. D. H. Cole and Raymond Postgate. [2d ed., reprinted with minor corrections] London, Methuen [1956] 742 p. illus. 19 cm. *1. Gt. Brit. — History. 2. Gt. Brit. — Social conditions. 3. Gt. Brit. — Economic conditions. 4. Labor and laboring classes — Gt. Brit. — History. 5. Middle classes — Gt. Brit. — History. I. Postgate, Raymond William 1896- joint author. II. T.*
DA470.C6 1956   330.942   56-4032

Maccoby, Simon. III. 1246
The English radical tradition, 1763-1914. [1st U.S. ed.] New York, New York University Press [1957] 236 p. 21 cm. *1. Gt. Brit. — Politics and government. 2. Gt. Brit. — Social conditions. I. T.*
DA472.M3 1957   942.07   57-6377

Foord, Archibald S. III. 1247
His Majesty's Opposition, 1714-1830. Oxford, Clarendon Press, 1964. xi, 494 p. 22 cm. *1. Gt. Brit. — Politics and government — 1714-1837. 2. Political parties — Gt. Brit. 3. Gt. Brit. — Constitutional history. I. T.*
DA480.F6 1964   942.07   64-4287

Laprade, William Thomas, 1883- III. 1248
Public opinion and politics in eighteenth century England, to the fall of Walpole. Westport, Conn., Greenwood Press [1971] 463 p. 23 cm. Reprint of the 1936 ed. *1. Great Britain — Politics and government — 18th century. 2. Press — Great Britain. 3. Public opinion — Great Britain. I. T.*
DA480.L3 1971   942.06   70-114538   ISBN:0837148065

Leadam, Isaac Saunders, 1848-1913. III. 1249
The history of England, from the accession of Anne to the death of George II, 1702-1760. New York, Greenwood Press [1969] xx, 557 p. maps. 23 cm. (The Political history of England, 9) Reprint of the 1912 impression of the work first published in 1909. *1. Great Britain — History — Anne, 1702-1714. 2. Great Britain — History — George I-II, 1714-1760. I. T. (S)*
DA480.L4x (DA30.P762 vol. 9)   942.07   69-13970

Lecky, William Edward Hartpole, 1838-1903. III. 1250
A history of England in the eighteenth century. New York, D. Appleton, 1892-[93] New York, AMS Press [1968] 7 v. 23 cm. *1. Great Britain — History — 18th century. 2. Great Britain — Social life and customs — 18th century. I. T.*
DA480.L462   942.07/1   68-57226

Marshall, Dorothy. III. 1251
Eighteenth century England. New York, D. McKay Co. [1962] 537 p. illus. 23 cm. (A History of England in ten volumes) *1. Gt. Brit. — History — 18th cent. I. T.*
DA480.M37   942.07   62-52772

Michael, Wolfgang, 1862-1945. III. 1252
England under George I: the beginnings of the Hanoverian dynasty, by Wolfgang Michael. Translated and adapted from the German. London, Macmillan, 1936. viii, 406 p. 23 cm. (Studies in modern history) Abridged translation of v.1, books 2-3, of the author's Englische Geschichte im achtzehnten Jahrhundert. Translated and adapted under the supervision of Professor L. B. Namier. *1. Gt. Brit. — History — 18th cent. I. T. II. T:The beginnings of the Hanoverian dynasty.*
DA480.M62   942.071   36-16361

Namier, Lewis Bernstein, Sir, 1888-1960. III. 1253
Crossroads of power; essays on eighteenth-century England. Freeport, N.Y., Books for Libraries Press [1970, c1962] viii, 234 p. 23 cm. (His Collected essays, v. 2. Essay index reprint series.) *1. Great Britain — History — 18th century — Addresses, essays, lectures. I. T.*
DA480.N3 1970   942.07/08   77-119604   ISBN:0836916905

DA483   BIOGRAPHY. MEMOIRS

Robertson, Charles Grant, Sir, 1869-1948. III. 1254
Chatham and the British empire, by Sir Charles Grant Robertson. London, Hodder & Stoughton for the English Universities Press [1946] xiii, 200 p. front. (port.) illus. (map) 18 cm. (Teach yourself history library) *1. Pitt, William, 1st earl of Chatham, 1708-1778. 2. Gt. Brit. — History — 18th cent. I. T.*
DA483.P6R65   942.072   47-15569

Sherrard, Owen Aubrey, 1887- III. 1255
Lord Chatham; a war minister in the making. [London] Bodley Head [1952] 323 p. plates, ports. 23 cm. *1. Pitt, William, 1st earl of Chatham, 1708-1778. I. T.*
DA483.P6S5   923.242   52-4029

Sherrard, Owen Aubrey, 1887- III. 1256
Lord Chatham and America. London, Bodley Head [1958] 395 p. 22 cm. *1. Pitt, William, 1st earl of Chatham, 1708-1778. I. T.*
DA483.P6S52   923.242   58-1749

Sherrard, Owen Aubrey, 1887- III. 1257
Lord Chatham; Pitt and the Seven Years' War. [London] Bodley Head [1955] 437 p. map. 23 cm. *1. Pitt, William, 1st earl of Chatham, 1708-1778. 2. Seven Years' War, 1756-1763.*
DA483.P6S53   923.242   55-4187

Williams, Basil, 1867-1950. III. 1258
The life of William Pitt, earl of Chatham. New York, Octagon Books, 1966. 2 v. illus., port. 23 cm. *1. Pitt, William, 1st earl of Chatham, 1708-1778. 2. Gt. Brit. — Politics and government — 18th cent. I. T.*
DA483.P6W5 1966a   942.07/3/0924 (B)   66-30301

Walpole, Horace, 4th earl of Orford, 1717-1797. III. 1259
The Yale edition of Horace Walpole's correspondence, edited by W. S. Lewis. [New Haven, Yale University Press, 1937-   v. in illus., facsims., ports. 27 cm. *I. T.*
DA483.W2A12   52-4945

Walpole, Horace, earl of Orford, 1717-1797. III. 1260
Letters, selected by W. S. Lewis, with an introd. by R. W. Ketton-Cremer. London, Folio Society, 1951. 283 p. ports. 23 cm.
DA483.W2A499   928.2   52-1184

Ketton-Cremer, Robert Wyndham, 1906- III. 1261
Horace Walpole; a biography, by R. W. Ketton-Cremer. Ithaca, N.Y., Cornell University Press [1966, c1964] xv, 317 p. geneal. table, plates, ports. 23 cm. *1. Walpole, Horace, 4th earl of Orford, 1717-1797.*
DA483.W2K4 1966   828.609 (B)   66-11431

DA485   CIVILIZATION

George, Mary Dorothy (Gordon) III. 1262
England in transition; life and work in the eighteenth century. London, G. Routledge, 1931. vii, 229 p. plates. 20 cm. *1. Gt. Brit. — Social conditions. 2. Gt. Brit. — Economic conditions. 3. Labor and laboring classes — Gt. Brit. — History. 4. Gt. Brit. — Industries — History. I. T.*
DA485.G4   914.2   32-3501

Humphreys, Arthur Raleigh. III. 1263
The Augustan world; life and letters in eighteenth-century England. London, Methuen [1954] x, 283 p. 21 cm. *1. Gt. Brit. — History — 18th cent. 2. English literature — 18th cent. — History and criticism. 3. Gt. Brit. — Intellectual life. I. T.*
DA485.H85   942.07   A55-1694

Turberville, Arthur Stanley, 1888-1945. III. 1264
English men and manners in the eighteenth century, an illustrated narrative. New York, Oxford University Press, 1957. xxiii, 539 p. illus., maps, ports, facsims. 20 cm. (A Galaxy book, GB10) *1. Gt. Brit. — Social life and customs. 2. Gt. Brit. — History — 18th cent. 3. Gt. Brit. — Biography. 4. Eighteenth century. I. T.*
DA485.T75 1957   942.07   57-14002

Turberville, Arthur Stanley, 1888- ed. III. 1265
Johnson's England; an account of the life & manners of his age, edited by A. S. Turberville. Oxford, Clarendon Press, 1933. 2 v. front., illus., plates, ports., maps, plans, facsims. 23 cm. *1. Johnson, Samuel, 1709-1784. 2. Gt. Brit. —*

Civilization. 3. Gt. Brit. — Social life and customs. 4. Gt. Brit. — History — 18th cent. 5. Gt. Brit. — Intellectual life. I. T.
DA485.T77   914.2   34-592

Woodforde, James, 1740-1803. III. 1266
The diary of a country parson, 1758-1802. Passages selected and edited by John Beresford. London, New York, Oxford University Press [1949] xviii, 622 p. geneal. table. 16 cm. (The World's classics, 514) 1. England — Social life and customs. I. T.
DA485.W62 1949   914.2   50-14450

DA490 – 497   Anne, 1702 – 1714

Trevelyan, George Macaulay, 1876- III. 1267
England under Queen Anne ... by George Macaulay Trevelyan. London, New York [etc.] Longmans, Green, 1930-34. 3 v. front. (v.3, port.) maps (part fold.) 23 cm. 1. Gt. Brit. — History — Anne, 1702-1714. 2. Spanish succession, War of 1701-1714. I. T:Ramillies and the union with Scotland. II. T. III. T:Blenheim.
DA495.T7   942.069   30-23326

Williams, Basil, 1867- III. 1268
Stanhope, a study in eighteenth-century war and diplomacy, by Basil Williams. Oxford, Clarendon Press, 1932. xv, 478 p. geneal. tab. front., pl., ports., fold. maps. 23 cm. 1. Stanhope, James Stanhope, 1st earl, 1673-1721. 2. Gt. Brit. — Foreign relations — 18th cent.
DA497.S8W5   923.242   32-24011

DA498 – 503   George I, 1714 – 1727.
George II, 1727 – 1760

Williams, Basil, 1867-1950. III. 1269
The Whig supremacy, 1714-1760. 2d ed. rev. by C. H. Stuart. Oxford, Clarendon Press, 1962. xix, 504 p. maps, plan. 23 cm. (The Oxford history of England, 11) 1. Great Britain — Politics and government — 1714-1760. 2. Great Britain — History — George I-II, 1714-1760. 3. Great Britain — Social conditions. I. T. (S)
DA498.W5 1962   942.071   62-2655

Gipson, Lawrence Henry, 1880- III. 1270
The British Empire before the American Revolution. [Completely rev.] New York, Knopf, 1958-   v.   maps. 25 cm. 1. Great Britain — History — 18th century. 2. Ireland — History — 18th century. 3. Great Britain — Colonies — America. 4. United States — History — Colonial period, ca. 1600-1775. I. T.
DA500.G52   942.072   58-9670

Owen, John Beresford. III. 1271
The rise of the Pelhams, by John B. Owen. New York, Barnes & Noble [1971] x, 357 p. 23 cm. Reprint of the 1957 ed. 1. Pelham, Henry, 1695?-1754. 2. Gt. Brit. — Politics and government — 1727-1760. I. T.
DA500.O85 1971   942.07/2   76-24488   ISBN:0389041459

Hervey, John Hervey, Baron, 1696-1743. III. 1272
Some materials towards memoirs of the reign of King George II. Edited by Romney Sedgwick. New York, AMS Press [1970] 3 v. (lx, 1003 p.) ports. 23 cm. Title on spine: Memoirs. Originally published in 1848 under title: Memoirs of the reign of George the Second. Reprint of the 1931 ed. 1. Gt. Brit. — History — George II, 1727-1760. 2. George II, King of Great Britain, 1683-1760. I. Sedgwick, Romney, 1894- ed. II. T.
DA501.A3H47 1970   942.07/2   79-119102   ISBN:404033008

Kramnick, Isaac. III. 1273
Bolingbroke and his circle; the politics of nostalgia in the age of Walpole. Cambridge, Mass., Harvard University Press, 1968. xiii, 321 p. port. 24 cm. (Harvard political studies) 1. Bolingbroke, Henry Saint-John, 1st viscount, 1678-1751. I. T. (S)
DA501.B6K7 1968   942.07/1   68-15639

Chesterfield, Philip Dormer Stanhope, 4th earl of, 1694-1773. III. 1274
The letters of Philip Dormer Stanhope, 4th earl of Chesterfield; edited, with an introduction, by Bonamy Dobrée. London, Eyre & Spottiswoode; New York, Viking Press, 1932. 6 v. front. (port.) fold. geneal. tab. 23 cm. "Previous important editions": v.1, p. xvii-xviii; "List of the chief authorities referred to in the Introduction": v.1, p. 3-4. I. Dobrée, Bonamy, 1891- ed.
DA501.C5A32   923.242   32-16739

Shellabarger, Samuel, 1888-1954. III. 1275
Lord Chesterfield and his world. New York, Biblo and Tannen, 1971 [c1951] 456 p. port. 23 cm. 1. Chesterfield, Philip Dormer Stanhope, 4th Earl of, 1694-1773. I. T.
DA501.C5S52 1971   942.07/1/0924   72-156737   ISBN:0819602728

Williams, Basil, 1867- III. 1276
Carteret and Newcastle; a contrast in contemporaries. [Hamden, Conn.] Archon Books, 1966. 240 p. fold. geneal. tables, ports. 22 cm. Reprint of the 1943 ed. 1. Granville, John Carteret, earl, 1690-1763. 2. Newcastle, Thomas Pelham-Holles, 1st duke of, 1693-1768. 3. Gt. Brit. — Politics and government — 18th cent. I. T.
DA501.G7W5 1966   942.070922   67-123

Montagu, Mary (Pierrepont) Wortley, Lady, 1689-1762. III. 1277
The complete letters of Lady Mary Wortley Montagu. Edited by Robert Halsband. Oxford, Clarendon Press, 1965-67. 3 v. illus., facsims., ports. 23 cm. I. Halsband, Robert, 1914- ed. II. T.
DA501.M7A48   826/.5   66-758

Halsband, Robert, 1914- III. 1278
The life of Lady Mary Wortley Montagu. Oxford, Clarendon Press, 1956 [i.e. 1957] 313 p. illus. 23 cm. 1. Montagu, Mary (Pierrepont) Wortley, Lady, 1689-1762.
DA501.M7H3   928.2   56-14373

Plumb, John Harold, 1911- III. 1279
Sir Robert Walpole [by] J. H. Plumb. Clifton [N.J.] A. M. Kelley, 1973-   v. illus. 23 cm. (Houghton Mifflin reprint editions) Reprint of the 1956-61 ed. 1. Walpole, Robert, Earl of Orford, 1676-1745.
DA501.W2P522   942.06/9/0924 (B)   72-128080
ISBN:0678035512 (v. 1)

DA505 – 522   George III, 1760 – 1820

Butterfield, Herbert, 1900- III. 1280
George III and the historians. Rev. ed. New York, Macmillan, 1959. 304 p. 22 cm. 1. George III, King of Great Britain, 1738-1820. 2. Gt. Brit. — History — George III, 1760-1820 — Historiography. I. T.
DA505.B974 1959   942.073   59-7967

Butterfield, Herbert, Sir, 1900- III. 1281
George III, Lord North, and the people, 1779-80, by H. Butterfield. New York, Russell & Russell [1968] 407 p. 23 cm. Reprint of the 1949 ed. 1. George III, King of Great Britain, 1738-1820. 2. North, Frederick North, Baron, 1732-1792. 3. Great Britain — Politics and government — 1760-1789. I. T.
DA505.B975 1968   942.07/3   68-10907

Harlow, Vincent Todd, 1898-1961. III. 1282
The founding of the Second British Empire, 1763-1793. London, New York, Longmans, Green [1952-64] 2 v. maps. 25 cm. 1. Gt. Brit. — Colonies — History. 2. Gt. Brit. — History — George III, 1760-1820. I. T:British Empire, 1763-1793.
DA505.H37   942.073   52-11742

Hunt, William, 1842-1931. III. 1283
The history of England from the accession of George III to the close of Pitt's first administration (1760-1801) New York, Greenwood Press [1969] xviii, 495 p. 3 maps. 23 cm. (The Political history of England, v. 10) Reprint of the 1905 ed. 1. Great Britain — History — George III, 1760-1820. I. T. (S)
DA505.H8x (DA30.P762 vol. 10)   942.07/03   69-13944

Namier, Lewis Bernstein, Sir, 1888-1960. III. 1284
England in the age of the American Revolution. 2d ed. New York, St Martin's Press, 1961 [i.e. 1962] 450 p. 23 cm. 1. Gt. Brit. — History — George II, 1727-1760. 2. Gt. Brit. — History — 1760-1789. 3. U.S. — History — Revolution — Causes. I. T.
DA505.N25 1962   942.072   62-2311

Pares, Richard, 1902-1958. III. 1285
King George III and the politicians; the Ford lectures delivered in the University of Oxford, 1951-2. London, New York [etc.] Oxford U.P., 1967. [7], 214 p. 21 cm. (Ford lectures, 1951-2. Oxford paperback no. 130.) 1. George III, King of Great Britain, 1738-1820. 2. Great Britain — Politics and government — 1760-1820. I. T. (S:Oxford. University. Ford lectures, 1951-52)
DA505.P3 1967   320.9/42   68-93556   ISBN:0198950131

Veitch, George Stead, 1885- III. 1286
The genesis of parliamentary reform. With an introd. by Ian R. Christie. [Hamden, Conn.] Archon Books, 1965. xxxv, 399 p. 23 cm. Reprint of a work first published in 1913. 1. Gt. Brit. Parliament — Reform. 2. Gt. Brit. — Politics and government — 1760-1820. 3. Political parties — Gt. Brit. 4. France — History — Revolution — Influence. I. T.
DA505.V5 1965   328.4209   66-959

Watson, John Steven. III. 1287
The reign of George III, 1760-1815. Oxford, Clarendon Press, 1960. xviii, 637 p. fold. maps. 23 cm. (The Oxford history of England, 12) 1. Great Britain — History — George III, 1760-1820. (S)
DA505.W38   942.073   60-50916

DA506   Biography. Memoirs

Brooke, John. III. 1288
King George III. With a foreword by H. R. H. the Prince of Wales. New York, McGraw-Hill [1972] xix, 411 p. col. front., illus. 26 cm. (American

| DA530 | Great Britain | III. 1312 |

Revolution bicentennial program) *1. George III, King of Great Britain, 1738-1820. I. T. (S)*
DA506.A2B75   942.07/3/0924 (B)   72-2011   ISBN:0070080593

George III, king of Great Britain, 1738-1820. III. 1289
Letters from George III to Lord Bute, 1756-1766; edited with an introduction by Romney Sedgwick. London, Macmillan, 1939. lxviii, 277 p. 23 cm. (Studies in modern history.) *1. Gt. Brit. — History — George III, 1760-1820. I. Sedgwick, Romney, 1894- ed. II. Bute, John Stuart, 3d earl of, 1713-1792.*
DA506.A2x   923.142   A41-4681

Burke, Edmund, 1729?-1797.   III. 1290
A letter to the sheriffs of Bristol; a speech at Bristol on parliamentary conduct; a letter to a noble lord; ed. by W. Murison. Cambridge [Eng.] The University Press, 1920. xxix, 312 p. 18 cm. (Pitt press series) *1. Bedford, Francis Russell, 5th duke of, 1765-1802. 2. U.S. — History — Revolution. 3. Gt. Brit. — Politics and government — 1760-1789. I. Murison, William, 1863- ed.*
DA506.B85 1921   22-6624

Burke, Edmund, 1729?-1797.   III. 1291
The correspondence of Edmund Burke. Edited by Thomas W. Copeland. Cambridge, University Press; Chicago, University of Chicago Press, 1958- v. port. 24 cm.
DA506.B9A18   923.242   58-5615

Cone, Carl B.   III. 1292
Burke and the nature of politics. [Lexington] University of Kentucky Press [1957-1964] 2 v. illus., port. 25 cm. *1. Burke, Edmund, 1729?-1797. 2. Gt. Brit. — Politics and government — 1760-1820. I. T.*
DA506.B9C54   942.07   57-11380

Magnus, Philip Montefiore, Sir, bart., 1906-   III. 1293
Edmund Burke, a life, by Sir Philip Magnus. 1st ed. London, J. Murray [1939] xiii, 367 p. illus., incl. facsim., plates, ports. 23 cm. *1. Burke, Edmund, 1729?-1797.*
DA506.B9M3   923.242   39-30394

Reid, Loren Dudley, 1905-   III. 1294
Charles James Fox: a man for the people [by] Loren Reid. [Columbia] University of Missouri Press [1969] xiv, 475 p. illus. 23 cm. *1. Fox, Charles James, 1749-1806. 2. Great Britain — Politics and government — 1760-1820.*
DA506.F7R38 1969   942.07/3/0924 (B)   69-19319   ISBN:0826200761

Walpole, Horace, 4th earl of Orford, 1717-1797.   III. 1295
Horace Walpole: memoirs and portraits. Edited by Matthew Hodgart. [Rev. ed.] New York, Macmillan [1963] xxxi, 264 p. illus., ports. 21 cm. (Historical memoirs) *1. Gt. Brit. — History — George II, 1727-1760. 2. Gt. Brit. — History — 1760-1789. I. Hodgart, Matthew John Caldwell, ed.*
DA506.W2A13 1963   942.073   63-17297

DA510 – 512   1760 – 1789

Brooke, John.   III. 1296
The Chatham administration, 1766-1768. London, Macmillan; New York, St. Martin's Press, 1956. 400 p. 23 cm. (England in the age of the American Revolution) *1. Pitt, William, 1st earl of Chatham, 1708-1778. 2. Gt. Brit. — Politics and government — 1760-1820. I. T.*
DA510.B7   942.073   56-14302

Christie, Ian R.   III. 1297
The end of North's ministry, 1780-1782. London, Macmillan; New York, St. Martin's Press, 1958. xiii, 428 p. 23 cm. (England in the age of the American Revolution) *1. North, Frederick North, baron, 1732-1792. 2. Gt. Brit. — Politics and government — 1760-1789. I. T. (S)*
DA510.C45   942.073   58-4847

Guttridge, George Herbert, 1898-   III. 1298
English whiggism and the American revolution, by G. H. Guttridge. Berkeley, University of California Press, 1942. 153 p. 24 cm. (University of California publications in history. Vol. XXVIII) *1. Whig party (Gt. Brit.) 2. Gt. Brit. — Politics and government — 1760-1789. 3. U.S. — History — Revolution. I. T.*
DA510.G87 (E173.C15)   942.073   A42-2021

Ritcheson, Charles R.   III. 1299
British politics and the American Revolution. [1st ed.] Norman, University of Oklahoma Press [1954] xv, 320 p. ports. 22 cm. *1. Gt. Brit. — Politics and government — 1760-1789. 2. U.S. — History — Revolution — Causes. I. T.*
DA510.R5   942.073   54-5933

Postgate, Raymond William, 1896-   III. 1300
That devil Wilkes, by R. W. Postgate. New York, Vanguard Press [c1929] 275 p. front. (port.) 24 cm. *1. Wilkes, John, 1727-1797. 2. Gt. Brit. — Politics and government — 1760-1789. I. T.*
DA512.W6P6   29-28532

Rudé, George F. E.   III. 1301
Wilkes and liberty; a social study of 1763 to 1774. Oxford, Clarendon Press, 1962. xvi, 240 p. front. 23 cm. *1. Wilkes, John, 1727-1797. 2. Gt. Brit. — Politics and government — 1760-1789. I. T.*
DA512.W6R8   923.242   62-1596

DA520 – 522   1789 – 1820.
The Regency

Cobban, Alfred, ed.   III. 1302
The debate on the French Revolution, 1789-1800. 2d ed. London, A. and C. Black [1963, c1960] xx, 495 p. 23 cm. (The British political tradition, book 2) Imprint covered by label: New York, Barnes & Noble. *1. France — History — Revolution — Foreign public opinion. 2. Gt. Brit. — Politics and government — 1789-1820. 3. Political science — History — Gt. Brit. I. T. (S)*
DA520.Cx (DA42.B75 bk.2 1963)   61-17763

Ginter, Donald E., comp.   III. 1303
Whig organization in the general election of 1790; selections from the Blair Adam papers, edited by Donald E. Ginter. Berkeley, University of California Press, 1967. lx, 276 p. 23 cm. *1. Adam, William, 1751-1839. 2. Portland, William Henry Cavendish Bentinck, 3d duke of, 1738-1809. 3. Whig Party (Gt. Brit.) 4. Gt. Brit. — Politics and government — 1789-1820. I. T.*
DA520.G5 1967   942.07/3   67-13999

Temperley, Harold William Vazeille, 1879-1939.   III. 1304
Life of Canning. New York, Haskell House, 1968. 293 p. illus. 24 cm. "Haskell House catalogue item #247." Reprint of the 1905 ed. *1. Canning, George, 1770-1827. I. T.*
DA522.C2T3 1968   942.07/4/0924 (B)   68-25269

Osborne, John Walter, 1927-   III. 1305
William Cobbett; his thought and his times, by John W. Osborne. New Brunswick, N.J., Rutgers University Press [1966] x, 272 p. port. 22 cm. *1. Cobbett, William, 1763-1835.*
DA522.C5O8   070.0924   66-18874

Brock, William Ranulf.   III. 1306
Lord Liverpool and Liberal Toryism, 1820 to 1827, by W. R. Brock. [2d ed. Hamden, Conn.] Archon Books, 1967. 300 p. ports. 20 cm. *1. Liverpool, Robert Banks Jenkinson, 2d Earl of, 1770-1828. 2. Gt. Brit. — Politics and government — 1820-1830. I. T.*
DA522.L7B7 1967a   942.07/4/0924 (B)   67-4292

Bartlett, Christopher John.   III. 1307
Castlereagh [by] C. J. Bartlett. New York, Scribner [1967, c1966] ix, 292 p. illus. ports. 22 cm. *1. Londonderry, Robert Stewart, 2d marquis of, 1769-1822. I. T.*
DA522.L8B3 1967   942.0730924 (B)   67-16525

Ehrman, John.   III. 1308
The younger Pitt. New York, Dutton [1969- v. illus., ports. (1 col.) 26 cm. *1. Pitt, William, 1759-1806. I. T.*
DA522.P6E36   942.07/3/0924   78-87178

DA530 – 565   19th Century

Briggs, Asa, 1921-   III. 1309
The age of improvement. London, New York, Longmans, Green [1959] 547 p. 23 cm. (A History of England) *1. Gt. Brit. — History — George III, 1760-1820. 2. Gt. Brit. — History — 19th cent. I. T.*
DA530.B68   942.07   59-816

Halévy, Élie, 1870-1937.   III. 1310
A history of the English people in the nineteenth century. Translated from the French by E. I. Watkin. [2d rev. ed.] London, E. Benn [1949-52] 6 v. in 7. ports. 23 cm. Vol.1 translated by E. I. Watkin and D. A. Barker, with an introduction by R. B. McCallum. Vol.4 "contains in part I a reprint of The age of Peel and Cobden and in part II Mr. R. B. McCallum's essay and chronological table." — p.v. *1. Gt. Brit. — History — 19th cent. 2. Gt. Brit. — Civilization. 3. Gt. Brit. — Economic conditions. 4. Gt. Brit. — History — 20th cent.*
DA530.H443   A52-9366

Seton-Watson, Robert William, 1879-1951.   III. 1311
Britain in Europe, 1789-1914; a survey of foreign policy. New York, H. Fertig, 1968. ix, 716 p. 24 cm. Reprint of the 1937 ed. *1. Great Britain — Foreign relations — 19th century. 2. Europe — Politics 1789-1900. 3. Great Britain — Foreign relations — 20th century. 4. Europe — Politics — 20th century. I. T.*
DA530.S4 1968   327.42   68-9599

Trevelyan, George Macaulay, 1876-1962.   III. 1312
British history in the nineteenth century and after, 1782-1919. New York,

Harper & Row [1966] xvi, 512 p. maps. 21 cm. (Harper Torchbooks. Academy library) First published in 1922 under title: British history in the nineteenth century (1782-1901) Reprint of second ed., 1937. *1. Gt. Brit. — History — 19th cent. 2. Gt. Brit. — History — 20th cent. I. T.*
DA530.T7 1966   942   66-1980

Woodward, Ernest Llewellyn, Sir, 1890-   III. 1313
The age of reform, 1815-1870. 2d ed. Oxford, Clarendon Press, 1962. xix, 681 p. maps (part fold.) 23 cm. (The Oxford history of England, 13) *1. Gt. Brit. — Politics and government — 19th cent. 2. Gt. Brit. — History — 19th cent. 3. Gt. Brit. — Social conditions. I. T. (S)*
DA530.W6 1962   942.07   62-4675

Himmelfarb, Gertrude.   III. 1314
Victorian minds. [1st ed.] New York, Knopf, 1968. xiii, 392, v. p. 22 cm. Essays. *1. Gt. Brit. — Intellectual life — 19th cent. I. T.*
DA533.H55   942.081   67-18617

Houghton, Walter Edwards, 1904-   III. 1315
The Victorian frame of mind, 1830-1870. New Haven, Published for Wellesley College by Yale University Press, 1957. 467 p. 24 cm. *1. Gt. Brit. — Civilization. I. T.*
DA533.H85   942.081   57-6339

Kitson Clark, George Sidney Roberts, 1900-   III. 1316
The making of Victorian England. Cambridge, Harvard University Press, 1962. xiii, 312 p. 23 cm. (Ford lectures, 1960) *1. Great Britain — Civilization. I. T. (S:Oxford University: Ford lectures, 1960.)*
DA533.K55   914.2   62-51827

Somervell, David Churchill, 1885-   III. 1317
English thought in the nineteenth century. 5th ed. London, Methuen [1947] x, 241 p. 20 cm. *1. Gt. Brit. — Intellectual life. 2. Nineteenth century. I. T.*
DA533.S65x   A50-7103

Williams, Raymond.   III. 1318
Culture and society, 1780-1950. New York, Columbia University Press, 1958. 363 p. 23 cm. *1. Gt. Brit. — Intellectual life. I. T.*
DA533.W6 1958   914.2   58-4388

DA535 – 542   1801 – 1837

Webster, Charles Kingsley, Sir, 1886-1961.   III. 1319
The foreign policy of Palmerston, 1830-1841; Britain, the liberal movement, and the Eastern question. New York, Humanities Press, 1969. 2 v. (xi, 914 p.) port. 22 cm. *1. Palmerston, Henry John Temple, 3d Viscount, 1784-1865. 2. Great Britain — Foreign relations — 19th century. 3. Europe — Politics — 1815-1871. I. T.*
DA535.W4 1969   327.42   72-10921

New, Chester William, 1882-   III. 1320
The life of Henry Brougham to 1830. Oxford, Clarendon Press, 1961. 458 p. illus. 23 cm. *1. Brougham and Vaux, Henry Peter Brougham, baron, 1778-1868.*
DA536.B7N4   923.242   61-66248

Woodham Smith, Cecil Blanche (FitzGerald) 1896-   III. 1321
The reason why, by Cecil Woodham-Smith. [2d ed.] New York, McGraw-Hill [1971, c1953] 287 p. illus., maps, ports. 24 cm. *1. Cardigan, James Thomas Brudenell, 7th Earl of, 1797-1868. 2. Lucan, George Charles Bingham, 3d Earl of, 1800-1888. 3. Balaklava, Battle of, 1854. I. T.*
DA536.C3W6 1971   942.081/0924   72-155886   ISBN:0070716706

Hobson, John Atkinson, 1858-1940.   III. 1322
Richard Cobden: the international man, by J. A. Hobson. New ed.; with introduction by Neville Masterman. London, Benn; New York, Barnes & Noble, 1968. ix, 421 p. port. 23 cm. Previous ed., London: Fisher Unwin, 1919. *1. Cobden, Richard, 1804-1965. I. The international man.*
DA536.C6H6 1968   942.081/0924   75-351313

Read, Donald.   III. 1323
Cobden and Bright: a Victorian political partnership. New York, St. Martin's Press, 1968 [c1967] ix, 275 p. illus., ports. 23 cm. *1. Cobden, Richard, 1804-1865. 2. Bright, John, 1811-1889. I. T.*
DA536.C6R4 1968   942.081/0922   68-15436

Greville, Charles Cavendish Fulke, 1794-1865.   III. 1324
The great world; portraits and scenes from Greville's memoirs, 1814-1860. Edited with an introd. by Louis Kronenberger. [1st ed.] Garden City, N.Y., Doubleday, 1963. 354 p. 22 cm. *1. Gt. Brit. — History — 19th cent. I. T.*
DA536.G8A423   942.08   63-7703

Macaulay, Thomas Babington Macaulay, 1st baron, 1800-1859.   III. 1325
Speeches by Lord Macaulay, with his Minute on Indian education; selected with an introduction and notes, by G. M. Young. London, Oxford University Press [1935] xxii, 361 p. 16 cm. (The world's classics. [CDXXXIII]) On cover: Selected speeches. *I. Young, George Malcolm, 1882-ed.*
DA536.M15A35   824.83   36-27128

Knowles, David, 1896-   III. 1326
Lord Macaulay, 1800-1859. Cambridge, [Eng.] University Press, 1960. 30 p. 19 cm. *1. Macaulay, Thomas Babington Macaulay, 1st baron, 1800-1859.*
DA536.M15K5   928.2   60-2407

Cecil, David, Lord, 1902-   III. 1327
Melbourne. Indianapolis, Bobbs-Merrill [1954] 450 p. ports. 22 cm. "Parts I and II were published in 1939 under the title of The young Melbourne." *1. Melbourne, William Lamb, 2d viscount, 1779-1848. 2. Lamb, Caroline (Ponsonby) Lady, 1785-1828. 3. Victoria, Queen of Great Britain, 1819-1901.*
DA536.M5C5 1954   923.242   54-9486

Kitson Clark, George Sidney Roberts, 1900-   III. 1328
Peel and the Conservative Party; a study in party politics, 1832-1841 [by] George Kitson Clark. [2d ed. Hamden, Conn.] Archon Books, 1964. xii, 515 p. illus., port. 23 cm. *1. Peel, Robert, Sir, bart., 1788-1850. 2. Gt. Brit. — Politics and government — 1830-1837. 3. Conservative Party (Gt. Brit.) I. T.*
DA536.P3C6 1964   942.075   65-7481

Gash, Norman.   III. 1329
Mr. Secretary Peel; the life of Sir Robert Peel to 1830. Cambridge, Harvard University Press, 1961. xiv, 693 p. ports. 23 cm. *1. Peel, Robert, Sir, bart., 1788-1850.*
DA536.P3G3   923.242   61-9686

Stanhope, John.   III. 1330
The Cato Street Conspiracy. London, J. Cape [1962] 190 p. facsims., ports. 21 cm. *1. Cato Street Conspiracy, 1820.*
DA537.S8   64-54787

DA550 – 565   VICTORIAN ERA (1837 – 1901)

Bourne, Kenneth.   III. 1331
The foreign policy of Victorian England, 1830-1902. Oxford, Clarendon P., 1970. xii, 531 p. 23 cm. *1. Gt. Brit. — Foreign relations — 1837-1901. 2. Gt. Brit. — History — Victoria, 1837-1901 — Sources. I. T.*
DA550.B68 1970   327.42   75-543411   ISBN:0198730071

Burn, William Laurence.   III. 1332
The age of equipoise; a study of the mid-Victorian generation. New York, Norton [1964] 340 p. 24 cm. *1. Great Britain — History — Victoria, 1837-1901. 2. Great Britain — Civilization. I. T.*
DA550.B8   914.2   64-2007

McDowell, Robert Brendan.   III. 1333
British conservatism, 1832-1914. London, Faber and Faber [1959] 191 p. 23 cm. *1. Gt. Brit. — Politics and government — 1837-1901. I. T.*
DA550.M27   942.08   60-1412

Southgate, Donald George.   III. 1334
The passing of the Whigs, 1832-1886, by Donald Southgate. London, Macmillan; New York, St Martin's Press, 1962. xvi, 488 p. illus., geneal. tables, ports. 23 cm. *1. Gt. Brit. — Politics and government — 1837-1901. I. T.*
DA550.S65 1962   942.08   62-51525

Young, George Malcolm, 1882-   III. 1335
Victorian England; portrait of an age. 2d ed. London, Oxford University Press [1960] 219 p. 20 cm. (Oxford paperbacks, no. 12) *1. Gt. Brit. — History — Victoria, 1837-1901. I. T.*
DA550.Y6 1960   942.08   60-51632

Longford, Elizabeth (Harman) Pakenham, countess of, 1906-   III. 1336
Queen Victoria: born to succeed, by Elizabeth Longford. [1st ed.] New York, Harper & Row [1965, c1964] 635 p. illus., fold. geneal. table, ports. 25 cm. First published in London in 1964 under title: Victoria R.I. *1. Victoria, Queen of Great Britain, 1819-1901. I. T.*
DA554.L6 1965   923.142   64-25117

Strachey, Giles Lytton, 1880-1932.   III. 1337
Queen Victoria, by Lytton Strachey. London, Chatto & Windus, 1969. [6], 257 p. 23 cm. *1. Victoria, Queen of Great Britain, 1819-1901.*
DA554.S7 1969   942.081/0924 (B)   72-435370   ISBN:701111313

Gash, Norman.   III. 1338
Reaction and reconstruction in English politics, 1832-1852. Oxford, Clarendon Press, 1965. 227 p. 22 cm. (The Ford lectures, 1964) *1. Gt. Brit. — Politics and government — 1830-1837. 2. Gt. Brit. — Politics and government — 1837-1901. I. T. (S:Oxford. University. Ford lectures, 1964)*
DA559.7.G35   66-609

Hovell, Mark, 1888-1916.   III. 1339
The Chartist movement. Edited and completed with a memoir by T. F. Tout.

[3d ed.] New York, A. M. Kelley, 1967. xxxvii, 327 p. 20 cm. *1. Chartism. I. Tout, Thomas Frederick, 1855-1929, ed. II. T.*
DA559.7H7 1967   329.9/42   67-4890

Ausubel, Herman. III. 1340
The late Victorians, a short history. New York, Van Nostrand [c1955] 188 p. 18 cm. (An Anvil original, no. 3) *1. Gt. Brit. — History — Victoria, 1837-1901. I. T.*
DA560.A88   942.081   55-6245

Briggs, Asa, 1921- III. 1341
Victorian people; a reassessment of persons and themes, 1851-67. Rev. ed. [Chicago] University of Chicago Press [1970] ix, 312 p. illus. 21 cm. *1. Great Britain — History — Victoria, 1837-1901. 2. Great Britain — Biography. I. T.*
DA560.B84 1970   914.2/03/810922 (B)   71-16973   ISBN:0226074900

Ensor, Robert Charles Kirkwood, 1877- III. 1342
England, 1870-1914, by R. C. K. Ensor. Oxford, The Clarendon Press, 1936. xxiii, 634 p., 1 l. 7 fold. maps. 23 cm. (The Oxford history of England) *1. Gt. Brit. — History — Victoria, 1867-1901. 2. Gt. Brit. — History — 20th cent. I. T.*
DA560.E6   942.08   36-10581

Howard, Christopher. III. 1343
Splendid isolation: a study of ideas concerning Britain's international position and foreign policy during the later years of the third Marquis of Salisbury. London, Melbourne [etc.] Macmillan; New York, St. Martin's P., 1967. xv, 120 p. 22 1/2 cm. *1. Gt. Brit. — Foreign relations — 1837-1901. I. T.*
DA560.H59   327.42   67-19736

Lowe, Cedric James. III. 1344
The reluctant imperialists; British foreign policy, 1878-1902 [by] C. J. Lowe. [1st American ed. New York] Macmillan [1969, c1967] xi, 417 p. maps. 21 cm. *1. Great Britain — Foreign relations — 1837-1901. I. T.*
DA560.L83 1969   327.42   69-10896

DA562 – 565   Biography. Memoirs

DA563 – 564   *Prime Ministers*

Gladstone, William Ewart, 1809-1898. III. 1345
The Gladstone diaries; edited by M. R. D. Foot. Oxford, Clarendon Press, 1968- v. illus., facsims., plates, ports. 24 cm. *I. Foot, Michael Richard Daniel, ed. II. T.*
DA563.A34   942.081/0924 (B)   68-59613

Knaplund, Paul, 1885- III. 1346
Gladstone and Britain's imperial policy. [Hamden, Conn.] Archon Books, 1966. 256 p. port. 23 cm. Reprint of the 1927 ed. *1. Gladstone, William Ewart, 1809-1898. 2. Gt. Brit. — Colonies. I. T.*
DA563.4.K5 1966   325.342   67-124

Magnus, Philip Montefiore, Sir, bart., 1906- III. 1347
Gladstone, a biography. New York, Dutton [1954] 482 p. illus. 22 cm. *1. Gladstone, William Ewart, 1809-1898.*
DA563.4.M3 1954a   923.242   54-11697

Morley, John Morley, Viscount, 1838-1923. III. 1348
The life of William Ewart Gladstone. New York, Greenwood Press [1968, c1903] 3 v. illus. 24 cm. *1. Gladstone, William Ewart, 1809-1898. 2. Great Britain — Politics and government — 1837-1901. I. T.*
DA563.4.M8 1968   942.081/092/4 (B)   68-5/630

Hammond, John Lawrence Le Breton, 1872-1949. III. 1349
Gladstone and liberalism, by J. L. Hammond and M. R. D. Foot. New York, Collier Books [1966] 180 p. 18 cm. *1. Gladstone, William Ewart, 1809-1898. 2. Liberal Party (Gt. Brit.) 3. Gt. Brit. — Politics and government — 1837-1901. I. Foot, Michael Richard Daniel, joint author. II. T.*
DA563.5.H28 1966   942.0810924 (B)   66-27708

Hammond, John Lawrence Le Breton, 1872-1949. III. 1350
Gladstone and the Irish nation, by J. L. Hammond. London, New York, Longmans, Green [1938] xvii, 768 p. front., ports. 23 cm. *1. Gladstone, William Ewart, 1809-1898. 2. Parnell, Charles Stewart, 1846-1891. 3. Irish question. 4. Ireland — Politics and government — 1837-1901. 5. Home rule (Ireland) I. T.*
DA563.5.H3   923.242   39-5001

Shannon, R. T. III. 1351
Gladstone and the Bulgarian agitation 1876. With an introd. by G. S. R. Kitson Clark. London, New York, Nelson [1963] xxviii, 308 p. 23 cm. (Nelson's studies in modern history) *1. Gladstone, William Ewart, 1809-1898. 2. Bulgarian massacres, 1876-1877. 3. Public opinion — Gt. Brit. I. T.*
DA563.5.S48 1963   942.08   64-1294

Blake, Robert, 1916- III. 1352
Disraeli. New York, St. Martin's Press [1967, c1966] xxiv, 819 p. illus., ports. 24 cm. *1. Beaconsfield, Benjamin Disraeli, 1st earl of, 1804-1881.*
DA564.B3B6 1967   942.081/0924 (B)   67-11837

Monypenny, William Flavelle, 1866-1912. III. 1353
The life of Benjamin Disraeli, Earl of Beaconsfield, by William Flavelle Monypenny and George Earle Buckle. New and rev. ed. New York, Russell & Russell [1968] 4 v. illus., port. 23 cm. Reprint of the 1929 ed. *1. Beaconsfield, Benjamin Disraeli, 1st Earl of, 1804-1881. 2. Great Britain — Politics and government — 1837-1901. I. Buckle, George Earle, 1854-1935. II. T.*
DA564.B3M9 1968   942.081/0924 (B)   68-25044

James, Robert Rhodes, 1933- III. 1354
Rosebery, a biography of Archibald Philip, fifth earl of Rosebery. [Reprinted, with some amendments] London, Weidenfeld and Nicolson [1963] xiv, 534 p. illus., ports., map. 23 cm. *1. Rosebery, Archibald Philip Primrose, 5th earl of, 1847-1929.*
DA564.R7J3 1963   63-24262

Cecil, Gwendolen, Lady, 1860- III. 1355
Life of Robert, marquis of Salisbury, by his daughter, Lady Gwendolen Cecil ... London, Hodder and Stoughton, 1921- v. fronts., ports. 24 cm. *1. Salisbury, Robert Arthur Talbot Gascoyne-Cecil, 3d marquis of, 1830-1903. 2. Gt. Brit. — Politics and government — 1837-1901. 3. Eastern question.*
DA564.S2C4   22-280

DA565   *Other Contemporaries*

Trevelyan, George Macaulay, 1876-1962. III. 1356
The life of John Bright. Westport, Conn., Greenwood Press [1971] x, [1], 480 p. illus. 23 cm. Reprint of the 1913 ed. *1. Bright, John, 1811-1889. 2. Great Britain — Politics and government — 19th century. I. T.*
DA565.B8T8 1971   942.081/0924 (B)   72-110873   ISBN:083714552X

Spender, John Alfred, 1862- III. 1357
The life of the Right Hon. Sir Henry Campbell-Bannerman, by J. A. Spender. London, Hodder and Stoughton [1923] 2 v. fronts., plates, ports., facsim. 23 cm. *1. Campbell-Bannerman, Henry, Sir, 1836-1908. 2. Gt. Brit. — Politics and government — 1837-1901. 3. Gt. Brit. — Politics and government — 1901-1910.*
DA565.C15S6   24-765

Chamberlain, Joseph, 1836-1914. III. 1358
A political memoir, 1880-92. Edited from the original manuscript by C. H. D. Howard. London, Batchworth Press [1953] xx, 340 p. ports. 22 cm. *1. Gt. Brit. — Politics and government — 1837-1901.*
DA565.C4A32   942.081   53-2236

Garvin, James Louis, 1868-1947. III. 1359
The life of Joseph Chamberlain, by J. L. Garvin. London, Macmillan, 1932-[69] 6 v. plates, ports, 23 cm. On spine, v.5-6: Joseph Chamberlain and the tariff reform campaign. Vols. 4-6 by Julian Amery. Vols. 5-6 have imprint: London, Macmillan; New York, St. Martin's Press. *1. Chamberlain, Joseph, 1836-1914. I. Amery, Julian, 1919-*
DA565.C4G3   942.081/0924 (B)   33-286

Churchill, Winston Leonard Spencer, Sir, 1874-1965. III. 1360
Lord Randolph Churchill. [New ed.] London, Odhams Press [1952] 840 p. illus., ports. 22 cm. *1. Churchill, Randolph Henry Spencer, Lord, 1849-1895.*
DA565.C6C6 1952   923.242   52-32352

Martin, Ralph G., 1920- III. 1361
Jennie: the life of Lady Randolph Churchill, by Ralph G. Martin. Englewood Cliffs, N.J., Prentice-Hall [1969-71] 2 v. illus., facsims., ports. 24 cm. *1. Churchill, Jennie (Jerome) Randolph Churchill, Lady, 1854-1921. I. T.*
DA565.C6M3   942.081/0924 (B)   68-54197

Koss, Stephen E. III. 1362
John Morley at the India Office, 1905-1910, by Stephen E. Koss. New Haven, Yale University Press, 1969. viii, 231 p. port. 24 cm. Based on the author's thesis, Columbia University. *1. Morley, John Morley, Viscount, 1838-1923. 2. India — Politics and government — 1765-1947. 3. Great Britain — Colonies. I. T.*
DA565.M78K66   325.3/1/0924   72-81423

DA566 – 592   20th Century

Amery, Leopold Charles Maurice Stennett, 1873-1955. III. 1363
My political life. London, Hutchinson [1953- v. illus., ports. 24 cm. *I. T.*
DA566.A65   923.242   53-32025

Pelling, Henry. III. 1364
Modern Britain, 1885-1955. Edinburgh, T. Nelson [1960] xii, 212 p. plates,

ports., maps, diagrs., tables. 23 cm. (A History of England, v.8) *1. Gt. Brit. — History — Victoria, 1837-1901. 2. Gt. Brit. — History — 20th cent. I. T. (S:A History of England (Edinburgh, T. Nelson) v.8)*
DA566.P45   942.082   A61-3048

Seaman, Lewis Charles Bernard. III. 1365
Post-Victorian Britain: 1902-1951 [by] L. C. B. Seaman. London, Methuen, 1966. xi, 531 p. illus., 16 plates (incl. ports) maps, tables. 22 cm. *1. Gt. Brit. — History — 20th cent. I. T.*
DA566.S4   942.082   66-71853

Taylor, Alan John Percivale, 1906- III. 1366
English history, 1914-1945 [by] A. J. P. Taylor. New York, Oxford University Press, 1965. xxvii, 708 p. maps. 23 cm. (The Oxford history of England, 15) *1. Gt. Brit. — History — 20th cent. I. T. (S)*
DA566.T38   942.083   65-27513

Marwick, Arthur, 1936- III. 1367
Britain in the century of total war; war, peace, and social change, 1900-1967. [1st American ed.] Boston, Little, Brown [1968] 511 p. 22 cm. "An Atlantic Monthly Press book." *1. Great Britain — Civilization — 20th century. 2. History, Modern — 20th century. I. T.*
DA566.4.M357 1968   942.082   68-17276

Williams, Raymond. III. 1368
The long revolution. New York, Columbia University Press, 1961. 369 p. 23 cm. *1. Gt. Brit. — Intellectual life. I. T.*
DA566.4.W48   914.2   61-6336

DA566.7   POLITICAL AND DIPLOMATIC HISTORY

Gt. Brit. Foreign Office. III. 1369
Documents on British foreign policy, 1919-1939. London, H. M. Stationery Off., 1946-   v. 25 cm. Edited by E. L. Woodward and others. *1. Gt. Brit. — Foreign relations — 20th century. I. Woodward, Ernest Llewellyn, 1890- ed. II. T.*
DA566.7.A18   327.42   47-2936

Beer, Samuel Hutchinson, 1911- III. 1370
British politics in the collectivist age, by Samuel H. Beer. [1st ed.] New York, Knopf, 1965. xii, 390, xiii p. 22 cm. *1. Gt. Brit. — Politics and government — 20th cent. 2. Political parties — Gt. Brit. I. T.*
DA566.7.B4   320.942   65-11116

Beloff, Max, 1913- III. 1371
Imperial sunset. [1st American ed.] New York, Knopf, 1970- [c1969-   v. illus., maps. 25 cm. *1. Great Britain — Foreign relations — 20th century. I. T.*
DA566.7.B442   327.42   69-11480

Lloyd, Trevor Owen. III. 1372
Empire to welfare state; English history 1906-1967 [by] T. O. Lloyd. [London] Oxford University Press, 1970. xv, 465 p. illus., maps. 24 cm. (The Short Oxford history of the modern world) *1. Gt. Brit. — Politics and government — 20th century. 2. Gt. Brit. — Economic conditions — 20th century. 3. Gt. Brit. — Social conditions — 20th century. I. T. (S)*
DA566.7.L56   309.1/42   78-134634

Medlicott, William Norton, 1900- III. 1373
British foreign policy since Versailles, 1919-1963 [by] W. N. Medlicott. 2nd ed. revised & enlarged. London, Methuen, 1968. xxi, 362 p. 22 cm. "Distributed in the U.S.A. by Barnes & Noble." *1. Great Britain — Foreign relations — 20th century. 2. Europe — Politics — 1918-1945. 3. World politics — 20th century. I. T.*
DA566.7.M4 1968   327.42   73-363297   ISBN:0416107702

Northedge, F. S. III. 1374
The troubled giant; Britain among the great powers, 1916-1939, by F. S. Northedge. New York, Published for the London School of Economics and Political Science [by] Praeger [1966, i.e. 1967] xi, 657 p. maps. 23 cm. *1. Gt. Brit. — Foreign relations — 1910-1936. 2. Gt. Brit. — Foreign relations — 1936-1945. 3. World politics — 1900-1945. I. London School of Economics and Political Science. II. T. III. T:Britain among the great powers, 1916-1939.*
DA566.7.N57   327.42   66-26556

Reynolds, Philip Alan. III. 1375
British foreign policy in the inter-war years. London, New York, Longmans, Green [1954] xi, 182 p. maps. 23 cm. *1. Gt. Brit. — Foreign relations — 1910-1936. I. T.*
DA566.7.R48   327.42   54-3303

Seton-Watson, Robert William, 1879-1951. III. 1376
Britain and the dictators; a survey of post-war British policy. New York, H. Fertig, 1968. xviii, 460 p. 24 cm. Reprint of the 1938 ed. *1. Great Britain — Foreign relations — 20th century. 2. Europe — Politics — 1918-1945. 3. Dictators. I. T.*
DA566.7.S4 1968   327.42   68-9600

Strang, William Strang, baron, 1893- III. 1377
Home and abroad. [London] Deutsch [1956] 320 p. illus. 23 cm. Autobiographical. *1. Gt. Brit. — Foreign relations — 20th cent. I. T.*
DA566.7.S74   923.242   56-14540

Watt, Donald Cameron. III. 1378
Personalities and policies; studies in the formulation of British foreign policy in the twentieth century, by D. C. Watt. [Notre Dame, Ind.] University of Notre Dame Press, 1965. xii, 275 p. 22 cm. (International studies of the Committee on International Relations, University of Notre Dame) *1. Gt. Brit. — Foreign relations — 20th cent. 2. Gt. Brit. — Foreign relations administration. 3. Diplomats, British. I. T. (S:Notre Dame, Ind. University. Committee on International Relations. International studies)*
DA566.7.W3   327.42   64-66347

DA566.9   BIOGRAPHY. MEMOIRS

A – J

Middlemas, Robert Keith, 1935- III. 1379
Baldwin; a biography [by] Keith Middlemas [and] John Barnes. [1st American ed. New York] Macmillan [1970, c1969] xvii, 1149 p. illus., facsim., ports. 25 cm. *1. Baldwin, Stanley Baldwin, 1st earl, 1867-1947. I. Barnes, Anthony John Lane, joint author.*
DA566.9.B15M5 1970   942.082/0924 (B)   70-87902

Young, George Malcolm, 1882- III. 1380
Stanley Baldwin. London, R. Hart-Davis, 1952. 266 p. illus. 23 cm. *1. Baldwin, Stanley Baldwin, 1st earl, 1867-1947. 2. Gt. Brit. — Politics and government — 1910-1936.*
DA566.9.B15Y6 1952   923.242   52-14968

Young, Kenneth, 1916- III. 1381
Arthur James Balfour; the happy life of the politician, prime minister, statesman, and philosopher, 1848-1930. London, G. Bell [1963] 516 p. illus. 26 cm. *1. Balfour, Arthur James Balfour, 1st earl of, 1848-1930.*
DA566.9.B2Y6   63-3177

Chandos, Oliver Lyttelton, 1st viscount, 1893- III. 1382
Memoirs; an unexpected view from the summit. [New York] New American Library [1963] xvi, 430 p. port., maps. 24 cm. *1. Gt. Brit. — History — 20th cent.*
DA566.9.C44A3 1963   923.242   63-21512

Churchill, Winston Leonard Spencer, Sir, 1874- III. 1383
The unwritten alliance: speeches 1953 to 1959. Edited by Randolph S. Churchill. London, Cassell [1961] xi, 332 p. 23 cm. *1. Gt. Brit. — Politics and government — 1945- — Addresses, essays, lectures. 2. Gt. Brit. — Relations (general) with the U.S. 3. U.S. — Relations (general) with Great Britain. I. T.*
DA566.9.C5A375 1961   63-6468

Broad, Lewis, 1900- III. 1384
Winston Churchill, a biography. Westport, Conn., Greenwood Press [1972, c1958-   ] v.   22 cm. *1. Churchill, Winston Leonard Spencer, Sir, 1874-1965.*
DA566.9.C5B6923   942.082/0924 (B)   74-138206
ISBN:0837155592 (v. 1)

Churchill, Randolph Spencer, 1911-1968. III. 1385
Winston S. Churchill [by] Randolph S. Churchill. Boston, Houghton Mifflin, 1966-   v. illus., geneal. tables, maps, ports. 24 cm. *1. Churchill, Winston Leonard Spencer, Sir, 1874-1965.*
DA566.9.C5C47   942.080924 (B)   66-12065

Schoenfeld, Maxwell Philip, 1936- III. 1386
The war ministry of Winston Churchill. [1st ed.] Ames, Iowa State University Press [1972]   p. *1. Churchill, Winston Leonard Spencer, Sir, 1874-1965. 2. World War, 1939-1945 — Great Britain. 3. Great Britain — Foreign relations — 1936-1945. I. T.*
DA566.9.C5S36   942.084   72-153159   ISBN:0813802601

Citrine, Walter McLennan Citrine, baron, 1887- III. 1387
Men and work; an autobiography [by] Lord Citrine. London, Hutchinson [1964] 384 p. ports. 24 cm. *1. Trades Union Congress. 2. Gt. Brit. — Politics and government — 20th cent. 3. Labor and laboring classes — Gt. Brit. I. T.*
DA566.9.C515A3   66-5366

Cooper, Duff, 1st viscount Norwich, 1890-1954. III. 1388
Old men forget; the autobiography of Duff Cooper (Viscount Norwich) London, Hart-Davis, 1953. 399 p. ports. 22 cm. *1. Gt. Brit. — Politics and government — 20th cent. I. T.*
DA566.9.C64A3   923.242   54-4615

Eden, Anthony, Sir, 1897- III. 1389
Facing the dictators; the memoirs of Anthony Eden, earl of Avon. Boston, Houghton Mifflin, 1962. 746 p. illus. 23 cm. "Companion with this volume [the author's] Full circle." *1. Gt. Brit. — Foreign relations — 1910-1936. I. T.*
DA566.9.E28A36   923.242   62-18265

Trevelyan, George Macaulay, 1876-1962. III. 1390
Grey of Fallodon, being the life of Sir Edward Grey, afterwards Viscount Grey of Fallodon. London, New York, Longmans, Green [1937] xiii, 393 p. plates, ports., map. 23 cm. *1. Grey, Edward Grey, 1st viscount, 1862-1933. 2. Gt. Brit. — Foreign relations.*
DA566.9.G8T7 1937a   923.242   48-40731

Koss, Stephen E. III. 1391
Lord Haldane; scapegoat for liberalism [by] Stephen E. Koss. New York, Columbia University Press, 1969. ix, 263 p. facsims., ports. 24 cm. *1. Haldane, Richard Burdon Haldane, 1st Viscount, 1856-1928. I. T.*
DA566.9.H27K6   942.083/0924   69-19460

Jones, Thomas, 1870-1955. III. 1392
Whitehall diary; edited by Keith Middlemas. London, New York [etc.] Oxford U.P., 1969- v. plates, ports. 25 cm. *1. Great Britain — Politics and government — 20th century. I. Middlemas, Robert Keith, 1935- ed. II. T.*
DA566.9.J66A3   942.083/0924   70-420453   ISBN:0192111930(v.1)

DA566.9   L – Z

Blake, Robert, 1916- III. 1393
The unknown Prime Minister; the life and times of Andrew Bonar Law, 1858-1923. London, Eyre & Spottiswoode, 1955. 556 p. illus. 23 cm. *1. Law, Andrew Bonar, 1858-1923. 2. Gt. Brit. — Politics and government — 20th cent. I. T.*
DA566.9.L35B55 1955   56-338

Beaverbrook, William Maxwell Aitken, baron, 1879- III. 1394
The decline and fall of Lloyd George. [1st ed.] New York, Duell, Sloan and Pearce [1963] 320 p. illus. 24 cm. *1. Lloyd George, David Lloyd George, 1st earl, 1863-1945. I. T.*
DA566.9.L5B4   923.242   63-14328

Jones, Thomas, 1870- III. 1395
Lloyd George. Cambridge, Harvard University Press, 1951. x, 330 p. illus., map, ports. 23 cm. (Makers of modern Europe) *1. Lloyd George, David Lloyd George, 1st earl, 1863-1945. (S)*
DA566.9.L5J6   923.242   51-12384

Lloyd George, Richard Lloyd George, 2d earl, 1889- III. 1396
My father, Lloyd George. New York, Crown Publishers [1961, c1960] 248 p. illus. 22 cm. First published in 1960 under title: Lloyd George. *1. Lloyd George, David Lloyd George, 1st earl, 1863-1945. I. T.*
DA566.9.L5L52 1961   923.242   61-10305

Lloyd George: twelve essays, III. 1397
edited by A. J. P. Taylor. [1st American ed.] New York, Atheneum, 1971. xiv, 393 p. 23 cm. *1. Lloyd George, David Lloyd George, 1st Earl, 1863-1945. 2. Great Britain — Politics and government — 20th century — Addresses, essays, lectures. I. Taylor, Alan John Percivale, 1906- ed.*
DA566.9.L5L55 1971   942.083/0924   70-139234

Morgan, Kenneth O. III. 1398
David Lloyd George, Welsh radical as world statesman. Cardiff, University of Wales Press, 1963. 85 p. 19 cm. *1. Lloyd George, David Lloyd George, 1st earl, 1863-1945. 2. Wales — Politics and government. I. T.*
DA566.9.L5M57   66-36373

Perham, Margery Freda, Dame, 1895- III. 1399
Lugard, by Margery Perham. Hamden, Conn., Archon Books, 1968. 2 v. illus., maps, ports. 23 cm. Reprint of the 1956 ed. *1. Lugard, Frederick John Dealtry, Baron, 1858-1945.*
DA566.9.L82P4   966.9/03/0924 (B)   68-6290

Macmillan, Harold, 1894- III. 1400
Riding the storm, 1956-1959. [1st U.S. ed.] New York, Harper & Row [1971] viii, 786 p. illus. 24 cm. (A Cass Canfield book) *1. Great Britain — Politics and government — 1945-1964. 2. Great Britain — Foreign relations — 1945- I. T.*
DA566.9.M33A27 1971b   942.085/0924 (B)   79-156535
ISBN:0060127749

Macmillan, Harold, 1894- III. 1401
Tides of fortune, 1945-1955. [1st U.S. ed.] New York, Harper & Row [1969] xxii, 729 p. ports. 24 cm. Autobiographical. *1. Great Britain — Politics and government — 20th century. 2. Great Britain — Foreign relations — 20th century. I. T.*
DA566.9.M33A28 1969   942.085/0924   78-83609

Gollin, Alfred M. III. 1402
Proconsul in politics; a study of Lord Milner in opposition and in power, by A. M. Gollin. With an introductory section, 1854-1905. New York, Macmillan, 1964. xi, 627 p. illus., ports. 23 cm. *1. Milner, Alfred Milner, 1st viscount, 1854-1925. I. T.*
DA566.9.M5G6 1964a   942.083   64-13121

Wrench, Evelyn, Sir, 1882- III. 1403
Alfred Lord Milner, the man of no illusions, 1854-1925. London, Eyre & Spottiswoode, 1958. 398 p. illus. 23 cm. *1. Milner, Alfred Milner, 1st viscount, 1854-1925.*
DA566.9.M5W7   923.242   59-186

Oxford and Asquith, Herbert Henry Asquith, 1st earl of, 1852-1928. III. 1404
Memories and reflections, 1852-1927, by the Earl of Oxford and Asquith, K.G. Boston, Little, Brown, 1928. 2 v. fronts., illus., ports., fold. map, facsims. 25 cm. The responsibility for the arrangement of the last third of this book and the final revision of the whole has been borne by the executors. The work has been carried out by Mr. Alexander Mackintosh, who assisted Lord Oxford throughout the preparation of the book. cf. Note by Lord Oxford's executors. *1. Gt. Brit. — Politics and government — 1837-1901. 2. Gt. Brit. — Politics and government — 20th cent. 3. Statesmen, British. 4. European war, 1914-1918 — Gt. Brit. I. Mackintosh, Alexander, Sir, 1858- ed. II. T.*
DA566.9.O7A55   28-21383

Jenkins, Roy. III. 1405
Asquith; portrait of a man and an era. New York, Chilmark Press [c1964] 572 p. ports. 24 cm. *1. Oxford and Asquith, Herbert Henry Asquith, 1st earl of, 1852-1928. I. T.*
DA566.9.O7J42   923.242   65-14596

Snowden, Philip Snowden, viscount, 1864-1937. III. 1406
An autobiography, by Philip, viscount Snowden. [1st ed.] London, Nicholson and Watson, 1934- v. front., plates, ports. 24 cm. *1. Independent labour party (Gt. Brit.) 2. Gt. Brit. — Politics and government — 20th cent.*
DA566.9.S55A3 1934   923.242   34-37977

Templewood, Samuel John Gurney Hoare, 1st viscount, 1880- III. 1407
Nine troubled years. London, Collins, 1954. 448 p. illus. 22 cm. *1. Gt. Brit. — Politics and government — 20th cent. 2. Gt. Brit. — Foreign relations — 20th cent. I. T.*
DA566.9.T4   55-496

Wedgwood, Cicely Veronica, 1910- III. 1408
The last of the radicals, Josiah Wedgwood, M.P. London, Cape [1951] 252 p. illus. 23 cm. *1. Wedgwood, Josiah Clement Wedgwood, baron, 1872-1943. I. T.*
DA566.9.W4W4   923.242   51-13163

DA567 – 570   Edward VII, 1901 – 1910

Magnus, Philip Montefiore, Sir, bart., 1906- III. 1409
King Edward the Seventh [by] Philip Magnus. [1st ed.] New York, Dutton, 1964. xv, 528 p. illus., geneal. tables, ports. (part col.) 24 cm. *1. Edward VII, King of Great Britain, 1841-1910.*
DA567.M26 1964   923.142   64-11062

Cross, Colin. III. 1410
The Liberals in power, 1905-1914. London, Barrie and Rockliff [1963] x, 198 p. ports. 22 cm. *1. Liberal Party (Gt. Brit.) 2. Gt. Brit. — Politics and government — 1901-1936. I. T.*
DA570.C7   64-9229

Monger, George W. III. 1411
The end of isolation; British foreign policy, 1900-1907. London, New York, T. Nelson [1963] vi, 343 p. 22 cm. (Nelson's studies in modern history) *1. Gt. Brit. — Foreign relations — 1901-1910. I. T.*
DA570.M6 1963   327.42   63-25315

DA573 – 568   George V, 1910 – 1936

Nicolson, Harold George, Hon., 1886- III. 1412
King George the Fifth; his life and reign. London, Constable, 1952. xxiii, 570 p. plates, ports. 24 cm. *1. George V, King of Great Britain, 1865-1936.*
DA573.N5   A52-10694

Keynes, John Maynard, 1883-1946. III. 1413
Essays in biography. New ed. with three additional essays, edited by Geoffrey Keynes. New York, Horizon Press, 1951. 354 p. port. 20 cm. *1. Gt. Brit. — Biography. 2. Statesmen, British. 3. Economists, British. I. T.*
DA574.A1K4 1951a   923.242   51-7759

Mosley, Oswald, Sir, bart., 1896- III. 1414
My life. New Rochelle, N.Y., Arlington House [1972, c1968] 521 p. illus. 24 cm. *I. T.*
DA574.M6A35 1972   942.084/0924 (B)   78-179718
ISBN:0870001604

Bettey, J. H. III. 1415
English historical documents, 1906-1939: a selection edited by J. H. Bettey.

London, Routledge & K. Paul, 1967. x, 198 p. tables. 22 1/2 cm. *1. Gt. Brit. — History — 20th cent. — Sources. I. T.*
DA576.B45 942.083/08 67-109889
ISBN:7100 6024 6 7100 2883 0 (pbk.)

Dangerfield, George, 1904-   **III. 1416**
The strange death of Liberal England. New York, Capricorn Books [1961, c1935] 449 p. 19 cm. (A Capricorn book, CAP50) *1. Liberal Party (Gt. Brit.) 2. Gt. Brit. — Politics and government — 1910-1936. 3. Liberalism. I. T. II. T:Liberal England.*
DA576.D3 1961   942.083   61-2982

Wilson, Trevor, 1928-   **III. 1417**
The downfall of the Liberal Party, 1914-1935 [by] Trevor Wilson. Ithaca, N.Y., Cornell University Press [1966] 415 p. illus., ports. 22 cm. *1. Liberal Party (Gt. Brit.) 2. Gt. Brit. — Politics and government — 1910-1936. I. T.*
DA576.W55 1966a   329.942   66-27932

Beaverbrook, William Maxwell Aitken, Baron, 1879-1964.   **III. 1418**
Men and power, 1917-1918. [Hamden, Conn.] Archon Books, 1968 [c1956] 447 p. illus., facsims., ports. 23 cm. *1. European War, 1914-1918 — Great Britain. 2. Great Britain — Politics and government — 1910-1936. I. T.*
DA577.B34 1968   320.9/42   68-7599

Marwick, Arthur, 1936-   **III. 1419**
The deluge; British society and the First World War. [1st American ed.] Boston, Little, Brown [1966, c1965] 336 p. illus. 22 cm. *1. European War, 1914-1918 — Great Britain. 2. Reconstruction (1914-1939) — Great Britain. 3. Great Britain — Social conditions. I. T.*
DA577.M37   914.20383   66-10818

Churchill, Winston Leonard Spencer, Sir, 1874-1965.   **III. 1420**
While England slept; a survey of world affairs, 1932-1938. With a pref. and notes by Randolph S. Churchill. Freeport, N.Y., Books for Libraries Press [1971] xii, 404 p. port. 24 cm. Speeches. Reprint of the 1938 ed. *1. Great Britain — Foreign relations — 20th century. 2. Europe — Politics — 1918-1945. 3. Germany — Politics and government — 1933-1945. 4. Disarmament. 5. Security, International. I. T.*
DA578.C48 1971   327.42   76-165621   ISBN:0836959280

George, Margaret.   **III. 1421**
The warped vision; British foreign policy, 1933-1939. [Pittsburgh] University of Pittsburgh Press [1965] xxiii, 238 p. 23 cm. *1. Gt. Brit. — Foreign relations — 1910-1936. 2. Gt. Brit. — Foreign relations — 1936-1945. I. T.*
DA578.G39   327.42   65-14623

Kennedy, John Fitzgerald, Pres. U.S., 1917-1963.   **III. 1422**
Why England slept. New York, W. Funk [1961] xxviii, 252 p. 22 cm. *1. Gt. Brit. — Politics and government — 1910-1936. 2. Gt. Brit. — Politics and government — 1936-1945. 3. Disarmament. I. T.*
DA578.K4 1961   942.083   61-66277

Lyman, Richard W.   **III. 1423**
The first Labour government, 1924. London, Chapman & Hall [1957] 302 p. illus. 23 cm. *1. Labour Party (Gt. Brit.) 2. Gt. Brit. — Politics and government — 1910-1936. I. T.*
DA578.L9   942.083   58-1703

McElwee, William Lloyd, 1907-   **III. 1424**
Britain's locust years, 1918-1940. London, Faber and Faber [1962] 292 p. fold. map. 22 cm. *1. Gt. Brit. — History — George V, 1910-1936. I. T.*
DA578.M26 1962   942.083   64-2577

Raymond, John, 1923- ed.   **III. 1425**
The Baldwin age. London, Eyre & Spottiswoode, 1960. 248 p. 22 cm. *1. Gt. Brit. — History — George V, 1910-1936. I. T.*
DA578.R38   942.083   61-1295

Rowse, Alfred Leslie, 1903-   **III. 1426**
Appeasement; a study in political decline, 1933-1939. New York, Norton [1961] 123 p. illus. 22 cm. *1. Oxford. University. All Souls College. 2. Gt. Brit. — Politics and government — 20th cent. I. T.*
DA578.R68   942.084   61-17123

DA584 – 592 George VI, 1937 – 1952.
Elizabeth II, 1952 –

Wheeler-Bennett, John Wheeler, 1902-   **III. 1427**
King George VI, his life and reign. New York, St Martin's Press [1958] xii, 891 p. illus., ports. (part col.) geneal. table. 24 cm. *1. George VI, King of Great Britain, 1895-1952.*
DA584.W45   923.142   58-13050

Attlee, Clement Richard Attlee, 1st earl, 1883-   **III. 1428**
As it happened. New York, Viking Press, 1954. viii, 312 p. ports. 22 cm. Autobiography. *I. T.*
DA585.A8A8 1954a   923.242   54-7570

Foot, Michael, 1913-   **III. 1429**
Aneurin Bevan, a biography. [1st American ed.] New York, Atheneum, 1963- [c1962-   v. illus. 22 cm. *1. Bevan, Aneurin, 1897-1960.*
DA585.B38F62   923.242   63-17846

Feiling, Keith Grahame, Sir, 1884-   **III. 1430**
The life of Neville Chamberlain, by Keith Feiling. Hamden, Conn., Archon Books, 1970. xi, 477 p. facsim., ports. 23 cm. Reprint of the 1946 ed. with a new pref. and bibliography (p. 467-468) *1. Chamberlain, Neville, 1869-1940. I. T.*
DA585.C5F4 1970   942.084/0924 (B)   75-95598

Macleod, Iain.   **III. 1431**
Neville Chamberlain. [1st American ed.] New York, Atheneum, 1962 [c1961] 319 p. illus. 20 cm. *1. Chamberlain, Neville, 1869-1940.*
DA585.C5M3 1962   923.242   62-13222

Watkins, K. W.   **III. 1432**
Britain divided; the effect of the Spanish Civil War on British political opinion. London, New York, T. Nelson [1963] ix, 270 p. 23 cm. *1. Gt. Brit. — Politics and government — 1936-1945. 2. Spain — History — Civil War, 1936-1939 — Foreign public opinion. 3. Public opinion — Gt. Brit. I. T.*
DA586.W3   942.084   63-6006

Calder, Angus.   **III. 1433**
The people's war; Britain, 1939-1945. [1st American ed.] New York, Pantheon Books [1969] 656 p. illus., ports. 24 cm. *1. World War, 1939-1945 — Great Britain. I. T.*
DA587.C28 1969b   940.5342   67-19178

Eden, Anthony, Sir, 1897-   **III. 1434**
Full circle; the memoirs of Anthony Eden. Boston, Houghton Mifflin, 1960. 676 p. illus. 22 cm. *1. Gt. Brit. — Politics and government — 1945- I. T.*
DA588.E42   923.242   59-8856

Northedge, F. S.   **III. 1435**
British foreign policy; the process of readjustment, 1945-1961. New York, Praeger [1962] 341 p. illus. 23 cm. (Minerva series of students handbooks, no. 7) Books that matter. *1. Gt. Brit. — Foreign relations — 1945- 2. World politics — 1945- I. T.*
DA588.N6   327.42   62-18270

Sissons, Michael, ed.   **III. 1436**
Age of austerity; [essays] Edited by Michael Sissons and Philip French. [London] Hodder and Stoughton [1963] 349 p. illus. 23 cm. *1. Gt. Brit. — History — George VI, 1936-1952 — Addresses, essays, lectures. I. French, Philip, joint ed. II. T.*
DA588.S5   914.2   65-359

Younger, Kenneth Gilmour, 1908-   **III. 1437**
Changing perspectives in British foreign policy, by Kenneth Younger. London, New York, Oxford University Press, 1964. viii, 139 p. 19 cm. (Chatham House essays, 7) *1. Gt. Brit. — Foreign relations — 1945- 2. World politics — 1945- I. T.*
DA588.Y59   327.42   65-302

Beloff, Max, 1913-   **III. 1438**
The future of British foreign policy. Foreword by Vera Micheles Dean. New York, Taplinger Pub. Co. [1969] v, 154 p. 21 cm. (World realities series) *1. Great Britain — Politics and government — 1964- 2. Great Britain — Foreign relations — 1945- I. T.*
DA592.B38 1969b   327.42   73-86970   ISBN:0800831209

Sampson, Anthony.   **III. 1439**
The new anatomy of Britain. New York, Stein and Day [1972, c1971] xviii, 773 p. illus. 24 cm. "A complete rewrite of the author's ... 1962 book 'Anatomy of Britain.'" *1. Great Britain — Civilization — 1945- 2. Great Britain — Politics and government — 1964- I. T.*
DA592.S23 1972   309.1/42/085   78-186150   ISBN:0812814568

DA600 – 690 Description. Local History

Beresford, Maurice Warwick, 1920-   **III. 1440**
Medieval England, an aerial survey, by M. W. Beresford & J. K. S. St. Joseph. Cambridge [Eng.] University Press, 1958. xiii, 274 p. illus., maps. 29 cm. (Cambridge air surveys, 2) *1. England — Historical geography. I. St. Joseph, John Kenneth Sinclair, joint author. II. T. (S)*
DA610.B4   942   58-1947

Darby, Henry Clifford, 1909-   **III. 1441**
The Domesday geography of eastern England, by H. C. Darby. [3d ed.] Cambridge [Eng.] University Press, 1971. xiv, 400 p. illus. 24 cm. *1. Domesday book. 2. England — Historical geography. I. T.*
DA610.D24 1971   911/.425   70-108106   ISBN:0521080223

Darby, Henry Clifford, 1909- ed.   **III. 1442**
The Domesday geography of midland England, edited by H. C. Darby and I. B. Terrett. 2d ed. Cambridge, University Press, 1971. xvii, 490 p. maps, facsim. 24 cm. *1. Domesday book. 2. England — Historical geography. I. Terrett, I. B., joint ed. II. T.*
DA610.D25 1971   911/.426   78-134626   ISBN:0521080789

Darby, Henry Clifford, 1909-   **III. 1443**
The Domesday geography of northern England, edited by H. C. Darby and I. S. Maxwell. Cambridge [Eng.] University Press, 1962. xv, 540 p. maps (part col.) col. facsim. 24 cm. (The Domesday geography of England, 4) *1. Domesday book. 2. England — Historical geography. I. Maxwell, Ian Stanley. II. T. (S)*
DA610.D255   914.27   62-53452

Darby, Henry Clifford, 1909- ed.   **III. 1444**
The Domesday geography of south-east England, edited by H. C. Darby and Eila M. J. Campbell. Cambridge [Eng.] University Press, 1962. xvi, 658 p. maps, facsim. 24 cm. (The Domesday geography of England, 3) *1. Domesday book. 2. England — Historical geography. I. Campbell, Eila M. J., joint ed. II. T. (S)*
DA610.D26   914.22   62-6262

Darby, Henry Clifford, 1909-   **III. 1445**
The Domesday geography of South-west England, edited by H. C. Darby and R. Weldon Finn. London, Cambridge U.P., 1967. xiv, 469 p. front. (facsim.), maps (some col.), tables. 24 cm. (The Domesday geography of England) *1. Domesday book. 2. England — Historical geography. I. Finn, Rex Welldon, joint author. II. T. (S)*
DA610.D27   914.23   67-11519

Defoe, Daniel, 1661?-1731.   **III. 1446**
A tour through England & Wales; divided into circuits or journies, by Daniel Defoe. London & Toronto, J. M. Dent; New York, E. P. Dutton [1928] 2 v. 18 cm. (Everyman's library. Travel and topography. [no. 820-821]) "This edition has been set up from the verbatim reprint of the first edition (including the Tour through Scotland) published in 1927 by Mr. Peter Davies." *1. England — Description and travel. 2. Wales — Description and travel.*
DA620.D31 1928   914.2   A29-103

Cobbett, William, 1763-1835.   **III. 1447**
Rural rides [by] William Cobbett. London, Dent; New York, Dutton [1932, '30] 2 v. illus. (map) 18 cm. (Everyman's library. Travel & topography. [no. 638-639]) "First published in this edition 1912." Vol. 1 reprinted 1932; v.2, 1930. With reproduction of t.-p. of London edition of 1853, edited by James Paul Cobbett. Introduction by Edward Thomas. *1. England — Description and travel. I. T.*
DA625.C654x (AC1.E8 no. 638-639)   914.2   37-5629

Gt. Brit. Central Office of Information.   **III. 1448**
Britain; an official handbook. London, 1949/50-   v. maps. 22-24 cm. Annual. Subtitle varies. *1. Great Britain. 2. Gt. Brit. — Statistics. I. T.*
DA630.A17   914.2   50-14073

James, Henry, 1843-1916.   **III. 1449**
English hours. With illus. by Joseph Pennell. New York, Horizon Press [1969, c1968] xxxiv, 336 p. illus. 24 cm. *1. England — Description and travel — 1801-1900. I. Pennell, Joseph, 1857-1926, illus. II. T.*
DA630.J27 1969   914.2/04/81   68-55315

Dury, George H., 1916-   **III. 1450**
The British Isles: a systematic and regional geography [by] G. H. Dury. 3rd ed. London, Heinemann, 1965. xiv, 503 p. 36 plates, maps, tables. 22 1/2 cm. *1. Gt. Brit. — Description and travel — 1946- I. T.*
DA631.D8 1965   914.20385   66-76862

Ekwall, Eilert, 1877-1964.   **III. 1451**
The concise Oxford dictionary of English place-names. 4th ed. Oxford, Clarendon Press, 1960. L, 546 p. 24 cm. *1. Names, Geographical — England. 2. English language — Etymology — Names. I. English place-names.*
DA645.E38 1960   914.2   60-2031

DA670 – 690   COUNTIES. CITIES

Rowse, Alfred Leslie, 1903-   **III. 1452**
Tudor Cornwall; portrait of a society, by A. L. Rowse. [New ed.] New York, C. Scribner [1969] 462 p. illus., maps, port. 22 cm. *1. Cornwall, Eng. — History. I. T.*
DA670.C8R6 1969b   914.23/7/035   69-17046

Wordsworth, William, 1770-1850.   **III. 1453**
A guide through the district of the lakes in the north of England, with a description of the scenery, &c., for the use of tourists and residents. With illus. by John Piper, and an introd. by W. M. Merchant. New York, Greenwood Press, 1968. 174 p. illus., map. 23 cm. Reprint of the 1952 ed. *1. Lake District, Eng. I. T.*
DA670.L1W67 1968   914.28   68-55639

Stow, John, 1525?-1605.   **III. 1453a**
Survey of London. Introduction by H. B. Wheatley. [Rev. ed.] London, Dent; New York, Dutton [1965] xxiv, 533 p. map. 19 cm. (Everyman's library, no. 589) *1. London — Description — To 1800. 2. London — History — To 1600. I. T.*
DA680.S87x

Rudé, George F. E.   **III. 1454**
Hanoverian London, 1714-1808 [by] George Rudé. Berkeley, University of California, 1971. xvi, 271 p. illus., plans. 25 cm. (The History of London) *1. London — History — 18th century. I. T.*
DA682.R8   914.21/03/7   69-10590   ISBN:0520017781

Jocelin de Brakelond, fl. 1200.   **III. 1455**
The chronicle of Jocelin of Brakelond, monk of St. Edmundsbury: a picture of monastic and social life in the XIIth century, newly translated and edited by L. C. Jane. Introd. by Cardinal Gasquet. New York, Cooper Square Publishers, 1966. xxxvi, 255 p. front. 17 cm. (The Medieval library) *1. Bury St. Edmunds Abbey. 2. Samson, Abbot of Bury St. Edmunds, 1135-1211. I. Jane, Lionel Cecil, 1879-1932, ed. II. T.*
DA690.B97J6 1966   942.6/4   66-23318

Walmsley, Robert, 1905-   **III. 1456**
Peterloo: the case reopened. New York, A. M. Kelley, 1969. xx, 585 p. illus. 25 cm. *1. Manchester, Eng. — Peterloo Massacre, 1819. I. T.*
DA690.M4W3 1969b   942.7/2   73-81146

Howell, Roger.   **III. 1457**
Newcastle upon Tyne and the Puritan Revolution: a study of the Civil War in North England [by] Roger Howell, Jr. Oxford, Clarendon P., 1967. xiv, 397 p. tables. 22 1/2 cm. *1. Newcastle-upon-Tyne — History. 2. Gt. Brit. — History — Civil War, 1642-1649. I. T.*
DA690.N6H6   942.8/2   67-85946

Anglo-Saxon chronicle.   **III. 1458**
The Peterborough chronicle, 1070-1154. Edited from Ms. Bodley Laud misc. 636, with introd., commentary, and an appendix containing the interpolations by Cecily Clark. [London] Oxford University Press, 1958. lxx, 120 p. 23 cm. (Oxford English monographs) *1. Peterborough Cathedral. 2. Gt. Brit. — History — To 1485 — Sources. I. Clark, Cecily, ed.*
DA690.P47A49   942.55   58-1160

DA700 – 745   WALES

Roderick, Arthur James, ed.   **III. 1459**
Wales through the ages. [Llandybie, Carmarthenshire] C. Davies [1959-60] 2 v. illus. 22 cm. *1. Wales — History.*
DA714.R6   942.9   61-2284

Williams, David, 1900-   **III. 1460**
A history of modern Wales. [1st ed.] London, Murray [1950] 308 p. plates, ports., map. 23 cm. *1. Wales — History.*
DA720.W48   942.9   50-11638

Borrow, George Henry, 1803-1881.   **III. 1461**
Wild Wales; its people, language and scenery. London, Oxford University Press, H. Milford [1934] xv, 622 p. 16 cm. (The World's classics, 224) *1. Wales — Description and travel. I. T.*
DA730.B74 1934   914.29   43-13547

Thomas, Dylan, 1914-1953.   **III. 1462**
A child's Christmas in Wales. Illustrated by Fritz Eichenberg. [New York, New Directions Pub. Corp., 1969, c1954] 31 p. illus. 21 x 28 cm. (A New Directions book) *1. Christmas — Wales. 2. Wales — Social life and customs. 3. Christmas — Wales. 4. Wales — Social life and customs. I. Eichenberg, Fritz, 1901- illus. II. T.*
DA730.T44 1969   821/.9/12   77-88732

DA750 – 890 SCOTLAND

Dickinson, William Croft, 1897- ed. III. 1463
A source book of Scottish history, edited by William Croft Dickinson, Gordon Donaldson [and] Isabel A. Milne. London, New York, Nelson [1952-54] 3 v. 19 cm. *1. Scotland — History — Sources.*
DA755.D5   941   53-32020

Donaldson, Gordon, comp. III. 1464
Scottish historical documents [compiled by] Gordon Donaldson. New York, Barnes & Noble [1970] xi, 287 p. 23 cm. *1. Scotland — History — Sources. I. T.*
DA755.D57   941   71-21537   ISBN:0389040479

Dickinson, William Croft, 1897- III. 1465
A new history of Scotland, by William Croft Dickinson and George S. Pryde. [London, New York, Nelson, 1962, c1961-62] 2 v. 2 fold. col. maps. 25 cm. Half-title; each vol. has special t.p. *1. Scotland — History. I. Pryde, George Smith. II. T.*
DA760.D5   941   62-2395

Donaldson, Gordon. III. 1466
Scotland: James V to James VII. New York, Praeger [1966, c1965] x, 449 p. maps. 23 cm. (The Edinburgh history of Scotland, v.3) *1. Scotland — History — 16th cent. 2. Scotland — History — 17th cent. I. T.*
DA760.E3 vol. 3   941   66-11446

Ferguson, William, 1924- III. 1467
Scotland: 1689 to the present. New York, Praeger [1968] ix, 464 p. map. 23 cm. (The Edinburgh history of Scotland, v.4) *1. Scotland — History. I. T.*
DA760.E3 vol. 4   941   67-26473

Mitchison, Rosalind. III. 1468
A history of Scotland; illustrated by George Mackie. London, Methuen, 1970. x, 468 p. illus., geneal. table, maps, music. 22 cm. "Distributed in the U.S.A. by Barnes & Noble, inc." *1. Scotland — History. I. T.*
DA760.M58 1970   941   75-476603   ISBN:416144500

Grant, Isabel Frances. III. 1469
The social and economic development of Scotland before 1603, by I. F. Grant. Edinburgh, London, Oliver and Boyd, 1930. xii, 594 p. front. (map) 23 cm. *1. Scotland — Social conditions. 2. Scotland — Economic conditions. 3. Scotland — Industries — History. 4. Scotland — History — To 1603. I. T.*
DA772.G7   330.941   30-16602

Smout, T. Christopher. III. 1470
A history of the Scottish people, 1560-1830, by T. C. Smout. New York, Scribner [1970, c1969] 576 p. illus., maps. 24 cm. *1. Scotland — Civilization. 2. Scotland — Economic conditions. I. T.*
DA772.S63 1970   914.1/03   75-92624

Henderson, Isabel. III. 1471
The Picts. New York, Praeger [1967] 228 p. illus., facsims., maps. 21 cm. (Ancient peoples and places, v.54) *1. Picts. 2. Art, Pictish. 3. Scotland — History — To 1057.*
DA774.H4   914.1/03/1   67-15744

Donaldson, Gordon. III. 1472
The Scots overseas. London, Hale, 1966. 232 p. plates (incl. ports.) 22 1/2 cm. *1. Scotch in foreign countries. 2. Scotland — Emigration and immigration. I. T.*
DA774.5.D6 1966   325.241   66-68133

DA775 – 826 by Period

Piggott, Stuart, ed. III. 1473
The prehistoric peoples of Scotland. London, Routledge and Paul [1962] ix, 165 p. illus., maps, diagr. 24 cm. (Studies in ancient history and archaeology) Imprint covered by label: New York, Humanities Press. *1. Scotland — History — To 1057. I. T.*
DA777.P55   941.01   63-3786

Barrow, G. W. S. III. 1474
Robert Bruce and the community of the realm of Scotland, by G. W. S. Barrow. Berkeley, University of California Press, 1965. xxiv, 502 p. illus., maps. 23 cm. *1. Robert I, King of Scotland, 1274-1329. 2. Scotland — History — War of Independence, 1285-1371. I. T.*
DA783.4.B34   941.02   65-2316

Mackie, Robert Laird, 1885- III. 1475
King James IV of Scotland, a brief survey of his life and times. Edinburgh, Oliver and Boyd [1958] 300 p. illus. 23 cm. *1. James IV, King of Scotland, 1473-1513.*
DA784.5.M25   923.141   58-2913

Donaldson, Gordon. III. 1476
The first trial of Mary, Queen of Scots. New York, Stein and Day [1969] 254 p. illus., ports. 23 cm. *1. Mary Stuart, Queen of the Scots, 1542-1587. I. T.*
DA787.A1D58 1969   343/.5/230924   77-87952   ISBN:812812689

Lee, Maurice. III. 1477
James Stewart, Earl of Moray; a political study of the Reformation in Scotland. Westport, Conn., Greenwood Press [1971, c1953] ix, 320 p. 23 cm. *1. Moray, James Stewart, 1st Earl of, 1531?-1570. 2. Reformation — Scotland.*
DA787.M6L4 1971   942.05   73-104251   ISBN:0837139759

Lee, Maurice. III. 1478
John Maitland of Thirlestane and the foundation of the Stewart despotism in Scotland. Princeton, N.J., Princeton University Press, 1959. 314 p. illus. 24 cm. (Princeton studies in history, 11) *1. Maitland, John, baron of Thirlestane, 1543-1595. 2. Scotland — History — To 1603.*
DA788.L4   941.05   59-9097

Buchan, John, 1875-1940. III. 1479
Montrose; a history, by John Buchan. Boston, Houghton Mifflin, 1928. xvii, 385 p. 2 port. (incl. front.) maps. 24 cm. *1. Montrose, James Graham, 1st marquis of, 1612-1650. 2. Scotland — History — Charles I, 1625-1649.*
DA803.7.A3B83   28-24618

Petrie, Charles Alexander, Sir, bart., 1895- III. 1480
The Jacobite movement. [3d ed., rev.] London, Eyre & Spottiswoode, 1959. 499 p. illus. 22 cm. *1. Jacobites. 2. Gt. Brit. — History. I. T.*
DA813.P4x   A60-2276

Prebble, John, 1915- III. 1481
Culloden. [1st American ed.] New York, Atheneum, 1962 [c1961] 367 p. illus. 22 cm. *1. Culloden, Battle of, 1746.*
DA814.5.P67 1962   941.07   62-7541

Hanham, H. J. III. 1482
Scottish nationalism [by] H. J. Hanham. London, Faber, 1969. 3-250 p. 23 cm. *1. Nationalism — Scotland. I. T.*
DA821.H3   320.158/0941   79-407512   ISBN:57109080X

Kellas, James G. III. 1483
Modern Scotland; the nation since 1870 [by] James G. Kellas. New York, Praeger [1968] 284 p. maps. 23 cm. *1. Scotland. I. T.*
DA821.K44 1968b   941/.08   68-9439

DA850 – 890 Description. Local History

Johnson, Samuel, 1709-1784. III. 1484
Johnson's Journey to the western islands of Scotland; and Boswell's Journal of a tour to the Hebrides with Samuel Johnson, LL.D; edited by R. W. Chapman. London, New York, Oxford U.P., 1970. xix, 475 p., fold. plate. facsims., map. 21 cm. (Oxford paperbacks, 205) *1. Hebrides — Description and travel. 2. Scotland — Description and travel — To 1800. I. Boswell, James, 1740-1795. Journal of a tour to the Hebrides. 1970. II. Chapman, Robert William, 1881-1960, ed. III. Journey to the western islands of Scotland. IV. Journal of a tour to the Hebrides with Samuel Johnson, LL.D.*
DA880.H4J6 1970   914.11/7/047   75-507901   ISBN:192810723

Mackenzie, William Cook, 1862- III. 1485
The Highlands and isles of Scotland; a historical survey, by W. C. Mackenzie. Edinburgh & London, The Moray Press [1937] 326 p. front., plates, ports. 22 cm. Map on lining-papers. *1. Highlands of Scotland — History. 2. Scotland — History. I. T.*
DA880.H6M247   941.1   38-21682

Gaskell, Philip. III. 1486
Morvern transformed: a Highland parish in the nineteenth century. London, Cambridge U.P., 1968. xix, 273 p. 17 plates, illus., tables, maps, ports. 24 cm. *1. Morvern — History. I. T.*
DA890.M87G3   941.3/8   67-24944   ISBN:521 05060 X

DA900 – 995 Ireland. Northern Ireland

DA900 – 990 IRELAND

Beckett, James Camlin, 1912-   III. 1487
A short history of Ireland, [by] J. C. Beckett. 3rd ed. London, Hutchinson, 1966. 191 p. maps. 22 cm. (Hutchinson university library: history) *1. Ireland — History. I. T.*
DA912.B4 1966   941.5   66-76529

Evans, Emyr Estyn.   III. 1488
Irish heritage; the landscape, the people and their work, by E. Estyn Evans. With illustrations by the author. Dundalk, W. Tempest, Dundalgan Press, 1942. xvi, 190 p. illus. (incl. maps) VI pl. 24 cm. *1. Country life — Ireland. 2. Ireland — Social life and customs. 3. Ireland — Description and travel. I. T.*
DA925.E9   914.15   42-20481

Heslinga, Marcus Willem.   III. 1489
The Irish border as a cultural divide; a contribution to the study of regionalism in the British Isles. Assen, Van Gorcum, 1962. 225 p. maps. 25 cm. Proefschrift — Utrecht. "Stellingen": [2] l. inserted at end. *1. Ireland — Civilization. 2. Ireland — History. 3. Regionalism — Ireland. I. T.*
DA925.H4   914.15   63-1978

DA930 – 965 by Period

De Paor, Máire.   III. 1490
Early Christian Ireland [by] Máire and Liam de Paor. New York, Praeger [1958] 263 p. illus. 21 cm. (Ancient peoples and places, v.8) Books that matter. *1. Ireland — History — To 1603. 2. Ireland — Civilization. I. De Paor, Liam, joint author. II. T.*
DA932.D4   941.5   58-9638

Otway-Ruthven, Annette Jocelyn, 1909-   III. 1491
A history of medieval Ireland [by] A. J. Otway-Ruthven; with an introduction by Kathleen Hughes. London, Benn; New York, Barnes & Noble, 1968. xv, 454 p. fold plate, maps (1 col.). 23 cm. *1. Ireland — History — 1172-1603. I. T.*
DA934.O8 1968   941.5   68-77860   ISBN:0510278019

Bagwell, Richard, 1840-1918.   III. 1492
Ireland under the Tudors; with a succinct account of the earlier history. [London] Holland Press [c1963] 3 v. maps. 23 cm. Reprint of the 1885-90 ed. *1. Ireland — History — 16th cent. I. T.*
DA935.B14 1963   67-9028

Falls, Cyril Bentham, 1888-   III. 1493
Elizabeth's Irish wars, by Cyril Falls. New York, Barnes & Noble [1970] 362 p. illus., facsims., map. 23 cm. Reprint of the 1950 ed. *1. Ireland — History — 1558-1603. I. T.*
DA937.F3 1970   941.5/5   72-13225   ISBN:389039616

Bagwell, Richard, 1840-1918.   III. 1494
Ireland under the Stuarts and during the interregnum. [London] Holland Press [c1963] 3 v. maps. 22 cm. Reprint of the 1909-1916 ed. *1. Ireland — History — 17th cent. I. T.*
DA940.B3x   67-8919

Clarke, Aidan.   III. 1495
The old English in Ireland, 1625-42. Ithaca, N.Y., Cornell University Press [1966] 287 p. 22 cm. *1. Ireland — History — 1625-1649. 2. English in Ireland. I. T.*
DA941.5.C5 1966a   941.56   66-15553

Simms, John Gerald.   III. 1496
The Williamite confiscation in Ireland, 1690-1703. London, Faber and Faber [1956] 207 p. maps. 23 cm. (Studies in Irish history, v.7) *1. Land grants — Ireland. I. T. (S)*
DA946.S5   941.57   57-3592

McDowell, Robert Brendan.   III. 1497
Irish public opinion, 1750-1800, by R. B. McDowell. London, Faber and Faber [1944] 306 p. 23 cm. (Studies in Irish history) "First published in Mcmxliv." *1. Ireland — Politics and government — 1760-1820. 2. Ireland — Social conditions. 3. Public opinion — Ireland. I. T.*
DA947.M2   941.57   44-6997

O'Connell, Maurice R., 1922-   III. 1498
Irish politics and social conflict in the age of the American Revolution, by Maurice R. O'Connell. Philadelphia, University of Pennsylvania Press [1965] 444 p. illus. 22 cm. *1. Ireland — Politics and government — 1760-1820. 2. U.S. — History — Revolution — Influence. 3. Ireland — Social conditions. I. T.*
DA947.O36   941.57   64-24494

Pakenham, Thomas, Hon., 1933-   III. 1499
The year of liberty; the story of the great Irish rebellion of 1798. [1st American ed.] Englewood Cliffs, N.J., Prentice-Hall [1970, c1969] 416 p. illus., facsims., maps, ports. 25 cm. *1. Ireland — History — Rebellion of 1798. I. T.*
DA949.P3 1970   941.5/7   79-96825   ISBN:139718958

DA950 – 958 19TH CENTURY

MacDonagh, Oliver.   III. 1500
Ireland. Englewood Cliffs, N.J., Prentice-Hall [1968] xi, 146 p. map. 21 cm. (The Modern nations in historical perspective. A Spectrum book.) *1. Ireland — History — 19th century. 2. Ireland — History — 20th century.*
DA950.M18   941.5/8   68-14461

McDowell, Robert Brendan.   III. 1501
The Irish administration, 1801-1914, by R. B. McDowell. London, Routledge & K. Paul, 1964. xi, 328 p. 23 cm. (Studies in Irish history, 2d ser., v.2) *1. Ireland — Politics and government — 19th cent. 2. Ireland — Politics and government — 20th cent. I. T.*
DA950.M2   65-3241

McDowell, Robert Brendan.   III. 1502
Public opinion and government policy in Ireland, 1801-1846. London, Faber and Faber [1952] 303 p. 23 cm. (Studies in Irish history, v.5) *1. Ireland — Politics and government — 19th cent. 2. Public opinion — Ireland. I. T. (S)*
DA950.2.M2 1952   941.58   53-21588

Gwynn, Denis Rolleston, 1893-   III. 1503
Daniel O'Connell. Rev. centenary ed. [Cork] Cork Univ. Press, 1947. 262 p. 22 cm. *1. O'Connell, Daniel, 1775-1847. 2. Ireland — Politics and government — 19th cent.*
DA950.22G85x   A48-8203

Nowlan, Kevin B.   III. 1504
The politics of repeal; a study in the relations between Great Britain and Ireland, 1841-50, by Kevin B. Nowlan. London, Routledge & K. Paul, 1965. viii, 248 p. 23 cm. (Studies in Irish history, 2d ser., v.3) *1. O'Connell, Daniel, 1775-1847. 2. Ireland — Politics and government — 1837-1901. 3. Home rule (Ireland) I. T. (S)*
DA950.5.N6   65-3974

Edwards, Robert Dudley, ed.   III. 1505
The great famine; studies in Irish history, 1845-52. Editors, R. Dudley Edwards [and] T. Desmond Williams. [1st U.S. ed. New York] New York University Press, 1957. xvi, 517 p. illus., maps. 22 cm. *1. Ireland — Famines. 2. Ireland — History — 1837-1901. I. Williams, Thomas Desmond, joint ed. II. T.*
DA950.7.E3 1957   941.58   57-8843

Mansergh, Nicholas.   III. 1506
Ireland in the age of reform and revolution; a commentary on Anglo-Irish relations and on political forces in Ireland, 1840-1921, by Nicholas Mansergh. London, G. Allen & Unwin [1940] 272 p. 22 cm. "First published in 1940." *1. Irish question. 2. Ireland — Politics and government. I. T.*
DA951.M3 1940   941.58   A41-630

Ireland. Northern Ireland

Thornley, David. **III. 1507**
Isaac Butt and home rule. London, MacGibbon & Kee, 1964. 413 p. port. 23 cm. *1. Butt, Isaac, 1813-1879. 2. Home rule (Ireland) I. T.*
DA952.B8T5   64-7039

Ó Broin, Leon, 1902- **III. 1508**
Fenian fever; an Anglo-American dilemma. New York, New York University Press, 1971. x, 264 p. illus. 23 cm. *1. Fenians. 2. Irish in the United States. I. T.*
DA954.O24 1971b   941.58   76-165471   ISBN:0814761518

Norman, Edward R. **III. 1509**
The Catholic Church and Ireland in the age of rebellion, 1859-1873 [by] E. R. Norman. Ithaca, N.Y., Cornell University Press [1965] xi, 485 p. illus., ports. 23 cm. *1. Ireland — Politics and government — 1837-1901. 2. Catholic Church in Ireland. I. T.*
DA955.N6 1965   941.58   64-25406

O'Brien, Conor Cruise, 1917- ed. **III. 1510**
Parnell and his party, 1880-90. Oxford, Clarendon Press, 1957. xii, 373 p. port., diagr., tables. 23 cm. "[Originated] as a thesis for the degree of doctor of philosophy in the University of Dublin." *1. Parnell, Charles Stewart, 1846-1891. 2. Irish question. I. T.*
DA958.P2O16   941.58   57-3208

O'Brien, Richard Barry, 1847-1918. **III. 1511**
The life of Charles Stewart Parnell, 1846-1891. New York, Greenwood Press [1969-   v. illus., facsim. 23 cm. Reprint of the 1898 ed. *1. Parnell, Charles Stewart, 1846-1891. I. T.*
DA958.P2O2 1969   941.5/8/0924 (B)   68-57635

DA959 – 965   20TH CENTURY

Bell, J. Bowyer, 1931- **III. 1512**
The secret army; the IRA, 1916-1970 [by] J. Bowyer Bell. [1st American ed.] New York, John Day Co. [1971, c1970] ix, 404 p. illus., maps, ports. 24 cm. *1. Irish Republican Army — History. 2. Ireland — History — 20th century. 3. Northern Ireland — History. I. T.*
DA959.B43 1971   941.5/9   79-143409

O'Brien, Conor Cruise, 1917- ed. **III. 1513**
The shaping of modern Ireland. Toronto, University of Toronto Press, 1960. 201 p. 23 cm. "Originally ... a series of Thomas Davis lectures broadcast by Radio Eireann in 1955-56." *1. Ireland — History — 20th century — Addresses, essays, lectures. I. T.*
DA959.O18 1960b   941.59   60-50646

Nowlan, Kevin B., comp. **III. 1514**
Ireland in the war years and after 1939-51, edited by Kevin B. Nowlan and T. Desmond Williams. [1st American ed. Notre Dame, Ind.] University of Notre Dame Press [1970, c1969] ix, 216 p. 21 cm. "Contributions ... were originally broadcast in the Thomas David lecture series from Radio Éireann between January and April 1967." *1. Ireland — Civilization — Addresses, essays, lectures. 2. Northern Ireland — History — Addresses, essays, lectures. I. Williams, Thomas Desmond, joint comp. II. T.*
DA959.1.N68 1970   941.5/9   74-98905

Williams, Desmond, ed. **III. 1515**
The Irish struggle, 1916-1926. Toronto, University of Toronto Press [1966] vii, 193 p. 23 cm. *1. Ireland — History — 20th cent. — Addresses, essays, lectures. I. T.*
DA960.W48 1966a   941.59   67-72956

Caulfield, Malachy Francis, 1915- **III. 1516**
The Easter rebellion. [1st ed.] New York, Holt, Rinehart and Winston [1963] 375 p. 22 cm. *1. Ireland — History — Sinn Fein Rebellion, 1916. I. T.*
DA962.C33   941.59   63-12078

Younger, Calton. **III. 1517**
Ireland's civil war. London, Muller, 1968. [1], viii, 534 p. 12 plates, illus., ports. 23 cm. *1. Ireland — History — Civil War, 1922-1923. I. T.*
DA962.Y6   941.5/9   70-367247

Coogan, Timothy Patrick. **III. 1518**
Ireland since the rising. New York, Praeger [1966] xii, 355 p. ports. 25 cm. *1. Ireland — History — 1920- I. T.*
DA963.C64   941.59   66-17363

Harkness, D. W. **III. 1519**
The restless Dominion; the Irish Free State and the British Commonwealth of Nations, 1921-31 [by] D. W. Harkness. New York, New York University Press, 1970 [c1969] xv, 312 p. 24 cm. *1. Irish question. 2. Ireland — History — 1922-1949. I. T.*
DA963.H28 1970   327.415/042   73-114761

Taylor, Rex, 1921- **III. 1520**
Michael Collins. London, Hutchinson [1958] 352 p. illus., ports., facsims. 22 cm. *1. Collins, Michael, 1890-1922.*
DA965.C6T3 1958   923.2415   58-4609

Greaves, C. Desmond. **III. 1521**
The life and times of James Connolly, by C. Desmond Greaves. New York, International Publishers [1971, c1961] 448 p. 20 cm. (New World paperbacks, NW-S-14) *1. Connolly, James, 1868-1916. I. T.*
DA965.C7G7 1971   335.4/092/4 (B)   78-188758

Longford, Frank Pakenham, 7th Earl of, 1905- **III. 1522**
Eamon de Valera [by] the Earl of Longford & Thomas P. O'Neill. [1st American ed.] Boston, Houghton Mifflin, 1971, [c1970] xix, 499 p. illus., maps, ports. 24 cm. *1. De Valera, Eamonn, 1882- I. O'Neill, Thomas P., joint author.*
DA965.D4L6 1971   941.5/9/0924 (B)   77-144076   ISBN:0395121019

DA969 – 990   Description

Young, Arthur, 1741-1820. **III. 1523**
A tour in Ireland, with general observations on the present state of that kingdom made in the years 1776, 1777 and 1778; selected & edited by Constantia Maxwell. Cambridge [Eng.] The University Press, 1925. xxii, 244 p. front., plates, fold. map. 20 cm. *1. Ireland — Description and travel. I. Maxwell, Constantia Elizabeth, ed.*
DA972.Y68 1925   26-22239

Freeman, Thomas Walter. **III. 1524**
Ireland, a general and regional geography, by T. W. Freeman. [3d ed.] London, Methuen; New York, Dutton [1965] xix, 560 p. illus., maps, plates. 23 cm. ([Methuen's advanced geographies]) First published in 1950 under title: Ireland, its physical, historical, social, and economic geography. *1. Ireland — Description and travel — 1901-1950. I. T.*
DA977.F72 1965   68-569

Encyclopaedia of Ireland. **III. 1525**
Dublin, A. Figgis; New York, McGraw-Hill, 1968. 463 p. illus., maps. 29 cm. *1. Ireland.*
DA979.E5   914.15   68-54316

Synge, John Millington, 1871-1909. **III. 1526**
The Aran Islands. London, Allen & Unwin [1961] 166 p. 19 cm. *1. Aran Islands.*
DA990.A8S82 1961   62-3119

DA990 – 995   NORTHERN IRELAND

Stewart, Anthony Terence Quincey. **III. 1527**
The Ulster crisis [by] A. T. Q. Stewart. London, Faber, 1967. 3-284 p. 12 plates (incl. ports.), 2 maps, tables. 22 1/2 cm. *1. Ulster — Politics and government. 2. Home rule (Ireland) I. Carson, Edward Henry Carson, Baron, 1854-1935. II. T.*
DA990.U46S78   941.6   67-84876

Wilson, Thomas, PH.D., ed. **III. 1528**
Ulster under home rule; a study of the political and economic problems of Northern Ireland. London, New York, Oxford University Press, 1955. xxiv, 229 p. 23 cm. *1. Northern Ireland — Politics and government. 2. Northern Ireland — Economic conditions. I. T.*
DA990.U46W5   941.6   56-1350

Jones, Emrys. **III. 1529**
A social geography of Belfast. London, New York, Oxford University Press, 1960. xiv, 299 p. illus., plates, maps, plans. 23 cm. *1. Belfast — Social conditions. I. T.*
DA995.B5J6   309.14161   60-51808

DB   Austria. Hungary. Czechoslovakia

DB 1 – 99 AUSTRIA. AUSTRO-HUNGARIAN EMPIRE

Kann, Robert A., 1906-   **III. 1530**
A study in Austrian intellectual history; from late baroque to romanticism. New York, Praeger [1960] 367 p. illus. 22 cm. (Books that matter) *1. Abraham a Sancta Clara, Father, 1644-1709. 2. Sonnenfels, Josef von, 1732 or 3-1817. 3. Austria — Civilization. I. Austrian intellectual history. (S)*
DB30.K3   914.36   60-9207

Crankshaw, Edward.   **III. 1531**
The Habsburgs: portrait of a dynasty. New York, Viking Press [1971] 272 p. illus. 27 cm. (A Studio book) *1. Habsburg, House of — History. 2. Austria — Politics and government. I. T.*
DB36.1.C7   943.6   72-156753   ISBN:0670361348

Wandruszka, Adam, 1914-   **III. 1532**
The House of Habsburg; six hundred years of a European dynasty. Translated from the original German by Cathleen and Hans Epstein. [1st ed. in the U.S.A.] Garden City, N.Y., Doubleday, 1964. xxiii, 212 p. maps. 22 cm. *1. Habsburg, House of. I. T.*
DB36.1.W313   943   64-11745

Tapié, Victor Lucien, 1900-   **III. 1533**
The rise and fall of the Habsburg monarchy [by] Victor-L. Tapié. Translated by Stephen Hardman. New York, Praeger [1971] viii, 430 p. 25 cm. Translation of: Monarchie et peuples du Danube. *1. Austria – Politics and government. 2. Hungary – Politics and government. 3. Bohemia – Politics and government. 4. Habsburg, House of. I. T.*
DB47.T313   943.6/03   77-137893

Gehl, Jürgen.   **III. 1534**
Austria, Germany, and the Anschluss, 1931-1938. Foreword by Alan Bullock. London, New York, Oxford University Press, 1963. x, 212 p. maps. 23 cm. Based on thesis, St. Antony's College, Oxford. *1. Austria – Foreign relations – Germany. 2. Germany – Foreign relations – Austria. 3. Anschluss movement, 1918-1938. I. T.*
DB48.G4 1963   943.605   63-25360

Leeper, Alexander Wigram Allen, 1887-1935.   **III. 1535**
A history of medieval Austria, by A. W. Leeper, edited by R. W. Seton-Watson & C. A. Macartney. [London, New York, etc.] Oxford University Press, 1941. vi, 429 p. 23 cm. *1. Austria – History – To 1273. I. Seton-Watson, Robert William, 1879- ed. II. Macartney, Carlile Aylmer, 1895- joint ed.*
DB51.L4   943.6   41-12960

Crankshaw, Edward.   **III. 1536**
Maria Theresa. New York, Viking Press [1970, c1969] 366 p. illus., geneal. table, fold. map, ports. 22 cm. *1. Maria Theresa, Empress of Austria, 1717-1780. 2. Austria — History — Maria Theresa, 1740-1780.*
DB71.C7 1970   943/.053/0924 (B)   70-94850   ISBN:0670456314

Gooch, George Peabody, 1873-   **III. 1537**
Maria Theresa, and other studies [by] G. P. Gooch. [Hamden, Conn.] Archon Books, 1965. viii, 432 p. ports. 22 cm. Reprint of 1951 ed. *1. Maria Theresia, Empress, of Austria, 1717-1780. 2. Joseph II, Emperor of Germany, 1741-1790. 3. Marie Antoinette, consort of Louis XVI, King of France, 1755-1793. 4. Historiography. 5. History — Study and teaching. I. T.*
DB71.G63 1965   908   65-25396

Bernard, Paul P.   **III. 1538**
Joseph II, by Paul P. Bernard. New York, Twayne Publishers [1968] 155 p. 21 cm. (Twayne's rulers and statesmen of the world series, 5) *1. Joseph II, Emperor of Germany, 1741-1790.*
DB74.B43   943/.057/0924 (B)   67-25205

Bernard, Paul P.   **III. 1539**
Jesuits and Jacobins; enlightenment and enlightened despotism in Austria [by] Paul P. Bernard. Urbana, University of Illinois Press [1971] ix, 198 p. 24 cm. *1. Austria — History — Joseph II, 1780-1790. 2. Enlightenment. 3. Austria — Intellectual life. 4. Jesuits in Austria. 5. Josephinism. I. T.*
DB74.3.B397 1971   914.36/03/3   78-151997   ISBN:025200180X

Wangermann, Ernst.   **III. 1540**
From Joseph II to the Jacobin trials: government policy and public opinion in the Habsburg dominions in the period of the French Revolution. 2nd ed. London, Oxford U.P., 1969. xiii, 218 p. 23 cm. (Oxford Historical monographs) *1. Joseph, II, Emperor of Germany, 1741-1790. 2. Leopold, II, Emperor of Germany, 1747-1792. 3. Austria — Politics and government — 18th century. I. T.*
DB74.3.W3 1969   943.6/03   74-444349   ISBN:19821832X

DB80 – 99   19th – 20th Centuries

Macartney, Carlile Aylmer, 1895-   **III. 1541**
The Habsburg Empire, 1790-1918 [by] C. A. Macartney. [1st American ed.] New York, Macmillan [1969] xiv, 886 p. 24 cm. *1. Austria — History — 1789-1900. 2. Austria — History — 1867-1918. I. T.*
DB80.M3 1969   943.6/04   69-12834

Taylor, Alan John Percivale, 1906-   **III. 1542**
The Habsburg monarchy, 1809-1918; a history of the Austrian Empire and Austria-Hungary. New ed. London, H. Hamilton [1948] 279 p. ports., maps (on lining-papers) 22 cm. "An entirely rewritten version of an earlier work with the same title ... published in 1941." *1. Austria — History — 1789-1900. 2. Austria — History — 20th century.*
DB80.T382   943.6   49-19763

Bertier de Sauvigny, Guillaume de, 1912-   **III. 1543**
Metternich and his times, by G. de Bertier de Sauvigny. Translated by Peter Ryde. London, Darton, Longman & Todd [1962] xviii, 315 p. illus., maps, ports. 23 cm. *1. Metternich-Winneburg, Clemens Lothar Wenzel, Fürst von, 1773-1859. I. T.*
DB80.8.M57B43   65-32777

Cecil, Algernon, 1879-1953.   **III. 1544**
Metternich, 1773-1859; a study of his period and personality. [3d ed.] London, Eyre and Spottiswoode [1947] x, 324 p. ports. 22 cm. *1. Metternich-Winneburg, Clemens Lothar Wenzel, Fürst von, 1773-1859. 2. Europe — Politics — 1789-1900.*
DB80.8.M57C4x   923.2436   A48-7443

Kraehe, Enno E.   **III. 1545**
Metternich's German policy. Princeton, N.J., Princeton University Press, 1963- v. map. 24 cm. *1. Metternich-Winneburg, Clemens Lothar Wenzel, Fürst von, 1773-1859. 2. Austria — Foreign relations — 1789-1900.*
DB80.8.M57K7   943.603   63-9994

Schroeder, Paul W.   **III. 1546**
Metternich's diplomacy at its zenith, 1820-1823, by Paul W. Schroeder. New York, Greenwood Press [1969, c1962] xii, 292 p. maps, port. 23 cm. *1. Metternich-Winneburg, Clemens Lothar Wenzel, Fürst von, 1773-1859. 2. Europe — Politics — 1815-1848. I. T.*
DB80.8.M57S33 1969   943.6/04   78-95135   ISBN:837124719

Rath, Reuben John, 1910-   **III. 1547**
The Viennese Revolution of 1848 [by] R. John Rath. New York, Greenwood Press [1969, c1957] ix, 424 p. maps. 23 cm. *1. Austria — History — Revolution, 1848-1849. 2. Vienna — History. I. T.*
DB83.R3 1969   943.6/04   70-94617   ISBN:0837124654

May, Arthur James, 1899-   **III. 1548**
The Hapsburg Monarchy, 1867-1914. Cambridge, Harvard University Press, 1951. x, 532 p. 25 cm. *1. Austria — History — 1867-1918. 2. Hungary — History — 1867-1918. I. T.*
DB85.M35   943.6   51-7368

Clark, Chester Wells. III. 1549
Franz Joseph and Bismarck; the diplomacy of Austria before the War of 1866. New York, Russell & Russell [1968, c1934] xv, 635 p. 23 cm. (Harvard historical studies, v. 36) *1. Austria — Foreign relations — 1848-1867. 2. Franz Joseph I, Emperor of Austria, 1830-1916. 3. Austria — Foreign relations — Prussia. 4. Prussia — Foreign relations — Austria. 5. Prussia — Foreign relations — 1815-1870. 6. Bismarck, Otto, Fürst von, 1815-1898. I. T. (S)*
DB86.C5 1968   327.436/043   68-15113

Kann, Robert A., 1906- III. 1550
The multinational empire; nationalism and national reform in the Habsburg monarchy, 1848-1918. New York, Octagon Books, 1964 [c1950] 2 v. maps. 24 cm. Vol.2 issued also as thesis, Columbia University. *1. Austria — Politics and government — 1848-1918. 2. Austria — History — 1848-1867. 3. Austria — History — 1867-1918. 4. Nationalism — Austria. 5. Minorities — Austria. I. T.*
DB86.K3 1964   943.6   64-16383

Dedijer, Vladimir. III. 1551
The road to Sarajevo. New York, Simon and Schuster [1966] 550 p. illus., col. map (on lining papers) ports. 25 cm. *1. Franz Ferdinand, Archduke of Austria, 1863-1914 — Assassination. 2. Austria — Politics and government — 1867-1918. I. T.*
DB89.F7D4   943.604   65-24282

Remak, Joachim, 1920- III. 1552
Sarajevo; the story of a political murder. New York, Criterion Books [1959] 301 p. illus. 22 cm. *1. Franz Ferdinand, Archduke of Austria, 1863-1914 — Assassination. I. T.*
DB89.F7R4   943.604   59-6557

Stadler, Karl R. III. 1553
Austria, by Karl R. Stadler. New York, Praeger [1971] 346 p. illus., maps (1 fold.), ports. 23 cm. (Nations of the modern world) *1. Austria — History — 20th century. I. T. (S)*
DB91.S72 1971   943.6/05   69-12307

Zeman, Zbyněk A. B. III. 1554
The break-up of the Habsburg Empire, 1914-1918; a study in national and social revolution [by] Z. A. B. Zeman. London, New York, Oxford University Press, 1961. xvi, 274 p. illus., maps., ports. 23 cm. *1. Austria — History — 20th cent. 2. Nationalism — Austria. I. T.*
DB91.Z4   943.604   61-66610

Gulick, Charles Adams, 1896- III. 1555
Austria from Habsburg to Hitler, with a foreword by Walther Federn. Berkeley, Univ. of California Press, 1948. 2 v. 24 cm. *1. Austria — History — 1918-1938. 2. Austria — Politics and government — 1918-1938.*
DB96.G8   943.6   48-1808

Shepherd, Gordon. III. 1556
The Anschluss. Philadelphia, Lippincott [1963] 222 p. illus. 22 cm. First published in London in 1963 under title: Anschluss: the rape of Austria. *1. Austria — History — 1938-1945. 2. Anschluss movement, 1918-1938. I. T.*
DB97.S5 1963a   943.605   63-15615

DB191 – 217
CZECHOSLOVAKIA

Keefe, Eugene K. III. 1557
Area handbook for Czechoslovakia. Co-authors: Eugene K. Keefe [and others. Washington, For sale by the Supt. of Docs., U.S. Govt. Print. Off.] 1972. xiv, 321 p. maps. 24 cm. "One of a series of handbooks prepared by Foreign Area Studies (FAS) of The American University." "DA pam 550-158." Supt. of Docs. no.: D101.22:550-158 *1. Czechoslovak Republic. I. American University, Washington, D.C. Foreign Area Studies. II. T.*
DB196.K4   914.37   77-185481

Wanklyn, Harriet Grace. III. 1558
Czechoslovakia. New York, F. A. Praeger [1954] xviii, 445 p. illus., maps (part col.) 23 cm. (Books that matter) *1. Czechoslovak Republic.*
DB196.W3 1954a   914.37   52-11993

Wiskemann, Elizabeth. III. 1559
Czechs & Germans: a study of the struggle in the historic provinces of Bohemia and Moravia. 2nd ed. London, Melbourne [etc.] issued under the auspices of the Royal Institute of International Affairs [by] Macmillan; New York, St. Martin's P., 1967. xiv, 299 p. 4 maps (1 col.), tables. 22 1/2 cm. *1. Czechoslovak Republic — Politics and government. 2. Germans in Bohemia. 3. Germans in Moravia. I. Royal Institute of International Affairs. II. T.*
DB200.7.W5 1967   943.7   67-10945

Bradley, John Francis Nejez. III. 1560
Czechoslovakia: a short history, by J. F. N. Bradley. Edinburgh, Edinburgh University Press, 1971. iii-xii, 212 p., 33 plates. illus., maps, ports. 23 cm. (Short histories of Europe, 2) *1. Czechoslovak Republic — History.*
DB205.B68 1971   943.7   78-159593   ISBN:0852241933

Seton-Watson, Robert William, 1879-1951. III. 1561
A history of the Czechs and Slovaks, by R. W. Seton-Watson. Hamden, Conn., Archon Books, 1965. 413 p. map. 23 cm. "Originally published 1943." *1. Bohemia — History. 2. Slovakia — History. 3. Czechoslovak Republic — History. I. T.*
DB205.S4 1965   943.7   65-16973

Thomson, Samuel Harrison, 1895- III. 1562
Czechoslovakia in European history. [2d ed., enl.] Princeton, Princeton University Press, 1953. 485 p. illus. 23 cm. *1. Czechs. 2. Slovaks. 3. Bohemia — History. 4. Czechoslovak Republic — History. I. T.*
DB205.1.T48 1953   943.7   52-8780

Heymann, Frederick Gotthold, 1900- III. 1563
Poland & Czechoslovakia [by] Frederick G. Heymann. Englewood Cliffs, N.J., Prentice-Hall [1966] viii, 181 p. maps. 21 cm. (Modern nations in historical perspective. A Spectrum book.) *1. Czechoslovak Republic — History. 2. Poland — History. I. T.*
DB205.3.H4   943.7   66-22803

Vondracek, Felix John, 1901- III. 1564
The foreign policy of Czechoslovakia, 1918-1935. New York, Columbia University Press; London, P. S. King, 1937. 451 p. fold. map. 23 cm. (Studies in history, economics and public law, ed. by the Faculty of political science of Columbia University. no. 426) Issued also as thesis (Ph.D.) Columbia University. *1. Czechoslovak republic — Foreign relations. I. T.*
DB205.7.V6x (H31.C7 no. 426)   37-20604

Heymann, Frederick Gotthold, 1900- III. 1565
John Žižka and the Hussite revolution, by Frederick G. Heymann. New York, Russell & Russell [1969, c1955] 521 p. illus., maps. 25 cm. *1. Žižka, Jan, 1360 (ca.)-1424. I. T.*
DB208.H4 1969   943.7/02/0924 (B)   71-77671

Kaminsky, Howard, 1924- III. 1566
A history of the Hussite revolution. Berkeley, University of California Press, 1967. xv, 580 p. illus., maps. 25 cm. *1. Hussites. I. T. II. T:The Hussite revolution.*
DB208.K3   943.7/02   67-12608

Heymann, Frederick Gotthold, 1900- III. 1567
George of Bohemia, King of Heretics, by Frederick G. Heymann. Princeton, N.J., Princeton University Press, 1965. xvi, 671 p. illus., maps, ports. 24 cm. *1. Jiří z Poděbrad, King of Bohemia, 1420-1471. 2. Bohemia — History — 1403-1526. I. T.*
DB209.H4   943.702   64-19821

Odložilík, Otakar, 1899- III. 1568
The Hussite King; Bohemia in European affairs, 1440-1471. New Brunswick, N.J., Rutgers University Press [1965] ix, 337 p. illus., maps (1 fold.) ports. 25 cm. *1. Jiří z Poděbrad, King of Bohemia, 1420-1471. 2. Europe — History — 476-1492. I. T.*
DB209.O3   943.702   65-19406

Kerner, Robert Joseph, 1887-1956. III. 1569
Bohemia in the eighteenth century; a study in political, economic, and social history, with special reference to the reign of Leopold II, 1790-1792. New York, AMS Press [1969] xii, 412 p. 24 cm. Reprint of the 1932 ed. *1. Bohemia — Politics and government. 2. Bohemia — Constitutional history. 3. Bohemia — Economic conditions. 4. Bohemia — History — 1618-1848. 5. Leopold II, Emperor of Germany, 1747-1792. I. T.*
DB212.K4 1969b   943.7/02   79-94315

DB214 – 217   19th – 20th
Centuries

Beneš, Edvard, Pres. Czechoslovak Republic, 1884-1948. III. 1570
Memoirs; from Munich to new war and new victory. Translated by Godfrey Lias. London, Allen & Unwin [1954] xi, 346 p. 24 cm. Translation of Paměti. "The present volume is the first of three which the late President Dr. Eduard Beneš intended to write ... only one of the three volumes was completed." *1.*

Czechoslovak Republic — Foreign relations. 2. *Europe — Politics — 1918-1945.*
DB215.B4144 1954a   923.1437   A55-4958

Kerner, Robert Joseph, 1887- ed.   **III. 1571**
Czechoslovakia; chapters by Gerald Druce [and others] ... edited by Robert J. Kerner. Berkeley, University of California Press, 1945. xxi, 504 p. front., illus. (maps) plates, ports. 23 cm. (The United nations series) 1. *Czechoslovak Republic — History.* 2. *Czechoslovak Republic — Civilization.*
DB215.K4 1945   943.7   46-4529

Wheeler-Bennett, John Wheeler, 1902-   **III. 1572**
Munich: prologue to tragedy. New York, Duell, Sloan and Pearce [1948] xiii, 507 p. illus., maps. 22 cm. 1. *Munich Four-Power Agreement, 1938.* 2. *Europe — Politics — 1918-1945.* I. T.
DB215.W45   940.52   48-8501

Zinner, Paul E.   **III. 1573**
Communist strategy and tactics in Czechoslovakia, 1918-48. New York, Praeger [1963] 264 p. 22 cm. (Praeger publications in Russian history and world communism, no. 129) 1. *Czechoslovak Republic — Politics and government.* 2. *Komunistická strana Československa.* 3. *Czechoslovak Republic — History — Coup d'état, 1948.* I. T.
DB215.Z55   943.703   63-10829

Mastny, Vojtech, 1936-   **III. 1574**
The Czechs under Nazi rule; the failure of national resistance, 1939-1942. New York, Columbia University Press, 1971. xiii, 274 p. 24 cm. (East Central European studies of Columbia University) 1. *Czechoslovak Republic — History — 1938-1945.* 2. *Bohemia and Moravia (Protectorate, 1939-1945) — Politics and government.* I. T. (S:Columbia University. Program on East Central Europe. East Central European studies)
DB215.3.M38   943.7/03   72-132065   ISBN:0231033036

Bušek, Vratislav, ed.   **III. 1575**
Czechoslovakia. Vratislav Bušek and Nicolas Spulber, editors. New York, Published for the Mid-European Studies Center of the Free Europe Committee by Praeger [1957] xvii, 520 p. maps, tables. 24 cm. (East-Central Europe under the Communists. Praeger publications in Russian history and world communism, no. 19.) 1. *Czechoslovak Republic.* I. Spulber, Nicolas, joint ed. II. Free Europe Committee. Mid-European Studies Center. (S)
DB215.5.B83   943.7   57-9333

Komunistická strana Československa. Ústřední výbor. Kommission für die Vollendung der Parteirehabilitierung.   **III. 1576**
The Czechoslovak political trials, 1950-1954; the suppressed report of the Dubček Government's commission of inquiry. Edited with a pref. and a postscript by Jiří Pelikán. Stanford, Calif., Stanford University Press, 1971. 360 p. 23 cm. German translation has title: Das unterdrückte Dossier. 1. *Czechoslovak Republic — Politics and government — 1945-* 2. *Political purges — Czechoslovak Republic.* I. T.
DB215.5.K633 1971   320.9/437/04   70-150328   ISBN:0804707693

Kusin, Vladimir V.   **III. 1577**
The intellectual origins of the Prague spring; the development of reformist ideas in Czechoslovakia, 1956-1967, by Vladimir V. Kusin. Cambridge [Eng.] University Press, 1971. v, 153 p. 23 cm. (Soviet and East European studies) 1. *Czechoslovak Republic — Politics and government, 1945-1968.* 2. *Czechoslovak Republic — History — Intervention, 1968-* I. T. (S)
DB215.5.K87   320.9/437/04   73-155582   ISBN:0521081246

Ripka, Hubert, 1895-1958.   **III. 1578**
Czechoslovakia enslaved; the story of the communist coup d'état. London, Gollancz, 1950. 339 p. 23 cm. 1. *Czechoslovak Republic — History — Coup d'état, 1948.* I. T.
DB215.5.R52   943.7   50-2995

Schwartz, Harry, 1919-   **III. 1579**
Prague's 200 days; the struggle for democracy in Czechoslovakia. New York, Praeger [1969] x, 274 p. map. 22 cm. 1. *Czechoslovak Republic — Politics and government.* 2. *Czechoslovak Republic — History — Intervention, 1968.* 3. *Komunistická strana Ceskoslovenika.* I. T.
DB215.6.S33   943.7/04   69-19700

Beneš, Edvard, Pres. Czechoslovak Republic, 1884-1948.   **III. 1580**
My war memoirs, by Eduard Beneš. Translated from the Czech by Paul Selver. Westport, Conn., Greenwood Press [1971] 512 p. port. 23 cm. Reprint of the 1928 ed. 1. *European War, 1914-1918 — Czechoslovak Republic.*
DB217.B3A4 1971   943.7/03/0924   70-114467   ISBN:0837147638

DB231 – 840 SPECIAL PROVINCES. REGIONS

Novak, Bogdan C.   **III. 1581**
Trieste, 1941-1954; the ethnic, political, and ideological struggle [by] Bogdan C. Novak. Chicago, University of Chicago Press [1970] xx, 526 p. maps. 23 cm. Based on the author's thesis, University of Chicago. 1. *Trieste — Politics and government.* 2. *World War, 1939-1945 — Territorial questions — Yugoslavia.* 3. *World War, 1939-1945 — Territorial questions — Italy.* I. T.
DB321.N68 1970   327.45/0497   73-96068   ISBN:0226596214

Eterovich, Francis H., ed.   **III. 1582**
Croatia: land, people, culture. Francis H. Eterovich, editor; Christopher Spalatin, associate editor. Foreword by Ivan Meštrović. [Toronto] Published for the Editorial Board by University of Toronto Press [1964-   v. illus., 10 fold. maps, ports. 24 cm. 1. *Croatia.* 2. *Croats.* I. T.
DB366.E8   914.394   65-2286

Hitchins, Keith.   **III. 1583**
The Rumanian national movement in Transylvania, 1780-1849. Cambridge, Harvard University Press, 1969. xi, 316 p. 21 cm. (Harvard historical monographs, 61) Based on the author's thesis, Harvard, 1964. 1. *Transylvania — Politics and government.* 2. *Romanians in Transylvania.* I. T. (S)
DB739.H57   320.1/58/094984   69-12724

Burghardt, Andrew Frank, 1924-   **III. 1584**
Borderland; a historical and geographical study of Burgenland, Austria. Madison, University of Wisconsin Press, 1962. xii, 365 p. illus., maps. 24 cm. Based on the author's thesis, University of Wisconsin, 1958. 1. *Burgenland.* I. T.
DB785.B8B8   914.3615   62-15992

DB901 – 975 HUNGARY

Helmreich, Ernst Christian, ed.   **III. 1585**
Hungary. New York, Published for the Mid-European Studies Center of the Free Europe Committee by Praeger [1957] xiv, 466 p. maps, tables. 24 cm. (East-Central Europe under the Communists. Praeger publications in Russian history and world communism, no. 49. Books that matter.) 1. *Hungary.* 2. *Communism — Hungary.* 3. *Hungary — History — Revolution, 1956.* I. Free Europe Committee. Mid-European Studies Center (S)
DB906.H4   943.91   57-9334

Macartney, Carlile Aylmer, 1895-   **III. 1586**
Hungary, a short history. Chicago, Aldine Pub. Co. [1962] 262 p. illus. 22 cm. 1. *Hungary — History.*
DB925.M16   943.9   62-19084

Sinor, Denis.   **III. 1587**
History of Hungary. New York, A. Praeger [1959] 310 p. 23 cm. (Books that matter) 1. *Hungary — History.*
DB925.1.S5   943.91   59-15752

Marczali, Henrik, 1856-1940.   **III. 1588**
Hungary in the eighteenth century [by] Henry Marczali. New York, Arno Press, 1971. lxiv, 377 p. map. 24 cm. (The Eastern Europe collection) Reprint of the 1910 ed. A rev. and updated English version of the original Hungarian ed., which first appeared in 1882, with an introductory essay on the earlier history of Hungary, by H. W. V. Temperley. 1. *Hungary — History — 1683-1848.* 2. *Hungary — Politics and government — 1683-1848.* I. Temperley, Harold William Vazeille, 1879-1939. II. T.
DB932.5.M325 1971   309.1/439/04   75-135818   ISBN:0405027605

Barany, George, 1922-   **III. 1589**
Stephen Széchenyi and the awakening of Hungarian nationalism, 1791-1841. Princeton, N.J., Princeton University Press, 1968. xviii, 487 p. illus., facsims., ports. 25 cm. A revision of the author's thesis, University of Colorado. 1. *Széchenyi, István, gróf, 1791-1860.* 2. *Nationalism — Hungary.* I. T.
DB933.3.S8B3 1968   943.9/1/040924 (B)   68-20865

DB947 – 957 20th Century

Kertesz, Stephen Denis, 1904-   III. 1590
Diplomacy in a whirlpool; Hungary between Nazi Germany and Soviet Russia. Notre Dame, Ind., University of Notre Dame Press [1953] xvi, 273 p. maps. 24 cm. (International studies of the Committee on International Relations, University of Notre Dame) *1. Hungary — Foreign relations. I. T. (S:Notre Dame, Ind. University. Committee on International Relations. International studies)*
DB948.K47   327.4391   53-7349

Horthy, Miklos, nagybányai, 1868-1957.   III. 1591
Memoirs. With an introd. by Nicholas Roosevelt. New York, R. Speller [1957] 268 p. illus. 22 cm. Translation of Ein Leben für Ungarn. *1. Hungary — History — 20th cent.*
DB950.H6A33   943.91   57-2991

Károlyi, Mihály, gróf, 1875-1955.   III. 1592
Memoirs of Michael Karolyi; faith without illusion. Translated from the Hungarian by Catherine Karolyi; with an introd. by A. J. P. Taylor. London, J. Cape [1956] 392 p. illus., ports., col. map (on lining papers) 24 cm.
DB950.K3A38 1959   923.24391   56-2747

Macartney, Carlile Aylmer, 1895-   III. 1593
October fifteenth; a history of modern Hungary, 1929-1945. 2d ed. Edinburgh, University Press [1961- v. maps. 25 cm. (Edinburgh University publications; history, philosophy, and economics, no. 6) *1. Hungary — History — 1918-1945. I. T.*
DB955.M223   943.91   62-2566

Nagy-Talavera, Nicholas M., 1929-   III. 1594
The Green Shirts and the others; a history of Fascism in Hungary and Rumania, by Nicholas M. Nagy-Talavera. Stanford, Calif., Hoover Institution Press, Stanford University [1970] xii, 427 p. maps (on lining papers) 23 cm. (Hoover Institution publications, 85) Based on the author's thesis, University of California. *1. Hungary — Politics and government — 1918-1945. 2. Romania — Politics and government — 1914-1944. 3. Szálasi Ferenc, 1897-1946. 4. Codreanu, Corneliu Zelea, 1899-1938. I. T. (S:Stanford University. Hoover Institution on War, Revolution, and Peace. Publications, 85)*
DB955.N37   943.9/05   74-98136   ISBN:0817918515

Völgyes, Iván, 1936-   III. 1595
Hungary in revolution, 1918-19: nine essays, edited by Ivan Völgyes. Lincoln, University of Nebraska Press [1971] x, 219 p. 25 cm. *1. Hungary — History — Revolution, 1918-1919 — Addresses, essays, lectures. I. T.*
DB955.V58   943.9/05   71-125855   ISBN:0803207883

Váli, Ferenc Albert, 1905-   III. 1596
Rift and revolt in Hungary; nationalism versus communism. Cambridge, Harvard University Press, 1961. xvii, 590 p. fold. map, diagrs. 25 cm. *1. Hungary — Politics and government — 1945- 2. Communism — Hungary. I. T.*
DB956.V3   943.9105   61-13745

Zinner, Paul E.   III. 1597
Revolution in Hungary. New York, Columbia University Press, 1962. xi, 380 p. 24 cm. *1. Communism — Hungary. 2. Hungary — Politics and government — 1945- 3. Hungary — History — Revolution, 1956. I. T.*
DB956.Z5   943.9105   62-17062

Kecskemeti, Paul.   III. 1598
The unexpected revolution; social forces in the Hungarian uprising. Stanford, Calif., Stanford University Press, 1961. 178 p. 23 cm. "Prepared as part of a continuing program of research undertaken by the Rand Corporation for the United States Air Force." *1. Hungary — History — Revolution, 1956. I. T.*
DB957.K38   943.9105   61-10927

Lasky, Melvin J., ed.   III. 1599
The Hungarian revolution; a white book. The story of the October uprising as recorded in documents, dispatches, eye-witness accounts, and world-wide reactions. Edited by Melvin J. Lasky. Freeport, N.Y., Books for Libraries Press [1970, c1957] 318 p. illus., maps, ports. 27 cm. *1. Hungary — History — Revolution, 1956. I. T.*
DB957.L3 1970   943.9/105   70-119936   ISBN:836953797

Lettis, Richard, ed.   III. 1600
The Hungarian revolt, October 23-November 4, 1956 [by] Richard Lettis and William E. Morris. New York, Scribner [1961] 219 p. illus. 24 cm. (A Scribner research anthology) *1. Hungary — History — Revolution, 1956. I. Morris, William E., joint ed. II. T.*
DB957.L48   943.9105   61-19091

DC   France

DC20 – 29 DESCRIPTION

Adams, Henry, 1838-1918. III. 1601
Mont-Saint-Michel and Chartres. With an introduction by Ralph Adams Cram. Boston & New York, Houghton Mifflin, 1936. xiv, 397 p. illus., plates. 22 cm. *1. Mont St. Michel, France. 2. Chartres, France. Notre-Dame (Cathedral) 3. Middle ages. I. Cram, Ralph Adams, 1863-1942, ed.*
DC20.A2 1936   914.4   36-27246

Conder, John J. III. 1602
A formula of his own; Henry Adam's literary experiment [by] John J. Conder. Chicago, University of Chicago Press [1970] xiv, 202 p. 21 cm. *1. Adams, Henry, 1838-1918. Mont-Saint-Michel and Chartres. 2. Adams, Henry, 1838-1918. The education of Henry Adams. I. T.*
DC20.A23C63   818/.4/08   79-103427   ISBN:0226114376

Young, Arthur, 1741-1820. III. 1603
Travels in France during the years 1787, 1788 & 1789. Edited by Constantia Maxwell. Cambridge [Eng.] The University Press, 1929. lvi, 428 p. fold. map. port. 21 cm. *1. France — Description and travel. 2. Agriculture — France. 3. France — Agriculture. I. Maxwell, Constantia Elizabeth, 1885- ed. II. T.*
DC25.Y68 1929   Agr29-1365

Du Pont de Nemours, Victor Marie, 1767-1827. III. 1604
Journey to France and Spain, 1801. Edited by Charles W. David. Port Washington, N.Y., Kennikat Press [1972, c1961] xxvi, 144 p. illus., map, ports. 23 cm. *1. France — Social life and customs. 2. Spain — Description and travel. I. T.*
DC26.D8 1972   914/.03/27   70-153259   ISBN:0804615659

James, Henry, 1843-1916. III. 1605
A little tour in France. With illus. by Joseph Pennell. New York, AMS Press [1969] xiii, 350 p. illus. 23 cm. Reprint of the 1900 ed. Originally appeared in the Atlantic monthly, 1883-84, under title: En Provence. *1. France — Description and travel. I. Pennell, Joseph, 1857-1926, illus. II. T.*
DC28.J27 1969   914.4   78-94312

DC30 – 34 CIVILIZATION

Padover, Saul Kussiel, 1905- III. 1606
French institutions: values and politics. With the collaboration of François Goguel, Louis Rosenstock-Franck [and] Eric Weil. [Stanford, Calif.] Stanford University Press, 1954. vi, 102 p. diagr. 23 cm. (Hoover Institute studies. Series E: Institutions, no. 2) *1. France — Civilization. 2. France — Politics and government — 1945- I. T. (S:Hoover Institution studies)*
DC33.P25   914.4   53-11875

Defourneaux, Marcelin. III. 1607
La vie quotidienne au temps de Jeanne d'Arc. [Paris] Hachette [1952] 315 p. 20 cm. (La Vie quotidienne) *1. France — Social life and customs. 2. France — Social conditions. I. T.*
DC33.2.Dx   64-9957

Faral, Edmond, 1882- III. 1608
La vie quotidienne au temps de saint Louis. [Paris] Hachette [1956, c1938] 277 p. 20 cm. *1. France — Social life and customs. I. T.*
DC33.2.F3x   A57-2755

Huizinga, Johan, 1872-1945. III. 1609
The waning of the Middle Ages; a study of the forms of life, thought, and art in France and the Netherlands in the XIVth and XVth centuries. Garden City, N.Y., 1954. 362 p. 19 cm. (Doubleday anchor books, A42) Translatio of Herfsttij der Middeleeuwen. *1. Civilization, Medieval. 2. Middle Ages. 3. France — Social life and customs. 4. Netherlands — Social life and customs. I. T.*
DC33.2.H83 1954   914.4   54-4529

Stone, Donald. III. 1610
France in the sixteenth century; a medieval society transformed, by Donald Stone, Jr. Englewood Cliffs, N.J., Prentice-Hall [1969] x, 180 p. 21 cm. (French literary backgrounds series) *1. France — Civilization — 1328-1600. 2. France — History — 16th century. 3. French literature — 16th century — History and criticism. I. T.*
DC33.3.S75   914.4/03/28   69-11352

Wiley, William Leon. III. 1611
The gentleman of Renaissance France, by W. L. Wiley. Westport, Conn., Greenwood Press [1971, c1954] xii, 303 p. illus. 23 cm. *1. France — Court and courtiers. I. T.*
DC33.3.W5 1971   914.4/03/2   75-152622   ISBN:083716169X

Ford, Franklin Lewis, 1920- III. 1612
Robe and sword; the regrouping of the French aristocracy after Louis XIV. Cambridge, Harvard University Press, 1953. xii, 280 p. illus. 22 cm. (Harvard historical studies, v.64) *1. France — Court and courtiers. 2. France — Nobility. 3. France — History — Bourbons, 1589-1789. I. T. (S)*
DC33.4.F7   944.034   52-12261

Havens, George Remington, 1890- III. 1613
The age of ideas; from reaction to revolution in eighteenth-century France. New York, Holt [1955] 474 p. illus. 25 cm. *1. France — Civilization. 2. Eighteenth century. I. T.*
DC33.4.H35   944.03   55-6056

Mandrou, Robert. III. 1614
La France aux XVIIe et XVIIIe siècles. Paris, Presses universitaires de France, 1967. 336 p. illus. 19 cm. (Nouvelle Clio. L'histoire et ses problèmes, 33) Cover illustrated in color. *1. France — History — Bourbons, 1589-1789. I. T. (S)*
DC33.4.M28   68-92490

Kohn, Hans, 1891- III. 1615
Making of the modern French mind. New York, Van Nostrand [c1955] 191 p. 18 cm. (An Anvil original, no. 1) *1. France — Intellectual life. I. T.*
DC33.7.K64   914.4   55-6243

Tannenbaum, Edward R. III. 1616
The new France. [Chicago] University of Chicago Press [1961] 251 p. illus. 24 cm. *1. National characteristics, French. 2. France — Intellectual life. 3. France — Civilization. I. T.*
DC33.7.T3   914.4   61-8076

Hayes, Carlton Joseph Huntley, 1882- III. 1617
France, a nation of patriots, by Carlton J. H Hayes. New York, Columbia University Press, 1930. x, 487 p. illus., map. 23 cm. (Social and economic studies of post-war France, prepared under the auspices of the Columbia university Council for research in the social sciences; ed. by C. J. H. Hayes ... vol. v) Appendices: A. Digest of typical textbooks in French schools for instruction in history, morals and civics, geography and reading. — B. Guide to teacher-societies. — C. Select list of French periodicals (other than dailies). — D. Guide to daily newspapers of Paris. — E. Guide to leading daily newspapers of provincial France. *1. Citizenship — France. 2. France — Nationality. 3. Education — France. 4. Propaganda, French. I. T.*
DC34.H3   30-4234

DC35 – 412 HISTORY

Boussard, Jacques. III. 1618
Atlas historique et culturel de la France. Préf. de Jean Alazard. Paris,

Elsevier [1957] viii, 214 p. illus., ports., col. maps. 35 cm. *1. France — History — Pictorial works. 2. France — Historical geography — Maps. 3. France — Civilization. I. T.*
DC35.5.B65   A59-146

Lavisse, Ernest, 1842-1922, ed.   **III. 1619**
Histoire de France depuis les origines jusqu'à la révolution; publiée avec la collaboration de mm. Bayet, Bloch [e.a.] Paris, Hachette et cie, 1900-[c11] 9 v. illus., maps (1 fold.) 24 x 20 cm. Each tome originally issued in 8 fascicules. *1. France — History. I. Vidal de La Blanche, Paul Marie Joseph, 1845-1918. II. Bloch, Gustave, 1848-1923. III. Bayet, Charles Marie Adolphe Louis, 1849-1918. IV. Pfister, Christian, 1857-1933. V. Kleinclausz, Arthur Jean, 1869-1947. VI. Luchaire, Achille, 1846-1908. VII. Coville, Alfred, 1860-1942. VIII. Langlois, Charles Victor, 1863-1929. IX. Petit-Dutaillis, Charles Edmond, 1868-1947.*
DC38.L41   F00-2488

McCloy, Shelby Thomas, 1898-   **III. 1620**
The Negro in France. [Lexington] University of Kentucky Press [1961] 278 p. 24 cm. *1. Negroes in France. I. T.*
DC41.N4M3   301.451   61-6554

DC55 – 59   Political and Diplomatic History

Carroll, Eber Malcolm, 1893-   **III. 1621**
French public opinion and foreign affairs, 1870-1914, by E. Malcolm Carroll. New York, London, Century [c1931] viii p., 2 l., 3-348 p. 23 cm. At head of title: The American historical association. "This volume is published from a fund contributed to the American historical association by the Carnegie corporation of New York." *1. Public opinion — France. 2. France — Foreign relations — 1870- 3. Europe — Politics — 1871- 4. Press — France. I. American historical association. II. T.*
DC58.C3   944.08   31-12228

Renan, Ernest, 1823-1892.   **III. 1622**
La Réforme intellectuelle et morale de la France ... Précédé de les Origines de la France contemporaine, par Jean-François Revel. Paris, Union générale d'éditions, 1967. 181 p. 18 cm. (Le Monde en 10/18, 361) Cover illustrated in color. First published in Paris, 1871, as the first essay in Renan's La réforme intellectuelle et morale. *1. France — Politics and government — 1852-1870. 2. France — Intellectual life. 3. France — Moral conditions. I. T.*
DC58.R395 1967   68-82912

Oncken, Hermann, 1869-1945.   **III. 1623**
Napoleon III and the Rhine; the origin of the War of 1870-1871. With an introd. by Ferdinand Schevill. Translated by Edwin H. Zeydel. New York, Russell & Russell [1967, c1928] xxiii, 209 p. 20 cm. A translation of the introductory essay in Die Rheinpolitik Kaiser Napoleons III. von 1863 bis 1870 und der Ursprung des Krieges von 1870-71, edited by the author. *1. Napoléon III, Emperor of the French, 1808-1873. 2. France — Boundaries. 3. Franco-German War, 1870-1871. 4. France — Foreign relations — 1852-1870. I. Zeydel, Edwin Hermann, 1893- II. T.*
DC59.O63 1967   943.08/2   66-24743

Carrias, Eugène.   **III. 1624**
Le danger allemand (1866-1945) Paris, Presses universitaires de France, 1952. 259 p. 19 cm. *1. France — Foreign relations — Germany. 2. Germany — Foreign relations — France. 3. Militarism. I. T.*
DC59.8.G3C37   52-40497

Digeon, Claude.   **III. 1625**
La crise allemande de la pensée française, 1870-1914. [1. éd.] Paris, Presses universitaires de France, 1959. viii, 568 p. 22 cm. "Lorsqu'il fut présenté comme thèse en Sorbonne cet ouvrage était intitulé: La question allemande dans la vie intellectuelle française, de l'avant-guerre de 1870 à celle de 1914." *1. France — Relations (general) with Germany. 2. Germany — Relations (general) with France. 3. Germany — Foreign opinion, French. I. T.*
DC59.8.G3D46   A60-5910

Willis, Frank Roy.   **III. 1626**
France, Germany, and the new Europe, 1945-1967 [by] F. Roy Willis. Rev. and expanded ed. Stanford, Calif., Stanford University Press, 1968. xiv, 431 p. 24 cm. *1. France — Relations (general) with Germany. 2. Germany — Relations (general) with France. 3. European federation. I. T.*
DC59.8.G3W5 1968   327.43/044   68-17142

DC60 – 412   By Period
DC60 – 109 EARLY.
MEDIEVAL TO 1515

Wallace-Hadrill, John Michael.   **III. 1627**
The long-haired kings, and other studies in Frankish history. New York, Barnes & Noble [1962] 261 p. illus. 23 cm. *1. Merovingians. 2. France — History — Carlovingian and early period to 987. 3. France — Kings and rulers. I. T.*
DC65.W3   944.01   63-1094

Fichtenau, Heinrich.   **III. 1628**
The Carolingian empire. Translated by Peter Munz. New York, Barnes & Noble, 1963 [i.e. 1965] xxiv, 196 p. 23 cm. (Studies in mediaeval history, 9) *1. Carlovingians. I. T. (S:Studies in mediaeval history (Oxford, Blackwell) v.9)*
DC70.F513 1963   944.01   65-2046

Halphen, Louis, 1880-   **III. 1629**
Charlemagne et l'empire carolingien. Nouv. éd., rev. et corr. Paris, A. Michel, 1949, [c1947] 532 p. illus. 20 cm. (L'Évolution de l'humanité, synthèse collective, 2. sect., 33) *1. France — History — Carlovingian and early period to 987. 2. Carlovingians.*
DC70.H3 1949   57-28333

Calmette, Joseph Louis Antoine, 1873-   **III. 1630**
Charlemagne. [1. éd.] Paris, Presses Universitaires de France, 1951. 127 p. map. 18 cm. ("Que sais-je?" Le point des connaissances actuelles, 471) *1. Charlemagne, 742-814.*
DC73.C212   51-5834

Ganshof, François Louis, 1895-   **III. 1631**
The Carolingians and the Frankish monarchy; studies in Carolingian history [by] F. L. Ganshof. Translated by Janet Sondheimer. Ithaca, N.Y., Cornell University Press [1971] ix, 314 p. 25 cm. A collection of articles originally in French or German. *1. Charlemagne, 742-814. 2. France — History — Carlovingian and early period to 987. I. T.*
DC73.G34   944/.01   72-147074   ISBN:0801406358

Einhard, 770 (ca.)-840.   **III. 1632**
The life of Charlemagne. With a foreword by Sidney Painter. [Translated by Samuel Epes Turner. Ann Arbor] University of Michigan Press [1960] 74 p. fold. map, geneal. table. 21 cm. (Ann Arbor paperbacks, AA35) *1. Charlemagne, 742-814.*
DC73.32.T8 1960   923.14   60-16107

Fawtier, Robert, 1885-   **III. 1633**
The Capetian kings of France; monarchy & nation, 987-1328. Translated into English by Lionel Butler and R. J. Adam. London, Macmillan; New York, St Martin's Press, 1960. 242 p. illus. 23 cm. Translation of Les Capétiens et la France. *1. France — History — Capetians, 987-1328.*
DC82.F313   944.021   60-1438

Petit-Dutaillis, Charles Edmond, 1868-1947.   **III. 1634**
The feudal monarchy in France and England, from the tenth to the thirteenth century. [Translated from the French by E. D. Hunt] New York, Barnes & Noble [1964] xx, 420 p. geneal. tables, maps. 25 cm. *1. France — History — Capetians, 987-1328. 2. Gt. Brit. — History — Medieval period, 1066-1485. 3. Monarchy. 4. Feudalism — France. 5. Feudalism — Gt. Brit. I. T.*
DC83.P42 1964   944.021   64-3684

Strayer, Joseph Reese, 1904-   **III. 1635**
The Albigensian Crusades [by] Joseph R. Strayer. New York, Dial Press, 1971. 201 p. map (on lining papers) 22 cm. (Crosscurrents in world history) *1. Albigenses. I. T.*
DC83.3.S87   944/.023   70-150404

Luchaire, Achille, 1846-1908.   **III. 1636**
Social France at the time of Philip Augustus. Translated by Edward B. Krehbiel. New York, F. Ungar Pub. Co. [1957?] 441 p. 22 cm. *1. France — History — Philip II Augustus, 1180-1223. 2. France — Social life and customs.*
DC90.L82 1957   944.023   57-12325

Joinville, Jean sire de, 1224?-1317?   **III. 1637**
The life of St. Louis; translated by René Hague from the text edited by Natalis de Wailly. New York, Sheed and Ward, 1955. 306 p. illus. 22 cm. (The Makers of Christendom) Translation of L'histoire et chronique du ... roy S. Loys. *1. Louis IX, Saint, King of France, 1214-1270. 2. Crusades — Seventh, 1248-1250.*
DC91.J7 1955   923.144   55-10924

DC96 – 105 Hundred Years' War. Jeanne d'Arc

Fowler, Kenneth Alan. III. 1638
The Hundred Years War; edited by Kenneth Fowler. London, Macmillan [New York] St. Martin's Press, 1971. ix, 229 p. 23 cm. (Problems in focus series) *1. Hundred Years' War, 1339-1453.*
DC96.F7 1971   944/.025   71-156288   ISBN:0333100115

Perroy, Édouard. III. 1639
The Hundred Years War. With an introd. to the English ed. by David C. Douglas. Bloomington, Indiana University Press, 1959. 376 p. maps. 23 cm. *1. Hundred Years' War, 1339-1453.*
DC96.Px   A63-283

Buchan, Alice. III. 1640
Joan of Arc and the recovery of France. London, Published by Hodder & Stoughton for the English Universities Press [1948] ix, 264 p. port., maps. 18 cm. (Teach yourself history library. London) *1. Jeanne d'Arc, Saint, 1412-1431. (S)*
DC103.Bx   923.544   A49-2729

DC110 – 412 MODERN (1515 –

Cobban, Alfred. III. 1641
A history of modern France. [New ed. rev. and enl.] New York, Braziller [1965] 3 v. in 1. maps. 22 cm. *1. France — History.*
DC110.C57 1965   944   65-14605

Grant, Arthur James, 1862- III. 1642
The French monarchy (1483-1789) by A. J. Grant. Cambridge [Eng.] The University Press, 1925. 2 v. fold. maps. 20 cm. (Cambridge historical series. [1]) *1. France — History — House of Valois, 1328-1589. 2. France — History — Bourbons, 1589-1789. I. T.*
DC110.G7 1925   25-16956

Guérard, Albert Léon, 1880- III. 1643
The life and death of an ideal; France in the classical age. New York, G. Braziller, 1956. 391 p. 21 cm. *1. France — History — 16th cent. 2. France — History — Bourbons, 1589-1789. 3. France — History — 1789-1815. I. France in the classical age. II. T.*
DC110.G8 1956   944.03   56-2497

Wright, Gordon, 1912- III. 1644
France in modern times: 1760 to the present. Chicago, Rand McNally [c1960] 621 p. illus. 24 cm. (Rand McNally history series) *1. France — History. I. T.*
DC110.W7   944   60-12278

DC111 – 120 16th Century (1515 – 1589)

Kingdon, Robert McCune, 1927- III. 1645
Geneva and the coming of the wars of religion in France, 1555-1563. Genève, E. Droz, 1956. 163 p. 26 cm. (Travaux d'humanisme et renaissance, 22) Issued also in microfilm form as thesis, Columbia University. *1. France — History — Wars of the Huguenots, 1562-1598. 2. Compagnie des pasteurs et professeurs de Genève. I. T.*
DC111.K5x   A59-1909

Livet, Georges. III. 1646
Les Guerres de religion (1559-1598). 2 édition ... Paris, Presses universitaires de France, 1966. 128 p. 18 cm. (Que sais-je? 1016) Illustrated cover. *1. France — History — Wars of the Huguenots, 1562-1598. I. T.*
DC111.L5 1966   944/.029   67-84971

Thompson, James Westfall, 1869-1941. III. 1647
The wars of religion in France, 1559-1576; the Huguenots, Catherine de Medici, Philip II. New York, F. Unger Pub. Co. [1957] xv, 635 p. illus., maps, geneal. tables. 23 cm. *1. France — History — Wars of the Huguenots, 1562-1598. 2. Holy League, 1576-1593. I. T.*
DC111.T4 1957   944.029   58-7725

Neale, John Ernest, Sir, 1890- III. 1648
The age of Catherine de Medici. New York, Barnes & Noble [1959, c1958] 111 p. 21 cm. *1. Catherine de Médicis, consort of Henry II, King of France, 1519-1589. 2. France — History — Wars of the Huguenots, 1562-1598. I. T.*
DC111.3.Nx   A59-8073

Renaudet, Augustin, 1880- III. 1649
Préréforme et humanisme à Paris pendant les premières guerres d'Italie, 1494-1517. 2. ed., rev. et corr. Paris, Librairie d'Argences, 1953. lxiv, 739 p. 25 cm. (Bibliothèque elzévirienne, nouv. sér. Études et documents) *1. Paris. Université — History. 2. Humanism. 3. Renaissance — France. 4. Reformation — France — Paris. I. T.*
DC111.3.R4 1953   A54-1572

Sutherland, Nicola Mary. III. 1650
The French Secretaries of State in the age of Catherine de Medici. [London] University of London, Athlone Press, 1962. 344 p. illus. 23 cm. (University of London historical studies, 10) *1. Cabinet officers — France. 2. France — Politics and government — 16th cent. I. T.*
DC111.5.S8   944.028   62-6638

Biron, Armand de Gontaut, baron de, 1524-1592. III. 1651
The letters and documents of Armand de Gontaut, baron de Biron, marshal of France (1524-1592) collected by the late Sidney Hellman Ehrman. Edited, with an introduction, by James Westfall Thompson. Berkeley, University of California Press, 1936. 2 v. fronts., 2 pl., ports., facsim. 22 cm. Paged continuously. *1. France — History — Wars of the Huguenots, 1562-1598. I. Ehrman, Sidney Hellman, 1905-1930, comp. II. Thompson, James Westfall, 1869- ed.*
DC112.B5A4   923.544   37-160

Héritier, Jean, 1892- III. 1652
Catherine de Médicis. Nouv. éd. entièrement refondue. Paris, A. Fayard [c1959] 626 p. 19 cm. *1. Catherine de Médicis, consort of Henry II, King of France, 1519-1589.*
DC119.8.H44 1959   60-33887

DC121 – 130 17th Century (1589 – 1715)

Esmonin, Edmond, 1877- III. 1653
Études sur la France des XVII et XVIII siècles. [1. éd.] Paris, Presses universitaires de France, 1964. 538 p. 25 cm. (Université de Grenoble. Publications de le Faculté des lettres et sciences humaines, 32) *1. France — Politics and government — 17th cent. 2. France — Politics and government — 18th cent. 3. Dauphine — History. I. T.*
DC121.E8   66-39929

Stankiewicz, W. J. III. 1654
Politics & religion in seventeenth-century France; a study of political ideas from the monarchomachs to Bayle, as reflected in the toleration controversy. Berkeley, University of California Press, 1960. x, 269 p. 25 cm. *1. Edict of Nantes. 2. France — Politics and government — 17th cent. 3. Religious liberty — France. I. T.*
DC121.3.S8   944.03   60-10648

Lough, John. III. 1655
An introduction to seventeenth century France. [U.S.A. ed. New York] McKay [1969] xxi, 296 p. illus., maps, ports. 22 cm. *1. France — Civilization — 17th-18th centuries. 2. France — History — 17th century. I. T.*
DC121.7.L6 1969   914.4/03/32   79-8758

Mousnier, Roland. III. 1656
L'assassinat d'Henri IV, 14 mai 1610. [Paris] Gallimard [1964] 410 p. maps, plates. 21 cm. (Trente journées qui ont fait la France, 13) *1. Henri IV, King of France, 1553-1610. 2. France — History — Henri IV, 1589-1610. 3. France — Church history — 16th cent. I. T.*
DC122.M6   65-39709

Liublinskaia, Aleksandra Dmitrievna. III. 1657
French absolutism: the crucial phase 1620-1629 [by] A. D. Lublinskaya; translated [from the Russian] by Brian Pearce, with a foreword by J. H. Elliot. London, Cambridge U.P., 1968. xvi, 350 p. map. 24 cm. Translation of Frantsuzskiĭ absoliutizm v pervoĭ treti semnadtsatogo v. (romanized form) *1. France — History — Louis XIII, 1610-1643. 2. France — Economic conditions. I. T.*
DC123.L5813   944/.032   68-21395   ISBN:0521071178

Tapié, Victor Lucien, 1900- III. 1658
La France de Louis XIII et de Richelieu [par] Victor L. Tapié. [Paris] Flammarion, 1967. 445 p. 21 cm. (L'Histoire) Cover illustrated in color. *1. France — History — Louis XIII, 1610-1643. I. T.*
DC123.T3 1967   944/.032   67-83564

Ranum, Orest A. III. 1659
Richelieu and the councillors of Louis XIII; a study of the secretaries of state and superintendents of finance in the ministry of Richelieu, 1635-1642. Oxford [Eng.] Clarendon Press, 1963. vi, 211 p. ports. 23 cm. *1. Richelieu, Armand Jean du Plessis, Cardinal, duc de, 1585-1642. 2. France — Politics and government — 1610-1643.*
DC123.3.R3 1963   944.032   63-3603

III. 1660 France

Burckhardt, Carl Jacob, 1891- **III. 1660**
Richelieu and his age: his rise to power [by] Carl J. Burckhardt; translated [from the German] and abridged by Edwin and Willa Muir. [1st ed.], 2nd impression. London, Allen & Unwin, 1967. 413 p. front., 14 plates (ports., map). 23 cm. Translation of Richelieu. *1. Richelieu, Armand Jean du Plessis, Cardinal, duc de, 1585-1642. I. Muir, Edwin, 1887-1959, tr. II. Muir, Willa, 1890- tr. III. T.*
DC123.9.R5B82 1967   67-94682

Church, William Farr, 1912- **III. 1661**
Richelieu and reason of state, by William F. Church. Princeton, N.J., Princeton University Press [1973, c1972] 554 p. 25 cm. *1. Richelieu, Armand Jean du Plessis, Cardinal, duc de, 1585-1642. 2. France — Politics and government — 1610-1643. I. T.*
DC123.9.R5C5   944/.032/0924   76-181518   ISBN:0691051992

Wedgwood, Cicely Veronica, 1910- **III. 1662**
Richelieu and the French monarchy. New, rev. ed. New York, Collier Books [1962] 155 p. 18 cm. (Men and history, BS130V) *1. Richelieu, Armand Jean du Plessis, Cardinal, duc de, 1585-1642.*
DC123.9.R5W4 1962   923.244   62-19197

Kunstler, Charles, 1887- **III. 1663**
La vie quotidienne sous la Régence. [Paris] Hachette [1960] 301 p. 21 cm. (La Vie quotidienne) *1. France — Social life and customs. I. T.*
DC124.K8   61-22584

Kossmann, Ernst Heinrich, 1922- **III. 1664**
La Fronde. Leiden, Universitaire Pers Leiden, 1954. 275 p. 25 cm. (Leidse historische reeks, deel 3) Issued also as thesis, Leyden. *1. Fronde.*
DC124.4.K67 1954   55-21638

DC125 – 130   Louis XIV, 1638 – 1715

Ashley, Maurice Percy. **III. 1665**
Louis XIV and the greatness of France. New York, Macmillan Co., 1948. ix, 263 p. port., maps. 18 cm. (Teach yourself history library.) *1. Louis XIV, King of France 1638-1715. 2. France — History — Louis XIV, 1643-1715. (S)*
DC125.A8 1948   944.033   48-11969

Méthivier, Hubert. **III. 1666**
Le Siècle de Louis XIV ... 4 édition .. Paris, Presses universitaires de France, 1966. 128 p. 18 cm. (Que sais-je? No 426) Cover illustrated in color. First ed. published in 1950 under title: Louis XIV. *1. Louis XIV, King of France, 1638-1715. I. T.*
DC125.M46 1966   944/.033   67-192847

Voltaire, François Marie Arouet de, 1694-1778. **III. 1667**
The age of Louis XIV. Translated by Martyn P. Pollack. London, Dent; New York, Dutton [1926] xiv, 475 p. 18 cm. (Everyman's library [no. 780] History) *1. France — History — Louis XIV, 1643-1715. I. T.*
DC125.V6x (AC1.E8 no. 780)   A26-193

Mongrédien, Georges, 1901- **III. 1668**
La vie quotidienne sous Louis XIV. [Paris] Hachette [1948] 250 p. 21 cm. *1. France — Social life and customs. I. T.*
DC126.M54   944.033   49-24648

André, Louis, 1867-1948. **III. 1669**
Louis XIV et l'Europe. Paris, Michel, 1950. xxix, 395 p. ports., fold. maps. 21 cm. (L'Évolution de l'humanité, synthèse, collective, 3. sect., 64) *1. Louis XIV, King of France, 1638-1715. (S)*
DC127.3.A6   944.033   50-11387

Lewis, Warren Hamilton. **III. 1670**
The splendid century; life in the France of Louis XIV. Garden City, N.Y., Doubleday, 1957 [c1953] 304 p. illus. 19 cm. (Doubleday anchor books, A122) *1. France — Social life and customs.*
DC128.L4   944.033   57-3377

Goubert, Pierre. **III. 1671**
Louis XIV and twenty million Frenchmen; translated [from the French] by Anne Carter. London, Allen Lane, 1970. 350 p. 23 cm. Translation of Louis XIV et vingt millions de Français. *1. Louis XIV, King of France, 1638-1715. 2. France — History — Louis XIV, 1643-1715 I. T.*
DC129.G613 1970b   944/.033   76-498058   ISBN:713901039

Louis XIV and the craft of kingship, **III. 1672**
edited by John C. Rule. [Columbus] Ohio State University Press [1970, c1969] x, 478 p. illus., port. 24 cm. Includes chiefly papers originally presented at a conference held at Ohio State University, Dec., 1964. *1. Louis XIV, King of France, 1638-1715. I. Rule, John C., ed.*
DC129.L68   944/.033/0924   72-79845

Wolf, John Baptist, 1907- **III. 1673**
Louis XIV, by John B. Wolf. [1st ed.] New York, Norton [1968] xix, 678 p. illus., coat of arms, maps, port. 25 cm. *1. Louis XIV, King of France, 1638-1715.*
DC129.W6 1968   944/.033/0924 (B)   67-20618

Saint-Simon, Louis de Rouvroy, duc de, 1675-1755. **III. 1674**
Historical memoirs of the duc de Saint-Simon; a shortened version. Edited and translated by Lucy Norton, with an introd. by D. W. Brogan. New York, McGraw-Hill [1968-72. v. 1, c. 1967] 3 v. illus., maps. 24 cm. *1. France — History — Louis XIV, 1643-1715. 2. France — History — Regency, 1715-1723. 3. France — Court and courtiers. I. Norton, Lucy, ed. II. T.*
DC130.S2A1992   944/.033/0924   67-24825   ISBN:007054459X (v. 3)

DC131 – 138   18th Century (1715 – 1789)

Behrens, Catherine Betty Abigail. **III. 1675**
The ancien régime [by] C. B. A. Behrens. [1st American ed. New York] Harcourt, Brace & World [1967] 215 p. illus. (part col.), maps, ports. 21 cm. *1. France — History — Louis XV, 1715-1774. 2. France — History — Louis XV, 1774-1793. 3. Europe — History — 18th cent. I. T.*
DC131.B4 1967   944/.034   67-11707

Gottschalk, Louis Reichenthal, 1899- **III. 1676**
The era of the French revolution (1715-1815) by Louis R. Gottschalk under the editorship of James T. Shotwell. Boston, New York [etc.] Houghton Mifflin [c1929] x, 509 p. maps (part double) diagr. 22 cm. "This book is based upon the six booklets covering the same field of history that were published by the author between 1923 and 1925." — Pref. *1. Napoléon I, emperor of the French, 1769-1821. 2. France — Politics and government. 3. France — History — Revolution. 4. France — History — Consulate and empire, 1799-1815. I. Shotwell, James Thomson, 1874- ed. II. T.*
DC131.G6   29-9131

Gaxotte, Pierre. **III. 1677**
Le siècle de Louis XV. Nouv. éd., rev. et augm. Paris, A Fayard [1958, c1933] 492 p. 19 cm. (Les Grandes études historiques) *1. France — History — Louis XV, 1715-1774. I. T.*
DC133.G3x   A60-1872

Gooch, George Peabody, 1873- **III. 1678**
Louis XV; the monarchy in decline. London, New York, Longmans, Green [1956] 285 p. illus. 23 cm. *1. Louis XV, King of France, 1710-1774.*
DC133.3.G6   923.144   56-59058

Wilson, Arthur McCandless, 1902- **III. 1679**
French foreign policy during the administration of Cardinal Fleury, 1726-1743; a study in diplomacy and commercial development. Westport, Conn., Greenwood Press [1972, c1936] ix, 433 p. 22 cm. Original ed. issued as vol. 40 of Harvard historical studies series. *1. France — Foreign relations. 2. Fleury, André Hercule de, Cardinal, 1653-1743. 3. France — History — Louis XV, 1715-1774. 4. France — Commerce — History. I. T. (S:Harvard historical studies, v. 40.)*
DC133.5.W5 1972   327.44   70-138193   ISBN:0837153336

Lough, John. **III. 1680**
An introduction to eighteenth century France. [London] Longmans [1960] 349 p. illus. 22 cm. *1. France — Civilization. 2. France — History — Bourbons, 1589-1789.*
DC133.8.L6   944.034   60-2946

Castelot, André. **III. 1681**
Queen of France; a biography of Marie Antoinette. Translated from the French by Denise Folliot. [1st ed.] New York, Harper [1957] 434 p. illus. 22 cm. Translation of Marie Antoinette. *1. Marie Antoinette, consort of Louis XVI, King of France, 1755-1793. I. T.*
DC137.1.C313 1957a   923.144   56-6021

Dakin, Douglas. **III. 1682**
Turgot and the ancien régime in France. New York, Octagon Books, 1965. xi, 361 p. map, port. 24 cm. "Originally published 1939 ... reprinted 1965." *1. Turgot, Anne Robert Jacques, baron de l'Aulne, 1727-1781. 2. France — Politics and government — 1774-1793. 3. Finance, Public — France — To 1789. 4. Taxation — France — History.*
DC137.5.T9D3 1965   923.344   65-16771

Godechot, Jacques Léon, 1907- **III. 1683**
France and the Atlantic revolution of the eighteenth century, 1770-1799 [by] Jacques Godechot. Translated by Herbert H. Rowen. New York, Free Press [1965] vii, 279 p. 22 cm. Translation of Les révolutions, 1770-1799. *1. France — History — Revolution — Causes and character. 2. History, Modern — 18th cent. 3. Europe — History — 1789-1815. I. T.*
DC138.G543   940.27   65-16268

Mornet, Daniel, 1878-1954. **III. 1684**
Les Origines intellectuelles de la Révolution française, 1715-1787. Préface de

René Pomeau ... 6 édition. Paris, A. Colin, 1967. xii, 552 p. 24 cm. *1. France — History — Revolution — Causes and character. 2. France — Intellectual life. I. T.*
DC138.M56 1967   68-86443

Tocqueville, Alexis Charles Henri Maurice Clérel de, 1805-1859.   **III. 1685**
The old régime and the French Revolution. Translated by Stuart Gilbert. [1st ed.] Garden City, N.Y., Doubleday, 1955. xv, 300 p. 18 cm. (Doubleday anchor books, A60) *1. France — History — Revolution — Causes and character. I. T.*
DC138.T6335   944.04   55-10160

Herr, Richard.   **III. 1686**
Tocqueville and the old regime. Princeton, N.J., Princeton University Press, 1962. 142 p. 23 cm. *1. Tocqueville, Alexis Charles Henri Maurice Clérel de, 1805-1859. L'ancien régime et la révolution.*
DC138.T6344H4   944.04   62-7404

DC139 – 249 Revolution. Napoleonic Period (1789 – 1815)

Roberts, John Morris, 1928- ed.   **III. 1687**
French Revolution documents. Editors: J. M. Roberts and R. C. Cobb. New York, Barnes & Noble, 1966-   v. 23 cm. English or French. *1. France — History — Revolution — Sources. I. Cobb, Richard Charles, 1917- joint ed. II. T.*
DC141.R6   944.04   66-6974

Thompson, James Matthew, 1878-1956, ed.   **III. 1688**
English witnesses of the French Revolution. Port Washington, N.Y., Kennikat Press [1970] xii, 267 p. 24 cm. Reprint of the 1938 ed. *1. France — History — Revolution — Personal narratives. 2. British in France. 3. France — History — Revolution — Foreign public opinion. I. T.*
DC142.T45 1970   944.04   71-110925   ISBN:804609071

Acton, John Emerich Edward Dalberg Acton, baron, 1834-1902.   **III. 1689**
Lectures on the French Revolution. Edited by John Neville Figgis and Reginald Vere Laurence. New York, Noonday Press [1959] 379 p. 21 cm. (Noonday paperbacks, N139) "Lectures ... delivered ... at Cambridge in the academical years 1895-96, 1896-97, 1897-98, 1898-99." *1. France — History — Revolution.*
DC143.A3 1959   944.04   59-9453

Cobban, Alfred.   **III. 1690**
Aspects of the French Revolution. New York, G. Braziller [1968] 328 p. 23 cm. *1. France — History — Revolution — Addresses, essays, lectures. I. T.*
DC143.C6   944.04/08   68-24195

DC146   BIOGRAPHY

Brucker, Gene A.   **III. 1691**
Jean-Sylvain Bailly, revolutionary mayor of Paris. Urbana, University of Illinois Press, 1950. vii, 134 p. 27 cm. (Illinois studies in the social sciences, v.31, no. 3) "Prepared as a thesis for a master's degree at the University of Illinois." *1. Bailly, Jean Sylvain, 1736-1793. (S:Illinois. University. Illinois studies in the social sciences, v.31, no. 3)*
DC146.B15B7   (H31.I4 vol. 31, no. 3)   923.244   50-62867

Gershoy, Leo, 1897-   **III. 1692**
Bertrand Barere; a reluctant terrorist. Princeton, N.J., Princeton University Press, 1962. 459 p. illus. 26 cm. *1. Barère de Vieuzac, Bertrand, 1755-1841.*
DC146.B2G43   923.244   61-11848

Rudé, George F. E., comp.   **III. 1693**
Robespierre, edited by George Rudé. Englewood Cliffs, N.J., Prentice-Hall [1967] vii, 181 p. 21 cm. (Great lives observed. A Spectrum book.) *1. Robespierre, Maximilien Marie Isidore de, 1758-1794.*
DC146.R6R8   944/.035/0924   67-18696

Thompson, James Matthew, 1878-   **III. 1694**
Robespierre and the French Revolution. New York, Macmillan, 1953. 180 p. 19 cm. (Teach yourself history) *1. Robespierre, Maximilien Marie Isidore de, 1758-1794. 2. France — History — Revolution, 1789-1794.*
DC146.R6T45 1953   923.244   53-4117

Bruun, Geoffrey, 1898-   **III. 1695**
Saint-Just, apostle of the terror. Hamden, Conn., Archon Books, 1966 [c1932] 168 p. 21 cm. *1. Saint-Just, Louis Antoine de, 1767-1794. 2. France — History — Revolution, 1793-1794. I. T.*
DC146.S135B7 1966   944.0440924   66-16083

Curtis, Eugene Newton, 1880-   **III. 1696**
Saint-Just, colleague of Robespierre. New York, Columbia University Press, 1935. xi, 402 p. illus. 22 cm. *1. Saint-Just, Louis Antoine de, 1767-1794. 2. France — History — Revolution, 1793 1794.*
DC146.S135C8   923.244   36-461

Van Deusen, Glyndon Garlock, 1897-   **III. 1697**
Sieyes: his life and his nationalism, by Glyndon G. Van Deusen. New York, AMS Press [1970] 170 p. 23 cm. (Studies in history, economics, and public law, no. 362) Reprint of the 1932 ed. *1. Sieyès, Emanuel Joseph, comte, 1748-1836. 2. France — Politics and government — 1774-1793. 3. France — Politics and government — 1789-1815. 4. Nationalism — France. I. T. (S:Columbia studies in the social sciences, no. 362)*
DC146.S5V3 1970   944.04/0924   68-58632   ISBN:40451362X

Herold, J. Christopher.   **III. 1698**
Mistress to an age; a life of Madame de Staël. [1st ed.] Indianapolis, Bobbs-Merrill Co. [1958] 500 p. illus. 22 cm. *1. Staël-Holstein, Anne Louise Germaine (Necker) baronne de, 1766-1817. I. T.*
DC146.S7H44   928.4   58-12385

DC147 – 150   GENERAL WORKS

Farmer, Paul, 1918-   **III. 1699**
France reviews its revolutionary origins; social politics and historical opinion in the Third Republic. New York, Octagon Books, 1963 [c1944] vi, 145 p. 24 cm. Issued also as thesis, Columbia University. *1. France — History — Revolution. 2. France — History — Historiography. 3. Historians, French. 4. France — Politics and government — 1870-1940. I. T.*
DC147.8.F3 1963   944   63-20890

Godechot, Jacques Léon, 1907-   **III. 1700**
La grande nation; l'expansion révolutionnaire de la France dans le monde de 1789 à 1799. Ouvrage publié avec le concours du Centre national de la recherche scientifique. [Paris] Aubier, 1956. 2 v. (758 p.) 20 cm. *1. France — History — Revolution. 2. Europe — History — 1789-1815. I. T.*
DC148.Gx   A57-5663

Gershoy, Leo, 1897-   **III. 1701**
The French Revolution and Napoleon, with new annotated bibliography. New York, Appleton-Century-Crofts [1964] xiii, 584 p. maps (3 fold. col.) plans. 22 cm. *1. France — History — Revolution. 2. Napoléon I, Emperor of the French, 1769-1821. 3. France — History — Consulate and Empire, 1799-1815. I. T.*
DC148.G4 1964   944.04   64-12378

Hampson, Norman.   **III. 1702**
A social history of the French Revolution. London, Routledge and K. Paul [1963] viii, 278 p. 22 cm. (Studies in social history) *1. France — History — Revolution. 2. Social classes — France. I. T.*
DC148.H26   64-1533

Lefebvre, Georges, 1874-1959.   **III. 1703**
The French Revolution. Translated from the French by Elizabeth Moss Evanson. London, Routledge & K. Paul; New York, Columbia University Press, 1962-64. 2 v. 23 cm. Vol. 2 translated by John Hall Stewart and James Friguglietti. *1. France — History — Revolution. I. T.*
DC148.L413   944.04   64-11939

Madelin, Louis, 1871-1956.   **III. 1704**
The French revolution (crowned by the French academy) (Gobert prize) by Louis Madelin; translated from the French. London, W. Heinemann, 1936. xiii, 661 p. 23 cm. (The national history of France, ed. by Fr. Funck-Brentano) Series title in part also at head of t.-p. "First published, September 1916 ... [10th reimpression] September 1936." Translation of La révolution. *1. France — History — Revolution.*
DC148.M256 1936   944.04   37-4405

Phipps, Ramsay Weston, 1838-1923.   **III. 1705**
The armies of the first French republic and the rise of the marshals of Napoleon I ... by the late Colonel Ramsay Weston Phipps. London, Oxford University Press, 1926-   v. fold. maps. 24 cm. *1. France. Armée. 2. France — History — Revolution, 1791-1797. 3. France — History, Military, 1789-1815. 4. Marshals — France.*
DC148.P5   27-14675

Soboul, Albert.   **III. 1706**
La Révolution française ... [Paris] Gallimard 196   v. 16 cm. (Collection Idées, 46) Illustrated cover. *1. France — History — Revolution. I. T.*
DC148.S6   68-100961

Tocqueville, Alexis Charles Henri Maurice Clérel de, 1805-1859.   **III. 1707**
The European revolution & correspondence with Gobineau. Introduced, edited, and translated by John Lukacs. Garden City, N.Y., Doubleday, 1959. xi, 340 p. 18 cm. (Doubleday anchor books, A163) *1. France — History — Revolution. 2. Europe — History — 1789-1900. I. Gobineau, Joseph Arthur, comte de, 1816-1882. II. T.*
DC148.T683   59-6275

Mathiez, Albert, 1874-1932.   **III. 1708**
The French Revolution. Translated from the French by Catherine Alison Phillips. New York, Russell & Russell, 1962 [c1956] 509 p. 25 cm. *1. France — History — Revolution.*
DC149.M26 1962   944.04   62-13841

Burke, Edmund, 1729?-1797.   **III. 1709**
Reflections on the Revolution in France. Edited with an introd. by Thomas H. D. Mahoney; with an analysis of the Reflections by Oskar Piest. New York, Liberal Arts Press [c1955] xliv, 307 p. 21 cm. (The Library of liberal arts, no. 46) *1. France — History — Revolution — Causes and character. I. T.*
DC150.B852   944.04   56-491

DC151 – 159 SPECIAL ASPECTS

Chandler, David G.   **III. 1710**
The campaigns of Napoleon [by] David G. Chandler. New York, Macmillan [1966] xliii, 1172 p. illus., facsims., maps (part col.), ports. 24 cm. *1. Napoléon I, Emperor of the French, 1769-1821. 2. Europe — History — 1789-1815. 3. France — History, Military — 1789-1815. I. T.*
DC151.C48   940.270924   66-12970

Mahan, Alfred Thayer, 1840-1914.   **III. 1711**
The influence of sea power upon the French Revolution and Empire, 1793-1812. New York, Greenwood Press [1968, c1892] 2 v. illus. 23 cm. "Originally published in 1898." *1. France — History — Revolution, 1793-1799. 2. France — History — Consulate and Empire, 1799-1815. 3. Sea-power. 4. France — History, Naval. I. T.*
DC153.M216 1968   944.04   69-10127

Aulard, François Victor Alphonse, 1849-1928.   **III. 1712**
The French Revolution; a political history, 1789-1804, by A. Aulard. Translated from the French of the 3d ed., with a pref., notes, and historical summary, by Bernard Miall. New York, Russell & Russell, 1965. 4 v. 21 cm. Translation of Histoire politique de la révolution française. *1. France — History — 1789-1815. 2. France — Politics and government — 1789-1815. 3. Republicanism in France. 4. Political parties — France. I. Miall, Bernard, 1876- ed. and tr. II. T.*
DC155.A92x   944.04   65-13947

Weiner, Margery.   **III. 1713**
The French exiles, 1789-1815. New York, Morrow, 1961 [c1960] 240 p. illus. 22 cm. *1. Émigrés. 2. French in England. 3. France — History — Revolution. I. T.*
DC158.W4 1961   325.2440942   61-16544

La Gorce, Pierre François Gustave de, 1846-1934.   **III. 1714**
Histoire religieuse de la révolution française ... Paris, Plon-Nourrit, 1909- v. 23 cm. Vol.3: 4.éd. *1. France — History — Revolution — Religious history.*
DC158.2.L2   09-19197

McManners, John.   **III. 1715**
The French Revolution and the Church. London, S.P.C.K. for the Church Historical Society, 1969. xiv, 161 p. 19 cm. (Church history outlines, 4) *1. France — History — Revolution — Religious history. I. Church Historical Society (Gt. Brit.) II. T.*
DC158.2.M3   322/.1/0944   70-465912   ISBN:281023352

Cobban, Alfred.   **III. 1716**
The social interpretation of the French Revolution. London, Cambridge U.P., 1968. xii, 178 p. 20 cm. (Wiles lectures, 1962) *1. France — History — Revolution. 2. France — Social conditions. I. T. (S)*
DC158.8.C6 1968   944.04   71-474746   ISBN:521095484

Rudé, George F. E.   **III. 1717**
The crowd in the French Revolution. Oxford, Clarendon Press, 1959. viii, 267 p. fold. map, tables. 23 cm. *1. Crowds. 2. France — History — Revolution — Economic aspects. I. T.*
DC158.8.R8   944.04   59-1108

Soboul, Albert.   **III. 1718**
The Parisian sans-culottes and the French Revolution, 1793-4. [English translation by Gwynne Lewis] Oxford, Clarendon Press, 1964. 280 p. 23 cm. "An abridgment of [the author's] doctoral thesis." — Dust jacket. *1. Sansculottes. 2. France — History — Revolution — 1793-1794. I. T.*
DC158.8.S613   914.4   64-5298

DC161 – 249 BY PERIOD

DC161 – 190 Assemblies.

Directory (1787/1789 – 1799)

Carlyle, Thomas, 1795-1881.   **III. 1719**
The French revolution; a history, by Thomas Carlyle. New York, Modern Library [1934] xxxi, 748 p. XVI pl. (incl. ports.) on 8 l. 21 cm. *1. France — History — Revolution, 1789-1794. I. T.*
DC161.C3 1934   944.04   34-27104

Michelet, Jules, 1798-1874.   **III. 1720**
History of the French Revolution. Translated by Charles Cooks. Edited and with an introd. by Gordon Wright. Chicago, University of Chicago Press [1967] xxi, 476 p. 21 cm. (Classic European historians) *1. France — History — Revolution — 1789-1795. 2. France — History — Revolution — Causes and character. I. Wright, Gordon, 1912- ed. II. T.*
DC161.M5153 1967   944.04   67-15315

Salvemini, Gaetano, 1873-   **III. 1721**
The French Revolution, 1788-1792. Translated from the Italian by I. M. Rawson. New York, Holt [1954] 343 p. 22 cm. "The present version has been made from a text carefully revised by the author. It differs in a number of ways from the latest Italian edition (1949) and contains many minor emendations as well as new material." *1. France — History — Revolution, 1789-1792.*
DC161.S313 1954   944.04   54-10529

Sydenham, M. J.   **III. 1722**
The French revolution [by] M. J. Sydenham. [1st American ed.] New York, Putnam [1965] 255 p. maps, plans. 21 cm. *1. France — History — Revolution, 1789-1794. I. T.*
DC161.S87 1965   320.944   65-20690

Thompson, James Matthew, 1878-1956.   **III. 1723**
The French Revolution. [5th ed.] Oxford, B. Blackwell, 1955. xvi, 544 p. illus., ports., maps, diagrs., facsims. 23 cm. *1. France — History — Revolution, 1789-1799. I. T.*
DC161.T47 1955   944.04   56-3363

Lefebvre, Georges, 1874-1959.   **III. 1724**
The coming of the French Revolution 1789. Translated from the French by R. R. Palmer. New York, Vintage Books, 1957 [c1947] xviii, 191, x p. 19 cm. (A Vintage book, K-43) "First published in French, under the title Quatre-vingt-neuf, in 1939." *1. France — History — Revolution — Causes and character. I. T.*
DC163.Lx   944.04   57-1034

Lefebvre, Georges, 1874-1959.   **III. 1725**
The Great Fear of 1789; rural panic in revolutionary France. Introd. by George Rudé. Translated from the French by Joan White. [1st American ed.] New York, Pantheon Books [1973] xvi, 234 p. maps. 22 cm. Translation of La grande peur de 1789. *1. France — History — Revolution, 1789. 2. France — History — Revolution — Causes and character. 3. France — Economic conditions. 4. Peasantry — France. 5. Panics. I. T.*
DC163.L413 1973   944.04/1   72-12379   ISBN:0394484944

Poncet-Delpech, Jean Baptiste, 1743-1817.   **III. 1726**
La première année de la Révolution, vue par un témoin, 1789-1790; les "Bulletins" de Poncet-Delpech, député du Quercy aux États généraux de 1789, par Daniel Ligou. Paris, Presses universitaires de France, 1961. 321 p. 24 cm. (Publications de la Faculté des lettres et science humaines d'Alger, 38) *1. France — History — Revolution, 1789-1790 — Sources. I. Ligou, Daniel, ed. II. T. (S:Algiers (City) Université. Faculté des lettres et sciences humaines. Publications, 38)*
DC165.P6x (AS651.A62 no. 38)   65-2370

Palmer, Robert Roswell, 1909-   **III. 1727**
Twelve who ruled; the year of the terror in the French Revolution. Princeton, Princeton University Press [1958, c1941] 417 p. ports., map. 22 cm. Originally published under title: Twelve who ruled; the Committee of Public Safety, during the terror. *1. France. Convention nationale, 1792-1795. Comité de salut public. 2. France — History — Revolution, 1793-1794. 3. France — History — Revolution — Biography. I. T.*
DC177.Px   A63-3

Brinton, Clarence Crane, 1898-   **III. 1728**
The Jacobins; an essay in the new history. New York, Russell & Russell, 1961 [c1957] 319 p. 22 cm. *1. Jacobins.*
DC178.B8 1961   944.04   61-13765

Sydenham, M. J.   **III. 1729**
The Girondins. [London] University of London, Athlone Press, 1961. viii, 252 p. ports., map. 23 cm. (University of London historical studies, 8) "An abridgment of work approved by the University of London for the award of the degree of doctor of philosophy." *1. France. Convention nationale, 1792-1795. 2. Girondists. 3. France — History — Revolution, 1789-1793. (S:London. University. Historical studies, 8)*
DC179.S92   944.041   61-19510

Sirich, John Black, 1910-   **III. 1730**
The revolutionary committees in the departments of France, 1793-1794. New York, H. Fertig, 1971 [c1943] xii, 238 p. 23 cm. *1. France — Politics and government — Revolution. 2. France — History — Revolution, 1793-1794. I. T.*
DC183.5.S57 1971   944.04   73-85082

Thomson, David, 1912- III. 1731
The Babeuf plot; the making of a Republican legend. London, K. Paul, Trench, Trubner [1947] xi, 112 p. ports. 19 cm. *1. Babeuf, François Noël, 1760-1797. 2. Socialism in France. I. T.*
DC187.8.T5 923.244 48-1024

DC191 – 219 Consulate (1799 – 1804)
First Empire (1804 – 1815)
Napoleon

Caulaincourt, Armand Augustin Louis, marquis de, duc de Vicence, 1773-1827. III. 1732
With Napoleon in Russia; the memoirs of General de Caulaincourt, duke of Vicenza. From the original memoirs as edited by Jean Hanoteau. Abridged, edited, and with an introd. by George Libaire. New York, Grosset & Dunlap [1959, c1935] 422 p. illus. 21 cm. (The Universal library, UL-55) Translation of Mémoires du général de Caulaincourt. *1. Napoléon I — Invasion of Russia, 1812. 2. France — History — Consulate and Empire, 1799-1815. I. T.*
DC198.C35A33 1959 923.544 59-2924

Madelin, Louis, 1871- III. 1733
Fouché, 1759-1820. Paris, Plon [1955] 396 p. 20 cm. *1. Fouché, Joseph, duc d'Otrante, 1759-1820.*
DC198.F7M2 1955 58-28799

Deutsch, Harold Charles. III. 1734
The genesis of Napoleonic imperialism, by Harold C. Deutsch. Cambridge, Harvard University Press; London, H. Milford, Oxford University Press, 1938. xxi, 460 p. 23 cm. (Harvard historical studies, vol.XLI) *1. Napoléon I, emperor of the French, 1769-1821. 2. France — History — Consulate and empire, 1799-1815. 3. Imperialism. I. T.*
DC201.D4 327.44 38-2656

Herold, J. Christopher. III. 1735
The age of Napoleon. [English-language ed.] New York, American Heritage Pub. Co.; book trade distribution by Harper & Row [c1963] 453 p. 16 illus. (incl. ports.) maps (on lining papers) 24 cm. *1. Napoléon I, Emperor of the French, 1769-1821. 2. France — History — Consulate and Empire, 1799-1815. I. T.*
DC201.H44 944.046 63-11132

Holtman, Robert B. III. 1736
The Napoleonic revolution [by] Robert B. Holtman. [1st ed.] Philadelphia, Lippincott [1967] 225 p. illus., maps. 21 cm. (Critical periods of history) *1. Napoléon I, Emperor of the French, 1769-1821. 2. Europe — Politics — 1789-1900. I. T.*
DC201.H675 940.2/7/0924 67-11308

Lefebvre, Georges, 1874-1959. III. 1737
Napoleon, from 18 Brumaire to Tilsit, 1799-1807. Translated from the French by Henry F. Stockhold. New York, Columbia University Press, 1969. x, 337 p. 22 cm. "Translation of the first three parts of Napoléon ... published in 1935 ... this translation is based on the fifth (1965) edition." *1. Napoléon I, Emperor of the French, 1769-1821. 2. France — History — Consulate and Empire, 1799-1815. 3. France — History, Military — 1789-1815. I. T.*
DC201.L3413 1969 944.05 68-29160

Lefebvre, Georges, 1874-1959. III. 1738
Napoleon; from Tilsit to Waterloo, 1807-1815. Translated from the French by J. E. Anderson. New York, Columbia University Press, 1969 [c1936] viii, 414 p. 22 cm. "Translation of the second three parts of Napoléon ... published in 1936 ... this translation is based on the fifth (1965) edition." *1. France — History — Consulate and Empire, 1799-1815. 2. France — History, Military — 1789-1815. 3. Napoléon I, Emperor of the French, 1769-1821. I. T.*
DC201.L3513 944.05 74-79193

Markham, Felix Maurice Hippisley. III. 1739
Napoléon and the awakening of Europe. London, English Universities Press [1954] 183 p. illus. 18 cm. (Teach yourself history library) *1. Napoléon, Emperor of the French, 1769-1821. 2. Europe — History — 1789-1815. I. T.*
DC201.M18 944.04 54-2259

Mackesy, Piers. III. 1740
The war in the Mediterranean, 1803-1810. Cambridge, Harvard University Press, 1957. xviii, 430 p. maps. 23 cm. *1. Gt. Brit. — History — 1789-1820. 2. France — History — Consulate and Empire, 1799-1815. 3. Mediterranean region — History. I. T.*
DC202.M2 940.27 66-57018

Holtman, Robert B. III. 1741
Napoleonic propaganda, by Robert B. Holtman. New York, Greenwood Press [1969, c1950] xv, 272 p. 23 cm. *1. Napoléon I, Emperor of the French, 1769-1821. 2. France — History — Consulate and Empire, 1799-1815. 3. Propaganda, French. I. T.*
DC202.5.H65 1969 944/.04/6 78-90530 ISBN:83712140X

Puryear, Vernon John, 1901- III. 1742
Napoleon and the Dardanelles. Berkeley, University of California Press, 1951. 437 p. 24 cm. *1. Napoléon I, Emperor of the French, 1769-1821. 2. France — Foreign relations — Turkey. 3. Turkey — Foreign relations — France. I. T.*
DC202.7.P8 327.4409496 51-10924

Cronin, Vincent. III. 1743
Napoleon Bonaparte; an intimate biography. New York, Morrow, 1972 [c1971] 480 p. illus. 25 cm. *1. Napoléon I, Emperor of the French, 1769-1821. I. T.*
DC203.C9 1972 944.05/092/4 (B) 72-166356

Madelin, Louis, 1871- III. 1744
Napoléon. Paris, Dunrod [1934] 450 p. 19 cm. (Collection "Les constructeurs") *1. Napoléon I, emperor of the French, 1769-1821. 2. France — Politics and government — 1799-1815. 3. France — Constitutional history.*
DC203.M177 923.144 35-5011

Thompson, James Matthew, 1878- III. 1745
Napoleon Bonaparte. New York, Oxford University Press, 1952. ix, 463 p. ports., maps (on lining papers) facsims. 25 cm. English ed. (Oxford, B. Blackwell) has title: Napoleon Bonaparte, his rise and fall. *1. Napoléon I, Emperor of the French, 1769-1821.*
DC203.T53 1952a 923.144 52-9576

Geyl, Pieter, 1887- III. 1746
Napoleon, for and against, translated from the Dutch by Olive Renier. New Haven, Yale University Press, 1949. 477 p. fold. col. maps. 23 cm. *1. Napoléon I, Emperor of the French, 1769-1821. 2. France — History — 1789-1815. 3. Historians, French. 4. France — History — Historiography.*
DC203.8G42 ~~923.144~~ A49-9829   944 .05
N16ge

Hales, Edward Elton Young, 1908- III. 1747
Napoleon and the Pope; the story of Napoleon and Pius VII [by] E. E. Y. Hales. London, Eyre & Spottiswoode [1962, c1961] xv, 207 p. map, ports. 21 cm. *1. Napoléon I, Emperor of the French, 1769-1821. 2. Pius VII, Pope, 1742-1823. I. T.*
DC203.9.H27 1962 940.27 65-632

Napoléon I, Emperor of the French, 1769-1821. III. 1748
Letters and documents. Selected and translated by John Eldred Howard. New York, Oxford University Press, 1961- v. illus., ports., maps, facsims., geneal. table. 23 cm. *I. Howard, John Eldred, ed. and tr.*
DC213.H6 923.144 61-4572

Napoléon I, Emperor of the French, 1769-1821. III. 1749
Letters. Selected, translated, and edited by J. M. Thompson. London, Dent; New York, Dutton [1954] 312 p. 19 cm. (Everyman's library, no. 995) *I. Thompson, James Matthew, 1878- ed. and tr.*
DC213.Tx (AC1.E8 no. 995) 923.144 54-2838

Napoléon I, Emperor of the French, 1769-1821. III. 1750
The mind of Napoleon; a selection from his written and spoken words, edited and translated by J. Christopher Herold. New York, Columbia University Press, 1955. 322 p. 23 cm. *I. T.*
DC214.H4 308.1 55-9068

Knapton, Ernest John. III. 1751
Empress Josephine. Cambridge, Mass., Harvard University Press, 1963. xiii, 359 p. illus., ports. 25 cm. *1. Josephine, consort of Napoleon I, 1763-1814. I. T.*
DC216.1.K55 923.144 63-17203

DC220 – 249 Napoleonic
Wars. Congress of Vienna

Tarle, Evgeniĭ Viktorovich, 1874-1955. III. 1752
Napoleon's invasion of Russia, 1812 [by] Eugene Tarle. New York, Octagon Books, 1971 [c1942] 422 p. plans (on lining paper) 23 cm. Translation of Nashestvie Napoleona na Rossiiu (romanized form) *1. Napoléon I, Emperor of the French, 1769-1821 — Invasion of Russia, 1812. I. T.*
DC235.T32 1971 940.2/7 77-120670

Gulick, Edward Vose. III. 1753
Europe's classical balance of power; a case history of the theory and practice of one of the great concepts of European statecraft. Ithaca, Cornell University Press for the American Historical Association [1955] xvii, 337 p. maps. 24 cm. *1. Vienna. Congress, 1814-1815. 2. Balance of power. 3. Europe — Politics — 1789-1815. I. T.*
DC249.G8 940.27 55-13999

Nicolson, Harold George, Hon., 1886- III. 1754
The Congress of Vienna, a study in allied unity: 1812-1822, by Harold Nicolson. London, Constable [1946] xiii, 312 p. ports. 23 cm. Maps on lining-papers. "First published 1946." *1. Vienna. Congress, 1814-1815. 2. Europe — Politics — 1789-1815.*
DC249.N5 1946 940.27 46-21112

Webster, Charles Kingsley, Sir, 1886-1961. III. 1755
The Congress of Vienna, 1814-1815. New York, Barnes & Noble [1963] 213 p. 23 cm. *1. Vienna. Congress, 1814-1815.*
DC249.W4 1963   940.27   63-4077

DC251 – 326 19th Century

Bury, John Patrick Tuer. III. 1756
France, 1814-1940 [by] J. P. T. Bury. 4th ed. revised. London, Methuen, 1969. xii, 348 p. geneal. table, 6 maps. 22 cm. *1. France — History — 1789- I. T.*
DC251.B8 1969   944   77-374947   ISBN:416122604

Lavisse, Ernest, 1842-1922, ed. III. 1757
Histoire de France contemporaine depuis la révolution jusqu'à la paix de 1919; ouvrage illustré de nombreuses gravures hors texte. [Paris] Hachette [c1920-22] 10 v. illus, map, ports. 24 cm. The index (v.10) covers also the author's Histoire de France depuis les origines jusqu'à la révolution. *1. France — History — 1789- I. Sagnac, Philippe, 1868-*
DC251.L35   21-3103

Taine, Hippolyte Adolphe, 1828-1893. III. 1758
The modern régime. Tr. by John Durand. New York, H. Holt, 1890-94. 2 v. 20 cm. (His Origins of contemporary France. [v.5-6]) *1. France — Civilization. 2. France — Politics and government. 3. France — Social life and customs. I. Durand, John, 1822-1908, tr. II. T.*
DC251.T14   944   04-17633

Rémond, René. III. 1759
The right wing in France from 1815 to De Gaulle. Translated from the French by James M. Laux. 2d American ed. Philadelphia, University of Pennsylvania Press [1969] 465 p. ports. 22 cm. Translation of La droite en France de 1815 à nos jours. *1. France — Politics and government. I. T.*
DC252.R413 1969   320.5/2/0944   72-87940   ISBN:812274903

Johnson, Douglas W. J. III. 1760
Guizot; aspects of French history, 1787-1874. London, Routledge & K. Paul, 1963. 469 p. illus. 22 cm. (Studies in political history) *1. Guizot, François Pierre Guillaume, 1787-1874.*
DC255.G8J6   63-5018

Brinton, Clarence Crane, 1898- III. 1761
The lives of Talleyrand. 1st ed. New York, W. W. Norton [c1936] xi, 316 p. front., ports. 21 cm. At head of title: Crane Brinton. *1. Talleyrand-Périgord, Charles Maurice de, Prince de Bénévent, 1754-1838. I. T.*
DC255.T3B7   923.244   36-22597

DC256 – 274 1815 – 1851

Artz, Frederick Binkerd, 1894- III. 1762
France under the Bourbon Restoration, 1814-1830. New York, Russell & Russell, 1963. 443 p. illus. 23 cm. *1. France — History — Restoration, 1814-1830.*
DC256.A7 1963   944.061   63-11027

Bertier de Sauvigny, Guillaume de, 1912- III. 1763
La Restauration. [Paris] Flammarion [1955] 652 p. 20 cm. (Collection "L'Histoire") *1. France — History — Restoration, 1814-1830. I. T.*
DC256.B46   56-17916

Ponteil, Félix. III. 1764
La monarchie parlementaire, 1815-1848. Paris, Colin, 1949. 224 p. 17 cm. (Collection Armand Colin, no. 256. Section d'histoire et sciences économiques) *1. France — History — Restoration, 1814-1830. 2. France — History — Louis Philip, 1830-1848. I. T.*
DC256.P6   944.06   50-237

Pinkney, David H. III. 1765
The French revolution of 1830, by David H. Pinkney. [Princeton] N.J., Princeton University Press [1972] ix, 397 p. 23 cm. *1. France — History — July Revolution, 1830. I. T.*
DC261.P56   944.07   72-39051   ISBN:0691052026 069110011X (pbk.)

Tocqueville, Alexis Charles Henri Maurice Clérel de, 1805-1859. III. 1766
Recollections. Translated by Alexander Teixeira de Mattos. Edited with many additions from the original text and an introd. by J. P. Mayer. New York, Columbia University Press, 1949. xxvi, 331 p. 23 cm. *1. France — History — February Revolution, 1948.*
DC270.T652 1949   944.07   49-50219

Price, Roger. III. 1767
The French Second Republic: a social history. London, Batsford, 1972. vii, 386 p. 23 cm. *1. France — Politics and government — 1848-1852. 2. France — Social conditions. I. T.*
DC272.P7 1972b   320.9/44/07   72-180282   ISBN:0713411171

Marx, Karl, 1818-1883. III. 1768
The eighteenth Brumaire of Louis Bonaparte. With explanatory notes. New York, International Publishers [1964] 161 p. facsim. 21 cm. *1. France — History — Coup d'etat, 1851. 2. France — History — February Revolution, 1848. 3. France — History — Second Republic, 1848-1852. I. T.*
DC274.M324   944.07   63-23036

DC275 – 326 SECOND EMPIRE. FRANCO-GERMAN WAR (1852 – 1871)

Simpson, Frederick Arthur, 1883- III. 1769
Louis Napoleon & the recovery of France. [3d ed.] London, New York, Longmans, Green [1951] xvi, 400 p. plates, ports. 23 cm. *1. Napoléon III, Emperor of the French, 1808-1873. 2. France — History — Second Empire, 1852-1870. 3. France — Politics and government — 1852-1870.*
DC276.S62 1951   944.07   51-14914

Zeldin, Theodore, 1933- III. 1770
The political system of Napoleon III. London, Macmillan; New York, St Martin's Press, 1958. 195 p. illus. 23 cm. *1. Napoléon III, Emperor of the French, 1808-1873. 2. France — Politics and government — 1852-1870. I. T.*
DC277.1.Z4   944.07   58-3067

Williams, Roger Lawrence, 1923- III. 1771
Gaslight and shadow; the world of Napoleon III, 1851-1870. New York, Macmillan, 1957. 321 p. 22 cm. *1. France — Civilization. 2. France — History — Second Empire, 1852-1870. I. T.*
DC278.W63   944.07   57-6555

Corley, Thomas Anthony Buchanan, 1923- III. 1772
Democratic despot; a life of Napoleon III. London, Barrie and Rockliff [1961] 402 p. illus. 23 cm. *1. Napoléon III Emperor of the French, 1808-1873. I. T.*
DC280.C6   61-66635

Guérard, Albert Léon, 1880- III. 1773
Napoleon III; a great life in brief. [1st ed.] New York, Knopf, 1955. 207 p. 19 cm. (Great lives in brief, a new series of biographies) *1. Napoléon III, Emperor of the French, 1808-1873. 2. France — History — Second Empire, 1852-1870.*
DC280.G842   944.07   55-5618

Simpson, Frederick Arthur, 1883- III. 1774
The rise of Louis Napoleon, by F. A. Simpson. 3rd ed., new impression. London, Cass, 1968. xvii, 400 p. 12 plates, illus., facsims., ports. 23 cm. *1. Napoléon III, Emperor of the French, 1808-1873. 2. Napoléon III, Emperor of the French, 1808-1873 — Bibliography. 3. France — Politics and government — 1830-1848. 4. Europe — Politics — 1815-1848. I. T.*
DC280.S6 1968   944.07/0924 (B)   77-403534

Thompson, James Matthew, 1878- III. 1775
Louis Napoleon and the Second Empire. Oxford, Blackwell, 1954. 342 p. illus. 23 cm. *1. Napoléon III, Emperor of the French, 1808-1873. 2. France — History — Second Empire, 1852-1870. I. T.*
DC280.T5   944.07   54-4946

Williams, Roger Lawrence, 1923- III. 1776
The mortal Napoleon III [by] Roger L. Williams. Princeton, N.J., Princeton University Press [1972, c1971] 226 p. ports. 23 cm. *1. Napoléon III, Emperor of the French, 1808-1873. I. T.*
DC280.W67   944.07/0924 (B)   75-155005   ISBN:0691051925

Kurtz, Harold. III. 1777
The Empress Eugénie, 1826-1920. Boston, Houghton Mifflin, 1964. xiii, 407 p. illus., ports. 23 cm. *1. Eugénie, consort of Napoléon III, 1826-1920. I. T.*
DC280.2.K85 1964a   923.144   64-55895

Gooch, George Peabody, 1873- III. 1778
The Second Empire. [London] Longmans [1960] 324 p. illus. 23 cm. *1. Napoléon III, Emperor of the French, 1808-1873. 2. France — History — Second Empire, 1852-1870. I. T.*
DC280.4.G6   944.07   60-3451

Steefel, Lawrence Dinkelspiel, 1894- III. 1779
Bismarck, the Hohenzollern candidacy, and the origins of the Franco-German War of 1870. Cambridge, Harvard University Press, 1962. xi, 281 p. 22 cm. *1. Bismarck, Otto, Fürst von, 1815-1898. 2. Franco-German War, 1870-1871 — Causes. I. T.*
DC292.S7   943.082   62-13271

Howard, Michael Eliot, 1922- III. 1780
The Franco-Prussian War; the German invasion of France, 1870-1871. New York, Macmillan, 1961. 512 p. illus. 23 cm. *1. Franco-German War, 1870-1871.*
DC293.H6   943.082   61-65482

Kranzberg, Melvin.   **III. 1781**
The siege of Paris, 1870-1871; a political and social history. Westport, Conn., Greenwood Press [1971, c1950] xi, 213 p. 23 cm. A revision of the author's thesis, Harvard University. *1. Paris — Siege, 1870-1871. I. T.*
DC312.K7 1971   944.08   78-112326   ISBN:083714714X

Mason, Edward Sagendorph, 1899-   **III. 1782**
The Paris Commune; an episode in the history of the Socialist movement [by] Edward S. Mason. New York, H. Fertig, 1967 [i.e. 1968] xiv, 386 p. 24 cm. Reprint of the 1930 ed. *1. Paris — History — Commune, 1871. 2. Socialism in France. I. T.*
DC316.M34 1968   944.081   67-24588

Greenberg, Louis M., 1933-   **III. 1783**
Sisters of liberty; Marseille, Lyon, Paris, and the reaction to a centralized state, 1868-1871, by Louis M. Greenberg. Cambridge, Mass., Harvard University Press, 1971. 391 p. 21 cm. (Harvard historical monographs, 62) *1. Paris — History — Commune, 1871. 2. Marseille — History. 3. Lyons — History. I. T. (S)*
DC317.G74   944.07   70-134952   ISBN:0674810007

DC330 – 412   19th – 20th Centuries

Brabant, Frank Herbert, 1892-   **III. 1784**
The beginning of the Third Republic in France; a history of the National Assembly (February-September 1871) New York, H. Fertig, 1972. xii, 555 p. 23 cm. Reprint of the 1940 ed., issued in series: Studies in modern history. *1. France — Politics and government — 1870-1940. 2. France. Assemblée nationale, 1871-1942 — History. 3. Thiers, Adolphe, 1797-1877. I. T.*
DC331.B76 1972   944.081   73-80524

Brogan, Denis William, Sir, 1900-   **III. 1785**
The development of modern France, 1870-1939 [by] D. W. Brogan. Rev. ed. New York, Harper & Row [1966] 2 v. 21 cm. (Harper torchbooks. The Academy library, TB1184-TB1185) *1. France — History — Third Republic, 1870-1940. 2. France — Politics and government — 1870-1940. I. T.*
DC335.B75 1966   944.08   66-2183

Chapman, Guy.   **III. 1786**
The Third Republic of France; the first phase 1871-1894. [New York] St Martin's Press, 1962 [i.e. 1963] 433 p. illus. 23 cm. *1. France — History — Third Republic, 1870-1940. I. T.*
DC335.C48   944.08   62-21077

Conference on Modern France, Princeton, N.J., 1950.   **III. 1787**
Modern France: problems of the Third and Fourth Republics. Edited by Edward Mead Earle. Contributors: Warren C. Baum [and others] New York, Russell & Russell, 1964 [c1951] xiv, 522 p. illus. 24 cm. Papers read at the conference sponsored by the Committee on International and Regional Studies, Harvard University, and other bodies, published with some additions and corrections. *1. France — History — Third Republic, 1870-1940. 2. France — Politics and government — 20th cent. I. Earle, Edward Mead, 1894-1954, ed. II. Harvard University. Committee on Regional Studies. III. T.*
DC335.C65 1950a   320.944   64-10387

Sedgwick, Alexander, 1930-   **III. 1788**
The Third French Republic, 1870-1914. New York, Crowell [c1968] x, 148 p. 21 cm. (Europe since 1500: a paperbound series) *1. France — History — Third Republic, 1870-1940. I. T.*
DC335.S4   944.081   68-13384

Joll, James, ed.   **III. 1789**
The decline of the Third Republic. New York, Praeger [1959] 127 p. map, diagr. 23 cm. (St. Antony's papers, no. 5) Books that matter. *1. France — History — Third Republic, 1870-1940. I. T. (S:St. Antony's papers (New York, Praeger) no. 5)*
DC337.J6   944.08   59-7824

Shattuck, Roger.   **III. 1790**
The banquet years; the origins of the avant garde in France, 1885 to World War I: Alfred Jarry, Henri Rousseau, Erik Satie [and] Guillaume Apollinaire. Rev. ed. New York, Vintage Books [1968] xiv, 397 p. illus., facsims., music, ports. 19 cm. First ed. published in 1958 under title: The banquet years, the arts in France, 1885-1918. *1. France — Intellectual life. 2. Jarry, Alfred, 1873-1907. 3. Rousseau, Henri Julien Félix, 1844-1910. 4. Satie, Erik, 1866-1925. 5. Apollinaire, Guillaume, 1880-1918. I. T.*
DC338.S48 1968   914.4/03/810922   68-12411

Buthman, William Curt, 1900-   **III. 1791**
The rise of integral nationalism in France, with special reference to the ideas and activities of Charles Maurras, by William Curt Buthman, PH.D. New York, Columbia University Press; London, P. S. King & Son, 1939. 355 p. 23 cm. (Studies in history, economics and public law, ed. by the Faculty of political science of Columbia University. no. 455) Issued also as thesis (PH.D.) Columbia University. *1. France — Nationality. I. Maurras, Charles, 1868- II. T.*
DC340.B9 1939a (H31.C7 no. 455)   944.08 (308.2)   39-32365

Curtis, Michael, 1923-   **III. 1792**
Three against the Third Republic: Sorel, Barrès, and Maurras. Princeton, Princeton University Press, 1959. 313 p. 23 cm. *1. Barrès, Maurice, 1862-1923. 2. Maurras, Charles, 1868-1952. 3. Sorel, Georges, 1847-1922. 4. France — History — Third Republic, 1870-1940. I. T.*
DC340.C8   944.08   59-11075

Schuman, Frederick Lewis, 1904-   **III. 1793**
War and diplomacy in the French Republic; an inquiry into political motivations and the control of foreign policy [by] Frederick L. Schuman. With an introd. by Quincy Wright. New York, H. Fertig, 1969. xvii, 452 p. 24 cm. Reprint of the 1931 ed. *1. France — Foreign relations — 1870-1940. 2. France — Politics and government — 1870-1940. 3. Europe — Politics — 1871-1918. 4. Diplomacy. I. T.*
DC340.S35 1969   327.44   68-9635

Shapiro, David Michael, ed.   **III. 1794**
The Right in France, 1890-1919; three studies. [1st American ed.] Carbondale, Southern Illinois University Press [1962] 144 p. illus. 23 cm. (St. Antony's papers, no. 13) *1. France — Politics and government — 1870-1940. I. T.*
DC340.S45 1962   944.08   62-15227

Thomson, David, 1912-   **III. 1795**
Democracy in France since 1870. 4th ed. New York, Oxford University Press, 1964. 346 p. 21 cm. "Issued under the auspices of the Royal Institute of International Affairs." *1. France — Politics and government — 1870-1940. 2. France — Politics and government — 1945- I. T.*
DC340.T5 1964   944.08   64-54597

DC342 – 354   BIOGRAPHY. DREYFUS CASE

Seager, Frederic H.   **III. 1796**
The Boulanger affair; political crossroad of France, 1886-1889 [by] Frederic H. Seager. Ithaca, N.Y., Cornell University Press [1969] xiv, 276 p. 22 cm. *1. Boulanger, Georges Ernest Jean Marie, 1837-1891. 2. France — Politics and government — 1870-1940. I. T.*
DC342.8.B7S4   944.081/0924   68-9753

Bruun, Geoffrey, 1898-   **III. 1797**
Clemenceau. Hamden, Conn., Archon Books, 1962 [c1943] 225 p. illus. 22 cm. (Makers of modern Europe) *1. Clemenceau, Georges Eugène Benjamin, 1841-1929. 2. France — History — Third Republic, 1870-1940.*
DC342.8.C6B7 1962   923.244   62-4985

Jackson, John Hampden, 1907-   **III. 1798**
Clemenceau and the Third Republic. New York, Macmillan Co., 1948. xiii, 266 p. port., maps (on lining-papers) 18 cm. (Teach yourself history library. New York) *1. Clemenceau, Georges Eugène Benjamin, 1841-1929. 2. France — History — Third Republic, 1870-1940. (S)*
DC342.8.C6J3 1948   944.08   49-1976

Bury, John Patrick Tuer.   **III. 1799**
Gambetta and the national defence; a republican dictatorship in France, by J. P. T. Bury. Westport, Conn., Greenwood Press [1971] xxiv, 341 p. illus., map, ports. 23 cm. Reprint of the 1936 ed. *1. Gambetta, Léon Michel, 1838-1882. 2. France — Politics and government — 1870-1940. 3. Franco-German War, 1870-1871. 4. France — Defenses. I. T.*
DC342.8.G3B8 1971   944.81/0924   77-114490   ISBN:0837148189

Goldberg, Harvey, 1923-   **III. 1800**
The life of Jean Jaurès. Madison, University of Wisconsin Press, 1962. 590 p. illus. 25 cm. *1. Jaurès, Jean Léon, 1859-1914. 2. Socialism in France.*
DC342.8.J4G63   923.244   62-7216

Chapman, Guy.   **III. 1801**
The Dreyfus case, a reassessment. New York, Reynal [1956, c1955] 400 p. illus. 22 cm. *1. Dreyfus, Alfred, 1859-1935. I. T.*
DC354.C47 1956   923.544   56-5250

Halasz, Nicholas, 1895-   **III. 1802**
Captain Dreyfus; the story of a mass hysteria. New York, Simon and Schuster, 1955. 274 p. 22 cm. *1. Dreyfus, Alfred, 1859-1935.*
DC354.H15   944.08   55-8810

DC361 – 412   20TH CENTURY

In search of France   **III. 1803**
[by] Stanley Hoffmann [and others] Cambridge, Harvard University Press, 1963. xiii, 443 p. 24 cm. "Prepared under the auspices of the Center for International Affairs, Harvard University." *1. France — Politics and*

government — 1945- 2. France — Social conditions. 3. National characteristics, French. I. Hoffmann, Stanley. II. Harvard University. Center for International Affairs.
DC361.I5   944.082   63-9549

Hughes, Henry Stuart, 1916-　　　　　　　　　　　　**III. 1804**
The obstructed path; French social thought in the years of desperation, 1930-1960 [by] H. Stuart Hughes. [1st ed.] New York, Harper & Row [1968] xi, 304 p. 21 cm. *1. France — Intellectual life. I. T.*
DC365.H8   914.4/03/8   67-28807

Weber, Eugen Joseph, 1925-　　　　　　　　　　　　**III. 1805**
Action française; royalism and reaction in twentieth century France. Stanford, Calif., Stanford University Press, 1962. 594 p. 25 cm. *1. L'Action française. 2. France — Politics and government — 1870-1940. I. T.*
DC369.W36   62-15267

Weber, Eugen Joseph, 1925-　　　　　　　　　　　　**III. 1806**
The nationalist revival in France, 1905-1914. Berkeley, University of California Press, 1959. viii, 237 p. 24 cm. (University of California publications in history, v.60) "Biographical notes": p. 219-231. *1. Nationalism — France. 2. France — Politics and government — 1870-1940. I. T. (S:California. University. University of California publications in history, v.60)*
DC369.W36x   (E173.C15 vol. 60)   342.44   A59-9362

Binion, Rudolph, 1927-　　　　　　　　　　　　**III. 1807**
Defeated leaders; the political fate of Caillaux, Jouvenel, and Tardieu. Morningside Heights, N.Y., Columbia University Press, 1960. 425 p. 24 cm. *1. Caillaux, Joseph, 1863-1944. 2. Jouvenel, Henry de, 1876-1935. 3. Tardieu, André Pierre Gabriel Amédée, 1876-1945. I. T.*
DC371.B5 1960   923.244   59-14524

Colton, Joel G., 1918-　　　　　　　　　　　　**III. 1808**
Léon Blum, humanist in politics [by] Joel Colton. [1st ed.] New York, Knopf, 1966. xiv, 512, xiv p. illus., ports. 25 cm. *1. Blum, Léon, 1872-1950.*
DC373.B5C6   944.08150924 (B)   65-18764

Gaulle, Charles de, Pres. France, 1890-　　　　　　　　　　　　**III. 1809**
De Gaulle: implacable ally [edited by] Roy C. Macridis. With a special introd. by Maurice Duverger. New York, Harper & Row [1966] xxxv, 248 p. 21 cm. *1. France — Politics and government — 20th cent. 2. France — Foreign relations — 1945- I. Macridis, Roy C., ed. II. T.*
DC373.G3A25   944.080924   66-12560

DePorte, Anton W.　　　　　　　　　　　　**III. 1810**
De Gaulle's foreign policy, 1944-1946 [by] A. W. DePorte. Cambridge, Harvard University Press, 1968 [i.e. 1967] xiii, 327 p. 22 cm. *1. Gaulle, Charles de, Pres. France, 1890- 2. France — Foreign relations — 1940-1945. I. T.*
DC373.G3D47   327.44   67-29624

Lacouture, Jean.　　　　　　　　　　　　**III. 1811**
De Gaulle. Translated by Francis K. Price. [New York] New American Library [1966] 215 p. 22 cm. *1. Gaulle, Charles de, Pres. France, 1890-*
DC373.G3L2513   944.080924 (B)   66-24425

Werth, Alexander, 1901-　　　　　　　　　　　　**III. 1812**
De Gaulle; a political biography. New York, Simon and Schuster [1966] 416 p. 23 cm. *1. Gaulle, Charles de, Pres. France, 1890- 2. France — Politics and government — 20th century.*
DC373.G3W4   944.080924   66-21828

Thomson, David, 1912-　　　　　　　　　　　　**III. 1813**
Two Frenchmen: Pierre Laval and Charles de Gaulle. London, Cresset Press, 1951. 255 p. 22 cm. *1. Laval, Pierre, 1883-1945. 2. Gaulle, Charles de, 1890- I. T.*
DC373.L35T47   944.08   51-6272

Miquel, Pierre, historian.　　　　　　　　　　　　**III. 1814**
Poincaré. Paris, Librairie A. Fayard [1961] 636 p. 19 cm. (Les Grands études historiques) *1. Poincaré, Raymond, Pres. France, 1860-1934.*
DC385.M5   62-44852

Wright, Gordon, 1912-　　　　　　　　　　　　**III. 1815**
Raymond Poincaré and the French presidency. New York, Octagon Books, 1967 [c1942] ix, 271 p. 24 cm. (The Hoover Library on War, Revolution, and Peace. Publication no. 19) *1. Poincaré, Raymond, Pres. France, 1860-1934. 2. France — Politics and government — 1914-1940. 3. France — Presidents. (S:Stanford University. Hoover Institution on War, Revolution, and Peace. Publication no. 19)*
DC385.W7 1967   944.081/0924   67-18792

DC387 – 396   1914 – 1940

King, Jere Clemens.　　　　　　　　　　　　**III. 1816**
Generals & politicians; conflict between France's high command, Parliament, and Government, 1914-1918. Westport, Conn., Greenwood Press [1971, c1951] 294 p. 23 cm. *1. France — Politics and government — 1914-1940. 2. European War, 1914-1918 — France. I. T.*
DC387.K38 1971   944.08   74-112325   ISBN:0837147131

Greene, Nathanael, 1935-　　　　　　　　　　　　**III. 1817**
From Versailles to Vichy: the Third French Republic, 1919-1940. New York, Crowell [1970] x, 160 p. 21 cm. (Europe since 1500; a paperbound series) *1. France — Politics and government — 1914-1940. I. T.*
DC389.G68   944.081/5   70-13854

Reynaud, Paul, 1878-　　　　　　　　　　　　**III. 1818**
In the thick of the fight, 1930-1945. Translated by James D. Lambert. New York, Simon and Schuster [1955] 684 p. illus. 23 cm. "Published in France under the title 'Au cœur de la mêlée' 1951 [rev. ed. of La France a sauvé l'Europe] This abridgment first published in Great Britain, 1955." *1. France — History — 1914-1940. 2. World War, 1939-1945 — France. I. T.*
DC389.R433   944.08   55-4907

Scott, William Evans.　　　　　　　　　　　　**III. 1819**
Alliance against Hitler; the origins of the Franco-Soviet pact. Durham, N.C., Duke University Press, 1962. x, 296 p. group port. 25 cm. (Duke historical publications) "Franco-Soviet treaty of mutual assistance": p. [272]-273; "Protocole de signature": p. [274]-275. *1. France — Foreign relations — Russia. 2. Russia — Foreign relations — France. I. France. Treaties, etc., 1932-1940 (Lebrun) Traité d'assistance mutuelle entre la France et l'Union des Republiques soviétiques socialistes, signé a Paris, le 2 mai 1935. II. France. Treaties, etc., 1932-1940 (Lebrun) Traité d'assistance mutuelle entre la France et l'Union des Républiques soviétiques socialistes, signé a Paris, le 2 mai 1935. Protocole de signature. III. T. (S)*
DC389.S43   327.44047   62-20214

Larmour, Peter J.　　　　　　　　　　　　**III. 1820**
The French Radical Party in the 1930's [by] Peter J. Larmour. Stanford, Calif., Stanford University Press, 1964. 327 p. illus. 24 cm. *1. Parti républicain radical et radical-socialiste. 2. France — Politics and government — 1914-1940. I. T.*
DC394.L3   944.08   64-14554

Micaud, Charles Antoine, 1910-　　　　　　　　　　　　**III. 1821**
The French Right and Nazi Germany, 1933-1939; a study of public opinion, by Charles A. Micaud. New York, Octagon Books, 1964 [c1943] x, 255 p. 24 cm. *1. Public opinion — France. 2. France — Politics and government — 1914-1940. I. T.*
DC396.M5 1964   327.43044   64-24855

Werth, Alexander, 1901-　　　　　　　　　　　　**III. 1822**
The twilight of France, 1933-1940. Edited with an introd. by D. W. Brogan. New York, H. Fertig, 1966 [c1942] xxii, 368 p. 24 cm. *1. France — Politics and government — 1914-1940. 2. France — Foreign relations — 1914-1940. 3. World War, 1939-1945 — France. I. Brogan, Denis William, 1900- ed. II. T.*
DC396.W42 1966   944.0815   66-24358

DC397   1940 – 1946

Aron, Robert, 1898-　　　　　　　　　　　　**III. 1823**
The Vichy regime, 1940-44. In collaboration with Georgette Elgey. Translated by Humphrey Hare. Boston, Beacon Press [1969] vi, 536 p. 21 cm. (Europe in the twentieth century. Beacon paperback, BP329.) Translation of author's abridgment of his Histoire de Vichy. The text is a reprint of the 1958 ed. *1. France — History — German occupation, 1940-1945. I. T.*
DC397.A71343 1969   944.081/6   70-89958

Farmer, Paul, 1918-　　　　　　　　　　　　**III. 1824**
Vichy: political dilemma. New York, Columbia University Press, 1955. vi, 376 p. 24 cm. *1. France — Politics and government — 1940-1945. I. T.*
DC397.F3 1955   944.081   55-6180

Michel, Henri, 1907-　　　　　　　　　　　　**III. 1825**
Les courants de pensée de la Résistance. [1. éd.] Paris, Presses universitaires de France, 1962. 842 p. 23 cm. (Esprit de la Résistance; la guerre, l'occupation, la déportation, la libération) *1. France — Politics and government — 1940-1945. I. T.*
DC397.M53   64-33359

Michel, Henri, 1907-　　　　　　　　　　　　**III. 1826**
Vichy, année 40. Paris, R. Laffont, 1966. 463 p. plates. 24 cm. (L'Histoire que nous vivons) Illustrated cover. *1. France — Politics and government — 1940-1945. 2. World War, 1939-1945 — France. I. T.*
DC397.M537   944.081/6   67-78846

Paxton, Robert O.　　　　　　　　　　　　**III. 1827**
Parades and politics at Vichy; the French officer corps under Marshal Pétain, by Robert O. Paxton. Princeton, N.J., Princeton University Press, 1966. xi, 472 p. ports. 21 cm. *1. France. Armée — Officers. 2. France — History — German occupation, 1940-1945. 3. France — Politics and government — 1940-1945. I. T.*
DC397.P36   944.0816   66-10557

Paxton, Robert O.   **III. 1828**
Vichy France: old guard and new order, 1940-1944 [by] Robert O. Paxton. [1st ed.] New York, Knopf; distributed by Random House, 1972. 399, xix p. illus. 25 cm. *1. France — Politics and government — 1940-1945. 2. France — History — German occupation, 1940-1945. I. T.*
DC397.P37   320.9/44/0816   74-171140   ISBN:0394473604

DC398 – 412   1947 –

Werth, Alexander, 1901-   **III. 1829**
France, 1940-1955. With a foreword by G. D. H. Cole. London, R. Hale [1956] 764 p. 22 cm. *1. France — History — German occupation, 1940-1945. 2. France — History — 1945-*
DC400.W4   56-3622

Aron, Raymond, 1905-   **III. 1830**
France steadfast and changing: the Fourth to the Fifth Republic. [Translated by J. Irwin and Luigi Einaudi] Cambridge, Harvard University Press, 1960. 201 p. 22 cm. Translation of Immuable et changeante. *1. France — History — 1945- 2. National characteristics, French. I. T.*
DC401.A813   944.082   60-11551

Goguel-Nyegaard, François.   **III. 1831**
France under the Fourth Republic [by] François Goguel. New York, Russell & Russell [1971, c1952] xiii, 198 p. maps. 23 cm. Translated from the French manuscript by Roy Pierce. *1. France — Politics and government — 1945-1958. I. T.*
DC404.G6 1971   320.9/44/082   76-139923

Hoffmann, Stanley.   **III. 1832**
Le Mouvement Poujade. Avec la collaboration de Michel des Accords [et al.] Préf. de Jean Meynaud. Paris, A. Colin, 1956. 417 p. illus. 24 cm. (Cahiers de la Fondation nationale des sciences politiques, 81) *1. Poujade, Pierre, 1920- 2. Union de défense des commerçants et artisans. I. T.*
DC404.H6x (H31.F6 no. 81)   57-27363

Pickles, Dorothy Maud.   **III. 1833**
French politics; the first years of the Fourth Republic [by] Dorothy Pickles. New York, Russell & Russell [1971] xii, 302 p. 23 cm. Reprint of the 1953 ed. *1. France — Politics and government — 1945-1958. I. T.*
DC404.P5 1971   320.9/44/082   72-122001

Wright, Gordon, 1912-   **III. 1834**
The reshaping of French democracy. New York, H. Fertig, 1970 [c1948] 277 p. 21 cm. *1. France — Politics and government — 1945- I. T.*
DC404.W7 1970   320.9/44   68-9654

Werth, Alexander, 1901-   **III. 1835**
Lost statesman, the strange story of Pierre Mendès-France. New York, Abelard-Schuman [1958] 428 p. illus. 23 cm. *1. Mendès-France, Pierre, 1907- 2. France — Politics and government — 1945- I. T.*
DC407.M4W4 1958   923.244   58-6091

Charlot, Jean.   **III. 1836**
The Gaullist phenomenon: the Gaullist movement in the Fifth Republic. Translated by Monica Charlot and Marianne Neighbour. New York, Praeger [1971] 205 p. illus. 23 cm. (Studies in political science, 6) Translation of Le phénomène gaulliste. *1. France — Politics and government — 1958- I. T.*
DC412.C51413 1971b   320.9/44/083   70-165527

Furniss, Edgar Stephenson, 1918-   **III. 1837**
De Gaulle and the French Army; a crisis in civil-military relations. New York, Twentieth Century Fund, 1964. x, 331 p. 25 cm. *1. Gaulle, Charles de, Pres. France, 1890- 2. France — Military policy. 3. France — Politics and government — 1958- I. T.*
DC412.F79   944.082   64-14079

Grosser, Alfred, 1925-   **III. 1838**
French foreign policy under De Gaulle. Translated by Lois Ames Pattison. Boston, Little, Brown [1967] xiv, 175 p. 21 cm. "A revision of La politique extérieure de la Cinquième République. The chapter 'And now ...' was written especially for the English version." *1. France — Foreign relations — 1945- I. T.*
DC412.G753   327.44   67-15419

Macridis, Roy C.   **III. 1839**
The De Gaulle republic: quest for unity [by] Roy C. Macridis [and] Bernard E. Brown. Homewood, Ill., Dorsey Press, 1960. 400 p. illus. 24 cm. (The Dorsey series in political science) Supplement. Homewood, Ill., Dorsey Press, 1963. 141 p. illus. 23 cm. (The Dorsey series in political science) *1. France — Politics and government — 1958- I. Brown, Bernard Edward, 1925- joint author. II. T.*
DC412.M3   944.082   60-14048

Pickles, Dorothy Maud.   **III. 1840**
Algeria and France; from colonialism to cooperation. New York, Praeger [1963] 215 p. 21 cm. (Books that matter) *1. France — Politics and government — 1945- 2. Algeria — History — 1945- 3. Algeria — Relations (general) — France. 4. France — Relations (general) — Algeria. I. T.*
DC412.P48 1963   965.04   63-12778

Pickles, Dorothy Maud.   **III. 1841**
The Fifth French Republic. New York, Praeger [1960] 222 p. 20 cm. (Books that matter. Praeger paperbacks, PPS-21.) *1. France — Politics and government — 1958- I. T.*
DC412.P5 1960   944.082   60-8738

Wahl, Nicholas.   **III. 1842**
The Fifth Republic; France's new political system. New York, Random House [1959] 130 p. 19 cm. (Studies in political science, PS31) "The Constitution of the Fifth Republic": p. 103-126. *1. France — Politics and government — 1958- I. France. Constitution, 1958. II. T.*
DC412.W3   944.082   59-15499

Williams, Philip Maynard.   **III. 1843**
De Gaulle's Republic [by] Philip M. Williams and Martin Harrison. [London] Longmans [1960] vii, 279 p. diagrs. 23 cm. "Constitution of the Fifth Republic": p. 232-249. *1. Gaulle, Charles de, Pres. France, 1890- 2. France — Politics and government — 1945- 3. Algeria — History — 1945- I. Harrison, Martin, joint author. II. France. Constitution, 1958. III. T.*
DC412.W5   944.082   60-4868

DC600 – 989   LOCAL HISTORY

Cartellieri, Otto, 1872-1930.   **III. 1844**
The Court of Burgundy. [Translated by Malcolm Letts] New York, Barnes & Noble [1972] xv, 282 p. illus. 24 cm. Translation of Am Hofe der Herzöge von Burgund. Reprint of the 1929 ed., issued in series: The History of civilization. *1. Burgundy — Court and courtiers. 2. Burgundy — Civilization. 3. Civilization, Medieval. I. T.*
DC611.B78C2813 1972   914.4/4/032   72-186144   ISBN:0389044563

Vaughan, Richard, 1927-   **III. 1845**
Philip the Bold; the formation of the Burgundian state. Cambridge, Mass., Harvard University Press, 1962. 278 p. illus. 23 cm. *1. Philippe le Hardi, Duke of Burgundy, 1342-1404. 2. Burgundy — History.*
DC611.B78V35   944.4   63-793

Strayer, Joseph Reese, 1904-   **III. 1846**
The administration of Normandy under Saint Louis. Cambridge, Mass., Mediaeval Academy of America, 1932. [New York, AMS Press, 1971] x, 133 p. 24 cm. *1. Normandy — Politics and government — Medieval. 2. France — Politics and government — 1226-1270. I. Normandy under Saint Louis. II. T.*
DC611.N88S7 1971   354.44/2   72-171362   ISBN:0404062970

Wylie, Laurence William, 1909-   **III. 1847**
Village in the Vaucluse, by Laurence Wylie. 2d ed., enl. Cambridge, Harvard University Press, 1964. xviii, 377 p. illus., maps, ports. 22 cm. *1. Vaucluse, France (Dept.) — Social life and customs. I. T.*
DC611.V357W9 1964b   914.49/2   64-23470

Easton, Malcolm.   **III. 1848**
Artists and writers in Paris; the Bohemian idea, 1803-1867. New York, St. Martin's Press, 1964 [i.e.1965] viii, 205 p. illus., port. 23 cm. *1. Paris — Intellectual life. 2. Bohemianism. 3. Artists in literature. 4. French fiction — 19th cent. — History and criticism. I. T.*
DC715.E2 1965   709.4436   64-24268

Pinkney, David H.   **III. 1849**
Napoleon III and the rebuilding of Paris. Princeton, N.J., Princeton University Press, 1958. xi, 245 p. illus., maps, plans. 25 cm. *1. Napoléon III, Emperor of the French, 1808-1873. 2. Cities and towns — Planning — Paris. 3. Paris — Public works.*
DC733.P59   944.07   58-6108

Flanner, Janet, 1892-   **III. 1850**
Paris journal [by] Janet Flanner (Genêt) Edited by William Shawn. [1st ed.] New York, Atheneum, 1965-71. 2 v. 25 cm. Selected from her series of letters first published in the New Yorker magazine. *1. Paris — History — 1944- 2. France — Politics and government — 1945- 3. Paris — Intellectual life. I. Shawn, William, ed. II. The New Yorker (1925-) III. T.*
DC737.F55 1965   944.082   65-25903

Walter, Gérard, 1896-   **III. 1851**
Paris under the occupation. Translated from the French by Tony White. New York, Orion Press [1960] 209 p. illus. 22 cm. Translation of La vie á Paris sous l'occupation. *1. Paris — History — 1940-1945. I. T.*
DC737.W283   940.534436   60-13616

Wylie, Laurence William, 1909- ed.   **III. 1852**
Chanzeaux, a village in Anjou. Edited by Lawrence Wylie. Cambridge, Mass., Harvard University Press, 1966. xx, 383 p. illus., maps. 25 cm. *1. Chanzeaux, France.*
DC801.C43W9   914.4/18   66-18258

Kaplow, Jeffry.   **III. 1853**
Elbeuf during the revolutionary period, history and social structure. Baltimore, Johns Hopkins Press, 1964. 278, x p. tables. 24 cm. (Johns Hopkins University. Studies in historical and political science, Series 81, no. 2) *1. Elbeuf, France — History. 2. Elbeuf, France — Social conditions. (S)*
DC801.E4K3 (H31.J6 ser. 81, no. 2)   309.14425   64-15091

Stewart, John Hall, 1904-   **III. 1854**
A documentary survey of the French Revolution. New York, Macmillan [1951] xxviii, 818 p. facsims. (on lining papers) 22 cm. *1. France — History — Revolution — Sources. I. T.*
DC1417.7.S8   944.04   51-10629

DD Germany

DD1 – 78 GENERAL WORKS. CIVILIZATION

Snyder, Louis Leo, 1907- ed. Ill. 1855
Documents of German history. New Brunswick, N.J., Rutgers University Press, 1958. xxiii, 619 p. fold. maps. 24 cm. 1. Germany — History — Sources. 2. Document sources — Germany. I. T.
DD3.S55   943.0082   57010-968

Gooch, George Peabody, 1873-1968. Ill. 1856
Studies in German history. New York, Russell & Russell [1969] vii, 515 p. 22 cm. Essays. Reprint of the 1948 ed. 1. Germany — History — Addresses, essays, lectures. I. T.
DD5.G66 1969   943   70-75465

Staël-Holstein, Anne Louise Germaine (Necker) baronne de, 1766-1817. Ill. 1857
De l'Allemagne. Nouv. éd., publiée d'après les manuscrits et les éditions originales avec des variantes, une introd., des notices et des notes par la comtesse Jean de Pange, avec le concours de Simone Balayé. Paris, Hachette, 1958. 2 v. 23 cm. (Les grands écrivains de la France) 1. Germany. 2. German literature — History and criticism. 3. Germany — Intellectual life. 4. National characteristics, German. I. Pange, Pauline Laure Marie (de Broglie) comtesse de, 1888-
DD35.Sx   A59-3495

Dickinson, Robert Eric, 1905- Ill. 1858
Germany; a general and regional geography, by Robert E. Dickinson. [2d ed.] London, Methuen [1964] xxiii, 716 p. illus., maps. 24 cm. On label on t.p.: Distributed in the United States by Barnes & Noble [New York] 1. Germany — Description and travel — 1945- 2. Physical geography — Germany.
DD43.D5 1964   67-59646

Bithell, Jethro, 1878- ed. Ill. 1859
Germany, a companion to German studies. [5th ed., rev., enl.] London, Methuen [1955] xii, 578 p. fold. col. map. 23 cm. (Methuen's companions to modern studies) 1. Germany — Civilization — History. 2. National characteristics, German. 3. Germany — History. 4. German literature — History and criticism. 5. Art, German. 6. Music, German. 7. Germany — Bibliography. 8. Guides to the literature — Germany. I. T.
DD61.B56 1955   914.3   55003-335

Plessner, Helmuth, 1892- Ill. 1860
Die verspätete Nation; über die politische Verführbarkeit bürgerlichen Geistes. [2. erweiterte Aufl. Stuttgart] W. Kohlhammer [1959] 174 p. 24 cm. First ed. published in 1935 under title: Das Schicksal deutschen Geistes im Ausgang seiner bürgerlichen Epoche. 1. Germany — Civilization. 2. Philosophy, German. I. T.
DD61.P5 1959   60-27769

Epstein, Klaus. Ill. 1861
The genesis of German conservatism. Princeton, N.J., Princeton University Press, 1966. xii, 733 p. 25 cm. 1. Germany — Intellectual life. 2. Conservatism — Germany. I. T.
DD65.E6   320.50943   66-11970

Anchor, Robert. Ill. 1862
Germany confronts modernization; German culture and society, 1790-1890. Lexington, Mass., Heath [1972] 151 p. illus. 23 cm. (Civilization and society. Studies in social, economic, and cultural history) 1. Germany — Intellectual life. 2. Germany — Social conditions. 3. Germany — Politics and government — 1789-1900. I. T.
DD66.A5   309.1/43   70-179800   ISBN:0669810347 0669810266 (pbk)

Veblen, Thorstein, 1857-1929. Ill. 1863
Imperial Germany and the industrial revolution, by Thorstein Veblen; with an introduction by Dr. Joseph Dorfman. New ed. New York, Viking Press, 1939. xxi, 343 p. 20 cm. 1. Germany — Civilization. 2. Germany — Economic policy. I. T.
DD67.V4 1939   943.08   39-27516

Ergang, Robert Reinhold, 1898- Ill. 1864
Herder and the foundations of German nationalism. New York, Octagon Books, 1966 [c1931] 288 p. 24 cm. (Studies in history, economics, and public law, no. 341) 1. Herder, Johann Gottfried von, 1744-1803. 2. Nationalism — Germany. I. T. (S:Columbia studies in the social sciences, no. 341)
DD76.E7 1966   193   66-19732

Ritter, Gerhard, 1888- Ill. 1865
The German problem; basic questions of German political life, past and present. [Translated from the German by Sigurd Burckhardt] Columbus, Ohio State University Press, 1965. ix, 233 p. 22 cm. (Publications of the Graduate Institute for World Affairs of the Ohio State University, no. 6) "A publication of the Mershon Center for Education in National Security." Translation of Das deutsche Problem, Grundfragen deutschen Staatslebens gestern und heute which was a revision and expansion of Europa und die deutsche Frage. 1. Nationalism — Germany. 2. Germany — History — 20th cent. 3. Germany — Politics and government. I. T. (S:Ohio. State University, Columbus. Graduate Institute for World Affairs. Publication no. 6)
DD76.R483   320.150943   65-63469

Stern, Fritz Richard, 1926- Ill. 1866
The politics of cultural despair; a study in the rise of the Germanic ideology. Berkeley, University of California Press, 1961. 367 p. 24 cm. Revision of the author's thesis, Columbia University, issued in microfilm form in 1954 under title: Cultural despair and the politics of discontent. 1. Lagarde, Paul Anton de, 1827-1891. 2. Langbehn, Julius, 1851-1907. 3. Moeller van den Bruck, Arthur, 1876-1925. 4. Nationalism — Germany. 5. National socialism. I. T.
DD76.S72 1961   943   61-7517

DD84 – 261 HISTORY

Iggers, Georg G. Ill. 1867
The German conception of history; the national tradition of historical thought from Herder to the present, by Georg G. Iggers. [1st ed.] Middletown, Conn., Wesleyan University Press [1968] xii, 363 p. 24 cm. 1. Germany — Historiography. I. T.
DD86.I34   914.3/0072   68-17147

Barraclough, Geoffrey, 1908- Ill. 1868
The origins of modern Germany, by G. Barraclough. Oxford, B. Blackwell, 1966. xi, 481 p. maps. 22 cm. Reprint of the 2d rev. ed., 1947. 1. Germany — History. I. T.
DD89.B27 1966   943   68-7947

Dill, Marshall. Ill. 1869
Germany; a modern history. New ed., rev. and enl. Ann Arbor, University of Michigan Press [1970] x, 490, xxiii p. maps. 25 cm. (The University of Michigan history of the modern world) 1. Germany — History. I. T. (S:Michigan. University. The University of Michigan history of the modern world)
DD89.D5 1970   943   70-124426   ISBN:472071017

Handbuch der deutschen Geschichte, Ill. 1870
begründet von Otto Brandt, fortgeführt von Arnold Oskar Meyer. Neu hrsg. von Leo Just unter Mitwirkung von Walter Bussmann [et al.] Konstanz, Akademische Verlagsgesellschaft Athenaion [c1956- v. 1, c1957] v. fold. col. map (in pocket) 27 cm. Each vol. has also special t.p. Issued also in parts. 1. Germany — History. I. Brandt, Otto, 1892-1935. II. Meyer, Arnold Oskar, 1877-1944, ed. III. Just, Leo, 1901-1969, ed.
DD89.H313   64-50340

Heer, Friedrich, 1916- Ill. 1871
The Holy Roman Empire. Translated by Janet Sondheimer. New York, Praeger [1968] xiv, 309 p. plates (part col.) 26 cm. Translation of Das Heilige Römische Reich. 1. Germany — History. 2. Austria — History. 3. Holy Roman Empire — History. I. T.
DD89.H3513 1968   943   68-30935

Valentin, Veit, 1885-1947. Ill. 1872
The German people, their history and civilization from the Holy Roman

III. 1873   *Germany*   **DD89**

empire to the Third Reich. [1st ed.] New York, Knopf, 1946. xx, 730, xxx p. fold. front., maps. 25 cm. "The translation ... from the original German was made by Olga Marx. The English text has been edited by Dorothy Teall in consultation with the author." *1. Germany — History. I. Marx, Olga, 1894- tr. II. Teall, Dorothy, ed. III. T.*
DD89.V3   943   46-5313

Bryce, James Bryce, viscount, 1838-1922.   **III. 1873**
The Holy Roman empire, by James Bryce ... A new ed., enl. and rev. throughout, with a chronological table of events and three maps. New York, The Macmillan company; London, Macmillan & co., ltd., 1904. lii p., 1 l., 575 p. 3 double maps. 21 cm. *1. Holy Roman empire — History.*
DD90.B952   04-34916

Gebhardt, Bruno, 1858-1905.   **III. 1874**
Handbuch der deutschen Geschichte. 9., neu bearb. Aufl. hrsg. von Herbert Grundmann. Stuttgart, Union Verlag, 1970- v. 25 cm. At head of title: Gebhardt. *1. Germany — History. I. Grundmann, Herbert, 1902- ed. II. T.*
DD90.G322   78-533119

Henderson, Ernest Flagg, 1861-   **III. 1875**
A short history of Germany, by Ernest F. Henderson ... New ed. with additional chapters. New York, Macmillan, 1937. 2 v. in 1. double maps. 22 cm. First published 1902. *1. Germany — History.*
DD90.H5 1967   38-33725

Kohn, Hans, 1891- ed.   **III. 1876**
German history; some new German views. London, Allen & Unwin [1954] 224 p. 23 cm. "The German texts were translated by Dr. Herbert H. Rowen." *1. Germany — History — Addresses, essays, lectures. 2. Germany — History — Historiography. I. T.*
DD93.K67 1954   943.004   54-2174

Görlitz, Walter, 1913-   **III. 1877**
History of the German General Staff, 1657-1945. Translated by Brian Battershaw. Introd. by Walter Millis. New York, Praeger [1953] xviii, 508 p. ports. 22 cm. *1. Germany. Heer. Generalstab. 2. Germany — History, Military. 3. Germany — History — 1871- 4. World War, 1939-1945 — Germany.*
DD101.G614 1953   943   52-13106

Ritter, Gerhard, 1888-1967.   **III. 1878**
The Schlieffen Plan; critique of a myth. Foreword by B. H. Liddell Hart. [Translated by Andrew and Eva Wilson] London, O. Wolff, 1958. 195 p. plans. 23 cm. Translation of Der Schlieffenplan. *1. Germany — History, Military. 2. Schlieffen, Alfred, Graf von, 1833-1913. I. T.*
DD101.5.Rx   943.08/4   68-7998

DD110 – 120   Political and Diplomatic History

Krieger, Leonard.   **III. 1879**
The German idea of freedom; history of a political tradition. Boston, Beacon Press [1957] xii, 540 p. 22 cm. *1. Germany — Politics and government. 2. Nationalism. 3. Liberalism. I. T.*
DD112.K82   943   57-9088

Ritter, Gerhard, 1888-1967.   **III. 1880**
The sword and the scepter; the problem of militarism in Germany. Translated from the German by Heinz Norden. Coral Gables, Fla., University of Miami Press [c1969- v. 25 cm. Translation of Staatskunst und Kriegshandwerk. *1. Germany — Politics and government. 2. Germany — History, Military. 3. Militarism — Germany. 4. Politics and war. I. T.*
DD112.R5213   320.9/43   68-31041   ISBN:0870241273 (v. 1) varies

Carroll, Eber Malcolm, 1893-1959.   **III. 1881**
Germany and the great powers, 1866-1914; a study in public opinion and foreign policy, by E. Malcolm Carroll. Hamden, Conn., Archon Books, 1966 [c1938] xv, 852 p. illus. 23 cm. *1. Public opinion — Germany. 2. Germany — Foreign relations — 1871-1918. 3. Europe — Politics — 1871-1918. 4. Press — Germany. I. T.*
DD117.C3 1966   327.43   66-13340

Wertheimer, Mildred Salz, 1896-   **III. 1882**
The Pan-German League, 1890-1914, by Mildred S. Wertheimer. New York, Octagon Books, 1971 [c1924] 256 p. port. 24 cm. (Studies in history, economics, and public law, no. 251) Originally presented as the author's thesis, Columbia University, 1924. *1. Alldeutscher Verband. 2. Pangermanism. (S:Columbia studies in the social sciences, no. 251.)*
DD119.W4 1971   320.5/4/0943   79-159257   ISBN:0374983526

Trumpener, Ulrich.   **III. 1883**
Germany and the Ottoman Empire, 1914-1918. Princeton, N.J., Princeton University Press, 1968. xv, 433 p. 22 cm. *1. Germany — Foreign relations — Turkey. 2. Turkey — Foreign relations — Germany. I. T.*
DD120.G3T7   327.43/0561   68-10395

Sontag, Raymond James, 1897-   **III. 1884**
Germany and England: background of conflict, 1848-1894. New York, Russell & Russell, 1964 [c1938] xvii, 362 p. 23 cm. *1. Germany — Foreign relations — Gt. Brit. 2. Gt. Brit. — Foreign relations — Germany. 3. Germany — Politics and government — 1848-1870. 4. Germany — Politics and government — 1871-1918. 5. Gt. Brit. — Politics and government — 1837-1901. I. T.*
DD120.G7S6 1964   327.420943   64-15034

Carr, Edward Hallett, 1892-   **III. 1885**
German-Soviet relations between the two World Wars, 1919-1939. Baltimore, Johns Hopkins Press, 1951. ix, 146 p. 23 cm. (The Albert Shaw lectures on diplomatic history, 1951) *1. Germany — Foreign relations — Russia. 2. Russia — Foreign relations — Germany. I. T. (S)*
DD120.R8C3   327.430947   51-12783

DD121 – 261   History, by Period
DD121 – 174 EARLY. MEDIEVAL, TO 1519. HOLY ROMAN EMPIRE

Barraclough, Geoffrey, 1908- tr.   **III. 1886**
Mediaeval Germany, 911-1250; essays by German historians, translated with an introduction by Geoffrey Barraclough. Oxford, B. Blackwell, 1938. 2 v. illus. (map) 23 cm. (Half-title: Studies in mediaeval history, edited by Geoffrey Barraclough. [1-2]) *1. Germany — Constitutional history. 2. Germany — History — 843-1273. 3. Investiture. 4. Church and state in Germany. I. T.*
DD126.B35   943.02   39-18883

Thompson, James Westfall, 1869-1941.   **III. 1887**
Feudal Germany. New York, F. Ungar Pub. Co. [1962] 2 v. illus. 22 cm. *1. Germany — History — 843-1273. 2. Holy Roman Empire — History — 843-1273. I. T.*
DD126.T5 1962   943.02   62-17093

Duckett, Eleanor Shipley.   **III. 1888**
Carolingian portraits; a study in the ninth century. Ann Arbor, University of Michigan Press [1962] 311 p. illus. 24 cm. *1. Carlovingians. 2. Germany — History — 843-918. I. T.*
DD131.D8   943.021   62-18441

Otto, Bp. of Freising, d. 1158.   **III. 1889**
The deeds of Frederick Barbarossa, by Otto of Freising and his continuator, Rahewin; translated and annotated, with an introd., by Charles Christopher Mierow with the collaboration of Richard Emery. New York, Columbia University Press, 1953. x, 366 p. front. 24 cm. (Records of civilization: sources and studies, no. 49) Translation of Gesta Friderici I. imperatoris. *1. Friedrich I, Barbarossa, Emperor of Germany, 1121-1190. 2. Germany — History — Frederick I, 1152-1190 — Sources. I. Rahewin, d. ca. 1177. II. Mierow, Charles Christopher, 1883- ed. and tr. III. T. (S)*
DD149.O784   943.024   53-7800

Kantorowicz, Ernst Hartwig, 1895-   **III. 1890**
Frederick the Second, 1194-1250. Authorized English version by E. O. Lorimer. New York, Ungar [1957] xxvii, 724 p. maps (part fold.) 22 cm. *1. Friedrich II, Emperor of Germany, 1194-1250. 2. Germany — History — Frederick II, 1215-1250. 3. Holy Roman Empire — History — Frederick II, 1215-1250.*
DD151.K33 1957   923.143   57-9408

DD175 – 261   1519 –

Holborn, Hajo, 1902-1969.   **III. 1891**
A history of modern Germany. [1st ed.] New York, A. A. Knopf, 1959-69. 3 v. illus., maps (part fold.) 24 cm. *1. Germany — History.*
DD175.H62   943   59-5991

Engels, Friedrich, 1820-1895.   **III. 1892**
The German revolutions: The Peasant War in Germany, and Germany: revolution and counter-revolution. Edited and with an introd. by Leonard

Krieger. Chicago, University of Chicago Press [1967] xlvii, 246 p. 21 cm. (Classic European historians) The Peasant War in Germany is a translation by Moissaye J. Olgin of Der deutsche Bauernkrieg. Germany: revolution and counter-revolution was originally published in the New York tribune, 1851-52, in a series of articles on which Marx and Engels collaborated. *1. Peasants' War, 1524-1525. 2. Germany — Social conditions. 3. Germany — History — Revolution, 1848-1849. 4. Austria — History — Revolution, 1848-1849. 5. Communism — Germany. I. Krieger, Leonard, ed. II. Engels, Friedrich, 1820-1895. Revolution and counter-revolution. III. T. (S)*
DD182.E52 1967   943/.008   67-15314

Bruford, Walter Horace, 1894-   III. 1893
Germany in the eighteenth century: the social background of the literary revival, by W. H. Bruford. Cambridge [Eng.] University Press, 1935. x, 354 p. front. (ports.) fold. map. 23 cm. *1. Germany — Social life and customs. 2. Germany — Politics and government — 18th cent. 3. Germany — Economic conditions. 4. German literature — 18th cent. — History and criticism. I. T.*
DD193.B7   914.3   35-7429

Droz, Jacques, 1909-   III. 1894
L'Allemagne et la Révolution française. [1. éd.] Paris, Presses universitaires de France, 1949. vi, [1] 500 p. 23 cm. *1. Germany — Politics and government — 1740-1806. 2. Germany — Politics and government — 1806-1815. 3. Romanticism — Germany. I. T.*
DD197.5.D7   943.06   50-3274

Fichte, Johann Gottlieb, 1762-1814.   III. 1895
Addresses to the German nation. Edited with an introd. by George Armstrong Kelly. New York, Harper & Row [1968] xxxv, 228 p. 21 cm. (European perspectives. Harper torchbooks, TB1366.) Translation of Reden an die deutsche Nation. *1. Germany — Politics and government — 1806-1815. 2. Education and state. 3. National characteristics, German. I. T.*
DD199.F413 1968   914.3/03/6   68-5895

DD201 – 261   19th – 20th Centuries

Brandenburg, Erich, 1868-   III. 1896
Die Reichsgründung, von Erich Brandenburg. Leipzig, Quelle & Mayer, 1916. 2 v. 24 cm. *1. Germany — History — 1815-1866. 2. Germany — History — 1866-1871. 3. Germany — Politics and government. I. T.*
DD203.B7   20-22140

Mann, Golo, 1909-   III. 1897
The history of Germany since 1789. Translated from the German by Marian Jackson. New York, Praeger [1968] xii, 547 p. 25 cm. Translation of Deutsche Geschichte des 19. und 20. Jahrhunderts. *1. Germany — History — 1789-1900. 2. Germany — History — 20th cent. I. T.*
DD203.M2713   943   67-24685

Pinson, Koppel Shub, 1904-1961.   III. 1898
Modern Germany; its history and civilization. Chapter 23 by Klaus Epstein. 2d ed. New York, Macmillan [1966] xv, 682 p. map (on lining papers) 25 cm. "General bibliographical note": p. 607-608. Bibliography: p. 609-620. *1. Germany — History — 1789-1900. 2. Germany — History — 20th cent. I. T.*
DD203.P5 1966   943.08   66-16925

Schnabel, Franz, 1887-1966.   III. 1899
Deutsche Geschichte im neunzehnten Jahrhundert, von Franz Schnabel. Freiburg im Breisgau, Herder, 1929- v. 24 cm. *1. Germany — History — 1789-1900. 2. Germany — Civilization.*
DD203.S33   30-3083

Taylor, Alan John Percivale, 1906-   III. 1900
The course of German history, a survey of the development of Germany since 1815, by A. J. P. Taylor ... London, H. Hamilton [1945] 229 p. maps. 21 1/2 cm. "First published 1945." *1. Germany — History — 1789-1900. 2. Germany — History — 20th cent. I. T.*
DD203.T3   943.07   45-8396

Treitschke, Heinrich Gotthard von, 1834-1896.   III. 1901
Treitschke's history of Germany in the nineteenth century, tr. by Eden & Cedar Paul, with an introduction by William Harbutt Dawson. London, Jarrold 1915-19. 7 v. 23 cm. *1. Germany — History — 1789-1900. 2. Germany — Intellectual life. 3. German literature — History and criticism. I. Paul Eden, 1865- tr. II. Paul, Cedar, tr.*
DD203.T8 1915a   16-16685

Ward, Adolphus William, Sir, 1837-1924.   III. 1902
Germany, 1815-1890, by Sir Adolphus William Ward ... Cambridge, The University Press, 1916-18. 3 v. maps (4 fold.) 20 cm. (Cambridge historical series, [8]) Vol. II: With sections by Spenser Wilkinson. *1. Germany — History — 1780-1900. I. Wilkinson, Spenser, 1853-1937.*
DD203.W3   16-17259

Gollwitzer, Heinz, 1917-   III. 1903
Die Standesherren; die politische und gesellschaftliche Stellung der Mediatisierten, 1815-1918. Ein Beitrag zur deutschen Sozialgeschichte. Stuttgart, F. Vorwerk [1957] 458 p. 22 cm. *1. Germany — Nobility. 2. Germany — Politics and government — 19th cent. 3. Germany — Constitutional history. I. T.*
DD204.G64   A58-4891

Mosse, Werner Eugen.   III. 1904
The European powers and the German question, 1848-71, with special reference to England and Russia, by W. E. Mosse. New York, Octagon Books, 1969. ix, 409 p. 24 cm. Reprint of the 1958 ed. *1. Germany — Politics and government — 1848-1870. 2. Germany — Foreign relations. 3. Nationalism — Germany. 4. Europe — Politics — 1815-1871. I. T.*
DD204.M6 1969   943/.07   74-76002

Oncken, Hermann, 1869-   III. 1905
Rudolf von Bennigsen, ein deutscher liberaler Politiker; nach seinen Briefen und hinterlassenen Papieren, von Hermann Oncken. Stuttgart und Leipzig, Deutsche Verlags-Anstalt, 1910. 2 v. fronts., plates, ports. 26 cm. *1. Bennigsen, Rudolf, 1824-1902. 2. Germany — Politics and government — 1848-1870. 3. Germany — Politics and government — 1871-*
DD205.B4O6   26-7756

Gagern, Heinrich, Freiherr von, 1799-1880.   III. 1906
Deutscher Liberalismus im Vormärz; Heinrich von Gagern: Briefe und Reden 1815-1848. Hrsg. vom Bundesarchiv und der Hessischen Historischen Kommission, Darmstadt, bearb. von Paul Wentzcke und Wolfgang Klötzer. Göttingen, Musterschmidt, [1959] 496 p. port., facsim. 25 cm. *1. Germany — Politics and government — 1806-1848. I. Wentzcke, Paul 1879- ed. II. Klötzer, Wolfgang, ed. III. T.*
DD205.G28A4   A59-5695

Hohenlohe-Schillingsfürst, Chlodwig Karl Viktor, Fürst zu, 1819-1901.   III. 1907
Memoirs of Prince Chlodwig of Hohenlohe-Schillingsfuerst, authorised by Prince Alexander of Hohenlohe-Schillingsfuerst and edited by Friedrich Curtius. English ed. supervised by George W. Chrystal. New York, AMS Press [1970] 2 v. facsim., ports. 23 cm. Reprint of the 1906 ed. Translation of the author's Denkwürdigkeiten. *1. Germany — History — 1848-1870. 2. Germany — History — 1871-1918. I. Curtius, Friedrich, 1851-1933, ed. II. Chrystal, George William, Sir, 1880-1944. III. T.*
DD205.H7A213 1970   943/.07/0924   75-111765
   ISBN:0404033067 (v. 1) 0404033075 (v. 2)

Lougee, Robert W.   III. 1908
Paul de Lagarde, 1827-1891; a study of radical conservatism in Germany. Cambridge, Harvard University Press, 1962. viii, 357 p. port. 22 cm. *1. Lagarde, Paul Anton de, 1827-1891.*
DD205.L3L6   923.743   62-17221

Thomas, Richard Hinton.   III. 1909
Liberalism, nationalism and the German intellectuals (1822-1847); an analysis of the academic and scientific conferences of the period. Cambridge [Eng.] W. Heffer, 1951. 148 p. 22 cm. *1. Germany — Learned institutions and societies. 2. Nationalism — Germany. 3. Germany — Politics and government — 1815-1866. I. T.*
DD206.T4   943.07   53-764

DD207   1848 – 1849

Droz, Jacques, 1909-   III. 1910
Les révolutions allemandes de 1848, d'après un manuscrit et des notes de E. Tonnelat. [1. éd.] Paris, Presses Universitaires de France, 1957. 656 p. diagrs. 25 cm. (Publications de la Faculté des lettres de l'Université de Clermont. 2. sér., fasc. 6) *1. Germany — History — Revolution, 1848-1849. I. Tonnelat, Ernest, 1877-1948. (S:Clermont-Ferrand, France. Université. Faculté des lettres et sciences humaines. Publications, 2. sér., fasc. 6)*
DD207.D7   A58-3478

Stadelmann, Rudolf, 1902-1949.   III. 1911
Soziale und politische Geschichte der Revolution von 1848. [München] Münchner Verlag, 1948. 216 p. 23 cm. *1. Germany — History — Revolution, 1848-1849.*
DD207.S8x   A50-3138

Valentin, Veit, 1885-1947.   III. 1912
1848; chapters of German history. Translated by Ethel Talbot Scheffauer. Hamden, Conn., Archon Books, 1965. 480 p. 21 cm. Reprint of the 1940 ed. An abridged translation of Geschichte der deutschen Revolution von 1848-49. *1. Germany — History — Revolution, 1848-1849. I. T.*
DD207.V352 1965   943.07   65-16974

Eyck, Frank.   III. 1913
The Frankfurt Parliament 1848-1849. London, Melbourne [etc.] Macmillan, New York, St. Martin's P., 1968. xiv, 425 p. 8 plates, 1 illus., map, ports. 23 cm. *1. Deutsche Nationalversammlung, Frankfurt am Main, 1848-1849. 2. Germany — History — Revolution, 1848-1849. 3. Germany — Politics and government — 1848-1849.*
DD207.5.E87   328.43/09   68-14232

Legge, James Granville, 1861-1940.   **III. 1914**
Rhyme and revolution in Germany; a study in German history, life, literature, and character, 1813-1850. [1st AMS ed.] New York, AMS Press [1970] xxiv, 584 p. 23 cm. Reprint of the 1918 ed. *1. Germany — History — 1815-1866. 2. Germany — History — Revolution, 1848-1849. 3. Political poetry, German. 4. German poetry — Translation into English. 5. English poetry — Translations from German. I. T.*
DD207.5.L4 1970   914.3/03/7   72-126646   ISBN:404039472

Noyes, P. H.   **III. 1915**
Organization and revolution; working-class associations in the German revolutions of 1848-1849, by P. H. Noyes. Princeton, N.J., Princeton University Press, 1966. x, 434 p. 21 cm. *1. Germany — History — Revolution, 1848-1849. 2. Labor and laboring classes — Germany — Societies, etc. I. T.*
DD207.5.N6   943.07   66-14313

DD210   1850 – 1871

Hamerow, Theodore S.   **III. 1916**
The social foundations of German unification, 1858-1871 [by] Theodore S. Hamerow. Princeton, N.J., Princeton University Press, 1969-72. 2 v. 23 cm. *1. Germany — Politics and government — 1848-1870. 2. Germany — Economic conditions. 3. Germany — Social conditions. 4. Bismarck, Otto von, 1815-1898. I. T.*
DD210.H25   320.9/43/07   75-75241   ISBN:0691051747

Sybel, Heinrich von, 1817-1895.   **III. 1917**
The founding of the German Empire by William I; based chiefly upon Prussian state documents. Translated by Marshall Livingston Perrin, assisted by Gamaliel Bradford, Jr. New York, Greenwood Press [1968] 7 v. maps, ports. 23 cm. Reprint of the 1890-97 ed. Translation of Die Begründung des Deutschen Reiches durch Wilhelm I. Vols. 6 and 7 translated by Helene Schimmelfennig White. *1. Germany — History — 1815-1866. 2. Germany — History — 1866-1871. 3. Germany — Politics and government — 1815-1866. 4. Germany — Politics and government — 1866-1871. I. T.*
DD210.S7132   943.08   68-31005

Windell, George G.   **III. 1918**
The Catholics and German unity, 1866-1871. Minneapolis, University of Minnesota Press [1954] xi, 312 p. 24 cm. *1. Germany — Politics and government — 1866-1871. 2. Catholics in Germany. I. T.*
DD210.W5   943.081   54-13011

DD217 – 231   NEW EMPIRE (1871 – 1918)

Simon, Walter Michael, 1922-   **III. 1919**
Germany in the age of Bismarck, by W. M. Simon. London, George Allen and Unwin; New York, Barnes and Noble, 1968. x, 246 p. 23 cm. (Historical problems: studies and documents, 2) *1. Germany — History — 1848-1870 — Sources. 2. Germany — History — 1871-1918 — Sources. 3. Bismarck, Otto, Fürst von, 1815-1898. I. T. (S)*
DD217.S5   943.08/3   68-117995

DD218   Bismarck

Bismarck, Otto, Fürst von, 1815-1898.   **III. 1920**
The memoirs, being the reflections and reminiscences of Otto, Prince von Bismarck, written and dictated by himself after his retirement from office. Translated from the German under the supervision of A. J. Butler. New York, H. Fertig, 1966. 2 v. illus., ports. 24 cm. Translation of Gedanken und Erinnerungen. *1. Germany — History — 1789-1900. 2. Germany — Politics and government — 1789-1900. 3. Europe — Politics — 1789-1900. 4. Prussia — Politics and government — 1815-1870. I. T.*
DD218.A2 1966   943.080924   66-24343

Becker, Otto, 1885-1955.   **III. 1921**
Bismarcks Ringen um Deutschlands Gestaltung; hrsg. und ergänzt von Alexander Scharff. Heidelberg, Quelle & Meyer [1958] 963 p. illus. 23 cm. *1. Bismarck, Otto, Fürst von, 1815-1898.*
DD218.B4   59-28340

Busch, Moritz, 1821-1899.   **III. 1922**
Bismarck; some secret pages of his history, being a diary kept by Moritz Busch during twenty-five years' official and private intercourse with the great chancellor. New York, Macmillan, 1898. St. Clair Shores, Mich., Scholarly Press [1971] 2 v. illus. 21 cm. *1. Bismarck, Otto, Fürst von, 1815-1898.*
DD218.B98 1971   943.08/0924   70-144925   ISBN:0403008158

Eyck, Erich, 1878-   **III. 1923**
Bismarck and the German Empire. London, Allen & Unwin [1950] 327 p. port. 22 cm. "A summary of [the author's] ... three-volume Bismarck, published in German." *1. Bismarck, Otto, Fürst von, 1815-1898.*
DD218.E92   923.243   50-9287

Marcks, Erich, 1861-1938.   **III. 1924**
Bismarck, eine biographie, 1815-1851 ... Mit drei Bildnissen. Stuttgart, Berlin, Deutsche Verlags-Anstalt [1941] xxiv, 623 p. 23 cm. "Neunzehnte, um den nachgelassenen Band 'Bismarck und die deutsche Revolution 1848-1851' erweiterte Auflage." *1. Bismarck, Otto, fürst von, 1815-1898. 2. Germany — History — 1848-1870. I. Andreas, Willy, 1884- ed.*
DD218.M252   923.243   46-30792

Pflanze, Otto.   **III. 1925**
Bismarck and the development of Germany; the period of unification, 1815-1871. Princeton, N.J., Princeton University Press, 1963. 510 p. illus. 25 cm. *1. Bismarck, Otto, Fürst von, 1815-1898. 2. Germany — History — 1815-1866. 3. Germany — History — 1866-1871. I. T.*
DD218.P44   943.604   63-7159

Richter, Werner, 1888-   **III. 1926**
Bismarck. Translated from the German by Brian Battershaw. Foreword by F. H. Hinsley. [1st American ed.] New York, Putnam [1965, c1964] 420 p. illus., ports. 22 cm. *1. Bismarck, Otto, Fürst von, 1815-1898. I. T.*
DD218.R513 1965   923.243   64-23090

Robertson, Charles Grant, Sir, 1869-1948.   **III. 1927**
Bismarck. New York, H. Fertig, 1969. xii, 520 p. 23 cm. *1. Bismarck, Otto, Fürst von, 1815-1898.*
DD218.R6 1969   943.08/0924 (B)   68-9604

Taylor, Alan John Percivale, 1906-   **III. 1928**
Bismarck, the man and the statesman. [1st American ed.] New York, Knopf, 1955. 286 p. illus. 22 cm. *1. Bismarck, Otto, Fürst von, 1815-1898.*
DD218.T33 1955a   923.243   55-10649

Medlicott, William Norton, 1900-   **III. 1929**
Bismarck and modern Germany, by W. N. Medlicott. Mystic, Conn., L. Verry [1965] vi, 200 p. 18 cm. (Teach yourself history library) *1. Bismarck, Otto, Fürst von, 1815-1898. 2. Germany — Politics and government — 1871-1918. I. T. (S)*
DD218.2.M4   943.080924   66-1243

Mitchell, Allan.   **III. 1930**
Bismarck and the French nation, 1848-1890. New York, Pegasus [c1971] 152 p. 22 cm. *1. Bismarck, Otto Fürst von, 1815-1898. 2. Germany — Foreign relations — France. 3. France — Foreign relations — Germany. I. T.*
DD218.2.M54   327.43/044 (B)   72-167692

Zechlin, Egmont, 1896-   **III. 1931**
Bismarck und die Grundlegung der deutschen Grossmacht. [2., vom Verfasser durchgesehene Aufl.] Stuttgart, Cotta [1960] xxi, 652 p. maps, facsims. 24 cm. *1. Bismarck, Otto, Fürst von, 1815-1898. 2. Prussia — History — 1815-1870. 3. Germany — History — 1848-1870. 4. Europe — Politics — 1848-1871.*
DD218.2.Z4x   A61-2440

Bismarck, Otto, Fürst von, 1815-1898.   **III. 1932**
Bismarck und der Staat: ausgewählte Dokumente, eingeleitet von Hans Rothfels. [3. Aufl. Stuttgart] Kohlhammer, 1958. 412 p. 23 cm. Previously published under title: Deutscher Staat. *1. Germany — Politics and government. I. Rothfels, Hans 1891- ed.*
DD218.3.R6 1958   59-51398

DD219   Other Biography

Holstein, Friedrich von, 1837-1909.   **III. 1933**
The Holstein papers, edited by Norman Rich & M. H. Fisher. Cambridge [Eng.] University Press, 1955-63. 4 v. ports., facsim. 26 cm. *1. Germany — Politics and government — 1871-1918. 2. Germany — Foreign relations — 1871-1918. I. Rich, Norman, ed. II. Fisher, M. H., ed.*
DD219.H6A3   55-3247

Rich, Norman.   **III. 1934**
Friedrich von Holstein, politics and diplomacy in the era of Bismarck and Wilhelm II. Cambridge [Eng.] University Press, 1965. 2 v. (870 p.) illus., ports. 26 cm. *1. Holstein, Friedrich von, 1837-1909. 2. Germany — Politics and government — 1871-1918. 3. Germany — Foreign relations — 1871-1918. I. T.*
DD219.H6R5   943.08   64-21565

Kessel, Eberhard, 1907-   **III. 1935**
Moltke. Stuttgart, K. F. Koehler [1957] 807 p. illus., ports. 23 cm. *1. Moltke, Helmuth Karl Bernhard, Graf von, 1800-1891.*
DD219.M7K49   A58-3416

Stadelmann, Rudolf, 1902-1949.   **III. 1936**
Moltke und der Staat. Krefeld, Scherpe-Verlag, 1950. 566 p. ports., facsims. 23 cm. *1. Moltke, Helmuth Karl Bernhard, Graf von, 1800-1891. 2. Germany — History — 1848-1870. 3. Germany — History — 1871-1918. 4. Prussia — History — 1789-1900. I. T.*
DD219.M7S7   51-22891

Hollyday, Frederic B. M.   **III. 1937**
Bismarck's rival; a political biography of general and admiral Albrecht von Stosch. Durham, N.C., Duke University Press, 1960. x, 316 p. port. 25 cm. (Duke historical publications) *1. Stosch, Albrecht von, 1818-1896. I. T. (S)*
DD219.S74H6   923.243   60-7077

Dorpalen, Andreas.   **III. 1938**
Heinrich von Treitschke. New Haven, Yale University Press, 1957. ix, 345 p. port., map. 24 cm. *1. Treitschke, Heinrich Gotthard von, 1834-1896.*
DD219.T7D6   928.3 (923.243)   57-6337

Waldersee, Alfred Heinrich Karl Ludwig, graf von, 1832-1904.   **III. 1939**
A field-marshal's memoirs: from the diary, correspondence, and reminiscences of Alfred, count von Waldersee ... Condensed and translated by Frederic Whyte ... London, Hutchinson, 1924. xxi, 22-286 p. front. (port.) 24 cm. Translation of Denkwürdigkeiten. *1. Germany — History — 1871- I. Whyte, Frederic, tr. II. T.*
DD219.W3A3   24-24582

DD220 – 229   1878 – 1918

Craig, Gordon Alexander, 1913-   **III. 1940**
The politics of the Prussian Army 1640-1945. New York, Oxford University Press, 1956 [c1955] xx, 536 p. 22 cm. *1. Germany. Heer. 2. Prussia. Armee. 3. Germany — Politics and government — 1871- 4. Prussia — Politics and government. I. T.*
DD221.C7 1956   943.08   56-8006

Dawson, William Harbutt, 1860-1948.   **III. 1941**
The German Empire, 1867-1914, and the unity movement. Hamden, Conn., Archon Books, 1966. 2 v. 24 cm. First published in 1919. *1. Germany — Politics and government — 1866-1871. 2. Germany — Politics and government — 1871-1918. I. T.*
DD221.D3 1966   943.08   66-16085

Ziekursch, Johannes, 1876-   **III. 1942**
Politische Geschichte des neuen deutschen Kaiserreiches, von Johannes Ziekursch. Frankfurt am Main, Frankfurter Societäts-Druckerei, 1925-30. 3 v. 24 cm. *1. Germany — History — 1848-1870. 2. Germany — History — 1871-*
DD221.Z5   26-2722

Craig, Gordon Alexander, 1913-   **III. 1943**
From Bismarck to Adenauer: aspects of German statecraft. Baltimore, Johns Hopkins Press, 1958. 156 p. 23 cm. (The Albert Shaw lectures on diplomatic history, 1958) *1. Bismarck, Otto, Fürst von, 1815-1898. 2. Adenauer, Konrad, 1876- 3. Germany — Foreign relations — 1871- 4. Statesmen, German. 5. Germany — Diplomatic and consular service. I. T.*
DD221.5.C7   327.43   58-59683

Fuller, Joseph Vincent.   **III. 1944**
Bismarck's diplomacy at its zenith, by Joseph Vincent Fuller. Cambridge, Harvard University Press, 1922. xii, 368 p. 23 cm. (Harvard historical studies ... Vol. XXVI) *1. Bismarck, Otto, fürst von, 1815-1898. 2. Germany — Foreign relations — 1871- I. T.*
DD221.5.F8   22-24464

Morsey, Rudolf.   **III. 1945**
Die oberste Reichsverwaltung unter Bismarck, 1867-1890. Münster, Westfalen, Aschendorff, 1957. 352 p. 24 cm. (Neue münstersche Beiträge zur Geschichtsforschung, Bd. 3) "Überarbeitete Fassung einer münsterischen phil. Diss. aus dem Jahre 1955." *1. Germany — Politics and government — 1871-1888. 2. Civil service — Germany. I. T. (S)*
DD222.Mx   A58-1926

Bennett, Daphne.   **III. 1946**
Vicky: Princess Royal of England and German Empress. [New York] St. Martin's Press [1972] 382 p. illus. 24 cm. *1. Victoria, consort of Frederick III, German Emperor, 1840-1901. I. T.*
DD224.9.B45 1972   943.08/4/0924 (B)   74-145442

Anderson, Pauline Safford (Relyea)   **III. 1947**
The background of anti-English feeling in Germany, 1890-1902, by Pauline Relyea Anderson. New York, Octagon Books, 1969 [c1939] xxii, 382 p. 24 cm. Issued also as thesis, Bryn Mawr College, 1937. *1. Public opinion — Germany. 2. Propaganda — Germany. 3. Germany — Foreign relations — Great Britain. 4. Great Britain — Foreign relations — Germany. I. T.*
DD228.2.A5 1969   329/.05/0943   78-86268

Puhle, Hans-Jürgen.   **III. 1948**
Agrarische Interessenpolitik und preussischer Konservatismus im wilhelminischen Reich (1893-1914) Ein Beitrag zur Analyse des Nationalismus in Deutschland am Beispiel des Bundes der Landwirte und der Deutsch-Konservativen Partei. Hannover, Verlag für Literatur u. Zeitgeschehen (1967) 365 p. 24 cm. (Schriftenreihe des Forschungsinstituts der Friedrich-Ebert-Stiftung. B: Historisch-politische Schriften) A revision of the author's thesis, Freie Universität, Berlin, 1965. *1. Deutsch-konservative Partei. 2. Germany — Politics and government — 1888-1918. 3. Agriculture and state — Germany. 4. Bund der Landwirte. I. T.*
DD228.2.P8   943.08/4   67-105307

Eyck, Erich, 1878-   **III. 1949**
Das persönliche Regiment Wilhelms II; politische Geschichte des deutschen Kaiserreiches von 1890 bis 1914. Erlenbach-Zürich, E. Rentsch [1948] 814 p. 24 cm. *1. Wilhelm II, German Emperor, 1859-1941. 2. Germany — Politics and government — 1888-1918. I. T.*
DD228.5.E9   48-25609

Kehr, Eckart, 1902-   **III. 1950**
Schlachtflottenbau und Partei-Politik 1894-1901; Versuch eines Querschnitts durch die innenpolitischen, sozialen und ideologischen Voraussetzungen des deutschen Imperialismus, von Eckart Kehr. Berlin, E. Ebering, 1930. ix, 463 p. 24 cm. (Historische Studien. hft. 197) *1. Germany — Politics and government — 1888-1918. 2. Germany — Navy — History. I. T.*
DD228.5.K4   943.084   35-10227

Nichols, John Alden, 1919-   **III. 1951**
Germany after Bismarck, the Caprivi era, 1890-1894. Cambridge, Harvard University Press, 1958. xii, 404 p. illus., port. 25 cm. "The present version of this study results from a considerable reworking of the original presented to Columbia University in 1951 for the Ph.D. degree." *1. Caprivi de Caprara de Montecuculi, Georg Leo, Graf von, 1831-1899. 2. Germany — History — 1871-1918. I. T.*
DD228.5.N5 1958   943.084   58-11554

Röhl, John C. G.   **III. 1952**
Germany without Bismarck; the crisis of government in the Second Reich, 1890-1900 [by] J. C. G. Röhl. Berkeley, University of California Press, 1967. 304 p. 23 cm. *1. Germany — History — William II, 1888-1918. 2. Bismarck, Otto, Fürst von, 1815-1898. 3. Germany — Politics and government — 1888-1918. I. T.*
DD228.5.R6 1967   943.08/4   67-26960

Brandenburg, Erich, 1868-   **III. 1953**
From Bismarck to the world war; a history of German foreign policy 1870-1914, by Erich Brandenburg, translated by Annie Elizabeth Adams. London, Oxford University Press, 1927. xiii, 542 p. 23 cm. "Based on documents in the German Foreign office." — Pref. *1. Germany — Foreign relations — 1871- 2. Germany — Politics and government — 1871- 3. European war, 1914-1918 — Causes. I. Adams, Annie Elizabeth, d. 1926, tr. II. Germany. Auswärtiges Amt. III. T.*
DD228.6.B72   27-17234

Gatzke, Hans Wilhelm, 1915-   **III. 1954**
Germany's drive to the west (Drang nach Westen) A study of Germany's western war aims during the First World War. Baltimore, Johns Hopkins Press, 1950. x, 316 p. 24 cm. A revision of the author's thesis — Harvard University. *1. Germany — Politics and government — 1888-1918. 2. European War, 1914-1918 — Germany. I. T.*
DD228.8.G3 1950   940.343   50-7516

Lutz, Ralph Haswell, 1886-1968, ed.   **III. 1955**
Fall of the German Empire, 1914-1918. Translations by David G. Rempel and Gertrude Rendtorff. New York, Octagon Books, 1969 [c1932] 2 v. 24 cm. (Hoover War Library publications, no. 1-2) *1. European War, 1914-1918 — Germany. 2. Germany — History — William II, 1888-1918 — Sources. 3. Germany — History — Revolution, 1918 — Sources. 4. Germany — Politics and government — 1888-1918. 5. European War, 1914-1918 — Sources. 6. European War, 1914-1918 — Diplomatic history. I. T. (S:Stanford University. Hoover Institution on War, Revolution, and Peace. Publications, no. 1-2)*
DD228.8.L8 1969   943.08/4   71-89977

Mendelssohn-Bartholdy, Albrecht, 1874-1936.   **III. 1956**
The war and German society; the testament of a liberal. New York, H. Fertig, 1971. xiv, 299 p. 24 cm. (Economic and social history of the World War. German series) Reprint of the 1937 ed. *1. European War, 1914-1918 — Germany. 2. European War, 1914-1918 — Economic aspects — Germany. 3. Germany — Politics and government — 1888-1918. I. T. (S:Carnegie Endowment for International Peace. Division of Economics and History. Wirtschafts- und Sozialgeschichte des Weltkrieges. Deutsche Serie.)*
DD228.8.M43 1971   943.08/4   74-114589

Wilhelm II, German emperor, 1859-1941.   **III. 1957**
The Kaiser's memoirs, Wilhelm II, emperor of Germany, 1888-1918; English translation by Thomas R. Ybarra. New York and London, Harper & brothers, 1922. 4 p. l., 365 [1] p. front. (port.) 22 1/2 cm. London edition (Cassell and company, ltd.) has title: My memoirs, 1878-1918. *1. Germany — Politics and government — 1888-1918. 2. European war, 1914-1918. I. Ybarra, Thomas Russell, 1880- tr. II. T.*
DD229.A45   22-21224

Balfour, Michael Leonard Graham, 1908-   **III. 1958**
The Kaiser and his times, by Michael Balfour. Boston, Houghton Mifflin, 1964. xi, 524 p. illus., geneal. table, ports. 22 cm. *1. Wilhelm II, German Emperor, 1859-1941. I. T.*
DD229.B26 1964a   923.143   64-22678

DD231 Biography. Memoirs

Bülow, Bernhard Heinrich Martin Karl, Fürst von, 1849-1929. III. 1959
Memoirs of Prince von Bülow. [Translated from the German by F. A. Voigt] New York, AMS Press [1972] 4 v. illus. 24 cm. Translation of Denkwürdigkeiten. Reprint of the 1931-32 ed. *1. Germany — Politics and government — 1871-1918. 2. Germany — Foreign relations — 1871-1918.*
DD231.B8A17 1972   943.08/4/0924 (B)   77-127900
ISBN:0404012302

Epstein, Klaus.   III. 1960
Matthias Erzberger and the dilemma of German democracy. New York, H. Fertig, 1971 [c1959] xiii, 473 p. port. 24 cm. *1. Erzberger, Matthias, 1875-1921.*
DD231.E7E6 1971   943.08/4/0924 (B)   75-80546

Wheeler-Bennett, John Wheeler, Sir, 1902-   III. 1961
Hindenburg: the wooden Titan [by] John W. Wheeler-Bennett. London, Melbourne [etc.] Macmillan; New York, St Martin's P., 1967. xviii, 507 p. front., 8 plates (incl. ports.) 22 1/2 cm. Original American ed. (New York, Morrow 1936) has title: Wooden titan, Hindenburg in twenty years of German history, 1914-1934. *1. Hindenburg, Paul von, Pres. Germany, 1847-1934. 2. Germany — History — 20th cent. I. T.*
DD231.H5W5 1967   943.085/0924   67-15778

Maximilian, prince of Baden, 1867-1929.   III. 1962
The memoirs of Prince Max of Baden; authorized translation by W. M. Calder and C. W. H. Sutton. London, Constable, 1928. 2 v. front. (port.) fold. map. 23 cm. *1. European war, 1914-1918. I. Calder, William Moir, 1881- tr. II. Sutton, C. W. H., tr.*
DD231.M3A4   29-83

Raeder, Erich, 1876-1960.   III. 1963
My life; translated from the German by Henry W. Drexel. Annapolis, United States Naval Institute, 1960. 430 p. illus. 24 cm. *1. Germany — History, Naval — 20th cent. I. T.*
DD231.R17A313   923.543   60-9236

Kessler, Harry Klemens Ulrich, Graf von, 1868-1937.   III. 1964
Walther Rathenau; his life and work. [Translated by W. D. Robson-Scott and Lawrence Hyde, and rev. by the author, with notes and additions for English readers] New York, H. Fertig, 1969 [c1928] 400 p. facsim., ports. 23 cm. *1. Rathenau, Walther, 1867-1922. 2. Germany — History — 20th century.*
DD231.R3K43 1969   943.085/0924 (B)   68-9663

Scheidemann, Philipp, 1865-1939.   III. 1965
The making of new Germany: memoirs of a Social Democrat, by Philip Scheidemann. Translated by J. E. Michell. Freeport, N.Y., Books for Libraries Press [1970, c1929] 2 v. (x, 688 p.) 23 cm. Translation of Memoiren eines Sozialdemokraten. *1. Germany — Politics and government — 20th century. 2. Sozialdemokratische Partei Deutschlands. I. Memoirs of a Social Democrat. II. T.*
DD231.S35A33 1970   320.9/43/084   73-140372   ISBN:083695615X

Stresemann, Gustav, 1878-1929.   III. 1966
Gustav Stresemann; his diaries, letters, and papers, edited and translated by Eric Sutton. London, Macmillan, 1935-40. 3 v. illus. (v. 1-2) plates, ports. 23 cm. The original, "Gustav Stresemann. Vermächtnis," was published in 3 v., 1932-34, under the general editorship of Henry Bernhard. The English edition has been slightly condensed. cf. Editor's note. *1. Germany — Politics and government — 20th cent. 2. Germany — Foreign relations — 20th cent. I. Bernhard, Henry, 1896- ed. II. Sutton, Eric, tr.*
DD231.S83A332   923.243   35-30709

Gatzke, Hans Wilhelm, 1915-   III. 1967
Stresemann and the rearmament of Germany. Baltimore, Johns Hopkins Press [1954] 132 p. port. 23 cm. *1. Stresemann, Gustav, 1878-1929. 2. Germany — History, Military. I. T.*
DD231.S83G3   943.085   54-11254

Thimme, Annelise.   III. 1968
Gustav Stresemann; eine politische Biographie zur Geschichte der Weimarer Republik. Hannover, O. Goedel, 1957. 132 p. 22 cm. (Goedelbuch, 104) *1. Stresemann, Gustav, 1878-1929.*
DD231.S83Tx   A58-1139

Tirpitz, Alfred Peter Friedrich von, 1849-1930.   III. 1969
My memoirs. New York, AMS Press [1970] 2 v. illus. 23 cm. Reprint of the 1919 ed. *1. Germany. Kriegsmarine. 2. European war, 1914-1918 — Germany. 3. European War, 1914-1918 — Naval operations, German. I. T.*
DD231.T5A5 1970   940.4/512/0924   77-111779   ISBN:0404064647

DD232 – 251 20TH CENTURY (1918 – 1934)

Dehio, Ludwig, 1888-   III. 1970
Germany and world politics in the twentieth century. Translated by Dieter Pevsner. New York, Knopf, 1959. 141 p. 23 cm. *1. Germany — History — 20th cent. 2. Nationalism — Germany. I. T.*
DD232.D413   943.08   59-1222

Holborn, Hajo, 1902-1969.   III. 1971
Germany and Europe: historical essays. [1st ed.] Garden City, N.Y., Doubleday, 1970. 327 p. plans. 22 cm. *1. Idealism, German. 2. Germany — Politics and government — 1871-1918 — Addresses, essays, lectures. 3. Germany — Politics and government — 20th century. I. T.*
DD232.H64   320.9/43   67-12869

Mosse, George Lachmann.   III. 1972
The crisis of German ideology; intellectual origins of the Third Reich, by George L. Mosse. [1st ed.] New York, Grosset & Dunlap [1964] vi, 373 p. 21 cm. *1. Germany — Intellectual life. 2. Nationalism — Germany. I. T.*
DD232.M6   320.943   64-21950

Passant, Ernest James.   III. 1973
A short history of Germany, 1815-1945. Economic sections by W. O. Henderson, and with contributions by C. J. Child and D. C. Watt. Cambridge [Eng.] University Press, 1959. 255 p. illus. 21 cm. *1. Germany — History — 1789-1900. 2. Germany — History — 20th century.*
DD232.P35   943.08   59-1749

Horkenbach, Cuno, ed.   III. 1974
Das Deutsche Reich von 1918 bis heute, hrsg. von Cuno Horkenbach mit sachlicher Unterstützung der Reichsbehörden, von Parlamentariern und Journalisten, Parteien, Körperschaften und Verbänden. Berlin, Verlag für Presse, Wirtschaft und Politik [1931-1935] 4 v. tables (part fold.) 26 cm. *1. Germany — History — Revolution, 1918- 2. Germany — Politics and government — 1918- 3. Germany — Statistics. 4. Germany — Biography. 5. Germany — History — 1933- 6. Germany — Politics and government — 1933- I. T.*
DD233.H6   943.085   38-22973

Rosenberg, Alfred, 1893-1946.   III. 1975
Race and race history, and other essays. Edited and introduced by Robert Pois. [1st U.S. ed.] New York, Harper & Row [1971, c1970] 204 p. 22 cm. (Roots of the right: readings in fascist, racist, and elitist ideology) *1. National socialism — Addresses, essays, lectures. 2. Race — Addresses, essays, lectures. 3. Germany — Politics and government — 1933-1945. I. T.*
DD236.R58 1970b   323.1/1   73-156571   ISBN:0060133643

Brecht, Arnold, 1884-   III. 1976
Prelude to silence; the end of the German Republic. New York, H. Fertig, 1968. xxi, 160 p. 21 cm. Reprint of the 1944 ed., with a new preface by the author. *1. Germany — History — 1918-1933. 2. Germany — History — 1933-1945. I. T.*
DD237.B7 1968   943.085   67-24580

Eyck, Erich, 1878-1964.   III. 1977
A history of the Weimar Republic. Translated by Harlan P. Hanson and Robert G. L. Waite. Cambridge, Harvard University Press, 1962-63. 2 v. 24 cm. *1. Germany — History — 1918-1933. I. Weimar Republic. II. T.*
DD237.E913   943.085   62-17219

Halperin, Samuel William.   III. 1978
Germany tried democracy, a political history of the Reich from 1918 to 1933. Hamden, Conn., Archon Books [1963, c1946] 567 p. 22 cm. *1. Germany — History — 1918-1933. I. T.*
DD237.H3 1963   943.085   63-11731

Carsten, Francis Ludwig.   III. 1979
The Reichswehr and politics: 1918-1933 [by] F. L. Carsten. Oxford, Clarendon P., 1966. viii, 427 p. 22 1/2 cm. Originally published as Reichswehr und Politik. Cologne, Kipenheuer & Witsch. *1. Germany. Reichswehr. 2. Germany — Politics and government — 1918-1933. I. T.*
DD238.C313   943.085   66-74192

Lebovics, Herman.   III. 1980
Social conservatism and the middle classes in Germany, 1914-1933. Princeton, N.J., Princeton University Press, 1969. xi, 248 p. 23 cm. *1. Conservatism — Germany. 2. Middle classes — Germany. 3. Germany — Politics and government — 1888-1918. 4. Germany — Politics and government — 1918-1933. I. T.*
DD238.L43   320.5/2   68-56316

Waite, Robert George Leeson, 1919-   III. 1981
Vanguard of nazism; the Free Corps movement in postwar Germany, 1918-1923. Cambridge, Harvard University Press, 1952. xii, 344 p. 22 cm. (Harvard historical studies, v.60) "Extensive revision of ... [the author's

thesis submitted to ... Harvard University." 1. Germany. Heer. Freikorps. 2. Germany — History — 1918-1933. I. T. (S)
DD238.W34   943.085   52-5045

Gay, Peter, 1923- III. 1982
Weimar culture: the outsider as insider. [1st ed.] New York, Harper & Row [1968] xv, 205 p. illus., ports. 22 cm. 1. Germany — Intellectual life. 2. Germany — Politics and government — 1918-1933. I. T.
DD239.G38   001.2/0943   68-29572

DD240 – 241 Political and Diplomatic History

Bracher, Karl Dietrich, 1922- III. 1983
Die Auflösung der Weimarer Republik; eine Studie zum Problem des Machtverfalls in der Demokratie. Mit einer Einleitung von Hans Herzfeld. 3., verb. und ergänzte Aufl. Villingen/Schwarzwald, Ring-Verlag, 1960. xxiii, 809 p. tables. 23 cm. (Schriften des Institutes für Politische Wissenschaft, Bd.4) 1. Germany — Politics and government — 1918-1933. I. T. (S:Berlin. Institut für Politische Wissenschaft. Schriften, Bd.4)
DD240.B67 1960   62-46211

Gordon, Harold J. III. 1984
The Reichswehr and the German Republic, 1919-1926, by Harold J. Gordon, Jr. Port Washington, N.Y., Kennikat Press [1972, c1957] xvi, 478 p. 23 cm. 1. Germany. Heer. 2. Germany — Military policy. 3. Germany — Politics and government — 1918-1933. I. T.
DD240.G66 1972   943.085   74-159087   ISBN:0804616299

Heiden, Konrad, 1901- III. 1985
A history of national socialism, by Konrad Heiden, translated from the German. [1st American ed.] New York, Knopf, 1935. xvi, 430, ix, p. 25 cm. "This translation has been made from Herr Heiden's two books, Geschichte des Nationalsozialismus (1932) and Geburt des dritten Reiches (1934)." — Translator's note. 1. Nationalsozialistische deutsche Arbeiter-Partei. 2. Germany — Politics and government — 1918-1933. I. Hitler, Adolf, 1889- II. National socialism, A theory of. III. T.
DD240.H373 1935   943.085   35-2984

Kaufmann, Walter H. III. 1986
Monarchism in the Weimar Republic. New York, Bookman Associates [1953] 305 p. 23 cm. 1. Germany — Politics and government — 1918-1933. I. T.
DD240.K34   943.085   53-8591

Stampfer, Friedrich, 1874- III. 1987
Die vierzehn Jahre der ersten deutschen Republik. Karlsbad, "Graphia," 1936. 636 p. 23 cm. 1. Germany — Politics and government — 1918-1933. 2. Germany — History — 1918-1933. I. T.
DD240.S75   Af47-6801

Turner, Henry Ashby. III. 1988
Stresemann and the politics of the Weimar Republic. Princeton, N.J., Princeton University Press, 1963. v, 287 p. 23 cm. 1. Stresemann, Gustav, 1879-1929. 2. Germany — Politics and government — 1918-1933.
DD240.T8   943.085   63-10002

Von Klemperer, Klemens, 1916- III. 1989
Germany's new conservatism, its history and dilemma in the twentieth century. Foreword by Sigmund Neumann. Princeton, Princeton University Press, 1957. xxvi, 250 p. 23 cm. 1. Germany — Politics and government — 1918-1933. 2. Germany — Politics and government — 20th cent. 3. Conservatism — Case studies. I. T.
DD240.V6   943.085   57-5462

Wheeler-Bennett, John Wheeler, Sir, 1902- III. 1990
The nemesis of power; the German Army in politics, 1918-1945 [by] John W. Wheeler-Bennett. 2d ed. London, Macmillan; New York, St. Martin's Press, 1964. xxii, 831 p. illus., ports. 23 cm. 1. Germany — Politics and government — 1918-1933. 2. Germany — Politics and government — 1933-1945. 3. Germany. Heer. 4. World War, 1939-1945 — Germany. I. T.
DD240.W5 1964   943.085   64-55914

Hilger, Gustav. III. 1991
The incompatible allies; a memoir-history of German-Soviet relations, 1918-1941 [by] Gustav Hilger [and] Alfred G. Meyer. New York, Macmillan, 1953. xiii, 350 p. illus., ports. 22 cm. 1. Germany — Foreign relations — Russia. 2. Russia — Foreign relations — Germany. 3. Diplomats — Correspondence, reminiscences, etc. I. Meyer, Alfred G., joint author. II. T.
DD241.R8H5   327.430947   53-12899

Kochan, Lionel. III. 1992
Russia and the Weimar Republic. [Cambridge, Eng.] Bowes & Bowes [1954] 190 p. 23 cm. 1. Russia — Foreign relations — Germany. 2. Germany — Foreign relations — Russia. 3. Germany — Foreign relations — 1918-1933. I. T.
DD241.R8K58   327.430947   54-1709

DD247 Biography

Arendt, Hannah. III. 1993
Eichmann in Jerusalem; a report on the banality of evil. New York, Viking Press [1963] 275 p. 22 cm. 1. Eichmann, Adolf, 1906-1962. 2. Jews in Europe — Persecutions.
DD247.E5A7   923.543   63-12361

Goebbels, Joseph, 1897-1945. III. 1994
The early Goebbels diaries, 1925-1926. With a pref. by Alan Bullock. Edited by Helmut Heiber. Translated from the German by Oliver Watson. New York, Praeger [1963, c1962] 156 p. 23 cm. (Books that matter) Translation of Das Tagebuch von Joseph Goebbels, 1925/26; mit weiteren Dokumenten hrsg. von Helmut Heiber. I. Heiber, Helmut, 1924- ed. II. T.
DD247.G6A223 1963   923.243   63-7570

Goebbels, Joseph, 1897-1945. III. 1995
The Goebbels diaries, 1942-1943. Edited, translated, and with an introd. by Louis P. Lochner. Westport, Conn., Greenwood Press [1970, c1948] ix, 566 p. group port. 23 cm. Translation of Goebbels Tagebücher. I. Lochner, Louis Paul, 1887- ed. and tr. II. T.
DD247.G6A25 1970   943.086/0924   74-108391   ISBN:837138159

Manvell, Roger, 1909- III. 1996
Dr. Goebbels, his life and death, by Roger Manvell and Heinrich Fraenkel. New York, Simon and Schuster, 1960. 306 p. illus. 23 cm. 1. Goebbels, Joseph, 1897-1945. I. Fraenkel, Heinrich, 1897- joint author.
DD247.G6M33   923.243   59-13878

Ritter, Gerhard, 1888- III. 1997
The German resistance; Carl Goerdeler's struggle against tyranny. Translated by R. T. Clark. New York, Praeger [1959] 330 p. 23 cm. Translation of Carl Goerdeler und die deutsche Widerstandsbewegung. 1. Goerdeler, Carl Friedrich, 1884-1944. 2. Germany — Politics and government — 1933-1945. 3. Anti-Nazi movement. I. T.
DD247.G63R513   943.086   58-8190

Bewley, Charles Henry, 1888- III. 1998
Hermann Göring and the Third Reich; a biography based on family and official records. [New York] Devin-Adair Co., 1962. xvi, 517 p. illus., ports. 22 cm. 1. Göring, Hermann, 1893-1946. 2. Germany — Politics and government — 1933-1945. I. T.
DD247.G67B4   943.086   62-20038

Hassell, Ulrich von, 1881-1944. III. 1999
The Von Hassell diaries, 1938-1944; the story of the forces against Hitler inside Germany, as recorded by Ambassador Ulrich von Hassell, a leader of the movement. With an introd. by Allen Welsh Dulles. [1st ed.] Garden City, N.Y., Doubleday, 1947. xiv, 400 p. 24 cm. Translation of Vom andern Deutschland. 1. Germany — Politics and government — 1933-1945. 2. World War, 1939-1945 — Germany. I. T.
DD247.H33A315   943.086   47-11273

Manvell, Roger, 1909- III. 2000
Himmler [by] Roger Manvell and Heinrich Fraenkel. [1st American ed.] New York, Putnam [1965] xvii, 285 p. illus., ports. 23 cm. First published in London under title: Heinrich Himmler. I. Himmler, Heinrich, 1900-1945. I. Fraenkel, Heinrich, 1897- joint author.
DD247.H46M3 1965a   923.243   64-18020

DD247 Hitler

Hitler, Adolf, 1889-1945. III. 2001
Mein Kampf, by Adolf Hitler, translated by Ralph Manheim. Boston, Houghton Mifflin, 1943. xxi, 694 p. 21 cm. 1. Nationalsozialistische deutsche Arbeiter-Partei. 2. Germany — Politics and government — 20th cent. I. Manheim, Ralph, 1907- tr. II. T.
DD247.H5A322   923.143   43-14343

Hitler, Adolf, 1889-1945. III. 2002
The testament of Adolf Hitler; the Hitler-Bormann documents, February-April 1945, edited by François Genoud. Translated from the German by R. H. Stevens. With an introd. by H. R. Trevor-Roper. [2d ed.] London, Cassell [1961, c1960] 115 p. port. 19 cm. "First published in France under the title: Le testament politique de Hitler." 1. Germany — Politics and government — 1933-1945. 2. National socialism. 3. World War, 1939-1945 — Germany. I. Bormann, Martin, 1900- II. Genoud, François, ed. III. T.
DD247.H5A664553 1961   940.53   65-7281

Hitler, Adolf, 1889-1945. III. 2003
Secret conversations, 1941-1944 [translated by Norman Cameron and R. H. Stevens] With an introductory essay on The mind of Adolf Hitler, by H. R. Trevor-Roper. New York, Farrar, Straus and Young [1953] 597 p. 22 cm. London ed. (Weidenfeld and Nicolson) has title: Table talk, 1941-1944. "The original Bormann-Vermerke ... translated in full." I. T.
DD247.H5A685 1953a   923.143   53-9116

Hitler, Adolf, 1889-1945.   **III. 2004**
The speeches of Adolf Hitler, April 1922-August 1939; An English translation of representative passages arranged under subjects and edited by Norman H. Baynes. New York, H. Fertig, 1969. 2 v. (xii, 1980 p.) 23 cm. Reprint of the 1942 ed. 1. National socialism. 2. Germany — Politics and government — 1933-1945. 3. Germany — Foreign relations — 1933-1945. I. Baynes, Norman Hepburn, 1877-1961, ed. II. T.
DD247.H5A73 1969   943.085/0924   68-57828

Bullock, Alan Louis Charles.   **III. 2005**
Hitler, a study in tyranny. Completely rev. ed. New York, Harper & Row [c1962] 848 p. illus., ports., maps, geneal. table. 22 cm. 1. Hitler, Adolf, 1889-1945. I. A study in tyranny.
DD247.H5B85 1962a   923.143   63-21045

Dietrich, Otto, 1897-1952.   **III. 2006**
Hitler. Translated by Richard and Clara Winston. Chicago, H. Regnery Co., 1955. 277 p. 22 cm. Translation of 12 Jahre mit Hitler. 1. Hitler, Adolf, 1889-
DD247.H5D565   923.143   55-10826

Heiden, Konrad, 1901-1966.   **III. 2007**
Der Fuehrer; Hitler's rise to power. Translated by Ralph Manheim. Boston, Beacon Press [1969, c1944] x, 788 p. 21 cm. (Europe in the twentieth century. A Beacon paperback no. 336.) 1. Hitler, Adolf, 1889-1945. 2. Nationalsozialistische Deutsche Arbeiter-Partei. I. T.
DD247.H5H344 1969   943.085/0924   79-89960

Jenks, William Alexander, 1918-   **III. 2008**
Vienna and the young Hitler. New York, Columbia University Press, 1960. 252 p. 24 cm. 1. Hitler, Adolf, 1889-1945. 2. Vienna — Social conditions. 3. Vienna — Intellectual life. I. T.
DD247.H5J38   923.143   60-5285

Jetzinger, Franz.   **III. 2009**
Hitler's youth. Translated from the German by Lawrence Wilson. Foreword by Alan Bullock. London, Hutchinson [1958] 200 p. illus. 22 cm. 1. Hitler, Adolf, 1889-1945. I. T.
DD247.H5J453   923.143   59-960

Kubizek, August.   **III. 2010**
The young Hitler I knew. Translated from the German by E. V. Anderson; with an introd. by H. R. Trevor-Roper. Boston, Houghton Mifflin, 1955 [c1954] 298 p. illus. 22 cm. Translation of Adolf Hitler, mein Jugendfreund. 1. Hitler, Adolf, 1889-1945.
DD247.H5K813 1955   923.143   55-5301

Peterson, Edward Norman.   **III. 2011**
The limits of Hitler's power [by] Edward N. Peterson. Princeton, N.J., Princeton University Press, 1969. xxiii, 472 p. 23 cm. 1. Hitler, Adolf, 1889-1945. 2. Germany — Politics and government — 1933-1945. I. T.
DD247.H5P39   320.9/43   69-18066   ISBN:691051755

Trevor-Roper, Hugh Redwald.   **III. 2012**
The last days of Hitler [by] H. R. Trevor-Roper. 4th ed. London, Macmillan, 1971. lxiii, 286 p., 5 plates. facsim., map, plan, port. 21 cm. 1. Hitler, Adolf, 1889-1945. I. T.
DD247.H5T7 1971   943.086/092/4 (B)   72-176406
ISBN:0333075277

DD247   H – Z

Papen, Franz von, 1879-   **III. 2013**
Memoirs. Translated by Brian Connell. London, A. Deutsch [1952] 630 p. illus. 22 cm. 1. Statesmen, German — Correspondence, reminiscences, etc.
DD247.P3A33   923.243   52-4947

Schacht, Hjalmar Horace Greeley, 1877-   **III. 2014**
Confessions of "the Old Wizard"; autobiography. Translated by Diana Pyke. Boston, Houghton Mifflin, 1956. xx, 484 p. illus., ports. 22 cm. Translation of 76 [i.e. Sechsundsiebzig] Jahre meines Lebens. 1. Finance — Germany. 2. Germany — Economic conditions — 1918-1945. I. T.
DD247.S335A352   923.343   55-11550

Speer, Albert, 1905-   **III. 2015**
Inside the Third Reich: memoirs, Translated from the German by Richard and Clara Winston. Introd. by Eugene Davidson. [New York] Macmillan [1970] xviii, 596 p. illus., facsims., plans, ports. 24 cm. Translation of Erinnerungen. 1. Germany — Politics and government — 1933-1945. 2. Hitler, Adolf, 1889-1945. I. T.
DD247.S63A313 1970   943.086/0924 (B)   70-119132

Sykes, Christopher, 1907-   **III. 2016**
Tormented loyalty; the story of a German aristocrat who defied Hitler. [1st U.S. ed.] New York, Harper & Row [1969] 477 p. illus., ports. 22 cm. First published in London in 1968 under title: Troubled loyalty. 1. Trott zu Solz, Adam von, 1909-1944. 2. Hitler, Adolf, 1889-1945 — Assassination attempt, July 20, 1944. 3. Anti-Nazi movement. I. T.
DD247.T7S95 1969   943.086/0924 (B)   69-15266

DD248 – 251   Special Topics, 1918 – 1934

Lutz, Ralph Haswell, 1886-1968.   **III. 2017**
The German Revolution, 1918-1919. New York, AMS Press [1968] 186 p. 22 cm. (Stanford University publications. University series: history, economics, and political science, v. I, no. 1) Reprint of the 1922 ed. 1. Germany — History — Revolution, 1918. I. T. (S:Stanford studies in history, economics, and political science, v. 1, no. 1)
DD248.L8 1968   943.085   68-54283

Angress, Werner T.   **III. 2018**
Stillborn revolution; the Communist bid for power in Germany, 1921-1923, by Werner T. Angress. Port Washington, N.Y., Kennikat Press [1972, c1963] 2 v. (xv, 513 p.) map. 23 cm. 1. Germany — Politics and government — 1918-1933. 2. Communism — Germany. I. T.
DD249.A78 1972   943.085   79-159080   ISBN:0804616221

Matthias, Erich, ed.   **III. 2019**
Das Ende der Parteien, 1933. Hrsg. von Erich Matthias und Rudolf Morsey. Düsseldorf, Droste Verlag [1960] xv, 816 p. illus., ports., maps (1 col. on lining paper) 26 cm. (Veröffentlichung der Kommission für Geschichte des Parlamentarismus und der Politischen Parteien) Erratum slip inserted. 1. Political parties — Germany. 2. Germany — Politics and government — 1918-1933. I. Morsey, Rudolf, joint ed. II. T. (S:Kommission für Geschichte des Parlamentarismus und der Politischen Parteien. Veröffentlichung)
DD251.M36   A61-219

DD253 – 256   NATIONAL SOCIALISM. THIRD REICH, 1933 – 1945

Loewenstein, Karl, 1891-   **III. 2020**
Hitler's Germany; the Nazi background to war, by Karl Loewenstein. New ed. completely rev. New York, Macmillan, 1940. xviii, 230 p. 20 cm. 1. Germany — Politics and government — 1933-. 2. National socialism. I. T.
DD253.L58 1940   943.085   40-34526

Neumann, Franz Leopold, 1900-1954.   **III. 2021**
Behemoth; the structure and practice of national socialism 1933-1944. [2d ed. with new appendix] New York, Octagon Books, 1963 [c1944] 649 p. 24 cm. 1. National socialism. I. T.
DD253.N43 1963   943.086   63-14347

Rauschning, Hermann, 1887-   **III. 2022**
The revolution of nihilism; warning to the West, by Hermann Rauschning. Translated from German by E. W. Dickes. New York, Alliance Book Corporation, Longmans, Green [c1939] xvii, 300 p. 24 cm. 1. Nationalsozialistische deutsche Arbeiter-Partei. 2. Germany — Politics and government — 1933-1945. I. Dickes, Ernest Walter, 1876- tr. II. T.
DD253.R38   943.085   39-21141

Thyssen, Fritz, 1873-1951.   **III. 2023**
I paid Hitler. [Translated from the original by Cesar Saerchinger] Port Washington, N.Y., Kennikat Press [1972, c1941] xxix, 281 p. 22 cm. Dictated to Emery Reves and, in part, revised, corrected and approved by the author. 1. Hitler, Adolf, 1889-1945. 2. Nationalsozialistische Deutsche Arbeiter-Partei. 3. Germany — Politics and government — 1918-1933. 4. Germany — Politics and government — 1933-1945. I. Saerchinger, César, 1889- tr. II. Reves, Emery, 1904- III. T.
DD253.T55 1972   943.086/0924 (B)   71-153243   ISBN:0804615535

Orlow, Dietrich.   **III. 2024**
The history of the Nazi Party. [Pittsburgh] University of Pittsburgh Press [1969-73] 2 v. 24 cm. 1. Nationalsozialistishe Deutsche Arbeiter-Partei — History. I. T.
DD253.25.O7   329.9/43   69-20026
ISBN:0822931834 (v. 1)   0822932539 (v. 2)

Burden, Hamilton Twombly, 1937-   **III. 2025**
The Nuremberg Party rallies: 1923-39 [by] Hamilton T. Burden. Foreword by Adolf A. Berle. New York, Praeger [1967] xv, 206 p. illus., maps, ports. 25 cm. 1. Nationalsozialistische Deutsche Arbeiter-Partei. Reichsparteitag. I. T.
DD253.27.B8   943.086   67-20473

Höhne, Heinz, 1926-   **III. 2026**
The Order of the Death's Head; the story of Hitler's S.S. Translated from the German by Richard Barry. [1st American ed.] New York, Coward-McCann [1970, c1969] xii, 690 p. illus., maps, ports. 25 cm. Translation of Der Orden unter dem Totenkopf. 1. Nationalsozialistische Deutsche Arbeiter-Partei. Schutzstaffel. I. T.
DD253.6.H613 1970   943.086   69-19032

Dulles, Allen Welsh, 1893-   **III. 2027**
Germany's underground, by Allen Welsh Dulles. [1st ed.] New York,

Macmillan, 1947. xiii, 207 p. 21 cm. *1. Hitler, Adolf, 1889-1945. 2. Anti-Nazi movement. I. T.*
DD256.D8   943.086   47-2566

Deutsch, Harold Charles.   III. 2028
The conspiracy against Hitler in the twilight war, by Harold C. Deutsch. Minneapolis, University of Minnesota Press [1968] x, 394 p. 24 cm. *1. Anti-Nazi movement. 2. Hitler, Adolf, 1889-1945. 3. Pius XII, Pope, 1876-1958. I. T.*
DD256.3.D43 1968   364.13/1   68-22365

Allen, William Sheridan.   III. 2029
The Nazi seizure of power; the experience of a single German town, 1930-1935. Chicago, Quadrangle Books, 1965. xi, 345 p. illus., map. 22 cm. *1. Germany — Politics and government — 1918-1933. 2. Local government — Germany — Case studies. 3. National socialism. I. T.*
DD256.5.A58   943.086   65-10378

Bracher, Karl Dietrich, 1922-   III. 2030
The German dictatorship; the origins, structure, and effects of national socialism. Translated from the German by Jean Steinberg. With an introd. by Peter Gay. New York, Praeger Publishers [1970] xv, 553 p. 25 cm. Translation of Die deutsche Diktatur; Entstehung, Struktur, Folgen des Nationalsozialismus. *1. National socialism — History. 2. Germany — Politics and government — 1933-1945. 3. Anti-Nazi movement. I. T.*
DD256.5.B66313 1970   329.943   70-95662

Bracher, Karl Dietrich, 1922-   III. 2031
Die nationalsozialistische Machtergreifung; Studien zur Errichtung des totalitären Herrschaftssystems in Deutschland 1933/34 [von] Karl Dietrich Bracher, Wolfgang Sauer [und] Gerhard Schulz. Köln, Westdeutscher Verlag, 1960. xx, 1034 p. 25 cm. (Schriften des Instituts für Politische Wissenschaft, Bd. 14) "Berichtigung": slip inserted. *1. Germany — Politics and government — 1933-1945. I. T. (S:Berlin. Institut für Politische Wissenschaft. Schriften, Bd. 14)*
DD256.5.B665   61-35850

Bramsted, Ernest Kohn.   III. 2032
Goebbels and National Socialist propaganda, 1925-1945, by Ernest K. Bramsted. [East Lansing] Michigan State University Press, 1965. xxxvii, 488 p. 24 cm. *1. Goebbels, Joseph, 1897-1945. 2. Germany. Reichsministerium für Volksaufklärung und Propaganda. 3. Propaganda, German. 4. World War, 1939-1945 — Propaganda. I. T.*
DD256.5.B674   301.15230943   64-19392

Broszat, Martin.   III. 2033
German National Socialism, 1919-1945. Translated from the German by Kurt Rosenbaum and Inge Pauli Boehm. Santa Barbara, Calif., Clio Press [1966] viii, 154 p. 22 cm. (Twentieth century series, no. 1) Translation of Der Nationalsozialismus. *1. National socialism. I. T.*
DD256.5.B6793   321.9/4   66-26137

Burdick, Charles Burton, 1927-   III. 2034
Germany's military strategy and Spain in World War II [by] Charles B. Burdick. [1st ed. Syracuse, N.Y.] Syracuse University Press [1968] xi, 228 p. illus., plans, ports. 24 cm. *1. World War, 1939-1945 — Germany. 2. World War, 1939-1945 — Spain. 3. Germany — History, Military — 20th century. I. T.*
DD256.5.B9   940.54/013   68-26994

Cohen, Élie Aron.   III. 2035
Human behavior in the concentration camp; translated from the Dutch by M. H. Braaksma. [1st ed.] New York, W. W. Norton [1953] 295 p. 22 cm. Translation of Het duitse concentratiekamp. *1. Nationalsozialistische Deutsche Arbeiter-Partei. Schutzstaffel. 2. Concentration camps — Germany. 3. Prison psychology. I. T.*
DD256.5.C612   940.547243   53-13294

François-Poncet, André, 1887-   III. 2036
The fateful years; memoirs of a French ambassador in Berlin, 1931-1938. Translated from the French by Jacques LeClercq. New York, H. Fertig, 1972 [c1946] xiii, 295 p. 21 cm. Translation of Souvenirs d'une ambassade à Berlin, septembre 1931-octobre 1938. *1. Germany — Politics and government — 1933-1945. 2. National socialism. 3. Hitler, Adolf, 1889-1945. I. T.*
DD256.5.F71513 1972   943.086   76-80549

Gisevius, Hans Bernd, 1904-   III. 2037
To the bitter end. Tr. from the German by Richard and Clara Winston. Boston, Houghton Mifflin Co., 1947. xv, 632 p. 22 cm. *1. Nationalsozialistische deutsche Arbeiter-Partei. 2. Germany — Politics and government — 1933-1945. I. Winston, Richard, tr. II. T.*
DD256.5.G52   943.086   47-5861

Kogon, Eugen, 1903-   III. 2038
The theory and practice of hell; the German concentration camps and the system behind them. Translated by Heinz Norden. New York, Farrar, Straus [1950?] 307 p. illus. 22 cm. Translation of Der SS-Staat, das System der deutschen Konzentrationslager. *1. Nationalsozialistische Deutsche Arbeiter-Partei. Schutzstaffel. 2. Concentration camps — Germany. I. T.*
DD256.5.K614   943.086   50-10716

Mau, Hermann.   III. 2039
German history, 1933-45; an assessment by German historians, by Hermann Mau and Helmut Krausnick. [Translated from the German by Andrew and Eva Wilson] London, O. Wolff, 1959. 157 p. 19 cm. Translation of Deutsche Geschichte der jüngsten Vergangenheit, 1933-1945. *1. Germany — History — 1933-1945. I. Krausnick, Helmut. II. T.*
DD256.5.M383   943.086   A60-425

Meinecke, Friedrich, 1862-1954.   III. 2040
The German catastrophe; reflections and recollections. Translated by Sidney B. Fay. Cambridge, Harvard University Press, 1950. xiii, 121 p. port. 22 cm. *1. Hitler, Adolf, 1889-1945. 2. Germany — History — 1933-1945. 3. National socialism. I. T.*
DD256.5.M42   943.086   50-5221

Reitlinger, Gerald, 1900-   III. 2041
The SS, alibi of a nation, 1922-1945. New York, Viking Press, 1957. xi, 502 p. illus., ports., maps. 23 cm. *1. Nationalsozialistische Deutsche Arbeiter-Partei. Schutzstaffel. 2. Germany — Politics and government — 1933-1945. I. T.*
DD256.5.R4x   943.086   57-7862

Rothfels, Hans, 1891-   III. 2042
The German opposition to Hitler, an appraisal. Hinsdale, Ill., Regnery, 1948. 172 p. 20 cm. (The Humanist library) *1. Germany — Politics and government — 1933-1945. I. T. (S)*
DD256.5.R6   943.086   48-3753

Schoenbaum, David.   III. 2043
Hitler's social revolution; class and status in Nazi Germany, 1933-1939. [1st ed.] Garden City, N.Y., Doubleday, 1966. xxiii, 336 p. 22 cm. Based on thesis, Oxford University. *1. Germany — History — 1933-1945. 2. Germany — Social conditions. I. T.*
DD256.5.S336   943.086   66-17420

Shirer, William Lawrence, 1904-   III. 2044
The rise and fall of the Third Reich; a history of Nazi Germany. New York, Simon and Schuster, 1960. 1245 p. 25 cm. *1. Germany — History — 1933-1945. I. T.*
DD256.5.S48   943.086   60-6729

Tenenbaum, Joseph, 1887-   III. 2045
Race and Reich; the story of an epoch. New York, Twayne Publishers [c1956] xvi, 554 p. facsim. 23 cm. *1. Germany — Race question. 2. National socialism. 3. Jewish question. I. T.*
DD256.5.T48   943.086   56-170

Weinberg, Gerhard L.   III. 2046
The foreign policy of Hitler's Germany; diplomatic revolution in Europe, 1933-36 [by] Gerhard L. Weinberg. Chicago, University of Chicago Press [1970] xi, 397 p. map (on lining papers) 24 cm. *1. Germany — Foreign relations — 1933-1945. I. T.*
DD256.5.W417   327.43   70-124733   ISBN:0226885097

DD257   ALLIED OCCUPATION, 1945 –

Clay, Lucius Du Bignon, 1897-   III. 2047
Decision in Germany. [1st ed.] Garden City, N.Y., Doubleday, 1950. xiv, 522 p. illus., ports., maps (on lining papers) 22 cm. *1. Germany — History — Allied occupation, 1945- I. T.*
DD257.C55   943.086   50-5813

Gimbel, John.   III. 2048
The American occupation of Germany; politics and the military, 1945-1949. Stanford, Calif., Stanford University Press, 1968. xiv, 335 p. map. 24 cm. *1. Germany (Territory under Allied occupation, 1945-1955. U.S. Zone) 2. Germany (Federal Republic, 1949-) — Politics and government. 3. Berlin — Blockade, 1948-1949. 4. Economic Assistance, American — History. I. T.*
DD257.2.G5   355.02/8/0943   68-26778

DD259   FEDERAL REPUBLIC, 1949 –

Grosser, Alfred, 1925-   III. 2049
La démocratie de Bonn, 1949-1957. Paris, A. Colin, 1958. 309 p. 23 cm. *1. Germany (Federal Republic, 1949-) — Politics and government. I. T.*
DD259.G68   320.943   65-2390

Conant, James Bryant, 1893-   III. 2050
Germany and freedom; a personal appraisal. Cambridge, Harvard University Press, 1958. 117 p. 21 cm. (The Godkin lectures at Harvard University, 1958) *1. Germany (Federal Republic, 1949-) I. T.*
DD259.2.C64   943.087   58-8994

Deutsch, Karl Wolfgang, 1912-   **III. 2051**
Germany rejoins the powers; mass opinion, interest groups, and elites in contemporary German foreign policy, by Karl W. Deutsch and Lewis J. Edinger. Stanford, Calif., Stanford University Press, 1959. xvi, 320 p. 25 cm. *1. Germany (Federal Republic, 1949-) — Foreign relations. 2. Public opinion — Germany (Federal Republic, 1949-) I. Edinger, Lewis Joachim, 1922- joint author. II. T.*
DD259.4.D46   327.43   59-10633

Grass, Günter, 1927-   **III. 2052**
Speak out; speeches, open letters, commentaries. Translated by Ralph Manheim. Introd. by Michael Harrington. New York, Harcourt, Brace & World [1969] xii, 142 p. 21 cm. Mainly selected from the author's Über das Selbstverständliche, published in 1968. *1. Germany (Federal Republic, 1949-) — Politics and government — Addresses, essays, lectures. I. T.*
DD259.4.G653   320.9/43   69-12035

Hanrieder, Wolfram F.   **III. 2053**
The stable crisis; two decades of German foreign policy [by] Wolfran F. Hanrieder. New York, Harper & Row [1970] xiv, 221 p. 21 cm. *1. Germany (Federal Republic, 1949-) — Foreign relations. I. T.*
DD259.4.H24 1970   327.43   72-109578

Adenauer, Konrad, 1876-   **III. 2054**
Memoirs. Translated by Beate Ruhm von Oppen. Chicago, H. Regnery Co. [c1966-   v. illus., ports. 25 cm. *1. Germany — Politics and government — 1945- 2. Germany (Federal Republic, 1949-) — Politics and government. 3. World politics — 1945-*
DD259.7.A3A333   943.0870924   65-26906

Hiscocks, Richard.   **III. 2055**
The Adenauer era. Philadelphia, Lippincott [1966] x, 312 p. 22 cm. *1. Adenauer, Konrad, 1876-1967. 2. Germany (Federal Republic, 1949-) — Politics and government. 3. Germany (Federal Republic, 1949-) — Social conditions. I. T.*
DD259.7.A3H5   943.0870924   66-23243

Heuss, Theodor, Pres. German Federal Republic, 1884-   **III. 2056**
Preludes to life; early memoirs. Translated from the German by Michael Bullock. [1st American ed.] New York, Citadel Press [1955] 183 p. illus. 22 cm. *I. T.*
DD259.7.H4A32   923.143   56-1976

DD261 DEMOCRATIC REPUBLIC, 1949 –

Smith, Jean Edward.   **III. 2057**
Germany beyond the wall; people, politics ... and prosperity. [1st ed.] Boston, Little, Brown [1969] xiv, 338 p. 25 cm. *1. Germany (Democratic Republic, 1949-) I. T.*
DD261.S53   309.1/431   69-12636

Baring, Arnulf.   **III. 2058**
Der 17. [i.e. siebzehnte] Juni 1953. Hrsg. vom Bundesministerium für Gesamtdeutsche Fragen. Bonn [Auslieferung: Deutscher Bundes-Verlag] 1957. 84 p. 21 cm. (Bonner Berichte aus Mittel- und Ostdeutschland.) *1. Germany (Democratic Republic, 1949-) — History — Uprising, June 1953. 2. Germany — History — Allied occupation, 1945- I. T. (S)*
DD261.4.B37   59-41322

Harpprecht, Klaus.   **III. 2059**
The East German rising, 17th June 1953 [by] Stefan Brant [pseud. Translated and adapted by Charles Wheeler] With a foreword by John Hynd. New York, Praeger [1957] 202 p. illus. 23 cm. (Books that matter) Translation of Der Aufstand. *1. Germany (Democratic Republic, 1949-) — History — Uprising, June, 1953. 2. Germany (Democratic Republic, 1949-) — Politics and government. 3. Germany — History — Allied occupation, 1945- I. T.*
DD261.4.H313 1957   943.1   57-5815

DD301 – 901 Local History
DD301 – 454 PRUSSIA

Schoeps, Hans Joachim, comp.   **III. 2060**
Das war Preussen. Zeugnisse der Jahrhunderte. Eine Anthologie. 3., erw. Aufl. Berlin, Haude u. Spener (1968). 269 p. 21 cm. *1. Prussia. 2. Prussia — History — Sources. I. T.*
DD303.S35 1968   78-388604

Anderson, Eugene Newton.   **III. 2061**
Nationalism and the cultural crisis in Prussia, 1806-1815; [essays] New York, Octagon Books, 1966 [c1939] ix, 303 p. 21 cm. *1. Nationalism — Prussia. I. T.*
DD331.A6 1966   943/.1   66-29328

Carsten, Francis Ludwig.   **III. 2062**
The origins of Prussia. Oxford, Clarendon Press, 1954. 309 p. fold. map. 23 cm. *1. Prussia — History. I. T.*
DD347.C3   A54-4860

Hintze, Otto, 1861-   **III. 2063**
Die Hohenzollern und ihr Werk; fünfhundert Jahre vaterländischer Geschichte, von Otto Hintze. Berlin, P. Parey, 1915. xvi, 704 p. 26 cm. *1. Hohenzollern, House of. 2. Prussia — History.*
DD347.H55   16-4403

Marriott, John Arthur Ransome, Sir, 1859-1945.   **III. 2064**
The evolution of Prussia, the making of an empire, by Sir J. A. R. Marriott and Sir Charles Grant Robertson. Rev. ed. Oxford, Clarendon Press [1946] 499 p. illus. 19 cm. "First published 1915." *1. Prussia — History. I. Robertson, Charles Grant, Sir, 1869- joint author. II. T.*
DD347.M3x   A47-5661

Schevill, Ferdinand, 1868-1954.   **III. 2065**
The Great Elector. Hamden, Conn., Archon Books, 1965 [c1947] ix, 442 p. illus., maps, ports. 23 cm. Reprint of the 1947 ed. *1. Friedrich Wilhelm, Elector of Brandenburg, called the Great Elector, 1620-1688. I. T.*
DD394.S4 1965   923.143   65-16972

Ranke, Leopold von, 1795-1886.   **III. 2066**
Memoirs of the House of Brandenburg and history of Prussia during the seventeenth and eighteenth centuries. Translated from the German by Sir Alexr. and Lady Duff Gordon. New York, Haskell House Publishers, 1969. 3 v. 23 cm. Reprint of the 1849 ed. Translation of Neun Bücher preussischen Geschichte. *1. Prussia — History — Frederick William I, 1713-1740. 2. Prussia — History — Frederick II, the Great, 1740-1786. I. T.*
DD397.R25 1969   943/.05   68-25278   ISBN:838301681

Ergang, Robert Reinhold, 1898-   **III. 2067**
The Potsdam führer, Frederick William I, father of Prussian militarism, by Robert Ergang. New York, Columbia University Press, 1941. 290 p. 23 cm. *1. Friedrich Wilhelm I, king of Prussia, 1688-1740. I. T.*
DD399.E7   923.143   41-19534

Easum, Chester Verne.   **III. 2068**
Prince Henry of Prussia, brother of Frederick the Great, by Chester V. Easum. Westport, Conn., Greenwood Press [1971, c1942] 403 p. illus., facsims., geneal. table, fold. map, ports. 23 cm. *1. Heinrich, Prince of Prussia, 1726-1802.*
DD402.H4E2 1971   943/.053/0924   75-113061   ISBN:0837146976

Gooch, George Peabody, 1873-   **III. 2069**
Frederick the Great, the ruler, the writer, the man. Hamden, Conn., Archon Books [1962] 363 p. illus. 22 cm. *I. Friedrich II, der Grosse, King of Prussia, 1712-1786.*
DD403.G6 1962   923.143   62-16045

Gaxotte, Pierre.   **III. 2070**
Frederick the Great, by Pierre Gaxotte, translated by R. A. Bell. New Haven, Yale University Press, 1942. 420 p. front., plates, ports. 25 cm. Translation of Frédéric II. *1. Friedrich II, der Grosse, king of Prussia, 1712-1786. 2. Friedrich Wilhelm I, king of Prussia, 1688-1740. 3. Prussia — History — Frederick II, the Great, 1740-1786. I. Bell, R. A., tr.*
DD404.G32 1942   923.143   A42-2150

Koser, Reinhold, 1852-1914.   **III. 2071**
Geschichte Friedrichs des Grossen. 6. und 7. Aufl. Stuttgart, Cotta, 1921- v. maps (part fold. col.) 24 cm. *1. Friedrich II, der Grosse, King of Prussia, 1712-1786.*
DD404.K82   50-43442

Lavisse, Ernest, 1842-1922.   **III. 2072**
The youth of Frederick the Great. Translated from the French by Mary Bushnell Coleman. Chicago, S. C. Griggs, 1892. [New York, AMS Press, 1972] p. Translation of La jeunesse du Grand Frédéric. *1. Friedrich II, der Grosse, King of Prussia, 1712-1786. I. T.*
DD404.L413 1972   943/.053/0924 (B)   71-172308   ISBN:0404038913

Ritter, Gerhard, 1888-   **III. 2073**
Frederick the Great; a historical profile. Translated, with an introd., by Peter Paret. Berkeley, University of California Press, 1968. xiv, 207 p. port. 23 cm. *1. Friedrich II, der Grosse, King of Prussia, 1712-1786. I. T.*
DD404.R513   943/.053/0924 (B)   68-15815

Ford, Guy Stanton, 1873-1962.   **III. 2074**
Stein and the era of reform in Prussia, 1807-1815. Gloucester, Mass., P. Smith, 1965 [c1922] vii, 336 p. 21 cm. *1. Stein, Heinrich Friedrich Karl, Freiherr vom und zum, 1757-1831. 2. Prussia — Politics and government — 1806-1848. I. T.*
DD416.S8F6 1965   943.060924 (B)   65-9668

Ritter, Gerhard, 1888-   **III. 2075**
Stein; eine politische Biographie. [3.] neugestaltete Aufl. Stuttgart, Deutsche Verlags-Anstalt [1958] 656 p. port. 24 cm. *1. Stein, Heinrich Friedrich Karl, Freiherr vom und zum, 1757-1831.*
DD416.S8R5 1958   A59-339

Schoeps, Hans Joachim.   **III. 2076**
Das andere Preussen; konservative Gestalten und Probleme im Zeitalter Friedrich Wilhelms IV. 3. Aufl. Berlin, Haude & Spencer [1964] 368 p. illus., ports. 24 cm. *1. Gerlach, Ernst Ludwig von, 1795-1877. 2. Leo, Heinrich, 1799-1878. 3. Prussia — Politics and government — 1815-1870. I. T.*
DD417.S3x

Friedjung, Heinrich, 1851-1920.   **III. 2077**
The struggle for supremacy in Germany, 1859-1866. Translated by A. J. P. Taylor and W. L. McElwee. New York, Russell & Russell, 1966. xxxi, 339 p. map. 23 cm. Reprint of the 1935 abridged translation of the 10th German ed. of 1916-17. *1. Austro-Prussian War, 1866. 2. Austro-Italian War, 1866. I. Taylor, Alan John Percivale, 1906- tr. II. McElwee, William Lloyd, 1907- tr. III. T.*
DD438.F92 1966   943.07   66-13169

Craig, Gordon Alexander, 1913-   **III. 2078**
The Battle of Königgrätz; Prussia's victory over Austria, 1866. [1st ed.] Philadelphia, Lippincott [1964] xii, 211 p. maps. 21 cm. (Great battles of history) *1. Königgrätz, Battle of, 1866. I. T.*
DD439.K7C7   943.604   64-14461

DD491 – 901 OTHER REGIONS

Fay, Sidney Bradshaw, 1876-   **III. 2079**
The rise of Brandenburg-Prussia to 1786, by Sidney Bradshaw Fay. New York, Holt [c1937] viii, 155 p. front. (map) double diagr. 20 cm. (The Berkshire studies in European history) *1. Brandenburg — History. I. T.*
DD491.B85F28   943.15   37-12570

Droz, Jacques.   **III. 2080**
Le libéralisme rhénan, 1815-1848; contribution à l'histoire du libéralisme allemand ... par Jacques Droz. Paris, F. Sorlot, 1940. xviii, 463 p. 25 cm. "Additifs": leaf inserted. *1. Rhine province — History. 2. Liberalism. 3. Germany — Politics and government — 1815-1866. I. T.*
DD491.R48D7   943.4   46-42542

Steefel, Lawrence Dinkelspiel, 1894-   **III. 2081**
The Schleswig-Holstein question, by Lawrence D. Steefel. Cambridge, Harvard University Press, 1932. xii, 400 p. geneal. tab., fold. mounted maps. 23 cm. (Harvard historical studies ... Vol. XXXII) "This monograph has grown out of a thesis presented in 1923 in partial fulfilment of the requirements for the degree of doctor of philosophy at Harvard university." — Pref. *1. Schleswig-Holstein question.*
DD491.S68S8   943.51   32-9250

Brandt, Willy, 1913-   **III. 2082**
My road to Berlin [by] Willy Brandt, as told to Leo Lania [pseud. 1st ed.] Garden City, N.Y., Doubleday, 1960. 287 p. illus. 22 cm. *1. Berlin — History — Allied occupation, 1945- I. Herrmann, Lazar, 1896- II. T.*
DD857.B7A3   923.243   60-10666

Kimmich, Christoph M.   **III. 2083**
The free city; Danzig and German foreign policy, 1919-1934, by Christoph M. Kimmich. New Haven, Yale University Press, 1968. 196 p. map (on lining papers) 23 cm. *1. Danzig — Politics and government. 2. Germany — Foreign relations — 1918-1933. 3. Stresemann, Gustav, 1878-1929. I. T.*
DD901.D283K5   320.9/438/2   68-27758

Gimbel, John.   **III. 2084**
A German community under American occupation: Marburg, 1945-52. Stanford, Calif., Stanford University Press, 1961. vi, 259 p. 23 cm. (Stanford studies in history, economics, and political science, 21) *1. Marburg — Politics and government. 2. Germany — History — Allied occupation, 1945- — Case studies. I. T. (S)*
DD901.M275G5   943.087   61-7798

Ford, Franklin Lewis, 1920-   **III. 2085**
Strasbourg in transition, 1648-1789. Cambridge, Harvard University Press, 1958. xvii, 321 p. illus., ports., maps. 22 cm. *1. Strassburg — History. I. T.*
DD901.S87F6   943.445   58-7247

Bruford, Walter Horace, 1894-   **III. 2086**
Culture and society in classical Weimar, 1775-1806. [London] Cambridge University Press, 1962. 465 p. illus. 23 cm. *1. Goethe, Johann Wolfgang von, 1749-1832. 2. Weimar — Intellectual life. I. T.*
DD901.W4B7   943.23   62-6747

DE – DG Greece. Italy

DE MEDITERRANEAN REGION. GRECO-ROMAN WORLD

Harvey, Paul, Sir, 1869-1948. III. 2087
The Oxford companion to classical literature, compiled and edited by Sir Paul Harvey. Oxford, The Clarendon Press, 1937. xl, [1], 468 p. plates, maps, plans. 19 cm. *1. Classical dictionaries. I. T.*
DE3.H3   913.38   38-1064

The New Century classical handbook. III. 2088
Edited by Catherine B. Avery; editorial consultant, Jotham Johnson. New York, Appleton-Century-Crofts [1962] xiii, 1162 p. illus., maps (on lining papers) 26 cm. *1. Classical dictionaries. I. Avery, Catherine B., ed. II. Classical handbook.*
DE5.N4   913.38   62-10069

The Oxford classical dictionary, III. 2089
edited by N. G. L. Hammond and H. H. Scullard. 2d ed. Oxford [Eng.] Clarendon Press, 1970. xxii, 1176 p. 26 cm. *1. Classical dictionaries. I. Hammond, Nicholas Geoffrey Lemprière, ed. II. Scullard, Howard Hayes, 1903- ed.*
DE5.O9 1970   913.38003   73-18819

Plutarchus. III. 2090
The lives of the noble Grecians and Romans, translated by John Dryden and revised by Arthur Hugh Clough. New York, Modern Library [1932] xxiv, 1309 p. 21 cm. (The Modern library of the world's best books. [Modern library giants]) At head of title: Plutarch. *1. Greece — Biography. 2. Rome — Biography. I. Dryden, John, 1631-1700. II. Clough, Arthur Hugh, 1819-1861, ed.*
DE7.P5 1932   920.03 (888.8)   32-17475

Plutarchus. III. 2091
Selected lives from the Lives of the noble Grecians and Romans. Compared together by that grave learned philosopher and historiographer Plutarch of Chaeronea; translated out of Greek into French by James Amyot and out of French into English by Thomas North. Now selected, edited and introduced by Paul Turner. Carbondale, Ill., Southern Illinois University Press [1963- v. 26 cm. ([Centaur classics]) Cover title: Plutarch's "Lives." *1. Greece — Biography. 2. Rome — Biography. I. Turner, Paul, 1917- ed.*
DE7.P7T8   920.03   63-8902

Grant, Michael, 1914- III. 2092
The ancient historians. New York, Scribner [1970] xviii, 486 p. illus., facsims., maps, ports. 24 cm. *1. Greek historians. 2. Latin historians. I. T.*
DE8.G7   938/.0072/022   70-106551

Cary, Max, 1881- III. 2093
The geographic background of Greek & Roman history. Oxford, Clarendon Press, 1949. vi, 331 p. maps (part fold.) 25 cm. *1. Classical geography. I. T.*
DE29.C35   913.38   49-3013

Heyden, A. A. M. van der, ed. III. 2094
Atlas of the classical world. Edited by A. A. M. van der Heyden and H. H. Scullard. [London, New York] Nelson, 1959 [i.e. 1960] 221 p. illus., col. maps (1 fold.) 36 cm. *1. Civilization, — Greek — Pictorial works. 2. Rome — Civilization — Pictorial works. 3. Classical geography — Maps. 1. Scullard, Howard Hayes, 1903- joint ed. II. T.*
DE29.H463   911.38   60-1130

Cary, Max, 1881- III. 2095
Life and thought in the Greek and Roman world, by M. Cary and T. J. Haarhoff. 12 plates and 4 maps in the text. London, Methuen [1940] x p., 1 l., 348 p. illus. (maps) 12 pl. on 6 l. 19 cm. "First published in 1940." *1. Civilization, Greco-Roman. I. Haarhoff, Theodore Johannes, 1892- joint author. II. T.*
DE71.C27 1940   913.38   A41-3107

Couch, Herbert Newell, 1899- III. 2096
Classical civilization [by] Herbert Newell Couch and Russel M. Geer. 2d ed. Westport, Conn., Greenwood Press [1973- c1951- v. illus. 22 cm. Vol. 1: Reprint of the 1951 ed. published by Prentice-Hall, New York. *1. Civilization, Greek. 2. Rome — Civilization. I. Geer, Russel Mortimer. II. T.*
DE71.C62 1973   913.38   76-156186   ISBN:0837161290

Ehrenberg, Victor, 1891- III. 2097
Society and civilization in Greece and Rome. Cambridge, Published for Oberlin College by Harvard University Press, 1964. xiv, 106 p. illus. 22 cm. (Martin classical lectures, v.18) *1. Greece — Social life and customs. 2. Rome — Social life and customs. I. T. (S)*
DE71.E5x (PA25.M3 vol. 18)   913.38   64-19580

Haarhoff, Theodore Johannes, 1892- III. 2098
The stranger at the gate; aspects of exclusiveness and cooperation in ancient Greece and Rome, with some reference to modern times. [2d ed.] Oxford, Blackwell, 1948. xii, 354 p. 22 cm. *1. Civilization, Greek. 2. Hellenism. 3. Rome — Civilization. 4. Civilization, Greco-Roman. 5. Nationalism and nationality. I. T.*
DE71.Hx   A50-9748

Toynbee, Arnold Joseph, 1889- III. 2099
Hellenism; the history of a civilization. New York, Oxford University Press, 1959. 272 p. illus. 21 cm. *1. Hellenism — History.*
DE71.T6   901.91   59-7810

Levi, Mario Attilio, 1902- III. 2101
Political power in the ancient world. Translation by Jane Costello. [New York] New American Library [1966, c1965] 194 p. 22 cm. Translation of La lotta politica nel mondo antico. *1. History, Ancient. I. T.*
DE83.L413 1966   320.5093   65-24023

DF GREECE

DF 10 – 289 Ancient Greece

Cary, Max, 1881-1958. III. 2102
The documentary sources of Greek history. New York, Greenwood Press [1969] xi, 140 p. 23 cm. Reprint of the 1927 ed. *1. Greece — History — Sources. I. T.*
DF12.C3 1969   938   78-90478   ISBN:837122155

Gomme, Arnold Wycombe. III. 2103
Essays in Greek history and literature, by A. W. Gomme. Freeport, N.Y., Books for Libraries Press [1967] viii, 298 p. illus. 22 cm. (Essay index reprint series) "First published 1937." *1. Thucydides. 2. Greece — History — Addresses, essays, lectures. 3. Greek literature — Addresses, essays, lectures. I. T.*
DF14.G49 1967   913.3/8   67-23222

Myres, John Linton, Sir, 1869-1954. III. 2104
Geographical history in Greek lands. Oxford, Clarendon Press, 1953. ix, 381 p. illus., maps. 23 cm. *1. Greece — Description, geography. I. T.*
DF30.M79   938   53-1115

DF75 – 135 ANTIQUITIES. CIVILIZATION

Botsford, George Willis, 1862-1917, ed.   III. 2105
Hellenic civilization. Edited by G. W. Botsford and E. G. Sihler. With contributions from William L. Westermann, Charles J. Ogden, and others. New York, Octagon Books, 1965 [c1915] xiii, 719 p. 24 cm. (Records of civilization; sources and studies, no. 1) *1. Civilization, Greek. I. Sihler, Ernest Gottlieb, 1853-1942, joint ed. II. T. (S)*
DF77.B7 1965   913.3803   65-20966

Bowra, Cecil Maurice, Sir, 1898-   III. 2106
The Greek experience. [1st ed.] Cleveland, World Pub. Co. [1958, c1957] 210 p. illus. 25 cm. (The World histories of civilization) *1. Civilization, Greek. I. T.*
DF77.B73   913.38   58-5772

Carpenter, Rhys, 1889-   III. 2107
The humanistic value of archaeology. Westport, Conn., Greenwood Press [1971, c1933] 134 p. 23 cm. *1. Greece — Antiquities. 2. Archaeology. I. T.*
DF77.C33 1971   913.3/8/03   72-138582   ISBN:0837157811

Ehrenberg, Victor, 1891-   III. 2108
From Solon to Socrates: Greek history and civilization during the sixth and fifth centuries B.C. London, Methuen, 1968. xvii, 493 p. maps. 22 cm. "Distributed in the USA by Barnes and Noble." *1. Civilization, Greek. 2. Greece — History. I. T.*
DF77.E35   913.3/8   68-107540

Finley, Moses I.   III. 2109
The ancient Greeks, an introduction to their life and thought. New York, Viking Press [1963] 177 p. illus. 22 cm. *1. Civilization, Greek. I. T.*
DF77.F5   913.38   63-8453

Finley, Moses I.   III. 2110
Early Greece; the Bronze and archaic ages [by] M. I. Finley. New York, Norton [1970] 155 p. illus., maps, plan. 21 cm. (Ancient culture and society) *1. Civilization, Greek. I. T.*
DF77.F53 1970   913.38/03/11   78-95884   ISBN:393054101

Hadas, Moses, 1900-   III. 2111
Hellenistic culture: fusion and diffusion. New York, Columbia University Press, 1959. 324 p. 24 cm. *1. Hellenism. 2. Civilization, Greek. I. T.*
DF77.H3   913.38   59-13777

Hamilton, Edith, 1867-1963.   III. 2112
The echo of Greece. [1st ed.] New York, W. W. Norton [c1957] 224 p. 22 cm. *1. Civilization, Greek. I. T.*
DF77.H33   913.38   57-5498

Hamilton, Edith, 1867-   III. 2113
The Greek way. New York, Modern Library [1961? c1942] 347 p. 19 cm. *1. Civilization, Greek. 2. Greek literature — History and criticism.*
DF77.H3414   880.9   61-66709

Jaeger, Werner Wilhelm, 1888-   III. 2114
Paideia: the ideals of Greek culture, by Werner Jaeger, translated ... by Gilbert Highet. 2d ed. New York, Oxford University Press, 1945-   3 v. 23 cm. *1. Education, Greek. 2. Civilization, Greek. 3. Greek literature — History and criticism. I. Highet, Gilbert, 1906- tr. II. T.*
DF77.J274   370.938   45-9752

Kitto, Humphrey Davy Findley.   III. 2115
The Greeks. London, Baltimore, Penguin Books [1954] 256 p. illus. 18 cm. (Pelican books, A220) *1. Civilization, Greek. 2. Greece — History.*
DF77.K5 1954   913.38   55-927

Livingstone, Richard Winn, Sir, 1880- ed.   III. 2116
The legacy of Greece; essays by Gilbert Murray, W. R. Inge, J. Burnet [and others] ed. by R. W. Livingstone. Oxford, Clarendon Press, 1921. xii, 424 p. illus., plates. 20 cm. *1. Greece. I. T.*
DF77.L6   913.38   22-10803

MacKendrick, Paul Lachlan, 1914-   III. 2117
The Greek stones speak; the story of archaeology in Greek lands. New York, St Martin's Press [1962] 470 p. illus. 22 cm. *1. Greece — Antiquities. I. T.*
DF77.M18   913.38   62-10902

Starr, Chester G., 1914-   III. 2118
The origins of Greek civilization, 1100-650 B. C. [1st ed.] New York, Knopf, 1961. xviii, 385, viii p. illus., maps. 25 cm. *1. Civilization, Greek.*
DF77.S62   913.38   60-53446

Tarn, William Woodthorpe, Sir, 1869-1957.   III. 2119
Hellenistic civilisation. 3d ed., rev. by the author and G. T. Griffith. London, E. Arnold [1952] xi, 372 p. maps. 22 cm. *1. Civilization, Greek. 2. Hellenism. I. T.*
DF77.T3 1952   913.38   52-8411

Whibley, Leonard, 1862 or 3-1941, ed.   III. 2120
A companion to Greek studies. 4th ed., rev. New York, Hafner Pub. Co., 1963. xxxviii, 790 p. illus., col. maps (part fold.) 24 cm. *1. Greek philology — Handbooks, manuals, etc. 2. Greece — Antiquities. 3. Greece — Description, geography. 4. Art — Greece. 5. Greek literature — History and criticism. I. T.*
DF77.W5 1963   913.38   63-10743

Bowra, Cecil Maurice, Sir, 1898-1971.   III. 2121
Classical Greece, by C. M. Bowra and the editors of Time-Life Books. New York, Time, inc. [1965] 192 p. illus. (part col.) col. maps, plan, ports. 28 cm. (Great ages of man) *1. Civilization, Greek — Pictorial works. 2. Art — Greece. I. T.*
DF78.B6   913.3803   65-17305

Flacelière, Robert, 1904-   III. 2122
Daily life in Greece at the time of Pericles. Translated from the French by Peter Green. [1st American ed.] New York, Macmillan, 1965. xvi, 310 p. illus., maps. 22 cm. (Daily life series) *1. Greece — Social life and customs. I. T.*
DF78.F5513 1965   913.8   65-13591

DF81 – 90 Politics

Freeman, Kathleen, 1897-   III. 2123
Greek city-states. [1st American ed.] New York, Norton [1950] 274 p. maps. 22 cm. *1. Greece — History, Local. 2. Greece — Politics and government. I. T.*
DF82.F68 1950a   938   50-10299

Meritt, Benjamin Dean, 1899-   III. 2124
The Athenian tribute lists, by Benjamin Dean Meritt, H. T. Wade-Gery, [and] Malcolm Francis McGregor. Cambridge, Mass., Harvard University Press, 1939-   v. illus., plates (part fold.) fold. map in pocket. 35 cm. "Published for the American school of classical studies at Athens." Vol. 2-   have imprint: Princeton, N.J., American School of Classical Studies at Athens. *1. Finance, Public — Athens. 2. Inscriptions, Greek — Athens. I. Wade-Gery, Henry Theodore, 1888- joint author. II. McGregor, Malcolm Francis, 1910- joint author. III. American school of classical studies at Athens. IV. T.*
DF83.M415   938.5   39-6671

Jones, Arnold Hugh Martin, 1904-1970.   III. 2125
The cities of the eastern Roman provinces. Rev. by Michael Avi-Yonah [and others] 2d ed. Oxford [Eng.] Clarendon Press, 1971. xvii, 595 p. fold. maps. 25 cm. *1. Cities and towns, Ancient. 2. Rome — Provinces — Administration. 3. Greece — Colonies. 4. Hellenism. I. T.*
DF85.J6 1971   938/.009/732   74-25037

Jones, Arnold Hugh Martin, 1904-   III. 2126
The Greek city from Alexander to Justinian, by A. H. M. Jones. Oxford, Clarendon Press, 1940. x, 393 p. 26 cm. *1. Cities and towns, Ancient. 2. Cities and towns — Greece. 3. Municipal government — Greece. 4. Municipal government — Rome. I. T.*
DF85.J615   352.038   40-29459

Griffith, Guy Thompson.   III. 2127
The mercenaries of the Hellenistic world, by G. T. Griffith. Hare prize essay, 1933. Cambridge [Eng.] The University Press, 1935. x, 340 p. 22 cm. A revision of the Hare prize essay, "The Greek soldier of fortune". *1. Mercenary troops. 2. Greece — History, Military. I. T.*
DF89.G7   938   35-12619

DF91 – 100 Social Life. Customs

Robinson, Cyril Edward, 1884-   III. 2128
Everyday life in ancient Greece, by C. E. Robinson. Oxford, Clarendon Press, 1933. 159 p. front., illus., double map. 19 cm. *1. Greece — Social life and customs. I. T.*
DF91.R6   913.38   34-2387

Slater, Philip Elliot.   III. 2129
The glory of Hera; Greek mythology and the Greek family, by Philip E. Slater. Boston, Beacon Press [1968] xxvi, 513 p. 24 cm. *1. Family — Greece. 2. Mythology, Greek. 3. Women in Greece. I. T.*
DF93.S55   301.42/7   68-24373

Rider, Bertha Carr.   III. 2130
The Greek house; its history and development from the Neolithic period to

the Hellenistic age, by Bertha Carr Rider. Cambridge [Eng.] University Press, 1916. xii, 272 p. illus., plans 23 cm. *1. Dwellings — Greece. 2. Architecture, Greek — History. 3. Classical antiquities. I. T.*
DF99.R5   16-24977

Kurtz, Donna C.   **III. 2131**
Greek burial customs [by] Donna C. Kurtz and John Boardman. Ithaca, N.Y., Cornell University Press [1971] 384 p. illus., maps, plans. 23 cm. (Aspects of Greek and Roman life) *1. Funeral rites and ceremonies — Greece. I. Boardman, John, 1927- joint author. II. T. (S)*
DF101.K87 1971   393   74-150980   ISBN:0801406439

DF207 – 241 HISTORY
DF209 – 212 Sources.
Historiography

Brown, Truesdell Sparhawk, 1906- ed.   **III. 2132**
Ancient Greece, edited by Truesdell S. Brown. [New York] Free Press of Glencoe [c1965] viii, 262 p. 21 cm. (Sources in Western civilization, 2) *1. Greece — History — Sources. 2. Civilization, Greek. I. T. (S)*
DF209.5.B7   913.38   65-11889

Hill, George Francis, Sir, 1867-1948, comp.   **III. 2133**
Sources for Greek history between the Persian and Peloponnesian wars. New ed. by R. Meiggs and A. Andrewes. Oxford, Clarendon Press, 1951. xx, 426 p. 23 cm. *1. Greece — History — Sources.*
DF209.5.H65 1951   938.04   52-6068

Tod, Marcus Niebuhr, 1878- ed.   **III. 2134**
A selection of Greek historical inscriptions. Oxford, Clarendon Press, 1933-48. 2 v. 23 cm. *1. Inscriptions, Greek. 2. Greece — History — Sources. I. T.*
DF209.5.T5   938   33-15667

Bury, John Bagnell, 1861-1927.   **III. 2135**
The ancient Greek historians. New York, Dover Publications [1958] 281 p. 21 cm. *1. Greece — History — Historiography. I. T.*
DF211.B8 1958   938.007   58-11272

Gomme, Arnold Wycombe.   **III. 2136**
The Greek attitude to poetry and history. Berkeley, University of California Press, 1954. vi, [2], 190 p. front. 24 cm. (Sather classical lectures, v.27) *1. Greece — History — Historiography. I. T. (S)*
DF211.G65   938.007   54-6471

Jacoby, Felix, 1876-   **III. 2137**
Atthis, the local chronicles of ancient Athens. Oxford, Clarendon Press, 1949. vi, 431 p. 25 cm. *1. Greece — History — Historiography. I. T.*
DF211.J3   938.007   50-722

Pearson, Lionel Ignacius Cusack.   **III. 2138**
The local historians of Attica, by Lionel Pearson. Westport, Conn., Greenwood Press [1972] xii, 167 p. 22 cm. Reprint of the 1942 ed., which was issued as no. 11 of Philological monographs. A revision of the author's thesis, Yale, 1939. *1. Greek historians. 2. Greece — Historiography. I. T. (S:Philological monographs, no. 11.)*
DF211.P4 1972   938/.5/0072   71-152621   ISBN:0837160200

Pearson, Lionel Ignacius Cusack.   **III. 2139**
Early Ionian historians, by Lionel Pearson. Oxford, Clarendon, 1939. vi, 240 p. 23 cm. *1. Hecataeus, of Miletus. 2. Xanthus, the Lydian. 3. Charon, of Lampsacus. 4. Hellanicus, of Lesbos. 5. Herodotus. 6. Greek historians. I. T.*
DF212.A2P4   928.8   39-31831

Barber, Godfrey Louis.   **III. 2140**
The historian Ephorus, by G. L. Barber, M.A. The Prince Consort prize essay, 1934. Cambridge [Eng.] The University Press, 1935. xii, 189, [1] p. 19 cm. *1. Ephorus. I. Prince Consort dissertation, 1934. II. T.*
DF212.E7B3   928.8   36-12221

Evans, Joan, 1893-   **III. 2141**
Time and chance; the story of Arthur Evans and his forbears. London, New York [etc.] Longmans, Green [1943] xi, 410 p. front., illus. (facsim.) plates, ports. 22 cm. Genealogical tables on lining-papers. "First published, 1943." *1. Evans, Arthur John, Sir, 1851-1941. 2. Evans family. I. T.*
DF212.E82E8   E43-3098

DF213 – 217 General Works

Bury, John Bagnell, 1861-1927.   **III. 2142**
A history of Greece to the death of Alexander the Great. 3d ed. rev. by Russell Meiggs. London, Macmillan, New York, St. Martin's Press, 1959. 925 p. illus. 20 cm. *1. Greece — History.*
DF214.B97 1959   938   A63-5094

De Sélincourt, Aubrey, 1894-   **III. 2143**
The world of Herodotus. [1st American ed.] Boston, Little, Brown [1963, c1962] 392 p. illus. 22 cm. *1. Greece — History. 2. Civilization, Greek. I. T.*
DF214.D4 1963   938   62-17957

Grote, George, 1794-1871.   **III. 2144**
A history of Greece, by George Grote. London, J. M. Dent; New York, E. P. Dutton [1906] 12 v. 18 cm. (Everyman's library. History) Title within ornamental border; illustrated lining-papers. Introduction by A. D. Lindsay. *1. Greece — History.*
DF214.Gx   A10-1823

Hammond, Nicholas Geoffrey Lemprière.   **III. 2145**
A history of Greece to 322 B.C., by N. G. L. Hammond. 2nd ed. Oxford, Clarendon P., 1967. xxiv, 691 p. front., illus., 13 plates, maps, plans, tables. 22 1/2 cm. *1. Greece — History. I. T.*
DF214.H28 1967   938   67-91674

Haywood, Richard Mansfield, 1905-   **III. 2146**
Ancient Greece and the Near East. New York, McKay Co. [1964] xii, 626 p. illus., maps. 22 cm. *1. Greece — History. I. T.*
DF214.H36   913.38   64-10476

Laistner, Max Ludwig Wolfram, 1890-   **III. 2147**
A history of the Greek world, from 479 to 323 B.C. [3d ed.] London, Methuen; New York, Barnes & Noble [1962] 492 p. illus. 23 cm. (Methuen's history of the Greek and Roman world, 2) *1. Greece — History.*
DF214.L6 1962   938.04   63-663

Robinson, Cyril Edward, 1884-   **III. 2148**
A history of Greece. New York, Barnes & Noble [1957] xii, 480 p. illus., maps, diagrs., tables. 19 cm. Ninth ed. "Chronological tables and summaries": p. 436-470. *1. Greece — History.*
DF214.R6x   A59-4216

Bengtson, Hermann, 1909-   **III. 2149**
Griechische Geschichte von den Anfängen bis in die römische Kaiserzeit. 2., durchgesehene und ergänzte Aufl. München, Beck, 1960. xix, 609. col. maps (part fold.) 25 cm. (Handbuch der Altertumswissenschaft, 3 Abt., 4 T.) In the series this vol. supersedes R. von Pöhlmann's Griechische Geschichte und Quellenkunde published in 1914. *1. Greece — History. I. T. (S)*
DF215.B45 (PA25.H24 Abt. 3, T. 4 1960)   A61-4654

Botsford, George Willis, 1862-1917.   **III. 2150**
Botsford and Robinson's Hellenic history. 5th ed. Rev. by Donald Kagan. [New York] Macmillan [1969] xxi, 533 p. illus., maps, plans. 24 cm. *1. Greece — History. I. Robinson, Charles Alexander, 1900-1965, joint author. II. Kagan, Donald. III. Hellenic history. IV. T.*
DF215.B74 1969   938   69-15096

Cook, Robert Manuel.   **III. 2151**
The Greeks until Alexander. New York, Praeger [1962] 264 p. illus. 22 cm. (Ancient peoples and places, v. 24. Books that matter.) *1. Greece — History. I. T.*
DF215.C6 1962   938   62-8380

Wilcken, Ulrich, 1862-1944.   **III. 2152**
Griechische Geschichte im Rahmen der Alterumsgeschichte. [8. Aufl.] Berlin, Rütten & Loening, 1958. 384 p. illus. 24 cm. *1. Greece — History.*
DF215.W5 1958   58-38626

DF220 – 241 by Period
DF220 – 221 MYTHICAL, MINOAN, MYCENAEAN AGES

Alsop, Joseph Wright, 1910-   **III. 2153**
From the silent earth, a report of the Greek bronze age. Introd. by Maurice Bowra. Photos. by Alison Frantz. [1st ed.] New York, Harper & Row [1964] xviii, 296 p. illus., map (on lining papers) table. 22 cm. *1. Bronze age — Greece. 2. Civilization, Mycenaean. I. T.*
DF220.A43   913.391   64-12666

Burn, Andrew Robert.   **III. 2154**
The world of Hesiod; a study of the Greek Middle Ages, c. 900-700 B.C. [2d

Cottrell, Leonard. III. 2155
Realms of gold; a journey in search of the Mycenaeans. [1st ed.] Greenwich, Conn., New York Graphic Society [1963] 278 p. illus. 22 cm. 1. Mycenae. 2. Greece, Modern — Description and travel — 1951- I. T.
DF220.C6   914.95   63-16278

Desborough, Vincent Robin d'Arba. III. 2156
The last Mycenaeans and their successors; an archaeological survey, c. 1200-c. 1000 B.C. Oxford, Clarendon Press, 1964. xviii, 288 p. 25 plates, map. 29 cm. 1. Mycenae. 2. Civilization, Mycenaean. I. T.
DF220.D45   913.391   64-1295

Dunbabin, Thomas James. III. 2157
The Greeks and their eastern neighbours; studies in the relations between Greece and the countries of the Near East in the eighth and seventh centuries B.C. With a foreword by Sir John Beazley. Edited by John Boardman. London, Society for the Promotion of Hellenic Studies, 1957. 96 p. illus., port., map. 22 cm. (Society for the Promotion of Hellenic Studies [London] Supplementary paper, no. 8) Six lectures delivered at Oxford in 1953-54, collected and prepared for publication as a memorial to the author. "Correction" slip mounted on t.p. 1. Greece — Relations (general) with Asia, Western. 2. Asia, Western — Relations (general) with Greece. I. T. (S)
DF220.D77   938.01   58-1788

Glotz, Gustave, 1862-1935. III. 2158
The Aegean civilization. New York, Barnes & Noble [1968] xvi, 422 p. illus., maps (part col.), plans. 24 cm. (The History of civilization) Reprint of the 1925 ed. Translation of La civilisation égéene. 1. Civilization, Mycenaean. 2. Crete — Antiquities. I. T.
DF220.G63 1968b   913.3/9/1031   68-5610

McDonald, William Andrew, 1913- III. 2159
Progress into the past; the rediscovery of Mycenaean civilization [by] William A. McDonald. New York, Macmillan [1967] xx, 476 p. illus., maps, plans, ports. 24 cm. 1. Civilization, Mycenaean. 2. Greece — Antiquities. I. T.
DF220.M23   913.38/8/03   67-19952

Palmer, Leonard Robert, 1906- III. 2160
Mycenaeans and Minoans; Aegean prehistory in the light of the Linear B tablets [by] Leonard R. Palmer. 2d ed., substantially rev. and enl. New York, Knopf, 1965. 369 p. illus., maps. 22 cm. 1. Civilization, Mycenaean. 2. Crete — Antiquities. I. T.
DF220.P3 1965   913.3918031   64-19093

Thompson, George Derwent. III. 2161
Studies in ancient Greek society. [New ed.] London, Lawrence & Wishart [1954-   v. illus., maps. 23 cm. 1. Civilization Greek. 2. Greece — Social conditions. 3. Bronze age — Greece. I. T.
DF220.T53   938   54-37081

Vermeule, Emily. III. 2162
Greece in the bronze age. Chicago, University of Chicago Press [1964] xix, 406 p. illus., maps, 48 plates. 25 cm. 1. Bronze age — Greece. 2. Civilization, Mycenaean. I. T.
DF220.V4   913.38   64-23427

Webster, Thomas Bertram Lonsdale, 1905- III. 2163
From Mycenae to Homer. New York, Praeger [1959, c1958] 311 p. illus. 23 cm. 1. Homerus. 2. Civilization, Mycenaean. 3. Art, Mycenaean. 4. Greek poetry — History and criticism. I. T.
DF220.W4 1959   913.391   59-8133

DF221 Special Localities

Evans, Arthur John, Sir, 1851-1941. III. 2164
The Palace of Minos; a comparative account of the successive stages of the early Cretan civilization as illustrated by the discoveries at Knossos. New York, Biblo and Tannen, 1964. 4 v. in 6. illus. (part col.) 2 fold. col. maps, plans. 27 cm. Part of illustrative matter folded in pocket, v. 3-6. Index, by Joan Evans, with special sections classified in detail and chronologically arranged, by Sir Arthur Evans. New York, Biblo and Tannen, 1964. vi, 221 p. 27 cm. 1. Crete — Antiquities. 2. Civilization, Greek. I. Evans, Joan, 1893- II. T.
DF221.C8E75 1964   913.3918   63-18048

Hutchinson, Richard Wyatt, 1894- III. 2165
Prehistoric Crete. Baltimore, Penguin Books [1962] 373 p. illus. 18 cm. (Pelican books, A501) 1. Crete — Antiquities. I. T.
DF221.C8H8   913.3918   62-6461

Palmer, Leonard Robert, 1906- III. 2166
On the Knossos tablets: The find-places of the Knossos tablets [by] L. R. Palmer. The date of the Knossos tablets [by] John Boardman. Oxford, Clarendon Press, 1963. xxvi, 251, x, 100 p. illus., plates, facsims., plans. 24 cm. Both works draw on the private notebooks of Sir Arthur Evans, and the daybooks of his assistant, Dr. Donald Mackenzie, which are in the Ashmolean Museum, Oxford. 1. Cnossus, Crete. I. Evans, Arthur John, Sir, 1851-1941. II. Boardman, John, 1927 III. T:The Knossos tablets.
DF221.C8P3   913.3918   64-1888

Pendlebury, John Devitt Stringfellow, 1904-1941. III. 2167
A handbook to the palace of Minos, Knossus, with its dependencies. Foreword: Sir Arthur Evans. Introduction: Sir John Myres, Sir John Forsdyke. London, M. Parrish [1954] 76 p. illus. 23 cm. 1. Crete — Antiquities.
DF221.C8P4x   A55-5631

Platōn, Nikolaos Eleutheriou, 1909- III. 2168
Zakros: the discovery of a lost palace of ancient Crete [by] Nicholas Platon. New York, Scribner [1971] 345 p. illus. (part col.) 26 cm. 1. Zakros site, Crete. I. T.
DF221.C8P586   913.3/9/18   70-123855   ISBN:0684311038

Mylonas, George Emmanuel, 1898- III. 2169
Ancient Mycenae: the capital city of Agamemnon. Princeton, Princeton University Press, 1957. viii, 201 p. plates, maps, plans. 25 cm. (The Page-Barbour lectures, for 1955, at the University of Virginia) 1. Mycenae. (S:Page-Barbour lectures, 1955)
DF221.M9M9   938.01   56-10826

Mylonas, George Emmanuel, 1898- III. 2170
Mycenae and the Mycenaean Age, by George E. Mylonas. Princeton, N.J., Princeton University Press, 1966. xvi, 251 p. illus., maps, plans. 29 cm. 1. Mycenae. 2. Civilization, Mycenaean. I. T.
DF221.M9M93   913.391031   65-17154

Wace, Alan John Bayard, 1879- III. 2171
Mycenae, an archaeological history and guide. Princeton, Princeton University Press, 1949. xviii, 150 p. 110 plates (incl. maps (part fold.)) 29 cm. 1. Mycenae.
DF221.M9W33   913.388   49-10867

Wace, Alan John Bayard, 1879- III. 2172
Prehistoric Thessaly; being some account of recent excavations and explorations in north-eastern Greece from lake Kopais to the borders of Macedonia, by A. J. B. Wace and M. S. Thompson ... Cambridge, University Press, 1912. xv, [1], 272 p. illus. (incl. map, plans) VI col. pl. 31 x 24 cm. 1. Thessaly. 2. Greece — Antiquities. I. Thompson, Maurice Scott, joint author. II. T.
DF221.T4W3   12-11099

Blegen, Carl William, 1887- III. 2173
Troy and the Trojans. New York, Praeger [1963] 240 p. illus., map, plans. 21 cm. (Ancient peoples and places, v.33) 1. Troy.
DF221.T8B55   939.21   63-8040

DF222 – 228   775 – 431 B.C.
ATHENS

Andrewes, Antony, 1910- III. 2174
The Greek tyrants. London, Hutchinson's University Library [1956] 167 p. (p. 165-167 advertisements) map (on lining papers) 20 cm. (Hutchinson's university library: Classical history and literature) 1. Greece — History. 2. Dictators. I. T.
DF222.A6   938   A56-8629

Burn, Andrew Robert. III. 2175
The lyric age of Greece. New York, St Martin's Press, 1960. 422 p. illus. 23 cm. 1. Civilization, Greek. I. T.
DF222.B85   938.02   60-13276

Freeman, Kathleen. III. 2176
The work and life of Solon, with a translation of his poems, by Kathleen Freeman. Cardiff, The University of Wales Press Board; London, H. Milford, 1926. 236 p. 23 cm. 1. Solon. 2. Athens — Politics and government.
DF224.S7F7   27-9448

Woodhouse, William John, 1866-1937. III. 2177
Solon the liberator; a study of the agrarian problem in Attika in the seventh century. New York, Octagon Books, 1965. xvi, 218 p. 21 cm. "Originally published 1938 ... reprinted 1965." 1. Solon. 2. Attica — History. 3. Land tenure — Greece. 4. Peasantry — Greece.
DF224.S7W6 1965   330.9385   65-16783

Burn, Andrew Robert. III. 2178
Persia and the Greeks: the defence of the West, c. 546-478 B.C. New York, St Martin's Press, 1962 [i.e. 1963] xvi, 586 p. maps. 23 cm. 1. Greece — History — Persian Wars, 500-449 B.C. I. T.
DF225.B8   938.03   62-21076

Grundy, George Beardoe, 1861-1948.   **III. 2179**
The great Persian War and its preliminaries; a study of the evidence, literary and topographical. New York, AMS Press [1969] xiii, 591 p. illus., maps (1 fold.) 23 cm. Reprint of the 1901 ed. *1. Greece — History — Persian Wars, 500-449 B.C. I. T.*
DF225.G88 1969   938/.03   71-84875

Hignett, Charles.   **III. 2180**
Xerxes' invasion of Greece. Oxford, Clarendon Press, 1963. xii, 496 p. 8 maps. 23 cm. *1. Greece — History — Persian Wars, 500-449 B.C. I. T.*
DF225.H5   938.03   63-2777

Berve, Helmut, 1896-   **III. 2181**
Miltiades; Studien zur Geschichte des Mannes und seiner Zeit. Berlin, Weidmann, 1937. vi p., 1 l., 101 p. 25 cm. (Hermes. Einzelschriften, hft.2) *1. Miltiades.*
DF226.M5Bx   Ac38-1160

Burn, Andrew Robert.   **III. 2182**
Pericles and Athens. New York, Macmillan, 1949. xxv, 253 p. front., maps (part col.) 18 cm. (Teach yourself history library) *1. Pericles, 499-429 B.C. 2. Athens — History. (S:Teach yourself history library (New York))*
DF227.B8   938.04   49-10369

Robinson, Charles Alexander, 1900-   **III. 2183**
Athens in the Age of Pericles. [1st ed.] Norman, University of Oklahoma Press, [1959] 165 p. 20 cm. (The Centers of civilization series) *1. Athens — History.*
DF227.R6   938.04   59-13472

DF229 – 232   431 – 362 B.C.
PELOPONNESIAN WAR

Thucydides.   **III. 2184**
Complete writings: The Peloponnesian War. The unabridged Crawley translation, with an introd. by John H. Finley, Jr. New York, Modern Library [1951] xxi, 516 p. map. 19 cm. (Modern Library college editions, T51) *1. Greece — History — Peloponnesian War, 431-404 B.C.*
DF229.T5C7 1951   888.2 (938.05)   51-2474

Thucydides.   **III. 2185**
History of the Peloponnesian War. Translated with an introd. by Rex Warner. Melbourne, Baltimore, Penguin Books [1954] 553 p. maps. 18 cm. (Penguin classics, L39) *1. Greece — History — Peloponnesian War, 431-404 B.C. I. Warner, Rex, 1905-*
DF229.T5W3x   A55-10440

Cornford, Francis Macdonald, 1874-1943.   **III. 2186**
Thucydides Mythistoricus. New York, Greenwood Press [1969] xvi, 252 p. 23 cm. Reprint of the 1907 ed. *1. Thucydides. 2. Greece — History — Peloponnesian War, 431-404 B.C. I. T.*
DF229.T6C8 1969   938/.05   69-13866   ISBN:837110556

Finley, John Huston, 1904-   **III. 2187**
Thucydides. [Ann Arbor] University of Michigan Press [1963, c1942] 344 p. maps. 21 cm. (Ann Arbor paperbacks) *1. Thucydides.*
DF229.T6F5x   888   63-14012

Grundy, George Beardoe, 1861-1948.   **III. 2188**
Thucydides and the history of his age. Oxford, Blackwell, 1948. 2 v. illus., maps 22 cm. Vol.1: 2d ed. First published 1911. *1. Thucydides. 2. Greece — History — Peloponnesian War, 431-404 B.C. 3. Greece — Economic conditions. 4. Military art and science — History.*
DF229.T6G7x   A50-819

Kagan, Donald.   **III. 2189**
The outbreak of the Peloponnesian War. Ithaca [N.Y.] Cornell University Press [1969] xvi, 420 p. 24 cm. *1. Greece — History — Peloponnesian War, 431-404 B. C. I. T.*
DF229.2.K3   938/.05   69-18212   ISBN:801405017

Woodhouse, William John, 1866-   **III. 2190**
King Agis of Sparta and his campaign in Arkadia in 418 B.C.; a chapter in the history of the art of war among the Greeks, by W. J. Woodhouse. Oxford, Clarendon Press, 1933. viii, 161 p. 23 cm. English translation of Thucydides' De bello peloponnesiaco, book V, chapters 61-75, followed by the author's interpretation of the events therein described. cf. Pref. *1. Greece — History — Peloponnesian war, B.C. 431-404. 2. Greece — Army. 3. Military art and science — History. I. Thucydides. De bello peloponnesiaco. V. II. T.*
DF229.6.W6   938.05   33-31399

Xenophon.   **III. 2191**
The march up country; a translation of Xenophon's Anabasis [by] W. H. D. Rouse. [1st American ed.] Ann Arbor, University of Michigan Press [1958] xiii, 205 p. map (on lining papers) 21 cm. *1. Cyrus the Younger, d. 401 B.C. 2. Iran — History — Ancient to 640 A.D. I. Rouse, William Henry Denham, 1863-1950, tr. II. T.*
DF231.32.A3 1958   888.3   58-5911

DF233 – 241   339 BC – 476 A.D.

Jaeger, Werner Wilhelm, 1888-1961.   **III. 2192**
Demosthenes: the origin and growth of his policy. New York, Octagon Books, 1963 [c1938] x, 273 p. 24 cm. (Sather classical lectures, v.13) "The translation of this book from the German manuscript has been made by Edward Schouten Robinson." *1. Demosthenes. (S)*
DF233.J313 1963   928.8   63-20891

Burn, Andrew Robert.   **III. 2193**
Alexander the Great and the Hellenistic Empire. New York, Macmillan Co., 1948. xiii, 297 p. port., maps (on lining-papers) 18 cm. (Teach yourself history library) *1. Alexander the Great, 356-323 B.C. 2. Greece — History. (S)*
DF234.B83x   A48-7413

Green, Peter, 1924-   **III. 2194**
Alexander the Great. New York, Praeger Publishers [1970] 272 p. illus. (part col.), geneal. table, maps, ports. 26 cm. *1. Alexander the Great, 356-323 B.C.*
DF234.G68 1970   938/.07/0924   72-100915

Robinson, Charles Alexander, 1900-   **III. 2195**
Alexander the Great; the meeting of East and West in world government and brotherhood. [1st ed.] New York, Dutton, 1947. 252 p. port. 23 cm. Map on lining-papers. *1. Alexander the Great, 356-323 B.C.*
DF234.R65   923.138   47-4203

Robinson, Charles Alexander, 1900-1965.   **III. 2196**
The history of Alexander the Great. Providence, R.I., Brown University, 1953-63. Millwood, N.Y., Kraus Reprint Co., 1967-72. 2 v. 26 cm. Vol. 2 originally published by Brown University Press. Original ed. issued as v. 16 and 26 of Brown University studies. *1. Alexander the Great, 356-323 B.C. I. T. (S:Brown University. Brown University studies, v. 16 [etc.])*
DF234.R663   938/.07/0924 (B)   72-5737

Wilcken, Ulrich, 1862-1944.   **III. 2197**
Alexander the Great. Translated by G. C. Richards. With pref., an introd. to Alexander studies, notes, and bibliography by Eugene N. Borza. New York, W. W. Norton [1967] xxxi, 365 p. map. 20 cm. *1. Alexander the Great, 356-323 B.C. 2. Macedonia — History — Ancient to 168 B.C. I. Borza, Eugene N., ed.*
DF234.W713 1967   938/.07   67-15823

Griffith, Guy Thompson, ed.   **III. 2198**
Alexander the Great: the main problems; edited by G. T. Griffith. Cambridge, Heffer; New York, Barnes & Noble, 1966. xii, 382 p. 22 cm. (Views and controversies about classical antiquity) *1. Alexander The Great, 356-323 B.C. (S)*
DF234.2.G7 1966   930.40924   66-72639

Stark, Freya.   **III. 2199**
Alexander's path, from Caria to Cilicia. London, J. Murray [1958] 283 p. illus. 24 cm. *1. Alexander the Great — Campaigns — Asia Minor. 2. Asia Minor — Description and travel. I. T.*
DF234.37.S8   915.6   59-24

Wheeler, Robert Eric Mortimer, Sir, 1890-   **III. 2200**
Flames over Persepolis, turning-point in history [by] Mortimer Wheeler. New York, Reynal in association with W. Morrow [1968] 180 p. illus. (part col.), maps, plans. 26 cm. *1. Persepolis. 2. Alexander the Great, 356-323 B.C. 3. Greeks in India. I. T.*
DF234.55.W5 1968b   935/.06   68-25488

Cary, Max, 1881-1958.   **III. 2201**
A history of the Greek world, from 323 to 146 B.C. With a new select bibliography by V. Ehrenberg. London, Methuen; New York, Barnes & Noble [1963] xvi, 446 p. maps (part fold.) 23 cm. (Methuen's history of the Greek and Roman world, 3) *1. Greece — History. 2. Hellenism. 3. Civilization, Greek. I. T.*
DF235.C3 1963   65-8802

Macurdy, Grace Harriet.   **III. 2202**
Hellenistic queens; a study of woman-power in Macedonia, Seleucid Syria, and Ptolemaic Egypt, by Grace Harriet Macurdy. Baltimore, Hopkins Press; London, H. Milford, Oxford University Press, 1932. xv, 250 p. 12 pl. 24 cm. (The John Hopkins university studies in archaeology, no. 14) "The publication of this book was made possible by a grant from the Lucy Maynard Salmon fund for research, established at Vassar college, June, 1926." — p. [vii] Errata slip laid in. *1. Macedonia — Queens. 2. Syria — Queens. 3. Egypt — Queens. I. Vassar college. Lucy Maynard Salmon fund for research. II. T. III. T:Woman-power in Macedonia, Seleucid Syria, and Ptolemaic Egypt.*
DF235.3.M3   923.13 (396.3093)   32-7515

Rostovtsev, Mikhail Ivanovich, 1870-1952. III. 2203
The social & economic history of the Hellenistic world, by M. Rostovtzeff. Oxford, The Clarendon press, 1941. 3 v. front., illus., plates (1 col.) ports., plans. 26 cm. Paged continuously. *1. Greece — History. 2. Greece — Social conditions. 3. Greece — Economic conditions. I. T.*
DF235.3.R6   938.08   A41-4669

Walbank, Frank William. III. 2204
Philip V of Macedon, by F. W. Walbank. [Hamden, Conn.] Archon Books, 1967. xii, 387 p. maps, 2 plates. 22 cm. First published 1940. *1. Philip V, King of Macedonia, 237-179 B.C. 2. Macedonia — History — Ancient to 168 B.C. 3. Rome — History — Republic, 265-30 B.C. I. T.*
DF238.9.P5W3 1967   938.108   67-12981

DF251 – 289   LOCAL HISTORY

Cook, John M. III. 2205
The Greeks in Ionia and the East. New York, Praeger, [1963] 268 p. illus. 21 cm. (Ancient peoples and places, v. 31. Books that matter.) *1. Greeks in Asia. I. T.*
DF251.C6   913.392   63-8041

Effenterre, Henri van, 1912- III. 2206
La Crète et le monde grec de Platon à Polybe. Paris, E. de Boccard, 1948. 340 p. illus., fold. maps. 25 cm. (Bibliothèque des écoles françaises d'Athènes et de Rome. [1. sér. (in 8°)] fasc. 163) *1. Crete — History. 2. Civilization, Greek. (S)*
DF261.C8Ex   (D5.B4 fasc. 163)   939.18   49-6932

Willetts, R. F., 1915- III. 2207
Ancient Crete; a social history from early times until the Roman occupation, by R. F. Willetts. London, Routledge and Paul [1965] ix, 197 p. illus., map. 22 cm. (Studies in social history) *1. Crete — History. I. T.*
DF261.C8W49   66-483

Willetts, R. F., 1915- III. 2208
Aristocratic society in ancient Crete. London, Routledge and Paul [1955] xv, 280 p. 22 cm. *1. Crete — Social life and customs. 2. Domestic relations — Crete. 3. Law — Crete. I. T.*
DF261.C8W5 1955   939.18   56-168

Parke, Herbert William, 1903- III. 2209
The Delphic oracle, by H. W. Parke [and] D. E. W. Wormell. Oxford, Blackwell, 1956. 2 v. 23 cm. Revised and enlarged edition of Parke's A history of the Delphic oracle. *1. Delphian oracle. I. Wormell, Donald Ernest Wilson, joint author.*
DF261.D35P3 1956   983.3   A57-3245

Mylonas, George Emmanuel, 1898- III. 2210
Eleusis and the Eleusinian mysteries. Princeton, N.J., Princeton University Press, 1961. xx, 346 p. illus., map. 25 cm. *1. Eleusis. 2. Eleusinian mysteries.*
DF261.E4M88   292.65   61-7421

Drees, Ludwig. III. 2211
Olympia; gods, artists, and athletes. [English translation by Gerald Onn] New York, Praeger [1968] 193 p. illus., maps, 98 plates (part col.) 26 cm. *1. Olympia. 2. Olympic games. 3. Art — Greece.*
DF261.O5D713 1968   913.3/8/8   68-8255

Huxley, George Leonard. III. 2212
Early Sparta. Cambridge, Harvard University Press, 1962. 164 p. map, geneal. tables. 23 cm. *1. Sparta — History. I. T.*
DF261.S8H8   938.9   62-3881

Jones, Arnold Hugh Martin, 1904- III. 2213
Sparta [by] A. H. M. Jones. Cambridge, Harvard University Press, 1967. viii, 189 p. geneal., table, maps. 23 cm. *1. Sparta — History. I. T.*
DF261.S8J6x   938./.9   67-7233

Michell, Humfrey, 1883- III. 2214
Sparta. Cambridge [Eng.] University Press, 1952. 348 p. 23 cm. *1. Sparta.*
DF261.S8M55   938.9   52-8225

Cloché, Paul, 1881- III. 2215
Thèbes de Béotie, des origines à la conquête romaine. Namur, Secrétariat des publications, Facultés universitaires [1952?] 289 p. map. 25 cm. (Bibliothèque de la Faculté de philosophie et lettres de Namur, fasc.13) *1. Thebes, Greece — History. (S)*
DF261.T3C5   A52-10369

Hill, Ida Carleton (Thallon) III. 2216
The ancient city of Athens: its topography and monuments. Chicago, Argonaut, 1969. xi, 258 p. illus., plans. 24 cm. First published 1953. *1. Athens — Antiquities. I. T.*
DF275.H5 1969   913.3/8/5   77-222359

Zimmern, Alfred Eckhard, Sir, 1879- III. 2217
The Greek commonwealth; politics and economics in fifth-century Athens. 5th ed., rev. [London] Oxford University Press [1961] 471 p. illus. 20 cm. (Oxford paperbacks, no. 13) *1. Greece. 2. Greece — Politics and government. 3. Greece — Economic conditions. I. T.*
DF277.Z5 1961   938.5   61-65321

Cloché, Paul, 1881- III. 2218
La démocratie athénienne. Ouvrage publié avec le concours du Centre nationale de la recherche scientifique. [1. éd.] Paris, Presses universitaires de France, 1951. 432 p. 23 cm. *1. Athens — History. 2. Athens — Politics and government. I. T.*
DF285.C58   52-19912

Ferguson, William Scott, 1875-1954. III. 2219
Hellenistic Athens; an historical essay. New York, H. Fertig, 1969. xviii, 487 p. 24 cm. Reprint of the 1911 ed. *1. Athens — History. I. T.*
DF285.F4 1969   938   68-9652

Gomme, Arnold Wycombe. III. 2220
The population of Athens in the fifth and fourth centuries B.C. [by] A. W. Gomme. Oxford, B. Blackwell, 1933. vii, 87 p. fold. map. 22 cm. (Glasgow university publications, XXVIII) *1. Athens — Population. I. T.*
DF289.G6   938.5   33-22738

DF501 – 649   Medieval Greece. Byzantine Empire (323 – 1453)

Baynes, Norman Hepburn, 1877- III. 2221
Byzantine studies and other essays. [London] University of London, Athlone Press, 1955. 392 p. illus. 23 cm. *1. Byzantine studies.*
DF503.B33   938   55-3149

Diehl, Charles, 1859-1944. III. 2222
Byzantine portraits, translated by Harold Bell. New York, Knopf, 1927. vii, 342 p. 23 cm. "Le grand palais de Constantinople, by Jean Ebersolt": folded plan in pocket. "Originally issued as Figures byzantines. Paris: Armand Colin, 1906." *1. Byzantine empire — Civilization. 2. Byzantine empire — Court and Courtiers. 3. Women in the Byzantine empire. I. Bell, Harold Wilmerding, 1885- tr. II. T.*
DF506.D52   27-3732

Hussey, Joan Mervyn. III. 2223
The Byzantine world. New York, Harper [1961] 188 p. illus. 21 cm. (Harper torchbooks, TB1057. The Academy library) *1. Byzantine Empire — Civilization. I. T.*
DF521.H8 1961   61-66665

Miller, Dean A. III. 2224
The Byzantine tradition [b] D. A. Miller. New York, Harper & Row [1966] xvii, 108 p. map. 21 cm. (Major traditions of world civilization) *1. Byzantine Empire — Civilization. I. T. (S)*
DF521.M5   914.9503   66-14169

Rice, David Talbot, 1903- III. 2225
The Byzantines. New York, Praeger [1962] 224 p. illus. 21 cm. (Ancient peoples and places, 27. Books that matter.) *1. Byzantine Empire — Civilization. I. T.*
DF521.R5 1962   949.501   62-15123

Sherrard, Philip. III. 2226
Byzantium, by Philip Sherrard and the editors of Time-Life Books. New York, Inc. [1966] 192 p. illus., maps, ports. 28 cm. (Great ages of man) Some of the illustrative matter is colored. *1. Byzantine Empire — Civilization. I. Time-Life Books. II. T.*
DF521.S4   66-28334

Diehl, Charles, 1859-1944. III. 2227
Byzantium: greatness and decline. Translated from the French by Naomi Walford. With an introd. and bibliography by Peter Charanis. New Brunswick, N.J., Rutgers University Press, 1957. xviii, 366 p. illus., facsims. 25 cm. (Rutgers Byzantine series) *1. Byzantine Empire — History. 2. Byzantine Empire — Civilization. I. T.*
DF531.D42   949.5   57-6223

Runciman, Steven, 1903- III. 2228
Byzantine civilisation, by Steven Runciman. New York, Longmans, Green, 1933. 320 p. 23 cm. *1. Byzantine empire — Civilization. I. T.*
DF531.R8   949.5   33-14676

Norden, Walter, 1876- III. 2229
Das Papsttum und Byzanz; die Trennung der beiden Mächte und das Problem ihrer Wiedervereinigung, bis zum Untergange des byzantinischen Reichs (1453). New York, Franklin [1958] xix, 764 p. 25 cm. Originally published in Berlin in 1903. *1. Orthodox Eastern Church — Relations — Catholic Church. 2. Catholic Church — Relations — Orthodox Eastern Church. 3. Byzantine Empire — History. 4. Papacy — History. I. T.*
DF548.N7 1958   63-6346

Baynes, Norman Hepburn, 1877-1961, ed. III. 2230
Byzantium; an introduction to East Roman civilization, edited by Norman H. Baynes and H. St. L. B. Moss. Oxford, Clarendon Press [1961] 436 p. plates, maps. 20 cm. (Oxford paperbacks, no. 16) *1. Byzantine Empire — Civilization. I. Moss, Henry St. Lawrence Beaufort, joint ed. II. T.*
DF552.B3x   A63-88

Obolensky, Dimitri, 1918- III. 2231
The Byzantine commonwealth; Eastern Europe, 500-1453. New York, Praeger Publishers [1971] xiv, 445 p. illus. 25 cm. (History of civilization) *1. Byzantine Empire. 2. Byzantine Empire — Civilization. I. T.*
DF552.O25 1971b   914.95/03   73-137892

Vasiliev, Alexander Alexandrovich, 1867-1953. III. 2232
History of the Byzantine Empire, 324-1453. 2d English ed., rev.] Madison, University of Wisconsin press, 1952. xi, 846 p. maps, geneal. tables. 26 cm. *1. Byzantine Empire — History.*
DF552.V3 1952   949.5   52-13951

Baynes, Norman Hepburn, 1877- III. 2233
The Byzantine empire, by Norman H. Baynes. New York, Holt [c1926] 256 p. 17 cm. (Home university library of modern knowledge, no. 114) *1. Byzantine empire.*
DF552.5.B3 1926   26-6916

Diehl, Charles, 1859-1944. III. 2234
History of the Byzantine empire, by Charles Diehl. Translated from the French by George B. Ives. Princeton, Princeton University Press, 1925. viii, 198 p. 25 cm. *1. Byzantine empire — History. I. Ives, George Burnham, 1856-1930, tr.*
DF552.5.D55   25-11973

Ostrogorski, Georgije. III. 2235
History of the Byzantine state [by] George Ostrogorsky. Translated from the German by Joan Hussey. With a foreword by Peter Charanis. Rev. ed. New Brunswick, N.J., Rutgers University Press, 1969. xl, 624 p. illus., col. maps. 25 cm. (Rutgers Byzantine series) Translation of Geschichte des byzantinischen Staates. *1. Byzantine Empire — History. I. T.*
DF552.5.O8153 1969   949.5   71-83571   ISBN:813505992

DF553 – 599 EASTERN EMPIRE (323/476 – 1057)

Vasiliev, Alexander Alexandrovich, 1867- III. 2236
Justin the First; an introduction to the epoch of Justinian the Great. Cambridge, Harvard University Press, 1950. viii, 439 p. 25 cm. (Dumbarton Oaks studies, 1) *1. Justinus I, Emperor of the East, 450?-527. (S)*
DF568.V3   949.501   50-7072

Procopius, of Caesarea. III. 2237
History of the wars, Secret history, and Buildings. Newly translated, edited, abridged, and with an introd. by Averil Cameron. New York, Washington Square Press [1967] xlii, 351 p. maps. 18 cm. (The Great histories) *1. Byzantine Empire — History — Justinian I, 525-565. I. Cameron, Averil, ed. II. T.*
DF572.P999 1967   949.5/01   67-28144

Ure, Percy Neville, 1879-1950. III. 2238
Justinian and his age. Harmondsworth, Middlesex, Penguin Books, [1951] 262 p. plates, maps. 18 cm. (Pelican books, A217) *1. Justinianus I, Emperor of the East, 483?-565. 2. Byzantine Empire — History — Justinian I, 527-565.*
DF572.Ux   A52-5006

Bury, John Bagnell, 1861-1927. III. 2239
A history of the Eastern Roman Empire from the fall of Irene to the accession of Basil I, A.D. 802-867. New York, Russell & Russell, 1965. xv, 530 p. 23 cm. "First published in 1912. Reissued 1965." "Continues ... on a larger scale ... [the author's History of the later Roman Empire from Arcadius to Irene." *1. Byzantine Empire — History. I. T.*
DF581.B8 1965   949.502   65-18794

Runciman, Steven. III. 2240
The Emperor Romanus Lecapenus and his reign; a study of tenth-century Byzantium, by Steven Runciman. Cambridge [Eng.] University Press, 1929. vi, 275 p. maps, fold. map, fold. geneal. tab. 23 cm. *1. Romanus I Lecapenus, co-emperor of the East, d. 948. 2. Byzantine empire — History — Constantine VII Porphyrogenitus, 912-959.*
DF593.R8   30-4070

DF600 – 649 1057 – 1453

Miller, William, 1864- III. 2241
The Latins in the Levant; a history of Frankish Greece (1204-1566) By William Miller. With maps. London, J. Murray, 1908. xx, 675 p. 4 maps (3 fold.) 23 cm. *1. Byzantine empire — History. 2. Latin Orient — History. 3. Greece, Medieval — History. I. T.*
DF601.M5   08-33802

Comnena, Anna, b. 1083. III. 2242
The Alexiad of the Princess Anna Comnena, being the history of the reign of her father, Alexius I, Emperor of the Romans, 1081-1118 A.D. Translated by Elizabeth A. S. Dawes. New York, Barnes & Noble [1967] viii, 439 p. 23 cm. Reprint of the 1928 ed. Translation of Alexias. *1. Alexius I Comnenus, Emperior of the East, 1048-1118. 2. Byzantine Empire — History — Alexius I Comnenus, 1081-1118. I. T.*
DF605.C6 1967a   949.5/03/0924 (B)   67-5910

Chronicle of Morea. III. 2243
Crusaders as conquerors: the Chronicle of Morea. Translated from the Greek, with notes and introd., by Harold E. Lurier. New York, Columbia University Press, 1964. 346 p. illus., map. 23 cm. (Records of civilization: sources and studies, no. 69) *1. Achaea (Principality) I. Lurier, Harold E., tr. II. T. (S)*
DF623.C563   949.52   62-9367

Bakalopoulos, Apostolos Euangelou, 1909- III. 2244
Origins of the Greek nation; the Byzantine period, 1204-1461, by Apostolos E. Vacalopoulos. New Brunswick, N.J., Rutgers University Press [1970] xxviii, 401 p. illus., maps. 25 cm. (Rutgers Byzantine series) Revised translation of Historia tou neou Hellēnismou. *1. Greece, Medieval — History. 2. Byzantine Empire — History. 3. Civilization, Greek. I. T. (S)*
DF631.B313 1970   949.504   75-119511   ISBN:0-8135-0659-X

Geanakoplos, Deno John. III. 2245
Emperor Michael Palaeologus and the West, 1258-1282; a study in Byzantine-Latin relations. Cambridge, Harvard University Press, 1959. xii, 434 p. illus., ports., maps, facsims. 24 cm. *1. Michael VIII Palaeologus, Emperor of the East, 1234-1282. 2. Byzantine Empire — Foreign relations.*
DF635.G4   949.504   59-7652

DF701 – 951 Modern Greece

Miller, Henry, 1891- III. 2246
The colossus of Maroussi. [New York, New Directions, 1958, c1941] 244 p. 19 cm. (A New Directions paperbook, no. 75) *1. Greece, Modern — Description and travel. I. T.*
DF726.M63 1958   914.95   58-9511

A Short history of Greece, from early times to 1964, III. 2247
by W. A. Heurtley [and others] Cambridge, University Press, 1965. viii, 202 p. maps. 23 cm. Based on the historical sections of A Handbook of Greece published by the Naval Intelligence Division of the Admiralty. *1. Greece — History. 2. Greece, Medieval — History. 3. Greece, Modern — History. I. Heurtley, W. A.*
DF757.S5   949.5   64-21551

Tsoucalas, Constantine, 1937- III. 2248
The Greek tragedy. Harmondsworth, Penguin, 1969. 208 p. map. 18 cm. (A Penguin special) *1. Greece, Modern — Politics and government. I. T.*
DF785.T86   949.5/07   70-457108   ISBN:140522778

Couloumbis, Theodore A. III. 2249
Greek political reaction to American and NATO influences [by] Theodore A. Couloumbis. New Haven, Yale University Press, 1966. x, 250 p. 25 cm. *1. North Atlantic Treaty Organization — Greece. 2. Greece, Modern — Relations (general) with the U.S. 3. U.S. — Relations (general) with Greece. I. T.*
DF787.U5C6   301.29495073   66-12491

Dakin, Douglas. III. 2250
The unification of Greece, 1770-1923. New York, St. Martin's Press [1972] xiv, 344 p. maps. 25 cm. *1. Greece, Modern — History. I. T.*
DF801.D3   949.5/06   76-187329

Forster, Edward Seymour, 1879-1950. III. 2251
A short history of modern Greece, 1821-1956. 3d ed., rev. and enl. by Douglas Dakin. London, Methuen [1958] 268 p. illus. 23 cm. *1. Greece, Modern — History — 1821-*
DF802.F6x   949.506   60-1923

Miller, William, 1864- III. 2252
A history of the Greek people (1821-1921) by William Miller. With an introduction by G. P. Gooch. London, Methuen [1922] x, 184 p. maps. 20 cm. (Histories of the peoples) *1. Greece, Modern — History — 1821-*
DF803.M5   23-7331

Makrygiannes, Iōannēs, 1797-1864. III. 2253
The memoirs of General Makriyannis, 1797-1864; edited and translated [from the Greek] by H. A. Lidderdale; foreword by C. M. Woodhouse. London, Oxford U.P., 1966. xxi, 234 p. front., 17 plates (incl. ports. maps) 22 1/2 cm. *1. Greece, Modern — History — War of Independence, 1821-1829. 2. Greece, Modern — History — Otho I, 1832-1862.*
DF803.9.M3A313   355.3320924 (B)   66-74119

Woodhouse, Christopher Montague, 1917- III. 2254
The Greek war of independence, its historical setting. London, Hutchinson's University Library [1952] 167 p. illus. 19 cm. (Hutchinson's University Library. History) *1. Greece, Modern — History — War of Independence, 1821-1829. I. T.*
DF805.W6   949.506   52-10008

Petropulos, John Anthony. III. 2255
Politics and statecraft in the kingdom of Greece, 1833-1843. Princeton, N.J., Princeton University Press, 1968. xix, 646 p. 24 cm. *1. Greece, Modern — Politics and government — 19th cent. I. T.*
DF823.P4   329.9/495   66-21837

Xydis, Stephen George. III. 2256
Greece and the Great Powers, 1944-1947; prelude to the "Truman doctrine," by Stephen G. Xydis. Thessaloniki, Institute for Balkan Studies, 1963. xxi, 758 p. illus., ports. 25 cm. (Hetaireia Makedonikōn Spoudōn. Hidryma Meletōn Chersonēsou tou Haimou. Publication no. 60) Errata slip inserted. *1. Greece, Modern — Foreign relations. I. T. (S:Hetaireia Makedonikōn Spoudōn. Hidryma Meletōn Chersonēsou tou Haimou. Ekdoseis, 60)*
DF849.X9   65-83320

Clogg, Richard, 1939- III. 2257
Greece under military rule; edited by Richard Clogg and George Yannopoulos. London, Secker & Warburg [1972] xxii, 272 p. 24 cm. *1. Greece, Modern — Politics and government — 1967- I. Yannopoulos, George, 1938- joint author. II. T.*
DF852.C56   309.1/495/07   73-150404   ISBN:0436102552

Papandreou, Andreas George. III. 2258
Democracy at gunpoint: the Greek front [by] Andreas Papandreou. [1st ed.] Garden City, N.Y., Doubleday, 1970. xv, 365 p. 25 cm. *1. Greece, Modern — Politics and government — 1935- I. T.*
DF852.P34   949.5/07   73-101714

Durrell, Lawrence. III. 2259
Prospero's cell, and Reflections on a marine Venus. New York, Dutton, 1960. 142, 198 p. illus. 21 cm. *1. Corfu — Description and travel. 2. Rhodes — Description and travel. I. Reflections on a marine Venus. II. T.*
DF901.C7D82   914.955   60-12104

Fermor, Patrick Leigh. III. 2260
Mani; travels in the southern Peloponnese. Photos. by Joan Eyres Monsell; front. by John Craxton. New York, Harper [c1958] 320 p. illus. 22 cm. *1. Peloponnesus — Description and travel.*
DF901.P4F45 1958a   914.952   60-7523

DG ITALY
DG11 – 265 Ancient Italy. Rome to 476

Lewis, Naphtali, ed. III. 2261
Roman civilization; selected readings, edited with an introd. and notes, by Naphtali Lewis & Meyer Reinhold. New York, Columbia University Press, 1951-   v. 24 cm. (Records of civilization: sources and studies, no. 45) *1. Rome — Civilization. 2. Rome — History — Sources. I. Reinhold, Meyer, 1909- joint ed. II. T. (S)*
DG13.L4   937   51-14589

Chilver, Guy Edward Farquhar. III. 2262
Cisalpine Gaul; social and economic history from 49 B.C. to the death of Trajan, by G. E. F. Chilver. Oxford, Clarendon Press, 1941. vi, [2], 235, [1] p. 2 fold. maps, diagrs. 25 cm. *1. Gaul, Cisalpine.*
DG51.C5   937.2   41-15357

Dunbabin, Thomas James. III. 2263
The western Greeks; the history of Sicily and South Italy from the foundation of the Greek colonies to 480 B.C., by T. J. Dunbabin. Oxford, Clarendon P., 1968. ix, 504 p. 25 cm. "An early version of this book was in 1937 submitted to All Souls College for examination for fellowship by thesis." *1. Greece — Colonies — Sicily. 2. Magna Grecia — History. I. T.*
DG55.M3D8 1968   913.3/7/8031   77-353250

Woodhead, Arthur Geoffrey. III. 2264
The Greeks in the West. New York, Praeger [1962] 243 p. illus. 21 cm. (Ancient peoples and places, v.28. Books that matter.) *1. Magna Grecia — History. I. T.*
DG55.M3W6   938   62-15539

Gjerstad, Einar, 1897- III. 2265
Early Rome. Lund, C. W. K. Gleerup, 1953-   v. illus. (part col.) 30 cm. (Skrifter utg. af Svenska institutet i Rom. Acta Instituti Romani Regni Sueciae, 4°, XVII:1) *1. Rome (City) — Antiquities. I. T. (S:Svenska institutet i Rom. Skrifter. Acta. Series prima XVII:1)*
DG63.Gx   (DG12.S8 vol. 17)   55-18753

Meiggs, Russell. III. 2266
Roman Ostia. Oxford, Clarendon Press, 1960. xvii, 598 p. illus., 41 plates, maps, plans. 24 cm. *1. Ostia, Italy. I. T.*
DG70.O8M4   937.6   60-2888

DG75 – 109 ANTIQUITIES. CIVILIZATION

Aymard, André. III. 2267
Rome et son empire, par André Aymard et Jeannine Auboyer. [1. éd.] Paris, Presses Universitaires de France, 1954. 793 p. 48 plates, maps, plans. 24 cm. (Histoire générale des civilisations, t.2) *1. Rome — History. 2. Rome — Civilization. 3. Civilization, Oriental. I. Auboyer, Jeannine. (S)*
DG77.A9x   A55-4935

Grimal, Pierre, 1912- III. 2268
The civilization of Rome. Translated by W. S. Maguinness. New York, Simon and Schuster, 1963. 531 p. illus., maps, facsims. 22 cm. *1. Rome — Civilization.*
DG77.G733   913.37   63-11905

Hamilton, Edith, 1867-1963. III. 2269
The Roman way. 1st ed. New York, Norton [c1932] x, 281 p. 22 cm. *1. Latin literature — History and criticism. 2. Rome — Civilization. I. T.*
DG77.H3   870.9   32-28015

Mattingly, Harold, 1884- III. 2270
Roman imperial civilisation. New York, St. Martin's Press, 1957 [i.e. 1958] 312 p. illus. 23 cm. *1. Rome — Civilization. I. T.*
DG77.M38   913.37   58-14525

Sandys, John Edwin, Sir, 1844-1922, ed. III. 2271
A companion to Latin studies, edited by Sir John Edwin Sandys. 3d ed. Cambridge [Eng.] University Press, 1938. xxxv, 891 p. illus. (incl. facsims.) 2 fold. plans. 23 cm. "First edition 1910 ... third edition 1921, reprinted 1925 ... 1938." *1. Latin philology. 2. Rome — Antiquities. 3. Rome — Description, Geography. 4. Art — Rome. 5. Latin literature — History and criticism. I. T.*
DG77.S3 1938   937 (913.37)   39-21366

Carcopino, Jérôme, 1881- III. 2272
Daily life in ancient Rome; the people and the city at the height of the empire, by Jérôme Carcopino. Edited with bibliography and notes by Henry T. Rowell. Translated from the French by E. O. Lorimer. New Haven, Yale University press, 1940. xv, 342 p. front., plates, plan. 25 cm. "Published on the foundation established in memory of Oliver Baty Cunningham of the class of 1917, Yale college." *1. Rome — Social life. and customs. 2. Rome (City) — History. I. Rowell, Henry T., ed. II. Lorimer, Emily (Overend) tr. III. T.*
DG78.C32   937.6   40-34290

Dill, Samuel, Sir, 1844-1924. III. 2273
Roman society from Nero to Marcus Aurelius, by Samuel Dill. [2d ed.] London, Macmillan; New York, Macmillan, 1905. xxii, 639 p. 24 cm. *1. Rome — Social life and customs. 2. Rome — Religion.*
DG78.D58   09-14379

Earl, Donald C.   III. 2274
The moral and political tradition of Rome [by] Donald Earl. Ithaca, N.Y., Cornell University Press [1967] 167 p. 23 cm. (Aspects of Greek and Roman life) *1. Rome — Politics and government. 2. Rome — Moral conditions. I. T. (S)*
DG78.E217   172.0937   67-20630

Friedländer, Ludwig, 1824-1909.   III. 2275
Roman life and manners under the early empire, by Ludwig Friedländer; authorized translation of the 7th enl. and rev. ed. of the Sittengeschichte Roms. London, G. Routledge; New York, E. P. Dutton [1908]-13. 4 v. 21 cm. Vol.1 translated by L. A. Magnus, v.2 by J. H. Freese and L. A. Magnus, v.3 by J. H. Freese, v.4 (Appendices and notes) by A. B. Gough. *1. Rome — Social life and customs. 2. Rome — Civilization. I. Magnus, Leonard Arthur, tr. II. Freese, John Henry, d. 1930, tr. III. Gough, Alfred Bradly, 1872- tr.*
DG78.F82   08-37054

Toynbee, Arnold Joseph, 1889-   III. 2276
Hannibal's legacy; the Hannibalic War's effects on Roman life, by Arnold J. Toynbee. London, New York, Oxford University Press, 1965. 2 v. 8 col. maps (fold. in pockets) 25 cm. *1. Rome — Civilization. I. T.*
DG78.T67   913.3703   65-29826

DG81 – 89 Politics. Military and Naval History

Frank, Tenney, 1876-1939.   III. 2277
Roman imperialism, by Tenney Frank. New York, Macmillan, 1914. xiii, 365 p. 23 cm. *1. Rome — History. 2. Rome — Politics and government. 3. Imperialism.*
DG81.F7   937   14-6613

Taylor, Lily Ross, 1886-   III. 2278
Party politics in the age of Caesar. Berkeley, University of Calif. Press, 1949. viii, 255 p. 24 cm. (Sather classical lectures, v.22) *1. Rome — Politics and government — 265-30 B.C. 2. Political parties — Rome. I. T. (S)*
DG81.T38   937.05   49-2564

Storoni Mazzolani, Lidia.   III. 2279
The idea of the city in Roman thought: from walled city to spiritual commonwealth. Translated by S. O'Donnell. Bloomington, Indiana University Press [1970] 288 p. 23 cm. Translation of L'idea di città nel mondo romano. *1. Rome — Civilization. 2. Cities and towns, Ancient. I. T.*
DG82.S8613   913.37/03   79-108947   ISBN:0253139805

Badian, E.   III. 2280
Foreign clientelae, 264-70 B.C. Oxford, Clarendon Press, 1958. x, 342 p. 25 cm. "This study was ... submitted for the degree of doctor of philosophy." *1. Patron and client. I. T.*
DG83.3.B3   937.04   58-2626

Gelzer, Matthias, 1886-   III. 2281
The Roman nobility. Translated with an introd. by Robin Seager. New York, Barnes & Noble, 1969. xiv, 164 p. 24 cm. Contains the author's The Nobility of the Roman Republic, a translation of Die Nobilität der römischen Republik and his The nobility of the principate, a translation of Die Nobilität der Kaiserzeit. *1. Rome — Nobility. I. Gelzer, Matthias, 1886- The nobility of the principate. Die Nobilität der Kaiserzeit. 1969. II. T.*
DG83.3.G413 1969b   929.7/5   68-59641

Hill, Herbert.   III. 2282
The Roman middle class in the Republican period. Oxford, Blackwell, 1952. xi, 226 p. 22 cm. *1. Equestrian order (Rome) I. T.*
DG83.3.H5   937.02   52-14367

Broughton, Thomas Robert Shannon, 1900-   III. 2283
The magistrates of the Roman Republic, by T. Robert S. Broughton with the collaboration of Marcia L. Patterson. New York, American Philological Association, 1951-52. 2 v. 24 cm. (Philological monographs, no. 15, v.1-2) *1. Rome — Registers. I. T. (S)*
DG83.5.A1B73   937.02   51-6071

Cheesman, George Leonard.   III. 2284
The auxilia of the Roman imperial army, by G. L. Cheesman. Oxford, Clarendon Press, 1914. 192 p. front. 23 cm. *1. Rome — Army. 2. Rome — Colonies. I. T.*
DG89.C5   15-8720

Parker, Henry Michael Denne.   III. 2285
The Roman legions. With a bibliography by G. R. Watson. [Reprinted, with corrections] New York, Barnes & Noble [1958] 296 p. maps. 22 cm. *1. Rome — Army. I. T.*
DG89.Px   A59-8201

Thiel, Johannes Hendrik, 1896-   III. 2286
Studies on the history of Roman sea-power in republican times, by J. H. Thiel. Amsterdam, North-Holland Publishing Company (N. v. Noord-hollandsche uitgevers mij.) 1946. 456 p. 2 illus. 25 cm. "Corrigenda": slip inserted. *1. Rome — History, Naval. 2. Sea-power.*
DG89.T5   937.02   47-682

DG90 – 109 Social Life. Customs

Balsdon, John Percy Vyvian Dacre, 1901-   III. 2287
Roman women: their history and habits. [1st American ed.] New York, John Day Co. [1963] 351 p. illus. 23 cm. *1. Women in Rome. I. T.*
DG91.B3 1963   913.37   63-10219

Toynbee, Jocelyn M. C.   III. 2288
Death and burial in the Roman world [by] J. M. C. Toynbee. Ithaca, N.Y., Cornell University Press [1971] 336 p. illus., plans. 23 cm. (Aspects of Greek and Roman life) *1. Funeral rites and ceremonies, Roman. 2. Rome (City) — Tombs. I. T. (S)*
DG103.T69   393/.0937   77-120603   ISBN:0801405939

DG201 – 365 HISTORY

Laistner, Max Ludwig Wolfram, 1890-   III. 2289
The greater Roman historians. Berkeley, Univ. of California Press, 1947. viii, 196 p. 24 cm. (Sather classical lectures, v.21, 1947) *1. Rome — History — Historiography. 2. Latin historians. I. T. (S)*
DG206.A2L3   937.007   48-5105

Hadas, Moses, 1900-1966, ed. and tr.   III. 2290
A history of Rome, from its origins to 529 A.D., as told by the Roman historians. [1st ed.] Garden City, N.Y., Doubleday, 1956. 305 p. illus. 18 cm. (Doubleday anchor books, A78) *1. Rome — History.*
DG207.A1H3   937   56-7540

Tacitus, Cornelius.   III. 2291
The complete works of Tacitus: The annals. The history. The life of Cnaeus Julius Agricola. Germany and its tribes. A dialogue on oratory. Translated from the Latin by Alfred John Church and William Jackson Brodribb; edited, and with an introduction, by Moses Hadas ... New York, The Modern Library [1942] xxv, [1], 773 p. geneal. tab. 19 cm. (The Modern library of the world's best books) *I. Church, Alfred John, 1829-1912, tr. II. Brodribb, William Jackson, 1829-1905, joint ed. III. Hadas, Moses, 1900- ed.*
DG207.T2C45   878.6   42-36137

Jones, Arnold Hugh Martin, 1904-1970, comp.   III. 2292
A history of Rome through the fifth century, edited by A. H. M. Jones. New York, Walker [1968- v. 24 cm. (Documentary history of Western civilization) *1. Rome — History. I. T.*
DG209.J652   937   68-13332

Mommsen, Theodor, 1817-1903.   III. 2293
The history of Rome. [Translation] Glencoe, Ill., Free Press [1957] 5 v. map. 20 cm. *1. Rome — History.*
DG209.M7444   937   57-7123

Rostovtsev, Mikhail Ivanovich, 1870-   III. 2294
Rome. Translated from the Russian by J. D. Duff. Galaxy book ed. prepared with the assistance of Elias J. Bickerman. New York, Oxford University Press, 1960. 347 p. illus. 21 cm. (A Galaxy book, GB42) Translation of v.2 of Ocherk istorii drevniago mira (romanized form) *1. Rome — History.*
DG209.R653   937   60-15102

Boak, Arthur Edward Romilly, 1888-1962.   III. 2295
A history of Rome to A.D. 565 [by] Arthur E. R. Boak [and] William G. Sinnigen. 5th ed. New York, Macmillan [1965] xv, 576 p. illus., maps (part col.), port. 25 cm. First ed. published in 1921 under title: A history of Rome to 565 A.D. *1. Rome — History. I. Sinnigen, William Gurnee, 1928- joint author. II. T.*
DG210.B6 1965   937   65-11481

Cary, Max, 1881-   III. 2296
A history of Rome down to the reign of Constantine. 2d ed. London, Macmillan; New York, St. Martin's Press, 1954. 820 p. illus. 19 cm. *1. Rome — History.*
DG210.C3 1954   937   55-4171

Starr, Chester G., 1914-   III. 2297
The emergence of Rome as ruler of the Western World. 2d ed. Ithaca, Cornell University Press, 1953. 122 p. illus. 22 cm. (The Development of Western civilization; narrative essays in the history of our tradition from the

time of the ancient Greeks and Hebrews to the present.) 1. Rome — History. I. T.
DG210.S8 1953 937 53-2022

Lintott, Andrew William. III. 2298
Violence in republican Rome, by A. W. Lintott. Oxford, Clarendon P., 1968. xi, 234 p. 23 cm. 1. Rome — History — Republic, 510-30 B.C. 2. Violence — Rome. 3. Criminal law (Roman law) I. T.
DG211.L5 362 78-363006 ISBN:0198142676

DG221 – 365 By Period
DG221 – 225 PRE-ROMAN
ITALY. ETRUSCANS

Bloch, Raymond, 1914- III. 2299
The origins of Rome. New York, Praeger [1960] 212 p. illus., plates, maps. 21 cm. (Ancient peoples and places, 15) 1. Rome — History — Aboriginal and early period.
DG221.B553 937.01 60-8075

Pallottino, Massimo. III. 2300
The Etruscans. Translated from the Italian by J. Cremona. [Harmondsworth, Middlesex] Penguin Books [1955] 295 p. illus. 18 cm. (Pelican books, A310) Translation of Etruscologia. 1. Etruria — History. 2. Civilization, Etruscan. 3. Etruscan language.
DG223.P283 913.375 56-53

Richardson, Emeline Hill. III. 2301
The Etruscans, their art and civilization, by Emeline Richardson. Chicago, University of Chicago Press [1964] xvii, 285 p. illus. 25 cm. 1. Civilization, Etruscan. 2. Art, Etruscan. I. T.
DG223.R5 913.375 64-15817

Vacano, Otto Wilhelm von, 1910- III. 2302
The Etruscans in the ancient world. Translated by Sheila Ann Ogilvie. New York, St Martin's Press, 1960 [i.e. 1961] 195 p. illus. 23 cm. 1. Etrurians. I. T.
DG223.V313 937.5 60-16881

DG231 – 233 753 – 510 B.C.

Heitland, William Emerton, 1847-1935. III. 2303
The Roman Republic. New York, Greenwood Press [1969] 3 v. maps. 24 cm. "First published in 1909." 1. Rome — History — Republic, 510-30 B.C. I. T.
DG231.H4 1969 937/.02 69-13930 ISBN:837120772(v.1)varies

Piganiol, André, 1883- III. 2304
La Conquête romaine ... 5 édition entièrement refondue. Paris, Presses Universitaires de France, 1967. 656 p. maps. 22 cm. (Peuples et civilisations; histoire générale, 3) 1. Rome — History — Republic, 510-30 B.C. 2. Italy — History — Ancient, to 476 A.D. I. T. (S)
DG231.Px (D20.P37 t. 3 1967) 937 67-93437

Scullard, Howard Hayes, 1903- III. 2305
A history of the Roman world from 753 to 146 B.C., by Howard H. Scullard. London, Methuen, 1969. xiv, 480 p. maps. 22 cm. (Methuen's history of the Greek and Roman world, 4. University paperbacks, UP301.) "Distributed in the U.S.A. by Barnes & Noble." 1. Rome — History — Kings, 753-510 B.C. 2. Rome — History — Republic, 510-30 B.C. I. T.
DG231.S35 1969 913.3/7/031 70-384646 ISBN:416436609

Adcock, Frank Ezra, Sir, 1886- III. 2306
The Roman art of war under the republic. New York, Barnes & Noble, 1960. 140 p. 22 cm. (Martin classical lectures, v.8) 1. Rome — Army. 2. Military art and science — History. 3. Rome — Navy. I. T. (S)
DG231.3.Ax (PA25.M3 vol. 8 1960) 355.0937 60-3785

Badian, E., ed. III. 2307
Studies in Greek and Roman history. New York, Barnes & Noble, 1964. viii, 290 p. 22 cm. 1. Alexander the Great, 356-323 B.C. 2. Rome — History — Addresses, essays, lectures. I. T.
DG231.3.B3 937 64-3632

Cowell, Frank Richard, 1897- III. 2308
Cicero and the Roman Republic; with a foreword by Allan Nevins, 56 illus. in photogravure and 15 isotype charts in colour. New York, Chanticleer Press [1948] xvii, 306 p. plates, ports., maps (part col.) diagrs. 23 cm. (The Measure of the ages) 1. Rome — Civilization. 2. Rome — History — Republic, 510-30 B.C. 3. Cicero, Marcus Tullius — Contemporary Rome.
DG231.3.C6 937.05 48-9161

DG235 – 269 REPUBLIC
(509 – 27 B.C.)

Errington, Robert Malcolm. III. 2309
The dawn of empire: Rome's rise to world power, by R. M. Errington. Ithaca, N.Y., Cornell University Press [1972] x, 318 p. maps. 23 cm. 1. Rome — History — Republic, 265-30 B.C. I. T.
DG241.E77 1972 937/.02 75-176296 ISBN:0801406897

Dorey, Thomas Alan. III. 2310
Rome against Carthage [by] T. A. Dorey and D. R. Dudley. [1st ed. in the U.S.A.] Garden City, N.Y., Doubleday, 1972 [c1971] xviii, 205 p. illus. 22 cm. 1. Rome — History — Republic, 265-30 B.C. 2. Carthage — History. 3. Punic wars. I. Dudley, Donald Reynolds, joint author. II. T.
DG242.D67 937/.04 76-157585

De Beer, Gavin Rylands, Sir, 1899- III. 2311
Hannibal: challenging Rome's supremacy [by] Sir Gavin de Beer. New York, Viking Press [1969] 319 p. illus. (part col.), facsims., maps, ports. 25 cm. (A Studio book) London ed. has sub-title: The struggle for power in the Mediterranean. 1. Hannibal.
DG249.D37 1969 939/.73/0924 (B) 75-80030

Scullard, Howard Hayes, 1903- III. 2312
Roman politics, 220-150 B.C. Oxford, Clarendon Press, 1951. xvi, 325 p. front. 24 cm. 1. Rome — Politics and government — 265-30 B.C. I. T.
DG250.S3 937.04 51-10700

Astin, A. E. III. 2313
Scipio Aemilianus, by A. E. Astin. Oxford, Clarendon P., 1967. xiii, 374 p. diagr. 24 1/2 cm. 1. Scipio Aemilianus Africanus, Publius Cornelius, minor.
DG253.S4A8 937/.05/0924 (B) 67-82263

Greenidge, Abel Hendy Jones, 1865-1906. III. 2314
Sources for Roman history, 133-70 B.C., collected and arr. by A. H. J. Greenidge and A. M. Clay. 2d ed., rev. by E. W. Gray. Oxford, Clarendon Press, 1960. viii, 318 p. 19 cm. 1. Rome — History — Republic, 510-30 B.C. — Sources. I. Clay, A. M., joint author.
DG254.G8 1960 937.02 60-2011

Marsh, Frank Burr, 1880- III. 2315
The founding of the Roman empire, by Frank Burr Marsh. Austin, University of Texas, 1922. vii, 329 p. 23 cm. 1. Rome — History — Republic, 265-30 B.C. 2. Rome — History — Augustus, 30 B.C.-14 A.D. I. T.
DG254.M3 22-23925

Marsh, Frank Burr, 1880-1940. III. 2316
A history of the Roman world from 146 to 30 B.C. Rev. with additional notes by H. H. Scullard. [3d ed.] London, Methuen; New York, Barnes & Noble [1963] 472 p. illus. 23 cm. (Methuen's history of the Greek and Roman world, 5) 1. Rome — History — Republic, 265-30 B.C.
DG254.M34 1963 937.05 63-3016

Scullard, Howard Hayes, 1903- III. 2317
From the Gracchi to Nero: a history of Rome from 133 B.C. to A.D. 68, by H. H. Scullard. 3rd ed. London, Methuen, 1970. xv, 484 p. map. 22 cm. "Distributed in the U.S.A. by Barnes and Noble." 1. Rome — History — Republic, 265-30 B.C. 2. Rome — History — The five Julii, 30 B.C.-68 A.D. I. T.
DG254.S35 1970 937/.05 71-560931 ISBN:0416077501

Syme, Ronald, Sir, 1903- III. 2318
The Roman revolution. [London] Oxford University Press [1960] xi, 568 p. geneal. tables. 20 cm. (Oxford paperbacks, no. 1) 1. Rome — Politics and government — 265-30 B.C. 2. Rome — Politics and government — 30 B.C.-68 A.D. I. T.
DG254.S9 1960 937.05 60-51198

Badian, E. III. 2319
Roman imperialism in the late republic, by E. Badian. [2d ed.] Ithaca, N.Y., Cornell University Press [1968] xii, 117 p. 22 cm. 1. Rome — Politics and government — 265-30 B.C. 2. Imperialism. I. T.
DG254.2.B3 1968b 937/.6/04 68-8998

Seager, Robin, comp. III. 2320
The crisis of the Roman republic: studies in political and social history; selected and introduced by Robin Seager. Cambridge, Heffer; New York, Barnes & Noble, 1969. xiii, 218 p. fold. plate. 23 cm. (Views and controversies about classical antiquity) Includes the pagination of the original articles. 1. Rome — Politics and government — 265-30 B.C. I. T. (S)
DG254.2.S4 309.1/37 73-427018 ISBN:852700245

Hardy, Ernest George, 1852-1925. III. 2321
The Catilinarian conspiracy in its context: a re-study of the evidence, by E. G. Hardy ... Oxford, B. Blackwell, 1924. 4 p. l., 115, [1] p. 22 cm. 1. Rome — History — Republic — Conspiracy of Catilina, B.C. 65-62.
DG259.H3 25-6237

Hutchinson, Lester, 1904-   **III. 2322**
The conspiracy of Catiline. New York, Barnes & Noble [1967] 182 p. 23 cm. *1. Catilina, Lucius Sergius, 108 (ca.)-62 B.C. 2. Rome — History — Conspiracy of Catiline, 65-62 B.C. I. T.*
DG259.H8 1967   937/.05   67-5533

Dorey, T A , ed.   **III. 2323**
Cicero. Chapters by H. H. Scullard [and others] Edited by T. A. Dorey. New York, Basic Books [1965] xii, 218 p. 22 cm. (Studies in Latin literature and its influence) *1. Cicero, Marcus Tullius.*
DG260.C5D6   928.7   65-10506

Hadas, Moses, 1900-1966.   **III. 2324**
Sextus Pompey, by Moses Hadas. New York, Columbia University Press, 1930. vii, 181 p. 24 cm. Published also as thesis (Ph.D.) Columbia university. *1. Pompeius Magnus, Sex.*
DG260.P3H3 1930a   923.237   30-28698

Gelzer, Matthias, 1886-   **III. 2325**
Caesar: politician and statesman. Translated by Peter Needham. Cambridge, Harvard University Press, 1968. viii, 359 p. map, ports. 23 cm. *1. Caesar, C. Julius. 2. Rome — History — Republic, 265-30 B.C.*
DG261.G414 1968   937/.05/0924 (B)   68-4657

Holmes, Thomas Rice Edwards, 1855-1933.   **III. 2326**
The architect of the Roman empire, by T. Rice Holmes. Oxford, Clarendon Press, 1928-31. 2 v. fold. maps. 23 cm. "Index of modern commentators": v.1, p. [284]-285; v.2, p. 191-192. *1. Augustus, emperor of Rome, 63 B.C.-14 A.D. 2. Rome — History — Augustus, 30 B.C.-14 A.D. 3. Rome — History — Republic, 263-30 B.C. I. T.*
DG268.H6   937.05   28-18233

DG270 – 365 EMPIRE
(27 B.C. – 476 A.D.)

Rostovtsev, Mikhail Ivanovich, 1870-   **III. 2327**
The social and economic history of the Roman Empire. 2d ed. rev. by P. M. Fraser. Oxford, Clarendon Press, 1957. 2 v. (xxxi, 847 p.) illus., ports. 25 cm. *1. Rome — History — Empire, 30 B.C.-476 A.D. 2. Rome — Social conditions. 3. Rome — Economic conditions. I. T.*
DG271.R6 1957   937.06   58-362

Starr, Chester G., 1914-   **III. 2328**
Civilization and the Caesars; the intellectual revolution in the Roman Empire. Ithaca, N.Y., Cornell University Press [1954] xiv, 413 p. illus., ports. 25 cm. *1. Rome — Civilization. I. T.*
DG272.S8   937.06   54-13378

Salmon, Edward Togo.   **III. 2329**
A history of the Roman world from 30 B.C. to A.D. 138, by Edward T. Salmon. 6th ed. London, Methuen, 1968. xv, 367 p. table, 5 maps. 23 cm. (Methuen's history of the Greek and Roman world, 6) *1. Rome — History — Empire, 30 B.C.-284 A.D. I. T.*
DG276.S26 1968   937/.07   73-355498   ISBN:0416107109

Suetonius Tranquillus, C.   **III. 2330**
The twelve Caesars. Translated by Robert Graves. [Harmondsworth, Middlesex, Baltimore] Penguin Books [1957] 315 p. illus. 19 cm. (The Penguin classics, L72) *1. Roman emperors. 2. Rome — History — Empire, 30 B.C.-284 A.D. I. T.*
DG277.S7T5 1957   937.07 (878.7)   57-9665

Bowersock, Glen Warren.   **III. 2331**
Augustus and the Greek world [by] G. W. Bowersock. Oxford [Eng.] Clarendon Press, 1965. xii, 176 p. 23 cm. *1. Rome — History — Augustus, 30 B.C.-14 A.D. 2. Rome — Relations (general) with Greece. 3. Greece — Relations (general) with Rome. I. T.*
DG279.B68   65-6502

Charles-Picard, Gilbert.   **III. 2332**
Augustus and Nero; the secret of empire. Translated from the French by Len Ortzen. New York, T. Y. Crowell Co. [1966, c1965] xviii, 190 p. 22 cm. *1. Augustus, Emperor of Rome, 63 B.C.-14 A.D. 2. Nero, Emperor of Rome, 37-68. I. T.*
DG279.C483   937.07   65-12832

Rowell, Henry Thompson.   **III. 2333**
Rome in the Augustan Age. [1st ed.] Norman, University of Oklahoma Press [1962] 242 p. illus. 20 cm. (The Centers of civilization series, 5) *1. Augustus, Emperor of Rome, 63 B.C.-14 A.D. 2. Rome — Civilization. I. T.*
DG279.R63   937.07   62-11377

Marsh, Frank Burr, 1880-1940.   **III. 2334**
The reign of Tiberius. New York, Barnes & Noble [1959] vi, 335 p. 22 cm. *1. Tiberius, Emperor of Rome, 42 B.C.-37 A.D. 2. Rome — History — Tiberius, 14-37. 3. Rome — History — Augustus, 30 B.C.-14 A.D. I. T.*
DG282.Mx   937.07   61-19842

Smith, Charles Edward, 1905-1959.   **III. 2335**
Tiberius and the Roman Empire. Port Washington, N.Y., Kennikat Press [1972, c1942] v, 281 p. 22 cm. *1. Rome — History — Tiberius, 14-37. I. T.*
DG282.S55 1972   937/.07   74-159060   ISBN:0804616833

Balsdon, John Percy Vyvian Dacre, 1901-   **III. 2336**
The Emperor Gaius (Caligula) by J. P. V. D. Balsdon ... Oxford, The Clarendon Press, 1934. xix, 243, [1] p. fold. geneal. tab. 20 cm. *1. Caligula, emperor of Rome, 12-41. I. T.*
DG283.B3   937.07   35-1068

Burn, Andrew Robert.   **III. 2337**
Agricola and Roman Britain. London, English Universities Press [1953] 182 p. illus. 19 cm. (Teach yourself history library) *1. Agricola, Cn. Julius, 37-93. 2. Gt. Brit. — History — Roman period.*
DG291.7.A2B8   923.537   54-1809

DG311 – 365 Decline and Fall (284 – 476)

Bury, John Bagnell, 1861-1927.   **III. 2338**
History of the later Roman Empire from the death of Theodosius I. to the death of Justinian. New York, Dover Publications [1958] 2 v. maps. 21 cm. "An unabridged and unaltered republication of the first edition." *1. Rome — History — Empire, 284-476. 2. Byzantine Empire — History.*
DG311.B98 1958   937.08   58-11273

Gibbon, Edward, 1737-1794.   **III. 2339**
The history of the decline & fall of the Roman empire, by Edward Gibbon, illustrated from the etchings by Gian Battista Piranesi. The text edited by J. B. Bury, with the notes by Mr. Gibbon, and the introduction and the index as prepared by Professor Bury; also with a letter to the reader from Philip Guedalla. New York, The Heritage press [1946] 3 v. front., plates, maps. 24 cm. Paged continuously. Part of the illustrative matter is folded. *1. Rome — History — Empire, B.C. 30-A.D. 476. 2. Byzantine empire — History. I. Bury, John Bagnell, 1861-1927, ed. II. Piranesi, Giovanni Battista, 1720-1778, illus.*
DG311.G56 1946   940.1   46-6725

Bond, Harold L.   **III. 2340**
The literary art of Edward Gibbon. Oxford, Clarendon Press, 1960. 167 p. 22 cm. "This study was originally prepared as a dissertation for the Ph.D. degree at Harvard ... [and] has been extensively revised." *1. Gibbon, Edward, 1737-1794. The history of the decline and fall of the Roman Empire. I. T.*
DG311.G6B6   937   60-2049

Jordan, David P., 1939-   **III. 2341**
Gibbon and his Roman Empire [by] David P. Jordan. Urbana, University of Illinois Press [1971] xv, 245 p. illus. 24 cm. *1. Gibbon, Edward, 1737-1794. The history of the decline and fall of the Roman Empire. I. T.*
DG311.G6J67   937.06   78-141515   ISBN:0252001524

Haywood, Richard Mansfield, 1905-   **III. 2342**
The myth of Rome's fall. New York, Crowell [1958] 178 p. illus. 21 cm. *1. Rome — History — Empire, 284-476. I. T.*
DG311.H37   937.08   58-12290

Jones, Arnold Hugh Martin, 1904-   **III. 2343**
The later Roman Empire, 284-602; a social economic and administrative survey by A. H. M. Jones. [1st American ed.] Norman, University of Oklahoma Press [1964] 2 v. (xv, 1518 p.) 7 fold. maps. 25 cm. *1. Rome — History — Empire, 284-476. 2. Byzantine Empire — History. I. T.*
DG311.J6 1964   913.7   64-20762

Jones, Arnold Hugh Martin, 1904-   **III. 2344**
The decline of the ancient world [by] A. H. M. Jones. New York, Holt, Rinehart and Winston [1966] viii, 414 p. 3 fold. maps. 22 cm. (A General history of Europe) *1. Rome — History — Empire, 284-476. 2. Byzantine Empire — History. I. T.*
DG311.J62 1966a   937.08   66-15446

Lot, Ferdinand, 1866-1952.   **III. 2345**
The end of the ancient world and the beginnings of the Middle Ages. [Translated by Philip Leon and Mariette Leon] New York, Barnes & Noble [1966] xxvi, 454 p. plates, 3 fold. maps. 25 cm. ([The History of Civilization]) *1. Europe — History — 392-814. 2. Civilization, Medieval. I. T. (S:The history of civilization (New York))*
DG311.L65 1966   940.1   66-5248

Boak, Arthur Edward Romilly, 1888-   **III. 2346**
Manpower shortage and the fall of the Roman Empire in the West. Ann Arbor, University of Michigan Press, 1955. vi, 169 p. map (on lining papers) 21 cm. (The Jerome lectures, 3d ser.) *1. Rome — Population. 2. Rome — History — Empire, 284-476. I. T. (S)*
DG312.B58   937.08   55-14610

Burckhardt, Jakob Christoph, 1818-1897.   **III. 2347**
The age of Constantine the Great; tr. by Moses Hadas. New York, Pantheon

Books [1949] 400 p. map (on lining-paper) geneal. table. 22 cm. *1. Rome — Civilization. 2. Rome — History — Empire, 284-476. I. T.*
DG315.B923   937.08   49-8918

MacMullen, Ramsay, 1928-   **III. 2348**
Constantine. New York, Dial Press, 1969. vi, 263 p. illus., map, ports. 22 cm. (Crosscurrents in world history) *1. Constantinus I, the Great, Emperor of Rome, d. 337.*
DG315.M3   937/.08/0924 (B)   77-91117

Alföldi, András, 1895-   **III. 2349**
A conflict of ideas in the late Roman Empire; the clash between the Senate and Valentinian I. Translated by Harold Mattingly. Oxford, Clarendon Press, 1952. vi, 151 p. 25 cm. *1. Valentinianus I, Emperor of Rome, 321-375. 2. Rome. Senate. 3. Rome — Civilization. I. T.*
DG319.A6   937.03   52-7543

Kaegi, Walter Emil.   **III. 2350**
Byzantium and the decline of Rome. Princeton, N.J., Princeton University Press, 1968. xi, 289 p. illus. 23 cm. A revision of the author's thesis, Harvard. *1. Rome — History — Empire — 284-476. 2. Byzantine Empire — Relations (general) with Rome. 3. Rome — Relations (general) with the Byzantine Empire. I. T.*
DG319.K3   937/.09   67-21026

DG401 – 999   Medieval and Modern Italy (476 –

Cole, John P., 1928-   **III. 2351**
Italy; an introductory geography, by J. P. Cole. New York, Praeger [1966] 271 p. maps. 21 cm. (Praeger introductory geographies) First published in London in 1964. *1. Italy.*
DG417.C6 1966   914.50392   66-17364

Olschki, Leonardo, 1885-   **III. 2352**
The genius of Italy. Ithaca, N.Y., Cornell University Press [1954 c1949] 481 p. 22 cm. *1. Italy — Civilization, — History. I. T.*
DG441.O55x   914.5   54-12760

Sforza, Carlo, conte, 1872-   **III. 2353**
Italy and Italians; tr. by Edward Hutton. [1st American ed.] New York, E. P. Dutton, 1949. ix, 165 p. 23 cm. *1. Italy — Civilization. 2. National characteristics, Italian. I. Hutton, Edward, 1875- tr. II. T.*
DG441.S428 1949   914.5   49-8837

DG461 – 579   HISTORY

Mack Smith, Denis, 1920-   **III. 2354**
Italy; a modern history. New ed. rev. and enl. Ann Arbor, University of Michigan Press [1969] xi, 542, xxx p. maps. 25 cm. (The University of Michigan history of the modern world) *1. Italy — History. (S:Michigan. University. The University of Michigan history of the modern world)*
DG467.M3 1969   945   69-15851

Salvatorelli, Luigi, 1886-   **III. 2355**
A concise history of Italy from prehistoric times to our own day; translated by Bernard Miall. London, Allen & Unwin [1940] 688 p. 24 cm. "The Italian original 'Sommario della storia d'Italia' was first published in Turin in 1938. First published in English in 1940." *1. Italy — History. I. Miall, Bernard, tr. II. T.*
DG467.S32 1940a   945   40-10737

Trevelyan, Janet Penrose (Ward) 1879-   **III. 2356**
A short history of the Italian people, from the barbarian invasions to the present day. Rev. [i.e. 4th] ed. with an epilogue by D. Mack Smith and a foreword by G. M. Trevelyan. London, Allen & Unwin [1956] 425 p. illus. 23 cm. *1. Italy — History. I. T.*
DG468.T7 1956   945   56-3772

Cassels, Alan, 1929-   **III. 2357**
Mussolini's early diplomacy. Princeton, N.J., Princeton University Press, 1970. xvii, 425 p. map. 23 cm. *1. Italy — Politics and government — 1922-1945. 2. Italy — Foreign relations — 1922-1945. I. T.*
DG498.C27   327.45   72-90944   ISBN:691051798

Kogan, Norman.   **III. 2358**
Italy and the Allies. Cambridge, Harvard University Press, 1956. 246 p. illus. 22 cm. *1. Italy — Foreign relations — 20th cent. 2. World War, 1939-1945 — Italy. I. T.*
DG498.K6   327.45   56-11282

Diggins, John P.   **III. 2359**
Mussolini and fascism; the view from America [by] John P. Diggins. Princeton, N.J., Princeton University Press [1972] xx, 524 p. illus. 25 cm. *1. Italy — Foreign opinion, American. 2. Fascism — Italy. 3. Italians in the United States. 4. Mussolini, Benito, 1883-1945. I. T.*
DG499.U5D5   914.5/03/91   78-153845   ISBN:0691046042

DG500 – 579   By Period

DG500 – 549 MEDIEVAL TO 1815

Pullan, Brian S.   **III. 2360**
A history of early Renaissance Italy: from the mid-thirteenth to the mid-fifteenth century [by] Brian Pullan. New York, St. Martin's Press [1973, c1972] 386 p. maps. 23 cm. *1. Italy — History — 1268-1492. 2. Italy — Civilization. I. T.*
DG530.P84 1973b   914.5/03/5   72-93030

Burckhardt, Jakob Christoph, 1818-1897.   **III. 2361**
The civilization of the Renaissance in Italy. [Translation by S. G. C. Middlemore] Introd. by Benjamin Nelson and Charles Trinkaus. New York, Harper [1958] 2 v. illus., ports. 21 cm. (Harper torchbooks, TB40-41) *1. Renaissance — Italy. 2. Italy — Civilization. I. T.*
DG533.B85 1958   945.05   58-10149

Garin, Eugenio, 1909-   **III. 2362**
Italian humanism; philosophy and civic life in the Renaissance. Translated by Peter Munz. New York, Harper & Row [1965] xxiv, 227 p. 23 cm. *1. Renaissance — Italy. I. T.*
DG533.G323 1965   195   66-10236

Hay, Denys.   **III. 2363**
The Italian Renaissance in its historical background. Cambridge [Eng.] University Press, 1961. 217 p. illus. 22 cm. (The Wiles lectures, 1960) *1. Renaissance — Italy. I. T.*
DG533.H39   945.05   61-65683

Horizon (New York, 1958-)   **III. 2364**
The Horizon book of the Renaissance, by the editors of Horizon magazine. Editor in charge: Richard M. Ketchum. Author: J. H. Plumb. With biographical essays by Morris Bishop [and others] New York, American Heritage Pub. Co.; book trade distribution by Doubleday [1961] 431 p. illus. (part col.) ports., col. map. 31 cm. *1. Renaissance — Italy. 2. Art — Italy. I. Ketchum, Richard M., 1922- ed. II. Plumb, John Harold, 1911-*
DG533.H6   945.05   61-11489

Jacob, Ernest Fraser, 1894- ed.   **III. 2365**
Italian Renaissance studies; a tribute to the late Cecilia M. Ady. New York, Barnes & Noble, 1960. 507 p. illus., port. 23 cm. *1. Ady, Cecilia Mary, 1881-1958. 2. Renaissance — Italy. I. T.*
DG533.J3 1960   945.05   60-50856

Symonds, John Addington, 1840-1893.   **III. 2366**
Renaissance in Italy, by John Addington Symonds. [1st Modern Library ed.] New York, Modern Library [1935] 2 v. 21 cm. *1. Catholic church — History. 2. Renaissance — Italy. 3. Italy — History. 4. Humanism. 5. Art, Italian. 6. Italian literature — History and criticism. I. T.*
DG533.S945 1935   945.05   35-27141

Bowsky, William M.   **III. 2367**
Henry VII in Italy; the conflict of empire and city-state, 1310-1313. Lincoln, University of Nebraska Press, 1960. xii, 301 p. plates, map (on lining papers) 24 cm. *1. Heinrich VII, Emperor of Germany, 1269?-1313. 2. Italy — History — 1268-1492. I. T.*
DG535.B6   945.05   60-7325

Baron, Hans, 1900-   **III. 2368**
The crisis of the early Italian Renaissance; civic humanism and republican liberty in an age of classicism and tyranny. Rev. 1 vol. ed. with an epilogue. Princeton, N.J., Princeton University Press, 1966. xviii, 584 p. illus. 21 cm. *1. Italy — Politics and government — 1268-1559. 2. Humanism. 3. Renaissance — Italy. I. T.*
DG537.B37 1966   945.05   66-10549

Vespasiano da Bisticci, Fiorentino, 1421-1498.   **III. 2369**
Renaissance princes, popes, and prelates; the Vespasiano memoirs, lives of illustrious men of the xvth century. Translated by William George and Emily Waters. Introd. to the Torchbook ed. by Myron P. Gilmore. New York, Harper & Row [1963] xvi, 475 p. illus., ports. 21 cm. (Harper torchbooks. The Academy library) *1. Italy — Biography. I. T. II. T:The Vespasiano memoirs.*
DG537.8.A1V6 1963   920.045   64-3339

Noether, Emiliana Pasca.   **III. 2370**
Seeds of Italian nationalism, 1700-1815. New York, AMS Press [1969] 202 p. 23 cm. (Columbia University studies in the social sciences, 570) Reprint of the 1951 ed., issued also as thesis, Columbia University. *1. Italy — Politics and government. 2. Nationalism — Italy. I. T. (S:Columbia studies in the social sciences, 570)*
DG545.N6 1969   320.1/58/0945   79-94926

DG551 – 759   1815 –

Albrecht-Carrié, René, 1904-   **III. 2371**
Italy from Napoleon to Mussolini. New York, Columbia University Press, 1950. xiii, 314 p. 24 cm. *1. Italy — History — 1815-1870. 2. Italy — History — 1870-1915. 3. Italy — History — 1914-1945. I. T.*
DG551.A6   945.08   49-50178

Berkeley, George Fitz-Hardinge, 1870-   **III. 2372**
Italy in the making ... By G. F.-H. Berkeley. Cambridge [Eng.] The University Press, 1932-[40] 3 v. fronts. (port.) maps (part fold.) 22 cm. Vols.2- : By G. F.-H. & J. Berkeley. *1. Italy — History — 1815-1870. I. Berkeley, Joan (Weld) II. T.*
DG551.B4   945.08   33-7256

DG552 – 554   Risorgimento
(1848 – 1871)

King, Bolton, 1860-   **III. 2373**
A history of Italian unity, being a political history of Italy from 1814 to 1871. New York, Russell & Russell [1967] 2 v. maps. 23 cm. Reprint of the rev. ed. of 1924. *1. Italy — History — 1815-1870. I. T.*
DG552.K52 1967   945/.08   66-24716

Mack Smith, Denis, 1920- comp.   **III. 2374**
The making of Italy, 1796-1870. New York, Walker [1968] viii, 428 p. maps. 24 cm. (Documentary history of Western civilization) *1. Italy — History — 19th century — Sources. I. T.*
DG552.M26   945/.08/08   68-13331

Grew, Raymond.   **III. 2375**
A sterner plan for Italian unity; the Italian National Society in the Risorgimento. Princeton, N.J., Princeton University Press, 1963. xiii, 500 p. fold. map. 25 cm. *1. Società nazionale italiana. 2. Italy — History — 1849-1870. I. T.*
DG552.6.G7   945.08   63-7068

Rudman, Harry William, 1908-   **III. 2376**
Italian nationalism and English letters; figures of the risorgimento and Victorian men of letters, by Harry W. Rudman. New York, AMS Press, 1966 [c1940] 444 p. 23 cm. Original ed. issued as v. 146 of Columbia University studies in English and comparative literature. Originally presented as the author's thesis, Columbia, 1940. *1. Mazzini, Giuseppe, 1805-1872. 2. Italians in London. 3. Garibaldi, Giuseppe, 1807-1882. 4. Great Britain — Intellectual life — 19th century. I. T. (S:Columbia University studies in English and comparative literature, v. 146.)*
DG552.7.R8 1966   72-182707

Thayer, William Roscoe, 1859-1923.   **III. 2377**
The life and times of Cavour. New York, H. Fertig, 1971 [c1911] 2 v. geneal. tables, maps, ports. 23 cm. *1. Cavour, Camillo Benso, conte di, 1810-1861. 2. Italy — History — 1849-1870. I. T.*
DG552.8.C3T5 1971   945/.08/0924 (B)   68-9634
C3168+

Whyte, Arthur James Beresford.   **III. 2378**
The early life and letters of Cavour, 1810-1848, by A. J. Whyte. [London] Oxford University Press, 1925. xix, 384 p. front., plates, ports., facsim. 23 cm. Sequel: The political life and letters of Cavour, 1848-1861. *1. Cavour, Camillo Benso, conte di, 1810-1861.*
DG552.8.C3W5   25-11099

Whyte, Arthur James Beresford.   **III. 2379**
The political life and letters of Cavour, 1848-1861, by A. J. Whyte. London, Oxford University Press, 1930. xv, 478 p. front. (port.) 23 cm. Sequel to The early life and letters of Cavour, 1810-1848. *1. Cavour, Camillo Benso, conte di, 1810-1861. I. T.*
DG552.8.C3W52   923.245   31-7360

Hibbert, Christopher, 1924-   **III. 2380**
Garibaldi and his enemies; the clash of arms and personalities in the making of Italy. [1st American ed.] Boston, Little, Brown [1966] xvi, 423 p. illus., maps, ports. 25 cm. *1. Garibaldi, Giuseppe, 1807-1882. 2. Italy — History — 19th cent. I. T.*
DG552.8.G2H5 1966   945.080924 (B)   66-10974

Mack Smith, Denis, 1920-   **III. 2381**
Garibaldi, a great life in brief. [1st ed.] New York, Knopf, 1956. 207 p. illus. 19 cm. (Great lives in brief; a new series of biographies) *1. Garibaldi, Giuseppe, 1807-1882.*
DG552.8.G2M24   923.245   56-5804

Trevelyan, George Macaulay, 1876-   **III. 2382**
Garibaldi and the making of Italy, by George Macaulay Trevelyan. With four maps and numerous illustrations. New York, Longmans, Green, 1911. xix, 390 p. front., plates, ports., 4 fold maps. 24 cm. *1. Garibaldi, Giuseppe, 1807-1882. 2. Italy — History — War of 1860-1861. I. T.*
DG552.8.G2T7   11-35882

Trevelyan, George Macaulay, 1876-   **III. 2383**
Garibaldi and the thousand, by George Macaulay Trevelyan. With five maps and numerous illustrations. 2d impression. London, New York [etc.] Longmans, Green, 1909. xv, 395 p. front., plates, ports., 5 maps (3 fold.) 24 cm. *1. Garibaldi, Giuseppe, 1807-1882. 2. Italy — History — War of 1860-1861. I. T.*
DG552.8.G2T75   10-1700

Mazzini, Giuseppe, 1805-1872.   **III. 2384**
Selected writings, edited and arranged with an introduction, by N. Gangulee. London, Drummond [1945] 253 p. front. (port.) 22 cm. In English. *I. Gangulee, Nagendranath, 1889- ed.*
DG552.8.M28x   A46-3080

Mazzini, Giuseppe, 1805-1872.   **III. 2385**
The living thoughts of Mazzini, presented by Ignazio Silone. Westport, Conn., Greenwood Press [1972, c1939] 130 p. front. 22 cm. Original ed. issued in series: The living thoughts library. "The selections are from Life and writings of Joseph Mazzini, published by Smith & Elder, 1864-1870." *I. T.*
DG552.8.M2918 1972   320.5   79-138163   ISBN:0837156203

Griffith, Gwilym Oswald, 1882-   **III. 2386**
Mazzini: prophet of modern Europe, by Gwilym O. Griffith. New York, H. Fertig, 1970. 381 p. 23 cm. Reprint of the 1932 ed. *1. Mazzini, Giuseppe, 1805-1872. 2. Italy — History — 1815-1870. I. T.*
DG552.8.M3G7 1970   320.1/0924 (B)   78-80552

Hales, Edward Elton Young, 1908-   **III. 2387**
Mazzini and the secret societies; the making of a myth. New York, P. J. Kenedy [1956] 226 p. illus. 24 cm. *1. Mazzini, Giuseppe, 1805-1872. I. T.*
DG552.8.M3H3   923.245   56-9830

Salvemini, Gaetano, 1873-   **III. 2388**
Mazzini. Translated from the Italian by I. M. Rawson. Stanford, Stanford University Press [1957] 192 p. 23 cm. *1. Mazzini, Giuseppe, 1805-1872.*
DG552.8.M3S253   923.245   57-7972

Abba, Giuseppe Cesare, 1838-1910.   **III. 2389**
The diary of one of Garibaldi's Thousand. Translated with an introd. by E. R. Vincent. London, New York, Oxford University Press, 1962. 166 p. illus. 20 cm. (The Oxford library of Italian classics) Translation of Noterelle d'uno dei Mille. *1. Garibaldi, Giuseppe, 1807-1882. 2. Italy — History — War of 1860-1861. I. T.*
DG554.A283   945.08   62-51310

Mack Smith, Denis, 1920-   **III. 2390**
Cavour and Garibaldi, 1860; a study in political conflict. Cambridge [Eng.] University Press, 1954. xii, 458 p. ports., map (on lining-papers) 24 cm. *1. Cavour, Camillo Benso, conte di, 1810-1861. 2. Garibaldi, Giuseppe, 1807-1882. 3. Italy — History — War of 1860-1861.*
DG554.M3   945.08   54-3061

DG555 – 575   Monarchy.
Fascism (1871 – 1947)

Croce, Benedetto, 1866-1952.   **III. 2391**
A history of Italy, 1871-1915. Translated by Cecilia M. Ady. New York, Russell & Russell, 1963. 333 p. 23 cm. *1. Italy — History — 1870-1915.*
DG555.C77 1963   945.09   63-15154

Hughes, Serge.   **III. 2392**
The fall and rise of modern Italy. New York, Macmillan [1967] xiv, 322 p. 22 cm. *1. Italy — Politics and government — 20th century. I. T.*
DG555.H8   320.9/45   67-26058

Seton-Watson, Christopher.   **III. 2393**
Italy from liberalism to fascism, 1870-1925. London, Methuen; New York, Barnes & Noble, 1967. x, 772 p. col. map, tables. 25 cm. *1. Italy — History — 1870-1915. 2. Italy — History — 1914-1945. I. T.*
DG555.S4 1967   945.09   67-114393

Salomone, Arcangelo William, 1915-   **III. 2394**
Italy in the Giolittian era; Italian democracy in the making, 1900-1914. Introductory essay by Gaetano Salvemini. Philadelphia, University of Pennsylvania Press [1960] xxiv, 206 p. illus., ports. 24 cm. "Section one,

entitled 'Italian democracy in the making' ... appeared as a separate volume under that title late in 1945 ... Section two will serve ... to bring up to date ... the materials." *1. Giolitti, Giovanni, 1842-1928. 2. Italy — Politics and government — 20th cent. I. T.*
DG566.S3 1960   945.09   59-13438

Rusinow, Dennison I.   **III. 2395**
Italy's Austrian heritage, 1919-1946, by Dennison I. Rusinow. Oxford, Clarendon P., 1969. xiii, 423 p. plate, maps. 23 cm. Based on author's thesis, Oxford. *1. Italy — History — 1914-1945. 2. Friuli-Venezia Giulia — History. 3. Trentino-Alto Adige, Italy — History. I. T.*
DG568.R8   945.3/091   74-439872   ISBN:198214774

Chabod, Federico.   **III. 2396**
A history of Italian fascism. Translated from the Italian by Muriel Grindrod. London, Weidenfeld and Nicolson [1963] 192 p. 22 cm. Translation of L'Italia contemporanea, originally published in French under title: L'Italie contemporaine. *1. Fascism — Italy. 2. Italy — History — 1914-1945. I. T.*
DG571.C4443   66-80589

Finer, Herman, 1898-   **III. 2397**
Mussolini's Italy. [Hamden, Conn.] Archon Books, 1964. 564 p. illus. 20 cm. *1. Mussolini, Benito, 1883-1945. 2. Fascism — Italy. 3. Italy — Politics and government — 1914-1945. 4. Partito nazionale fascista. I. T.*
DG571.F5 1964   945.091   64-18538

Macartney, Maxwell Henry Hayes.   **III. 2398**
Italy's foreign and colonial policy, 1914-1937, by Maxwell H. H. Macartney and Paul Cremona. New York, H. Fertig, 1972. vii, 353 p. 22 cm. Reprint of the 1938 ed. *1. Italy — Foreign relations — 1914-1945. 2. Europe — Politics — 1918-1945. 3. Italy — Colonies. 4. Mediterranean region — Politics. I. Cremona, Paul, joint author. II. T.*
DG571.M2 1972   327.45   75-80570

Mussolini, Benito, 1883-1945.   **III. 2399**
Fascism; doctrine and institutions. New York, H. Fertig, 1968. 313 p. 21 cm. Reprint of the 1935 ed. "The doctrine of fascism" (p. [5]-42) is a translation of an article originally published in v. 14 (1932), p. 847-851, of the Enciclopedia italiana. *1. Fascism — Italy. 2. Partito nazionale fascista. I. Italy. Laws, statutes, etc. II. T.*
DG571.M764 1968   321.9/4/0945   68-9636

Salvemini, Gaetano, 1873-1957.   **III. 2400**
The fascist dictatorship in Italy. New York, Fertig, 1967. ix, 319 p. illus., ports. 21 cm. *1. Fascism — Italy. 2. Italy — Politics and government — 1922-1945. I. T.*
DG571.S2 1967   945.091   66-24352

Villari, Luigi, 1876-   **III. 2401**
Italian foreign policy under Mussolini. New York, Devin-Adair Co., 1956. xii, 396 p. illus., ports. 22 cm. *1. Mussolini, Benito, 1883-1945. 2. Italy — Foreign relations — 1922-1945. I. T.*
DG571.V535   327.45   56-5712

Deakin, Frederick William Dampier, 1913-   **III. 2402**
The brutal friendship: Mussolini, Hitler, and the fall of Italian fascism. [1st American ed.] New York, Harper & Row [c1962] 896 p. 25 cm. *1. Mussolini, Benito, 1883-1945. 2. Hitler, Adolf, 1889-1945. 3. World War, 1939-1945 — Italy. 4. Germany — Foreign relations — Italy. 5. Italy — Foreign relations — Germany. I. T.*
DG572.D38 1962a   945.091   62-14527

Ciano, Galeazzo, conte, 1903-1944.   **III. 2403**
Ciano's diary, 1939-1943. Edited, with an introduction, by Malcolm Muggeridge. Foreword by Sumner Welles. London, Toronto, W. Heinemann [1947] xxii, 575 p. ports. 24 cm. *1. World War, 1939-1945 — Italy. 2. Italy — Foreign relations — 1922-1945. I. Muggeridge, Malcolm, 1903- ed. II. T.*
DG575.C52A32   940.5345   47-28173

Ciano, Galeazzo, conte, 1903-1944.   **III. 2404**
Ciano's diplomatic papers, being a record of nearly 200 conversations held during the years 1936-42 with Hitler, Mussolini, Franco, Goering, Ribbentrop, Chamberlain, Eden, Sumner Welles, Schuschnigg, Lord Perth, François-Poncet, and many other world diplomatic and political figures, together with important memoranda, letters, telegrams, etc. Ed. by Malcolm Muggeridge. Tr. by Stuart Hood. London, Odhams Press [1948] xxii, 490 p. 22 cm. "The original Italian edition ... is entitled L'Europa verso la catastrofe." *1. Europe — Politics — 1918-1945. 2. Italy — Foreign relations — 1922-1945. I. Muggeridge, Malcolm, 1903- ed. II. Hood, Stuart O., tr.*
DG575.C52A413   940.532445   49-19765

Carrillo, Elisa A.   **III. 2405**
Alcide de Gasperi; the long apprenticeship, by Elisa A. Carrillo. [Notre Dame, Ind.] University of Notre Dame Press [1965] vii, 189 p. 25 cm. (Studies in Christian democracy) *1. Gasperi, Alcide de, 1881-1954. I. T. (S)*
DG575.G3C27   945.0920924 (B)   65-23517

Mussolini, Benito, 1883-1945.   **III. 2406**
My autobiography. With a foreword by Richard Washburn Child. Westport, Conn., Greenwood Press [1970] xix, 318 p. illus., ports. 23 cm. Reprint of the 1928 ed. *1. Italy — Politics and government — 1914-1945. I. Child, Richard Washburn, 1881-1935.*
DG575.M8A2 1970   945,091/0924 (B)   78-109803   ISBN:837142946

Mussolini, Benito, 1883-1945.   **III. 2407**
The fall of Mussolini, his own story. Tr. from the Italian by Frances Frenaye; edited and with a pref. by Max Ascoli. New York, Farrar, Straus, 1948. 212 p. map. 22 cm. Translation of Il tempo del bastone e della carota. *1. World War, 1939-1945 — Italy. 2. Italy — History — 1922-1945 — Sources. I. Frenaye, Frances, 1912- tr. II. Ascoli, Max, 1888- ed. III. T.*
DG575.M8A542   940.5345   48-10400

Fermi, Laura.   **III. 2408**
Mussolini. [Chicago] University of Chicago Press [1961] 477 p. illus. 23 cm. *1. Mussolini, Benito, 1883-1945.*
DG575.M8F42   923.245   61-17075

Kirkpatrick, Ivone, Sir.   **III. 2409**
Mussolini, a study in power. [1st ed.] New York, Hawthorn Books [1964] 726 p. illus., ports., maps, geneal. table. 24 cm. *1. Mussolini, Benito, 1883-1945. I. T.*
DG575.M8K5   923.245   64-13278

DG576 – 579   1948 –

Carlyle, Margaret.   **III. 2410**
Modern Italy. Rev. ed. New York, Praeger [1965] ix, 154 p. 22 cm. *1. Italy — Politics and government — 1945- 2. Italy — Economic conditions — 1945- I. T.*
DG577.C35 1965   309.145   65-15652

Grindrod, Muriel.   **III. 2411**
The rebuilding of Italy:politics and economics, 1945-1955. London, New York, Royal Institute of International Affairs [1955] vii, 269 p. maps (part fold.) tables. 22 cm. *1. Italy — Politics and government — 1945- 2. Italy — Economic conditions — 1945- I. T.*
DG577.G7   945.092   56-13528

Hughes, Henry Stuart, 1916-   **III. 2412**
The United States and Italy [by] H. Stuart Hughes. Rev. ed. Cambridge, Harvard University Press, 1965. xii, 297 p. maps. 22 cm. (The American foreign policy library) *1. Italy — Politics and government — 1945- 2. Italy — Economic conditions — 1945- I. T. (S)*
DG577.H8 1965   945.09   65-13845

Kogan, Norman.   **III. 2413**
A political history of postwar Italy. London, Pall Mall P., 1966. x, 252 p. front., maps, 15 tables. 22 cm. *1. Italy — History — 1945- I. T.*
DG577.K6 1966a   945.092   67-72567

DG600 – 999   Local History

DG651 – 679   LOMBARDY. VENICE

Greenfield, Kent Roberts, 1893-   **III. 2414**
Economics and liberalism in the Risorgimento; a study of nationalism in Lombardy, 1814-1848. Introductory essay by Rosario Romeo. Rev. ed. Baltimore, Johns Hopkins Press, 1965. xxiii, 303 p. 24 cm. *1. Lombardy — Economic conditions. 2. Journalism — Lombardy. 3. Italy — History — 1815-1870. I. T.*
DG658.5.G7 1965   945.208   65-27721

Davis, James Cushman.   **III. 2415**
The decline of the Venetian nobility as a ruling class. Baltimore, Johns Hopkins Press, 1962. 155 p. illus. 24 cm. (Johns Hopkins University. Studies in historical and political science, ser. 80, no. 2) *1. Venice — Nobility. 2. Venice — History — 1508-1797. 3. Venice — Social conditions. I. T. (S)*
DG678.D3   (H31.J6 ser. 80, no. 2)   945.31   62-20558

DG731 – 760 FLORENCE

Machiavelli, Niccolò, 1469-1527.   III. 2416
Opere. [Milano, Feltrinelli, 1961-68; v.1, 1968] 8 v. 19 cm. (Biblioteca di classici italiani, 3, 8, 19, 6, 12, 21. Universale economica, 320/321) Vol.1-5 edited by S. Bertelli; v.6-8 by F. Gaeta. Vol.1: 2, ed.; v.2-8: 1. ed. Vols.2-8 lack series no. for second series. I. Bertelli, Sergio, ed. II. Gaeta, Franco, ed.
DG731.5.M3 1961   66-51549

Schevill, Ferdinand, 1868-1954.   III. 2417
History of Florence, from the founding of the city through the Renaissance. New York, Ungar [1961] 536 p. illus. 24 cm. 1. Florence — History. 2. Renaissance — Italy.
DG736.S3 1961   945.5   60-8571

Machiavelli, Niccolò, 1469-1527.   III. 2418
History of Florence and of the affairs of Italy, from the earliest times to the death of Lorenzo the Magnificent. Introd. to the Torchbook ed. by Felix Gilbert. New York, Harper [1960] xxv, 417 p. 21 cm. (Harper torchbooks, TB1027. The Academy library) 1. Florence — History.
DG737.A2M4 1960   945.51   60-51391

Brucker, Gene A.   III. 2419
Renaissance Florence [by] Gene Brucker. New York, Wiley [1969] xiii, 306 p. illus., maps. 22 cm. (New dimensions in history: historical cities) 1. Florence — History — To 1421. I. T. (S)
DG737.B74   914.5/5   77-82972   ISBN:471113700

Brucker, Gene A.   III. 2420
Florentine politics and society, 1343-1378. Princeton, N.J., Princeton University Press, 1962. xiii, 431 p. map. 25 cm. (Princeton studies in history, 12) "Originated as a doctoral dissertation at Princeton University ... thoroughly revised." 1. Florence — Politics and government. I. T. (S:Princeton University. Princeton studies in history, 12)
DG737.26.B7 1962   945.41   62-7035

Acton, Harold Mario Mitchell, 1904-   III. 2421
The last Medici. [Rev. ed.] London, Methuen [1958] 327 p. illus. 23 cm. 1. Cosimo III, de' Medici, grand duke of Tuscany, 1642-1723. 2. Giovanni Gastone, de' Medici, grand duke of Tuscany, 1671-1737. 3. Medici, House of. I. T.
DG737.42.A3 1958   923.1455   59-551

Schevill, Ferdinand, 1868-1954.   III. 2422
The Medici. New York, Harper [1960, c1949] 240 p. illus. 21 cm. (Harper torchbooks. The academy library) 1. Medici, House of.
DG737.42.S3x   945.5   A63-5089

Young, George Frederick, 1846-1919.   III. 2423
The Medici, by Colonel G. F. Young, C.B.; with 32 illustrations reproduced in aquatone. [1st Modern Library ed.] New York, The Modern library [1933] xxi, 824 p. XXXII pl. on 16 l. (incl. ports.) fold. geneal. tab. 21 cm. 1. Medici, House of.
DG737.42.Y8 1933   929.7501   33-8805

Martines, Lauro.   III. 2424
The social world of the Florentine humanists, 1390-1460. Princeton, N.J., Princeton University Press, 1963. x, 419 p. 25 cm. 1. Florence — Intellectual life. 2. Florence — Social life and customs. 3. Humanists. I. T.
DG737.55.M3   914.551   63-7073

Ridolfi, Roberto, 1899-   III. 2425
The life of Girolamo Savonarola. Translated from the Italian by Cecil Grayson. London, Routledge and Paul [c1959] 325 p. illus. 25 cm. 1. Savonarola, Girolamo Maria Francesco Matteo, 1452-1498.
DG737.97.R533 1959a   922.245   60-898

Prezzolini, Giuseppe, 1882-   III. 2426
Machiavelli. [Translated by Gioconda Savine. 1st ed.] New York, Farrar, Straus & Giroux [1967] 372 p. 22 cm. 1. Machiavelli, Niccolò, 1469-1527.
DG738.14.M2P5913   320.10924   67-10921

Ridolfi, Roberto, 1899-   III. 2427
The life of Niccolò Machiavelli. Translated from the Italian by Cecil Grayson. [Chicago] University of Chicago Press [1963] 337 p. illus. 25 cm. 1. Machiavelli, Niccolò, 1469-1527.
DG738.14.M2R513   923.245   62-15048

DG797 – 799 PAPAL STATES

Gregorovius, Ferdinand Adolf, 1821-1891.   III. 2428
Lucretia Borgia, according to original documents and correspondence of her day. Translated from the 3d German ed., by John Leslie Garner. New York, B. Blom [1968] xxiii, 378 p. illus. 20 cm. Reprint of 1903 ed. 1. Borgia, Lucrezia, 1480-1519. 2. Italy — History — 1492-1559. 3. Renaissance — Italy. I. Garner, John Leslie, tr.
DG797.83.G71 1968   945/.06/0924 (B)   68-20226

Trevelyan, George Macaulay, 1876-1962.   III. 2429
Garibaldi's defence of the Roman Republic, 1848-9. Westport, Conn., Greenwood Press [1971] xv, 387 p. illus. 23 cm. Reprint of the 1912 ed. 1. Garibaldi, Giuseppe, 1807-1882. 2. Rome (City) — History — Revolution of 1848-1849. I. T.
DG798.5.T8 1971   945/.08/0924 (B)   76-156214   ISBN:0837161657

Halperin, Samuel William.   III. 2430
Italy and the Vatican at war; a study of their relations from the outbreak of the Franco-Prussian War to the death of Pius IX, by S. William Halperin. New York, Greenwood Press [1968, c1939] xvii, 483 p. 23 cm. 1. Roman question. 2. Church and state in Italy. I. T.
DG799.H3 1968   322/.1/0945   68-57606

DG840 – 875 NAPLES. SICILY

Acton, Harold Mario Mitchell, 1904-   III. 2431
The Bourbons of Naples, 1734-1825. New York, St Martin's Press [1958, c1956] 731 p. illus. 23 cm. 1. Naples (Kingdom) — History. I. T.
DG848.3.A3 1958   945.7   58-14637

Acton, Harold Mario Mitchell, 1904-   III. 2432
The last Bourbons of Naples (1825-1861) New York, St. Martin's Press [1962, c1961] 559 p. illus. 23 cm. 1. Ferdinando II, King of the Two Sicilies, 1810-1859. 2. Francesco II, King of the Two Sicilies, 1836-1894. I. T.
DG848.46.A25 1962   923.145   62-7507

Romani, George T.   III. 2433
The Neapolitan revolution of 1820-1821. Evanston, Northwestern University Press, 1950. vii, 190 p. map. 23 cm. (Northwestern University studies. Social studies series, no. 6) 1. Naples (Kingdom) — History — Revolution, 1820-1821. I. T.
DG848.51.R6   945.7   50-10812

Finley, Moses I.   III. 2434
A history of Sicily [by] M. I. Finley. New York, Viking Press [1968- v. illus., maps. 23 cm. 1. Sicily — History. I. T.
DG866.F5   937/.8   68-31396   ISBN:670122726

Runciman, Steven, 1903-   III. 2435
The Sicilian Vespers; a history of the Mediterranean world in the later thirteenth century. Cambridge [Eng.] University Press, 1958. xiii, 355 p. illus., ports., maps (1 fold.) geneal. tables. 22 cm. 1. Sicily — History — 1189-1282. 2. Mediterranean region — History. I. T.
DG867.28.R8   945.8   58-2158

DG975 OTHER CITIES, A – Z

Ashby, Thomas, 1874-1931.   III. 2436
The Roman campagna in classical times. New ed. with introd. by J. B. Ward-Perkins. London, E. Benn; New York, Barnes & Noble [1970] x, 258 p. illus. 23 cm. 1. Campagna di Roma — Description. 2. Rome — Antiquities. 3. Roads — Rome. I. T.
DG975.C17A8 1970   913.37/6   70-513332
    ISBN:389039977 (Barnes & Noble) 51003151X

Levi, Carlo, 1902-   III. 2437
Christ stopped at Eboli; the story of a year, by Carlo Levi, translated from the Italian by Frances Frenaye. New York, Farrar, Straus, 1947. 268 p. 21 cm. Map on lining-papers. 1. Lucania — Social life and customs. I. Frenaye, Frances, 1912- tr. II. T.
DG975.L78L43   914.577   47-3385

Waley, Daniel Philip.   III. 2438
Mediaeval Orvieto; the political history of an Italian city-state, 1157-1334. Cambridge [Eng.] University Press, 1952. xxv, 170 p. plates. fold. map. geneal. tables. 23 cm. 1. Orvieto — History.
DG975.O7W34   945.6   52-8823

DG975   *Greece. Italy*   III. 2441

Herlihy, David.   **III. 2439**
Pisa in the early Renaissance; a study of urban growth. New Haven, Yale University Press, 1958. xx, 229 p. map. 23 cm. (Yale historical publications. Miscellany 68) "This book grew of a dissertation written at Yale University." *1. Pisa — History. I. T. (S)*
DG975.P615H4   945.5   58-6933

Herlihy, David.   **III. 2440**
Medieval and Renaissance Pistoia; the social history of an Italian town, 1200-1430. New Haven, Yale University Press, 1967. xviii, 297 p. maps. 24 cm. *1. Pistoia — History. 2. Pistoia — Social conditions. I. T.*
DG975.P65H4   914.5/52/03   67-13437

Schevill, Ferdinand, 1868-1954.   **III. 2441**
Siena, the history of a mediaeval commune. New York, Harper & Row [1964] xlii, 433 p. illus., maps. 21 cm. (Harper torchbooks. The Academy library) "Originally published in 1909." *1. Siena — History. I. T.*
DG975.S5S35 1964   914.558   64-56203

DH – DJ   Netherlands

DH1 – 207 GENERAL WORKS

Timmers, J. J. M., 1907- III. 2442
A history of Dutch life and art. Translated by Mary F. Hedlund. [London] Nelson, 1959. 201 p. illus., ports., col. map. 36 cm. "Originally published as Atlas van de Nederlandse beschaving." *1. Netherlands — Civilization. 2. Art — Netherlands.*
DH71.T513   709.492   60-427

Iongh, Jane de. III. 2443
Margaret of Austria, regent of the Netherlands; translated by M. D. Herter Norton. [1st ed.] New York, Norton [1953] 256 p. illus. 22 cm. *1. Margaretha, of Austria, regent of the Netherlands, 1480-1530.*
DH183.I55   923.1492   53-13087

Haley, Kenneth Harold Dobson. III. 2444
The Dutch in the seventeenth century [by] K. H. D. Haley. [1st American ed. New York] Harcourt Brace Jovanovich [1972] 216 p. illus. (part col.) 22 cm. *1. Netherlands — History — Wars of Independence, 1556-1648. 2. Netherlands — History — 1648-1795. I. T.*
DH186.5.H33 1972   914.92/03/4   72-157880
   ISBN:015126855X 0155184733 (pbk)

Motley, John Lothrop, 1814-1877. III. 2445
The rise of the Dutch republic. A history by John Lothrop Motley. London, Dent; New York, Dutton [1928-30] 3 v. 18 cm. (Everyman's library. History. [no.86-88]) First published in this edition, 1906. Introduction signed: V. R. R. *1. Netherlands — History — Wars of independence, 1556-1648.*
DH186.5.M7x   949.203   36-37650

Parker, Geoffrey, 1933- III. 2446
The Army of flanders and the Spanish road, 1567-1659; the logistics of Spanish victory and defeat in the Low Countries' Wars. Cambridge [Eng.] University Press, 1972. xviii, 309 p. illus. 24 cm. (Cambridge studies in early modern history) *1. Netherlands — History — Wars of Independence, 1556-1648. I. T.*
DH186.5.P28   949.2/03   76-180021   ISBN:0521084628

Wedgwood, Cicely Veronica, 1910- III. 2447
William the Silent, William of Nassau, prince of Orange, 1533-1584, by C. V. Wedgwood. London, J. Cape [1944] 256 p. 2 port., fold. map. 23 cm. "First published 1944." *1. Willem I, prince of Orange, 1533-1584. 2. Netherlands — History — Wars of independence, 1556-1648.*
DH188.W7W4   ~~923.1492~~ 949.202 w67w   44-7864

DH401 – 811   BELGIUM

Lyon, Margot. III. 2448
Belgium [by] Margot Lyon. New York, Walker [1971] 204 p. 28 illus., 4 maps. 22 cm. (Nations and peoples) *1. Belgium.*
DH418.L9 1971   914.93/03/4   68-13971   ISBN:0802721112

Mallinson, Vernon. III. 2449
Belgium. New York, Praeger [1970] 240 p. illus., geneal. table, 2 maps (1 fold.), ports. 23 cm. (Nations of the modern world) *1. Belgium. (S)*
DH418.M25 1970   949.3   72-104772

Kalken, Frans van, 1881- III. 2450
Histoire de la Belgique et de son expansion coloniale. Bruxelles, Office de publicité, 1954. 869 p. illus., ports., maps. 20 cm. *1. Belgium — History.*
DH521.K278   54-24324

Meeüs, Adrien de, 1900- III. 2451
History of the Belgians. Translated from the French by G. Gordon. New York, Praeger [1962] 378 p. 24 cm. (Books that matter) *1. Belgium — History.*
DH521.M423   949.3   62-13755

Pirenne, Henri, 1862-1935. III. 2452
Histoire de Belgique des origines à nos jours. L'iconographie de l'ouvrage a été rassemblée et commentée par Franz Schauwers et Jacques Paquet. Bruxelles, Renaissance Du Livre [1948-52] 4 v. illus., col. plates, ports. (part col.) maps, facsims. (part col.) 32 cm. "Compléments à l'Histoire de Belgique de 1914 à 1940, par John Bartier [et al.]": 93 p. at end of v.4. *1. Belgium — History. I. Schauwers, Franz, ed.*
DH521.P58   949.3   48-27764

Ascherson, Neal. III. 2453
The king incorporated; Leopold II in the age of trusts. London, Allen & Unwin [1963] 310 p. illus., ports., maps. 22 cm. *1. Leopold II, King of the Belgians, 1835-1909. I. T.*
DH671.A8 1963   64-56680

Miller, Jane Kathryn. III. 2454
Belgian foreign policy between two wars, 1919-1940. New York, Bookman [1951] 337 p. 23 cm. *1. Belgium — Foreign relations — 1914- 2. Belgium — History — 1914- I. T.*
DH677.M5   327.493   51-4901

Arango, Ergasto Ramón. III. 2455
Leopold III and the Belgian royal question. Baltimore, Johns Hopkins Press [1963, c1961] xiv, 234 p. 22 cm. *1. Léopold III, King of the Belgians, 1901 I. T.*
DH687.A82   949.304   63-19557

Kieft, David Owen. III. 2456
Belgium's return to neutrality; an essay in the frustration of small power diplomacy. Oxford, Clarendon Press, 1972. xv, 201 p. 22 cm. *1. Belgium — Politics and government — 1914-1951. 2. Belgium — Foreign relations — 1914- I. T.*
DH687.K53   327.493   72-183279   ISBN:0198214979

Annales Gandenses. III. 2457
Annals of Ghent. Translated from the Latin with introd. and notes by Hilda Johnstone. New York, Oxford University Press, 1951. xxix, 100, 100, 101-105 p. map, geneal. tables. 23 cm. (Medieval classics) Latin and English on opposite pages numbered in duplicate. *1. Flanders — History — Sources. I. Johnstone, Hilda, 1882- ed. and tr. (S:Medieval classics (New York))*
DH801.F46A6 1951   949.3   52-7544

Wegg, Jervis. III. 2458
The decline of Antwerp under Philip of Spain, by Jervis Wegg. With twelve illustrations and two plans. London, Methuen [1924] xv, 352 p. plates, ports., plan. 23 cm. Plans on lining-papers. *1. Antwerp — History. 2. Netherlands — History — Wars of independence, 1556-1648. I. T.*
DH811.A6W4   25-13195

DJ1 – 411   HOLLAND

Landheer, Bartholomeus, 1904- ed. III. 2459
The Netherlands; chapters by Johan Willem Albarda, Adriaan Jacob Barnouw, Hendrik Nicolaas Boon [and others]. Edited by Bartholomew Landheer. Berkeley, Los Angeles, University of California press, 1943. 5 p. l., ix-xviii p., 3 l., 3-464 p. incl. illus. (maps) tables. front., plates, ports. 23 cm. ([The United nations series]) *1. Netherlands — History. 2. Netherlands — Civilization. (S)*
DJ5.L3   949.2   A44-255

Sitwell, Sacheverell, 1897- III. 2460
The Netherlands; a study of some aspects of art, costume and social life. [2d ed., rev.] London, New York, Batsford [1952] 168 p. illus. 23 cm. *1. Netherlands — Description and travel. 2. Netherlands — Social life and customs.*
DJ24.S5 1952   914.92   52-33506

Huizinga, Johan, 1872-1945. **III. 2461**
Dutch civilisation in the seventeenth century, and other essays [by] J. H. Huizinga. Selected by Pieter Geyl and F. W. N. Hugenholtz. Translated by Arnold J. Pomerans. New York, F. Ungar Pub. Co. [1968] 288 p. 21 cm. *1. Netherlands — Civilization. 2. History — Philosophy. I. Geyl, Pieter, 1887-1966, comp. II. Hugenholtz, F. W. N., comp. III. T.*
DJ71.H92 1968b   914.92/03   68-22778

Zumthor, Paul, 1915- **III. 2462**
Daily life in Rembrandt's Holland. Translated from the French by Simon Watson Taylor. London, Weidenfeld and Nicolson [1962] 353 p. illus. 23 cm. (Daily life series) *1. Netherlands — Civilization. 2. Netherlands — Social life and customs. I. T.*
DJ71.Z913   62-51617

Barnouw, Adriaan Jacob, 1877- **III. 2463**
The making of modern Holland, a short history. London, G. Allen & Unwin [1948] 224 p. maps (part fold.) 20 cm. *1. Netherlands — History. I, T.*
DJ111.B32 1948   949.2   49-14153

Vandenbosch, Amry, 1894- **III. 2464**
Dutch foreign policy since 1815; a study in small power politics. The Hague, M. Nijhoff, 1959. 318 p. 25 cm. *1. Netherlands — Foreign relations. I. T.*
DJ147.V3   327.492   59-2211

Geyl, Pieter, 1887- **III. 2465**
The Netherlands in the seventeenth century. Rev. and enl. ed. New York, Barnes & Noble [1961-   v. illus. 23 cm. First published in 1936 under title: The Netherlands divided (1609-1648) *1. Netherlands — History — Wars of Independence, 1556-1648. 2. Netherlands — History — 1648-1714. 3. Netherlands — Civilization. I. T.*
DJ156.G482   949.203   61-66073

Wilson, Charles Henry. **III. 2466**
The Dutch Republic and the civilization of the seventeenth century [by] Charles Wilson. New York, McGraw-Hill [1968] 255 p. illus., facsims., maps, ports, (all part col.) 20 cm. (World university library) *1. Netherlands — History — Wars of Independence, 1556-1648. 2. Netherlands — History — 1648-1714. 3. Netherlands — Civilization. I. T.*
DJ156.W55   914.92/03/4   68-14342

Geyl, Pieter, 1887- **III. 2467**
The revolt of the Netherlands (1555-1609) [2d ed.] New York, Barnes & Noble [c1958] 310 p. maps 22 cm. *1. Netherlands — History — Wars of Independence, 1556-1648. I. T.*
DJ156.9.G48x   A59-3543

Haley, Kenneth Harold Dobson. **III. 2468**
William of Orange and the English opposition, 1672-4. Oxford, Clarendon Press, 1953. 231 p. 23 cm. *1. William III, King of Great Britain, 1650-1702. 2. Du Moulin, Pierre, d. 1676. 3. Anglo-Dutch War, 1672-1674.*
DJ193.H3   949.204   53-4330

Cobban, Alfred. **III. 2469**
Ambassadors and secret agents; the diplomacy of the First Earl of Malmesbury at the Hague. London, Cape [1954] 255 p. ports., map. 23 cm. *1. Malmesbury, James Harris, 1st earl of, 1746-1820. 2. Netherlands — Foreign relations — 1714-1795. I. T.*
DJ202.C55   54-4990

Warmbrunn, Werner. **III. 2470**
The Dutch under German occupation, 1940-1945. Stanford, Calif., Stanford University Press, 1963. xiii, 338 p. 24 cm. *1. Netherlands — History — German occupation, 1940-1945. I. T.*
DJ287.W3   940.5337   63-10738

DK Russia. Poland. Finland

DK 1 – 276 RUSSIA

Walsh, Warren Bartlett, 1909- ed.   **III. 2471**
Readings in Russian history from ancient times to the post-Stalin era. 4th ed., extensively rev. [Syracuse, N.Y.] Syracuse University Press, 1963. 3 v. (x, 867 p.) illus. 24 cm. *1. Russia — History — Sources. I. T.*
DK3.W3 1963   947.0082   63-14771

Harcave, Sidney Samuel, 1916- ed.   **III. 2472**
Readings in Russian history. New York, Crowell [1962] 2 v. illus. 23 cm. *1. Russia — History — Addresses, essays, lectures. I. T.*
DK4.H3   947.082   62-12198

Pokrovskiĭ, Mikhail Nikolaevich, 1868-1932.   **III. 2473**
Russia in world history; selected essays. Edited, with an introd. by Roman Szporluk. Translated by Roman and Mary Ann Szporluk. Ann Arbor, University of Michigan Press [c1970] 241 p. 22 cm. *1. Russia — History — Addresses, essays, lectures. 2. Russia — History — Revolution, 1917-1921 — Addresses, sermons, etc. I. T.*
DK5.P653 1970   947.084/1   75-107981   ISBN:0472087371

McGraw-Hill encyclopedia of Russia and the Soviet Union. Editor: **III. 2474**
Michael T. Florinsky; consultants: Harry Schwartz [and others. 1st ed.] New York, McGraw-Hill [1961] xiv, 624 p. illus., ports., maps. 29 cm. *1. Russia — Dictionaries and encyclopedias. I. Florinsky, Michael T., 1894- ed.*
DK14.M26   914.7   61-18169

Maxwell, Robert, 1923- ed.   **III. 2475**
Information U.S.S.R.; an authoritative encyclopaedia about the Union of Soviet Socialist Republics. Oxford, New York, Pergamon Press, 1962. xii, 982 p. illus., ports., maps (part fold., 1 fold. col.) tables. 27 cm. (Countries of the world. Information series, v. 1) "Pages 1-763 ... were translated from volume 50 of the Great Soviet encyclopaedia by J. T. McDermott." *1. Russia — Dictionaries and encyclopedias. I. Bolʹshaia sovetskaia entsiklopediia. II. T.*
DK14.M38 1962   947.003   62-9879

Gregory, James Stothert, 1912-   **III. 2476**
Russian land, Soviet people: a geographical approach to the U.S.S.R., by James S. Gregory. London, Harrap, 1968. 947 p. 26 fold. plates, illus., maps. 24 cm. *1. Russia. 2. Russia — History. I. T.*
DK17.G75   914.7   68-122679

The Soviet Union and Eastern Europe;   **III. 2477**
a handbook, edited by George Schöpflin. New York, Praeger [1970] xii, 614 p. maps (part col.) 24 cm. (Handbooks to the modern world) *1. Russia. 2. Europe, Eastern. I. Schöpflin, George, ed.*
DK17.S64 1970b   914.7   70-100941

Keefe, Eugene K.   **III. 2478**
Area handbook for the Soviet Union. Co-authors: Eugene K. Keefe [and others. Washington; For sale by the Supt. of Docs., U.S. Govt. Print. Off.] 1971. xviii, 827 p. illus., maps. 24 cm. "DA pam 550-95." "One of a series of handbooks prepared by Foreign Area Studies (FAS) of the American University." *1. Russia. I. American University, Washington, D.C. Foreign Area Studies. II. T.*
DK18.K43   914.7/03/85   71-609246

DK 19 – 28 Description

Cross, Anthony Glenn, comp.   **III. 2479**
Russia under Western eyes, 1517-1825. Edited with an introd. by Anthony Cross. New York, St. Martin's Press [1971] 400 p. illus., maps (on lining papers) 25 cm. *1. Russia — Description and travel. 2. Russia — Foreign opinion. I. T.*
DK19.C76   914.7/03   71-159500

Wallace, Donald Mackenzie, Sir, 1841-1919.   **III. 2480**
Russia; on the eve of war and revolution. Edited and introduced by Cyril E. Black. New York, Vintage Books [1961] xiv, 528 p. 19 cm. (Vintage Russian library, V724) *1. Russia.*
DK26.W2 1961   947.08   62-810

Wallace, Donald Mackenzie, Sir, 1841-1919.   **III. 2481**
Russia. Entirely new and much enlarged ed., rev. and in great part rewritten. New York, Praeger Publishers [c1970] ix, xx, 672 p. maps, port. 22 cm. (Praeger scholarly reprints. Source books and studies in Russian and Soviet history) Reprint of the 1905 ed. *1. Russia — Description and travel.*
DK26.W2 1970   914.7/03/8   74-105286

Lydolph, Paul E.   **III. 2482**
Geography of the U.S.S.R. [by] Paul E. Lydolph. Randall Sale, cartographer. 2d ed. New York, J. Wiley [1970] xv, 683 p. illus., maps. 26 cm. *1. Russia — Description and travel — 1945- I. T.*
DK28.L9 1970   914.7   78-112594   ISBN:471557250

Mellor, Roy E. H.   **III. 2483**
Geography of the U.S.S.R., by R. E. H. Mellor. London, Macmillan; New York, St. Martin's Press, 1964. xv, 402 p. illus., maps. 23 cm. *1. Russia — Description and travel — 1945- I. T.*
DK28.M444 1964   914.7   64-25713

Shabad, Theodore.   **III. 2484**
Geography of the USSR; a regional survey. New York, Columbia University Press, 1951. xxxii, 584 p. maps. 24 cm. *1. Russia — Description and travel — 1945- I. T.*
DK28.S46   914.7   51-9701

Utechin, Sergej, 1921-   **III. 2485**
A concise encyclopaedia of Russia, by S. V. Utechin. New York, Dutton, 1964 [c1961] xxvi, 623 p. illus., ports., fold. map. 19 cm. First published in 1961 under title: Everyman's concise encyclopaedia of Russia. *1. Russia — Dictionaries and encyclopedias. I. T.*
DK28.U83 1964   914.7   64-55967

DK 30 – 35 Civilization. Ethnography

Blinoff, Marthe, ed. and tr.   **III. 2486**
Life and thought in old Russia. [University Park] Pennsylvania State University Press [1961] 222 p. illus. 25 cm. *1. Russia — Civilization. I. T.*
DK32.B67   914.7   61-11415

Cherniavsky, Michael.   **III. 2487**
Tsar and people; studies in Russian myths. New Haven, Yale University Press, 1961. 258 p. illus. 23 cm. *1. National characteristics, Russian. I. T.*
DK32.C523   914.7   61-14431

Masaryk, Thomáš Garrigue, Pres. Czechoslovak Republic, 1850-1937.   **III. 2488**
The spirit of Russia; studies in history, literature and philosophy. Translated from the German original by Eden and Cedar Paul, with additional chapters and bibliographies by Jan Slavik; the former translated and the latter condensed and translated by W. R. & Z. Lee. [2d ed., 3d impression] London, Allen & Unwin; New York, Macmillan [1961-67] 3 v. 22 cm. Imprint covered by label: Barnes & Noble, New York; v. 3 has imprint: New York, Barnes & Noble, issued without edition statement. Vol. 3 edited by George Gibian and translated by Robert Bass. Translation of Russland und Europa. *1. Russia — Civilization. 2. Philosophy, Russian. 3. Russian literature — History and criticism. 4. Russia — History. I. Gibiah, George, ed. II. T.*
DK32.M412   914.7/03/8   68-31931

Miliukov, Pavel Nikolaevich, 1859-1943. III. 2489
Outlines of Russian culture ... by Paul Miliukov, edited by Michael Karpovich; translated by Valentine Ughet and Eleanor Davis. Philadelphia, University of Pennsylvania Press, 1942. 3 v. illus., pl. 23 cm. "An authorized abridged version of the original, specially prepared for the American edition." — Editor's foreword. *1. Russia — Civilization. I. Karpovich, Michael, 1888- ed. II. Davis, Eleanor (Goodrich) 1876- tr. III. Ughet, Valentine, joint tr. IV. T.*
DK32.M54   914.7   42-6909

Strakhovsky, Leonid Ivan, 1898- ed. III. 2490
A handbook of Slavic studies. Cambridge, Harvard Univ. Press, 1949. xxi, 753 p. 24 cm. *1. Slavic studies.*
DK32.S86   936.7   49-3015

Berdiaev, Nikolaĭ Aleksandrovich, 1874-1948. III. 2491
The Russian idea. [Translated from the Russian by R. M. French] New York, Macmillan, 1948. 255 p. 21 cm. *1. Russia — Civilization. I. French, Reginald Michael, 1884- tr. II. T.*
DK32.7.B415 1948   914.7   48-5698

Billington, James H. III. 2492
The icon and the axe; an interpretive history of Russian culture, by James H. Billington. [1st ed.] New York, Knopf, 1966. xviii, 786, xxxiii p. illus., map, ports. 25 cm. *1. Russia — Intellectual life. I. T.*
DK32.7.B5   914.703   66-18687

Plekhanov, Georgiĭ Valentinovich, 1856-1918. III. 2493
History of Russian social thought. Translated from the Russian by Boris M. Bekkar and others. New York, H. Fertig, 1967. 224 p. 25 cm. Reprint of the 1938 edition. Translation of Istoriia russkoĭ obshchestvennoĭ mysli (romanized form) *1. Russia — Civilization. 2. Russia — Social conditions. I. T.*
DK32.7.P512 1967   914.7/03   66-25858

Tompkins, Stuart Ramsay, 1886- III. 2494
The Russian intelligentsia: makers of the revolutionary state. [1st ed.] Norman, University of Oklahoma Press [1957] 282 p. illus. 23 cm. Sequel to the Russian mind. *1. Russia — intellectual life. I. T.*
DK32.7.T58   914.7   57-11200

Conquest, Robert. III. 2495
The Soviet deportation of nationalities. London, Macmillan; New York, St Martin's Press, 1960. 203 p. illus. 23 cm. *1. Minorities — Russia. 2. Population transfers. I. T.*
DK33.C6   323.147   60-16198

Goldhagen, Erich. III. 2496
Ethnic minorities in the Soviet Union. [New York] Published for the Institute of East European Jewish Studies of the Philip W. Lown School of Near Eastern and Judaic Studies. Brandeis University, by Praeger [1968] xiv, 351 p. 22 cm. Essays read at a symposium held in fall, 1965 at the Institute of East European Jewish Studies of Philip W. Lown School of Near Eastern and Judaic Studies of Brandeis University. *1. Minorities — Russia. 2. Russia — Languages. I. Brandeis University, Waltham, Mass. Institute of East European Jewish Studies. II. T.*
DK33.G62   301.451/0947   67-20478

Gorer, Geoffrey, 1905- III. 2497
The people of great Russia; a psychological study by Geoffrey Gorer and John Rickman. New York, Norton [1962] 235 p. 20 cm. (The Norton library, N112) *1. Russians. 2. Russia — Social life and customs. I. Rickman, John, 1891- II. T.*
DK33.G67 1962   914.7   62-4043

Kolarz, Walter. III. 2498
Russia and her colonies. [Hamden, Conn.] Archon Books, 1967. xiv, 334 p. maps. 22 cm. Reprint of the 1953 ed. *1. Minorities — Russia. 2. Russia — Colonies. I. T.*
DK33.K64 1967   325.3/47   67-15926

Soviet nationality problems. III. 2499
Authors: Edward Allworth [and others] Editor: Edward Allworth. New York, Columbia University Press, 1971. xiv, 296 p. illus., facsims., maps. 24 cm. Based on papers from a research seminar on Soviet nationality problems, given at Columbia University in 1968-69 school year. *1. Minorities — Russia. I. Allworth, Edward.*
DK33.S67 1971   301.45/0947   77-166211   ISBN:0231034938

Sulimirski, Tadeusz, 1898- III. 2500
The Sarmatians [by] T. Sulimirski. New York, Praeger [1970] 267 p. illus., maps, plan. 21 cm. (Ancient peoples and places, v. 73) *1. Sarmatians. 2. Russia — Antiquities.*
DK34.S3S84 1970b   913.3/9/5   70-121076

Zenkovsky, Serge A. III. 2501
Pan-Turkism and Islam in Russia. Cambridge, Harvard University Press, 1960. 345 p. illus. 24 cm. (Harvard University. Russian Research Center. Russian Research Center studies, 36) *1. Turks in Russia. 2. Minorities — Russia. 3. Mohammedans in Russia. I. T.*
DK34.T8Z4   947   60-5399

DK36 – 276   History

Aksakov, Sergeĭ Timofeevich, 1791-1859. III. 2502
The family chronicle. Translated by M. C. Beverly. Introd. by Ralph E. Matlaw. New York, Dutton, 1961. 227 p. 19 cm. (A Dutton paperback, D86) *1. Aksakov family. 2. Russia — Social life and customs. I. T.*
DK37.8.A3A3 1961   891.783   61-65198

Black, Cyril Edwin, 1915- ed. III. 2503
Rewriting Russian history; Soviet interpretations of Russia's past. 2d ed., rev. New York, Vintage Books [1962] 431 p. 19 cm. (Vintage Russian library) *1. Russia — History — Historiography. I. T.*
DK38.B5 1962   947   63-1520

Christoff, Peter K. III. 2504
An introduction to nineteenth-century Russian Slavophilism; a study in ideas. 's-Gravenhage, Moulton, 1961- v. ports. 25 cm. (Slavistic printings and reprintings, 23) *1. Slavophilism. I. T. (S)*
DK38.C45   63-45564

Mazour, Anatole Gregory, 1900- III. 2505
Modern Russian historiography. 2d ed. Princeton, N.J., Van Nostrand [1958] 260 p. illus. 22 cm. First ed. published in 1939 under title: An outline of modern Russian historiography. *1. Russia — History — Historiography. I. T.*
DK38.M3 1958   947.007   58-13572

Mazour, Anatole Gregory, 1900- III. 2506
The writing of history in the Soviet Union, by Anatole G. Mazour. Stanford, Calif., Hoover Institution Press [1971] xvi, 383 p. 24 cm. (Hoover Institution publications) *1. Russia — Historiography. I. T. (S:Stanford University. Hoover Institution on War, Revolution and Peace. Publications.)*
DK38.M325   947/.0072/047   76-99084   ISBN:081791871X

Riasanovsky, Nicholas Valentine, 1923- III. 2507
Russia and the West in the teaching of the Slavophiles; a study of romantic ideology. Cambridge, Harvard University Press, 1952. 244 p. 22 cm. (Harvard historical studies, v.61) "Original version ... was written as a doctoral dissertation at Oxford University." *1. Slavophilism. I. T. (S)*
DK38.R5   914.7   52-9394

Florinsky, Michael T., 1894- III. 2508
Russia: a history and an interpretation. New York, Macmillan, 1953. 2 v. maps. 22 cm. *1. Russia — History.*
DK40.F6 1953   947   53-11899

Kliuchevskiĭ, Vasiliĭ Osipovich, 1841-1911. III. 2509
A history of Russia, by V. O. Kluchevsky. Translated by C. J. Hogarth. New York, Russell & Russell, 1960. 5 v. 23 cm. *1. Russia — History.*
DK40.K613   947   60-6033

Mirskiĭ, Dmitriĭ Petrovich, 1890- III. 2510
Russia, a social history, by D. S. Mirsky, edited by Professor C. G. Seligman, F.R.S. London, Cresset, 1931. xix, 312, xxi p. illus., maps, plates. 26 cm. (Cresset historical series.) *1. Russia — History. 2. Russia — Social conditions. I. Seligman, Charles Gabriel, 1873- ed.*
DK40.M5   947   31-14833

Pares, Bernard, Sir, 1867-1949. III. 2511
A history of Russia. Definitive ed., with a new introd. by Richard Pares. New York, Knopf, 1953. xxxvii, 611, xxxi p. maps. 25 cm. *1. Russia — History.*
DK40.P3 1953   947   52-5077

Pokrovskiĭ, Mikhail Nikolaevich, 1868-1932. III. 2512
History of Russia, from the earliest times to the rise of commercial capitalism. Translated and edited by J. D. Clarkson [and] M. R. M. Griffiths. New York, Russell & Russell, 1966. xvi, 383 p. maps. 24 cm. *1. Russia — History. I. Clarkson, Jesse Dunsmore, 1897- ed. and tr. II. Griffiths, Mary Rose Millie, 1898- ed. and tr. III. T.*
DK40.P612 1966a   947   66-24751

Riasanovsky, Nicholas Valentine, 1923- III. 2513
A history of Russia [by] Nicholas V. Riasanovsky. 2d ed. New York, Oxford University Press, 1969. xviii, 748 p. illus., geneal. tables, maps (1 col. on lining papers), ports. 24 cm. *1. Russia — History. I. T.*
DK40.R5 1969   947   69-17179

Vernadsky, George, 1887-   **III. 2514**
A history of Russia, by George Vernadsky and Michael Karpovich. [New Haven, Yale university press; London, H. Milford, Oxford university press, 1943- v. maps (part fold.) 25 cm. Half-title; Each volume has special t.-p. *1. Russia — History. I. Karpovich, Michael, 1888-*
DK40.V44   947   A43-1903

Clarkson, Jesse Dunsmore, 1897-   **III. 2515**
A history of Russia, by Jesse D. Clarkson. 2d ed. New York, Random House [1969] xxii, 886 p. illus., maps, ports. 25 cm. *1. Russia — History. I. T.*
DK41.C55 1969   947   69-11101

Platonov, Sergeĭ Fedorovich, 1860-1933.   **III. 2516**
History of Russia, by S. F. Platonov, translated by E. Aronsberg, edited by F. A. Golder. New York, Macmillan, 1925. vii, 435 p. maps (part double) geneal. tables. 21 cm. *1. Russia — History. I. Aronsberg, Emanuel, tr. II. Golder, Frank Alfred, 1877-1929, ed.*
DK41.P6   25-24285

Sumner, Benedict Humphrey, 1893-   **III. 2517**
A short history of Russia [by] B. H. Sumner ... New York, Reynal & Hitchcock [1943] 5 p. l., 469 p. illus. (maps) plates, ports. 22 cm. *1. Russia — History.*
DK41.S8   947   43-17185

Kerner, Robert Joseph, 1887-   **III. 2518**
The urge to the sea; the course of Russian history. The role of rivers, portages, ostrogs, monasteries, and furs, by Robert J. Kerner. Berkeley and Los Angeles, University of California Press, 1942. xvii, 212 p. illus., maps (part fold.) 24 cm. (Publications of the Northeastern Asia seminar of the University of California) *1. Russia — History. I. T.*
DK43.K47   947   42-36949

Curtiss, John Shelton, 1899-   **III. 2519**
The Russian Army under Nicholas I, 1825-1855. Durham, N.C., Duke University Press, 1965. x, 386 p. maps. 24 cm. *1. Russia. Armiia — History. 2. Russia — History, Military — 1801-1917. I. T.*
DK53.C85   355.0330947   65-24927

DK60 – 69 POLITICAL AND DIPLOMATIC HISTORY

Conference on a Century of Russian Foreign Policy, Yale University, 1961.   **III. 2520**
Russian foreign policy; essays in historical perspective. Edited by Ivo J. Lederer. New Haven, Yale University Press, 1962. xxiii, 620 p. 24 cm. *1. Russia — Foreign relations — Congresses. I. Lederer, Ivo J., ed. II. Yale University. III. T.*
DK61.C65   327.47   62-8251

Beloff, Max, 1913-   **III. 2521**
The foreign policy of Soviet Russia, 1929-1941. Issued under the auspices of the Royal Institute of International Affairs. London, New York, Oxford University Press, 1947-49. 2 v. maps (1 fold.) 23 cm. *1. Russia — Foreign relations — 1917-1945. I. T.*
DK63.B4   327.47   48-478

Eudin, Xenia Joukoff.   **III. 2522**
Soviet foreign policy, 1928-1934; documents and materials, by Xenia Joukoff Eudin and Robert M. Slusser. University Park, Pennsylvania State University Press [1967, c1966- v. 25 cm. (Hoover Institution publications) "A continuation of the two Hoover Institution collections published in 1957; Soviet Russia and the West, 1920-1927; a documentary survey, by X. J. Eudin and H. H. Fisher, and Soviet Russia and the East, 1920-1927; a documentary survey, by X. J. Eudin and R. C. North." *1. Russia — Foreign relations — 1917-1945. I. Slusser, Robert M., joint author. II. T.*
DK63.E8   327.47   66-25465

Kennan, George Frost, 1904-   **III. 2523**
Soviet foreign policy, 1917-1941. Princeton, N.J., Van Nostrand [1960] 192 p. 19 cm. (Van Nostrand anvil books, no.47) *1. Russia — Foreign relations — 1917-1945. I. T.*
DK63.K4   327.47   60-13459

Barghoorn, Frederick Charles, 1911-   **III. 2524**
The Soviet cultural offensive; the role of cultural diplomacy in Soviet foreign policy. Princeton, N.J., Princeton University Press, 1960. 353 p. 25 cm. *1. Russia — Foreign relations — 1945- 2. Cultural relations. I. T.*
DK63.3.B35   327.47   60-12227

Dallin, Alexander, comp.   **III. 2525**
Soviet conduct in world affairs; a selection of readings. New York, Columbia University Press, 1960. 318 p. 24 cm. *1. Russia — Foreign relations — 1917-1945. 2. Russia — Foreign relations — 1945- I. T.*
DK63.3.D32   327.47   59-15509

Dallin, David J., 1889-1962.   **III. 2526**
Soviet foreign policy after Stalin. [1st ed.] Philadelphia, Lippincott, 1961 [c1960] xii, 543 p. maps. 24 cm. *1. Russia — Foreign relations — 1953- I. T.*
DK63.3.D33   327.47   60-14257

Fleming, Denna Frank, 1893-   **III. 2527**
The cold war and its origins, 1917-1960. Garden City, N.Y., Doubleday [1961] 2 v. (xx, 1158 p.) 25 cm. *1. Russia — Foreign relations — 1917-1945. 2. Russia — Foreign relations — 1945- I. T.*
DK63.3.F55   327.47   61-9193

Gehlen, Michael P.   **III. 2528**
The politics of coexistence; Soviet methods and motives, by Michael P. Gehlen. Bloomington, Indiana University Press [1967] 334 p. 21 cm. (Indiana University international studies) *1. Russia — Foreign relations — 1953- 2. Communist strategy. I. T. (S:Indiana. University. International studies)*
DK63.3.G4   327.47   67-13023

Kennan, George Frost, 1904-   **III. 2529**
Russia and the West under Lenin and Stalin. [1st ed.] Boston, Little, Brown [1961] 411 p. 22 cm. *1. Russia — Foreign relations — 1917-1945. I. T.*
DK63.3.K38   327.47   61-9292

Mackintosh, John Malcolm.   **III. 2530**
Strategy and tactics of Soviet foreign policy. London, New York, Oxford University Press, 1962. 332 p. 23 cm. *1. Russia — Foreign relations — 1945- I. T.*
DK63.3.M23 1962   327.47   62-6989

Rubinstein, Alvin Z., ed.   **III. 2531**
The foreign policy of the Soviet Union. Edited, with introductory essays, by Alvin Z. Rubinstein. 3d ed. New York, Random House [1972] xviii, 474 p. 24 cm. *1. Russia — Foreign relations — 1917-1945. 2. Russia — Foreign relations — 1945- I. T.*
DK63.3.R8 1972   327.47   71-38820   ISBN:0394316991

Shulman, Marshall Darrow.   **III. 2532**
Stalin's foreign policy reappraised. Cambridge, Harvard University Press, 1963. vi, 320 p. 22 cm. (Russian Research Center studies, 48) *1. Russia — Foreign relations — 1945- I. T.*
DK63.3.S368   327.47   63-13816

Triska, Jan F.   **III. 2533**
Soviet foreign policy [by] Jan F. Triska [and] David D. Finley. New York, Macmillan [1968] xix, 518 p. 24 cm. *1. Russia — Foreign relations — 1917-1945. 2. Russia — Foreign relations — 1945- I. Finley, David D., joint author. II. T.*
DK63.3.T74   327.47   68-12288

DK67   Russia and Europe

Blackstock, Paul W., ed.   **III. 2534**
The Russian menace to Europe; a collection of articles, speeches, letters, and news dispatches, by Karl Marx and Friedrich Engels. Selected and edited by Paul W. Blackstock and Bert F. Hoselitz. Glencoe, Ill., Free Press [1952] 288 p. 22 cm. *1. Europe — Politics — 1789-1900. 2. Russia — Foreign relations — Europe. I. Hoselitz, Berthold Frank, 1913- joint ed. II. Marx, Karl, 1818-1883. III. Engels, Friedrich, 1820-1895. IV. T.*
DK67.B5   947.07   52-13423

Eudin, Xenia Joukoff.   **III. 2535**
Soviet Russia and the West, 1920-1927; a documentary survey, by Xenia Joukoff Eudin and Harold H. Fisher in collaboration with Rosemary Brown Jones. Stanford, Stanford University Press, 1957. xxxvii, 450 p. illus. 25 cm. (The Hoover Library on War, Revolution, and Peace. Publication no. 26) *1. Russia — Foreign relations — Europe. 2. Europe — Politics — 1918-1945. I. Fisher, Harold Henry, 1890- joint author. II. T. (S:Stanford University. Hoover Institute and Library on War, Revolution, and Peace, Publication no. 26)*
DK67.E85   327.47094   57-6013

Lobanov-Rostovsky, Andrei, 1892-   **III. 2536**
Russia and Europe, 1825-1878. Ann Arbor, Mich., G. Wahr Pub. Co., 1954. 330 p. 24 cm. *1. Russia — Foreign relations — 19th cent. 2. Europe — Politics — 1789-1900. I. T.*
DK67.L6   940.28   55-1181

Jelavich, Charles.   **III. 2537**
Tsarist Russia and Balkan nationalism; Russian influence in the internal affairs of Bulgaria and Serbia, 1879-1886. Berkeley, University of California Press, 1958. x, 304 p. map. 25 cm. (Russian and East European studies) *1. Russia — Foreign relations — Bulgaria. 2. Bulgaria — Foreign relations —*

Russia. 3. Russia — Foreign relations — Serbia. 4. Serbia — Foreign relations — Russia. I. T. (S)
DK67.4.J4   327.4709497   58-12830

DK68   Russia and Asia

Eudin, Xenia Joukoff.   III. 2538
Soviet Russia and the East, 1920-1927; a documentary survey, by Xenia Joukoff Eudin and Robert C. North. Stanford, Stanford University Press, 1957. xviii, 478 p. illus. 25 cm. (The Hoover Library on War, Revolution, and Peace. Publication no. 25) 1. Russia — Foreign relations — Asia. 2. Asia — Politics. I. North, Robert Carver, joint author. II. T. (S:Stanford University. Hoover Institute and Library on War, Revolution, and Peace. Publication no. 25)
DK68.E85   327.47095   56-8690

Lobanov-Rostovsky, Andrei, 1892-   III. 2539
Russia and Asia. Ann Arbor, G. Wahr Pub. Co., 1951. 342 p. illus. 23 cm. 1. Russia — Foreign relations — Asia.
DK68.L6 1951   327.47   51-5701

McLane, Charles B.   III. 2540
Soviet policy and the Chinese Communists, 1931-1946. New York, Columbia University Press, 1958. viii, 310 p. 24 cm. (Studies of the Russian Institute, Columbia University) 1. Russia — Foreign relations — China. 2. China — Foreign relations — Russia. 3. Communism — China. I. T. (S:Columbia University. Russian Institute. Studies)
DK68.7.C5M27   327.470951   58-11903

Mancall, Mark.   III. 2541
Russia and China; their diplomatic relations to 1728. Cambridge, Harvard University Press, 1971. xii, 396 p. 25 cm. (Harvard East Asian series 61) 1. Russia — Foreign relations — China. 2. China — Foreign relations — Russia. 3. Siberia — Discovery and exploration. I. T. (S)
DK68.7.C5M29   327.47/051   74-85077   ISBN:0674781155

Zagoria, Donald S.   III. 2542
The Sino-Soviet Conflict, 1956-1961. Princeton, N.J., Princeton University Press, 1962. 484 p. 25 cm. 1. Russia — Foreign relations — China (People's Republic of China, 1949-   ) 2. China (People's Republic of China, 1949-   ) 3. Communism — History. I. T.
DK68.7.C5Z3   327.47051   62-10890

DK70 – 276   HISTORY, BY PERIOD
DK70 – 112   Early. Medieval, to 1613

Chadwick, Nora (Kershaw) 1891-   III. 2543
The beginnings of Russian history: an enquiry into sources, by N. K. Chadwick. Cambridge [Eng.] The University Press, 1946. xi, 180 p. front. 20 cm. 1. Nestor, annalist, d. 1115? 2. Russia — History — To 1533 — Sources.
DK70.A2C5   947.92   46-6223

Povest' vremennykh let. English.   III. 2544
The Russian Primary chronicle: Laurentian text. Translated and edited by Samuel Hazzard Cross and Olgerd P. Shobowitz-Wetzor. Cambridge, Mass., Mediaeval Academy of America [1953] 313 p. maps, geneal. table. 24 cm. (Mediaeval Academy of America. Publication no. 60) Part of the chronicle is believed to have been written by Nestor in the 11th century. 1. Russia — History — To 1533. I. Nestor, annalist, d. 1115? II. Cross, Samuel Hazzard, 1891-1946, ed. and tr. III. Sherbowitz-Wetzor, Olgerd P., ed. and tr. IV. T. (S)
DK70.P612   947   53-10264

Karamzin, Nikolaĭ Mikhaĭlovich, 1766-1826.   III. 2545
Memoir on ancient and modern Russia. A translation and analysis [by] Richard Pipes. Cambridge, Harvard University Press, 1959. xiv, 266 p. port. 22 cm. (Russian Research Center studies, 33) Translation of O drevneĭ i novoĭ Rossii (romanized form) 1. Russia — History. I. Pipes, Richard, ed. and tr. II. T. (S:Harvard University. Russian Research Center. Studies, 33)
DK71.K343   947   59-6162

Paszkiewicz, Henryk, 1897-   III. 2546
The making of the Russian nation. [Chicago] H. Regnery Co. [1963] 509 p. fold. maps. 26 cm. 1. Russia — History — To 1533. I. T.
DK71.P29 1963a   947   65-1517

Vernadsky, George, 1887-   III. 2547
The origins of Russia. Oxford, Clarendon Press, 1959. x, 354 p. illus. 22 cm. 1. Russia — History — To 1533.
DK72.V4   947.01   59-1228

Presniakov, Aleksandr Evgen'evich, 1870-1929.   III. 2548
The formation of the great Russian state; a study of Russian history in the thirteenth to fifteenth centuries. Translated from the Russian by A. E. Moorhouse. Introd. by Alfred J. Rieber. Chicago, Quadrangle Books [c1970] xlii, 414 p. 22 cm. (The Quadrangle series in Russian history) Translation of Obrazovanie Velikorusskago gosudarstva (romanized form) 1. Russia — History — 1237-1480. I. T.
DK90.P713   947/.03   75-78314

Kurbskiĭ, Andreĭ Mikhaĭlovich, kniaz', d. 1583.   III. 2549
The correspondence between Prince A. M. Kurbsky and Tsar Ivan IV, of Russia, 1564-1579. Edited with a translation and notes by J. L. I. Fennell. Cambridge [Eng.] University Press, 1955. xi, 275 p. 22 cm. 1. Russia — History — Ivan IV, 1533-1584 — Sources. I. Ivan IV, the Terrible, Czar of Russia, 1530-1584.
DK106.A25   947.04   A56-4698

Fennell, John Lister Illingworth.   III. 2550
Ivan the Great of Moscow. London, Macmillan; New York, St Martin's Press, 1961 [i.e. 1962] 386 p. illus. 23 cm. 1. Russia — History — Ivan III, 1462-1505.
DK106.F4   947.04   62-1391

Graham, Stephen, 1884-   III. 2551
Ivan the Terrible; life of Ivan IV of Russia. [Hamden, Conn.] Archon Books, 1968. x, 335 p. illus., ports. 22 cm. Reprint of the 1933 ed. 1. Ivan IV, the Terrible, Czar of Russia, 1530-1584. 2. Russia — History — Ivan IV, 1533-1584.
DK106.G7 1968   947/.04/0924   (B)   68-8020   ISBN:0208006834

Graham, Stephen, 1884-   III. 2552
Boris Godunof. With a pref. by George Vernadsky. [Hamden, Conn.] Archon Books, 1970 [c1933] ix, 290 p. ports. 22 cm. 1. Boris Godunov, Czar of Russia, 1551?-1605. 2. Russia — History — Boris Godunov, 1598-1605.
DK109.G7 1970   947/.04/0924   (B)   74-120368   ISBN:208009698

Platonov, Sergeĭ Fedorovich, 1860-1933.   III. 2553
The time of troubles; a historical study of the internal crises and social struggle in sixteenth- and seventeenth-Century Muscovy [by] S. F. Platonov. Translated by John T. Alexander. Lawrence, University Press of Kansas [c1970] xvii, 197 p. maps. 22 cm. (Kansas paperback, KP-8) Translation of Smutnoe vremia (romanized form) 1. Russia — History — Epoch of confusion, 1605-1613. I. T.
DK111.P5813   947/.04   79-97029   ISBN:700600620

DK113 – 264   1613 – 1917

Bain, Robert Nisbet, 1854-1909.   III. 2554
The first Romanovs, 1613-1725; a history of Moscovite civilization and the rise of modern Russia under Peter the Great and his forerunners. New York, Russell & Russell [1967] xii, 413 p. illus., ports. 22 cm. Reprint of ed. first published in 1905. 1. Russia — History — 1613-1689. 2. Russia — History — Peter I, 1689-1725. 3. Romanov, House of. I. T.
DK114.B2 1967   947/.04   66-24666

Kliuchevskiĭ, Vasiliĭ Osipovich, 1841-1911.   III. 2555
A course in Russian history: the seventeenth century, by V. O. Kliuchevsky. Translated from the Russian by Natalie Duddington. Introd. by Alfred J. Rieber. Chicago, Quadrangle Books [1968] xl, 400 p. 22 cm. (Quadrangle series in Russian history) Translation of v. 3 of Kurs russkoĭ istorii (romanized form) 1. Russia — History — 1613-1689 2. Russia — History — Epoch of confusion, 1605-1613. I. T.
DK114.K573   947/.04   68-26442

Rogger, Hans.   III. 2556
National consciousness in eighteenth-century Russia. Cambridge, Harvard University Press, 1960. viii, 319 p. 22 cm. (Russian Research Center studies, 38) 1. Nationalism — Russia. 2. Russia — History — 1689-1800. I. T. (S:Harvard University. Russian Research Center. Studies, 38)
DK127.R6   947.06   60-8450

Grey, Ian, 1918-   III. 2557
Peter the Great, Emperor of all Russia. [1st ed.] Philadelphia, Lippincott [1960] 505 p. 22 cm. 1. Peter I, the Great, Emperor of Russia, 1672-1725.
DK131.G75   923.147   60-5109

Schuyler, Eugene, 1840-1890.   III. 2558
Peter the Great, Emperor of Russia; a study of historical biography. New York, Russell & Russell [1967] 2 v. illus., geneal. table, maps (1 fold.), ports. 22 cm. Reprints of the 1884 ed. 1. Peter I, the Great, Emperor of Russia, 1672-1725. I. T.
DK131.S39 1967   947/.05/0924   (B)   66-24757

Sumner, Benedict Humphrey, 1893-   III. 2559
Peter the Great and the emergence of Russia. New York, Macmillan, 1951. vii, 216 p. port., maps (on lining papers) geneal. table. 18 cm. (Teach yourself

history library) Addendum slip mounted on p. 211. *1. Peter I, the Great, Emperor of Russia, 1672-1725. 2. Russia — History — Peter I, 1689-1725. I. T. (S)*
DK131.S88 947.05 A52-973

Waliszewski, Kazimierz, 1849-1935. III. 2560
Peter the Great. Translated from the French by Lady Mary Loyd. [2d ed.] New York, Greenwood Press [1968] x, 562 p. port. 23 cm. Reprint of the 1897 ed. *1. Russia — History — Peter I, 1689-1725. 2. Peter I, the Great, Emperor of Russia, 1672-1725.*
DK131.W173 1968 947/.05/0924 (B) 69-14133

Grunwald, Constantin de. III. 2561
Peter the Great; translated from the French by Viola Garvin. London, D. Saunders with MacGibbon & Kee, 1956. 224 p. illus. 22 cm. Translation of La Russie de Pierre le Grand. *1. Russia — Civilization. 2. Russia — History — Peter I, 1689-1725.*
DK142.G72 1956 56-23112

Bain, Robert Nisbet, 1854-1909. III. 2562
The daughter of Peter the Great. New York, AMS Press [1970] xviii, 328 p. ports. 23 cm. Reprint of the 1899 ed. *1. Elizabeth, Empress of Russia, 1709-1762. 2. Russia — History — Elizabeth, 1741-1762. I. T.*
DK161.B18 1970 947/.06 72-136407 ISBN:0404004474

Bain, Robert Nisbet, 1854-1909. III. 2563
Peter III, Emperor of Russia; the story of a crisis and a crime. Westminster, A. Constable, 1902. St. Clair Shores, Mich., Scholarly Press, 1972. xvi, 208 p. ports. 23 cm. *1. Peter III, Emperor of Russia, 1723-1762.*
DK166.B2 1972 947/.06/0924 (B) 71-108456 ISBN:0403004659

DK170 – 183 CATHARINE II, 1762 – 1796

Catharine II, Empress of Russia, 1729-1796. III. 2564
The memoirs of Catherine the Great. Edited by Dominique Maroger, with an introd. by G. P. Gooch; translated from the French by Moura Budberg. New York, Macmillan [1955] 400 p. ports. 23 cm. *I. Maroger, Dominique, ed.*
DK170.A262 923.147 55-1967

Anthony, Katharine Susan, 1877- III. 2565
Catherine the Great, by Katharine Anthony. Garden City, N.Y., Garden City Publishing Company, Inc. [1927?] 3 p. l., 3-331 p. front., ports. 22 cm. (The star series) *1. Catharine II, empress of Russia, 1729-1796.*
DK170.A6 1927 923.147 33-5911

Gooch, George Peabody, 1873- III. 2566
Catherine the Great, and other studies [by] G. P. Gooch. Hamden, Conn., Archon Books, 1966. xi, 292 p. ports. 22 cm. First published in 1954. *1. Catharine II, Empress of Russia, 1729-1796. 2. Voltaire, François Marie Arouet de, 1694-1778. 3. Bismarck, Otto, Fürst von, 1815-1898. 4. France — Intellectual life. I. T.*
DK170.G65 1966 920.02 66-18227

Grey, Ian, 1918- III. 2567
Catherine the Great: autocrat and Empress of all Russia. Philadelphia, Lippincott, 1962 [c1961] 254 p. illus. 22 cm. *1. Catherine II, Empress of Russia, 1729-1796.*
DK170.G68 1962 923.147 62-7180

Thomson, Gladys Scott. III. 2568
Catherine the Great and the expansion of Russia. New York, Macmillan, 1950. x, 294 p. port., col. map, geneal. table. 19 cm. (Teach yourself history library) Map and geneal. table on lining papers. *1. Catharine II, Empress of Russia, 1729-1796. (S:Teach yourself history library (New York))*
DK170.T5 1950 947.06 50-6988

Waliszewski, Kazimierz, 1849-1935. III. 2569
The romance of an empress; Catherine II of Russia. [Hamden, Conn.] Archon Books, 1968. viii, 458 p. port. 21 cm. Reprint of the 1894 ed. *1. Catharine II, Empress of Russia, 1729-1796. 2. Russia — History — Catharine II, 1762-1796. I. T.*
DK170.W27 1968 947/.06/0924 (B) 68-26929

DK188 – 243 19TH CENTURY

Kornilov, Aleksandr Aleksandrovich, 1862-1926. III. 2570
Modern Russian history; from the age of Catherine the Great to the end of the nineteenth century, Translated from the Russian by Alexander S. Kaun. With a bibliography by John S. Curtiss. New York, Russell & Russell [1970, c1944] 310, 284, x p. illus. 22 cm. Translation of Kurs istorii Rossii XIX vieka. "Reproduced from the revised one-volume edition of 1943." *1. Russia — History — 19th century. I. T.*
DK189.K7 1970 947/.07 74-102513

Venturi, Franco. III. 2571
Roots of revolution; a history of the populist and socialist movements in nineteenth century Russia. Translated from the Italian by Francis Haskell. With an introd. by Isaiah Berlin. New York, Knopf, 1960. 850 p. 25 cm. Translation of Il populismo russo. *1. Populism in Russia (Narodnichestvo) I. T.*
DK189.V413 947.08 59-5423

Yarmolinsky, Avrahm, 1890- III. 2572
Road to revolution; a century of Russian radicalism. London, Cassell [1957] 369 p. illus. 22 cm. *1. Russia — Politics and government — 19th cent. I. T.*
DK189.Y3 947.07 57-3572

Paléologue, Georges Maurice, 1859-1966. III. 2573
The enigmatic czar; the life of Alexander I of Russia. Translated from the French by Edwin and Willa Muir. [Hamden, Conn.] Archon Books, 1969. 325 p. ports., fold map. 22 cm. Translation of Alexandre 1er. Unabridged and unaltered reprint of the 1938 ed. *1. Alexander I, Emperor of Russia, 1777-1825. I. T.*
DK191.P32 1969 947/.07/0924 (B) 69-18274 ISBN:208007482

Strakhovsky, Leonid Ivan, 1898-1963. III. 2574
Alexander I of Russia; the man who defeated Napoleon. Westport, Conn., Greenwood Press [1970, c1947] 302 p. illus., ports. 23 cm. *1. Alexander I, Emperor of Russia, 1777-1825.*
DK191.S75 1970 947/.07/0924 (B) 77-100245 ISBN:083714034X

Grimsted, Patricia Kennedy. III. 2575
The foreign ministers of Alexander I; political attitudes and the conduct of Russian diplomacy, 1801-1825. Berkeley, University of California Press, 1969. xxvi, 367 p. ports. 24 cm. (Russian and East European studies) *1. Russia — Foreign relations — 1801-1825. 2. Alexander I, Emperor of Russia, 1777-1825. 3. Statesmen, Russian. I. T. (S)*
DK197.G7 1969 327.47 69-11615 ISBN:520013875

Lobanov-Rostovsky, Andrei, 1892- III. 2576
Russia and Europe, 1789-1825. by Andrei A. Lobanov-Rostovsky. New York, Greenwood Press, 1968 [c1947] xviii, 448 p. 24 cm. *1. Russia — Foreign relations — 1801-1825. I. T.*
DK197.L6 1968 327.47 68-30825

Raeff, Marc. III. 2577
Michael Speransky, statesman of imperial Russia, 1772-1839. The Hague, M. Nijhoff, 1957. viii, 387 p. port. 25 cm. *1. Speranskiĭ, Mikhail Mikhaĭlovich, graf, 1772-1839. 2. Russia — Politics and government — 19th cent.*
DK201.R3 923.247 A58-1656

Hertzen, Aleksandr Ivanovich, 1812-1870. III. 2578
The memoirs of Alexander Herzen, parts I and II, translated from the Russian by J. D. Duff. New Haven, Yale University Press, 1923. xvi, 384 p. 21 cm. "The present volume is the seventh work published by the Yale University Press on the Theodore L. Glasgow Memorial Publication Fund." *1. Duff, James Duff, 1860-1940, tr. II. Yale University. Theodore L. Glasgow Memorial Publication Fund.*
DK209.6.H4A32 928.917 23-13462

Hertzen, Aleksandr Ivanovich, 1812-1870. III. 2579
My past and thoughts, the memoirs of Alexander Herzen; the authorised translation; translated from the Russian by Constance Garnett ... London, Chatto & Windus, 1924-27. 6 v. 16 cm. "This translation has been made by arrangement from the sole complete and copyright edition of My past and thoughts, that published in the original Russian at Berlin, 1921." Translation of Byloe i dumy (romanized form) *I. Garnett, Constance (Black) 1862-1946, tr. II. T.*
DK209.6.H4A33 928.917 24-17707

Grunwald, Constantin de. III. 2580
Tsar Nicholas I. Translated from the French by Brigit Patmore. New York, Macmillan, 1955. ix, 294 p. port. 22 cm. Translation of La vie de Nicolas I. *1. Nicholas I, Emperor of Russia, 1796-1855.*
DK210.G72 1955 923.147 55-13563

Riasanovsky, Nicholas Valentine, 1923- III. 2581
Nicholas I and official nationality in Russia, 1825-1855. Berkeley, University of California Press, 1959. viii, 296 p. 24 cm. (Russian and East European studies) *1. Nicholas I, Emperor of Russia, 1796-1855. 2. Nationalism — Russia. (S)*
DK210.R5 947.07 59-11316

Mazour, Anatole Gregory, 1900- III. 2582
The first Russian revolution, 1825; the Decembrist movement, its origins, development, and significance. Stanford, Calif., Stanford University Press [1961, c1937] 328 p. illus. 23 cm. *1. Russia — History — Conspiracy of December, 1825. I. T.*
DK212.M3 1961 947.07 61-11048

Raeff, Marc. III. 2583
The Decembrist movement. Englewood Cliffs, N.J., Prentice-Hall [1966] x, 180 p. 21 cm. (Russian civilization series) *1. Russia — History — Conspiracy of December, 1825. 2. Secret societies — Russia. I. T.*
DK212.R22 947.07 66-11188

Lampert, Evgeniĭ, 1913-   III. 2584
Sons against fathers; studies in Russian radicalism and revolution [by] E. Lampert. Oxford, Clarendon Press, 1965. vi, 405 p. illus., ports. 23 cm. *1. Chernyshevskiĭ, Nikolaĭ Gavrilovich, 1828-1889. 2. Dobroliubov, Nikolaĭ Aleksandrovich, 1836-1861. 3. Pisarev, Dmitriĭ Ivanovich, 1840-1868. 4. Revolutions — Russia. I. T.*
DK219.3.L3   65-2412

Almedingen, Martha Edith, 1898-   III. 2585
The Emperor Alexander II; a study by E. M. Almedingen. London, Bodley Head [1962] 367 p. illus. 23 cm. *1. Alexander II, Emperor of Russia, 1818-1881.*
DK220.A4   63-2170

Graham, Stephen, 1884-   III. 2586
Tsar of freedom, the life and reign of Alexander II. [Hamden, Conn.] Archon Books, 1968 [c1963] xii, 324 p. illus., ports. 22 cm. *1. Alexander II, Emperor of Russia, 1818-1881. I. T.*
DK220.G7 1968   947.08/0924 (B)   68-15345

Mosse, Werner Eugen.   III. 2587
Alexander II and the modernization of Russia. New, rev. ed. New York, Collier Books [1962] 159 p. 18 cm. (Men and history, AS443V) *1. Alexander II, Emperor of Russia, 1818-1881.*
DK220.M6 1962   923.147   62-19202

Wortman, Richard.   III. 2588
The crisis of Russian populism. London, Cambridge U.P., 1967. xii, 211 p. front. (ports.). 22 1/2 cm. *1. Populism in Russia. I. T.*
DK221.W66   320.9/47   67-12849

Seton-Watson, Hugh.   III. 2589
The decline of imperial Russia, 1855-1914. With 8 maps. New York, F. A. Praeger [1952] 406 p. illus. 22 cm. (Books that matter) *1. Russia — History — 19th century. 2. Russia — History — 1904-1914. I. T.*
DK223.S4   947.08   52-7488

Byrnes, Robert Francis.   III. 2590
Pobedonostsev, his life and thought [by] Robert F. Byrnes. Bloomington, Indiana University Press [1968] xiii, 495 p. ports. 25 cm. (Indiana University international studies) *1. Pobedonostsev, Konstantine Petrovich, 1827-1907. (S:Indiana. University. International studies.)*
DK236.P6B8   947.08/0924 (B)   68-14598

DK246 – 276 20TH CENTURY

Pares, Bernard, Sir, 1867-1949.   III. 2591
My Russian memoirs. [1st AMS ed.] New York, AMS Press [1969] 623 p. ports. 23 cm. Reprint of the 1931 ed. *1. Russia — History — Nicholas II, 1894-1917. 2. Russia — History — Revolution, 1917-1921. 3. European War, 1914-1918 — Russia. I. T.*
DK246.P3 1969   947.08   78-96471

Treadgold, Donald W., 1922-   III. 2592
Twentieth century Russia [by] Donald W. Treadgold. 2d ed. Chicago, Rand McNally [1964] xiii, 576 p. illus., maps. ports. 24 cm. (Rand McNally history series) *1. Russia — History — 20th century. I. T.*
DK246.T65 1964   947.084   64-14118

Ulam, Adam Bruno, 1922-   III. 2593
The Bolsheviks; the intellectual and political history of the triumph of communism in Russia [by] Adam B. Ulam. New York, Macmillan [1965] ix, 598 p. ports. 24 cm. *1. Communism — Russia — History. 2. Lenin, Vladimir Il'ich, 1870-1924. I. T.*
DK246.U4   335.430947   65-18463

Golder, Frank Alfred, 1877-1929, ed.   III. 2594
Documents of Russian history 1914-1917; translated by Emanuel Aronsberg. New York, London, Century [c1927] xvi, 663 p. 23 cm. (The Century historical series) "The material for this book is taken from various places, but largely from two newspapers, the 'Reich' and the 'Izvestiia'." — Pref. *1. Russia — History — Revolution, 1917- — Sources. 2. Russia — Politics and government — 1917- 3. European war, 1914-1918 — Russia. I. Aronsberg, Emanuel, tr.*
DK251.G6   28-1054

DK253 – 254 Biography. Memoirs

Lunacharskiĭ, Anatoliĭ Vasil'evich, 1875-1933.   III. 2595
Revolutionary silhouettes [by] Anatoly Vasilievich Lunacharsky. Translated from the Russian and edited by Michael Glenny. With an introd. by Issac Deutscher. [1st American ed.] New York, Hill and Wang [1968, c1967] 155 p. illus., ports. 22 cm. Translation of the 1923 ed. of Revoliutsionnye siluety (romanized form) *1. Revolutionists, Russian. I. T.*
DK253.L813 1968   947.08/0922   68-30764

Lenin, Vladimir Il'ich, 1870-1924.   III. 2596
Collected works of V. I. Lenin. Completely revised, edited and annotated. The only edition authorized by the V. I. Lenin institute, Moscow. [New York, International publishers, c1927-   v. 23 cm. "This will be the only authorized English translation of Lenin's writings from 1893 to 1924." — Editor's note, v. 13. *I. Moscow. Institut V. I. Lenina.*
DK254.L3A5   28-6510

Lenin, Vladimir Il'ich, 1870-1924.   III. 2597
The essentials of Lenin. London, Lawrence & Wishart, 1947. 2 v. illus. 23 cm. "Follows in every respect the latest Russian edition published by the Marx-Engels-Lenin Institute, Moscow, the only difference being that 'What is to be done?' and 'One step forward, two steps back,' are given in the abridged form published by the author in 1908."
DK254.L3A572   308.1   48-12478

Lenin, Vladimir Il'ich, 1870-1924.   III. 2598
Selected works [of] V. I. Lenin; one-volume edition. [1st ed.] New York, International Publishers [1971] 798 p. 22 cm. (New World paperbacks, NW-133) Reprint of the 1968 ed.
DK254.L3A578 1971   335.4/08   75-175177   ISBN:0717803007

Fischer, Louis, 1896-1970.   III. 2599
The life of Lenin. [1st ed.] New York, Harper & Row [1964] viii, 703 p. ports. 24 cm. *1. Lenin, Vladimir Il'ich, 1870-1924. I. T.*
DK254.L4F53   923.247   64-14385

Shub, David, 1887-   III. 2600
Lenin: a biography. Revised ed. Harmondsworth, Penguin, 1966. 496 p. 18 1/2 cm. (Political leaders of the twentieth century. Pelican book A809.) *1. Lenin, Vladimir Ilich, 1870-1924.*
DK254.L4S48 1966   66-78539

Stalin, Iosif, 1879-1953.   III. 2601
Leninism; selected writings by Joseph Stalin. New York, International Publishers [1942] 479 p. 22 cm. Reissue, with some omissions, of the author's Problems of Leninism, published in Moscow, 1940, as a translation of the 11th Russian edition. *1. Lenin, Vladimir Il'ich, 1870-1924. 2. Kommunisticheskaia partiia Sovetskogo Soiuza. 3. Russia — Politics and government — 1917- 4. Communisim — Russia. 5. Proletariat. I. T.*
DK254.L4S75 1942   947.084   42-24314

Trotskiĭ, Lev, 1879-1940.   III. 2602
Lenin; notes for a biographer [by] Leon Trotsky. With an introd. by Bertram D. Wolfe. Translated from the Russian and annotated by Tamara Deutscher. New York, G. P. Putnam's Sons [c1971] 224 p. 22 cm. Translation of O Lenine (romanized form) *1. Lenin, Vladimir Il'ich, 1870-1924.*
DK254.L4T7 1971   947.084/1/0924   75-136807

Wolfe, Bertram David, 1896-   III. 2603
Three who made a revolution; a biographical history. [4th rev. ed.] New York, Dial Press, 1964. viii, 659 p. ports. 22 cm. *1. Lenin, Vladimir Il'ich, 1870-1924. 2. Trotskiĭ, Lev, 1879-1940. 3. Stalin, Iosif, 1879-1953. I. T.*
DK254.L4W6 1964   947.08   64-3227

Deutscher, Isaac, 1907-1967.   III. 2604
Lenin's childhood. London, New York, Oxford University Press, 1970. vii, 67 p. 23 cm. *1. Lenin, Vladimir Il'ich, 1870-1924. I. T.*
DK254.L44D48 1970   947.084/1/0924 (B)   79-18168
    ISBN:192117041

Pipes, Richard.   III. 2605
Struve, liberal on the left. Cambridge, Mass., Harvard University Press, 1970-   v. ports. 24 cm. (Russian Research Center studies, 64) *1. Struve, Petr Berngardovich, 1870-1944. (S:Harvard University. Russian Research Center. Studies, 64)*
DK254.S597P5   914.7/03/80924 (B)   77-131463
    ISBN:0674845951(v.1)

Trotskiĭ, Lev, 1879-1940.   III. 2606
Basic writings. Edited and introduced by Irving Howe. New York, Random House [c1963] 427 p. 22 cm. *1. Russia — Politics and government — 1917- 2. Communism. I. Howe, Irving, ed.*
DK254.T6A25 1963   63-16157

Deutscher, Isaac, 1907-   III. 2607
The prophet armed: Trotsky, 1879-1921. New York, Oxford University Press, 1954. viii, 540 p. fold. map. 23 cm. *1. Trotskiĭ, Lev, 1879-1940. I. T.*
DK254.T6D4   947.083   54-5291

Deutscher, Isaac, 1907-1967.   III. 2608
The prophet outcast: Trotsky, 1929-1940. London, New York, Oxford University Press, 1963. xv, 543 p. illus., ports., facsim. 23 cm. The 3d vol. of author's trilogy, the 1st of which is The prophet armed; the 2d of which is The prophet unarmed: Trotsky, 1921-1929. *1. Trotskiĭ, Lev, 1879-1940. I. T.*
DK254.T6D415   923.247   63-24133

Deutscher, Isaac, 1907-   III. 2609
The prophet unarmed: Trotsky, 1921-1929. London, New York, Oxford University Press, 1959. 490 p. illus. 23 cm. The 2d vol. of the author's trilogy, the 1st of which is The prophet armed: Trotsky, 1879-1921, the 3d of which is The prophet outcast: Trotsky, 1929-1940. *1. Trotskiĭ, Lev, 1879-1940. I. T.*
DK254.T6D42   923.247   59-3695

Witte, Sergeĭ IUl'evich, graf, 1849-1915.   III. 2610
The memoirs of Count Witte. Translated from the original Russian manuscript and edited by Abraham Yarmolinsky. New York, H. Fertig, 1967 [c1921] xi, 445 p. port. 24 cm. Selections translated from Vospominaniia (romanized form) *1. Russia — Politics and government — 1894-1917. I. Yarmolinsky, Avrahm, 1890- ed. and tr. II. T.*
DK254.W5A5 1967   947.08/0924   (B)   67-24601

Mehlinger, Howard D.   III. 2611
Count Witte and the Tsarist government in the 1905 revolution [by] Howard D. Mehlinger and John M. Thompson. Bloomington, Indiana University Press [1972] xiv, 434 p. 25 cm. (Indiana University international studies) *1. Witte, Sergeĭ IUl'evich, graf, 1849-1915. 2. Russia — Politics and government — 1894-1917. 3. Russia — History — Revolution of 1905. I. Thompson, John M., joint author. II. T. (S:Indiana. University. International studies.)*
DK254.W5M44 1972   947.08/092/4   (B)   77-165048
ISBN:0253314704

DK260 – 264   1894 – 1917

Gurko, Vladimir Iosifovich, 1863-1927.   III. 2612
Features and figures of the past; government and opinion in the reign of Nicholas II, by V. I. Gurko. Edited by J. E. Wallace Sterling, Xenia Joukoff Eudin [and] H. H. Fisher. Translated by Laura Matveev. New York, Russell & Russell [1970, c1967] xix, 760 p. port. 23 cm. (The Hoover Library on War, Revolution, and Peace. Publication no. 14) *1. Russia — Politics and government — 1894-1917. 2. Agriculture — Russia. I. T. (S:Stanford University. Hoover Institution on War, Revolution, and Peace. Publications, no. 14)*
DK260.G82 1970   320.9/47   70-102501

Pares, Bernard, Sir, 1867-1949.   III. 2613
The fall of the Russian monarchy; a study of evidence, by Bernard Pares. [1st ed.] London, J. Cape [1939] 510 p. pl., ports., VI plans (part fold.) 23 cm. Erratum slip inserted. *1. Russia — History — Nicholas II, 1894-1917. 2. Russia — Politics and government — 1894-1917. 3. European war, 1914-1918 — Russia. 4. Russia — History — Revolution, 1917-1921 — Causes. I. Rasputin, Grigoriĭ Efimovich, 1871-1916. II. T.*
DK260.P3 1939   947.08   39-19181

Maynard, John, Sir, 1865-1943.   III. 2614
Russia in flux. Edited and abridged by S. Haden Guest, from "Russia in flux" and "The Russian peasant and other studies." With a foreword by Sir Bernard Pares. New York, Macmillan, 1948. xviii, 564 p. 22 cm. *1. Russia — History. 2. Peasantry — Russia. I. Maynard, John, Sir, 1865-1943. The Russian peasant and other studies. II. Guest, Stephen Haden, 1902- III. T.*
DK262.M37   947.08   48-5810

Miliukov, Pavel Nikolaevich, 1859-1943.   III. 2615
Russia and its crisis. With a new foreword by Donald W. Treadgold. New York, Collier Books [1962] 416 p. 18 cm. (Collier books, BS88) "Based on ... lectures [given] in America in 1903 and 1904." *1. Russia. 2. Russia — Politics and government.*
DK262.M66 1962   947   62-16982

Pares, Bernard, Sir, 1867-1949.   III. 2616
Russia: between reform and Revolution. Edited and with an introd. by Francis B. Randall. New York, Schocken Books [1962] 425 p. 21 cm. (Schocken paperbacks, SB34) First published in 1907 under title: Russia and reform. *1. Russia — Politics and government. 2. Russia — Social conditions. I. T.*
DK262.P26 1962   947   62-19395

Russia enters the twentieth century, 1894-1917.   III. 2617
Edited by Erwin Oberländer [and others] New York, Schocken Books [1971] 352 p. 23 cm. First issued in German under title: Russlands Aufbruch ins 20. Jahrhundert. *1. Russia — History — Nicholas II, 1894-1917. I. Oberländer, Erwin, 1937- ed.*
DK262.R8813 1971   914.7/03/8   70-148837   ISBN:0805234047

Hough, Richard Alexander, 1922-   III. 2618
The Potemkin mutiny. [1st American ed. New York] Pantheon Books [1961, c1960] 190 p. illus. 22 cm. *1. Kniaz' Potemkin Tavricheskiĭ (Armored cruiser) 2. Russia — History — Revolution of 1905. I. T.*
DK263.H6 1961   947.08   61-10421

Robinson, Geroid Tanquary, 1892-   III. 2619
Rural Russia under the old régime; a history of the landlord-peasant world and a prologue to the peasant revolution of 1917. New York, Macmillan Co., 1949 [c1932] ix, 342 p. maps. 22 cm. *1. Land tenure — Russia. 2. Peasantry —*
Russia. *3. Serfdom — Russia. 4. Russia — Social conditions. 5. Russia — History — Revolution of 1905. I. T.*
DK263.R6 1949   333   (914.7)   49-5682

Treadgold, Donald W., 1922-   III. 2620
Lenin and his rivals; the struggle for Russia's future, 1898-1906. New York, Praeger, 1955. 291 p. 24 cm. (Praeger publications in Russian history and world communism, no. 33) *1. Lenin, Vladimir Il'ich, 1870-1924. 2. Russia — Politics and government — 1894-1917. I. T.*
DK263.T74   947.08   54-13231

Smith, Clarence Jay.   III. 2621
The Russian struggle for power, 1914-1917; a study of Russian foreign policy during the First World War, by C. Jay Smith, Jr. New York, Greenwood Press [1969, c1956] xv, 553 p. 23 cm. *1. Russia — Foreign relations — 1894-1917. 2. European War, 1914-1918 — Russia. I. T.*
DK264.8.S5 1969   327.47   75-90709   ISBN:837122821

DK265   Revolution (1917 – 1921)

Conference on the Russian Revolution, Harvard University, 1967.   III. 2622
Revolutionary Russia [by] Oskar Anweiler [and others] Edited by Richard Pipes. Cambridge, Mass., Harvard University Press, 1968. x, 365 p. 25 cm. (Russian Research Center studies, 55) Cosponsored by the Joint Committee for Slavic Studies of the American Council of Learned Societies and the Russian Research Center of Harvard University. *1. Russia — History — Revolution, 1917-1921. 2. Russia — History — Congresses. I. Anweiler, Oskar. II. Pipes, Richard, ed. III. Harvard University. Russian Research Center. IV. Joint Committee on Slavic Studies. V. T. (S:Harvard University. Russian Research Center. Studies, 55)*
DK265.A135 1967aa   947.084/1   68-15641

Bunyan, James, 1898- comp.   III. 2623
The Bolshevik revolution, 1917-1918; documents and materials, by James Bunyan and H. H. Fisher. Stanford University, Calif., Stanford University Press, 1934. xii, 735 p. 23 cm. ([Leland Stanford Junior University. Library] Hoover War Library publications. no. 3) "This volume follows chronologically the Documents of Russian history, 1914-1917, published by the late Professor Frank A. Golder ... A considerable number of the documents of the present volume were selected and translated by Mr. Golder." — Pref. *1. Russia — History — Revolution, 1917-1921 — Sources. 2. Russia — Politics and government — 1917-1936. 3. European war, 1914-1918 — Documents, etc., sources. I. Fisher, Harold Henry, 1890- joint comp. II. Golder, Frank Alfred, 1877-1929. III. T.*
DK265.B93   947.084   34-35285

Bunyan, James, 1898- comp.   III. 2624
Intervention, civil war, and communism in Russia, April-December 1918; documents and materials, by James Bunyan. Baltimore, The Johns Hopkins Press, 1936. xv, 594 p. double map. 24 cm. At head of title: The Walter Hines Page school of international relations, the Johns Hopkins university. "Follows chronologically The Bolshevik revolution 1917-1918." — Foreword. *1. Russia — History — Revolution, 1917-1921 — Sources. 2. Russia — Politics and government — 1917-1936. 3. Russia — Foreign relations — 1917-1945. I. Johns Hopkins university. Walter Hines Page school of international relations. II. T.*
DK265.B94   947.084   37-51

Chamberlin, William Henry, 1897-   III. 2625
The Russian revolution, 1917-1921, by William Henry Chamberlin. New York, Macmillan, 1935. 2 v. fronts., illus. (maps) plates, ports., facsim. 24 cm. "Documents of the revolution": v.1, p. 429-511: v.2, p. 465-503. *1. Russia — History — Revolution, 1917-1921. I. T.*
DK265.C43   947.084   35-7577

Chernov, Viktor Mikhaĭlovich, 1873-1952.   III. 2626
The great Russian revolution, by Victor Chernov. Translated and abridged by Philip E. Mosely. New York, Russell & Russell, 1966 [c1936] viii, 466 p. illus., ports. 23 cm. *1. Russia — History — Revolution, 1917-1921. I. Mosely Philip Edward, 1905- ed. and tr. II. T.*
DK265.C48 1966   947.0841   66-13165

Daniels, Robert Vincent.   III. 2627
Red October; the Bolshevik Revolution of 1917 [by] Robert V. Daniels. New York, Scribner [1967] xiv, 269 p. illus., maps (on lining papers), ports. 24 cm. *1. Russia — History — Revolution, 1917-1921. I. T.*
DK265.D27   947.084/1   67-24060

Florinsky, Michael T., 1894-   III. 2628
The end of the Russian Empire. New York, Collier Books [1961] 254 p. 18 cm. (Collier books, BS3) *1. Russia — History — Nicholas II, 1894-1917. 2. Russia — Politics and government — 1894-1917. 3. European War, 1914-1918 — Russia. 4. Russia — Social conditions. 5. Russia — Economic conditions. I. T.*
DK265.F5 1961   947.08   61-17492

Footman, David, 1895-   III. 2629
Civil War in Russia. New York, Praeger [1962, c1961] 328 p. illus. 23 cm.

(Praeger publications in Russian history and world communism, no. 114. Books that matter.) *1. Russia — History — Revolution, 1917-1921. I. T.*
DK265.F578 1962   947.0841   62-17560

Kautsky, Karl, 1854-1938.   III. 2630
The dictatorship of the proletariat. Introd. by John H. Kautsky. [Translated by H. J. Stenning. Ann Arbor] University of Michigan Press [1964] xxxvii, 149 p. 21 cm. (Ann Arbor paperbacks for the study of communism and Marxism) "AA96." *1. Communism — Russia. 2. Dictatorship of the proletariat. 3. Democracy. I. T.*
DK265.K33 1964   335.413   64-55366

Kerenskiĭ, Aleksandr Fedorovich, 1881-   III. 2631
The catastrophe; Kerensky's own story of the Russian revolution, by Alexander F. Kerensky. New York, Appleton, 1927. xi, 376 p. front. (port.) 23 cm. *1. Russia — History — Revolution, 1917-1921. I. T.*
DK265.K393   27-23536

Luxemburg, Rosa, 1870-1919.   III. 2632
The Russian Revolution, and Leninism or Marxism? New introd. by Bertram D. Wolfe. [Ann Arbor] University of Michigan Press [1961] 109 p. 21 cm. (Ann Arbor paperbacks, AA57) *1. Russia — History — Revolution, 1917-1921. 2. Communism — Russia. I. Leninism or Marxism?*
DK265.L882 1961   947.0841   61-44218

Moorehead, Alan, 1910-   III. 2633
The Russian revolution. [1st ed.] New York, Harper [1958] 301 p. illus. 22 cm. *1. Russia — History — Revolution, 1917-1921. I. T.*
DK265.M79   947.08   58-6154

Paléologue, Georges Maurice, 1859-1944.   III. 2634
An ambassador's memoirs. Translated by F. A. Holt. New York, Octagon Books, 1972. 3 v. illus. 24 cm. Translation of La Russie des tsars pendant la grande guerre. *1. Russia — History — Nicholas II, 1894-1917. 2. European War — 1914-1918 — Russia. 3. Russia — Social conditions. I. T.*
DK265.P255 1972   320.9/47/08   77-159219   ISBN:0374961859

Radkey, Oliver Henry.   III. 2635
The sickle under the hammer; the Russian Socialist Revolutionaries in the early months of Soviet rule. New York, Columbia University Press, 1963. xiii, 525 p. 24 cm. (Studies of the Russian Institute, Columbia University) *1. Partiia sotsialistov-revoliutsionerov. 2. Russia — History — Revolution, 1917-1921. I. T. (S:Columbia University. Russian Institute. Studies)*
DK265.R228   947.0844   62-18352

Reed, John, 1887-1920.   III. 2636
Ten days that shook the world. With a foreword by V. I. Lenin, a pref. by N. K. Krupskaya, and a new introd. by John Howard Lawson. New York, International Publishers [1967] l, 395 p. illus. 21 cm. "Text ... reproduced from the first edition ... New York," 1919. "Lenin's introduction ... reproduced" from edition of 1922. *1. Russia — History — Revolution, 1917-1921. I. T.*
DK265.R38 1967   947.084/1   67-27252

Rosenberg, Arthur, 1889-1943.   III. 2637
A history of bolshevism from Marx to the first Five years' plan. Translated from the German by Ian F. D. Morrow. New York, Russell & Russell, 1965. viii, 250 p. 23 cm. A reprint of the 1934 ed. Translation of Geschichte des Bolschewismus von Marx bis zur Gegenwart. *1. Communism — History. 2. Communism — Russia. I. T.*
DK265.R69 1965   335.43   65-17919

Stalin, Iosif, 1879-1953.   III. 2638
The October revolution; a collection of articles and speeches by Joseph Stalin. New York, International Publishers [1934] 168 p. 22 cm. (Marxist library. [v.21]) Printed in Russia. *1. Vsesoiuznia kommunisticheskaia partiia (bol'shevikov) 2. Russia — History — Revolution, 1917- 3. Communism — Russia. I. T.*
DK265.S668   947.084   35-6324

Stewart, George, 1892-   III. 2639
The White Armies of Russia; a chronicle of counter-revolution and Allied intervention. New York, Russell & Russell [1970] xiii, 469 p. illus., maps (part fold.), ports. 23 cm. Reprint of the 1933 ed. L.C. copy imperfect: leaf of illus. following p. 326 mutilated. *1. Russia — History — Revolution, 1917-1921 — Campaigns. 2. Russia — History — Allied intervention, 1918-1920. I. T.*
DK265.S75 1970   947.084/1   73-81477

Sukhanov, Nikolaĭ Nikolaevich.   III. 2640
The Russian Revolution, 1917, a personal record. Edited, abridged, and translated by Joel Carmichael from Zapiski o revolutsii. London, New York, Oxford University Press, 1955. 691 p. illus. 23 cm. *1. Russia — History — Revolution, 1917-1921. I. Carmichael, Joel. II. T.*
DK265.S8475   947.083   55-14322

Trotskiĭ, Lev, 1879-1940.   III. 2641
The history of the Russian Revolution. Translated from the Russian by Max Eastman. Ann Arbor, University of Michigan Press [1957, c1932] 3 v. in 1. 25 cm. *1. Russia — History — Revolution, 1917-1921.*
DK265.T773 1957   947.084 (947.083)   57-13948

DK265.19 – 265.9   Special Topics

Katkov, George.   III. 2642
Russia, 1917; the February revolution. [1st U.S. ed.] New York, Harper & Row [1967] xxviii, 489 p. illus., facsim., maps, ports. 22 cm. *1. Russia — History — Revolution, 1917-1921. I. T.*
DK265.19.K3 1967   947.084/1   66-20739

Bradley, John, 1930-   III. 2643
Allied intervention in Russia. New York, Basic Books [1968] xix, 251 p. maps. 22 cm. *1. Russia — History — Allied intervention, 1918-1920. I. T.*
DK265.4.B67 1968   940.4/147   68-19845

Strakhovsky, Leonid Ivan, 1898-1963.   III. 2644
Intervention at Archangel; the story of allied intervention and Russian counter-revolution in North Russia, 1918-1920. New York, H. Fertig, 1971 [c1944] vii, 336 p. maps. 21 cm. *1. Russia — History — Allied intervention, 1918-1920. I. T.*
DK265.4.S87 1971   940.4/38   74-80594

Strakhovsky, Leonid Ivan, 1898-1963.   III. 2645
The origins of American intervention in North Russia (1918). With a foreword by James Brown Scott. New York, H. Fertig, 1972 [c1937] ix, 140 p. map. 24 cm. *1. Russia — History — Allied intervention, 1918-1920. 2. Russia — Foreign relations — United States. 3. United States — Foreign relations — Russia. I. T.*
DK265.42.U5S73 1972   940.4/38   78-80595

Unterberger, Betty Miller.   III. 2646
America's Siberian expedition, 1918-1920; a study of national policy. New York, Greenwood Press [1969, c1956] 271 p. maps. 24 cm. *1. Russia — History — Allied intervention, 1918-1920. 2. United States — Foreign relations — Russia. 3. Russia — Foreign relations — United States. I. T.*
DK265.42.U5U52 1969   947.084/1   69-14128

Ellis, Charles Howard, 1895-   III. 2647
The British "intervention" in Transcaspia, 1918-1919. Berkeley, University of California Press, 1963. 175 p. illus., ports., maps (on lining papers) 22 cm. *1. European War, 1914-1918 — Transcaspian Province. 2. Transcaspian Province — History. I. T.*
DK265.8.T67E55 1963   940.415   63-6226

Adams, Arthur E.   III. 2648
Bolsheviks in the Ukraine; the second campaign, 1918-1919. New Haven, Yale University Press, 1963. 440 p. illus. 23 cm. *1. Ukraine — History — Revolution, 1917-1921. I. T.*
DK265.8.U4A6   947.71   63-7930

Carr, Edward Hallett, 1892-   III. 2649
The Soviet impact on the Western World. New York, H. Fertig, 1973 [c1947] xii, 113 p. 22 cm. "Lectures delivered in Oxford in February and March 1946, for the Estlin Carpenter Trust." *1. Russia — History — Revolution, 1917-1921 — Influence. 2. Communism. I. T.*
DK265.9.I5C3 1973   335.43   73-80532

DK266   Soviet Regime.

Lenin, 1918 – 1924

Bauer, Raymond Augustine, 1916-   III. 2650
How the Soviet system works: cultural, psychological, and social themes [by] Raymond A. Bauer, Alex Inkeles, and Clyde Kluckhohn. Cambridge, Harvard University Press, 1956. xiv, 274 p. 22 cm. (Russian Research Center studies, 24) "Final report [of the] ... Harvard Project on the Soviet Social System." "Reports and publications of the Harvard Project on the Soviet Social System": p. [252]-258. "References": p. [259]-265. *1. Russia — Economic policy. 2. Communism — Russia. I. T. (S:Harvard University. Russian Research Center. Russian Research Center studies, 24)*
DK266.B26   947.085   56-8549

Carr, Edward Hallett, 1892-   III. 2651
A history of Soviet Russia. New York, Macmillan, 1951 [c1950]-   v. 22 cm. *1. Russia — History — Revolution, 1917-1921. 2. Communism — Russia. I. T.*
DK266.C263   947.084   51-1610

Deutscher, Isaac, 1907-   III. 2652
Russia in transition, and other essays. [1st American ed.] New York, Coward-McCann [1957] 245 p. 22 cm. *1. Russia — History — 1917- — Addresses, essays, lectures. I. T.*
DK266.D47   947.084 (947.083)   57-7057

Fischer, Louis, 1896-   III. 2653
Russia's road from peace to war: Soviet foreign relations, 1917-1941. [1st

III. 2654   Russia. Poland. Finland   DK266

ed.] New York, Harper & Row [1969] vi, 499 p. illus., ports. 25 cm. *1. Russia — Foreign relations — 1917-1945. I. T.*
DK266.F49   327.47   69-15306

Nettl, J. P.   **III. 2654**
The Soviet achievement [by] J. P. Nettl. London, Thames & Hudson [1967]. 288 p. col. front., illus. (some col.), facsims., maps, tables, diagrs. 22 cm. (Library of European civilization) *1. Russia — Politics and government — 1917- 2. Russia — Social conditions — 1917- I. T.*
DK266.N47   947.08   67-105072

Pipes, Richard.   **III. 2655**
The formation of the Soviet Union; Communism and nationalism, 1917-1923. Rev. ed. Cambridge, Harvard University Press, 1964. xii, 365 p. illus., maps, ports. 25 cm. (Russian Research Center studies, 13) *1. Russia — History — 1917- I. T. (S:Harvard University. Russian Research Center, Studies, 13)*
DK266.P53 1964   947.084   64-21284

Rauch, Georg von.   **III. 2656**
A history of Soviet Russia. Translated by Peter and Annette Jacobsohn. 6th ed. New York, Praeger [1972] xiv, 541 p. maps. 21 cm. Translation of Geschichte des bolschewistischen Russland. *1. Russia — History — 1917- I. T.*
DK266.R372 1972   947.084   76-185777

Salisbury, Harrison Evans, 1908-   **III. 2657**
The Soviet Union, by Harrison E. Salisbury. [Chicago] Encyclopaedia Britannica Educational Corp. [1967] 90 p. illus., maps, ports. 23 cm. (A Byline book. World affairs workshop.) First ed. published in 1965 under title: Russia. *1. Russia — Politics and government — 1917- I. T.*
DK266.S25 1967   914.7   68-393

Ulam, Adam Bruno, 1922-   **III. 2658**
Expansion and coexistence; the history of Soviet foreign policy, 1917-67 [by] Adam B. Ulman. New York, Praeger [1968] viii, 775 p. 24 cm. *1. Russia — Foreign relations — 1917-1945. 2. Russia — Foreign relations — 1945- I. The history of Soviet foreign policy, 1917-67. II. T.*
DK266.U49   327.47   68-11323

Lewin, Moshé.   **III. 2659**
Lenin's last struggle. Translated from the French by A. M. Sheridan Smith. [1st American ed.] New York, Pantheon Books [c1968] xxiv, 193 p. 22 cm. Translation of Le dernier combat de Lénine. *1. Russia — Politics and government — 1917-1936. 2. Lenin, Vladimir Il'ich, 1870-1924. I. T.*
DK266.5.L4513   947.084/1/0924   68-20892

Schapiro, Leonard Bertram, 1908-   **III. 2660**
The origin of the communist autocracy; political opposition in the Soviet state, first phase, 1917-1922. [Published for the London School of Economics and Political Science (University of London)] Cambridge, Harvard University Press, 1955. xvii, 397 p. 22 cm. *1. Russia — Politics and government — 1917-1936. 2. Russia — History — Revolution, 1917-1921. I. T.*
DK266.5.S3   A55-8644

DK267 – 273   Stalin, 1925 – 1953

Brzezinski, Zbigniew K., 1928-   **III. 2661**
The permanent purge; politics in Soviet totalitarianism. Cambridge, Harvard University Press, 1956. 256 p. 22 cm. (Russian Research Center studies, 20) *1. Political purges. I. T. (S:Harvard. University. Russian Research Center. Studies, 20)*
DK267.B76   947.084 (947.083)   56-5342

Kohn, Hans, 1891-   **III. 2662**
Nationalism in the Soviet Union. [Translated by E. W. Dickes.] London, Routledge, 1933. xi, 164 p. 19 cm. "First published in Germany in 1932 under the title Der Nationalismus in der Sowjetunion ..." *1. Russia — Nationality. 2. Soviet. 3. Russia — Politics and government — 1917- 4. Nationalism and nationality. I. Dickes, Ernest Walker, 1876- tr. II. T.*
DK267.K62   947.084   33-19510

Leites, Nathan Constantin, 1912-   **III. 2663**
A study of bolshevism. Glencoe, Ill., Free Press [1953] 639 p. 25 cm. *1. Communism — Russia.*
DK267.L415   335.4   53-7396

Medvedev, Roĭ Aleksandrovich.   **III. 2664**
Let history judge: the origins and consequences of Stalinism [by] Roy A. Medvedev. Translated by Colleen Taylor. Edited by David Joravsky and by Georges Haupt. [1st ed.] New York, Knopf, 1971. xxxiv, 566, xviii p. 25 cm. *1. Russia — Politics and government — 1917-1936. 2. Russia — Politics and government — 1936-1953. 3. Stalin, Iosif, 1879-1953. I. T.*
DK267.M41413   947.084/2   70-31702   ISBN:0394446453

Schwartz, Harry, 1919-   **III. 2665**
The red phoenix; Russia since World War II. New York, Praeger [1961] 427 p. 22 cm. (Praeger publications in Russian history and world communism, no. 90) *Books that matter. 1. Russia — History — 1925-1953. 2. Russia — History — 1953- I. T.*
DK267.S335   947.0842   61-11062

Werth, Alexander, 1901-   **III. 2666**
Russia; the post-war years. Epilogue by Harrison E. Salisbury. New York, Taplinger Pub. Co. [1971] xvii, 446 p. 23 cm. Continuation of the author's Russia at war, 1941-1945. *1. Russia — History — 1925-1953. I. T.*
DK267.W414 1971   914.7/03/842   75-143223   ISBN:0800869303

DK268   Biography. Memoirs

Stalin, Iosif, 1879-1953.   **III. 2667**
Works. Moscow, Foreign Languages Pub. House, 1952- v. mounted port. 20 cm. Label mounted on t.p. of v.1: London, Lawrence and Wishart, 1953. Added t.p., in Russian.
DK268.S75A267   308.1   54-23357

Stalin, Iosif, 1879-1953.   **III. 2668**
Selected writings. Westport, Conn., Greenwood Press [1970] 479 p. 23 cm. Includes addresses, articles, and reports on the Communist program in Russia. "Reprinted from an edition published ... in 1942." *1. Russia — Politics and government — 1917- Addresses, essays, lectures. 2. Communism — Russia — Addresses, essays, lectures. I. T.*
DK268.S75A34 1970   335.43   78-109976   ISBN:0837144825

Deutscher, Isaac, 1907-   **III. 2669**
Stalin; a political biography. 2d ed. New York, Oxford University Press, 1967 [c1966] xvi, 661 p. illus., ports. 22 cm. *1. Stalin, Iosif, 1879-1953.*
DK268.S8D48 1967   947.084/2/0924   67-4373

Khrushchev, Nikita Sergeevich, 1894-   **III. 2670**
The anatomy of terror; Khrushchev's revelations about Stalin's regime. Introd. by Nathaniel Weyl. Washington, Public Affairs Press [1956] 73 p. 24 cm. *1. Stalin, Iosif, 1879-1953. 2. Russia — Politics and government — 1936-1953. I. T.*
DK268.S8K7   947.083   56-11668

Souvarine, Boris.   **III. 2671**
Stalin, a critical survey of bolshevism, by Boris Souvarine. Translated by C. L. R. James. New York, Alliance Book Corporation, Longmans, Green [c1939] xiv, 690 p. 25 cm. *1. Stalin, Iosif, 1879-1953. 2. Communism — Russia. I. James, Cyril Lionel Robert, 1901- tr.*
DK268.S8S62 1939   923.247   39-22569

Trotskiĭ, Lev, 1879-1940.   **III. 2672**
Stalin: an appraisal of the man and his influence, by Leon Trotsky; edited and translated from the Russian by Charles Malamuth. New ed. London, MacGibbon & Kee, 1968. xv, 516 p. 16 plates, illus., ports. 25 cm. *1. Stalin, Iosif, 1879-1953. I. T.*
DK268.S8T7 1968   947.084/2/0924 (B)   77-386055   ISBN:261620762

Wolfe, Bertram David, 1896-   **III. 2673**
Khrushchev and Stalin's ghost; text, background, and meaning of Khrushchev's secret report to the Twentieth Congress on the night of February 24-25, 1956. New York, Praeger [c1957] 322 p. 22 cm. (Books that matter) *1. Stalin, Iosif, 1879-1953. 2. Russia — Politics and government — 1936- 3. Khrushchev, Nikita Sergeevich, 1894- II. T.*
DK268.S8W6   947.085   56-12224

Zhukov, Georgiĭ Konstantinovich, 1896-   **III. 2674**
The memoirs of Marshal Zhukov. [1st American ed.] New York, Delacorte Press [1971] 703, viii p. illus., plans (part col.), ports. 23 cm. Translation of Vospominaniia i razmyshleniia (romanized form) "A Seymour Lawrence book." *1. World War, 1939-1945 — Russia. I. T.*
DK268.Z52A313 1971   940.542/1/0924   73-120846

DK268.3   Social Life.
Customs

Barghoorn, Frederick Charles, 1911-   **III. 2675**
Soviet Russian nationalism. New York, Oxford University Press, 1956. ix, 330 p. 22 cm. *1. Nationalism — Russia. I. T.*
DK268.3.B32   947.085   56-7176

Bauer, Raymond Augustine, 1916-   **III. 2676**
Nine soviet portraits [by] Raymond A. Bauer with the assistance of Edward Wasiolek. [Cambridge] Published jointly by the Technology Press of Massachusetts Institute of Technology, and Wiley, New York [1955] 190 p. illus. 24 cm. (Technology Press books in the social sciences) *1. Russia — Social conditions — 1945- I. T.*
DK268.3.B35   914.7   55-14307

Ginzburg, Evgeniĭa Semenovna.   **III. 2677**
Journey into the whirlwind. Translated by Paul Stevenson and Max Hayward. [1st ed.] New York, Harcourt, Brace & World [1967] 418 p. map.

22 cm. "A Helen and Kurt Wolff book." Translation of Krutoĭ marshrut (romanized form) 1. Prisoners, Russian. 2. Russia — Social conditions — 1917- I. T.
DK268.3.G513   365/.64/0924   67-26000

Joint Committee on Slavic Studies. III. 2678
Continuity and change in Russian and Soviet thought. Edited, with an introd. by Ernest J. Simmons. New York, Russell & Russell [1967, c1955] xii, 563 p. 25 cm. "Result of an ... effort which took the initial form of a conference held at Arden House, March 26-28, 1954, under the auspices of the Joint Committee on Slavic Studies." 1. Russia — Economic policy. 2. Authority. 3. Russia — Politics and government — 1917- 4. Philosophy, Russian. 5. Russian literature — 20th cent. — History and criticism. 6. Messianism, Russian. I. Simmons, Ernest Joseph, 1903- ed. II. T.
DK268.3.J6 1967   914.7/03   66-27108

Mead, Margaret, 1901- III. 2679
Soviet attitudes toward authority; an interdisciplinary approach to problems of Soviet character. New York, Morrow, 1955 [c1951] 148 p. 24 cm. 1. Communism — Russia. 2. Russia — Civilization. 3. Russia — Social conditions. I. T.
DK268.3.M4x   914.7   A63-5053

Mehnert, Klaus, 1906- III. 2680
Soviet man and his world. Translated from the German by Maurice Rosenbaum. New York, Praeger [1962, c1961] 310 p. 23 cm. (Praeger publications in Russian history and world communism, no. 100. Books that matter.) Translation of Der Sowjetmensch. 1. National characteristics, Russian. 2. Russia — Description and travel — 1917- I. T.
DK268.3.M453   914.7   62-8964

Swayze, Harold. III. 2681
Political control of literature in the USSR, 1946-1959. Cambridge, Harvard University Press, 1962. ix, 301 p. 25 cm. (Russian Research Center studies, 44) 1. Russian literature — 20th cent. — History and criticism. 2. Censorship — Russia. 3. Communism and literature. I. T. (S:Harvard University. Russian Research Center. Studies, 44)
DK268.3.S95   891.70904   62-9432

DK273   1939 – 1945

Fischer, Louis, 1896-1970. III. 2682
The road to Yalta: Soviet foreign relations, 1941-1945. [1st ed.] New York, Harper & Row [1972] xv, 238 p. port. 25 cm. 1. Russia — Foreign relations — 1917-1945. 2. World War, 1939-1945 — Diplomatic history. I. T.
DK273.F53 1972   940.53/22/47   72-185899   ISBN:006011262X

Gallagher, Matthew P. III. 2683
The Soviet history of World War II: myths, memories, and realities. New York, Praeger [1963] 205 p. 21 cm. (Praeger publications in Russian history and world communism, no. 121) 1. World War, 1939-1945 — Russia. I. T.
DK273.G3   940.5347   63-9908

Moore, Barrington, 1913- III. 2684
Terror and progress USSR: some sources of change and stability in the Soviet dictatorship. Cambridge, Harvard University Press, 1954. xvii, 261 p. 22 cm. (Russian Research Center Studies, 12) 1. Communism — Russia. I. T. (S:Harvard University. Russian Research Center. Russian Research Center studies, 12)
DK273.M68   947.085   54-5995

DK274 – 276   1953 –

Brumberg, Abraham, comp. III. 2685
In quest of justice; protest and dissent in the Soviet Union today. New York, Praeger [1970] xiv, 477 p. 25 cm. 1. Russia — Politics and government — 1953- 2. Russia — Social conditions — 1945- I. T.
DK274.B78 1970   914.7/03/85   69-12700

Conquest, Robert. III. 2686
Power and policy in the U.S.S.R.; the study of Soviet dynastics. New York, St Martin's Press, 1961. x, 485 p. 23 cm. 1. Kommunisticheskaia partiia Sovetskogo Soiuza. 2. Russia — Politics and government — 1945- I. T.
DK274.C62   947.0842   61-15941

Conquest, Robert. III. 2687
Russia after Khrushchev. New York, Praeger [1965] viii, 267 p. 22 cm. (Praeger publications in Russian history and world communism, no. 164) 1. Russia — Politics and government — 1953- I. T.
DK274.C63   947.085   65-15645

Dallin, Alexander. III. 2688
Soviet politics since Khrushchev, edited by Alexander Dallin and Thomas B. Larson. Englewood Cliffs, N.J., Prentice-Hall [1968] viii, 181 p. 21 cm. (A Spectrum book) 1. Russia — Politics and government — 1953- I. Larson, Thomas B., joint author. II. T.
DK274.D28   300/.947   68-14468

Hooson, David J. M. III. 2689
The Soviet Union; people and regions [by] David Hooson. Belmont, Calif., Wadsworth Pub. Co. [1966] 376 p. illus., maps. 22 cm. 1. Russia. I. T.
DK274.H63   914.7   66-25892

Khrushchev, Nikita Sergeevich, 1894- III. 2690
For victory in peaceful competition with capitalism. With a special introd. written for the American ed. New York, Dutton, 1960. xxxi, 783 p. 21 cm. "A collection of speeches and statements made in the course of 1958 on various questions relating to the international situation and foreign policy of the Soviet Union." 1. Russia — Relations (general) with foreign countries. I. T.
DK274.K483   327.47   60-6004

Leonhard, Wolfgang. III. 2691
The Kremlin since Stalin. Translated from the German by Elizabeth Wiskemann and Marian Jackson. New York, Praeger [1962] 403 p. 21 cm. (Books that matter) Translation of Kreml ohne Stalin. 1. Russia — Politics and government — 1953- I. T.
DK274.L413 1962   947.085   62-14888

Mosely, Philip Edward, 1905- III. 2692
The Kremlin and world politics; studies in Soviet policy and action. [1st ed.] New York, Vintage Books, 1960. viii, 557, x p. 19 cm. (Vintage Russian library, R-1002) 1. World politics — 1955- 2. Russia — Foreign relations — 1945- I. T.
DK274.M59   327.47   60-9146

Problems of communism. III. 2693
Russia under Khrushchev; an anthology from Problems of communism, edited by Abraham Brumberg. New York, Praeger [1962] ix, 660 p. 21 cm. (Books that matter. Praeger publications in Russian history and world communism, no. 105.) 1. Russia. I. Brumberg, Abraham, ed. II. T.
DK274.P7   947.085   62-13165

Reve, Karel van het, comp. III. 2694
Dear comrade; Pavel Litvinov and the voices of Soviet citizens in dissent. Edited and annotated by Karel van het Reve. New York, Pitman Pub. Corp. [1969] xvii, 199 p. 25 cm. "Originally published in the Netherlands ... under title: Letters and telegrams to Pavel Litvinov December 1967-May 1968." Parallel text in English and Russian. 1. Public opinion — Russia. 2. Censorship — Russia. I. Litvinov, Pavel Mikhaĭlovich, 1940- II. T.
DK274.R38 1969   301.15/4   71-79049

Tatu, Michel, 1933- III. 2695
Power in the Kremlin: from Krushchev to Kosygin. Translated by Helen Katel. New York, Viking Press [1969, c1968] 570 p. 24 cm. Translation of Le pouvoir en U.R.S.S. 1. Russia — Politics and government — 1953- I. T.
DK274.T3613 1969b   320.9/47   67-10216   ISBN:0670570281

Werth, Alexander, 1901- III. 2696
Russia under Khrushchev. [1st American ed.] New York, Hill and Wang [1962, c1961] 352 p. 21 cm. 1. Khrushchev, Nikita Sergeevich, 1894- 2. Russia — Politics and government — 1953- 3. Russia — Foreign relations — 1953- I. T.
DK274.W4 1962   914.7   62-11998

Werth, Alexander, 1901- III. 2697
Russia: hopes and fears. New York, Simon and Schuster [1969] 352 p. 22 cm. 1. Russia. I. T.
DK274.W43 1969b   914.7/03/85   71-79641   ISBN:671203339

Juviler, Peter H., ed. III. 2698
Soviet policy-making; studies of communism in transition, edited by Peter H. Juviler and Henry W. Morton. New York, Praeger [1967] xiv, 274 p. 21 cm. (Praeger publications in Russian history and world communism, no. 182) 1. Russia — Politics and government — 1953- — Addresses, essays, lectures. 2. Russia — Social conditions — 1945- — Addresses, essays, lectures. I. Morton, Henry W., 1929- joint ed. II. T.
DK274.3 1967.J8   914.7/03/85   66-18913

Khrushchev, Nikita Sergeevich, 1894- III. 2699
Khrushchev speaks; selected speeches, articles, and press conferences, 1949-1961. Edited, with commentary, by Thomas P. Whitney. Ann Arbor, University of Michigan Press [1963] 466 p. 24 cm. I. Whitney, Thomas P., ed.
DK275.K5A36   947.085   63-8075

Crankshaw, Edward. III. 2700
Khrushchev; a career. New York, Viking Press [1966] 311 p. ports. 24 cm. 1. Khrushchev, Nikita Sergeevich, 1894- I. T.
DK275.K5C7   947.085 (B)   66-15880

Frankland, Mark, 1934- III. 2701
Khrushchev. Introd. by Harry Schwartz. New York, Stein and Day [1967, c1966] 213 p. 25 cm. 1. Khrushchev, Nikita Sergeevich, 1894- I. T.
DK275.K5F7 1967   947/.085 (B)   67-16690

Kellen, Konrad. III. 2702
Khrushchev, a political portrait. New York, Praeger [1961] 271 p. 21 cm.

(Praeger publications in Russian history and world communism, no. 93. Books that matter.) *1. Khrushchev, Nikita Sergeevich, 1894-*
DK275.K5K4   923.247   61-10511

Linden, Carl A. **III. 2703**
Khrushchev and the Soviet leadership, 1957-1964 [by] Carl A. Linden. Baltimore, Johns Hopkins Press [1966] x, 270 p. 22 cm. "Published in co-operation with the Institute for Sino-Soviet Studies, George Washington University." *1. Khrushchev, Nikita Sergeevich, 1894- 2. Russia — Politics and government — 1953- I. George Washington University, Washington, D.C. Institute for Sino-Soviet Studies. II. T.*
DK275.K5L5   320.924   66-16035

Conquest, Robert. **III. 2704**
The politics of ideas in the U.S.S.R. New York, Praeger [1967] 175, [1] p. 23 cm. (Praeger publications in Russian history and world communism, no. 197. Contemporary Soviet Union series: institutions and policies) *1. Propaganda, Communist. 2. Russia — Intellectual life. 3. Mass media — Russia. 4. Kommunisticheskaia partiia sovetskogo soiuza. I. T. (S)*
DK276.C6 1967   327.1/4   67-27314

Miller, Wright Watts. **III. 2705**
Russians as people. With a pref. by Alexander Dallin. [1st ed.] New York, Dutton, 1961 [c1960] 205 p. illus. 21 cm. *1. Russia — Social life and customs. I. T.*
DK276.M5 1961   914.7   61-10642

DK400 – 443   POLAND

Barnett, Clifford R. **III. 2706**
Poland, its people, its society, its culture [by] Clifford R. Barnett in collaboration with Robert J. Feldman [and others] New Haven, HRAF Press [1958] 470 p. illus. 22 cm. (Survey of world cultures) *1. Poland.*
DK404.B3   914.38   58-11469

Szczepański, Jan, 1913- **III. 2707**
Polish society. New York, Random House [1970] ix, 214 p. illus., maps. 21 cm. (Studies in modern societies, SS39. A Random House study in sociology.) *1. Poland — Social conditions. 2. Poland — Civilization. I. T.*
DK411.S95   309.1/438   73-108924

Horak, Stephan M., 1920- **III. 2708**
Poland and her national minorities, 1919-39; a case study, by Stephan Horak. [1st ed.] New York, Vantage Press [1961] 259 p. illus. 21 cm. *1. Minorities — Poland. I. T.*
DK412.H59   323.1438   60-15582

The Cambridge history of Poland. **III. 2709**
Edited by W. F. Reddaway [and others] New York, Octagon Books, 1971- v. illus., maps (part col.), ports. 25 cm. Vol. 1 first published 1950; v. 2, 1941. *1. Poland — History. I. Reddaway, William Fiddian, 1872-1949, ed.*
DK414.C32   943.8   73-119437

Halecki, Oskar, 1891- **III. 2710**
A history of Poland. New York, Roy Publishers [1961] 370 p. 22 cm. Translation of La Pologne de 963 à 1914; with additional material up to 1960. *1. Poland — History.*
DK414.H232 1961   943.8   61-14442

Wandycz, Piotr Stefan. **III. 2711**
Czechoslovak-Polish Confederation and the Great Powers, 1940-43. [Bloomington, Indiana University] 1956. 152 p. 26 cm. (Indiana University publications. Slavic and East European series, v.3) *1. Czechoslovak-Polish Confederation (Proposed)*
DK418.5.C9W34   327.4370438   60-3358

Budurowycz, Bohdan Basil, 1921- **III. 2712**
Polish-Soviet relations, 1932-1939. New York, Columbia University Press, 1963. xi, 229 p. 25 cm. (East Central European studies of Columbia University) Revision of thesis, Columbia University, issued in 1958 in microfilm form. *1. Russia — Foreign relations — Poland. 2. Poland — Foreign relations — Russia. I. T. (S:Columbia University. Program on East Central Europe. East Central European studies)*
DK418.5.R8B8 1963   327.438047   63-7509

Shotwell, James Thomson, 1874- **III. 2713**
Poland and Russia, 1919-1945 [by] James T. Shotwell ... [and] Max M. Laserson. New York, Pub. for the Carnegie Endowment for International Peace by King's Crown Press, 1945. vi, 114 p. front. (map) 24 cm. *1. Poland — Foreign relations — Russia. 2. Russia — Foreign relations — Poland. 3. World war, 1939-1945 — Territorial questions — Poland. 4. Reconstruction (1939-1951) — Poland. 5. Curzon line. I. Laserson, Max M., 1887-1951, joint author. II. Carnegie Endowment for International Peace. Division of Economics and History.*
DK418.5.R9S48   327.4380947   A45-4954

Kaplan, Herbert H. **III. 2714**
The first partition of Poland [by] Herbert H. Kaplan. New York, Columbia University Press, 1962. [New York, AMS Press, 1972] xvi, 215 p. 23 cm. Original ed. issued in series: East Central European studies of Columbia University. *1. Poland — History — First partition, 1772. I. T. (S:East Central European studies.)*
DK434.K33 1972   943.8/02   76-171548   ISBN:0404036368

Lord, Robert Howard, 1885-1954. **III. 2715**
The second partition of Poland; a study in diplomatic history. New York, AMS Press [1969] xxx, 586 p. 23 cm. Reprint of the 1915 ed. *1. Poland — History — Second partition, 1793. I. T.*
DK434.L7 1969   943.8/02   73-101268

Kukiel, Marian, 1885- **III. 2716**
Czartoryski and European unity, 1770-1861. Princeton, Princeton University Press, 1955. 354 p. illus. 23 cm. (Poland's millennium series of the Kościuszko Foundation) *1. Czartoryski, Adam Jerzy, Książę, 1770-1861. 2. Poland — Politics and government — 1796-1918. 3. Europe — Politics — 1789-1900. I. T.*
DK435.5.C83K8   923.2438   54-6076

Leslie, R. F. **III. 2717**
Polish politics and the Revolution of November 1830, by R. F. Leslie. Westport, Conn., Greenwood Press [1969] xii, 307 p. geneal. table, maps. 23 cm. (University of London historical studies, 3) Reprint of the 1956 ed. "Represents in part the work done for a Ph.D. thesis of the University of London." *1. Poland — History — Revolution, 1830-1832. I. T. (S:London. University. Historical studies, 3)*
DK436.L545 1969   943.8/03   79-91766   ISBN:837124166

Leslie, R. F. **III. 2718**
Reform and insurrection in Russian Poland, 1856-1865. Westport, Conn., Greenwood Press [1969, c1963] ix, 272 p. 23 cm. *1. Poland — History — 1830-1866. I. T.*
DK437.L48 1969   943.8/03   72-91767   ISBN:837124158

Dębicki, Roman. **III. 2719**
Foreign policy of Poland, 1919-39, from the rebirth of the Polish Republic to World War II. With a foreword by Oscar Halecki. New York, Praeger [1962] 192 p. 22 cm. *1. Poland — Foreign relations. I. T.*
DK440.D45   327.438   62-13732

Komarnicki, Titus. **III. 2720**
Rebirth of the Polish Republic; a study in the diplomatic history of Europe, 1914-1920. London, W. Heinemann [1957] xiii, 776 p. maps. 22 cm. *1. European War, 1914-1918 — Poland. 2. Poland — History — 1918-1945. I. T.*
DK440.K575 1957   943.8   57-3573

Korbel, Josef. **III. 2721**
Poland between East and West; Soviet and German diplomacy toward Poland, 1919-1933. Princeton, N.J., Princeton University Press, 1963. xi, 321 p. 23 cm. *1. Poland — Foreign relations — Russia. 2. Russia — Foreign relations — Poland. 3. Poland — Foreign relations — Germany. 4. Germany — Foreign relations — Poland. I. T.*
DK440.K577   327.438047   63-9993

Piłsudski, Józef, 1867-1935. **III. 2722**
Joseph Pilsudski; the memories of a Polish revolutionary and soldier, translated and edited by D. R. Gillie. London, Faber & Faber [1931] x, 377 p. front., plates, ports., fold. maps. 24 cm. *1. Socialism in Poland. 2. Poland — Politics and government. 3. European war, 1914-1918 — Poland. I. Gillie, Darsie Rutherford, ed. and tr.*
DK440.5.P5A42   923.1438 (923.5438)   31-15807

Mikołajczyk, Stainsław, 1901-1966. **III. 2723**
The rape of Poland; pattern of Soviet aggression. Westport, Conn., Greenwood Press [1972, c1948] xiii, 309 p. illus. 24 cm. *1. Poland — Foreign relations — Russia. 2. Russia — Foreign relations — Poland. 3. Poland — History — Occupation, 1939-1945. 4. Poland — History — 1945- I. T.*
DK441.M5 1972   943.8/05   73-141282   ISBN:0837158796

Syrop, Konrad. **III. 2724**
Spring in October; the story of the Polish revolution, 1956. New York, Praeger [1958, c1957] 207 p. illus. 23 cm. *1. Poland — Politics and government — 1945- I. T.*
DK441.S9   943.8   57-14803

Staar, Richard Felix, 1923- **III. 2725**
Poland, 1944-1962; the Sovietization of a captive people. [Baton Rouge] Louisiana State University Press [1962] xviii, 300 p. illus., maps. 25 cm. *1. Communism — Poland. 2. Poland — History — 1945-*
DK443.S7   943.805   62-15027

DK450 – 465 FINLAND

Platt, Raye Roberts, 1891- ed. III. 2726
Finland and its geography. [1st ed.] New York, Duell, Sloan and Pearce [1955] xxv, 510 p. illus., maps. 26 cm. (An American Geographical Society handbook) *1. Finland — Description and travel — 1945- (S:American Geographical Society of New York. Handbook)*
DK450.P53   914.71   (914.895*)   55-7472

Poutvaara, Matti. III. 2727
Suomi. Finland. [6 painos. Porvoossa] W. Söderström [1960] 295 p. chiefly illus. 20 x 22 cm. English, Finnish, French, German, and Swedish. *1. Finland — Description and travel — Views. I. T.*
DK450.2.P63 1960   914.71   61-40521

Jutikkala, Eino Kaarlo Ilmari, 1907- III. 2728
A history of Finland [by] Eino Jutikkala, with Kauko Pirinen. Translated by Paul Sjöblom. New York, Praeger [1962] 291 p. illus. 25 cm. (Books that matter) *1. Finland — History.*
DK451.J783   947.1   62-13488

Mazour, Anatole Gregory, 1900- III. 2729
Finland between East and West. Princeton, N.J., Van Nostrand [1956] xiv, 298 p. illus., ports., maps (part col.) 24 cm. *1. Finland — History. I. T.*
DK451.M33   947.1 (948.95)   56-8220

Wuorinen, John Henry, 1897- III. 2730
A history of Finland, by John H. Wuorinen. New York, Published for American-Scandinavian Foundation by Columbia University Press, 1965. xv, 548 p. illus., maps, ports. 24 cm. *1. Finland — History. I. T.*
DK451.W8   947.1   65-13618

Shearman, Hugh. III. 2731
Finland: the adventures of a small power. Published under the auspices of the London Institute of World Affairs. London, Stevens, 1950. xi, 114 p. maps. 22 cm. (The Library of world affairs, no. 13) *1. Finland — History. 2. Finland. (S)*
DK451.3.S4x   A51-9000

Jakobson, Max. III. 2732
Finnish neutrality; a study of Finnish foreign policy since the Second World War. New York, Praeger [1969, c1968] 116 p. illus., map, 23 cm. Includes a chapter on the period 1917-1944. *1. Finland — Foreign relations — 1945- 2. Finland — Neutrality. I. T.*
DK451.7.J3 1969   327.471   69-16085

Chew, Allen F. III. 2733
The white death: the epic of the Soviet-Finnish Winter War, by Allen F. Chew. [East Lansing] Michigan State University Press [1971] x, 313 p. plans. 24 cm. *1. Russo-Finnish War, 1939-1940. I. T.*
DK459.5.C48   947/.103   76-169986   ISBN:0870131672

Schwartz, Andrew J. III. 2734
America and the Russo-Finnish War. Introd. by Quincy Wright. Washington, Public Affairs Press [1960] 103 p. 24 cm. *1. Russo-Finnish War, 1939-1940 — Diplomatic history. 2. U.S. — Foreign relations — 1933-1945. I. T.*
DK459.5.S37   947.103   59-15839

Tanner, Väinö Alfred, 1881- III. 2735
The winter war: Finland against Russia, 1939-1940. Stanford, Calif., Stanford University Press [1957] 274 p. illus. 25 cm. Translation of Olin ulkoministerinä talvisodan aikana. *1. Russo-Finnish War, 1939-1940. I. T.*
DK459.5.T312   947.1 (948.95)   57-5904

Mannerheim, Carl Gustaf Emil, friherre, 1867-1951. III. 2736
Memoirs. Translated by Count Eric Lewenhaupt. [1st American ed.] New York, Dutton, 1954. 540 p. port., maps. 22 cm.
DK461.M32A33 1954a   923.5471   54-5060

Poutvaara, Matti. III. 2737
Lappi; keskiyön auringon. maa. Lappland; midnattssolens land. The land of the midnight sun. [2. painos. Helsinki] W. Söderström [1957] 191 p. illus. (part col.) fold. map. 30 cm. Finnish, Swedish, English, and German. *1. Lapin Lääni, Finland — Description and travel.*
DK465.L28P6 1957   914.71 (914.895)   58-40501

DK501 – 973 LOCAL HISTORY

DK507 Belorussia

Vakar, Nicholas P. III. 2738
Belorussia: the making of a nation, a case study. Cambridge, Harvard University Press, 1956. xii, 297 p. ports., maps. 25 cm. (Russian Research Center studies, 21) *1. White Russia — History. I. T. (S:Harvard University. Russian Research Center. Russian Research Center studies, 21)*
DK507.V3   947.6   54-8634

DK508 Ukraine

Allen, William Edward David, 1901- III. 2739
The Ukraine; a history. New York, Russell & Russell, 1963. 404 p. illus. 23 cm. *1. Ukraine — History.*
DK508.5.A79 1963   947.71   63-8355

Hrushevs'kyĭ, Mykhaĭlo, 1866-1934. III. 2740
A history of Ukraine, by Michael Hrushevsky. Edited by O. J. Frederiksen. Pref. by George Vernadsky. Published for the Ukrainian National Association. [Hamden, Conn.] Archon Books, 1970 [c1941] xviii, 629 p. 23 cm. Translation of Istoriia Ukraïny-Rusy (romanized form) *1. Ukraine — History. I. T.*
DK508.5.H683 1970   947.7/1   72-120370   ISBN:208009671

Armstrong, John Alexander, 1922- III. 2741
Ukrainian nationalism. 2d ed. New York, Columbia University Press, 1963. 361 p. illus. 25 cm. (Studies of the Russian Institute, Columbia University) *1. Nationalism — Ukraine. 2. World War, 1939-1945 — Ukraine. I. T.*
DK508.8.A78 1963   947.71   62-18367

Sullivant, Robert S., 1925- III. 2742
Soviet politics and the Ukraine, 1917-1957. New York, Columbia University Press, 1962. 438 p. illus. 24 cm. Issued, with variations, in microfilm form in 1958 as thesis, University of Chicago, under title: Soviet politics in the Ukraine, 1917-1957. *1. Ukraine — Politics and government — 1917- 2. Nationalism — Ukraine. I. T.*
DK508.8.S75   320.158   62-10455

DK511 Baltic States

Page, Stanley W. III. 2743
The formation of the Baltic States; a study of the effects of great power politics upon the emergence of Lithuania, Latvia, and Estonia, by Stanley W. Page. New York, H. Fertig, 1970 [c1959] ix, 193 p. 21 cm. (Harvard historical monographs [39]) *1. Baltic States — History. I. T. (S)*
DK511.B3P28 1970   947.4   74-80578

Pick, Frederick Walter, 1912- III. 2744
The Baltic nations: Estonia, Latvia and Lithuania, by F. W. Pick. London, Boreas [1945] 172 p. maps. 19 cm. "First published 1945." *1. Baltic states — History.*
DK511.B3P5   947.4   45-7863

Reddaway, William Fiddian, 1872-1949. III. 2745
Problems of the Baltic, by W. F. Reddaway. Cambridge [Eng.] The University Press, 1940. 120 p. illus. (map) 18 cm. (Current problems.) *1. Baltic States. I. T.*
DK511.B3R37   947   41-4258

Royal institute of international affairs. Information dept. III. 2746
The Baltic states; a survey of the political and economic structure and the foreign relations of Estonia, Latvia, and Lithuania, prepared by the Information department of the Royal institute of international affairs. London, New York [etc.] Oxford University Press, 1938. 194 p. fold. map. 22 cm. *1. Baltic states.*
DK511.B3R6   947.4   39-8235

Jackson, John Hampden, 1907-   **III. 2747**
Estonia. [2d ed. with a postscript on the years 1940-1947] London, G. Allen & Unwin [1948] 272 p. maps, diagrs. 22 cm. *1. Estonia. I. T.*
DK511.E5J2 1948   947.4   49-1421

Bilmanis, Alfreds, 1887-1948.   **III. 2748**
A history of Latvia. Westport, Conn., Greenwood Press [1970, c1951] x, 441 p. maps, port. 24 cm. *1. Latvia — History. I. T.*
DK511.L17B48 1970   947/.43   69-13827   ISBN:837114462

Gerutis, Albertas, 1905-   **III. 2749**
Lithuania 700 years. Edited by Dr. Albertas Gerutis. Translated by Algirdas Budreckis. Introd. by Raphael Sealey. New York, Manyland Books [1969] xii, 474 p. illus., map, ports. 24 cm. *1. Lithuania — History — Addresses, essays, lectures. I. T.*
DK511.L2G5   947/.5   75-80057

Senn, Alfred Erich.   **III. 2750**
The emergence of modern Lithuania. New York, Columbia University Press, 1959. 272 p. illus. 24 cm. (Studies of the Russian Institute, Columbia University) Thesis statement on label mounted on t.p. *1. Lithuania — History. I. T.*
DK511.L27S4   947.5   59-6606

DK511 – 973   Other Regions

Lang, David Marshall.   **III. 2751**
A modern history of Soviet Georgia. New York, Grove Press [1962] 298 p. illus. 23 cm. *1. Georgia (Transcaucasia) — History.*
DK511.G4L3   947.95   62-13057

Soloukhin, Vladimir Alekseevich.   **III. 2752**
A walk in rural Russia, by Vladimir Soloukhin. Translated from the Russian by Stella Miskin. New York, Dutton [1967, c1966] 254 p. illus., maps. 23 cm. Translation of Vladimirskie proselki (romanized form) *1. Vladimir, Russia (Province) — Description and travel. I. T.*
DK511.V6S653 1967   914.70485   66-28087

Golder, Frank Alfred, 1877-1929.   **III. 2753**
Russian expansion on the Pacific, 1641-1850; an account of the earliest and later expeditions made by the Russians along the Pacific coast of Asia and North America; including some related expeditions to the Arctic regions. Gloucester, Mass., P. Smith, 1960 [c1914] 368 p. illus. 21 cm. *1. Discoveries (in geography) — Russian. 2. Northeast Passage. 3. Siberia — Discovery and exploration. 4. Russia — Colonies — North America. I. T.*
DK753.G7 1960   957   60-52264

Kennan, George, 1845-1924.   **III. 2754**
Siberia and the exile system. New York, Russell & Russell [1970] 2 v. illus., maps, ports. 25 cm. "First published in 1891." *1. Siberia — Description and travel. 2. Siberia — Exiles. I. T.*
DK755.K34122   915.7   76-77675

Akademiia nauk SSSR. Institut ėtnografii.   **III. 2755**
The peoples of Siberia. Edited by M. G. Levin and L. P. Potapov. [Translated from the Russian by Scripta Technica, inc. English translation edited by Stephen P. Dunn] Chicago, University of Chicago Press [1964] viii, 948 p. illus., maps (1 fold. in pocket) ports. 24 cm. "Originally published by the Russian Academy of Science, Moscow, 1956." *1. Ethnology — Siberia. I. Levin, Maksim Grigor'evich, ed. II. Potapov, Leonid Pavlovich, 1905- ed. III. Dunn, Stephen Porter, 1928- ed. IV. T.*
DK758.A4813   915.7   62-18118

Kolarz, Walter.   **III. 2756**
The peoples of the Soviet Far East. [Hamden, Conn.] Archon Books, 1969. xii, 193 p. illus., maps. 23 cm. Reprint of the 1954 ed. *1. Ethnology — Soviet Far East. I. T.*
DK758.K6 1969   323.1/57   69-12416   ISBN:208007016

Allworth, Edward, ed.   **III. 2757**
Central Asia; a century of Russian rule, edited by Edward Allworth. Contributors: Edward Allworth [and others] New York, Columbia University Press, 1967. xiv, 552 p. illus., maps, music, ports. 25 cm. *1. Soviet Central Asia. I. Carrère d'Encausse, Hélène. II. T.*
DK851.A4   958   66-16288

Krader, Lawrence.   **III. 2758**
Peoples of central Asia. Bloomington, Indiana University, 1963. xiv, 319 p. 2 fold. maps (in pocket) tables. 26 cm. (Uralic and Altaic series, v.26. Indiana University publications.) "American Council of Learned Societies. Research and studies in Uralic and Altaic languages. Project nos. 12 and 62." *1. Ethnology — Soviet Central Asia. I. T. (S:Indiana. University. Uralic and Altaic series, v.26)*
DK855.4.K7   63-63330

Wheeler, Geoffrey.   **III. 2759**
The modern history of Soviet Central Asia. New York, Praeger [1964] xi, 272 p. illus., maps, ports. 23 cm. (Asia-Africa series of modern histories) *1. Soviet Central Asia — History. I. T.*
DK856.W5 1964   958.4   64-19966

Becker, Seymour.   **III. 2760**
Russia's protectorates in Central Asia: Bukhara and Khiva, 1865-1924. Cambridge, Harvard University Press, 1968. xiv, 416 p. illus., maps, ports. 25 cm. (Russian Research Center studies, 54) *1. Bokhara — Politics and government. 2. Khiva — Politics and government. I. T. (S:Harvard University. Russian Research Center. Studies, 54)*
DK879.B4   325.3/47/0958   67-30825

DL   Scandinavia

DL1 – 42 GENERAL WORKS

Sømme, Axel Christian Zetlitz, 1899-   **III. 2761**
The geography of Norden: Denmark, Finland, Iceland, Norway, Sweden. London, Heinemann [1961] 363 p. illus., maps (part col.) diagrs. 27 cm. (Scandinavian university books) *1. Scandinavia. 2. Finland. I. T.*
DL5.S6 1961a   914.8   62-5819

Lauring, Palle.   **III. 2762**
Land of the Tollund man; the prehistory and archaeology of Denmark. Translated by Reginald Spink; photos. by Lennart Larsen. [1st English ed.] London, Lutterworth Press [1957] 160 p. illus., maps. 26 cm. Translation of De byggede riget. *1. Denmark — Antiquities. I. T.*
DL21.Lx   A58-3946

Shetelig, Haakon, 1877-   **III. 2763**
Scandinavian archeology, by Haakon Shetelig and Hjalmar Falk. Translated by E. V. Gordon. Oxford, Clarendon Press, 1937. xix, 458 p. illus., 62 pl. on 38 l., diagrs. 23 cm. *1. Scandinavia — Antiquities. 2. Archaeology. I. Falk, Hjalmar Sejersted, 1859-1928, joint author. II. Gordon, Eric Valentine, 1896-1938, tr. III. T.*
DL21.S57   913.48   38-8139

Friis, Henning Kristian, 1911- ed.   **III. 2764**
Scandinavia, between East and West. Ithaca, Cornell University Press, 1950. x, 388 p. 24 cm. "A publication of the New School for Social Research." *1. Scandinavia — Politics. 2. Scandinavia — Economic conditions. 3. Scandinavia — Social conditions. I. T.*
DL30.F75 1950   914.8   50-8531

Shirer, William Lawrence, 1904-   **III. 2765**
The challenge of Scandinavia: Norway, Sweden, Denmark, and Finland in our time. [1st ed.] Boston, Little, Brown [1955] 437 p. 23 cm. *1. Scandinavia — Civilization. 2. Finland — Civilization. I. T.*
DL30.S45   948   55-7466

Jones, Gwyn, 1907-   **III. 2766**
A history of the Vikings. London, New York [etc.] Oxford U.P., 1968. xvi, 504 p. illus., maps, plates. 23 cm. *1. Civilization, Scandinavian. 2. Vikings. I. T.*
DL31.J6   914.8/03/2   68-124332

Olrik, Axel, 1864-1917.   **III. 2767**
Viking civilization, by Axel Olrik, revised after the author's death by Hans Ellekilde. New York, American-Scandinavian Foundation; W. W. Norton [c1930] 246 p. plates. 22 cm. (Scandinavian classics. vol.XXXIV) "The English version follows the Danish edition of 1927 ... The translation is the work of Professor Jacob Wittmer Hartmann ... and Hanna Astrup Larsen." — Editorial note. Translation of Nordisk aandsliv i vikingetid og tidlig middelalder. *1. Civilization, Scandinavian. 2. Civilization, Medieval. 3. Northmen. I. Ellekilde, Hans Lavrids, 1891- ed. II. Hartmann, Jacob Wittmer, 1881- tr. III. Larsen, Hanna Astrup, 1873-1945, joint tr. IV. T.*
DL31.O53   948.01   30-30010

DL43 – 85 HISTORY

Kirchner, Walther.   **III. 2768**
The rise of the Baltic question. Westport, Conn., Greenwood Press [1970, c1954] xi, 283 p. 23 cm. *1. Baltic States — Politics. 2. Europe — Politics. 3. Livonia — History. I. T.*
DL59.K5 1970   947.4   77-100237   ISBN:837130093

Scott, Franklin Daniel, 1901-   **III. 2769**
The United States and Scandinavia. Cambridge, Harvard University Press, 1950. xviii, 359 p. maps (part col.) 20 cm. (The American foreign policy library) *1. U.S. — Foreign relations — Scandinavia. 2. Scandinavia — Foreign relations — U.S. 3. Scandinavia. I. T. (S)*
DL59.S35 1950   948   50-7563

Turville-Petre, Edward Oswald Gabriel.   **III. 2770**
The heroic age of Scandinavia. London, New York, Hutchinson's University Library [1951] 196 p. illus. 20 cm. (Hutchinson's university library: history) *1. Scandinavia — History. I. T.*
DL61.T8   948.01   51-14881

Arbman, Holger, 1904-   **III. 2771**
The Vikings. Translated and edited, with an introd., by Alan Binns. New York, Praeger [1961] 212 p. illus. 21 cm. (Ancient peoples and places, v. 21. Books that matter.) *1. Vikings.*
DL65.A723   948.02   61-10520

Brondsted, Johannes, 1890-   **III. 2772**
The Vikings; [an illustrated history of the Vikings: their voyages, battles, customs, and decorative arts] Translated by Kalle Skov. Baltimore, Penguin Books [1965] 347 p. illus. 18 cm. *1. Vikings.*
DL65.B7x

Foote, Peter Godfrey.   **III. 2773**
The Viking achievement; a survey of the society and culture of early medieval Scandinavia [by] Peter G. Foote [and] David M. Wilson. New York, Praeger [1970] xxv, 473 p. illus., maps. 25 cm. *1. Northmen. I. Wilson, David McKenzie, joint author. II. T.*
DL65.F6 1970   914.8/03/2   75-108560

Ingstad, Helge Marcus, 1899-   **III. 2774**
Westward to Vinland; the discovery of pre-Columbian Norse house-sites in North America [by] Helge Ingstad. Translated from the Norwegian by Erik J. Friis. [1st American ed.] New York, St. Martin's Press [1969] 249 p. illus. 24 cm. Translation of Vesterveg til Vinland. *1. Vikings. 2. America — Discovery and exploration — Norse. I. T.*
DL65.I513 1969   973.1/3   67-10089

Kendrick, Thomas Downing, Sir.   **III. 2775**
A history of the Vikings [by] T. D. Kendrick. New York, Barnes & Noble [1968] xi, 412 p. illus., maps. 22 cm. Reprint of the 1930 ed. *1. Vikings. I. T.*
DL65.K27 1968   948/.01   68-4261

Klindt-Jensen, Ole.   **III. 2776**
The world of the Vikings. Illustrated by Svenolov Ehrén. Washington, R. B. Luce [1970] 238 p. illus. (part col.), maps (part col.) 28 cm. Translation of Vikingernes verden. *1. Vikings. I. T.*
DL65.K513   948/.03/1   73-119528

Sawyer, P. H.   **III. 2777**
The age of the Vikings [by] P. H. Sawyer. 2d ed. New York, St. Martin's Press [1972, c1971] vi, 275 p. illus. 23 cm. *1. Vikings. I. T.*
DL65.S25 1972   948/.02   79-185487

DL101 – 291 DENMARK

Jones, W. Glyn.   **III. 2778**
Denmark, by W. Glyn Jones. New York, Praeger [1970] 256 p. illus., facsims., fold. map, plates, ports. 23 cm. (Nations of the modern world) *1. Denmark. (S)*
DL109.J6 1970   948/.9   77-109476

Lauring, Palle.   **III. 2779**
A history of the kingdom of Denmark. Translated from the Danish by David Hohnen. Drawings by Vibeke Lind. 3rd. ed. Copenhagen, Høst, 1968. 274 p. illus., 16 plates. 24 cm. *1. Denmark — History. I. T.*
DL148.L353 1968   948/.9   68-118267

Danstrup, John.   **III. 2780**
A history of Denmark. [Tr. into English by Verner Lindberg] Copenhagen, Wivel, 1948. 195 p. col. maps. 21 cm. *1. Denmark — History. I. Lindberg, Verner, tr.*
DL149.D32   948.9   48-22609

Larson, Laurence Marcellus, 1868-1938.   **III. 2781**
Canute the Great, 995 (circ)-1035, and the rise of Danish imperialism during the Viking Age. New York, AMS Press [1970] xviii, 375 p. illus., facsim., maps. 23 cm. (Heroes of the nations) Reprint of the 1912 ed. *1. Canute, the Great, King of England and Denmark, 995?-1035. (S)*
DL165.L3 1970   948.901/0924   71-111764   ISBN:404038794

DL301 – 398 ICELAND

Malmström, Vincent Herschel, 1926-   **III. 2782**
A regional geography of Iceland. Washington, National Academy of Sciences-National Research Council, 1958. 255 p. illus., maps, diagrs., tables. 28 cm. (National Research Council. Division of Earth Sciences. Foreign field research program, report no. 1. National Research Council. Publication 584.) *1. Physical geography — Iceland. 2. Iceland — Industries. I. T. (S:National Research Council. Publication 584)*
DL305.M27   914.91   58-60026

Gjerset, Knut, 1865-1936.   **III. 2783**
History of Iceland, by Knut Gjerset. New York, Macmillan, 1924. vi, 482 p. col. front. 23 cm. *1. Iceland — History. 2. Iceland — Civilization.*
DL338.G5   24-2336

Nuechterlein, Donald Edwin, 1925-   **III. 2784**
Iceland, reluctant ally. Ithaca, N.Y., Cornell University Press [1961] 213 p. illus. 24 cm. *1. Iceland — Politics and government. 2. Iceland — Foreign relations.*
DL375.N8   949.104   61-12044

DL401 – 596 NORWAY

Gathorne-Hardy, Geoffrey Malcolm, 1878-   **III. 2785**
Norway, by G. Gathorne Hardy, with an introduction by the Right Hon. H. A. L. Fisher. New York, Scribner, 1925. 324 p. 23 cm. (The modern world) *1. Norway.*
DL411.G3 1925a   914.81   33-30481

Popperwell, Ronald G.   **III. 2786**
Norway, by Ronald G. Popperwell. New York, Praeger [1972] 335 p. illus. 23 cm. (Nations of the modern world) *1. Norway — Civilization. (S)*
DL431.P66   914.81/03   72-154357

Falnes, Oscar Julius, 1898-   **III. 2787**
National romanticism in Norway, by Oscar J. Falnes. New York, AMS Press [1968] 398 p. 22 cm. (Studies in history, economics, and public law, no. 386) Reprint of the 1933 ed., which was issued also as thesis, Columbia, 1933. *1. Norway — Nationality. 2. Romanticism — Norway. 3. Norway — Historiography. 4. Historians, Norwegian. 5. Folk literature — Norway — History and criticism. 6. Norwegian language. I. T. (S:Columbia studies in the social sciences, no. 386)*
DL441.F3 1968   320.1/58/09481   68-54263

Derry, Thomas Kingston, 1905-   **III. 2788**
A short history of Norway. London, G. Allen & Unwin [1957] 281 p. maps (on lining papers) 23 cm. *1. Norway — History.*
DL448.D4   948.1   57-3947

Gjerset, Knut, 1865-1936.   **III. 2789**
History of the Norwegian people. [1st AMS ed.] New York, AMS Press [1969] 2 v. in 1. illus., maps, ports. 23 cm. Reprint of the 1932 ed. *1. Norway — History. I. T.*
DL449.G5 1969   914.81/03   79-101272   ISBN:404028187

Koht, Halvdan, 1873-1965.   **III. 2790**
The voice of Norway, by Halvdan Koht and Sigmund Skard. New York, AMS Press, 1967 [c1944] x, 313 p. 23 cm. *1. Norway — History. 2. Norway — Politics and government. 3. Norwegian literature — History and criticism. I. Skard, Sigmund, 1903- II. T.*
DL449.K5 1969   914.81/03   75-181941

Eckstein, Harry.   **III. 2791**
Division and cohesion in democracy; a study of Norway. Princeton, N.J., Princeton University Press, 1966. xvii, 293 p. 23 cm. "Published for the Center of International Studies, Princeton University." *1. Norway — Politics and government. I. Princeton University. Center of International Studies. II. T.*
DL458.E25   320.9481   66-17700

DL601 – 876 SWEDEN

Sweden. Riksarkivet.   **III. 2792**
Sweden and the world; documents from the Swedish National Archives. Introd. by Ingvar Andersson. [Stockholm] Swedish Institute [1960] [94] p. illus., facsims., 2 col. plates. 33 cm. *1. Sweden — History — Sources. 2. Sweden — Relations (general) with foreign countries. I. Andersson, Ingvar, 1899- II. T.*
DL603.A57   65-2363

Roberts, Michael, 1908-   **III. 2793**
Sweden as a great power, 1611-1697: government, society, foreign policy. Edited by Michael Roberts. New York, St. Martin's Press, 1968. vi, 182, [1] p. 21 cm. (Documents of modern history) *1. Sweden — History — 1523-1718 — Sources. I. T.*
DL603.R6 1968b   948.5/02   68-29381

Introduction to Sweden, by Ingvar Andersson and others.   **III. 2794**
Published by the Swedish Institute. [Translation by Nils G. Sahlin. 5th ed.] Stockholm, Forum [1961] 210 p. illus. 22 cm. *1. Sweden. I. Andersson, Ingvar, 1899- II. Svenska institutet för kulturellt utbyte med utlandet, Stockholm.*
DL609.I52 1961   914.85   62-9409

Scobbie, Irene.   **III. 2795**
Sweden. New York, Praeger [1972] 254 p. illus. 23 cm. (Nations of the modern world) *1. Sweden. (S)*
DL609.S37 1972   948.5   72-78336

Andersson, Ingvar, 1899-   **III. 2796**
A history of Sweden. Translated from the Swedish by Carolyn Hannay. New York, Praeger [1956] xxvi, 461 p. illus., ports., maps, facsims. 23 cm. *1. Sweden — History.*
DL648.A612   55-10489

Moberg, Vilhelm, 1898-   **III. 2797**
A history of the Swedish people. Translated from the Swedish by Paul Britten Austin. [1st American ed.] New York, Pantheon [1972- v. 22 cm. Translation of Min svenska historia. *1. Sweden — History. I. T.*
DL648.M613   948.5   72-3411   ISBN:0394481925

Roberts, Michael, 1908-   **III. 2798**
Essays in Swedish history. Minneapolis, University of Minnesota Press [1967, c1966] ix, 358 p. 22 cm. *1. Sweden — History — Addresses, essays, lectures. I. T.*
DL648.R6 1967b   948.5   68-4928

Abrahamsen, Samuel, 1917-   **III. 2799**
Sweden's foreign policy. Including an introd. by Alvin Johnson. Washington, Public Affairs Press [1957] 99 p. 24 cm. *1. Sweden — Foreign relations — 1905- I. T.*
DL658.8.A58   327.485   57-6907

Tingsten, Herbert Lars Gustav, 1896-   **III. 2800**
The debate on the foreign policy of Sweden, 1918-1939. Translated by Joan Bulman. London, New York, Oxford University Press, 1949. 324 p. 23 cm. "Correction" slip inserted. *1. League of Nations. 2. Sweden — Foreign relations — 1905- 3. Åland question. I. T.*
DL658.8.T513   948.5   50-14521

Stenberger, Mårten Karl Herman, 1898-   **III. 2801**
Sweden. Translated from the Swedish by Alan Binns. New York, Praeger [1963, c1962] 229 p. illus. 21 cm. (Ancient peoples and places, v.30. Books that matter.) *1. Sweden — History — To 1397. 2. Sweden — Antiquities.*
DL661.S73 1963   948.501   62-19107

Roberts, Michael.   **III. 2802**
The early Vasas: a history of Sweden 1523-1611. Cambridge, London, Cambridge U.P., 1968. xiv, 509 p. 5 plates, table, 3 maps, 5 ports. 24 cm. *1. Sweden — History — 1523-1654. 2. Vasa, House of. I. T.*
DL701.R6   948.5/02   68-10332   ISBN:0521069300

Ahnlund, Nils Gabriel, 1889-   **III. 2803**
Gustav Adolf, the great, by Nils Ahnlund, translated from the Swedish by Michael Roberts. Princeton, Princeton University Press; New York, American-Scandinavian Foundation, 1940. ix, 314 p. illus., maps, pl., ports. 24 cm. *1. Gustaf II Adolf, king of Sweden, 1594-1632. I. Roberts, Michael, 1902- tr. II. T.*
DL706.A34   923.1485   40-11226

Roberts, Michael, 1908-   **III. 2804**
Gustavus Adolphus; a history of Sweden, 1611-1632. London, New York, Longmans, Green [1953-58] 2 v. ports., maps (2 fold.) geneal. table. 23 cm. *1. Sweden — History — Gustavus II Adolphus, 1611-1632.*
DL706.R75   948.5   53-2040

Bengtsson, Frans Gunnar, 1894-1954.   **III. 2805**
The sword does not jest; the heroic life of King Charles XII of Sweden. Translated from the Swedish by Naomi Walford. With an introd. by Eric Linklater. New York, St Martin's Press, 1960. 495 p. illus. 23 cm. Translation of Karl XII:s levnad. *1. Karl XII, King of Sweden, 1682-1718. I. T.*
DL732.B413   923.1485   60-13877

Hatton, Ragnhild Marie.   **III. 2806**
Charles XII of Sweden [by] R. M. Hatton. New York, Weybright and Talley [1969, c1968] xvii, 656 p. illus., maps, plan, ports. 25 cm. *1. Karl XII, King of Sweden, 1682-1718.*
DL732.H35 1969   948.5/03/0924 (B)   69-10605

Scott, Franklin Daniel, 1901-   **III. 2807**
Bernadotte and the fall of Napoleon, by Franklin D. Scott. Cambridge, Harvard University Press, 1935. 190 p. 21 cm. (Harvard historical monographs. VII) "This monograph is a condensation of a doctoral dissertation [Harvard university, 1932] under the same title." Prefatory note. *1. Karl XIV Johan, king of Sweden and Norway, 1763-1844. 2. Napoléon I, emperor of the French, 1769-1821. 3. Europe — History — 1789-1815. I. T.*
DL820.S33 1935   948.07   35-17803

DL971   LAPLAND

Bosi, Roberto, 1924-   **III. 2808**
The Lapps. [Translated by James Cadell] New York, Praeger [1960] 220 p. illus. 21 cm. (Ancient peoples and places, v.17. Books that matter.) *1. Lapps.*
DL971.L2B673   947.17   60-15600

Collinder, Björn, 1894-   **III. 2809**
The Lapps. New York, Greenwood Press [1969, c1949] 252 p. illus. 23 cm. *1. Lapps.*
DL971.L2C6 1969   914.71/7/03   73-90490   ISBN:837122139

Manker, Ernst Mauritz, 1893-   **III. 2810**
People of eight seasons; the story of the Lapps. [Translated by Kathleen McFarlane] New York, Viking Press [1964, c1963] 214, [17] p. illus. (part col.) 29 cm. (A Studio book) *1. Lapps. I. T.*
DL971.L2M29223 1964   914.7   64-15063

DP Spain. Portugal

DP1 – 402 SPAIN

Ford, Richard, 1796-1858. III. 2811
A hand-book for travellers in Spain and readers at home, describing the country and cities, the natives and their manners, the antiquities, religion, legends, fine arts, literature, sports, and gastronomy, with notices on Spanish history. Foreword by Sir John Balfour. Edited and with an introd. by Ian Robertson. Carbondale, Ill., Southern Illinois University Press [1966] 3 v. (xviii, 1507 p.) illus., fold. maps, port. 23 cm. (Centaur classics) Cover title: Handbook for Spain, 1845. *1. Spain — Description and travel — Guide-books. I. T. II. T:Handbook for Spain, 1845.*
DP14.F6 1966a   914.6047   65-10028

Fisher, William Bayne. III. 2812
Spain; an introductory geography, by W. B. Fisher and H. Bowen-Jones. New York, Praeger [1966] 222 p. illus., maps. 21 cm. (Praeger introductory geographies) *1. Spain — Description and travel — 1951- I. Bowen-Jones, Howard, joint author.*
DP17.F5 1966   914.6   66-17362

Madariaga, Salvador de, 1886- III. 2813
Spain, a modern history. New York, Praeger [1958] 736 p. 25 cm. (Books that matter) *1. Spain. 2. Spain — History.*
DP26.M3 1958   946   58-9695

Borrow, George Henry, 1803-1881. III. 2814
The Bible in Spain; or, The journeys, adventures, and imprisonments of an Englishman, in an attempt to circulate the Scriptures in the peninsula. Edited, with an introd. and notes, by Peter Quennell. London, Macdonald [1959] L, 586 p. plates, ports. 19 cm. (Macdonald illustrated classics, 39) *1. Spain — Description and travel. I. T.*
DP41.B7 1959   914.6   62-1934

Brenan, Gerald. III. 2815
The face of Spain. New York, Grove Press [1957, c1956] 310 p. illus. 21 cm. (An Evergreen book, E-51) *1. Spain — Description and travel — 1951- I. T.*
DP42.B646x   914.6   57-5548

Sitwell, Sacheverell, 1897- III. 2816
Spain. [2d ed.] London, Batsford [1953] 148 p. illus. 22 cm. *1. Spain — Description and travel.*
DP42.S665 1953   914.6   53-30606

Michener, James Albert, 1907- III. 2817
Iberia; Spanish travels and reflections [by] James A. Michener. Photos. by Robert Vavra. New York, Random House [1968] 818 p. illus., geneal. table, maps (part col.), ports. 25 cm. *1. Spain — Description and travel — 1951- 2. Spain — Civilization — 20th century. I. T.*
DP43.M45   914.6/04/82   67-22623

Way, Ruth. III. 2818
A geography of Spain and Portugal, by Ruth Way, assisted by Margaret Simmons. London, Methuen [1962] xi, 362 p. illus., plates, maps. 22 cm. *1. Spain — Description and travel — 1951- 2. Portugal — Description and travel — 1951-*
DP43.W3   914.6   62-5701

DP44 – 53 Civilization

Castro, Américo, 1885- III. 2819
The structure of Spanish history; translated by Edmund L. King. Princeton, Princeton University Press, 1954. xiii, 689 p. illus., ports. 25 cm. A translation, with modifications and additions, of España en su historia. *1. Spain — Civilization. I. T.*
DP48.C3383   914.6   53-10149

Pritchett, Victor Sawdon, 1900- III. 2820
The Spanish temper. [1st American ed.] New York, Knopf, 1954. 269 p. illus. 21 cm. *1. Spain — Civilization. 2. National characteristics, Spanish. I. T.*
DP48.P8   914.6   53-6857

Sarrailh, Jean. III. 2821
La españa ilustrada de la segunda mitad del siglo XVIII. México, Fondo de Cultura Económica [1957] 784 p. illus. 24 cm. (Sección de obras de historia) Translation of L'Espagne éclairée de la seconde moitié du XVIII siècle. *1. Spain — Civilization. I. T.*
DP48.S38x

Trend, John Brande, 1887- III. 2822
The origins of modern Spain, by J. B. Trend. New York, Russell & Russell, 1965. x, 220 p. 23 cm. "First published in 1934." *1. Spain — Intellectual life. 2. Spain — Biography. 3. Education — Spain — History. 4. Spain — History — Revolutionary period, 1868-1875. I. T.*
DP48.T72 1965   946.08   65-17925

Vicens Vives, Jaime, ed. III. 2823
Historia social y económica de España y América. Barcelona, Editorial Teide [1957-59] 4 v. in 5. illus. (part col.) ports., maps, diagrs., facsims. 26 cm. *1. Spain — Civilization — History. 2. Spanish America — Civilization — History. I. T.*
DP48.V45   58-19380

Díaz-Plaja, Fernando. III. 2824
The Spaniard and the seven deadly sins. Translated from the Spanish by John Inderwick Palmer. New York, Scribner [1967] 223 p. map (on lining papers) 21 cm. Translation of El español y los siete pecados capitales. *1. National characteristics, Spanish. 2. Deadly sins. I. T.*
DP52.D513   914.6/03   67-21337

Ganivet, Angel, 1865-1898. III. 2825
Spain: an interpretation. [Translated by J. R. Carey] with introduction by R. M. Nadal. London, Eyre & Spottiswoode, 1946. 136 p. 22 cm. Translation of 'Idearium español'. *1. National characteristics, Spanish. I. Carey, J. R., tr.*
DP52.G29   914.6   47-20750

Ramsden, Herbert. III. 2826
Angel Genivet's Idearium Espanōl: a critical study, by H. Ramsden. Manchester, Manchester U.P., 1967. vi, 196 p. 20 cm. (Publications of the Faculty of Arts of the University of Manchester, no. 16) *1. Ganivet, Angel, 1865-1898. Idearium español. I. Ganivet, Angel, 1865-1898. Iderium español. (S:Victoria University of Manchester. Faculty of Arts. Publications, no. 16)*
DP52.G32R3   68-111682

Menéndez Pidal, Ramón, 1869- III. 2827
The Spaniards in their history; translated with a prefatory essay on the author's work by Walter Starkie. New York, Norton [1950] viii, 251 p. maps. 22 cm. Translated from the introd. to the first volume of the author's Historia de España, published in 1947. *1. National characteristics, Spanish. I. Starkie, Walter Fitzwilliam, 1894- II. T.*
DP52.M4 1950a   914.6   50-9474

DP56 – 271 History

Diccionario de historia de España, desde sus orígenes hasta el fin del reinado de Alfonso XIII. III. 2828
Madrid, Revista de Occidente [1952] 2 v. maps. 22 cm. *1. Spain — History — Dictionaries.*
DP56.D5   52-43873

Ubieto Arteta, Antonio. III. 2829
Introducción a la historia de España [por] Antonio Ubieto, Juan Reglá [y] José María Jover. [1. ed.] Barcelona, Editorial Teide [1963] 798 p. illus.,

facsims., maps, ports. 23 cm. *1. Spain — History. I. Reglá Campistol, Juan. II. Jover, José María.*
DP58.U2   64-51814

Altamira y Crevea, Rafael, 1866-1951.   **III. 2830**
A history of Spain from the beginnings to the present day; translated by Muna Lee. [1st ed.] New York, Van Nostrand Co. [1949] xxx, 748 p. illus., ports., maps. 24 cm. Translation of the 2d ed. of Manual de historia de España. *1. Spain — History.*
DP66.A672   946   49-11695

Atkinson, William Christopher, 1902-   **III. 2831**
A history of Spain & Portugal. [Harmondsworth, Middlesex, Baltimore] Penguin Books [1960] 382 p. illus. 18 cm. (The Pelican history of the world) *1. Spain — History. 2. Portugal — History.*
DP66.A9   946   60-3356

Hills, George.   **III. 2832**
Spain. New York, Praeger [1970] 480 p. illus., 1 fold. map, ports. 23 cm. (Nations of the modern world) *1. Spain — History. (S)*
DP66.H55 1970b   946/.009   70-100936

Merriman, Roger Bigelow, 1876-1945.   **III. 2833**
The rise of the Spanish Empire in the Old World and in the New. New York, Cooper Square Publishers, 1962 [c1918] 4 v. maps, facsim., geneal. tables (part fold.) 24 cm. *1. Spain — History. I. T.*
DP66.M42   946   61-13267

Soldevila Zubiburu, Fernando, 1894-   **III. 2834**
Historia de España. [Versión castellana. Ed. ilustrada, pies de grabado e índice alfabético por J. Sales] Barcelona, Ediciones Ariel [1952- v. illus., ports. (part col.) fold. col. maps, col. coats of arms, facsims.] geneal. tables. 25 cm. *1. Spain — History.*
DP66.S6   946   53-29179

Vicens Vives, Jaime.   **III. 2835**
Approaches to the history of Spain. Translated and edited by Joan Connelly Ullman. Berkeley, University of California Press, 1967. xxviii, 189 p. illus., maps. 21 cm. Translation of Aproximación a la historia de España. *1. Spain — History. I. T.*
DP66.V513   946   67-27127

Vilar, Pierre, 1906-   **III. 2836**
Spain; a brief history. Translated by Brian Tate. [1st ed.] Oxford, New York, Pergamon Press [1967] vii, 140 p. map. 20 cm. (Pergamon Oxford Spanish series) Commonwealth and international library. Translation of Histoire de l'Espagne. *1. Spain — History. I. T.*
DP68.V5513 1967   946   67-26694

Ortega y Gasset, José, 1883-   **III. 2837**
Invertebrate Spain, by José Ortega y Gasset; translation and foreword by Mildred Adams. New York, Norton [c1937] 212 p. 23 cm. The first three essays ... were taken from the volume whose Spanish title, España invertebrada, provided the subject as well as the title for this book. The others were chosen from other volumes of Señor Ortega's work ..." Foreword. *1. Spain — Politics and government. 2. Spain — Civilization. I. Adams, Mildred, 1894- tr. II. T.*
DP84.O7   946   37-27312

DP91 – 271   BY PERIOD
DP91 – 96   To   711

Sutherland, Carol Humphrey Vivian.   **III. 2838**
The Romans in Spain, 217 B.C.-A.D. 117, by C. H. V. Sutherland. London, Methuen & Co., Ltd. [1939] xi, 264 p. illus., 3 maps (2 fold.) 19 cm. "First published in 1939." *1. Spain — History — Roman period, B.C. 218-A.D. 414. 2. Rome — Provinces — Hispania. I. T.*
DP94.S8   946.01   40-13199

Thompson, E. A.   **III. 2839**
The Goths in Spain, by E. A. Thompson. Oxford, Clarendon P., 1969. xiv, 358 p. 23 cm. *1. Visigoths in Spain. 2. Spain — History — Gothic period, 414-711. I. T.*
DP96.T48   946/.01   78-399622   ISBN:198142714

DP98 – 160   Moorish Domination.
Reconquest (711 – 1516)

Jackson, Gabriel.   **III. 2840**
The making of Medieval Spain. [1st American ed. New York] Harcourt Brace Jovanovich [1972] 216 p. illus. (part col.) 21 cm. (History of European civilization library) *1. Spain — History — Arab period, 711-1492. I. T.*
DP99.J32 1972b   914.6   73-151307
ISBN:0151559759   0155546422 (pbk.)

Lévi-Provençal, Évariste, 1894-1956.   **III. 2841**
Histoire de l'Espagne musulmane. Nouv. éd. rev. et augm. Paris, G.-P. Maisonneuve, 1950- v. illus., plates, maps, geneal. tables. 24 cm. *1. Arabs in Spain. 2. Spain — History — Arab period, 711-1492.*
DP99.L55   A51-4381

Scholberg, Kenneth R., ed. and tr.   **III. 2842**
Spanish life in the late Middle Ages, selected and translated by Kenneth R. Scholberg. Chapel Hill, University of North Carolina Press [1966] 180 p. 23 cm. (University of North Carolina. Studies in the Romance languages and literatures, no. 57) *1. Spain — History — 711-1516. 2. Spain — Social life and customs. I. T. (S: North Carolina. University. Studies in the Romance languages and literatures, no. 57)*
DP99.Sx (PC13.N67 no. 57)   914.6   66-64140

Sánchez-Albornoz y Menduiña, Claudio, 1893-   **III. 2843**
España y el Islam. Buenos Aires, Editorial sudamericana [1943] 199 p. 17 cm. *1. Spain — History — Arab period, 711-1492. I. T.*
DP99.S3   946.02   44-27201

Lane-Poole, Stanley, 1854-1931.   **III. 2844**
The Moors in Spain. With the collaboration of Arthur Gilman. Beirut, Khayats, 1967. xx, 285 p. illus., maps. 20 cm. (Khayats oriental reprint no. 23) Previous ed., 1886, has title: The story of the Moors in Spain. *1. Spain — History — Arab period, 711-1492. 2. Arabs in Spain. I. Gilman, Arthur, 1837-1909. II. T.*
DP102.L3 1967   914.6/03/2   67-9727

Chaytor, Henry John, 1871-1954.   **III. 2845**
A history of Aragon and Catalonia. New York, AMS Press [1969] xvi, 322 p. maps. 23 cm. Reprint of the 1933 ed. *1. Aragon — History. 2. Catalonia — History. 3. Spain — History — Arab period, 711-1492. I. T.*
DP125.C5 1969   946/.02   73-92610

Shneidman, Jerome Lee, 1929-   **III. 2846**
The rise of the Aragonese-Catalan empire, 1200-1350 [by] J. Lee Shneidman. New York, New York University Press, 1970. 2 v. (xv, 624 p.) geneal. tables, maps. 25 cm. *1. Aragon — History. 2. Aragon — Foreign relations. I. T.*
DP128.S25   946/.02   70-92525   ISBN:0814703844

Procter, Evelyn Stefanos, 1897-   **III. 2847**
Alfonso X of Castile, patron of literature and learning. Oxford, Clarendon Press, 1951. vi, 149 p. 19 cm. (Norman Maccoll lectures, 1949) *1. Alfonso X, el Sabio, King of Castile and Leon, 1221-1284. (S)*
DP140.3.Px   A53-1055

DP161 – 232   1459/1516 – 1885

Díaz-Plaja, Fernando, ed.   **III. 2848**
La historia de España en sus documentos. Madrid, Instituto de Estudios Políticos, 1954-58. 4 v. 25 cm. *1. Spain — History — Sources. I. T.*
DP161.D5   55-21660

Davies, Reginald Trevor.   **III. 2849**
The golden century of Spain, 1501-1621, by R. Trevor Davies. London, Macmillan, 1937. xi, 327 p. front., illus. (maps) plates, port. 23 cm. *1. Spain — History — Ferdinand and Isabella, 1479-1516. 2. Spain — History — House of Austria, 1516-1700. I. T.*
DP162.D3   946.03   38-14927

Mariéjol, Jean Hippolyte, 1855-1934.   **III. 2850**
The Spain of Ferdinand and Isabella. Translated and edited by Benjamin Keen. New Brunswick, N.J., Rutgers University Press [1961] xxiv, 429 p. illus., maps, geneal. tables. 22 cm. *1. Spain — History — Ferdinand and Isabella, 1479-1516. I. T.*
DP162.M333   946.03   60-14206

Miller, Townsend.   **III. 2851**
The castles and the Crown; Spain: 1451-1555. New York, Coward-McCann [1963] 379 p. illus. 22 cm. *1. Isabel I, Católica, Queen of Spain, 1451-1504. 2. Fernando V, el Católico, King of Spain, 1452-1516. 3. Juana, la Loca, Queen of Castile, 1479-1555. 4. Felipe I, King of Castille, 1478-1506. I. T.*
DP162.M5   946.03   63-8207

Prescott, William Hickling, 1796-1859.   **III. 2852**
History of the reign of Ferdinand and Isabella, the Catholic. Abridged and edited by C. Harvey Gardiner. Carbondale, Ill., Southern Illinois University Press [1962] 303 p. illus. 23 cm. *1. Fernando v., el Católico, King of Spain, 1452-1516. 2. Isabel I, la Católica, Queen of Spain, 1451-1504. 3. Spain — History — Ferdinand and Isabella, 1479-1516.*
DP162.P8 1962a   946.03   62-16246

Domínguez Ortiz, Antonio. III. 2853
The golden age of Spain, 1516-1659. Translated by James Casey. New York, Basic Books [1971] 361 p. map. 22 cm. (The History of Spain) *1. Spain — History — House of Austria, 1516-1700. 2. Spain — Civilization — 1516-1700. I. T.*
DP171.D6513   914.6/03/4   70-167765

Elliott, John Huxtable. III. 2854
Imperial Spain, 1469-1716. New York, St. Martin's Press [1964, c1963] 411 p. 22 plates (incl. ports., facsims.) maps, diagrs., geneal. tables. 22 cm. *1. Spain — History — House of Austria, 1516-1700. 2. Spain — History — 711-1516. I. T.*
DP171.E4 1964   946.04   64-13365

Lynch, John, 1927- III. 2855
Spain under the Habsburgs. New York, Oxford University Press, 1964- v. illus., ports., maps (part fold.) 23 cm. *1. Spain — History — House of Austria, 1516-1700. I. T.*
DP171.L9   946.04   64-1472

Herr, Richard. III. 2856
The eighteenth-century revolution in Spain. Princeton, N.J., Princeton University Press, 1958. 454 p. illus. 22 cm. Index paging not available at time of cataloging. *1. Spain — History — Bourbons, 1700- 2. Spain — Intellectual life. I. T.*
DP192.H4   946.054   58-7126

Carr, Raymond. III. 2857
Spain: 1808-1939. Oxford, Clarendon P., 1966. xxix, 766 p. plate, maps, tables, diagrs. 22 1/2 cm. (Oxford history of modern Europe) *1. Spain — Politics and government — 19th cent. 2. Spain — Politics and government — 20th cent. 3. Spain — Social conditions. I. T. (S)*
DP203.C3   946   66-72222

Clarke, Henry Butler, 1863-1904. III. 2858
Modern Spain, 1815-1898. With a memoir by W. H. Hutton. New York, AMS Press [1969] xxvi, 510 p. fold. map. 23 cm. Reprint of the 1906 ed. *1. Spain — History — 19th century. I. Hutton, William Holden, 1860-1930. II. T.*
DP203.C6 1969   945/.08   70-90098

Marx, Karl, 1818-1883. III. 2859
Revolution in Spain, by Karl Marx and Frederick Engels. New York, International Publishers [c1939] 255 p. 22 cm. *1. Spain — History — 19th cent. 2. Spain — History, Military. 3. Revolutions. 4. Spain — Social conditions. I. Engels, Friedrich, 1820-1895. II. T.*
DP203.M35   946.07   39-12572

Ramos Oliveira, Antonio, 1907- III. 2860
Politics, economics and men of modern Spain, 1808-1946, by A. Ramos Oliveira, translated by Teener Hall. London, V. Gollancz ltd, 1946. 720 p. fold. map. 19 cm. *1. Spain — History — 19th cent. 2. Spain — History — 20th cent. 3. Spain — Economic conditions. I. Hall, Teener, tr. II. T.*
DP203.R3 1946   946.06   46-22635

Lovett, Gabriel H. III. 2861
Napoleon and the birth of modern Spain, by Gabriel H. Lovett. [New York] New York University Press, 1965. 2 v. (vii, 884 p.) map. 25 cm. *1. Spain — History — Napoleonic Conquest, 1808-1813. I. T.*
DP205.L65   946.06   65-11764

Oyarzun, Román. III. 2862
La historia del carlismo. Madrid, Alianza Editorial [1969] 553 p. 18 cm. (El Libro de bolsillo, 180. Sección Humanidades) *1. Carlists. I. T.*
DP218.O9 1969   70-261519

Hennessy, Charles Alistair Michael. III. 2863
The Federal Republic in Spain; Pi y Margall and the Federal Republican movement, 1868-74. Oxford, Clarendon Press, 1962. xvi, 299 p. 22 cm. *1. Pi y Margall, Francisco, 1824-1901. 2. Spain — Politics and government — 1868-1875. I. T.*
DP222.H4   946.08   62-4984

DP233 – 271   20th Century

Brenan, Gerald. III. 2864
The Spanish labyrinth; an account of the social and political background of the Civil War. [2d ed.] Cambridge [Eng.] University Press, 1950. xx, 384 p. maps. 23 cm. *1. Spain — Politics and government — 1886-1931. 2. Spain — Politics and government — 1931-1939. 3. Spain — Social conditions. I. T.*
DP233.B7 1950   946.08   51-3672

Rama, Carlos M., 1921- III. 2865
La crisis española del siglo XX. [1 ed.] México, Fondo de Cultura Económica [1960] 376 p. 22 cm. *1. Spain — Politics and government — 20th cent. 2. Spain — History — Philosophy. I. T.*
DP233.R3   60-46306

Laín Entralgo, Pedro. III. 2866
La generación del noventa y ocho. 5. ed. [Madrid] Espasa-Calpe [1963] 259 p. 18 cm. (Colección Austral, 784) *1. Spain — Civilization. I. T. (S)*
DP243.L34x

Arrarás, Joaquín. III. 2867
Historia de la Segunda República Española; [texto abreviado] Madrid, Editora Nacional, 1965. 525 p. illus., ports. 22 cm. (Libros de historia) *1. Spain — History — Republic, 1931-1939. I. T.*
DP254.A752   65-66328

Jackson, Gabriel. III. 2868
The Spanish Republic and the Civil War, 1931-1939. Princeton, N.J., Princeton University Press, 1965. xiii, 578 p. illus., maps. 22 cm. *1. Spain — History — Republic, 1931-1939. I. T.*
DP254.J3   946.081   65-10826

Carr, Raymond. III. 2869
The Republic and the Civil War in Spain; edited by Raymond Carr. London, Macmillan; New York, St. Martin's Press, 1971. x, 275 p. 23 cm. (Problems in focus series) *1. Spain — Politics and government — 1931-1939. 2. Spain — History — Civil War, 1936-1939. I. T.*
DP257.C295 1971   946.081   79-148464   ISBN:0333006321

Payne, Stanley G. III. 2870
Falange; a history of Spanish fascism. Stanford, Calif., Stanford University Press, 1961. ix, 316 p. 23 cm. (Stanford studies in history, economics, and political science, 22) *1. Fascism — Spain. 2. Spain — Politics and government — 1931-1939. 3. Spain — Politics and government — 1939- (S)*
DP257.P34 (AS36.L54 vol. 22)   946.081   61-12391

Payne, Stanley G. III. 2871
The Spanish Revolution [by] Stanley G. Payne. [1st ed.] New York, Norton [1970] xvi, 398 p. maps. 21 cm. (Revolutions in the modern world) *1. Spain — History — 20th century. 2. Spain — History — Civil War, 1936-1939 — Causes. I. T.*
DP257.P35 1970   946.081   73-78891

Robinson, Richard Alan Hodgson. III. 2872
The origins of Franco's Spain; the Right, the Republic and revolution, 1931-1936 [by] Richard A. H. Robinson. [Pittsburgh] University of Pittsburgh Press [1971, c1970] 475 p. 23 cm. (Library of politics and society) *1. Spain — Politics and government — 1931-1939. 2. Political parties — Spain. I. T.*
DP257.R58 1971   320.9/46/081   77-133417   ISBN:0822910993

Crozier, Brian. III. 2873
Franco. [1st American ed.] Boston, Little, Brown [c1967] xx, 589 p. illus., maps, ports. 25 cm. *1. Franco Bahamonde, Francisco, 1892- I. T.*
DP264.F7C75 1967   946.082/0924 (B)   68-13880

DP269   CIVIL WAR (1936 – 1939)

Bolloten, Burnett, 1909- III. 2874
The grand camouflage; the Spanish Civil War and revolution, 1936-39. Introd. by H. R. Trevor-Roper. New York, Praeger [1968] xi, 350 p. ports. 22 cm. *1. Spain — History — Civil War, 1936-1939. 2. Communism — Spain. I. T.*
DP269.B656 1968   946.081   67-29697

Borkenau, Franz, 1900-1957. III. 2875
The Spanish cockpit; an eye-witness account of the political and social conflicts of the Spanish Civil War. Foreword by Gerald Brenan. [Ann Arbor] University of Michigan Press [1963, c1937] xi, 303 p. 21 cm. *1. Spain — History — Civil War, 1936-1939. 2. Spain — Politics and government — 1931-1939. I. T.*
DP269.B66 1963   946.081   63-23723

Thomas, Hugh, 1931- III. 2876
The Spanish Civil War. New York, Harper [1961] 720 p. illus. 23 cm. *1. Spain — History — Civil War, 1936-1939. I. T.*
DP269.T5   946.081   61-6177

Cattell, David Tredwell, 1923- III. 2877
Communism and the Spanish Civil War, by David T. Cattell. New York, Russell & Russell, 1965. xii, 290 p. 23 cm. "First published in 1955." *1. Spain — History — Civil War, 1936-1939. 2. Communism — Spain. 3. Spain — History — Civil War, 1936-1939 — Foreign participation — Russian. I. T.*
DP269.47.R8C3 1965   946.081   65-17881

Orwell, George, 1903-1950. III. 2878
Homage to Catalonia. [1st American ed.] New York, Harcourt, Brace [1952] 232 p. 21 cm. *1. Spain — History — Civil War, 1936-1939 — Personal narratives. 2. Spain — Politics and government — 1931-1939. I. T.*
DP269.9.O7 1952   946.081   52-6442

DP270 1939 –

Feis, Herbert, 1893-   **III. 2879**
The Spanish story; Franco and the nations at war. New York, W. W. Norton [1966] xii, 282, vi p. 20 cm. (The Norton library, N339) First published in 1948. *1. Spain — Foreign relations — 1939- 2. World War, 1939-1945 — Spain. I. T.*
DP270.F37 1966   946.082   66-15307

DP285 – 402 Local History

Lee, Laurie.   **III. 2880**
A rose for winter; travels in Andalusia. New York, Morrow [1956?] 160 p. 21 cm. *1. Andalusia — Description and travel. I. T.*
DP302.A46L4x   914.68   55-12945

Elliot, John Huxtable.   **III. 2881**
The revolt of the Catalans, a study in the decline of Spain, 1598-1640. Cambridge [Eng.] University Press, 1963. xvi, 623 p. illus., ports., fold. maps. 24 cm. *1. Catalonia — History. 2. Spain — History — Philip IV, 1621-1665. 3. Spain — History — Philip III, 1598-1621. I. Olivares, Gaspar de Guzmán, conde-duque de, 1587-1645. II. T.*
DP302.C66E4   946.7   63-3426

Burns, Robert Ignatius.   **III. 2882**
The crusader kingdom of Valencia; reconstruction on a thirteenth-century frontier. Cambridge, Harvard University Press, 1967. 2 v. (xviii, 561 p. illus., maps. 24 cm. *1. Valencia — History. 2. Valencia — Church history. I. T.*
DP302.V205B8   946/.76/02   67-10902

Pitt-Rivers, Julian Alfred.   **III. 2883**
The people of the Sierra. Introd. by E. E. Evans-Pritchard. New York, Criterion Books [c1954] 232 p. illus. 23 cm. *1. Alcalá de la Sierra, Spain — Social life and customs. 2. Cities and towns — Spain — Andalusia — Case studies. I. T.*
DP402.A33P5 1954a   914.68   55-2571

DP501 – 776 PORTUGAL

Marques, Antonio Henrique R. de Oliveira.   **III. 2884**
Daily life in Portugal in the late Middle Ages [by] A. H. de Oliveira Marques. Translated by S. S. Wyatt. Drawings by Vítor André. Madison, University of Wisconsin Press, 1971. xvi, 355 p. illus., geneal. tables, maps, plan, ports. 25 cm. Translation of A sociedade medieval portuguesa. *1. Portugal — Social life and customs. I. T.*
DP532.3.M3413   914.69/03/2   78-106040   ISBN:0299055809

Livermore, Harold Victor, 1914-   **III. 2885**
A new history of Portugal [by] H. V. Livermore. Cambridge, Cambridge U.P., 1966. xi, 365 p. front., 13 plates, maps, table. 24 cm. *1. Portugal — History. I. T.*
DP538.L72   946.9   65-19147

Marques, Antonio Henrique R. de Oliveira.   **III. 2886**
History of Portugal [by] A. H. de Oliveira Marques. New York, Columbia University Press, 1972. 2 v. illus. 23 cm. A completely rewritten and enlarged version in Portuguese was published in 1972- under title História de Portugal. *1. Portugal — History. I. T.*
DP538.M37   946.9   77-184748
    ISBN:0231031599 (v. 1) 0231087004 (v. 2)

Nowell, Charles E.   **III. 2887**
A history of Portugal. New York, Van Nostrand [1952] xii, 259 p. illus., ports., maps. 24 cm. *1. Portugal — History.*
DP538.N68   946.9   52-6387

Stanislawski, Dan.   **III. 2888**
The individuality of Portugal; a study in historical-political geography. Austin, University of Texas Press [1959] xiv, 248 p. illus., maps (part fold.) 24 cm. *1. Portugal — History. 2. Portugal — Historical geography. 3. Spain — History. 4. Spain — Historical geography. I. T.*
DP538.S75   911.469   59-8119

Diffie, Bailey Wallys, 1902-   **III. 2889**
Prelude to empire: Portugal overseas before Henry the Navigator. [Lincoln] University of Nebraska Press, 1960. 127 p. illus. 21 cm. (A Bison book original, BB108) *1. Portugal — History — To 1385. 2. Portugal — Commerce. I. T.*
DP559.D5   946.901   60-14301

Bovill, E. W.   **III. 2890**
The Battle of Alcazar; an account of the defeat of Don Sebastian of Portugal at El-Ksar el-Kebir. London, Batchworth Press [1952] xiii, 198 p. illus., port., maps. 23 cm. *1. Sebastião, King of Portugal, 1554-1578. 2. Kassr-el-Kebir, Battle of, 1578.*
DP614.B68   946.9   53-7377

Kay, Hugh.   **III. 2891**
Salazar and modern Portugal. New York, Hawthorn Books [1970] xxii, 478 p. illus., maps, ports. 24 cm. *1. Salazar, Antonio de Oliveira, 1889-1970. 2. Portugal — History — 1910- I. T.*
DP676.S25K3   946.9/04/0924   73-115919

Fryer, Peter.   **III. 2892**
Oldest ally; a portrait of Salazar's Portugal [by] Peter Fryer & Patricia McGowan Pinheiro. London, D. Dobson [1961] 280 p. illus. 22 cm. *1. Portugal — Description and travel — 1951- 2. Portugal — Politics and government — 1933- I. Pinheiro, Patricia McGowan, joint author. II. T.*
DP680.F7   61-66638

Kendrick, Thomas Downing, Sir.   **III. 2893**
The Lisbon earthquake. [Authorized American ed.] Philadelphia, Lippincott [1957?] 255 p. illus. 21 cm. *1. Lisbon — Earthquake, 1755. I. T.*
DP762.K4x   946.94   57-6239

DQ   Switzerland

Lunn, Arnold Henry Moore, Sir, 1888-   **III. 2894**
The Swiss and their mountains; a study of the influence of mountains on man. Chicago, Rand McNally [1963] 167 p. plates (part col.) ports. 23 cm. *1. Switzerland. I. T.*
DQ17.L86   301.30914   63-20089

Siegfried, André, 1875-1959.   **III. 2895**
Switzerland, a democratic way of life. Translated from the French by Edward Fitzgerald. London, Cape [1950] 223 p. maps (1 fold. col.) 21 cm. *1. Switzerland.*
DQ17.S52   914.94   50-4860

Soloveytchik, George, 1902-   **III. 2896**
Switzerland in perspective. London, New York, Oxford University Press, 1954. 306 p. illus. 22 cm. *1. Switzerland. 2. Switzerland — Foreign relations.*
DQ17.S64   914.94   55-2613

Kohn, Hans, 1891-   **III. 2897**
Nationalism and liberty; the Swiss example. New York, Macmillan, 1956. 133 p. 23 cm. *1. Nationalism — Switzerland. I. T.*
DQ36.K58   949.4   56-14643

Sorell, Walter, 1905-   **III. 2898**
The Swiss; a cultural panorama of Switzerland. New York, Bobbs-Merrill [1972] xvi, 303 p. 24 cm. *1. Switzerland — Intellectual life. 2. National characteristics, Swiss. I. T.*
DQ36.S66   914.94/03/7   78-173225

Bonjour, Edgar, 1898-   **III. 2899**
A short history of Switzerland, by E. Bonjour, H. S. Offler, and G. R. Potter. Oxford, Clarendon Press, 1952. 388 p. maps. 23 cm. *1. Switzerland — History. I. Offler, Hilary Seton.*
DQ54.B65   949.4   52-12224

Herold, J. Christopher.   **III. 2900**
The Swiss without halos. New York, Columbia Univ. Press, 1948. 271 p. illus., maps. 24 cm. *1. Switzerland — History. 2. Switzerland — Civilization. I. T.*
DQ54.H4   949.4   48-8907

Gilliard, Charles, 1879-   **III. 2901**
A history of Switzerland, with concluding pages brought up-to-date by J. C. Biaudet. Translated by D. L. B. Hartley. London, Allen & Unwin [1955] 116 p. illus. 21 cm. *1. Switzerland — History.*
DQ55.G52   949.4   56-1453

Lloyd, William Bross, 1908-   **III. 2902**
Waging peace, the Swiss experience. Foreword by Quincy Wright. Pref. by William E. Rappard. Washington, Public Affairs Press [1958] vii, 101 p. map. 24 cm. *1. Switzerland — Politics and government. 2. Federal government — Switzerland. I. T.*
DQ70.L55   949.4   58-13403

Rappard, William Emmanuel, 1883-   **III. 2903**
Collective security in Swiss experience, 1291-1948. London, Allen & Unwin [1948] xvi, 150 p. 23 cm. Primarily an abridged English version of the author's Cinq siècles de sécurité collective, 1291-1798. *1. Switzerland — Politics and government. I. T.*
DQ70.R33   949.4   49-3427

Engel, Claire Éliane.   **III. 2904**
A history of mountaineering in the Alps. With a foreword by F. S. Smythe. London, Allen and Unwin [1950] 296 p. 24 plates. 25 cm. *1. Alps — Description and travel. 2. Mountaineering.*
DQ824.E5 1950a   796.52   A50-5881

DR Eastern Europe. Balkan Peninsula

DR1 – 48 GENERAL WORKS

Fischer-Galaţi, Stephen A., comp.   **III. 2905**
Man, state, and society in East European history. Edited by Stephen Fischer-Galati. New York, Praeger [1970] xiii, 343 p. 24 cm. (Man, state, and society) *1. Europe, Eastern — History — Collections. I. T.*
DR1.F56   309.1/47   69-10516

Osborne, Richard Horsley.   **III. 2906**
East-Central Europe; an introductory geography [by] R. H. Osborne. New York, Praeger [1967] 384 p. maps. 21 cm. (Praeger introductory geographies) *1. Europe, Eastern. I. T.*
DR10.O75 1967   914   67-21456

Singleton, Frederick Bernard.   **III. 2907**
Background to Eastern Europe, by F. B. Singleton. [1st ed.] Oxford, New York, Pergamon Press [1965] viii, 226 p. maps. 20 cm. (The Commonwealth and international library of science, technology, engineering, and liberal studies. Liberal studies division) *1. Europe, Eastern. I. T.*
DR10.S55 1965   940.5   65-22917

Stoianovich, Traian.   **III. 2908**
A study in Balkan civilization. New York, Knopf [1967] vi, 215, vi p. maps. 21 cm. (Borzoi studies in history, BH3) *1. Balkan Peninsula — Civilization. 2. Balkan Peninsula — Social life and customs. I. T.*
DR22.S75   914.96/03   67-10715

Portal, Roger.   **III. 2909**
The Slavs; a cultural and historical survey of the Slavonic peoples. Translated from the French by Patrick Evans. [1st U.S. ed.] New York, Harper & Row [c1969] xvii, 508 p. illus., maps, ports. 25 cm. (Studies in world history) *1. Slavs.*
DR25.P613 1969b   910.09/175/918   72-93911

Language and area studies, East Central and Southeastern Europe;   **III. 2910**
a survey.
Edited by Charles Jelavich. Chicago, University of Chicago Press [1969] xix, 483 p. 24 cm. Survey prepared by the Subcommittee on East Central and Southeast European Studies of the Joint Committee on Slavic Studies of the American Council of Learned Societies and the Social Science Research Council. *1. East European studies — U.S. 2. Balkan studies — U.S. 3. Languages, Modern — Study and teaching — U.S. I. Jelavich, Charles, ed. II. Joint Committee on Slavic Studies. Subcommittee on East Central and Southeast European Studies.*
DR34.8.L33   914.7   72-81222   ISBN:226396150

Jelavich, Charles.   **III. 2911**
The Balkans [by] Charles and Barbara Jelavich. Englewood Cliffs, N.J., Prentice-Hall [1965] xi, 148 p. maps. 21 cm. (The Modern nations in historical perspective. A Spectrum book.) *1. Balkan Peninsula — History. I. Jelavich, Barbara (Brightfield) joint author. II. T.*
DR36.J38   949.6   65-14999

Jelavich, Charles, ed.   **III. 2912**
The Balkans in transition; essays on the development of Balkan life and politics since the eighteenth century. Edited by Charles and Barbara Jelavich. Berkeley, University of California Press, 1963. xvii, 451 p. maps, diagrs., tables. 25 cm. (Russian and East European studies) Papers presented at a conference held at the University of California, Berkeley, June 13-15, 1960 and sponsored by the Center for Slavic and East European Studies. *1. Balkan Peninsula — History. I. Jelavich, Barbara (Brightfields) joint ed. II. California. University. Center for Slavic and East European Studies. III. T. (S)*
DR36.J4   949.6   63-19230

Palmer, Alan Warwick.   **III. 2913**
The lands between; a history of East-Central Europe since the Congress of Vienna [by] Alan Palmer. [1st American ed. New York] Macmillan [1970] ix, 405 p. illus., maps, ports. 25 cm. *1. Europe, Eastern — History. 2. Central Europe — History. I. T.*
DR36.P3 1970b   943   74-83064

Stavrianos, Leften Stavros.   **III. 2914**
The Balkans since 1453. New York, Rinehart [1958] xxi, 970 p. illus., ports., maps, facsims. 24 cm. (Rinehart books in European history) *1. Balkan Peninsula — History. I. T.*
DR36.S83   949.6   58-7242

Sugar, Peter F.   **III. 2915**
Nationalism in Eastern Europe. Edited by Peter F. Sugar and Ivo J. Lederer. Seattle, University of Washington Press [1969] ix, 465 p. 25 cm. (Publications on Russia and Eastern Europe, no. 1) *1. Nationalism — Europe, Eastern. I. Lederer, Ivo J., joint author. II. T. (S)*
DR37.S94   320.1/58/0947   74-93026

Hoffman, George Walter, 1914-   **III. 2916**
The Balkans in transition. Princeton, N.J., Van Nostrand [c1963] 124 p. maps, tables. 20 cm. (Van Nostrand searchlight book, 20) *1. Balkan Peninsula — History. I. T.*
DR38.H6   63-23579

Kovrig, Bennett.   **III. 2917**
The myth of liberation; East-Central Europe in U.S. diplomacy and politics since 1941. Baltimore, Johns Hopkins University Press [c1973] xi, 360 p. 24 cm. *1. United States — Foreign relations — Europe, Eastern. 2. Europe, Eastern — Foreign relations — United States. I. T.*
DR38.3.U6K68   327.73/047   72-4028   ISBN:0801813611

DR39 – 48 by Period

McNeill, William Hardy, 1917-   **III. 2918**
Europe's steppe frontier, 1500-1800 [by] William H. McNeill. Chicago, University of Chicago Press [1964] 252 p. maps. 23 cm. "End-paper map errata": fold. leaf inserted. *1. Europe, Eastern — History. 2. Central Europe — History. 3. Turkey — History. I. T.*
DR41.M3 1964   943   64-22248

Ristelhueber, René, 1881-1960.   **III. 2919**
A history of the Balkan peoples. Edited and translated by Sherman David Spector. New York, Twayne Publishers [1971] 470 p. maps. 21 cm. Translation of Histoire des peuples balkaniques. *1. Balkan Peninsula — History. 2. Ethnology — Balkan Peninsula. I. T.*
DR43.R513 1971   949.6   78-147184

Stavrianos, Leften Stavros.   **III. 2920**
The Balkans, 1815-1914. New York, Holt, Rinehart and Winston [1963] 135 p. 19 cm. (Berkshire studies in European history) *1. Balkan Peninsula. I. T.*
DR43.S8   914.96   63-12627

Helmreich, Ernst Christian.   **III. 2921**
The diplomacy of the Balkan wars, 1912-1913. New York, Russell & Russell [1969, c1938] xvi, 523 p. 23 cm. (Harvard historical studies, v. 42) "Study originated in a doctoral dissertation on The diplomacy of the first Balkan war, 1912-1913, which was presented at Harvard in 1932." *1. Balkan Peninsula — History — War of 1912-1913. I. T. (S)*
DR46.3.H4 1969   949.6   68-27063

Lukacs, John A., 1923-   **III. 2922**
The great powers & Eastern Europe. New York, American Book Co. [1953] xii, 878 p. maps. 23 cm. *1. Europe, Eastern — History. I. T.*
DR48.L8   949.6   53-13369

Macartney, Carlile Aylmer, 1895-   **III. 2923**
Independent Eastern Europe, a history, by C. A. Macartney and A. W. Palmer. London, Macmillan; New York, St Martin's Press, 1962. 499 p. illus. 23 cm. *1. Europe, Eastern — History. I. Palmer, Alan Warwick, joint author. II. T.*
DR48.M25 1962   947   62-3631

Seton-Watson, Hugh.   **III. 2924**
Eastern Europe between the wars, 1918-1941. With a new pref. written for

this ed. [3d ed. Hamden, Conn.] Archon Books, 1962. 425 p. illus. 23 cm. *1. Europe, Eastern — History. I. T.*
DR48.S38 1962   914.7   62-53112

DR48.5   1945 –

Brown, James F., 1928-   III. 2925
The new Eastern Europe; the Khrushchev era and after [by] J. F. Brown. New York, Praeger [1966] vii, 306 p. 21 cm. (Praeger publications in Russian history and world communism, no.169) *1. Europe, Eastern — Politics. 2. Europe, Eastern — Economic conditions. 3. Europe, Eastern — Biography. I. T.*
DR48.5.B7   320.947   65-24939

Fischer-Galati, Stephen A., ed.   III. 2926
Eastern Europe in the sixties. New York, Praeger [1963] xiii, 239 p. illus. 21 cm. (Praeger publications in Russian history and world communism, no. 137) *1. Europe, Eastern. I. T.*
DR48.5.F5   309.147   63-18532

Ionescu, Ghita.   III. 2927
The break-up of the Soviet Empire in Eastern Europe. Baltimore, Penquin Books [1965] 168 [1] p. 19 cm. (A Penguin special) *1. Europe, Eastern — Politics. 2. Communism — Europe, Eastern. I. T.*
DR48.5.I6   320.947   65-6872

Lendvai, Paul, 1929-   III. 2928
Eagles in cobwebs; nationalism and communism in the Balkans. [1st ed.] Garden City, N.Y., Doubleday, 1969. xii, 396 p. map (on lining papers) 22 cm. *1. Europe; Eastern — Politics. I. Nationalism and communism in the Balkans. II. T.*
DR48.5.L43   320.9/496   69-10952

Pethybridge, Roger William, 1934- ed.   III. 2929
The development of the Communist bloc. Edited with an introd. by Roger Pethybridge. Boston, Heath [1965] xii, 244 p. 24 cm. (Studies in history and politics) *1. Communist countries — History. I. T.*
DR48.5.P45   909.097170825   65-25436

Seton-Watson, Hugh.   III. 2930
The East European revolution. [3d ed.] London, Methuen [1956] 435 p. illus. 23 cm. *1. Europe, Eastern — Politics. 2. Europe, Eastern — History. I. T.*
DR48.5.S4 1956   940.55   57-1670

Staar, Richard Felix, 1923-   III. 2931
The Communist regimes in Eastern Europe, by Richard F. Staar. 2d rev. ed. Stanford, Calif., Hoover Institution on War, Revolution, and Peace [1971] xiv, 304 p. 23 cm. (Hoover Institution publications, 94) *1. Europe, Eastern — Politics. 2. Communism — Europe, Eastern. I. T. (S:Stanford University. Hoover Institution on War, Revolution, and Peace. Publications, 94)*
DR48.5.S74 1971   320.9/171/7   70-148364

Wolff, Robert Lee.   III. 2932
The Balkans in our time. Cambridge, Harvard University Press, 1956. xxi, 618 p. maps, tables. 25 cm. (Russian Research Center studies [23]. The American foreign policy library.) *1. Balkan Peninsula — History. 2. Communism — Balkan Peninsula. I. T. (S:Harvard University. Russian Research Center. Russian Research Center studies, 23.) (S:The American foreign policy library)*
DR48.5.W6   949.6   56-6529

DR51 – 98   BULGARIA

Dellin, L. A. D., ed.   III. 2933
Bulgaria. New York, Published for the Mid-European Studies Center of the Free Europe Committee, by F. A. Praeger [1957] xvii, 457 p. illus., maps. 24 cm. (East-Central Europe under the Communists. Praeger publications in Russian history and world communism, no. 47.) *1. Bulgaria. I. Free Europe Committee. Mid-European Studies Center. (S)*
DR55.D4   914.97   57-9332

Khristov, Khristo A.   III. 2934
A short history of Bulgaria [by] D. Kossev, H. Hristov [and] D. Angelov. [Translated by Marguerite Alexieva and Nicolai Koledarov. Illustrated by Ivan Bogdanov and Vladislav Paskalev] Sofia, Foreign Languages Press; [distributor: A. Vanous, New York, 1963] 461 p. illus., ports., fold. maps, facsims. 21 cm. "The original work in its Bulgarian form was edited by Professor H. Hristov." *1. Bulgaria — History. I. Kosev, Dimitŭr. II. T.*
DR67.K453   949.77   64-705

Macdermott, Mercia.   III. 2935
A history of Bulgaria, 1393-1885. New York, Praeger [1962] 354 p. illus. 23 cm. (Books that matter) *1. Bulgaria — History — 1393-1878.*
DR82.M3 1962a   949.7701   62-10304

Corti, Egon Caesar, conte, 1886-1953.   III. 2936
Alexander von Battenberg. Translated by E. M. Hodgson. London, Cassell, 1954. 319 p. illus. 22 cm. Translation of Leben und Liebe Alexanders von Battenberg. *1. Alexander I, Prince of Bulgaria, 1857-1893.*
DR86.C632   923.2497   56-850

Oren, Nissan.   III. 2937
Revolution administered: Agrarianism and communism in Bulgaria. Baltimore, Johns Hopkins University Press [1973] xv, 204 p. 24 cm. (Integration and community building in Eastern Europe, EE8) *1. Bulgaria – Politics and government. 2. Bulgaria — Politics and government — 1944. 3. Communism — Bulgaria. I.\ T. (S)*
DR89.O68   320.9/4977/03   72-8831
ISBN:0801812097 0801812100 (pbk)

Brown, James F., 1928-   III. 2938
Bulgaria under Communist rule [by] J. F. Brown. New York, Praeger [1970] ix, 339 p. 22 cm. *1. Bulgaria — History — 1944- 2. Bulgaria — Economic policy — 1944- 3. Communism — Bulgaria. I. T.*
DR90.B7   320.9/497/7   78-83329

Sanders, Irwin Taylor, 1909-   III. 2939
Balkan village. Lexington, Univ. of Kentucky Press, 1949. xiii, 291 p. illus., maps. 25 cm. *1. Dragalevtsi, Bulgaria. I. T.*
DR98.D7S3   914.97   49-9009

DR201 – 298   ROMANIA

Riker, Thad Weed, 1880-1952.   III. 2940
The making of Roumania. New York, Arno Press, 1971. viii, 592 p. map. 24 cm. (The Eastern Europe collection) Reprint of the 1931 ed. *1. Romania — Politics and government. I. T.*
DR244.R5 1971   949/.801   70-135830   ISBN:0405027729

Fischer-Galați, Stephen A.   III. 2941
Twentieth century Rumania [by] Stephen Fischer-Galați. New York, Columbia University Press, 1970. ix, 248 p. illus., map. 24 cm. *1. Romania — Politics and government. I. T.*
DR250.F5   320.9/498   77-108838   ISBN:0231028482

Fischer-Galați, Stephen A.   III. 2942
The new Rumania: from people's democracy to socialist republic [by] Stephen Fischer-Galati. Cambridge, Mass., M.I.T. Press [1967] xi, 126 p. 24 cm. (Studies in international communism, 10) *1. Rumania — History — 1944- 2. Rumania — Politics and government — 1945- I. T. (S:Massachusetts Institute of Technology. Center for International Studies. Studies in international communism)*
DR267.F5   949.8/03   67-15603

Ionescu, Ghita.   III. 2943
Communism in Rumania, 1944-1962. London, New York, Oxford University Press, 1964. xvi, 378 p. 23 cm. *1. Rumania — History — 1944- 2. Communism — Rumania. I. T.*
DR267.I65   949.803   64-55367

DR301 – 396   YUGOSLAVIA

Halpern, Joel Martin.   III. 2944
A Serbian village. Illus. by Barbara Kerewsky Halpern. New York, Columbia University Press, 1958. xxii, 325 p. illus., maps. 24 cm. A condensed version of the author's doctoral dissertation published in 1956 under title: Social and cultural change in a Serbian village. *1. Orašac, Yugoslavia. 2. Yugoslavia — Social life and customs. I. T.*
DR312.H32   914.97   57-11449

Palmer, Alan Warwick. III. 2945
Yugoslavia, by A. W. Palmer. [London] Oxford University Press, 1964. 127 p. illus., maps (on lining papers) ports. 19 cm. (The Modern world, 6) *1. Yugoslavia — History.*
DR318.P3 1964   914.97   64-4724

MacKenzie, David. III. 2946
The Serbs and Russian Pan-Slavism, 1875-1878. Ithaca, N.Y., Cornell University Press [1967] xx, 365 p. maps, ports. 24 cm. *1. Serbia — Foreign relations — Russia. 2. Russia — Foreign relations — Serbia. 3. Panslavism. 4. Balkan Peninsula — Politics. I. T.*
DR327.R9M3   327.47/0497/1   67-12306

Djilas, Milovan. III. 2947
Memoir of a revolutionary [by] Milovan Djilas. Translated by Drenka Willen. [1st ed.] New York, Harcourt Brace Jovanovich [c1973] 402 p. 24 cm. *1. Djilas, Milovan. 2. Communism — Yugoslavia. I. T.*
DR359.D5A33   322.4/2/0924 (B)   72-91835   ISBN:0151588503

Dilas, Milovan. III. 2948
Conversations with Stalin. Translated from the Serbo-Croat by Michael B. Petrovich. [1st ed.] New York, Harcourt, Brace & World [1962] 211 p. 21 cm. Translation of Susreti sa Staljinom. *1. Communist countries — Politics. I. Stalin, Iosif, 1879-1953. II. T.*
DR359.D513   949.702   62-14470

Auty, Phyllis. III. 2949
Tito; a biography. New York, McGraw-Hill [1970] xiv, 343 p. illus., maps, ports. 23 cm. *1. Tito, Josip Broz, Pres. Yugoslavia, 1892-*
DR359.T5A9 1970b   949/.702/0924 (B)   75-107283

Dedijer, Vladimir. III. 2950
Tito. New York, Simon and Schuster, 1953 [i.e.1952] 443 p. 22 cm. *1. Tito, Josip Broz, known as, 1892-*
DR359.T5D4   923.5497   53-6161

Vucinich, Wayne S. III. 2951
Serbia between East and West; the events of 1903-1908 [by] Wayne S. Vucinich. New York, AMS Press [1968] x, 304 p. map, ports. 22 cm. (Stanford University publications. University series. History, economics, and political science, v. 9) Reprint of the 1954 ed. *1. Serbia — History — 1804-1918. I. T. (S:Stanford studies in history, economics, and political science, v. 9)*
DR360.V83 1968   949.7/1/01   68-54304

Hoptner, Jacob B., 1911- III. 2952
Yugoslavia in crisis, 1934-1941. New York, Columbia University Press, 1962. xv, 328 p. 24 cm. (East Central European studies of Columbia University) *1. Yugoslavia — Foreign relations — 1918-1945. 2. Yugoslavia — History — 1918-1941. I. T. (S)*
DR366.H59 1962   949.702   61-7174

Kerner, Robert Joseph, 1887- ed. III. 2953
Yugoslavia; chapters by Griffith Taylor [and others] Berkeley, University of California Press, 1949. xxi, 558 p. illus., ports., maps. 23 cm. (The United Nations series) *1. Yugoslavia. (S)*
DR366.K47   949.7   49-1741

West, Rebecca, pseud. III. 2954
Black lamb and grey falcon; a journey through Yugoslavia, by Rebecca West. New York, Viking Press, 1943. 1181 p. plates, ports. 24 cm. First published in 1941. Maps on lining-papers. *1. Yugoslavia — Description and travel. 2. Yugoslavia — History. 3. Serbia — History. 4. Eastern question (Balkan) I. T.*
DR366.W48x   914.17   A43-3813

Rubinstein, Alvin Z. III. 2955
Yugoslavia and the nonaligned world, by Alvin Z. Rubinstein. Princeton, N.J., Princeton University Press, 1970. xv, 353 p. 23 cm. *1. Yugoslavia — Foreign relations — 1945- 2. Yugoslavia — Politics and government — 1945- I. T.*
DR367.A1R8   327.497   78-90959   ISBN:691051801

Campbell, John Coert, 1911- III. 2956
Tito's separate road; America and Yugoslavia in world politics, by John C. Campbell. [1st ed.] New York, Published for the Council on Foreign Relations by Harper & Row [1967] viii, 180 p. 21 cm. (Policy book series of the Council on Foreign Relations) *1. Yugoslavia — Politics and government — 1945- 2. Yugoslavia — Foreign relations — 1945- I. Council on Foreign Relations. II. T.*
DR370.C33   949.7/02   67-15967

Hoffman, George Walter, 1914- III. 2957
Yugoslavia and the new communism [by] George W. Hoffman [and] Fred Warner Neal. New York, Twentieth Century Fund, 1962. xvi, 546 p. maps, diagrs., tables. 24 cm. *1. Communism — Yugoslavia. 2. Yugoslavia — Economic conditions — 1945- I. Neal, Fred Warner, joint author. II. T.*
DR370.H58   949.702   62-13485

Ulam, Adam Bruno, 1922- III. 2958
Titoism and the Cominform [by] Adam B. Ulam. Westport, Conn., Greenwood Press [1971, c1952] viii, 243 p. 23 cm. *1. Communism — Yugoslavia. 2. Communism — History. I. T.*
DR370.U4 1971   321.9/2   70-100246   ISBN:0837134048

Vucinich, Wayne S. III. 2959
Contemporary Yugoslavia; twenty years of Socialist experiment [by] Jozo Tomasevich [and others] Edited by Wayne S. Vucinich. Berkeley, University of California Press, 1969. xiii, 441 p. maps. 24 cm. Based on a conference on contemporary Yugoslavia, held at Stanford University, Dec. 4-5, 1965. *1. Yugoslavia — Politics and government — 1945- — Addresses, essays, lectures. I. Tomasevich, Jozo, 1908- II. Stanford University. III. T.*
DR370.V8   320.9/497   69-16512

DR401 – 592   TURKEY

Gökalp, Ziya, 1875-1924. III. 2960
Turkish nationalism and Western civilization; selected essays. Translated and edited with an introd. by Niyazi Berkes. New York, Columbia University Press, 1959. 336 p. 23 cm. *1. Nationalism — Turkey. 2. Turkey — Civilization — Occidental influences. I. T.*
DR405.G613 1959   915.61   59-65081

Dewdney, John C. III. 2961
Turkey: an introductory geography [by] J. C. Dewdney. New York, Praeger [1971] x, 214 p. maps. 23 cm. (Praeger introductory geographies) *1. Turkey. I. T.*
DR417.D48 1971   915.61   79-101658

Roberts, Thomas Duval, 1903- III. 2962
Area handbook for the Republic of Turkey [by] Thomas D. Roberts [and others] Prepared for the American University by Systems Research Corporation. Washington, U.S. Govt. Print. Off., 1970. xvi, 438 p. illus., maps. 24 cm. "DA pam 550-59." "One of a series of studies prepared by Foreign Area Studies (FAS) of the American University." *1. Turkey. I. Systems Research Corporation. II. American University, Washington, D.C. Foreign Area Studies. III. T.*
DR417.R54   309.1/561   76-607576

Creasy, Edward Shepherd, Sir, 1812-1878. III. 2963
History of the Ottoman Turks [by] Edward S. Creasy. With a new introd. by Zeine N. Zeine. Beirut, Khayats, 1961. xix, 560 p. facsim. 20 cm. (Oriental reprints, no. 1) Reprint of 2d ed., published in 1878. *1. Turkey — History. 2. Eastern question (Balkan) I. Ottoman Turks. II. T.*
DR440.C91x   Ne65-981

Eliot, Charles Norton Edgecumbe, Sir, 1862-1931. III. 2964
Turkey in Europe [by] Sir Charles Eliot. New York, Barnes & Noble [1965] 459 p. 2 fold. col. maps. 23 cm. *1. Turkey — History. 2. Islam. 3. Christians in Turkey. 4. Eastern question (Balkan) I. T.*
DR441.E5 1965   914.96   65-6973

Lewis, Geoffrey L. III. 2965
Turkey, by Geoffrey Lewis. 3d ed. New York, Praeger [1965] 230 p. fold. map. 23 cm. (Nations of the modern world) *1. Turkey — History. 2. Turkey — Description and travel. (S)*
DR441.L45 1965   956.1   65-14182

Vaughan, Dorothy Margaret. III. 2966
Europe and the Turk: a pattern of alliances, 1350-1700. Liverpool, University Press [1954] 305 p. front., maps. 23 cm. *1. Europe — Politics. 2. Turkey — Foreign relations. 3. Turkey — History. I. T.*
DR471.Vx   A56-4710

Cahen, Claude. III. 2967
Pre-Ottoman Turkey; a general survey of the material and spiritual culture and history, c. 1071-1330. Translated from the French by J. Jones-Williams. New York, Taplinger Pub. Co. [1968] xx, 458 p. illus., maps. 24 cm. *1. Turkey — History — To 1453. I. T.*
DR481.C3313 1968b   915.61/03/1   68-24744

Wittek, Paul, 1894- III. 2968
The rise of the Ottoman Empire. New York, B. Franklin [1971] vii, 54 p. 23 cm. (Burt Franklin research and source works series, 769. Byzantine series, 30) Reprint of the 1938 ed. which was issued as v. 23 of Royal Asiatic Society monographs. Lectures delivered at the University of London, May 4-6, 1937. *1. Turkey — History — 1288-1453. I. T. (S:Asiatic Society monographs, v. 23.)*
DR481.W5 1971   956.1/01   70-153023   ISBN:0833738550

Schwoebel, Robert.   III. 2969
The shadow of the crescent: The Renaissance image of the Turk (1453-1517). Nieuwkoop, B. de Graaf, 1967 [1968] xiv, 260 p. with illus. 24 cm. *1. Turkey — History — 1453-1683. I. T.*
DR486.S3 1968   956.1/01   67-27189

Merriman, Roger Bigelow, 1876-   III. 2970
Suleiman the Magnificent, 1520-1566, by Roger Bigelow Merriman. Cambridge, Mass., Harvard University Press, 1944. viii, 325 p. double pl., ports. 22 cm. Map on lining-papers. Rewritten from the unfinished manuscript on Sulaimān the Magnificent, by Archibald Cary Coolidge. cf. Pref. *1. Sulaimān I, the Magnificent, sultan of the Turks, 1494-1566. 2. Turkey — History — 1453-1683. I. Coolidge, Archibald Cary, 1866-1928.*
DR506.M4   923.1496   A44-5977

Lybyer, Albert Howe, 1876-   III. 2971
The government of the Ottoman Empire in the time of Suleiman the Magnificent. Cambridge, Harvard University Press, 1913. x, 349 p. 23 cm. (Harvard historical studies, vol.18) *1. Sulaimān I, the Magnificent, Sultan of the Turks, 1494-1566. 2. Turkey — Politics and government.*
DR507.L8   13-7898

Barker, Thomas Mack.   III. 2972
Double eagle and crescent; Vienna's second Turkish siege and its historical setting [by] Thomas M. Barker. [Albany] State University of New York Press [1967] xviii, 447 p. illus., maps (on lining papers) 24 cm. *1. Vienna — Siege, 1683. I. T.*
DR536.B38   943.6/03   67-63760

Stoye, John Walter.   III. 2973
The Siege of Vienna [by] John Stoye. [1st ed.] New York, Holt, Rinehart and Winston [1965, c1964] 349 p. illus., facsim., maps (part col.) plans, ports. 24 cm. *1. Vienna — Siege, 1683. I. T.*
DR536.S76 1965a   943.603   65-15134

DR556 – 592   19th – 20th Centuries

Berkes, Niyazi.   III. 2974
The development of secularism in Turkey. Montreal, McGill University Press, 1964. xiii, 537 p. map. 26 cm. *1. Turkey — History. 2. Islam and state — Turkey. I..T.*
DR557.B4   320.9561   64-8158

Mardin, Şerif Arif.   III. 2975
The genesis of young Ottoman thought; a study in the modernization of Turkish political ideas. Princeton, N.J., Princeton University Press, 1962. viii, 456 p. 23 cm. (Princeton Oriental studies, v.21) *1. Turkey — Intellectual life. 2. Turkey — Politics and government — 19th century. I. T. (S:Oriental studies series, v.21.)*
DR557.M3 (PJ25.P7 vol. 21)   320.9561   61-7420

Miller, William, 1864-1945.   III. 2976
The Ottoman Empire and its successors, 1801-1927. New York, Octagon Books, 1966. xv, 616 p. fold. maps. 23 cm. Reprint of the 3d edition, first published in 1927. *1. Turkey — History. 2. Eastern question (Balkan) I. T.*
DR557.M6 1966a   956.101   66-26861

Shaw, Stanford Jay.   III. 2977
Between old and new; the Ottoman Empire under Sultan Selim III, 1789-1807 [by] Stanford J. Shaw. Cambridge, Mass., Harvard University Press, 1971. xiii, 535 p. illus., port. 25 cm. (Harvard Middle Eastern studies, 15) *1. Turkey — History — Selim III, 1789-1808. I. T. (S)*
DR559.S5   949.6   74-131465   ISBN:0674068300

Davison, Roderic H.   III. 2978
Reform in the Ottoman Empire, 1856-1876. Princeton, N.J., Princeton University Press, 1963. xiii, 479 p. 25 cm. *1. Turkey — Politics and government — 1829-1878. I. T.*
DR569.D3   956.101   63-12669

Ramsaur, Ernest Edmondson.   III. 2979
The Young Turks; prelude to the revolution of 1908. New York, Russell & Russell [1970, c1957] xii, 180 p. 23 cm. *1. İttihad ve Terakki Cemiyeti. 2. Turkey — Politics and government — 1878-1909. I. T.*
DR572.R3 1970   956.1/01   79-81465

Howard, Harry Nicholas, 1902-   III. 2980
The partition of Turkey; a diplomatic history, 1913-1923, by Harry N. Howard. Norman, University of Oklahoma Press, 1931. 486 p. maps (part fold.) 24 cm. *1. Turkey — History — 1909- 2. European war, 1914-1918 — Territorial questions — Turkey. 3. Eastern question (Balkan) 4. European war, 1914-1918 — Turkey. I. T.*
DR577.H6   949.6   31-24861

Lewis, Bernard.   III. 2981
The emergence of modern Turkey. 2nd ed. London, New York [etc.] issued under the auspices of the Royal Institute of International Affairs [by] Oxford U.P., 1968. xi, 530 p. maps. 21 cm. (Oxford paperbacks no. 135) *1. Turkey — History — 1909- I. Royal Institute of International Affairs. II. T.*
DR583.L48 1968   956.1   68-139021

Kedourie, Elie.   III. 2982
England and the Middle East; the destruction of the Ottoman Empire, 1914-1921. [London] Bowes & Bowes [1956] 236 p. 23 cm. *1. Gt. Brit. — Foreign relations — Near East. 2. Near East — Politics. 3. Turkey — History — 1909- I. T.*
DR588.K4   327.420956   56-4094

Bisbee, Eleanor.   III. 2983
The new Turks; pioneers of the Republic, 1920-1950. Philadelphia, University of Pennsylvania Press, 1951. xiv, 298 p. illus., ports., maps (on lining papers) 25 cm. *1. Turks. 2. Turkey — History — 1918-1960. I. T.*
DR590.B5   956   51-10780

Frey, Frederick W.   III. 2984
The Turkish political elite [by] Frederick W. Frey. Cambridge, Mass., M.I.T. Press [1965] xxvi, 483 p. fold. map. 25 cm. (M.I.T. studies in comparative politics series]) *1. Turkey — Politics and government — 1918-1960. 2. Turkey — Politics and government — 1960- 3. Political parties — Turkey. 4. Leadership. I. T. (S)*
DR590.F7   956.102   65-13834

Mango, Andrew.   III. 2985
Turkey. London, Thames and Hudson, 1968. 192 p. 16 plates. 29 illus., 4 maps, 6 ports. 22 cm. (New nations and peoples) *1. Turkey — History — 1918-1960. 2. Turkey — History — 1960- 3. Turkey — Politics and government — 1918-1960. 4. Turkey — Politics and government — 1960- I. T.*
DR590.M35   956.1/02   68-92250

Robinson, Richard D., 1921-   III. 2986
The First Turkish Republic; a case study in national development. Cambridge, Harvard University Press, 1963. xii, 367 p. illus., ports. 22 cm. (Harvard Middle Eastern studies, 9) *1. Turkey — History — 1918-1960. I. T. (S)*
DR590.R62   956.102   63-17210

Weiker, Walter F.   III. 2987
The Turkish Revolution 1960-1961; aspects of military politics. Washington, Brookings Institution [1963] 172 p. 23 cm. *1. Turkey — History — 1960- I. T.*
DR590.W4   956.101   63-17303

DR701 – 743 SPECIAL REGIONS. CITIES

DR701   Macedonia

Barker, Elisabeth.   III. 2988
Macedonia, its place in Balkan power politics. London, New York, Royal Institute of International Affairs [1950] 129 p. maps. 22 cm. *1. Macedonian question. I. T.*
DR701.M4B3   949.7   50-6759

DR701   Albania

Keefe, Eugene K.   III. 2989
Area handbook for Albania. Co-authors: Eugene K. Keefe [and others. Washington; For sale by the Supt. of Docs., U.S. Govt. Print. Off.] 1971. xiv, 223 p. map. 24 cm. "DA pam 550-98." "One of a series of handbooks

prepared by Foreign Area Studies (FAS) of the American University." *1. Albania. I. American University, Washington, D.C. Foreign Area Studies. II. T.*
DR701.S5K36   914.96/5   73-609651

Skendi, Stavro.   **III. 2990**
The Albanian national awakening, 1878-1912. Princeton, N.J., Princeton University Press, 1967. xvi, 498 p. 23 cm. *1. Albania — History. 2. Nationalism — Albania. I. T.*
DR701.S5S66   949.6/501   66-17710

Swire, Joseph, 1903-   **III. 2991**
Albania; the rise of a kingdom [by] J. Swire. New York, Arno Press, 1971. xxiv, 560 p. illus., maps, ports. 24 cm. (The Eastern Europe collection) Reprint of the 1929 ed. *1. Albania — History.*
DR701.S5S83 1971   949.6/501   79-135835   ISBN:040502777X

Griffith, William E.   **III. 2992**
Albania and the Sino-Soviet rift. Cambridge, M.I.T. Press, 1963. xv, 423 p. 25 cm. (Massachusetts Institute of Technology. Center for International Studies. Studies in international communism) *1. Albania — Foreign relations — Russia. 2. Russia — Foreign relations — Albania. I. T. (S)*
DR701.S86G65   327.4704965   63-10880

Pano, Nicholas C.   **III. 2993**
The People's Republic of Albania [by] Nicholas C. Pano. Baltimore, Johns Hopkins Press [1968] xvi, 185 p. map. 22 cm. (Integration and community building in Eastern Europe) *1. Albania — Politics and government — 1944- (S)*
DR701.S86P3   949.6/5/03   68-27736

Skendi, Stavro, ed.   **III. 2994**
Albania. Stavro Skendi, editor, with the assistance of Mehmet Beqiraj [and others] New York, Published for the Mid-European Studies Center of the Free Europe Committee, by F. A. Praeger [1956] xiv, 389 p. maps. 24 cm. (East-Central Europe under the Communists. Praeger publications in Russian history and world communism, no. 46.) *1. Albania. I. Free Europe Committee. Mid-European Studies Center. (S)*
DR701.S86S56   949.65*   55-11625

DR726 – 729   Istanbul

Lewis, Bernard.   **III. 2995**
Istanbul and the civilization of the Ottoman Empire. [1st ed.] Norman, University of Oklahoma Press [1963] xiii, 189 p. illus., map. 20 cm. (The Centers of civilization series, 9) *1. Istanbul — Civilization. (S)*
DR726.L4   914.961   63-17161

Downey, Glanville, 1908-   **III. 2996**
Constantinople in the age of Justinian. [1st ed.] Norman, University of Oklahoma Press [1960] 181 p. illus. 20 cm. (The Centers of civilization series) *1. Istanbul — History. I. T.*
DR729.D6   949.501   60-13473

DS Asia

DS1 – 11 GENERAL WORKS. DESCRIPTION.

Asia Society. III. 2997
American institutions and organizations interested in Asia, a reference directory. Editor: Ward Morehouse; assistant editor: Edith Ehrman. 2d ed. New York, Taplinger Pub. Co., 1961. xii, 581 p. 24 cm. First ed., 1957, compiled by the Conference on Asian Affairs. *1. Asia — Societies, etc. — Directories. I. Morehouse, Ward, 1929- ed. II. Conference on Asian Affairs, New York. American institutions and organizations interested in Asia. III. T.*
DS1.C572   950.06273   61-11435

The Far East and Australasia. III. 2998
1st- ed.; 1969- London, Europa Publications. v. maps (part col.) 26 cm. Annual. *1. Asia — Yearbooks. 2. Oceanica — Yearbooks.*
DS1.F3   915/.03/05   74-417170

Cressey, George Babcock, 1896- III. 2999
Asia's lands and peoples, a geography of one-third of the earth and two-thirds of its people. 3d ed. New York, McGraw-Hill [1963] 663 p. illus. 26 cm. (McGraw-Hill series in geography) *1. Asia. I. T.*
DS5.C7 1963   915   62-22087

Ginsburg, Norton Sydney, ed. III. 3000
The pattern of Asia. Co-authors: John E. Bush [and others] Englewood Cliffs, N.J., Prentice-Hall, 1958. 929 p. illus. 24 cm. *1. Asia. I. Brush, John E. II. T.*
DS5.G5   915   58-8513
G435

Wint, Guy, 1910- ed. III. 3001
Asia; a handbook. New York, Praeger [1966] xiii, 856 p. maps (part fold.) 24 cm. Appendix (p. [737]-802): Post-war treaties and agreements. *1. Asia. I. T.*
DS5.W5   915   65-13263

Dawson, Christopher Henry, 1889- ed. III. 3002
The Mongol mission: narratives and letters of the Franciscan missionaries in Mongolia and China in the thirteenth and fourteenth centuries. Translated by a nun of Stanbrook Abbey. New York, Sheed and Ward, 1955. xxxix, 246 p. illus., fold. map 22 cm. (The Makers of Christendom) *1. Asia — Description and travel. 2. Mongols — History. I. Giovanni da Piau del Carpine, Abp. of Antivari, d. 1252. History of the Mongols. II. Ruysbroek, Willem van, 13th century. The journey of William of Rubruck. III. T. (S)*
DS6.D3   951.7   55-10925

Fa-hsien, fl. 339-414. III. 3003
The travels of Fa-hsien (399-414 A.D.) or, Record of the Buddhistic kingdoms. Re-translated by H. A. Giles. London, Routledge & Paul [1956] xx, 96 p. illus., fold. map. 17 cm. Translation of Fo kuo chi (romanized form) *1. Asia — Description and travel. 2. Buddha and Buddhism. I. T.*
DS6.F35 1956   915   59-42037

Olschki, Leonardo, 1885- III. 3004
Marco Polo's Asia; an introduction to his "Description of the world" called "Il milione." Translated from the Italian by John A. Scott, and rev. by the author. Berkeley, University of California Press, 1960. ix, 459 p. plates, fold. map, facsims. 24 cm. Translation of L'Asia di Marco Polo. *1. Polo, Marco, 1254-1323? 2. Asia — Description and travel. I. T.*
DS6.O373   950.1   60-8315

Dobby, Ernest Henry George. III. 3005
Monsoon Asia [by] E. H. G. Dobby. 3rd ed. London, University of London P., [1967]. 381 p. plates, maps, tables. 22 cm. (A Systematic regional geography, v.5) *1. Asia — Description and travel. I. T. (S:Unstead, John Frederick, 1876- ed. A systematic regional geography, v.5)*
DS10.D59 1967   915   67-111124

Childe, Vere Gordon, 1892-1957. III. 3006
New light on the most ancient East. [4th ed.] New York, F. A. Praeger [1953] xiii, 255 p. illus., maps. 23 cm. (Books that matter) First published 1928 under title: The most ancient East. *1. Oriental antiquities. 2. Man, Prehistoric. 3. Civilization, Ancient. I. T.*
DS11.C52 1953   913.3   52-13107

DS17 – 27 ETHNOGRAPHY. MONGOLS

Permanent International Altaistic Conference. 5th, Bloomington, Ind., 1962. III. 3007
Aspects of Altaic civilization; proceedings of the Fifth Meeting of the Permanent International Altaistic Conference held at Indiana University, June 4-9, 1962. Edited by Denis Sinor, assisted by David Francis. Bloomington, Indiana University [1963] ix, 263 p. illus. 22 cm. (Indiana University publications. Uralic and Altaic series, v.23) English, German, or French. *1. Ural-Altaic tribes. I. Sinor, Denis, ed. II. Indiana. University. III. T. (S:Indiana. University. Uralic and Altaic series, v.23)*
DS17.P4 1962   572.894   63-63140

Charol, Michael, 1894- III. 3008
The Mongol Empire; its rise and legacy, by Michael Prawdin. Translated by Eden and Cedar Paul. [Rev. 4th impression] London, G. Allen and Unwin [1961] 581 p. maps, port. 23 cm. Translation of Tschingis-Chan und sein Erbe. *1. Jenghis Khan, 1162-1227. 2. Mongols — History. I. T.*
DS19.C522 1961   951.7   64-7297

Howorth, Henry Hoyle, Sir, 1842-1923. III. 3009
History of the Mongols, from the 9th to the 19th century. New York, B. Franklin [1965] 4 v. in 5. maps. 24 cm. (Burt Franklin research and source work series, #85) L.C. set imperfect: maps in v. 1 wanting. Reprint of the 1876-1927 ed. "Sources from which the history of the Mongols ... has been collected": pt. 1, p. xvi-xxviii. *1. Mongols — History. 2. Asia — History. I. T.*
DS19.H862   909/.09/74942   70-6598

Saunders, John Joseph, 1910- III. 3010
The history of the Mongol conquests [by] J. J. Saunders. New York, Barnes & Noble [1971] xix, 275 p. illus. 22 cm. *1. Mongols — History, Military. I. T.*
DS19.S27 1971   950/.2   72-193146   ISBN:0389044512

Spuler, Bertold, 1911- comp. III. 3011
History of the Mongols, based on Eastern and Western accounts of the thirteenth and and fourteenth centuries. Translated from the German by Helga and Stuart Drummond. Berkeley, University of California Press, 1972. x, 221 p. maps. 23 cm. (The Islamic world series) Translation of Geschichte der Mongolen, nach östlichen und europäischen Zeugnissen des 13. und 14. Jahrhunderts. *1. Mongols — History. I. T. (S)*
DS19.S5613 1972   950/.2   68-8720   ISBN:0520019601

Martin, Henry Desmond, 1908- III. 3012
The rise of Chingis Khan and his conquest of North China, by H. Desmond Martin. Introd. by Owen Lattimore. Edited by Eleanor Lattimore. New York, Octagon Books, 1971 [c1950] xvii, 360 p. 3 maps (fold. in pocket), plans, port. 24 cm. *1. Jenghis Khan, 1162-1227. 2. China — History — Yuan dynasty, 1260-1368. I. T.*
DS22.M3 1971   951/.025/0924   70-120647

Vladimirtsov, Borīs IAkovlevīch. III. 3013
The life of Chingis-Khan, by B. Ya. Vladimirtsov. Translated from the Russian by Prince D. S. Mirsky. Boston, Houghton Mifflin, 1930. xii, 172 p. 20 cm. *1. Jenghis Khan, 1162-1227. 2. Mongols — History. I. Mirsky, Dmitry Svyatopolk-, 1890- tr.*
DS22.V6 1930a   923.15   31-12544

DS31–35 HISTORY: GENERAL

London. University. School of Oriental and African Studies. III. 3014
Historical writing on the peoples of Asia. London, New York, Oxford University Press, 1961-62. 4 v. 25 cm. *1. Asia — History — Historiography. I. T.*
DS32.5.L6   950.072   61-4093

Kirk, George Eden, 1911- III. 3015
A short history of the Middle East, from the rise of Islam to modern times, by George E. Kirk. 7th rev. ed. New York, Praeger [1964] 340 p. maps. 21 cm. *1. Near East — History. I. T.*
DS33.K57 1964   309.156   64-25427

Lach, Donald Frederick, 1917- III. 3016
Asia in the making of Europe [by] Donald F. Lach. Chicago, University of Chicago Press [1965-   v. illus., maps, ports. 24 cm. *1. East and West — History. 2. Asia — History. I. T.*
DS33.1.L3   901.93   64-19848

London. University. School of Oriental and African Studies. III. 3017
Handbook of oriental history, by members of the Dept. of Oriental history, School of Oriental and African Studies, University of London. Edited by C. H. Philips. London, Offices of the Royal Historical Society, 1951. viii, 265 p. 24 cm. (Royal Historical Society [London] Guides and handbooks, no. 6) *1. Asia — History — Outlines, syllabi, etc. I. Philips, Cyril Henry, 1912- ed. (S)*
DS33.1.L6   950.02   51-4902

Lamb, Alastair, 1930- III. 3018
Asian frontiers; studies in a continuing problem. New York, Praeger [1968] ix, 246 p. maps. 22 cm. *1. Asia — Boundaries. 2. Asia — Politics. I. T.*
DS33.3.L3 1968b   327.5   68-18543

Martin, Laurence W., ed. III. 3019
Neutralism and nonalignment; the new States in world affairs. New York, Praeger [1962] xxi, 250 p. 21 cm. (Books that matter) *1. States, New — Politics. 2. World politics — 1955- I. T.*
DS33.3.M3 1962   909.82   62-18684

Barnett, A. Doak, ed. III. 3020
Communist strategies in Asia; a comparative analysis of governments and parties. New York, Praeger [1963] ix, 293 p. 21 cm. (Praeger publications in Russian history and world communism, no. 132) "Originally presented, in briefer form, as papers for a symposium on 'Communism in Asia' held during the 1962 Annual Meeting of the Association for Asian Studies." *1. Communism — Asia. 2. Asia — Politics. I. T.*
DS35.B3   950   63-10823

East, William Gordon, ed. III. 3021
The changing map of Asia, a political geography, edited by W. Gordon East and O. H. K. Spate. [3d ed. rev.] London, Methuen; New York, Dutton [1958] xviii, 434 p. maps (part fold.) 23 cm. *1. Asia — Politics. 2. Asia — Historical geography. I. Spate, Oskar Hermann Khristian, joint ed. II. T.*
DS35.E3 1958   915   59-1411

Romein, Jan Marius, 1893- III. 3022
The Asian century; a history of modern nationalism in Asia, by Jan Romein in collaboration with Jan Erik Romein. Translated by R. R. Clark. With a foreword by K. M. Panikkar. Berkeley, University of California Press, 1962. 448 p. 25 cm. "First published in Dutch ... This edition translated from the German and with an additional section ('Last period') first published 1962." *1. Asia — History. I. T.*
DS35.R583   950.4   62-51755

DS35.3–40 ISLAMIC COUNTRIES. ARAB COUNTRIES

The Cambridge history of Islam; III. 3023
edited by P. M. Holt, Ann K. S. Lambton [and] Bernard Lewis. Cambridge [Eng.] University Press, 1970. 2 v. illus., maps. 24 cm. *1. Islamic countries — History. 2. Civilization, Islamic. I. Holt, Peter Malcolm, ed. II. Lambton, Ann Katharine Swynford, ed. III. Lewis, Bernard, ed.*
DS35.6.C3   910.03/176/7   73-77291
ISBN:52107567X(v.1) 521076013(v.2)

Khalil, Muhammad, ed. III. 3024
The Arab States and the Arab League; a documentary record. Beirut, Khayats [1962] 2 v. 25 cm. *1. Arab countries — History — Sources. I. League of Arab States. II. T.*
DS36.2.K45   Ne63-705

Watt, William Montgomery. III. 3025
The influence of Islam on Medieval Europe [by] W. Montgomery Watt. Edinburgh, University Press [1972] viii, 125 p. 21 cm. (Islamic surveys, 9) *1. Europe — Relations (general) with the Islamic Empire. 2. Islamic Empire — Relations (general) with Europe. 3. Civilization, Occidental — Islamic influences. I. T. (S)*
DS36.85.I8 no. 9 (CB251)   910/.031/17671 s (914/.03/1)   70-182902
ISBN:0852242182

Shorter encyclopaedia of Islam. III. 3026
Edited on behalf of the Royal Netherlands Academy, by H. A. R. Gibb and J. H. Kramers. Ithaca, N.Y., Cornell University Press [c1953] viii, 671 p. illus. 27 cm. "Includes all the articles contained in the first edition and Supplement of the Encyclopaedia of Islam which relate particularly to the religion and law of Islam." *1. Islam — Dictionaries. I. Gibb, Hamilton Alexander Rosskeen, 1895- ed. II. Kramers, Johannes Hendrik, 1891-1951, ed. III. Akademie van Wetenschappen, Amsterdam. IV. The Encyclopedia of Islam.*
DS37.E52 1953a   297.03   57-59109

The Encyclopaedia of Islam. III. 3027
New ed., prepared by a number of leading orientalists. Edited by an editorial committee consisting of H. A. R. Gibb [and others] Leiden, Brill, 1960-   v. illus., plates, fold. maps (part col.) diagrs., plans. 26 cm. *1. Islam — Dictionaries. 2. Islamic countries — Dictionaries and encyclopedias. I. Gibb, Hamilton Alexander Rosskeen, Sir 1895- , ed.*
DS37.E523   956.003   61-4395

Hitti, Philip Khuri, 1886- III. 3028
History of the Arabs from the earliest times to the present [by] Philip K. Hitti. 10th ed. [London] Macmillan; [New York] St Martin's Press [1970] xxiv, 822 p. illus. geneal. tables, maps. 23 cm. *1. Arabs. 2. Islamic Empire — History. 3. Civilization, Arab. I. T.*
DS37.7.H58 1970   953   74-102765

Brockelmann, Carl, 1868-1956. III. 3029
History of the Islamic peoples. With a review of events, 1939-1947, by Moshe Perlman. Tr. by Joel Carmichael and Moshe Perlmann. New York, Putnam [1947] xx, 582 p. 8 maps. 22 cm. "Published and distributed in the public interest by authority of the Alien Property Custodian under license no. A-704." *1. Islamic countries — History. I. Perlmann, Hoshe. II. Carmichael, Joel, tr.*
DS38.B72   953   47-5836

Gabrieli, Francesco, 1904- III. 3030
The Arab revival. [Translated from the Italian by Lovett F. Edwards. London] Thames and Hudson [1961] 178 p. illus. 21 cm. (The Great revolutions) *1. Arab countries — History. I. T.*
DS38.G243   956   61-2298

Gaudefroy-Demombynes, Maurice, 1862-1957. III. 3031
Muslim institutions, translated from the French by John P. MacGregor. London, Allen & Unwin [1950] 216 p. 23 cm. *1. Islam. I. T.*
DS38.G314   297   50-11430

Gibb, Hamilton Alexander Rosskeen, Sir, 1895- III. 3032
Islamic society and the West; a study of the impact of western civilization on Moslem culture in the Near East, by H. A. R. Gibb and Harold Bowen. London, New York, Oxford University Press, 1950-   v. in 23 cm. "Issued under the auspices of the Royal Institute of International Affairs." *1. Civilization, Islamic — Occidental influences. I. Bowen, Harold, joint author.*
DS38.G485   949.6   50-9162

Goitein, Solomon Dob Fritz, 1900- III. 3033
Studies in Islamic history and institutions, by S. D. Goitein. Leiden, E. J. Brill, 1966. ix, [3], 391 p. 25 cm. *1. Islamic countries. 2. Islam — Addresses, essays, lectures. I. T.*
DS38.G58   909.09767   66-9057

Kerr, Malcolm H. III. 3034
The Arab cold war, 1958-1967; a study of ideology in politics, by Malcolm Kerr. 2nd edition. London, New York [etc.] Issued under the auspices of the Royal Institute of International Affairs [by] Oxford U.P., 1967. vi, 169 p. 18 cm. (Chatham House essays, 10) "First edition published in 1965 under the title: The Arab cold war, 1958-1964." Third ed. published in 1970 under title: The Arab cold war, 1959-1970. *1. Arab countries — Politics. I. T.*
DS38.K38 1967   320.9/174/927   67-25461

Lammens, Henri, 1862-1937. III. 3035
Islām: beliefs and institutions, by H. Lammens, translated from the French by Sir. E. Denison Ross. London, Methuen [1929] ix, 256 p. 20 cm. *1. Islam. I. Ross, Edward Denison, Sir, 1871-1940, tr. II. T.*
DS38.L3   29-16695

O'Leary, De Lacy Evans, 1872- III. 3036
How Greek science passed to the Arabs. London, Routledge and K. Paul [1949] vi, 196 p. 23 cm. *1. Civilization, Arabic — Greek influences. 2. Hellenism. 3. Church history — Primitive and early church. I. T.*
DS38.O38   915   49-6444

Sharabi, Hisham Bashir, 1927- III. 3037
Nationalism and revolution in the Arab World (the Middle East and North Africa); by Hisham Sharabi. Princeton, N.J., Van Nostrand [1966] ix, 176 p. map, ports. 21 cm. (New perspectives in political science series, 7) Part 2 (p. 107-173) contains translations of documentary material. *1. Arab countries — Politics. I. T.*
DS38.S44   320.9174927   66-1254

Smith, Wilfred Cantwell, 1916- III. 3038
Islam in modern history. Princeton,N.J., Princeton University Press, 1957. 317 p. 25 cm. *1. Islam. 2. Civilization, Islamic. I. T.*
DS38.S56   297   57-5458

Spuler, Bertold, 1911- III. 3039
The Muslim world; a historical survey. Translated from the German by F. R. C. Bagley. Leiden, E. J. Brill, 1960- v. col. maps (part fold.) 25 cm. Translation of Geschichte der islamischen Länder. *1. Mohammedan countries — History. I. T.*
DS38.S643   A61-1030

Von Grunebaum, Gustave Edmund, 1909- ed. III. 3040
Unity and variety in Muslim civilization. Edited by Gustave E. von Grunebaum, with papers by Armand Abel [and others. Chicago] University of Chicago Press [1955] xii, 385 p. illus., map (on lining papers) 25 cm. (Comparative studies of cultures and civilizations) *1. Civilization, Islamic. I. T. (S)*
DS38.V6   915   55-11191

al-Balâdhurî, Aḥmad ibn Yaḥyā, d. 892. III. 3041
The origins of the Islamic state, being a translation from the Arabic, accompanied with annotations, geographic and historic notes of the Kitâb futûḥ al-buldân of al-Imâm Abu-l 'Abbâs, Aḥmad ibn-Jâbir al-Balâdhuri, by Philip Khûri Hitti. [1st AMS ed.] New York, AMS Press [1968-69] 2 v. 23 cm. (Studies in history, economics and public law, 163-163a) Series statement also appears as: Columbia University studies in the social sciences. Vol. 1 translated by P. K. Hitti, vol. 2 translated by F. C. Murgotten; each volume originally presented as the respective translator's thesis, Columbia University. Reprint of the 1916-24 ed. *1. Islamic Empire — History. I. Hitti, Philip Khuri, 1886- tr. II. Murgotten, Francis Clark, 1880- tr. III. T. (S:Columbia studies in the social sciences, 163-163a)*
DS38.2.B313   909/.0974/927   76-82247

Von Grunebaum, Gustave Edmund, 1909- III. 3042
Classical Islam; a history, 600-1258, by G. E. Von Grunebaum. Translated by Katherine Watson. [1st U.S. ed.] Chicago, Aldine Pub. Co. [1970] 243 p. illus., maps. 22 cm. Translation of Der Islam first published in Propyläen Weltgeschichte in 1963. *1. Islamic Empire. I. T.*
DS38.3.V6413 1970b   909.09/767   78-75049   ISBN:20215016X

DS41 – 326 SOUTHWEST ASIA. ANCIENT ORIENT. NEAR EAST

Hurewitz, Jacob Coleman, 1914- ed. III. 3043
Diplomacy in the Near and Middle East; a documentary record. Princeton, N.J., Van Nostrand [1956] 2 v. 24 cm. *1. Near East — History — Sources. 2. Eastern question. I. T.*
DS42.H78   956   56-9728

Coon, Carleton Stevens, 1904- III. 3044
Caravan: the story of the Middle East. Rev. ed. New York, Holt [1958] 386 p. illus. 22 cm. *1. Near East. I. T.*
DS44.C6 1958   950   58-13740

Longrigg, Stephen Hemsley. III. 3045
The Middle East: a social geography. Chicago, Aldine Pub. Co. [1964, c1963] 291 p. illus., maps. 23 cm. *1. Near East. I. T.*
DS44.L56 1964   309.156   63-21832

The Middle East; a political and economic survey. III. 3046
4th ed., edited by Peter Mansfield. London, New York, Oxford University Press, 1973. xi, 591 p. maps 22 cm. Previous editions prepared by the Royal Institute of International Affairs, Information Dept. *1. Near East. I. Mansfield, Peter, 1928- ed. II. Royal Institute of International Affairs. Information Dept. The Middle East; a political and economic survey.*
DS44.M5 1973   915.6/03/4   73-159442   ISBN:019215933X

Le Strange, Guy, 1854-1933. III. 3047
The lands of the Eastern Caliphate: Mesopotamia, Persia, and Central Asia from the Moslem conquest to the time of Timur. New York, Barnes & Noble [1966] xvii, 536 p. 10 maps. 23 cm. First published in 1905. *1. Mesopotamia — Historical geography. 2. Iran — Historical geography. 3. Asia, Central — Historical geography. 4. Asia Minor — Historical geography. I. T.*
DS44.9.L6 1966   911.56   66-1733

Fisher, William Bayne. III. 3048
The Middle East: a physical, social and regional geography [by] W. B. Fisher. 6th ed. completely revised and reset. London, Methuen, 1971. xii, 571 p. illus., maps. 25 cm. *1. Near East — Description and travel. I. T.*
DS49.F56 1971   915.6   78-597190   ISBN:0416091407

Rostovtsev, Mikhail Ivanovich, 1870-1952. III. 3049
Caravan cities, by M. Rostovtzeff. Translated by D. and T. Talbot Rice. New York, AMS Press [1971] xiv, 232 p. map, plans, plates. 19 cm. "Reprinted from the edition of 1932." *1. Palmyra, Syria. 2. Gerasa. 3. Petrá, Arabia. 4. Dura, Syria. I. T.*
DS49.R83 1971   915.6   75-137287   ISBN:0404054455

Royal Institute of International Affairs. Information Dept. III. 3050
The Middle East; a political and economic survey. 3d ed. edited by Reader Bullard. Issued under the auspices of the Royal Institute of International Affairs. London, New York, Oxford University Press, 1958. xviii, 569 p. maps (2 fold. col.) tables. 23 cm. Previous editions prepared in the institute's Information Dept. *1. Near East. I. Bullard, Reader William, Sir, 1885- ed.*
DS49.R87 1958   950   58-3353

Brice, William Charles. III. 3051
South-west Asia [by] William C. Brice. London, University of London P. [1967] 448 p. 16 plates, maps, tables, diagrs. 22 cm. (A Systematic regional geography, v.8) Maps on endpapers. *1. Asia, Western — Description and travel. I. T. (S:Unstead, John Frederick, 1876- ed. A Systematic regional geography, v.8)*
DS49.7.B7x (G126.U67 vol.8)   915.6   67-75420

Cressey, George Babcock, 1896- III. 3052
Crossroads; land and life in southwest Asia. Chicago, Lippincott [1960] xiv, 593 p. illus., maps (1 col. on lining papers) 26 cm. (The Lippincott geography series) *1. Asia, Western — Description and travel. 2. Levant — Description and travel. I. T.*
DS49.7.C7   915.6   60-11518

DS51 – 54 Special Cities. Peoples. Regions

Le Strange, Guy, 1854- III. 3053
Baghdad during the Abbasid caliphate from contemporary Arabic and Persian sources, by G. Le Strange ... with eight plans. London, Oxford University Press, [1942] xxxi, 381 p. fold. map, plans (part fold.) 23 cm. Part of the plans accompanied by a leaf containing descriptive letterpress, not included in the collation. "Impression of 1924. First edition 1900. This impression has been produced photographically ... from sheets of the first edition." *1. Bagdad.*
DS51.B3L4 1924   26-2950

Wiet, Gaston, 1887- III. 3054
Baghdad; metropolis of the Abbasid caliphate. Translated by Seymour Feiler. [1st ed.] Norman, University of Oklahoma Press [1971] vii, 184 p. map. 20 cm. (The Centers of civilization series) *1. Bagdad — History. I. T. (S)*
DS51.B3W5   956.7   72-123348   ISBN:080610922X

Bois, Thomas, 1900- III. 3055
The Kurds. Translated from the French by M. W. M. Welland. [1st English

ed.] Beirut, Khayats, 1966. 159 p. 23 cm. Translation of Connaissance des Kurdes. *1. Kurds.*
DS51.K7B613   915.66/7/03   67-66415

Edmonds, Cecil John.   **III. 3056**
Kurds, Turks, and Arabs; politics, travel, and research in north-eastern Iraq, 1919-1925. London, New York, Oxford University Press, 1957. xiii, 457 p. illus., ports., maps (part fold.) geneal. tables. 22 cm. *1. Kurds. 2. Mosul. 3. Iraq. I. T.*
DS51.M7E4   956.7   58-761

DS54   CYPRUS

Keefe, Eugene K.   **III. 3057**
Area handbook for Cyprus. Co-authors: Eugene K. Keefe [and others. Washington; For sale by the Supt. of Docs., U.S. Govt. Print. Off.] 1971. xiv, 241 p. maps. 25 cm. "DA pam 550-22." "One of a series of handbooks prepared by Foreign Area Studies (FAS) of the American University." 1964 ed. issued by American University, Washington, D.C., Foreign Areas Studies Division. *1. Cyprus. I. American University, Washington, D.C. Foreign Area Studies. II. American University, Washington, D.C. Foreign Areas Studies Division. Area handbook for Cyprus. III. T.*
DS54.K4 1971   915.645/03/4   79-610125

Purcell, Hugh Dominic, 1932-   **III. 3058**
Cyprus, by H. D. Purcell. New York, Praeger [1969, c1968] 416 p. illus., maps. 23 cm. (Nations of the modern world) "Books of Cyprus": p. 403-406. *1. Cyprus. (S)*
DS54.5.P8 1969b   956.45   68-9731

Stephens, Robert Henry, 1920-   **III. 3059**
Cyprus, a place of arms; power politics and ethnic conflict in the eastern Mediterranean [by] Robert Stephens. New York, Praeger [1966] 232 p. 23 cm. *1. Cyprus — History. I. T.*
DS54.5.S68 1966a   956.45   66-12987

Luke, Harry Charles Joseph, Sir, 1884-   **III. 3060**
Cyprus under the Turks, 1571-1878: a record based on the archives of the English Consulate in Cyprus under the Levant Company and after, by Sir Harry Luke. [1st ed.], facsimile reprint with a new introduction by the author. London, C. Hursk, 1969. xi, iii-ix, 281 p. 2 plates, 1 illus., map. 20 cm. "First published in 1921." *1. Cyprus — History. I. T.*
DS54.7.L8 1921a   956.45/02   73-417344   ISBN:900966092

Durrell, Lawrence.   **III. 3061**
Bitter lemons. [1st American ed.] New York, Dutton [c1957] 256 p. illus. 22 cm. *1. Cyprus — Social life and customs. 2. Cyprus — Politics and government. I. T.*
DS54.8.D8 1957a   915.64   58-5225

DS56 – 64 Near East: History and Civilization (General)

Moscati, Sabatino.   **III. 3062**
The face of the ancient Orient; a panorama of Near Eastern civilizations in pre-classical times. Chicago, Quadrangle Books [1960] 328 p. illus. 23 cm. *1. Civilization, Ancient. I. T.*
DS56.M563   901.91   59-15207

Von Grunebaum, Gustave Edmund, 1909-   **III. 3063**
Modern Islam; the search for cultural identity. Berkeley, University of California Press, 1962. viii, 303 p. 24 cm. Articles by the author, which have appeared previously in various collections. *1. Civilization, Islamic. 2. Nationalism — Arab countries. I. T.*
DS57.V6   915.6   62-17178

Cleveland, William L.   **III. 3064**
The making of an Arab nationalist; Ottomanism and Arabism in the life and thought of Sati' al-Husri, by William L. Cleveland. Princeton, N.J., Princeton University Press, 1971 [i.e. 1972] xvi, 211 p. port. 23 cm. (Princeton studies on the Near East) *1. al-Ḥuṣarī, Abū Khaldūn Sāṭiʿ. I. T. (S)*
DS61.52.H87C55   320.5/4/0924 (B)   78-155961   ISBN:069103088X

Fisher, Sydney Nettleton, 1906-   **III. 3065**
The Middle East, a history. 2d ed. [rev. and enl.] New York, Knopf [1968, c1969] xiv, 749, xxx p. maps. 24 cm. *1. Near East — History. I. T.*
DS62.F5 1969   956   68-24673

Hitti, Philip Khuri, 1886-   **III. 3066**
The Near East in history, a 5000 year story. Princeton, N.J., Van Nostrand [1961] 574 p. illus. 24 cm. *1. Near East — History.*
DS62.H68   956   61-1098

Hottinger, Arnold.   **III. 3067**
The Arabs: their history, culture and place in the modern world. Berkeley, University of California Press, 1963. 344 p. illus., maps, facsims. 25 cm. "For the English language edition, the original book has been revised and brought up to date." *1. Arab countries. 2. Nationalism — Arab countries. I. T.*
DS62.H8233   953   64-1108

Lenczowski, George.   **III. 3068**
The Middle East in world affairs. 3d ed. Ithaca, N.Y., Cornell University Press [1962] 723 p. illus. 25 cm. *1. Near East — History. 2. Near East — Politics. I. T.*
DS62.L53 1962   956   62-16343

The Conflict of traditionalism and modernism in the Muslim Middle East.   **III. 3069**
Edited with an introd. by Carl Leiden. [Austin, Humanities Research Center, University of Texas; distributed by University of Texas Press, 1968, c1966] 160 p. illus., map. 26 cm. Eleven papers delivered at a symposium, March 29-31, 1965, sponsored by the Middle East Center of the University of Texas. *1. Near East — Addresses, essays, lectures. I. Leiden, Carl, ed. II. Texas. University. Middle East Center.*
DS62.4.C6   915.6/03   68-59178

Peretz, Don, 1922-   **III. 3070**
The Middle East today. 2d ed. New York, Holt Rinehart and Winston [1971] ix, 496 p. maps. 25 cm. *1. Near East — Politics. I. T.*
DS62.8.P45 1971   309.1/56/03   71-135127   ISBN:003085556X

Sachar, Howard Morley, 1928-   **III. 3071**
The emergence of the Middle East: 1914-1924 [by] Howard M. Sachar. [1st ed.] New York, Knopf, 1969. xiii, 518, xxix p. maps. 25 cm. *1. Near East — History — 20th century. I. T.*
DS62.9.S23 1969   956   76-79349

Antonius, George.   **III. 3072**
The Arab awakening; the story of the Arab national movement. London, H. Hamilton [1945] 470 p. fold. col. maps. 22 cm. Addenda slip inserted. *1. Nationalism — Arab countries. 2. European War, 1914-1918 — Arabia. I. T.*
DS63.A5 1945   950   48-42337

Berger, Morroe.   **III. 3073**
The Arab world today. [1st ed.] Garden City, N.Y., Doubleday, 1962. 480 p. illus. 22 cm. *1. Arab countries — Politics. 2. Arab countries — Economic conditions. I. T.*
DS63.B43   956   62-7601

Cremeans, Charles Davis, 1915-   **III. 3074**
The Arabs and the world; Nasser's Arab nationalist policy. [1st ed.] New York, Published for the Council on Foreign Relations by Praeger [1963] 338 p. illus. 22 cm. *1. Arab countries — Politics. I. T.*
DS63.C74   327.53   63-10459

Frye, Richard Nelson, 1920- ed.   **III. 3075**
The Near East and the Great Powers. With an introd. by Ralph Bunche. Edited by Richard N. Frye. Port Washington, N.Y., Kennikat Press [1969, c1951] viii, 214 p. 21 cm. "The substance of the book was first presented in the form of papers ... in a conference entitled The Great Powers and the Near East, held at Harvard University ... August 7, 8 and 9 of 1950." *1. Near East — Politics. I. T.*
DS63.F7 1969   956   77-79309   ISBN:804605300

Holt, Peter Malcolm.   **III. 3076**
Egypt and the Fertile Crescent, 1516-1922; a political history [by] P. M. Holt. Ithaca, N.Y., Cornell University Press [1966] xii, 337 p. illus., geneal. tables, maps. 23 cm. *1. Turkey — History. 2. Egypt — Relations (general) with Western Asia. 3. Asia, Western — Relations (general) with Egypt. I. T.*
DS63.H62 1966a   956   66-18429

Kirk, George Eden, 1911-   **III. 3077**
Contemporary Arab politics: a concise history. New York, F. A. Praeger [1961] 231 p. illus. 22 cm. (Books that matter) *1. Arab countries — Politics. I. T.*
DS63.K48   956   61-8176

Laqueur, Walter Ze'ev, 1921- ed.   **III. 3078**
The Middle East in transition; studies in contemporary history. Contributors: Hamilton A. R. Gibb [and others] New York, Praeger [1958] xix, 513

p. 23 cm. *1. Near East — Politics. 2. Near East — Social conditions. 3. Russia — Foreign relations — Near East. I. T.*
DS63.L36 1958   956   58-8181

Sachar, Howard Morley, 1928-   **III. 3079**
Europe leaves the Middle East, 1936-1954 [by] Howard M. Sachar. With an introd. by William L. Langer. [1st ed.] New York, Knopf, 1972. xviii, 687, xxxviii p. maps 25 cm. *1. Near East — History — 20th century. I. T.*
DS63.S2   956/.03   72-2157   ISBN:0394460642

Sharabi, Hisham Bashir, 1927-   **III. 3080**
Governments and politics of the Middle East in the twentieth century. Princeton, N.J., Van Nostrand [1962] 296 p. illus. 24 cm. (Van Nostrand political science series) *1. Near East — Politics. I. T.*
DS63.S52   956   62-3407

Spencer, William.   **III. 3081**
Political evolution in the Middle East. Philadelphia, Lippincott [1962] 440 p. illus. 24 cm. (The Lippincott college series in political science) *1. Near East — Politics. I. T.*
DS63.S62   956   63-7028

Thompson, Jack Howell, 1940- ed.   **III. 3082**
Modernization of the Arab world, edited by Jack H. Thompson and Robert D. Reischauer for the Journal of international affairs. Princeton, N.J., Van Nostrand [1966] xiii, 249 p. 21 cm. (New perspectives in political science, 11) A number of the articles originally appeared in v.19, no. 1 of the Journal of international affairs. *1. Near East — Politics. 2. Arab countries — Economic conditions. I. Reischauer, Robert Danton, 1941- joint ed. II. Journal of international affairs. III. T.*
DS63.T49   915.6   67-548

Glubb, John Bagot, Sir, 1897-   **III. 3083**
Britain and the Arabs; a study of fifty years, 1908 to 1958. London, Hodder and Stoughton [1959] 496 p. maps (part fold.) 23 cm. *1. Gt. Brit. — Foreign relations — Near East. 2. Near East — Politics. I. T.*
DS63.2.G7G5 1959   327.420956   59-1659

DeNovo, John A.   **III. 3084**
American interests and policies in the Middle East, 1900-1939. Minneapolis, University of Minnesota Press [1963] xii, 447 p. maps. 24 cm. *1. U.S. — Relations (general) with the Near East. 2. Near East — Relations (general) with the U.S. I. T.*
DS63.2.U5D4   327.73056   63-21129

Field, James A.   **III. 3085**
America and the Mediterranean world, 1776-1882, by James A. Field, Jr. Princeton, N.J., Princeton University Press, 1969. xv, 485 p. maps. 25 cm. *1. United States — Foreign relations — Near East. 2. Near East — Foreign relations — United States. 3. United States — Foreign relations — Mediterranean region. 4. Mediterranean region — Foreign relations — United States. I. T.*
DS63.2.U5F47   327.56/073   68-11440

Polk, William Roe, 1929-   **III. 3086**
The United States and the Arab world [by] William R. Polk. Rev. ed. Cambridge, Harvard University Press, 1969. xix, 377 p. maps. 22 cm. (The American foreign policy library) *1. United States — Relations (general) with Arab countries. 2. Arab countries — Relations (general) with the United States. 3. Arab countries — Politics. I. T. (S)*
DS63.2.U5P6 1969   327.73/056   69-18042

Zeine, Zeine N.   **III. 3087**
The emergence of Arab nationalism; with a background study of Arab-Turkish relations in the Near East [by] Zeine N. Zeine. [3d ed.] Delmar, N.Y., Caravan Books [1973] viii, 192 p. illus. 23 cm. First ed. published in 1958 under title: Arab-Turkish relations and the emergence of Arab nationalism. *1. Nationalism — Arab countries. 2. Turkey — Foreign relations — Arab countries. 3. Arab countries — Foreign relations — Turkey. I. T.*
DS63.6.Z44 1973   327.496/1/056   76-39576   ISBN:0882060007

Fisher, Sydney Nettleton, 1906- ed.   **III. 3088**
The military in the Middle East; problems in society and government. Columbus, Ohio State University Press, 1963. 138 p. 23 cm. ([Ohio. State University, Columbus] Graduate Institute for World Affairs. [Publication] no. 1) "A publication of the Mershon Center for Education in National Security." "Papers ... presented at the Graduate Institute for World Affairs of the Ohio State University during a three-day conference, November 30-December 2, 1961." *1. Militarism — Near East. 2. Near East — Politics. 3. Near East — Social conditions. I. Ohio. State University, Columbus. Graduate Institute for World Affairs. II. T. (S)*
DS64.F5   355   63-9001

DS66   Hittites

Gurney, Oliver Robert.   **III. 3089**
The Hittites. London, Baltimore, Penguin Books [1952] 239 p. illus. 19 cm. (Pelican books, A259) *1. Hittites.*
DS66.G8   939   52-14552

DS67 – 79   Iraq (Assyria. Babylonia)

Luckenbill, Daniel David, 1881-1927.   **III. 3090**
Ancient records of Assyria and Babylonia. New York, Greenwood Press [1968, c1926] 2 v. 22 cm. *1. Assyria — History — Sources. I. T.*
DS68.L8 1968   935/.03/08   68-57626

Chiera, Edward, 1885-1933.   **III. 3091**
They wrote on clay; the Babylonian tablets speak today. Edited by George G. Cameron. [Chicago] University of Chicago Press [1956, c1938] 234 p. illus. 21 cm. (Phoenix books, P2) *1. Mesopotamia — Antiquities. 2. Excavations (Archaeology) — Mesopotamia. 3. Cuneiform inscriptions. I. T.*
DS69.5.C5x   913.358   56-163

Oppenheim, A. Leo, 1904-   **III. 3092**
Ancient Mesopotamia: portrait of a dead civilization, by A. Leo Oppenheim. Chicago, University of Chicago Press [1964] ix, 433 p. illus., maps (1 fold. in pocket) port. 24 cm. *1. Civilization, Assyro-Babylonian. I. T.*
DS69.5.O6 1964   913.35   64-19847

Lloyd, Seton.   **III. 3093**
Foundations in the dust; a story of Mesopotamian exploration. London, New York, Oxford University Press [1949] xii, 237 p. illus., ports., maps. (1 fold.) 22 cm. *1. Excavations (Archaeology) — Mesopotamia. 2. Mesopotamia — Antiquities. 3. Archaeologists, British. I. T.*
DS70.L48 1949   913.358   50-769

Harris, George Lawrence, 1910-   **III. 3094**
Iraq: its people, its society, its culture. In collaboration with Moukhtar Ani [and others] New Haven, HRAF Press [1958] 350 p. maps., tables. 22 cm. (Survey of world cultures) *1. Iraq. (S)*
DS70.6.H3   915.67   58-14179

Smith, Harvey Henry, 1892-   **III. 3095**
Area handbook for Iraq. Co-authors: Harvey H. Smith and others. Rev. ed. Washington, U.S. Govt. Print. Off., 1971. lvi, 413 p. Supersedes DA Pam 550-31, March, 1969. *1. Iraq. I. American University, Washington, D.C. Foreign Area Studies Division. II. T.*
DS70.6.S6x

Olmstead, Albert Ten Eyck, 1880-1945.   **III. 3096**
History of Assyria. [Chicago] University of Chicago Press [1960, c1951] 695 p. illus. 23 cm. (Chicago reprint series) *1. Assyria — History. 2. Civilization, Assyro-Babylonian.*
DS71.O6 1960   935   60-51197

Oppenheim, A. Leo, 1904- comp.   **III. 3097**
Letters from Mesopotamia: official business, and private letters on clay tablets from two millennia. Translated and with an introd. by A. Leo Oppenheim. Chicago, University of Chicago Press [1967] viii, 217 p. illus., map. 24 cm. *1. Mesopotamia — Civilization. I. T.*
DS71.O7   913.3/5/03   67-20576

Kramer, Samuel Noah, 1897-   **III. 3098**
History begins at Sumer. Garden City, N.Y., Doubleday, 1959. 247 p. illus. 19 cm. (Doubleday anchor books, A175) Published in 1956 under title: From the tablets of Sumer. *1. Sumerians. I. T.*
DS72.K7 1959   935   59-2276

Kramer, Samuel Noah, 1897-   **III. 3099**
The Sumerians: their history, culture, and character. [Chicago] University of Chicago Press [1963] xiv, 355 p. illus., plates. 25 cm. *1. Sumerians.*
DS72.K73   913.35   63-11398

Contenau, Georges, 1877-   **III. 3100**
Everyday life in Babylon and Assyria. [Authorized translation by K. R. & A.

R. Maxwell-Hyslop] New York, St Martin's Press, 1954. xv, 324 p. illus., 24 plates, maps. 22 cm. *1. Babylonia — Social life and customs. 2. Assyria Social life and customs. I. T.*
DS75.S6C63   913.352   54-10269

Khadduri, Majid, 1909-   **III. 3101**
Independent Iraq, 1932-1958; a study in Iraqi politics. 2d ed. London, New York, Oxford University Press, 1960. viii, 388 p. fold. map. 23 cm. *1. Iraq — Politics and government. I. T.*
DS79.K43 1960   956.7   60-50855

DS80 – 89 Lebanon (Phenicia)

Smith, Harvey Henry, 1892-   **III. 3102**
Area handbook for Lebanon. Co-authors: Harvey H. Smith [and others] Washington, For sale by the Supt. of Docs., U.S. Govt. Print. Off., 1969. xviii, 352 p. maps. 24 cm. "DA pam no. 550-24." "Supersedes DA pam 550-24, 1 May 1964." "This volume is one of a series of handbooks prepared by Foreign Area Studies (FAS) of the American University." *1. Lebanon. I. American University, Washington, D.C. Foreign Area Studies. II. T.*
DS80.S63   915.692   72-603935

Hitti, Philip Khuri, 1886-   **III. 3103**
Lebanon in history: from the earliest times to the present [by] Philip K. Hitti. 3rd ed. London, Melbourne [etc.] Macmillan; New York, St. Martin's P., 1967. xx, 550 p. front., illus. (incl. ports.) col. plate, maps, tables. 22 1/2 cm. *1. Lebanon — History. I. T.*
DS80.9.H5 1967   956.92   67-21542

Moscati, Sabatino.   **III. 3104**
The world of the Phoenicians. Translated from the Italian by Alastair Hamilton. New York, Praeger [1968] xxii, 281 p. illus., maps, plans. 26 cm. (Praeger history of civilization) Translation of Il mondo dei Fenici. *1. Phenicians. I. T.*
DS81.M613 1968b   913.3/9/4403   68-27432

Polk, William Roe, 1929-   **III. 3105**
The opening of south Lebanon, 1788-1840; a study of the impact of the West on the Middle East. Cambridge, Harvard University Press, 1963. xx, 299 p. illus., maps, geneal. tables. 22 cm. (Harvard Middle Eastern studies, 8) *1. Lebanon — History. I. T. (S)*
DS84.P6 1963   956.92   63-13815

Salibi, Kamal Suleiman, 1929-   **III. 3106**
The modern history of Lebanon [by] K. S. Salibi. New York, Praeger [1965] xxvii, 227 p. illus., maps, ports. 23 cm. (The Praeger Asia-Africa series) *1. Lebanon — History. I. T.*
DS84.S25   956.92   65-14186

Meo, Leila M. T.   **III. 3107**
Lebanon, improbable nation; a study in political development [by] Leila M. T. Meo. Bloomington, Indiana University Press [1965] x, 246 p. maps. 21 cm. (Indiana. University. International studies) *1. Lebanon — Politics and government. I. T. (S)*
DS86.M4   320.95692   65-63610

Qubain, Fahim Issa, 1924-   **III. 3108**
Crisis in Lebanon. Washington, Middle East Institute, 1961. 243 p. 24 cm. *1. Lebanon — Politics and government. I. T.*
DS86.Q8   956.92   61-19686

DS92 – 99 Syria

American University, Washington, D.C. Foreign Areas Studies Division.   **III. 3109**
Area handbook for Syria. Washington, For sale by the Supt. of Docs., U.S. Govt. Print. Off. [1970] x, 393 p. maps. 24 cm. "DA pam no. 550-47." Reprint of the 1965 ed. *1. Syria. I. T.*
DS93.A65 1970   915.691/03/4   71-26943

Fedden, Henry Romilly, 1908-   **III. 3110**
Syria; an historical appreciation, by Robin Fedden. Illustrated from photos. mainly by A. Costa. Rev. ed. London, Hale [1955] 243 p. illus. 23 cm. *1. Syria — Description and travel. 2. Syria — History.*
DS94.F4 1955   956.9   55-4421

Hitti, Philip Khûri, 1886-   **III. 3111**
History of Syria, including Lebanon and Palestine. 2d ed. London, Macmillan; New York, St Martin's Press, 1957. xxv, 750 p. illus. (part col.) maps (part fold.) 22 cm. *1. Syria — History. 2. Lebanon. 3. Palestine — History.*
DS95.H5x   A59-3552

Bevan, Edwyn Robert, 1870-1943.   **III. 3112**
The house of Seleucus. New York, Barnes & Noble [1966] 2 v. illus., 3 fold. col. maps, ports. 23 cm. "First published in 1902" *1. History, Ancient. 2. Seleucids. I. T.*
DS96.B57 1966   935.06   66-782

Usāmah ibn Murshid ibn Munqidh, 1095-1188.   **III. 3113**
An Arab-Syrian gentleman and warrior in the period of the crusades; memoirs of Usāmah ibn-Munqidh (Kitāb ali'tibār) translated from the original manuscript by Philip K. Hitti. New York, Columbia University Press, 1929. x, 265 p. map, facsims. front., pl. 23 cm. (Records of civilization: sources and studies, ed. under the auspices of the Dept. of history, Columbia university) *1. Syria — History. 2. Crusades. I. Ḥitti, Philip Khûri, 1886- tr. II. T.*
DS97.U69   29-16940

Hourani, Albert Habib.   **III. 3114**
Syria and Lebanon, a political essay by A. H. Hourani. Issued under the auspices of the Royal institute of international affairs. London, New York [etc.] Oxford University Press [1946] x, 402 p. maps (1 double) 22 cm. *1. Syria — Politics and government. 2. Lebanon — Politics and government. I. Royal institute of international affairs.*
DS98.H65   956.9   47-3024

Zeine, Zeine N.   **III. 3115**
The struggle for Arab independence; Western diplomacy & the rise and fall of Faisal's kingdom in Syria. Beirut [Khayat's] 1960. xiii, 297 p. maps (1 fold. col.) facsims. 23 cm. *1. Syria — History. 2. Gt. Brit. — Foreign relations — Near East. 3. France — Foreign relations — Near East. 4. Near East — Politics. I. T.*
DS98.Z4x   A61-142

Downey, Glanville, 1908-   **III. 3116**
A history of Antioch in Syria: from Seleucus to the Arab conquest. Princeton, N.J., Princeton University Press, 1961. xvii, 752 p. illus., maps. 24 cm. *1. Antioch — History.*
DS99.A6D6   939.42   61-6288

Rostovtsev, Mikhaĭl Ivanovich, 1870-   **III. 3117**
Dura-Europos and its art, by M. Rostovtzeff. Oxford, Clarendon Press, 1938. xiv, 162 p. front., illus., plates, fold. map, fold. plan. 25 cm. *1. Dura, Syria. 2. Mural painting and decoration. 3. Decoration and ornament — Dura, Syria. 4. Art — Dura, Syria. I. T.*
DS99.D8R7   913.3943   39-8531

DS101 Palestine. Israel. Jews

Finkelstein, Louis, 1895- ed.   **III. 3118**
The Jews: their history, culture, and religion. 3d ed. New York, Harper [1960] 2 v. (xxxvi, 1859 p.) illus., ports., maps (part col.), facsims., music. 24 cm. Fourth ed. (1970-71) published as a 3 v. work. Vol. 1 has title: The Jews: their history; v. 2: The Jews: their religion and culture; v. 3: The Jews: their role in civilization. *1. Jews — History. 2. Judaism — History. 3. Jewish literature — History and criticism. 4. Civilization — Jewish influences. I. T.*
DS102.4.F5 1960   956.93   60-7383

Encyclopaedia Judaica.   **III. 3119**
Jerusalem, Encyclopaedia Judaica; [New York] Macmillan [c1971-72, v. 1, c1972] 16 v. illus. (part col.) 32 cm. Part of illustrative matter in pocket. *1. Jews — Dictionaries and encyclopedias.*
DS102.8.E496   296/.03   72-177492

The Jewish encyclopedia; a descriptive record of the history, religion, literature, and customs of the Jewish people from the earliest times.   **III. 3120**
Prepared under the direction of Cyrus Adler [and others] Isidore Singer, projector and managing editor, assisted by American and foreign boards of consulting editors. [New York] Ktav Pub. House [1964?] 12 v. illus., ports., maps, facsims., geneal. tables, music. 26 cm. *1. Jews — Dictionaries*

encyclopedias. I. Singer, Isidore, 1859-1939, ed. II. Adler, Cyrus, 1863-1940, ed.
DS102.8.Jx   915.693   64-9604

The New standard Jewish encyclopedia.   III. 3121
Cecil Roth and Geoffrey Wigoder, editors-in-chief. New, rev. ed. Jerusalem, Massada Pub. Co., 1970. 30, 2027 columns. illus. (part col.), facsims., ports. 27 cm. Previous editions have title: The Standard Jewish encyclopedia. *1. Jews — Dictionaries and encyclopedias. I. Roth, Cecil, 1899-1970, ed. II. Wigoder, Geoffrey, 1922- ed.*
DS102.8.S73 1970   910.09/174/924   70-16986   ISBN:491003641

Universal Jewish encyclopedia; an authoritative and popular   III. 3122
presentation of Jews and Judaism since the earliest times;
edited by Isaac Landman. New York, The Universal Jewish encyclopedia, inc. [c1939-43] 10 v. fronts., illus., plates, ports., maps, facsims., diagrs. 28 cm. The illustrative material is partly colored and partly folded. *1. Jews — Dictionaries and encyclopedias. I. Landman, Isaac, 1880- , ed.*
DS102.8.U5   296.03   40-5070

DS103 – 113 DESCRIPTION. ANTIQUITIES. CIVILIZATION

Harman, Abraham, ed.   III. 3123
Israel. Editors: Abe Harman [and] Yigael Yadin. Pref.: David Ben-Gurion. Garden City, N.Y., Doubleday [1958] 1 v. (chiefly illus., part col.) 30 cm. *1. Israel — Description and travel — Views. I. Yadin, Yigael, 1917- joint ed.*
DS108.5.H28   915.694   58-2753

Kenyon, Kathleen Mary.   III. 3124
Jerusalem; excavating 3000 years of history by Kathleen M. Kenyon. New York, McGraw-Hill [c1967] 211 p. illus. (part col.), plans. 26 cm. (New aspects of archaeology) Based on the results of an expedition sponsored by the British School of Archaeology in Jerusalem, the Dominican école biblique et archéologique de St. Étienne, and the Royal Ontario Museum. *1. Jerusalem — Antiquities. I. British School of Archaeology in Jerusalem. II. T.*
DS109.K4   913.3/3/03   67-22045

Parrot, André, 1901-   III. 3125
The Temple of Jerusalem. [Translated by Beatrice E. Hooke] London, SCM Press [1957] 112 p. illus., plans. 19 cm. (Studies in Biblical archaeology, no. 5) *1. Jerusalem. Temple. I. T. (S)*
DS109.3.Px   913.3   64-7340

Yadin, Yigael, 1917-   III. 3126
Masada; Herod's fortress and the Zealot's last stand. [Translated from the Hebrew by Moshe Pearlman] New York, Random House [1966] 272 p. illus. (part col.) map, plans (part col.) 26 cm. *1. Mezada (Fortress), Israel. I. T.*
DS110.M33Y33   913.031028   66-23094

Glubb, John Bagot, 1897-   III. 3127
The story of the Arab Legion. London, Hodder & Stoughton [1948] 371 p. plates, ports., maps. 23 cm. *1. Trans-Jordan. Arab Legion. 2. Trans-Jordan — History.*
DS110.4.G5   956.9   49-1942

Dayan, Moshe, 1915-   III. 3128
Diary of the Sinai Campaign. [1st ed.] New York, Harper & Row [1966] 236 p. illus., maps, ports. 22 cm. *1. Sinai Campaign, 1956 — Personal narratives. I. T.*
DS110.5.D313 1966a   953.1050924   66-15731

Glueck, Nelson, 1900-   III. 3129
Deities and dolphins; the story of the Nabataeans. New York, Farrar, Straus and Giroux [1965] xii, 650 p. illus., maps, plans. 27 cm. *1. Nabataeans. 2. Jordan — Antiquities. 3. Petra, Arabia. 4. Dolphin (in religion, folk-lore, etc.) I. T.*
DS110.5.G55   913.39403   64-19808

Goodenough, Erwin Ramsdell, 1893-   III. 3130
Jewish symbols in the Greco-Roman period. [New York] Pantheon Books [1953-1969] 13 v. illus. 32 cm. (Bollingen series, 37) *1. Jews — Antiquities. I. T. (S)*
DS111.G65   913.33   52-10031

Kenyon, Kathleen Mary.   III. 3131
Archaeology in the Holy Land, by Kathleen M. Kenyon. 3d ed. New York, Praeger [1970] 360 p. illus., maps, plans. 23 cm. *1. Palestine — Antiquities. I. T.*
DS111.K4 1970b   913.33/03   70-88898

Kenyon, Kathleen Mary.   III. 3132
Royal cities of the Old Testament [by] Kathleen Kenyon. New York, Schocken Books [1971, i.e. 1972, c1971] xi, 164 p. illus. 25 cm. *1. Cities and towns, Ancient. 2. Palestine — Antiquities. I. T.*
DS111.1.K46 1972   913.3   79-159482   ISBN:0805234128

Baron, Salo Wittmayer, 1895-   III. 3133
A social and religious history of the Jews. 2d ed., rev. and enl. New York, Columbia University Press, 1952- v. 24 cm. *1. Jews — History. 2. Judaism — History. 3. Jews — Political and social conditions. I. T.*
DS112.B3152   296   52-404

Katz, Jacob, 1904-   III. 3134
Tradition and crisis; Jewish society at the end of the Middle Ages. [New York] Free Press of Glencoe [1961] 280 p. 22 cm. *1. Jews — Social life and customs. 2. Jews — History — 70-1789. I. T.*
DS112.K373   915.693   61-9168

Vaux, Roland de, 1903-   III. 3135
Ancient Israel: its life and institutions. Translated by John McHugh. New York, McGraw-Hill [1961] xxiii, 592 p. 25 cm. Translation of Les institutions de l'Ancien Testament. *1. Jews — Social life and customs. I. T.*
DS112.V313   913.33   61-12360

Zborowski, Mark.   III. 3136
Life is with people; the Jewish little-town of eastern Europe [by] Mark Zborowski and Elizabeth Herzog. Foreword by Margaret Mead. New York, International Universities Press [1952] 456 p. 23 cm. *1. Jews — Social life and customs. I. Herzog, Elizabeth (Greenebaum) joint author. II. T.*
DS112.Z37   296   52-7181

Ginzberg, Louis, 1873-1953.   III. 3137
Students, scholars, and saints; [lectures] New York, Meridian Books [1958, c1928] 291 p. 21 cm. *1. Jews — Education. 2. Jews — Biography. I. T.*
DS113.G7 1958   296   58-8532

Pedersen, Johannes, 1883-   III. 3138
Israel, its life and culture, I-[IV] London, Oxford University Press [1953-54; v.2, 1953] 2 v. 22 cm. Photoprint of the translation by Mrs. A. Møller and A. I. Fausbell in collaboration with the author, first published 1926-40. *1. Bible. O.T. — Criticism, interpretation, etc. 2. Jews — Social life and customs. I. T.*
DS113.P42   933   58-29360

Schwarz, Leo Walder, 1906- ed.   III. 3139
Great ages and ideas of the Jewish people, by Salo W. Baron [and others] New York, Modern Library [c1956] 515 p. 21 cm. (The Modern library of the world's best books [G-85]) *1. Judaism — History. I. Baron, Salo Wittmayer, 1895- II. T.*
DS113.S38 1956   956.93   62-4323

Landau, Jácob M.   III. 3140
The Arabs in Israel: a political study [by] Jacob M. Landau. London, New York, [etc.] published under the auspices of the Royal Institute of International Affairs [by] Oxford U.P., 1969. xiii, 301 p. form, map. 23 cm. *1. Arabs in Israel. I. Royal Institute of International Affairs. II. T.*
DS113.7.L3   323.1/19/2705694   70-392686   ISBN:192149776

DS114 – 127 HISTORY

Abraham ben David, ha-Levi, ca. 1110-ca. 1180.   III. 3141
A critical edition with a translation and notes of the book of tradition (Sefer ha-qabbalah) by Abraham Ibn Daud. By Gerson D. Cohen. [1st ed.] Philadelphia, Jewish Publication Society of America, 1967. lxii, 348, 74, 22 p. 24 cm. (Judaica texts and translations, 1st ser. no. 3) *1. Jews — History — Chronology. 2. Tradition (Judaism) I. Cohen, Gerson David, 1924- ed. II. T:Sefer ha-kabalah. III. T:The book of tradition. (S)*
DS114.A513   909/.09/74924   65-17048

Dubnov, Semen Markovich, 1860-1941.   III. 3142
History of the Jews. Translated from the Russian 4th definitive rev. ed. vols. 1 & 2 by Moshe Spiegel. South Brunswick [N.J.] T. Yoseloff [1967- v. 24 cm. Translation of Istorii evreĭskogo naroda na Vostoke. *1. Jews — History. I. T.*
DS117.D7213   933   66-14785

Robinson, Theodore Henry, 1881-   III. 3143
A history of Israel. Oxford, Clarendon Press, 1932. 2 v. maps (part fold.) 23 cm. *1. Jews — History. I. Oesterley, William Oscar Emil, 1866-*
DS117.R57   933   33-1497

Sachar, Abram Leon, 1899-   III. 3144
A history of the Jews. 5th ed., rev. and enl. New York, Knopf, 1965. xvi, 478, xiv p. 4 fold maps. 25 cm. *1. Jews — History. I. T.*
DS117.S3 1965   956.93   64-17704

The World history of the Jewish people.　　　　　　III. 3145
Tel-Aviv? Jewish History Publications [1964- c1963-　v. *1. Jews — History.*
DS117.W6　　Ne64-3260

Aharoni, Yohanan, 1919-　　　　　　　　　　　　III. 3146
The land of the Bible; a historical geography, by Yohanan Aharoni. Translated from the Hebrew by A. F. Rainey. Philadelphia, Westminster Press [1967] xiv, 409 p. maps. 25 cm. Translation of Erets-Yisrael bi-tekufat ha-Mikra (romanized form) *1. Bible — Geography. 2. Palestine — History — To 70 A.D. I. T.*
DS118.A3313　　220.91　　67-11273

Goldberg, Israel, 1887-1964.　　　　　　　　　　III. 3147
Israel: a history of the Jewish people, by Rufus Learsi. Westport, Conn., Greenwood Press [1972, c1949] 715 p. maps. 23 cm. *1. Jews — History. I. T.*
DS118.G56 1972　　909/.04/924　　72-162629　　ISBN:0837161977

Margolis, Max Leopold, 1866-1932.　　　　　　III. 3148
A history of the Jewish people, by Max L. Margolis and Alexander Marx. New York, Meridian Books and the Jewish Publication Society of America, Philadelphia [1958, c1927] 752 p. 21 cm. *1. Jews — History. I. Marx, Alexander, 1878-1953, joint author.*
DS118.M3 1958　　933　　58-11935

Noth, Martin, 1902-　　　　　　　　　　　　　III. 3149
The history of Israel. 2d ed. [Translation rev. by P. R. Ackroyd] London, A. & C. Black [1960] 487 p. 24 cm. *1. Jews — History.*
DS118.N553 1960　　933　　60-50534

Parkes, James William, 1896-　　　　　　　　　III. 3150
A history of the Jewish people. Chicago, Quadrangle Books [1963, c1962] 254 p. 22 cm. *1. Jews — History. I. Jewish people.*
DS118.P32 1963　　956.93　　62-19984

Roth, Cecil, 1899-　　　　　　　　　　　　　III. 3151
A bird's-eye view of Jewish history. [Rev. ed.] New York, Union of American Hebrew Congregations, 1954. 466 p. illus. 21 cm. (Union adult series) *I. T.*
DS118.R6 1954　　296　　55-31939

Goitein, Solomon Dob Fritz, 1900-　　　　　　III. 3152
Jews and Arabs, their contacts through the ages. New York, Schocken Books [1955] 257 p. 22 cm. *1. Jewish-Arab relations. 2. Jews — History. I. T.*
DS119.G58　　956.94　　55-7968

Kobler, Franz, 1882- ed.　　　　　　　　　　　III. 3153
A treasury of Jewish letters; letters from the famous and the humble. [2d ed. New York] Publication of the East and West Library issued by Farrar, Straus, and Young [1953] 2 v. (lxxix, 670 p.) illus., ports. 22 cm. *1. Jewish letters. I. T.*
DS119.K58 1953　　296　　53-8849

Dodd, Charles Harold, 1884- comp.　　　　　　III. 3154
Israel and the Arab world [by] C. H. Dodd and M. E. Sales. New York, Barnes & Noble [1970] xvi, 247 p. illus., maps. 23 cm. (The World studies series) *1. Jewish-Arab relations — History — Sources. I. Sales, Mary E., joint comp. II. T.*
DS119.7.D62　　956　　70-13191　　ISBN:38901091X

Khouri, Fred John.　　　　　　　　　　　　　III. 3155
The Arab-Israeli dilemma [by] Fred J. Khouri. [1st ed. Syracuse, N.Y.] Syracuse University Press [1968] xi, 436 p. 24 cm. *1. Jewish-Arab relations. I T.*
DS119.7.K48　　956　　68-20483

Peretz, Don, 1922-　　　　　　　　　　　　　III. 3156
A Palestine entity? [By] Don Peretz, Evan M. Wilson and Richard J. Ward. Washington, Middle East Institute [1970] v, 119 p. 23 cm. (Middle East Institute, Washington, D.C. Special study, no. 1) Background reading for the 24th Annual Conference of the Middle East Institute. *1. Arabs in Palestine. 2. Jewish-Arab relations. I. Wilson, Evan M., 1910- II. Ward, Richard Joseph, 1921- III. T. (S)*
DS119.7.P45　　320.1/58/095694　　73-139243

Rodinson, Maxime.　　　　　　　　　　　　　III. 3157
Israel and the Arabs. Translated from the French by Michael Perl. [1st American ed.] New York, Pantheon Books [c1968] 239 p. 22 cm. Translation of Israël et le refus arabe. *1. Jewish-Arab relations. I. T.*
DS119.7.R613 1968b　　956　　68-13013

Safran, Nadav.　　　　　　　　　　　　　　III. 3158
From war to war: the Arab-Israeli confrontation, 1948-1967; a study of the conflict from the perspective of coercion in the context of inter-Arab and big power relations. New York, Pegasus [1969] 464 p. illus., maps. 22 cm. *1. Jewish-Arab relations. 2. Near East — Politics. 3. Israel-Arab War, 1967- I. T.*
DS119.7.S32　　956　　68-27991

The Transformation of Palestine; essays on the origin and development of the Arab-Israeli conflict.　　　III. 3159
Edited by Ibrahim Abu-Lughod. With a foreword by Arnold J. Toynbee. Evanston [Ill.] Northwestern University Press, 1971. xv, 522 p. facsim., maps. 24 cm. *1. Jewish-Arab relations — Addresses, essays, lectures. I. Abu-Lughod, Ibrahim A., ed.*
DS119.7.T7　　956　　71-137791　　ISBN:0810103451

DS121 – 127 By Period

DS121 – 122 TO 70 A.D.

Bright, John, 1908-　　　　　　　　　　　　III. 3160
A history of Israel. Philadelphia, Westminster Press [1959] 500 p. illus. 24 cm. (Westminster aids to the study of the Scriptures) *1. Jews — History — To 70 A.D.*
DS121.B72　　933　　59-9314

Wellhausen, Julius, 1844-1918.　　　　　　　　III. 3161
Prolegomena to the history of ancient Israel. With a reprint of the article, Israel, from the Encyclopaedia Britannica. Pref. by W. Robertson Smith. New York, Meridian Books, 1957. 552 p. 21 cm. (Meridian library, ML6) *1. Bible. O.T. — Criticism, interpretation, etc. 2. Jews — History — To 953 B.C. 3. Judaism — History — Ancient period.*
DS121.W48 1957　　932　　57-10843

Josephus, Flavius.　　　　　　　　　　　　　III. 3162
The Jewish war [by] Josephus. Translated with an introd. by G. A. Williamson. [Harmondsworth, Middlesex; Baltimore] Penguin Books [1959] 411 p. maps, geneal. table. 18 cm. (The Penguin classics, L90) *1. Jews — History — 586 B.C.-70 A.D. I. T.*
DS122.J723　　933　　59-4945

Mathews, Shailer, 1863-1941.　　　　　　　　III. 3163
A history of New Testament times in Palestine, 175 B.C.-70 A.D., by Shailer Mathews. Rev. ed. New York, Macmillan, 1910. xi, 234 p. front. (map) 19 cm. (New Testament handbooks) *1. Jews — History — 586 B.C.-70 A.D. 2. Bible. N.T. — History of contemporary events, etc. (S)*
DS122.M44　　933　　10-20654

Schürer, Emil, 1844-1910.　　　　　　　　　　III. 3164
A history of the Jewish people in the time of Jesus. Edited and introduced by Nahum N. Glatzer. New York, Schocken Books [1961] 428 p. 21 cm. "An abridgement of the first division [Political history of Palestine from B. C. 175 to A. D. 135] of Schürer's work. The English rendition of the work was first published in 1886-1890, by T. & T. Clark, Edinburgh." Translation of Geschichte der judischen Volkes im Zeitalter Jesu Christi. *1. Jews — History — 586 B. C.-70 A. D. I. Jewish people in the time of Jesus.*
DS122.S423　　933　　61-8195

Tcherikover, Avigdor, 1895-　　　　　　　　　III. 3165
Hellenistic civilization and the Jews. Translated by S. Applebaum. 1st ed. Philadelphia, Jewish Publication Society of America, 1959. vii, 566 p. 2 maps (on lining papers) 22 cm. Translation of ha-Yehudim veha-Yevanim ba-tekufah ha-Helenistit (romanized form) *1. Jews — History — 586 B.C.-70 A.D. 2. Greece — History. 3. Hellenism. I. T.*
DS122.T313　　933　　59-8518

Zeitlin, Solomon, 1892-　　　　　　　　　　　III. 3166
The rise and fall of the Judaean state; a political, social and religious history of the Second Commonwealth. [1st ed.] Philadelphia, Jewish Publication Society of America, 1962-　v. illus. 22 cm. *1. Jews — History — 586 B.C.-70 A.D. I. T.*
DS122.Z43　　933　　61-11708

Josephus, Flavius.　　　　　　　　　　　　　III. 3167
The great Roman-Jewish war: A.D. 66-70 (De bello Judaico) The William Whiston translation as rev. by D. S. Margoliouth. Edited with an introd. by William R. Farmer. Including The life of Josephus. Gloucester, Mass., Peter Smith, 1970. xv, 332 p. geneal. tables, maps, port. 22 cm. The texts used in this ed. were first published in The works of Flavius Josephus in 1906. Translation of De bello Judaico. *1. Jews — History — Rebellion, 66-73. I. Whiston, William, 1667-1752, tr. II. Farmer, William Reuben, ed. III. Josephus, Flavius, The life of Flavius Josephus. 1970. IV. The life of Flavius Josephus. V. T.*
DS122.8.J73 1970　　933　　70-23319

DS123 – 126.4 70 – 1948

Parkes, James William, 1896-　　　　　　　　III. 3168
Whose land? A history of the peoples of Palestine. New York, Taplinger [1971, c1970] 333 p. maps. 22 cm. "Based on A History of Palestine from 135 A.D. to modern times, 1949." *1. Palestine — History. I. T.*
DS123.P36 1971　　956.94　　70-148829　　ISBN:0800882601

Wirth, Louis, 1897-   III. 3169
The ghetto, by Louis Wirth; illustrations from woodcuts by Todros Geller. Chicago, Ill., University of Chicago Press [1928] xvi, 306 p. illus. 20 cm. (The University of Chicago sociological series) *1. Jews. 2. Jews — Political and social conditions. 3. Jews in Chicago. I. T.*
DS123.W5   29-2559

Baron, Salo Wittmayer, 1895-   III. 3170
The Jewish community: its history and structure to the American Revolution. Westport, Conn., Greenwood Press [1972, c1942] 3 v. 23 cm. Original ed. issued in series: The Morris Loeb series. *1. Jews — Politics and government. 2. Jews — Bibliography. I. T. (S:The Morris Loeb series.)*
DS124.B29 1972   917.3/06/924   74-97269   ISBN:0837132746

Sharf, Andrew.   III. 3171
Byzantine Jewry from Justinian to the Fourth Crusade. New York, Schocken Books [1971] xiv, 239 p. maps. 23 cm. (The Littman Library of Jewish civilization) *1. Jews in the Byzantine Empire — History. I. T.*
DS124.S45 1971   914.95/06/924   74-135519   ISBN:0805233873

Mahler, Raphael, 1899-   III. 3172
A history of modern Jewry. New York, Schocken Books [1971- v. 25 cm. Abridged translation of Divre yeme Yisrael, dorot aḥaronim. *1. Jews — History — 1789-1945. I. T.*
DS125.M322132   909.04/924/07   74-148838   ISBN:0805233989

Sachar, Howard Morley, 1928-   III. 3173
The course of modern Jewish history. [1st ed.] Cleveland, World Pub. Co. [1958] 617 p. maps. 24 cm. *1. Jews — History — 1789-1945. 2. Jews — History — 1945- I. T.*
DS125.S3   296.09   58-6757

Sykes, Christopher, 1907-   III. 3174
Crossroads to Israel. Cleveland, World Pub. Co. [1965] xii, 404 p. illus., maps. 22 cm. *1. Israel — History. 2. Zionism. 3. Palestine — History — 1917-1948. I. T.*
DS125.S86   956.9404   65-23372

Ben-Gurion, David, 1886-   III. 3175
Days of David Ben-Gurion, seen in photographs and with text from his speeches and writings. Edited by Ohad Zmora [and others] Design: Eliezer Weishoff. Introd. by S. Y. Agnon. New York, Grossman, 1967. 157 p. illus., ports. 31 cm. *I. Zmora, Ohad, ed. II. T.*
DS125.3.B37A5 1967   956.94/05/0924   67-15209

Chaim Weizmann,   III. 3176
a biography by several hands. With a preface by David Ben-Gurion. Edited by Meyer W. Weisgal and Joel Carmichael. London, Weidenfeld and Nicolson [c1962] xi, 364 p. illus. 22 cm. *1. Weizmann, Hayyim, Pres. Israel, 1874-1952. I. Weisgal, Meyer Wolfe, 1894- ed. II. Carmichael, Joel, ed.*
DS125.3.W45C5

Hurewitz, Jacob Coleman, 1914-   III. 3177
The struggle for Palestine. [1st ed.] New York, Norton [1950] 404 p. maps. 24 cm. Issued also as thesis, Columbia University, under title: The road to partition. *1. Palestine — History — 1929-1948. I. T.*
DS126.H87   956.9   50-9773

Horowitz, David, 1899-   III. 3178
State in the making; translated from the Hebrew by Julian Meltzer. [1st American ed.] New York, Knopf, 1953. 349 p. 22 cm. *1. Palestine — Politics and government. I. T.*
DS126.4.H6   956.94   52-12197

Sacher, Harry, 1881-   III. 3179
Israel; the establishment of a state. London, G. Weidenfeld & Nicolson [1952] 332 p. illus. 23 cm. *1. Palestine — History — 1929-1948.*
DS126.4.S33   956.94   52-11245

Sherf, Zeev.   III. 3180
Three days [by] Zeev Sharef. Translated by Julian Louis Meltzer from the Hebrew. [1st ed.] Garden City, N.Y., Doubleday, 1962. 298 p. 23 cm. *1. Palestine — History — 1929-1948. 2. Mandates — Palestine. I. T.*
DS126.4.S48153 1962   956.94   62-8911

DS126 – 127   1948 –

Ben-Gurion, David, 1886-   III. 3181
Israel: years of challenge. [1st ed.] New York, Holt, Rinehart and Winston [1963] vi, 240 p. illus., ports., maps. 22 cm. *1. Israel — History. 2. Israel — Social policy. I. T.*
DS126.5.B44   956.94   63-18431

Crossman, Richard Howard Stafford, 1907-   III. 3182
A nation reborn; a personal report on the roles played by Weizmann, Bevin, and Ben-Gurion in the story of Israel. [1st ed.] New York, Atheneum Publishers, 1960. 171 p. 21 cm. *1. Weizmann, Chaim, Pres. Israel, 1874-1952. 2. Bevin, Ernest, 1881-1951. 3. Ben-Gurion, David, 1887- 4. Israel — History. I. T.*
DS126.5.C7   956.94   60-11034

Elon, Amos.   III. 3183
The Israelis: founders and sons. [1st ed.] New York, Holt, Rinehart and Winston [1971] 359 p. 24 cm. *1. National characteristics, Israeli. 2. Jewish-Arab relations. I. T.*
DS126.5.E4195   915.694/03   75-138887   ISBN:0030859670

Peretz, Don, 1922-   III. 3184
Israel and the Palestine Arabs. With a foreword by Roger Baldwin. Washington, Middle East Institute, 1958 [c1956] 264 p. 24 cm. *1. Refugees, Arabic. 2. Arabs in Palestine. 3. Arabs in Israel. I. T.*
DS126.5.P4   956.94   58-2533

Smith, Harvey Henry, 1892-   III. 3185
Area handbook for Israel. Co-authors Harvey H. Smith [and others] [Washington; For sale by the Supt. of Docs., U.S. Govt. Print. Off.] 1970. xvi, 456 p. illus., maps. 24 cm. "DA pam no. 550-25." "Supersedes DA pam 550-25, May 1964." "One of a series of handbooks prepared by Foreign Area Studies (FAS) of the American University." *1. Israel. I. American University, Washington, D.C. Foreign Area Studies. II. T.*
DS126.5.S6   309.1/5694/05   78-607520

Kimche, Jon.   III. 3186
A clash of destinies; the Arab-Jewish War and the founding of the State of Israel, by Jon and David Kimche. New York, Praeger [1960] 287 p. illus. 22 cm. (Books that matter) *1. Israel-Arab War, 1948-1949. I. Kimche, David, joint author. II. T.*
DS126.9.K5   956.94   60-6996

Zurayq, Qusṭanṭin, 1909-   III. 3187
The meaning of the disaster, by Constantine K. Zurayk. Translated from the Arabic by R. Bayly Winder. Beirut, Khayat's College Book Cooperative, 1956. xi, 74 p. 20 cm. *1. Arabs in Palestine. 2. Refugees, Arab. 3. Arab Countries — Politics. I. T.*
DS126.92.Z813   64-36006

Bar-Zohar, Michel.   III. 3188
Embassies in crisis; diplomats and demagogues behind the Six-Day War, by Michael Bar-Zohar. Translated from the French by Monroe Stearns. Englewood Cliffs, N.J., Prentice-Hall [1970] vi, 279 p. 24 cm. *1. Israel-Arab War, 1967- I. T.*
DS127.B34   956   71-102278   ISBN:132745062

DS133 – 135   JEWS OUTSIDE ISRAEL

Neusner, Jacob, 1932-   III. 3189
A history of the Jews in Babylonia. 2nd printing revised. Leiden, E. J. Brill, 1969- v. 24 1/2 cm. (Studia post-Biblica, v. 9) *1. Jews in Babylonia — History. I. T. (S)*
DS135.B2N42   913.35/09/74924   70-468047

Tcherikover, Avigdor, 1895-1958, ed.   III. 3190
Corpus papyrorum Judaicarum, edited by Victor A. Tcheridover, in collaboration with Alexander Fuks. Cambridge, Published for the Magnes Press, Hebrew University [by] Harvard University Press, 1957-64. 3 v. 28 cm. Transcriptions of documents relating to Jews and Judaism in Egypt, with English translations and commentaries. Vol.2 edited by Victor A. Tcherikover and Alexander Fuks; v.3 edited by Victor A. Tcherikover, Alexander Fuks [and] Menahem Stern, with an epigraphical contribution by David M. Lewis. *1. Jews in Egypt — History — Sources. I. Fuks, Alexander, 1917- joint ed. II. Stern, Menahem, joint ed.*
DS135.E4T35   58-864

Richardson, Henry Gerald, 1884-   III. 3191
The English Jewry under Angevin kings. London, Methuen [1960] 313 p. 22 cm. *1. Jews in Gt. Brit. — History. 2. Gt. Brit. — History — Angevin period, 1154-1216. I. T.*
DS135.E5R5   942.031   61-286

Roth, Cecil, 1899-   III. 3192
A history of the Jews in England. 3d ed. Oxford, Clarendon Press, 1964. xiii, 311 p. 23 cm. *1. Jews in Great Britain. I. T.*
DS135.E5R62 1964   301.451   64-6814

Dawidowicz, Lucy S.   III. 3193
The olden tradition; Jewish life and thought in Eastern Europe [by] Lucy S. Dawidowicz. [1st ed.] New York, Holt, Rinehart and Winston [1967] 502 p. maps. 22 cm. *1. Jews in Eastern Europe. I. T.*
DS135.E8D3   914.70974924   66-13203

Hilberg, Raul, 1926-   **III. 3194**
The destruction of the European Jews. Chicago, Quadrangle Books [1961] x, 788 p. maps. 25 cm. *1. Jews in Europe — Persecutions. 2. Genocide — Case studies. 3. Germany — Politics and government — 1933-1945. I. T.*
DS135.E83H5   943.086   61-7931

Reitlinger, Gerald, 1900-   **III. 3195**
The final solution; the attempt to exterminate the Jews of Europe, 1939-1945. [1st American ed.] New York, Beechhurst Press [1953] xii, 622 p. maps. 23 cm. *1. Jews in Europe. 2. Germany — Politics and government — 1933-1945. 3. World War, 1939-1945 — Jews. 4. World War, 1939-1945 — Atrocities. I. T.*
DS135.E83R4 1953   940.5315296   53-13001

323.14
R278

Hertzberg, Arthur.   **III. 3196**
The French Enlightenment and the Jews. New York, Columbia University Press, 1968. viii, 420 p. 24 cm. *1. Jews in France — Political and social conditions — History. 2. Enlightenment. I. T.*
DS135.F82H4   301.45/296/044   68-18996

Byrnes, Robert Francis.   **III. 3197**
Antisemitism in modern France, by Robert F. Byrnes. New York, H. Fertig, 1969- [c1950- v. 24 cm. *1. Antisemitism — France. 2. Dreyfus, Alfred, 1859-1935. I. T.*
DS135.F83B93   301.451/924/044   68-9613

Kisch, Guido, 1889-   **III. 3198**
The Jews in medieval Germany; a study of their legal and social status. 2d ed. New York, Ktav Pub. House, 1970. xxviii, 655 p. 24 cm. *1. Jews — Legal status, laws, etc. — Germany. 2. Jews in Germany — History — 1096-1800. I. T.*
DS135.G31K58x   340   74-86311   ISBN:87068017X

Massing, Paul W.   **III. 3199**
Rehearsal for destruction; a study of political anti-Semitism in imperial Germany, by Paul W. Massing. New York, H. Fertig, 1967 [c1949] xiv, 341 p. 24 cm. *1. Antisemitism — Germany. I. T.*
DS135.G33M35 1967   323.1/19/24043   66-24348

Schorsch, Ismar.   **III. 3200**
Jewish reactions to German anti-Semitism, 1870-1914. New York, Columbia University Press, 1972. vii, 291 p. 23 cm. (Columbia University studies in Jewish history, culture, and institutions, no. 3) Revision of the author's thesis, Columbia. *1. Jews in Germany — History — 1800-1933. 2. Antisemitism — Germany. I. T. (S:Columbia University. Center of Israel and Jewish Studies. Columbia University studies in Jewish history, culture, and institutions, no. 3.)*
DS135.G33S3x (DS102.C56 no. 3)   915.694/008 s (323.1/1924/043)   74-190193   ISBN:0231036434

Roth, Cecil, 1899-   **III. 3201**
The history of the Jews of Italy, by Cecil Roth. Philadelphia, The Jewish Publication Society of America, 5706-1946. xiv p., 1 l., 575 p. plates, ports. 22 cm. Map on lining-papers. *1. Jews in Italy — History.*
DS135.I8R6   46-6577

Leon, Harry Joshua.   **III. 3202**
The Jews of ancient Rome. [1st ed.] Philadelphia, Jewish Publication Society of America, 1960. ix, 378 p. illus. 24 cm. (The Morris Loeb series) *1. Jews in Rome — History. 2. Inscriptions, Jewish. 3. Inscriptions, Greek. 4. Inscriptions, Latin. I. T.*
DS135.I85R64   937   60-9793

Dubnov, Semen Markovich, 1860-1941.   **III. 3203**
History of the Jews in Russia and Poland, from the earliest times until the present day, by S. M. Dubnov; tr. from the Russian by I. Friedlaender. Philadelphia, The Jewish Publication Society of America, 1916-20. 3 v. 20 cm. *1. Jews in Russia. 2. Jews in Poland. I. Friedlaender, Israel, 1876-1920, tr. II. T.*
DS135.R9D8   16-16352

Goldberg, Ben Zion, 1895-   **III. 3204**
The Jewish problem in the Soviet Union: analysis and solution. With a foreword by Daniel Mayer. New York, Crown Publishers [1961] 374 p. illus. 22 cm. *1. Jews in Russia — History — 1917- I. T.*
DS135.R9G46   325.256930947   61-10311

The Jews in Soviet Russia since 1917,   **III. 3205**
edited by Lionel Kochan. London, New York, Published for the Institute of Jewish Affairs [by] Oxford University Press, 1970. ix, 357 p. 23 cm. *1. Jews in Russia — History — 1917- — Collections. I. Kochan, Lionel, ed. II. Institute of Jewish Affairs.*
DS135.R9J47 1970   914.7/09/74924   71-490841   ISBN:192151738

Gilboa, Jehoshua A.   **III. 3206**
The black years of Soviet Jewry, 1939-1953 [by] Yehoshua A. Gilboa. Translated from the Hebrew by Yosef Shachter and Dov Ben-Abba. [1st ed.] Boston, Little, Brown [1971] x, 418 p. 25 cm. *1. Jews in Russia — History — 1917. I. T.*
DS135.R92G5413   914.7/06/924   70-143716

Baer, Yitzhak, Fritz, 1888-   **III. 3207**
A history of the Jews in Christian Spain. Translated from the Hebrew by Louis Schoffman. [1st ed.] Philadelphia, Jewish Publication Society of America, 1961-66. 2 v. map (on lining papers of v.2) 22 cm. "May be regarded as a translation of the second [Hebrew] edition. Here and there ... the text has been slightly abridged ... Elsewhere, ... principally in the notes, the translation contains material not found in either of the Hebrew editions." *1. Jews in Spain — History.*
DS135.S7B343   946.009174924   61-16852

Caro Baroja, Julio.   **III. 3208**
Los judíos en la España moderna y contemporánea. [Madrid] Ediciones Arión [1962, c1961] 3 v. illus., ports., maps, facsims. 24 cm. *1. Jews in Spain.*
DS135.S7C28   63-54304

Neuman, Abraham Aaron, 1890-   **III. 3209**
The Jews in Spain, their social, political and cultural life during the middle ages, by Abraham A. Neuman. Philadelphia, The Jewish Publication Society of America, 1942- 2 v. fronts., plates, maps, facsims. 23 cm. (The Morris Loeb series) *1. Jews in Spain. I. Jewish publication society of America. II. T.*
DS135.S7N4   296.0946   42-21783

Yerushalmi, Yosef Hayim, 1932-   **III. 3210**
From Spanish court to Italian ghetto; Isaac Cardoso; a study in seventeenth-century marranism and Jewish apologetics. New York, Columbia University Press, 1971. xx, 524 p. facsims. 24 cm. (Columbia University studies in Jewish history, culture, and institutions, no. 1) Based on the author's thesis, Columbia University, 1966. *1. Cardoso, Isaac, 1603 or 4-1683. 2. Maranos. I. T. (S:Columbia University. Center of Israel and Jewish Studies. Columbia University studies in Jewish history, culture, and institutions, no. 1.)*
DS135.S7Y4x (DS102.C56 no. 1)   914.6/06/9240924 (B)   76-109544   ISBN:0231032862

DS141 – 151 ANTISEMITISM. ZIONISM

Glock, Charles Y.   **III. 3211**
Christian beliefs and anti-Semitism [by] Charles Y. Glock and Rodney Stark. [1st ed.] New York, Harper & Row [1966] xxi, 266, 24 p. facsims., form. 24 cm. "Volume one in a series based on the University of California Five-year study of anti-Semitism in the United States, being conducted by the Survey Research Center under a grant from the Anti-defamation League of B'nai Brith." *1. Antisemitism and Christianity. 2. Antisemitism — United States. I. Stark, Rodney, joint author. II. California. University. Survey Research Center. III. T.*
DS145.G49   261.2   65-21002

Poliakov, Léon, 1910-   **III. 3212**
The history of anti-Semitism. Translated from the French by Richard Howard. New York, Vanguard Press [1965- v. 24 cm. *1. Antisemitism. I. T.*
DS145.P4613   301.451924   65-10228

Lendvai, Paul, 1929-   **III. 3213**
Anti-Semitism without Jews; Communist Eastern Europe. [1st ed.] Garden City, N.Y., Doubleday [1971] vi, 393 p. 22 cm. *1. Antisemitism — Europe, Eastern. 2. Jews in Eastern Europe. I. T.*
DS146.E8L35   914.7/06/924   70-131089

Mosse, George Lachmann.   **III. 3214**
Germans and Jews; the Right, the Left, and the search for a "Third Force" in pre-Nazi Germany [by] George L. Mosse. [1st ed.] New York, H. Fertig, 1970. 260 p. 21 cm. *1. Antisemitism — Germany. 2. Jews in Germany — Intellectual life. 3. Germany — Politics and government — 20th century. I. T.*
DS146.G4M66   301.451/924/043   68-9631

Pulzer, Peter G. J.   **III. 3215**
The rise of political anti-Semitism in Germany and Austria [by] P. G. J. Pulzer. New York, Wiley [1964] xiv, 364 p. illus., ports. 21 cm. (New dimensions in history: essays in comparative history) Based on the author's thesis, Cambridge, 1960. *1. Antisemitism — Germany. 2. Antisemitism — Austria. I. T. (S)*
DS146.G4P8   323.143   64-23858

P968

Selznick, Gertrude Jaeger.   **III. 3216**
The tenacity of prejudice; anti-Semitism in contemporary America [by] Gertrude J. Selznick and Stephen Steinberg. [1st ed.] New York, Harper & Row [1969] xxi, 248 p. forms. 25 cm. (Patterns of American prejudice series, 4) *1. Antisemitism — U.S. I. Steinberg, Stephen, joint author. II. T. (S)*
DS146.U6S4 1969   301.451/924/073   69-15261

Laqueur, Walter Ze'ev, 1921-   III. 3217
A history of Zionism [by] Walter Laqueur. London, Weidenfeld and Nicolson [1972] xvi, 640 p. illus. 24 cm. *1. Zionism — History. I. T.*
DS149.L315   956.94/001   72-188323   ISBN:0297994123

Samuel, Maurice, 1895-   III. 3218
Harvest in the desert [by] Maurice Samuel. Philadelphia, The Jewish Publication Society of America, 1944. 316 p. 22 cm. *1. Zionism — History. I. Jewish Publication Society of America. II. T.*
DS149.S47   44-5171

DS153 – 154   Jordan

Patai, Raphael, 1910-   III. 3219
The Kingdom of Jordan. Princeton, Princeton University Press, 1958. ix, 315 p. plates, ports., maps, tables. 23 cm. *1. Jordan.*
DS153.P32   956.95*   58-6107

Systems Research Corporation.   III. 3220
Area handbook for the Hashemit Kingdom of Jordan. Co-authors: Howard C. Reese [and others] Prepared for the American University [Foreign Area Studies] by Systems Research Corp. Washington, For sale by the Supt. of Docs., U.S. Govt. Print. Off., 1969. xvi, 370 p. maps. 24 cm. "DA pam 550-34." *1. Jordan. I. American University, Washington, D.C. Foreign Area Studies. II. Reese, Howard C. III. T.*
DS153.S95   309.1/5695   79-606088

Shwadran, Benjamin.   III. 3221
Jordan, a state of tension. New York, Council for Middle Eastern Affairs Press, 1959. 436 p. illus. 21 cm. *1. Jordan — Politics and government. 2. Jordan — History.*
DS154.15.S4   956.95   59-11043

'Abdallāh, King of Jordan, 1882-1951.   III. 3222
Memoirs of King Abdullah of Transjordan. [New York] Philosophical Library [1950] 278 p. ports. 21 cm. Edited by Philip P. Graves; translated by G. Khuri. *1. Arabia — History — Sources. 2. Jordan — History — Sources.*
DS154.52.A3A27 1950   956.95   51-103

Glubb, John Bagot, Sir, 1897-   III. 3223
A soldier with the Arabs. New York, Harper [c1957] 458 p. illus. 22 cm. "Personal narrative." *1. Jordan — History. I. T.*
DS154.52.G5A3   956.95   57-11782

DS155 – 199   Asia Minor. Armenia

Woolley, Charles Leonard, Sir, 1880-1960.   III. 3224
A forgotten kingdom, being a record of the results obtained from the excavation of two mounds, Atchana and Al Mina, in the Turkish Hatay, by C. Leonard Woolley. New York, Norton [1968] 191 p. illus., maps. 20 cm. (The Norton library) *1. Alalakh. 2. Near East — Civilization. I. T.*
DS156.A47W6 1968   913.39/35   68-3240

Bean, George Ewart.   III. 3225
Aegean Turkey; an archaeological guide [by] George E. Bean. New York, F. A. Praeger [1966] 288 p. illus., maps (1 fold.), plans, plates. 23 cm. *1. Ionia, Asia Minor. I. T.*
DS156.I6B4 1966a   914.96104103   66-22350

Hovannisian, Richard G.   III. 3226
The Republic of Armenia [by] Richard G. Hovannisian. Berkeley, University of California Press, 1971- v. illus. 25 cm. *1. Armenia — History — 1917-1921. I. T.*
DS195.5.H56   956.6/2   72-129613   ISBN:0520018052

DS201 – 248   Arabian Peninsula. Saudi Arabia

Walpole, Norman C.   III. 3227
Area handbook for Saudi Arabia. Co-authors: Norman C. Walpole [and others. Washington; For sale by the Supt. of Docs., U.S. Govt. Print. Off.] 1971. xlviii, 373 p. maps. 24 cm. "DA pam 550-51." "One of a series of handbooks prepared by Foreign Area Studies (FAS) of the American University." *1. Saudi Arabia. I. American University, Washington, D.C. Foreign Area Studies. II. T.*
DS204.W34 1971   309.1/53/805   74-614218

Hansen, Thorkild, 1927-   III. 3228
Arabia Felix, the Danish expedition of 1761-1767. Translated by James and Kathleen McFarlane. [1st ed.] New York, Harper & Row [1964] 381 p. illus., charts, facsims., plans. 25 cm.
DS206.H313   915.3   63-20289

Burton, Richard Francis, Sir, 1821-1890.   III. 3229
Narrative of a pilgrimage to El-Medinah and Meccah. Introduction by J. M. Scott. [London] Distributed by Heron Books [1969?] 517 p. illus., plates, port. 21 cm. First published in 1854 under title: Personal narrative of a pilgrimage to El-Medinah and Meccah. *1. Arabia — Description and travel. 2. Mecca — Description. 3. Medina — Description. 4. Pilgrims and pilgrimages, Muslim — Mecca. I. T.*
DS207.B964 1969   915.3/8   77-518026

Doughty, Charles Montagu, 1843-1926.   III. 3230
Travels in Arabia Deserta; with an introd. by T. E. Lawrence. New and definitive ed. New York, Random House [1936] 2 v. in 1. illus., plates, port., fold. map (in pocket) 24 cm. *1. Arabia — Description and travel. 2. Arabia — Social life and customs.*
DS207.D73x   915.3   A48-46

Philby, Harry St. John Bridger, 1885-   III. 3231
Sheba's daughters; being a record of travel in Southern Arabia, by H. St. J. B. Philby, with an appendix on the rock inscriptions by A. F. L. Beeston. 47 plates, folding map, and rock pictures in the text. London, Methuen [1939] xix, 485 p. front., illus., plates (1 double) ports., fold. map. 24 cm. "First published in 1939." *1. Arabia — Description and travel. 2. Inscriptions, South Arabian. I. Beeston, Alfred Felix Landon. II. T.*
DS207.P527   915.3   40-33626

Sanger, Richard Harlakenden, 1905-   III. 3232
The Arabian Peninsula. Freeport, N.Y., Books for Libraries Press [1970, c1954] xiv, 295 p. illus., maps, ports. 24 cm. *1. — Arabia Description and travel. I. T.*
DS207.S3 1970   915.3/03/5   76-117891   ISBN:836953444

Thesiger, Wilfred, 1910-   III. 3233
Arabian sands. [1st ed.] New York, Dutton, 1959. 326 p. illus. 23 cm. *1. Arabia — Description and travel. I. T.*
DS208.T48   915.3   59-5809

Faris, Nabih Amin, 1906- ed.   III. 3234
The Arab heritage, by Philip K. Hitti, Giorgio Levi della Vida, Julian Obermann ... [and others] Ed. by Nabih Amin Faris. Princeton, N.J., Princeton University Press, 1944. x, 279 p. plates. 23 cm. A popular adaptation of lectures delivered at the third Summer seminar in Arabic and Islamic studies at Princeton university, 1941. *1. Civilization, Arabic. I. Hitti, Philip Khûri, 1886- II. T.*
DS215.F3   915.3   A44-1926

DS221 – 248   HISTORY

Gabrieli, Francesco, 1904-   III. 3235
The Arabs, a compact history. Translated by Salvator Attanasio. New York, Hawthorn Books [1963] viii, 215 p. illus., group ports. 22 cm. (Peoples of the world: past and present) *1. Arabs — History.*
DS223.G313   953   62-15687

Glubb, John Bagot, Sir, 1897-   III. 3236
The Empire of the Arabs [by] Sir John Glubb. [1st American ed.] Englewood Cliffs, N.J., Prentice-Hall [1965, c1963] 384 p. geneal. tables, maps. 23 cm. *1. Arab countries — History. I. T.*
DS223.G55 1965   953.02   65-22941

Hitti, Philip Khuri, 1886- III. 3237
The Arabs; a short history [by] Philip K. Hitti. 5th ed. London, Melbourne,[etc.] Macmillan, 1968. viii, 212 p. 8 maps. 21 cm. (Papermac 234) *1. Arabs — History. 2. Civilization, Arab.*
DS223.H48 1968b   910.09/174/927   70-401353

Lane-Poole, Stanley, 1854-1931. III. 3238
The Mohammadan dynasties: chronological and genealogical tables with historical introductions. New York, F. Ungar Pub. Co. [1965] xxviii, 361 p. 21 cm. *1. Islamic countries — History — Chronology. 2. Islamic countries — Kings and rulers — General. I. T.*
DS223.L3 1965   956   64-21615

Lewis, Bernard. III. 3239
The Arabs in history. 4th ed. London, Hutchinson, 1966. 200 p. maps. 22 cm. (Hutchinson university library: History) *1. Arabia — History. 2. Arabs. 3. Islamic Empire — History. I. T.*
DS223.L4 1966   910.909174927   66-75479

Nutting, Anthony. III. 3240
The Arabs; a narrative history from Mohammed to the present. [1st ed.] New York, C. N. Potter [1964] 424 p. geneal. tables, maps. 24 cm. *1. Arabs. 2. Arabia — History.*
DS223.N8   953   63-19899

Glubb, John Bagot, Sir, 1897- III. 3241
The great Arab conquests. [1st American ed.] Englewood Cliffs, N.J., Prentice-Hall [1964, c1963] 384 p. maps, geneal. table. 24 cm. *1. Arabs — History. I. T.*
DS232.G55 1964   953   64-12094

Bishai, Wilson B., 1923- III. 3242
Islamic history of the Middle East; backgrounds, development, and fall of the Arab Empire [by] Wilson B. Bishai. Boston, Allyn and Bacon [1968] xvi, 399 p. maps. 24 cm. *1. Islamic Empire. I. T.*
DS236.B5   915.6/03/1   68-12977

Muir, William, Sir, 1819-1905. III. 3243
The caliphate: its rise, decline, and fall. With a new introd. by Zeine N. Zeine. Beirut, Khayats, 1963. xvi, 628 p. 3 fold. maps. 23 cm. (Khayats oriental reprints no. 5) "Reprinted from the edition of 1898." *1. Caliphs. 2. Islamic countries — History. I. T.*
DS236.M9x   Ne65-2182

Wellhausen, Julius, 1844-1918. III. 3244
The Arab kingdom and its fall, by J. Wellhausen; translated by Margaret Graham Weir. [Calcutta] University of Calcutta, 1927. xv, 592 p. 22 cm. *1. Arabia — History. I. Weir, Margaret Graham, tr. II. Calcutta. University. III. T.*
DS236.W452   953   44-24942

Buckler, Francis William, 1891- III. 3245
Harunu'l-Rashid and Charles the Great [by] F. W. Buckler. Cambridge, Mass., The Mediaeval Academy of America, 1931. vii, 64 p. 26 cm. (Monographs of the Mediaeval academy of America, no. 2. "Academy publications, no. 7.") Appendices: I. Charles the Great and Harun ar-Rashid, by W. W. Barthold. — II. The chronology of Cosmas, patriarch of Alexandria. — III. Propter elephantem bestiam. — IV. An extract from "The pallium of Saint Cuthbert." *1. Hārūn al-Rashīd, caliph, 763 (ca.)-809. 2. Charlemagne, 742-814. 3. Islamic countries — Politics. 4. France — Foreign relations — Islamic countries.*
DS238.H3B8   953   31-11708

Twitchell, Karl Saben, 1885- III. 3246
Saudi Arabia, with an account of the development of its natural resources. With the collaboration of Edward J. Jurji and R. Bayly Winder. 3d ed. Princeton, Princeton University Press, 1958. 281 p. illus. 22 cm. *1. Saudi Arabia.*
DS244.T9 1958   915.3   58-7133

Philby, Harry St. John Bridger, 1885-1960. III. 3247
Sa'udi Arabia. New York, Arno Press, 1972. xix, 393 p. illus. 23 cm. (World affairs: national and international viewpoints) Reprint of the 1955 ed., issued in series: Nations of the modern world. *1. Saudi Arabia — History. 2. Ibn Sa'ūd, King of Saudi Arabia, 1880-1953. I. T. (S) (S:Nations of the modern world.)*
DS244.53.P48 1972   953.8   72-4289   ISBN:0405045816

Little, Tom. III. 3248
South Arabia; arena of conflict. New York, Praeger [1968] xi, 196 p. maps. 22 cm. *1. Arabia, Southern — Politics and government. 2. Aden — History. I. T.*
DS247.A14L5 1968b   953/.32   68-19644

Stanford Research Institute. III. 3249
Area handbook for the Peripheral States of the Arabian Peninsula. Prepared for the American University. [Washington; For sale by the Supt. of Docs., U.S. Govt. Print. Off.] 1971. xiv, 201 p. maps. 24 cm. "DA pam no. 550-92." "One of a series of handbooks prepared under the auspices of Foreign Area Studies (FAS) of the American University." *1. Arabia, Southern. 2. Persian Gulf States. I. American University, Washington, D.C. Foreign Area Studies. II. T.*
DS247.A14S78   915.36   76-608679

Rihani, Ameen Fares, 1876-1940. III. 3250
Maker of modern Arabia, by Ameen Rihani. Boston, Houghton, Mifflin, 1928. xvii, 370 p. front., illus. (incl. maps) plates, ports. 23 cm. London edition, 1928, has title: Ibn Sa'oud of Arabia, his people and his land. *1. Ibn Sa'ūd, king of Saudi Arabia, 1880- 2. Nejd — Description and travel. I. T.*
DS247.N4R5   28-26638

Hawley, Donald. III. 3251
The Trucial States [with a foreword by Sir William Luce]. London, Allen & Unwin, 1970. 3-379 p., 4 plates. illus., geneal. tables, maps. 23 cm. Map on lining paper. *1. Trucial States — History. I. T.*
DS247.T87H38   953/.5   71-574568   ISBN:0049530054

DS251 – 318   Iran (Persia)

Elwell-Sutton, Laurence Paul. III. 3252
A guide to Iranian area study. Ann Arbor, Published for the American Council of Learned Societies by J. W. Edwards, 1952. 235 p. 22 cm. *1. Iran. 2. Iran — History — Chronology. 3. Iran — Bibliography.*
DS254.5.E4   915.5   52-4643

Frye, Richard Nelson, 1920- III. 3253
Iran. New York, Holt [1953] 126 p. illus. 20 cm. *1. Iran.*
DS254.5.F7   955   52-13895

Smith, Harvey Henry, 1892- III. 3254
Area handbook for Iran. Co-authors: Harvey H. Smith [and others. Washington; For sale by the Supt. of Docs., U.S. Govt. Print. Off.] 1971. xxii, 653 p. maps. 25 cm. "DA pam no. 550-68." "One of a series of handbooks prepared by Foreign Area Studies (FAS) of the American University." Revision of 1964 ed. issued by the Foreign Areas Studies Division of American University. *1. Iran. I. American University, Washington, D.C. Foreign Area Studies. II. American University, Washington, D.C. Foreign Areas Studies Division. Area handbook for Iran. III. T.*
DS254.5.S6 1971   915.5/03/5   72-608678

Browne, Edward Granville, 1862-1926. III. 3255
A year amongst the Persians; impressions as to the life, character, & thought of the people of Persia, received during twelve months' residence in that country in the years 1887-1888. With a memoir by Sir E. Denison Ross and a foreword by Sir Ellis H. Minns. [3d ed.] London, A. and C. Black, 1950. xxii, 650 p. port., fold. map. 23 cm. *1. Iran — Description and travel.*
DS258.B88 1950   915.5   51-19601

Arberry, Arthur John, 1905- ed. III. 3256
The legacy of Persia. Oxford, Clarendon Press, 1953. xvi, 421 p. illus. 19 cm. (The Legacy series) *1. Iran — Civilization. I. T.*
DS266.A7   915.5   53-2314

Armajani, Yahya. III. 3257
Iran. Englewood Cliffs, N.J., Prentice-Hall [1972] viii, 182 p. map. 21 cm. (The Modern nations in historical perspective. A Spectrum book) *1. Iran — History. I. T.*
DS272.A9   955   70-168738   ISBN:0135061393 0135061210 (pbk)

Bausani, Alessandro, 1921- III. 3258
The Persians, from the earliest days to the twentieth century. Translated from the Italian by J. B. Donne. New York, St. Martin's Press [1971] 204 p. illus. 23 cm. Translation of I Persiani. *1. Iran — History. I. T.*
DS272.B3813 1971b   915.5/03   71-149313

The Cambridge history of Iran. III. 3259
Cambridge, University Press, 1968. v. illus., maps, plates. 24 cm. *1. Iran — History. I. Fisher, William Bayne, ed. II. Boyd, John Andrew, ed.*
DS272.C34   955   67-12845   ISBN:0521060351 (v. 1)

Huart, Clément Imbault, 1854-1926. III. 3260
Ancient Persia and Iranian civilization, by Clément Huart. Translated by M. R. Dobie. London, K. Paul, Trench, Trubner; New York, Knopf, 1927. xix, 249 p. illus., IV pl., double map. 25 cm. (The history of civilization. [Pre-history and antiquity]) *1. Persia — History — Ancient to A.D. 640. 2. Persia — Civilization. I. Dobie, Marryat Ross, 1888- tr. II. T.*
DS272.H8   27-13414

Sykes, Percy Molesworth, Sir, 1867-1945. III. 3261
A history of Persia, by Brigadier-General Sir Percy Sykes. 3d ed., with supplementary essay. London, Macmillan, 1930. 2 v. fronts., illus. (incl.

facsims.) plates, ports., fold. maps (1 in pocket) 23 cm. *1. Iran — History.*
DS272.S8 1930   955 (935.5)   31-9610

Wilber, Donald Newton. III. 3262
Iran, past and present. [5th ed.] Princeton, N.J., Princeton University Press, 1963. vii, 312 p. illus., port., maps. 23 cm. *1. Iran.*
DS272.W49 1963   63-15832

Frye, Richard Nelson, 1920- III. 3263
The heritage of Persia. [1st ed.] Cleveland, World Pub. Co. [1963] 301 p. illus. 25 cm. (The World histories of civilization) *1. Iran — History — Ancient to 640 A.D. I. T.*
DS275.F7   935   62-15708

Ghirshman, Roman. III. 3264
Iran from the earliest times to the Islamic conquest. [Harmondsworth, Middlesex] Penguin Books [1954] 368 p. illus., maps. 18 cm. (Pelican archaeology series.) *1. Iran — History — Ancient to 640 A.D. I. T.*
DS275.G5x   A55-8406

Olmstead, Albert Ten Eyck, 1880-1945. III. 3265
History of the Persian Empire, Achaemenid period. Chicago, University of Chicago Press [1948] xix, 576 p. plates, maps, plan. 25 cm. *1. Persia — History — Ancient to 640 A.D. I. T.*
DS281.O4   935   48-7317

Avery, Peter. III. 3266
Modern Iran. New York, F. A. Praeger [1965] xvi, 527 p. fold. map. 23 cm. (Nations of the modern world) *1. Iran — History — 19th century. 2. Iran — History — 1909- I. T.*
DS307.A95   955.05   65-14176

Browne, Edward Granville, 1862-1926. III. 3267
The Persian revolution of 1905-1909. New York, Barnes & Noble [1966] xxvi, 470 p. facsims., maps, plates, ports. 23 cm. Reprint of a work first published in 1910. *1. Iran — History — 1905-1911. I. T.*
DS313.B7 1966   955.05   66-3160

Upton, Joseph M. III. 3268
The history of modern Iran; an interpretation. Cambridge, Distributed for the Center for Middle Eastern Studies of Harvard University by Harvard University Press, 1960. 163 p. illus. 21 cm. (Harvard Middle Eastern monographs, 2) *1. Iran — History — 1909- I. T:Modern Iran.*
DS315.U75   955.05   60-7207

Banani, Amin. III. 3269
The modernization of Iran, 1921-1941. Stanford, Stanford University Press, 1961. 191 p. illus. 23 cm. *1. Iran — History — 1909- I. T.*
DS317.B3   955.05   61-5504

Marlowe, John. III. 3270
Iran, A short political guide. New York, Praeger [1963] 144 p. map. 23 cm. (The Pall Mall series of short political guides, 5. Books that matter.) *1. Iran — History — 1909-*
DS317.M3   955.05   63-13660

Binder, Leonard. III. 3271
Iran; political development in a changing society. Berkeley, University of California Press, 1962. xii, 362 p. 24 cm. *1. Iran — Politics and government — 1945-*
DS318.B5   955.05   62-14944

Iran faces the seventies. III. 3272
Edited by Ehsan Yar-Shater. Foreword by John S. Badeau. New York, Praeger Publishers [1971] xx, 391 p. 25 cm. (Modern Middle East series of the Middle East Institute, Columbia University no. 4. Praeger special studies in international economics and development) Papers presented at a conference held in Nov. 1968 at Columbia University. *1. Iran — Addresses, essays, lectures. I. Yar-Shater, Ehsan, ed. (S:Modern Middle East series, no. 4.)*
DS318.I7   915.5/03/5   70-158106

Lenczowski, George. III. 3273
Russia and the West in Iran, 1918-1948; a study in big-power rivalry. New York, Greenwood Press, 1968 [c1949] xv, 383 p. illus., maps (1 fold.), ports. 24 cm. *1. Iran — History — 1909- 2. Iran — Foreign relations. I. T.*
DS318.L46 1968   955.05   68-23307

Mohammed Reza Pahlavi, Shah of Iran, 1919- III. 3274
Mission for my country. [1st ed.] New York, McGraw-Hill [1961, c1960] 336 p. illus. 24 cm. *1. Iran — Politics and government — 1945- I. T.*
DS318.M6 1961   955.05   61-7241

DS326   Persian Gulf

Hay, Rupert, Sir, 1893- III. 3275
The Persian Gulf States. With a foreword by E. M. Eller. Washington, Middle East Institute, 1959. 160 p. illus. 24 cm. *1. Persian Gulf States.*
DS326.H35   915.383   59-4460

Wellhausen, Julius, 1844-1918. III. 3276
The Arab kingdom and its fall, by J. Wellhausen. Translated by Margaret Graham Weir. Beirut, Khayats, 1963. xvii, 592 p. 23 cm. (Khayats oriental reprints, no. 6) Originally published in German in 1902. "Reprinted from the edition of 1927." *1. Arabia — History. I. T.*
DS326.Wx   65-7745

Wilson, Arnold Talbot, Sir, 1884-1940. III. 3277
The Persian Gulf; an historical sketch from the earliest times to the beginning of the twentieth century. With a foreword by L. S. Amery. London, Allen & Unwin [1954] xi, 327 p. port., fold. col. map. 23 cm. *1. Persian Gulf. 2. Asia, Western — History.*
DS326.W5 1954   55-30846

DS329   Parthia

Colledge, Malcolm A. R. III. 3278
The Parthians [by] Malcolm A. R. Colledge. New York, Praeger [1967] 243 p. illus., maps. 21 cm. (Ancient peoples and places, 59) *1. Parthia. I. T.*
DS329.P2C6 1967   935/.06   67-28295

DS335 – 498   SOUTH ASIA

Palmer, Norman Dunbar. III. 3279
South Asia and United States policy [by] Norman D. Palmer. Boston, Houghton Mifflin [1966] x, 332 p. map. 24 cm. *1. South Asia — Foreign relations — United States. 2. United States — Foreign relations — South Asia. I. T.*
DS335.P28   327.54073   66-3463

Tinker, Hugh. III. 3280
South Asia; a short story. New York, Praeger [1966] 287 p. illus., maps, ports. 21 cm. *1. South Asia — History. I. T.*
DS335.T55   950   66-17368

Weiner, Myron. III. 3281
Political change in South Asia. [1st ed.] Calcutta, Firma K. L. Mukhopadhyay, 1963. viii, 285 p. tables. 23 cm. *1. South Asia — Politics. I. T.*
DS335.W4   Sa63-4765

DS350 – 375   Afghanistan

Humlum, Johannes, 1911- III. 3282
La géographie de l'Afghanistan; étude d'un pays aride. Avec des chapitres de M. Køie & K. Ferdinand. [Éd. A] Copenhague, Gyldendal, 1959. 421 p. illus., maps. (1 fold. col. in portfolio) 31 cm. (Scandinavian university books) *1. Afghanistan — Description and travel.*
DS352.H79   60-25143

Smith, Harvey Henry, 1892- III. 3283
Area handbook for Afghanistan. Co-authors: Harvey H. Smith [and others] Washington, For sale by the Supt. of Docs., U.S. Govt. Print. Off., 1969. xiv, 435 p. 24 cm. "DA pam no. 550-65." "Revision of the second edition of the

1959 Area handbook for Afghanistan, which was prepared ... by the Foreign Area Studies Division, Special Operations Research Office, the American University." *1. Afghanistan. I. American University, Washington, D.C. Foreign Area Studies. II. American University, Washington, D.C. Foreign Areas Studies Division. Area handbook for Afghanistan. III. T.*
DS352.S55   915.81   79-601329

Fletcher, Arnold.   **III. 3284**
Afghanistan, highway of conquest. Ithaca, N. Y., Cornell University Press [1965] vii, 325 p. illus., ports. 24 cm. *1. Afghanistan — History. I. T.*
DS356.F57   958.1   65-17709

Fraser-Tytler, William Kerr, Sir, 1886-   **III. 3285**
Afghanistan: a study of political developments in central and southern Asia, by W. K. Fraser-Tytler. 3rd ed., revised by M. C. Gillett. London, New York [etc.] Oxford U.P., 1967. xvi, 362 p. front., plates, maps, diagrs. 22 1/2 cm. *1. Afghanistan — History. 2. Eastern question (Central Asia) I. Gillett, Michael Cavenagh, Sir, 1907- II. T.*
DS356.F7 1967   958.1   67-88066

Wilber, Donald Newton.   **III. 3286**
Afghanistan: its people, its society, its culture. In collaboration with Elizabeth E. Bacon [and others] New Haven, HRAF Press [1962] 320 p. illus. 22 cm. (Survey of world cultures [11]) *1. Afghanistan.*
DS356.W5 1962   915.81   62-18167

Gregorian, Vartan.   **III. 3287**
The emergence of modern Afghanistan; politics of reform and modernization, 1880-1946. Stanford, Calif., Stanford University Press, 1969. viii, 586 p. illus., maps, ports. 25 cm. *1. Afghanistan — History. I. T.*
DS361.G68   958.1   69-13178   ISBN:804707065

Griffiths, John Charles.   **III. 3288**
Afghanistan [by] John C. Griffiths. With a historical note by Sir Olaf Caroe. New York, Praeger [1967] viii, 179 p. maps. 23 cm. *1. Afghanistan — Politics and government.*
DS361.G7   67-19582

Seaman, Lewis Charles Bernard.   **III. 3289**
From Vienna to Versailles. New York, Harper & Row [1963] viii, 216 p. maps. 22 cm. (Harper Colophon books. CN8) *1. Europe — Politics — 1815-1871. 2. Europe — Politics — 1871-1918. I. T.*
DS363.54.Sx

Newell, Richard S., 1933-   **III. 3290**
The politics of Afghanistan [by] Richard S. Newell. Ithaca [N.Y.] Cornell University Press [1972] xiv, 236 p. 21 cm. (South Asian political systems) *1. Afghanistan — Politics and government. 2. Afghanistan — Economic conditions. I. T. (S)*
DS369.4.N44   320.9/581/04   78-176487   ISBN:0801406889

DS375 – 393 Pakistan. Bangladesh

Nyrop, Richard F.   **III. 3291**
Area handbook for Pakistan. Co-authors: Richard F. Nyrop [and others]. Washington; For sale by the Supt. of Docs., U.S. Govt. Print. Off.] 1971. xvi, 691 p. illus., maps. 24 cm. "DA pam 550-48." "One of a series of handbooks prepared by Foreign Area Studies (FAS) of the American University." 1965 ed. issued by Foreign Areas Studies Division of American University. *1. Pakistan. I. American University, Washington, D.C. Foreign Area Studies. II. American University, Washington, D.C. Foreign Areas Studies Division. Area handbook for Pakistan. III. T.*
DS377.N97   309.1/549   79-608677

Ikram, Sheikh Mohamad, 1908- ed.   **III. 3292**
The cultural heritage of Pakistan, edited by S. M. Ikram and Percival Spear. [Karachi, New York] Oxford University Press [1955] 204 p. illus. 21 cm. *1. Pakistan — Civilization. I. Spear, Thomas George Percival, joint ed. II. T.*
DS379.I39   56-13679

Wilber, Donald Newton.   **III. 3293**
Pakistan, its people, its society, its culture [by] Donald N. Wilber, in collaboration with Donald Atwell [and others] New Haven, HRAF Press [1964] 487 p. illus., maps. 22 cm. (Survey of world cultures [13]) *1. Pakistan. I. Atwell, Donald. II. T. (S)*
DS379.W5   915.491   64-8647

Feldman, Herbert.   **III. 3294**
From crisis to crisis: Pakistan 1962-1969. London, Oxford University Press, 1972. xvi, 340 p. 23 cm. Sequel to the author's Revolution in Pakistan. *1. Pakistan — Politics and government. I. T.*
DS384.F36   320.9/549/04   72-189488   ISBN:0192151924

Wilcox, Wayne Ayres.   **III. 3295**
Pakistan; the consolidation of a nation. New York, Columbia University Press, 1963. 276 p. illus. 23 cm. *1. Pakistan — Politics and government.*
DS384.W5   954.91   63-9873

Ayub Khan, Mohammad, Pres. Pakistan, 1907-   **III. 3296**
Friends not masters, a political autobiography. New York, Oxford University Press, 1967. xiv, 275 p. illus., maps, ports. 24 cm. *1. Pakistan — Politics and government. I. T.*
DS385.A9A3   954.9/04/0924 (B)   67-25583

Nicholas, Marta R.   **III. 3297**
Bangladesh: the birth of a nation; a handbook of background information and documentary sources. Compiled by Marta Nicholas and Philip Oldenburg. (With contributions from Shamsul Bari [and others.] Madras, M. Seshachalam, 1972. xii, 156 p. illus. 22 cm. *1. Bangladesh. I. Oldenburg, Philip, joint author. II. Bari, Shamsul.*
DS393.4.N52   915.49/2/034   73-929521   ISBN:0882532014

DS401 – 498 India

Garrett, John, fl. 1845-1873.   **III. 3298**
A classical dictionary of India. Graz, Akademische Druck- u. Verlagsanstalt, 1971. x, 793, 160 p. 20 cm. Reprint of the Madras, 1871 ed. Includes reprint of the supplement, published in Madras, 1873. *1. India — Dictionaries and encyclopedias. 2. Mythology, Indic — Dictionaries. I. T.*
DS405.G3 1971   913.3/4/003   72-176849

Lamb, Beatrice (Pitney) 1904-   **III. 3299**
India: a world in transition. Rev. ed. New York, F. A. Praeger [1966] xi, 382 p. fold. map. 21 cm. (Praeger paperbacks, P116) *1. India. I. T.*
DS407.L28 1966   915.4   66-14163

Mehta, Ved Parkash.   **III. 3300**
Portrait of India, by Ved Mehta. New York, Farrar, Straus and Giroux [1970] xi, 544 p. map (on lining paper) 24 cm. *1. India. I. T.*
DS407.M4 1970   915.4/03   76-97615

Moreland, William Harrison, 1868-1938.   **III. 3301**
A short history of India, by W. H. Moreland and Atul Chandra Chatterjee. 4th ed. London, New York, Longmans, Green [1957] xii, 594 p. maps (1 col.) 23 cm. *1. India — History. I. Chatterjee, Atul Chandra, Sir, 1874-1955, joint author.*
DS407.M7 1957   A59-5016

Shinn, Rinn-Sup.   **III. 3302**
Area handbook for India. Co-authors: Rinn-Sup Shinn [and others]. Washington; For sale by the Supt. of Docs., U.S. Govt. Print. Off.] 1970. xx, 791 p. illus., maps. 24 cm. "DA pam 550-21." "One of a series of handbooks prepared by Foreign Area Studies (FAS) of the American University." A revision of the 1964 ed. prepared by Foreign Areas Studies Division, American University, Washington, D.C." *1. India. I. American University, Washington, D.C. Foreign Area Studies. II. American University, Washington, D.C. Foreign Areas Studies Division. Area handbook for India. III. T.*
DS407.S46 1970   915.4/03/4   76-608601

Spate, Oskar Hermann Khristian.   **III. 3303**
India and Pakistan: a general and regional geography [by] O. H. K. Spate & A. T. A. Learmonth with the collaboration of A. M. Learmonth and a chapter on Ceylon by B. H. Farmer. 3rd ed. revised and completely reset. London, Methuen, 1967. xxxiii, 877 p. front., plate, maps, tables, diagrs. 25 cm. "Distributed in the USA by Barnes & Noble." *1. India. 2. Pakistan. 3. Ceylon. I. Learmonth, A. T. A., joint author. II. T.*
DS407.S67 1967   915.4   68-86324

Majumdar, Ramesh Chandra, ed.   **III. 3304**
The classical accounts of India, being a compilation of the English translations of the accounts left by Herodotus, Megasthenes, Arrian, Strabo, Quintus, Diodorus Siculus, Justin, Plutarch, Frontinus, Nearchus, Apollonius, Pliny, Ptolemy, Aelian and others, with maps, editorial notes, comments, analysis and introduction. [1st ed.] Calcutta, Firma K. L. Mukhopadhyay, 1960. xxvi, 504 p. fold. maps. 23 cm. *1. India — Description and Travel — To 1000. I. T.*
DS409.M3   915.4   62-30287

Heber, Reginald, Bp. of Calcutta, 1783-1826.   **III. 3305**
Bishop Heber in northern India; selections from Heber's journal, edited by M. A. Laird. London, Cambridge U.P., 1971. x, 324 p., plate; illus, maps, ports. 23 cm. (The European understanding of India) *1. India — Description and travel — 1762-1858. 2. India — Social life and customs. I. T.*
DS412.H443 1971   915/.4   70-123673   ISBN:0521078733

Trevelyan, George Otto, Sir, bart., 1838-1928. III. 3306
The competition wallah. By G. O. Trevelyan. 2d ed., with omissions and corrections. London, Macmillan, 1866. xii, 355 p. 20 cm. *1. Civil service — India. 2. India — Description and travel. I. T.*
DS413.T81 1866   915.4   37-23598

Fairservis, Walter Ashlin, 1921- III. 3307
The roots of ancient India; the archaeology of early Indian civilization [by] Walter A. Fairservis, Jr. Drawings by Jan Fairservis. New York, Macmillan [1971] xxv, 482 p. illus., maps. 24 cm. *1. India — Antiquities. 2. India — Civilization. I. T.*
DS418.F24   913.34/03   69-10610

DS421 – 422 SOCIAL LIFE. CUSTOMS. CASTE

Chaudhuri, Nirad C., 1897- III. 3308
The autobiography of an unknown Indian, by Nirad C. Chaudhuri. Berkeley, University of California Press, 1968 [c1951] xii, 506 p. 21 cm. *1. India — Social life and customs. I. T.*
DS421.C47 1968   915.4/03/350924   68-25418

Dubois, Jean Antoine, 1765-1848. III. 3309
Hindu manners, customs and ceremonies, by the Abbé J. A. Dubois, translated from the author's later French ms. and edited with notes, corrections, and biography by Henry K. Beauchamp. With a prefatory note by the Right Hon. F. Max Müller, and a portrait. 3d ed. Oxford, Clarendon Press [1924] xxxiv, 741 p. port. 19 cm. "Impression of 1924. First edition, 1897." *1. India — Social life and customs. 2. India — Civilization. 3. India — Religion. I. Beauchamp, Henry King, 1866-1907, ed. and tr.*
DS421.D825 1924   45-41402

Lajpat Rai, Lala, 1865-1928. III. 3310
Unhappy India, Lajpat Rai. 2d ed., rev. & enl. Calcutta, Banna Pub. Co., 1928. [New York, AMS Press, 1972] lxx, 565 p. 23 cm. A reply to K. Mayo's Mother India. *1. India — Social conditions. 2. India — Economic conditions — 1918-1947. 3. Women in India. 4. Mayo, Katherine, 1868?-1940. Mother India. I. T.*
DS421.M42 1972   915.4/03/35   72-171642   ISBN:0404038034

Rawlinson, Hugh George, 1880- III. 3311
India, a short cultural history. New York, F. A. Praeger [1952] xiv, 454 p. illus., maps. 26 cm. (The Cresset historical series) *1. India — Civilization. 2. India — History.*
DS421.R35 1952   934   52-11243

Sen, Gertrude (Emerson) III. 3312
Voiceless India [by] Gertrude Emerson (Gertrude Sen) Westport, Conn., Greenwood Press [1971] 458 p. illus., map. 23 cm. Reprint of the 1930 ed. *1. India — Social life and customs. 2. India — Social conditions. 3. Pachperwa, India. I. T.*
DS421.S47 1971   915.4/2/035   74-109975   ISBN:0837144817

Wiser, Charlotte Melina (Viall) III. 3313
Behind mud walls, 1930-1960, by William H. Wiser and Charlotte Viall Wiser. With a foreword by David G. Mandelbaum. [Rev. and enl.] Berkeley, University of California Press, 1963. xv, 249 p. 21 cm. Authors' names in reverse order in previous editions. *1. Country life — India. 2. India — Social life and custom. 3. Missions — India. I. Wiser, William Henricks, 1890- joint author. II. T.*
DS421.W73 1963   915.4   63-19178

Béteille, André. III. 3314
Caste, class, and power; changing patterns of stratification in a Tanjore village. Berkeley, University of California Press, 1965. 238 p. illus., map. 24 cm. *1. Caste — India — Tanjore (District) I. T.*
DS422.C3B4   301.44095482   65-25628

Bouglé, Célestin Charles Alfred, 1870-1940. III. 3315
Essays on the caste system. Translated with an introd. by D. F. Pocock. Cambridge [Eng.] University Press, 1971. xiv, 228 p. 23 cm. (European understanding of India) Translation of Essais sur le régime des castes. *1. Caste — India. 2. India — Social conditions. I. T.*
DS422.C3B6513 1971   301.44/0954   79-154506   ISBN:0521080932

Ghurye, Govind Sadashiv, 1893- III. 3317
Caste and race in India [by] G. S. Ghurye. [5th ed.] Bombay, Popular Prakashan [1969] vi, 504 p. 23 cm. (Popular library of Indian sociology and social thought) Second and 3d editions (1950, 1956) have title: Caste and class in India; 4th ed., 1961, has title: Caste, class, and occupation. *1. Caste — India. 2. Ethnology — India. 3. Hindus. I. T.*
DS422.C3G5 1969   301.44/0954   71-905700

Hutton, John Henry, 1885- III. 3318
Caste in India, its nature, function and origins [by] J. H. Hutton. 4th ed. [London] Indian Branch, Oxford University Press [1963] xvi, 324 p. illus., fold. maps. 25 cm. *1. Caste — India. I. T.*
DS422.C3H8 1963   301.440954   64-5242

Isaacs, Harold Robert, 1910- III. 3319
India's ex-Untouchables [by] Harold R. Isaacs. New York, John Day Co. [1965] 188 p. 21 cm. "A study from the Center for International Studies, Massachusetts Institute of Technology." *1. Untouchables. 2. Social mobility. I. Massachusetts Institute of Technology. Center for International Studies. II. T.*
DS422.C3I8   301.45   65-10790

DS423 – 428 CIVILIZATION

Davids, Thomas William Rhys, 1843-1922. III. 3320
Buddhist India. [3d Indian ed. Calcutta] S. Gupta [1957] 158 p. illus. 23 cm. *1. India — History. 2. India — Civilization. 3. Buddha and Buddhism. I. T.*
DS423.D2 1957   934 (954)   57-59485

De Bary, William Theodore, 1918- ed. III. 3321
Sources of Indian tradition. Compiled by Wm. Theodore De Bary [and others] New York, Columbia University Press, 1958. xxvii, 961 p. maps. 24 cm. (Records of civilization: sources and studies, 56. Introduction to oriental civilizations) Translations from various sources and by various individuals. *1. India — Religion. 2. India — Civilization. 3. Pakistan — Civilization. I. T. (S:Records of civilization: sources and studies, 56.) (S:Introduction to oriental civilizations)*
DS423.D33   915.4   58-4146

Elder, Joseph Walter. III. 3322
Civilization of India syllabus [by] Joseph W. Elder, editor, Willard L. Johnson [and] Christopher R. King. Madison, Dept. of Indian Studies, University of Wisconsin, 1965. unpaged. illus. *1. India — Civilization. I. Wisconsin. University. Dept. of Indian Studies. II. T.*
DS423.E5x

Gordon, Leonard A. III. 3323
A syllabus of Indian civilization, by Leonard A. Gordon and Barbara Stoler Miller. New York, Columbia University Press, 1971. viii, 182 p. maps. 24 cm. *1. India — Civilization — History — Outlines, syllabi, etc. I. Miller, Barbara Stoler, joint author. II. T.*
DS423.G68   915.4/03/0202   70-168868   ISBN:0231035608

Lannoy, Richard. III. 3324
The speaking tree: a study of Indian culture and society. London, New York, Oxford University Press, 1971. xxvii, 466 p., 25 plates; illus. (incl. 1 col.) 24 cm. *1. Art, Indic. 2. Family — India. 3. India — Social conditions. 4. Religion and state — India. I. T.*
DS423.L27 1971   915.4/03   74-158205   ISBN:0192151770

Sarkar, Jadunath, Sir, 1870-1960. III. 3325
India through the ages, a survey of the growth of Indian life and thought [by] Jadunath Sarkar. 5th ed. enlarged. Calcutta, M. C. Sarkar [1960] 96 p. 19 cm. (Sir William Meyer lectures, 1928, Madras University) *1. India — Civilization. I. T.*
DS423.S3x

Singer, Milton B., ed. III. 3326
Traditional India: structure and change. Philadelphia, American Folklore Society, 1959. xxiii, 332 p. illus. 26 cm. (Publications of the American Folklore Society; bibliographical series, v. 10) *1. India — Civilization. 2. Social change. I. T. (S:American Folklore Society. Bibliographical and special series, v. 10)*
DS423.S57   915.4   58-59652

Taylor, Edmond, 1908- III. 3327
Richer by Asia. 2d ed. Boston, Houghton Mifflin, 1964. xvi, 420 p. 22 cm. *1. India — Civilization. I. T.*
DS423.T3 1964   915.4   64-57023

Allchin, Bridget. III. 3328
The birth of Indian civilization; India and Pakistan before 500 B.C. [by] Bridget and Raymond Allchin. Baltimore, Penguin Books [1968] 365 p. illus. 18 cm. (Pelican books, A950) *1. India — Civilization. I. Allchin, Frank Raymond, 1923- joint author. II. T.*
DS425.A65 1968b   913.3/4/03   79-1722

Auboyer, Jeannine. III. 3329
Daily life in ancient India, from approximately 200 BC to 700 AD. Translated from the French by Simon Watson Taylor. [1st American ed.] New York, Macmillan, 1965. xv, 344 p. illus., map. 23 cm. (Daily life series) *1. India — Civilization. I. T. (S)*
DS425.A953 1965   913.3403   65-17835

Basham, Arthur Llewellyn. III. 3330
The wonder that was India; a survey of the history and culture of the Indian sub-continent before the coming of the Muslims [by] A. L. Basham. 3d rev. ed. New York, Taplinger Pub. Co. [1968] xxiii, 572 p. illus. (part col.), maps. 24 cm. *1. India — Civilization. 2. India — History — Early to 324 B.C. 3. India — History — 324B.C.-1000 A.D. I. T.*
DS425.B33 1968   913.34/03   68-10737

al-Bīrūnī, 973?-1048. III. 3331
Alberuni's India. Translated by Edward C. Sachau. Abridged ed. edited with introd. and notes by Ainslie T. Embree. New York, Norton [1971] xix, 246 p. illus. 20 cm. (The Norton library, N568) Translation of Tarīkh al-hind. *1. Civilization, Hindu. I. Embree, Ainslie Thomas, ed. II. T.*
DS425.B5713 1971   915.4/03/22   79-29490   ISBN:0393005682

Davids, Thomas William Rhys, 1843-1922. III. 3332
Buddhist India. Freeport, N.Y., Books for Libraries Press [1972] xv, 332 p. illus. 23 cm. Reprint of the 1903 ed. issued in series: The story of the nations. *1. India — History — Early to 324 BC. 2. India — History — 324 BC to 1000 AD. 3. India — Civilization. 4. Buddha and Buddhism — India. I. T. (S:The Story of the nations.)*
DS425.D37 1972   915.4/03   78-38349   ISBN:0836967666

Drekmeier, Charles. III. 3333
Kingship and community in early India. Stanford, Calif., Stanford University Press, 1962. xii, 369 p. map. 24 cm. "A version of this study was submitted as a dissertation to Harvard University." *1. India — Civilization. 2. India — Religion. I. T.*
DS425.D7   915.4   62-9565

Fick, Richard, 1867- III. 3334
The social organisation in north-east India in Buddha's time, by Richard Fick; translated by Shishirkumar Maitra. [Calcutta] University of Calcutta, 1920. xvii, 365 p. 22 cm. *1. India — Social life and customs. 2. Caste — India. I. Śiśira-Kumāra Maitra, tr. II. T.*
DS425.F5   25-1752

Renou, Louis, 1896- III. 3335
The civilization of ancient India. Translated from the French by Philip Spratt. [2d ed.] Calcutta, Susil Gupta (India) Private Ltd. [1959] 189 p. 23 cm. *1. India — Civilization. 2. Civilization, Hindu.*
DS425.R433 1959   913.4   59-16386

Ikram, Sheikh Mohamad, 1908- III. 3336
Muslim civilization in India, by S. M. Ikram. Edited by Ainslie T. Embree. New York, Columbia University Press, 1964. x, 325 p. maps. 25 cm. "An abridgment of the author's fuller History of Muslim civilization in India and Pakistan (712-1858), published in Lahore in 1962." *1. Civilization, Mohammedan. I. T.*
DS427.I42   915.4   64-14656

Qureshi, Ishtiaq Husain. III. 3337
The Muslim community of the Indo-Pakistan subcontinent, 610-1947; a brief historical analysis. 's-Gravenhage, Mouton, 1962. 334 p. 25 cm. (Columbia University. Publications in Near and Middle East studies. Ser. A, 1) *1. Mohammedans in India. I. T. (S)*
DS427.Q8   63-2042

Spear, Thomas George Percival. III. 3338
The nabobs; a study of the social life of the English in eighteenth century India, by Percival Spear. Gloucester, Mass., P. Smith, 1971 [c1963] xxi, 213 p. illus. 21 cm. *1. British in India. 2. India — Social life and customs. 3. India — Politics and government — 1765-1947. I. T.*
DS428.S6 1971   915.4/06/2   71-22849

DS430 – 432 ETHNOGRAPHY

India (Republic) Anthropological Survey. III. 3339
Peasant life in India; a study in Indian unity & diversity. Calcutta [1961] 60 p. illus., maps. 32 cm. (Its Memoir, no. 8) *1. Ethnology — India. 2. Peasantry — India. I. T. (S)*
DS430.A5   Sa66-5983

Gorer, Geoffrey, 1905- III. 3340
Himalayan village; an account of the Lepchas of Sikkim. With a new foreword by the author. 2d ed. New York, Basic Books [1967] 488 p. illus., map, ports. 24 cm. *1. Lepchas. I. T.*
DS432.L4G6 1967   390   67-22188

Sardesai, Govind Sakharam, rao bahadur, 1865- III. 3341
New history of the Marathas. Bombay, Phoenix Publications [1946 48] 3 v. plate, ports. (2 col.) 2 maps (1 fold.) 23 cm. *1. Mahrattas.*
DS432.M2S38   954   48-17390

Orans, Martin. III. 3342
The Santal; a tribe in search of a great tradition. Detroit, Wayne State University Press, 1965. xiv, 154 p. 23cm. *1. Santals.*
DS432.S2O7   309.1541   65-12595

DS433 – 485 HISTORY

Bhattacharya, Sachchidananda. III. 3343
A dictionary of Indian history. [1st American ed.] New York, G. Braziller [c1967] xii, 888 p. 22 cm. *1. India — History — Dictionaries. I. T.*
DS433.B48 1967b   954/.003   68-19984

Hardy, Peter. III. 3344
Historians of medieval India; studies in Indo-Muslim historical writing. London, Luzac, 1960. v, 146 p. 22 cm. "Revised version of a thesis ... for the degree of doctor of philosophy of the University of London." *1. India — History — Historiography. 2. Historians, Indic. 3. Mohammedans in India. I. T.*
DS435.Hx   A61-4650

Philips, Cyril Henry, 1912- ed. III. 3345
Historians of India, Pakistan and Ceylon. London, Oxford University Press, 1961. 504 p. (School of Oriental and African Studies, University of London. Historical writing on the peoples of Asia [1]) *1. India — History — Historiography. 2. Pakistan — History — Historiography. 3. Ceylon — History — Historiography. I. T.*
DS435.Px

Warder, Anthony Kennedy. III. 3346
An introduction to Indian historiography [by] A. K. Warder. Bombay, Popular Prakashan [1972] xii, 196 p. 22 cm. (Monographs of the Department of Sanskrit and Indian Studies, University of Toronto, 1) *1. India — Historiography. I. T. (S:Toronto. University. Dept. of Sanskrit and Indian Studies. Monographs, 1.)*
DS435.W37   954/.007/2   72-904916

Crane, Robert I. III. 3347
The history of India; its study and interpretation. Washington, Service Center for Teachers of History [1958] 46 p. 23 cm. (Service Center for Teachers of History. Publication no. 17) *1. India — History — Study and teaching.*
DS435.8.C7   954.007   58-59932

Singer, Milton B., ed. III. 3348
Introducing India in liberal education; proceedings of a conference held at the University of Chicago, May 17, 18, 1957. Chicago, University of Chicago [1957] xiii, 287 p. 23 cm. *1. India — Civilization — Study and teaching. I. Chicago. University. II. T.*
DS435.8.S5   915.4   57-4500

Allan, John, 1884-1955. III. 3349
The Cambridge shorter history of India, by J. Allan, Sir T. Wolseley Haig [and] H. H. Dodwell. Edited by H. H. Dodwell. With additional chapters on The last phase, 1919-1947 by R. R. Sethi. Delhi, S. Chand, 1964. xxi, 784, xxxxvii p. maps. 23 cm. *1. India — History. I. Haig, Wolseley, Sir, 1865-1938, joint author. II. Dodwell, Henry Herbert, 1879-1946, joint author. III. T.*
DS436.A36 1964   954   Sa66-5822

The Cambridge history of India. Supplementary volume: The Indus civilization, III. 3350
by Mortimer Wheeler. 3d ed. Cambridge [Eng.] University Press, 1968. xi, 143 p. illus., maps (1 fold) plans (1 fold.) 36 plates. 24 cm. *1. India — History. I. Wheeler, Robert Eric Mortimer, Sir, 1890- . II. The Indus Civilization.*
DS436.C22 Suppl. 1968   22-11272

Griffiths, Percival Joseph, Sir, 1899- III. 3351
Modern India, by Sir Percival Griffiths. 4th ed. New York, F. A. Praeger [1965] 311 p. maps (1 fold.) 23 cm. (Nations of the modern world) *1. India — History. 2. India — Politics and government — 1947- 3. India — Economic conditions — 1947- I. T. (S)*
DS436.G7 1965   320.954   65-14181

Smith, Vincent Arthur, 1848-1920. III. 3352
The Oxford history of India. 3rd ed., edited by Percival Spear. Pt. 1 rev. by Mortimer Wheeler and A. L. Basham; pt. 2 rev. by J. B. Harrison; pt. 3 rewritten by Percival Spear. Oxford, Clarendon Press, 1967 [i.e. 1968] xv, 898 p. 41 plates (incl. 2 fold.), illus., maps, plan, ports. 19 cm. *1. India — History I. Spear, Thomas George Percival, ed. II. T.*
DS436.S55 1967   954   78-354084

Spear, Thomas George Percival. III. 3353
India, a modern history. Ann Arbor, University of Michigan Press [1961] x, 491, xix p. maps. 25 cm. (The University of Michigan history of the modern world) *1. India — History. (S:Michigan. University. The University of Michigan history of the modern world)*
DS436.S68   954   61-10988

Thapar, Romila. III. 3354
A history of India. Baltimore, Penguin Books [1965-66, v.2, 1965] 2 v. maps, plans. 19 cm. (Pelican books, A769-A770) Vol. 2 by Percival Spear. *1. India — History. I. Spear, Thomas George Percival. II. T.*
DS436.T37   954   66-31497

Wolpert, Stanley A., 1927- III. 3355
India [by] Stanley Wolpert. Englewood Cliffs, N.J., Prentice-Hall [1965] x, 178 p. maps. 21 cm. (The Modern nations in historical perspective, S-613) A Spectrum book. *1. India — History. I. T.*
DS436.W65   954   65-20603

DS444 – 450 Political and Diplomatic History

Diver, Katherine Helen Maud (Marshall) 1867-1945. III. 3356
Royal India; a descriptive and historical study of India's fifteen principal states and their rulers. Freeport, N.Y., Books for Libraries Press [1971, c1942] x, 278 p. illus., ports. 23 cm. (Essay index reprint series) *1. India — Politics and government. 2. India — Kings and rulers. I. T.*
DS445.D5 1971   954   76-142620   ISBN:0836921526

Keith, Arthur Berriedale, 1879-1944, ed. III. 3357
Speeches & documents on Indian policy, 1750-1921, edited by Professor A. Berriedale Keith. London, New York, Oxford University Press [1922] 2 v. 16. (The world's classics. 231-232)) *1. East India company (English) 2. India — Politics and government — 1765-1947. I. T.*
DS446.3.K4   23-10033

Lajpat, Rai, Lala, 1865-1928. III. 3358
Young India; an interpretation and a history of the nationalist movement from within. New York, Howard Fertig, 1968. xxvi, 257 p. ports. 21 cm. Reprint of the 1916 ed. *1. India — Politics and government — 1765-1947. I. T.*
DS448.L35 1968   320.9/54   67-24593

Lovett, Harrington Verney, Sir, 1864-1945. III. 3359
A history of the Indian nationalist movement. [3d ed.] New York, A. M. Kelley, 1969. 303 p. 23 cm. (Reprints of economic classics) Reprint of the 1921 ed. *1. India — Politics and government — 1765-1947. I. T.*
DS448.L7 1969   954.035   79-94540   ISBN:678051003

Neale, Walter C. III. 3360
India: the search for unity, democracy, and progress, by Walter C. Neale. Princton, N. J., Van Nostrand [1965] 128 p. maps. 21 cm. (Van Nostrand searchlight book, no. 24) *1. India — Politics and government — 1947- 2. India — Economic conditions — 1945- I. T.*
DS448.N36   309.154   65-3615

Woodman, Dorothy. III. 3361
Himalayan frontiers: a political review of British, Chinese, Indian and Russian rivalries. London, Barrie & Rockliff the Cresset P., 1969. xv, 423 p., 3 fold. plates. facsim., maps. 23 cm. *1. Himalaya region — Politics. 2. India — Boundaries — China. 3. China — Boundaries — India. I. T.*
DS450.C5W6   327.54   76-464891   ISBN:248997270

DS451 – 481 History, by Period

DS451 TO 997

Majumdar, Ramesh Chandra. III. 3362
Ancient India, by R. C. Majumdar. [Rev. i.e. 2d ed.] Delhi, Motilal Banarsidass [1964] xvi, 538 p. 19 plates. 23 cm. *1. India — History. I. T.*
DS451.M25 1964   Sa65-2341

Mookerji, Radha Kumud, 1884- III. 3363
The Gupta Empire. [4th ed.] Delhi, Motilal Banarsidass [1969] viii, 174 p. illus., geneal. tables. 25 cm. Label mounted on t.p.: Distributed by Lawrence Verry, Mystic, Conn. *1. Gupta dynasty. I. T.*
DS451.M66 1969   934/.06   74-17404

Narain, A. K. III. 3364
The Indo-Greeks by A. K. Narain. Oxford, Clarendon Press [1962] xvi, 201 p. maps, plates. 22 cm. Reprinted from corrected sheets of the 1st ed. *1. Greeks in India. 2. Bactria — History. 3. Numismatics — India. I. T.*
DS451.N28 1962   Sa65-2373

Piggott, Stuart. III. 3365
Prehistoric India to 1000 B.C. Harmondsworth, Middlesex, Penguin Books [1950] 293 p. illus., maps. 19 cm. (Pelican books, A205) *1. India — Antiquities. 2. India — History — Early. I. T.*
DS451.P46   934   51-3580

Rawlinson, Hugh George, 1880- III. 3366
Intercourse between India and the Western World; from the earliest times to the fall of Rome, by H. G. Rawlinson. 2d ed. New York, Octagon Books, 1971. vi, 196 p. illus. 24 cm. Reprint of the 1926 ed. *1. India — History — Early to 324 B.C. 2. India — History — 324 B.C.-1000 A.D. 3. India — Relations (general) with foreign countries. 4. India — Commerce — History. I. T.*
DS451.R3 1971   934   75-159221   ISBN:0374967210

Wheeler, Robert Eric Mortimer, Sir, 1890- III. 3367
Early India and Pakistan: to Ashoka [by] Sir Mortimer Wheeler. Rev. ed. New York, Praeger [1968, c1959] 241 p. illus., maps, plans. 21 cm. (Ancient peoples and places, v. 12) *1. India — History — Early to 324 B.C. I. T.*
DS451.W48 1968   934   68-28335

Mookerji, Radha Kumud, 1884- III. 3368
Asoka. 3d ed. rev. and enl. Delhi, Motilal Banarsidass, 1962. xii, 289 p. illus., fold. map, facsims. 23 cm. *1. Aśoka, King of Magadha, fl. 259 B.C.*
DS451.5.M6 1962   Sa63-3136

Thapar, Romila. III. 3369
Aśoka and the decline of the Mauryas. [London] Oxford University Press, 1961. viii, 283 p. illus., maps (part fold.) facsims. 24 cm. *1. Aśoka, King of Magadha, fl. 259 B.C. 2. Maurya dynasty.*
DS451.5.T5   934   61-19541

Mookerji, Radha Kumud, 1884- III. 3370
Chandragupta Maurya and his times. [4th ed.] Delhi, Motilal Banarsidass [1966] xvi, 263 p. 25 cm. (Madras. University. Sir William Meyer lectures, 1940-41) *1. Chandragupta Maurya, Emperor of Northern India. 2. India — History — Early to 324 B.C. 3. India — Politics and government — Ancient period. (S:Sir William Meyer lectures, Madras University, 1940-41)*
DS451.9.C5M6 1966   913/.34   Sa67-3518

DS452 – 462 MOSLEM RULE (997 – 1761)
MOGUL EMPIRE (1526 – 1761)

Elliot, Henry Miers, Sir, 1808-1853. III. 3371
The history of India, as told by its own historians: the Muhammadan period; the posthumous papers of the late Sir H. M. Elliot. Edited and continued by John Dowson. [1st Indian ed.] Allahabad, Kitab Mahal, Wholesale Division [1963-1964] 8 v. 23 cm. *1. India — History — 1000-1526. I. Dowson, John, 1820-1881, ed. II. T.*
DS457.E553   Sa65-2362

Lal, Kishori Saran, 1920- III. 3372
History of the Khaljis, A.D. 1290-1320. [Rev. ed.] Bombay, New York, Asia Pub. House [1967] xii, 388 p. illus., geneal. table, maps. 22 cm. *1. Khilji dynasty. I. T.*
DS459.2.L3 1967   954/.023   Sa67-6818

Edwardes, Stephen Meredyth, 1873-1927. III. 3373
Mughal rule in India, by ... S. M. Edwardes and H. L. O. Garrett. London, Oxford University Press, 1930. vi, 374 p., plates, 2 port. (incl. front.) map, fold. geneal. tab. 20 cm. *1. Mogul empire. 2. India — History — European settlements, 1500-1765. I. Garrett, Herbert Leonard Offley, 1881- joint author. II. T.*
DS461.E4   954   30-30942

Gascoigne, Bamber. III. 3374
The great Moghuls [by] Bamber Gascoigne. Photos. by Christina Gascoigne. [1st U.S. ed.] New York, Harper & Row [1971] 264 p. illus., col. plates. 26 cm. *1. Mogul empire. 2. India — History — 1500-1765. I. Gascoigne, Christina, 1938 or 9- illus. II. T.*
DS461.G3 1971   954/.025   77-152348   ISBN:0060114673

Spear, Thomas George Percival. III. 3375
Twilight of the Mughuls; studies in late Mughul Delhi. Cambridge [Eng.] University Press, 1951. x, 269 p. plates, fold. map. 23 cm. *1. Mogul Empire. 2. Delhi — History. I. T.*
DS461.S6   954.5   51-7304

Smith, Vincent Arthur, 1848-1920. III. 3376
Akbar, the Great Mogul, 1542-1605. 2d ed., rev. Delhi, A. Chand, 1966

[c1958] xii, 379 p. illus., maps (part fold.) plans, ports. 23 cm. *1. Akbar, Emperor of Hindustan, 1542-1605. 2. Mogul Empire. I. T.*
DS461.3.S5 1966   915.40325   Sa66-5974

Bernier, Francois, 1620-1688. III. 3377
Travels in the Mogul empire, A.D. 1656-1668. A rev. and improved [2d] ed. based upon Irving Brock's translation, by Archibald Constable. Delhi, S. Chand [1968] xxvii, 497 p. illus., maps, ports. (part col.) 23 cm. *1. Mogul Empire. 2. India — History — 1500-1765. 3. India — Description and travel — 1498-1761. 4. India — Social life and customs. I. Brock, Irving, tr. II. Constable, Archibald, ed. III. T.*
DS461.7.B53 1968   954.025   Sa68-10515

Sarkar, Jadunath, Sir, 1870- III. 3378
A short history of Aurangzib, 1618-1707. 3d ed., abridged. Calcutta, M. C. Sarkar, 1962. 478 p. 22 cm. *1. Aurangzib, Emperor of Hindustan, 1619-1707. 2. Mogul Empire. 3. India — History — European settlements — 1500-1765.*
DS461.7.S32 1962   Sa62-647

Irvine, William, 1840-1911. III. 3379
Later Mughals. Edited and augmented with the History of Nadir Shah's invasion, by Jadunath Sarkar. New Delhi, Oriental Books Reprint Corp.; [exclusively distributed by Munshiram Manoharlal, Delhi, 1971] 2 v. in 1. (xxxi, 432, 392 p.) port. 23 cm. First published in 1921-22 in 2 v. *1. Mogul Empire. 2. India — History — 18th century. I. Sarkar, Jadunath, Sir, 1870-1958, ed. II. T.*
DS461.8.I72   73-919253

Hutchinson, Lester, 1904- III. 3380
European freebooters in Moghul India. New York, Asia Pub. House [1964?] vii, 192 p. map, ports. 23 cm. *1. India — History — 18th cent. I. T.*
DS462.H87   954.029   65-16107

DS463 – 480.83 ENGLISH RULE
(1761 – 1947)

Ali, Abdullah Yusuf, 1872- III. 3381
A cultural history of India during the British period. Bombay, D. B. Taraporevala Sons [c1940] vi, 334 p. 22 cm. *1. India — History — British occupation, 1765-1947. 2. India — Civilization. 3. British in India. I. T.*
DS463.A56   915.4   41-16776

Bearce, George Donham, 1922- III. 3382
British attitudes towards India, 1784-1858. [London, New York] Oxford University Press, 1961. 315 p. 23 cm. *1. Gt. Brit. — Relations (general) with India. 2. India — Relations (general) with Great Britain. I. T.*
DS463.B35   327.42054   61-66608

Hardy, Peter. III. 3383
The Muslims of British India [by] P. Hardy. [London] Cambridge University Press, 1972. ix, 306 p. maps 22 cm. (Cambridge South Asian studies, no. 13) *1. Muslims in India. 2. India — Politics and government — 1765-1947. I. T. (S)*
DS463.H37 1972   320.9/54/03   77-184772
ISBN:0521084881 0521097835 (pbk)

Mason, Philip. III. 3384
The men who ruled India, by Philip Woodruff [pseud.] New York, Schocken Books [1964] 2 v. maps. 21 cm. (Schocken paperbacks) "SB68"-"SB69." *1. India — History — 1500-1765. 2. India — History — British occupation, 1765-1947. I. T.*
DS463.M263   954.03   64-13320

Thompson, Edward John, 1886- III. 3385
Rise and fulfillment of British rule in India, by Edward Thompson and G. T. Garratt. London, Macmillan, 1934. xii, 690 p. maps (part fold.) 23 cm. *1. India — History — European settlements, 1500-1765. 2. India — History — British occupation, 1765- I. Garratt, Geoffrey Theodore, 1888- joint author. II. British rule in India. II. T.*
DS463.T516 1934   954   34-21637

Moon, Penderel, 1905- III. 3386
Warren Hastings and British India. New York, Macmillan, 1949. ix, 361 p. port., maps (on lining papers) 18 cm. (Teach yourself history library) *1. Hastings, Warren, 1732-1818. (S:Teach yourself history library (New York))*
DS473.M82 1949   923.254   49-10373

Seal, Anil. III. 3387
The emergence of Indian nationalism: competition and collaboration in the later nineteenth century. London, Cambridge U.P., 1968. xvi, 416 p. maps. 23 cm. (Political change in modern South Asia) *1. Nationalism — India. 2. India — Politics and government — 19th century. I. T. (S)*
DS475.S4   320.9/54   68-18344   ISBN:0521062748

Embree, Ainslie Thomas. III. 3388
Charles Grant and British rule in India. New York, Columbia University Press, 1962. 320 p. 23 cm. (Columbia studies in the social sciences, no. 606)

1. Grant, Charles, 1746-1823. 2. East India Company (English) 3. India — History — British occupation, 1765-1947.
DS475.2.G7E4 1962a (H31.C7 no. 606)   954.03   62-7591

Metcalf, Thomas R., 1934- III. 3389
The aftermath of revolt: India, 1857-1870, by Thomas R. Metcalf. Princeton, N. J., Princeton University Press, 1964. xi, 352 p. maps (1 fold.) 21 cm. *1. India — Politics and government — 1765-1947. I. T.*
DS479.M46   954.035   63-23412

Philips, Cyril Henry, 1912- ed. III. 3390
The evolution of India and Pakistan, 1858 to 1947; select documents. With the co-operation of H. L. Singh and B. N. Pandey. London, New York, Oxford University Press, 1962. xxi, 786 p. 25 cm. (Select documents on the history of India and Pakistan, v.4) *1. India — History — 1765-1947 — Sources. I. T. (S)*
DS479.P5   954.03   62-52888

Lajpat Rai, Lala, 1865-1928. III. 3391
Writings and speeches, edited by Vijaya Chandra Joshi. [1st ed.] Delhi, University Publishers [1966] 2 v. 23 cm. *I. Joshi, Vijaya Chandra, ed. II. T.*
DS479.1.L27A25 1966   Sa66-6206

Azad, Abul Kalam, maulana, 1888-1958. III. 3392
India wins freedom; an autobiographical narrative. With introd. and explanatory notes by Louis Fischer. [1st American ed.] New York, Longmans, Green, 1960. 293 p. illus. 22 cm. *1. India — History — 20th cent. I. T.*
DS480.45.A9 1960   954.03   60-10882

Bose, Subhas Chandra, 1897-1945. III. 3393
The Indian struggle, 1920-1942. Compiled by the Netaji Research Bureau, Calcutta. Bombay, New York, Asia Pub. House [1964] xii, 476 p. illus., facsims., port. 23 cm. Another issue, published in New York. DS480.45.B6 1964a *1. India — Politics and government — 1919-1947. I. Netaji Research Bureau, Calcutta. II. T.*
DS480.45.B6 1964   954.035   Sa64-5232

Hodson, Henry Vincent, 1906- III. 3394
The great divide: Britain—India—Pakistan [by] H. V. Hodson. [1st American ed.] New York, Atheneum, 1971 [c1969] xii, 543 p. illus., group ports., fold. col. map. 24 cm. *1. India — Politics and government — 1919-1947. 2. Pakistan movement — History. I. T.*
DS480.45.H57 1971   954.03/5   79-130812

The Partition of India: policies and perspectives, 1935-1947. III. 3395
Edited by C. H. Philips and Mary Doreen Wainwright. Cambridge, M.I.T. Press [1970, c1969] 607 p. 25 cm. Proceedings of a conference held in London in 1967. *1. India — Politics and government — 1919-1947 — Addresses, essays, lectures. 2. Muslims in India. I. Philips, Cyril Henry, 1912- ed. II. Wainwright, Mary Doreen, ed.*
DS480.45.P33 1970b   320.9/54   77-118351   ISBN:262160439

Wallbank, Thomas Walter, 1901- ed. III. 3396
The partition of India; causes and responsibilities, edited with an introd. by T. Walter Wallbank. Boston, Heath [1966] xiv, 103 p. 24 cm. (Problems in Asian civilizations) *1. India — Politics and government — 1919-1947. 2. Pakistan. I. T. (S)*
DS480.45.W34   320.954   66-26814

The Transfer of power 1942-7; III. 3397
editor-in-chief Nicholas Mansergh, assistant editor E. W. R. Lumby. London, H.M.S.O., 1970- v. facsims., col. maps. 28 cm. At head of title: Constitutional relations between Britain and India. On spine: India; the transfer of power 1942-7. Unpublished documents drawn either from the official archives of the India Office in the custody of the India Office Records or from the private collections of the Vicaregal papers in the India Office Library. *1. India — Politics and government — 1919-1947 — Sources. 2. India — History — British occupation, 1765-1947 — Sources. I. Mansergh, Nicholas, ed. II. Lumby, Esmond Walter Rawson, ed. III. India Office Records. IV. India Office Library. V. Constitutional relations between Britain and India. VI. India; the transfer of power 1942-7.*
DS480.83.T7   327.42/054   72-129254   ISBN:0115800166 (v. 1)

DS480.84 – 481   1947 –

Brown, William Norman, 1892- III. 3398
The United States and India, Pakistan, Bangladesh, by W. Norman Brown. [3d ed.] Cambridge, Harvard University Press, 1972. ix, 462 p. map. 25 cm. (The American foreign policy library) Previous editions published under title: The United States and India and Pakistan. *1. India — History — 1947- 2. Pakistan — History. 3. Bangladesh — History. I. T. (S)*
DS480.84.B73 1972   954./4   72-81270   ISBN:0674924460

Dean, Vera (Micheles) 1903- III. 3399
New patterns of democracy in India. 2d ed. Cambridge, Mass., Harvard University Press, 1969. xii, 255 p. illus., map. 22 cm. *1. India — Politics and*

government — 1947- 2. India — Economic conditions — 1947- I. T.
DS480.84.D38 1969   954.04   79-78516

Morris-Jones, Wyndraeth Humphreys. III. 3400
The Government and politics of India [by] W. H. Morris-Jones. London, Hutchinson University Library [1964] 236 p. maps. 20 cm. (Hutchinson university library: Politics) Label mounted on t. p. : Hillary House, New York. *1. India — Politics and government — 1947- I. T.*
DS480.84.M59   320.954   65-3425

Tinker, Hugh. III. 3401
India and Pakistan; a political analysis. Rev. ed. New York, F. A. Praeger [1968, c1967] 248 p. maps. 21 cm. (Praeger university series, U-526) *1. India — Politics and government — 1947- 2. Pakistan — Political and government. I. T.*
DS480.84.T5 1968   320.9/54   68-16097

Maxwell, Neville George Anthony. III. 3402
India's China war [by] Neville Maxwell. London, Cape, 1970. 475 p., 6 fold. plates. 6 maps. 23 cm. Maps on lining papers. *1. Sino-Indian Border Dispute, 1957- I. T.*
DS480.85.M38   954/.04   77-536579   ISBN:0224618873

Keer, Dhananjay. III. 3403
Dr. Ambedkar, life and mission. [2d ed.] Bombay, Popular Prakashan [1962] 528 p. illus. 23 cm. *1. Ambedkar, Bhimrao Ramji, 1892-1956.*
DS481.A6K4 1962   Sa63-3134

Bose, Subhas Chandra, 1897-1945. III. 3404
An Indian pilgrim; an unfinished autobiography, and collected letters, 1897-1921. [Translations from the Bengali by Sisir Kumar Bose] New York, Asia Pub. House [1965] viii, 199 p. facsims., geneal. tables, port. 23 cm. *I. T.*
DS481.B6A3 1965   954.0350924 (B)   65-5400

Gandhi, Mohandas Karamchand, 1869-1948. III. 3405
The essential Gandhi, an anthology. Edited by Louis Fischer, New York, Random House [1962] 369 p. 21 cm. *I. Fischer, Louis, 1896- ed. II. T.*
DS481.G3A17 1962   923.254   62-8458

Bhattacharyya, Sailendra Nath, 1921- III. 3406
Mahatma Gandhi, the journalist [by] S. N. Bhattacharyya. Bombay, New York, Asia Pub. House [1965] x, 195 p. illus., facsim., ports. 23 cm. *1. Gandhi, Mohandas Karamchand, 1869-1948.*
DS481.G3B45 1965   Sa66-5405

Fischer, Louis, 1896- III. 3407
The life of Mahatma Gandhi. [1st ed.] New York, Harper [1950] ix, 558 p. illus., ports., map (on lining papers) 22 cm. *1. Gandhi, Mohandas Karamchand, 1869-1948.*
DS481.G3F44   923.254   50-9391   954.03
                                          615 f

The Meanings of Gandhi. III. 3408
Edited by Paul F. Power. [1st ed. Honolulu] University Press of Hawaii [c1971] 199 p. port. 23 cm. "An East-West Center book." *1. Gandhi, Mohandras Karamchand, 1869-1948 — Addresses, essays, lectures. 2. Passive resistance — Addresses, essays, lectures. I. Power, Paul F., ed.*
DS481.G3M387   954.03/5/0924   72-170180   ISBN:0824801040

Rolland, Romain, 1866-1944. III. 3409
Mahatma Gandhi; the man who became one with the universal being, by Romain Rolland, translated by Catherine D. Groth. New York, Century [c1924] 250 p. port. 19 cm. *1. Gandhi, Mohandas Karamchand, 1869-1948. 2. India — Politics and government — 1919-1947. I. Groth, Catherine Daae, 1888- tr.*
DS481.G3R6   24-4346

Bolitho, Hector, 1898- III. 3410
Jinnah, creator of Pakistan. [1st ed.] London, J. Murray [1954] 244 p. illus. 23 cm. *1. Jinnah, Mahomed Ali, 1876-1948.*
DS481.J5B6 1954   54-14996

Menon, Kumara Padmanabha Sivasankara, 1898- III. 3411
Many worlds; an autobiography [by] K. P. S. Menon. London, New York, Oxford University Press, 1965. viii, 324 p. illus., ports. 23 cm. *1. India — Politics and government — 20th cent. 2. World politics — 1945- I. T.*
DS481.M4A3   320.954 (B)   66-1547

Nehru, Jawaharlal, 1889- III. 3412
Jawaharlal Nehru, an autobiography; with musings on recent events in India. Bombay, Allied Publishers [1962] xiii, 623 p. port. 23 cm. *1. Gandhi, Mohandas Karamchand, 1869-1948. 2. India — Politics and government — 1919-1947.*
DS481.N35A3 1962   Sa64-1400

Nehru, Jawaharlal, 1889-1964. III. 3413
Nehru, the first sixty years; presenting in his own words the development of the political thought of Jawaharlal Nehru and the background against which it evolved ... Selected and edited, with introductory, historical and other interpretative commentary by Dorothy Norman, with a foreword by Jawaharlal Nehru. New York, John Day Co. [1965] 2 v. ports. 23 cm. *1. India — Politics and government. I. Norman, Dorothy, 1905- ed. II. T.*
DS481.N35A3 1965   320.954   64-14203

Crocker, Walter Russell, 1902- III. 3414
Nehru; a contemporary's estimate, by Walter Crocker. With a foreword by Arnold Toynbee. New York, Oxford University Press, 1966. 186 p. port. 23 cm. *1. Nehru, Jawaharlal, 1889-1964.*
DS481.N35C7   954.040924   66-31908

Sultan Muhammad Shah, Sir, agha khan, 1877- III. 3415
The memoirs of Aga Khan; world enough and time. New York, Simon and Schuster, 1954. 367 p. illus. 24 cm. *I. T.*
DS481.S8A3   923.254   54-8644

Tandon, Prakash. III. 3416
Beyond Punjab, 1937-1960. London, Chatto and Windus, 1971. 3-222 p. 23 cm. *1. India — Social life and customs. I. T.*
DS481.T24A3   915.4/03/40924   73-882980   ISBN:0701117796

DS484 – 490 Local History

DS484 SOUTH INDIA

Irschick, Eugene F. III. 3417
Politics and social conflict in South India; the non-Brahman movement and Tamil separatism, 1916-1929 [by] Eugene F. Irschick. Berkeley, University of California Press, 1969. 414 p. maps. 24 cm. Sponsored by the Center for South and Southeast Asia Studies, University of California, Berkeley. *1. South India — Politics and government. 2. Tamils. I. California. University. Center for South and Southeast Asia Studies. II. T.*
DS484.I7   320.9/54/8   68-31595

Nilakanta Sastri, Kallidaikurichi Aiyah Aiyar, 1892- III. 3418
A history of South India from prehistoric times to the fall of Vijayanagar [by] K. A. Nilakanta Sastri. 3d ed. [Madras] Indian Branch, Oxford University Press, 1966. xiv, 520 p. col. map, plates (1 col.) 22 cm. *1. South India — History. I. T.*
DS484.N5 1966   954.802   Sa67-255

DS485 BENGAL

Chattopadhyaya, Gautam, ed. III. 3419
Awakening in Bengal in early nineteenth century; selected documents. Edited by Goutam Chattopadhyay. Calcutta, Progressive Publishers, 1965. 2v. 23 cm. English and Bengali. *1. Bengal — Intellectual life. I. T.*
DS485.B44C53   915.414033   Sa66-6865

Kopf, David. III. 3420
British Orientalism and the Bengal renaissance; the dynamics of Indian modernization, 1773-1835. Berkeley, University of California Press, 1969. xii, 324 p. 25 cm. *1. Bengal — Intellectual life. I. T.*
DS485.B44K6   915.4/14/0331   69-13135

Broomfield, J. H. III. 3421
Elite conflict in a plural society; twentieth-century Bengal [by] J. H. Broomfield. Berkeley, University of California Press, 1968. xv, 349 p. maps. 25 cm. *1. Bengal — Politics and government. 2. Hindus. 3. Muslims in Bengal. I. T.*
DS485.B49B76   320.9/54/14   68-13822

DS485 BHUTAN

Karan, Pradyumna Prasad. III. 3422
The Himalayan kingdoms: Bhutan, Sikkim, and Nepal, by Pradyumna P. Karan and William M. Jenkins, Jr. Princeton, N.J., Van Nostrand [1963] 144 p. illus. 21 cm. (Van Nostrand searchlight book #13) *1. Bhutan. 2. Nepal. 3. Sikkim, India. I. Jenkins, William M., joint author. II. T.*
DS485.B503K3   915.49   63-4420

DS485 BURMA

American University, Washington, D.C. Foreign Area Studies. III. 3423
Area handbook for Burma. Co-authors: John W. Henderson [and others. Washington, For sale by the Supt. of Docs., U.S. Govt. Print. Off.] 1971. xiv, 341 p. maps. 24 cm. "DA pam 550-61." *1. Burma. I. Henderson, John William, 1910- II. T.*
DS485.B81A348 1971   309.1/591/05   75-612066

Bixler, Norma. III. 3424
Burma, a profile. New York, Praeger Publishers [1971] xii, 244 p. illus., maps. 22 cm. (Praeger country profiles) *1. Burma. I. T.*
DS485.B81B55   915.91/03/5   77-118047

Scott, James George, Sir, 1851-1935. III. 3425
The Burman; his life and notions, by Shway Yoe [pseud.] New York, Norton [1963] 609 p. illus. 20 cm. (The Norton library, N212) 1. Burma — Social life and customs. I. T.
DS485.B81S4 1963   915.91   63-5970

Mi Mi Khaing, Daw. III. 3426
Burmese family. Illustrated by E. G. N. Kinch. [1st American ed.] Bloomington, Indiana University Press [1962] 200 p. illus. 24 cm. 1. Burma — Social life and customs. 2. Women in Burma. I. T.
DS485.B84M5 1962   915.91   62-8981

Nash, Manning. III. 3427
The golden road to modernity; village life in contemporary Burma. New York, Wiley [1965] viii, 333 p. illus., maps. 24 cm. 1. Burma — Social life and customs. I. T.
DS485.B84N3   390.09591   65-21437

Cady, John Frank, 1901- III. 3428
A history of modern Burma. Ithaca, N.Y., Cornell University Press [1958] 682 p. illus. 24 cm. 1. Burma — History.
DS485.B86C2   959.1   58-1545

Harvey, Godfrey Eric, 1889- III. 3429
History of Burma from the earliest times to 10 March 1824, the beginning of the English conquest [by] G. E. Harvey. New York, Octagon Books, 1967. xxxi, 415 p. maps, plates. 23 cm. Reprint of The 1925 ed. 1. Burma — History. I. T.
DS485.B86H3x   959.1/02   67-13860

Hmannān mahā yazawintawkyī. III. 3430
The Glass Palace chronicle of the kings of Burma, translated by Pe Maung Tin and G. H. Luce. London, Oxford University Press, 1923. xxiii, 179 p. map. 23 cm. "Issued by the Text Publication Fund of the Burma Research Society." "In the year 1829 King Bagyidaw of Burma appointed a committee of scholars to write a chronicle of the Burmese kings ... The name of the chronicle was taken from the Palace of glass, in ... which the compilation was made ... The present translation is based on the Mandalay edition of 1907. It begins with the third part ... [which] opens with the history of the three Burmese kingdoms of Tagaung, Tharehkittara, and Pagan. The fourth and fifth parts continue the history of Pagan until the time of its fall." 1. Burma — History. I. Pe Maung Tin, U, 1888- tr. II. Luce, Gordon Hannington, 1889- tr. III. Burma Research Society. Text Publication Fund. IV. T.
DS485.B87H48   23-16557

Ba Maw, U, 1892- III. 3431
Breakthrough in Burma; memoirs of a revolution, 1939-1946 [by] Ba Maw. New Haven, Yale University Press, 1968. xxiii, 460 p. maps, ports. 24 cm. 1. Burma — History. I. T.
DS485.B89B28   959.1/04/0924   67-24504

Furnivall, John Sydenham. III. 3432
Colonial policy and practice; a comparative study of Burma and Netherlands India. New York, New York University Press [1956] xii, [1], 568 p. map. 24 cm. 1. Burma — Politics and government. 2. Indonesia — Politics and government. 3. Colonies — Administration. I. T.
DS485.B89F8 1956   959.1   56-10677

Butwell, Richard A. III. 3433
U Nu of Burma [by] Richard Butwell. Stanford, Calif., Stanford University Press [1969] viii, 327 p., illus., ports. 23 cm. 1. Nu, U.
DS485.B892B8 1969   959.1/05/0924 (B)   76-97911   ISBN:804701555

Johnstone, William Crane, 1901- III. 3434
Burma's foreign policy; a study in neutralism. Cambridge, Harvard University Press, 1963. ix, 338 p. 25 cm. "Burma research project papers": p. [303]-304. 1. Burma — Foreign relations. I. T.
DS485.B892J6   327.591   63-9550

DS485   KASHMIR

Lamb, Alastair, 1930- III. 3435
The Kashmir problem; a historical survey. New York, Praeger [1967] 163 p. 4 maps (1 fold.) 23 cm. First published in 1966 under title: Crisis in Kashmir, 1947-1966. 1. Kashmir — History. I. T.
DS485.K2L33 1967   954.6   67-11660

DS485   NEPAL

American University, Washington, D.C. Foreign Areas Studies Division. III. 3436
Area handbook for Nepal (with Sikkim and Bhutan). Washington, For sale by the Supt. of Docs., U.S. Govt. Print Off., 1964. xv, 448 p. maps. 24 cm. At head of title: U.S. Army. "Department of the Army pamphlet no. 550-35." 1. Nepal. 2. Sikkim. 3. Bhutan. I. U.S. Army. II. T.
DS485.N4A8   67-115014

Bista, Dor Bahadur. III. 3437
People of Nepal. [1st ed. Kathmandu] Dept. of Publicity, Ministry of Information and Broadcasting, His Majesty's Govt. of Nepal [1967] xvi, 176 p. illus., ports. (part col.) 23 cm. 1. Ethnology — Nepal. I. Nepal. Dept. of Publicity. II. T.
DS485.N4B53   390/.09549/6   Sa67-7774

Fürer-Haimendorf, Christoph von, 1909- III. 3438
The Sherpas of Nepal, Buddhist highlanders. Berkeley, University of California Press, 1964. xix, 298 p. illus., fold. map, ports. 23 cm. 1. Sherpas. 2. Nepal — Social life and customs. I. T.
DS485.N4F8 1964   309.15496   64-25908

Hagen, Toni, 1917- III. 3439
Nepal; the kingdom in the Himalayas [by] Toni Hagen, Friedrich Traugott Wahlen [and] Walter Robert Corti. [Translated by Britta M. Charleston and Toni Hagen; rev. by Ewald Osers. 3d ed.] Chicago, Distributed in the U.S.A. by Rand McNally [1971] 180 p. 84 illus. (part col.) maps. 31 cm. Translation of Nepal; Königreich am Himalaya. 1. Nepal — Description and travel. I. T.
DS485.N4H283 1971   915.49/6/03   79-28765

Joshi, Bhuwan Lal. III. 3440
Democratic innovations in Nepal; a case study of political acculturation [by] Bhuwan Lal Joshi and Leo E. Rose. Berkeley, University of California Press, 1966. xvi, 551 p. maps. 25 cm. 1. Nepal — Politics and government. I. Rose, Leo E., joint author. II. T.
DS485.N4J65   320.95496   66-14092

Karan, Pradyumna Prasad. III. 3441
Nepal, a cultural and physical geography. With the collaboration of William M. Jenkins. Lexington, University of Kentucky Press, 1960. 100, [1] p. illus., ports., 36 maps (1 col., 1 fold. col. in pocket) 28 x 36 cm. 1. Nepal — Description and travel.
DS485.N4K3   915.426   60-8518

DS485   PUNJAB

Tandon, Prakash. III. 3442
Punjabi century, 1857-1947. With a foreword by Maurice Zinkin. Berkeley, University of California Press, 1968. 274 p. map. 20 cm. Sequel: Beyond Punjab, 1937-1960. 1. Punjab — Social life and customs. I. T.
DS485.P19T3 1968   309.1/54/5   68-25959

Singh, Khushwant. III. 3443
A history of the Sikhs. Princeton, N.J., Princeton University Press, 1963-66. 2 v. illus., geneal. tables, maps (part fold.) ports. 23 cm. 1. Sikhs — History. 2. Punjab — History.
DS485.P3S493   954.97   63-7550

DS485   UTTAR PRADESH

Brass, Paul R. III. 3444
Factional politics in an Indian state; the Congress Party in Uttar Pradesh [by] Paul R. Brass. Berkeley, University of California Press, 1965. xiv, 262 p. illus., maps. 24 cm. 1. Uttar Pradesh, India — Politics and government. I. T.
DS485.U6B7   329.9542   65-23109

Berreman, Gerald Duane, 1930- III. 3445
Hindus of the Himalayas; ethnography and change, by Gerald D. Berreman. [2d ed., rev. and enlarged] Berkeley, University of California Press, 1972. lvii, 440 p. illus. 23 cm. Based on the author's thesis, Cornell University, 1959. 1. Sirkanda, India. 2. Ethnology — India — Uttar Pradesh. 3. Villages — India — Uttar Pradesh. I. T.
DS486.S56B4 1972   301.29/54/2   73-156468
    ISBN:0520014235 0520020359 (pbk)

DS488 – 490   SRI LANKA (CEYLON)

Cook, Elsie Kathleen. III. 3446
Ceylon; its geography, its resources and its people. New [i.e. 2d] ed. of "A geography of Ceylon" rev. and brought up to date by K. Kularatnam. Maps and diagrs. drawn by Maurice Weightman. Madras, Macmillan, 1951. 360 p. illus. 21 cm. 1. Ceylon — Description and travel.
DS489.C7 1951   915.48   52-17432

Nyrop, Richard F. III. 3447
Area handbook for Ceylon. Co-authors: Richard F. Nyrop [and others. Washington; For sale by the Supt. of Docs., U.S. Govt. Print. Off.] 1971. xvi, 525 p. maps. 25 cm. "DA pam 550-96." "One of a series of handbooks prepared by the Foreign Area Studies (FAS) of the American University." 1. Ceylon. I. American University, Washington, D.C. Foreign Area Studies. II. T.
DS489.N9   915.493/03/3   71-609526

Seligmann, Charles Gabriel, 1873-1940. III. 3448
The Veddas, by C. G. Seligmann and Brenda Z. Seligmann with a chapter by C. S. Myers and an appendix by A. Mendis Gunasekara. Costerhout,

Anthropological Publications, 1969. xiii, 463 p. illus. geneal. tables, fold map, music, plan, ports. 24 cm. (Cambridge Archaeological and ethnological series) Distributed by Humanities Press, New York. "Photomechanic reprint after the edition of 1911. *1. Veddahs. I. Seligman, Brenda Z. (Salaman) joint author. II. Myers, Charles Samuel, 1873- III. Gunasĕkara, Abraham Mendis, d. 1931. (S)*
DS489.2.S4 1969   915.493   71-405524

Arasaratnam, Sinnappah. III. 3449
Ceylon [by] S. Arasaratnam. Englewood Cliffs, N.J., Prentice-Hall [1964] vi, 182 p. maps. 21 cm. (The Modern nations in historical perspective) *1. Ceylon — History. I. T.*
DS489.5.A778   954.89   64-20750

Pakeman, Sidney Arnold, 1891- III. 3450
Ceylon. New York, Praeger [1964] 256 p. 1 fold. map. 23 cm. (Nations of the modern world) *1. Ceylon — History. I. T. (S)*
DS489.5.P3   954.89   64-16684

Zeylanicus. III. 3451
Ceylon: between Orient and Occident; with a foreword by S. A. Pakeman. London, Elek, 1970. 288 p., 8 plates. illus., maps. 23 cm. *1. Ceylon — History. I. T.*
DS489.5.Z46   915.493/03   71-541625   ISBN:0236176579

DS501 – 689
EAST ASIA (GENERAL)
SOUTHEAST ASIA
DS501 – 518 General Works

Lasker, Bruno, 1880- III. 3452
Peoples of southeast Asia, by Bruno Lasker; prepared under the auspices of the American Council of the Institute of Pacific Relations. [1st ed.] New York, Knopf, 1944. viii, 288, x p. front., plates. 22 cm. *1. East (Far East) — Description and travel. 2. East (Far East) — Social conditions. 3. World war, 1939-1945 — East (Far East) I. Institute of Pacific relations. American council. II. T.*
DS508.L26   915.9   44-877

Fisher, Charles Alfred. III. 3453
South-East Asia: a social, economic and political geography [by] Charles A. Fisher. 2nd ed. London, Methuen; New York, Dutton, 1966. xix, 831 p. maps, tables. 24 cm. Map on endpapers. *1. Asia, Southeastern — Description and travel. I. T.*
DS508.2.F5 1966   915.9   66-72859

Kolb, Albert, 1906- III. 3454
East Asia: China, Japan, Korea, Vietnam; geography of a cultural region. Translated by C. A. M. Sym. London, Methuen, 1971. xvi, 591 p. maps (part fold. col., 1 in pocket) 26 cm. (Methuen's advanced geographies) Translation of Ostasien. Distributed in the U.S.A. by Barnes & Noble. *1. East (Far East) — Civilization. 2. Vietnam — Civilization. I. T.*
DS509.3.K6313 1971   915/.03/42   72-175950   ISBN:0416184206

Burling, Robbins. III. 3455
Hill farms and padi fields; life in mainland Southeast Asia. Englewood Cliffs, N.J., Prentice-Hall [1965] viii, 180 p. map. 21 cm. (A Spectrum book, S-110) *1. Ethnology — Asia, Southeastern. I. T.*
DS509.5.B8   572.959   65-13575

Purcell, Victor William Williams Saunders, 1896-1965. III. 3456
The Chinese in Southeast Asia. 2d ed. London, Oxford University Press, 1965. xvi, 623 p. maps (1 fold.) 25 cm. "Issued under the auspices of the Royal Institute of International Affairs." *1. Chinese in Southeastern Asia. I. Royal Institute of International Affairs. II. T.*
DS509.5.C5P87 1965   301.451   65-4234

LeBar, Frank M. III. 3457
Ethnic groups of mainland Southeast Asia [by] Frank M. LeBar, Gerald C. Hickey [and] John K. Musgrave. Contributing authors: Robbins Burling [and others] New Haven, Human Relations Area Files Press [1964] x, 288 p. 2 fold. col. maps (in pocket) 30 cm. Published as a result of a grant to the Human Relations Area Files from the National Science Foundation. *1. Ethnology — Asia, Southeastern — Dictionaries. I. Hickey, Gerald Cannon, 1925- II. Musgrave, John K. III. Human Relations Area Files, inc. IV. T.*
DS509.5.L4   572.959   64-25414

Murdock, George Peter, 1897- ed. III. 3458
Social structure in Southeast Asia. Chicago, Quadrangle Books, 1960. ix, 182 p. maps, diagrs., tables. 26 cm. (Viking Fund publications in anthropology, no. 29) Papers presented at a symposium on social structure in Southeast Asia, held at the 9th Pacific Science Congress, Bangkok, Thailand, 1957. *1. Ethnology — Asia, Southeastern. I. T. (S)*
DS509.5.M8   572.959   61-981

Southeast Asian tribes, minorities, and nations, III. 3459
edited by Peter Kunstadter. Princeton, N.J., Princeton University Press, 1967. 2 v. (xiii, 902 p.) illus., maps. 24 cm. Consists of papers from a conference held at Princeton University under the auspices of the Center of International Studies, May 10-15, 1965; papers from a panel session held at the annual convention of the American Anthropological Association, Denver, Nov. 1965; and 3 other papers. *1. Minorities — Asia, Southeastern — Addresses, essays, lectures. 2. Minorities — China. 3. Minorities — India. I. Kunstadter, Peter, ed. II. Princeton University. Center of International Studies. III. American Anthropological Association.*
DS509.5.S63   301.35/0954   66-17703

DS511 – 517 HISTORY

Buchanan, Keith M. III. 3460
The Southeast Asian world; an introductory essay [by] Keith Buchanan. New York, Taplinger [1967] 176 p. illus., maps. 23 cm. *1. Asia, Southeastern. I. T.*
DS511.B8   309.0/59   67-20243

Cady, John Frank, 1901- III. 3461
Southeast Asia: its historical development. New York, McGraw-Hill [c1964] xvii, 657 p. maps. 24 cm. *1. Asia, Southeastern — History. I. T.*
DS511.C26   959   63-15888

Clyde, Paul Hibbert, 1896- III. 3462
The Far East; a history of the Western impact and the Eastern response (1830-1970) [by] Paul H. Clyde [and] Burton F. Beers. 5th ed. Englewood Cliffs, N.J., Prentice-Hall [1971] xxiii, 536 p. illus., maps (part col.) 24 cm. *1. East (Far East) — History. I. Beers, Burton F., joint author. II. T.*
DS511.C67 1971   950   72-144100   ISBN:013302976X

Cœdès, George. III. 3463
The Indianized states of Southeast Asia, by G. Coedès. Edited by Walter F. Vella. Translated by Susan Brown Cowing. Honolulu, East-West Center Press [1968] xxi, 403 p. maps. 24 cm. Translation of Les états hindouisés d'Indochine et d'Indonésie, which was first published under title: Histoire ancienne des états hindouisés d'Extrême Orient. *1. Asia, Southeastern — History. 2. East Indians in Southeastern Asia. I. T.*
DS511.C7713 1968   959   67-29224

Hall, Daniel George Edward, 1891- III. 3464
A history of South-east Asia, by D. G. E. Hall. 3rd ed. London, Melbourne [etc.] Macmillan; New York, St. Martin's P., 1968. xxiv, 1019 p. illus., (part fold., part col.), ports. 22 cm. *1. Asia, Southeastern — History. I. T.*
DS511.H15 1968   959   68-15302

Harrison, Brian. III. 3465
South-East Asia: a short history. 3rd ed. London, Macmillan; New York, St Martin's P., 1966. xi, 278 p. 4 plates, 8 maps, table. 22 1/2 cm. Maps on endpapers. *1. Asia, Southeastern — History. I. T.*
DS511.H3 1966   959   66-13529

In search of Southeast Asia; a modern history III. 3466
[by] David Joel Steinberg [and others] Edited by David Joel Steinberg. New York, Praeger Publishers [1971] xii, 522 p. illus., maps. 24 cm. (Praeger paperbound texts) *1. Asia, Southeastern — History. I. Steinberg, David Joel, ed.*
DS511.I5 1971   915.9/03   70-121850

Latourette, Kenneth Scott, 1884-1968. III. 3467
A short history of the Far East. 4th ed. New York, Macmillan [1964] viii, 776 p. maps. 25 cm. *1. East (Far East) — History. I. T.*
DS511.L3 1964   950   64-14965

Le May, Reginald Stuart, 1885- III. 3468
The culture of South-east Asia, the heritage of India. Foreword by R. A. Butler. London, Allen & Unwin [1954] 218 p. plates, maps (part fold.) 24 cm. *1. Asia, Southeastern — Civilization. I. T.*
DS511.L4   915.9   54-1347

Morse, Hosea Ballou, 1855-1934. III. 3469
Far Eastern international relations, by Hosea Ballou Morse and Harley Farnsworth MacNair. New York, Russell & Russell [1967, c1931] 2 v. (xvii, 1128 p.) illus., maps. 23 cm. *1. Eastern question (Far East) 2. China — Foreign relations. 3. Japan — Foreign relations — 1912-1945. I. MacNair, Harley Farnsworth, 1891- joint author. II. T.*
DS511.M88 1967   327.5   67-15998

DS518 POLITICS. FOREIGN RELATIONS

Iriye, Akira. III. 3470
After imperialism; the search for a new order in the Far East, 1921-1931. Cambridge, Harvard University Press, 1965. viii, 375 p. map. 24 cm. (Harvard East Asian series, 22) 1. East (Far East) — History. I. T. (S)
DS518.I75   327.5   65-22052

Brimmell, Jack Henry. III. 3471
Communism in South East Asia; a political analysis. Issued under the auspices of the Royal Institute of International Affairs. London, New York, Oxford University Press, 1959. 415 p. illus. 23 cm. 1. Communism — Asia, Southeastern. I. T.
DS518.1.B7   959   60-61

Gordon, Bernard K., 1932- III. 3472
The dimensions of conflict in Southeast Asia [by] Bernard K. Gordon. Englewood Cliffs, N.J., Prentice-Hall [1966] xiv, 201 p. maps. 21 cm. (A Spectrum book) 1. Asia, Southeastern — Politics. I. T.
DS518.1.G6   327.0959   66-14699

Mills, Lennox Algernon. III. 3473
Southeast Asia; illusion and reality in politics and economics [by] Lennox A. Mills. Minneapolis, University of Minnesota Press [1964] viii, 365 p. map. 23 cm. 1. Asia, Southeastern — Politics. 2. Asia, Southeastern — Economic conditions. I. T.
DS518.1.M55   309.159   64-17805

Shaplen, Robert, 1917- III. 3474
Time out of hand; revolution and reaction in Southeast Asia. [1st ed.] New York, Harper & Row [1969] xii, 455 p. 23 cm. 1. Asia, Southeastern — Politics. I. T.
DS518.1.S47   320.9/59   68-28217

Trager, Frank N., ed. III. 3475
Marxism in Southeast Asia; a study of four countries. Edited, with an introd. and conclusion. With contributions by Jeanne S. Mintz [and others] Stanford, Calif., Stanford University Press, 1959. 381 p. 24 cm. 1. Communism — Asia, Southeastern. 2. Asia, Southeastern — Politics. I. T.
DS518.1.T7   335.40959   59-12469

Cady, John Frank, 1901- III. 3476
The roots of French imperialism in Eastern Asia. Ithaca, N.Y., Published for the American Historical Association [by] Cornell University Press [1954] xii, 322 p. maps. 24 cm. 1. French in the East. 2. France — Colonies — East (Far East)
DS518.2.C3   325.344095   54-13440

Dallin, David J., 1889-1962. III. 3477
Soviet Russia and the Far East. [Hamden, Conn.] Archon Books, 1971 [c1948] vii, 398 p. maps. 23 cm. 1. Russia — Foreign relations — Asia. 2. Asia — Foreign relations — Russia. I. T.
DS518.7.D3 1971   327.47/05   76-150769   ISBN:0208009965

American-East Asian relations: a survey. III. 3478
Contributions by Burton F. Beers [and others] Edited by Ernest R. May and James C. Thomson Jr. Cambridge, Mass., Harvard University Press, 1972. xv, 425 p. 25 cm. (Harvard studies in American-East Asian relations, 1) 1. United States — Foreign relations — East (Far East) — Addresses, essays, lectures. 2. East (Far East) — Foreign relations — United States — Addresses, essays, lectures. I. Beers, Burton F. II. May, Ernest R., ed. III. Thomson, James Claude, 1931- ed. (S)
DS518.8.A858   327.73/05   70-188970   ISBN:0674022858

Fifield, Russell Hunt, 1914- III. 3479
Southeast Asia in United States policy. [1st ed.] New York, Published for the Council on Foreign Relations by Praeger [1963] xi, 488 p. map. 22 cm. 1. Asia, Southeastern. 2. United States — Foreign relations — Asia, Southeastern. I. Council on Foreign Relations. II. T.
DS518.8.F48   327.73059   63-20144

Iriye, Akira. III. 3480
Across the Pacific; an inner history of American-East Asian relations. Introd. by John K. Fairbank. [1st ed.] New York, Harcourt, Brace & World [1967] xvii, 361 p. 24 cm. 1. U.S. — Relations (general) with the East (Far East). 2. East (Far East) — Relations (general) with the U.S. I. T.
DS518.8.I73   301.29/5/073   67-19202

DS521 – 558 Indochina

Cœdès, George. III. 3481
The making of South East Asia, by G. Cœdès. Translated by H. M. Wright. Berkeley, University of California Press, 1966. xvi, 268 p. illus. 23 cm. Translation of Les peuples de la péninsule indochinoise. 1. Asia, Southeastern — History. I. T.
DS527.C613   959   66-4402

Lancaster, Donald. III. 3482
The emancipation of French Indochina. London, New York, Oxford University Press, 1961. xii, 445 p. fold. map. 23 cm. "Issued under the auspices of the Royal Institute of International Affairs." 1. Indochina, French — History. I. T.
DS541.L28   959.7   61-1998

Thompson, Virginia McLean, 1903- III. 3483
French Indo-China, by Virginia Thompson. New York, Octagon Books, 1968. 516 p. map. 24 cm. Reprint of the 1937 ed. 1. Indochina, French — History. 2. French in Indochina.
DS541.T5 1968   959   68-17756

Eastman, Lloyd E. III. 3484
Throne and mandarins: China's search for a policy during the Sino-French controversy, 1880-1885 [by] Lloyd E. Eastman. Cambridge, Harvard University Press, 1967. xiii, 254 p. map. 22 cm. (Harvard historical studies, v.79) 1. Chinese-French War, 1884-1885. 2. China — Foreign relations — To 1912. I. T. (S)
DS549.E2   951/.03   67-12098

Hammer, Ellen Joy, 1921- III. 3485
The struggle for Indochina, 1940-1955 [by] Ellen J. Hammer. Stanford, Calif., Stanford University Press [1966, c1955] ix, 373 p. map. 24 cm. 1. Indochina, French — History. I. T.
DS550.H353   959.703   66-24065

Randle, Robert F. III. 3486
Geneva 1954; the settlement of the Indochinese War, by Robert F. Randle. Princeton, N.J., Princeton University Press, 1969. xviii, 639 p. map, ports. 24 cm. 1. Indochina, French — History — Indochinese War, 1946-1954 — Peace. 2. Geneva Conference, 1954. I. Geneva Conference, 1954. II. T.
DS550.R3   327/.09597   69-18069   ISBN:0691075298

DS557 VIETNAM

American University, Washington, D.C. Foreign Area Studies Division. III. 3487
Area handbook for South Vietnam. Co-authors: Harvey H. Smith [and others] Washington, for sale by the Supt. of Docs., U.S. Govt. Print. Off., 1967. xiv, 510 p. maps. 24 cm. "DA pam no. 550-54." 1. Vietnam. I. Smith, Harvey Henry, 1892- II. T.
DS557.A5A717   915.97/03/4   67-62089

Buttinger, Joseph. III. 3488
Vietnam; a political history. New York, Praeger [1968] viii, 565 p. maps. 22 cm. A combined and abridged ed. of the author's The smaller dragon (1958) and Vietnam: a dragon embattled (1967) 1. Vietnam — History. I. T.
DS557.A5B84   959.7   68-23351

Fall, Bernard B., 1926-1967. III. 3489
The two Viet-Nams; a political and military analysis [by] Bernard B. Fall. 2d rev. ed. New York, Praeger [1967] xii, 507 p. maps. 22 cm. 1. Vietnam — History. I. T.
DS557.A5F34 1967   959.7   66-14505

Gurtov, Melvin. III. 3490
The first Vietnam crisis; Chinese Communist strategy and United States involvement, 1953-1954. New York, Columbia University Press, 1967. xxiv, 228 p. 23 cm. (Studies of the East Asian Institute, Columbia University) 1. China (People's Republic of China, 1949- — Foreign relations — Vietnam. 2. Vietnam — Foreign relations — China (People's Republic, 1949-) 3. U.S. — Foreign relations — Vietnam. 4. Vietnam — Foreign relations — U.S. I. T. (S:Columbia University. East Asian Institute. East Asian Institute studies)
DS557.A5G8   327.510597   67-12207

Hickey, Gerald Cannon, 1925- III. 3491
Village in Vietnam. New Haven, Yale University Press, 1964. 314 [i.e. xxviii],

325 p. illus., geneal. tables, maps, plans, ports. 27 cm. *1. Ethnology — Vietnam. 2. Khanh Hau, Vietnam. I. T.*
DS557.A5H5   309.1597   64-20923

McAlister, John T., 1936- III. 3492
Viet Nam; the origins of revolution [by] John T. McAlister, Jr. [1st ed. Princeton, N.J.] Published for the Center of International Studies, Princeton University [by] Knopf, New York, 1969. xix, 377, xii p. maps. 22 cm. *1. Vietnam — Politics and government. I. Princeton University. Center of International Studies. II. T.*
DS557.A5M17 1969   959.7   69-10690

Smith, Ralph Bernard. III. 3493
Viet-Nam and the West [by] Ralph Smith. Ithaca, N.Y., Cornell University Press [1971] ix, 206 p. maps. 22 cm. *1. Vietnam — History. I. T.*
DS557.A5S58 1971   915.97/03   78-148717   ISBN:0801406366

FitzGerald, Frances, 1940- III. 3494
Fire in the lake; the Vietnamese and the Americans in Vietnam. [1st ed.] Boston, Little, Brown [1972] xiv, 491 p. maps. 24 cm. "An Atlantic Monthly Press book." "Portions ... appeared originally in the New Yorker, in slightly different form." *1. Vietnam — Politics and government. 2. Vietnamese Conflict, 1961- — United States. I. T.*
DS557.A6F53   320.9/597/043   72-186966

Nhat-Hanh, Thich. III. 3495
Vietnam: the lotus in the sea of fire. London, S.C.M. Press, 1967. 128 p. 18 cm. *1. Vietnam — Politics and government. 2. Religion and state — Vietnam. I. T.*
DS557.A6N495 1967   959.7/04   67-81292

Pike, Douglas, 1924- III. 3496
Viet Cong; the organization and techniques of the National Liberation Front of South Vietnam. Cambridge, Mass., M.I.T. Press [1966] xx, 490 p. illus., maps (on lining papers) ports. 24 cm. (Massachusetts Institute of Technology. Center for International Studies. Studies in international communism, no. 7) *1. South Viet Nam National Front for Liberation. I. T. (S)*
DS557.A6P54   959.704   66-28896

Pike, Douglas Eugene, 1924- III. 3497
War, peace, and the Viet Cong. Cambridge, Mass., M.I.T. Press [1969] xii, 186 p. 22 cm. *1. South Viet Nam National Front for Liberation. 2. Vietnamese Conflict, 1961- I. T.*
DS557.A6P553   959.7/04   70-83403

South Vietnam; a political history, 1954-1970. III. 3498
New York, Scribner [1970] viii, 168 p. maps. 21 cm. (Keesing's research report [5]) "Written by the editorial staff of Keesing's contemporary archives" — Dust jacket. *1. Vietnam — Politics and government. I. Keesing's contemporary archives.*
DS557.A6S658   959.7/04   70-134360

Meyerson, Harvey. III. 3499
Vinh Long. With an introd. by Congressman John V. Tunney. Illustrated with maps by Adam Nakamura. Boston, Houghton Mifflin, 1970. xxiv, 220 p. illus., maps. 22 cm. *1. Vietnamese Conflict, 1961- — Campaigns — Vinh Long (Province)*
DS557.A62V5 1970   959.7/04   70-91063

Cooper, Chester L. III. 3500
The lost crusade; America in Vietnam, by Chester L. Cooper. With a foreword by W. Averell Harriman. New York, Dodd, Mead [1970] xi, 559 p. 24 cm. *1. Vietnamese Conflict, 1961- — United States. 2. United States — Foreign relations — Vietnam. 3. Vietnam — Foreign relations — United States. I. T.*
DS557.A63C66   959.7/04   79-135539   ISBN:0396062415

Draper, Theodore, 1912- III. 3501
Abuse of power. New York, Viking Press [1967] ix, 244 p. 21 cm. *1. Vietnamese Conflict, 1961- — U.S. I. T.*
DS557.A63D7   959.7/04   66-18668

Hoopes, Townsend, 1922- III. 3502
The limits of intervention; an inside account of how the Johnson policy of escalation in Vietnam was reversed. New York, D. McKay Co. [1969] ix, 245 p. 21 cm. *1. Vietnamese Conflict, 1961- — United States. I. T.*
DS557.A63H6   959.7/04   78-94505

Schell, Jonathan, 1943- III. 3503
The village of Ben Suc. [1st ed.] New York, Knopf, 1967. 132 p. map. 22 cm. *1. Vietnamese Conflict, 1961- — Destruction and pillage — Ben Suc. I. T.*
DS557.A68S33   959.7/04   67-29479

DS557 DEMOCRATIC REPUBLIC OF VIETNAM

American University, Washington, D.C. Foreign Area's Studies Division. III. 3504
Area handbook for North Vietnam. Co-authors: Harvey H. Smith [and others] Washington, For sale by the Supt. of Docs., U.S. Govt. Print. Off., 1967. xii, 494 p. illus., maps. 24 cm. "DA pam no. 550-57." 1957 and 1962 editions published under title: Area handbook for Vietnam. The present revision is in two separate studies, South Vietnam and North Vietnam. *I. Smith, Harvey Henry, 1892- II. T.*
DS557.A7A63   915.97   68-60367

Ho-chi-Minh, Pres. Democratic Republic of Vietnam, 1894?- III. 3505
On revolution; selected writings, 1920-66. Edited and with an introd. by Bernard F. Fall. New York, Praeger [1967] xix, 389 p. 22 cm. (Praeger publications in Russian history and world communism, no. 190) *I. Fall, Bernard B., 1926-1967. II. T.*
DS557.A7H533   959.7008   67-20481

Huyen, N. Khac. III. 3506
Vision accomplished? The enigma of Ho Chi Minh [by] N. Khac Huyen. New York, Macmillan [1971] xviii, 377 p. 22 cm. *1. Ho-chi-Minh, President Democratic Republic of Vietnam, 1894?-1969. 2. Communism — Vietnam. I. T.*
DS557.A76H679 1971b   959.7/04/0924 (B)   77-30932

Race, Jeffrey. III. 3507
War comes to Long An; revolutionary conflict in a Vietnamese Province. Berkeley, University of California Press, 1972. xxiii, 299 p. illus. 24 cm. *1. Long An, Vietnam — History. 2. Vietnamese Conflict, 1961- I. T.*
DS557.A8L657 1972   959.704/31   79-145793   ISBN:0520019148

DS557 CAMBODIA

Munson, Frederick P. III. 3508
Area handbook for Cambodia. Co-authors: Frederick P. Munson [and others] Washington, For sale by the Supt. of Docs., U.S. Govt. Print. Off., 1968. xvi, 364 p. illus., maps. 24 cm. "DA pam no. 550-50." "Supersedes DA pam 550-50, April 1963." "One of a series of handbooks prepared by Foreign Area Studies (FAS) of the American University." "A revision of the U.S. Army area handbook for Cambodia." *1. Cambodia. I. American University, Washington, D.C. Foreign Area Studies. II. American University, Washington, D.C. Foreign Area Studies Division. U.S. Army area handbook for Cambodia. III. T.*
DS557.C2M94 1968   915.96/03/4   72-600172

Briggs, Lawrence Palmer. III. 3509
The ancient Khmer Empire. Philadelphia, American Philosophical Society, 1951. 295 p. illus., maps. 30 cm. (Transactions of the American Philosophical Society, new ser., v.41, pt.1) *1. Khmers — Antiquities. 2. Cambodia — History. I. T. (S:American Philosophical Society, Philadelphia. Transactions, new ser., v.41, pt. 1)*
DS557.C23B7x (Q11.P6 n.s., vol. 41, pt. 1)   959.6   51-2328

Willmott, William E. III. 3510
The political structure of the Chinese community in Cambodia, by W. E. Willmott. [London] Univeristy of London, Athlone Press; New York, Humanities Press, 1970. viii, 211 p. map. 23 cm. (London School of Economics. Monographs on social anthropology, no. 42) *1. Chinese in Cambodia. I. T. (S:Monographs on social anthropology, no. 42)*
DS557.C242W52   301.451/951/0596   70-584141   ISBN:0391001140

Dauphin-Meunier, Achille, 1906- III. 3511
Histoire du Cambodge, par A. Dauphin-Meunier ... 2 édition mise à jour. Paris, Presses Universitaires de France, 1968. 128 p. maps. 17 cm. (Que sais-je? No. 916) Cover illustrated in color. *1. Cambodia — History. I. T.*
DS557.C25D3 1968   68-133571

Smith, Roger M. III. 3512
Cambodia's foreign policy, by Roger M. Smith. Ithaca, N.Y., Cornell University Press [1965] x, 273 p. fold. map. 23 cm. *1. Cambodia — Foreign relations. I. T.*
DS557.C28S6   327.596   65-15375

Osborne, Milton E. III. 3513
The French presence in Cochinchina and Cambodia; rule and response (1859-1905), by Milton E. Osborne. Ithaca [N.Y.] Cornell University Press [1969] xvi, 379 p. illus., maps, ports. 22 cm. *1. Cochin China — Politics and government. 2. Cambodia — Politics and government. 3. French in Cochin China. 4. French in Cambodia. I. T.*
DS557.C7O76   325.3/44/09597   78-87021   ISBN:0801405122

DS557 LAOS

Berval, René de. III. 3514
Kingdom of Laos; the land of the million elephants and of the white parasol, by René de Berval in collaboration with Their Highnesses Princes Phetsarath and Souvanna Phouma [and others. English translation by Mrs. Teissier du Cros and others. 1st ed.] Saigon, Viêt-Nam, France-Asie [1959] 506 p. illus., ports., maps. 24 cm. Translation of Présence du royaume Lao, published in March, April and May 1956, as special issues of France-Asie. *1. Laos.*
DS557.L2B43   915.94   59-2790

Roberts, Thomas Duval, 1903- III. 3515
Area handbook for Laos. Co-authors: T. D. Roberts [and others] Washington, For sale by the Supt. of Docs., U.S. Govt. Print. Off., 1967. ix, 349 p. maps. 24 cm. "DA pam no. 550-59." "One of a series of handbooks prepared by Foreign Area Studies (FAS) of the American University." *1. Laos. I. American University, Washington, D.C. Foreign Area Studies.*
DS557.L2R6   915.95   68-60604

Laos: war and revolution. III. 3516
Edited by Nina S. Adams and Alfred W. McCoy. [1st ed.] New York, Harper & Row [c1970] xxiii, 482 p. maps. 21 cm. (Harper colophon books, CN 221) "A publication of the Committee of Concerned Asian Scholars." *1. Laos — History — Addresses, essays, lectures. I. Adams, Nina S., ed. II. McCoy, Alfred W., ed. III. Committee of Concerned Asian Scholars.*
DS557.L25L3 1970   959.4/04   76-140188   ISBN:0060902213

Toye, Hugh. III. 3517
Laos: buffer state or battleground. London, New York [etc.] Oxford U.P., 1968. xvii, 245 p. 8 plates, illus., tables, 8 maps, ports. 23 cm. *1. Laos — Politics and government. 2. Laos — History. I. T.*
DS557.L25T6 1968   959.4/04   68-115716   ISBN:0192151584

Dommen, Arthur J. III. 3518
Conflict in Laos; the politics of neutralization [by] Arthur J. Dommen. Rev. ed. New York, Praeger [1971] xvi, 454 p. maps. 22 cm. *1. Laos — Politics and government. 2. Laos — Foreign relations. I. T.*
DS557.L28D6 1971   959.4   76-145945

Langer, Paul Fritz, 1915- III. 3519
North Vietnam and the Pathet Lao; partners in the struggle for Laos [by] Paul F. Langer and Joseph J. Zasloff. Cambridge, Harvard University Press, 1970. xiv, 262 p. illus., maps. 22 cm. *1. Laos — Politics and government. 2. Vietnam (Democratic Republic, 1946-) — Foreign relations — Laos. 3. Laos — Foreign relations — Vietnam (Democratic Republic, 1946-) I. Zasloff, Joseph Jermiah, joint author. II. T.*
DS557.L28L3   959.7/04   73-134326   ISBN:0674626753

DS557 – 558 SPECIAL LOCALITIES

Gourou, Pierre, 1900- III. 3520
The peasants of the Tonkin Delta, a study of human geography. [Translated by Richard R. Miller] New Haven, Human Relations Area Files, 1955. 2 v. (xiii, 889 p.) illus., maps, diagrs., profiles. 21 cm. (Behavior science translations) *1. Tongking. I. T. (S)*
DS557.T7G62 1955   915.99   56-1826

Groslier, Bernard Philippe. III. 3521
Angkor: art and civilization [by] Bernard Groslier [and] Jacques Arthaud. [Translated from the French by Eric Ernshaw Smith. Rev. ed.] New York, Praeger [1966] 236 p. illus., fold. maps, plans, col. plates. 28 cm. Translation of Angkor: hommes et pierres. *1. Angkor, Cambodia. I. Arthaud, Jacques, joint author. II. T.*
DS558.A6G73 1966   913.59603   66-20910

DS560 – 589 Thailand (Siam)

Seidenfaden, Erik, 1881-1958. III. 3522
The Thai peoples. Bangkok, Siam Society, 1958-   v. illus. 24 cm. *1. Tai race.*
DS560.S4   959.3   62-858

Pendleton, Robert Larimore, 1890-1957. III. 3523
Thailand; aspects of landscape and life, by Robert L. Pendelton, with the assistance of Robert C. Kingsbury and others. [1st ed.] New York, Duell, Sloan and Pearce [1962] xv, 321 p. illus., maps. 26 cm. (An American Geographical Society handbook) *1. Thailand. (S:American Geographical Society of New York. Handbook)*
DS566.P4 1962   915.93   62-12164

Anuman Rajathon, Phrayā, 1888- III. 3524
Life and ritual in old Siam; three studies of Thai life and customs. Translated and edited by William J. Gedney. New Haven, HRAF Press [1961] 191 p. illus., plates. 23 cm. *1. Farm life — Thailand. 2. Buddha and Buddhism — Thailand. 3. Birth (in religion, folk-lore, etc.) I. Gedney, William J., ed. and tr. II. T.*
DS568.A7   915.93   61-13465

Coughlin, Richard J. III. 3525
Double identity; the Chinese in modern Thailand. [Hong Kong] Hong Kong University Press, 1960. 222 p. illus. 23 cm. *1. Chinese in Thailand. I. T.*
DS570.C5C6 1960   301.45   60-4015

Skinner, George William, 1925- III. 3526
Chinese society in Thailand: an analytical history. Ithaca, N.Y., Cornell University Press [1957] xvii, 459 p. maps (part fold.) diagrs., tables. 24 cm. *1. Chinese in Thailand. I. T.*
DS570.C5S54   325.25109593   57-3051

Henderson, John William, 1910- III. 3527
Area handbook for Thailand. Co-authors: John W. Henderson [and others. 3d revision. Washington; For sale by the Supt. of Docs., U.S. Govt. Print. Off.] 1971. xiv, 413 p. map. 24 cm. "DA Pam 550-53." "One of a series of handbooks prepared by Foreign Area Studies (FAS) of the American University." Issued in 1963 by American University, Foreign Areas Studies Division. *1. Thailand. I. American University, Washington, D.C. Foreign Area Studies. II. American University, Washington, D.C. Foreign Areas Studies Division. Area handbook for Thailand. III. T.*
DS571.H45 1971   915.93   72-611403

Wood, William Alfred Rae, 1878- III. 3528
A history of Siam, from the earliest times to the year A.D. 1781, with a supplement dealing with more recent events, by W. A. R. Wood. Rev. ed. Bangkok, The Siam Barnakich Press [1933] 300 p. front., plates (part col.) ports., fold. map. 23 cm. Illustrated lining-papers. *1. Thailand — History.*
DS571.W6 1933   959.3   41-22868

Damrong Rajanubhab, Prince, 1862-1943. III. 3529
Miscellaneous articles written for the journal of the Siam Society by Prince Damrong. Published by permission of the Siam Society for the centenary of the Prince. [Bangkok, Kuruspha Press] B. E. 2505 [1962] 124 p. 24 plates. 26 cm. *1. Siam Society.*
DS572.D3x

Chula Chakrabongse, Prince, 1908-1963. III. 3530
Lords of life; the paternal monarchy of Bangkok, 1782-1932, with the earlier and more recent history of Thailand. New York, Taplinger Pub. Co., 1960. 352 p. illus. (part col) ports., 3 maps on fold. leaf, geneal. table. 23 cm. *1. Thailand — History. I. T.*
DS578.C48   959.3   60-11970

Moffat, Abbot Low, 1901- III. 3531
Mongkut, the King of Siam. Ithaca, N.Y., Cornell University Press [1961] 254 p. illus. 23 cm. *1. Mongkut, King of Thailand, 1804-1868.*
DS581.M6   923.1593   61-16666

Landon, Kenneth Perry, 1903- III. 3532
Siam in transition; a brief survey of cultural trends in the five years since the revolution of 1932. New York, Greenwood Press [1968] ix, 328 p. fold. map. 24 cm. Reprint of the 1939 ed. *1. Thailand. I. T.*
DS584.L3 1968   915.93/03/4   68-57615

DS591 – 605 Malaysia

Henderson, John William, 1910- III. 3533
Area handbook for Malaysia. Co-authors: John W. Henderson [and others. Washington; For sale by the Supt. of Docs., U.S. Govt. Print. Off.] 1970. xvi, 639 p. maps. 24 cm. "DA pam 550-45." "One of a series of handbooks prepared by Foreign Area Studies (FAS) of the American University." "Supersedes DA pam 550-45, July 1965." 1965 ed. by B. C. Maday, and others, published under title: Area handbook for Malaysia and Singapore. *1. Malaysia. I. American University, Washington, D.C. Foreign Area Studies. II. Maday, Bela C. Area handbook for Malaysia and Singapore. III. T.*
DS592.H45 1970   915.95/03/5   71-608971

Ooi, Jin-Bee. III. 3534
Land, people, and economy in Malaya. [London] Longmans [1963] xix, 426

III. 3535   Asia   DS592

p. illus., maps. 23 cm. (Geographies for advanced study) *1. Malaysia. I. T.*
DS592.O5   919.1   64-1693

Blythe, Wilfred.   **III. 3535**
The impact of Chinese secret societies in Malaya: a historical study. London, Kuala Lumpur [etc.] Issued under the auspices of the Royal Institute of International Affairs [by] Oxford U.P., 1969. xiv, 570 p. 9 plates, illus., facsims., maps. 25 cm. *1. Chinese in Malaya. 2. Hung Mên. 1. Royal Institute of International Affairs. II. T.*
DS595.B54   364.14/06   71-396881   ISBN:192149747

Newell, William Hare.   **III. 3536**
Treacherous river: a study of rural Chinese in North Malaya. Kuala Lumpur, University of Malaya Press; [sole ditributors: Oxford University Press, London, New York] 1962. xxv, 233 p. illus., maps, tables. 23 cm. *1. Chinese in Malaya. I. T.*
DS595.N45   301.45   63-2972

Vaughan, Jonas Daniel, 1825-1891.   **III. 3537**
The manners and customs of the Chinese of the Straits Settlements. With an introd. by Wilfred Blythe. Kuala Lumpur, Oxford University Press, 1971. vii, 126 p. illus. (part col.) 25 cm. (Oxford in Asia historical reprints) "First published in 1879." *1. Chinese in the Straits Settlements — Social life and customs. I. T.*
DS595.V38 1971   79-942279

Bastin, John Sturgus, 1927- comp.   **III. 3538**
Malaysia; selected historical readings, compiled by John Bastin and Robin W. Winks. Kuala Lumpur, New York, Oxford University Press, 1966. xiv, 484 p. maps. 24 cm. *1. Malaysia — History — Addresses, essays, lectures. I. Winks, Robin W., joint comp.*
DS596.B33   959.5   Sa67-771

Gullick, J. M.   **III. 3539**
Malaysia, by J. M. Gullick. New York, Praeger [1969] 304 p. illus., fold. map, ports. 23 cm. (Nations of the modern world) 1963-1964 editions published under title: Malaya. *1. Malaysia — History. 2. Malaysia — Politics and government. I. T. (S)*
DS596.G83 1969b   991.1/52   69-11867

Pye, Lucian W., 1921-   **III. 3540**
Guerrilla communism in Malaya, its social and political meaning. Princeton, Princeton University Press [1956] 369 p. illus. 23 cm. *1. Communism — Malay Peninsula. I. T.*
DS596.P9   959.5   56-10827

Roff, William R.   **III. 3541**
The origins of Malay nationalism, by William R. Roff. New Haven, Yale University Press, 1967. xx, 297 p. illus., facsims., ports. 24 cm. (Yale Southeast Asia studies, 2) *1. Nationalism — Malay Peninsula. 2. Elite (Social sciences) 3. Malay Peninsula — History. I. T. (S)*
DS596.5.R6   320.1/58/095951   67-13447

Barber, Noël.   **III. 3542**
The war of the running dogs; the Malayan Emergency: 1948-1960. [1st American ed.] New York, Weybright and Talley [1972, c1971] 284 p. illus. 22 cm. *1. Malaya — History — Malayan Emergency, 1948-1960. I. T.*
DS597.B37 1972   959.5/04   78-188017

Hanna, Willard Anderson, 1911-   **III. 3543**
Sequel to colonialism; the 1957-1960 foundations for Malaysia; an on-the-spot examination of the geographic, economic, and political seedbed where the idea of a Federation of Malaysia was germinated, by Willard A. Hanna. New York, American Universities Field Staff [1965] 288 p. map (on lining papers) 24 cm. "Originally written as reports for serial publication by the American Universities Field Staff, these chapters are now collected, rearranged, and republished in a close approximation of the original form." *1. Malaysia — History. I. American Universities Field Staff. II. T.*
DS597.H3 1965   959.5   65-12895

Means, Gordon Paul.   **III. 3544**
Malaysian politics [by] Gordon P. Means. New York, New York University Press [1970] 447 p. illus., maps. 23 cm. Based on the author's thesis, University of Washington. *1. Malaysia — Politics and government. I. T.*
DS597.M4 1970b   320.9/595/04   78-91692   ISBN:0814704697

Hanna, Willard Anderson, 1911-   **III. 3545**
The formation of Malaysia; new factor in world politics; an analytical history and assessment of the prospects of the newest state in Southeast Asia, based on a series of reports written for the American Universities Field Staff, by Willard A Hanna. New York, American Universities Field Staff [1964] 247 p. map (on lining paper) 29 cm. *1. Malaysia. I. T.*
DS597.2.H3   915.95   64-19390

Wang, Gungwu, ed.   **III. 3546**
Malaysia, a survey. New York, F. A. Praeger [1964] 466 p. maps. 26 cm. *1. Malaysia — History. I. T.*
DS597.2.W3 1964   959.5   64-24586

Firth, Rosemary.   **III. 3547**
Housekeeping among Malay peasants. 2nd ed. London, Athlone P.; New York, Humanities P., 1966. xvi, 242 p. front., 8 plates, 2 maps, tables, diagrs. 22 1/2 cm. (Monographs on social anthropology, no. 7) *1. Kelantan — Social life and customs. 2. Home economics — Kelantan. I. T. (S)*
DS598.K3F5 1966   309.15951   66-10914

Cole, Fay Cooper, 1881-   **III. 3548**
The peoples of Malaysia [by] Fay-Cooper Cole. New York, Van Nostrand, 1945. xiv, 354 p. plates, maps, diagrs. 22 cm. "Authorities from whom data for the graphs and discussion was drawn": p. 335-337. *1. Malay archipelago — Social life and customs. 2. Malay race. 3. Ethnology — Malay archipelago. I. T.*
DS601.C63   919.1   45-5386

Robequain, Charles, 1897-   **III. 3549**
Malaya, Indonesia, Borneo, and the Philippines; a geographical, economic, and political description of Malaya, the East Indies, and the Philip[p]ines. Translated by E. D. Laborde. Issued in co-operation with the International Secretariat, Institute of Pacific Relations. [2d ed.] London, New York, Longmans, Green [1958] xi, 466 p. illus., maps, diagrs. 23 cm. Translation of Le monde malais. *1. Malay Archipelago. I. T.*
DS601.R752 1958   991   58-4431

Wallace, Alfred Russel, 1823-1913.   **III. 3550**
The Malay Archipelago, the land of the orang-utan and the bird of paradise; a narrative of travel, with studies of man and nature. New York, Dover Publications [1962] xvii, 515 p. illus., maps (1 fold.) 21 cm. "Unabridged republication of the last revised edition ... first published in 1869." *1. Natural history — Malay Archipelago. 2. Malay Archipelago — Description and travel. 3. Ethnology — Malay Archipelago.*
DS601.W18 1962   574.991   62-2568

DS611 – 649   Indonesia

Alisjahbana, Sutan Takdir, 1908-   **III. 3551**
Indonesia: social and cultural revolution, by S. Takdir Alispahbana. [Translated from the Indonesian by Benedict R. Anderson. 2d ed.] Kuala Lumpur, Oxford University Press, 1966. ix, 206 p. map (on lining papers) 23 cm. First published in 1961 under title: Indonesia in the modern world. *1. Indonesia. I. T.*
DS615.A68 1966   919.1033   Sa66-7740

Grant, Bruce.   **III. 3552**
Indonesia. [2nd ed. Carlton, Melbourne] Melbourne University; London, New York, Cambridge University Press [1966] ix, 204 p. maps (on lining-papers) ports. 23 cm. *1. Indonesia.*
DS615.G67 1966   919.1   66-29036

Henderson, John William, 1910-   **III. 3553**
Area handbook for Indonesia. Co-authors: John W. Henderson [and others. Washington; For sale by the Supt. of Docs., U.S. Govt. Print. Off., 1970. xviii, 569 p. illus., maps. 25 cm. "DA pam 550-39." "One of a series of handbooks prepared by Foreign Area Studies (FAS) of the American University." Supersedes 1964 ed. prepared by Foreign Area Studies Division, American University, Washington, D.C. *1. Indonesia. I. American University, Washington, D.C. Foreign Area Studies. II. American University, Washington, D.C. Foreign Areas Studies Division. Area handbook for Indonesia. III. T.*
DS615.H44   309.1/91   73-608279

McVey, Ruth Thomas, ed.   **III. 3554**
Indonesia [by] Herbert Feith [and others] New Haven, Southeast Asia studies, Yale University, by arrangement with HRAF Press [1963] 600 p. maps (2 fold. col.) tables. 22 cm. (Survey of world cultures [12]) *1. Indonesia. (S)*
DS615.M3   919.1   62-21842

Furnivall, John Sydenham.   **III. 3555**
Netherlands India: a study of plural economy, by J. S. Furnivall; with an introduction by A. C. D. De Graeff. [1st ed.] reprinted. London, Cambridge U.P., 1967. xxiv, 502 p. maps. 22 cm. (Cambridge University Press. Library editions) First published 1939. *1. Indonesia — History. 2. Indonesia — Politics and government. 3. Indonesia — Economic conditions. I. T.*
DS634.F8 1967   309.1/91   68-88337

Vlekke, Bernard Hubertus Maria, 1899-   **III. 3556**
Nusantara, a history of Indonesia. Rev. ed. Chicago, Quadrangle Books, 1960 [c1959] 479 p. illus. 22 cm. *1. Indonesia — History. I. T.*
DS634.V55 1960   62-58200

Kahin, George McTurnan. III. 3557
Nationalism and revolution in Indonesia. Ithaca, Cornell University Press [1952] xii, 490 p. maps. 25 cm. "Published under the auspices of the International Secretariat of the Institute of Pacific Relations and the Southeast Asia Program, Cornell University." *1. Nationalism — Indonesia. 2. Indonesia — Politics and government — 1950- I. T.*
DS644.K32   991   52-4383

Dahm, Bernhard. III. 3558
Sukarno and the struggle for Indonesian independence. Translated from the German by Mary F. Somers Heidhues. Ithaca, [N.Y.] Cornell University Press [1969] xvii, 374 p. maps. 24 cm. "Revised and updated edition of Sukarnos Kampf um Indonesiens Unabhängigkeit." *1. Sukarno, Pres. Indonesia, 1901- I. T.*
DS644.1.S8D283   991/.03/0924 (B)   69-18356   ISBN:801404886

Hughes, John, 1930- III. 3559
Indonesian upheaval. New York, D. McKay Co. [1967] ix, 304 p. 21 cm. *1. Indonesia — Politics and government — 1966. I. T.*
DS644.4.H8   991/.03   67-26500

Kartini, raden adjeng, 1879-1904. III. 3560
Letters of a Javanese princess. Translated from the Dutch by Agnes Louise Symmers. Edited and with an introd. by Hildred Geertz. Pref. by Eleanor Roosevelt. New York, W. W. Norton [1964] 246 p. 20 cm. (UNESCO collection of representative works: Indonesian series. The Norton library, N207.) *1. Women in Java. I. T. (S)*
DS646.23.K3 1964   309.1922   64-5470

Day, Clive, 1871-1951. III. 3561
The Dutch in Java. [1st ed. reprinted] with an introduction by John Bastin. Kuala Lumpur, New York [etc.] Oxford U.P., 1966. xxii, 434 p. front. (facsim.) tables. 21 1/2 cm. (Oxford in Asia. Historical reprints) 1st ed. published as The policy and administration of the Dutch in Java. *1. Netherlands — Colonies — Administration. 2. Java — Politics and government. I. T.*
DS646.27.D27 1966   325.349209922   66-67566

Tregonning, K. G. III. 3562
A history of modern Sabah (North Borneo, 1881-1963) by K. G. Tregonning. 2d ed. [Singapore] Published for the University of Singapore by the University of Malaya Press, 1965. 275 p. illus., maps, ports. 22 cm. First ed. published in 1958 under title: Under chartered company rule: North Borneo, 1881-1946. *1. British North Borneo Company. 2. Sabah — History. I. T.*
DS646.33.T7 1965   991.152   66-1275

Runciman, Steven, Sir, 1903- III. 3563
The white rajahs; a history of Sarawak from 1841 to 1946. Cambridge, University Press, 1960. 319 p. illus. 24 cm. *1. Sarawak — History. I. T.*
DS646.36.R9   991.15   60-50589

Ormeling, Ferdinand Jan. III. 3564
The Timor problem; a geographical interpretation of an underdeveloped island. Djakarta, J. B. Wolters, 1955. xv, 284 p. illus., maps, tables. 24 cm. Disertasi — Universitas Indonesia, Djakarta. Errata leaf inserted. *1. Timor, Dutch — Description and travel. I. T.*
DS646.5.O7   919.24   56-43948

Belo, Jane, comp. III. 3565
Traditional Balinese culture; essays. New York, Columbia University Press, 1970. xxvii, 421 p. illus., map, music. 28 cm. *1. Bali (Island) — Civilization — Addresses, essays, lectures. I. T.*
DS647.B2B4   919.2/3   68-54454   ISBN:231030843

Covarrubias, Miguel, 1904-1957. III. 3566
Island of Bali [by] Miguel Covarrubias; with an album of photographs by Rose Covarrubias. 1st ed. New York, A. A. Knopf, 1937. xxv, 417 p. illus., plates (part col.) fold. map. 24 cm. *1. Bali (Island)*
DS647.B2C6   919.2   37-34623

DS651 – 689   Philippine Islands

Chaffee, Frederic H. III. 3567
Area handbook for the Philippines. Co-authors: Frederic H. Chaffee [and others] Washington, For sale by the Supt. of Docs., U.S. Govt. Print. Off., 1969. xiv, 413 p. maps. 24 cm. "DA pam no. 550-72." "One of a series of handbooks prepared by Foreign Area Studies (FAS) of the American University." *1. Philippine Islands. I. American University, Washington, D.C. Foreign Area Studies. II. T.*
DS655.C4   919.14/03   78-601326

Corpuz, Onofre D. III. 3568
The Philippines [by] Onofre D. Corpuz. Englewood Cliffs, N.J., Prentice-Hall [1966, c1965] viii, 149 p. map. 21 cm. (The Modern nations in historical perspective, S-616. A Spectrum book.) *1. Philippine Islands. I. T.*
DS655.C67   309.1914   65-23299

Wickberg, Edgar. III. 3569
The Chinese in Philippine life, 1850-1898. New Haven, Yale University Press, 1965. x, 280 p. illus., maps, port. 24 cm. (Yale Southeast Asia studies, 1) *1. Chinese in the Phillippine Islands. I. T. (S)*
DS666.C5W5   301.451510914   65-22475

Barton, Roy Franklin, 1883-1947. III. 3570
Ifugao law. With a new foreword by Fred Eggan. Berkeley, University of California Press, 1969. xviii, [6], 120 p. map, 26 plates. 24 cm. First published in 1919. "Publications of Roy Franklin Barton": p. [1]-[2] (2d group) *1. Ifugaos. 2. Law, Primitive — Philippine Islands. 3. Ethnology — Philippine Islands. I. T.*
DS666.I15B3 1969   340/.09914/1   78-76334

Barton, Roy Franklin, 1883- III. 3571
The religion of the Ifugaos. [Menasha, Wis.] American Anthropological Assn. [1946-   v. 25 cm. (Memoir series of the American Anthropological Association, no. 65) American anthropologist. New ser., v.48, no. 4, pt.2, October 1946. *1. Ifugaos — Religion. I. American anthropologist. (S:American Anthropological Association. Memoirs, no. 65)*
DS666.I15B3x (GN2.A22 no. 65)   299.921   48-3664

Taylor, George Edward, 1905- III. 3572
The Philippines and the United States: problems of partnership. [1st ed.] New York, Published for the Council on Foreign Relations by Praeger [1964] x, 325 p. 22 cm. *1. Philippine Islands — History. 2. U.S. — Foreign relations — Philippine Islands. 3. Philippine Islands — Foreign relations — U.S. I. T.*
DS672.8.T3 1964   327.730914   64-12080

Phelan, John Leddy, 1924- III. 3573
The Hispanization of the Philippines: Spanish aims and Filipino responses, 1565-1700. Madison, University of Wisconsin Press, 1959. xiv, 218 p. illus., maps. 22 cm. *1. Catholic Church in the Philippine Islands. 2. Spaniards in the Philippine Islands. 3. Philippine Islands — History — 1521-1812. 4. Philippine Islands — Civilization — Spanish influences. I. T.*
DS674.P5   991.402   A59-8602

Coates, Austin. III. 3574
Rizal, Philippine nationalist and martyr. Hong Kong, New York, Oxford University Press, 1968. xxxii, 378 p. illus., facsims., maps, ports. 23 cm. *1. Rizal y Alonso, José, 1861-1896. I. T.*
DS675.8.R5C57   991.4/02/0924 (B)   78-304

Elliott, Charles Burke, 1861-1935. III. 3575
The Philippines to the end of the commission government; a study in tropical democracy. New York, Greenwood Press, 1968 [c1917] 541 p. ports. 24 cm. *1. Philippine Islands — Politics and government. I. T.*
DS685.E4 1968   991.4/032   69-10088

Friend, Theodore. III. 3576
Between two empires; the ordeal of the Philippines, 1929-1946. New Haven, Yale University Press, 1965. xviii, 312 p. illus., maps, ports. 25 cm. (Yale historical publications. Studies, 22) *1. Philippine Islands — History — 1898- 2. Nationalism — Philippine Islands. I. T. (S)*
DS685.F7   991.403   65-12541

Roosevelt, Nicholas, 1893- III. 3577
The Philippines; a treasure and a problem. New York, AMS Press [1970] xii, 315 p. 23 cm. Reprint of the 1926 ed. *1. Philippine Islands. 2. Philippine Islands — Politics and government — 1898-1935. I. T.*
DS685.R7 1970   309.1/914   71-100510   ISBN:0404006183

Hayden, Joseph Ralston, 1887-1945. III. 3578
The Philippines, a study in national development, by Joseph Ralston Hayden. New York, Macmillan, 1942. xxvi, 984 p. front., plates, ports., maps (1 fold.) 24 cm. *1. Philippine islands — Politics and government — 1935-1946. 2. Philippine islands — Social conditions. 3. Philippine islands — Foreign relations.*
DS686.H3   991.4   42-2760

Ravenholt, Albert. III. 3579
The Philippines; a young Republic on the move. Drawings by Manuel Rey Isip. Map by Dorothy deFontaine. Princeton, N.J., Van Nostrand [1962] 204 p. illus. 21 cm. (The Asia library) *1. Philippine Islands.*
DS686.5.R3   991.4   62-51874

DS701 – 798 CHINA

De Bary, William Theodore, 1918- , ed. III. 3580
Sources of Chinese tradition, compiled by W. Theodore de Bary, Wing-tsit Chan [and] Burton Watson. With contributions by Yi-pao Mei [and others] New York, Columbia University Press [1960] xxiv, 967 p. illus., maps. 24 cm. (Records of civilization; sources and studies, 55. Introduction to oriental civilizations) Translated from various sources and by various individuals. *1. China — History — Sources. 2. China — Civilization. I. T. (S:Records of civilization: sources and studies, 55) (S:Introduction to oriental civilizations)*
DS703.D4   951.0082   60-9911

Harvard University. East Asian Research Center. III. 3581
Papers on China. v.1- Cambridge, 1947-   v. 28 cm. Annual. Vols. for 1947-56 issued by the East Asia Program of the university's Committee on Regional Studies (called in 1947-54 Committee on International and Regional Studies) 1957-59 issued by the center under an earlier name: Center for East Asian Studies. *1. China. I. Harvard University. Committee on Regional Studies. Papers on China. II. T.*
DS703.4.H3   56-2493

Hinton, Harold C. ed. III. 3582
Major topics on China and Japan; a handbook for teachers. Edited by Harold C. Hinton and Marius B. Jansen. New York] Institute of Pacific Relations, 1957. 326 p. illus. 28 cm. *1. China. 2. Japan. I. Jansen, Marius B., joint ed. II. T.*
DS706.H53   951.0082   57-4216

Latourette, Kenneth Scott, 1884- III. 3583
The Chinese, their history and culture. 4th ed., thoroughly rev. New York, Macmillan [1964] 2 v. in 1 (xii, 714 p.) map (on lining papers) 24 cm. *1. China. 2. China — History. 3. China — Civilization. I. T.*
DS706.L3 1964   915.1   64-17372

Whitaker, Donald P. III. 3584
Area handbook for the People's Republic of China [by] Donald P. Whitaker, Rinn-Sup Shinn [and others. Washington, For sale by the Supt. of Docs., U.S. Govt. Print. Off.] 1972. xvi, 729 p. maps. 24 cm. "DA pam. 550-60." "One of a series of handbooks prepared by Foreign Area Studies (FAS) of the American University." "Replaces the 1967 Area handbook for Communist China, which was prepared by a team headed by Frederic H. Chaffee." *1. China. I. Shinn, Rinn-Sup, joint author. II. American University, Washington, D.C. Foreign Area Studies. III. Chaffee, Frederic H. Area handbook for Communist China. IV. T.*
DS706.W46   915.1/03/5   72-600022

Lattimore, Owen, 1900- III. 3585
Inner Asian frontiers of China. [2d ed.] Irvington-on-Hudson, N.Y., Capitol Pub. Co., and American Geographical Society, New York, 1951. lxi, 585 p. maps. 21 cm. (American Geographical Society [of New York] Research series no. 21) "This study has been made with the coöperation of the Secretariat of the Institute of Pacific Relations and constitutes a report in its International research series." *1. China — Historical geography. 2. China — Boundaries. I. T. (S) (S:Institute of Pacific Relations. International research series)*
DS706.5.L3 1951   915.1   52-655

Ennin, 793 or 4-864. III. 3586
Diary; the record of a pilgrimage to China in search of the law; translated from the Chinese by Edwin O. Reischauer. New York, Ronald Press Co. [1955] xvi, 454 p. col. port., maps (on lining papers) 25 cm. Translation of Nittō guhō junrei gyōki. *1. China — Description and travel. 2. China — History — T'ang dynasty, 618-907. — Sources. 3. Buddha and Buddhism — China. I. Reischauer, Edwin Oldfather, 1910- tr. II. T:A pilgrimage to China in search of the law.*
DS707.E512   951.016   55-5553

Li Chih-ch'ang, 1193-1278. III. 3587
The travels of an alchemist; the journey of the Taoist, Ch'ang-ch'un, from China to the Hindukush at the summons of Chingiz Khan, recorded by his disciple, Li Chih-ch'ang. Translated, with an introduction, by Arthur Waley. London, Routledge [1931] xi, 166 p. double front. (map) 23 cm. (The Broadway travelers) Translation of Hsi yu chi. *1. Ch'iu Ch'ang-ch'un, 1148-1227. 2. Mongolia — Description and travel. 3. Asia, Central — Description and travel. 4. China — Description and travel. I. Waley, Arthur, ed. and tr. II. T.*
DS707.L5   915.1   31-31754

Reischauer, Edwin Oldfather, 1910- III. 3588
Ennin's travels in T'ang China. New York, Ronald Press Company [1955] xii, 341 p. 24 cm. *1. Ennin, 793-864. 2. China — Description and travel. I. T.*
DS707.R45   951.016   55-6273

Macartney, George Macartney, earl, 1737-1806. III. 3589
An embassy to China; being the journal kept by Lord Macartney during his embassy to the Emperor Ch'ien-lung, 1793-1794. Edited with an introd. and notes By J. L. Cranmer-Byng. Hamden, Conn., Archon Books, 1963. 421 p. illus. 23 cm. *1. China — Description and travel. I. T.*
DS708.M14   915.1   63-6504

Cressey, George Babcock, 1896- III. 3590
Land of the 500 million; a geography of China. New York, McGraw-Hill, 1955. xv, 387 p. illus., maps, tables. 26 cm. (McGraw-Hill series in geography) *1. China — Description and travel — 1949- I. T.*
DS710.C73   915.1   55-8895

Greene, Felix. III. 3591
Awakened China; the country Americans don't know. [1st ed.] Garden City, N.Y., Doubleday, 1961. 425 p. 22 cm. *1. China — Description and travel — 1949- I. T.*
DS711.G7   915.1   61-9512

Tregear, Thomas R. III. 3592
A geography of China, by T. R. Tregear. Chicago, Aldine Pub. Co. [1966, c1965] xvii, 342 p. illus., maps. 22 cm. *1. China — Description and travel. I. T.*
DS711.T68 1966   915.1   65-26752

Andersson, Johan Gunnar, 1874- III. 3593
Children of the yellow earth; studies in prehistoric China, by J. Gunnar Andersson. Translated from the Swedish by Dr. E. Classen. New York, Macmillan, 1934. xxi, 345 p. illus. 32 pl. double map, 22 cm. *1. China — Antiquities. 2. Man, Prehistoric — China. 3. Excavations (Archaeology) — China. I. Classen, Ernest, 1881- tr. II. T.*
DS715.A52 1934a   913.31   35-2425

Watson, William, 1917- III. 3594
Early civilization in China. New York, McGraw-Hill [1966] 143 p. illus. (part col.) maps. 22 cm. (Library of the early civilizations.) *1. China — Antiquities. I. T.*
DS715.W32 1966a   915.103   66-16974

Granet, Marcel, 1884-1940. III. 3596
Festivals and songs of ancient China. Translated from the French by E. D. Edwards. New York, Dutton, 1932. ix, 281 p. 22 cm. (The Broadway oriental library.) *1. China — Religion. 2. Chinese poetry — History and criticism. 3. Shih ching. 4. Folk-lore, Chinese. 5. Festivals — China. I. Edwards, Evangeline Dora, tr. II. T.*
DS719.G72   915.1   33-4631

DS721 – 727
Civilization. Ethnography

Balazs, Étienne, 1905-1963. III. 3597
Chinese civilization and bureaucracy; variations on a theme. Translated by H. M. Wright. Edited by Arthur F. Wright. New Haven, Yale University Press, 1964. xix, 309 p. 25 cm. Essays. "Sponsored by the East Asian Research Center, Harvard University, and the Council on East Asian Studies, Yale University." *1. China — Civilization. I. T.*
DS721.B213   915.1   64-20909

Burkhardt, Valentine Rodolphe, 1884- III. 3598
Chinese creeds & customs. Illus. by the author. [1st ed. Taipei, Taiwan, Book World, 1958] 3 v. in 1. illus. 21 cm. Vol.1: 12th impression; v.2: 5th impression. *1. China — Social life and customs. I. T.*
DS721.B95x

Dawson, Raymond Stanley. III. 3599
The Chinese chameleon: an analysis of European conceptions of Chinese civilization [by] Raymond Dawson. London, New York, [etc.] Oxford U.P., 1967. xvi, 235 p. front., illus., 15 plates (incl. ports., map, facsims.) 22 1/2 cm. *1. China — Civilization. I. T.*
DS721.D357   915.1/03   67-81516

Fairbank, John King, 1907- ed. III. 3600
Chinese thought and institutions. With contributions by T'ung-tsu Ch'ü [and others]. Chicago] University of Chicago Press [1957] xiii, 438 p. map, diagrs., tables. 25 cm. (Comparative studies of cultures and civilizations) 1. China — Intellectual life. I. T. (S:Comparative studies in cultures and civilizations)
DS721.F26   915.1   57-5272

Fitzgerald, Charles Patrick, 1902- III. 3601
China: a short cultural history. [4th rev. ed.] New York, Praeger [1954] xviii, 621 p. illus., maps (1 fold.) 26 cm. 1. China — Civilization — History. 2. China — History. 3. Art, Chinese. 4. China — Religion.
DS721.F55 1954   915.1   54-6804

Gentzler, J. Mason. III. 3602
A syllabus of Chinese civilization, by J. Mason Gentzler. New York, Columbia University Press, 1968. x, 107 p. maps. 23 cm. (Companions to Asian studies) "Prepared under the auspices of the University Committee on Oriental Studies." 1. China — Civilization. I. Columbia University. Committee on Oriental Studies. II. T. (S)
DS721.G37   915.1/03/0202   68-55814

Gernet, Jacques. III. 3603
Daily life in China, on the eve of the Mongol invasion, 1250-1276. Translated from the French by H. M. Wright. Stanford, Calif., Stanford University Press [1962] 254 p. illus., maps. 22 cm. Translation of La vie quotidienne en Chine, à la veille de l'invasion mongole, 1250-1276. 1. China — Social life and customs. I. T.
DS721.G413 1962b   915.1/03/2   73-110281   ISBN:804707200

Granet, Marcel, 1884-1940. III. 3604
Chinese civilization. Translated by Kathleen E. Innes and Mabel R. Brailsford. New York, Meridian Books [1958] 444 p. illus. 21 cm. (Meridian books, MG14) 1. China — Social life and customs. 2. China — History — Early to 1643.
DS721.G788 1958   951   58-8529

Hsu, Francis L. K., 1909- III. 3605
Americans and Chinese: purpose and fulfillment in great civilizations. Garden City, N.Y., Published for the American Museum of Natural History [by] the Natural History Press [1970] xxviii, 493 p. 25 cm. Revision of the 1953 ed., published under title: Americans and Chinese: two ways of life. 1. China — Civilization. 2. United States — Civilization — 20th century. I. T.
DS721.H685 1970   915.1   72-116215

Isaacs, Harold Robert, 1910- III. 3606
Images of Asia; American views of China and India [by] Harold R. Isaacs. New York, Capricorn Books [1962, c1958] 416 p. illus. 21 cm. (Cap giant 223) "Published originally as Scratches on our minds. 1958." I. T.
DS721.I8 1962   301.154   64-7499

Levenson, Joseph Richmond, 1920- III. 3607
Confucian China and its modern fate [by] Joseph R. Levenson. Berkeley, University of California Press, 1958-65. 3 v. 23 cm. 1. China — Intellectual life. 2. China — Civilization — History. 3. Communism — China. I. T.
DS721.L538   915.1   58-2791

Liang, Ch'i-ch'ao, 1873-1939. III. 3608
Intellectual trends in the Ch'ing period (Ch'ing-tai hsüeh-shu kai-lun) Translated with introd. and notes by Immanuel C. Y. Hsü. Foreword by Benjamin I. Schwartz. Cambridge, Harvard University Press, 1959. xxii, 147, lii p. 24 cm. (Harvard East Asian studies, 2) 1. China — Intellectual life. I. T.
DS721.L5483   915.1   59-6158

Lin, Yutang, 1895- III. 3609
My country and my people. Rev. illustrated ed. New York, J. Day Co. [1939] xxvi, 440 p. illus., plates, port., facsim. 23 cm. 1. China — Civilization. 2. National characteristics, Chinese. I. T.
DS721.L58 1939   915.1   39-7059

Needham, Joseph, 1900- III. 3610
Science and civilization in China, by Joseph Needham with the research assistance of Wang Ling. Cambridge [Eng.] University Press, 1954-   v. illus., maps (2 fold.) 26 cm. 1. China — Civilization — History. 2. China — Intellectual life. 3. Science — History — China. I. T.
DS721.N39   54-4723

Scott, Adolphe Clarence, 1909- III. 3611
Literature and the arts in twentieth century China. [1st ed.] Garden City, N.Y., Doubleday [1963] 212 p. illus. 18 cm. (Anchor books) 1. China — Intellectual life. I. T.
DS721.S37   915.1   63-8760

Self and society in Ming thought, III. 3612
by Wm. Theodore de Bary and the Conference on Ming Thought. New York, Columbia University Press, 1970. xii, 550 p. 24 cm. (Studies in Oriental culture, no. 4) "Most of the papers appearing herein were presented at [the Conference on Ming Thought] and subsequently revised for publication." 1. China — Civilization — Addresses, essays, lectures. 2. China — History — Ming dynasty, 1368-1644. I. De Bary, William Theodore, 1918- ed. II. Conference on Ming Thought, Champaign, Ill., 1966. (S)
DS721.S39   915.1/03/2   78-101229   ISBN:231032714

Wang, Yi Chu, 1916- III. 3613
Chinese intellectuals and the West, 1872-1949, by Y. C. Wang. Chapel Hill, University of North Carolina Press [1966] xiv, 557 p. 24 1. China — Civilization — Occidental influences. 2. Intercultural education. 3. Returned students — China. I. T.
DS721.W334   915.1033   66-10207

Creel, Herrlee Glessner, 1905- III. 3614
The birth of China; a study of the formative period of Chinese civilization. New York, F. Ungar Pub. Co. [1954, c1937] 402 p. illus., map (on lining papers) 24 cm. 1. China — Civilization. 2. China — Antiquities. 3. Excavations (Archaeology) — China. 4. Bronze age — China. I. T.
DS723.C7x   913.31   54-5633

Li, Chi, 1896- III. 3615
The beginnings of Chinese civilization; three lectures illustrated with finds at Anyang. Seattle, University of Washington Press [1957] xvii, 123 p. illus., plates, map. 25 cm. 1. China — Antiquities. I. T.
DS723.L5   913.31 (951)   57-5285

Croizier, Ralph C., comp. III. 3616
China's cultural legacy and communism. Edited by Ralph C. Croizier. New York, Praeger Publishers [1970] xiii, 313 p. illus., ports. 21 cm. (Praeger library of Chinese affairs. Praeger university series.) 1. China — Civilization — 1949- — Addresses, essays, lectures. I. T.
DS724.C7 1970   915.1/03/5   77-83334

Li, Chi, 1896- III. 3617
The formation of the Chinese people; an anthropological inquiry. New York, Russell & Russell [1967] 283 p. illus., geneal. table, maps. 24 cm. Reprint of the 1928 ed. 1. Ethnology — China. I. T.
DS730.L5 1967   572.9/51   66-27117

Uchida, Naosaku, 1905- III. 3618
The overseas Chinese; a bibliographical essay based on the resources of the Hoover Institution. With a supplementary bibliography by Eugene Wu, with the collaboration of Chün-tu Hsüeh. [Stanford University, Calif.] Hoover Institution on War, Revolution, and Peace, Stanford University, 1959. ix, 134 p. 28 cm. (Hoover Institution. Bibliographical series, 7) 1. Chinese in foreign countries — History. 2. Chinese in foreign countries — Bibliography. I. T. (S:Stanford University. Hoover Institution on War, Revolution, and Peace. Bibliographical series, 7)
DS732.U32   325.251   60-1670

DS733 – 798   History

United States. Library of Congress. Orientalia division. III. 3619
Eminent Chinese of the Ch'ing period (1644-1912) Edited by Arthur W. Hummel. Washington, U.S. Govt. print. off., 1943-44. 2 v. 28 cm. At head of title: The Library of Congress. Paged continuously. Prepared by the Asiatic division of the Library of Congress, cf. v. 1, p. viii. 1. China — Biography. I. Hummel, Arthur William, 1884- ed.
DS734.U65   920.051   43-53640

Feuerwerker, Albert. III. 3620
Chinese Communist studies of modern Chinese history, by Albert Feuerwerker and S. Cheng. Cambridge, East Asian Research Center, Harvard University; distributed by Harvard University Press, 1961. xxv, 287 p. 28 cm. (Chinese Economic and Political Studies. Special series) 1. China — History — Historiography. I. Cheng, S., joint author. II. T. (S:Harvard University. Chinese Economic and Political Studies. Special series)
DS734.7.F4   951.0072   61-19595

Gardner, Charles Sidney, 1900- III. 3621
Chinese traditional historiography, by Charles S. Gardner. Cambridge, Harvard University Press, 1938. xi, 120 p. 21 cm. (Harvard historical monographs. XI) 1. China — History — Historiography. I. T.
DS734.7.G3   907 (951)   38-13532

History in communist China, III. 3622
edited by Albert Feuerwerker. Cambridge, M.I.T. Press [1968] xiv, 382 p. 21 cm. "In their original drafts most of ... [the essays] were prepared for ... a conference on Chinese communist historiography ... and held at Ditchley Manor, Oxfordshire, September 6-12, 1964." 1. China — Historiography — Addresses, essays, lectures. I. Feuerwerker, Albert, ed.
DS734.7.H56   951/.0072   68-18238

Watson, Burton, 1925-   III. 3623
Ssu-ma Ch'ien, grand historian of China. New York, Columbia University Press, 1958. xi, 276 p. 24 cm. A revision of the author's thesis, Columbia University, published in 1956 under title: Ssu-ma Ch'ien: the historian and his work. 1. Ssŭ-ma, Ch'ien, ca. 145-ca. 86 B.C. 2. China — History — Historiography.
DS734.9.S8W3   951.007   57-13030

Meskill, John Thomas, ed.   III. 3624
The pattern of Chinese history: cycles, development, or stagnation? Edited with an introd. by John Meskill. Boston, Heath [1965] xx, 108 p. 24 cm. (Problems in Asian civilizations) 1. China — History — Philosophy. I. T. (S)
DS734.95.M4   951.001   65-17466

Eberhard, Wolfram, 1909-   III. 3625
A history of China. [3d ed. rev. and enl.] Berkeley, University of California Press, 1969. xv, 367 p. illus. 22 cm. (Campus 16) Translation of Chinas Geschichte. 1. China — History. I. T.
DS735.E214 1969   951   69-16627

Fairbank, John King, 1907-   III. 3626
The United States and China. 3d ed. Cambridge, Mass., Harvard University Press, 1971. xvi, 500 p. maps. 22 cm. (The American foreign policy library) 1. China — History. 2. United States — Foreign relations — China. 3. China — Foreign relations — United States. I. T. (S)
DS735.F3 1971   327.51/073   71-152270   ISBN:0674924010

Goodrich, Luther Carrington, 1894-   III. 3627
A short history of the Chinese people [by] L. Carrington Goodrich. 3rd ed., with a final chapter by W. A. C. Adie. London, Allen & Unwin, 1969. xv, 295 p. 17 maps. 23 cm. 1. China — History. I. Adie, W. A. C. II. T.
DS735.G58 1969   951   73-454308   ISBN:049510150

Grousset, René, 1885-   III. 3628
The rise and splendour of the Chinese Empire. [Translated by Anthony Watson-Gandy and Terence Gordon. 1st American ed.] Berkeley, University of California Press, 1953. 312 p. illus., port., maps. 23 cm. Translation of Histoire de la Chine. 1. China — History. I. T.
DS735.G85x   A53-9939

Wint, Guy, 1910-   III. 3629
Common sense about China. New York, Macmillan, 1960. 176 p. 22 cm. (The Common sense series) 1. China — History. 2. Communism — China. I. T.
DS736.W5 1960a   951.05   60-15049

Liu, Frederick Fu, 1919-   III. 3630
A military history of modern China, 1924-1949, by F. F. Liu. Princeton, Princeton University Press, 1956. 312 p. illus. 25 cm. 1. China — History, Military.
DS738.L5   951.04   56-8386

DS740 POLITICAL AND DIPLOMATIC HISTORY

Chiang, Kai-shek, 1886-   III. 3631
China's destiny, by Chiang Kai-shek; authorized translation by Wang Chung-hui ... with an introduction by Lin Yutang. New York, Macmillan, 1947. xi, 260 p. 21 cm. "First edition (in Chinese), Chungking, March 1943 ... First English edition, New York, 1947." "The translation was prepared by a group of Chinese scholars under the supervision of Dr. Wang Chung-hui." — Introd., p. ix. 1. China — Foreign relations. 2. China — Politics and government — 1912- 3. Reconstruction (1939-) — China. I. Wang, Chung-hui, 1882- tr. II. T.
DS740.C5   951.04   47-30071

Li, Chien-nung.   III. 3632
The political history of China, 1840-1928. Translated and edited by Ssu-yu Teng and Jeremy Ingalls. Princeton, N.J., D. Van Nostrand Co. [1956] 545 p. 24 cm. 1. China — History. I. Têng, Ssŭ-yü, 1906- ed. and tr. II. Ingalls, Jeremy, 1911- ed. and tr.
DS740.L463   951.03   56-12095

Israel, John.   III. 3633
Student nationalism in China, 1927-1937. Stanford, Calif., Published for the Hoover Institution on War, Revolution, and Peace by Stanford University Press, 1966. ix, 253 p. illus., maps. 24 cm. (Hoover Institution publications) 1. China — Politics and government — 1912-1949. 2. Students — China. I. Stanford University. Hoover Institution on War, Revolution, and Peace. II. T.
DS740.2.I8   951.042   66-15300

Têng, Ssŭ-yü, 1906-   III. 3634
China's reponse to the West; a documentary survey, 1839-1923 [by] Ssŭ-yü Teng [and] John. K. Fairbank, with E-tu Zen Sun, Chaoying Fang, and others. [Prepared in Coöperation with the International Secretariat of the Institute of Pacific Relations] Cambridge, Harvard University Press, 1954. vi, 296 p. 25 cm. 1. China — Relations (general) with foreign countries. I. Fairbank, John King, 1907- joint author. II. T.
DS740.2.T4   327.51   53-5061

Morse, Hosea Ballou, 1855-1934.   III. 3635
The international relations of the Chinese empire, by Hosea Ballou Morse. London, New York [etc.] Longmans, Green, 1910-18. 3 v. fronts., plates, ports. (1 col.) fold. maps, diagrs. (part fold.) 23 cm. 1. China — Foreign relations. 2. China — Politics and government. 3. China — History. 4. Opium trade. I. T.
DS740.4.M6   11-2033

Van Ness, Peter.   III. 3636
Revolution and Chinese foreign policy; Peking's support for wars of national liberation. Berkeley, University of California Press, 1970. xii, 266 p. 24 cm. 1. China — Foreign relations — 1949- I. T.
DS740.4.V34 1970   327.51   73-89893

Schrecker, John E.   III. 3637
Imperialism and Chinese nationalism; Germany in Shantung [by] John E. Schrecker. Cambridge, Mass., Harvard University Press, 1971. xiv, 322 p. 25 cm. (Harvard East Asian series, 58) 1. China — Foreign relations — Germany. 2. Germany — Foreign relations — China. I. T. (S)
DS740.5.G3S33 1971   327.51/043   73-129119   ISBN:0674445201

Pelcovits, Nathan Albert, 1912-   III. 3638
Old China Hands and the Foreign Office [by] Nathan A. Pelcovits. New York, Octagon Books, 1969 [c1948] xi, 349 p. map. 24 cm. 1. Great Britain — Foreign relations — China. 2. China — Foreign relations — Great Britain. 3. Merchants, British. 4. China Association, London. I. T.
DS740.5.G5P4 1969   327.51/042   78-76003

Bagchi, Prabodh Chandra.   III. 3639
India and China; a thousand years of cultural relations. 2d ed., rev. and enl. Westport, Conn., Greenwood Press [1971] vi, 234 p. map. 23 cm. 1. China — Relations (general) with India. 2. India — Relations (general) with China. I. T.
DS740.5.I5B3 1971   301.29/51/054   71-136053   ISBN:0837152038

Brandt, Conrad.   III. 3640
Stalin's failure in China, 1924-1927. Cambridge, Harvard University Press, 1958. xv, 226 p. 22 cm. (Russian Research Center studies, 31) 1. Stalin, Iosif, 1879-1953. 2. China — Foreign relations — Russia. 3. Russia — Foreign relations — China. I. T. (S:Harvard University. Russian Research Center. Russian Research Center studies, 31)
DS740.5.R8B7   951.042   58-12963

Clemens, Walter C.   III. 3641
The arms race and Sino-Soviet relations [by] Walter C. Clemens, Jr. Stanford, Calif., Hoover Institution on War, Revolution and Peace, Stanford University, 1968. xi, 335 p. illus. 24 cm. (Hoover Institution publications 72) 1. China — Foreign relations — 1949- — Russia. 2. Russia — Foreign relations — China. 3. Atomic weapons and disarmament. I. T.
DS740.5.R8C6   327.47/051   68-21253

Clubb, Oliver Edmund, 1901-   III. 3642
China & Russia; the "great game" [by] O. Edmund Clubb. New York, Columbia University Press, 1971. xii, 578 p. illus., maps, ports. 24 cm. (Studies of the East Asian Institute, Columbia University) 1. Russia — Foreign relations — China. 2. China — Foreign relations — Russia. I. T. (S:Columbia University. East Asian Institute. Studies)
DS740.5.R8C63   327.47/051   72-155362   ISBN:0231027400

Garthoff, Raymond L., ed.   III. 3643
Sino-Soviet military relations, edited by Raymond L. Garthoff. New York, F. A. Praeger [1966] xii, 285 p. 22 cm. 1. China (People's Republic of China, 1949-) — Relations (military) with Russia. 2. Russia — Relations (military) with China (People's Republic of China, 1949-). I. T.
DS740.5.R8G3   327.47051   66-18900

Gittings, John.   III. 3644
Survey of the Sino-Soviet dispute: a commentary and extracts from the recent polemics 1963-1967. London, New York [etc.] issued under the auspices of the Royal Institute of International Affairs [by] Oxford U.P., 1968. xix, 410 p. 25 cm. 1. China — Foreign relations — 1949- — Russia. 2. Russia — Foreign relations — China. I. Royal Institute of International Affairs. II. T.
DS740.5.R8G5   327.51/047   75-356659

Jackson, William Arthur Douglas, 1923-   III. 3645
The Russo-Chinese borderlands: zone of peaceful contact or potential conflict? By W. A. Douglas Jackson. 2d ed. Princeton, N.J., Van Nostrand [1968] 156 p. maps. 21 cm. (Von Nostrand searchlight book no. 2) 1. Russia — Boundaries — China. 2. China — Boundaries — Russia. I. T.
DS740.5.R8J3 1968   327.47/051   68-9548

North, Robert Carver.   III. 3646
Moscow and Chinese Communists. 2d ed. Stanford, Calif., Stanford

University Press [1963] 310 p. 24 cm. *1. Communism — China. 2. China — Foreign relations — Russia. 3. Russia Foreign relations — China. I. T.*
DS740.5.R8N6 1963   951.04   62-18742

Whiting, Allen Suess, 1926-   **III. 3647**
Soviet policies in China, 1917-1924, by Allen S. Whiting. Stanford, Calif., Stanford University Press [1968, c1953] viii, 350 p. 24 cm. *1. China — Foreign relations — Russia. 2. Russia — Foreign relations — China. I. T.*
DS740.5.R8W5 1968   327.47/051   68-12335

Fitzgerald, Charles Patrick, 1902-   **III. 3648**
The southern expansion of the Chinese people, by C. P. FitzGerald. New York, Praeger [1972] xxi, 230 p. illus. 23 cm. *1. China — Relations (general) with Southeastern Asia. 2. Asia, Southeastern — Relations (general) with China. I. T.*
DS740.6.F58   301.29/51/059   73-185594

DS741 – 778 HISTORY, BY PERIOD
DS741 – 753 Early to 1644

Bodde, Derk, 1909-   **III. 3649**
China's first unifier: a study of the Ch'in dynasty as seen in the life of Li Ssŭ, 280?-208 B.C. Hong Kong, Hong Kong U.P.; London, Oxford U.P., 1967. xii, 270 p. front. 25 cm. (Sinica Leidensia, v.3) *1. Li Ssŭ, 280?-208 B.C. 2. Ch'in shih-huang-ti, Emperor of China, 259-210 B.C. I. T. (S)*
DS747.5.B6 1967b   931   67-108881

Ssŭ-ma, Ch'ien, ca. 145-ca. 86 B.C.   **III. 3650**
Records of the grand historian of China. Translated from the Shih chi of Ssu-ma Ch'ien by Burton Watson. New York, Columbia University Press, 1961. 2 v. maps. 24 cm. (Records of civilization: sources and studies, no. 65) UNESCO collection of representative works: Chinese series. *1. China — History — 1766 B.C.-220 A.D. I. Watson, Burton, 1925- tr. II. T. (S:UNESCO collection of representative works: Chinese series)*
DS748.S7453   931   60-13348

Fitzgerald, Charles Patrick, 1902-   **III. 3651**
Son of heaven [a biography of Li Shih-Min, founder of the T'ang dynasty, by C. P. Fitzgerald] New York, AMS Press [1971] ix, 232 p. illus., geneal. table, maps, plans, port. 23 cm. Reprint of the 1933 ed. *1. T'ang T'ai-tsung, Emperor of China, 597-649. I. T.*
DS749.3.F5 1971   951/.01/0924 (B)   74-136382   ISBN:0404024041

Pulleyblank, E. G.   **III. 3652**
The background of the rebellion of An Lu-shan. London, New York, Oxford University Press, 1955. 264 p. maps. tables. 23 cm. (London oriental series, v.4) *1. China — History — Early to 1643. I. T. (S)*
DS749.3.P8x   A58-1352

Schafer, Edward H.   **III. 3653**
The vermilion bird; T'ang images of the South [by] Edward H. Schafer. Berkeley, University of California Press, 1967. viii, 380 p. illus., maps. 27 cm. *1. China — History — T'ang dynasty, 618-907. 2. China — Description and travel. 3. Natural history — China. I. T.*
DS749.3.S3   915.1   67-10463

Wang, Gungwu.   **III. 3654**
The structure of power in North China during the five dynasties. Kuala Lumpur, University of Malaya Press, 1963. viii, 257 p. maps. 23 cm. "Originally submitted as a thesis ... at the University of London." *1. China — Politics and government — Early to 1643. I. T.*
DS749.5.W3   951.01   Sa64-2651

Hucker, Charles O.   **III. 3655**
The traditional Chinese state in Ming times (1368-1644) Tucson, University of Arizona Press, 1961. 85 p. 16 cm. "In ... slightly different form this essay was prepared as a contribution to a conference on political power in traditional China ... held at Laconia, New Hampshire, in September, 1959." *1. China — Politics and government — Early to 1643. I. T.*
DS753.H83   951.026   61-15391

Michael, Franz H.   **III. 3656**
The origin of Manchu rule in China; frontier and bureaucracy as interacting forces in the Chinese Empire. New York, Octagon Books, 1965 [c1942] viii, 127 p. fold. map. 24 cm. *1. Manchus. 2. China — History — Early to 1643. 3. China — History — Tatar Conquest, 1643-1644. I. T.*
DS753.M5 1965   320.951   65-25880

DS754 – 773 Manchu Dynasty (1644 – 1912)

Marsh, Robert Mortimer.   **III. 3657**
The mandarins; the circulation of elites in China, 1600-1900. Glencoe [Ill.] Free Press of Glencoe [1961] 300 p. 22 cm. *1. Bureaucracy. 2. Social mobility — China. I. T.*
DS754.M37   951.03   60-10899

Fu, Lo-shu, 1920- ed.   **III. 3658**
A documentary chronicle of Sino-Western relations, 1644-1820, compiled, translated, and annotated by Lo-shu Fu. Tucson, Published for the Association for Asian Studies by the University of Arizona Press [1966] 2 v. (xviii, 792 p.) 24 cm. (Association for Asian Studies. Monographs and papers, no. 22) *1. China — History — Ch'ing dynasty, 1644-1912 — Sources. 2. China — Relations (general) with foreign countries. I. T. (S)*
DS754.2.F8   951.03   66-18529

Kahn, Harold L.   **III. 3659**
Monarchy in the emperor's eyes; image and reality in the Ch'ien-lung reign [by] Harold L. Kahn. Cambridge, Mass., Harvard University Press, 1971. ix, 314 p. illus. 25 cm. (Harvard East Asian series, 59) *1. Ch'ing Kao-tsung, Emperor of China, 1711-1799. 2. China — History — Ch'ien-lung, 1736-1795. I. T. (S)*
DS754.4.C5K3   951/.03/0924   75-135546   ISBN:0674582306

Spence, Jonathan D.   **III. 3660**
Ts'ao Yin and the K'ang-hsi Emperor; bondservant and master, by Jonathan D. Spence. New Haven, Yale University Press, 1966. xiv, 329 p. map. 24 cm. (Yale historical publications. Miscellany 85) *1. Ts'ao, Yin, 1658-1712. 2. Ch'ing Shêng-tsu, Emperor of China. 1654-1722. I. T. (S)*
DS754.4.T72S66   951.030924   66-21537

Kuhn, Philip A.   **III. 3661**
Rebellion and its enemies in late imperial China, militarization and social structure, 1796-1864 [by] Philip A. Kuhn. Cambridge, Mass., Harvard University Press, 1970. 254 p. illus., maps. 25 cm. (Harvard East Asian series, 49) *1. China — History — 19th century. I. T. (S)*
DS755.K77   951/.03   75-115476   ISBN:674749510

Chang, Hsin-pao, 1922-   **III. 3662**
Commissioner Lin and the Opium War. Cambridge, Harvard University Press, 1964. xiv, 319 p. illus., maps, port. 24 cm. (Harvard East Asian series, 18) *1. Lin, Tsê-hsü, 1785-1850. 2. China — History — War of 1840-1842. I. T. (S)*
DS757.5.C45   951.03   64-21786

Waley, Arthur.   **III. 3663**
The Opium War through Chinese eyes. Stanford, Calif., Stanford University Press [1968, c1958] 256 p. 22 cm. *1. China — History — War of 1840-1842. I. T.*
DS757.5.W3 1968   951/.03   68-12334

Boardman, Eugene Powers.   **III. 3664**
Christian influence upon the ideology of the Taiping Rebellion, 1851-1864. New York, Octagon Books, 1972 [c1952] xi, 188 p. facsim. 23 cm. *1. Taiping Rebellion, 1850-1864. 2. Christians in China. I. T.*
DS759.B6 1972   951/.03   71-159168   ISBN:0374906971

Meadows, Thomas Taylor.   **III. 3665**
The Chinese and their rebellions, viewed in connection with their national philosophy, ethics, legislation, and administration. To which is added, an essay on civilization and its present state in the East and West. Stanford, Calif., Academic Reprints [1953] lx, 656 p. maps (part fold.) 22 cm. *1. China — History — Taiping Rebellion, 1850-1864. 2. China — Civilization. 3. Civilization. I. T.*
DS759.M48 1953   951.037   54-2175

Michael, Franz H.   **III. 3666**
The Taiping Rebellion; history and documents, by Franz Michael, in collaboration with Chung-li Chang [Translations by Margery Anneberg and others] Seattle, University of Washington Press, 1966-1971. 3 v. maps. 25 cm. (University of Washington publications on Asia) "A product of the Modern Chinese History Project carried on by the Far Eastern and Russian Institute of the University of Washington." *1. Taiping Rebellion, 1850-1864. I. Washington (State) University. Far Eastern and Russian Institute. II. T. (S:Washington (State) University. University of Washington publications on Asia)*
DS759.M57   951.03   66-13538

Shih, Vincent Yu-chung, 1902-   **III. 3667**
The Taiping ideology; its sources, interpretations, and influences, by Vincent Y. C. Shih. Seattle, University of Washington Press [1967] xix, 553 p. 24 cm. (Far Eastern and Russian Institute. Publications on Asia, no. 15) *1.*

Taiping Rebellion, 1850-1864. I. T. (S:Washington (State) University. Far Eastern and Russian Institute. Publications on Asia, no. 15)
DS759.S48   951/.03   66-19571

Chiang, Siang-tseh. III. 3668
The Nien Rebellion. Seattle, University of Washington Press, 1954. xvi, 159 p. maps. 23 cm. (University of Washington publications on Asia) "Written ... as a doctoral dissertation at the University of Washington in 1951 ... now presented in its original dissertation form [with the addition of a preface]" *1. Nien Rebellion, 1853-1868. I. T. (S:Washington (State) University. University of Washington publications on Asia)*
DS759.5.C5 1954   951.037   54-3971

Têng, Ssŭ-yü, 1906- III. 3669
The Nien army and their guerrilla warfare, 1851-1868 [by] S. Y. Teng. Paris, Mouton, 1961. 254 p. illus., maps, plans. 24 cm. (Le Monde d'outre-mer, passé et présent. 1. sér.: Études, 13) *1. Nien Rebellion, 1853-1868. I. T. (S)*
DS759.5.T43   951/.03   73-249839

Banno, Masataka. III. 3670
China and the West, 1858-1861: the origins of the Tsungli yamen. Cambridge, Harvard University Press, 1964. x, 367, xiv p. 22 cm. (Harvard East Asian series 15) *1. China. Tsun li ko kuo shih wu ya mên. 2. China — History — Foreign intervention, 1857-1861. I. T. (S)*
DS760.B3   327.51   64-13419

DS761 – 773   1861 – 1912

Cameron, Meribeth Elliott, 1905- III. 3671
The reform movement in China, 1898-1912, by Meribeth E. Cameron, PH.D. Stanford University, Calif., Stanford University Press, 1931. 223 p. 26 cm. (Stanford University publications. University series. History, economics, and political science. vol.III, no. 1) "Originally submitted as a thesis for the degree of doctor of philosophy at Stanford university [1928]" — Pref. *1. Tzŭ-hsi, empress dowager of China, 1835-1908. 2. China — Politics and government — 1900-1949. I. T.*
DS761.C3 (AS36.L54 vol. 3, no. 1)   951   31-32244

Powell, Ralph L. III. 3672
The rise of Chinese military power, 1895-1912, by Ralph L. Powell. Port Washington, N.Y., Kennikat Press [1972, c1955] x, 383 p. map. 23 cm. *1. China — History, Military. I. T.*
DS761.P69 1972   355/.00951   76-159102   ISBN:0804616450

Purcell, Victor William Williams Saunders, 1896- III. 3673
The Boxer Uprising, a background study. Cambridge [Eng.] University Press, 1963. 348 p. illus. 24 cm. *1. China — History — 1862-1899. 2. Boxers. I. T.*
DS761.P8   951.03   63-26

Cohen, Paul A. III. 3674
China and Christianity; the missionary movement and the growth of Chinese antiforeignism, 1860-1870. Cambridge, Harvard University Press, 1963. xiv, 392 p. illus., port. 22 cm. (Harvard East Asian series, 11) Based on thesis, Harvard University. *1. Missions — China. 2. China — Foreign relations — To 1912. I. T. (S)*
DS762.C6   63-19135

Wright, Mary (Clabaugh) III. 3675
The last stand of Chinese conservatism; the T'ung-chih restoration, 1862-1874. Stanford, Stanford University Press [1957] x, 426 p. 25 cm. (Stanford studies in history, economics, and political science, 13) Subtitle also in Chinese on t.p. *1. T'ung-chih, Emperor of China, 1856-1875. 2. China — History — 1862-1899. I. T. (S:Stanford University. Stanford studies in history, economics and political science, 13)*
DS762.W7   951.038   57-5946

Tan, Chester C. III. 3676
The Boxer catastrophe, by Chester C. Tan. New York, Octagon Books, 1967. ix, 276 p. 24 cm. (Columbia studies in the social sciences, no. 583) Reprint of the 1955 ed. *1. Boxers. 2. Manchuria — History. 3. China — Foreign relations — Russia. 4. Russia — Foreign relations — China. I. T.*
DS771.T3x (H31.C7 no. 583 1967)   951/.03   66-18057

Giles, Lancelot, 1878-1934. III. 3677
The siege of the Peking legations; a diary. Edited with introduction, Chinese anti-foreignism and the Boxer uprising, by L. R. Marchant. Foreword by Sir Robert Scott. [Nedlands, W.A.] University of Western Australia Press [1970] xxvii, 212 p. illus., facsims., maps. 25 cm. *1. Peking — Siege, 1900. I. Marchant, Leslie Ronald, ed. II. T.*
DS772.G54 1970   951/.03   78-123328   ISBN:0855640413

China in revolution: the first phase, 1900-1913. III. 3678
Edited and with an introd. by Mary Clabaugh Wright. New Haven, Yale University Press, 1968. xiii, 505 p. 24 cm. Papers from a research conference held at Wentworth-by-the-Sea, Portsmouth, New Hampshire, Aug. 1965. *1. China — History — Revolution, 1911-1912. I. Wright, Mary (Clabaugh) ed. T.*
DS773.C5145   951/.03   68-27770

Gasster, Michael, 1930- III. 3679
Chinese intellectuals and the revolution of 1911; the birth of modern Chinese radicalism. Seattle, University of Washington Press [1969] xxix, 288 p. 24 cm. (Far Eastern and Russian Institute. Publications on Asia, no. 19) *1. China — History — Revolution, 1911-1912. I. T. (S:Washington (State). University. Far Eastern and Russian Institute. Publications on Asia, no. 19)*
DS773.G35   915.1/03   66-19568

DS774 – 778   1912 –

Clubb, Oliver Edmund, 1901- III. 3680
20th century China, by O. Edmund Clubb. 2d ed. New York, Columbia University Press, 1972. xiv, 526 p. illus. 23 cm. *1. China — History — 1900-. I. T.*
DS774.C57 1972   951.04   78-187028
ISBN:0231036485 0231083009 (pbk)

Isaacs, Harold Robert, 1910- III. 3681
The tragedy of the Chinese revolution. 2d rev. ed. Stanford, Calif., Stanford University Press [1961] 392 p. 24 cm. *1. China — History — 1912-1937. 2. Communism — China. I. T.*
DS774.I7 1961   951.042   61-11101

Schwartz, Benjamin Isadore, 1916- III. 3682
Chinese communism and the rise of Mao. Cambridge, Harvard University Press, 1951. 258 p. 22 cm. (Russian Research Center studies, 4) *1. Mao, Tsê-tung, 1893- 2. Communism — China. 3. China — History — 1900- I. T. (S:Harvard University. Russian Research Center. Russian Research Center studies, 4)*
DS774.S37   951.04   51-12067

Bianco, Lucien. III. 3683
Origins of the Chinese revolution, 1915-1949. Translated from the French by Muriel Bell. Stanford, Calif., Stanford University Press [1971] xiii, 223 p. maps. 23 cm. Translation of Les origines de la révolution chinoise, 1915-1949, revised by the author. *1. China — Politics and government — 1912-1949. I. T.*
DS775.B513   951.04   75-150321   ISBN:0804707464

Brandt, Conrad. III. 3684
A documentary history of Chinese communism, by Conrad Brandt, Benjamin Schwartz, and John K. Fairbank. New York, Atheneum, 1966. 552 p. 21 cm. (Atheneum paperbacks, 87) Reprint of the work first published in 1952. *1. Chung-kuo kung ch'an tang — History. 2. Communism — China — History. I. Schwartz, Benjamin Isadore, 1916- joint author. II. Fairbank, John King, 1907- joint author. III. T.*
DS775.B7x   951.04   66-6102

Chou, Ts'ê-tsung, 1916- III. 3685
The May fourth movement: intellectual revolution in modern China. Cambridge, Harvard University Press, 1960. xv, 486 p. tables. 25 cm. (Harvard East Asian studies, 6) Added t.p. in Chinese. *1. May fourth movement. (S)*
DS775.C5386 1960   951.041   60-10034

Chou, Ts'ê-tsung, 1916- III. 3686
Research guide to the May fourth movement; intellectual revolution in modern China, 1915-1924. Cambridge, Harvard University Press, 1963. xi, 297 p. 24 cm. (Harvard East Asian series, 13) *1. May fourth movement. I. Chou, Ts'ê-tsung, 1916- The May fourth movement. II. T. (S)*
DS775.C53862   951.041   63-22745

Snow, Edgar, 1905- III. 3687
Red star over China. 1st rev. and enl. ed. New York, Grove Press [1968] 543 p. illus., col. maps (on lining papers), ports. 24 cm. *1. Communism — China. 2. China — History — Republic, 1912-1949. I. T.*
DS775.S72 1968   951.04   68-17724

Stuart, John Leighton, 1876- III. 3688
Fifty years in China; the memoirs of John Leighton Stuart, missionary and ambassador. New York, Random House [1954] 346 p. illus. 22 cm. *1. China — History — 1900- I. T.*
DS775.S84   951.04   54-7808

Trotskiĭ, Lev, 1879-1940. III. 3689
Problems of the Chinese revolution. With appendices by Zinoviev, Vuyovitch, Nassunov & others. Translated with an introd. by Max Shachtman. 3d ed., with a new introd. by Benjamin Schwartz. New York, Paragon Book Reprint Corp., 1966. vi, 432 p. 21 cm. *1. Chung-kuo min tang. 2. Communism — China. 3. China — Politics and government — 1912-1949. I. T.*
DS775.T7 1966   951.04   66-17378

Sun, Yat-sen, 1866-1925. III. 3690
Memoirs of a Chinese revolutionary; a programme of national recon-

struction for China. New York, AMS Press [1970] 254 p. port. 23 cm. Reprint of the 1927 ed. *1. China — History — 1912-1937. I. T.*
DS777.A32 1970   951.04/1/0924   73-111786   ISBN:404063055

Jansen, Marius B.   **III. 3691**
The Japanese and Sun Yat-sen. Cambridge, Harvard University Press, 1954. viii, 274 p. group port., facsims. 21 cm. (Harvard historical monographs, 27) *1. Sun, Yat-sen, 1866-1925. 2. China — Foreign relations — Japan. 3. Japan — Foreign relations — China. I. T. (S)*
DS777.J3   951.041   53-8021

Leng, Shao Chuan, 1921-   **III. 3692**
Sun Yat-sen and communism, by Shao Chuan Leng and Norman D. Palmer. New York, F. A. Praeger [1961, c1960] viii, 234 p. 22 cm. (The Foreign Policy Research Institute series, no. 10. Praeger publications in Russian history and world communism, no. 91. Books that matter.) *1. Sun, Yat-sen, 1866-1925. 2. Communism — China. I. Palmer, Norman Dunbar, joint author. II. T. (S)*
DS777.L4 1961   951.041   60-16426

Sharman, Lyon, 1872-1957.   **III. 3693**
Sun Yat-sen; his life and its meaning; a critical biography. Stanford, Calif., Stanford University Press [1968, c1934] xxi, 420 p. 23 cm. *1. Sun, Yat-sen, 1866-1925. 2. China — History — Revolution, 1911-1912. 3. China — History — Republic, 1912-1949. 4. Chung-Kuo Kuo min tang.*
DS777.S5 1968   951.04/1/0924 (B)   68-17141

Ch'ên, Jerome, 1919-   **III. 3694**
Yuan Shih-k'ai. 2d ed. Stanford, Calif., Stanford University Press, 1972. 258 p. map. 23 cm. *1. Yüan, Shih-k'ai, 1859-1916.*
DS777.2.C48 1972   951/.03/0924 (B)   76-153815   ISBN:0804707899

Ch'en, Kung-po, 1892-1946.   **III. 3695**
The Communist movement in China; an essay written in 1924. Edited with an introd. by C. Martin Wilbur. New York, Octagon Books, 1966 [c1960] vi, 138 p. 24 cm. "Issued under the auspices of the East Asian Institute, Columbia University." Appendices (p. 102-136): 1. The first program of the Communist Party of China, 1921. — 2. The first decision as to the object of the Communist Party of China, 1921. — 3. The manifesto of the Communist Party of China adopted in July 1922 by the second congress. — 4. The decisions of the second conference of the Communist Party of China 1922. — 5. The organization of the Communist Party of China. — 6. The manifesto of the third conference of the Chinese Communist Party, 1923. *1. Communism — China. I. Wilbur, Clarence Martin, 1908- ed. II. Columbia University. East Asian Institute. III. Chung-kuo kung ch'an tang. IV. T.*
DS777.44.C5 1966   951.041   65-28873

White, Theodore Harold, 1915-   **III. 3696**
Thunder out of China [by] Theodore H. White and Annalee Jacoby. [1st ed.] New York, William Sloane Associates [1946] xvi, 331 p. maps. 22 cm. *1. China — History — 1937-1945. 2. World War, 1939-1945 — China. 3. Reconstruction (1939-1951) — China. I. Jacoby, Annalee, 1916- joint author. II. T.*
DS777.47.W5   951.042   46-11919

DS777.53 SINO-JAPANESE CONFLICT, 1937 – 1945

Barnett, A. Doak.   **III. 3697**
China on the eve of Communist takeover. New York, Praeger [1963] 371 p. illus. 22 cm. (Praeger publications in Russian history and world communism, no. 130) *1. China — Politics and government — 1937-1949. 2. China — Social conditions. 3. China — Economic conditions — 1912-1949. I. T.*
DS777.53.B32 1963   354.51   63-10824

Belden, Jack, 1910-   **III. 3698**
China shakes the world. New York [Monthly Review Press, 1970] xvii, 524 p. 21 cm. Reprint of the 1949 ed., with an introd. by Owen Lattimore. *1. China — Politics and government — 1937-1949. 2. Communism — China. I. T.*
DS777.53.B38 1970   951.04/2   77-105312

Boyle, John Hunter.   **III. 3699**
China and Japan at war, 1937-1945; the politics of collaboration. Stanford, Calif., Stanford University Press, 1972. ix, 430 p. illus. 24 cm. *1. Sino-Japanese Conflict, 1937-1945 — Collaborationists. 2. Communism — China. I. T.*
DS777.53.B65   952.03/3   76-183886   ISBN:0804708002

Frillmann, Paul, 1911-   **III. 3700**
China; the remembered life, by Paul Frillmann and Graham Peck. Introd. by John K. Fairbank. Boston, Houghton Mifflin, 1968. xvii, 291 p. illus., maps, ports. 22 cm. *1. Sino-Japanese Conflict, 1937-1945 — Personal narratives, American. I. Peck, Graham, 1914- joint author. II. T.*
DS777.53.F73   67-15527

Johnson, Chalmers A.   **III. 3701**
Peasant nationalism and communist power; the emergence of revolutionary China. Stanford, Calif., Stanford University Press, 1962. xii, 256 p. maps, tables. 24 cm. *1. Communism   China. 2. Nationalism — China. 3. Peasantry — China. 4. World War, 1939-1945 — Yugoslavia. I. T.*
DS777.53.J58   951.042   62-16949

Peck, Graham, 1914-   **III. 3702**
Two kinds of time; illustrated by the author. Boston, Houghton, Mifflin, 1950. viii, 725 p. illus., maps. 22 cm. *1. China — Description and travel. 2. World War, 1939-1945 — China. I. T.*
DS777.53.P37   940.5351   50-10600

Snow, Edgar, 1905-   **III. 3703**
Random notes on Red China (1936-1945) Cambridge, Chinese Economic and Political Studies, Harvard University; distributed by Harvard University Press, 1957. 148 p. 28 cm. (Harvard University. Chinese Economic and Political Studies. Special series) *1. China — History — 1937-1949. 2. Communism — China. I. T.*
DS777.53.S562   951.05   58-146

Tsou, Tang, 1918-   **III. 3704**
America's failure in China, 1941-50. [Chicago] University of Chicago Press [1963] 614 p. 25 cm. *1. China — Politics and government — 1937-1949. 2. U.S. — Foreign relations — China. 3. China — Foreign relations — U.S. I. T.*
DS777.53.T866   327.73051   63-13072

Young, Arthur Nichols, 1890-   **III. 3705**
China's wartime finance and inflation, 1937-1945 [by] Arthur N. Young. Cambridge, Harvard University Press, 1965. xviii, 421 p. illus. 25 cm. (Harvard East Asian series, 20) *1. Sino-Japanese Conflict, 1937-1945. 2. Inflation (Finance) — China. I. T. (S)*
DS777.53.Y62   336.51   65-22049

DS777.55 – 778 PEOPLE'S REPUBLIC OF CHINA (1949 –

Barcata, Louis, 1906-   **III. 3706**
China in the throes of the cultural revolution; an eye witness report. New York, Hart Pub. Co. [1968] 299 p. illus., map (on lining papers), ports. 25 cm. Translation of China in der Kulturrevolution. *1. China. I. T.*
DS777.55.B2753   915.1/03/5   68-24731

Barnett, A. Doak.   **III. 3707**
China after Mao, with selected documents, by A. Doak Barnett. Princeton, N.J., Princeton University Press, 1967. 287 p. 21 cm. (The Walter E. Edge lectures) *1. Mao, Tsê-tung, 1893- 2. China (People's Republic of China, 1949-) — Politics and government. 3. Chung-kuo kung ch'an tang — Purges. I. T. (S)*
DS777.55.B29   320.9/51   67-14406

Barnett, A. Doak.   **III. 3708**
Communist China and Asia; challenge to American policy. [1st ed. New York] Published for the Council on Foreign Relations by Harper, 1960. 575 p. 22 cm. *1. China. 2. China — Foreign relations — 1949- I. T.*
DS777.55.B3   951.05   60-5956

Barnett, A. Doak.   **III. 3709**
Communist China: the early years, 1949-55 [by] A. Doak Barnett. New York, F. A, Praeger [1964] xiv, 336 p. 21 cm. (Praeger publications in Russian history and world communism, no 152) *1. China (People's Republic of China, 1949-) — History. I. T.*
DS777.55.B322   951.05   64-22487

Baum, Richard, 1940- comp.   **III. 3710**
China in ferment; perspectives on the cultural revolution. Edited by Richard Baum, with Louise B. Bennett. Englewood Cliffs, N.J., Prentice-Hall [1971] viii, 246 p. 21 cm. (A Spectrum book) *1. China — Politics and government — 1949- — Addresses, essays, lectures. I. Bennett, Louise B., joint comp. II. T.*
DS777.55.B346   951.05   70-153433   ISBN:0131326880

Bloodworth, Dennis.   **III. 3711**
The Chinese looking glass. New York, Farrar, Straus and Giroux [1967] xii, 432 p. 22 cm. *1. China (People's Republic of China, 1949-) I. T.*
DS777.55.B55   915.1/03/5   67-22047

Bodde, Derk, 1909-   **III. 3712**
Peking diary, a year of revolution. New York, Schuman [1950] xxi, 292 p. illus., ports. 24 cm. *1. Peking — History. 2. China — Description and travel. 3. Communism — China. I. T.*
DS777.55.B6   951.156   50-10426

China in crisis.   **III. 3713**
Edited by Ping-ti Ho and Tang Tsou. With a foreword by Charles U. Daly. [Chicago] University of Chicago Press [1968- v. 23 cm. Contains papers presented at two five-day conferences held at the University of Chicago, Center for Policy Study, Feb. 1967. *1. China. I. Ho, Ping-ti, ed. II. Tsou, Tang, 1918- ed. III. Chicago. University. Center for Policy Study.*
DS777.55.C44684   915.1/03   68-20981

Goldman, Merle.   **III. 3714**
Literary dissent in Communist China. Cambridge, Harvard University Press, 1967. xvii, 343 p. 24 cm. (Harvard East Asian series, 29) *1. China (People's Republic of China, 1949-) — Intellectual life. I. T. (S)*
DS777.55.G67   895/.109005   67-17311

The Great cultural revolution in China,   **III. 3715**
compiled and edited by the Asia Research Centre. Rutland, Vt., C. E. Tuttle Co. [1968] 507 p. 22 cm. Sequel: The Great power struggle in China. *1. China — Intellectual life. 2. Chung-kuo kung ch'an tang — Purges. I. Asia Research Centre.*
DS777.55.G686 1968   951.05   68-15016

Halpern, Abraham Meyer, 1914- ed.   **III. 3716**
Policies toward China; views from six continents. Edited by A. M. Halpern. [1st ed.] New York, Published for the Council on Foreign Relations by McGraw-Hill [1965] xiv, 528 p. maps (1 fold.) 22 cm. (The United States and China in world affairs) "One in a series ... being published by the Council on Foreign Relations ... under a ... grant from the Ford Foundation." *1. China (People's Republic of China, 1949-) — Foreign relations. I. Council on Foreign Relations. II. T. (S)*
DS777.55.H295   327.51   65-24892

Hunter, Neale.   **III. 3717**
Shanghai journal; an eyewitness account of the cultural revolution. New York, Praeger [1969] v, 311 p. illus. 22 cm. *1. Shanghai — Politics and government. I. T.*
DS777.55.H83   951/.05   71-76954

Lifton, Robert Jay, 1926-   **III. 3718**
Revolutionary immortality; Mao Tse-tung and the Chinese cultural revolution. New York, Random House [1968] xviii, 178 p. 22 cm. *1. China — Politics and government — 1949- 2. Mao, Tse-tung, 1893- I. T.*
DS777.55.L457   320.9/51   68-28545

Mao, Tsê-tung, 1893-   **III. 3719**
On the correct handling of contradictions among the people. [1st ed.] Peking, Foreign Languages Press, 1957. 69 p. 19 cm. "Text of a speech made on February 27, 1957 at the eleventh session (enlarged) of the Supreme State Conference." *1. Communism — China.*
DS777.55.M33 1957a   59-33565

Myrdal, Jan.   **III. 3720**
Report from a Chinese village. Illustrated and with photos. by Gun Kessle. Translated from the Swedish by Maurice Michael. New York, Pantheon Books [1965] xxxiv, 373 p. illus., ports. 22 cm. Translation of Rapport från kinesisk by. Sequel: China: the revolution continued. *1. China — Social life and customs. I. T.*
DS777.55.M913   309.151   64-18346

Schurmann, Herbert Franz.   **III. 3721**
Ideology and organization in Communist China [by] Franz Schurmann. 2d ed., enl. Berkeley, University of California Press, 1968. lii, 642 p. illus. 25 cm. *1. China — Politics and government — 1949- 2. Chung-kuo kung ch'an tang — Party work. I. T.*
DS777.55.S35 1968   335.43/4/0951   68-26124

Shabad, Theodore.   **III. 3722**
China's changing map; national and regional development, 1949-71. Completely rev. ed. New York, Praeger [1972] xiii, 370 p. maps. 23 cm. (Praeger library of Chinese affairs) *1. Physical geography — China. 2. China — Economic conditions — 1949- 3. China — Politics and government — 1949- I. T.*
DS777.55.S455 1972   330.951/05   71-178868

Snow, Edgar, 1905-   **III. 3723**
Red China today. [1st American ed.] New York, Random House [1971] 749 p. illus., maps, ports. 25 cm. First published in 1962 under title: The other side of the river. *1. China. I. T.*
DS777.55.S6 1971   915.1/03/5   73-102336   ISBN:0394462610

Tsang, Chiu-sam, 1901-   **III. 3724**
Society, schools & progress in China. [1st ed.] Oxford, New York, Pergamon Press [1968] xx, 333 p. 20 cm. (The Commonwealth and international library. Education and educational research) *1. China. 2. Education — China. I. T.*
DS777.55.T73 1968   370/.951   68-21109   ISBN:0080128440

Van Slyke, Lyman P.   **III. 3725**
Enemies and friends; the united front in Chinese Communist history [by] Lyman P. Van Slyke. Stanford, Calif., Stanford University Press, 1967. viii, 330 p. 24 cm. *1. China (People's Republic of China, 1949-) 2. Communism — China. I. T.*
DS777.55.V36   951.05   67-26351

MacFarquhar, Roderick, ed.   **III. 3726**
The hundred flowers campaign and the Chinese intellectuals. With an epilogue by G. F. Hudson. New York, Praeger [1960] 324 p. 25 cm. *1. Communist self-criticism. 2. China — Politics and government — 1949- I. T.*
DS777.57.M3   951.05   60-10877

Yü, Tê-chi, 1921-   **III. 3727**
Mass persuasion in Communist China [by] Frederick T. C. Yu. New York, Praeger [1964] viii, 186 p. 22 cm. (Praeger publications in Russian history and world communism, no.145) *1. Propaganda, Chinese. 2. Public opinion — China (People's Republic of China, 1949-) I. T.*
DS777.57.Y78   301.15230951   64-13389

DS778   Biography. Memoirs

Biographical dictionary of Republican China.   **III. 3728**
Howard L. Boorman, editor; Richard C. Howard, associate editor. New York, Columbia University Press, 1967- v. 28 cm. *1. China — Biography. I. Boorman, Howard L., ed. II. Howard, Richard C., ed.*
DS778.A1B5   951/.00922   67-12006

Klein, Donald W.   **III. 3729**
Biographic dictionary of Chinese communism, 1921-1965 [by] Donald W. Klein [and] Anne B. Clark. Cambridge, Mass., Harvard University Press, 1971. 2 v. (1194 p.) maps. 27 cm. (Harvard East Asian series, 57) *1. China — Biography. 2. Communists, Chinese. I. Clark, Anne., joint author. II. T. (S)*
DS778.A1K55 1971   951.04/922 (B)   69-12725   ISBN:0674074106

Snow, Helen (Foster) 1907-   **III. 3730**
The Chinese Communists: sketches and autobiographies of the Old Guard. Book 1: Red dust. Book 2: Autobiographical profiles and biographical sketches. Introd. to book 1 by Robert Carver North. Westport, Conn., Greenwood Pub. Co. [1972] xxi, 398 p. illus. 24 cm. First published in 1952 under title: Red Dust. *1. Communists, Chinese. 2. China — Biography. I. Snow, Helen (Foster) 1907- Red dust. 1972. II. T.*
DS778.A1S499   335.43/4 (B)   77-104236   ISBN:0837163218

Hsu, Kai-yu, 1922-   **III. 3731**
Chou En-lai: China's gray eminence. [1st ed.] Garden City, N.Y., Doubleday, 1968. xviii, 294 p. illus., maps (part col.), ports. 22 cm. *1. Chou, Én-lai, 1898-*
DS778.C593H8   951.04/0924 (B)   68-10566

Smedley, Agnes, 1890-1950.   **III. 3732**
The great road; the life and times of Chu Teh. New York, Monthly Review Press, 1956. 461 p. illus. 22 cm. *1. Chu, Tê, 1886- 2. Communism — China. I. T.*
DS778.C6S5   923.551   56-11272

Bennett, Gordon A.   **III. 3733**
Red Guard; the political biography of Dai Hsiao-ai, by Gordon A. Bennett and Ronald N. Montaperto. [1st ed.] Garden City, N.Y., Doubleday, 1971. xx, 267 p. 22 cm. *1. Dai, Hsiao-ai. 2. Hung wei ping. I. Montaperto, Ronald N., joint author. II. T.*
DS778.D34B45   951.05/0924   70-116236

Sheridan, James E.   **III. 3734**
Chinese warlord; the career of Feng Yü-hsiang [by] James E. Sheridan. Stanford, Calif., Stanford University Press, 1966. x, 386 p. maps. 24 cm. *1. Feng, Yü-hsiang, 1882-1948. I. T.*
DS778.F45S45   951.040924 (B)   65-18978

Hsüeh, Chün-tu, 1922-   **III. 3735**
Huang Hsing and the Chinese revolution. Stanford, Calif., Stanford University Press, 1961. 260 p. 23 cm. (Stanford studies in history, economics, and political science, 20) *1. Huang, Hsing, 1874-1916. 2. China — History — Revolution, 1911-1912.*
DS778.H85H7 (AS36.L54 vol. 20)   951.03   61-6531

Levenson, Joseph Richmond, 1920-   **III. 3736**
Liang Ch'i-ch'ao and the mind of modern China. Cambridge, Harvard University Press, 1959. 256 p. 21 cm. *1. Liang, Ch'i-ch'ao, 1873-1929. 2. China — Civilization.*
DS778.L45L4 1959   923.251   59-16503

DS778   Mao Tse-tung

Mao, Tsê-tung, 1893-   **III. 3737**
Mao papers, anthology and bibliography edited by Jerome Ch'en. London, New York, Oxford University Press, 1970. xxxiii, 221 p. ports. 23 cm. *1. Mao, Tsê-tung, 1893- — Bibliography. I. Ch'ên, Jerome, 1919- ed. II. T.*
DS778.M3A4295   016.95105/0924   76-147091   ISBN:192151886

Mao, Tsê-tung, 1893-   **III. 3738**
Maoism, a sourcebook; selections from the writings of Mao Tse-tung. Introduced and edited by H. Arthur Steiner. [Los Angeles] University of California at Los Angeles. 1952. 142 p. 29 cm. *1. Communism — China. I. Steiner, H. Arthur, 1905- ed. II. T.*
DS778.M3A5   951.042   52-1681

Mao, Tsê-tung, 1893-   **III. 3739**
Selected military writings. [1st ed.] Peking, Foreign Languages Press, 1963.

408 p. port. 23 cm. *1. China — Politics and government — 1912-1949. 2. Guerrilla warfare. I. T.*
DS778.M3A515   355.081   65-1840

Mao, Tse-tung, 1893- III. 3740
Quotations from Chairman Mao Tse-Tung; edited and with an introductory essay and notes by Stuart R. Schram, foreword by A. Doak Barnett. New York, Praeger [c1967] xxxiv, 182 p. 22 cm. *I. Schram, Stuart R., ed. II. T.*
DS778.M3A5155x

Mao, Tsê-tung, 1893- III. 3741
Mao Tse-tung: an anthology of his writings. Edited with an introd. by Anne Fremantle. [New York] New American Library [1962] 300 p. 18 cm. (A Mentor book, MT379) *1. Communism — China.*
DS778.M3A516   951.05   62-14315

Mao, Tsê-tung, 1893- III. 3742
Selected works. New York, International Publishers [1954-   v. 23 cm. *1. Communism — China. 2. China — Politics and government — Addresses, essays, lectures. I. T.*
DS778.M3A52   951.05   54-9751

Mao, Tsê-tung, 1893- III. 3743
The political thought of Mao Tse-tung [by] Stuart R. Schram. Rev. and enl. ed. New York, Praeger [1969] 479 p. 22 cm. *1. Communism — China. I. Schram, Stuart R., ed. II. T.*
DS778.M3A538 1969   320.9/51   68-16093

Ch'ên, Jerome, 1919- comp. III. 3744
Mao. Englewood Cliffs, N.J., Prentice-Hall [1969] x, 176 p. 22 cm. (Great lives observed) *1. Mao, Tsê-tung, 1893-*
DS778.M3C473   951.05/0924 (B)   69-15346   ISBN:13555912X

Ch'ên, Jerome, 1919- III. 3745
Mao and the Chinese revolution. With thirty-seven poems by Mao Tse-tung translated from the Chinese by Michael Bullock and Jerome Ch'ên. London, New York, Oxford University Press, 1965. ix, 419 p. maps, port. 23 cm. *1. Mao, Tsê-tung, 1893- 2. Communism — China. I. Mao, Tsê-tung, 1893- II. T.*
DS778.M3C474   923.151   65-2375

Hsiao, Yü, 1894- III. 3746
Mao Tse-tung and I were beggars. Illustrated by the author, Siao-yu. With a foreword by Lin Yutang, pref. by Raymond F. Piper, and historical commentary and notes by Robert C. North. [Syracuse, N.Y.] Syracuse University Press [1959] 266 p. illus. 24 cm. *1. Mao, Tsê-tung, 1893-*
DS778.M3H75   923.551   59-15411

Rue, John E. III. 3747
Mao Tse-tung in opposition, 1927-1935 [by] John E. Rue, with the assistance of S. R. Rue. Stanford, Calif., Published for the Hoover Institution on War, Revolution, and Peace by Stanford University Press, 1966. viii, 387 p. maps. 24 cm. *1. Mao, Tsê-tung, 1893- 2. Chung-kuo kung ch'an tang. 3. China — Politics and Government — 1912-1949. I. Stanford University. Hoover Institution on War, Revolution, and Peace. II. T.*
DS778.M3R8   951.90430924   66-15302

Schram, Stuart R. III. 3748
Mao Tsê-tung [by] Stuart Schram. New York, Simon and Schuster [1967, c1966] 351 p. illus., ports. 22 cm. *1. Mao, Tsê-tung, 1893-*
DS778.M3S3 1967   951/.05/0924 (B)   67-12918

DS778   N - Z

Liew, K. S. III. 3749
Struggle for democracy; Sung Chiao-jen and the 1911 Chinese revolution [by] K. S. Liew. Berkeley, University of California Press, 1971. ix, 260 p. illus. 23 cm. *1. Sung, Chiao-jên, 1882?-1913. 2. China — History — Revolution, 1911-1912. I. T.*
DS778.S8L5 1971b   951/.03/0924 (B)   74-123623   ISBN:0520017609

Bunker, Gerald E. III. 3750
The peace conspiracy; Wang Ching-wei and the China war, 1937-1941 [by] Gerald E. Bunker. Cambridge, Mass., Harvard University Press, 1972. 327 p. illus. 25 cm. (Harvard East Asian series 67) *1. Wang, Chao-ming, 1883-1944. 2. Sino-Japanese Conflict, 1937-1945. I. T. (S)*
DS778.W3B85   940.53/12/0924   78-180149   ISBN:0-674-65915-5

Gillin, Donald G. III. 3751
Warlord: Yen Hsi-shan in Shansi Province, 1911-1949, by Donald G. Gillin. Princeton, N.J., Princeton University Press, 1967. xiv, 334 p. maps, ports. 22 cm. *1. Yen, Hsi-shan, 1883-1960. I. T.*
DS778.Y4G6   951.040924 (B)   66-14308

DS781 – 798   LOCAL HISTORY

Lattimore, Owen, 1900- III. 3752
The Mongols of Manchuria; their tribal divisions, geographical distribution, historical relations with Manchus and Chinese, and present political problems. New York, H. Fertig, 1969 [c1934] 311 p. maps. 21 cm. *1. Mongols — History. 2. Mongols in Manchuria. 3. Chinese in Manchuria. 4. Mongolia — History. 5. Eastern question (Far East) I. T.*
DS783.7.L3 1969   951/.7   68-9626

Ogata, Sadako N. III. 3753
Defiance in Manchuria; the making of Japanese foreign policy, 1931-1932, by Sadako N. Ogata. Berkeley, University of California Press, 1964. xvi, 259 p. map. 25 cm. (Publications of the Center for Japanese and Korean studies) *1. Japan. Rikugun Kantōgun. 2. Manchuria — History — 1931-1945. I. T. (S:California. University. Center for Japanese and Korean Studies Publications)*
DS783.7.O4   327.52   64-18645

Stimson, Henry Lewis, 1867- III. 3754
The Far Eastern crisis; recollections and observations, by Henry L. Stimson. New York, Pub. for the Council on Foreign Relations by Harper, 1936. xii, 293 (i.e. 295) p. front., illus. (maps) plates, ports. 25 cm. "First edition." *1. Eastern question (Far East) 2. Manchuria. 3. Japanese in Manchuria. I. Council on foreign relations, inc. II. T.*
DS783.7.S8   951.8   36-20072

Willoughby, Westel Woodbury, 1867-1945. III. 3755
The Sino-Japanese controversy and the League of Nations. New York, Greenwood Press, 1968 [c1935] xxv, 733 p. 22 cm. *1. Manchuria. 2. Japanese in Manchuria. 3. League of Nations — China. 4. League of Nations — Japan. 5. Japan — Foreign relations — China. 6. China — Foreign relations — Japan. 7. League of Nations. Council. 8. League of Nations. Special Assembly, 1932- I. T.*
DS783.7.W5 1968   951/.8   68-54995

Yoshihashi, Takehiko, 1912- III. 3756
Conspiracy at Mukden; the rise of the Japanese military. New Haven, Yale University Press, 1963. xvi, 274 p. maps. 23 cm. (Yale studies in political science, 9) *1. Manchuria — History — 1931-1945. 2. Japanese in Manchuria. I. T. (S)*
DS783.7.Y57   952.033   63-17025

Borg, Dorothy, 1902- III. 3757
The United States and the Far Eastern crisis of 1933-1938; from the Manchurian incident through the initial stage of the undeclared Sino-Japanese war. Cambridge, Harvard University Press, 1964. x, 674 p. 25 cm. (Harvard East Asian series, 14) *1. Manchuria — History — 1931-1945. 2. China — Foreign relations — Japan. 3. Japan — Foreign relations — China. 4. U.S. — Foreign relations — 1933-1945. I. T. (S)*
DS784.B65 1964   64-13421

DS785 – 786   Tibet. Central Asia

Grousset, René, 1885-1952. III. 3758
The empire of the steppes; a history of central Asia. Translated from the French by Naomi Walford. New Brunswick, N.J., Rutgers University Press [1970] xxx, 687 p. maps. 25 cm. *1. Asia, Central — History. I. T.*
DS785.G8313   958   77-108759   ISBN:813506271

Hambis, Louis. III. 3759
La Haute-Asie. [1. éd.] Paris, Presses universitaires de France, 1953. 134 p. illus. 18 cm. ("Que sais-je?" Le point des connaissances actuelles, 573) *1. Asia, Central — History. I. T.*
DS785.H197   54-26938

Lamb, Alastair, 1930- III. 3760
Britain and Chinese Central Asia; the road to Lhasa, 1767 to 1905. London, Routledge and Paul [1960] 387 p. illus. 23 cm. *1. Gt. Brit. — Foreign relations — Tibet. 2. Tibet — Foreign relations — Gt. Brit. I. T.*
DS785.L17   327.420515   61-1070

Ginsburgs, George. III. 3761
Communist China and Tibet: the first dozen years, by George Ginsburgs and Michael Mathos. The Hague, M. Nijhoff, 1964. 218 p. 25 cm. *1. Tibet — History — 1951- 2. Tibet — Politics and government — 1951- I. Mathos, Michael, joint author. II. T.*
DS786.G55   65-84502

Richardson, Hugh Edward, 1905-   **III. 3762**
A short history of Tibet. [1st American ed.] New York, Dutton, 1962. 308 p. illus. 22 cm. "Published in England under the title of Tibet and its history." *1. Tibet — History.*
DS786.R5 1962   951.5   61-6023

Sinor, Denis.   **III. 3763**
Inner Asia: history, civilization, languages; a syllabus. Bloomington, Indiana University [c1969] xvi, 261 p. 23 cm. (Indiana University publications. Uralic and Altaic series, v. 96) *1. Asia, Central. I. T. (S:Indiana. University. Uralic and Altaic series, v. 96)*
DS786.S545   915.8/03   67-66168

Snellgrove, David L.   **III. 3764**
A cultural history of Tibet [by] David Snellgrove [and] Hugh Richardson. New York, F. A. Praeger [1968] 291 p. illus., maps. 26 cm. *1. Tibet — Civilization — History. I. Richardson, Hugh Edward, 1905- joint author. II. T.*
DS786.S6 1968b   915.15/03   68-26668

Stein, Rolf Alfred, 1911-   **III. 3765**
Tibetan civilization [by] R. A. Stein. Translated by J. E. Stapleton Driver. With original drawings by Lobsang Tendzin. Stanford, Calif., Stanford University Press, 1972. 333 p. illus. 23 cm. "With minor revisions [of the original French ed.] by the author." *1. Tibet — Civilization. I. T.*
DS786.S7713 1972b   915.1/5/03   72-183893   ISBN:0804708061

Tucci, Giuseppe, 1894-   **III. 3766**
Tibet, land of snows. Photos. by Wim Swaan, Edwin Smith, and others. Translated by J. E. Stapleton Driver. New York, Stein and Day [1967] 216 p. illus. (part col.), facsims., map. 28 cm. *1. Tibet. I. Swaan, Wim, illus. II. T.*
DS786.T8   915.15/03   67-24403

DS793   Provinces, A – Z

Wakeman, Frederic E.   **III. 3767**
Strangers at the gate; social disorder in South China, 1839-1861 [by] Frederic Wakeman, Jr. Berkeley, University of California Press [c1966] 276 p. maps. 24 cm. *1. Kwangtung, China (Province) — History. 2. China — History — War of 1840-1842. I. T.*
DS793.K7W3   951.512703   66-25349

DS796   Hongkong

Endacott, G. B.   **III. 3768**
A history of Hong Kong. London, Oxford University Press, 1958. 322 p. illus. 23 cm. *1. Hongkong — History.*
DS796.H7E5   951.25   58-4392

Lo, Hsiang-lin, 1905-   **III. 3769**
Hong Kong and Western cultures. Toyko, Centre for East Asian Cultural Studies; Honolulu, East West Center Press, [1964, c1963] vi, 289, 56 p. illus., facsims., ports. 19 cm. Translation of Hsiang-kang yü Chung Hsi wên hua chih chiao liu (romanized form) *1. Hongkong — Relations (general) with China. 2. China — Relations (general) with Hongkong. 3. Hongkong — Relations (general) with Europe. 4. Europe — Relations (general) with Hongkong. I. T.*
DS796.H7L593   65-7535

Rand, Christopher.   **III. 3770**
Hongkong, the island between. New York, Knopf, 1952. [New York, AMS Press, 1973] 244 p. 19 cm. *1. Hongkong — Description and travel. 2. Communism — China.*
DS796.H7R35 1973   915.1/25   74-161781   ISBN:0404090370

DS798   Mongolia

Historical Evaluation and Research Organization, Washington, D.C.   **III. 3771**
Area handbook for Mongolia. Co-authors: Trevor N. Dupuy [and others] Prepared for the American University by Historical Evaluation and Research Organization. Washington, For sale by the Supt. of Docs., U.S. Govt. Print. Off., 1970. xiv, 500 p. maps 24 cm. "DA pam. no. 550-76." "One of a series of handbooks prepared by Foreign Area Studies (FAS) of the American Unversity." *1. Mongolia (Mongolian People's Republic) I. Dupuy, Trevor Nevitt, 1916- II. American University, Washington, D.C. Foreign Area Studies. III. T.*
DS798.H57   309.1/517/3   74-607921

DS801 – 897   JAPAN

Asakawa, Kanichi, 1874- ed.   **III. 3772**
The documents of Iriki, illustrative of the development of the feudal institutions of Japan, translated and edited by K. Asakawa. New Haven, Yale University Press; London, H. Milford, Oxford University Press, 1929. xvi, 442, 134, 6, 2 p. geneal. tables. maps, facsims. 26 cm. (Yale historical publications. Manuscripts and edited texts, x) "Published under the direction of the Department of history on the Kingsley trust association publication fund, established by the Scroll and key society of Yale College." The Japanese section is paged with Japanese numerals. "Japanese text of documents": 134 pages at end. *1. Shibuya family. 2. Shimadzu family. 3. Iriki, Kyushu, Japan. 4. Feudalism — Japan. 5. Land tenure — Kyushu, Japan. 6. Iriki-in. I. Kingsley trust association. II. T.*
DS803.A7   29-10899

The New official guide: Japan. 1964-   **III. 3773**
Tokyo, Japan Travel Bureau. v. fold. maps (part col.) 19 cm. Supersedes Japan, the official guide. Vols. for 1964- issued by Kokusai Kankō Shinkōkai under an English form of name: Japan National Tourist Organization. *1. Japan — Description and travel — Guide-books. I. Nihon Kōtsu Kōsha. II. Kokusai Kankō Shinkōkai.*
DS805.2.N47   66-19335

Japan. Mombushō. Nihon Yunesuko Kokunai Iinkai.   **III. 3774**
Japan: its land, people, and culture, compiled by Japanese National Commission for UNESCO. [Tokyo] Print. Bureau, Ministry of Finance [1958] 1077 p. illus., ports., maps. 26 cm. *1. Japan. I. T.*
DS806.A54   915.2   59-2236

Borton, Hugh, ed.   **III. 3775**
Japan. Ithaca, Cornell University Press [1951, c1950] viii, 320 p. 24 cm. Articles first published in the 1951 ed. of the Encyclopedia Americana. *1. Japan.*
DS806.B6   952.0082   51-12514

Chaffee, Frederic H.   **III. 3776**
Area handbook for Japan. Co-authors: Frederic H. Chaffee [and others. Revision] Washington, For sale by the Supt. of Docs., U.S. Govt. Print. Off., 1969. xvi, 628 p. maps. 24 cm. "DA pam 550-30." "This pamphlet supersedes DA pam 550-30, February 1961 [issued by Foreign Area Studies Division, American University]." "This volume is one of a series of handbooks prepared by Foreign Area Studies (FAS) of the American University." *1. Japan. I. American University, Washington, D.C. Foreign Area Studies Division. Area handbook for Japan. II. American University, Washington, D.C. Foreign Area Studies. III. T.*
DS806.C48   309.1/51   73-605269

Hall, John Whitney, 1916-   **III. 3777**
Twelve doors to Japan, by John Whitney Hall and Richard K. Beardsley. With chapters by Joseph K. Yamagiwa [and] B. James George, Jr. New York, McGraw-Hill [1965] xxi, 649 p. maps. 24 cm. *1. Japan. I. Beardsley, Richard King, 1918- joint author. II. T.*
DS806.H25   915.203   64-66015

Webb, Herschel.   **III. 3778**
An introduction to Japan. 2d ed. New York, Columbia University Press, 1957. 145 p. illus. 21 cm. *1. Japan.*
DS806.W35 1957   915.2   57-9552

Alcock, Rutherford, Sir, 1809-1897.   **III. 3779**
The capital of the tycoon: a narrative of a three years' residence in Japan. London, Longman, Green, Longman, Roberts, & Green, 1863. St. Clair Shores, Mich., Scholarly Press [1969] 2 v. illus. 23 cm. *1. Japan — Description and travel — 1801-1900. 2. Japan — Foreign relations — To 1868. I. T.*
DS809.A35 1969   915.2   73-8881

Hearn, Lafcadio, 1850-1904.   **III. 3780**
Glimpses of unfamiliar Japan, by Lafcadio Hearn. Boston and New York, Houghton, Mifflin, 1894. 2 v. 4 pl. 21 cm. Paged continuously. *1. Japan — Description and travel. I. T.*
DS809.H43   915.2   04-16699

Perry, Matthew Calbraith, 1794-1858.   **III. 3781**
Narrative of the expedition of an American squadron to the China Seas and Japan, performed in the years 1852, 1853, and 1854, under the command of Commodore M. C. Perry, United States Navy, by order of the Government of the United States. Compiled from the original notes and journals of Commodore Perry and his officers, at his request, and under his supervision, by Francis L. Hawks. Washington, B. Tucker, 1856. New York, AMS Press, 1967. 3 v. illus., charts, facsims., maps, plates and portfolio (15 fold. charts,

maps) 29 cm. (33d Cong., 2d sess. Senate. Ex. doc. no. 79) On spine: United States Japan Expedition. "List of charts of the United States Japan Expedition" (15 fold sheets)) issued in portfolio, to accompany v.2. Vol.2 (Natural history reports) by D. S. Green and others; v.3 has title: Observation on the zodiacal light, from April 2, 1853 to April 22, 1855, made chiefly on board the United States Steam-Frigate Mississippi ... with conclusions from the data thus obtained, by George Jones. *1. Unites States Naval Expedition to Japan, 1852-1854. 2. Japan — Description and travel — 1801-1900. I. Hawks, Francis Lister, 1798-1866, comp. II. Jones, George, 1800-1870. III. United States Japan Expedition. IV. T. (S:U.S. 33d Cong., 2d sess., 1854-1855. Senate. Executive document no. 79)*
DS809.P456 1967   952.02/5   67-31019

Hearn, Lafcadio, 1850-1904. III. 3782
Japan; an attempt at interpretation. Tokyo, Rutland, Vt., Tuttle [1955, c1904] 498 p. 19 cm. *1. Japan — Civilization.*
DS810.H43 1955   915.2   56-249

Ōkuma, Shigénobu, count, 1838-1922, comp. III. 3783
Fifty years of new Japan (Kaikoku gojūnen shi) comp. by Count Shingénobu Ōkuma. English version ed. by Marcus B. Huish. London, Smith, Elder, & co., 1909. 2 v. fold. map. 23 cm. *1. Japan. 2. Japan — Civilization. I. Huish, Marcus Bourne, 1845- ed. II. T.*
DS810.O4 1909   20-7617

Isida, Ryuziro, 1904- III. 3784
Geography of Japan. Tokyo, Kokusai Bunka Shinkokai; [Distributed by Japan Publications Trading Co., San Francisco] 1969. xi, 124 p. illus. (part col.), maps. 24 cm. (Japanese life and culture ser.) *1. Japan — Description and travel — 1945- I. T.*
DS811.I7 1969   309.1/52   70-75821

Trewartha, Glenn Thomas, 1896- III. 3785
Japan, a geography [by] Glenn T. Trewartha. Madison, University of Wisconsin Press, 1965. x, 652 p. illus., maps. 24 cm. *1. Japan — Description and travel — 1945-. I. T.*
DS811.T72   915.2   65-11200

DS815 – 832   Civilization

Komatsu, Isao, 1919- III. 3786
The Japanese people; origins of the people and the language. Tokyo, Kokusai Bunka Shinkokai; [distributed by East West Center, Honolulu] 1962. xi, 64 p. illus., plates, maps. 25 cm. (Series on Japanese life and culture, v.1) *1. Japanese — Origin. 2. Japanese language — History. I. T. (S)*
DS815.K65   64-562

Japan. Mombushō. III. 3787
Kokutai no hongi. Cardinal principles of the national entity of Japan. Tr. by John Owen Gauntlett and ed. with an introd. by Robert King Hall. Cambridge, Harvard University Press, 1949. viii, 200 p. 22 cm. *1. Japan — Civilization. 2. National characteristics, Japanese. I. Cardinal principles of the national entity of Japan. II. T.*
DS821.A16 1949   915.2   49-9335

Benedict, Ruth (Fulton) 1887- III. 3788
The chrysanthemum and the sword; patterns of Japanese culture, by Ruth Benedict. Boston, Houghton Mifflin, 1946. 324 p. 22 cm. *1. Japan — Social life and customs. 2. Japan — Civilization. I. T.*
DS821.B46   915.2   46-11843

Chamberlain, Basil Hall, 1850-1935. III. 3789
Japanese things; being notes on various subjects connected with Japan, for the use of travelers and others. Rutland, Vt., Tuttle [c1971] x, 568 p. fold. col. map (in pocket) 19 cm. Previous editions have title: Things Japanese. *1. Japan. I. T.*
DS821.C43 1971   915.2/03/3103   76-87791   ISBN:804807132

Gibney, Frank, 1924- III. 3790
Five gentlemen of Japan; the portrait of a nation's character. New York, Farrar, Straus and Young [1953] 373 p. illus. 22 cm. *1. National characteristics, Japanese. I. T.*
DS821.G5   915.2   53-7052

Jansen, Marius B., ed. III. 3791
Changing Japanese attitudes toward modernization. Edited by Marius B. Jansen. Contributors: Robert N. Bellah [and others] Princeton, N. J., Princeton University Press, 1965. x, 546 p. illus. 21 cm. Papers prepared for a seminar held in Bermuda under the auspices of the Conference on Modern Japan of the Association for Asian Studies in Jan. 1962. *1. Japan — Civilization — Addresses, essays, lectures. I. Bellah, Robert Neelly, 1927- II. Conference on Modern Japan. III. T.*
DS821.J334   915.2   63-23406

Keene, Donald. III. 3792
The Japanese discovery of Europe, 1720-1830. Rev. ed. Stanford, Calif., Stanford University Press, 1969. xiii, 255 p. illus., map, ports. 23 cm. 1954 ed. published under title: The Japanese discovery of Europe. *1. Honda, Toshiaki, 1744-1821. 2. Japan — Relations (general) with Europe. 3. Europe — Relations (general) with Japan. I. T.*
DS821.K32 1969   301.29/51/04   69-13180

Keene, Donald. III. 3793
Living Japan. Garden City, N.Y., Doubleday [1959] 224 p. plates (part col.) map. 29 cm. *1. Japan — Civilization. I. T.*
DS821.K33   915.2   59-10088

Maraini, Fosco. III. 3794
Meeting with Japan; translated from the Italian by Eric Mosbacher. 2nd ed. London, Hutchinson, 1969. 463 p., 64 plates. illus. (some col.), charts, maps. 25 cm. Originally published as 'Ore Giapponesi', Bari, Leonardo da Vinci, 1957. Maps on lining papers. *1. Japan — Social life and customs — 1945- I. T.*
DS821.M273 1969   915.2   72-457078   ISBN:090517318

Plath, David W. III. 3795
The after hours; modern Japan and the search for enjoyment [by] David W. Plath. Berkeley, University of California Press, 1964. xi, 222 p. illus. 22 cm. *1. Japan — Social life and customs. 2. Recreation — Japan. I. T. II. T:Modern Japan and the search for enjoyment.*
DS821.P55   309.152   64-16133

Riesman, David, 1909- III. 3796
Conversations in Japan: modernization, politics, and culture [by] David Riesman [and] Evelyn Thompson Riesman. New York, Basic Books [1967] xii, 371 p. 25 cm. *1. Japan — Civilization. 2. National characteristics, Japanese. I. Riesman, Evelyn Thompson. II. T.*
DS821.R52   915.2/03/4   67-17861

Sansom, George Bailey, Sir, 1883- III. 3797
Japan, a short cultural history. Rev. ed. New York, Appleton-Century-Crofts [1962] 558 p. illus. 24 cm. *1. Japan — Civilization. 2. Japan — History.*
DS821.S3 1962   952   62-2310

Sansom, George Bailey, Sir, 1883- III. 3798
The Western World and Japan, a study in the interaction of European and Asiatic cultures. [1st ed.] New York, Knopf, 1950 [i.e. 1949] xvi, 504, xi p. illus., ports., maps. 25 cm. *1. Japan — Relations (general) with Europe. 2. Europe — Relations (general) with Japan. 3. Japan — Civilization — Occidental influences. I. T.*
DS821.S313   952.025   50-5199

Silberman, Bernard S., 1930- ed. III. 3799
Japanese character and culture; a book of selected readings. Tucson, University of Arizona Press, 1962. 421 p. 24 cm. *1. National Characteristics, Japanese. I. T.*
DS821.S57   915.2   61-63840

Tsunoda, Ryūsaku, ed. III. 3800
Sources of the Japanese tradition, compiled by Ryūsaku Tsunoda, Wm. Theodore de Bary [and] Donald Keene. New York, Columbia University Press [1958] xxvi, 928 p. maps. 24 cm. (Records of civilization: sources and studies, 54. Introduction to oriental civilizations) Translations from various sources and by various individuals. *1. Japan — Civilization. 2. Japan — History — Sources. I. T. (S:Records of civilization: sources and studies, 54.) (S:Introduction to oriental civilizations)*
DS821.T76   952.0082   58-7167

Arima, Tatsuo. III. 3801
The failure of freedom; a portrait of modern Japanese intellectuals. Cambridge, Harvard University Press, 1969. xiii, 296 p. 22 cm. (Harvard East Asian series, 39) *1. Intellectuals — Japan. 2. Liberalism — Japan. I. T. (S)*
DS822.4.A7   915.2/03/320922   74-82292   ISBN:674291301

Morris, Ivan I. III. 3802
The world of the shining prince; court life in ancient Japan [by] Ivan Morris. [1st American ed.] New York, Knopf, 1964. xv, 336 p. illus. 22 cm. *1. Japan — Court and courtiers. I. T.*
DS824.M6 1964   915.2   64-12310

Katō, Shizue, 1897- III. 3803
Facing two ways; the story of my life, by Baroness Shidzué Ishimoto. New York, Farrar & Rinehart [c1935] vi, 373 p. illus., plates, ports. 22 cm. *1. Japan — Social life and customs — 1912-1945. 2. Women in Japan. 3. Woman — Rights of women. I. T.*
DS825.K29   920.7   35-14203

Shisō no Kagaku Kenkyūkai. III. 3804
Japanese popular culture; studies in mass communication and cultural

change made at the Institute of Science of Thought, Japan. Edited and translated by Hidetoshi Kato. [1st ed.] Toyko, Rutland, Vt., C. E. Tuttle Co. [1959] 223 p. illus., tables. 22 cm. (Massachusetts Institute of Technology. Center for International Studies. Studies of the program in international communication, 4) *1. Japan — Popular culture. I. Katō, Hidetoshi, 1930- ed. and tr. II. T. (S)*
DS827.P6S48   915.2   58-5088

Bennett, John William, 1915-   **III. 3805**
In search of identity; the Japanese overseas scholar in America and Japan [by] John W. Bennett, Herbert Passin [and] Robert K. McKnight. Minneapolis, University of Minnesota Press [1958] 369 p. illus. 24 cm. *1. Returned students — Japan. 2. Japan — Civilization — American influences. 3. Japan — Intellectual life. I. T.*
DS827.R4B4   915.2   58-10879

DS833 – 897 History

Goedertier, Joseph M.   **III. 3806**
A dictionary of Japanese history [by] Joseph M. Goedertier. [1st ed.] New York, Walker/Weatherhill [i.e. J. Weatherhill; distributed by Walker, 1968] 415 p. 24 cm. "Compiled under the auspices of the Oriens Institute for Religious Research." *1. Japan — History — Dictionaries. 2. Japanese language — Dictionaries — English. I. Oriensu Shūkyō Kenkyūjo. II. T.*
DS833.G63   952/.003   68-15703

Varley, H. Paul.   **III. 3807**
A syllabus of Japanese civilization, by H. Paul Varley. New York, Columbia University Press, 1968. ix, 98 p. maps. 23 cm. (Companions to Asian studies) *1. Japan — History — Outlines, syllabi, etc. 2. Japan — Civilization — History — Outlines, syllabi, etc. I. T. (S)*
DS833.V3   915.2/03/0202   68-55815

The Japan biographical encyclopedia & who's who.   **III. 3808**
Tokyo, Japan Biographical Research Dept., Rengo Press, 1958-   v. col. maps. 27 cm. *1. Japan — Biography — Dictionaries.*
DS834.J7   920.052   58-1808

Borton, Hugh.   **III. 3809**
Japan's modern century; from Perry to 1970. 2d ed. New York, Ronald Press [1970] x, 610 p. illus., maps, ports. 24 cm. Appendices (p. 567-590): The Potsdam proclamation. — Text of Japan's two constitutions, 1889-1946. — The Security treaty of 1960. *1. Japan — History. I. T.*
DS835.B6 1970   952.03   70-110544

Kaempfer, Engelbert, 1651-1716.   **III. 3810**
The history of Japan, together with a description of the Kingdom of Siam, 1690-92. Translated by J. G. Scheuchzer. [1st AMS ed.] Glasgow, J. MacLehose, 1906. [New York, AMS Press, 1971] 3 v. illus., fold. maps, port. 23 cm. *1. Japan — History — To 1868. 2. Japan — Description and travel — To 1800. 3. Thailand — Description and travel. I. Scheuchzer, John Gaspar, 1702-1729, tr. II. T.*
DS835.K2 1971   915.2/03/25   78-137313   ISBN:0404036309 (set)

Kuno, Yoshi Saburo, 1865-1941.   **III. 3811**
Japanese expansion on the Asiatic continent; a study in the history of Japan with special reference to her international relations with China, Korea, and Russia. Port Washington, N.Y., Kennikat Press [1967, c1940] 2 v. illus., maps, ports. 22 cm. *1. Japan — History. 2. Japan — Foreign relations. I. T.*
DS835.K8 1967   952   67-27615

Latourette, Kenneth Scott, 1884-   **III. 3812**
The history of Japan. Rev. ed. New York, Macmillan, 1957. 299 p. illus. 21 cm. First published in 1918 under title: The development of Japan. *1. Japan — History. I. T.*
DS835.L3 1957   952   57-5775

Murdoch, James, 1856-1921.   **III. 3813**
A history of Japan. Foreword and selected bibliography by John L. Mish. New York, F. Ungar Pub. Co. [1964] 3 v. in 6. geneal. tables. 26 cm. *1. Japan — History — To 1867. I. T.*
DS835.M82 1964   952   64-15695

Reischauer, Edwin Oldfather, 1910-   **III. 3814**
Japan; the story of a nation [by] Edwin O. Reischauer. [1st ed.] New York, Knopf [1970] xv, 345, xx p. maps. 21 cm. *1. Japan — History. I. T.*
DS835.R38 1970   952   77-108925

Sansom, George Bailey, Sir, 1883-   **III. 3815**
A history of Japan. Stanford, Calif., Stanford University Press, 1958-63. 3 v. illus., maps, facsims. 26 cm. (Stanford studies in the civilizations of eastern Asia) *1. Japan — History. (S)*
DS835.S27   952   58-11694

Boxer, Charles Ralph, 1904-   **III. 3816**
Jan Compagnie in Japan, 1600-1817; an essay on the cultural, artistic and scientific influence exercised by the Hollanders in Japan from the seventeenth to the nineteenth centuries [by] C. R. Boxer. Authorized reprint (with corrections) of 2nd rev. ed. Tokyo, New York [etc.] Oxford U.P., 1968. viii, 198 p. illus. (part col.), facsims., map. 26 cm. (Oxford in Asia. Historical reprints) *1. Nederlandsche Oost-Indische Compagnie. 2. Dutch in Japan. 3. Titsingh, Issac, 1744-1812. I. T.*
DS836.B6 1968   915.2/03/25   73-415000

Mitchell, Richard H.   **III. 3817**
The Korean minority in Japan [by] Richard H. Mitchell. Berkeley, University of California Press. 1967. 186 p. 23 cm. *1. Koreans in Japan. I. T.*
DS836.M5   301.453/519/052   67-18074

The Southern barbarians; the first Europeans in Japan   **III. 3818**
[by] Michael Cooper [and others] Edited by Michael Cooper. Tokyo, Palo Alto, Calif., Kodansha International in cooperation with Sophia University [1971] 216 p. facsims. (part col.), maps, plates (part col.), ports. (part col.) 31 cm. *1. Europeans in Japan. 2. Japan — Church history — To 1868. 3. Japan — Civilization — Occidental influences. 4. Art, Japanese — Occidental influences. I. Cooper, Michael, S.J., ed.*
DS836.S68   915.2   74-128689   ISBN:0870111388

Ienaga, Saburō, 1913-   **III. 3819**
History of Japan. [4th ed.] Tōkyō, Japan Travel Bureau [1959] 262 p. illus. 19 cm. (Tourist library, 15) *1. Japan — History.*
DS837.I3 1959   952   59-15650

Sansom, George Bailey, Sir, 1883-   **III. 3820**
Japan in world history. Issued under the auspices of the Institute of Pacific Relations. London, Allen & Unwin [1952] 94 p. illus. 19 cm. *1. Japan — History — Philosophy. I. T.*
DS837.S3 1952   952   53-19137

DS840 – 849 POLITICAL AND DIPLOMATIC HISTORY

Beasley, William G. ed. and tr.   **III. 3821**
Select documents on Japanese foreign policy, 1853-1868, translated and edited by W. G. Beasley. London, New York, Oxford University Press, 1955. xi, 359 p. 25 cm. *1. Japan — Foreign relations — To 1867. I. T:Japanese foreign policy, 1853-1868.*
DS840.B4   55-4067

Reischauer, Robert Karl, 1907-1937.   **III. 3822**
Japan, government-politics, by Robert Karl Reischauer. New York, T. Nelson and sons, 1939. 221 p. diagrs. 20 cm. Maps on lining-papers. *1. Japan — Politics and government.*
DS841.R4   39-3379

Asakawa, Kan'ichi, 1873-1948.   **III. 3823**
The early institutional life of Japan; a study in the reform of 645 A.D. 2d ed. New York, Paragon Book Reprint Corp., 1963. 6, 355 p. 24 cm. "Based upon the author's doctoral diss., completed at Yale University." *1. Japan — Politics and government — To 794. 2. Japan — History — To 1867. I. T.*
DS842.A8 1963   952.01   63-21051

Brown, Delmer Myers, 1909-   **III. 3824**
Nationalism in Japan; an introductory historical analysis [by] Delmer M. Brown. New York, Russell & Russell [1971, c1955] viii, 336 p. 24 cm. *1. Nationalism — Japan — History. I. T.*
DS843.B76 1971   952   79-143555

Takeuchi, Tatsuji, 1904-   **III. 3825**
War and diplomacy in the Japanese empire, by Tatsuji Takeuchi, introd. by Quincy Wright. [1st ed.] Garden City, N.Y., Doubleday, Doran, 1935. xix, 505 p. 23 1/2 cm. "The constitution of the empire of Japan": p. 477-484. *1. Japan. Constitution. 2. Japan — Politics and government. 3. Japan — Foreign relations. 4. Japan — Foreign relations — Treaties. I. Japan. Constitution. II. T.*
DS845.T3   952.03   36-10

Dennis, Alfred Lewis Pinneo, 1874-1930.   **III. 3826**
The Anglo-Japanese alliance, by Alfred L. P. Dennis. Berkeley, University of California Press, 1923. 111 p. 25 cm. (University of California publications. Bureau of International Relations. v.1, no. 1) Cover-title. Appendix I. The Anglo-Japanese treaties. A. Treaty of 1902. B. Treaty of 1905. 3. Treaty of 1911. — Appendix II. The four power pact. — Appendix III. Reading list (p. 110-111) *1. Gt. Brit. — Foreign relations — Japan. 2.*

Japan — Foreign relations — Gt. Brit. I. Gt. Brit. Treaties, etc. II. Japan. Treaties, etc. III. T.
DS849.G7D4   A23-1030

Lensen, George Alexander, 1923- III. 3827
The Russian push toward Japan; Russo-Japanese relations, 1697-1875. New York, Octagon Books, 1971 [c1959] xv, 553 p. illus. 25 cm. *1. Russia — Foreign relations — Japan. 2. Japan — Foreign relations — Russia. 3. Siberia, Eastern — History. I. T.*
DS849.R7L39 1971   327.47/052   75-120640   ISBN:0374949360

Lensen, George Alexander, 1923- III. 3828
Russia's Japan expedition of 1852 to 1855. Gainesville, University of Florida Press, 1955. xxvii, 208 p. illus., ports. 23 cm. Title also in Japanese on cover and half title. *1. Putiatin, Evfimiĭ Vasil'evich, graf, 1803-1883. 2. Russia — Foreign relations — Japan. 3. Japan — Foreign relations — Russia. I. T. II. T:Japan expedition of 1852 to 1855.*
DS849.R7L4 1955   327.520947   55-8081

Grew, Joseph Clark, 1880- III. 3829
Ten years in Japan, a contemporary record drawn from the diaries and private and official papers of Joseph C. Grew, United States ambassador to Japan, 1932-1942. New York, Simon and Schuster, 1944. xii, 554 p., 1 l. front., plates, ports. 22 cm. *1. U.S. — Foreign relations — Japan. 2. Japan — Foreign relations — U.S. 3. Japan — Politics and government. 4. World war, 1939-1945 — Causes. I. T.*
DS849.U6G7   327.730952   44-40123

Moore, Frederick, 1877- III. 3830
With Japan's leaders; an intimate record of fourteen years as counsellor to the Japanese government, ending December 7, 1941, by Frederick Moore. New York, Scribner, 1942. 365 p. 21 cm. *1. Japan — Foreign relations — U.S. 2. U.S. — Foreign relations — Japan. I. T.*
DS849.U6M68   327.520973   42-17502

DS851 – 890 BY PERIOD
DS851 – 871 Early to 1868

Kojiki. English. III. 3831
Kojiki. Translated with an introd. and notes by Donald L. Philippi. [Princeton, N.J.] Princeton University Press, 1969 [c1968] v, 655 p. 24 cm. *1. Japan — History — To 645 — Sources. 2. Mythology, Japanese. 3. Shinto. I. Philippi, Donald L., tr. II. T.*
DS851.A2K643 1969   915.2/03/1   69-17446

Nihon shoki. English. III. 3832
Nihongi; chronicles of Japan from the earliest times to A.D. 697. Translated from the original Chinese and Japanese by W. G. Aston. With an introd. to the new ed. by Terence Barrow. [1st Tuttle ed.] Rutland, Vt., C. E. Tuttle Co. [1972] 2 v. in 1. illus. 19 cm. (Tut books. H) *1. Japan — History — To 645. 2. Mythology, Japanese. I. Aston, William George, 1841- tr. II. T.*
DS851.A2N53 1972   915.2/03/1   70-152110   ISBN:0804809844

Tsunoda, Ryūsaku, tr. III. 3833
Japan in the Chinese dynastic histories: Later Han through Ming dynasties. Editor: L. Carrington Goodrich. South Pasadena [Calif.] P. D. and I. Perkins, 1951. vii, 187 l. maps. 28 cm. (Perkins Asiatic monographs, no. 2) "Prepared under the auspices of the Columbia University Council for Research in the Social Sciences." *1. Japan — History — To 1867 — Sources. I. Goodrich, Luther Carrington, 1894- ed. II. T. (S)*
DS851.A2T7   952.01   53-67

Kidder, Jonathan Edward. III. 3834
Japan before Buddhism [by] J. E. Kidder, Jr. [Rev. ed.] New York, F. A. Praeger [1966] 284 p. illus., maps. 22 cm. (Ancient peoples and places, 10) *1. Japan — History — To 645. 2. Japan — Antiquities. I. T.*
DS851.K5 1966   915.2031   66-12521

Reischauer, Robert Karl, 1907-1937. III. 3835
Early Japanese history, c. 40 B.C.-A.D. 1167. Gloucester, Mass., P. Smith, 1967 [c1937] 2 v. illus., maps. 24 cm. At head of title: Princeton University, School of Public and International Affairs. Pt. B. by Jean Reischauer and Robert Karl Reischauer. *1. Japan — History — To 1868. I. Reischauer, Jean, joint author. II. Princeton University. Woodrow Wilson School of Public and International Affairs. III. T.*
DS851.R4 1967   952/.01   67-8701

Shinoda, Minoru. III. 3836
The founding of the Kamakura shogunate, 1180-1185. With selected translations from the Azuma kagami. New York, Columbia University Press, 1960. xii, 385 p. maps, geneal. tables. 25 cm. (Records of civilization: sources and studies, no. 57) "Substantial revision of the dissertation submitted in January, 1957 ... Columbia University." *1. Japan — History — Kamakura period, 1185-1333. I. Azumakagami. II. T. (S)*
DS859.S48 1960   952.02   59-10433

Taiheiki. III. 3837
The Taiheiki: a chronicle of medieval Japan. Translated, with an introd. and notes, by Helen Craig McCullough. New York, Columbia University Press, 1959. xlix, 401 p. illus. 24 cm. (Records of civilization: sources and studies, no. 59) "[Ascribed] in the diary of Tōin Kinsada (1340-1399) ... [to] the monk Kojima." *1. Godaigo, Emperor of Japan, 1288-1338. 2. Japan — History — To 1867. I. Kojima Hōshi, d. 1374, supposed author. II. McCullough, Helen Craig, ed. and tr. (S)*
DS861.T313   952.02   59-6662

Dening, Walter, 1846-1913. III. 3838
The life of Toyotomi Hideyoshi. 4th ed., with pref., notes and an appendix. Tokyo, Hokuseido Press, 1955. xiv, 360 p. illus. (part col.) fold. col. maps. 22 cm. *1. Toyotomi, Hideyoshi, 1536?-1598.*
DS868.D4 1955   923.252   56-1288

Earl, David Magarey, 1911- III. 3839
Emperor and nation in Japan; political thinkers of the Tokugawa period. Seattle, University of Washington Press [1964] x, 270 p. 22 cm. "In its original form ... submitted as a doctoral dissertation to the Faculty of Political Science of Columbia University." *1. Yoshida, Shōin, 1830-1859. 2. Japan — History — Tokugawa period, 1600-1867. 3. Patriotism — Japan. I. T.*
DS871.E3   320.952   63-20539

Hall, John Whitney, 1916- III. 3840
Tanuma Okitsugu, 1719-1788, forerunner of modern Japan. Cambridge, Harvard University Press, 1955. xii, 208 p. 24 cm. (Harvard-Yenching Institute. Monograph series, 14) *1. Tanuma, Okitsugu, 1719-1788. (S)*
DS871.H3   952.0252   52-5396

Norman, E. Herbert, 1909- III. 3841
Andō Shōeki and the anatomy of Japanese feudalism. Tokyo [1949] 2 v. 22 cm. (The Transactions of the Asiatic Society of Japan, 3d ser., v.2, 1949) [Vol.2] "Supplementary volume containing the original text of passages quoted in volume I from the Shizen shineidō and the Tōdō shinden." *1. Andō, Shōeki, 18th cent. 2. Feudalism — Japan. I. Andō, Shōeki, 18th cent. Shizen shin'eidō. II. Andō, Shōeki, 18th cent. Tōdō shinden.*
DS871.N6x   A51-2181

Sadler, Arthur Lindsay, 1882- III. 3842
The maker of modern Japan; the life of Tokugawa Ieyasu. London, G. Allen & Unwin, ltd. [1937] 429 p. illus. (incl. plans) plates, ports., fold. geneal. tab. 23 cm. *1. Tokugawa, Ieyasu, 1542-1616. 2. Japan — History. I. T.*
DS871.S3   923.252   37-7531

Totman, Conrad D. III. 3843
Politics in the Tokugawa bakufu, 1600-1843 [by] Conrad D. Totman. Cambridge, Harvard University Press, 1967. 346 p. illus., maps. 24 cm. (Harvard East Asian series, 30) *1. Tokugawa family. 2. Japan — Politics and government — 1600-1868. I. T. (S)*
DS871.T6   952.02/5   67-22873

Webb, Herschel. III. 3844
The Japanese imperial institution in the Tokugawa period. New York, Columbia University Press, 1968. xi, 296 p. 22 cm. (Studies of the East Asian Institute, Columbia University) *1. Japan — Emperors. 2. Japan — Politics and government — 1600-1868. I. T. (S:Columbia University. East Asian Institute. Studies)*
DS871.W3   320.9/52   68-11912

DS881 – 884 19th Century

Beasley, William G. III. 3845
The modern history of Japan. New York, Praeger [1963] xi, 352 p. illus., ports., maps. 23 cm. (The Praeger Asia-Africa series) *1. Japan — History. I. T.*
DS881.B4 1963   952   63-20665

Black, John R. d. 1880. III. 3846
Young Japan: Yokohama and Yedo, 1858-79, by John R. Black. With an introduction by Grace Fox. Tokyo, New York, Oxford Univ. P., 1968. 2 v. col. front. 23 cm. (Oxford in Asia. Historical reprints) Reprint of 1883 ed. *1. Japan — History — Meiji period, 1868-1912. I. T.*
DS881.B62 1968   952.031   77-437868

Norman, E. Herbert, 1909- III. 3847
Japan's emergence as a modern state; political and economic problems of the Meiji period, by E. Herbert Norman. New York, International Secretariat, Institute of Pacific Relations, 1940. xvi, 254 p. 24 cm. (I.P.R. inquiry series) *1. Japan — Politics and government — 1867-1912. 2. Japan — Economic conditions. 3. Japan — Economic policy. I. T.*
DS881.N6   952.031   40-8128

Harootunian, Harry D., 1929-   **III. 3848**
Toward restoration; the growth of political consciousness in Tokugawa Japan [by] H. D. Harootunian. Berkeley, University of California Press, 1970. xviii, 421 p. 24 cm. (Publications of the Center for Japanese and Korean studies) *1. Japan — History — Restoration, 1853-1870. 2. Japan — Politics and government — 1600-1868. I. T. (S:California. University. Center for Japanese and Korean studies. Publications)*
DS881.3.H28 1970   915.2/03/25   79-94993   ISBN:520015665

Jansen, Marius B.   **III. 3849**
Sakamoto Ryōma and the Meiji Restoration. Princeton, N.J., Princeton University Press, 1961. xii, 423 p. illus., fold. map, ports. 25 cm. *1. Sakamoto, Ryōma, 1836-1867. 2. Japan — History — Restoration, 1853-1870. I. T.*
DS881.3.J28   952.031   61-6909

Norman, E. Herbert, 1909-   **III. 3850**
Soldier and peasant in Japan: the origins of conscription, by E. Herbert Norman. New York, International Secretariat, Institute of Pacific Relations, 1943. xiv, 76 p. 3 plates (incl. ports.) 21 cm. *1. Military service, Compulsory — Japan. 2. Japan — Politics and government. 3. Peasantry — Japan. 4. Militarism. I. Institute of Pacific relations. II. T.*
DS881.3.N6   355.22   43-18424

Satow, Ernest Mason, Sir, 1843-1929.   **III. 3851**
A diplomat in Japan, by Sir Ernest Satow; with an introduction by Gordon Daniels. Tokyo, New York, Oxford U.P., 1968. xii, 427 p. illus., maps, ports. 23 cm. (Oxford in Asia. Historical reprints) Reprint of 1921 ed. *1. Japan — History — Restoration, 1853-1870. 2. Japan — Foreign relations — To 1868. I. T.*
DS881.3.S3 1968   327.42/052   72-430540

Straelen, Henricus van, 1903-   **III. 3852**
Yoshida Shōin, forerunner of the Meiji restoration; a biographical study. Leiden, E. J. Brill, 1952. 149 p. 25 cm. (T'oung pao; archives concernant l'histoire, les langues, la géographie, l'ethnologie et les arts de l'Asie orientale. Monographie 2) *1. Yoshida, Shōin, 1830-1859. (S)*
DS881.5.Y6S7   923.252   52-12675

Storry, George Richard, 1913-   **III. 3853**
A history of modern Japan, by Richard Storry. [Harmondsworth, Middlesex; Baltimore] Penguin Books [1960] 287 p. illus. 19 cm. (A Pelican book, A475) *1. Japan — History — 1868- I. T.*
DS881.9.S8 1960   952   60-4354

McLaren, Walter Wallace, 1877-   **III. 3854**
A political history of Japan during the Meiji era, 1867-1912. New York, Russell & Russell, 1965. 379 p. 22 cm. "First published in 1916." *1. Japan — History — Meiji period, 1867-1912. I. T.*
DS882.M3 1965   952.031   65-17910

Wilson, Robert Arden, 1910-   **III. 3855**
Genesis of the Meiji government in Japan, 1868-1871. Berkeley, University of California Press, 1957. iv, 149 p. 24 cm. (University of California publications in history, v.56) *1. Japan — History — Meiji period, 1867-1912. I. T. (S:California. University. University of California publications in history, v.56)*
DS882.5.W5 (E173.C15 vol. 56)   952.031   A58-9047

Harada, Kumao, 1888-1946.   **III. 3856**
Fragile victory; Prince Saionji and the 1930 London treaty issue, from the memoirs of Baron Harada Kumao. Translated with an introd. and annotations by Thomas Francis Mayer-Oakes. Detroit, Wayne State University Press, 1968. 330 p. illus., map (on lining-papers), ports. 26 cm. At head of title: Saionji-Harada memoirs. Translation of v. 1 of Saionji Kō to seikyoku (romanized form) Originally published as the translator's thesis, University of Chicago, 1955, under title: Prince Saionji and the London Naval Conference. *1. Saionji, Kimmochi, 1849-1940. 2. Japan — Politics and government — 1868-1912. 3. Japan — Politics and government — 1912-1945. 4. London Naval Conference, 1930. I. Mayer-Oakes, Thomas Francis, 1912- ed. II. Prince Saionji and the 1930 London treaty issue. III. Saionji-Harada memoirs. IV. T.*
DS884.S3H333 1968   327.52/042   66-22988

DS885 – 890   20th Century

Yanaga, Chitoshi, 1903-   **III. 3857**
Japan since Perry. Hamden, Conn., Archon Books, 1966 [c1949] x, 723 p. maps. 23 cm. *1. Japan — History. I. T.*
DS885.Y3 1966   952.03   66-16779

Wilson, George M.   **III. 3858**
Radical nationalist in Japan: Kita Ikki, 1883-1937, [by] George M. Wilson. Cambridge, Mass., Harvard University Press, 1969. xii, 230 p. port. 22 cm. (Harvard East Asian series, 37) Developed from author's thesis, Harvard University. *1. Kita, Ikki, 1883-1937. I. T. (S)*
DS885.5.K52W5   322/.4 (B)   69-12740

Duus, Peter, 1933-   **III. 3859**
Party rivalry and political change in Taishō Japan. Cambridge, Mass., Harvard University Press, 1968. viii, 317 p. 25 cm. (Harvard East Asian series, 35) Based on thesis, Harvard University. *1. Japan — Politics and government — 1912-1945. 2. Political parties — Japan. I. T. (S)*
DS886.D88   329.9/51   68-21972

Young, Arthur Morgan, 1874-   **III. 3860**
Japan in recent times, 1912-1926, by A. Morgan Young. Westport, Conn., Greenwood Press [1973] 347 p. 22 cm. Reprint of the 1929 ed. *1. Japan — History — Taishō period, 1912-1926. I. T.*
DS886.Y6 1973   952.03/2   76-136554   ISBN:0837154804

Crowley, James B.   **III. 3861**
Japan's quest for autonomy; national security and foreign policy, 1930-1938, by James B. Crowley. Princeton, N.J., Princeton University Press, 1966. xviii, 428 p. 21 cm. Elaboration of a doctoral thesis, Yale University. *1. Japan — Foreign relations — 1912-1945. 2. Eastern question (Far East) I. T.*
DS888.5.C7   327.52   66-10552

Storry, George Richard, 1913-   **III. 3862**
The double patriots; a study of Japanese nationalism [by] Richard Storry. Westport, Conn., Greenwood Press [1973] 335 p. 22 cm. Reprint of the 1957 ed. *1. Japan — Foreign relations — 1912-1945. 2. Japan — Politics and government — 1912-1945. I. T.*
DS888.5.S7 1973   952.03/3   72-10982   ISBN:0837166438

DS889   1926 –

Baerwald, Hans H.   **III. 3863**
The purge of Japanese leaders under the occupation. Berkeley, University of California Press, 1959. 111 p. 24 cm. (University of California publications in political science, v.8) *1. Japan — History — Allied occupation, 1945-1952. I. T. (S:California. University. University of California publications in political science, v.8)*
DS889.B2 (JA37.C3 vol. 8)   952.04   59-63933

Borton, Hugh.   **III. 3864**
Japan since 1931, its political and social developments, by Hugh Borton ... New York, International Secretariat, Institute of Pacific Relations, 1940. xii, 149 p. 24 cm. (I.P.R. inquiry series) *1. Japan — Politics and government — 1912-1945. 2. Japan — Social conditions. 3. Japan — Economic conditions — 1918-1945. I. T.*
DS889.B65   952.033   41-51526

Emmerson, John K.   **III. 3865**
Arms, yen & power: the Japanese dilemma [by] John K. Emmerson. Foreword by Edwin O. Reischauer. New York, Dunellen [1971] xiv, 420 p. 22 cm. *1. Japan — Politics and government — 1945- 2. Japan — Foreign relations — 1945- 3. Japan — Defenses. I. The Japanese dilemma. II. T.*
DS889.E57   320.9/52/04   70-168683   ISBN:0842400575

Japan between East and West   **III. 3866**
[by] Hugh Borton [and others] Foreword by Ernest A. Gross. [1st ed.] New York, Published for the Council on Foreign Relations by Harper, 1957. xxii, 327 p. tables. 22 cm. *1. Japan — Foreign relations — 1945- 2. Japan — Relations (general) with the Occident. I. Borton, Hugh. II. Council on Foreign Relations.*
DS889.J32   327.52   57-7977

Kawai, Kazuo, 1904-   **III. 3867**
Japan's American interlude. [Chicago] University of Chicago Press [1960] 257 p. 22 cm. *1. Japan — History — Allied occupation, 1945-1952. I. T.*
DS889.K38   952.04   59-14111

Martin, Edwin M.   **III. 3868**
The Allied occupation of Japan [by] Edwin M. Martin. Westport, Conn., Greenwood Press [1972, c1948] xiv, 155 p. 22 cm. *1. Japan — History — Allied occupation, 1945-1952. I. T.*
DS889.M29 1972   952.04   76-169848   ISBN:0837162483

Maruyama, Masao, 1914-   **III. 3869**
Thought and behavior in modern Japanese politics. Expanded ed. Edited by Ivan Morris. London, New York, Oxford University Press [1969] xvii, 407 p. 21 cm. (A Galaxy book, 291) *1. Nationalism — Japan. 2. National characteristics, Japanese. I. Morris, Ivan, 1., ed. II. T.*
DS889.M34 1969   320.9/52   74-90162

Maxon, Yale Candee, 1906-   **III. 3870**
Control of Japanese foreign policy; a study of civil-military rivalry, 1930-1945. Berkeley, University of California Press, 1957. vi, 286 p. 24 cm. (University of California publications in political science, v.5) *1. Japan — Foreign relations — 1912-1945. 2. Japan — Politics and government — 1912-1945. 3. Militarism — Japan. I. T. (S:California. University. University of California publications in political science, v.5)*
DS889.M38 (JA37.C3 vol. 5)   327.52   A57-9540

Morley, James William, 1921-   **III. 3871**
Japan and Korea: America's allies in the Pacific [by James W. Morley. New York, Walker [1965] 152 p. 22 cm. *1. Japan — Politics and government — 1945- 2. Korea — Politics and government — 1948- 3. Japan — Foreign relations — Korea. 4. Korea — Foreign relations — Japan. 5. U.S. — Foreign relations. I. T.*
DS889.M5873   320.95   64-23055

Morris, Ivan I.   **III. 3872**
Nationalism and the right wing in Japan; a study of postwar trends. With an introd. by Maruyama Masao. Issued under the auspices of the Royal Institute of International Affairs. London, New York, Oxford University Press, 1960. 476 p. illus. 23 cm. *1. Japan — Politics and government — 1945- I. T.*
DS889.M589   952.04   60-2705

Olson, Lawrence Alexander, 1918-   **III. 3873**
Dimensions of Japan; a collection of reports written for the American Universities Field Staff. New York, American Universities Field Staff [1963] x, 403 p. 24 cm. *1. Japan — Politics and government — 1945- 2. Japan — Economic conditions — 1945- 3. Japan — Foreign relations — 1945- I. American Universities Field Staff. II. T.*
DS889.O47   915.2   63-14762

Ward, Robert Edward, ed.   **III. 3874**
Five studies in Japanese politics. Ann Arbor, University of Michigan Press, 1957. 121 p. maps, diagr., tables. 28 cm. (University of Michigan. Center for Japanese Studies. Occasional papers, no. 7) *1. Japan — Politics and government — 1945- 2. Police — Japan. 3. Sakhalin. (S:Michigan. University. Center for Japanese studies. Occasional papers, no. 7)*
DS889.W338x (DS801.M5 no. 7)   354.52   57-63486

Wildes, Harry Emerson, 1890-   **III. 3875**
Typhoon in Tokyo; the occupation and its aftermath. New York, Macmillan, 1954. 356 p. 22 cm. *1. Japan — History — Allied occupation, 1945-1952. I. T.*
DS889.W5   940.5352 (952.033)   54-10175

Yoshida, Shigeru, 1878-   **III. 3876**
The Yoshida memoirs; the story of Japan in crisis. Translated by Kenichi Yoshida. [1st American ed.] Boston, Houghton Mifflin, 1962 [c1961] 305 p. 23 cm. *1. Japan — History — Allied occupation, 1945-1952.*
DS889.Y583 1962   952.04   61-10350

Young, Arthur Morgan, 1874-   **III. 3877**
Imperial Japan, 1926-1938, by A. Morgan Young. New York, W. Morrow, 1938. 328 p. 22 cm. *1. Japan — History. 2. Japan — Politics and government. 3. Japan — Foreign relations. 4. Japanese in Manchuria. 5. Manchuria — History. I. T.*
DS889.Y6   925.033   38-27898

DS890   BIOGRAPHY. MEMOIRS

Kurzman, Dan.   **III. 3878**
Kishi and Japan; the search for the sun. Foreword by James A. Michener. New York, I. Obolensky [1960] 394 p. 25 cm. *1. Kishi, Nobusuke, 1896- 2. Japan — Politics and government — 1945-*
DS890.K5K8   923.252   60-9041

Shigemitsu, Mamoru, 1887-1957.   **III. 3879**
Japan and her destiny; my struggle for peace. Edited by F. S. G. Piggott. Translated by Oswald White. New York, Dutton, 1958. 392 p. port. 24 cm. *1. Japan — History — 1912-1945. 2. Japan — Foreign relations — 1912-1945. I. T.*
DS890.S513A23   952.033   57-5005

Butow, Robert Joseph Charles, 1924-   **III. 3880**
Tojo and the coming of the war [by] Robert J. C. Butow. Stanford, Calif., Stanford University Press [1969, c1961] 584 p. illus., ports. 25 cm. *1. Tōjō, Hideki, 1884-1948. 2. World War, 1939-1945 — Japan. I. T.*
DS890.T57B8 1969   952.03/0924 (B)   73-93492

DS895 – 897   LOCAL HISTORY

Craig, Albert M.   **III. 3881**
Chōshū in the Meiji restoration. Cambridge, Harvard University Press, 1961. 385, xxxix p. chart, tables. 21 cm. (Harvard historical monographs, 47) *1. Chōshū, Japan — History. 2. Japan — History — Restoration, 1853-1870. I. T. (S)*
DS895.C5C7   952.025   61-8839

Hsieh, Chiao-min, 1918-   **III. 3882**
Taiwan—ilha formosa; a geography in perspective. Washington, Butterworths, 1964. viii, 372 p. illus., maps. 26 cm. *1. Formosa — Description and travel. 2. Formosa — History. I. T.*
DS895.F7H68   915.1249   64-22305

Kerr, George H., 1911-   **III. 3883**
Formosa betrayed [by] George H. Kerr. Boston, Houghton Mifflin, 1965. xxii, 514 p. maps. 22 cm. *1. Formosa — Politics and government. 2. Formosa — Native races. 3. Chinese in Formosa. I. T.*
DS895.F75K43   951.05   65-20221

Mendel, Douglas Heusted, 1921-   **III. 3884**
The politics of Formosan nationalism [by] Douglas Mendel. Berkeley, University of California Press, 1970. 315 p. map. 25 cm. *1. Taiwan — Politics and government. I. T.*
DS895.F75M4   320.9/512/49   78-94982   ISBN:0520015576

Glacken, Clarence J.   **III. 3885**
The Great Loochoo; a study of Okinawan village life. Berkeley, University of California Press, 1955. xiv, 324 p. illus., maps. 23 cm. Based on the author's Studies in Okinawan village life. *1. Ethnology — Okinawa Island. I. T.*
DS895.R9G5   572.95281   55-9880

Norbeck, Edward, 1915-   **III. 3886**
Takashima, a Japanese fishing community. Salt Lake City, University of Utah Press, 1954. 231 p. illus. 24 cm. Issued also as thesis, University of Michigan, in microfilm form, under title: Takashima, a fishing community of Japan. *1. Takashima Island, Japan (Okayama Prefecture: Kojima City)*
DS895.T33N6 1954   309.152   54-3502

Statler, Oliver.   **III. 3887**
Japanese inn. New York, Random House [1961] xii, 365 p. illus. 24 cm. *1. Minaguchiya, Okitsu, Japan. 2. Japan — Social life and customs. I. T.*
DS897.O4S7   915.2   61-6236

DS901 – 925   KOREA

Clare, Kenneth G., 1918-   **III. 3888**
Area handbook for the Republic of Korea. Co-authors: Kenneth G. Clare [and others] Prepared for the American University by Westwood Research, inc. Washington; For sale by the Supt. of Docs., U.S. Govt. Print. Off., 1969. xiv, 492 p. maps. 25 cm. "One of a series of handbooks prepared under the auspices of Foreign Area Studies (FAS) of the American University. Previous ed. issued in 1964 by American University Foreign Areas Studies Division under title Area handbook for Korea. Supersedes DA Pam 550-41, Nov. 1964. *1. Korea. I. Westwood Research, inc. II. American University, Washington, D.C. Foreign Areas Studies Division. Area handbook for Korea. III. American University, Washington, D.C. Foreign Area Studies. IV. T.*
DS902.C59 1969   915.19/03/43   78-604178

Korea: its land, people and culture of all ages.   **III. 3889**
[2d ed.] Seoul, Hakwon-sa [1963] 739 p. illus. (part col.) ports., fold. col. map. 27 cm. *1. Korea.*
DS902.K54 1963   63-50369

McCune, Shannon Boyd-Bailey, 1913-   **III. 3890**
Korea, land of broken calm, by Shannon McCune. Drawings by Kim Foon. Princeton, N.J., Van Nostrand [1966] ix, 221 p. illus., maps. 21 cm. (The Asia library) *1. Korea. I. T.*
DS902.M22 1966   915.19   66-16903

McCune, Shannon Boyd-Bailey, 1913-   **III. 3891**
Korea's heritage; a regional & social geography. [1st ed.] Tokyo, Rutland, Vt., C. E. Tuttle Co. [1956] xiii, 250 p. illus., maps., diagrs., tables. 22 cm. *1. Korea — Description and travel. I. T.*
DS902.M23   915.19   56-6807

Jo, Yung-hwan, 1932- comp.   **III. 3892**
Korea's response to the West. Kalamazoo, Mich., Korea Research and Publications; [distributed by Cellar Book Shop, Detroit, 1971] xi, 254 p. 28 cm. (Series on contemporary Korean problems, 6) *1. Korea — Civilization — Occidental influences — Addresses, essays, lectures. 2. Korea — Relations (general) with foreign countries — Addresses, essays, lectures. I. T. (S)*
DS904.J57   327.519/018/21   73-28403

Kang, Younghill, 1903-   **III. 3893**
The grass roof, by Younghill Kang. New York, London, Scribner, 1931. viii, 367 p. 22 cm. Autobiography of a young Korean. *1. Korea — Social life and customs. I. T.*
DS904.K3   920   31-26699

Osgood, Cornelius, 1905-   **III. 3894**
The Koreans and their culture. New York, Ronald Press Co. [1951] xvi, 387 p. illus., maps. 24 cm. *1. Korea — Civilization. I. T.*
DS904.O8   915.19   51-271

Rutt, Richard.   **III. 3895**
Korean works and days: notes from the diary of a country priest. [1st ed.] Rutland, Vt., C. E. Tuttle Co. [1964] 231 p. illus. 22 cm. Title also in Korean. Based on the author's series of articles about Korean village life, which were published anonymously in 1957 and 1958 by the Korea times. *1. Korea — Social life and customs. I. T.*
DS904.R8   915.19   63-15271

Choy, Bong Youn, 1914-   **III. 3896**
Korea; a history. Foreword by Younghill Kang. Rutland, Vt., C. E. Tuttle Co. [1971] 474 p. maps. 22 cm. *1. Korea — History. I. T.*
DS907.C62   915.19/03   73-147180   ISBN:0804802491

Griffis, William Elliot, 1843-1928.   **III. 3897**
Corea, the hermit nation. 9th ed., rev. and enl. [1st AMS ed.] New York, AMS Press [1971] xxvii, 526 p. illus., maps. 23 cm. Reprint of the 1911 ed. *1. Korea — History. 2. Korea — Social life and customs. I. T.*
DS907.G8 1971   951.9/01   74-158615   ISBN:0404029167

Han, U-gŭn.   **III. 3898**
The history of Korea, by Han Woo-keun. Translated by Lee Kyung-shik. Edited by Grafton K. Mintz. Seoul, Eul-Yoo Pub. Co. [1970] xii, 548 p. illus. (part col.), maps (part col.), ports. 23 cm. Translation of Han'guk t'ongsa (romanized form) *1. Korea — History. I. T.*
DS907.H299813   71-275357

Henthorn, William E.   **III. 3899**
A history of Korea [by] William E. Henthorn. New York, Free Press [1971] xiv, 256 p. illus. 24 cm. *1. Korea — History. I. T.*
DS907.H45 1971   915.19/03   75-143511

Hulbert, Homer Bezaleel, 1863-1949.   **III. 3900**
History of Korea. Edited by Clarence Norwood Weems. New York, Hillary House Publishers, 1962. 2 v. illus. 24 cm. *1. Korea — History. I. Weems, Clarence Norwood, 1907- ed.*
DS907.H8 1962   951.9   62-9992

Henderson, Gregory.   **III. 3901**
Korea, the politics of the vortex. Cambridge, Harvard University Press, 1968. xvi, 479 p. illus., col. maps (on lining papers), ports. 25 cm. "Written under the auspices of the Center for International Affairs, Harvard University." *1. Korea — Politics and government. I. Harvard University. Center for International Affairs. II. T.*
DS910.H4   320.9/519   68-25611

McCune, George McAfee, 1908-1948, ed.   **III. 3902**
Korean-American relations; documents pertaining to the Far Eastern diplomacy of the United States. Edited, with an introd., by George M. McCune and John A. Harrison. Berkeley, University of California Press, 1951-   v. 24 cm. Vol. 2 edited, with an introd. by Spencer J. Palmer. *1. Korea — Foreign relations — U.S. 2. U.S. — Foreign relations — Korea. I. Harrison, John Arnold, joint ed. II. Palmer, Spencer J., ed. III. T.*
DS910.M3   327.7309519   51-1111

Nelson, Melvin, Frederick, 1907-   **III. 3903**
Korea and the old orders in eastern Asia, by M. Frederick Nelson. New York, Russell & Russell [1967] xvi, 326 p. 22 cm. "This study was originally made and submitted as a thesis in partial fulfillment of requirements for the degree of doctor of philosophy at Duke University." *1. Korea — Foreign relations. 2. East (Far East) I. T.*
DS910.N4 1967   327.519   66-27132

DS915 – 922   19th – 20th Centuries

Conroy, Francis Hilary, 1919-   **III. 3904**
The Japanese seizure of Korea, 1868-1910; a study of realism and idealism in international relations. Philadelphia, University of Pennsylvania Press [1960] 544 p. illus., ports., map (on lining papers) 22 cm. *1. Korea — History — 1868-1910. I. T.*
DS915.C6 1960   951.902   60-6936

Lee, Chong-sik.   **III. 3905**
The politics of Korean nationalism. Berkeley, University of California Press, 1963. xiv, 342 p. 24 cm. Based on the author's doctoral dissertation, Korean nationalist movement, 1905-1945, submitted to the University of California, Berkeley, in 1961. *1. Nationalism — Korea. I. T.*
DS916.L4   951.9   63-19029

McCune, George McAfee, 1908-1948.   **III. 3906**
Korea today, by George M. McCune with the collaboration of Arthur L. Grey, Jr. Cambridge, Harvard University Press, 1950. xxi, 372 p. map (on lining papers) 21 cm. "Issued under the auspices of the International Secretariat, Institute of Pacific Relations." A revision and expansion of the author's Korea's postwar political problems, submitted as a document for the Tenth Conference of the Institute of Pacific Relations in 1947. *1. Korea — Politics and government. I. Institute of Pacific Relations. II. T.*
DS916.M13 1950   951.9   50-8875

Allen, Richard C.   **III. 3907**
Korea's Syngman Rhee, an unauthorized portrait. [1st ed.] Tokyo, Rutland, Vt., C. E. Tuttle Co. [1960] 259 p. illus. 23 cm. *1. Rhee, Syngman, 1875- I. T.*
DS916.5.R5A65   923.1519   60-15606

Chung, Kyung Cho.   **III. 3908**
New Korea; new land of the morning calm [by] Kyung Cho Chung. New York, Macmillan [1962] 274 p. illus. 22 cm. *1. Korea — Politics and government — 1948- I. T.*
DS917.C573   951.904   62-15611

Goodrich, Leland Matthew, 1899-   **III. 3909**
Korea; a study of U.S. policy in the United Nations. [1st ed.] New York, Council on Foreign Relations, 1956. 235 p. illus. 23 cm. *1. United Nations — Korea. 2. Korean War, 1950-1953. 3. Korea — History — 1945-*
DS917.G6   951.9   56-9751

Oh, John Kie-chiang, 1930-   **III. 3910**
Korea; democracy on trial. Ithaca, N.Y., Cornell University Press [1968] xiv, 240 p. map. 23 cm. *1. Korea — Politics and government — 1948- I. T.*
DS917.O28   320.9/519/5   68-26693

Reeve, W. D.   **III. 3911**
The Republic of Korea: a political and economic study. London, New York, Oxford University Press, 1963. ix, 197 p. 22 cm. "Law concerning extraordinary measures for national reconstruction (promulgated on 6 June 1961)": p. [179]-185. "Law no. 643, Anti-communist law (promulgated on 3 July 1961)": p. [186]-189. *1. Korea — History — 1945- I. Korea (Republic) Laws, statutes, etc. II. T.*
DS917.R37 1963   951.904   63-25579

United States. Dept. of State. Office of Public Affairs.   **III. 3912**
Korea, 1945 to 1948; a report on political developments and economic resources with selected documents. New York, Greenwood Press [1969] iv, 124 p. maps. 27 cm. Reprint of the 1948 ed. *1. Korea — Politics and government — 1945-1948. 2. Korea — Economic conditions — 1945. I. T.*
DS917.U54 1969   309.1/519   68-55125   ISBN:0837117313

DS918 – 921   KOREAN WAR, 1950 – 1953

Berger, Carl, Jan. 28, 1925-   **III. 3913**
The Korea knot, a military-political history. Rev. ed. Philadelphia, University of Pennsylvania Press [1965, c1964] 255 p. map. 22 cm. *1. Korean War, 1950-1953. I. T.*
DS918.B4 1965   951.9042   64-24503

Collins, Joseph Lawton, 1896-   **III. 3914**
War in peacetime; the history and lessons of Korea, by J. Lawton Collins. Boston, Houghton Mifflin, 1969. xiii, 416 p. illus., maps, ports. 24 cm. *1. Korean War, 1950-1953. I. T.*
DS918.C62   951.9/042   69-15008

Fehrenbach, T. R.   **III. 3915**
This kind of war; a study in unpreparedness. New York, Macmillan [1963] xii, 688 p. illus., ports., maps. 25 cm. *1. Korean War, 1950-1953. I. T.*
DS918.F37   951.9042   63-9972

Kahn, Ely Jacques, 1916-   **III. 3916**
The peculiar war; impressions of a reporter in Korea. New York, Random House [1952] 211 p. 21 cm. *1. Korean — War, 1950-1953. I. T.*
DS918.K3   951.9   52-5554

Leckie, Robert.   **III. 3917**
Conflict; the history of the Korean War, 1950-53. New York, Putnam [1962] 448 p. illus. 22 cm. *1. Korean War, 1950-1953. I. T.*
DS918.L36   951.9042   62-10975

Ridgway, Matthew Bunker, 1895-   **III. 3918**
The Korean war: How we met the challenge. How all-out Asian war was

averted. Why MacArthur was dismissed. Why today's war objectives must be limited. [By] Matthew B. Ridgway. [1st ed.] Garden City, N.Y., Doubleday, 1967. xvii, 291 p. illus., maps, plans, ports. 24 cm. Bibliography: p. 275-279. *1. Korean War, 1950-1953. I. T.*
DS918.R49   951.9/042   67-11172

Stone, Isidor F., 1907-   **III. 3919**
The hidden history of the Korean War [by] I. F. Stone. New York, Monthly Review Press [1969, c1952] xvi, 368 p. map. 21 cm. Includes new appendix (p. 349-352) *1. Korean War, 1950-1953. 2. United States — Foreign relations — 1945-1953. I. T.*
DS918.S8 1969   951.9/042   79-81788

U.S. Congress. Senate. Committee on Armed Services.   **III. 3920**
Inquiry into the military situation on the Far East and the facts surrounding the relief of General of the Army Douglas MacArthur from his assignment in that area; report of proceedings. Hearing held before Committee on Armed Services and Committee on Foreign Relations. Washington, Ward & Paul, official reporters [1951] 43 v. 29 cm. Cover title. At head of title: The United States Senate. Richard B. Russell, chairman. Hearings held May 3-June 27, 1951. *1. MacArthur, Douglas, 1880- 2. Korean War, 1950- I. U.S. Congress. Senate. Committee on Foreign Relations. II. Ward and Paul, Washington, D.C. III. T.*
DS918.U5 1951d   951.9   51-6188

U.S. Dept. of the Army. Office of Military History.   **III. 3921**
United States Army in the Korean War. Washington, 1961- v. illus., maps (part fold., part col.) 26 cm. *1. Korean War, 1950-1953.*
DS918.U5246   951.9042   61-61568

Marshall, Samuel Lyman Atwood, 1900-   **III. 3922**
The river and the gauntlet; defeat of the Eighth Army by the Chinese Communist forces, November, 1950, in the Battle of the Chongchon River, Korea, by S. L. A. Marshall. Westport, Conn., Greenwood Press [1970, c1953] x, 385 p. illus., maps. 23 cm. *1. Ch'ŏngch'ŏn-gang, Battle of, 1950. 2. United States. Army. Eighth Army. 3. Korean War, 1950-1953 — Regimental histories — United States — Eighth Army. I. T.*
DS918.2.C4M3 1970   951.9/042   74-100239   ISBN:0837130115

United States. Marine Corps.   **III. 3923**
U.S. Marine operations in Korea, 1950-1953. Washington, Historical Branch, G-3, Headquarters, U.S. Marine Corps, 1954- . Grosse Pointe, Mich., Scholarly Press [1969?-   v. illus., maps, ports. 23 cm. *1. Korean War, 1950-1953 — Regimental histories — United States — Marine Corps. I. Montross, Lynn, 1895-1961. II. Canzona, Nicholas A. III. T.*
DS919.A517   951.9   77-8614

Paige, Glenn D.   **III. 3924**
The Korean decision, June 24-30, 1950 [by] Glenn D. Paige. New York, Free Press [1968] xxv, 394 p. 22 cm. *1. Korean War, 1950-1953 — United States. I. T.*
DS919.P33   951.9/042   68-10794

Spanier, John W.   **III. 3925**
The Truman-MacArthur controversy and the Korean War. Cambridge, Mass., Belknap Press, 1959. xii, 311 p. illus. 24 cm. *1. Korean War, 1950-1953. 2. Civil supremacy over the military — U.S. I. T.*
DS919.S62   951.9042   59-12976

Whiting, Allen Suess, 1926-   **III. 3926**
China crosses the Yalu; the decision to enter the Korean War [by] Allen S. Whiting. Stanford, Calif., Stanford University Press [1968, c1960] x, 219 p. maps. 24 cm. *1. Korean War, 1950-1953 — China. I. T.*
DS919.5.W5 1968   951.9/042   68-13744

Field, James A.   **III. 3927**
History of United States Naval operations: Korea. With a foreword by Ernest McNeill Eller. Washington [U.S. Govt. Print. Off.] 1962. xv, 499 p. illus., maps. 26 cm. *1. Korean War, 1950-1953 — Naval operations.*
DS920.A2F5   951.9042   62-60083

Kinkead, Eugene, 1906-   **III. 3928**
In every war but one. [1st ed.] New York, Norton [1959] 219 p. 22 cm. Expanded from an article published in the New Yorker magazine, Oct. 26, 1957, under title: The study of something new in history. *1. Korean War, 1950-1953 — Prisoners and prisons. 2. Turncoats. I. T.*
DS921.K46   951.9042   58-11107

Geneva. Conference, 1954.   **III. 3929**
The 1954 Geneva Conference; Indo-China and Korea. With a new introd. written especially for the Greenwood reprint by Kenneth T. Young. New York, Greenwood Press [1968] vi, 168, 42 p. 26 cm. "Combining Documents relating to the discussion of Korea and Indo-China at the Geneva Conference, April 27-June 15, 1954, and Further documents relating to the discussion of Indo-China at the Geneva Conference, June 16-July 21, 1954." Each reprint includes facsim. of the original t.p. *1. Korean War, 1950-1953 — Peace. 2. Indochina, French — History — 1945- I. Geneva. Conference, 1954. Documents relating to the discussion of Korea and Indo-China at the Geneva Conference. II. Geneva. Conference, 1954. Further documents relating to the discussion of Indo-China at the Geneva Conference. III. T.*
DS921.7.G4 1954ab   951.9/042   68-57791

Vatcher, William Henry.   **III. 3930**
Panmunjom; the story of the Korean military armistice negotiations. New York, Praeger [1958] ix, 322 p. illus., map, ports. 22 cm. "Text of Armistice agreement": p. 281-312. *1. Korean War, 1950-1953 — Armistices.*
DS921.7.V3   951.9   58-7887

DS922   1960 –

Chung, Kyung Cho.   **III. 3931**
Korea; the third Republic. New York, Macmillan [1971] xii, 269 p. illus., map, port. 21 cm. "The Constitution of the Republic of Korea": p. 231-256. *1. Korea — Politics and government — 1960- I. Korea (Republic). Constitution. English. 1971. II. T.*
DS922.C69   320.9/519/04   74-165110

DS930 – 935 KOREA (DEMOCRATIC PEOPLE'S REPUBLIC)

Shinn, Rinn-Sup.   **III. 3932**
Area handbook for North Korea. Co-authors: Rinn-Sup Shinn [and others] Washington; For sale by the Supt. of Docs., U.S. Govt. Print. Off., 1969. xvi, 481 p. maps. 24 cm. "DA pam no. 550-81." "This volume is one of a series of handbooks prepared by Foreign Area Studies (FAS) of the American University." *1. Korea (Democratic People's Republic) I. American University, Washington, D.C. Foreign Area Studies. II. T.*
DS932.S5   915.19/03/43   75-605343

Kim, Il-sŏng, 1912-   **III. 3933**
Revolution and socialist construction in Korea; selected writings of Kim Il Sung. [1st ed.] New York, International Publishers [1971] 225 p. 21 cm. Selections from the author's writings, speeches, and reports, 1955 to 1970. *I. T.*
DS934.K5A254   320.9/519/3043   75-152910   ISBN:0717803244

Scalapino, Robert A., ed.   **III. 3934**
North Korea today. New York, Praeger [1963] 141 p. diagr. 22 cm. (Praeger publications in Russian history and world communism, no. 135) First published in Great Britain in 1963 as a special issue of the China quarterly. *1. Korea (Democratic People's Republic) I. T.*
DS935.S25   951.904   63-20152

Koh, Byung Chul.   **III. 3935**
The foreign policy of North Korea. New York, F. A. Praeger [1969] xxi, 237 p. 24 cm. (Praeger special studies in international politics and public affairs) *1. Korea (Democratic People's Republic) — Foreign relations. I. T.*
DS935.5.K6   327.519/3   68-55009

DT Africa

DT1 – 6 GENERAL WORKS

Africa. 1968-   **III. 3936**
[Tunis?] v. illus., maps. 29 cm. "A reference volume on the African Continent prepared by Jeune afrique and published as a special annual issue." *1. Africa — Yearbooks. I. Jeune afrique (Tunis)*
DT1.A14   915/.005   68-6810

Aspects of West African Islam.   **III. 3937**
Edited by Daniel F. McCall [and] Norman R. Bennett. Boston, African Studies Center, Boston University, 1971. xiv, 234 p. illus. 23 cm. (Boston University papers on Africa, v.5) *1. Africa, West — History — Addresses, essays, lectures. 2. Islam — Africa, West — Addresses, essays, lectures. I. McCall, Daniel F., ed. II. Bennett, Norman Robert, 1932- ed. (S:Boston University. African Studies Center. Papers on Africa, v.5.)*
DT1.B6 vol. 5   916/.03/08s (916.6/03)   72-176492

Hailey, William Malcolm Hailey, baron, 1872-   **III. 3938**
An African survey; a study of problems arising in Africa south of the Sahara, by Lord Hailey. Rev. 1956. London, New York, Oxford University Press, 1957. xxvi, 1676 p. maps (part fold., 1 col.) tables. 25 cm. "Issued under the auspices of the Royal Institute of International Affairs." "Index ... compiled by Miss D. E. Marshall." *1. Africa, Sub-Saharan. 2. Colonies — Administration. I. T.*
DT3.H3 1957   309.16   57-14073

Hallett, Robin.   **III. 3939**
The penetration of Africa; European exploration in North and West Africa to 1815. New York, Praeger [1965] xxii, 458 p. illus., maps, ports. 23 cm. *1. Africa, North — Discovery and exploration. 2. Africa, West — Discovery and exploration. I. T.*
DT3.H33   916   65-25279

Perham, Margery Freda, 1895- ed.   **III. 3940**
African discovery; an anthology of exploration [by] Margary Perham and J. Simmons. [Evanston] Northwestern University Press [1963] 280 p. illus., ports., maps. 23 cm. "From the works of the British explorers of Africa, covering the period from 1769 to 1873." *1. Africa — Discovery and exploration. I. Simmons, Jack, 1915- joint ed. II. T.*
DT3.P4 1963   960   63-13480

Davidson, Basil, 1914-   **III. 3941**
The African genius; an introduction to African cultural and social history. [1st American ed.] Boston, Little, Brown [1970, c1969] 367 p. illus., map 22 cm. "An Atlantic monthly press book." Published in 1969 under title: The Africans: an entry to cultural history. *1. Africa, Sub-Saharan — Civilization. 2. Africa, Sub-Saharan — Social conditions. I. T.*
DT4.D38 1970   916.7   70-80751

Fitzgerald, Walter, 1898-1949.   **III. 3942**
Africa: a social, economic, and political geography of its major regions. 10th ed. revised by W. C. Brice. London, Methuen, 1967. xii, 503 p. maps. 23 cm. On label on t.p.: Distributed in the United States by Barnes & Noble. *1. Africa. I. Brice, William Charles.*
DT5.F5 1967   916   67-99393

Legum, Colin, ed.   **III. 3943**
Africa; a handbook to the continent. Rev. and enl. ed. New York, Praeger [1966] xii, 558 p. illus., maps. 24 cm. *1. Africa. I. T.*
DT5.L35 1966a   916   66-12478

DT7 – 16 DESCRIPTION. ETHNOGRAPHY

Oliver, Roland Anthony, ed.   **III. 3944**
Africa in the days of exploration. Edited by Roland Oliver and Caroline Oliver. Englewood Cliffs, N.J., Prentice-Hall [1965] vi, 152 p. map. 21 cm. (The Global history series. A Spectrum book, S-123.) *1. Africa — History — Sources. 2. Africa — Description and travel. I. Oliver, Caroline, joint ed. II. T.*
DT7.O4   916.097496   65-23297

Stamp, Laurence Dudley, Sir, 1898-1966.   **III. 3945**
Africa, a study in tropical development [by] L. Dudley Stamp. 2d ed. New York, Wiley [1964] x, 534 p. illus., maps. 25 cm. *1. Africa — Description and travel — 1951- I. T.*
DT12.S7 1964   916   64-20087

Africa and the islands,   **III. 3946**
by R. J. Harrison Church [and others. 2d ed.] New York, Wiley [1967] xiv, 494 p. illus., maps. 22 cm. (Geographies: an intermediate series) *1. Africa — Description and travel — 1951- 2. Africa — History. I. Church, Ronald James Harrison.*
DT12.2.A55 1967   916   67-24326

Hance, William Adams, 1916-   **III. 3947**
The geography of modern Africa, by William A. Hance. New York, Columbia University Press, 1964. xiv, 653 p. illus., maps, port. 26 cm. *1. Africa — Description and travel — 1951- I. T.*
DT12.2.H28   916   64-14239

The African experience.   **III. 3948**
Edited by John N. Paden and Edward W. Soja. Evanston, Northwestern University Press, 1970- v. maps (part col.) 26 cm. Prepared at Northwestern University with the support of the U.S. Office of Education. *1. Africa — Civilization — Addresses, essays, lectures. 2. Africa — Civilization — Study and teaching. I. Paden, John N., ed. II. Soja, Edward W., ed. III. Northwestern University, Evanston, Ill.*
DT14.A37   916/.03/3   70-98466   ISBN:0810102935

Murdock, George Peter, 1897-   **III. 3949**
Africa: its peoples and their culture history. New York, McGraw-Hill, 1959. xiii, 456 p. illus., maps (1 fold. in pocket) 24 cm. *1. Africa — Civilization.*
DT14.M8   572.96   59-8552

Gibbs, James L., ed.   **III. 3950**
Peoples of Africa. Edited by James L. Gibbs, Jr. New York, Holt, Rinehart and Winston [1965] xiv, 594 p. illus., maps. 24 cm. *1. Ethnology — Africa, Sub-Saharan. 2. Ethnology — Africa, South. I. T.*
DT15.G53   309.16   65-10276

International African Institute.   **III. 3951**
African worlds; studies in the cosmological ideas and social values of African peoples. London, New York, Oxford University Press, 1954. xvii, 243 p. diagrs., tables. 26 cm. On slip mounted on t.p.: Edited with an introduction by Daryll Forde. *1. Ethnology — Africa. I. Forde, Cyril Daryll, 1902- ed. II. T.*
DT15.I5   572.96   A54-5828

Seligman, Charles Gabriel, 1873-1940.   **III. 3952**
Races of Africa [by] C. G. Seligman. 4th ed. London, New York, Oxford University Press, 1966. 170 p. maps. 20 cm. (Oxford paperbacks university series, opus 9) *1. Ethnology — Africa. I. T.*
DT15.S45 1966   916.033   66-8534

DT17 – 38 HISTORY

Segal, Ronald, 1932-   **III. 3953**
African profiles. Baltimore, Penguin Books [1962] 351 p. illus. 19 cm. (Penguin African library, AP1) *1. Africa — Biography. 2. Africa — Politics. I. T.*
DT18.S38   920.06   62-51585

Segal, Ronald, 1932-   **III. 3954**
Political Africa; a who's who of personalities and parties. In collaboration with Catherine Hoskyns [and] Rosalynde Ainslie. New York, Praeger [1961] ix, 475 p. map. 25 cm. (Books that matter) *1. Africa — Biography. 2. Political parties — Africa. I. A who's who of personalities and parties. II. T.*
DT18.S4   920.06   61-16754

Lystad, Robert A., ed.   **III. 3955**
The African world; a survey of social research. Edited for the African Studies Association by Robert A. Lystad. New York, Praeger [1965] xvi, 575 p. 26 cm. *1. African studies. 2. Africa — Bibliography. I. African Studies Association. II. T.*
DT19.8.L9   916   65-10753

Bohannan, Paul.   **III. 3956**
Africa and Africans [by] Paul Bohannan & Philip Curtin. Rev. ed. Garden City, N.Y., Published for the American Museum of Natural History [by] Natural History Press [1971] vi, 391 p. maps. 22 cm. *1. Africa — History. 2. Africa — Civilization. I. Curtin, Philip D., joint author. II. T.*
DT20.B6 1971   916/.03   79-139006

Davidson, Basil, 1914-   **III. 3957**
Africa in history; themes and outlines. [1st American ed. New York] Macmillan [1969, c1968] 318 p. illus., maps. 22 cm. Published in 1966 under title: Africa: history of a continent. *1. Africa — History. I. T.*
DT20.D28 1969   960   69-16910

Davidson, Basil, 1914- ed.   **III. 3958**
The African past; chronicles from antiquity to modern times. [1st ed.] Boston, Little, Brown [1964] xix, 392 p. illus. 22 cm. *1. Africa — History. I. T.*
DT20.D3   916   64-13182

July, Robert William.   **III. 3959**
A history of the African people [by] Robert W. July. New York, Scribner [1970] xxii, 650 p. illus., maps, ports. 25 cm. *1. Africa — History. I. T.*
DT20.J8   960   74-93897

Oliver, Roland Anthony.   **III. 3960**
Africa since 1800, by Roland Oliver and Anthony Atmore. London, Cambridge U.P., 1967. ix, 304 p. maps. 22 cm. *1. Africa — History. I. Atmore, Anthony, joint author. II. T.*
DT20.O38   960   67-11527

Oliver, Roland Anthony.   **III. 3961**
A short history of Africa [by] Roland Oliver and J. D. Fage. [New York] New York University Press, 1963. 279 p. illus. 25 cm. *1. Africa — History. I. Fage, J. D., joint author.*
DT20.O4 1963   960   63-11304

Wauthier, Claude, 1923-   **III. 3962**
The literature and thought of modern Africa; a survey [by] Claude Wauthier. Translated by Shirley Kay. New York, F. A. Praeger [1967, c1966] 323 p. 23 cm. (Praeger library of African affairs) Revised version of work first published under title: L'Afrique des africains, inventaire de la négritude. *1. Nationalism — Africa. 2. Africa in literature. I. T.*
DT21.W313 1967   809.896   67-11467

Oliver, Roland Anthony.   **III. 3963**
The dawn of African history, edited by Roland Oliver. 2nd ed. London, Oxford U.P., 1968. vi, 106 p. 18 plates, 10 illus., 13 maps. 21 cm. *1. Africa — History — To 1884. I. T.*
DT25.O4 1968   960/.2   68-109382

Shinnie, Margaret.   **III. 3964**
Ancient African kingdoms. New York, St Martin's Press, 1965. 126 p. illus., maps. 23 cm. *1. Africa — History. 2. Africa — Civilization. I. T.*
DT25.S5   916.032   65-18634

Anene, Joseph C., ed.   **III. 3965**
Africa in the nineteenth and twentieth centuries: a handbook for teachers and students; edited by Joseph C. Anene and Godfrey N. Brown; with a foreword by K. O. Dike. Ibadan, Ibadan U.P.; London, Nelson, 1966. xviii, 555 p. illus., 15 plates (incl. 7 col.) maps, plans, diagrs. 23 cm. Col. maps on endpapers. *1. Africa — History. I. Brown, Godfrey N., joint ed. II. T.*
DT28.A8 1966   960   66-71921

Collins, Robert O., comp.   **III. 3966**
Problems in the history of colonial Africa, 1860-1960. Edited by Robert O. Collins. Englewood Cliffs, N.J., Prentice-Hall [1970] xiii, 389 p. map. 23 cm. *1. Africa — History — 1884-1960 — Addresses, essays, lectures. I. T.*
DT29.C57   960/.2   70-113845   ISBN:137166052

DT30   1945 –

Abraham, Willie E.   **III. 3967**
The mind of Africa. [Chicago] University of Chicago Press [1962] 206 p. 23 cm. (The Nature of human society) *1. Africa — Civilization. 2. Africa — Economic conditions. 3. Pan-Africanism. I. T.*
DT30.A33   916   63-9733

American Society of African Culture.   **III. 3968**
Pan-Africanism reconsidered. Berkeley, University of California Press, 1962. xix, 376 p. tables. 25 cm. "Speeches, papers, and comments given at the Third Annual Conference of the American Society of African Culture, which was held in Philadelphia at the University of Pennsylvania from June 22 to June 26, 1960." *1. Pan-Africanism — Addresses, essays, lectures. 2. Africa — Civilization — Addresses, essays, lectures. 3. Negro race. I. T.*
DT30.A53   301.451   62-11491

Carter, Gwendolen Margaret, 1906- ed.   **III. 3969**
African one-party states. Edited by Gwendolen M. Carter. Contributors: Charles F. Gallagher [and others] Ithaca, N.Y., Cornell University Press [1962] xii, 501 p. map. 25 cm. *1. Africa — Politics. I. Gallagher, Charles F. II. T.*
DT30.C32   960   62-19165

Carter, Gwendolen Margaret, 1906- ed.   **III. 3970**
Five African States; responses to diversity: the Congo, Dahomey, the Cameroun Federal Republic, the Rhodesias and Nyasaland [and] South Africa. Contributors: Edouard Bustin [and others] Ithaca, N.Y., Cornell University Press [1963] xiv, 643 p. maps (1 fold.) 24 cm. *1. Congo (Leopoldville) 2. Dahomey. 3. Cameroun. 4. Rhodesia and Nyasaland. 5. Africa, South. I. T.*
DT30.C33   916   63-18867

Carter, Gwendolen Margaret, 1906- ed.   **III. 3971**
National unity and regionalism in eight African states: Nigeria, Niger, the Congo, Gabon, Central African Republic, Chad, Uganda [and] Ethiopia, edited by Gwendolen M. Carter. Contributors: Richard L. Sklar [and others] Ithaca, N.Y., Cornell University Press [1966] xiii, 565 p. maps. 25 cm. *1. Regionalism — Africa. I. T.*
DT30.C335   320.158096   66-12113

Duffy, James, 1923- ed.   **III. 3972**
Africa speaks. Edited by James Duffy and Robert A. Manners. Princeton, N.J., Van Nostrand [1961] 223 p. 23 cm. *1. Nationalism — Africa, Sub-Saharan. 2. Africa, South — Race question. I. Manners, Robert Alan, joint ed. II. T.*
DT30.D8   960.3   61-3312

Emerson, Rupert, 1899- ed.   **III. 3973**
The political awakening of Africa, edited by Rupert Emerson and Martin Kilson. Englewood Cliffs, N.J., Prentice-Hall [1965] x, 175 p. 21 cm. (The Global history series, S-124) A Spectrum book. *1. Africa — Politics — 1960- I. Kilson, Martin, joint ed. II. T.*
DT30.E46   320.96   65-20605

Hatch, John Charles.   **III. 3974**
A history of postwar Africa [by] John Hatch. New York, Praeger [1965] 432 p. maps. 21 cm. *1. Africa — Politics — 1960- I. T.*
DT30.H313   960.3   65-18078

Junod, Violaine I., ed.   **III. 3975**
The handbook of Africa, edited by Violaine I. Junod, assisted by Idrian N. Resnick. [New York] New York University Press, 1963. 472 p. illus. 25 cm. *1. Africa. I. Resnick, Idrian N., joint ed.*
DT30.J82   916   63-11303

Legum, Colin.   **III. 3976**
Pan-Africanism; a short political guide. Rev. ed. New York, F. A. Praeger [1965] 326 p. fold. map. 22 cm. *1. Pan-Africanism.*
DT30.L39 1965   320.1596   65-15641

Lewis, William Hubert, 1928- ed.   **III. 3977**
French-speaking Africa; the search for identity. Edited by William H. Lewis.

III. 3978

New York, Walker [1965] 256 p. map. 24 cm. Papers presented at a colloquim held in Washington, D.C., Aug. 17-21, 1964, sponsored by the U.S. Dept. of State and others. *1. France — Colonies — Africa. 2. Africa — Politics — 1960- 3. States, New. I. U.S. Dept. of State. II. T.*
DT30.L46   309.16   65-15988

McKay, Vernon. III. 3978
Africa in world politics. New York, Harper & Row [c1963] 468 p. 22 cm. *1. Africa — Politics — 1960- 2. World politics — 1955- I. T.*
DT30.M24   327.6   62-18877

Nkrumah, Kwame, Pres. Ghana, 1909- III. 3979
Africa must unite. [New ed.] New York, International Publishers [1970] xvii, 229 p. 21 cm. *1. Pan-Africanism. 2. Africa — History — 1960- 3. Ghana — History. I. T.*
DT30.N45 1970   960   70-140209   ISBN:717802957

Rivkin, Arnold. III. 3980
The African presence in world affairs; national development and its role in foreign policy. [New York] Free Press of Glencoe [1963] xvi, 304 p. 22 cm. "A publication in a series of studies on African economic and political development from the Center for International Studies, Massachusetts Institute of Technology." *1. Africa — Politics — 1960- 2. Africa — Economic conditions — 1918- 3. World politics — 1945- I. Massachusetts Institute of Technology. Center for International Studies. II. T.*
DT30.R52   960.3   63-13542

Wallerstein, Immanuel Maurice, 1930- III. 3981
Africa: the politics of unity; an analysis of a contemporary social movement [by] Immanuel Wallerstein. New York, Random House [1967] xi, 274 p. map. 22 cm. *1. Pan-Africanism. I. T.*
DT30.W34   320.1/59/6   66-22247

DT31 – 38 Political and Diplomatic History (General)

Azikiwe, Nnamdi, 1904- III. 3982
Renascent Africa. New York, Negro Universities Press [1969] 313 p. port. 23 cm. "Originally published in 1937 by the author, Nigeria." *1. Nationalism — Africa. I. T.*
DT31.A95 1969   320.1/58/096   79-94488   ISBN:837123658

Buell, Raymond Leslie, 1896-1946. III. 3983
The native problem in Africa. [Hamden, Conn.] Archon Books, 1965. 2 v. maps. 25 cm. "First edition 1928, second impression 1965." *1. Africa — Politics. 2. Africa — Native races. 3. Africa — Economic conditions — 1918- I. T.*
DT31.B8 1965   301.4519606   65-8096

Collins, Robert O., comp. III. 3984
The partition of Africa: illusion or necessity? Edited by Robert O. Collins. New York, J. Wiley [1969] xi, 239 p. maps. 22 cm. (Major issues in history) *1. Africa — Colonization — Addresses, essays, lectures. I. T.*
DT31.C55   325.3/1/094   75-81334   ISBN:471165794

Gann, Lewis H., 1924- III. 3985
Burden of empire; an appraisal of Western colonialism in Africa south of the Sahara, by L. H. Gann and Peter Duignan. New York, F. A. Praeger [1967] xii, 435 p. maps. 22 cm. (Hoover Institution publications) *1. Africa, Sub-Saharan — Politics. I. Duignan, Peter, joint author. II. T.*
DT31.G345   967   67-26216

Gann, Lewis H., 1924- comp. III. 3986
Colonialism in Africa, 1870-1960: edited by L. H. Gann & Peter Duignan. London, Cambridge U.P., 1969- v. maps. 24 cm. (Hoover Institution publications) *1. Africa — Colonization — Addresses, essays, lectures. 2. Africa — Politics — Addresses, essays, lectures. I. Duignan, Peter, joint comp. II. The history and politics of colonialism 1870-1914. III. T. (S)*
DT31.G35   960   75-77289   ISBN:521073731 (v. 1)

Hodgkin, Thomas Lionel, 1910 III. 3987
Nationalism in colonial Africa. [1st U.S.ed. New York] New York University Press [1957] 216 p. illus. 21 cm. *1. Nationalism — Africa. I. T.*
DT31.H56 1957   323.16   57-8133

Nicol, Davidson. III. 3988
Africa, a subjective view. [London] Longmans [1964] viii, 88 p. 21 cm. *1. Africa — Politics — Addresses, essays, lectures. I. T.*
DT31.N47   66-59313

Perham, Margery Freda, 1895- III. 3989
The colonial reckoning; the end of imperial rule in Africa in the light of British experience. [1st ed.] New York, Knopf, 1962. 203 p. 20 cm. *1. Nationalism — Africa. I. T.*
DT31.P37 1962   960.3   62-11049

Sithole, Ndabaningi, 1920- III. 3990
African nationalism. 2nd ed. London, New York [etc.] Oxford U.P., 1968. vi, 196 p. plate, port. 21 cm. *1. Nationalism — Africa. I. T.*
DT31.S55 1968   320.1/58/096   68-133467

Thiam, Doudou. III. 3991
The foreign policy of African States: ideological bases, present realities, future prospects. Pref. by Roger Decottignies. [Translation with revisions by the author] New York, Praeger [1965] xv, 134 p. 23 cm. *1. Africa — Politics — 1960- 2. Pan-Africanism. I. T.*
DT31.T513   327.6   65-21345

Zartman, I. William. III. 3992
International relations in the new Africa [by] I. William Zartman. Englewood Cliffs, N.J., Prentice-Hall [1966] xi, 175 p. illus., map. 21 cm. (A Spectrum book) *1. Africa — Foreign relations. I. T.*
DT31.Z3   327.096   66-16339

DT32 – 38 RELATIONS WITH PARTICULAR COUNTRIES

Batten, Thomas Reginald. III. 3993
Problems of African development. 2d ed. London, Oxford University Press, 1954. 2 v. 18 cm. *1. Gt. Brit. — Colonies — Africa. 2. Africa — Social conditions. 3. Africa — Economic conditions. 4. Africa — Native races. I. T.*
DT32.Bx   A56-295

Britain and Germany in Africa: imperial rivalry and colonial rule. III. 3994
Edited by Prosser Gifford and Wm. Roger Louis. With the assistance of Alison Smith. New Haven, Yale University Press, 1967. xvii, 825 p. maps. 24 cm. "Essays presented at a conference on imperial rivalry and colonial rule held at Yale University in the spring of 1965." The conference was sponsored by the university's Concilium on International Studies. A related work, France and Britain in Africa: imperial rivalry and colonial rule, was published in 1971, containing papers of a second conference. *1. Great Britain — Colonies — Africa — Congresses. 2. Germany — Colonies — Africa — Congresses. I. Gifford, Prosser, ed. II. Louis, Wm. Roger, ed. III. Smith, Alison. IV. Yale University. Concilium on International Studies.*
DT32.B73   325.6   67-24500

Robinson, Ronald. III. 3995
Africa and the Victorians; the climax of imperialism in the Dark Continent, by Ronald Robinson and John Gallagher, with Alice Denny. New York, St Martins Press, 1961. xi, 491 p. maps (part fold.) 22 cm. *1. Gt. Brit. — Colonies — Africa. 2. British in Africa. 3. Imperialism. I. Gallagher, John, 1919- joint author. II. T.*
DT32.R55   325.342096   61-18110

Lugard, Frederick John Dealtry, baron, 1858-1945. III. 3996
The dual mandate in British tropical Africa [by] Lord Lugard. With a new introd. by Margery Perham. [5th ed. Hamden, Conn.] Archon Books, 1965. xlix, 643 p. 23 cm. *1. Gt. Brit. — Colonies — Africa. 2. Gt. Brit. — Colonies — Administration. 3. Africa — Economic conditions — 1918- 4. Africa, Sub-Saharan — Native races. 5. European War, 1914-1918 — Territorial questions — Africa. I. Mandate in British tropical Africa. II. British tropical Africa. III. T.*
DT32.5.L8 1965   309.16   63-15494

Fanon, Frantz, 1925-1961. III. 3997
The wretched of the earth. Pref. by Jean-Paul Sartre. Translated from the French by Constance Farrington. New York, Grove Press [1965, c1963] 255 p. 21 cm. *1. France — Colonies — Africa. 2. Algeria — History — 1945- 3. Offenses against the person. I. T.*
DT33.F313   301.24   65-14196

France and Britain in Africa: imperial rivalry and colonial rule. III. 3998
Edited by Prosser Gifford and Wm. Roger Louis. New Haven, Yale University Press, 1971. xix, 989 p. maps. 25 cm. Rev. papers of a conference held by the Concilium on International Studies in March 1968. A related work, Britain and Germany in Africa: imperial rivalry and colonial rule, contains the papers of the 1965 conference. *1. France — Colonies — Africa — Congresses. 2. Great Britain — Colonies — Africa — Congresses. 3. Great Britain — Foreign relations — France — Congresses. 4. France — Foreign relations — Great Britain — Congresses. I. Gifford, Prosser, ed. II. Louis, William Roger, ed. III. Yale University. Concilium on International Studies.*
DT33.F7   325.6   70-151574   ISBN:0300012896

DT83   Africa   III. 4021

Suret-Canale, Jean.   **III. 3999**
French colonialism in tropical Africa, 1900-1945. Translated from the French by Till Gottheiner. New York, Pica Press [1971] xvii, 521 p. illus., maps. 23 cm. Translation of Afrique noire: occidentale et centrale, v. 2: L'ère coloniale (1900-1945) *1. France — Colonies — Africa. I. T.*
DT33.S9533   325.3/1   75-95756   ISBN:0876637020

Chilcote, Ronald H.   **III. 4000**
Portuguese Africa [by] Ronald H. Chilcote. Englewood Cliffs, N.J., Prentice-Hall [1967] x, 149 p. maps. 21 cm. (A Spectrum book: The modern nations in historical perspective) *1. Portugal — Colonies — Africa. I. T.*
DT36.C45   325.3/469/096   67-14849

Duffy, James, 1923-   **III. 4001**
Portugal in Africa. [Cambridge] Harvard University Press, 1962. 239 p. maps. 21 cm. *1. Portugal — Colonies — Africa. I. T.*
DT36.D79 1962   325.3469   62-6988

Duffy, James, 1923-   **III. 4002**
Portuguese Africa. Cambridge, Harvard University Press, 1959. 389 p. illus. 25 cm. *1. Portugal — Colonies — Africa. I. T.*
DT36.D8   325.3469096   59-7650

Hammond, Richard James, 1911-   **III. 4003**
Portugal and Africa, 1815-1910; a study in uneconomic imperialism [by] R. J. Hammond. Stanford, Calif., Stanford University Press, 1966. xv, 384 p. illus., maps. 24 cm. (A Publication of the Food Research Institute, Stanford University. Studies in tropical development) *1. Portugal — Colonies — Africa. 2. British in Africa. I. T. (S:Stanford University. Food Research Institute. Studies in tropical development)*
DT36.H3   325.3469096   66-17561

Portuguese Africa; a handbook.   **III. 4004**
Edited by David M. Abshire and Michael A. Samuels. New York, Published in cooperation with the Center for Strategic and International Studies, Georgetown University, by Praeger [1969] xiii, 480 p. illus., maps. 24 cm. (Handbooks to the modern world) *1. Portugal — Colonies — Africa. I. Abshire, David M., ed. II. Samuels, Michael A., ed. III. Georgetown University, Washington, D.C. Center for Strategic and International Studies.*
DT36.P62 1969   916.7   69-15740

Emerson, Rupert, 1899-   **III. 4005**
Africa and United States policy. Englewood Cliffs, N.J., Prentice-Hall [1967] 117 p. map. 23 cm. (America's role in world affairs series) *1. Africa, Sub-Saharan — Foreign relations — U.S. 2. U.S. — Foreign relations — Africa, Sub-Saharan. I. T.*
DT38.E4   327.67/073   67-13354

Larkin, Bruce D., 1936-   **III. 4006**
China and Africa, 1949-1970; the foreign policy of the People's Republic of China [by] Bruce D. Larkin. Berkeley, University of California Press, 1971. 268 p. 24 cm. *1. Africa — Foreign relations — China. 2. China — Foreign relations — 1949- — Africa. I. T.*
DT38.9.C5L38 1971   327.51/06   78-123624   ISBN:0520017617

Brzezinski, Zbigniew K., 1928- ed.   **III. 4007**
Africa and the communist world. Contributors: Alexander Dallin [and others] Stanford, Calif., Published for the Hoover Institution on War, Revolution, and Peace by Stanford University Press, 1963. xii, 272 p. map (on lining papers) 23 cm. (Hoover Institution publications) *1. Communist strategy. 2. Communism — Africa, Sub-Saharan. 3. Africa, Sub-Saharan — Foreign economic relations — Communist countries. 4. Communist countries — Foreign economic relations — Africa, Sub-Saharan. I. T. (S:Stanford University. Hoover Institution on War, Revolution, and Peace. Publications)*
DT38.9.R8B7   327.47067   63-17816

DT43 – 154   EGYPT. SUDAN

Conference on the Modern History of Egypt, University of London, 1965.   **III. 4008**
Political and social change in modern Egypt: historical studies from the Ottoman conquest to the United Arab Republic; edited by P. M. Holt. London, New York [etc.] Oxford U.P., 1968. xx, 400 p. 3 plates, 1 illus., facsims., map. 25 cm. English or French. "The essays printed in this volume represent, in revised form, papers contributed to a Conference on the Modern History of Egypt, held in April 1965 at the School of Oriental and African Studies in the University of London." *1. Egypt — History — 1517-1882 — Congresses. 2. Egypt — History — 1798- — Congresses. I. Holt, Peter Malcolm, ed. II. London. University. School of Oriental and African Studies. III. T.*
DT43.C63 1965a   962   68-121481

Breasted, James Henry, 1865-1935, ed. and tr.   **III. 4009**
Ancient records of Egypt; historical documents from the earliest times to the Persian conquest, collected, edited, and translated with commentary. New York, Russell & Russell, 1962. 5 v. 23 cm. *1. Egypt — History — Sources. I. T.*
DT57.B76x   932   62-13827

Wilson, John Albert, 1899-   **III. 4010**
Signs & wonders upon Pharaoh; a history of American Egyptology [by] John A. Wilson. Chicago, University of Chicago Press [1964] xxv, 243 p. illus. ports. 24 cm. *1. Egyptology. I. T.*
DT60.W65   913.32   64-23535

Baumgartel, Elise J., 1892-   **III. 4011**
The cultures of prehistoric Egypt. London, Published on behalf of the Griffith Institute, Ashmolean Museum, Oxford, by Oxford University Press, 1947-60. 2 v. illus., plates, maps. 31 cm. *1. Egypt — Antiquities. 2. Egypt — Civilization. I. T.*
DT61.B35   913.32   48-13407

Cottrell, Leonard.   **III. 4012**
Life under the Pharaohs. [1st ed.] New York, Holt, Rinehart and Winston [1960] 255 p. illus. 22 cm. *1. Egypt — Social life and customs. I. T.*
DT61.C6 1960   913.32   60-13042

Glanville, Stephen Ranulph Kingdom, 1900-1956, ed.   **III. 4013**
The legacy of Egypt; edited by S. R. K. Glanville. Oxford, Clarendon Press, 1942. xx, 424 p. illus. (incl. plans) 34 pl. (incl. map) on 19 l. 19 cm. *1. Egypt — Civilization. I. T.*
DT61.G552   913.32   A42-4963

Wilson, John Albert, 1899-   **III. 4014**
The burden of Egypt; an interpretation of ancient Egyptian culture. [Chicago] University of Chicago Press [1951] xix, 332 p. illus., ports., map (on lining papers) 25 cm. (An Oriental Institute essay) *1. Egypt — Civilization. I. T. (S:Chicago. University. Oriental Institute. Oriental Institute essay)*
DT61.W56   913.32   51-9735

Fakhry, Ahmed.   **III. 4015**
The pyramids. [Chicago] University of Chicago Press [1961] 260 p. illus., maps, plans. 24 cm. *1. Pyramids.*
DT63.F3   913.32   61-8645

Lane, Edward William, 1801-1876.   **III. 4016**
The manners & customs of the modern Egyptians; by Edward William Lane. [3d ed.] London, Dent; New York, Dutton [1908] xxix, 630 p. illus. 18 cm. (Everyman's library. Travel and topography. [No. 315]) Includes music (melodies unaccompanied) "Editor's preface (edition of 1860)" signed: Edward Stanley Poole. Complete list of Lane's published works: p. ix. *1. Egypt — Social life and customs.*
DT70.L27 1908   W08-104

Crawford, Dorothy J.   **III. 4017**
Kerkeosiris; an Egyptian village in the Ptolemaic period, by Dorothy J. Crawford. Cambridge [Eng.] University Press, 1971. xv, 238 p. illus., map. 26 cm. (Cambridge classical studies) *1. Kerkeosiris, Egypt. I. T. (S)*
DT73.K49C7   913.3/2   70-96083   ISBN:0521076072

DT74 – 107   History

Collins, Robert O.   **III. 4018**
Egypt & the Sudan [by] Robert O. Collins [and] Robert L. Tignor. Englewood Cliffs, N.J., Prentice-Hall [1967] vi, 180 p. map. 21 cm. The Modern nations in historical perspective. *1. Egypt — History. I. Tignor, Robert L., joint author. II. T.*
DT77.C6   962   67-14846

Breasted, James Henry, 1865-1935.   **III. 4019**
A history of Egypt from the earliest times to the Persian conquest, by James Henry Breasted ... with two hundred illustrations and maps. 2d ed., fully rev. New York, C. Scribner's sons, 1909. xxix p., 2 l., 3-634 p. col. front., illus., plates, maps. 24 1/2 cm. *1. Egypt — History, Ancient.*
DT83.B782   09-3526

Gardiner, Alan Henderson, Sir, 1879-1963.   **III. 4020**
Egypt of the Pharaohs, an introduction. Oxford, Clarendon Press, 1961. 461 p. illus. 25 cm. *1. Egypt — History — To 332 B.C.*
DT83.G2   932.01   61-1371

Bell, Harold Idris, Sir, 1879-   **III. 4021**
Egypt, from Alexander the Great to the Arab conquest; a study in the

diffusion and decay of Hellenism. Oxford, Clarendon Press, 1948. vii, 168 p. 19 cm. (Gregynog lectures for 1946) "Delivered ... in the University College of Wales, Aberystwyth, in November 1946." *1. Egypt — History — Greco-Roman period, 332 B.C.-640 A.D. (S)*
DT92.B46   932   49-9355

Lane-Poole, Stanley, 1854-1931.   III. 4022
A history of Egypt in the Middle Ages. New York, Haskell House, 1969. vii, 382 p. illus., map. 23 cm. "First published 1901." *1. Egypt — History — 640-1882. I. T.*
DT95.L35 1969   962/.02   68-25246   ISBN:838302106

Muir, William, Sir, 1819-1905.   III. 4023
The Mameluke; or, Slave dynasty of Egypt, 1260-1517, A.D. By Sir William Muir. London, Smith, Elder, 1896. xxxii, 245 p. front., plates (part double) fold. map. 23 cm. *1. Egypt — History — 640-1882. 2. Mamelukes.*
DT96.M95   01-18811

Berger, Morroe.   III. 4024
Military elite and social change: Egypt since Napoleon. [Princeton, N.J.] Center for [i.e. of] International Studies, Wilson [i.e. Woodrow] Wilson School of Public and International Affairs, Princeton University, 1960. 35 p. 28 cm. (Princeton University. Center of International Studies. Research monograph no. 6) Erratum slip inserted. *1. Egypt. al-Jaysh — History. 2. Egypt — Social conditions. I. T. (S)*
DT100.B38   962   60-2581

Dodwell, Henry Herbert, 1879-   III. 4025
The founder of modern Egypt; a study of Muhammad Ali by Henry Dodwell. Cambridge [Eng.] University Press, 1931. viii, 276 p. 22 cm. *1. Muhammad 'Ali, khedive of Egypt, 1769-1849. 2. Egypt — History — Mohammed Ali, 1805-1849. I. T.*
DT104.D58   962   31-22265

Safran, Nadav.   III. 4026
Egypt in search of political community; an analysis of the intellectual and political evolution of Egypt, 1804-1952. Cambridge, Harvard University Press, 1961. 298 p. 24 cm. (Harvard Middle Eastern studies, 5. Harvard political studies.) *1. Egypt — Politics and government. I. T. (S)*
DT107.S2   962   61-13742

Dekmejian, R. Hrair, 1933-   III. 4027
Egypt under Nasir; a study in political dynamics, by R. Hrair Dekmejian. [1st ed.] Albany, State University of New York Press, 1971. xvi, 368 p. illus., port. 25 cm. *1. Egypt — Politics and government — 1952- 2. Nasser, Gamal Abdel, Pres. United Arab Republic, 1918-1970. I. T.*
DT107.83.D43   962/.05   70-152520   ISBN:0873950801

Haykal, Muḥammad Ḥasanayn.   III. 4028
Nasser - the Cairo documents [by] Mohamed Heikal. London, New English Library, 1972. 328, [16] p. illus., facsims., ports. 25 cm. American ed. published under title: The Cairo documents. *1. Egypt — Foreign relations. 2. Nasser, Gamal Abdel, Pres. United Arab Republic, 1918-1970. I. The Cairo documents. II. T.*
DT107.83.H367 1972   962/.05/0924 (B)   73-152425
ISBN:0450012239

Neguib, Mohammed, 1901-   III. 4029
Egypt's destiny; a personal statement. [1st American ed.] Garden City, N.Y., Doubleday, 1955. 256 p. 22 cm. *1. Egypt — History — 1952- I. T.*
DT107.83.N44 1955a   962   55-5271

Smith, Harvey Henry, 1892-   III. 4030
Area handbook for the United Arab Republic (Egypt) Co-authors: Harvey H. Smith [and others]. Washington, For sale by the Supt. of Docs., U.S. Govt. Print. Off.] 1970. xx, 555 p. maps. 24 cm. "DA pam 550-43." "One of a series of handbooks prepared by Foreign Area Studies (FAS) of the American University." Supersedes 1964 ed. prepared by Foreign Areas Studies Division, American University. *1. Egypt. I. American University, Washington, D.C. Foreign Area Studies. II. American University, Washington, D.C. Foreign Area Studies Division. Area handbook for the United Arab Republic (Egypt) III. T.*
DT107.83.S59 1970   916.2/03/5   71-608841

DT108   Sudan

Fabunmi, L. A.   III. 4031
The Sudan in Anglo-Egyptian relations; a case study in power politics, 1800-1956. [London] Longmans [1960] xx, 466 p. illus., maps. 23 cm. "This book has evolved from work done for the degree of doctor of philosophy ...

University of London." *1. Sudan — History. 2. Egypt — Foreign relations — Gt. Brit. 3. Gt. Brit. — Foreign relations — Egypt. I. T.*
DT108.F3   962.403   61-19917

Gray, Richard, 1929-   III. 4032
A history of the Southern Sudan, 1839-1889. [London] Oxford University Press, 1961. viii, 219 p. maps. 23 cm. *1. Sudan — History.*
DT108.G7 1961   962.403   61-66800

Henderson, Kenneth David Druitt, 1903-   III. 4033
Sudan Republic, by K. D. D. Henderson. New York, F. A. Praeger [1966, c1965] 256 p. maps (part fold.) 23 cm. (Nations of the modern world) *1. Sudan — History — 1820- I. T. (S)*
DT108.H4   309.1624   65-27084

Holt, Peter Malcolm.   III. 4034
A modern history of the Sudan, from the Funj Sultanate to the present day. New York, Grove Press [1961] 241 p. illus. 23 cm. *1. Sudan — History — 1820- I. T.*
DT108.H72   962.4   61-11858

Arkell, Anthony John, 1898-   III. 4035
A history of the Sudan: from the earliest times to 1821. With a foreword by Harold MacMichael. [2d ed., rev. London] University of London, Athlone Press, 1961. 252 p. illus. 21 cm. *1. Sudan — History.*
DT108.1.A7 1961   962.402   62-16

Hill, Richard Leslie.   III. 4036
Egypt in the Sudan, 1820-1881. London, New York, Oxford University Press, 1959. xi, 188 p. fold. map. 23 cm. (Middle Eastern monographs, 2) "Issued under the auspices of the Royal Institute of International Affairs." *1. Sudan — History. I. T. (S)*
DT108.2.H5   962.403   59-861

American University, Washington, D.C. Foreign Areas Studies Division.   III. 4037
Area handbook for the Republic of the Sudan. [Co-authors: John A. Cookson and others] 2d ed. Washington [Dept. of the Army] for sale by the Superintendent of Documents, U.S. Govt. Print. Office, 1964. xi, 473 p. illus., maps (part fold.) 24 cm. At head of title: U.S. Army. "Department of the Army pamphlet no. 550-27." *1. Sudan. I. Cookson, John A. II. U.S. Army. III. T.*
DT108.7.A7 1964   65-60681

DT115 – 154   Local History of Egypt and the Sudan. Nile River

Moorehead, Alan, 1910-   III. 4038
The Blue Nile. [Rev. ed.] New York, Harper & Row [1972] 336 p. illus. 27 cm. *1. Nile Valley — History. 2. Blue Nile River.*
DT115.M6 1972   962   73-186776   ISBN:0060130113

Burton, Richard Francis, Sir, 1821-1890.   III. 4039
The Nile basin [by] Richard F. Burton and Captain Speke's discovery of the source of the Nile, by James MacQueen. New introd. by Robert O. Collins. New York, Da Capo Press, 1967. xxxvii, 195 p. maps. 22 cm. Reprint of the 1864 ed. *1. Speke, John Hanning, 1827-1864. Journal of the discovery of the source of the Nile. 2. Nile River. 3. Africa, Central — Description and travel. I. MacQueen, James, 1778-1870. II. T.*
DT117.B97 1967   916.7/04   65-23403

Moorehead, Alan, 1910-   III. 4040
The White Nile. [Rev. ed.] New York, Harper & Row [1971] 368 p. illus., maps, ports. 26 cm. Part of the illustrative matter is colored. *1. Nile Valley — History. I. T.*
DT117.M6 1971   962.9/3   78-160663   ISBN:0060130490

Barbour, Kenneth Michael.   III. 4041
The Republic of the Sudan: a regional geography. London, University of London Press [1961] 292 p. illus., maps. 26 cm. *1. Sudan — Description and travel.*
DT124.B28   916.24   61-65685

Evans-Pritchard, Edward Evan, 1902-   III. 4042
The Nuer, a description of the modes of livelihood and political institutions of a Nilotic people, by E. E. Evans-Pritchard. Oxford, Clarendon Press, 1940. viii, 271 p. illus., plates, maps, diagrs. 23 cm. "A considerable part of

the facts related ... have been previously recorded, chiefly in Sudan notes and records, and Africa." — Pref. *1. Nuer (African tribe)*
DT132.E8   A40-3181

DT139 – 152   CAIRO

Abū Lughd, Jānit.   **III. 4043**
Cairo: 1001 years of the city victorious [by] Janet L. Abu-Lughod. Princeton, N.J., Princeton University Press, 1971. xiv, 284 p. illus., maps. 29 cm. (Princeton studies on the Near East) *1. Cairo. I. T. (S)*
DT143.A26   946.2/1603   73-112992   ISBN:0691030855

Lane-Poole, Stanley, 1854-1931.   **III. 4044**
The story of Cairo, by Stanley Lane-Poole. London, Dent, 1902. xx, 339 p. front., pl., plans. 18 cm. (The Mediæval town series) *1. Cairo. I. T.*
DT143.L33   02-15622

Wiet, Gaston, 1887-   **III. 4045**
Cairo, city of art and commerce. Translated by Seymour Feiler. [1st ed.] Norman, University of Oklahoma Press [1964] xiii, 170 p. map. 19 cm. (The Centers of civilization series) *1. Cairo — History. 2. Cairo — Social life and customs. I. T. (S)*
DT146.W513   916.216   64-20764

DT160 – 346   NORTH AFRICA

Charles-Picard, Gilbert.   **III. 4046**
The life and death of Carthage; a survey of Punic history and culture from its birth to the final tragedy, by Gilbert Charles Picard and Colette Picard. Translated from the French by Dominique Collon. New York, Tapiinger Pub. Co. [1969, c1968] vi, 362 p. illus., maps. 24 cm. *1. Carthage — History. I. Charles-Picard, Colette, joint author. II. T.*
DT168.C4823 1969   939/.73   69-12303

Warmington, Brian Herbert.   **III. 4047**
The North African provinces from Diocletian to the Vandal conquest, by B. H. Warmington. Westport, Conn., Greenwood Press [1971] vii, 126 p. illus. 23 cm. Reprint of the 1954 ed. *1. Africa, North — History — To 647. I. T.*
DT170.W3 1971   939/.7   78-135615   ISBN:083715202X

Ronart, Stephan.   **III. 4048**
Concise encyclopaedia of Arabic civilization: the Arab West [by] Stephan and Nandy Ronart. New York, Praeger [1966] vii, 410 p. maps. 22 cm. *1. Arabs in North Africa. 2. Arabs in Spain. I. Ronart, Nandy, joint author. II. T.*
DT173.R6   910.03174927   66-13401

Zartman, I. William.   **III. 4049**
Government and politics in northern Africa. New York, Praeger [1963] x, 205 p. maps. 21 cm. *1. Africa, North — Politics. 2. Ethiopia — Politics and government. 3. Somalia — Politics and government. I. T.*
DT176.Z35 1963   961   63-10828

Barbour, Nevill, 1895- ed.   **III. 4050**
A survey of North West Africa (the Maghrib) 2d ed. London, New York, Oxford University Press, 1962. xi, 411 p. maps (1 fold.) chart. 23 cm. *1. Africa, North. I. T.*
DT185.B3 1962   916.1   62-51256

Gallagher, Charles F.   **III. 4051**
The United States and North Africa: Morocco, Algeria, and Tunisia. Cambridge, Harvard University Press, 1963. xii, 275 p. maps (1. col.) 20 cm. (The American foreign policy library) *1. Africa, North — History. I. T. (S)*
DT194.G15   63-20766

Julien, Charles André, 1891-   **III. 4052**
History of North Africa: Tunisia, Algeria, Morocco. From the Arab Conquest to 1830, edited and rev. by R. Le Tourneau. Translated by John Petrie. Edited by C. C. Stewart. New York, Praeger [1970] xvi, 446 p. illus., maps. 23 cm. Translation of v.2 of Histoire de l'Afrique du Nord: De la conquête arabe à 1830. *1. Africa, North — History. I. T.*
DT194.J82213   961   79-104771

Fisher, Godfrey, Sir, 1885-   **III. 4053**
Barbary legend; war, trade, and piracy in North Africa, 1415-1830. Oxford, Clarendon Press, 1957. x, 349 p. front., fold. map. 22 cm. *1. Barbary States — History — 1516-1830. 2. Algeria — History — 1516-1830. 3. Pirates. I. T.*
DT201.F5   961   57-59619

al-Fāsī, 'Allāl, 1910-   **III. 4054**
The independence movements in Arab North Africa [by] Alāl al Fāsī. Translated from the Arabic by Hazem Zaki Nuseibeh. New York, Octagon Books, 1970 [c1954] xi, 414 p. 22 cm. (American Council of Learned Societies. Near Eastern Translation Program. [Publication] no. 8) Translation of al-Ḥarakāt al-istiqlālīyah fī al-Maghrib al-'Arabī (romanized form) *1. Morocco — Politics and government. 2. Nationalism — Africa, North. 3. Africa, North — Politics and government. I. T. (S:American Council of Learned Societies Devoted to Humanistic Studies. Near Eastern Translation Program. [Publication] no. 8)*
DT204.F323 1970   320.1/59/61   70-96201

DT211 – 239   Libya

Stanford Research Institute.   **III. 4055**
Area handbook for Libya. Prepared for the American University. Washington; For sale by the Supt. of Docs., U.S. Govt. Print. Off., 1969. xiii, 307 p. illus., maps, 25 cm. "DA pam no. 550-85." "One of a series of handbooks prepared under the auspices of Foreign Area Studies (FAS) of the American University." *1. Libya. I. American University, Washington, D.C. Foreign Area Studies. II. T.*
DT215.S73   309.1/61/2   77-606555

Wright, John L.   **III. 4056**
Libya, by John Wright. New York, Praeger [1969] 304 p. illus., maps. 23 cm. (Nations of the modern world) *1. Libya — History. I. T. (S)*
DT224.W7 1969b   961.2   79-79075

Khadduri, Majid, 1909-   **III. 4057**
Modern Libya: a study in political development. Baltimore, Johns Hopkins Press, 1963. vii, 404 p. ports., map (on lining papers) 23 cm. *1. Libya — Politics and government. I. T.*
DT236.K5   961.204   62-18509

Villard, Henry Serrano, 1900-   **III. 4058**
Libya, the new Arab kingdom of North Africa. Ithaca, N.Y., Cornell University Press [1956] xvi, 169 p. illus., ports., map. 23 cm. *1. Libya — History.*
DT236.V5   961.2   56-13846

DT241 – 269   Tunisia

Knapp, Wilfrid.   **III. 4059**
Tunisia. New York, Walker [1970] 224 p. illus., maps. 22 cm. (Nations and peoples) *1. Tunisia.*
DT245.K59 1970b   309.1/61/1   68-13998

Reese, Howard C.   **III. 4060**
Area handbook for the Republic of Tunisia. Co-authors: Howard C. Reese [and others]. Prepared for the American University by Systems Research Corp. [Washington; For sale by the Supt. of Docs., U.S. Govt. Print. Off.] 1970. xvi, 415 p. maps. 24 cm. "DA pam 550-89." "One of a series of handbooks prepared under the auspices of Foreign Area Studies." *1. Tunisia. I. Systems Research Corporation. II. American University, Washington, D.C. Foreign Area Studies. III. T.*
DT245.R4   309.1/61/1   70-607904

Bourguiba, Habib, Pres. Tunisia, 1903-   **III. 4061**
La Tunisie et la France; vingt-cinq ans de lutte pour une coopération libre. Paris, Julliard [1954] 462 p. illus. 21 cm. *1. Tunisia — History — French occupation, 1881-1956. I. T.*
DT264.B64   54-43912

Micaud, Charles Antoine, 1910-   **III. 4062**
Tunisia: the politics of modernization, by Charles A. Micaud, with Leon Carl Brown and Clement Henry Moore. New York, F. A. Praeger [1964] xiii, 205 p. map. 22 cm. *1. Tunisia — Politics and government. 2. Tunisia — Social conditions. I. T.*
DT264.M5   961.104   64-13384

Moore, Clement Henry.   **III. 4063**
Tunisia since independence; the dynamics of one-party government. Berkeley, University of California Press, 1965. xiv, 230 p. 24 cm. *1. Tunisia — Politics and government. 2. Bourguiba, Habib, Pres. Tunisia, 1903- I. T.*
DT264.M64   961.104   65-12926

DT271 – 299 Algeria

Nyrop, Richard F. III. 4064
Area handbook for Algeria. Co-authors: Richard F. Nyrop [and others. 2d. revision. Washington. For sale by the Supt. of Docs. U.S. Govt. Print. Off.] 1972. xiv, 401 p. maps. 24 cm. "One of a series of handbooks prepared by Foreign Area Studies (FAS) of the American University." Previous editions by American University, Foreign Areas Studies Division. "DA pam 550-44." 1. Algeria. I. American University, Washington, D.C. Foreign Areas Studies. II. American University, Washington, D.C. Foreign Areas Studies Division. Area handbook for Algeria. III. T.
DT275.N9 1972   916.5/03/5   72-600149

Tillion, Germaine. III. 4065
France and Algeria; complementary enemies. Translated from the French by Richard Howard. [1st American ed.] New York, Knopf, 1961. 183 p. 20 cm. Translation of Les ennemis complémentaires. 1. Algeria — History — 1945-
DT285.T513   965.04   61-14763

Alleg, Henri. III. 4066
The question. Introd. by Jean Paul Sartre. [American ed.] New York, G. Braziller, 1958. 123 p. 20 cm. 1. Algeria — History — 1945- I. T.
DT295.A6   965   58-11898

Behr, Edward, 1926- III. 4067
The Algerian problem. [1st American ed.] New York, W. W. Norton [1962, c1961] 260 p. illus. 22 cm. 1. Algeria — History — 1945- I. T.
DT295.B38 1962   965.04   62-9687

Camus, Albert, 1913-1960. III. 4068
Actuelles, III. Chronique algérienne, 1939-1958. Paris, Gallimard [1958] 212 p. 19 cm. 1. Algeria — Politics and government. I. T.
DT295.C29   A59-1220

Gillespie, Joan. III. 4069
Algeria, rebellion and revolution. New York, Praeger [1961, c1960] 208 p. illus. 23 cm. (Nations of the modern world. Books that matter.) Based partly on the author's thesis, Fletcher School of Law and Diplomacy. 1. Algeria — History — 1945. 2. Nationalism — Algeria.
DT295.G5 1961   965.04   60-14956

Gordon, David C. III. 4070
The passing of French Algeria [by] David C. Gordon. London, New York, Oxford University Press, 1966. 265 p. 23 cm. 1. Algeria — History. 2. Algeria — Relations (general) with France. 3. France — Relations (general) with Algeria. I. T.
DT295.G58 1966   965   66-2149

Tillion, Germaine. III. 4071
Algeria: the realities. Translated from the French by Ronald Matthews. [1st American ed.] New York, Knopf, 1958. 115 p. 20 cm. Translation of L'Algérie en 1957. 1. Algeria — History — 1830-
DT295.T513   965   58-10980

DT301 – 330 Morocco

American University, Washington, D.C. Foreign Areas Studies Division. III. 4072
Area handbook for Morocco. Co-authors: Norman C. Walpole [and others. Washington, For sale by the Supt. of Docs., U.S. Govt. Print. Off., 1970] x, 461 p. maps. 25 cm. "DA Pam 550-49." Reprint of the 1965 (i.e. 1966) ed. with list of published area handbooks added (p. 461) 1. Morocco. I. Walpole, Norman C. II. T.
DT305.A74 1970   309.1/64/05   74-27240

Barbour, Nevill, 1895- III. 4073
Morocco. New York, Walker [1965] 239 p. illus., facsims., maps (part fold.) ports. 22 cm. (New nations and peoples) 1. Morocco.
DT305.B33   916.4   65-19258

Mikesell, Marvin W. III. 4074
Northern Morocco: a cultural geography. Berkeley, University of California Press, 1961. vi, 135 p. illus., plates, maps. 26 cm. (University of California publications in geography, v.14) "A preliminary version of this study was prepared as a doctoral dissertation [University of California]" 1. Morocco — History. 2. Morocco — Description and travel. (S:California. University. University of California publications in geography, v.14)
DT310.2.M5x (G58.C3 vol. 14)   916.42   62-62686

Terrasse, Henri. III. 4075
Histoire du Maroc des origines à l'établissement du Protectorat français. Casablanca, Éditions Atlantides [1950, c1949-50] 2 v. maps (part fold.) 23 cm. "Errata": 3 p. inserted in v.2. 1. Morocco — History.
DT314.T47   964   50-25194

Ashford, Douglas Elliott. III. 4076
Political change in Morocco. Princeton, N.J., Princeton University Press, 1961. xi, 432 p. maps, tables. 25 cm. (Princeton oriental studies; social sciences, 3) 1. Morocco — Politics and government. 2. Political parties — Morocco. I. T. (S:Princeton oriental studies: social science, 3)
DT324.A777   964.04   61-6285

Le Tourneau, Roger. III. 4077
Fez in the age of the Marinides. Translated from the French by Besse Alberta Clement. [1st ed.] Norman, University of Oklahoma Press [1961] 158 p. illus. 20 cm. (The Centers of civilization series, 4) 1. Fez — History. 2. Beni Marin dynasty.
DT329.F4L423   964.31   61-6496

DT331 – 346 Sahara

Gautier, Émile Felix, 1864-1940. III. 4078
Sahara, the great desert, by E. F. Gautier. Authorized translation by Dorothy Ford Mayhew, with a foreword by Douglas Johnson. New York, Columbia University Press, 1935. xvii, 264 p. illus., maps (1 fold.) plates. 25 cm. "Translated from the second French edition of E.-F. Gautier's Le Sahara (Paris, Payot, 1928) and from hitherto unpublished material supplied by the author": p. [iv] 1. Sahara. I. Mayhew, Dorothy Ford, tr.
DT333.G32   916   35-17669

Wellard, James Howard, 1909- III. 4079
The great Sahara [by] James Wellard. [1st ed.] New York, Dutton, 1965 [c1964] 350 p. illus., maps, ports. 22 cm. 1. Sahara — History. I. T.
DT333.W39 1965   966.11   64-19541

Briggs, Lloyd Cabot, 1909- III. 4080
Tribes of the Sahara. Cambridge, Harvard University Press, 1960. xx, 295 p. illus., maps. 24 cm. 1. Ethnology — Sahara. 2. Sahara — Description and travel. I. T.
DT337.B7   572.96611   60-7988

DT351 – 364 CENTRAL AFRICA. SUB-SAHARAN AFRICA

Stanley, Henry Morton, Sir 1841-1904. III. 4081
The exploration diaries of H. M. Stanley, now first published from the original manuscripts. Edited by Richard Stanley and Alan Neame. New York, Vanguard Press [c1961] 208 p. illus., ports., maps. 25 cm. I. T.
DT351.S73 1961a   916.7   62-11208

Vansina, Jan. III. 4082
Kingdoms of the savanna. Madison, University of Wisconsin Press, 1966. ix, 364 p. maps (part fold.) 22 cm. 1. Africa, Central — History. I. T.
DT351.V36   967   65-16367

Balandier, Georges. III. 4083
Ambiguous Africa; cultures in collision. Translated from the French by Helen Weaver. New York, Pantheon Books [1966] ix, 276 p. illus., maps, plans. 22 cm. 1. Africa, Sub-Saharan — Civilization. I. T.
DT352.B313 1966a   916.033   65-10211

Davidson, Basil, 1914- III. 4084
Black mother; the years of the African slave trade. [1st American ed.] Boston, Little, Brown [1961] 311 p. illus. 22 cm. 1. Congo — History. 2.

Guinea (Region) — History. 3. Africa, East — History. 4. Slave-trade — Africa. I. T.
DT352.D33 1961a   967   61-13894

De Blij, Harm J. III. 4085
A geography of Subsaharan Africa [by] Harm J. de Blij. Chicago, Rand McNally [1964] 435 p. illus., maps. 26 cm. (Rand McNally geography series) 1. Africa, Sub-Saharan — Description and travel. I. T.
DT352.D4   916   64-14110

Foreign affairs (New York) III. 4086
Africa; a Foreign affairs reader, edited by Philip W. Quigg. Foreword by Hamilton Fish Armstrong. [1st ed.] New York, Published for the Council on Foreign Relations by Praeger [1964] xii, 346 p. 25 cm. 1. Africa, Sub-Saharan — Politics — Addresses, essays, lectures. 2. Nationalism — Africa, Sub-Saharan. 3. Africa, South — Native races — Addresses, essays, lectures. I. Quigg, Philip W., ed. II. T.
DT352.F6 1964   960.3082   64-12589

Herskovits, Melville Jean, 1895-1963. III. 4087
The human factor in changing Africa. London, Routledge & K. Paul, 1962. 500 p. illus. 22 cm. 1. Africa, Sub-Saharan. I. T.
DT352.H43 1962   63-3194

Jahn, Janheinz. III. 4088
Muntu; an outline of the new African culture. Translated by Marjorie Grene. New York, Grove Press [1961] 267 p. illus. 21 cm. 1. Africa, Sub-Saharan — Civilization. I. T.
DT352.J313   916.7   61-5522

Kimble, George Herbert Tinley, 1908- III. 4089
Tropical Africa. New York, Twentieth Century Fund, 1960. 2 v. illus., port., maps (1 fold. col.) 25 cm. 1. Africa, Sub-Saharan. I. T.
DT352.K48   916.7   60-15160

The New Africans; a guide to the contemporary history of emergent Africa and its leaders. III. 4090
Written by 50 correspondents of Reuters news agency. Edited by Sidney Taylor. [1st American ed.] New York, Putnam [1967] 504 p. illus., maps, ports. 23 cm. 1. Africa, Sub-Saharan. 2. Africa, Sub-Saharan — Biography. I. Taylor, Sidney, ed. II. Reuters ltd.
DT352.N49 1967   967   67-23596

Wiedner, Donald Lawrence, 1930- III. 4091
A history of Africa south of the Sahara. New York, Random House [1962] 578 p. illus. 22 cm. 1. Africa, Sub-Saharan — History. 2. Africa, South — History.
DT352.W48   967   62-8441

Davidson, Basil, 1914- III. 4092
The lost cities of Africa. Rev. ed. Boston, Little, Brown [1970] xxiii, 366 p. illus., maps. 22 cm. 1. Africa, Sub-Saharan — Civilization — History. I. T.
DT352.4.D3 1970   916/.03   70-126061

Stevenson, Robert F. III. 4093
Population and political systems in tropical Africa [by] Robert F. Stevenson. New York, Columbia University Press, 1968. xii, 306 p. maps. 24 cm. 1. Ethnology — Africa, Sub-Saharan. 2. Africa, Sub-Saharan — Population. 3. Fortes, Meyer, ed. African political systems. I. T.
DT352.42.S72   320.1/55/0967   68-11435

Rotberg, Robert I. III. 4094
Protest and power in black Africa. Edited by Robert I. Rothberg and Ali A. Mazrui. New York, Oxford University Press, 1970. xxx, 1274 p. maps. 24 cm. 1. Africa, Sub-Saharan — History — Addresses, essays, lectures. 2. Nationalism — Africa, Sub-Saharah — Addresses, essays, lectures. I. Mazrui, Ali Al'Amin, joint author. II. T.
DT353.R6   967   76-83051

Boahen, A. Adu. III. 4095
Britian, the Sahara and the western Sudan, 1788-1861, by A. Adu Boahen. Oxford, Clarendon Press, 1964. ix, 268 p. maps (part fold.) 23 cm. (Oxford studies in African affairs) 1. Sahara — History. 2. British in the Sahara. 3. British in West Africa. I. T. (S)
DT356.B57   327.420661   64-54602

DT365 – 469   EAST AFRICA

Coupland, Reginald, Sir, 1884-1952. III. 4096
East Africa and its invaders, from the earliest times to the death of Seyyid Said in 1856. New York, Russell & Russell, 1965. vi, 584 p. maps. 23 cm.

"First published in 1938." 1. Sa'īd bin Sultān, sultan of Zanzibar, 1791-1856. 2. Africa, East — History. 3. Slave-trade — Africa, East. 4. Arabs in Africa. 5. Oman — History. I. T.
DT365.C58 1965   967   65-17886

Coupland, Reginald, Sir, 1884-1952. III. 4097
The exploitation of East Africa, 1856-1890; the slave trade and the scramble. With an introd. by Jack Simmons. [Evanston, Ill.] Northwestern University Press, 1967. xiii, 507 p. fold. col. map, ports. 23 cm. 1. Kirk, John, Sir, 1832-1922. 2. Africa, East — History. 3. Slave-trade — Africa, East. 4. Arabs in Africa. I. T.
DT365.C6 1967   967.8   67-31335

Freeman-Grenville, Greville Stewart Parker, comp. III. 4098
The East African coast; select documents from the first to the earlier nineteenth century. Oxford, Clarendon Press, 1962. 314 p. illus. 23 cm. 1. Africa, East — History — Sources. I. T.
DT365.F7   967.6   63-662

Gann, Lewis H., 1924- III. 4099
White settlers in tropical Africa [by] Lewis H. Gann and Peter Duignan. Baltimore, Penguin Books [1962] 169 p. illus. 19 cm. (Penguin African series, WA13) 1. Europeans in East Africa. 2. Europeans in West Africa. I. Duignan, Peter, joint author. II. T.
DT365.G3   325.24096   62-4509

History of East Africa, III. 4100
edited by Roland Oliver [and others] Oxford, Clarendon Press, 1963-   v. maps. 22 cm. Errata slip mounted on p. 178 of v.1. 1. Africa, East — History. I. Oliver, Roland Anthony, ed.
DT365.H55   967.6   63-4375

Ingham, Kenneth. III. 4101
A history of East Africa. Rev. ed. New York, Praeger [1965] xii, 462 p. illus., maps, ports. 23 cm. 1. Africa, East — History. I. T.
DT365.I5 1965   967   65-17934

Mair, Lucy Philip, 1901- III. 4102
Primitive government. Baltimore, Penguin Books [1962] 288 p. illus. 19 cm. (Pelican books, A542) 1. Tribal government — Africa, East. I. T.
DT365.M25   321.2096   62-3405

Davidson, Basil, 1914- III. 4103
A history of East and Central Africa to the late nineteenth century. Garden City, N.Y., Anchor Books, 1969. xxi, 338 p. maps. 19 cm. A revised version of East and Central Africa to the late nineteenth century, published in 1967. 1. Africa, East — History. 2. Africa, Central — History. I. T.
DT365.65.D37 1969   967   69-20103

DT371 – 398   Ethiopia

Kaplan, Irving, 1923- III. 4104
Area handbook for Ethiopia. Co-authors: Irving Kaplan [and others. Washington; For sale by the Supt. of Docs., U.S. Govt. Print. Off.] 1971. xiv, 543 p. maps. 24 cm. "DA pam 550-28." "One of a series of handbooks prepared by Foreign Area Studies (FAS) of the American University." "This pamphlet supersedes DA pam 550-28, October 1960." 2d ed., 1964, issued by American University, Foreign Areas Studies Division. 1. Ethiopia. I. American University, Washington, D.C. Foreign Area Studies. II. American University, Washington, D.C. Foreign Areas Studies Division. Area handbook for Ethiopia. III. T.
DT373.K33 1971   309.1/63/06   79-609351

Lipsky, George Arthur, 1912- III. 4105
Ethiopia: its people, its society, its culture [by] George A. Lipsky in collaboration with Wendell Blanchard, Abraham M. Hirsch [and] Bela C. Maday. New Haven, HRAF Press [1962] 376 p. maps, diagrs., tables. 22 cm. (Survey of world cultures, 9) "Prepared under the auspices of the American University." 1. Ethiopia. (S)
DT373.L56   916.3   62-13515

Ullendorff, Edward. III. 4106
The Ethiopians; an introduction to country and people. 2d ed. London, New York; Oxford University Press, 1965 [c1960] xiv, 235 p. illus., fold. map, ports. 23 cm. 1. Ethiopia — Civilization. I. T.
DT379.5.U4 1965   916.3   65-3205

Simoons, Frederick J. III. 4107
Northwest Ethiopia; peoples and economy. Madison, University of Wisconsin Press, 1960. xvii, 250 p. illus., maps. 24 cm. Revision of thesis — University of California. 1. Ethnology — Ethiopia. I. T.
DT380.S5   572.963   60-5660

Greenfield, Richard.   **III. 4108**
Ethiopia; a new political history. New York, F. A. Praeger [1965] viii, 515 p. illus., maps. 22 cm. (Praeger library of African affairs) *1. Ethiopia — History. I. T.*
DT381.G7   963   65-14180

Hess, Robert L.   **III. 4109**
Ethiopia; the modernization of autocracy [by] Robert L. Hess. Ithaca, Cornell University Press [1970] xx, 272 p. illus., maps. 21 cm. (Africa in the modern world) *1. Ethiopia — History. I. T.*
DT381.H47   963   79-120290   ISBN:0801405734

Jones, Arnold Hugh Martin, 1904-   **III. 4110**
A history of Ethiopia, by A. H. M. Jones and Elizabeth Monroe. Oxford, Clarendon Press [1955] 196 p. illus. 19 cm. First published in 1935 under title: A history of Abyssinia. *1. Ethiopia — History. 2. Ethiopia — Religion. I. Monroe, Elizabeth, joint author. II. T.*
DT381.J6 1955   963   55-13861

Pankhurst, Estelle Sylvia, 1882-   **III. 4111**
Ethiopia, a cultural history. With a foreword by Canon John A. Douglas. Essex [Eng.] Lalibela House [1955] xxxviii, 747 p. illus. (part col.) ports., facsims., music, plans. 23 cm. *1. Ethiopia — History.*
DT381.P35   963   56-22371

DT401 – 420   Somalia

Kaplan, Irving, 1923-   **III. 4112**
Area handbook for Somalia. Co-authors: Irving Kaplan [and others. Washington; For sale by the Supt. of Docs., U.S. Govt. Print. Off.] 1969 [i.e. 1970] xiv, 455 p. illus., maps. 24 cm. "DA pam 550-86." "Prepared by Foreign Area Studies (FAS) of the American University." *1. Somalia. I. American University, Washington, D.C. Foreign Area Studies. II. T.*
DT401.K33   309.1/67/73   73-607519

Lewis, I. M.   **III. 4113**
The modern history of Somaliland, from nation to state [by] I. M. Lewis. New York, F. A. Praeger [1965] xi, 234 p. illus., maps, ports. 22 cm. (The Praeger Asia-Africa series) *1. Somalia — History. I. T.*
DT401.L4   967.73   65-14183

Touval, Saadia.   **III. 4114**
Somali nationalism; international politics and the drive for unity in the Horn of Africa. Cambridge, Harvard University Press, 1963. x, 214 p. diagr., map, tables. 22 cm. "This book ... grew out of a Ph.D. thesis presented at Harvard." *1. Somalia — Politics and government. 2. Nationalism — Somalia. I. T.*
DT401.T6   967.73   63-13817

Castagno, Alphonso Anthony, 1920-   **III. 4115**
Somalia. [New York] Carnegie Endowment for International Peace, 1959. 339-400 p. 20 cm. (International conciliation no. 522) *1. Somaliland, Italian. (S)*
DT416.C3x   (JX1907.A8 no. 522)   967.73   59-2255

DT421 – 433   East Africa (General)

Colson, Elizabeth, 1917- ed.   **III. 4116**
Seven tribes of British Central Africa, edited by Elizabeth Colson and Max Gluckman. [Reprinted with minor corrections. Manchester, Eng.] Published on behalf of the Rhodes-Livingstone Institute, Northern Rhodesia by Manchester University Press [1959] xix, 409 p. illus., maps, geneal. table. 23 cm. *1. Ethnology — Africa, Central. 2. Ethnology — Africa, British East. I. Gluckman, Max, 1911- joint ed. II. T.*
DT429.C6 1959   572.967   61-1359

Delf, George.   **III. 4117**
Asians in east Africa. Issued under the auspices of the Institute of Race Relations. London, New York, Oxford University Press, 1963. 73 p. illus. 19 cm. *1. East Indians in east Africa. I. T.*
DT429.D4   325.25409676   63-2567

Mangat, J. S.   **III. 4118**
A history of the Asians in East Africa, c.1886 to 1945, by J. S. Mangat. Oxford, Clarendon P., 1969. xviii, 216 p. 2 maps. 23 cm. (Oxford studies in African affairs) *1. East Indians in East Africa. I. T. (S)*
DT429.M3   967.6/09/74914   70-390011   ISBN:198216475

Hughes, Anthony John, 1933-   **III. 4119**
East Africa: Kenya, Tanzania, Uganda [by] A. J. Hughes. [Rev. ed.] Baltimore, Penguin Books [1969] 270 p. 19 cm. (Penguin African library, AP11) 1963 ed. has title: East Africa: the search for unity; Kenya, Tanganyika, Uganda, and Zanzibar. *1. Africa, East — Politics. I. T.*
DT431.H8 1969   320.9/676   76-8575

Nye, Joseph S.   **III. 4120**
Pan-Africanism and East African integration [by] Joseph S. Nye, Jr. Cambridge, Mass., Harvard University Press, 1965. x, 307 p. maps 22 cm. *1. Africa, East — Politics. 2. Africa, East — Economic conditions. 3. Pan-Africanism. I. T.*
DT431.N9   320.15967   65-22063

Ogot, Bethwell A.   **III. 4121**
Zamani; a survey of East African history, edited by B. A. Ogot and J. A. Kieran. [Nairobi] EAPH [1968] 407 p. maps. 22 cm. "Published for the Historical Association of Kenya." *1. Africa, East — History. I. Kieran, J. A., joint author. II. Historical Association of Kenya. III. T.*
DT431.O37   967.6   78-385251

Miller, Charles, 1918-   **III. 4122**
The lunatic express; an entertainment in imperialism. New York, Macmillan [1971] xii, 559 p. illus., maps (on lining papers), ports. 24 cm. *1. Africa, East — History. 2. Great Britain — Colonies — Africa. 3. Railroads — Africa, East. I. T.*
DT432.M53   916.7/03   71-153759

Lugard, Frederick John Dealtry, baron, 1858-1945.   **III. 4123**
The diaries of Lord Lugard. Edited by Margery Perham; assistant editor: Mary Bull. Evanston, Ill., Northwestern University Press [1959-63] 4 v. illus., ports., maps, facsim. 23 cm. (Northwestern University [Evanston, Ill.] African studies, no. 3) *1. Africa, British East. I. Perham, Margery Freda, 1895- ed. (S)*
DT433.L8A3 1959   967.6   59-9328

DT434   Kenya

Blixen, Karen, 1885-1962.   **III. 4124**
Out of Africa [by] Isak Dinesen [pseud.] With an introd. by Bernardine Kielty. New York, Modern Library [1952] 389 p. 19 cm. (The Modern library of the world's best books) *1. Country life — Kenya. 2. Kenya — Native races. I. T.*
DT434.E2B6 1952   916.762   52-5952

Huxley, Elspeth Joscelin (Grant) 1907-   **III. 4125**
Race and politics in Kenya; a correspondence between Elspeth Huxley and Margery Perham. With an introd. by Lord Lugard. New and rev. [i.e. 2d] ed. London, Faber and Faber [1956] 302 p. illus. 23 cm. *1. Kenya Colony and Protectorate — Politics and government. 2. Kenya Colony and Protectorate — Native races. I. Perham, Margery Freda, 1896- II. T.*
DT434.E2H78 1956   967.62   56-2071

Huxley, Elspeth Joscelin (Grant) 1907-   **III. 4126**
White man's country; Lord Delamere and the making of Kenya, by Elspeth Huxley. [New ed.] New York, Praeger [1968, c1967] 2 v. illus., maps, ports. 23 cm. *1. Delamere, Hugh Cholmondeley, Baron, 1870-1931. 2. Kenya — Politics and government. 3. Frontier and pioneer life — Kenya. I. T.*
DT434.E2H8 1968   325.2/42/096762   68-12424

Kaplan, Irving, 1923-   **III. 4127**
Area handbook for Kenya. Co-authors: Irving Kaplan [and others. Washington] 1967. vii, 707 p. illus., maps. 24 cm. "DA pam no. 550-56." "One of a series of handbooks prepared by Foreign Area Studies (FAS) of the American University." *1. Kenya. I. American University, Washington, D.C. Foreign Area Studies. II. T.*
DT434.E2K34   916.76/1   67-62739

Kenyatta, Jomo.   **III. 4128**
Facing Mount Kenya; the tribal life of Gikuyu, by Jomo Kenyatta, with an introduction by B. Malinowski. London, Secker and Warburg [1938] xxv, 339 p. illus. (incl. map) VIII pl. (incl. front. (port.)) 23 cm. "Glossary": p. 319-329. *1. Kikuyu tribe. 2. Ethnology — Africa, East. 3. Society, Primitive. I. T.*
DT434.E2K45   572.96765   39-3764

Goldschmidt, Walter Rochs, 1913- III. 4129
Kambuya's cattle; the legacy of an African herdsman [by] Walter Goldschmidt. Berkeley, University of California Press, 1969. viii, 242 p. illus., geneal. tables, ports. 24 cm. *1. Sabing (African tribe) 2. Inheritance and succession — Kenya. I. T.*
DT434.E242G6   301.29/676/2   68-31589

Kenyatta, Jomo. III. 4130
Harambee! The Prime Minister of Kenya's speeches 1963-1964, from the attainment of internal self-government to the threshold of the Kenya Republic. Foreword by Malcolm MacDonald. The text edited and arr. by Anthony Cullen on instructions of the Permanent Secretary, Prime Minister's Office. Nairobi, New York, Oxford University Press, 1964 [i.e. 1965] xi, 114 p. illus., ports. 22 cm. *1. Kenya — Politics and government — Addresses, essays, lectures. I. T. II. T:The Prime Minister of Kenya's speeches, 1963-1964.*
DT434.E26K4   354.6762035   65-4596

Mboya, Tom. III. 4131
Freedom and after. [1st ed.] Boston, Little, Brown [1963] x, 288 p. illus., ports., map (on lining papers) 22 cm. Autobiographical. *1. Kenya. 2. Africa — Politics — 1960- 3. Pan-Africanism. I. T.*
DT434.E27M35   967.62   63-20102

Rosberg, Carl Gustav. III. 4132
The myth of "Mau Mau"; nationalism in Kenya, by Carl G. Rosberg, Jr. and John Nottingham. Stanford, Calif., Published for the Hoover Institution on War, Revolution, and Peace by Praeger, New York [1966] xviii, 427 p. illus., maps (2 fold. in pocket), ports. 23 cm. (Hoover Institution publications) *1. Nationalism — Kenya. I. Nottingham, John Cato, 1928- joint author. II. T.*
DT434.E27R6   967.6203   66-21793

DT434   Uganda

Beattie, John. III. 4133
Bunyoro, an African kingdom. New York, Holt [1960] ix, 86 p. illus., port., map. 24 cm. (Case studies in cultural anthropology) *1. Banyoro. 2. Ethnology — Uganda. (S)*
DT434.U2B4   572.8963   60-7331

Herrick, Allison Butler. III. 4134
Area handbook for Uganda. Co-authors: Allison Butler Herrick [and others] Washington, For sale by the Supt. of Docs., U.S. Govt. Print. Off., 1969. xvi, 456 p. maps 24 cm. "DA pam no. 550-74." "One of a series of handbooks prepared by Foreign Area Studies (FAS) of the American Univeristy." *1. Uganda. I. American University, Washington, D.C. Foreign Area Studies. II. T.*
DT434.U2H4   916.76/1/03   73-601330

Ingham, Kenneth. III. 4135
The making of modern Uganda. London, Allen & Unwin [1958] 303 p. illus. 23 cm. *1. Uganda — History. I. T.*
DT434.U2I5   967.61   58-1807

Apter, David Ernest, 1924- III. 4136
The political kingdom in Uganda; a study in bureaucratic nationalism, by David E. Apter. [2d ed.] Princeton, N.J., Princeton University Press [1967] xxii, 498 p. illus., maps, port. 21 cm. *1. Uganda — Politics and government. 2. Buganda — Politics and government. I. T.*
DT434.U25A6 1967   320.9/676/1   67-18831

DT435   Zanzibar

Gray, John Milner, Sir, 1889- III. 4137
History of Zanzibar, from the Middle Ages to 1856. London, Oxford University Press, 1962. 314 p. illus. 23 cm. *1. Saʻīd bin Sulṭān, sultan of Zanzibar, 1791-1856. 2. Zanzibar — History.*
DT435.G7   967.81   62-52499

Middleton, John, 1921- III. 4138
Zanzibar, its society and its politics [by] John Middleton & Jane Campbell. London, New York, Oxford University Press, 1965. 71 p. maps. 19 cm. "Issued under the auspices of the Institute of Race Relations, London." *1. Zanzibar — Description and travel. 2. Zanzibar — Politics and government. I. Campbell, Jean M'Comb, 1934- joint author. II. Institute of Race Relations. III. T.*
DT435.M5   309.16781   65-21925

DT436 – 446   Tanzania

Herrick, Allison Butler. III. 4139
Area handbook for Tanzania. Co-authors: Allison Butler Herrick [and others] Washington, For sale by the Supt. of Docs., U.S. Govt. Print. Off., 1968. xvi, 522 p. maps. 24 cm. "Prepared by Foreign Area Studies (FAS) of the American University." *1. Tanzania. I. American University, Washington, D.C. Foreign Area Studies. II. T.*
DT438.H4   309.1/678   68-67374

Nyerere, Julius Kambarage, Pres. Tanzania, 1922- III. 4140
Freedom and unity: Uhuru na umoja; a selection from writings and speeches, 1952-65 [by] Julius K. Nyerere. London, Nairobi [etc.] Oxford U.P., 1967. xiii, 366 p. front., 8 plates (incl. ports.) 22 1/2 cm. *1. Africa — Politics — Addresses, essays, lectures. I. T. II. T:Uhuru na umoja.*
DT446.N9A5   320.9/6   67-77497

DT449 – 469   Other East African Countries

McDonald, Gordon C. III. 4141
Area handbook for Burundi. Co-authors: Gordon C. McDonald [and others] Washington, For sale by the Supt. of Docs., U.S. Govt. Print. Off., 1969. xiv, 203 p. maps. 24 cm. "DA pam no. 550-83." "Prepared by Foreign Area Studies (FAS) of The American University." *1. Burundi. I. American University, Washington, D.C. Foreign Area Studies. II. T.*
DT449.B8M3   916.7/572   70-605915

Louis, William Roger. III. 4142
Ruanda-Urundi, 1884-1919. Oxford, Clarendon Press, 1963. xvii, 290 p. map. 23 cm. *1. Ruanda-Urundi — History.*
DT449.R8L6   967.57   64-1021

Nyrop, Richard F. III. 4143
Area handbook for Rwanda. Co-authors: Richard F. Nyrop [and others] Washington, For sale by the Supt. of Docs., U.S. Govt. Print. Off., 1969. xiv, 212 p. maps. 25 cm. "DA pam 550-84." "Prepared by Foreign Area Studies (FAS) of The American University." *1. Rwanda. I. American University, Washington, D.C. Foreign Area Studies. II. T.*
DT449.R9N9   916.7/571   72-606089

Herrick, Allison Butler. III. 4144
Area handbook for Mozambique. Co-authors: Allison Butler Herrick [and others] Washington, For sale by the Supt. of Docs., U.S. Govt. Print. Off., 1969. xiv, 351 p. maps. 24 cm. "DA pam no. 550-64." "Prepared by Foreign Area Studies (FAS) of the American University." *1. Mozambique. I. American University, Washington, D.C. Foreign Area Studies. II. T.*
DT453.I14   916.7/9   72-601780

Axelson, Eric Victor. III. 4145
Portuguese in south-east Africa, 1600-1700. Johannesburg, Witwatersrand University Press, 1960. 226 p. illus. 25 cm. *1. Portuguese in East Africa.*
DT459.A93 1960   967.9   61-22909

Stoddard, Theodore Lothrop, 1926- III. 4146
Area handbook for the Indian Ocean territories. Co-authors: Theodore L. Stoddard [and others] Prepared for the American University by the Institute for Cross-Cultural Research. [Washington; For sale by the Supt. of Docs., U.S. Govt. Print. Off. 1971. xvi, 160 p. illus., maps. 24 cm. "DA pam 550-154." "One of a series of handbooks prepared under the auspices of Foreign Area Studies (FAS) of the American University." *1. Maldive Islands. 2. Seychelles. 3. Mauritius. 4. Réunion. I. Institute for Cross-Cultural Research. II. American University, Washington, D.C. Foreign Area Studies. III. T.*
DT468.S76   916.9   73-171984

Kent, Raymond K. III. 4147
From Madagascar to the Malagasy Republic. New York, Praeger [1962] 182 p. illus. 22 cm. (Books that matter.) *1. Madagascar — History. 2. Ethnology — Madagascar. I. T.*
DT469.M34K4   969.1   62-11772

Thompson, Virginia McLean, 1903- III. 4148
The Malagasy Republic: Madagascar today [by] Virginia Thompson and Richard Adloff. Stanford, Calif., Stanford University Press, 1965. xvi, 504 p.

illus., map., ports. 24 cm. *1. Madagascar. I. Adloff, Richard joint author. II. T.*
DT469.M343T5   309.1691   65-21495

DT471 – 507 West Africa (Former British Areas, General)

Davies, Oliver. III. 4149
West Africa before the Europeans: archeology & prehistory. London, Methuen, 1967. iii-xix, 364 p. illus., 24 plates, maps, tables, diagrs. 24 1/2 cm. (Methuen's handbooks of archeology) *1. Africa, West — Antiquities. I. T.*
DT471.D34   916.6/03   67-99828

Hargreaves, John D. III. 4150
Prelude to the partition of West Africa. London, Macmillan; New York, St Martin's Press, 1963. xi, 383 p. maps (1 fold.) 22 cm. *1. Africa, West — Colonization. 2. Africa, West — Commerce — History. 3. Europeans in West Africa. I. T.*
DT471.H29   966   63-22836

July, Robert William. III. 4151
The origins of modern African thought; its development in West Africa during the nineteenth and twentieth centuries. New York, Praeger [1968, c1967] 512 p. illus., map, ports. 22 cm. *1. Nationalism — Africa, West. 2. Africa, West — Biography. I. T.*
DT471.J84   916.6/03   67-24684

Lewis, William Arthur, 1915- III. 4152
Politics in West Africa [by] W. Arthur Lewis. Toronto, New York, Oxford University Press, 1965. 90 p. map. 19 cm. *1. Africa, West — Politics. 2. States, New. I. T.*
DT471.L57   320.966   65-8469

Newbury, Colin W. III. 4153
The western slave coast and its rulers: European trade and administration among the Yoruba and Adja-speaking peoples of South-western Nigeria, southern Dahomey and Togo. Oxford, Clarendon Press, 1961. ix, 234 p. maps (part fold.) tables. 22 cm. (Oxford studies in African affairs) *1. Slave coast — History. 2. Europeans in West Africa. I. T. (S)*
DT471.N38   966.8   62-180

Post, Kenneth William John, 1935- III. 4154
The new States of West Africa [by] Ken Post. Baltimore, Penguin Books [1964] 206 p. maps. 18 cm. (Penguin African library) "AP14." *1. States, New. 2. Africa, West. I. T.*
DT471.P6   309.166   64-55917

Welch, Claude Emerson. III. 4155
Dream of unity; Pan-Africanism and political unification in West Africa, by Claude E. Welch, Jr. Ithaca, N.Y., Cornell University Press [1966] xv, 396 p. maps. 22 cm. *1. Africa, West — Politics. 2. Pan-Africanism. 3. Regionalism — Africa, West. I. T.*
DT471.W38   320.1596   66-16290

Zolberg, Aristide R. III. 4156
Creating political order; the party-states of West Africa [by] Aristide R. Zolberg. Chicago, Rand McNally [1966] vi, 168 p. 22 cm. (Studies in political change) *1. Africa, West — Politics. I. T.*
DT471.Z6   320.966   66-19458

Fage, J. D. III. 4157
A history of West Africa: an introductory survey, by J. D. Fage. 4th ed. London, Cambridge U.P., 1969. xii, 239 p. maps. 23 cm. First-3d ed. published under title: An introduction to the history of West Africa. *1. Africa, West — History. I. T.*
DT475.F3 1969   966   71-85742   ISBN:521074061

Crowder, Michael, 1934- III. 4158
West Africa under colonial rule. Evanston [Ill.] Northwestern University Press, 1968. xv, 540 p. maps (1 fold.) 24 cm. *1. Africa, West — History. I. T.*
DT476.2.C76 1968b   966   68-27618

Lystad, Robert A. III. 4159
The Ashanti; a proud people [by] Robert A. Lystad. New York, Greenwood Press, 1968[c1958] 212 p. illus. 23 cm. *1. Ashantis.*
DT507.L9 1968   301.29/667   69-10125

DT509 Gambia

Gailey, Harry A. III. 4160
A history of the Gambia, by Harry A. Gailey. New York, Praeger [1965] xi, 244 p. illus., fold. map. 23 cm. *1. Gambia — History. I. T.*
DT509.G3 1965   966.51   65-11999

DT510 – 512 Ghana

Boateng, E. A. III. 4161
A geography of Ghana, by E. A. Boateng. 2nd ed. Cambridge, Cambridge U.P., 1966. xv, 212 p. 24 plates, maps, tables, diagrs. 23 cm. *1. Ghana — Description and travel. I. T.*
DT510.B6 1966   916.67   65-22922

Kaplan, Irving, 1923- III. 4162
Area handbook for Ghana. Co-authors: Irving Kaplan [and others. Rev. 2d ed. Washington; For sale by the Supt. of Docs., U.S. Govt. Print. Off.] 1971. xiv, 449 p. map. 24 cm. "DA Pam 550-153." "One of a series of handbooks prepared by Foreign Area Studies (FAS) of the American University." Supersedes Special warfare area handbook for Ghana, issued in 1962 by American University, Foreign Areas Studies Division. *1. Ghana. I. American University, Washington, D.C. Foreign Area Studies. II. American University, Washington, D.C. Foreign Areas Studies Division. Special warfare area handbook for Ghana. III. T.*
DT510.K37 1971   916.67   74-611338

Wolfson, Freda. III. 4163
Pageant of Ghana. London, Oxford University Press, 1958. 266 p. illus. 23 cm. (West African history series) *1. Ghana — History.*
DT510.W6   966.7   58-3099

Jahoda, Gustav. III. 4164
White man; a study of the attitudes of Africans to Europeans in Ghana before independence. London, New York, Oxford University Press, 1961. 144 p. 22 cm. *1. Ghana — Race question. 2. Prejudices and antipathies. I. T.*
DT510.42.J3   301.451   61-2090

Nkrumah, Kwame, Pres. Ghana, 1909- III. 4165
Ghana; the autobiography of Kwame Nkrumah. New York, International Publishers [1971, c1957] xiii, 310 p. maps, port. 21 cm. *1. Ghana — Politics and government — To 1957.*
DT510.6.N5A33 1971   966.7/05/0924 (B)   70-148514
    ISBN:0717802930

Omari, T. Peter. III. 4166
Kwame Nkrumah; the anatomy of an African dictatorship, by T. Peter Omari. With a foreword by Nii Amaa Ollennu. New York, Africana Pub. Corp. [1970] xix, 229 p. 23 cm. Appendices (p. 179-220): — A. Speech in Parliament by J. A. Braimah during debate on Preventive detention bill, 1958. — B. Nkrumaism — African socialism: Ghana's conception of socialism, by K. Baako — C. Eulogy on Dr. J. B. Danquah, by N. Azikiwe. — D. Last wills of Kwame Nkrumah. *1. Nkrumah, Kwame, Pres. Ghana, 1909- 2. Ghana — Politics and government — 1957-*
DT510.6.N5O43   966.7/05/0924   74-103939   ISBN:841900361

Austin, Dennis, 1922- III. 4167
Politics in Ghana, 1946-1960. Issued under the auspices of the Royal Institute of International Affairs. London, New York, Oxford University Press, 1964. xiv, 459 p. maps. 22 cm. "The Constitution of the Republic of Ghana": p. [430]-446. *1. Ghana — Politics and government. I. Ghana. Constitution. II. T.*
DT511.A84   966.7   64-55703

Bourret, F. M. III. 4168
Ghana, the road to independence, 1919-1957. [Rev. ed.] Stanford, Calif., Stanford University Press, 1960. 246 p. illus. 24 cm. First published in 1949 under title: The Gold Coast; a survey of the Gold Coast and British Togoland, 1919-1946. *1. Ghana — History. I. T.*
DT511.B68 1960   966.7   60-13872

Fage, J. D. III. 4169
Ghana: a historical interpretation. Madison, University of Wisconsin Press, 1959. 122 p. illus. 23 cm. *1. Ghana — History.*
DT511.F3   966.7   59-13698

Kimble, David.   III. 4170
A political history of Ghana; the rise of Gold Coast nationalism, 1850-1928. Oxford, Clarendon Press, 1963. xviii, 587 p. ports., maps, tables. 24 cm. "In substance ... the dissertation for which I was awarded the degree of Ph.D. in the University of London." *1. Ghana — Politics and government. I. T.*
DT511.K42 1963   966.7   63-4374

Ward, William Ernest Frank, 1900-   III. 4171
A history of Ghana. New York, Praeger [1963, c1958] 434 p. illus., ports., maps. 23 cm. First published in 1948 under title: A history of the Gold Coast. *1. Ghana — History. 2. Ashanti — History.*
DT511.W28 1963   966.7   63-18837

Wright, Richard, 1908-   III. 4172
Black power; a record of reactions in a land of pathos. [1st ed.] New York, Harper [1954] 358 p. illus. 22 cm. *1. Gold Coast — Description and travel. 2. Gold Coast — Social conditions. I. T.*
DT511.W7   916.67   54-10082

Nkrumah, Kwame, Pres. Ghana, 1909-   III. 4173
I speak of freedom; a statement of African ideology. New York, Praeger [1961] 291 p. illus. 21 cm. (Books that matter) *1. Ghana — History. 2. Africa — Politics. I. T.*
DT512.N55 1961   966.7   61-14200

DT515   Nigeria

Hodgkin, Thomas Lionel, 1910-   III. 4174
Nigerian perspectives, an historical anthology. London, Oxford University Press, 1960. 340 p. illus. 23 cm. (West African history series) *1. Nigeria — History — Sources.*
DT515.A3H6   966.9   60-51097

Buchanan, Keith M.   III. 4175
Land and people in Nigeria: the human geography of Nigeria and its environmental background [by] K. M. Buchanan and J. C. Pugh, with a contribution by A. Brown and a foreword by L. Dudley Stamp. London, University of London Press [1955] xii, 252 p. illus., maps, charts. 26 cm. *1. Nigeria. I. Pugh, John Charles, joint author. II. T.*
DT515.B75   916.69   56-23583

Burns, Alan Cuthbert, Sir, 1887-   III. 4176
History of Nigeria [by] Sir Alan Burns. 7th ed. London, Allen & Unwin, 1969. 366 p. 9 plates, 2 tables, maps (1 col.), ports. 23 cm. *1. Nigeria — History. I. T.*
DT515.B8 1969   966/.9   79-410228   ISBN:049660098

Coleman, James Smoot.   III. 4177
Nigeria: background to nationalism. Berkeley, University of California Press, 1958. xiv, 510 p. illus., ports., maps. 24 cm. *1. Nationalism — Nigeria.*
DT515.C685   966.9   58-10286

Nadel, Siegfried Frederick, 1903-   III. 4178
A black Byzantium; the kingdom of Nupe in Nigeria, by S. F. Nadel. With a foreword by Right Hon. Lord Lugard. London, New York [etc.] Pub. for the International Institute of African Languages & Cultures by Oxford University Press, 1942. xiv, 420 p. illus., tables, diagrs. front., plates, maps (part fold.) 23 cm. *1. Nupe. I. International Institute of African Languages and Cultures. II. T.*
DT515.N27   916.696   43-6377

Nelson, Harold D.   III. 4179
Area handbook for Nigeria, co-authors: Harold D. Nelson [and others. Rev. 3d ed. Washington; For sale by the Supt. of Docs., U.S. Govt. Print. Off.] 1972. xvi, 485 p. maps. 24 cm. "DA pam 550-157." "One of a series of handbooks prepared by Foreign Area Studies (FAS) of the American University." 1964 ed. issued by American University, Foreign Areas Studies Division. *1. Nigeria. I. American University, Washington, D.C. Foreign Area Studies. II. American University, Washington, D.C. Foreign Areas Studies Division. Area handbook for Nigeria. III. T.*
DT515.N37 1972   309.1/669   77-183909

Crowder, Michael, 1934-   III. 4180
A short history of Nigeria. Rev. and enl. ed. New York, F. A. Praeger [1966] 416 p. illus., maps (1 fold.), ports. 21 cm. *1. Nigeria — History. I. T.*
DT515.5.C68 1966   966.9   66-13679

Flint, John E.   III. 4181
Nigeria and Ghana [by] John E. Flint. Englewood Cliffs, N.J., Prentice-Hall [1966] viii, 176 p. maps. 21 cm. (A Spectrum book: The modern nations in historical perspective) *1. Nigeria — History. 2. Ghana — History. I. T.*
DT515.5.F5   966   66-16343

Awolowo, Obafemi, 1909-   III. 4182
Awo; the autobiography of Chief Obafemi Awolowo. Cambridge [Eng.] University Press, 1960. 315 p. illus. 23 cm. *I. T.*
DT515.6.A9A3   923.2669   60-50987

Azikiwe, Nnamdi, 1904-   III. 4183
Zik, a selection from the speeches of Nnamdi Azikiwe. Cambridge [Eng.] University Press, 1961. 344 p. illus. 23 cm. *1. Nigeria — Politics and government. I. T.*
DT515.6.A9A5   923.2669   61-1177

Jones-Quartey, K. A. B.   III. 4184
A life of Azikiwe [by] K. A. B. Jones-Quartey. Baltimore, Penguin Books [1965] 272 p. maps. 18 cm. (Penguin African series, WA14) *1. Azikiwe, Nnamdi, 1904- I. T.*
DT515.6.A9J6   966.9030924   66-1652

Bello, Ahmadu, Sir, 1909-   III. 4185
My life. Cambridge [Eng.] University Press, 1962. 245 p. illus. 23 cm. *1. Nigeria — Politics and government.*
DT515.6.B4A3   966.9   63-6

Balewa, Abubakar Tafawa, Sir, 1912-   III. 4186
Nigeria speaks; speeches made between 1957 and 1964. Selected and introduced by Sam Epelle. Foreword by T. O. S. Benson. Ikeja, Longmans of Nigeria [1964] xiii, 178 p. ports. 23 cm. *1. Nigeria — Foreign relations. 2. Nigeria — Politics and government. I. T.*
DT515.8.B27   65-66598

Schwarz, Frederick August Otto, 1935-   III. 4187
Nigeria: the tribes, the nation, or the race; the politics of independence [by] Frederick A.O. Schwarz, Jr. Cambridge, M.I.T. Press [1965] xiii, 316 p. illus., maps, port. 24 cm. *1. Nigeria — Politics and government. I. T.*
DT515.8.S3   320.9669   65-26840

Sklar, Richard L.   III. 4188
Nigerian political parties; power in an emergent African nation. Princeton, Princeton University Press, 1963. xi, 578 p. maps, tables. 25 cm. *1. Nigeria — Politics and government. 2. Political parties — Nigeria. I. T.*
DT515.8.S55   329.9669   62-21107

DT516   Sierra Leone

Lewis, Roy.   III. 4189
Sierra Leone; a modern portrait. London, H. M. Stationery Off., 1954. ix, 263 p. illus., maps (1 fold. col.) music. 23 cm. (The Corona library [2]) *1. Sierra Leone — Social life and customs. (S)*
DT516.L4   916.64   54-1967

Fyfe, Christopher.   III. 4190
A history of Sierra Leone. [London] Oxford University Press, 1962. vii, 773 p. fold. maps. 24 cm. *1. Sierra Leone — History.*
DT516.5.F85   966.4   62-4324

Kup, Alexander Peter.   III. 4191
A history of Sierra Leone, 1400-1787, by A. P. Kup. Cambridge [Eng.] University Press, 1961. 211 p. illus. 22 cm. *1. Sierra Leone — History.*
DT516.65.K85   966.4   61-1075

DT521 – 546   West Africa (Former French Areas, General) Ivory Coast.

Thompson, Virginia McLean, 1903-   III. 4192
French West Africa [by] Virginia Thompson and Richard Adloff. Stanford, Calif., Stanford University Press [1957?] 626 p. illus., maps, tables. 23 cm. *1. Africa, French West. I. Adloff, Richard, joint author.*
DT524.T5   966   58-7722

Adloff, Richard.   III. 4193
West Africa; the French-speaking nations, yesterday and today. New York,

Holt, Rinehart and Winston [1964] v, 361 p. illus., maps, ports. 19 cm. (Contemporary civilization series) *1. Africa, French West. I. T.*
DT532.A57   916.61   64-25653

Hargreaves, John D.   **III. 4194**
West Africa: the former French states [by] John D. Hargreaves. Englewood Cliffs, N.J., Prentice-Hall [1967] viii, 183 p. maps. 21 cm. (A Spectrum book: The modern nations in historical perspective) *1. Africa, French West — History. I. T.*
DT532.H3   966   67-14841

Morgenthau, Ruth Schachter.   **III. 4195**
Political parties in French-speaking West Africa. Oxford, Clarendon Press, 1964   xxii, 445 p. illus., maps. 23 cm. (Oxford studies in African affairs) *1. Africa, French West — Politics. 2. Political parties — Africa, French West. I. T. (S)*
DT532.M6   320.966   65-357

Neres, Philip.   **III. 4196**
French-speaking West Africa; from colonial status to independence. Issued under the auspices of the Institute of Race Relations. London, New York, Oxford University Press, 1962. 101 p. illus. 19 cm. *1. Africa, French West — History. I. T.*
DT532.N4 1962   966.1   62-53619

Laye, Camara, 1928-   **III. 4197**
The dark child. With an introd. by Philippe Thoby-Marcellin. [Translated from the French by James Kirkup and Ernest Jones] New York, Farrar, Straus and Giroux [1969, c1954] 188 p. 21 cm. Translation of L'enfant noir. Autobiographical. *I. T.*
DT543.4.L313 1969   916.6/52/0330924 (B)   73-5733

American University, Washington, D. C. Foreign Areas Studies Division.   **III. 4198**
Area handbook for Ivory Coast. Washington, 1962. xii, 485 p. maps. 24 cm. At head of title: U.S. Army Prepared under contract with the Dept. of the Army. *1. Ivory Coast. I. U.S. Army. II. T.*
DT545.A64   67-115012

Delavignette, Robert Louis, 1897-   **III. 4199**
French Equatorial Africa. Photos. by Michel Huet, Michel Mako and Pierre Ichac. Geographical, ethnological, and economic notes by Jacques Vulaines. [Paris] Librairie Hachette [1957] 126 p. illus. 22 cm. (Hachette world albums, 5) *1. Africa, French Equatorial — Description and travel — Views.*
DT546.D42   916.72   58-33720

Gide, André Paul Guillaume, 1869-1951.   **III. 4200**
Travels in the Congo. Translated from the French by Dorothy Bussy. [2d ed.] Berkeley, University of California Press, 1962 [c1957] 375 p. illus. 21 cm. "Originally published as Voyage au Congo and Le retour du Tchad." *1. Africa, French Equatorial — Description and travel. 2. Cameroons — Description and travel. I. T.*
DT546.G483 1962   916.72   62-3221

Thompson, Virginia McLean, 1903-   **III. 4201**
The emerging states of French Equatorial Africa [by] Virginia Thompson and Richard Adloff. Stanford, Calif., Stanford University Press, 1960. xii, 595 p. illus., ports., maps. 24 cm. *1. Africa, French Equatorial — Politics. I. Adloff, Richard, joint author. II. T.*
DT546.T48 1960   967.2   60-13871

DT546.1 – 584   Gabon Congo (Brazzaville). Chad Senegal. Mauritania. Cameroons

Schweitzer, Albert, 1875-1965.   **III. 4202**
African notebook. Translated by Mrs. C. E. B. Russell. Bloomington, Indiana University Press, 1958 [c1939] 144 p. illus. 20 cm. (A Midland book, MB/14) Translation of Afrikanische Geschichten. *1. Gabon — Social life and customs. I. T.*
DT546.1.S42x   916.721   58-12209

McDonald, Gordon C.   **III. 4203**
Area handbook for People's Republic of the Congo (Congo Brazzaville). Co-authors: Gordon C. McDonald [and others. Washington; For sale by the Supt. of Docs., U.S. Govt. Print. Off.] 1971. xiii, 255 p. maps. 25 cm. "DA pam no. 550-91." "One of a series of handbooks prepared by Foreign Area Studies (FAS) of the American University." *1. Congo (Brazzaville) I. American University, Washington, D.C. Foreign Area Studies. II. T.*
DT546.2.M25   309.1/67/24   75-608676

Nelson, Harold D.   **III. 4204**
Area handbook for Chad. Co-authors: Harold D. Nelson [and others. Washington; For sale by the Supt. of Docs., U.S. Govt. Print. Off.] 1972. xiv, 261 p. illus. 24 cm. "DA Pam 550-159." "One of a series of handbooks prepared by Foreign Area Studies (FAS) of the American University." *1. Chad. I. American University, Washington, D.C. Foreign Area Studies. II. T.*
DT546.4.N44   916.7/43   72-600075

American University, Washington, D.C. Foreign Areas Studies Division.   **III. 4205**
Area handbook for Senegal. [Washington, For sale by the Supt. of Docs., U.S. Govt. Print. Off.] 1963. xiv, 489 p. maps. 24 cm. At head of title: U.S. Army. "Operating under contract with Department of the Army." *1. Senegal. I. U.S. Dept. of the Army. II. T.*
DT549.A58   67-117133

Crowder, Michael, 1934-   **III. 4206**
Senegal: a study of French assimilation policy. Revised ed. London, Methuen, Distributed in the U.S.A. by Barnes & Noble, 1967. x, 151 p. map, tables. 18 1/2 cm. (Studies in African history, no. 1) *1. Senegal — Politics and government. 2. French in Senegal. 3. Acculturation. I. T.*
DT549.5.C7 1967   325.3/44/09663   67-108497

Gerteiny, Alfred G.   **III. 4207**
Mauritania [by] Alfred G. Gerteiny. New York, Praeger [1967] x, 243 p. map. 22 cm. (Praeger library of African affairs) *1. Mauritania.*
DT553.M2G4   916.6/1   67-23574

Le Vine, Victor T.   **III. 4208**
The Cameroons, from mandate to independence, by Victor T. Le Vine. Berkeley, University of California Press, 1964. xi, 329 p. geneal. table, maps. 25 cm. *1. Cameroun — History. 2. Cameroons — History. I. T.*
DT572.L4 1964   967.11   64-24585

Rudin, Harry Rudolph, 1898-   **III. 4209**
Germans in the Cameroons, 1884-1914; a case study in modern imperialism, by Harry R. Rudin. [Hamden, Conn.] Archon Books, 1968. 456 p. fold. map. 22 cm. Reprint of the 1938 ed. "This study ... originated in a doctoral dissertation at Yale University in 1931." *1. Cameroons. 2. Germany — Colonies — Administration. 3. Imperialism. I. T.*
DT572.R8 1968   325.3/43/096711   68-54380   ISBN:020800680X

Gardinier, David E.   **III. 4210**
Cameroon, United Nations challenge to French policy. London, New York, Oxford University Press, 1963. x, 142 p. map. 19 cm. "Issued under the auspices of the Institute of Race Relations, London." *1. Cameroons, French — History. I. Institute of Race Relations. II. T.*
DT574.G3   967.11   63-23620

DT591 – 617   Angola

Birmingham, David.   **III. 4211**
Trade and conflict in Angola: the Mbundu and their neighbours under the influence of the Portuguese, 1483-1790. Oxford, Clarendon P., 1966. xvii, 178 p. maps, tables. 22 1/2 cm. (Oxford studies in African affairs) *1. Angola — History. 2. Africa, West — History. 3. Slave-trade — Africa, West. 4. Mbundu (Bantu tribe) 5. Portuguese in West Africa. I. T. (S)*
DT604.B5   967.302   66-75626

Herrick, Allison Butler.   **III. 4212**
Area handbook for Angola. Co-authors: Allison Butler Herrick [and others] Washington, For sale by the Supt. of Docs., U.S. Govt. Print. Off., 1967. xii, 439 p. illus., maps. 24 cm. "DA PAM no. 550-59." "One of a series of handbooks prepared by Foreign Area Studies (FAS) of The American University." *1. Angola. I. American University, Washington, D.C. Foreign Areas Studies Division. II. T.*
DT611.H47   916.7/3   68-61155

Wheeler, Douglas L.   **III. 4213**
Angola [by] Douglas L. Wheeler and René Pélissier. New York, Praeger Publishers [1971] ix, 296 p. illus., maps, port. 23 cm. (Praeger library of African affairs) *1. Angola — Politics and government. I. Pélissier, René. II. T.*
DT611.62.W54   916.7/3/033   75-77309

Angola: a symposium; views of a revolt.   **III. 4214**
London, New York, Oxford University Press, 1962. 160 p. fold. map. 19 cm.

"Issued under the auspices of the Institute of Race Relations, London." *1. Portuguese in Angola. I. Institute of Race Relations.*
DT611.8.A6   967.3   62-3375

DT621 – 637   Liberia

American University, Washington, D.C. Foreign Areas Studies Division.   III. 4215
Area handbook for Liberia. Washington, For sale by the Supt. of Docs., U.S. Govt. Print Off., 1964. xiii, 419 p. maps. 24 cm. At head of title: U.S. Army. "Department of the Army pamphlet no. 550-38." *1. Liberia. I. U.S. Army. II. T.*
DT624.A62   67-115013

Anderson, Robert Earle, 1881-   III. 4216
Liberia, America's African friend. Chapel Hill, University of North Carolina Press [1952] x, 305 p. illus., ports., maps. 25 cm. *1. Liberia.*
DT624.A64   966.6   52-9731

Richardson, Nathaniel R.   III. 4217
Liberia's past and present. London, Diplomatic Press and Pub. Co., 1959. 348 p. illus. 29 cm. *1. Liberia — History. 2. Liberia — Politics and government. 3. Liberia — Biography.*
DT631.R5   966.6   59-4459

Buell, Raymond Leslie, 1896-1946.   III. 4218
Liberia: a century of survival, 1847-1947, by Raymond Leslie Buell. Philadelphia, University of Pennsylvania Press, the University Museum, 1947. vi p., 1 l., 140 p. 22 cm. (African handbooks, 7) *1. Liberia.*
DT632.B8   966.6   47-1714

Tubman, William V. S., Pres. Liberia, 1895-   III. 4219
The official papers of William V. S. Tubman, President of the Republic of Liberia: covering addresses, messages, speeches and statements 1960-1967; edited by E. Reginald Townsend, assisted by Abeodu Bowen Jones. London, published for the Department of Information and Cultural Affairs, Monrovia, Liberia, by Longmans, 1968. xxi, 687 p. 9 plates, 17 illus., 2 maps. 26 cm. *I. Townsend, E. Reginald, ed. II. Jones, Abeodu Bowen, ed. III. Liberia. Dept. of Information and Cultural Affairs.*
DT636.T8A5   966/.603/08   68-115801

DT641 – 665   Zaire (Congo Kinhasa). Congo (Leopoldville)

American University, Washington, D.C. Foreign Areas Studies Division.   III. 4220
Area handbook for the Republic of the Congo (Léopoldville) Washington, 1962. xii, 657 p. maps. 24 cm. At head of title: U.S. Army. Prepared under contract with the Dept. of the Army. *1. Congo (Democratic Republic) I. U.S. Army. II. T.*
DT644.A75   67-115016

McDonald, Gordon C.   III. 4221
Area handbook for the Democratic Republic of the Congo (Congo Kinshasa). Co-authors: Gordon C. McDonald [and others]. Washington; For sale by the Supt. of Docs., U.S. Govt. Print. Off.] 1971. xviii, 587 p. maps. 24 cm. "DA pam 550-67." "One of a series of handbooks prepared by Foreign Area Studies (FAS) of the American University." "In part a revision of the 1962 Area handbook for the Republic of the Congo (Léopoldville) [issued by the Foreign Areas Studies Division of American University]" *1. Zaire. I. American University, Washington, D.C. Foreign Area Studies. II. American University, Washington, D.C. Foreign Areas Studies Division. Area handbook for the Republic of the Congo (Léopoldville) III. T.*
DT644.M24   309.1/675   70-608680

Turnbull, Colin M.   III. 4222
The lonely African. New York, Simon and Schuster, 1962. 251 p. illus. 22 cm. *1. Congo (Leopoldville) — Social life and customs. 2. Social change.*
DT647.T8   916   62-9611

Turnbull, Colin M.   III. 4223
The forest people. New York, Simon and Schuster, 1961. 288 p. illus. 25 cm. *1. Bambute. 2. Ethnology — Congo (Leopoldville) I. T.*
DT650.T8   572.9675   61-12850

Crowe, Sybil Eyre.   III. 4224
The Berlin West African Conference, 1884-1885, by S. E. Crowe. Westport, Conn., Negro Universities Press [1970] x, 249 p. fold. maps. 23 cm. Reprint of the 1942 ed. *1. Berlin. Conference, 1884-1885. 2. Congo — Politics. I. T.*
DT652.C87 1970   967.5/01   75-106870   ISBN:0837132878

Anstey, Roger.   III. 4225
Britain and the Congo in the nineteenth century. Oxford, Clarendon Press, 1962. 260 p. illus. 23 cm. *1. Congo (Leopoldville) — History — Early period to 1908. 2. British in the Congo (Leopoldville) I. T.*
DT655.A7   967.5   63-156

Slade, Ruth M.   III. 4226
King Leopold's Congo; aspects of the development of race relations in the Congo Independent State. London, New York, Oxford University Press, 1962. xi, 230 p. illus., ports., maps (part fold.) 23 cm. "Issued under the auspices of the Institute of Race Relations, London." *1. Congo (Leopoldville) — History — Early to 1908. I. T.*
DT655.S55   967.5   62-4981

Anstey, Roger.   III. 4227
King Leopold's legacy: the Congo under Belgian rule, 1908-1960. London, Oxford U. P., issued under the auspices of the Institute of Race Relations, 1966. xv, 293 p. front. (map) 8 plates (incl. ports., facsim.) 22 1/2 cm. *1. Congo (Leopoldville) — History — 1908-1960. I. T.*
DT657.A6x   967.502   66-70025

Brausch, Georges.   III. 4228
Belgian administration in the Congo. Issued under the auspices of the Institute of Race Relations, London. London, New York, Oxford University Press, 1961. 92 p. 19 cm. *1. Congo (Leopoldville) — History — 1908-1960. I. T.*
DT657.B7   967.5   62-4986

Legum, Colin.   III. 4229
Congo disaster. [Harmondsworth, Middlesex]; Baltimore, Penguin Books [1961] 174 p. 18 cm. (A Penguin special S191) *1. Congo, Belgian — History. 2. Nationalism — Congo, Belgian. I. T.*
DT657.L4   967.5   61-2498

Lemarchand, René.   III. 4230
Political awakening in the Belgian Congo [by] René Lemarchand. Berkeley, University of California Press, 1964. x, 357 p. illus., maps, ports. 25 cm. *1. Congo (Leopoldville) — Politics and government. I. T.*
DT657.L45   320.9675   64-21774

Lumumba, Patrice, 1925-1961.   III. 4231
Congo, my country. With a foreword by Colin Legum. New York, Praeger [1962] 195 p. illus. 23 cm. (Books that matter) Translation of Le Congo, terre d'avenir, est-il menacé? *1. Congo (Leopoldville) — Politics and government. I. T.*
DT657.L813 1962   967.5   62-18269

Merriam, Alan P., 1923-   III. 4232
Congo, background of conflict. [Evanston, Ill.] Northwestern University Press, 1961. 368 p. illus. 23 cm. (Northwestern University African studies, no. 6) *1. Congo (Leopoldville) — Politics and government. I. T.*
DT657.M4   967.5   61-11381

Epstein, Howard M., ed.   III. 4233
Revolt in the Congo, 1960-1964, edited by Howard M. Epstein. New York, Facts on File [1965] 187 p. 21 cm. (Interim history.) A Facts on File publication. *1. Congo (Leopoldville) — History — 1960- I. Facts on File, inc., New York. II. T.*
DT658.E68   967.503   65-29769

Lefever, Ernest W.   III. 4234
Crisis in the Congo; a United Nations force in action [by] Ernest W. Lefever. Washington, Brookings Institution [1965] xii, 215 p. maps (on lining papers) 24 cm. (Studies of U.S. policy and the U.N.) *1. Congo (Leopoldville) — History — 1960- 2. Katanga, Congo (Province) — History. I. T. (S)*
DT658.L4   967.5   65-19040

Young, Crawford.   III. 4235
Politics in the Congo; decolonization and independence. Princeton, N.J., Princeton University Press, 1965. xii, 659 p. maps. 21 cm. *1. Congo (Leopoldville) — Politics and government. I. T.*
DT658.Y6   320.9675   65-10843

Hempstone, Smith, 1929-   III. 4236
Rebels, mercenaries, and dividends; the Katanga story. New York, Praeger [1962] 250 p. illus. 22 cm. (Books that matter) *1. Katanga, Congo (Province) — History. I. T.*
DT665.K3H4   967.5   62-15792

O'Brien, Conor Cruise, 1917- III. 4237
To Katanga and back, a UN case history. [New York] Simon and Schuster [1963, c1962] 370 p. illus. 24 cm. 1. United Nations — Zaire. 2. Katanga, Zaire (Province) I. T.
DT665.K3O27   967.5   63-9271

DT701 – 720   Southwest Africa

Wellington, John H. III. 4238
South West Africa and its human issues, by John H. Wellington. Oxford, Clarendon P., 1967. xxiv, 461 p. front., 13 plates, maps, tables. 22 1/2 cm. 1. Africa, Southwest. 2. Africa, Southwest — Native races. I. T.
DT703.W4   968/.8   67-108668

First, Ruth. III. 4239
South West Africa. Baltimore, Penguin Books [1963] 269 p. maps. 18 cm. (Penguin African library, AP10) 1. Africa, Southwest — History. 2. Africa, Southwest — Native races.
DT711.F48   968.8   64-2821

Aydelotte, William Osgood. III. 4240
Bismarck and British colonial policy; the problem of South West Africa, 1883-1885. [2d ed., rev.] New York, Russell & Russell [1970] xvii, 207 p. ports. 23 cm. 1. Bismarck, Otto, Fürst von, 1815-1898. 2. Africa, Southwest. 3. Germany — Foreign relations — Great Britain. 4. Great Britain — Foreign relations — Germany. I. T.
DT714.A85 1970   327.42/043   73-113161

Rosenthal, Eric. III. 4241
Encyclopaedia of Southern Africa; compiled and edited by Eric Rosenthal. 5th ed. London, New York, F. Warne, 1970. xii, 653 p., 59 plates. illus. (some col.), maps. 21 cm. 1. Africa, Southern — Dictionaries and encyclopedias. I. T.
DT729.R65 1970   916.8   75-114791   ISBN:723212600

DT730 – 995   SOUTHERN AFRICA

Axelson, Eric Victor, ed. III. 4242
South African explorers; selected and introduced by Eric Axelson. London, New York, Oxford University Press [1954] xxv, 346 p. fold. map. 16 cm. (The World's classics, 538) 1. Africa, South — Discovery and exploration. I. T.
DT731.A79   968   A56-643

Livingstone, David, 1813-1873. III. 4243
African journal, 1853-1856. Edited with an introd. by I. Schapera. Berkeley, University of California Press, 1963. 2 v. (xxiii, 495 p.) maps, facsims. 23 cm. 1. Africa, Central — Description and travel. 2. Africa, South — Description and travel.
DT731.L732 1963   916   63-5724

Walker, Eric Anderson, 1886- III. 4244
A history of southern Africa. [London] Longmans [1962] 973 p. maps. "New impression with corrections 1962." Earlier editions published under title: A history of South Africa. 1. Africa, South — History. 2. Africa, South — Politics and government.
DT732.W3x

Wellington, John H. III. 4245
Southern Africa; a geographical study. Cambridge [Eng.] University Press, 1955. 2 v. illus., ports., maps (8 fold. in pockets, part col.) tables. 24 cm. 1. Africa, South — Description and travel. I. T.
DT732.W4   916.8   55-4501

Cole, Monica M. III. 4246
South Africa, by Monica M. Cole. 2nd ed. London, Methuen; New York, Dutton, 1966. xxx, 706 p. plates, maps, tables, diagrs. 24 cm. ([Methuen's advanced geographies]) 1. Africa, South — Description and travel. 2. Africa, South — Industries.
DT733.C6 1966   916.8   67-70598

De Blij, Harm J. III. 4247
Africa South. [Evanston] Northwestern University Press [1962] 399 p. illus. 25 cm. 1. Africa, South — History. 2. Africa, South — Description and travel.
DT733.D4   967   62-14295

DT751 – 995   South Africa (Republic of South Africa)

Kaplan, Irving, 1923- III. 4248
Area handbook for the Republic of South Africa. Co-authors: Irving Kaplan [and others. Washington, For sale by the Supt. of Docs., U.S. Govt. Print. Off.] 1971. xvi, 845 p. maps. 24 cm. "DA pam 550-93." "One of a series of handbooks prepared by Foreign Area Studies (FAS) of the American University." 1. Africa, South. I. American University, Washington, D.C. Foreign Area Studies. II. T.
DT753.K3   916.8   75-608712

Marquard, Leopold, 1897- III. 4249
The peoples and policies of South Africa [by] Leo Marquard. 4th ed. London, New York, Oxford U.P., 1969. xi, 266 p. 21 cm. (Galaxy, book, 296) 1. Africa, South. I. T.
DT753.M37 1969   968   74-453713   ISBN:19285030X

DT759 – 764   ETHNOGRAPHY

Jabavu, Noni. III. 4250
Drawn in color: African contrasts. New York, St Martin's Press [1962, c1960] 208 p. 22 cm. "A personal account of ... [the author's] experiences and impressions of the differences between East and South Africa in their contact with westernisation." 1. Africa, South — Social life and customs. 2. Uganda — Social life and customs. I. T.
DT761.J25 1962   916.8   62-8319

Abrahams, Peter, 1919- III. 4251
Return to Goli. London, Faber and Faber [1953] 224 p. 19 cm. Autobiographical. 1. Africa, South — Native races. 2. Johannesburg — Description. I. T.
DT763.A62 1953   325.260968 (301.451)   53-30755

Cowen, Denis Victor. III. 4252
The foundations of freedom, with special reference to southern Africa. Cape Town, New York, Oxford University Press, 1961. 258 p. 23 cm. 1. Africa, South — Race question. 2. Civil rights — Africa, South. I. T.
DT763.C73   323.40968   61-4332

De Beer, Z. J. III. 4253
Multi-racial South Africa; the reconciliation of forces. Issued under the auspices of the Institute of Race Relations. London, New York, Oxford University Press, 1961. 68 p. 19 cm. 1. Africa, South — Race question. 2. Africa, South — Politics and government. I. T.
DT763.D39   323.168   61-19456

De Kiewiet, Cornelius William, 1902- III. 4254
The anatomy of South African misery. London, New York, Oxford University Press, 1956. viii, 88 p. 19 cm. (The Whidden lectures, 1956) 1. Africa, South — Native races. I. T. (S)
DT763.D4   968   57-13658

Hellmann, Ellen, ed. III. 4255
Handbook on race relations in South Africa. Ed. by Ellen Hellmann, assisted by Leah Abrahams. Pub. for the South African Institute of Race Relations. Cape Town, New York, Oxford Univ. Press, 1949. xii, 778 p. fold. map, diagrs., tables. 25 cm. 1. Africa, South — Race question.
DT763.H4   323.168   49-10258

Kuper, Leo. III. 4256
Passive resistance in South Africa. New Haven, Yale University Press. New York, Kraus Reprint Co., 1971 [c1957] 256 p. illus. 23 cm. 1. Passive resistance — Africa, South. 2. Africa, South — Race question. I. T.
DT763.K8 1971   301.451/968   73-148843

Macmillan, William Miller, 1885- III. 4257
Bantu, Boer, and Briton; the making of the South African native problem. Rev. and enl. ed. Oxford, Clarendon Press, 1963. xviii, 382 p. maps. 22 cm. 1. Africa, South — History. 2. Africa, South — Race question. 3. Bantus. I. T.
DT763.M3 1963   968   63-24832

Neame, Lawrence Elwin. III. 4258
The history of apartheid; the story of the colour war in South Africa. New

York, London House & Maxwell [1963, c1962] 200 p. illus. 23 cm. *1. Africa, South — Race question.*
DT763.N4 1963   323.1   63-12826

Ngubane, Jordan K.   **III. 4259**
An African explains apartheid. New York, Praeger [1963] 243 p. illus. 22 cm. (Books that matter) *1. Africa, South — History. 2. Segregation — Africa, South. 3. Communism — Africa, South. I. T.*
DT763.N45   968.06   63-7569

Patterson, Sheila, 1918-   **III. 4260**
Colour and culture in South Africa; a study of the status of the Cape coloured people within the social structure of the Union of South Africa. London, Routledge and Paul [1953] vi, 402 p. 23 cm. (International library of sociology and social reconstruction) *1. Colored people (South Africa) I. T. (S:International library of sociology and social reconstruction (London))*
DT763.P35 1953   572.968   53-24278

Roux, Edward.   **III. 4261**
Time longer than rope; a history of the black man's struggle for freedom in South Africa. [2d ed.] Madison, University of Wisconsin Press, 1964. xviii, 469 p. maps. 20 cm. *1. Africa, South — Native races. 2. Communism — Africa, South. I. T.*
DT763.R6 1964   968   64-12728

Richards, Audrey Isabel, 1899-   **III. 4262**
Hunger and work in a savage tribe; a functional study of nutrition among the southern Bantu. [1st American ed.] With a pref. by B. Malinowski. Glencoe, Ill., Free Press [1948] xvi, 238 p. 22 cm. *1. Bantus. 2. Food. 3. Society, Primitive. I. T.*
DT764.B2R5x   572.968   A50-9056

Schapera, Isaac, 1905- ed.   **III. 4263**
The Bantu-speaking tribes of South Africa; an ethnographical survey, edited for the (South African) Inter-university committee for African studies by I. Schapera. Contributors: Raymond A. Dart, Clement M. Doke [and others] London, Routledge, 1937. xv, 453 p. illus. (music) XXIV pl. (incl. front.) double map. 25 cm. *1. Bantus. 2. Ethnology — Africa, South. 3. Africa, South — Native races. 4. Bantu languages. I. Inter-university committee for African studies. II. T.*
DT764.B2S39   572.968   38-90

Thomas, Elizabeth Marshall, 1931-   **III. 4264**
The harmless people. [1st ed.] New York, Knopf, 1959. 266 p. illus. 22 cm. *1. Bushmen. 2. Kalahari Desert. I. T.*
DT764.B8T4   916.81   59-5437

Huttenback, Robert A.   **III. 4265**
Gandhi in South Africa; British imperialism and the Indian question, 1860-1914, by Robert A. Huttenback. Ithaca [N.Y.] Cornell University Press [1971] ix, 368 p. illus., map, ports. 22 cm. *1. East Indians in South Africa — History. 2. Gandhi, Mohandas Karamchand, 1869-1948. 3. Great Britain — Colonies — Africa — Administration. I. T.*
DT764.E3H84   320.5   73-124723   ISBN:0801405866

Wilson, Monica (Hunter)   **III. 4266**
Reaction to conquest; effects of contact with Europeans on the Pondo of South Africa. With an introd. by J. C. Smuts. 2d ed. London, New York, Published for the International African Institute by Oxford University Press, 1961. xxiii, 582 p. illus., maps. 22 cm. *1. Pondos. 2. Society, Primitive. I. T.*
DT764.P6W5 1961   572.9686   61-19154

DT765 – 779 HISTORY

Galbraith, John S.   **III. 4267**
Reluctant empire; British policy on the South African frontier, 1834-1854. Berkeley, University of California Press, 1963. 293 p. 25 cm. *1. Africa, South — History. I. T.*
DT766.G3   968.04   63-9801

Keppel-Jones, Arthur.   **III. 4268**
South Africa; a short history. [3d (rev.) ed.] London, Hutchinson University Library [1962, c1961; covered by label: New York, Hillary House] 232 p. 19 cm. (Commonwealth history) *1. Africa, South — History.*
DT766.K4 1962   968   62-6097

Marquard, Leopold, 1897-   **III. 4269**
The story of South Africa, by Leo Marquard. 3rd ed. (revised). London, Faber, 1968. 272 p. 8 plates, illus. 8 maps, ports. 23 cm. 1968 American ed. (New York, Praeger) has title: A short history of South Africa. *1. Africa, South — History. I. T.*
DT766.M4 1968   968   68-101494

Wilson, Monica (Hunter)   **III. 4270**
The Oxford history of South Africa, edited by Monica Wilson and Leonard Thompson. New York, Oxford University Press, 1969-   v. illus. 24 cm. *1. Africa, South — History. I. Thompson, Leonard Monteath, joint author. II. T*
DT766.W762   968   74-77602

Walker, Eric Anderson, 1886-   **III. 4271**
The great trek. 4th ed. London, A. & C. Black [1960] viii, 388 p. illus., 3 col. maps. (2 fold.) port. 23 cm. *1. Africa, South — History — Great trek, 1836-1840. I. T.*
DT773.W3 1960   64-57879

De Kiewiet, Cornelius William, 1902-   **III. 4272**
The imperial factor in South Africa; a study in politics and economics [by] C. W. de Kiewiet. New York, Russell & Russell, 1966. 341 p. 23 cm. "First published in 1937." *1. Africa, South — History. 2. Africa, South — Race question. 3. Africa, South — Economic conditions. I. T.*
DT775.D4 1966   968.04   66-11637

Lockhart, John Gilbert, 1891-   **III. 4273**
Cecil Rhodes; the colossus of southern Africa, by J. G. Lockhart and C. M. Woodhouse. New York, Macmillan [1963] 525 p. illus. 25 cm. *1. Rhodes, Cecil John, 1853-1902. 2. Africa, South — Politics and government — 1836-1909. I. Woodhouse, Christopher Montague, 1917- joint author.*
DT776.R4L62   923.242   63-11803

Williams, Basil, 1867-1950.   **III. 4274**
Cecil Rhodes. New York, Greenwood Press [1968] xi, 353 p. fold. map. 24 cm. Reprint of the 1921 ed. *1. Rhodes, Cecil John, 1853-1902.*
DT776.R4W5 1968   968/.04/0924 (B)   69-14152

Hailey, William Malcolm Hailey, baron, 1872-   **III. 4275**
The Republic of South Africa and the High Commission territories. London, New York, Oxford University Press, 1963. vii, 136 p. map. 20 cm. *1. Basutoland. 2. Bechuanaland. 3. Swaziland. 4. Africa, South — Politics and government — 1909- 5. Africa, South — Native races. I. T. II. T:The High Commission territories.*
DT779.H3   327.680681   64-307

Carter, Gwendolen Margaret, 1906-   **III. 4276**
The politics of inequality; South Africa since 1948 [by] Gwendolen M. Carter. [3d] rev. ed. London, Thames and Hudson [1962, c1958] 541 p. illus., maps. 25 cm. *1. Africa, South — Politics and government — 1948- I. T.*
DT779.7.C3 1962   65-84528

Pienaar, S.   **III. 4277**
South Africa; two views of separate development: Safeguarding the nations of South Africa, by S. Pienaar. Old fallacies with a new look; ignoring the Africans, by Anthony Sampson. London, New York, Oxford University Press, 1960. 81 p. illus. 19 cm. *1. Africa, South — Native races. I. Sampson, Anthony. Old fallacies with a new look.*
DT779.7.P5   323.168   60-2916

Sampson, Anthony.   **III. 4278**
The treason cage; the opposition on trial in South Africa. London, Heinemann [1958] 242 p. illus. 21 cm. *1. Africa, South — Race question. 2. Africa, South — Politics and government. I. T.*
DT779.7.S25   323.1   58-3351

Paton, Alan.   **III. 4279**
South African tragedy; the life and times of Jan Hofmeyr. Abridgment by Dudley C. Lunt. New York, Scribner [c1965] xii, 424 p. col. maps (on lining-papers) ports. 24 cm. First published in 1964 under title: Hofmeyr. *1. Hofmeyr, Jan Hendrik, 1894-1948. 2. Africa, South — Politics and government — 1909- I. T.*
DT779.8.H6P35 1965   968.050924 (B)   65-25406

Luthuli, Albert John, 1898-   **III. 4280**
Let my people go. New York, McGraw-Hill [1962] 255 p. illus. 22 cm. Autobiography. *1. Africa, South — Race question. I. T.*
DT779.8.L8A3   323.168   62-13819

Hancock, William Keith, 1898-   **III. 4281**
Smuts. Cambridge [Eng.] University Press, 1962-68. 2 v. ports., fold. maps (part col.), facsim. 24 cm. *1. Smuts, Jan Christiaan, 1870-1950.*
DT779.8.S6H28   968/.05/0924 (B)   62-52102

Hepple, Alexander, 1904-   **III. 4282**
Verwoerd. Harmondsworth, Penguin, 1967. 253 p. 18 cm. (Political leaders of the twentieth century. Pelican book A913.) *1. Verwoerd, Hendrik Frensch, 1901-1966.*
DT779.8V4H4   968/.05/0924 (B)   67-108656

DT781–995 Other Countries and Regions of Southern Africa

DT781–848 LESOTHO. BOTSWANA

Ashton, Edmund Hugh, 1911-   III. 4283
The Basuto: a social study of traditional and modern Lesotho, by Hugh Ashton. 2nd ed. London, New York [etc.] published for the International African Institute by the Oxford U.P., 1967. xxxii, 359 p. front., 17 plates (incl. map), tables, diagrs. 22 1/2 cm. *1. Basuto (African people) I. International African Institute.*
DT782.A8 1967   916.8/6/03   67-95012

Coates, Austin.   III. 4284
Basutoland. London, H. M. S. O., 1966. xii, 135 p. col. front., illus., 17 plates (incl. col. map) 22 1/2 cm. *1. Basutoland.*
DT782.C6   916.8603   66-2387

Sillery, Anthony.   III. 4285
The Bechuanaland Protectorate. Cape Town, New York, Oxford University Press, 1952. xii, 236 p. maps (1 fold.) tables. 22 cm. *1. Bechuanaland.*
DT791.S5   968.785   52-12752

Young, Bertram Alfred, 1912-   III. 4286
Bechuanaland, by B. A. Young. London, H. M. S. O., 1966. xv, 128 p. col. front., illus., 17 plates (incl. ports., map) 22 1/2 cm. *1. Botswana.*
DT791.Y68   916.81   66-66611

Benson, Mary.   III. 4287
Tshekedi Khama. London, Faber and Faber [1960] 318 p. illus. 23 cm. *1. Tshekedi Khama, 1905-1959.*
DT795.T75B4   923.2687   61-4393

DT850–935 CENTRAL AFRICA (FORMER BRITISH AREAS. DUTCH REPUBLICS. BOER WAR)

Cairns, H. Alan C.   III. 4288
The clash of cultures; early race relations in Central Africa, by H. Alan C. Cairns. New York, Praeger [1965] xvi, 330 p. 23 cm. Revision of thesis, Oxford University. *1. Africa, Central — Race question. 2. Africa, Central — History. 3. British in Africa. I. T.*
DT853.C36   301.2942067   65-25487

Hanna, Alexander John.   III. 4289
The story of the Rhodesias and Nyasaland [by] A. J. Hanna. [2d ed.] London, Faber and Faber [1965] 331 p. illus., maps (part col.) 23 cm. *1. Rhodesia, Northern — History. 2. Rhodesia, Southern — History. 3. Nyasaland — History. I. T.*
DT853.5.H35 1965   66-33124

Wills, Alfred John.   III. 4290
An introduction to the history of Central Africa [by] A. J. Wills. 2nd ed. London, Oxford U.P., 1967. ix, 412 p. 10 maps, table. 23 cm. Map on endpaper. *1. Rhodesia — History. 2. Malawi — History. I. The history of central Africa. II. T.*
DT853.5.W5 1967   968.9   67-77852

Rhodesia and Nyasaland. Federal Information Dept.   III. 4291
Handbook to the Federation of Rhodesia and Nyasaland. Edited by W. V. Brelsford, Director of Information. [London, Cassell, 1960] 803 p. plates (part col.) ports., maps (3 fold. (2 col.) 2 fold. col. charts, coat of arms, diagrs., tables. 25 cm. *1. Rhodesia and Nyasaland. I. Brelsford, William Vernon, ed. II. T.*
DT856.A47   916.89   60-52345

Clegg, Edward Marshall.   III. 4292
Race and politics; partnership in the Federation of Rhodesia and Nyasaland. London, New York, Oxford University Press, 1960. x, 280 p. maps (1 fold.) 23 cm. *1. Rhodesia and Nyasaland — Native races. 2. Rhodesia and Nyasaland — Politics and government. I. T.*
DT856.C58   968.9   60-51033

Gray, Richard, 1929-   III. 4293
The two nations; aspects of the development of race relations in the Rhodesias and Nyasaland. Issued under the auspices of the Institute of Race Relations. London, New York, Oxford University Press, 1960. xvii, 373 p. maps (1 fold.) 23 cm. *1. Rhodesia and Nyasaland — Native races. I. T.*
DT856.G72   968.9   60-53484

Keatley, Patrick.   III. 4294
The politics of partnership. Baltimore, Penguin Books [1963] 527 p. illus. 18 cm. (Penguin African library, AP5) *1. Rhodesia and Nyasaland — Politics and government. 2. Rhodesia and Nyasaland — Native races. 3. Rhodesia — Economic conditions. I. T.*
DT856.K38   968.9   63-5623

Leys, Colin, ed.   III. 4295
A new deal in Central Africa, edited by Colin Leys and Cranford Pratt. New York, Praeger [1960] 226 p. illus. 22 cm. (Books that matter) *1. Rhodesia and Nyasaland. I. Pratt, Cranford, joint ed. II. T.*
DT856.L4   968.9   60-12201

Mason, Philip.   III. 4296
Year of decision; Rhodesia and Nyasaland in 1960. London, New York, Oxford University Press, 1960. 282 p. illus. 20 cm. "Issued under the auspices of the Institute of Race Relations." *1. Rhodesia and Nyasaland — Politics and government. 2. Rhodesia and Nyasaland — Race problems. I. T.*
DT856.M3   342.689   60-50025

Debenham, Frank, 1883-   III. 4297
Nyasaland, the Land of the Lake. London, H. M. Stationery Off., 1955. 239 p. illus. 23 cm. (The Corona library [3]) *1. Nyasaland — Description and travel.*
DT858.D4   916.897   56-25497

Hanna, Alexander John.   III. 4298
The beginnings of Nyasaland and North-eastern Rhodesia, 1859-95. Oxford, Clarendon Press, 1956. viii, 281 p. 2 fold. maps, facsim. 23 cm. A revision of the author's thesis, University of London. *1. Nyasaland — History. 2. Rhodesia, Northern — History.*
DT858.H3 1956   968.97   56-13672

Pike, John G.   III. 4299
Malawi; a geographical study [by] J. G. Pike and G. T. Rimmington. London, Oxford University Press, 1965. xiv, 229 p. illus., maps (part fold.) 26 cm. *1. Malawi — Description and travel. I. Rimmington, Gerald T., joint author. II. T.*
DT858.P5   65-2172

Shepperson, George.   III. 4300
Independent African; John Chilembwe and the origins, setting, and significance of the Nyasaland native rising of 1915, by George Shepperson and Thomas Price. Edinburgh, University Press, 1958. x, 564 p. illus., ports., maps. 23 cm. (Edinburgh University Publications; history, philosophy and economics [no. 8]) *1. Chilembwe, John, d. 1915. 2. Booth, Joseph, 1851-1932. 3. Nyasaland — History. 4. Missions — Nyasaland. I. Price, Thomas, 1907- joint author. II. T. (S:Edinburgh. University. Edinburgh University publications; history, philosophy, and economics, no. 8)*
DT862.S4   968.97   59-420

Kuper, Hilda.   III. 4301
Indian people in Natal. [Pietermaritzburg] Natal, University Press, 1960. 305 p. illus. 22 cm. *1. East Indians in Natal. I. T.*
DT872.K8   301.45   61-725

Krige, Eileen (Jensen) 1904-   III. 4302
The social system of the Zulus. [4. ed.] Pietermaritzburg, Shuter & Shooter [1962] xix, 420 p. illus., maps. 23 cm. *1. Zulus.*
DT878.Z9K7x

Morris, Donald R.   III. 4303
The washing of the spears; a history of the rise of the Zulu nation under Shaka and its fall in the Zulu War of 1879 [by] Donald R. Morris. New York, Simon and Schuster [1965] 655 p. illus., maps, ports. 24 cm. *1. Zululand — History. 2. Chaka, Zulu chief, 1787?-1828. 3. Zulu War, 1879. 4. Cettiwayó, King of Zululand, 1826 (ca.)-1884. I. T.*
DT878.Z9M67   968.3   65-12594

Ritter, E. A., 1890-   III. 4304
Shaka Zulu; the rise of the Zulu Empire. London, New York, Longmans, Green [1955] 383 p. illus. 23 cm. *1. Chaka, Zulu chief, 1787?-1828. 2. Zulus — History.*
DT878.Z9R68   923.1683   55-3983

Patterson, Sheila, 1918-   III. 4305
The last trek; a study of the Boer people and the Afrikaner nation. London,

Routledge & Paul [1957] 336 p. 23 cm. *1. Boers, 2. Africa, South — Race question. I. T.*
DT888.P3 1957   968   57-1319

Van der Poel, Jean. III. 4306
The Jameson Raid. Cape Town, New York, Oxford University Press, 1951. 271 p. map. 22 cm. *1. Jameson's Raid, 1895-1896.*
DT929.V3   968.2   52-12756

Kruger, Rayne, 1922- III. 4307
Good-bye Dolly Gray; the story of the Boer War. Philadelphia, Lippincott, 1960. 507 p. illus. 22 cm. *1. South African War, 1899-1902. I. T.*
DT930.K8 1960   968.2   60-7851

Price, Richard. III. 4308
An imperial war and the British working class; working-class attitudes and reactions to the Boer War, 1899-1902. London, Routledge & K. Paul [1972] 279 p. 23 cm. (Studies in social history) *1. South African War, 1899-1902 — Public opinion. 2. Labor and laboring classes — Great Britain. I. T.*
DT935.P75 1972   968/.204   72-195499   ISBN:0710072295

DT946 – 963   RHODESIA

Mason, Philip. III. 4309
The birth of a dilemma; the conquest and settlement of Rhodesia. Issued under the auspices of the Institute of Race Relations. London, New York, Oxford University Press, 1958. 366 p. illus. 23 cm. *1. Rhodesia — History. 2. Rhodesia — Native races. I. T.*
DT948.M28   968.9   58-4475

Turner, Victor Witter. III. 4310
Schism and continuity in an African society; a study of Ndembu village life, by V. W. Turner. [Manchester, Eng.] Published on behalf of the Rhodes-Livingstone Institute, Northern Rhodesia, by Manchester University Press [1957] xxiii, 348 p. plates, maps, geneal. tables, tables. 22 cm. *1. Ndembu (African tribe) I. T.*
DT955.T83   A58-5778

Creighton, Thomas Richmond Mandell. III. 4311
Southern Rhodesia and the Central African Federation; the anatomy of partnership. New York, Praeger [1961, c1960] 257 p. illus. 23 cm. (Books that matter) First published under title: The anatomy of partnership. *1. Rhodesia, Southern — Native races. 2. Rhodesia and Nyasaland — Native races. I. T.*
DT962.C7 1961   968.9   61-8997

Gann, Lewis H., 1924- III. 4312
A history of Southern Rhodesia; early days to 1934, by L. H. Gann. London, Chatto & Windus, 1965. x, 354 p. fold. col. map. 25 cm. Imprint covered by label: New York, Humanities Press. *1. Rhodesia, Southern — History. I. T.*
DT962.G33   968.9102   66-1288

Leys, Colin. III. 4313
European politics in Southern Rhodesia. Oxford, Clarendon Press, 1959. xi, 323 p. maps, diagrs., tables. 22 cm. *1. Rhodesia, Southern — Politics and government. I. T.*
DT962.L48   968.91   59-1520

Rayner, William. III. 4314
The tribe and its successors; an account of African traditional life and European settlement in Southern Rhodesia. New York, Praeger [1962] 239 p. illus. 23 cm. (Books that matter) *1. Mashona. 2. Matabele. 3. Rhodesia, Southern — History. 4. Rhodesia, Southern — Native races. I. T.*
DT962.R3   968.91   62-9462

Ranger, Terence O. III. 4315
The African voice in Southern Rhodesia, 1898-1930 [by] T. O. Ranger. Evanston [Ill.] Northwestern University Press [1970] xii, 252 p. 23 cm. (The African voice) *1. Rhodesia, Southern — Native races. 2. Rhodesia, Southern — Politics and government. I. T.*
DT962.42.R35 1970b   325.3/42/096891   71-135510
ISBN:0810103206

Rogers, Cyril A. III. 4316
Racial themes in Southern Rhodesia: the attitudes and behavior of the white population, by Cyril A. Rogers and C. Frantz. With a foreword by Sir Robert C. Tredgold. Port Washington, N.Y., Kennikat Press [1973, c1962] xviii, 427 p. illus. 22 cm. *1. Rhodesia, Southern — Race question. 2. Attitude (Psychology) I. Frantz, Charles, joint author. II. T.*
DT962.42.R6 1973   301.45/1042/096891   72-85295
ISBN:0-8046-1724-4

Shamuyarira, Nathan M., 1929- III. 4317
Crisis in Rhodesia [by] Nathan M. Shamuyarira. With a foreword by Sir Hugh Foot. [1st American ed.] New York, Transatlantic Arts [1966, c1965] 240 p. map. 23 cm. *1. Rhodesia, Southern — Politics and government. I. T.*
DT962.7.S5x   968.91/03   67-4336

DT963   ZAMBIA

Cunnison, Ian George, 1923- III. 4318
The Luapula peoples of Northern Rhodesia: custom and history in tribal politics. [Manchester, Eng.] Published on behalf of the Rhodes-Livingstone Institute, Northern Rhodesia, by Manchester University Press [c1959] xiii, 258 p. illus., maps, geneal. tables, tables. 22 cm. *1. Ethnology — Rhodesia, Northern. 2. Lunda (Bantu tribe) I. T.*
DT963.C83   968.94   60-51227

Gann, Lewis H., 1924- III. 4319
The birth of a plural society; the development of Northern Rhodesia under the British South Africa Company, 1894-1914. [Manchester] Published in behalf of the Rhodes-Livingstone Institute, Northern Rhodesia, by Manchester University Press [1958] xxi, 230 p. illus., fold. col. map. 23 cm. *1. Rhodesia, Northern — History. I. T.*
DT963.G3   968.94   59-65059

Gelfand, Michael. III. 4320
Northern Rhodesia in the days of the charter; a medical and social study, 1878-1924. With a foreword by Lord Robins. Oxford, B. Blackwell, 1961. 291 p. illus. 23 cm. *1. British South Africa Company. 2. Rhodesia, Northern. I. T.*
DT963.G4   63-1497

Hall, Richard Seymour, 1925- III. 4321
Zambia [by] Richard Hall. New York, Praeger [1966, c1965] viii, 357 p. maps. 22 cm. (Praeger library of African affairs) *1. Zambia.*
DT963.H3 1966   916.894   65-18325

Kaplan, Irving, 1923- III. 4322
Area handbook for Zambia [by] Irving Kaplan [and others] Washington, For sale by the Supt. of Docs., U.S. Govt. Print. Off., 1969. xvi, 482 p. maps. 24 cm. "DA pam no. 550-75." "This volume is one of a series of handbooks prepared by Foreign Area Studies (FAS) of the American University." *1. Zambia. I. American University, Washington, D.C. Foreign Area Studies. II. T.*
DT963.K26   916.89/4   79-604730

Kaunda, Kenneth David, Pres. Zambia, 1924- III. 4323
Zambia shall be free; an autobiography. New York, Praeger [1963, c1962] 202 p. illus. 19 cm. *1. Zambia — Politics and government. I. T.*
DT963.K3   968.94   63-8622

Gann, Lewis H., 1924- III. 4324
A history of Northern Rhodesia; early days to 1953, by L. H. Gann. New York, Humanities Press, 1969 [c1963] xiv, 478 p. 24 cm. *1. Zambia — History. I. T.*
DT963.5.G3 1969   968.94   73-8132

DT964 – 995   OTHER COUNTRIES, REGIONS

Tabler, Edward E., ed. III. 4325
Trade and travel in early Barotseland; the diaries of George Westbeech, 1885-1888, and Captain Norman MacLeod, 1875-1876. Illustrated with the sketches of William Fairlie. Berkeley, University of California Press, 1963. xii, 125 p. illus. (part. col.) ports., fold. map. 24 cm. (Robins series, no. 2) *1. Barotseland — History — Sources. I. Westbeech, George. II. MacLeod, Norman Magnus, 1839-1929. III. T. (S)*
DT964.B3T3   916.89   63-1720

Barker, Dudley. III. 4326
Swaziland. London, H. M. Stationery Off., 1965. xiii, 145 p. illus. (part col.) fold. map, port. 23 cm. (The Corona library) Label mounted on lining paper: Sales Section, British Information Services, agents for H. M. Stationery Off., New York. *1. Swaziland. (S)*
DT971.B3   916.83036   65-8788

Kuper, Hilda. III. 4327
The Swazi, a South African Kingdom. New York, Holt, Rinehart and

III. 4328

Winston [c1963] vi, 87 p. illus., map. 24 cm. (Case studies in cultural anthropology) *1. Swazi (African tribe) (S)*
DT971.K793   916.834   63-22023

Kuper, Hilda. III. 4328
The uniform of colour; a study of white-black relationships in Swaziland. New York, Negro Universities Press [1969] xii, 160 p. map, 32 plates. 23 cm. Reprint of the 1947 ed. *1. Swaziland — Native races. I. T.*
DT971.K8 1969   301.29/68/3   70-97371   ISBN:837124220

Van der Post, Laurens. III. 4329
The lost world of the Kalahari. New York, Morrow, 1958. 279 p. illus. 21 cm. An account of the author's search for the vanishing Bushmen of South Africa. *1. Bushmen. 2. Kalahari Desert. I. T.*
DT995.K2V3   916.81   58-12303

DU Australia. New Zealand Oceania

DU1 – 65 OCEANIA (GENERAL)
DU1 – 28 Description

Osborne, Charles, 1927-   **III. 4330**
Australia, New Zealand, and the South Pacific; a handbook, edited by Charles Osborne. New York, Praeger [1970] xi, 580 p. illus., maps (part col.) 23 cm. (Handbooks to the modern world) *1. Oceanica. I. T.*
DU15.O8 1970b   919.4   69-12899

Henderson, John William, 1910-   **III. 4331**
Area handbook for Oceania. Co-authors: John W. Henderson [and others. Washington; For sale by the Supt. of Docs., U.S. Govt. Print. Off.] 1971. xiv, 555 p. maps (2 fold.) 24 cm. "DA pam 550-94." "One of a series of handbooks prepared by Foreign Area Studies (FAS) of the American University." *1. Islands of the Pacific. I. American University, Washington, D.C. Foreign Area Studies. II. T.*
DU17.H45   919   75-609070

Beaglehole, John Cawte.   **III. 4332**
The exploration of the Pacific, by J. C. Beaglehole. [3d ed.] Stanford, Calif., Stanford University Press, 1966. x, 346 p. fold. maps. 23 cm. *1. Oceanica — Discovery and exploration. I. T.*
DU19.B4 1966   919.9   66-22429

Sharp, Andrew.   **III. 4333**
The discovery of the Pacific Islands. Oxford, Clarendon Press, 1960. xiii, 259 p. maps. 23 cm. *1. Oceanica — Discovery and exploration. I. T.*
DU19.S48   990   60-50621

Lloyd, Christopher, 1906-   **III. 4334**
Pacific horizons, the exploration of the Pacific before Captain Cook, by Christopher Lloyd. [1st ed.] London, Allen and Unwin [1946] 188 p. front., pl., port., maps (1 double) 22 cm. *1. Oceanica — Discovery and exploration. 2. Pacific ocean. I. T.*
DU20.L72   990   46-8139

Cumberland, Kenneth Brailey.   **III. 4335**
Southwest Pacific; a geography of Australia, New Zealand, and their Pacific island neighbors, by Kenneth B. Cumberland. [Rev. ed.] New York, Praeger [1968] xviii, 423 p. illus., maps. 23 cm. *1. Oceanica — Description and travel — 1951- I. T.*
DU22.C85 1968   919   68-14558

Keesing, Felix Maxwell, 1902-   **III. 4336**
The South seas in the modern world, by Felix M. Keesing with a foreword by J. B. Condliffe. Rev. ed., 1945. New York, Day [1945] xxiv, 391 p. illus. (maps) tables (1 fold.) diagrs. 22 cm. (Institute of Pacific relations. International research series) "Issued under the auspices of the Secretariat, Institute of Pacific relations and the University of Hawaii." *1. Oceanica. I. T.*
DU22.K4 1945   45-9899

Oliver, Douglas L.   **III. 4337**
The Pacific Islands. Illus. by Sheila Mitchell Oliver. Rev. ed. Garden City, N.Y., Doubleday [1961] xxiii, 456 p. illus., maps. 19 cm. (The Natural history library, N14) Anchor books. *1. Islands of the Pacific. I. T. (S)*
DU20.O6 1961   990   61-19508

Wood, Gordon Leslie, 1890-   **III. 4338**
The Pacific Basin; a human and economic geography, by Gordon L. Wood and Patricia McBride. 3d ed. Melbourne, Oxford University Press [1950] xx, 393 p. illus., maps. 20 cm. *1. Pacific area. I. McBride, Patricia Ross, joint author. II. T.*
DU22.W6 1950   919   51-10695

Friis, Herman Ralph, 1905-   **III. 4339**
The Pacific basin; a history of its geographical exploration, edited by Herman R. Friis. New York, American Geographical Society. 1967. xi, 457 p. illus., maps. 26 cm. (American Geographical Society. Special publication no. 38) Some of the papers are revised and enlarged versions of papers presented at a symposium held as part of the Tenth Pacific Science Congress meeting at the University of Hawaii, Aug. 21-Sept. 6, 1961. *1. Pacific area. I. T. (S:American Geographical Society of New York. Special publication no. 38)*
DU23.F7   910.09/18/23   67-12957

Robinson, Kenneth W.   **III. 4340**
Australia, New Zealand and the Southwest Pacific [by] K. W. Robinson. [2nd ed. London] University of London Press [1968] xi, 344 p. maps, plates, tables. 22 cm. (A Systematic regional geography, v. 4) *1. Oceanica — Description and travel — 1951- I. T.*
DU23.R62 1968   919   70-421067   ISBN:340091355

Roberts, Stephen Henry, Sir, 1901-   **III. 4341**
Population problems of the Pacific, by Stephen H. Roberts. New York, AMS Press [1969] xx, 411 p. illus., maps. 23 cm. Reprint of the 1927 ed. *1. Ethnology — Islands of the Pacific. 2. Islands of the Pacific — Population. 3. Islands of the Pacific — Social conditions. I. T.*
DU28.R6 1969   309.1/9   71-99884   ISBN:404005993

Yanaihara, Tadao, 1893-   **III. 4342**
Pacific islands under Japanese mandate, by Tadao Yanaihara. London, and New York, Oxford University Press, 1940. x, 312 p. tables (part fold.) fold. map. 23 1/2 cm. (Institute of Pacific relations. International research series) "The original Japanese edition of this report was published in June 1935." — p. vii. *1. Islands of the Pacific. 2. Mandates — Islands of the Pacific. 3. Caroline islands. 4. Ladrone islands. 5. Marshall islands. I. T.*
DU28.Y32   309.196   41-5535

DU28.3 – 65   History

Grattan, Clinton Hartley, 1902-   **III. 4343**
The Southwest Pacific since 1900, a modern history; Australia, New Zealand, the islands, Antarctica. Ann Arbor, University of Michigan Press [1963] x, 759, xxviii p. maps. 24 cm. (The University of Michigan history of the modern world) *1. Oceanica — History. 2. Antarctic regions — History. I. T. (S:Michigan. University. The University of Michigan history of the modern world)*
DU28.3.G69   990   63-14013

Grattan, Clinton Hartley, 1902-   **III. 4344**
The Southwest Pacific to 1900; a modern history: Australia, New Zealand, the islands, Antarctica. Ann Arbor, University of Michigan Press [1963] 558 p. illus. 25 cm. (The University of Michigan history of the modern world) *1. Oceanica — History. I. T.*
DU28.3.G7   990   60-5670

Maude, Henry Evans, 1906-   **III. 4345**
Of islands and men; studies in Pacific history [by] H. E. Maude. Melbourne, New York [etc.] Oxford University Press, 1968. xxii, 397 p. illus., maps, tables. 23 cm. *1. Islands of the Pacific — History. I. T.*
DU28.3.M38   990   76-365876

West, Francis James.   **III. 4346**
Political advancement in the South Pacific, a comparative study of colonial practice in Fiji, Tahiti, and American Samoa. Melbourne, New York, Oxford University Press, 1961. 188 p. 23 cm. *1. Fiji Islands — Politics and government. 2. Tahiti — Politics and government. 3. American Samoa — Politics and government. 4. Colonies — Administration. I. T.*
DU28.3.W8   325.31   62-3326

Brookes, Jean Ingram.   **III. 4347**
International rivalry in the Pacific islands, 1800-1875. New York, Russell & Russell [1972, c1941] ix, 454 p. fold. map. 25 cm. *1. Oceanica — History. 2. Competition, International. I. T.*
DU29.B75 1972   327/.1/099   77-173529

Grattan, Clinton Hartley, 1902-   **III. 4348**
The United States and the Southwest Pacific. Cambridge, Harvard University Press 1961. 273 p. illus. 20 cm. (The American foreign policy library) *1. U.S. — Foreign relations — Oceanica. 2. Oceanica — Politics.*
DU30.G7   327.7309   61-5583

Morrell, William Parker, 1899-   **III. 4349**
Britain in the Pacific Islands. Oxford, Clarendon Press 1960. xii, 454 p. maps. 23 cm. *1. Gt. Brit. — Colonies — Oceanica. I. T.*
DU40.M6   990   60-3001

Scarr, Deryck.   **III. 4350**
Fragments of empire; a history of the Western Pacific High Commission, 1877-1914. Canberra, Australian National University Press [1967] xviii, 367 p. illus., maps, ports. 25 cm. *1. Gt. Brit. High Commission for Western Pacific Islands. 2. Gt. Brit. — Colonies — Oceanica — Administration. I. T.*
DU40.S32   325.3/42/0996   67-28349

Stanner, W. E. H.   **III. 4351**
The South Seas in transition; a study of post-war rehabilitation and reconstruction in three British Pacific dependencies. Sydney, Australasian Pub. Co. [1953] xiv, 448 p. maps (on lining papers) tables. 22 cm. "Issued under the joint auspices of the Australian Institute of International Affairs and the International Secretariat, Institute of Pacific Relations." *1. Papua. 2. Fiji Islands. 3. Western Samoa. I. T.*
DU40.S8   995   53-10748

Ward, John M.   **III. 4352**
British policy in the South Pacific, 1786-1893; a study in British policy towards the South Pacific Islands prior to the establishment of governments by the great powers. With a foreword by S. H. Roberts. Sydney, Australasian Pub. Co. [1948] xii, 364 p. maps. 23 cm. *1. Oceanica — History. 2. British in Oceanica. I. T.*
DU40.W3   990   48-11775

DU80 – 398   AUSTRALIA

Clark, Charles Manning Hope, ed.   **III. 4353**
Select documents in Australian history. Selected and edited by C. M. H. Clark with the assistance of L. J. Pryor. Sydney, Angus and Robertson [1950- v. 22 cm. *1. Australia — History — Sources. I. T.*
DU80.C58   994   51-2907

Clark, Charles Manning Hope, ed.   **III. 4354**
Sources of Australian history. London, New York, Oxford University Press, 1957. 622 p. 16 cm. (The World's classics, 558) *1. Australia — History — Sources. I. T.*
DU80.C59   994   58-1543

Who's who in Australia.   **III. 4355**
v. [1]- 1922, 1927, 1929 Melbourne, The Herald and Weekly Times, 1922- v. ports. 19-21 cm. Supersedes Fred John's annual...(incorporating Who is who in Australasia) Title varies: 1922, Who's who in the commonwealth of Australia. 1927- Who's who in Australia. Imprint varies: 1922, Sydney, Angus & Robertson Ltd. — 1927- Melbourne, The Herald and Weekly Times Ltd. *1. Australia — Biography.*
DU82.W5   23-288

Learmonth, A. T. A.   **III. 4356**
Encyclopaedia of Australia; compiled by A. T. A. & A. M. Learmonth. London, New York, F. Warne, 1968. viii, 606 p. 31 plates, illus. (incl. 1 col.), col. coat of arms, maps. 21 cm. Maps on lining papers. *1. Australia — Dictionaries and encyclopedias. I. Learmonth, Agnes Moffat, 1925- joint author. II. T.*
DU90.L4   919.4/003   71-367396   ISBN:723209898

The Modern encyclopaedia of Australia and New Zealand.   **III. 4357**
Sydney, Horwitz-Grahame [c1964] 1199 p. illus. (part col.) col. coats of arms, fold. maps. 24 cm. *1. Australia — Dictionaries and encyclopedias. 2. New Zealand — Dictionaries and encyclopedias.*
DU90.M6   65-2387

Fitzpatrick, Kathleen Elizabeth (Pitt) 1905- ed.   **III. 4358**
Australian explorers; a selection from their writings; with an introd. London, New York, Oxford University Press, 1958. 503 p. illus. 16 cm. (The World's classics, 559) *1. Australia — Discovery and exploration. I. T.*
DU97.F53   919.4   58-3255

Moorehead, Alan, 1910-   **III. 4359**
Cooper's Creek. [1st ed.] New York, Harper & Row [c1963] x, 222 p. illus.,

ports., maps. 22 cm. *1. Burke and Wills Expedition, 1860-1861. I. T.*
DU102.M8 1963a   919.4   63-20295

Wood, Thomas, 1892-1950.   **III. 4360**
Cobbers; a personal record of a journey from Essex, in England, to Australia, Tasmania and some of the reefs and islands in the Coral Sea, made in the years 1930, 1931, and 1932. 3d ed. London, New York, Oxford University Press, 1953. 256 p. illus. 23 cm. *1. Australia — Description and travel. I. T.*
DU104.W6 1953   919.4   55-31697

McKnight, Thomas Lee, 1928-   **III. 4361**
Australia's corner of the world; a geographical summation [by] Thomas L. McKnight. Englewood Cliffs, N.J., Prentice-Hall [1970] x, 116 p. maps. 23 cm. (Foundations of world regional geography series) *1. Australia — Description and travel — 1951- 2. Australia — History. 3. New Zealand — Description and travel — 1951- I. T.*
DU105.M26   919.4   73-104897   ISBN:130538019

Farwell, George, 1911-   **III. 4362**
Vanishing Australians. Illustrated by Douglas Maxted. Adelaide, Rigby [1961] 190 p. illus. 22 cm. *1. Frontier and pioneer life — Australia. I. T.*
DU107.F3 1961   62-30440

McLeod, Alan Lindsey, 1928- ed.   **III. 4363**
The pattern of Australian culture. Ithaca, N.Y., Cornell University Press [1963] x, 486 p. illus., ports. 24 cm. *1. Australia — Civilization. I. T.*
DU107.M16   919.4   63-14902

Nadel, George H., 1923-   **III. 4364**
Australia's colonial culture; ideas, men and institutions in mid-nineteenth century eastern Australia. With a foreword by C. Hartley Grattan. Cambridge, Harvard University Press, 1957. xiii, 304 p. illus., facsims. 22 cm. *1. Australia — Civilization. 2. Education — Australia. I. T.*
DU107.N3x   A58-2135

Ward, Russel Braddock.   **III. 4365**
The Australian legend [by] Russel Ward. 2nd ed. Melbourne, London, New York [etc.] Oxford U.P., 1966 [i.e. 1967] xi, 283 p. tables. 20 cm. *1. National characteristics, Australian. I. T.*
DU107.W3 1967   919.4/03   67-87923

DU110 – 117   History

Barnard, Marjorie Faith, 1897-   **III. 4366**
A history of Australia. New York, Praeger [1963] 710 p. illus. 25 cm. (Books that matter) *1. Australia — History.*
DU110.B3 1963   63-12493

Blainey, Geoffrey.   **III. 4367**
The tyranny of distance; how distance shaped Australia's history. Melbourne, Sun Books [1966] x, 365 p. illus., maps. 18 cm. *1. Australia — History. 2. Transportation — Australia. 3. Anthropogeography — Australia. I. T.*
DU110.B54   994   67-89825

Clark, Charles Manning Hope.   **III. 4368**
A history of Australia. [Carlton, Victoria] Melbourne University Press; London, New York, Cambridge University Press [1962, i.e., 1963- v. illus. 24 cm. *1. Australia — History.*
DU110.C48   994   63-5969

Crawford, Raymond Maxwell, 1906-   **III. 4369**
Australia, by R. M. Crawford. 3rd (revised) ed. London, Hutchinson, 1970. 190 p. maps. 23 cm. *1. Australia — History.*
DU110.C73 1970   919.4/03   77-543397   ISBN:009105110X

Fitzpatrick, Brian.   **III. 4370**
The Australian people, 1788-1945. [2d ed. Carlton] Melbourne University Press [1951] viii, 279 p. map (on lining papers) table. 22 cm. *1. Australia — History. I. T.*
DU110.F5 1951   994   52-35541

Grattan, Clinton Hartley, 1902- ed.   **III. 4371**
Australia. Berkeley, Univ. of California Press, 1947. xxviii, 444 p. illus., ports., maps. 23 cm. (The United Nations series) *1. Australia. (S)*
DU110.G8   994   47-12116

Spate, Oskar Hermann Khristian.   **III. 4372**
Australia, by O. H. K. Spate. London, Benn; Melbourne, Lothian, 1968. 328 p. 17 plates (1 fold), illus., 3 maps, ports. 23 cm. (Nations of the modern

Ward, John M.   III. 4373
Earl Grey and the Australian colonies, 1846-1857; a study of self-government and self-interest. [Carlton, Victoria] Melbourne University Press [1958] 496 p. illus. 22 cm. *1. Grey, Henry George Grey, 3d earl, 1802-1894. 2. Australia — Politics and government. I. T.*
DU110.W3   58-59633

Clark, Charles Manning Hope.   III. 4374
A short history of Australia. [New York] New American Library [1963] 256 p. 18 cm. (A Mentor book, MT522) *1. Australia — History. I. T.*
DU112.C54   64-696

Greenwood, Gordon, ed.   III. 4375
Australia; a social and political history. Sydney, Angus and Robertson [1955] xii, 432 p. illus.,ports., maps (2 fold. on lining papers) facsims. 24 cm. *1. Australia — History.*
DU112.G7   994   55-4936

Pike, Douglas.   III. 4376
Australia: the quiet continent. 2nd ed. London, Cambridge U.P., 1970. iii-xii, 244 p., 24 plates. illus., maps, ports. 19 cm. *1. Australia — History. I. T.*
DU112.P5 1970   919.4/3   73-100027   ISBN:521077451

Scott, Ernest, Sir, 1868-1939.   III. 4377
A short history of Australia. 7th ed. rev. by Herbert Burton. Melbourne, G. Cumberlege [1947] xxxii, 462 p. plate, maps (part fold.) 20 cm. *1. Australia — History. I. Burton, Herbert, 1900- ed. II. T.*
DU112.S4 1947   994   48-15394

Shaw, Alan George Lewers, 1916-   III. 4378
The story of Australia. [2d ed., rev.] London, Faber and Faber [1961] 320 p. illus., map. 22 cm. *1. Australia — History.*
DU112.S5 1961   64-238

Ward, Russel Braddock.   III. 4379
Australia [by] Russel Ward. Englewood Cliffs, N.J., Prentice-Hall [1965] viii, 152 p. map. 21 cm. (A Spectrum book: The modern nations in historical perspective) *1. Australia — History.*
DU112.W3   994   65-14998

DU113   DIPLOMATIC HISTORY

Australia in world affairs. 1950-55-   III. 4380
Melbourne, F. W. Cheshire. v. maps. 25 cm. Sponsored by the Australian Institute of International Affairs. Editors: 1950-55- G. Greenwood and N. Harper. *1. Australia — Foreign relations. I. Greenwood, Gordon, ed. II. Harper, Norman Denholm, ed.*
DU113.A7   327.94   58-206

Casey, Richard Gardiner Casey, baron, 1890-   III. 4381
Friends and neighbors. East Lansing, Michigan State College Press [1955] 181 p. illus. 21 cm. *1. Australia — Foreign relations. I. T.*
DU113.C37 1955   327.94   55-7676

Levi, Werner, 1912-   III. 4382
Australia's outlook on Asia. Sydney, Angus and Robertson [1958] 246 p. 23 cm. *1. Australia — Foreign relations — Asia. 2. Asia — Politics. I. T.*
DU113.L45 1958a   327.94095   58-45409

Rosecrance, Richard N.   III. 4383
Australian diplomacy and Japan, 1945-1951. [Parkville] Melbourne University Press; New York, Cambridge University Press [1962] 288 p. 23 cm. *1. Australia — Foreign relations — Japan. 2. Japan — Foreign relations — Australia. I. T.*
DU113.5.J3R6 1962   327.52094   62-5347

DU114   BIOGRAPHY

La Nauze, John Andrew, 1911-   III. 4384
Alfred Deakin; a biography [by] J. A. La Nauze. [Melbourne] Melbourne University Press; New York, Cambridge University Press [1965] 2 v. (xiv, 695 p.) ports. 25 cm. *1. Deakin, Alfred, 1856-1919.*
DU114.D35L29 1965   994.040924 (B)   65-25718

Whyte, William Farmer, 1879-   III. 4385
William Morris Hughes, his life and times. Sydney, Angus and Robertson [1957] 537 p. illus. 25 cm. *1. Hughes, William Morris, 1864- 2. Australia — Politics and government.*
DU114.H8W5   923.294   58-15472

Lang, John Dunmore, 1799-1878.   III. 4386
John Dunmore Lang, chiefly autobiographical, 1799 to 1878, cleric, writer, traveller, statesman, pioneer of democracy in Australia; an assembling of contemporary documents compiled and edited by Archibald Gilchrist. [Limited ed.] Melbourne, Jedgarm Publications, 1951. 2 v. (xviii, 768 p.) illus. 34 cm. *I. T.*
DU114.L3A3   52-35173

DU116 – 117   HISTORY, 20TH CENTURY

Andrews, Eric Montgomery.   III. 4387
Isolationism and appeasement in Australia; reactions to the European crises, 1935-1939 [by] E. M. Andrews. Columbia, University of South Carolina Press [1970] xv, 236 p. illus., maps. 22 cm. *1. Australia — Foreign relations. I. T.*
DU116.A5 1970b   327.94   77-118824   ISBN:872491293

Fitzpatrick, Brian.   III. 4388
The Australian Commonwealth; a picture of the community, 1901-1955. Melbourne, F. W. Cheshire [1956] 337 p. 23 cm. *1. Australia — History.*
DU116.F5   994   57-31383

DU120 – 122   Ethnography

Elkin, Adolphus Peter, 1891-   III. 4389
The Australian aborigines, by A. P. Elkin. Garden City, N.Y., Anchor Books, 1964. xxvi, 369 p. map, plates. 19 cm. (The Natural history library, N37) *1. Ethnology — Australia. 2. Australia — Native races. I. T. (S)*
DU120.E4 1964   572.994   64-19226

Lockwood, Douglas.   III. 4390
We, the aborigines. [Melbourne] Cassell Australia [1963] 259 p. illus., ports. 25 cm. *1. Australia — Native races. I. T.*
DU120.L6   572.994   64-4090

Price, Charles Archibald.   III. 4391
Southern Europeans in Australia. Melbourne, New York, Published in association with the Australian National University [by] Oxford University Press, 1963. xvi, 342 p. maps. 23 cm. *1. Minorities — Australia. I. T.*
DU120.P72   325.94   64-751

DU145 – 398   Local History

Harris, Alexander, 1805-1874.   III. 4392
Settlers and convicts, or, Recollections of sixteen years' labour in the Australian backwoods, by an emigrant mechanic (Alexander Harris?) Foreword by Manning Clark. [Melbourne] Melbourne University Press [1969] xiii, 245 p. 22 cm. Stamped on t.p.: "Distributed in the Western Hemisphere by International Scholarly Book Services, Inc., Zion, Illinois." *1. New South Wales — Social life and customs. I. T.*
DU160.H35 1969   919.4/4   73-462525   ISBN:522839444

Evatt, Herbert Vere, 1894-   III. 4393
Rum rebellion; a study of the overthrow of Governor Bligh by John Macarthur and the New South Wales Corps, including the John Murtagh Macrossan memorial lectures delivered at the University of Queensland, June 1937. Sydney, Angus and Robertson [1955] xvi, 240 p. col. front. 24 cm. *1. Bligh, William, 1754-1817. 2. Macarthur, John, 1767-1834. 3. New South Wales — History. 4. Trials — New South Wales. I. T.*
DU172.B5Ex   A56-6176

Browne, Thomas Alexander, 1826-1915.   III. 4394
Old Melbourne memories [by] Rolf Boldrewood. Introduction and editorial commentary by C. E. Sayers. Melbourne, Heinemann [1969] xviii, 210 p. 22 cm. ([Heinemann pioneer series]) First published by George Robertson,

III. 4395   *Australia. New Zealand. Oceania*   DU212

Melbourne, 1884. *1. Victoria, Australia — Description and travel. 2. Victoria, Australia — Social life and customs. I. T.*
DU212.B75 1969   919.4/5   70-505044

Deakin, Alfred, 1856-1919.   **III. 4395**
The crisis in Victorian politics, 1879-1881; a personal retrospect. Edited by J. A. La Nauze and R. M. Crawford. [Carlton] Melbourne University Press [1957] 94 p. 22 cm. *1. Victoria, Australia — Politics and government. I. T.*
DU222.D4A3   994.03   58-14655

Pike, Douglas Henry, 1908-   **III. 4396**
Paradise of dissent; South Australia 1829-1857. [2nd ed.] Melbourne, Melbourne University Press; London, New York, Cambridge University Press [1967] xii, 580 p. maps (on lining-papers) 25 cm. *1. South Australia — History. I. T.*
DU320.P5 1967   994/.2/02   67-29759

Crowley, Francis Keble.   **III. 4397**
Australia's western third; a history of Western Australia from the first settlements to modern times. London, Macmillan; New York, St Martin's Press, 1960. 404 p. illus. 22 cm. *1. Western Australia — History. I. T.*
DU370.C7 1960   994.1   60-50715

DU400 – 430 NEW ZEALAND

Taylor, Nancy M., ed.   **III. 4398**
Early travellers in New Zealand. Oxford, Clarendon Press, 1959. xxx, [ii], 594 p. maps (1 fold.) 23 cm. *1. New Zealand — Description and travel — Collections. I. T.*
DU400.T3   919.31   60-502

Burdon, Randal Mathews, 1896-   **III. 4399**
New Zealand notables, by R. M. Burdon ... [Christchurch, N.Z.] The Caxton Press, 1941-   v. 22 cm. *1. New Zealand — Biography. I. T.*
DU402.B8   920.0931   A42-3699

Belshaw, Horace, 1898- ed.   **III. 4400**
New Zealand; chapters by W. T. G. Airey [and others] Berkeley, University of California Press, 1947. xvii, 329 p. illus., ports., maps. 23 cm. (The United Nations series) *1. New Zealand. (S)*
DU405.B4   919.31   47-31349

An Encyclopaedia of New Zealand.   **III. 4401**
A. H. McLintock: editor. Wellington, N.Z., R. E. Owen, Govt. printer, 1966. 3 v. illus., maps. 25 cm. *1. New Zealand — Dictionaries and encyclopedias. I. McLintock, Alexander H., ed.*
DU405.E5   919.31/003   67-4443

Beaglehole, John Cawte.   **III. 4402**
The discovery of New Zealand. 2d ed. London, Oxford University Press, 1961. 102 p. illus. 23 cm. *1. New Zealand — Discovery and exploration. I. T.*
DU410.B4 1961   993.101   61-1997

Clark, Andrew Hill, 1911-   **III. 4403**
The invasion of New Zealand by people, plants and animals: the South Island. New Brunswick, Rutgers University Press, 1949. xiv, 465 p. illus., maps. 24 cm. (Rutgers University studies in geography, no.1) *1. South Island, N.Z. — Population. 2. Natural history — South Island, N.Z. I. T. (S:Rutgers University, New Brunswick, N.J. Rutgers University studies in geography, no.1)*
DU410.C5   993.1   49-50393

Dumont d'Urville, Jules Sébastien César, 1790-1842.   **III. 4404**
The voyage of the Astrolabe, 1840; an English rendering of the journals of Dumont d'Urville and his officers of their visit to New Zealand in 1840, together with some account of Bishop Pompallier and Charles, Baron de Thierry, by Olive Wright. Wellington, A. H. & A. W. Reed [1955] 180 p. illus. 25 cm. *1. Astrolabe Expedition, 1837-1840. 2. New Zealand — Discovery and exploration. I. Wright, Olive. II. T.*
DU410.D815   919.31   55-4069

Cumberland, Kenneth Brailey.   **III. 4405**
New Zealand, a regional view [by] Kenneth B. Cumberland [and] James W. Fox. [Christchurch, N.Z.] Whitcombe and Tombs [1959] xvii, 280 p. illus., maps, diagrs., tables. 22 cm. Based on the Post-primary school bulletins of the New Zealand Dept. of Education. *1. New Zealand — Description and travel. I. Fox, James W., joint author.*
DU412.C8   919.31   60-39597

DU420 – 422 History. Biography

Cameron, William James.   **III. 4406**
New Zealand [by] William J. Cameron. Englewood Cliffs, N.J., Prentice-Hall [1965] x, 180 p. maps. 21 cm. (The Modern nations in historical perspective. A Spectrum book.) "Suggested readings": p. 173-175. *1. New Zealand — History. I. T.*
DU420.C3   919.31   64-23570

Cowan, James, 1870-1943.   **III. 4407**
The New Zealand wars: a history of the Maori campaigns and the pioneering period. New York, AMS Press [1969] 2 v. illus., maps, ports. 23 cm. Reprint of the 1922 ed. *1. New Zealand — History — 1843-1870. I. T.*
DU420.C652   993.1/02   76-100514   ISBN:404006000

McClymont, W. G.   **III. 4408**
The exploration of New Zealand. 2d ed. London, Oxford University Press, 1959. 125 p. illus. 23 cm. *1. New Zealand — Discovery and exploration. I. T.*
DU420.M15 1959   993.1   59-3248

Marais, Johannes Stephanus.   **III. 4409**
The colonisation of New Zealand, by J. S. Marais. [1st ed.] reprinted. London, Dawsons, 1968. xii, 384 p. 23 cm. (The Colonial history series) *1. New Zealand — History — To 1843. 2. New Zealand Company, London. I. T.*
DU420.M3 1968   325.3/42/09931   72-385038   ISBN:712901353

Miller, Harold Gladstone, 1898-   **III. 4410**
New Zealand. London, New York, Hutchinson's University Library, 1950. 155 p. map (on lining papers) 19 cm. (Hutchinson's university library: British Empire history, 32) *1. New Zealand — History.*
DU420.M55   993.1   51-3103

Miller, John Owen.   **III. 4411**
Early Victorian New Zealand; a study of racial tension and social attitudes, 1839-1852. London, New York, Oxford University Press, 1958. 217 p. illus. 23 cm. *1. New Zealand — History — 1843-1870. 2. New Zealand — Native races. 3. New Zealand — Social conditions. I. T.*
DU420.M56 1958   993.1   58-3820

Reeves, William Pember, 1857-   **III. 4412**
The Long white cloud (Ao tea roa) by the Hon. William Pember Reeves. 3d ed. rev. and with new matter by the author; to which is added a sketch of recent events in New Zealand, by Cecil J. Wray. London, Allen & Unwin [1924] 390 p. front., illus., plates, ports., 2 fold. maps. 22 cm. "Ao tea roa" the Maori name of New Zealand. *1. New Zealand. 2. Ethnology — New Zealand. I. Wray, Cecil J. II. T.*
DU420.R33 1924   25-5983

Sinclair, Keith.   **III. 4413**
A history of New Zealand. London, New York, Oxford University Press, 1961. 305 p. illus. 23 cm. *1. New Zealand — History.*
DU420.S53 1961   993.1   61-66687

Sinclair, Keith.   **III. 4414**
The origins of the Maori wars. Wellington, New Zealand University Press, 1957. 297 p. illus. 22 cm. *1. New Zealand — History — 1843-1870.*
DU420.S55   993.102   61-35767

Wright, Harrison M.   **III. 4415**
New Zealand, 1769-1840; early years of western contact. Cambridge, Mass., Harvard University Press, 1959. x, 225 p. map. 21 cm. (Harvard historical monographs, 42) Based on thesis, Harvard University. *1. New Zealand — History — To 1843. (S)*
DU420.W75   993.101   59-12979

Gordon, Bernard K., 1932-   **III. 4416**
New Zealand becomes a Pacific power. [Chicago] University of Chicago Press [1960] 283 p. 23 cm. *1. New Zealand — Foreign relations. I. T.*
DU421.G65   327.931   60-15106

Sinclair, Keith.   **III. 4417**
William Pember Reeves, New Zealand Fabian. Oxford, Clarendon Press, 1965. x, 356 p. ports. 23 cm. *1. Reeves, William Pember, 1857-1932. I. T.*
DU422.R45S5   354.931000924 (B)   65-9091

Burdon, Randal Mathews, 1896-   **III. 4418**
King Dick, a biography of Richard John Seddon. [Christchurch, N.Z.] Whitcombe and Tombs, 1955. 339 p. illus. 23 cm. *1. Seddon, Richard John, 1845-1906. I. T.*
DU422.S4B8   923.2931   56-30649

Bloomfield, Paul, 1898-   **III. 4419**
Edward Gibbon Wakefield, builder of the British Commonwealth. [London] Longmans [1961] xi, 378 p. illus., maps. *1. Wakefield, Edward Gibbon, 1796-1862. 2. Gt. Brit. — Colonies — Australia. 3. Gt. Brit. — Colonies — New Zealand.*
DU422.W2B5x

DU423 Ethnography

Buck, Peter Henry, Sir, 1880-   **III. 4420**
The coming of the Maori, by Te Rangi Hiroa, Sir Peter Buck. [2d ed.] Wellington, Maori Purposes Fund Board; [distributed by] Whitcombe and Tombs, 1950. 551 p. illus. 26 cm. *1. Maoris. I. T.*
DU423.B83 1950   993.1   51-25987

Metge, Alice Joan.   **III. 4421**
The Maoris of New Zealand, by Joan Metge. New York, Humanities Press [1967] x, 245 p. illus., map. 19 cm. (Societies of the world) *1. Maoris. I. T.*
DU423.M4x   390/.09931   67-17669

Miller, Harold Gladstone, 1898-   **III. 4422**
Race conflict in New Zealand, 1814-1865 [by] Harold Miller. Auckland, Blackwood & J. Paul, 1966. xxvii, 238 p. illus., maps, ports. 23 cm. "Tri-ocean books." *1. New Zealand — Native races. 2. Maoris. I. T.*
DU423.M5   993.101   66-9283

Williams, John Adrian, 1935-   **III. 4423**
Politics of the New Zealand Maori; protest and cooperation, 1891-1909 [by] John A. Williams. Seattle, University of Washington Press [1969] xi, 204 p. illus., maps, ports. 22 cm. *1. New Zealand — Native races. 2. New Zealand — Politics and government. I. T.*
DU423.W63   320.9/93/1   69-14208

DU490 – 950 OCEANIA (ISLAND GROUPS)

Rivers, William Halse Rivers, 1864-1922, ed.   **III. 4424**
Essays on the depopulation of Melanesia. With a pref. by Sir Everard im Thurn. Cambridge, At the University Press, 1922. [New York, AMS Press, 1972] xviii, 116 p. 19 cm. *1. Melanesia — Social conditions. I. T.*
DU490.R5 1972   301.32/9/93   74-96470   ISBN:0404053572

Elkin, Adolphus Peter, 1891-   **III. 4425**
Social anthropology in Melanesia; a review of research. Published under the auspices of the South Pacific Commission. London, New York, Oxford University Press, 1953. xiii, 166 p. maps. 23 cm. *1. Melanesia. 2. Melanesia — Bibliography. I. T.*
DU500.E4   919.3   53-3743

Trumbull, Robert.   **III. 4426**
Paradise in trust; a report on Americans in Micronesia 1946-1958. New York, W. Sloane Associates, 1959. 222 p. 22 cm. *1. Micronesia. 2. Pacific Islands (Ter.) — Politics and government. I. T.*
DU500.T73   996.5   59-6173

Wiens, Herold Jacob, 1912-   **III. 4427**
Pacific island bastions of the United States. Princeton, N.J., Van Nostrand [1962] 127 p. illus. 20 cm. (Van Nostrand searchlight books, #4) *1. Micronesia. I. T.*
DU500.W5   919.65   62-4182

Buck, Peter Henry, Sir, 1880-1951.   **III. 4428**
Vikings of the sunrise. [Christchurch, N.Z.] Whitcombe and Tombs, 1954. 339 p. illus. 23 cm. *1. Polynesians. 2. Ethnology — Polynesia. I. T.*
DU510.B77 1954   572.996   55-24268

Goldman, Irving, 1911-   **III. 4429**
Ancient Polynesian society. Chicago, University of Chicago Press [1970] xxviii, 625 p. illus., maps. 24 cm. *1. Ethnology — Polynesia. 2. Society, Primitive. I. T.*
DU510.G58 1970   301.29/96   74-116028   ISBN:0226301141

Golson, Jack, ed.   **III. 4430**
Polynesian navigation; a symposium on Andrew Sharp's theory of accidental voyages. [Rev. ed.] Wellington, Polynesian Society, 1963. 153, viii, p. illus., maps (part fold.) 25 cm. ([Polynesian Society, Wellington] Memoir[s] no. 34) Label mounted on t.p.: distributed by Cellar Book Shop, Detroit. Supplement to the Journal of the Polynesian Society, v.71. *1. Polynesia — Discovery and exploration. 2. Navigation, Primitive. I. Polynesian Society, Wellington. Journal. Supplement. II. T. (S)*
DU510.G6 1963   996   64-4236

Heyerdahl, Thor.   **III. 4431**
Sea routes to Polynesia; with editorial notes by Karl Jettmar and a foreword by Hans W:son Ahlman. London, Allen & Unwin, 1968. 3-232 p. 24 plates, illus., col. charts (on lining papers), maps, port. 23 cm. *1. Polynesians. 2. Ethnology — Polynesia. I. T.*
DU510.H453 1968b   301.29/96   68-143823

Keesing, Felix Maxwell, 1902-   **III. 4432**
Social anthropology in Polynesia; a review of research. Published under the auspices of the South Pacific Commission. London, New York, Oxford University Press, 1953. x, 126 p. map (on lining papers) 23 cm. *1. Polynesia. 2. Polynesia — Bibliography. I. T.*
DU510.K43   919.6   53-3744

Sahlins, Marshall David, 1930-   **III. 4433**
Social stratification in Polynesia. Seattle, University of Washington Press, 1958. xiii, 306 p. 23 cm. At head of title: American Ethnological Society. *1. Social classes — Polynesia. I. American Ethnological Society, New York. II. T.*
DU510.S29   572.996   58-10482

Sharp, Andrew.   **III. 4434**
Ancient voyagers in Polynesia. Berkeley, University of California Press, 1964 [c1963] 159 p. illus., maps. 23 cm. *1. Polynesia — Discovery and exploration. 2. Navigation, Primitive. I. T.*
DU510.S5 1964   996   64-2478

Bates, Marston, 1906-   **III. 4435**
Coral Island; portrait of an atoll [by] Marston Bates and Donald P. Abbott. New York, Scribner [1958] 254 p. 24 cm. *1. Ifalik Atoll. I. Abbott, Donald Putnam. II. T.*
DU568.I3B3   919.66   58-10527

Goodenough, Ward Hunt.   **III. 4436**
Property, kin, and community on Truk [by] Ward H. Goodenough. Hamden, Conn., Archon Books [1967] 192 p. maps. 25 cm. Reprint of the 1951 ed. *1. Ethnology — Truk Islands. 2. Property — Truk Islands. 3. Kinship. I. T.*
DU568.T7G6 1967   572.996/6   66-30556

Fortune, Reo Franklin, 1903-   **III. 4437**
Sorcerers of Dobu; the social anthropology of the Dobu Islanders of the Western Pacific. By R. F. Fortune. With an introd. by B. Malinowski. [Rev. ed.] London, Routledge & K. Paul [1963] xxx, 318 p. illus., maps. 25 cm. "Australasian National Research Council Expedition to New Guinea, 1927-8." *1. Dobu Island. 2. Tewara Island. 3. Ethnology — Papua — D'Entrecasteaux Islands. 4. Magic — Papua — D'Entrecasteaux Islands. I. Australian National Research Council. II. T.*
DU580.F6 1963   66-646

Burns, Alan Cuthbert, Sir, 1887-   **III. 4438**
Fiji. London, H. M. Stationery Off., 1963. 255 p. illus. 22 cm. (Corona library [8]) *1. Fiji Islands.*
DU600.B78   919.611   63-4125

Derrick, Ronald Albert, 1892-   **III. 4439**
A history of Fiji. 2d ed. Suva, Print. and Stationery Dept. [1950- v. illus., ports., maps (1 fold.) 26 cm. *1. Fiji Islands — History.*
DU600.D45   996.11   52-40961

Mayer, Adrian C.   **III. 4440**
Peasants in the Pacific; a study of Fiji Indian rural society. Berkeley, University of California Press, 1961. xiii, 202 p. illus., maps. 23 cm. *1. East Indians in the Fiji Islands. I. T.*
DU600.M34   301.45   61-16216

Grimble, Arthur, Sir.   **III. 4441**
A pattern of islands. London, J. Murray [1954] 250 p. illus. 23 cm. American ed. (New York, Morrow) has title: We chose the islands. *1. Gilbert Islands — Description and travel. I. T.*
DU615.G83 1954   919.681   54-4053

DU620 – 629   Hawaii

Pukui, Mary (Wiggin) 1895- III. 4442
Place names of Hawaii and Supplement to the third edition of the Hawaiian-English dictionary, by Mary Kawena Pukui and Samuel H. Elbert. [Honolulu] University of Hawaii Press, 1966. x, 53 p. col. maps. 14 x 21 cm. *1. Names, Geographical — Hawaii. 2. Hawaiian language — Dictionaries — English. I. Elbert, Samuel H., 1907- joint author. II. Pukui, Mary (Wiggin) 1895- Hawaiian-English dictionary. III. T.*
DU622.P8   919.69   66-19326

Clemens, Samuel Langhorne, 1835-1910. III. 4443
Letters from the Sandwich Islands, written for the Sacramento Union by Mark Twain. Introd. & conclusion by G. Ezra Dane. Illus. by Dorothy Grover. Stanford University Press. New York, Haskell House [1972, c1938] xii, 224 p. illus. 23 cm. Reprint of the 1938 ed. *1. Hawaii — Description and travel — To 1950. 2. Hawaii — Social life and customs. I. Sacramento Union. II. T.*
DU623.C6 1972   919.69   72-2113   ISBN:0838314716

Conroy, Francis Hilary, 1919- III. 4444
The Japanese frontier in Hawaii, 1868-1898. Berkeley, University of California Press, 1953. vi, 175 p. 24 cm. (University of California publications in history, v.46) Based on thesis — University of California. *1. Japanese in the Hawaiian Islands. 2. Japan — Foreign relations — Hawaiian Islands. 3. Hawaiian Islands — Foreign relations — Japan. 4. Hawaiian Islands — Emigration and immigration. I. T. (S:California. University. University of California publications in history, v.46)*
DU624.7.C65   (E173.C15 vol. 46 996.9)   A53-9799

Daws, Gavan. III. 4445
Shoal of time; history of the Hawaiian Islands. New York, Macmillan [1968] xiii, 494 p. 24 cm. *1. Hawaii — History. I. T.*
DU625.D28   996.9   68-23630

Joesting, Edward, 1925- III. 4446
Hawaii: an uncommon history. [1st ed.] New York, Norton [1972] 353 p. map. 23 cm. *1. Hawaii — History. I. T.*
DU625.J63   919.69   66-11646   ISBN:0393053822

Kuykendall, Ralph Simpson, 1885-1963. III. 4447
Hawaii: a history, from Polynesian kingdom to American State, by Ralph S. Kuykendall and A. Grove Day. Rev. ed. Englewood Cliffs, N.J., Prentice-Hall [1961] 331 p. illus. 21 cm. *1. Hawaii — History. I. Day, Arthur Grove, 1904- joint author.*
DU625.K778 1961   996.9   61-8894

Bradley, Harold Whitman. III. 4448
The American frontier in Hawaii; the pioneers 1789-1843. Gloucester, Mass., P. Smith, 1968 [c1942] xi, 488 p. map (on lining papers) 21 cm. *1. Hawaii — History — To 1893. I. T.*
DU627.B7 1968   996.9/02   70-3572

Kuykendall, Ralph Simpson, 1885- III. 4449
The Hawaiian Kingdom. Honolulu, University of Hawaii, 1938-   v. illus., ports., maps (on lining papers) 24 cm. Vol.2 published by University of Hawaii Press. *1. Hawaii — History. I. T.*
DU627.K8   996.9   38-28602

Mellen, Kathleen (Dickenson) III. 4450
An island kingdom passes; Hawaii becomes American. New York, Hastings House [1958] 387 p. illus. 21 cm. *1. Hawaiian Islands — History. I. T.*
DU627.16.M4   996.9   58-8276

Russ, William Adam, 1903- III. 4451
The Hawaiian Republic, 1894-98, and its struggle to win annexation. Selinsgrove, Pa., Susquehanna University Press, 1961. viii, 398 p. 24 cm. Sequel to The Hawaiian Revolution, 1893-94. *1. Hawaiian Islands — Politics and government — 1893-1898. I. T.*
DU627.2.R79   996.903   61-6689

Tate, Merze, 1905- III. 4452
Hawaii: reciprocity or annexation. East Lansing, Michigan State University Press, 1968. xii, 303 p. map. 25 cm. *1. Hawaii — Annexation. I. T.*
DU627.4.T27   996.9/02   68-15011

DU647   Guam

Carano, Paul. III. 4453
A complete history of Guam, by Paul Carano and Pedro C. Sanchez. [1st ed.] Rutland, Vt., C. E. Tuttle [1964] xvii, 452 p. illus., maps (1 fold.) ports. 22 cm. *1. Guam — History. I. Sanchez, Pedro C., joint author. II. T.*
DU647.C3   996.7   64-21619

Pomeroy, Earl Spencer, 1915- III. 4454
Pacific outpost; American strategy in Guam and Micronesia, by Earl S. Pomeroy. New York, Russell & Russell [1970, c1951] xx, 198 p. 25 cm. *1. Guam — Politics and government. 2. Micronesia. 3. United States — Foreign relations — 1945-1953. I. T.*
DU647.P6 1970   327.73/0965   73-102529

DU650 – 720   Marquesas. Nauru

Suggs, Robert Carl, 1932- III. 4455
The hidden worlds of Polynesia; the chronicle of an archaeological expedition to Nuku Hiva in the Marquesas Islands. [1st ed.] New York, Harcourt, Brace [1962] 247 p. illus. 22 cm. *1. Marquesas Islands. I. T.*
DU700.S83   919.63   62-9445

Viviani, Nancy. III. 4456
Nauru, phosphate and political progress. Canberra, Australian National University Press, 1970. xiv, 215 p. illus., maps. 23 cm. *1. Nauru. I. T.*
DU715.V55   996/.85   78-93784   ISBN:708107656

DU740   New Guinea

Belshaw, Cyril S. III. 4457
The great village; the economic and social welfare of Hanuabada, an urban community in Papua. Foreword by Raymond Firth. London, Routledge & K. Paul [1957] xviii, 302 p. illus., tables. 22 cm. *1. Hanuabada. 2. Papua — Economic conditions. 3. Papua — Social conditions. I. T.*
DU740.B46 1957   572.995   57-37874

Essai, Brian, 1922- III. 4458
Papua and New Guinea, a contemporary survey. Melbourne, Oxford University Press, 1961. 255 p. illus. 23 cm. *1. Papua. 2. New Guinea (Ter.) I. T.*
DU740.E8   309.195   62-51953

Fisk, Ernest Kelvin, ed. III. 4459
New Guinea on the threshold; aspects of social, political, and economic development, edited by E. K. Fisk. [Pittsburgh,] University of Pittsburgh Press [1968] xii, 290 p. illus., maps. 24 cm. *1. Papua-New Guinea (Ter.) — Politics and government. 2. Papua-New Guinea (Ter.) — Social life and customs. 3. Papua-New Guinea (Ter.) — Economic conditions. I. T.*
DU740.F55 1968   309.1/95   68-21625

Gordon, Donald Craigie, 1911- III. 4460
The Australian frontier in New Guinea, 1870-1885. [1st AMS ed.] New York, AMS Press [1968] 301 p. fold. map. 23 cm. (Studies in history, economics, and public law, no. 562) Series statement also appears as: Columbia University studies in the social sciences, 562. Reprint of the 1951 ed. *1. Papua — History. I. T. (S:Columbia studies in the social sciences, 562.)*
DU740.G55 1968   995   68-58583

Hastings, Peter. III. 4461
Papua/New Guinea; Prospero's other island. Photography by Kerry Dundas and others. [Sydney] Angus and Robertson, 1971. 226 p. col. illus., maps (1 fold.) 24 cm. *1. Papua-New Guinea (Ter.) — Addresses, essays, lectures. I. T.*
DU740.H363   919.5/3/03   79-883696   ISBN:0207121095

Hogbin, Herbert Ian, 1904- III. 4462
Transformation scene; the changing culture of a New Guinea village. London, Routledge & Paul [1951] xii, 326 p. illus., maps. 23 cm. (International library of sociology and social reconstruction) *1. Ethnology — New Guinea. 2. Busama, New Guinea (Ter.) I. T. (S:International library of sociology and social reconstruction (London))*
DU740.H55 1951   572.995   51-8863

Mead, Margaret, 1901- III. 4463
Sex and temperament in three primitive societies. New York, Morrow [c1963] xiv, 335 p. illus. First published 1935. This 1963 edition contains new preface and preface to the 1950 edition. *1. New Guinea — Native races. 2. Society, Primitive. I. T.*
DU740.M39x

Rappaport, Roy A. III. 4464
Pigs for the ancestors; ritual in the ecology of a New Guinea people, by Roy A. Rappaport. New Haven, Yale University Press, 1967 [i.e. 1968] xx, 311 p. illus., map. 25 cm. *1. Tsembaga Maring. 2. Agriculture — Papua-New Guinea (Ter.) I. T.*
DU740.R27   301.29/955   68-13926

Rowley, Charles Dunford. III. 4465
The New Guinea villager; the impact of colonial rule on primitive society and economy [by] Charles Rowley. New York, Praeger [1966] 225 p. front. 25 cm. Maps on lining papers. *1. New Guinea (Ter.) — Politics and government. 2. New Guinea (Ter.) — Economic conditions. 3. Australians in New Guinea (Ter.) I. T.*
DU740.R77 1966   301.29955   66-15452

Souter, Gavin, 1929- III. 4466
New Guinea: the last unknown. New York, Taplinger Pub. Co. [1966, c1963] 296 p. illus., maps (1 fold. col.) ports. 25 cm. *1. New Guinea — History. I. T.*
DU740.S67 1966   995   66-10431

DU744 – 950 Other Islands, A – Z

Matthiessen, Peter. III. 4467
Under the mountain wall; a chronicle of two seasons in the stone age. New York, Viking Press [1962] 256 p. illus. 24 cm. *1. Ethnology — Indonesia-Irian Barat. I. T.*
DU744.M32   919.51   62-16796

Barnett, Homer Garner, 1906- III. 4468
Palauan society, a study of contemporary native life in the Palau Islands. Eugene, Or., 1949. iv, 223 l. map. 28 cm. (University of Oregon publications) *1. Pelew Islands — Social life and customs. I. T. (S:Oregon. University. University of Oregon publication)*
DU780.B3   919.66   49-47200

Danielsson, Bengt. III. 4469
What happened on the Bounty. Translated from the Swedish by Alan Tapsell. London, G. Allen & Unwin [1962] 230 p. illus., maps. 22 cm. Translation of Med Bounty til Söderhavet. *1. Bounty (Ship) I. T.*
DU800.D313   64-56073

Shapiro, Harry Lionel, 1902- III. 4470
The heritage of the Bounty. Rev. with a new postscript. Garden City, N.Y., Doubleday [1962] 301 p. illus. 19 cm. (The Natural history library, N23) Anchor books. *1. Pitcairn Island. I. T.*
DU800.S53 1962   919.618   62-3006

Copp, John Dixon. III. 4471
The Samoan dance of life; an anthropological narrative, by John Dixon Copp with the help of Faafouina I. Pula, and with a pref. by Margaret Mead. Boston, Beacon Press, 1950. xvi, 176 p. 22 cm. *1. Samoan Islands — Social life and customs. I. T.*
DU813.C65   919.61   50-10744

Mead, Margaret, 1901- III. 4472
Coming of age in Samoa; a psychological study in primitive youth for western civilisation, by Margaret Mead ... foreword by Franz Boas ... New York, W. Morrow & company, 1928. xv p., 1 l., 297 p. front., plates. 21 cm. *1. Samoan islands — Social life and customs. 2. Girls. 3. Children in the Samoan islands. 4. Women in the Samoan islands. 5. Adolescence. I. T.*
DU813.M4   919.61   28-20670

Keesing, Felix Maxwell, 1902- III. 4473
Elite communication in Samoa; a study of leadership [by] Felix M. Keesing [and] Marie M. Keesing. Stanford, Calif., Stanford University Press [1956] vii, 318 p. maps, diagrs. 23 cm. (Stanford anthropological series, no. 3) *1. Leadership. 2. Acculturation. 3. Samoan Islands — Civilization. I. Keesing, Marie Margaret (Martin) joint author. II. T. (S)*
DU817.K36   572.9961   56-10904

Davidson, James Wightman, 1915- III. 4474
Samoa mo Samoa; the emergence of the independent state of Western Samoa [by] J. W. Davidson. Melbourne, New York [etc.] Oxford University Press, 1967. xii, 467 p. maps (on lining-papers) 23 cm. *1. Western Samoa — Politics and government. 2. Western Samoa — History. I. T.*
DU819.A2D3   996/.14   68-79458

Oliver, Douglas L. III. 4475
A Solomon Island society; kinship and leadership among the Siuai of Bougainville. Cambridge, Harvard University Press, 1955. xxii, 533 p. illus., ports., maps, music. 25 cm. *1. Siuai (Papuan people) 2. Leadership. I. T.*
DU850.O4   572.9935   54-9776

Adams, Henry, 1838-1918. III. 4476
Tahiti, by Henry Adams; Memoirs of Arii Taimai e Marama of Eimeo, Teriirere of Tooarai, Terrinui of Tahiti, Tauraatua i Amo; Memoirs of Marau Taaroa, last queen of Tahiti. Edited, with an introduction, by Robert E. Spiller. New York, Scholars' Facsimiles and Reprints, 1947. vii, [1] p., facsim.: 2 p. l., 196 p. incl. VII geneal. tables. double map. 25 cm. (Scholars' facsimiles & reprints) Facsimile of the Clements library copy of the Paris (1901) edition. *1. Tahiti — History. I. Arii Taimai, afterwards Mrs. Salmon, b. ca. 1824. II. Spiller, Robert Ernest, 1896- ed.*
DU870.A3 1901a   996.2   47-3845

E1 – 143   America (General)

E11 – 45 GENERAL WORKS. NORTH AMERICA
(Central and South America: see: F1401 – 3799)

Griffin, Charles Carroll, 1902-   **III. 4477**
Program of the history of the New World; III: The national period in the history of the New World, an outline and commentary, by Charles C. Griffin. [1st ed. México, 1961] xxvii, 267 p. illus., maps (part fold.) ports. 23 cm. (Instituto Panamericano de Geografía e Historia. Comisión de Historia. Publicaciones, 103. Instituto Panamericano de Geografía e Historia. Publicación no. 240.) Summary report of the coordinator of the National period of the Program of the history of the New World (Program of the history of America) *1. America — History — Outlines, syllabi, etc. 2. America — History — Bibliography. I. The national period in the history of the New World. II. T. (S: Pan American Institute of Geography and History. Publicación no. 240)*
E16.Gx (F1401.P153 no. 103)   65-4702

Bolton, Herbert Eugene, 1870-   **III. 4478**
History of the Americas; a syllabus with maps, by Herbert Eugene Bolton. New ed. Boston, New York [etc.] Ginn and Company [c1935] xxiii, 365 p. illus., maps. 21 cm. *1. America — History.*
E18.B7 1935   970   35-12171

Bolton, Herbert Eugene, 1870-1953.   **III. 4479**
Wider horizons of American history [by] Herbert E. Bolton. Notre Dame, University of Notre Dame Press [1967, c1939] xiii, 191 p. 21 cm. Reprint of the 1939 ed. *1. America — History. 2. Spain — Colonies — America. 3. America — Discovery and exploration — Spanish. 4. Missions — America. 5. Jesuits in North America. I. T.*
E18.B75 1967   910.03/18/12   67-14884

Greater America; essays in honor of Herbert Eugene Bolton.   **III. 4480**
Berkeley and Los Angeles, University of California Press, 1945. ix, 723 p. port., maps (part fold.) 23 cm. "The essays here presented are abridgments of complete monographs, and as a unit illustrate the scope of the historical studies which Professor Bolton has stimulated ... Their subjects range geographically from Patagonia to Alaska, and chronologically from the age of discovery to the twentieth century." — Pref. Edited by Dr. Adele Ogden and Professor Engel Sluiter. *1. Bolton, Herbert Eugene, 1870- 2. America — History — Collections. 3. Spanish America — History — Collections. I. Ogden, Adele, 1902- ed. II. Sluiter, Engel, 1906- joint ed.*
E18.B76   970.04   A46-509

Zavala, Silvio Arturo, 1909-   **III. 4481**
Program of the history of the New World; II: The colonial period in the history of the New World. Abridgement by Max Savelle. [1. ed. México, Instituto Panamericano de Geografía e Historia, 1962] xxviii, 359 p. illus., ports., maps (part fold.) 24 cm. (Instituto Panamericano de Geografía e Historia. Comisión de Historia. Publicaciones, 102. Instituto Panamericano de Geografía e Historia. Publication no. 239.) *1. America — History — To 1810. I. The colonial period in the history of the New World. II. T. (S: Pan American Institute of Geography and History. Publicación no. 239)*
E18.Zx (F1401.P153 no. 239)   63-3931

Eccles, William John.   **III. 4482**
France in America, by W. J. Eccles. [1st ed.] New York, Harper & Row [1972] xii, 297 p. illus. 22 cm. (The New American Nation series) *1. France — Colonies — America. 2. French in America. 3. America — History — To 1810. I. T.*
E18.82.E25 1972   970.02   72-79657   ISBN:0060111526

Gibson, Charles, 1920-   **III. 4483**
Spain in America. [1st ed.] New York, Harper & Row [1966] xiv, 239 p. illus., maps, ports. 22 cm. (The New American Nation series) *1. America — History — To 1810. 2. Spain — Colonies — America. 3. America — Civilization — Spanish influences. I. T.*
E18.82.G5   980.01   66-21705

Gottmann, Jean.   **III. 4484**
L'Amérique. Paris, Hachette [1954] 470 p. illus. 23 cm. (Les Cinq parties du monde) *1. America — Description and travel.*
E27.G7 1954   54-43950

Mirsky, Jeannette, 1903-   **III. 4485**
The westward crossings; Balboa, Mackenzie, Lewis and Clark. Chicago, University of Chicago Press [1970, c1946] xv, 365, xiii p. illus., facsims., maps, ports. 21 cm. *1. America — Discovery and exploration. 2. North America — Description and travel. 3. Explorers. I. T.*
E27.M5 1970   973.1   70-116434   ISBN:0226531805

Wagley, Charles, 1913-   **III. 4486**
Minorities in the new world; six case studies [by] Charles Wagley and Marvin Harris. New York, Columbia University Press, 1958. xvi, 320 p. 24 cm. *1. Minorities — America. I. Harris, Marvin, 1927- joint author. II. T.*
E29.A1W3   325.73   58-12214

Tannenbaum, Frank, 1893-   **III. 4487**
Slave and citizen, the Negro in the Americas [by] Frank Tannenbaum. New York, Knopf, 1947 [i.e. 1946] xi, 128 p. double tab. 19 cm. "First edition." *1. Negroes in America. 2. Slavery in America. I. T.*
E29.N3T3   326.973   47-61

Jones, Llewellyn Rodwell, 1881-1947.   **III. 4488**
North America; an historical, economic and regional geography, by Ll. Rodwell Jones and P. W. Bryan. [10th ed. rev.] London, Methuen; New York, Dutton [1954] 582 p. illus. 23 cm. *1. North America — Historical geography. 2. North America — Economic conditions. 3. North America — Industries. 4. North America — Description and travel. I. Bryan, Patrick Walter, 1885- joint author.*
E38.J75 1954   917   56-51

Paterson, John Harris.   **III. 4489**
North America: a geography of Canada and the United States [by] J. H. Paterson. 4th ed. London, Oxford U.P., 1970. [16], 319 p., 16 plates. illus., facsim., maps. (some col.) 26 cm. *1. United States — Description and travel — 1940-1960. 2. Canada — Description and travel — 1951- I. T.*
E41.P3 1970   917   77-129101   ISBN:0199130124

Watson, James Wreford.   **III. 4490**
North America, its countries and regions, by J. Wreford Watson. [London] Longmans [1963] xxi, 854 p. illus., maps. 23 cm. (Geographies for advanced study) *1. North America — Description and travel — 1951- 2. Canada — Description and travel — 1951- 3. United States — Description and travel — 1960-*
E41.W25   64057-181

Graham, Gerald Sandford, 1903-   **III. 4491**
Empire of the North Atlantic; the maritime struggle for North America. 2d ed. [Toronto] University of Toronto Press, 1958. xvii, 338 p. maps. 24 cm. Issued under the auspices of the Canadian Institute of International Affairs. *1. North America — History. 2. Gt. Brit. — History, Naval. 3. North Atlantic Ocean. I. T.*
E45.Gx   A59-8093

E51 – 99   PRE-COLUMBIAN AMERICA

Steward, Julian Haynes, 1902- ed.   **III. 4492**
Handbook of South American Indians. Julian H. Steward, editor. Prepared in cooperation with the U.S. Dept. of State as a project of the Interdepartmental Committee on Scientific and Cultural Cooperation. New York, Cooper Square Publishers, 1963- v. illus., maps (part fold.) 24 cm. ([U.S.] Bureau of American Ethnology. Bulletin 143) *1. Indians of South America. I. U.S. Interdepartmental Committee on Scientific and Cultural Cooperation. II. T. (S)*
E51.Sx   980.1   63-17285

Society for American Archaeology. III. 4493
Seminars in archaeology: 1955. Organized and edited by Robert Wauchope, chairman, Richard K. Beardsley [and others] Salt Lake City, 1956. ix, 158 p. illus., maps, tables, 26 cm. (Its Memoirs, no. 11. American antiquity, v.22, no. 2, pt.2.) *1. Archaeology — Congresses. I. Wauchope, Robert, 1909- ed. II. T. (S)*
E51.S7 no. 11   913.082   57-44052

Willey, Gordon Randolph, 1913- ed. III. 4494
Prehistoric settlement patterns in the New World. New York, Wenner-Gren Foundation for Anthropological Research, 1956. viii, 202 p. illus., maps. 26 cm. (Viking Fund publications in anthropology, no. 23) *1. America — Antiquities. 2. Cities and towns, Ruined, extinct, etc. 3. Indians — Antiquities. I. T. (S)*
E53.W5   913.7 (970)   57-134

Judd, Neil Merton, 1887- III. 4495
Men met along the trail; adventures in archaeology, by Neil M. Judd. [1st ed.] Norman, University of Oklahoma Press [1968] x, 162 p. illus., ports. 22 cm. *1. Archaeologists — Correspondence, reminiscences, etc. I. T.*
E57.J8A3   970.1/072/024   68-10300

Anthropological Society of Washington, Washington, D.C. III. 4496
New interpretations of aboriginal American culture history. 75th anniversary volume. Washington, 1955. viii, 135 p. maps., diagr. 24 cm. *1. America — Antiquities. 2. Indians — Culture. 3. Man, Prehistoric — America. I. T.*
E58.A59   913.7 (970)   55-3752

Driver, Harold Edson, 1907- ed. III. 4497
The Americas on the eve of discovery, edited by Harold E. Driver. Englewood Cliffs, N.J., Prentice-Hall [1964] x, 179 p. map. 22 cm. (The Global history series, S-93) A Spectrum book. *1. Indians. I. T.*
E58.D67   970.1   64-15468

Driver, Harold Edson, 1907- III. 4498
Indians of North America [by] Harold E. Driver. 2d ed., rev. Chicago, University of Chicago Press [1969] xvii, 632 p. illus., maps (1 fold. in pocket) 24 cm. *1. Indians of North America. 2. Indians of Mexico. 3. Indians of Central America. 4. Indians of the West Indies.*
E58.D68 1969   970.1   79-76207   ISBN:226164667

Josephy, Alvin M., 1915- III. 4499
The Indian heritage of America [by] Alvin M. Josephy, Jr. [1st ed.] New York, Knopf, 1968. xiii, 384, xiv p. illus., facsims., maps, ports. 25 cm. *1. Indians — History. I. T.*
E58.J6   970.1   68-12661

Sanders, William T. III. 4500
New world prehistory; archaeology of the American Indian [by] William T. Sanders [and] Joseph Marino. Englewood Cliffs, N.J., Prentice-Hall [1970] viii, 120 p. illus., maps. 24 cm. (Foundations of modern anthropology series) *1. Indians — History. I. Marino, Joseph, joint author. II. T.*
E58.S25   970.1   70-98458   ISBN:136161936

Wissler, Clark, 1870-1947. III. 4501
The American Indian, an introduction to the anthropology of the New World. 3d ed. New York, P. Smith, 1950. xvii, 466 p. illus., maps (1 fold.) 21 cm. *1. Indians. I. T.*
E58.W832   970.1   A51-3696

Disselhoff, Hans Dietrich. III. 4502
The art of ancient America; civilizations of Central and South America, by H. D. Disselhoff and S. Linné. [Translated by Ann E. Keep] New York, Crown Publishers [1961] 274 p. illus. (part mounted col.) maps. 24 cm. (Art of the world, non-European cultures; the historical, sociological and religious backgrounds) Translation of Alt-Amerika; die Hochkulturen der Neuen Welt. *1. Indians of Mexico — Art. 2. Indians of Central America — Art. 3. Indians of South America — Art. I. Linné, Sigvald, 1899- joint author. II. T. (S:Art of the world; the historical, sociological and religious backgrounds)*
E59.A7D513   970.67   61-16973

Essays in pre-Columbian art and archaeology, III. 4503
by Samuel K. Lothrop and others. Cambridge, Harvard University Press, 1961. 507 p. illus., maps. 25 cm. *1. Indians — Art. 2. Latin America — Antiquities. 3. Art — Latin America. I. Lothrop, Samuel Kirkland, 1892-*
E59.A7E8   970.67   61-18531

Kelemen, Pál. III. 4504
Medieval American art; masterpieces of the New World before Columbus. 3d rev. ed. New York, Dover Publications [1969] 2 v. (xli, 418 p.) illus., map. 28 cm. *1. Indians — Art. 2. Indians — Antiquities. 3. America — Antiquities. I. T.*
E59.A7K4 1969   709.7   68-28248   ISBN:486219933 (v. 1)

Kubler, George, 1912- III. 4505
The art and architecture of ancient America; the Mexican, Maya, and Andean peoples. Baltimore, Penguin Books [1962] xxv, 396 p. illus., 168 plates, maps. 27 cm. (The Pelican history of art, Z21) *1. Indians — Art. 2. Spanish America — Antiquities. 3. Art — Spanish America. I. T. (S)*
E59.A7K8   970.67   62-5022

Meggers, Betty Jane. III. 4506
Prehistoric America [by] Betty J. Meggers. Chicago, Aldine·Atherton [1972] vi, 200 p. illus. 22 cm. "Based on the chapter entitled Prehistoric New World cultural development, which is included in volume III of the History of mankind: cultural and scientific development." *1. Indians — Culture. 2. Anthropo-geography — America. I. T.*
E59.C95M4   970.1   78-169504   ISBN:0202330273

Rosenblat, Angel. III. 4507
La población indígena de América, desde 1492 hasta la actualidad, por Ángel Rosenblat. Buenos Aires, Institución Cultural Española, 1945. 292 p., 3 l. illus., diagrs. 31 cm. (Stirps quaestionis) "Este trabajo apareció, en su primera elaboración, en Tierra firme, revista de la Sección hispano-americana del Centro de estudios históricos de Madrid, en 1935." — p. 9. *1. Indians — Statistics. I. T.*
E59.S7R6   970.63128   46-23538

E61 – 74 Archaeology

Alcina Franch, José. III. 4508
Manual de arqueología americana. [Madrid] Aguilar [1965] xx, 821 p. illus., maps, plans, ports. 25 cm. *1. America — Antiquities. 2. Indians — Antiquities.*
E61.A46   66-40058

Bosch y Gimpera, Pedro, 1891- III. 4509
L'Amérique avant Christophe Colomb, préhistoire et hautes civilisations [par] Pedro Bosch-Gimpera. Traduit de l'espagnol et préfacé par Raymond Lantier. Paris, Payot, 1967. 237 p. illus. 23 cm. (Bibliothèque historique) Illustrated cover. *1. America — Antiquities. 2. Indians — Antiquities. I. T.*
E61.B7314   67-86417

Bushnell, Geoffrey Hext Sutherland. III. 4510
The first Americans; the pre-Columbian civilizations [by] G. H. S. Bushnell. New York, McGraw-Hill [1968] 144 p. illus. (part col.), maps. 22 cm. (Library of the early civilizations) *1. America — Antiquities. 2. Indians — Antiquities. I. T.*
E61.B95 1968b   970.1   68-17503

Meggers, Betty Jane, ed. III. 4511
Aboriginal cultural development in Latin America; an interpretative review. Edited by Betty J. Meggers and Clifford Evans. Washington, Smithsonian Institution, 1963. vi, 148 p. maps, diagrs., tables. 25 cm. (Smithsonian miscellaneous collections, v.146, no. 1. Smithsonian Institution. Publication 4517.) Part of illustrative matter fold. in pocket. "The papers are revisions of those delivered on August 22, 1962, at the 35th International Congress of Americanists in Mexico City." *1. Latin America — Antiquities. 2. Indians — Antiquities. I. Evans, Clifford, 1920- joint ed. II. International Congress of Americanists, 35th, Mexico City, 1962. III. T. (S:Smithsonian Institution. Smithsonian miscellaneous collections, v. 146, no. 1)*
E61.M4x (Q11.S7 vol. 146, no. 1)   970.1   63-61831

Wauchope, Robert, 1909- III. 4512
Lost tribes & sunken continents; myth and method in the study of American Indians. [Chicago] University of Chicago Press [1962] 155 p. illus. 21 cm. *1. Indians — Origin. I. T.*
E61.W33   970.1   62-18112

Wormington, Hannah Marie, 1914- III. 4513
Ancient man in North America. 4th ed., rev. Denver, Denver Museum of Natural History, 1957. 322 p. illus., fold. map. 23 cm. (Denver. Museum of Natural History. Popular series, no. 4) *1. Man, Prehistoric — America. I. T. (S)*
E61.W6x (QH1.D43 no. 4)   A59-4798

Willey, Gordon Randolph, 1913- III. 4514
An introduction to American archaeology [by] Gordon R. Willey. Englewood Cliffs, N.J., Prentice-Hall [1966-1971] 2 v. illus., maps. 26 cm. (Prentice-Hall anthropology series) *1. America — Antiquities. 2. Indians — Antiquities. I. T.*
E61.W68   970.1   66-10096

William Marsh Rice University, Houston, Tex. III. 4515
Prehistoric man in the New World. [Contributors: Pedro Armillas and others. Editors: Jesse D. Jennings and Edward Norbeck. Chicago] Published for William Marsh Rice University by the University of Chicago Press [1964] x, 633 p. illus., maps, tables. 24 cm. (Rice University semicentennial publications) "The papers ... are lengthier versions of addresses delivered at Rice University on November 9 and 10, 1962, in a symposium entitled 'Prehistoric Man in the New World.'" *1. Indians — Antiquities — Addresses,*

essays, lectures. 2. Man, Prehistoric — America — Addresses, essays, lectures. 3. America — Antiquities — Addresses, essays, lectures. I. Jennings, Jesse David, 1909- ed. II. Norbeck, Edward, 1915- ed. III. T.
E61.W717   913.7082   63-18852

Von Hagen, Victor Wolfgang, 1908-   **III. 4516**
The ancient sun kingdoms of the Americas: Aztec, Maya, Inca. Illustrated by Alberto Beltrán. [1st ed.] Cleveland, World Pub. Co. [1961] 617 p. illus. 25 cm. 1. Aztecs. 2. Mayas — Antiquities. 3. Incas. I. T.
E65.V6   972.01   60-6695

Silverberg, Robert.   **III. 4517**
Mound builders of ancient America; the archaeology of a myth. Greenwich, Conn., New York Graphic Society [1968] viii, 369 p. illus., maps. 26 cm. 1. United States — Antiquities. 2. Mound-builders. 3. Mounds — United States. I. T.
E73.S57   970.4/3   68-12370

E77 – 99 Indians of North America

Driver, Harold Edson, 1907-   **III. 4518**
Comparative studies of North American Indians [by] Harold E. Driver and William C. Massey. Philadelphia, American Philosophical Society, 1957. 165-456 p. illus., maps (1 fold. in pocket) tables. 30 cm. (Transactions of the American Philosophical Society, new ser., v.47, pt. 2) 1. Indians of North America. I. Massey, William C., joint author. II. T. (S:American Philosophical Society, Philadelphia. Transactions, new ser., v.47, pt. 2)
E77.Dx (Q11.P6 n. s., vol. 47, pt. 2)   970.1   57-11239

Debo, Angie, 1890-   **III. 4519**
A history of the Indians of the United States. [1st ed.] Norman, University of Oklahoma Press [1970] xvii, 386 p. illus., ports. 24 cm. (Civilization of the American Indian series) 1. Indians of North America — History. I. T. (S)
E77.D34   970.1   73-108802   ISBN:806109114

Interuniversity Summer Research Seminar, University of New Mexico, 1956.   **III. 4520**
Perspectives in American Indian culture change, edited by Edward H. Spicer. [Chicago] University of Chicago Press [1961] x, 549 p. maps, tables. 24 cm. 1. Acculturation. 2. Indians of North America — The West. 3. Yaqui Indians. 4. Kwakiutl Indians. I. Spicer, Edward Holland, 1906-   , ed. II. Social Science Research Council. III. T.
E77.I55 1956   970.1   60-14358

McNickle, D'Arcy, 1904-   **III. 4521**
The Indian tribes of the United States: ethnic and cultural survival. London, New York, Oxford University Press, 1962. 79 p. illus. 19 cm. Issued under the auspices of the Institute of Race Relations, London. 1. Indians of North America — History. I. T.
E77.M176   970.1   62-5075

Spencer, Robert F.   **III. 4522**
The native Americans; prehistory and ethnology of the North American Indians [by] Robert F. Spencer, Jesse D. Jennings, et al. New York, Harper & Row [1965] xi, 539 p. illus., maps. 26 cm. 1. Indians of North America. 2. North America — Antiquities. I. Jennings, Jesse David, 1909- joint author. II. T.
E77.S747   970.1   65-12683

Swanton, John Reed, 1873-1958.   **III. 4523**
The Indian tribes of North America. Washington, U.S. Govt. Print. Off., 1952. Grosse Pointe, Mich., Scholarly Press, 1968. vi, 726 p. maps (part fold.) 24 cm. (Smithsonian Institution. Bureau of American Ethnology. Bulletin 145) 1. Indians of North America. I. T. (S:United States. Bureau of American Ethnology. Bulletin 145)
E77.S94 1968   970.1   71-9481

Underhill, Ruth Murray, 1884-   **III. 4524**
Red Man's America; a history of Indians in the United States. Illus. by Marianne Stoller. [Chicago] University of Chicago Press [1953] x, 400 p. illus., maps. 25 cm. 1. Indians of North America — History. I. T.
E77.U456   970.1   53-10535

Wissler, Clark, 1870-1947.   **III. 4525**
Indians of the United States. Rev. ed. Revisions prepared by Lucy Wales Kluckhohn. Garden City, N.Y., Doubleday, 1966. 336 p. maps, plates, ports. 24 cm. 1. Indians of North America — History. 2. Indians of North America — Social life and customs. I. Kluckhohn, Lucy Wales, ed. II. T.
E77.W779 1966   970.43   66-12215

Wissler, Clark, 1870-   **III. 4526**
The relation of nature to man in aboriginal America, by Clark Wissler ... New York, Oxford University Press, 1926. xx, 248 p. illus., maps, diagrs. 23 cm. "Lectures ... delivered under the Richard B. Westbrook Free Lectureship Foundation at the Wagner Free Institute of Science, Philadelphia." 1. Indians of North America. 2. Anthropo-geography — North America. I. Wagner free institute of science of Philadelphia. Richard B. Westbrook free lectureship foundation. II. T.
E77.W82   26-9831

Owen, Roger C., comp.   **III. 4527**
The North American Indians; a sourcebook, edited, and with introd., by Roger C. Owen, James J. F. Deetz [and] Anthony D. Fisher. New York, Macmillan [1967] xv, 752 p. illus. 24 cm. 1. Indians of North America — Collections. I. Deetz, James J. F., joint comp. II. Fisher, Anthony D., joint comp. III. T.
E77.2.O93   970.1/08   67-16712

Jennings, Jesse David, 1909-   **III. 4528**
Prehistory of North America [by] Jesse D. Jennings. New York, McGraw-Hill [1968] xi, 391 p. illus., maps. 26 cm. 1. North America — Antiquities. 2. Indians of North America — Antiquities. I. T.
E77.9.J4   970.1   68-13517

E78   BY REGION, A – Z

Giddings, James Louis, 1909-   **III. 4529**
The archeology of Cape Denbigh [by] J. L. Giddings. Providence, Brown University Press, 1964. xv, 331 p. illus., maps, plans, 73 plates. 26 cm. 1. Eskimos — Alaska — Antiquities. 2. Alaska — Antiquities. 3. Excavations (Archaeology) — Alaska. I. T.
E78.A3G5   571.097984   63-10231

Wasley, William Warwick, 1919-   **III. 4530**
Salvage archaeology in Painted Rocks Reservoir, western Arizona [by] William W. Wasley and Alfred E. Johnson. With appendices by Hugh C. Cutler [and] Mary Elizabeth King. Tucson. University of Arizona Press, 1965. xi, 123 p. illus., map, plans. 27 cm. (University of Arizona. Anthropological papers, no. 9) 1. Arizona — Antiquities. 2. Hohokam culture. 3. Excavations (Archaeology) — Arizona. 4. Painted Rocks Reservoir. I. Johnson, Alfred E., joint author. II. T. (S:Arizona. University. Anthropological papers no. 9)
E78.A7W3   970.491   64-63815

Kroeber, Alfred Louis, 1876-1960.   **III. 4531**
Handbook of the Indians of California. Washington, Govt. Print. Off., 1925. St. Clair Shores, Mich., Scholarly Press, 1972. 2 v. (xviii, 995 p.) illus. 22 cm. Original ed. issued as Bulletin 78 of the U.S. Bureau of American Ethnology. 1. Indians of North America — California. I. T. (S:United States. Bureau of American Ethnology. Bulletin 78.)
E78.C15K78 1972   970.4/94   75-108501   ISBN:0403003695

Quimby, George Irving, 1913-   **III. 4532**
Indian culture and European trade goods; the archaeology of the historic period in the western Great Lakes region. Madison, University of Wisconsin Press, 1966. xiv, 217 p. illus., map. 25 cm. 1. Great Lakes region — Antiquities. 2. Indians of North America — Great Lakes region — Antiquities. 3. Indians of North America — Implements. I. T.
E78.G7Q49   970.47   66-13805

Quimby, George Irving, 1913-   **III. 4533**
Indian life in the Upper Great Lakes, 11,000 B.C. to A.D. 1800. [Chicago] University of Chicago Press [1960] 182 p. illus. 25 cm. 1. Indians of North America — Great Lakes region. 2. Great Lakes region — Antiquities. I. T.
E78.G7Q5   970.477   60-11799

Holder, Preston, 1907-   **III. 4534**
The hoe and the horse on the Plains; a study of cultural development among North American Indians. Lincoln, University of Nebraska Press [1970] xii, 176 p. illus., map. 22 cm. 1. Indians of North America — Great Plains. I. T.
E78.G73H6   970.1   70-98474   ISBN:803207301

Ritchie, William Augustus, 1903-   **III. 4535**
The archaeology of New York State [by] William A. Ritchie. Rev. ed. Garden City, N.Y., Published for the American Museum of Natural History [by] the Natural History Press [1969] xxxiv, 357 p. illus., maps. 27 cm. 1. New York (State) — Antiquities. 2. Indians of North America — New York (State) — Antiquities. I. American Museum of Natural History, New York. II. T.
E78.N7R476 1969   970.4/47   68-22501

Drucker, Philip, 1911-   **III. 4536**
Cultures of the north Pacific coast. With an introd. by Harry B. Hawthorn. San Francisco, Chandler Pub. Co. [1965] xvi, 243 p. illus. (part col.) maps. 26

cm. (Chandler publications in anthropology and sociology) *1. Indians of North America — Northwest coast of North America. I. T.*
E78.N78D67   970.49   63-20546

McFeat, Tom, comp.   III. 4537
Indians of the North Pacific Coast, edited and with an introd. by Tom McFeat. Seattle, University of Washington Press [1967, c1966] xv, 268 p. 21 cm. *1. Indians of North America — Northwest coast of North America. I. T.*
E78.N78M3   970.4/98/2   67-13112

Foreman, Grant, 1869-   III. 4538
The Five civilized tribes [by] Grant Foreman; introductory note by John R. Swanton. Norman, University of Oklahoma Press, 1934. 455 p. front., plates, ports., fold. map, facsim. 24 cm. (The civilization of the American Indian) "First edition." "The present volume takes up the narrative where Advancing the frontier left it." — Introductory note. *1. Indians of North America — Oklahoma. 2. Choctaw Indians. 3. Chickasaw Indians. 4. Creek Indians. 5. Seminole Indians. 6. Cherokee Indians. I. T.*
E78.O45F6   34-38511

Haeberlin, Herman Karl, 1890-   III. 4539
The Indians of Puget sound, by Hermann Haeberlin and Erna Gunther. Seattle, Wash., University of Washington Press, 1930. 83 p. illus., map, 2 pl. 25 cm. (University of Washington publications in anthropology. v.4, no. 1) "Originally printed in the Zeitschrift für ethnologie, jahrgang 1924, heft 1-4." — Pref. "The tribes which are the most fully described in these notes are the Snohomish, the Snuqualmi and the Nisqually. There is some information about ... other ... groups." *1. Indians of North America — Puget sound. I. Gunther, Erna, 1896- joint author.*
E78.P8H13   970.4   30-27636

Cotterill, Robert Spencer, 1884-   III. 4540
The southern Indians; the story of the civilized tribes before removal. [1st ed.] Norman, University of Oklahoma Press [1954] xiii, 255 p. ports., maps, facsim. 24 cm. (The Civilization of the American Indian [38]) *1. Indians of North America — Southern States. 2. Five Civilized Tribes. I. T. (S)*
E78.S55C6   970.4 (970.1)   54-5931

Dale, Edward Everett, 1879-   III. 4541
The Indians of the Southwest; a century of development under the United States. [1st ed.] Norman, Pub. in cooperation with the Huntington Library [San Marino, Calif.] by the Univ. of Oklahoma Press, 1949. xvi, 283 p. illus., ports., maps. 24 cm. (The Civilization of the American Indian) *1. Indians of North America — Southwest, New. 2. Indians of North America — Government relations. I. T. (S)*
E78.S7D28   970.4   49-10762

Forbes, Jack D.   III. 4542
Apache, Navaho, and Spaniard. [1st ed.] Norman, University of Oklahoma Press [1960] 304 p. illus. 24 cm. *1. Indians of North America — Southwest, New. 2. Athapascan Indians. 3. Spaniards in the Southwest, New. 4. Southwest, New — History. I. T.*
E78.S7F6   979   60-13480

Kidder, Alfred Vincent, 1885-   III. 4543
An introduction to the study of Southwestern archaeology, with a preliminary account of the excavations at Pecos. And a summary of Southwestern archaeology today, by Irving Rouse. [Rev. ed.] New Haven, Yale University Press, 1962. 377 p. illus. 21 cm. (A Yale paperbound, YW-5) *1. Southwest, New — Antiquities. 2. Pecos, N.M. 3. Pueblo Indians — Antiquities. I. Southwestern archaeology.*
E78.S7K5 1962   970.49   62-6993

McGregor, John Charles, 1905-   III. 4544
Southwestern archaeology, by John C. McGregor. 2d ed. Urbana, University of Illinois Press, 1965. vii, 511 p. illus. 27 cm. *1. Southwest, New — Antiquities. 2. Indians of North America — Southwest, New — Antiquities. I. T.*
E78.S7M15 1965   970.491   65-10079

Spicer, Edward Holland, 1906-   III. 4545
Cycles of conquest; the impact of Spain, Mexico, and the United States on the Indians of the Southwest, 1533-1960. Drawings by Hazel Fontana. Tucson, University of Arizona Press [1962] xii, 609 p. illus., maps. 28 cm. *1. Indians of North America — Southwest, New. 2. Indians of North America, Civilization of. 3. Southwest, New — History. I. T.*
E78.S7S6   970.49   61-14500

Hyde, George E., 1882-   III. 4546
Indians of the High Plains: from the prehistoric period to the coming of Europeans [1st ed.] Norman, University of Oklahoma Press [1959] 231 p. illus. 24 cm. (The Civilization of the American Indian series, 54) *1. Indians of North America — The West — History. I. T.*
E78.W5H97   970.1   59-7963

Wedel, Waldo Rudolph, 1908-   III. 4547
Prehistoric man on the Great Plains. Norman, University of Oklahoma Press [1961] xviii, 355 p. illus., maps. 24 cm. *1. Great Plains — Antiquities. 2. Indians of North America — Antiquities. 3. Indians of North America — Great Plains. I. T.*
E78.W5W4   571   61-9002

E81 – 87   INDIAN WARS

Brown, Dee Alexander.   III. 4548
Bury my heart at Wounded Knee; an Indian history of the American West, by Dee Brown. [1st ed.] New York, Holt, Rinehart & Winston [1971, c1970] xvii, 487 p. illus., music, ports. 25 cm. *1. Indians of North America — The West — Wars. 2. The West — History. 3. Indians of North America — The West. I. T.*
E81.B75 1971   970.5   70-121633   ISBN:0030853222

Lincoln, Charles Henry, 1869- ed.   III. 4549
Narratives of the Indian wars, 1675-1699. New York, Barnes & Noble [1952] xii, 316 p. 2 maps (1 fold.) facsim. 22 cm. (Original narratives of early American history) *1. King Philip's War, 1675-1676. 2. U.S. — History — King William's War, 1689-1697. 3. New England — History — Colonial period — Sources. I. T. (S)*
E82.Lx   A53-9819

Leach, Douglas Edward, 1920-   III. 4550
Flintlock and tomahawk; New England in King Philip's War. New York, Macmillan, 1958. x, 304 p. ports., maps. 22 cm. *1. King Philip's War, 1675-1676. I. T.*
E83.67.L4   973.24   58-5467

Parkman, Francis, 1823-1893.   III. 4551
The Conspiracy of Pontiac; with a new introd. by Samuel Eliot Morison. [10th ed., rev., with additions] New York, Collier Books [1962] 544 p. 18 cm. ([Collier books] BS93) First published under title: History of the conspiracy of Pontiac. *1. Pontiac's Conspiracy, 1763-1765.*
E83.76.P279   973.27   62-16980

Peckham, Howard Henry, 1910-   III. 4552
Pontiac and the Indian uprising [by] Howard H. Peckham. New York, Russell & Russell [1970] xviii, 346 p. illus., facsims., maps, ports. 22 cm. "Reproduced from the second edition of 1961." *1. Pontiac's Conspiracy, 1763-1765. 2. Pontiac, Ottawa chief, d. 1769. I. T.*
E83.76.P4 1970   973.2/7/0924 (B)   70-102528

E90   BIOGRAPHY

Kroeber, Theodora.   III. 4553
Ishi in two worlds; a biography of the last wild Indian in North America. With a foreword by Lewis Gannett. Berkeley, University of California Press, 1961. 255 p. illus., ports., maps. 24 cm. *1. Ishi, d. 1916. 2. Yana Indians.*
E90.I8K7   970.3   61-7530

Two Leggings, ca. 1847-1923.   III. 4554
Two Leggings; the making of a Crow warrior [edited by] Peter Nabokov. Based on a field manuscript prepared by William Wildschut for the Museum of the American Indian, Heye Foundation. New York, Crowell [1967] xxv, 226 p. 22 cm. *1. Crow Indians — Social life and customs. I. Nabokov, Peter, ed. II. Wildschut, William. III. New York. Museum of the American Indian, Heye Foundation. IV. The making of a Crow warrior.*
E90.T9A3   970.3   67-15412

E91 – 95   GOVERNMENT RELATIONS

Jacobs, Wilbur R.   III. 4555
Dispossessing the American Indian; Indians and whites on the colonial frontier, by Wilbur R. Jacobs. New York, Scribner [1972] xiv, 240 p. illus. 24 cm. *1. Indians of North America — Government relations — To 1789. 2. Indians, Treatment of — North America. I. T.*
E91.J3 1972   970.5   72-37179   ISBN:0684128608 0684128594 (pbk.)

Cardinal, Harold, 1945-   III. 4556
The unjust society; the tragedy of Canada's Indians. Edmonton, M. G. Hurtig [c1969] x, 171 [2] p. 21 cm. *1. Indians of North America — Canada — Government relations. I. T.*
E92.C35   970.5   71-857038

Foreman, Grant, 1869-1953. III. 4557
The last trek of the Indians. New York, Russell & Russell [1972, c1946] 382 p. illus. 23 cm. *1. Indians of North America — Government relations. 2. Indians of North America — Land transfers. 3. Indians of North America — Ohio valley. 4. Indians of North America — Indian Territory. I. T.*
E93.F65 1972   970.5   73-173536

Fritz, Henry Eugene. III. 4558
The movement for Indian assimilation, 1860-1890. Philadelphia, University of Pennsylvania Press [1963] 244 p. illus. 22 cm. *1. Indians of North America — Government relations. 2. Indians, Treatment of — U.S. 3. Assimilation (Sociology) I. T.*
E93.F96   970.5   62-11272

Hagan, William Thomas. III. 4559
American Indians. [Chicago] University of Chicago Press [1961] 190 p. illus. 21 cm. (The Chicago history of American civilization) *1. Indians, Treatment of — U.S. 2. Indians of North America — Government relations.*
E93.H2   970.5   61-1555

Mardock, Robert Winston. III. 4560
The reformers and the American Indian. [Columbia] University of Missouri Press, 1971. vii, 245 p. 25 cm. *1. Indians, Treatment of. I. T.*
E93.M37   970.1   79-113815   ISBN:0826200907

Pearce, Roy Harvey. III. 4561
The savages of America; a study of the Indian and the idea of civilization. Rev. ed. Baltimore, Johns Hopkins Press, 1965. xv, 260 p. illus. 24 cm. *1. Indians of North America, Civilization of. 2. Indians in literature. I. T.*
E93.P4 1965   970.1   65-2719

Prucha, Francis Paul. III. 4562
American Indian policy in the formative years: the Indian trade and intercourse acts, 1790-1834. Cambridge, Harvard University Press, 1962. viii, 303 p. 25 cm. *1. Indians of North America — Government relations — 1789-1869. I. T.*
E93.P965   970.5   62-9428

Sorkin, Alan L. III. 4563
American Indians and Federal aid [by] Alan L. Sorkin. Washington, Brookings Institution [1971] viii, 231 p. 24 cm. (Studies in social economics) *1. Indians of North America — Government relations. 2. Indians of North America — Economic conditions. I. T. (S)*
E93.S66   970.5   78-150957   ISBN:0815780443

E98   SPECIAL TOPICS, A – Z

Dockstader, Frederick J. III. 4564
Indian art in America; the arts and crafts of the North American Indian. Greenwich, Conn., New York Graphic Society [1961] 224 p. illus. (part mounted col.) map. 29 cm. *1. Indians of North America — Art. 2. Indians of North America — Industries. I. T.*
E98.A7D57   970.67   60-8921

Inverarity, Robert Bruce, 1909- III. 4565
Art of the Northwest Coast Indians. Berkeley, University of California Press, 1950. xiv, 243 p. illus. (part col.) map (on lining papers) 29 cm. *1. Indians of North America — Art. 2. Indians of North America — Northwest, Pacific. I. T.*
E98.A7I5   970.67   50-62872

Kroeber, Alfred Louis, 1876-1960. III. 4566
Cultural and natural areas of native North America, by A. L. Kroeber. Berkeley, University of California Press, 1939. xi, 242 p. illus., maps (8 fold. in pocket) tables (1 fold. in pocket) 27 cm. (University of California publications in American archaeology and ethnology, v.38) *1. Indians of North America — Culture. 2. Anthropo-geography — North America. I. T.*
E98.C9K73 (E51.C15 vol. 38)   970.6   A40-56

Language, culture, and personality; essays in memory of Edward Sapir. III. 4567
Edited by Leslie Spier, A. Irving Hallowell [and] Stanley S. Newman. Menasha, Wis., Sapir memorial publication fund, 1941. x, 298 p. front. (port.) illus. (maps) plates, diagrs. (1 fold.) 27 x 21 cm. *1. Sapir, Edward, 1884-1939. 2. Indians of North America — Culture. 3. Indians of North America — Languages. I. Spier, Leslie, 1893- ed. II. Hallowell, Alfred Irving, 1892- joint ed. III. Newman, Stanley Stewart, 1905- joint ed.*
E98.C9L25   970.6   42-2294

Morgan, Lewis Henry, 1818-1881. III. 4568
Houses and house-life of the American aborigines. With an introd. by Paul Bohannan. Chicago, University of Chicago Press [1965] xxxi, 319 p. illus., plans. 23 cm. (Classics in anthropology) "Originally published as volume 4 of Contributions to North American ethnology ... 1881." *1. Indians of North America — Social life and customs. 2. Indians of North America — Dwellings. I. T.*
E98.D9M65 1965   970.1   66-13881

Schoolcraft, Henry Rowe, 1793-1864. III. 4569
Indian legends from Algic researches (The myth of Hiawatha, Oneóta, the red race in America) and historical and statistical information respecting the Indian tribes of the United States; edited by Mentor L. Williams. [East Lansing] Michigan State University Press, 1956. xxii, 322 p. 24 cm. *1. Hiawatha. 2. Indians of North America — Legends. 3. Folk-lore, Indian. I. Williams, Mentor Lee, 1901- ed. II. T.*
E98.F6S32   398.22   55-11688

Thompson, Stith, 1885- ed. III. 4570
Tales of the North American Indians, selected and annotated by Stith Thompson. Bloomington, Indiana University Press [1966] xxiii, 386 p. fold. map. 22 cm. (Midland books, MB-91) Reprint of the work first published in 1929. *1. Indians of North America — Legends. 2. Folk-lore, Indian. I. T.*
E98.F6T32 1966   398.2   66-22898

Berkhofer, Robert F. III. 4571
Salvation and the savage; an analysis of Protestant missions and American Indian response, 1787-1862. [Lexington] University of Kentucky Press [1965] xiv, 186 p. 23 cm. *1. Indians of North America — Missions. 2. Protestant churches — Missions — History. 3. Missions — U.S. — History. I. T.*
E98.M6B37   277.3   65-11826

La Barre, Weston, 1911- III. 4572
The peyote cult. With a new pref. by the author. Enl. ed. New York, Schocken Books [1969] xvii, 260 p. illus. 21 cm. *1. Peyotism. 2. Indians of North America — Religion and mythology. 3. Indians of North America — Rites and ceremonies. I. T.*
E98.R3L3 1969   299/.7   78-91546

Slotkin, James Sydney, 1913- III. 4573
The Peyote religion; a study in Indian-white relations. Glencoe, Ill., Free Press, 1956. vii, 195 p. illus., group port., tables. 25 cm. *1. Peyote. 2. Native American Church of North America. 3. Indians of North America — Government relations. I. T.*
E98.R3S5   970.5   56-10583

Underhill, Ruth Murray, 1884- III. 4574
Red man's religion; beliefs and practices of the Indians north of Mexico [by] Ruth M. Underhill. Chicago, University of Chicago Press [1965] x, 301 p. illus., maps, plates. 25 cm. "Intended as a companion to the author's Red man's America." *1. Indians of North America — Religion and mythology. I. T.*
E98.R3U57   299.7   65-24985

Waddell, Jack O., 1933- comp. III. 4575
The American Indian in urban society. Edited by Jack O. Waddell [and] O. Michael Watson. Boston, Little, Brown [1971] xiv, 414 p. maps. 21 cm. (The Little, Brown series in anthropology) *1. Indians of North America — Urban residence. I. Watson, O. Michael, joint comp. II. T.*
E98.S67W3   301.3/6   78-155318

Edmonson, Munro S. III. 4576
Status terminology and the social structure of North American Indians. Seattle, University of Washington Press, 1958. vii, 84 p. 23 cm. At head of title: American Ethnological Society. *1. Indians of North America — Social life and customs. 2. Social classes. 3. Kinship. I. American Ethnological Society. II. T.*
E98.S7E3   970.63233   58-11938

Eggan, Frederick Russell, 1906- III. 4577
The American Indian; perspectives for the study of social change, by Fred Eggan. Chicago, Aldine Pub. Co. [1966] xi, 193 p. 22 cm. (The Lewis Henry Morgan lectures, 1964.) *1. Indians of North America — Social life and customs. 2. Social change. I. T. (S)*
E98.S7E4   970.1   66-15202

Social anthropology of North American tribes, III. 4578
by Fred Eggan [and others] Fred Eggan, editor. Enl. [i.e. 2d] ed. [Chicago] University of Chicago Press [1955] 574 p. illus. 22 cm. "Originally presented to Professor A. R. Radcliffe-Brown." *1. Indians of North America — Social life and customs. 2. Kinship. I. Radcliffe-Brown, Alfred Reginald, 1881- II. Eggan, Frederick Russell, 1906- ed.*
E98.S7S6 1955   572.97   55-5123

E99   TRIBES, A – E

Goodwin, Grenville, 1907-1940. III. 4579
The social organization of the western Apache. With a pref. by Keith H. Basso. Tucson, University of Arizona Press [1969] xxii, 701 p. illus., maps. 24 cm. Reprint of the 1942 ed. *1. Apache Indians — Social life and customs. I. T.*
E99.A6G65 1969   970.3   76-75453

Opler, Morris Edward, 1907- III. 4580
An Apache life-way; the economic, social, and religious institutions of the Chiricahua Indians. New York, Cooper Square Publishers, 1965 [c1941] xvii, 500 p. illus., map. 22 cm. *1. Apache Indians — Social life and customs. I. T.*
E99.A6O73 1965   65-23533

Gulick, John, 1924- III. 4581
Cherokees at the crossroads. Chapel Hill, Institute for Research in Social Science, University of North Carolina, 1960. xv, 202 p. maps, diagrs., tables. 26 cm. (University of North Carolina. Institute for Research in Social Science. Monographs) *1. Cherokee Indians. 2. Indians of North America — North Carolina. I. T. (S:North Carolina. University. Institute for Research in Social Science. Monographs)*
E99.C5G8   970.3   60-63087

Wardell, Morris L., 1889- III. 4582
A political history of the Cherokee nation, 1838-1907, by Morris L. Wardell. [Norman, University of Oklahoma Press, 1938] 72 p. 23 cm. Part of thesis — University of Chicago, 1938. "Private edition, distributed by the University of Chicago libraries, Chicago, Illinois." "Reprinted from A political history of the Cherokee nation, 1838-1907, no. 17 of the Civilization of the American Indian series, University of Oklahoma Press, Norman, Oklahoma." *1. Cherokee Indians — History. I. T.*
E99.C5W28   970.3   38-39084

Llewellyn, Karl Nickerson, 1893- III. 4583
The Cheyenne way; conflict and case law in primitive jurisprudence, by K. N. Llewellyn and E. Adamson Hoebel. Norman, University of Oklahoma Press, 1941. ix, 360 p. front., plates, ports. 24 cm. (The Civilization of the American Indian [21]) *1. Law, Cheyenne. I. Hoebel, Edward Adamson, 1906- joint author. II. T.*
E99.C53L55   970.634   41-23735

Gibson, Arrell Morgan. III. 4584
The Chickasaws, by Arrell M. Gibson. Norman, University of Oklahoma Press [1971] xv, 312 p. illus., maps, ports. 24 cm. (The Civilization of the American Indian series, v. 109) *1. Chickasaw Indians. I. T. (S)*
E99.C55G5   970.3   76-145499   ISBN:0806109459

Debo, Angie, 1890- III. 4585
The rise and fall of the Choctaw Republic. [2d ed.] Norman, University of Oklahoma Press [1961] xviii, 314 p. illus., ports., maps, facsim. 24 cm. (The Civilization of the American Indian [6]) *1. Choctaw Indians. 2. Choctaw Indians — Government relations. I. T. (S:The Civilization of the American Indian series [6])*
E99.C8D4 1961   970.3   61-7973

Lowie, Robert Harry, 1883- III. 4586
The Crow Indians, by Robert H. Lowie. New York, Farrar & Rinehart [c1935] xxii, 350 p. front., illus., plates, ports. 24 cm. *1. Crow Indians. 2. Indians of North America — Social life and customs.*
E99.C92L913   970.3   35-9409

Hassrick, Royal B. III. 4587
The Sioux; life and customs of a warrior society. In collaboration with Dorothy Maxwell and Cile M. Bach. [1st ed.] Norman, University of Oklahoma Press [1964] xx, 337 p. illus., maps. 23 cm. (The Civilization f the American Indian series, 72) *1. Dakota Indians. I. T. (S)*
E99.D1H3   970.3   64-11331

Balikci, Asen, 1929- III. 4588
The Netsilik Eskimo. [1st ed.] Garden City, N.Y., Natural History Press, 1970. xxiv, 264 p. illus., col. map (on lining papers) 22 cm. Published for the American Museum of Natural History. *1. Eskimos — Northwest Territories, Can. I. American Museum of Natural History, New York. II. T.*
E99.E7B16   970.4/12/2   71-114660

Bandi, Hans Georg. III. 4589
Eskimo prehistory. Translated by Ann E. Keep. College, University of Alaska Press; distributed by University of Washington Press. Seattle [1969] xii, 226 p. illus., maps. 24 cm. (Studies of northern peoples, no. 2) Translation of Urgeschichte der Eskimo. *1. Arctic regions — Antiquities. 2. Eskimos — Antiquities. I. T. (S:Alaska. University. Dept. of Anthropology and Geography. Studies of northern peoples, no. 2)*
E99.E7B173   970.3   75-101405

Honigmann, John Joseph. III. 4590
Eskimo townsmen, by John J. and Irma Honigmann. Ottawa, Canadian Research Centre for Anthropology, University of Ottawa, 1965. xix, 278 p. illus., maps, ports. 23 cm. "Material for this report was collected ... from March 1 to August 27, 1963 [in Frobisher Bay] while under contract to the Northern Coordination and Research Centre, Department of Northern Affairs and National Resources." *1. Eskimos — Baffin Island — Social life and customs. 2. Frobisher Bay, Northwest Territories (Trading Post — Social life and customs. I. Honigmann, Irma, joint author. II. Canada. Northern Co-ordination and Research Centre. III. Ottawa. University. Canadian Research Centre for Anthropology. IV. T.*
E99.E7H77   970.4129   66-75766

Oswalt, Wendell H. III. 4591
Alaskan Eskimos [by] Wendell H. Oswalt. San Francisco, Chandler Pub. Co.; distributors: Science Research Associates, Chicago [1967] xv, 297 p. illus., maps. 21 cm. (Chandler publications in anthropology and sociology) *1. Eskimos — Alaska. I. T.*
E99.E7O783   970.4/98   67-18215

Ray, Dorothy Jean. III. 4592
Eskimo masks: art and ceremony. Photos. by Alfred A. Blaker. Seattle, University of Washington Press [1967] vii, 246 p. illus. (part col.), map. 25 cm. Text includes illustrations of the entire Lowie Museum collection. *1. Eskimos — Art. 2. Eskimos — Religion and mythology. 3. Indians of North America — Masks — Exhibitions. I. California. University. Robert H. Lowie Museum of Anthropology. II. T.*
E99.E7R28   970.1   66-19570

Spencer, Robert F. III. 4593
The North Alaskan Eskimo; a study in ecology and society. Washington, U.S. Govt. Print. Off., 1959. vi, 490 p. illus., maps (part fold.) 24 cm. ([U.S.] Bureau of American Ethnology. Bulletin 171) *1. Eskimos — Alaska. I. T. (S)*
E99.E7S65 (E51.U6 no. 171)   572.9798   59-61386

Weyer, Edward Moffat, 1904- III. 4594
The Eskimos; their environment and folkways. [Hamden, Conn.] Archon Books, 1969 [c1932] xvii, 491 p. illus., maps (part fold.) 24 cm. *1. Eskimos.*
E99.E7W48 1969   919.8   77-91393   ISBN:208008373

E99   TRIBES, F – M

Dockstader, Frederick J. III. 4595
The kachina and the white man; a study of the influences of white culture on the Hopi kachina cult. Illustrated by the author. [Bloomfield Hills, Cranbrook Institute of Science, 1954] xiv, 185 p. illus. (part col.) maps. 24 cm. (Cranbrook Institute of Science [Bloomfield Hills, Mich.] Bulletin 35) An earlier version was published as the author's dissertation, Western Reserve University, under title: White influences on the Hopi kachina cult. *1. Katcinas. 2. Hopi Indians — Religion and mythology. 3. Acculturation. I. T. (S)*
E99.H7D65 1954 (Q11.C95 no. 35)   970.62 (970.1 299.7)   54-6199

Nagata, Shuichi, 1931- III. 4596
Modern transformations of Moenkopi pueblo. Urbana, University of Illinois Press [1970] xvii, 336 p. illus., maps. 23 cm. (Illinois studies in anthropology, no. 6) "Originally submitted to ... the University of Illinois ... for a Ph.D. degree in anthropology." *1. Moenkopi. 2. Hopi Indians — Social conditions. I. T. (S)*
E99.H7N3   301.29/791/3   70-76829   ISBN:0252000315

O'Kane, Walter Collins, 1877- III. 4597
The Hopis: portrait of a desert people; with photos. in color by the author. [1st ed.] Norman, University of Oklahoma Press [1953] xii, 267 p. col. ports. 26 cm. (The Civilization of the American Indian) *1. Hopi Indians. 2. Indians of North America — Portraits. (S)*
E99.H7O54   970.3 (970.1)   53-5477

Thompson, Laura, 1905- III. 4598
Culture in crisis; a study of the Hopi Indians. With a foreword by John Collier, & a chapter from the writings of Benjamin Lee Whorf. New York, Harper [1950] xxiv, 221 p. illus., col. map. 25 cm. *1. Hopi Indians. I. T.*
E99.H7T42   970.3   50-10993

Thompson, Laura, 1905- III. 4599
The Hopi way, by Laura Thompson and Alice Joseph. With a foreword by John Collier. New York, Russell & Russell, 1965. 151 p. illus., maps. 24 cm. "The work is part of the results of the Indian Education Research Project, sponsored jointly by the Committee on Human Development of the University of Chicago and the United States Office of Indian Affairs." "First published in 1944." *1. Hopi Indians. I. Joseph, Alice. II. Chicago. University. Committee on Human Development. III. U.S. Bureau of Indian Affairs. IV. T.*
E99.H7T45 1965   970.3   65-18836

Osgood, Cornelius, 1905- III. 4600
Ingalik material culture. New Haven, Human Relations Area Files Press, 1970. 500 p. illus. (part col.), maps. 25 cm. (Yale University publications in anthropology, no. 22) Reprint of the 1940 ed. *1. Ingalik Indians. I. T. (S:Yale University. Dept. of Anthropology. Yale University publications in anthropology, no. 22)*
E99.I5O8x (GN2.Y3 no. 22, 1970)   670   77-118248

Graymont, Barbara. III. 4601
The Iroquois in the American Revolution. [1st ed.] [Syracuse, N.Y.] Syracuse University Press, 1972. x, 359 p. illus. 23 cm. (A New York State study) *1. Iroquois Indians — History. 2. New York (State) — History — Revolution. I. T.*
E99.I7G67   973.3/43   73-170096   ISBN:0815600836

Hunt, George T. III. 4602
The wars of the Iroquois; a study in intertribal trade relations [by] George T. Hunt. Madison, The University of Wisconsin Press [c1940] 209 p. 24 cm. Map on lining-papers. *1. Iroquois Indians — Wars. 2. Indians of North America — Commerce. I. Intertribal trade relations. II. T.*
E99.I7H8   970.3   40-3755

Honigmann, John Joseph. III. 4603
The Kaska Indians: an ethnographic reconstruction. New Haven, Published for the Dept. of Anthropology, Yale University, by the Yale University Press, 1954. 163 p. illus., maps. 25 cm. (Yale University publications in anthropology, no. 51) *1. Kaska Indians. (S:Yale University. Dept. of Anthropology. Yale University publications in anthropology, no. 51)*
E99.K26H6x (GN2.Y3 no. 51)   A55-8638

Cressman, Luther Sheeleigh, 1897- III. 4604
Klamath prehistory; the prehistory of the culture of the Klamath Lake area, Oregon. With appendices by William G. Haag and William S. Laughlin. Philadelphia, American Philosophical Society, 1956. 375-513 p. illus., maps, diagrs., profiles, tables. 30 cm. (Transactions of the American Philosophical Society, new ser., v.46, pt. 4) *1. Klamath Indians. 2. Klamath Valley — Antiquities. I. T. (S:American Philosophical Society, Philadelphia. Transactions, new ser., v.46, pt. 4)*
E99.K7Cx (Q11.P6 n. s., vol. 46, pt. 4)   913.795 (979.5)   56-12508

Spier, Leslie, 1893- III. 4605
Klamath ethnography, by Leslie Spier. Berkeley, Calif., University of California Press, 1930. 338 p. illus., fold. map. 28 cm. (University of California publications in American archaeology and ethnology. vol. XXX) *1. Klamath Indians. 2. Indians of North America — Oregon. 3. Indians of North America — Social life and customs. 4. Indians of North America — Culture. I. T.*
E99.K7S75 (E51.C15 vol. 30)   A30-1456

Boas, Franz, 1858-1942. III. 4606
Kwakiutl ethnography. Edited by Helen Codere. Chicago, University of Chicago Press [1966] xxxvii, 439 p. illus., facsim., maps, ports. 24 cm. (Classics in anthropology) Contains a previously unpublished manuscript, together with selections from published materials. *1. Kwakiutl Indians. I. Codere, Helen, ed. II. T.*
E99.K9B49   970.3   66-13861

Boas, Franz, 1858-1942. III. 4607
The religion of the Kwakiutl Indians. New York, AMS Press [1969] 2 v. 24 cm. (Columbia University contributions to anthropology, v. 10) Reprint of the 1930 ed. *1. Kwakiutl Indians — Religion and mythology. 2. Kwakiutl language — Texts. I. T. (S:Columbia University. Columbia University contributions to anthropology, v. 10)*
E99.K9B495 1969   299/.7   72-82368

Colson, Elizabeth, 1917- III. 4608
The Makah Indians; a study of an Indian tribe in modern American society. Minneapolis, University of Minnesota Press [1953] 308 p. maps, diagrs. 22 cm. *1. Makah Indians.*
E99.M19Cx   A53-5275

E99   Tribes, N – Z

Kluckhohn, Clyde, 1905-1960. III. 4609
The Navaho [by] Clyde Kluckhohn and Dorothea Leighton. Rev. ed., by Lucy H. Wales and Richard Kluckhohn. Published in cooperation with the American Museum of Natural History. Garden City, N.Y., Natural History Library [1962] 355 p. illus. 18 cm. (Natural history library, N28. A Doubleday anchor book.) *1. Navaho Indians. I. Leighton, Dorothea (Cross) 1908- joint author. II. T.*
E99.N3K54 1962   970.3   62-6779

Leighton, Dorothea (Cross) 1908- III. 4610
Children of the people; the Navaho individual and his development, by Dorothea Leighton and Clyde Kluckhohn. New York, Octagon Books, 1969 [c1947] xi, 277 p. illus., maps. 24 cm. "Written as a part of the Indian Education Research Project undertaken jointly by the Committee on Human Development of the University of Chicago and the United States Office of Indian Affairs." *1. Navaho Indians. 2. Indians of North America — Children. I. Kluckhohn, Clyde, 1905-1960, joint author. II. Chicago. University. Committee on Human Development. III. United States. Bureau of Indian Affairs. IV. The Navaho individual and his development. V. T.*
E99.N3L57 1969   970.3   77-96199

Mills, George Thompson. III. 4611
Navaho art and culture. [Colorado Springs] Taylor Museum of the Colorado Springs Fine Arts Center, 1959. 273 p. illus. (1 col.) 23 cm. Revision of thesis — Harvard University. *1. Navaho Indians — Art. 2. Navaho Indians — Culture. I. T.*
E99.N3M58   970.67   59-8524

Underhill, Ruth Murray, 1884- III. 4612
The Navajos. Norman, University of Oklahoma Press [1956] xvi, 299 p. illus., ports., maps. 24 cm. (The Civilization of the American Indian series, 43) *1. Navaho Indians. (S)*
E99.N3U32   970.3   56-5996

Olson, James C. III. 4613
Red Cloud and the Sioux problem [by] James C. Olson. Lincoln, University of Nebraska Press [1965] xiii, 375 p. illus., map. (on lining papers) ports. 24 cm. *1. Red Cloud, Sioux chief, 1822-1909. 2. Oglala Indians — History. 3. Indians of North America — Government relations. I. T.*
E99.O3O4   970.50924   65-10048

Eggan, Frederick Russell, 1906- III. 4614
Social organization of the western pueblos. Chicago, University of Chicago Press [1950] xvii, 373 p. map, diagrs. 22 cm. (The University of Chicago publications in anthropology. Social anthropological series) "Originally presented as ... [the author's] doctoral thesis ... [at] the University of Chicago in 1933." *1. Pueblos. 2. Pueblo Indians — Social life and customs. I. T. (S:Chicago. University. The University of Chicago publications in anthropology. Social anthropological series)*
E99.P9E27 1950   970.3   50-9388

Wallace, Anthony F. C., 1923- III. 4615
The death and rebirth of the Seneca, [by] Anthony F. C. Wallace, with the assistance of Sheila C. Steen. [1st ed.] New York, Knopf, 1970 [c1969] xiii, 384, xi p. illus. 25 cm. *1. Seneca Indians. 2. Handsome Lake, 1735-1815. I. Steen, Sheila C., joint author. II. T.*
E99.S3W3 1970   970.3   79-88754

Ewers, John Canfield. III. 4616
The Blackfeet; raiders on the Northwestern Plains. [1st ed.] Norman, University of Oklahoma Press [1958] xviii, 348 p. plates, ports., maps (1 fold.) plan. 24 cm. (The Civilization of the American Indian series, 49) *1. Siksika Indians. 2. Piegan Indians. 3. Kainah Indians. (S)*
E99.S54E78   970.3   58-7778

De Laguna, Frederica, 1906- III. 4617
The story of a Tlingit community: a problem in the relationship between archeological, ethnological, and historical methods. Washington, U.S. Govt. Print. Off., 1960. x, 254 p. illus., maps. 24 cm. ([U.S.] Bureau of American Ethnology. Bulletin 172) *1. Tlingit Indians. 2. Angoon, Alaska. (S)*
E99.T6D4 (E51.U6 no. 172)   970.3   60-60629

Krause, Aurel, 1848- III. 4618
The Tlingit Indians; results of a trip to the northwest coast of America and the Bering Straits. Translated by Erna Gunther. Seattle, Published for the American Ethnological Society by the University of Washington Press, 1956. viii, 310 p. illus., ports. 23 cm. *1. Tlingit Indians. 2. Alaska — History. 3. Alaska — Description and travel. 4. Tlingit language.*
E99.T6K92   970.3   56-3408

Garfield, Viola Edmundson, 1899- III. 4619
The Tsimshian: their arts and music. New York, J. J. Augustin [1951] xii, 290 p. illus., maps, music. 25 cm. (Publications of the American Ethnological Society, 18) *1. Tsimshian Indians. 2. Tsimshian Indians — Art. 3. Indians of North America — Music. (S:American Ethnological Society, New York. Publications, 18)*
E99.T8Gx (PM101.A5 vol. 18)   970.3   51-14382

Radin, Paul, 1883-1959. III. 4620
The trickster; a study in American Indian mythology, by Paul Radin. With commentaries by Karl Kerényi and C. G. Jung. New York, Greenwood Press [1969, c1956] xi, 211 p. 23 cm. *1. Winnebago Indians — Religion and mythology. I. Kerényi, Károly, 1897- II. Jung, Carl Gustav, 1875-1961. III. T.*
E99.W7R142 1969   299/.7   74-88986   ISBN:837121124

Castaneda, Carlos. III. 4621
The teachings of Don Juan; a Yaqui way of knowledge. Berkeley, University of California Press, 1968. viii, 196 p. 24 cm. *1. Juan, Don, 1891- 2. Yaqui Indians — Religion and mythology. 3. Hallucinogenic drugs and religious experience. I. T.*
E99.Y3C3 1968   299/.7   68-17303

Spicer, Edward Holland, 1906- III. 4622
Pascua, a Yaqui village in Arizona, by Edward H. Spicer. Chicago, Ill., The University of Chicago Press [1940] xxxi, 319 p. xiii pl. (incl. front.) fold. map, 2 fold. plans, diagrs. 21 cm. (The University of Chicago publications in anthropology. Ethnological series) *1. Yaqui Indians. I. T.*
E99.Y3S6   970.3   40-12408

Forbes, Jack D. III. 4623
Warriors of the Colorado; the Yumas of the Quechan Nation and their neighbors, by Jack D. Forbes. [1st ed.] Norman, University of Oklahoma Press [1965] xx, 378 p. illus., maps, ports. 24 cm. (The Civilization of the American Indian series [76]) *1. Yuma Indians — History. I. T. (S)*
E99.Y94F59   970.3   65-11222

Leighton, Dorothea (Cross) 1908-   **III. 4624**
People of the middle place; a study of the Zuni Indians [by] Dorothea C. Leighton [and] John Adair. [New Haven, Conn., Human Relations Area Files Press, 1966] xvi, 171 p. illus., maps. 22 cm. (Behavior science monographs) "Last of a series of tribal monographs reporting the results of the Indian education research project ... undertaken jointly in 1941 by the Committee on Human Development of the University of Chicago and the United States Office of Indian Affairs." 1. Zuñi Indians. I. Adair, John, ethnologist, joint author. II. Chicago. University. Committee on Human Development. III. U.S. Bureau of Indian Affairs. IV. T. (S)
E99.Z9L4   970.3   65-28463

E101 – 135   DISCOVERY OF AMERICA. EARLY EXPLORATION

Brebner, John Bartlet, 1895-   **III. 4625**
The explorers of North America, 1492-1806. New York, Macmillan, 1933. xv, 502 p. 4 fold. maps. 23 cm. (The pioneer histories) "Narratives" at end of each chapter. 1. America — Discovery and exploration. 2. North America — History. 3. Explorers.
E101.B83   973.1   33-31647

Morison, Samuel Eliot, 1887-   **III. 4626**
The European discovery of America; the northern voyages A.D. 500-1600. New York, Oxford University Press, 1971. xviii, 712 p. illus., coats of arms., facsims., maps, col. plate, ports. 24 cm. 1. America — Discovery and exploration. 2. Voyages and travels. I. T.
E101.M85   973.1/3   71-129637   ISBN:0195013778

Oleson, Tryggvi J.   **III. 4627**
Early voyages and northern approaches, 1000-1632 [by] Tryggvi J. Oleson. [Toronto] McClelland and Stewart; New York, Oxford University Press, 1964 [c1963] xii, 211 p. illus., maps, ports. 24 cm. (The Canadian centenary series, 1) 1. America — Discovery and exploration — Norse. 2. Eskimos — Canada. 3. Canada — History — To 1763 (New France) I. T. (S)
E105.O48   973.11   64-5213

Reman, Edward, 1887-1945.   **III. 4628**
The Norse discoveries and explorations in America. Berkeley, University of California Press, 1949. xi, 201 p. map. 23 cm. Rev. and edited from the author's ms. by Arthur G. Brodeur. 1. America — Discovery and exploration — Norse.
E105.R4   973.13   49-9107

O'Gorman, Edmundo, 1906-   **III. 4629**
The invention of America; an inquiry into the historical nature of the New World and the meaning of its history. Bloomington, Indiana University Press [1961] 177 p. illus. 21 cm. 1. America — Discovery and exploration — Historiography. 2. America — History — Philosophy. I. T.
E110.O42   973.1   61-8084

E111 – 120   Columbus

Colón, Fernando, 1488-1539.   **III. 4630**
The life of the Admiral Christopher Columbus by his son Ferdinand. Translated and annotated by Benjamin Keen. New Brunswick, N.J., Rutgers University Press [1959] xxxii, 316 p. illus., maps. 25 cm. Translation of Historie del S. D. Fernando Colombo; nelle quali s'ha particolare, & vera relatione della vita, & de' fatti dell'Ammiraglio D. Cristoforo Colombo, suo padre ... 1. Colombo, Cristoforo. 2. Indians of the West Indies. I. Keen, Benjamin, 1913- ed. and tr.
E111.C737   923.9   58-6288

Madariaga, Salvador de, 1886-   **III. 4631**
Christopher Columbus; being the life of the very magnificent lord, Don Cristóbal Colón. [1st ed.] New York, F. Ungar Pub. Co. [1967] xviii 524 p. port., maps (part fold.) 25 cm. 1. Colombo, Cristoforo.
E111.M172 1967   973.1/5/0924 (B)   67-25588

Morison, Samuel Eliot, 1887-   **III. 4632**
Admiral of the ocean sea; a life of Christopher Columbus, by Samuel Eliot Morison. Maps by Erwin Raisz. Drawings by Bertram Greene. [1st ed.] Boston, Little, Brown, 1942. 2 v. illus., fold. maps, plates, port. 24 cm. "An Atlantic monthly press book." Map on lining-papers. "Salve regina" (words and melody): v.1, p. [235] 1. Colombo, Cristoforo. I. T.
E111.M86 1942   923.9   42-5605

Morison, Samuel Eliot, 1887-   **III. 4633**
The Caribbean as Columbus saw it, by Samuel Eliot Morison and Mauricio Obregón. Photos. by David L. Crofoot, Cristina Martinez-Irujo de Obregón, members of the Harvard Columbus Expedition, and other friends. [1st ed.] Boston, Little, Brown [1964] xxxv, 252 p. illus., maps, ports. 26 cm. "An Atlantic Monthly Press book." 1. Colombo, Cristoforo. 2. America — Discovery and exploration — Spanish. 3. West Indies — Description and travel — 1951- 4. Central America — Description and travel — 1951- I. Obregón, Mauricio, joint author. II. T.
E112.M84   973.15   64-17483

O'Gorman, Edmundo, 1906-   **III. 4634**
La idea del descubrimiento de América; historia de esa interpretación y crítica de sus fundamentos. [México] Centro de Estudios Filosóficos, 1951. 417 p. 24 cm. (Ediciones del IV centenario de la Universidad de México, v.5.) 1. Colombo, Cristoforo. 2. America — Discovery and exploration. 3. America — Discovery and exploration — Historiography. 1. T. (S:Mexico (City) Universidad Nacional. Ediciones del IV centenario de la Universidad de México, v.5)
E112.O37   51-32164

Colombo, Cristoforo.   **III. 4635**
Journal. Translated by Cecil Jane [rev. and annotated by L. A. Vigneras] with an appendix by R. A. Skelton. 90 illus. from prints and maps of the period. New York, C. N. Potter [1960] xxiii, 227 p. illus. (part mounted, part col.) ports., maps (part col.) charts, coat of arms, facsims. 25 cm. Detail of French portulan chart from dust jacket inserted. "Letter of Columbus, describing the results of his first voyage": p. [189]-202. 1. America — Discovery and exploration.
E118.C725 1960   973.15   60-14430

E121 – 143   Other Explorers

Sauer, Carl Ortwin, 1889-   **III. 4636**
Sixteenth century North America; the land and the people as seen by the Europeans. Berkeley, University of California Press, 1971. xii, 319 p. illus. 24 cm. 1. America — Discovery and exploration. I. T.
E121.S26   973.1   75-138635   ISBN:0520018540

Bolton, Herbert Eugene, 1870-1953.   **III. 4637**
The Spanish borderlands; a chronicle of old Florida and the Southwest, by Herbert E. Bolton. New Haven, Yale University Press; [etc., etc.] 1921. xiii, 320 p. col. front. (port.) fold. map. 18 cm. (The Chronicles of America series, v.23) "Roosevelt edition." 1. America — Discovery and exploration — Spanish. 2. Spain — Colonies — North America. 3. Florida — History — Spanish exploration to 1565. 4. Southwest, New — History. I. T.
E123.B72 (E173.C56 vol. 23)   22-12145

Bourne, Edward Gaylord, 1860-1908.   **III. 4638**
Spain in America, 1450-1580. With new introd. and supplementary bibliography by Benjamin Keen. New York, Barnes & Noble [1962] 366 p. illus. 21 cm. (American nation series, v.3. University paperbacks, UP-38.) 1. America — Discovery and exploration — Spanish. 2. Spain — Colonies — America. I. T.
E123.B76 1962   973.16   62-10840

Horgan, Paul, 1903-   **III. 4639**
Conquistadors in North American history. New York, Farrar, Straus [1963] 303 p. 22 cm. 1. America — Discovery and exploration — Spanish. 2. Mexico — History — To 1810. 3. U.S. — History — Colonial period. I. T.
E123.H65   973.16   63-9068

Lowery, Woodbury, 1853-1906.   **III. 4640**
The Spanish settlements within the present limits of the United States, 1513-1561. New York, Russell & Russell, 1959. xiii, 515 p. illus. 24 cm. 1. America — Discovery and exploration — Spanish. 2. Mexico — History — Spanish colony, 1540-1810. 3. Spain — Colonies — North America. 4. Indians of North America.
E123.L91 1959   973.16   59-6235

Spanish explorers in the southern United States, 1528-1543: The   **III. 4641**
narrative of Alvar Nuñez Cebeça de Vaca,
ed. by Frederick W. Hodge. The narrative of the expedition of Hernando de Soto by the gentleman of Elvas, ed. by Theodore H. Lewis. The narrative of the expedition of Coronado, by Pedro de Castañeda, ed. by Frederick W. Hodge; with maps and a facsimile reproduction. New York, Scribner, 1907.

III. 4642　　　　　　　　　　　　　　　　　　　　*America (General)*　　　　　　　　　　　　　　　　　　　　**E123**

xx, 411 p. facsim., 2 fold. maps. 23 cm. (Original narratives of early American history ...) Series title also at head of t.-p. *1. Soto, Hernando de, 1500 (ca.)-1542. 2. Vázquez de Coronado, Francisco, 1510-1549. 3. America — Discovery and exploration — Spanish. 4. Indians of North America. 5. Florida — History — Spanish exploration to 1565. I. Núñez Cabeza de Vaca, Alvar, 16th cent. II. Castañeda de Nágera, Pedro de, 16th cent. III. Hodge, Frederick Webb, 1864- ed. IV. Lewis, Theodore H., ed. V. Relaçam verdadeira dos trabalhos.*
E123.S75　(E187.O7S7)　　　07-10607

Hallenbeck, Cleve.　　　　　　　　　　　　　　　　　　　　**III. 4642**
Álvar Núñez Cabeza de Vaca; the journey and route of the first European to cross the continent of North America, 1534-1536. Port Washington, N.Y., Kennikat Press [1970] 326 p. maps. 22 cm. (Kennikat Press scholarly reprints. Series in Latin-American history and culture) Pt. 1 is a paraphrase in English of Núñez Cabeza de Vaca's La relación y comentarios. *1. Núñez Cabeza de Vaca, Alvar, 16th cent. 2. America — Discovery and exploration — Spanish. I. Núñez Cabeza de Vaca, Alvar, 16th cent. La relación y comentarios.*
E125.N9H3 1970　　973.1/6　　78-123490　　ISBN:80461377X

Garcilaso de la Vega, el Inca, 1539-1616.　　　　　　　　　**III. 4643**
The Florida of the Inca; a history of the adelantado, Hernando de Soto, Governor and Captain General of the kingdom of Florida, and of other heroic Spanish and Indian cavaliers, written by the Inca, Garcilaso de la Vega, an officer of His Majesty, and a native of the great city of Cuzco, capital of the realms and provinces of Peru. Translated and edited by John Grier Varner and Jeannette Johnson Varner. Austin, University of Texas Press, 1951. xlv, 655 p. port., map (on lining papers) 25 cm. *1. Soto, Hernando de, 1500 (ca.)-1542.*
E125.S7G26　　973.16　　51-10292

Day, Arthur Grove.　　　　　　　　　　　　　　　　　　　**III. 4644**
Coronado's quest; the discovery of the southwestern states, by A. Grove Day. Berkeley and Los Angeles, University of California Press, 1940. xvi, 419 p. illus., fold. map. 21 cm. *1. Vazquez de Coronado, Francisco, 1510-1549. 2. Southwest, New — Description and travel. I. T.*
E125.V3D28　　40-28531

Hammond, George Peter, 1896- ed. and tr.　　　　　　　　**III. 4645**
Narratives of the Coronado expedition, 1540-1542 [edited and translated by] George P. Hammond ... and Agapito Rey. Albuquerque, University of New Mexico Press, 1940. xii, 413 p. front. 28 cm. (Coronado cuarto centennial publications, 1540-1940. Vol.2) *1. Vázquez de Coronado, Francisco, 1510-1539. 2. Southwest, New — Discovery and exploration. I. Rey, Agapito, 1892- joint ed. and tr. II. T:The Coronado expedition, 1540-1542, Narratives of.*
E125.V3H4　　973.16　　40-12409

Arciniegas, Germán, 1900-　　　　　　　　　　　　　　　**III. 4646**
Amerigo and the New World; the life & times of Amerigo Vespucci. Translated from the Spanish by Harriet de Onís. [1st ed.] New York, Knopf, 1955. 322 p. illus. 22 cm. *1. Vespucci, Amerigo, 1451-1512. I. T.*
E125.V5A65　　923.945　　53-9487

Burrage, Henry Sweetser, 1837-1926, ed.　　　　　　　　　**III. 4647**
Early English and French voyages, chiefly from Hakluyt, 1534-1608, ed. by Henry S. Burrage. New York, Barnes & Noble [1952] xx, 451 p. 23 cm. (Original narratives of early American history) *1. America — Discovery and exploration — English. 2. America — Discovery and exploration — French. I. Hakluyt, Richard, 1552?-1616. II. T. (S)*
E127.Bx　　A54-10008

McCann, Franklin Thresher, 1903-　　　　　　　　　　　**III. 4648**
English discovery of America to 1585, by Franklin T. McCann. New York, Octagon Books, 1969 [c1951] xiv, 246 p. illus. 23 cm. *1. America — Discovery and exploration — English. 2. America in literature. 3. English literature — History and criticism. 4. Cosmography. I. T.*
E127.M15 1969　　973.1/7　　73-86280

Oviedo y Valdés, Gonzalo Fernández de, 1478-1557.　　　**III. 4649**
Natural history of the West Indies. Translated and edited by Sterling A. Stoudemire. Chapel Hill, University of North Carolina Press [1959] xvii, 140 p. illus., map, facsim. 23 cm. (North Carolina. University. Studies in the Romance languages and literatures, no. 32) *1. America — Early accounts to 1600. 2. Indians of the West Indies. 3. Indians of Central America. 4. Natural history — West Indies. 5. Natural history — Central America. (S)*
E141.O913 (PC13.N67 no. 32)　　973.16　　59-63487

Vázquez de Espinosa, Antonio, d. 1630.　　　　　　　　　**III. 4650**
Description of the Indies, c. 1620. Translated by Charles Upson Clark. Washington, Smithsonian Institution Press [1968] xii, 862 p. 24 cm. (Smithsonian miscellaneous collections, v. 102. Smithsonian publication 3646.) Reprint of the 1942 ed. published under title: Compendium and description of the West Indies. Translation of Compendio y descripción de las Indias Occidentales, from the Vatican Library manuscript Barberinianus Latinus 3584. *1. Latin America — Description and travel. 2. Spain — Colonies — America. 3. Indians. 4. Philippine Islands — Description and travel. I. T. (S:Smithsonian Institution. Smithsonian miscellaneous collections, v. 102)*
E143.Vx (Q11.S7 vol. 102 1968)　　918　　68-25124

E151 – F970 United States

E151 – 161 GENERAL WORKS. SOCIAL LIFE. CUSTOMS

Shankle, George Earlie. III. 4651
State names, flags, seals, songs, birds, flowers, and other symbols; a study based on historical documents giving the origin and significance of the state names, nicknames, mottoes, seals, flags, flowers, birds, songs, and descriptive comments on the capitol buildings and on some of the leading state histories, with facsimiles of the state flags and seals. Rev. ed. Westport, Conn., Greenwood Press [1970] 522 p. illus. 23 cm. Reprint of the 1938 ed. *1. Names, Geographical — United States. 2. Seals (Numismatics) — United States. 3. Flags — United States. 4. Capitols. 5. Mottoes. 6. State flowers. 7. State birds. 8. State songs. 9. United States — History, Local — Bibliography. I. T.*
E155.S43 1970   917.3   73-109842   ISBN:0837143330

Stewart, George Rippey, 1895- III. 4652
American place-names; a concise and selective dictionary for the continental United States of America [by] George R. Stewart. New York, Oxford University Press, 1970. xl, 550 p. 25 cm. *1. Names, Geographical — U.S. I. T.*
E155.S79   917.3/003   72-83018

Long, Edward John, 1900- III. 4653
America's national monuments and historic sites; a guide in pictures and text to our magnificient natural and historic treasures. Introd. by Nelson Beecher Keyes; 8 maps by Rafael Palacios. Garden City, N.Y., Doubleday [1960] 256 p. illus. 22 cm. *1. U.S. — Description and travel — Guide-books. 2. U.S. — Description and travel — Views. 3. Canada — Description and travel — Guide-books. 4. Canada — Description and travel — Views. I. T.*
E158.L58   917.3   60-9498

Tilden, Freeman, 1883- III. 4654
The national parks. Foreword by George B. Hartzog, Jr. [2d rev. ed.] New York, Knopf, 1970 [c1951] xviii, 584, xx p. illus., map. 23 cm. "A revised & enlarged edition ... with new information & evaluation on all of the national parks, national monuments, & historic sites." *1. National parks and reserves — United States. I. T.*
E160.T5 1970   917.3   79-16092

Tilden, Freeman, 1883- III. 4655
The State parks, their meaning in American life. Foreword by Conrad L. Wirth. [1st ed.] New York, Knopf, 1962. 496, xi p. illus. 25 cm. *1. Parks — U.S. I. T.*
E160.T53   917.3   62-17547

Beard, Mary (Ritter) 1876-1958, ed. III. 4656
America through women's eyes. New York, Greenwood Press [1969, c1933] 558 p. 23 cm. *1. Women in the United States. 2. United States — Social conditions. 3. United States — History. I. T.*
E161.B42 1969   301.41/2/0973   68-54772

Blegen, Theodore Christian, 1891- III. 4657
Grass roots history [by] Theodore C. Blegen. Port Washington, N.Y., Kennikat Press [1969, c1947] x, 266 p. 22 cm. *1. United States — Social life and customs. 2. Frontier and pioneer life — Minnesota. 3. Norwegians in the United States. I. T.*
E161.B55 1969   917.3   75-85987   ISBN:0804606021

Carson, Gerald. III. 4658
The polite Americans; a wide-angle view of our more or less good manners over 300 years. New York, Morrow, 1966. xvi, 346 p. illus., facsims., ports. 24 cm. *1. U.S. — Social life and customs. 2. Etiquette — U.S. I. T.*
E161.C3 1966   395.0973   66-12087

Clark, Thomas Dionysius, 1903- III. 4659
The rampaging frontier; manners and humors of pioneer days in the South and the Middle West [by] Thomas D. Clark. Bloomington, Indiana University Press [1964] 350 p. 20 cm. (A Midland book, MB/66) *1. Frontier and pioneer life. I. T.*
E161.C57 1964   917.7   64-55418

Dulles, Foster Rhea, 1900- III. 4660
A history of recreation; America learns to play. 2d ed. New York, Appleton-Century-Crofts [1965] xvii, 446 p. illus., facsims. 21 cm. Previously published under title: America learns to play; a history of popular recreation. *1. United States — Social life and customs. 2. Recreation — United States. I. T.*
E161.D852 1965   790.0973   65-25489

Handlin, Oscar, 1915- ed. III. 4661
This was America; true accounts of people and places, manners and customs, as recorded by European travelers to the western shore in the eighteenth, nineteenth and twentieth centuries. Cambridge, Harvard Univ. Press, 1949. ix, 602 p. illus., maps. 25 cm. *1. U.S. — Description and travel. 2. U.S. — Social life and customs. I. T.*
E161.H3   917.3   49-7940

Schlesinger, Arthur Meier, 1888-1965. III. 4662
Learning how to behave; a historical study of American etiquette books. New York, Cooper Square Publishers, 1968. ix, 95 p. 21 cm. "A Marandell book." Reprint of the 1946 ed. *1. United States — Social life and customs. 2. Etiquette — United States. 3. Etiquette — Bibliography. I. T.*
E161.S25 1968   395   68-28296

Tryon, Warren Stenson, 1901- ed. III. 4663
A mirror for Americans; life and manners in the United States, 1790-1870, as recorded by American travelers. [Chicago] University of Chicago Press [1952] 3 v. (xx, 793, v. p.) illus., ports. 25 cm. *1. U.S. — Description and travel. 2. U.S. — Social life and customs. 3. Frontier and pioneer life — U.S. I. T.*
E161.T78   917.3   52-13949

Wecter, Dixon, 1906-1950. III. 4664
The saga of American society; a record of social aspiration, 1607-1937. New York, Scribner [1970] xxii, 504 p. illus., ports. 25 cm. Reprint of the 1937 ed., with an introd. by Louis Auchincloss. *1. United States — Social life and customs. 2. Virginia — Social life and customs. 3. New York (City) — Social life and customs. 4. Portraits, American. 5. United States — Historic houses, etc. I. T.*
E161.W43 1970   917.3/03   78-103633

E162 – 169 DESCRIPTION. TRAVEL, BY PERIOD
E162 – 163   1607 – 1783

Andrews, Charles McLean, 1863-1943. III. 4665
Colonial folkways; a chronicle of American life in the reign of the Georges, by Charles M. Andrews. New Haven, Yale University Press; [etc., etc.] 1921. ix, 255 p. col. front. 18 cm. (The Chronicles of America series, v.9) "Roosevelt edition." *1. U.S. — Social life and customs — Colonial period. I. T.*
E162.A58 (E173.C56 vol. 9)   22-12131

Bridenbaugh, Carl. III. 4666
Cities in revolt; urban life in America, 1743-1776. [1st ed.] New York, Knopf, 1955. xiii, 433, [1], xxi p. illus., ports., map, facsims. 25 cm. *1. United States — Social life and customs — Colonial period. 2. Cities and towns — United States. I. T.*
E162.B85   917.4   55-7399

Earle, Alice (Morse) 1851-1911. III. 4667
Home life in colonial days, written by Alice Morse Earle in the year MDCCCXCVIII; ilustrated by photographs, gathered by the author. New York, London, Macmillan, 1913. xvi, 470 p. illus., plates. 19 cm. (The Macmillan standard library) *1. U.S. — Social life and customs — Colonial period. 2. Home economics — History. I. T.*
E162.Ex   A13-2290

Eggleston, Edward, 1837-1902.   **III. 4668**
The transit of civilization from England to America in the seventeenth century. New York, P. Smith, 1933. ix, 344 p. 21 cm. *1. U.S. — History — Colonial period. 2. U.S. — Civilization. I. T.*
E162.E283   973.2   A34-396

Gummere, Richard Mott, 1883-   **III. 4669**
The American colonial mind and the classical tradition; essays in comparative culture. Cambridge, Harvard University Press, 1963. xiii, 228 p. 22 cm. *1. United States — Civilization — To 1783. 2. United States — Civilization — Greek influences. 3. United States — Civilization — Roman influences. I. T.*
E162.G88   917.3   63-20767

Hamilton, Alexander, 1712-1756.   **III. 4670**
Gentleman's progress; the Itinerarium of Dr. Alexander Hamilton, 1744; ed. with an introd. by Carl Bridenbaugh. Chapel Hill, Pub. for the Institute of Early American History and Culture at Williamsburg, Va., by the Univ. of North Carolina Press, 1948. xxxii, 267 p. illus., maps (on lining-papers) 25 cm. *1. U.S. — Description and travel. I. Bridenbaugh, Carl, ed. II. Institute of Early American History and Culture, Williamsburg, Va. III. T.*
E162.H21 1948   917.3   48-28157

Kammen, Michael G.   **III. 4671**
People of paradox; an inquiry concerning the origins of American civilization. [1st ed.] New York, Knopf, 1972. xvii, 316, xii p. illus. 22 cm. *1. United States — Civilization — To 1783. 2. National characteristics, American. I. T.*
E162.K2   917.3/03   72-376   ISBN:0394460774

Rossiter, Clinton Lawrence, 1917-   **III. 4672**
The first American Revolution; the American Colonies on the eve of independence. New York, Harcourt, Brace [c1956] 245 p. 19 cm. (A Harvest book, 17) "Revised version of part I of Seedtime of the Republic." *1. U.S. — History — Colonial period. 2. U.S. — Civilization — History. 3. U.S. — History — Revolution — Causes. I. T.*
E162.R7   973.2   56-13741

Smith, James Morton, ed.   **III. 4673**
Seventeenth-century America; essays in colonial history. Chapel Hill, Published for the Institute of Early American History and Culture at Williamsburg, Va., by the University of North Carolina Press [1959] xv, 238 p. 24 cm. Based upon original papers presented at a symposium sponsored by the Institute of Early American History and Culture at Williamsburg, Va., in 1957. *1. U.S. — History — Colonial period. 2. U.S. — Social life and customs — Colonial period. 3. U.S. — Church history — Colonial period. I. Institute of Early American History and Culture, Williamsburg, Va. II. T.*
E162.S66   973.02   59-16299

Wertenbaker, Thomas Jefferson, 1879-   **III. 4674**
The golden age of colonial culture. [2d ed., rev.] New York, New York Univ. Press [1949] 171 p. 22 cm. (New York University. Stokes Foundation. Anson G. Phelps lectureship on early American history) *1. U.S. — Civilization. 2. U.S. — Social life and customs — Colonial period. I. T. (S)*
E162.W48 1949   973.2   49-4583

Wright, Louis Booker, 1899-   **III. 4675**
The cultural life of the American Colonies, 1607-1763. [1st ed.] New York, Harper [1957] xiv, 292 p. illus., ports., map. 22 cm. (The New American Nation series) *1. U.S. — Social life and customs — Colonial period. 2. U.S. — Intellectual life. I. T.*
E162.W89   973.2   57-250

Chastellux, François Jean, marquis de, 1734-1788.   **III. 4676**
Travels in North-America [in the years 1780, 1781, and 1782. Translated from the French by an English gentleman. With notes by the translator. New York] New York times [1968] 2 v. fold. illus., fold. maps. 23 cm. (Eyewitness accounts of the American Revolution) Translation of Voyages dans l'Amérique septentrionale. Reprint of the 1787 ed. *1. United States — Description and travel — To 1783. I. T. (S)*
E163.C59 1968   917.3   67-29046
C389

Crèvecœur, Michel Guillaume St. John de, called Saint John de Crèvecœur, 1735-1813.   **III. 4677**
Letters from an American farmer, by J. Hector St. John de Crèvecœur. London & Toronto, J. M. Dent; New York, E. P. Dutton [1926] xxiii, 256 p. 18 cm. (Everyman's library, edited by Ernest Rhys. Travel and topography. [no. 640] "First issue of this edition 1912. Reprinted 1926." Title-page and page facing it (with quotation) have ornamental border. Includes reproduction of t.-p. of orginal edition, London, 1782. "Introduction and notes by Warren Barton Blake." *1. United States — Description and travel. 2. Nantucket, Mass. I. Blake, Warren Barton, 1883-1918, ed. II. T.*
E163.C826x   (AC1.E8 no. 640)   917.4   36-37597

Crèvecœur, Michel Guillaume St. Jean de, called Saint John de Crèvecœur, 1735-1813.   **III. 4678**
Sketches of eighteenth century America; more "Letters from an American farmer," by St. John de Crèvecœur, edited by Henri L. Bourdin, Ralph H. Gabriel and Stanley T. Williams. New Haven, Yale University Press; London, H. Milford, Oxford University Press, 1925. 342 p. port., facsim. 24 cm. "The present volume is the third work published by the Yale university press on the Phillip Hamilton McMillan memorial publication fund." *1. U.S. — Social life and customs — Colonial period. 2. Farm life. I. Bourdin, Henri Louis, ed. II. Gabriel, Ralph Henry, 1890- ed. III. Williams, Stanley Thomas, 1888- ed. IV. Yale university. Philip Hamilton McMillian memorial publication fund. V. T.*
E163.C873   25-23064

E164 – 166   1784 – 1860

Adams, Henry, 1838-1918.   **III. 4679**
The United States in 1800. Ithaca, N.Y., Great Seal Books [1955] x, 132 p. 19 cm. "Consists of the first six chapters of volume I of Henry Adams' History of the United States of America during the first administration of Thomas Jefferson, published ... in 1889." *1. U.S. — Intellectual life. 2. National characteristics, American. 3. U.S. — Social conditions. I. T.*
E164.Ax   917.3   55-14865

Foster, Augustus John, Sir, bart., 1780-1848.   **III. 4680**
Jeffersonian America: notes on the United States of America, collected in the years 1805-6-7 and 11-12. Edited with an introd. by Richard Beale Davis. San Marino, Calif., Huntington Library, 1954. xx, 356 p. port. 24 cm. (Huntington Library publications) *1. U.S. — Social life and customs. 2. Washington, D.C. — Social life and customs. I. T. (S:Henry E. Huntington Library and Art Gallery, San Marino, Calif. Huntington Library publications)*
E164.F76 1954   917.3   54-8926

Moreau de Saint-Méry, Médéric Louis Élie, 1750-1819.   **III. 4681**
Moreau de St. Méry's American journey (1793-1798) translated and edited by Kenneth Roberts [and] Anna M. Roberts. 1st ed. Preface by Kenneth Roberts. Introduction by Stewart L. Mims. Frontispiece painting by James Bingham. Garden City, N.Y., Doubleday, 1947. xxi, 394 p. col. front. 24 cm. Translation of Voyage aux États-Unis de l'Amérique, 1793-1798. *1. U.S. — Description and travel — 1783-1848. I. Roberts, Kenneth Lewis, 1885- ed. and tr. II. Roberts, Anna S. (Mosser) joint ed. and tr. III. Mims, Stewart Lea, 1880- IV. American journey.*
E164.M832   917.3   47-3941

Chevalier, Michel, 1806-1879.   **III. 4682**
Society, manners, and politics in the United States; being a series of letters on North America, by Michael Chevalier. New York, B. Franklin [1969] iv, 467 p. 23 cm. (Burt Franklin research and source works series, 352. American classics in history and social science, 79.) Translation of Lettres sur l'Amérique du Nord. *1. United States — Description and travel — 1783-1848. 2. United States — Politics and government — 1829-1837. 3. United States — Social conditions — To 1865. I. T.*
E165.C54 1969   309.1/73   69-18620

Cobbett, William, 1763-1835.   **III. 4683**
A year's residence in the United States of America. New York, A. M. Kelley, 1969. vii, 610 p. 22 cm. (America through European eyes. Reprints of economic classics.) Reprint of the 1818-19 ed. *1. United States — Description and travel — 1783-1848. 2. Agriculture — United States. 3. United States — Social life and customs — 1783-1865. I. T.*
E165.C669   917.3   70-85139   ISBN:0678005168

D'Arusmont, Frances (Wright) 1795-1852.   **III. 4684**
Views of society and manners in America. Edited by Paul R. Baker. Cambridge, Mass., Belknap Press of Harvard University Press, 1963. xxiii, 292 p. 24 cm. (The John Harvard Library) "Text ... used ... is that of the first London edition of 1821." *1. U.S. — Description and travel — 1783-1848. 2. U.S. — Social life and customs. I. T. (S)*
E165.D2303   917.3   63-10878

Dickens, Charles, 1812-1870.   **III. 4685**
American notes and Pictures from Italy. With 12 illus. by Marcus Stone, Samuel Palmer, and Clarkson Stanfield, and an introd. by Sacheverell Sitwell. London, New York, Oxford University Press, 1957. xiv, 433 p. illus. 19 cm. (The New Oxford illustrated Dickens) *1. U.S. — Description and travel — 1783-1848. 2. U.S. — Social life and customs. 3. Italy — Description and travel. I. Pictures from Italy. II. T.*
E165.D614   917.3   57-4815

Grund, Francis Joseph, 1805-1863.   **III. 4686**
Aristocracy in America, from the sketch-book of a German nobleman. With an introd. by George E. Probst. [1st American ed.] New York, Harper [1959] 302 p. 21 cm. (Harper torchbooks, TB1001. The Academy library) *1. U.S. — Social life and customs. 2. New York (City) — Social life and customs. 3. Boston — Social life and customs. 4. Philadelphia — Social life and customs. 5. Washington, D.C. — Social life and customs. I. T.*
E165.G91 1959   917.3   59-13839

E169   United States   III. 4711

Lyell, Charles, Sir, bart., 1797-1875.   **III. 4687**
A second visit to the United States of North America. By Sir Charles Lyell. New York, Harper, 1850. 2 v. illus. 19 cm. First published, London, 1849. *1. U.S. — Description and travel. 2. Geology — U.S.*
E165.L984   08-7107

Marryat, Frederick, 1792-1848.   **III. 4688**
A diary in America, with remarks on its institutions. Edited, with notes and an introd., by Sydney Jackman. [1st Borzoi ed.] New York, Knopf, 1962. xxvi 487, ix p. port. 22 cm. "[First] appeared in June 1839 ... in three volumes, with three supplementary volumes appearing later in the year ... In preparing this edition ... I have used both the first and second series." *1. U.S. — Description and travel — 1783-1848. 2. U.S. — Social life and customs. 3. Canada — Description and travel. I. Jackman, Sydney, ed. II. T.*
E165.M373   917.3   61-18120

Martineau, Harriet, 1802-1876.   **III. 4689**
Society in America. Edited, abridged and with an introductory essay of Seymour Martin Lipset. [1st ed.] Garden City, N.Y., Anchor Books, 1962. 357 p. 18 cm. (A Doubleday anchor original, A302) *1. U.S. — Social life and customs. 2. U.S. — Economic conditions. 3. U.S. — Politics and government. I. T.*
E165.M393   917.3   62-15241

Miller, Douglas T.   **III. 4690**
The birth of modern America, 1820-1850, by Douglas T. Miller. New York, Pegasus [1970] xvi, 192 p. illus. 21 cm. *1. United States — Civilization — 19th century. 2. United States — Social conditions — To 1865. I. T.*
E165.M62   973.5   79-114173

Sanford, Charles L., 1920-   **III. 4691**
Quest for America, 1810-1824, edited with an introd. by Charles L. Sanford. [New York] New York University Press, 1964. xxxvii, 474 p. illus., ports. 24 cm. (Documents in American civilization series) Includes 2 songs. *1. U.S. — Civilization — 1783-1865. I. T. (S)*
E165.S25 1964a   917.3035   64-25921

Tocqueville, Alexis Charles Henri Maurice Clérel de, 1805-1859.   **III. 4692**
Journey to America. Translated by George Lawrence. Edited by J. P. Mayer. Rev. and augm. ed. in collaboration with A. P. Kerr. Garden City, N.Y., Doubleday, 1971. xvi, 424 p. 18 cm. "Based on fourteen notebooks, details of which can be found in [the author's] Œvres complètes, ed. J. P. Mayer, vol. V, 1, p. 57." *1. United States — Description and travel — 1783-1848. I. T.*
E165.T5433 1971   917.3/03/56   78-157643

Pierson, George Wilson, 1904-   **III. 4693**
Tocqueville in America. Abridged by Dudley C. Lunt from "Tocqueville and Beaumont in America." Garden City, N.Y., Doubleday, 1959. 506 p. 19 cm. (Anchor books, A189) *1. Tocqueville, Alexis Charles Henri Maurice Clérel de, 1805-1859. 2. Beaumont de La Bonninière, Gustave Auguste de, 1802-1866. 3. U.S. — Description and travel — 1783-1848. I. T.*
E165.T547 1959   917.3   59-13981

Trollope, Frances (Milton) 1780-1863.   **III. 4694**
Domestic manners of the Americans; edited, with a history of Mrs. Trollope's adventures in America, by Donald Smalley. [1st Borzoi ed.] New York, A. A. Knopf, 1949. lxxxiii, 454, xix p. illus., port. 25 cm. *1. U.S. — Social life and customs. I. Smalley, Donald Arthur, 1907- ed. II. T.*
E165.T84 1949   917.3   49-11380

Cobden, Richard, 1804-1865.   **III. 4695**
The American diaries of Richard Cobden. Edited, with an introd. and notes, by Elizabeth Hoon Cawley. New York, Greenwood Press [1969, c1952] xii, 233 p. illus., facsim., maps, ports. 23 cm. 1952 ed. published under title: American diaries. The mss. of the two diaries are in the British Museum (Add. mss. 43807 and 43808) *1. United States — Description and travel — 1848-1865. 2. National characteristics, American. I. T.*
E166.C6 1969   917.3/04/6   75-90488   ISBN:0837122619

E167 – 169.02   1861 –

Russell, William Howard, Sir, 1820-1907.   **III. 4696**
My diary, North and South. Edited and introduced by Fletcher Pratt. Gloucester, Mass., P. Smith, 1969 [c1954] xiii, 268 p. port. 21 cm. *1. Southern States — Description and travel. 2. United States — History — Civil War. I. T.*
E167.R96 1969   917.3   79-10920

Trollope, Anthony, 1815-1882.   **III. 4697**
North America. New ed. [reprinted]. London, Dawsons, 1968. 2 v. 20 cm. (Colonial history series) Facsimile reprint of new ed., 1869. *1. United States — Description and travel — 1848-1865. 2. United States — Politics and government — Civil War. 3. Canada — Description and travel — 1763-1867. I. T.*
E167.T8425 1869a   917   79-350542   ISBN:0712903003

Giner, Ray.   **III. 4698**
Age of excess; the United States from 1877 to 1914. New York, Macmillan [1965] x, 386 p. 21 cm. *1. United States — Civilization — 1865-1918. I. T.*
E168.G48   917.3   65-12151

Morgan, Howard Wayne, ed.   **III. 4699**
The gilded age, a reappraisal. [Syracuse, N.Y.] Syracuse University Press, 1963. 286 p. 24 cm. *1. United States — Civilization — 1856-1918 — Addresses, essays, lectures. I. T.*
E168.M84   973.8   63-13886

Nathan, George Jean, 1882-   **III. 4700**
The American credo; a contribution toward the interpretation of the national mind. Rev. and enl. ed. By George Jean Nathan and H. L. Mencken. New York, A. A. Knopf, 1921. 266 p. 20 cm. *1. National characteristics, American. I. Mencken, Henry Louis, 1880- joint author. II. T.*
E168.N272   26-9256

Offenbach, Jacques, 1819-1880.   **III. 4701**
Orpheus in America: Offenbach's diary of his journey to the New World. Translated by Lander MacClintock. Drawings by Alajálov. New York, Greenwood Press [1969, c1957] 200 p. illus. 23 cm. Translation of Offenbach en Amérique. *1. United States — Description and travel — 1865-1900. 2. United States — Social life and customs — 1865-1918. 3. Music — United States. I. T.*
E168.O332 1969   917.3/04/82   69-14015

Sienkiewicz, Henryk, 1846-1916.   **III. 4702**
Portrait of America; letters. Edited & translated by Charles Morley. New York, Columbia University Press, 1959. 300 p. illus. 23 cm. Translation of selections from Listy z podróży do Ameryki. *1. U.S. — Description and travel — 1865-1900. I. T.*
E168.S5763   917.3   59-7371

Webb, Beatrice (Potter) 1858-1943.   **III. 4703**
American diary, 1898. Edited by David A. Shannon. Madison, University of Wisconsin Press, 1963. 181 p. illus. 22 cm. *1. U.S. — Description and travel — 1865-1900. 2. Municipal government — U.S. I. T.*
E168.W4   917.3   63-8436

Cooke, Alistair, 1908-   **III. 4704**
One man's America. [1st American ed.] New York, Knopf, 1952. 268 p. illus. 22 cm. Twenty-nine of a series of weekly talks of Britain called Letters from America, broadcast by the British Broadcasting Corp. and first published in London in 1951 under title: Letters from America. *1. United States. I. Letters from America (Radio program) II. T.*
E169.C75 1952   917.3   52-7542

Frank, Robert.   **III. 4705**
The Americans; photographs. Introd. by Jack Kerouac. [1st ed.] New York, Grove Press [1959] unpaged (chiefly illus.) 20 x 22 cm. *1. U.S. — Social life and customs — Illustrations. I. T.*
E169.F8233   917.3   59-13885

Gunther, John, 1901-   **III. 4706**
Inside U.S.A. Rev. ed. New York, Harper [1951] 1121 p. illus. 17 cm. *1. U.S. — Description and travel — 1940- I. T.*
E169.G97 1951   917.3   51-13816

Maritain, Jacques, 1882-   **III. 4707**
Reflections on America. New York, Scribner [1958] 205 p. 21 cm. *1. U.S. — Civilization. I. T.*
E169.M35   917.3   58-5719

Morris, James, 1926-   **III. 4708**
As I saw the U.S.A. [New York] Pantheon [1956] 245 p. 22 cm. London ed. (Faber and Faber) has title: Coast to coast. *1. U.S. — Description and travel — 1940- I. T.*
E169.M874 1956a   917.3   56-10414

Stearns, Harold Edmund, 1891-1943, ed.   **III. 4709**
Civilization in the United States: an inquiry by thirty Americans. Westport, Conn., Greenwood Press [1971] viii, 577 p. 23 cm. Reprint of the 1922 ed. *1. United States — Civilization — 1918-1945. I. T.*
E169.S78 1971   917.3/03/913   71-109977   ISBN:0837144833

Stewart, George Rippey, 1895-   **III. 4710**
U.S. 40; cross section of the United States of America. Maps by Edwin Raisz. Boston, Houghton Mifflin, 1953. viii, 311 p. illus., maps (1 col. on lining papers) 25 cm. *1. U.S. Highway 40. 2. U.S. — Description and travel — 1940-*
E169.S85   917.3   52-5249

White, Charles Langdon, 1897-   **III. 4711**
Regional geography of Anglo-America [by] C. Langdon White, Edwin J.

219

| III. 4712 | United States | E169 |

Foscue [and] Tom L. McKnight. 3d ed. Englewood Cliffs, N.J., Prentice-Hall [1964] xvii, 524 p. illus., maps. 26 cm. *1. U.S. — Description and travel. 2. Canada — Description and travel. I. T.*
E169.W54 1964   917   64-10071

Wilson, Edmund, 1895-   III. 4712
The American earthquake; a documentary of the twenties and thirties. New York, Octagon Books, 1971 [c1958] 576 p. 22 cm. *1. United States — Civilization — Addresses, essays, lectures. I. T.*
E169.W658 1971   917.3/03/91   78-139823

Baker, Russell, 1925-   III. 4713
All things considered. [1st ed.] Philadelphia, Lippincott [1965] 213 p. 22 cm. A collection of articles from the author's New York Times column. *1. U.S. — Social life and customs — Anecdotes, facetiae, satire. I. New York times. II. T.*
E169.02.B27   817.54   65-24477

Starkey, Otis Paul, 1906-   III. 4714
The Anglo-American realm [by] Otis P. Starkey, with the collaboration of J. Lewis Robinson. Cartography by Gerald D. Ruth. New York, McGraw-Hill [1968, c1969] ix, 533 p. illus., maps. 26 cm. (McGraw-Hill series in geography) *1. United States — Description and travel — 1960- 2. Canada — Description and travel — 1951- I. Robinson, John Lewis, 1918- II. T.*
E169.02.S78   917   68-28421

Wolfe, Tom.   III. 4715
The pump house gang. New York, Farrar, Straus & Giroux [1968] x, 309 p. illus. 22 cm. *1. U.S. — Social life and customs — 1945- 2. Social status. 3. England — Social life and customs — 20th cent. I. T.*
E169.02.W6   917.3/03/923   67-10922

E169.1 CIVILIZATION. INTELLECTUAL LIFE A – B

Adams, James Truslow, 1878-1949.   III. 4716
The American; the making of a new man, by James Truslow Adams. New York, Scribner, 1943. ix, 404 p. 22 cm. *1. National characteristics, American. 2. U.S. — History. I. T.*
E169.1.A2   917.3   43-51259

Adams, James Truslow, 1878-1949.   III. 4717
Our business civilization; some aspects of American culture. New York, AMS Press [1969] ix, 9-306 p. 23 cm. Reprint of the 1929 ed. *1. United States — Civilization — 1918-1945. 2. National characteristics, American. 3. United States — Social conditions — 1918-1932. I. T.*
E169.1.A216 1969   917.3/03/16   75-92608

Allen, Frederick Lewis, 1890-   III. 4718
The big change: America transforms itself, 1900-1950. [1st ed.] New York, Harper [1952] 308 p. 22 cm. *1. U.S. — Social conditions. 2. U.S. — Economic conditions. 3. National characteristics, American. I. T.*
E169.1.A4717   973.91   52-8455

American Academy of Arts and Sciences, Boston. Commission on the Year 2000.   III. 4719
Toward the year 2000; work in progress. Edited by Daniel Bell. Boston, Houghton Mifflin Co., 1968. ix, 400 p. 24 cm. (The Dædalus library, v. 11) "With the exception of 'Violence' by James Q. Wilson, which is published here for the first time, the essays in this book appeared in the summer 1967 issue of Dædalus, the journal of the American Academy of Arts and Sciences." *1. United States — History — Prophecies — Addresses, essays, lectures. 2. Twenty-first century — Forecasts. I. Bell, Daniel, ed. II. Dædalus. III. T.*
E169.1.A47192   973   68-17173

American Studies Association.   III. 4720
American perspectives; the national self-image in the twentieth century. Edited by Robert E. Spiller and Eric Larrabee; associate editors: Ralph Henry Gabriel, Henry Nash Smith [and] Edward N. Waters. Cambridge, Harvard University Press, 1961. vii, 216 p. 22 cm. (Library of Congress series in American civilization) *1. U.S. — Intellectual life. 2. U.S. — Economic policy. 3. National characteristics, American. I. Spiller, Robert Ernest, 1896- ed. II. Larrabee, Eric, ed. III. T. (S)*
E169.1.A49   917.3   61-8841

Bowers, David Frederick, 1906- ed.   III. 4721
Foreign influences in American life, essays and critical bibliographies. Edited for the Princeton program of study in American civilization. New York, P. Smith, 1952 [c1944] x, 254 p. plates. 21 cm. (Princeton studies in American civilization) *1. U.S. — Foreign population. 2. U.S. — Civilization. 3. U.S. — Nationality. I. Princeton University. Program of study in American civilization. II. T. (S)*
E169.1.Bx   A54-10011

Beard, Charles Austin, 1874-1948.   III. 4722
The rise of American civilization, by Charles A. Beard & Mary R. Beard. Decorations by Wilfred Jones. New ed., two volumes in one, rev. and enl. New York, Macmillan [1949] xi, 824, 903 p. illus., col. maps. 21 cm. *1. U.S. — Civilization. 2. U.S. — History. I. Beard, Mary (Ritter) 1876- joint author. II. T.*
E169.1.Bx   A51-2586

Baldwin, Leland Dewitt, 1897-   III. 4723
The meaning of America; essays toward an understanding of the American spirit. [Pittsburgh] University of Pittsburgh Press [1955] 319 p. illus. 24 cm. *1. U.S. — Civilization. 2. National characteristics, American. I. T.*
E169.1.B216   973   55-10721

Baritz, Loren, 1928-   III. 4724
City on a hill; a history of ideas and myths in America. New York, Wiley [1964] xi, 367 p. ports. 24 cm. *1. United States — Intellectual life. 2. Philosophy, American. I. T.*
E169.1.B225   917.3   64-25896

Barker, Charles Albro, 1904-   III. 4725
American convictions; cycles of public thought, 1600-1850, by Charles A. Barker. [1st ed.] Philadelphia, Lippincott [1970] xix, 632 p. illus., ports. 25 cm. *1. United States — Intellectual life. 2. United States — Religion. 3. United States — Civilization — To 1783. 4. United States — Civilization — 1783-1865. I. T.*
E169.1.B228   917.3/03   69-16960

Beard, Charles Austin, 1874-1948.   III. 4726
America in midpassage, by Charles A. Beard & Mary R. Beard. Drawings by Wilfred Jones. Gloucester, Mass., P. Smith, 1966 [c1939] 977 p. illus. 21 cm. Vol.3 of the authors' The rise of American civilization. *1. U.S. — Civilization — 1918-1945. 2. U.S. — History — 20th cent. I. Beard, Mary (Ritter) 1876-1958, joint author. II. T.*
E169.1.B282   917.3039   66-3464

Beard, Charles Austin, 1874-1948.   III. 4727
The American spirit, a study of the idea of civilization in the United States, by Charles A. Beard and Mary R. Beard. New York, Macmillan, 1942. vii, 696 p. 22 cm. Vol.4 of the authors' The rise of American civilization. "First printing." *1. U.S. — Civilization. 2. Civilization — Philosophy. I. Beard, Mary (Ritter) 1876- joint author. II. T.*
E169.1.B285   917.3   42-50003

Becker, Carl Lotus, 1873-1945.   III. 4728
Freedom and responsibility in the American way of life; five lectures delivered at the University of Michigan, December 1944; with an introductory essay by George H. Sabine. [1st ed.] New York, A. A. Knopf, 1945. xlii, 122, iv p. 22 cm. (Michigan. University. William W. Cook Foundation. Lectures, v.1) *1. U.S. — Civilization. I. T. (S)*
E169.1.B385   323.44   45-9854

Berman, Ronald.   III. 4729
America in the sixties; an intellectual history. New York, Free Press [1968] ix, 291 p. 21 cm. *1. United States — Intellectual life. I. T.*
E169.1.B49   917.3/03/92   68-10365

Bode, Carl, 1911-   III. 4730
The anatomy of American popular culture, 1840-1861. Berkeley, University of California Press, 1959. 292 p. illus. 24 cm. *1. U.S. — Civilization. 2. U.S. — Intellectual life. I. T.*
E169.1.B657   917.3   59-8759

Boorstin, Daniel Joseph, 1914-   III. 4731
America and the image of Europe: reflections on American thought. New York, Meridian Books [1960] 192 p. 19 cm. (Meridian books, M89) *1. United States — Civilization. 2. National characteristics, American. 3. United States — Relations (general) with foreign countries. I. T.*
E169.1.B75   917.3   60-6769

Boorstin, Daniel Joseph, 1914-   III. 4732
The image; or, What happened to the American dream. [1st ed.] New York, Atheneum, 1962 [c1961] 315 p. 22 cm. *1. United States — Civilization — 1945- 2. National characteristics, American. I. T.*
E169.1.B752   917.3   62-7936

Brogan, Denis William, 1900-   III. 4733
America in the modern world. New Brunswick, N.J., Rutgers University Press [1960] 117 p. 22 cm. *1. U.S. — Civilization. 2. National characteristics, American. 3. U.S. — Relations (general) with foreign countries. I. T.*
E169.1.B7968   917.3   59-13541

Brogan, Denis William, 1900-   III. 4734
The American character, by D. W. Brogan. New York, Knopf, 1944. xxi, 168 p. 22 cm. "First edition." *1. National characteristics, American. I. T.*
E169.1.B797   44-8534

Bryce, James Bryce, viscount, 1838-1922.   III. 4735
Reflections on American institutions; selections from The American Commonwealth. With an introd. by Henry Steele Commager. Greenwich, Conn., Fawcett Publications [1961] 272 p. 18 cm. (Premier Americana) "Chapters selected from parts 4, 5 and 6 of The American Commonwealth." *1. U.S. — Civilization — 1865-1918. I. Commager, Henry Steele, 1902- ed. II. T.*
E169.1.B893   917.3   61-66422

Burns, Edward McNall, 1897-   III. 4736
The American idea of mission; concepts of national purpose and destiny. New Brunswick, N.J., Rutgers University Press, 1957. 385 p. illus. 25 cm. *1. U.S. — Civilization. 2. National characteristics, American. 3. U.S. — History — Philosophy. I. T.*
E169.1.B943   917.3   57-10961

E169.1   C – F

Changing patterns in American civilization,   III. 4737
by Dixon Wecter [and others] Pref. by Robert E. Spiller. Philadelphia, Univ. of Pennsylvania Press, 1949. xi, 176 p. 23 cm. (Benjamin Franklin lectures of the University of Pennsylvania, inaugural ser., 1948) *1. U.S. — Civilization. I. Wecter, Dixon, 1906- (S:Pennsylvania. University. Benjamin Franklin lectures, 1948)*
E169.1.C445   917.3   49-3802

Chase, Richard Volney, 1914-   III. 4738
The democratic vista: a dialogue on life and letters in contemporary America. [1st ed.] Garden City, N.Y., Doubleday, 1958. 180 p. 22 cm. (Doubleday anchor books) *1. U.S. — Civilization. I. T.*
E169.1.C452   917.3   58-7351

Commager, Henry Steele, 1902- ed.   III. 4739
America in perspective; the United States through foreign eyes. Ed., with an introd. and notes, by Henry Steele Commager. New York, Random House [1947] xxiv, 389 p. 22 cm. *1. U.S. — Civilization. 2. National characteristics, American. I. T.*
E169.1.C67   917.3   47-6240

Commager, Henry Steele, 1902-   III. 4740
The American mind; an interpretation of American thought and character since the 1880's. New Haven, Yale University Press, 1950. ix, 476 p. port. 24 cm. *1. U.S. — Civilization. 2. U.S. — Intellectual life. 3. National characteristics, American. I. T.*
E169.1.C673   917.3   50-6338

The Cultural migration; the European scholar in America,   III. 4741
by Franz L. Neumann [and others] Introd. by W. Rex Crawford. Philadelphia, University of Pennsylvania Press, 1953. 156 p. 23 cm. (The Benjamin Franklin lectures of the University of Pennsylvania, 5th ser., 1952) *1. U.S. — Intellectual life. 2. Refugees, Political. 3. Intellectuals. I. Neumann, Franz Leopold, 1900- (S:Pennsylvania. University. Benjamin Franklin lectures, 1952)*
E169.1.C84 1953   917.3   53-6930

Curti, Merle Eugene, 1897-   III. 4742
American paradox: the conflict of thought and action. New Brunswick, N.J., Rutgers University Press, 1956. 116 p. 20 cm. *1. Intellectuals. 2. U.S. — Civilization. I. T.*
E169.1.C86   917.3   56-7610

Curti, Merle Eugene, 1897-   III. 4743
The growth of American thought, by Merle Curti. 3d ed. New York, Harper & Row [1964] xx, 939 p. illus., facsims., ports. 22 cm. *1. U.S. — Intellectual life. 2. U.S. — Civilization. I. T.*
E169.1.C87 1964   917.3   64-12796

Curti, Merle Eugene, 1897-   III. 4744
Probing our past. New York, Harper [c1955] 294 p. 22 cm. Essays. *1. U.S. — Intellectual life — Addresses, essays, lectures. 2. U.S. — History — Historiography. 3. U.S. — Relations (general) with foreign countries. I. T.*
E169.1.C885   973.04   54-11009

Curti, Merle Eugene, 1897-   III. 4745
The roots of American loyalty, by Merle Curti. New York, Atheneum, 1968 [c1946] xvi, 267 p. 21 cm. (Atheneum 115) *1. Patriotism — United States. 2. United States — History. I. T.*
E169.1.C89 1968   973   68-16409

Davidson, Donald, 1893-   III. 4746
The attack on leviathan; regionalism and nationalism in the United States. Chapel Hill, The University of North Carolina Press, 1938. x, 368 p. 23 cm. *1. Sectionalism (U.S.) 2. U.S. — Nationality. 3. U.S. — Civilization. I. Regionalism and nationalism in the United States. II. T.*
E169.1.D34   38-9614

Dudden, Arthur Power, 1921-   III. 4747
The United States of America, a syllabus of American studies. Philadelphia, University of Pennsylvania Press [1963] 2 v. illus. 22 cm. *1. U.S. — Civilization — Outlines, syllabi, etc.*
E169.1.D82 1963   917.3   63-5574

Echeverria, Durand.   III. 4748
Mirage in the West; a history of the French image of American society to 1815. Foreword by Gilbert Chinard. New York, Octagon Books, 1966 [c1957] xvii, 300 p. 24 cm. *1. U.S. — Civilization. 2. U.S. — Foreign opinion, French. 3. U.S. — Relations (general) with France. 4. France — Relations (general) with the U.S. I. T.*
E169.1.E23 1966   917.3   66-17509

Ekirch, Arthur Alphonse, 1915-   III. 4749
The civilian and the military. New York, Oxford University Press, 1956. 340 p. 24 cm. *1. Militarism — U.S. 2. Civil supremacy over the military — U.S. I. T.*
E169.1.E49   973   56-5160

Fiedler, Leslie A.   III. 4750
An end to innocence; essays on culture and politics. Boston, Beacon Press [1955] 214 p. 21 cm. *1. United States — Civilization — Addresses, essays, lectures. 2. United States — Politics and government — 1945- — Addresses, essays, lectures. I. T.*
E169.1.F5   973.9204*   55-7798

Fleming, Donald Harnish, 1923-   III. 4751
The intellectual migration; Europe and America, 1930-1960, edited by Donald Fleming and Bernard Bailyn. Cambridge, Belknap Press of Harvard University Press, 1969. 748 p. illus. 24 cm. "An expansion of the second volume of Perspectives in American history, an annual journal." — book jacket. *1. United States — Civilization — Foreign influences. 2. Europe — Emigration and immigration. 3. Intellectuals — United States. 4. Refugees, Political. I. Bailyn, Bernard, joint author. II. Perspectives in American history. III. T.*
E169.1.F6   001.2/0973   78-75432

Fortune.   III. 4752
U.S.A., the permanent revolution, by the editors of Fortune in collaboration with Russell W. Davenport. [1st ed.] New York, Prentice-Hall, 1951. xvii, 267 p. 24 cm. "Originally published as the February, 1951, issue of Fortune magazine." *1. U.S. — Civilization. 2. U.S. — Social conditions. 3. U.S. — Foreign relations — 1945- I. Davenport, Russell Wheeler, 1899- II. T.*
E169.1.F75   917.3   51-10804

Frank, Waldo David, 1889-   III. 4753
The re-discovery of America; an introduction to a philosophy of American life, by Waldo Frank. New York, London, Scribner, 1929. x, 353 p. 22 cm. *1. U.S. — Civilization. I. T.*
E169.1.F824   29-6953

E169.1   G – L

Gabriel, Ralph Henry, 1890-   III. 4754
The course of American democratic thought. 2d ed. New York, Ronald Press Co. [1956] xiv, 508 p. 24 cm. *1. U.S. — Civilization. 2. U.S. — Intellectual life. 3. Philosophy, American. 4. Philosophy — History — U.S. Democracy. I. T.*
E169.1.G23 1956   917.3   56-6263

Greene, Theodore P., 1920-   III. 4755
America's heroes; the changing models of success in American magazines [by] Theodore P. Greene. New York, Oxford University Press, 1970. vi, 387 p. 22 cm. The periodicals covered were published between 1757 and 1918 inclusive. *1. United States — Social life and customs. 2. United States — Intellectual life. 3. American periodicals — History. 4. Heroes in literature. I. T.*
E169.1.G754   051   70-117214

Guttmann, Allen.   III. 4756
The conservative tradition in America. New York, Oxford University Press,

1967. viii, 214 p. 22 cm. *1. U.S. — Civilization. 2. Conservatism — U.S. I. T.*
E169.1.G97   917.3/03   67-25460

Handlin, Oscar, 1915- III. 4757
The American people in the twentieth century. Boston, Beacon Press [1963] 248 p. 21 cm. *1. U.S. — Civilization — 20th cent. 2. Minorities — U.S. I. T.*
E169.1.H265 1963   917.3   63-2687

Hartshorne, Thomas L. III. 4758
The distorted image; changing conceptions of the American character since Turner [by] Thomas L. Hartshorne. Cleveland, Press of Case Western Reserve University, 1968. xiv, 226 p. 24 cm. *1. National characteristics, American. I. Changing conceptions of the American character since Turner. II. T.*
E169.1.H278   917.3/03/92   68-9429   ISBN:082950141X

Wertenbaker, Thomas Jefferson, 1879- III. 4759
The first Americans, 1607-1690, by Thomas Jefferson Wertenbaker New York, Macmillan, 1938. xx, 358 p. front., plates, ports., map, plan, facsims. 22 cm. (A history of American life. vol.II) "Published November, 1927; reprinted June, 1929; reprinted May, 1938." *1. U.S. — Social life and customs — Colonial period. 2. U.S. — Civilization. I. T.*
E169.1.H673 vol. 2   917.3   38-34436

Fish, Carl Russell, 1876-1932. III. 4760
The rise of the common man, 1830-1850, by Carl Russell Fish ... New York, The Macmillan Company, 1937. xix p., 1 l., 391 p. front., plates. 22 cm. (A history of American life. vol. VI) *1. U.S. — Social conditions. 2. U.S. — Economic conditions. 3. U.S. — Civilization. I. T.*
E169.1.H673 vol. 6   38-34437

Hofstadter, Richard, 1916-1970. III. 4761
Anti-intellectualism in American life. [1st ed.] New York, Knopf, 1963. 434, xiii p. 25 cm. *1. United States — Civilization. 2. Intellectuals — United States. I. T.*
E169.1.H74   917.3   63-14086

Is the common man too common? An informal survey of our cultural resources and what we are doing about them III. 4762
[by] Joseph Wood Krutch [and others. 1st ed.] Norman, University of Oklahoma Press [1954] xii, 146 p. 23 cm. *1. U.S. — Intellectual life. I. Krutch, Joseph Wood, 1893-*
E169.1.I8   917.3   54-5938

Jones, Howard Mumford, 1892- III. 4763
The age of energy; varieties of American experience, 1865-1915. New York, Viking Press [1971] xix, 545 p. illus. 23 cm. *1. United States — Civilization — 1865-1918. I. T.*
E169.1.J6435 1971   917.3/03/8   75-146599   ISBN:0670109665

Jones, Howard Mumford, 1892- III. 4764
O strange new world; American culture: the formative years. New York, Viking Press [1964] xiv, 464 p. illus., facsim. 23 cm. *1. United States — Civilization — To 1783. 2. United States — Civilization — 1783-1865. 3. United States — Civilzation — European influences. I. T.*
E169.1.J644 1964   917.3   64-15062

Kallen, Horace Meyer, 1882- III. 4765
Cultural pluralism and the American idea; an essay in social philosophy. With comments by Stanley H. Chapman [and others] Philadelphia, University of Pennsylvania Press [1956] 208 p. 22 cm. (Albert M. Greenfield Center for Human Relations. Studies in human relations, no. 1) *1. U.S. — Civilization — Addresses, essays, lectures. 2. U.S. — History — Philosophy. I. T. (S)*
E169.1.K26   917.3   56-11801

Kaplan, Abraham, 1918- III. 4766
American ethics and public policy. [With corrections] New York, Oxford University Press, 1963. 110 p. 21 cm. (A Galaxy book) "GB99." "Originally published in The American style: essays in value and performance, edited by Elting Morison." *1. National characteristics, American. 2. Political ethics. I. T.*
E169.1.K315   172   63-5685

Kirk, Russell. III. 4767
The American cause. Chicago, H. Regnery Co., 1957. 172 p. 22 cm. *1. U.S. — Civilization. 2. U.S. — History — Philosphy. 3. Communism. I. T.*
E169.1.K55   917.3   57-12748

Knoles, George Harmon. III. 4768
The jazz age revisited; British criticism of American civilization during the 1920's Stanford, Calif., Stanford University Press, 1955. vii, 171 p. 23 cm. (Stanford University publications. University series. History, economics, and political science, v.11) *1. U.S. — Civilization. 2. National characteristics, American. 3. Public opinion — Gt. Brit. I. T. (S:Stanford University. Stanford studies in history, economics, and political science, v.11)*
E169.1.K6 (AS36.L54 vol. 11)   973.91   55-10016

Kohn, Hans, 1891- III. 4769
American nationalism; an interpretative essay. New York, Macmillan, 1957. 272 p. 22 cm. *1. U.S. — Civilization — History. 2. National characteristics, American. 3. Nationalism — U.S. 4. Nationalism. I. T.*
E169.1.K63   917.3   57-8101

Kraus, Michael, 1901- III. 4770
Intercolonial aspects of American culture on the eve of the Revolution, with special reference to the northern towns. New York, Octagon Books, 1964 [c1928] 251 p. 24 cm. *1. U.S. — Civilization — To 1783. I. American culture on the eve of the Revolution. II. T.*
E169.1.K688 1964   917.3   64-24838

Laski, Harold Joseph, 1893- III. 4771
The American democracy, a commentary and an interpretation. New York, Viking Press, 1948. x, 785 p. 25 cm. *1. U.S. — Civilization. 2. U.S. — Politics and government. 3. U.S. — Social conditions. I. T.*
E169.1.L38 1948   917.3   48-2654

Leighton, Isabel, ed. III. 4772
The aspirin age, 1919-1941, written by Samuel Hopkins Adams [and others] New York, Simon and Schuster, 1949. ix, 491 p. 22 cm. *1. U.S. — Civilization. I. T.*
E169.1.L526   917.3   49-9336

Lerner, Max, 1902- III. 4773
America as a civilization; life and thought in the United States today. New York, Simon and Schuster, 1957. xiii, 1036 p. 25 cm. *1. U.S. — Civilization. 2. National characteristics, American. I. T.*
E169.1.L532   917.3   57-10979

Lipset, Seymour Martin. III. 4774
The first new Nation; the United States in historical and comparative perspective. New York, Basic Books [1963] xv, 366 p. 25 cm. *1. United States — Civilization. 2. National characteristics, American. 3. Comparative government. I. T.*
E169.1.L546   917.3   63-17345

Lynes, Russell, 1910- III. 4775
The tastemakers. [1st ed. New York] Harper [1954] 362 p. illus. 25 cm. *1. U.S. — Civilization. 2. U.S. — Social life and customs. 3. Aesthetics. 4. Art — U.S. I. T.*
E169.1.L95   917.3   54-8968

E169.1   M – N

Macdonald, Dwight. III. 4776
Against the American grain. New York, Random House [1962] 427 p. 22 cm. Essays. *1. U.S. — Popular culture. I. T.*
E169.1.M136   917.3   62-17170

Marx, Leo, 1919- III. 4777
The machine in the garden; technology and the pastoral ideal in America. New York, Oxford University Press, 1964. 392 p. illus. 21 cm. *1. United States — Civilization. 2. Nature. I. Technology and the pastoral ideal in America. II. T.*
E169.1.M35   917.3   64-24864

May, Henry Farnham, 1915- III. 4778
The end of American innocence; a study of the first years of our own time, 1912-1917. [1st ed.] New York, Knopf, 1959. 412 p. 22 cm. *1. United States — Intellectual life. 2. United States — Civilization — 1865-1918. I. T.*
E169.1.M496   917.3   59-11236

Mead, Margaret, 1901- III. 4779
And keep your powder dry; an anthropologist looks at America. Freeport, N.Y., Books for Libraries Press [1971, c1965] x, 274 p. 23 cm. (Essay index reprint series) *1. National characteristics, American. I. T.*
E169.1.M5 1971   917.3/03/917   77-156694   ISBN:0836924169

Miller, Perry, 1905-1963. III. 4780
The life of the mind in America, from the Revolution to the Civil War. [1st ed.] New York, Harcourt, Brace & World [1965] xi, 338 p. 24 cm. Contains books 1-2, and part of book 3, of a work intended to be complete in 9 books. The parts after book 3, chapter 1, were never completed. *1. U.S. — Intellectual life. 2. U.S. — Civilization — 1783-1865. I. T.*
E169.1.M6273   917.303   65-19065

Miller, Raymond Curtis, ed. III. 4781
Twentieth-century pessimism and the American dream. Detroit, Wayne State University Press, 1961. 104 p. illus. 21 cm. (The Leo M. Franklin

memorial lectures (1958) v.8) *1. U.S. — Civilization. 2. U.S. — Economic conditions. 3. Big business — U.S. I. T.*
E169.1.M6275   917.3   60-14908

Miller, Perry, 1905- III. 4782
Errand into the wilderness. Cambridge, Belknap Press of Harvard University Press, 1956. x, 244 p. 24 cm. *1. U.S. — Civilization. 2. U.S. — Religion. 3. Philosophy, American. I. T.*
E169.1.M628   917.3   56-11285

Miller, Perry, 1905-1963. III. 4783
Nature's nation. Cambridge, Belknap Press of Harvard University Press, 1967. xvi, 258 p. 24 cm. *1. U.S. — Intellectual life. 2. U.S. — Religion. 3. Philosophy, American. I. T.*
E169.1.M635   917.3/03   67-17316

Mills, Charles Wright. III. 4784
The power elite. New York, Oxford University Press, 1956. 423 p. 22 cm. *1. U.S. — Civilization. 2. U.S. — Social conditions. I. T.*
E169.1.M64   917.3   56-5427

Morris, Clarence, 1903- ed. III. 4785
Trends in modern American society, by John M. Blum [and others] Philadelphia, University of Pennsylvania Press [1962] 191 p. 22 cm. (The Benjamin Franklin lectures of the University of Pennsylvania, 7th ser.) *1. U.S. — Civilization — 1945- I. T.*
E169.1.M818   917.3   62-11262

Mumford, Lewis, 1895- III. 4786
The golden day; a study in American literature and culture. With a new introd. Boston, Beacon Press [1957, c1953] 144 p. 21 cm. (Beacon paperback, no. 38) *1. U.S. — Civilization. 2. U.S. — Intellectual life. 3. American literature — 19th cent. — History and criticism. I. T.*
E169.1.M943 1957   917.3 (810.9)   57-59151

Nagel, Paul C. III. 4787
This sacred trust; American nationality, 1798-1898 [by] Paul C. Nagel. New York, Oxford University Press, 1971. xvi, 376 p. 22 cm. *1. Nationalism — U.S. 2. U.S. — Civilization — 19th century. I. T.*
E169.1.N25   917.3/03   78-159648

Nash, Roderick. III. 4788
Wilderness and the American mind. New Haven, Yale University Press, 1967. viii, 256 p. 24 cm. "A note on the sources": p. [237]-246. Bibliographical footnotes. *1. U.S. — Civilization. 2. Frontier and pioneer life — U.S. I. T.*
E169.1.N37   917.3/03   67-24506

Niebuhr, Reinhold, 1892- III. 4789
Pious and secular America. New York, Scribner [1958] viii, 150 p. 21 cm. *1. U.S. — Civilization — Addresses, essays, lectures. I. T.*
E169.1.N67   917.3   58-5721

Noble, David W. III. 4790
The paradox of progressive thought. Minneapolis, University of Minnesota [1958] 272 p. 23 cm. *1. U.S. — Intellectual life. 2. U.S. — Biography. I. T.*
E169.1.N7   917.3   58-8765

Nye, Russel Blaine, 1913- III. 4791
The cultural life of the new Nation, 1776-1830. [1st ed.] New York, Harper [1960] xii, 324 p. illus. 22 cm. (The New American Nation series) *1. U.S. — Intellectual life. 2. U.S. — History — 1783-1865. I. T.*
E169.1.N9   973.3   60-16496

E169.1   P – Z

Parkes, Henry Bamford, 1904- III. 4792
The American experience; an interpretation of the history and civilization of the American people. 2d ed. rev. New York, Knopf, 1955. 345, viii p. 22 cm. *1. U.S. — Civilization. I. T.*
E169.1.P23 1955   917.3   55-3076

Perry, Ralph Barton, 1876-1957. III. 4793
Puritanism and democracy [by] Ralph Barton Perry. New York, Vanguard Press [1944] xvi, 688 p. 22 cm. *1. U.S. — Civilization. 2. Puritans. 3. Democracy. I. T.*
E169.1.P47   917.3   44-41893

Peyre, Henri, 1901- III. 4794
Observations on life, literature, and learning in America. Carbondale, Southern Illinois University Press [1961] 253 p. 23 cm. *1. U.S. — Civilization — Addresses, essays, lectures. 2. U.S. — Intellectual life. 3. Education — U.S.*

4. U.S. — Foreign opinion — French. I. T:Life, literature, and learning in America.
E169.1.P5   917.3   61-8218

Pochmann, Henry August, 1901- III. 4795
German culture in America; philosophical and literary influences, 1600-1900 [by] Henry A. Pochmann. With the assistance of Arthur R. Schultz and others. Madison, University of Wisconsin Press, 1957. xv, 865 p. 26 cm. *1. U.S. — Civilization — German influences. 2. Literature, Comparative — German and American. 3. Literature, Comparative — American and German. I. T.*
E169.1.P596   325.2430973   55-6791

Potter, David Morris. III. 4796
People of plenty; economic abundance and the American character. [Chicago] University of Chicago Press [1954] xxvii, 219 p. illus. 22 cm. (Charles R. Walgreen Foundation lectures) *1. National characteristics, American. 2. U.S. — Economic conditions. I. T. (S:Chicago. University. Charles R. Walgreen Foundation for the study of American Institutions. Lectures)*
E169.1.P6   917.3   54-12797

The Reporter (New York, 1949- III. 4797
Our times; the best from the Reporter. Edited by Max Ascoli. New York, Farrar, Straus and Cudahy [1960] 502 p. 22 cm. *1. U.S. — Civilization — Addresses, essays, lectures. 2. History, Modern — 20th cent. I. Ascoli, Max, 1888- ed. II. T.*
E169.1.R46   917.3   59-15071

Rourke, Constance Mayfield, 1885-1941. III. 4798
The roots of American culture and other essays, by Constance Rourke. Edited, with a preface, by Van Wyck Brooks. 1st ed. New York, Harcourt, Brace [1942] xii, 305 p. 22 cm. *1. U.S. — Civilization. I. Brooks, Van Wyck, 1886- ed. II. T.*
E169.1.R78   917.3   42-19827

Savelle, Max, 1896- III. 4799
Seeds of liberty; the genesis of the American mind. Seattle, University of Washington Press, 1965 [c1948] xvii, 618 p. illus., facsims., fold. map, music, ports. 22 cm. "Chapter nine ... entitled 'Of music, and of America singing,' was written by Cyclone Covey." *1. U.S. — Civilization — To 1783. I. Covey, Cyclone. II. T.*
E169.1.S27 1965   917.3032   65-23913

Schmitt, Peter J. III. 4800
Back to nature; the Arcadian myth in urban America [by] Peter J. Schmitt. New York, Oxford University Press, 1969. xxiii, 230 p. 22 cm. (The Urban life in America series) *1. United States — Civilization — 1865-1918. 2. Nature in literature. I. T.*
E169.1.S343   917.3/03/9   70-83052

Siegfried, André, 1875- III. 4801
America at mid-century. Translated by Margaret Ledésert. [1st American ed.] New York, Harcourt, Brace [1955] 357 p. illus. 22 cm. *1. U.S. — Civilization. I. T.*
E169.1.S568   917.3   55-7422

Siegfried, André, 1875-1959. III. 4802
America comes of age; a French analysis. Translated by H. H. Hemming and Doris Hemming. New foreword by George H. Knoles. New York, Da Capo Press, 1973. p. (The American scene: comments and commentators) Translation of Les États-Unis d'aujourd'hui. Reprint of the 1927 ed. published by Harcourt, Brace, New York. *1. United States — Civilization — 1918-1945. 2. United States — Race question. 3. United States — Economic conditions — 1918-1945. 4. United States — Politics and government — 1901-1953. I. T.*
E169.1.S58   917.3/03/91   68-16244   ISBN:0306710250

Somkin, Fred. III. 4803
Unquiet eagle; memory and desire in the idea of American freedom, 1815-1860. Ithaca, N.Y., Cornell University Press [1967] xi, 233 p. facism. 23 cm. *1. U.S. — Civilization — 1783-1865. I. T.*
E169.1.S68   917.3/03/5   67-23763

The Times literary supplement. III. 4804
The American imagination; a critical survey of the arts from the Times Literary supplement. With a foreword by Alan Pryce-Jones. New York, Atheneum, 1960. 209 p. 22 cm. *1. U.S. — Intellectual life. 2. Creation (Literary, artistic, etc.) I. T.*
E169.1.T56   917.3   60-11945

Torrielli, Andrew Joseph, 1912- III. 4805
Italian opinion on America as revealed by Italian travelers, 1850-1900, by Andrew J. Torrielli. Cambridge, Mass., Harvard University Press, 1941. vi, 330 p. 24 cm. (Harvard studies in Romance languages ... vol.XV) Based on thesis (PH.D.) — Harvard university, 1940. Without thesis note. *1. U.S. — Civilization. 2. U.S. — History — 1783-1865. 3. U.S. — History — 1865-1898. I. T.*
E169.1.T66 1941   917.3   A41-3270

Toynbee, Arnold Joseph, 1889-   **III. 4806**
America and the world revolution, and other lectures. New York, Oxford University Press, 1962. 231 p. 20 cm. *1. U.S. — Civilization. 2. U.S. — Relations (general) with foreign countries. 3. Latin America — Social conditions. 4. Civilization, Occidental. I. T.*
E169.1.T69   327.73   62-19209

Warner, William Lloyd, 1898-   **III. 4807**
The living and the dead; a study of the symbolic life of Americans. New Haven, Yale University Press, 1959. xii, 528 p. illus. 24 cm. (Yankee City series, v.5) *1. U.S. — Civilization. 2. U.S. — Social life and customs. 3. Symbolism. I. T. (S)*
E169.1.W28   917.3   59-6804

Weyl, Nathaniel, 1910-   **III. 4808**
The creative elite in America. Washington, Public Affairs Press [1966] vii, 236 p. 24 cm. *1. Intellectuals — U.S. 2. Creation (Literary, artistic, etc.) 3. Jews in the U.S. — Intellectual life. I. T.*
E169.1.W395   301.44   66-23828

Wish, Harvey, 1909-   **III. 4809**
Society and thought in America. 2d ed. New York, D. McKay Co. [19   v. illus. 22 cm. *1. United States — Civilization — History. 2. United States — Intellectual life. I. T.*
E169.1.W652   917.3   61-18349

Wolfe, Tom.   **III. 4810**
The kandy-kolored tangerine-flake streamline baby. [New York, Farrar, Straus and Giroux, 1965] xvii, 339 p. illus. 22 cm. *1. United States — Popular culture. 2. Social status. I. T.*
E169.1.W685   309.173   65-19050

Wylie, Philip, 1902-   **III. 4811**
Generation of vipers, newly annotated by the author ... New York, Rinehart [1955] 331 p. 22 cm. *1. U.S. — Civilization. I. T.*
E169.1.W9 1955   917.3   55-6424

Zelomek, A. Wilbert, 1900-   **III. 4812**
A changing America: at work and play. New York, Wiley [1959] 181 p. 22 cm. *1. U.S. — Civilization. 2. U.S. — Social life and customs. I. T.*
E169.1.Z4   917.3   59-6754

E169.12   CIVILIZATION, 1945 –

Rosenberg, Bernard, 1923- comp.   **III. 4813**
Mass culture revisited. Edited by Bernard Rosenberg [and] David Manning White. New York, Van Nostrand Reinhold [1971] xii, 473 p. 25 cm. *1. United States — Popular culture. 2. Mass media — United States. I. White, David Manning, joint comp. II. T.*
E169.12.R65   301.16/1/0973   71-164986

Slater, Philip Elliot.   **III. 4814**
The pursuit of loneliness; American culture at the breaking point [by] Philip E. Slater. Boston, Beacon Press [1970] xiii, 154 p. 24 cm. *1. U.S. — Civilization — 1945- 2. National characteristics, American. I. T.*
E169.12.S53 1970   917.3/03/92   79-101327   ISBN:807041807

E169.5   AMERICANIZATION

Antin, Mary, 1881-1949.   **III. 4815**
The promised land. With a foreword by Oscar Handlin. 2d ed. Boston, Houghton Mifflin, 1969 [c1912] xxii, 373 p. 22 cm. Autobiographical. *I. T.*
E169.5.A66 1969   917.3/03/910924 (B)   74-2734

E171 – 856   HISTORY
E171 – 172   Yearbooks. Societies

The American year book; a record of events and progress. 1910-   **III. 4816**
New York and London, D. Appleton, 1911-   v. 21 cm. Editors: 1910, S. N. D. North. — 1911-1919, F. G. Wickware. — 1925- A. B. Hart, Wm. Schuyler. Publication suspended from 1920-1924, inclusive. *1. Statistics — Yearbooks. 2. United States. I. North, Simon Newton Dexter, 1849-1924, ed. II. Wickware, Francis Graham, 1883-1940, ed. III. Hart, Albert Bushnell, 1854-1943, ed.*
E171.A585   11-1626

Directory of historical societies and agencies in the United States and Canada.   **III. 4817**
1956- [Madison, Wis.] American Association for State and Local History. v. 26 cm. *1. Historical societies — United States — Directories. 2. Historical societies — Canada — Directories. I. American Association for State and Local History.*
E172.A538   970.62   56-4164

Dunlap, Leslie Whittaker, 1911-   **III. 4818**
American historical societies, 1790-1860, by Leslie W. Dunlap. Madison, Wis., Priv. Print. [Cantwell Printing Co., 1944] ix, 238 p. 24 cm. *1. Historical societies — U.S. I. T.*
E172.D8   973.062   44-7046

Whitehill, Walter Muir, 1905-   **III. 4819**
Independent historical societies, an enquiry into their research and publication functions and their financial future. [Boston] The Boston Athenaeum; distributed by Harvard University Press, 1962. xviii, 593 p. 24 cm. *1. Historical societies — U.S. I. T.*
E172.W5   973.06973   63-1190

Davies, Wallace Evan.   **III. 4820**
Patriotism on parade; the story of veterans' and hereditary organizations in America, 1783-1900. Cambridge, Harvard University Press, 1955. xiv, 388 p. 22 cm. (Harvard historical studies, v.66) *1. Patriotic societies. I. T. (S)*
E172.7.D3   369.1   55-11951

E173   Sources. Documents

Angle, Paul McClelland, 1900- ed.   **III. 4821**
By these words; great documents of American liberty, selected and placed in their contemporary settings. Illustrated by Edward A. Wilson. New York, Rand, McNally [1954] 560 p. illus. 22 cm. *1. U.S. — History — Sources. I. T.*
E173.A79   973   54-10616

Billington, Ray Allen, 1903- ed.   **III. 4822**
The making of American democracy; readings and documents, edited by Ray Allen Billington [and others] Rev. ed. New York, Holt, Rinehart and Winston [1962- v. 25 cm. *1. U.S. — Hist — Sources. I. T.*
E173.B52   973.082   62-12126

Commager, Henry Steele, 1902- ed.   **III. 4823**
Documents of American history. 8th ed. New York, Appleton-Century-Crofts [1968] xxiii, 634, 746 p. 24 cm. *1. United States — History — Sources. I. T.*
E173.C66 1968   973/.08   68-17410

Commager, Henry Steele, 1902- ed.   **III. 4824**
Living ideas in America. New, enl. ed. New York, Harper & Row [1964] xx, 872 p. 22 cm. *1. U.S. — Civilization — Addresses, essays, lectures. 2. U.S. — History — Sources. 3. U.S. — Politics and government — Addresses, essays, lectures. I. T.*
E173.C67 1964   917.3   64-23898

Emery, Edwin, ed.   **III. 4825**
The story of America as reported by its newspapers, 1690-1965. New York, Simon and Schuster [1965] 311 p. illus., facsims., maps, ports. 43 cm. *1. United States — History — Sources. 2. American newspapers — Facsimiles. I. T.*
E173.E5   973.08   64-22412

Emery, Michael C., comp.   **III. 4826**
America's front page news, 1690-1970. Edited by Michael C. Emery, R. Smith Schuneman [and] Edwin Emery. Minneapolis, Vis-Com, inc.; trade distribution: Doubleday, New York; educational multi-media distribution: 3M IM/Press, St. Paul [1970] 280 p. 41 cm. Consists chiefly of facsim. reproductions of over 300 newspaper front pages, each with an annotation. *1. United States — History — Sources. 2. American newspapers — Facsimiles. I. Schuneman, R. Smith, joint comp. II. Emery, Edwin, joint comp. III. T.*
E173.E53   917.3/03   71-136211

Essays in American history dedicated to Frederick Jackson Turner.   **III. 4827**
New York, H. Holt, 1910. vii, 293 p. 22 cm. Edited by Guy Stanton Ford. *1. Turner, Frederick Jackson, 1861-1932. 2. U.S. — History — Addresses, essays, lectures. 3. Spanish America — History — Addresses, essays, lectures. I. Ford, Guy Stanton, 1873- ed.*
E173.E78   11-620

Hart, Albert Bushnell, 1854-1943, ed. III. 4828
American history told by contemporaries ... Edited by Albert Bushnell Hart ... New York, The Macmillan company; London, Macmillan, 1897-1929. 5 v. 20 cm. Sources at the beginning of each volume. Vol. V edited by A. B. Hart with the collaboration of J. G. Curtis. Vol. V. has imprint: New York, The Macmillan company. *1. U.S. — History — Sources. I. Curtis, John Gould, joint ed. II. T.*
E173.H32   02-5830

Historiography and urbanization; essays in American history in honor of W. Stull Holt, III. 4829
edited by Eric F. Goldman. Baltimore, Johns Hopkins Press, 1941. 9, 220 p. 21 cm. *1. U.S. — History — Addresses, essays, lectures. 2. Historiography. I. Holt, William Stull, 1896- II. Goldman, Eric Frederick, 1915- ed.*
E173.H67   973.04   41-6873

Leopold, Richard William, ed. III. 4830
Problems in American history, edited by Richard W. Leopold, Arthur S. Link [and] Stanley Coben. 3d ed. Englewood Cliffs, N.J., Prentice-Hall [1966] 2 v. 23 cm. *1. United States — History — Sources. I. Link, Arthur Stanley, joint ed. II. Coben, Stanley, joint ed. III. T.*
E173.L45 1966   973   66-19879

Nevins, Allan, 1890-1971. III. 4831
American press opinion; Washington to Coolidge. A documentary record of editorial leadership and criticism, 1785-1927. Port Washington, N.Y., Kennikat Press [1969] 2 v. (xxv, 598 p.) illus. 22 cm. Reprint of the 1928 ed. *1. Public opinion — United States. 2. Press — United States. 3. United States — History — Sources. I. T.*
E173.N52 1969   973/.08   68-8206   ISBN:0804603324

E174 Encyclopedias. Chronologies

Adams, James Truslow, 1878-1949, ed. III. 4832
Dictionary of American history; James Truslow Adams, editor-in-chief; R. V. Coleman, managing editor. 2d ed. rev. New York, Scribner, 1942-   v. 26 cm. On t. p. of v. 6: Supplement 1; issued without ed. statement. *1. United States — History — Dictionaries. I. Coleman, Roy V., 1885-   , joint ed. II. T.*
E174.A43 1942   973.03   44-1876

Adams, James Truslow, 1878-1949, ed. III. 4833
Concise dictionary of American history. Advisory editor: Thomas C. Cochran. Editor: Wayne Andrews. New York, Scribner [1962] vii,1156 p. 27 cm. A concise version of Adams' Dictionary of American history. *1. U.S. — History — Dictionaries. I. Cochran, Thomas Childs, 1902-   , ed. II. Andrews, Wayne, ed. III. T.*
E174.A45   973.03   62-9635

Carruth, Gorton. III. 4834
The encyclopedia of American facts and dates. Edited by Gorton Carruth and associates. 5th ed. New York, Crowell [c1970] vi, 890 p. 24 cm. (A Crowell reference book) *1. U.S. — History — Chronology. I. American facts and dates. II. T.*
E174.5.C3 1970   973.02   72-137822   ISBN:0690263015

Kull, Irving Stoddard. III. 4835
A short chronology of American history, 1492-1950 [by] Irving S. and Nell M. Kull. New Brunswick, Rutgers University Press, 1952. 388 p. 25 cm. *1. U.S. — History — Chronology. I. Kull, Nell M., joint author. II. T.*
E174.5.K8   973.02   52-9371

Morris, Richard Brandon, 1904-   , ed. III. 4836
Encyclopedia of American history. Updated, rev. New York, Harper [c1953, 1965] xiv, 843 p. illus., maps. 25 cm. *1. U. S. — History — Chronology. 2. U. S. — History — Dictionaries. I. T.*
E174.5.M847 1965   65-22859

E175 Historiography. Philosophy

Bellot, Hugh Hale, 1890- III. 4837
American history and American historians; a review of recent contributions to the interpretation of the history of the United States. [1st American ed.] Norman, University of Oklahoma Press [1952] x, 336 p. fold. maps. 23 cm. *1. U.S. — History — Historiography. 2. U.S. — History — 1898- 3. Historians, American. I. T.*
E175.B44 1952a   973.07   52-12131

Bernstein, Barton J. III. 4838
Towards a new past: dissenting essays in American history, edited by Barton J. Bernstein. London, Chatto & Windus, 1970. xvi, 364 p. 23 cm. *1. United States — Historiography — Addresses, essays, lectures.*
E175.B46 1970   973/.072   77-852882   ISBN:0701114827

Billington, Ray Allen, 1903- ed. III. 4839
The reinterpretation of early American history; essays in honor of John Edwin Pomfret. San Marino, Calif., Huntington Library, 1966. viii, 264 p. port. 22 cm. *1. Pomfret, John Edwin, 1898- 2. U.S. — Historiography — Addresses, essays, lectures. I. Pomfret, John Edwin, 1898- II. T.*
E175.B5   973.20722   66-31501

Callcott, George H., 1929- III. 4840
History in the United States, 1800-1860; its practice and purpose [by] George H. Callcott. Baltimore, Johns Hopkins Press [1970] viii, 239 p. 22 cm. *1. United States — Historiography. 2. United States — History — Study and teaching. I. T.*
E175.C3   907   74-88115   ISBN:080181099X

Craven, Wesley Frank, 1905- III. 4841
The legend of the Founding Fathers. New York, New York University Press, 1956. 191 p. 24 cm. (New York University. Stokes Foundation. Anson G. Phelps lectureship on early American history) *1. U.S. — History — Historiography. 2. U.S. — History — Colonial period. 3. National characteristics, American. I. T.*
E175.C7   973.2   56-8593

Higham, John, ed. III. 4842
The reconstruction of American history. London; Hutchinson [1962] 244 p. 22 cm. *1. U.S. — History — Historiography. I. T.*
E175.H65 1962b   62-66696

Higham, John. III. 4843
Writing American history; essays on modern scholarship. Bloomington, Indiana University Press [1970] x, 207 p. 22 cm. *1. United States — Historiography. I. T.*
E175.H654   973/.072   70-108209   ISBN:0253197007

Jameson, John Franklin, 1859-1937. III. 4844
The history of historical writing in America. New York, Antiquarian Press, 1961. 160 p. 19 cm. "First published 1891. Reprinted 1961." *1. U.S. — History — Historiography. I. T.*
E175.Jx   A63-6001

Kraus, Michael, 1901- III. 4845
The writing of American history. [1st ed.] Norman, University of Oklahoma Press [1953] x, 387 p. 25 cm. *1. U.S. — History — Historiography. I. T.*
E175.K75   973.07   53-8815

Loewenberg, Bert James, 1905- III. 4846
American history in American thought: Christopher Columbus to Henry Adams. New York, Simon and Schuster [1972] 731 p. 22 cm. First 15 chapters previously published under title: Historical writing in American culture. *1. United States — Historiography. 2. America — Historiography. I. Loewenberg, Bert James, 1905- Historical writing in American culture. II. T.*
E175.L6   973/.07/2073   79-139641   ISBN:067120856X

McDermott, John Francis, 1902- ed. III. 4847
Research opportunities in American cultural history. [Lexington] University of Kentucky Press [1961] viii, 205 p. 24 cm. A revision of papers delivered at a round table conference held at Washington University, St. Louis, Oct. 23-24, 1959. *1. U. S. — History — Historiography. 2. Historical research. 3. U.S. — Civilization. I. T.*
E175.M3   973.072   61-15623

Saveth, Edward Norman. III. 4848
American historians and European immigrants, 1875-1925. New York, Columbia Univ. Press, 1948. 244 p. 23 cm. (Columbia University. Faculty of Political Science. Studies in history, economics and public law, no. 540) *1. Historians, American. 2. U.S. — Emigration and immigration. 3. U.S. — History — Historiography. I. T. (S)*
E175.S35 (H31.C7 no. 540)   973.07   48-7605

Sheehan, Donald Henry, 1917- ed. III. 4849
Essays in American historiography; papers presented in honor of Allan Nevins, edited by Donald Sheehan & Harold C. Syrett. New York, Columbia University Press, 1960. x, 320 p. port. 25 cm. *1. Nevins, Allan, 1890- 2. U.S. — History — Historiography. I. Syrett, Harold Coffin, 1913- joint ed. II. T:American historiography.*
E175.S48   973.072   60-8187

The State of American history. III. 4850
Edited with an introd. by Herbert J. Bass. Chicago, Quadrangle Books, 1970. xiv, 426 p. 25 cm. A selection of essays originally presented at the 1969 meeting of the Organization of American Historians in Philadelphia. 1. United States — Historiography — Addresses, essays, lectures. I. Bass, Herbert J., ed. II. Organization of American Historians.
E175.S7 1970   973/.072   77-101068

Van Tassel, David Dirck, 1928- III. 4851
Recording America's past; an interpretation of the development of historical studies in America, 1607-1884. [Chicago] University of Chicago Press [1960] 222 p. 24 cm. 1. U.S. — History — Historiography. 2. U.S. — History — Societies, etc. I. T.
E175.V3 1960   973.072   60-14404

Wish, Harvey, 1909- III. 4852
The American historian; a social-intellectual history of the writing of the American past. New York, Oxford University Press, 1960. 366 p. 24 cm. 1. U.S. — History — Historiography. I. T.
E175.W5   973.072   60-13202

Mangione, Jerre Gerlando, 1909- III. 4853
The dream and the deal; the Federal Writers' Project, 1935-1943, by Jerre Mangione. [1st ed.] Boston, Little, Brown [1972] xvi, 416 p. illus. 24 cm. 1. Federal Writers' Project. I. T.
E175.4.W9M3   917.3/006/173   75-187787   ISBN:0316545007

E175.45 HISTORIANS: COLLECTIVE BIOGRAPHY

Cunliffe, Marcus. III. 4854
Pastmasters; some essays on American historians. Edited by Marcus Cunliffe and Robin W. Winks. [1st ed.] New York, Harper & Row [1969] xv, 492 p. 22 cm. 1. Historians, American. I. Winks, Robin W., joint author. II. T.
E175.45.C8   973/.072/073   77-81380

Hofstadter, Richard, 1916- III. 4855
The progressive historians: Turner, Beard, Parrington. [1st ed.] New York, Knopf, 1968. xvii, 498, xiii p. ports. 22 cm. 1. Turner, Frederick Jackson, 1861-1932. 2. Beard, Charles Austin, 1874-1948. 3. Parrington, Vernon Louis, 1871-1929. 4. United States — Historiography. I. T.
E175.45.H6   973/.072/022   68-23944

Levin, David, 1924- III. 4856
History as romantic art: Bancroft, Prescott, Motley, and Parkman. Stanford, Calif., Stanford University Press, 1959. 260 p. 24 cm. (Stanford studies in language and literature, 20) 1. History — Historiography. 2. Historians, American. I. T.
E175.45.L4   907.2   59-10634

Skotheim, Robert Allen. III. 4857
American intellectual histories and historians. Princeton, N.J., Princeton University Press, 1966. xi, 326 p. 21 cm. 1. Historians, American. 2. United States — Historiography. 3. United States — History — Philosophy. I. T.
E175.45.S5   973.072   66-11960

E175.5 HISTORIANS, A – Z

Adams, Henry, 1838-1918. III. 4858
The education of Henry Adams; an autobiography. Boston, Houghton, Mifflin [1930] x, 517 p. 22 cm. (The Riverside library) Privately printed 1907, first published in 1918 by the Massachusetts historical society, with editor's preface signed, Henry Cabot Lodge. I. Lodge, Henry Cabot, 1850-1924, ed. II. T.
E175.5.A17423   32-23054

Adams, Henry, 1838-1918. III. 4859
Henry Adams and his friends: a collection of his unpublished letters, compiled, with a biographical introd., by Harold Dean Cater. New York, Octagon Books, 1970 [c1947] cxix, 797 p. ports. 24 cm. I. Cater, Harold Dean, 1908- ed. II. T.
E175.5.A17428 1970   973/.072/024   78-96175

Adams, Henry, 1838-1918. III. 4860
Letters of Henry Adams, edited by Worthington Chauncey Ford. Boston and New York, Houghton Mifflin, 1930-38. 2 v. ports. 25 cm. I. Ford, Worthington Chauncey, 1858-1941, ed.
E175.5.A1743   928.1   30-25080

Baym, Max Isaac. III. 4861
The French education of Henry Adams. New York, Columbia University Press, 1951. xiv, 358 p. 23 cm. 1. Adams, Henry, 1838-1918. I. T.
E175.5.A1747   928.1   51-11489

Donovan, Timothy Paul. III. 4862
Henry Adams and Brooks Adams; the education of two American historians. [1st ed.] Norman, University of Oklahoma Press [1961] 220 p. illus. 23 cm. 1. Adams, Henry, 1838-1918. 2. Adams, Brooks, 1848-1927.
E175.5.A1748   973.072   61-6500

Jordy, William H. III. 4863
Henry Adams: scientific historian, by William H. Jordy. [Hamden, Conn.] Archon Books, 1970 [c1952] xv, 327 p. 23 cm. 1. Adams, Henry, 1838-1918.
E175.5.A1755 1970   973/.072/024 (B)   77-114423   ISBN:208008284

Levenson, Jacob Claver, 1922- III. 4864
The mind and the art of Henry Adams, by J. C. Levenson. Stanford, Calif., Stanford University Press [1968, c1957] x, 430 p. illus., ports. 22 cm. 1. Adams, Henry, 1838-1918. I. T.
E175.5.A1765 1968   973/.072/024   68-13745

Samuels, Ernest, 1903- III. 4865
Henry Adams; the major phase. Cambridge, Mass., Belknap Press of Harvard University Press, 1964. xv, 687 p. 22 cm. 1. Adams, Henry, 1838-1918.
E175.5.A1776   928.1   64-21790

Samuels, Ernest, 1903- III. 4866
Henry Adams, the middle years. Cambridge, Belknap Press of Harvard University Press, 1958. xiv, 514 p. 22 cm. 1. Adams, Henry, 1838-1918.
E175.5.A1777   928.1   58-12975

Samuels, Ernest, 1903- III. 4867
The young Henry Adams. Cambridge, Harvard Univ. Press, 1948. xvi, 378 p. 22 cm. 1. Adams, Henry, 1838-1918. I. T.
E175.5.A178   928.1   48-10525

Stevenson, Elizabeth, 1919- III. 4868
Henry Adams, a biography. New York, Macmillan, 1955. xiv, 425 p. illus., ports. 22 cm. 1. Adams, Henry, 1838-1918.
E175.5.A1782   928.1   55-13825

Wagner, Vern. III. 4869
The suspension of Henry Adams; a study of manner and matter. Detroit, Wayne State University Press, 1969. 268 p. front. 24 cm. 1. Adams, Henry, 1838-1918. I. T.
E175.5.A1784   818/.4/08   68-26875

Adams, Herbert Baxter, 1850-1901. III. 4870
Historical scholarship in the United States, 1876-1901: as revealed in the correspondence of Herbert B. Adams. Edited by W. Stull Holt. Westport, Conn., Greenwood Press [1970, c1938] 314 p. 23 cm. On spine: Historic scholarship in the United States, 1876-1901. 1. United States — Historiography. I. T.
E175.5.A1797 1970   973/.07/2   71-113060   ISBN:083714695X

Nye, Russel Blaine, 1913- III. 4871
George Bancroft, Brahmin rebel, by Russel B. Nye. New York, Octagon Books, 1972 [c1944] x, 340, xii p. illus. 24 cm. 1. Bancroft, George, 1800-1891.
E175.5.B186 1972   973/.072/024 (B)   72-4400   ISBN:0374961336

Caughey, John Walton, 1902- III. 4872
Hubert Howe Bancroft, historian of the West. New York, Russell & Russell [1970, c1946] 422 p. illus., facsims., ports. 23 cm. 1. Bancroft, Hubert Howe, 1832-1918. 2. California. University. Bancroft Library. I. T.
E175.5.B199 1970   978/.0072024   77-102475

Beale, Howard Kennedy, 1899- ed. III. 4873
Charles A. Beard: an appraisal, by Eric F. Goldman [and others. Lexington] University of Kentucky Press [1954] x, 312 p. port. 24 cm. 1. Beard, Charles Austin, 1874-1948.
E175.5.B37   928.1   53-5517

Borning, Bernard C. III. 4874
The political and social thought of Charles A. Beard. Seattle, University of Washington Press, 1962. xxv, 315 p. 25 cm. 1. Beard, Charles Austin, 1874-1948. I. T.
E175.5.B382   973.9   62-12129

Berman, Milton. III. 4875
John Fiske; the evolution of a popularizer. Cambridge, Harvard University Press, 1961. 297 p. illus. 21 cm. (Harvard historical monographs, 48) 1. Fiske, John, 1842-1901.
E175.5.F49   928.1   62-7334

The Marcus W. Jernegan essays in American historiography, by III. 4876
his former students at the University of Chicago,
edited by William T. Hutchinson. Chicago, Ill., The University of Chicago

Parkman, Francis, 1823-1893. III. 4877
The journals of Francis Parkman, ed. by Mason Wade. [1st ed.] New York, Harper, 1947. 2 v. (xxv, 718 p.) illus., ports., maps. 25 cm. *I. Wade, Mason, 1913- ed.*
E175.5.P202   ~~928.1~~   47-11938

973.2
P231j

Parkman, Francis, 1823-1893. III. 4878
Letters of Francis Parkman. Edited and with an introd. by Wilbur R. Jacobs. [1st ed.] Norman, University of Oklahoma Press [1960] 2 v. illus., ports., map, facsims. 25 cm. "Published in co-operation with the Massachusetts Historical Society."
E175.5.P205   928.1   60-8754

Doughty, Howard, 1904- III. 4879
Francis Parkman. New York, Macmillan, 1962. 414 p. 23 cm. *1. Parkman, Francis, 1823-1893.*
E175.5.P212   928.1   61-12191

Pease, Otis A. III. 4880
Parkman's history; the historian as literary artist [by] Otis A. Pease. [Hamden, Conn.] Archon Books, 1968 [c1953] xi, 86 p. 22 cm. (The Wallace Notestein essays, v. 1) *1. Parkman, Francis, 1823-1893. I. T. (S)*
E175.5.P23 1968   973/.072/024   68-16334

Wade, Mason, 1913- III. 4881
Francis Parkman, heroic historian, by Mason Wade. New York, Viking Press, 1942. xiii, 466 p. plates, ports., facsims. 24 cm. Maps on lining-papers. *1. Parkman, Francis, 1823-1893.*
E175.5.P28   928.1   42-25856

Flower, Milton Embick. III. 4882
James Parton, the father of modern biography [by] Milton E. Flower. New York, Greenwood Press, 1968 [c1951] ix, 253 p. illus., ports. 24 cm. *1. Parton, James, 1822-1891.*
E175.5.P3F6 1968   920/.00924   (B)   68-29742

Cruden, Robert. III. 4883
James Ford Rhodes: the man, the historian, and his work. With a complete bibliography of the writings of James Ford Rhodes. [Cleveland] Press of Western Reserve University, 1961. 290 p. 24 cm. *1. Rhodes, James Ford, 1848-1927.*
E175.5.R436   928.1   61-16743

E175.7 METHODOLOGY

Benson, Lee. III. 4884
Toward the scientific study of history; selected essays of Lee Benson. Philadelphia, Lippincott [1972] xi, 352 p. 22 cm. *1. United States — Historiography — Addresses, essays, lectures. 2. Historiography — Addresses, essays, lectures. I. T.*
E175.7.B4   907/.2   73-161415   ISBN:039747265X 0397472234 (pbk)

Hockett, Homer Carey, 1875- III. 4885
The critical method in historical research and writing. New York, Macmillan, [1955] 330 p. 22 cm. "A rewritten and expanded edition of the author's Introduction to research in American history." *1. U.S. — History — Historiography. 2. Historical research. I. T.*
E175.7.H6446   973.072   55-13664

Parker, Donald Dean, 1899- III. 4886
Local history; how to gather it, write it, and publish it, by Donald Dean Parker. Revised and edited by Bertha E. Josephson for the Committee on guide for study of local history of the Social science research council. [n. p., 1944] xiv, 186 p. 23 cm. *1. U.S. — History — Historiography. 2. Local history. I. Josephson, Bertha E., ed. II. Social science research council. Committee on guide for study of local history.*
E175.7.P3   973.07   A45-1091

E175.9 PHILOSOPHY OF AMERICAN HISTORY

Adams, Ephraim Douglass, 1865-1930. III. 4887
The power of ideals in American history. New York, AMS Press [1969] xiii, 159 p. 23 cm. (Yale lectures on the responsibilities of citizenship) Reprint of the 1913 ed. *1. United States — History — Philosophy. 2. National characteristics, American. 3. Idealism, American. I. T. (S)*
E175.9.A3 1969b   973~~.01~~   75-98025

Benson, Lee. Ad17   III. 4888
Turner and Beard; American historical writing reconsidered. Glencoe, Ill., Free Press [1960] 241 p. 22 cm. *1. Loria, Achille, 1857-1943. 2. Turner, Frederick Jackson, 1861-1932. 3. Beard, Charles Austin, 1874-1948. 4. U.S. — History — Philosophy. 5. U.S. — History — Historiography.*
E175.9.B4   973.072   60-10890

Fox, Dixon Ryan, 1887-1945, ed. III. 4889
Sources of culture in the Middle West; backgrounds versus frontier. New York, Russell & Russell, 1964 [c1961] 110 p. 22 cm. Three papers appraising F. J. Turner's historical theory relative to the influence of the frontier on American history, read at a special session of the 1933 annual meeting of the American Historical Association. *1. Turner, Frederick Jackson, 1861-1932. 2. U.S. — History — Philosophy. 3. The West — History. 4. U.S. — Civilization — 1865-1918. I. Culture in the Middle West. II. T.*
E175.9.F69 1964   977   64-15019

Handlin, Oscar, 1915- III. 4890
Chance or destiny; turning points in American history. [1st ed.] Boston, Little, Brown [1955] 220 p. 22 cm. *1. U.S. — History — Philosophy. I. T.*
E175.9.H35   973.04   55-7461

Hartz, Louis, 1919- III. 4891
The liberal tradition in America; an interpretation of American political thought since the Revolution. [1st ed.] New York, Harcourt, Brace [1955] 329 p. 21 cm. *1. U.S. — History — Philosophy. 2. U.S. — Politics and government. 3. Liberalism. I. T.*
E175.9.H37   973   55-5242

Koch, Adrienne, 1912- III. 4892
Power, morals, and the Founding Fathers; essays in the interpretation of the American enlightenment. Ithaca, N.Y., Great Seal Books [1961] 158 p. 19 cm. *1. U.S. — History — Philosophy. 2. Statesmen, American. I. T.*
E175.9.K6   973.01   61-12995

Niebuhr, Reinhold, 1892- III. 4893
A Nation so conceived; reflections on the history of America from its early visions to its present power, by Reinhold Niebuhr and Alan Heimert. New York, Scribner [1963] 155 p. 21 cm. *1. U.S. — History — Philosophy. 2. U.S. — Civilization. I. Heimert, Alan E., joint author. II. T.*
E175.9.N5   973.01   63-9458

Schlesinger, Arthur Meier, 1888- III. 4894
New viewpoints in American history, by Arthur Meier Schlesinger. New York, Macmillan, 1922. x, 299 p. 21 cm. Reprinted in part from various periodicals. *1. U.S. — History — Philosophy. 2. U.S. — History. 3. U.S. — Politics and government. I. T.*
E175.9.S34   22-7401

Strout, Cushing. III. 4895
The pragmatic revolt in American history: Carl Becker and Charles Beard. New Haven, Yale University Press, 1958. ix, 182 p. 23 cm. (Yale historical publications. The Wallace Notestein essays, no. 3) *1. Becker, Carl Lotus, 1873-1945. 2. Beard, Charles Austin, 1874-1948. 3. U.S. — History — Philosophy. I. T. (S:The Wallace Notestein essays, no. 3)*
E175.9.S8   973.01   58-11262

E176 Biography (General. Collective)

Aaron, Daniel, 1912- III. 4896
Men of good hope; a story of American progressives. New York, Oxford University Press, 1951. xiv, 329 p. 22 cm. *1. U.S. — Biography. I. T.*
E176.A2   920.073   51-1402

Appleton's cyclopaedia of American biography. III. 4897
Edited by James Grant Wilson and John Fiske. New York, Appleton, 1888. Detroit, Gale Research Co., 1968. 7 v. ports. 24 cm. Vol. 7 edited by J. G. Wilson. *1. America — Biography — Dictionaries. 2. United States — Biography — Dictionaries. I. Wilson, James Grant, 1832-1914, ed. II. Fiske, John, 1842-1901, joint ed.*
E176.A666   920.07   67-14061   Reference

Bradford, Gamaliel, 1863-1932. III. 4898
As God made them; portraits of some nineteenth-century Americans. Port Washington, Kennikat Press [1969, c1929] 294 p. illus., ports. 23 cm. (Essay and general literature index reprint series) *1. Webster, Daniel, 1782-1852. 2. Clay, Henry, 1777-1852. 3. Calhoun, John Caldwell, 1782-1850. 4. Greeley,*

Horace, 1811-1872. 5. Booth, Edwin, 1833-1893. 6. Child, Francis James, 1825-1896. 7. Gray, Asa, 1810-1888. I. T.
E176.B798 1969 973 (B) 74-85992

Bradford, Gamaliel, 1863-1932. **III. 4899**
Damaged souls. Port Washington, N.Y., Kennikat Press [1969, c1923] xi, 276 p. 22 cm. (Essay and general literature index reprint series) *1. United States — Biography. I. T.*
E176.B8 1969 973 77-85990 ISBN:0804605416

The Twentieth century biographical dictionary of notable **III. 4900**
Americans.
Editor-in-chief: Rossiter Johnson. Managing editor: John Howard Brown. Boston, Biographical Society, 1904. Detroit, Gale Research Co., 1968. 10 v. illus., ports. 24 cm. "Corrected edition of a work previously published under the titles: The Cyclopaedia of American biography, 1897-1903, and Lamb's biographical dictionary of the United States, 1900-1903." *1. United States — Biography — Dictionaries. I. Johnson, Rossiter, 1840-1931, ed. II. Brown, John Howard, 1840-1917, ed. III. The Cyclopaedia of American biography.*
E176.C993 920.073 68-19657

Dictionary of American biography. **III. 4901**
New York, Scribner [c1932-v.1, c1957] v. 26 cm. Edited by Allen Johnson and others. "Published under the auspices of the American Council of Learned Societies." "Volume I contains corrections of fact and additional data which have come to the attention of the editors from the first publication of the work up to the present." Vol. 11: Supplement 1, to Dec. 31, 1935. Supplement 2, to Dec. 31, 1940. *1. U.S. — Biography — Dictionaries. I. American Council of Learned Societies Devoted to Humanistic Studies.*
E176.D563 920.073 60-2195

Fishwick, Marshall William. **III. 4902**
American heroes, myth and reality. Introd. by Carl Carmer. Washington, Public Affairs Press [1954] 242 p. 24 cm. *1. U.S. — Biography. 2. Heroes. I. T.*
E176.F53 920.073 54-12693

Kennedy, John Fitzgerald, Pres. U.S., 1917-1963. **III. 4903**
Profiles in courage. [Memorial ed.] New York, Harper & Row [c1964] 287 p. port. 24 cm. *1. United States. Congress. Senate — Biography. 2. Courage. I. T.*
E176.K4 1964 923.273 64-16194

Koenig, Louis William, 1916- **III. 4904**
The invisible presidency. New York, Rinehart [1960] 438 p. 24 cm. *1. U.S. — Biography. 2. Executive power — U.S. 3. Presidents — U.S. I. T.*
E176.K6 973.91 60-5341

Madison, Charles Allan. **III. 4905**
Critics & crusaders; a century of American protest. 2d ed. New York, Ungar [1959] 662 p. illus. 22 cm. *1. U.S. — Biography. 2. Liberty. I. T.*
E176.M22 1959 920.073 58-14283

The National cyclopædia of American biography, being the history **III. 4906**
of the United States as illustrated in the lives of the founders, builders, and defenders of the republic, and of the men and women who are doing the work and moulding the thought of the present time;
edited by distinguished biographers, selected from each state, revised and approved by most eminent historians, scholars, and statesmen of the day. v.1- New York, J. T. White & Company, 1893-19   v. fronts., illus., ports. 28 1/2 cm. Supplement 1- New York, J. T. White & company, 1910- v. front., illus., ports. 28 1/2 cm. E176.N27 Suppl. Current volume A- New York, J. T. White & company, 1927- v. ports. 28 cm. Loose-leaf. Vol. A published 1930; vol.B, 1927. E176.N27 Curr. vol. A conspectus of American biography; being an analytical summary of American history and biography, containing also the complete indexes of The national cyclopædia of American biography. [v.1-13] Compiled by George Derby ... New York, J. T. White & company, 1906. 4 p. l., 752 p. 28 1/2 cm. "Character lessons in American biography. Adapted for the use of the public schools. By James T. White": p. 717-752. E176.N27 Conspectus 1906 White's conspectus of American biography, a tabulated record of American history and biography. 2d ed. A revised and enlarged edition of A conspectus of American biography. Compiled by the editorial staff of the National cyclopædia of American biography. New York, J. T. White & company, 1937. viii, 455 p. 28 cm. E176.N27 Conspectus 1937 Indexes. Personal and topical indexes to ... the National cyclopedia of American biography, including the first and revised editions ... New York, J. T. White & company, 1935- v. 28 cm. Loose-leaf. E176.N27 Index *1. U.S. — Biography. I. Derby, George. II. White, James Terry, 1845-1920. III. T:A conspectus of American biography.*
E176.N27 06-38537

Nye, Russel Blaine, 1913- **III. 4907**
A baker's dozen: thirteen unusual Americans. East Lansing, Michigan State University Press [1956] 300 p. 22 cm. *1. U.S. — Biography. I. T.*
E176.N95 920.073 56-11739

Wecter, Dixon, 1906-1950. **III. 4908**
The hero in America; a chronicle of hero-worship. With headings by Woodi Ishmael. [Ann Arbor] University of Michigan Press [1963, c1941] 524 p. illus., ports. 21 cm. (Ann Arbor paperbacks) *1. Heroes. 2. U.S. — Biography. I. T.*
E176.Wx 920.073 64-9847

Who was who in America; a companion biographical reference **III. 4909**
work to Who's who in America.
1607/1896- . Chicago, Marquis Who's Who. v. 27 cm. Vol. for 1607/1896 called Historical volume, published in 1963; vols. for 1897/1942-1951/60 called v.1-3, were published prior to this volume. "A component volume of Who's who in American history," 1607/1897- . Subtitle varies slightly. *1. U.S. — Biography — Dictionaries. I. Who's who in American history.*
E176.W64 920.073 43-3789

Who's who in America. **III. 4910**
v. [1]- ; 1899/1900- . Chicago, Marquis Who's Who. v. 31 cm. biennial. "A biographical dictionary of notable living men and women" (varies slightly) "A component volume of Who's who in American history," 1966/67- Founded 1899 by A. N. Marquis. Vols. 28-30 accompanied by separately published parts with title: Indices and necrology. *1. U.S. — Biography — Dictionaries. I. Marquis, Albert Nelson, d. 1943. II. Who's who in American history.*
E176.W642 920.073 04-16934

Who's who in American politics. **III. 4911**
1st- ed.; 1967/68- New York, Bowker. v. 29 cm. Biennial. "A biographical directory of United States political leaders." Editors: 1967/68- P. A. Theis and E. L. Henshaw. *1. U.S. — Biography. I. Theis, Paul A., ed. II. Henshaw, Edmund Lee, ed.*
E176.W6424 320/.0922 67-25024

Who's who in the East and Eastern Canada. **III. 4912**
1st- ed.; 1942/43- . Chicago, Marquis Who's Who. v. 27 cm. Biennial. "A biographical dictionary of noteworthy men and women of the Middle Atlantic and Northeastern States and Eastern Canada (varies) Title varies slightly. Includes names from the States of Connecticut, Delaware, Maine, Maryland, Massachusetts, New Hampshire, New Jersey, Pennsylvania, Rhode Island, Vermont and West Virginia, and in Canada from the Provinces of New Brunswick, Newfoundland, Nova Scotia, Prince Edward Island and Quebec. *1. Middle States — Biography — Dictionaries. 2. New England — Biography — Dictionaries. 3. Canada — Biography — Dictionaries.*
E176.W643 920.07 43-18522

Who's who in the Midwest and Central Canada. **III. 4913**
Chicago, Marquis-Who's Who [etc.] 1947- v. 24-27 cm. Biennial (irregular) "A biographical dictionary of noteworthy men and women of the Central and Midwestern States and Central Canada." Title varies: 1947, Who's who in the Central States.-1949-1963, 64, Who's who in the Midwest. Contains names from the States of Illinois, Indiana, Iowa, Kansas, Michigan, Minnesota, Missouri, Nebraska, North Dakota, Ohio, South Dakota and Wisconsin, and in Canada, Manitoba, Western Ontario and the District of Keewatin. *1. Middle West — Biography — Dictionaries. 2. Canada — Biography — Dictionaries. I. Who's who in the Central States.*
E176.W644 920.07 50-289

Who's who in the South and Southwest. **III. 4914**
1st ed.; 1947- Chicago, Marquis-Who's Who [etc.] v. 24-27 cm. Biennial (irregular) "A biographical dictionary of noteworthy men and women of the Southern and Southwestern States." Vol. for 1947 published also under title: Who's who in Alabama, Who's who in Arizona, Who's who in Florida, Who's who in Georgia, Who's who in Kentucky, Who's who in Louisiana, Who's who in Mississippi, Who's who in New Mexico, Who's who in North Carolina, Who's who in the Northwest, Who's who on the Pacific Coast, Who's who in South Carolina, Who's who in Tennessee, Who's who in Texas, and Who's who in Virginia. Vol. for 1947 published by Larkin, Roosevelt & Larkin. Includes names from the States of Alabama, Arkansas, the District of Columbia, Florida, Georgia, Kentucky, Louisiana, Mississippi, North Carolina, Oklahoma, South Carolina, Tennessee, Texas and Virginia, and Puerto Rico and the Virgin Islands. *1. Southern States — Biography — Dictionaries. 2. Southwest, New — Biography — Dictionaries. 3. Washington, D.C. — Biography — Dictionaries.*
E176.W645 920.075 50-58231

Who's who in the West and Western Canada. **III. 4915**
1st ed.; 1947- Chicago, Marquis-Who's Who [etc.] v. 24-27 cm. Biennial (irregular) "A biographical directory of noteworthy men and women of the Pacific Coastal and the Western States, and Western Canada." Title varies: 1947, Who's who on the Pacific Coast — 1949-1963/64, Who's who in the West. Vols. for 1949-51 published also under title: Who's who on the Pacific Coast. Vol. for 1947 published by Larkin, Roosevelt & Larkin, and pub. also under title: Who's who in the South and Southwest. Includes names from the States of Alaska, Arizona, California, Colorado, Hawaii, Idaho, Montana, Nevada, New Mexico, Oregon, Utah, Washington and Wyoming, and in Canada the Provinces of Alberta, British Columbia and Saskatchewan, the Districts of Franklin and Mackenzie and Yukon Territory. *1. The West — Biography. 2. Northwest, Canadian — Biography. I. T:Who's who on the Pacific Coast.*
E176.W646 920.078 49-48186

Willard, Frances Elizabeth, 1839-1898, ed. III. 4916
A woman of the century, fourteen hundred-seventy biographical sketches accompanied by portraits of leading American women in all walks of life. Edited by Frances E. Willard and Mary A. Livermore, assisted by a corps of able contributors. With a new introd. by Leslie Shepard. Detroit, Gale Research Co., 1967. 812 p. ports. 26 cm. Title page includes original imprint: Buffalo, C. W. Moulton, 1893. *1. Women in the United States — Biography. 2. United States — Biography. I. Livermore, Mary Ashton (Rice), 1820-1905, joint ed. II. T.*
E176.W691 1967   920.073   67-21361

Bailey, Thomas Andrew, 1902- III. 4917
Presidential greatness; the image and the man from George Washington to the present, by Thomas A. Bailey. [1st ed.] New York, Appleton-Century [1966] xi, 368 p. 22 cm. *1. Presidents — U.S. I. T.*
E176.1.B17   973   66-19996

Borden, Morton, ed. III. 4918
America's ten greatest Presidents. Chicago, Rand McNally [1961] 269 p. 22 cm. (Rand McNally history series) *1. Presidents — U.S. — Biography. I. T.*
E176.1.B77   923.173   61-6579

Kane, Joseph Nathan, 1899- III. 4919
Facts about the Presidents: a compilation of biographical and historical data. 2d ed. New York, H. W. Wilson Co., 1968. viii, 384 p. ports. 27 cm. *1. Presidents — United States. I. T.*
E176.1.K3 1968   973   67-17468

White, William Allen, 1868-1944. III. 4920
Masks in a pageant. Westport, Conn., Greenwood Press [1971] xv, 507 p. illus., ports. 23 cm. Reprint of the 1928 ed. *1. Presidents — United States — Biography. 2. Statesmen — United States. 3. United States — Politics and government. I. T.*
E176.1.W58 1971   973/.099   73-110884   ISBN:0837145686

E178 – 179 American History: General Works

Adams, James Truslow, 1878-1949. III. 4921
The epic of America, by James Truslow Adams; illustrated by M. J. Gallagher. Boston, Little, Brown, 1933. ix, 446 p. 23 cm. Head-pieces. "New edition printed November, 1933." *1. U.S. — History. I. T.*
E178.A2592   973   33-32199

American heritage. III. 4922
Times of trial. Edited by Allan Nevins for American Heritage. [1st ed.] New York, Knopf, 1958. x, 254, iv p. illus., plates (part col.) ports., maps, facsims. 25 cm. *1. U.S. — History. I. Nevins, Allan, 1890- ed. II. T.*
E178.A48   973.082   58-10978

Greene, Evarts Boutell, 1870- III. 4923
Provincial America, 1690-1740, by Evarts Boutell Greene. New York Harper, 1905. xxi, 356 p. front. (port.) 7 maps. 22 cm. (The American nation: a history ... v.6) Series title also at head of t.-p. *1. U.S. — History — Colonial period.*
E178.A54   05-19270

Bancroft, George, 1800-1891. III. 4924
History of the United States of America, from the discovery of the continent. The author's last revision. New York, Appleton, 1891-92. 6 v. front. (port.) 23 cm. Vols.1, 4-6, 1892. Extends to the adoption of the Constitution in 1789. *1. U.S. — History — Colonial period. 2. U.S. — History — Revolution. 3. U.S. — History — Confederation, 1783-1763.*
E178.B2276   18-8245

Benét, Stephen Vincent, 1898-1943. III. 4925
America. New York, Toronto, Farrar & Rinehart [1944] 122 p. 22 cm. *I. T.*
E178.B43   973   44-4140

Carman, Harry James, 1884-1964. III. 4926
A history of the American people, by Harry J. Carman, Harold C. Syrett & Bernard W. Wishy. 3d ed. New York, Knopf [1967] 2 v. illus., maps, ports. 22 cm. *1. U.S. — History. I. Syrett, Harold Coffin, 1913- joint author. II. Wishy, Bernard W., 1925- joint author. III. T.*
E178.C284 1967   973   67-20622

Channing, Edward, 1856-1931. III. 4927
A history of the United States, by Edward Channing. New York, Macmillan, 1905-25. 6 v. illus., maps (part fold.) 23 cm. A history of the United States, by Edward Channing; supplementary volume, general index, compiled by Eva G. Moore. New York, The Macmillan company, 1932. v, 155 p. 23 cm. E178.C44 Index *1. U.S. — History. I. Moore, Eva G.*
E178.C44   05-11649

Clark, Dan Elbert, 1884- III. 4928
The West in American history, by Dan Elbert Clark. New York, Thomas Y. Crowell company [c1937] xi, 682 p. 23 cm. *1. U.S. — History. 2. The West — History. 3. U.S. — Territorial expansion. I. T.*
E178.C57   978   37-4445

Commager, Henry Steele, 1902- ed. III. 4929
The heritage of America; edited by Henry Steele Commager and Allan Nevins. Rev. and enl. ed. Boston, Little, Brown, 1949. xxiv, 1227 p. illus. 21 cm. *1. United States — History. 2. American literature (Selections: Extracts, etc.) I. Nevins, Allan, 1890- joint ed. II. T.*
E178.C7274   973.082   49-48565

Degler, Carl N. III. 4930
Out of our past; the forces that shaped modern America [by] Carl N. Degler. Rev. ed. New York, Harper & Row [1970] xx, 546 p. 22 cm. *1. United States — History. I. T.*
E178.D37 1970   973   77-88637

Dulles, Foster Rhea, 1900- III. 4931
The United States since 1865. New ed. rev. and enl. Ann Arbor, University of Michigan Press [1969] ix, 562, xx p. illus. 25 cm. (The University of Michigan history of the modern world) *1. United States — History — 1865- I. T. (S:Michigan. University. The University of Michigan history of the modern world)*
E178.D87 1969   973   69-15850

Hacker, Louis Morton, 1899- III. 4932
The shaping of the American tradition; text by Louis M. Hacker; documents ed. by Louis M. Hacker and Helene S. Zahler. [Trade ed.] New York, Columbia University Press, 1947. 2 v. (xxiv, 1247 p.) 26 cm. *1. U.S. — History. 2. U.S. — History — Sources. 3. U.S. — Civilization — History. I. Zahler, Helene Sara, 1911- II. T.*
E178.H14 1947a   973   47-4680

Handlin, Oscar, 1915- III. 4933
The Americans; a new history of the people of the United States. With illus. by Samuel H. Bryant. [1st ed.] Boston, Little, Brown [1963] 434 p. illus. 22 cm. *1. U.S. — History. I. T.*
E178.H24   973   63-8951

Hildreth, Richard, 1807-1865. III. 4934
The history of the United States of America. Rev. ed. New York, A. M. Kelley, 1969. 6 v. 22 cm. (Reprints of economic classics) This ed. was first published in 1880. *1. United States — History. 2. United States — Politics and government. I. T.*
E178.H6823   973   69-16308

Kraus, Michael, 1901- III. 4935
The United States to 1865. New ed. rev. and enl. Ann Arbor, University of Michigan Press [1969] xiii, 548, xi p. illus. 25 cm. (The University of Michigan history of the modern world) *1. United States — History. I. T. (S:Michigan. University. The University of Michigan history of the modern world)*
E178.K7 1969   973   69-15849

Morison, Samuel Eliot, 1887- III. 4936
The growth of the American Republic [by] Samuel Eliot Morison, Henry Steele Commager, and William E. Leuchtenburg. [6th ed., rev., and enl.] New York, Oxford University Press, 1969-   v.   illus., maps, ports. 24 cm. *1. U.S. — History. I. Commager, Henry Steele, 1902- II. Leuchtenburg, William Edward, 1922- III. T.*
E178.M852   973   69-10494

Morison, Samuel Eliot, 1887- III. 4937
The Oxford history of the American people. New York, Oxford University Press, 1965. xxvii, 1150 p. illus., coats of arms, facsims., maps, ports. 24 cm. Includes unacc. melodies. *1. U.S. — History. I. T.*
E178.M855   973   65-12468

Schlesinger, Arthur Meier, 1888- III. 4938
Paths to the present. New York, Macmillan Co., 1949-   vii, 317 p. 22 cm. *1. U.S. — History. 2. U.S. — Civilization — History. 3. National characteristics, American. 4. U.S. — Politics and government. I. T.*
E178.S33   917.3   49-7676

Turner, Frederick Jackson, 1861-1932. III. 4939
The significance of sections in American history; with an introd. by Max Farrand. New York, P. Smith, 1950 [c1932] ix, 347 p. maps. 21 cm. Essays, edited by Max Farrand and Avery Craven. *1. U.S. — History. 2. Sectionalism (U.S.) I. T.*
E178.Tx   973   A51-9831

Wilson, Woodrow, Pres. U.S., 1856-1924. III. 4940
Division and reunion, 1829-1889. [11th ed.] New York, Collier Books [1961] xvii, 256 p. 18 cm. *1. U.S. — History — Civil War. 2. U.S. — History. 3. U.S. — Politics and government. I. T.*
E178.Wx   973   63-22872

Bailey, Thomas Andrew, 1902- III. 4941
The American pageant; a history of the Republic [by] Thomas A. Bailey. 3d ed. Boston, Heath [1965, c1966] xiv, 998, lx p. illus., maps (part col.) 25 cm. *1. United States — History. I. T.*
E178.1.B15 1966   973   66-11587

Hofstadter, Richard, 1916-1970. III. 4942
The United States [by] Richard Hofstadter, William Miller [and] Daniel Aaron. 3d ed. Englewood Cliffs, N.J., Prentice-Hall [1972] xvi, 879, xvia-lxiii p. illus. 25 cm. *1. United States — History. I. Miller, William, 1912- joint author. II. Aaron, Daniel, 1912- joint author. III. T.*
E178.1.H7 1972   973   79-160528   ISBN:0139384235

E178.4 – 178.5 HUMOR. PICTORIAL WORKS

Armour, Richard Willard, 1906- III. 4943
It all started with Columbus, being an unexpurgated, unabridged, and unlikely history of the United States from Christopher Columbus to John F. Kennedy for those who, having perused a volume of history in school, swore they would never read another. Lavishly illustrated by Campbell Grant. [Rev. ed.] New York, McGraw-Hill [1961] 121 p. illus. 20 cm. *1. United States — History, comic, satirical, etc. I. T.*
E178.4.A7 1961   973.088   61-17597

Nevins, Allan, 1890- III. 4944
A century of political cartoons; caricature in the United States from 1800 to 1900, by Allan Nevins and Frank Weitenkampf. With 100 reproductions of cartoons. New York, Scribner, 1944. 190 p. illus. 26 cm. *1. U.S. — History — Humor, caricatures, etc. 2. Caricatures and cartoons — U.S. I. Weitenkampf, Frank, 1866- joint author. II. T.*
E178.4.N47   973.5084   44-3029

Album of American history III. 4945
[by] James Truslow Adams, editor in chief [and others] New York, Scribner, 1944-[61] 6 v. illus., ports., maps. 29 cm. "The intent of the present work is to tell the history of America through pictures made at the time the history was being made." *1. United States — History — Pictorial works. I. Adams, James Truslow, 1878-1949, ed. II. Hopkins, J. G. E., ed.*
E178.5.A48   973.022/2   44-706

Davidson, Marshall B. III. 4946
Life in America. Boston, Houghton Mifflin, 1951. 2 v. illus., ports., maps. 26 cm. "Published in association with the Metropolitan Museum of Art." *1. U.S. — History — Pictorial works. 2. U.S. — Civilization — History. I. T.*
E178.5.D3   973   51-7084

E178 – 179 ESSAYS

Aaron, Daniel, 1912- ed. III. 4947
America in crisis; fourteen crucial episodes in American history [by] Perry Miller [and others] Edited by Daniel Aaron. Hamden, Conn., Archon Books, 1971 [c1952] xiv, 363 p. 22 cm. *1. United States — History — Addresses, essays, lectures. I. Miller, Perry, 1905-1963. II. T.*
E178.6.A17 1971   973.08   72-131372   ISBN:0208010432

Adams, Henry, 1838-1918. III. 4948
The great secession winter of 1860-61, and other essays. Edited and with an introd. by George Hochfield. New York, Sagamore Press [1958] xx, 428 p. 24 cm. *1. U.S. — Politics and government — 1849-1877 — Addresses, essays, lectures. 2. U.S. — History — Addresses, essays, lectures. I. T.*
E178.6.A2   973.704   58-9144

Allen, Harry Cranbrook, ed. III. 4949
British essays in American history, edited by H. C. Allen and C. P. Hill. London, E. Arnold [1957] ix, 348 p. 2 maps (1 col., on lining papers) 23 cm. *1. U.S. — History — Addresses, essays, lectures. I. Hill, Charles Peter, joint ed. II. T.*
E178.6.A37 1957   973.04   57-2671

Bryce, James Bryce, Viscount, 1838-1922. III. 4950
The study of American history. With an appendix relating to the foundation. Westport, Conn., Greenwood Press [1971, c1922] 118 p. 17 cm. (Lecture of the Sir George Watson chair of American History, Literature and Institutions, 1921) *1. United States — History — Addresses, essays, lectures. I. T. (S:Sir George Watson Foundation for American History, Literature and Institutions. Lectures, 1921.)*
E178.6.B92 1971   973/.07   72-136056   ISBN:0837152062

Eisenstadt, Abraham Seldin, 1920- ed. III. 4951
American history: recent interpretations. New York, Crowell [1962] 2 v. 23 cm. *1. U.S. — History — Addresses, essays, lectures. I. T.*
E178.6.E44   973.082   62-10281

Fine, Sidney A., 1920- ed. III. 4952
The American past; conflicting interpretations of the great issues. Edited by Sidney Fine & Gerald S. Brown. 2d ed. New York, Macmillan [1965] 2 v. 24 cm. Vol. 1, edited by Gerald S. Brown. *1. United States — History — Addresses, essays, lectures. 2. United States — History — Philosophy. I. Brown, Gerald Saxon, ed. II. T.*
E178.6.F522   973.082   65-15184

Garraty, John Arthur, 1920- III. 4953
Interpreting American history; conversations with historians [by] John A. Garraty. Drawings from life by Gail Garraty. [New York] Macmillan [1970] 2 v. in 1. ports. 24 cm. *1. U.S. — History — Addresses, essays, lectures. 2. U.S. — History — Philosophy. I. T.*
E178.6.G27   973/.01   70-97761

Saveth, Edward Norman, 1915- ed. III. 4954
Understanding the American past; American history and its interpretation. [1st ed.] Boston, Little, Brown [1954] 613 p. 22 cm. *1. U.S. — History — Addresses, essays, lectures. 2. U.S. — History — Historiography. I. T.*
E178.6.S3 1954   973.02   53-7320

Hofstadter, Richard, 1916- comp. III. 4955
American violence; a documentary history, edited by Richard Hofstadter and Michael Wallace. [1st ed.] New York, Knopf, 1970. xiv, 478, xiii p. 25 cm. *1. Violence — U.S. 2. U.S. — History. I. Wallace, Michael, joint comp. II. T.*
E179.H8 1970   973   73-111238   ISBN:394414861

E179 – 180 Historical Geography. The Frontier

Shankle, George Earlie. III. 4956
American nicknames; their origin and significance. 2d ed. New York, Wilson, 1955. vii, 524 p. 26 cm. *1. Nicknames. 2. Epithets. 3. Names, Geographical — U.S. 4. Names, Personal. I. T.*
E179.S545 1955   929.4   55-5038

Barrows, Harlan Harland, 1877-1960. III. 4957
Lectures on the historical geography of the United States as given in 1933. Edited by William A. Koelsch. Chicago, 1962. 248 p. 23 cm. (University of Chicago. Dept. of Geography. Research paper no. 77) *1. U.S. — Historical geography. 2. U.S. — Territorial expansion. I. T.*
E179.5.B3x (H31.C514 no. 77)   911.73   62-19702

Billington, Ray Allen, 1903- III. 4958
America's frontier heritage. [1st ed.] New York, Holt, Rinehart and Winston [1966] xiv, 302 p. 24 cm. (Histories of the American frontier) *1. Frontier and pioneer life — U.S. 2. National characteristics, American. I. T.*
E179.5.B62   917.303   66-13289

Billington, Ray Allen, 1903- ed. III. 4959
The frontier thesis: valid interpretation of American history? New York, Holt, Rinehart and Winston [1966] 122 p. port. 24 cm. (American problem studies) *1. Turner, Frederick Jackson, 1861-1932. The frontier in American history. 2. U.S. — History — Philosophy. I. T.*
E179.5.B625   973.01   66-21640

Billington, Ray Allen, 1903- III. 4960
Westward expansion; a history of the American frontier. 3d ed. New York, Macmillan [c1967] xvii, 933 p. maps. 25 cm. *1. U.S. — Territorial expansion. 2. U.S. — History. 3. Mississippi Valley — History — 1803-1865. 4. The West — History. I. T.*
E179.5.B63 1967   973   67-12337

Brown, Ralph Hall, 1898- III. 4961
Historical geography of the United States, by Ralph H. Brown, under the editorship of J. Russell Whitaker. New York, Harcourt, Brace [1948] viii, 596 p. illus., maps. 24 cm. *1. U.S. — Historical geography. I. Whitaker, Joe Russell, 1900- ed.*
E179.5.B9   973   48-1500

Clark, Thomas Dionysius, 1903- III. 4962
Frontier America; the story of the westward movement [by] Thomas D. Clark. 2d ed. New York, Scribner [1969] xii, 836 p. illus., maps. 25 cm. *1. United States — Territorial expansion. 2. Frontier and pioneer life — United States. I. T.*
E179.5.C48 1969   973   69-11124

De Voto, Bernard Augustine, 1897-1955. III. 4963
The course of empire; with maps by Erwin Raisz. Boston, Houghton Mifflin, 1952. xvii, 647 p. maps (part col.) 22 cm. *1. North America — Discovery and exploration. 2. U.S. — Territorial expansion. 3. Indians of North America — History. I. T.*
E179.5.D4   973.1   52-5261

Graebner, Norman A. III. 4964
Empire on the Pacific; a study in American continental expansion. New York, Ronald Press Co. [1955] ix, 278 p. maps. 21 cm. *1. U.S. — Territorial expansion. 2. Pacific States — History. 3. U.S. — Politics and government — 1845-1849. I. T.*
E179.5.G7   973.61   55-10664

Hofstadter, Richard, 1916- comp. III. 4965
Turner and the sociology of the frontier. Edited by Richard Hofstadter and Seymour Martin Lipset. New York, Basic Books [1968] vi, 232 p. illus. 22 cm. (The Sociology of American history) *1. Turner, Frederick Jackson, 1861-1932. 2. United States — Historiography. 3. Frontier and pioneer life — United States. I. Lipset, Seymour Martin, joint comp. II. T.*
E179.5.H62   301.29/73   68-22859

Merk, Frederick, 1887- III. 4966
Manifest destiny and mission in American history; a reinterpretation. With the collaboration of Lois Bannister Merk. [1st ed.] New York, Knopf, 1963. 265 p. 25 cm. *1. U.S. — Territorial expansion. 2. Public opinion — U.S. — Imperialism. I. T.*
E179.5.M4   973.6   63-8204

Odum, Howard Washington, 1884- III. 4967
American regionalism; a cultural-historical approach to national integration, by Howard W. Odum and Harry Estill Moore. New York, H. Holt [c1938] x, 693 p. illus., maps, diagrs. 24 cm. *1. Regionalism — U.S. I. Moore, Harry Estill, joint author. II. T.*
E179.5.O43   917.3   38-15648

Paxson, Frederic Logan, 1877-1948. III. 4968
History of the American frontier, 1763-1893. Dunwoody, Ga., N. S. Berg [1967, c1924] xvii, 598 p. maps (part fold.) 23 cm. *1. U.S. — History. 2. The West — History. I. American frontier, 1763-1893. II. T.*
E179.5.P344   973   67-9407

Philbrick, Francis Samuel, 1876- III. 4969
The rise of the West, 1754-1830, by Francis S. Philbrick. [1st ed.] New York, Harper & Row [1965] xvii, 398 p. illus., maps, ports. 22 cm. (New American Nation series) *1. Northwest, Old — History. 2. Southwest, Old — History. 3. U.S. — Territorial expansion. I. T.*
E179.5.P45   973   65-21377

Semple, Ellen Churchill, 1863-1932. III. 4970
American history and its geographic conditions. Rev. in collaboration with the author by Clarence Fielden Jones. New York, Russell & Russell [1968, c1933] x, 541 p. maps (part fold.) 22 cm. *1. United States — Historical geography. 2. Physical geography — United States. 3. Anthropo-geography — United States. I. Jones, Clarence Fielden, 1893- II. T.*
E179.5.S47 1968   911/.73   68-25039

Turner, Frederick Jackson, 1861-1932. III. 4971
The frontier in American history. With a foreword by Ray Allen Billington. New York, Holt, Rinehart and Winston [1962] xx, 375 p. 19 cm. *1. U.S. — History. 2. The West — History. I. T.*
E179.5.T956 1962   973   62-12340

Taylor, George Rogers, 1895- ed. III. 4972
The Turner thesis concerning the role of the frontier in American history. Rev. ed. Boston, Heath [1956] 109 p. 24 cm. (Problems in American civilization; readings selected by the Dept. of American Studies, Amherst College) *1. Turner, Frederick Jackson, 1861-1932. The frontier in American history. 2. U.S. — History — Philosophy. I. T.*
E179.5.T96T3 1956   973   56-14601

Weinberg, Albert Katz. III. 4973
Manifest destiny; a study of nationalist expansionism in American history [by] Albert K. Weinberg. Baltimore, The Johns Hopkins Press, 1935. xiii, 559 p. 24 cm. At head of title: The Walter Hines Page school of international relations, the John Hopkins university. "Notes": p. 487-542. *1. U.S. — Territorial expansion. 2. U.S. — Nationality. 3. Political science — History — U.S. 4. Public opinion — U.S. 5. Political ethics. I. Johns Hopkins university. Walter Hines Page school of international relations. II. T. III. T:Expansionism in American history.*
E179.5.W45   973   35-9403

Winks, Robin W. III. 4974
The myth of the American frontier; its relevance to America, Canada and Australia, by Robin W. Winks. [Leicester, Eng.] Leicester University Press, 1971. 39 p. 22 cm. (Sir George Watson lecture, 1971) *1. Frontier thesis. 2. Frontier and pioneer life — United States. 3. Frontier and pioneer life — Canada. 4. Frontier and pioneer life — Australia. I. T. (S)*
E179.5.W54 1971   917/.03   72-185991   ISBN:0718511107

Wisconsin. University. III. 4975
Regionalism in America. Edited by Merrill Jensen; with a foreword by Felix Frankfurter. The contributors: Vernon Carstensen [and others] Madison, University of Wisconsin Press, 1951. xvi, 425 p. maps. 24 cm. "Papers 6 delivered at a symposium on American regionalism held at the University of Wisconsin April 14 and 15, 1949 ... sponsored by the Committee on the Study of American Civilization, of the University of Wisconsin." *1. Regionalism — U.S. I. Jensen, Merrill, ed. II. T.*
E179.5.W56   973.082   51-6901

Kane, Joseph Nathan, 1899- III. 4976
The American counties; a record of the origin of the names of the 3,072 counties, dates of creation and organization, area, 1960 population, historical data, etc. of the fifty States. Rev. ed. New York, Scarecrow Press, 1962. 540 p. 22 cm. *1. U.S. — History, Local. I. T.*
E180.K3 1962   917.3   62-16064

E181 – 182 Military and Naval History

Jacobs, James Ripley, 1886- III. 4977
The beginning of the U.S. Army, 1783-1812. Princeton, Princeton University Press, 1947. ix, 419 p. illus., ports., maps, plans. 23 cm. *1. U.S. Army — History. 2. U.S. — History, Military. I. T.*
E181.J2   973.4   47-5140

Matloff, Maurice, 1915- III. 4978
American military history. Washington, Office of the Chief of Military History, U.S. Army; [for sale by the Supt. of Docs., U.S. Govt. Print. Off.] 1969. xvi, 701 p. illus., maps, ports. 26 cm. (Army historical series) Replaces earlier publications issued by the U.S. Dept. of the Army under the same title. *1. United States — History, Military. I. United States. Dept. of the Army. American military history. II. T. (S:United States Army historical series)*
E181.M33 1969   355/.00973   76-600410

Millis, Walter, 1899-1968. III. 4979
Arms and men; a study in American military history. New York, Putnam [1956] 382 p. 22 cm. *1. United States — History, Military. 2. United States — Armed Forces — History. 3. United States — Military policy. I. T.*
E181.M699   973   56-10240

Palmer, Frederick, 1873-1958. III. 4980
John J. Pershing, General of the Armies; a biography. Westport, Conn., Greenwood Press [1970, c1948] xiii, 380 p. ports. 23 cm. *1. Pershing, John Joseph, 1860-1948.*
E181.P512 1970   355.3/32/0924 (B)   77-100253   ISBN:0837129869

Prucha, Francis Paul. III. 4981
The sword of the Republic; the United States Army on the frontier, 1783-1846. [New York] Macmillan [1968, c1969] xvii, 442 p. illus., maps, ports. 24 cm. (The Wars of the United States) *1. United States — History, Military — To 1900. 2. United States. Army — History. I. T. (S)*
E181.P86   977/.02   69-10292

Hagedorn, Hermann, 1882- III. 4982
Leonard Wood, a biography, by Hermann Hagedorn. 1st ed. New York and London, Harper, 1931. 2 v. illus., plates, ports. 25 cm. *1. Wood, Leonard, 1860-1927.*
E181.W83   923.573   31-24003

Braisted, William Reynolds. III. 4983
The United States Navy in the Pacific, 1897-1909. New York, Greenwood Press [1969, c1958] xii, 282 p. 23 cm. *1. United States — History, Naval. 2. United States — Foreign relations — 1897-1901. 3. United States — Foreign relations — 1901-1909. I. T.*
E182.B73 1969   327.73/018/23   70-90473   ISBN:0837121329

King, Ernest Joseph, 1878- III. 4984
Fleet Admiral King, a naval record by Ernest J. King and Walter Muir Whitehill. [1st ed.] New York, W. W. Norton [1952] xv, 674 p. illus., ports., maps. 24 cm. *1. U.S. Navy — History. 2. World War, 1939-1945 — Naval operations, American. I. Whitehill, Walter Muir, 1905- joint author. II. T.*
E182.K53   923.573   52-13493

Livezey, William Edmund, 1903-   **III. 4985**
Mahan on sea power, by William E. Livezey. 1st ed. Norman, University of Oklahoma Press, 1947. xiii, 334 p. illus., maps, facsims., plates, ports. 22 cm. *1. Mahan, Alfred Thayer, 1840-1914. 2. Sea-power. 3. U.S. — History, Naval. I. T.*
E182.M254   923.573   47-2156

O'Gara, Gordon Carpenter, 1920-   **III. 4986**
Theodore Roosevelt and the rise of the modern Navy. New York, Greenwood Press [1969, c1943] x, 138 p. illus. 23 cm. *1. Roosevelt, Theodore, Pres. U.S., 1858-1919. 2. United States. Navy — History. I. T.*
E182.O34 1969   359/.00973   69-14016   ISBN:0837114802

Smelser, Marshall.   **III. 4987**
The Congress founds the Navy, 1787-1798. [Notre Dame, Ind.] University of Notre Dame Press, 1959. ix, 229 p. 24 cm. *1. U.S. Navy — History. 2. U.S. — History, Naval. I. T.*
E182.S57   359.0973   58-14181

cole

Sprout, Harold Hance, 1901-   **III. 4988**
The rise of American naval power, 1776-1918, by Harold & Margaret Sprout. Princeton, Princeton University Press, 1939. vii, 398 p. front., plates, map. 24 cm. "First edition." *1. U.S. — Navy — History. I. Sprout, Margaret (Tuttle) Mrs., joint author. II. American naval power, The rise of. III. T.*
E182.S78   973   39-27471

Sprout, Harold Hance, 1901-   **III. 4989**
Toward a new order of sea power; American naval policy and the world scene, 1918-1922, by Harold and Margaret Sprout. New York, Greenwood Press [1969, c1943] xii, 336 p. illus., maps. 24 cm. Continuation of the author's The rise of American naval power. *1. United States. Navy — History. 2. United States — History, Naval — 20th century. 3. Sea-power. I. Sprout, Margaret (Tuttle) 1903- joint author. II. T.*
E182.S79 1969   359/.009   69-14092

West, Richard Sedgewick, 1902-   **III. 4990**
Admirals of American empire; the combined story of George Dewey, Alfred Thayer Mahan, Winfield Scott Schley, and William Thomas Sampson, by Richard S. West, Jr. Westport, Conn., Greenwood Press [1971, c1948] 354 p. illus. 23 cm. *1. Dewey, George, 1837-1917. 2. Mahan, Alfred Thayer, 1840-1914. 3. Schley, Winfield Scott, 1839-1911. 4. Sampson, William Thomas, 1840-1902. 5. United States — History, Naval — To 1900. I. T.*
E182.W45 1971   359/.00922 (B)   73-156216   ISBN:0837161673

E183   Political History (General)

Brock, William Ranulf.   **III. 4991**
The character of American history, by W. R. Brock. 2d ed. London, Macmillan; New York, St Martin's Press, 1965. xii, 302 p. 23 cm. *1. U.S. — Politics and government. I. T.*
E183.B86 1965   973   66-12687

Brock, William Ranulf.   **III. 4992**
The evolution of American democracy [by] William R. Brock. New York, Dial Press, 1970. 272 p. 24 cm. (Two centuries of American life: a bicentennial history) *1. United States — Politics and government. 2. Democracy. I. T.*
E183.B88   320.9/73   79-111451

Burns, James MacGregor.   **III. 4993**
The deadlock of democracy; four-party politics in America. Englewood Cliffs, N.J., Prentice-Hall [1963] 388 p. 24 cm. *1. United States — Politics and government. 2. Political parties — United States. I. Four-party politics in America. II. T.*
E183.B96   329   63-8455

Ekirch, Arthur Alphonse, 1915-   **III. 4994**
The decline of American liberalism [by] Arthur A. Ekirch, Jr. New York, Atheneum, 1967. 401 p. 19 cm. (Atheneum paperbacks, 111) *1. U.S. — Politics and government. 2. Liberalism — U.S. I. T.*
E183.E4 1967   973   67-13171

Lipset, Seymour Martin.   **III. 4995**
The politics of unreason; right wing extremism in America, 1790-1970 [by] Seymour Martin Lipset and Earl Raab. [1st ed.] New York, Harper & Row [1970] xxiv, 547 p. 25 cm. (Patterns of American prejudice series, v. 5) *1. United States — Politics and government. 2. Right and left (Political science) I. Raab, Earl, joint author. II. T. (S)*
E183.L56   320.5   67-22529

Martin, Ralph G., 1920-   **III. 4996**
The bosses [by] Ralph G. Martin. New York, Putnam [1964] 349 p. 23 cm. *1. U.S. — Politics and government. 2. Corruption (in politics) — U.S. I. T.*
E183.M25   329.02   64-18010

Roseboom, Eugene Holloway, 1892-   **III. 4997**
A history of presidential elections, from George Washington to Richard M. Nixon [by] Eugene H. Roseboom. [3d ed. New York] Macmillan [1970] viii, 639 p. 21 cm. An abridged and updated version was published in 1967 under title: A short history of presidential elections. *1. Presidents — United States — Election. 2. United States — Politics and government. I. T.*
E183.R69 1970   329/.023   78-101726

324.73
R721

Rossiter, Clinton Lawrence, 1917-   **III. 4998**
Parties and politics in America. Ithaca, N.Y., Cornell University Press [1960] vii, 205 p. 23 cm. *1. Political parties — U.S. I. T.*
E183.R7   329   60-16163

Schlesinger, Arthur Meier, 1917-   **III. 4999**
History of American presidential elections, 1789-1968. Arthur M. Schlesinger, Jr., editor. Fred L. Israel, associate editor. William P. Hansen, managing editor. New York, Chelsea House [1971] 4 v. (xxxvii, 3959 p.) 24 cm. *1. Presidents — U.S. — Election — History. 2. U.S. — Politics and government. I. Israel, Fred L., joint author. II. T.*
E183.S28   329/.023/73   70-139269   ISBN:0070797862

Smith, William Raymond.   **III. 5000**
The rhetoric of American politics; a study of documents. Westport, Conn., Greenwood Pub. Corp. [c1969] xv, 464 p. 22 cm. *1. United States — Politics and government — Addresses, essays, lectures. 2. Rhetoric — Addresses, essays, lectures. 3. Debates and debating — Addresses, essays, lectures. I. T.*
E183.S67   320.9/73   71-95503   ISBN:0837114950

E183.7   Diplomatic History (General)

Bailey, Thomas Andrew, 1902-   **III. 5001**
A diplomatic history of the American people [by] Thomas A. Bailey. 8th ed. New York, Appleton-Century-Crofts [1969] xl, 1015 p. illus., maps. 24 cm. *1. United States — Foreign relations. I. T.*
E183.7.B29 1969   327.73   79-77535   ISBN:039005027X

Bailey, Thomas Andrew, 1902-   **III. 5002**
The man in the street; the impact of American public opinion on foreign policy, by Thomas A. Bailey. Gloucester, Mass., P. Smith, 1964 [c1948] v, 334 p. 21 cm. *1. U.S. — Foreign relations. 2. Public opinion — U.S. I. T.*
E183.7.B33 1964   327.73   64-56381

Bartlett, Ruhl Jacob, 1897- ed.   **III. 5003**
The record of American diplomacy; documents and readings in the history of American foreign relations, edited by Ruhl J. Bartlett. 4th ed. enl. New York, Knopf, 1964. xxiv, 892, xxii p. 25 cm. *1. U.S. — Foreign relations — Collections. I. T.*
E183.7.B35 1964   327.73   64-23887

Bemis, Samuel Flagg, 1891- ed.   **III. 5004**
The American Secretaries of State and their diplomacy. New York, Cooper Square Publishers, 1963- [v.1-10, c1928] v. ports., map. 22 cm. Vol.11- edited by Robert H. Ferrell. *1. Cabinet officers — United States. 2. United States — Foreign relations. 3. Statesmen, American. I. Ferrell, Robert H., ed. II. Secretaries of State. III. T.*
E183.7.B462   327.73   62-20139

Bemis, Samuel Flagg, 1891-   **III. 5005**
A diplomatic history of the United States. 5th ed. New York, Holt, Rinehart and Winston [1965] x, 1062 p. illus., maps (part col.) 24 cm. *1. U.S. — Foreign relations. I. T.*
E183.7.B4682 1965   327.73   65-11841

Cole, Wayne S.   **III. 5006**
An interpretive history of American foreign relations [by] Wayne S. Cole. Homewood, Ill., Dorsey Press, 1968. xiii, 598 p. illus., maps, ports. 24 cm. (The Dorsey series in American history) *1. U.S. — Foreign relations. I. T.*
E183.7.C63   327.73   67-26281

De Conde, Alexander.   **III. 5007**
A history of American foreign policy. Maps from first ed. by Edward A. Schmitz. New maps by Robert Sugar. 2d ed. New York, Scribner [1971] x, 988 p. illus., maps, plans, ports. 24 cm. *1. United States — Foreign relations. I. American foreign policy.*
E183.7.D4 1971   327.73   78-143911   ISBN:0684123908

D3582

E183.8   **United States**   III. 5027

Dulles, Foster Rhea, 1900-   **III. 5008**
The imperial years. New York, Crowell [1956] 340 p. illus. 22 cm. *1. U.S. — Foreign relations — 1865-1898. 2. U.S. — Foreign relations — 1897-1901. 3. U.S. — Foreign relations — 1901-1909. 4. U.S. — Territorial expansion. I. T.*
E183.7.D78   327.73   56-7790

Ferrell, Robert H.   **III. 5009**
American diplomacy; a history [by] Robert H. Ferrell. Rev., and expanded ed. New York, Norton [1969] xiv, 930 p. illus., maps, ports. 25 cm. *1. United States — Foreign relations. I. T.*
E183.7.F4 1969   327.73   69-13018

Leopold, Richard William.   **III. 5010**
The growth of American foreign policy; a history. [1st ed.] New York, Knopf, 1962. xxii, 848, xxix p. maps. 25 cm. *1. U.S. — Foreign relations. I. T.*
E183.7.L47   327.73   62-13894

Parenti, Michael, 1933-   **III. 5011**
The anti-communist impulse. New York, Random House [1970, c1969] xi, 333 p. 22 cm. *1. United States — Foreign relations — Communist countries. 2. Communist countries — Foreign relations — United States. I. T.*
E183.7.P2 1970   327.73/0171/7   72-85615

Perkins, Dexter, 1889-   **III. 5012**
The American approach to foreign policy. Rev. ed. Cambridge, Harvard University Press, 1962. 247 p. 22 cm. *1. U.S. — Foreign relations. I. T.*
E183.7.P46 1962   327.73   62-11400

Perkins, Dexter, 1889-   **III. 5013**
The evolution of American foreign policy. 2d ed. New York, Oxford University Press, 1966. 168 p. 21 cm. (A Galaxy book) *1. United States — Foreign relations. I. T.*
E183.7.P47 1966   327.73   66-10824

Spykman, Nicholas John, 1893-1943.   **III. 5014**
America's strategy in world politics, the United States and the balance of power [by] Nicholas John Spykman, maps by Richard Edes Harrison. [1st ed.] New York, Harcourt, Brace and company [1942] 500 p. maps (part double) 24 cm. Map on lining-papers. Half-title: Institute of international studies, Yale university. *1. U.S. — Foreign relations. 2. Pan-Americanism. 3. World politics. I. Yale university. Institute of international studies. II. T.*
E183.7.S7   327.73   42-7980

Williams, William Appleman.   **III. 5015**
From colony to empire; essays in the history of American foreign relations. Edited by William Appleman Williams. New York, J. Wiley [1972] viii, 506 p. illus. 23 cm. *1. United States — Foreign relations — Addresses, essays, lectures. 2. United States — Territorial expansion — Addresses, essays, lectures. I. T.*
E183.7.W725   327.73   72-545   ISBN:0471946850

E183.8 Relations with Particular Countries, A – Z
E183.8.A   .B ARGENTINA. BRAZIL

Peterson, Harold F.   **III. 5016**
Argentina and the United States, 1810-1960. [Albany] State University of New York; [University Publishers, New York, sole distributors] 1964. xxii, 627 p. maps. 25 cm. *1. U.S. — Foreign relations — Argentine Republic. 2. Argentine Republic — Foreign relations — U.S. I. T.*
E183.8.A7P46   327.73082   62-21414

Burns, E. Bradford.   **III. 5017**
The unwritten alliance: Rio-Branco and Brazilian-American relations [by] E. Bradford Burns. New York, Columbia University Press, 1966. xiv, 305 p. illus., map, ports. 24 cm. A publication of Columbia University's Institute of Latin American Studies. *1. Rio Branco, José Maria da Silva Paranhos, barão do, 1845-1912. 2. U.S. — For relations — Brazil. 3. Brazil — Foreign relations — U.S. I. Columbia University. Institute of Latin American Studies. II. T.*
E183.8.B7B85   327.73081 81   65-25661
B937

Hill, Lawrence Francis, 1890-   **III. 5018**
Diplomatic relations between the United States and Brazil, by Lawrence F. Hill. New York, AMS Press [1971] x, 322 p. 23 cm. Reprint of the 1932 ed. *1. United States — Foreign relations — Brazil. 2. Brazil — Foreign relations — United States. I. T.*
E183.8.B7H56 1971   327.73/081   76-169489   ISBN:0404032680

E183.8.C2   CANADA

Tansill, Charles Callan, 1890-   **III. 5019**
Canadian-American relations, 1875-1911. Gloucester, Mass., P. Smith, 1964 [c1943] xviii, 507 p. map. 21 cm. (The Relations of Canada and the United States) *1. Canada — Foreign relations — U.S. 2. U.S. — Foreign relations — Canada. I. T. (S:Carnegie Endowment for International Peace. Division of Economics and History. The relations of Canada and the United States)*
E183.8.C2   327.73071   65-7269

Brebner, John Bartlet, 1895-1957.   **III. 5020**
North Atlantic triangle; the interplay of Canada, the United States, and Great Britain. New York, Russell & Russell [1970, c1945] xxii, 344, [43] p. illus., maps (part fold.) 25 cm. (The Relations of Canada and the United States) *1. United States — Foreign relations — Canada. 2. Canada — Foreign relations — United States. 3. United States — Foreign relations — Great Britain. 4. Great Britain — Foreign relations — United States. I. T. (S:Carnegie Endowment for International Peace. Division of Economics and History. The relations of Canada and the United States)*
E183.8.C2B74 1970   327.73/071   77-110676

Brown, Robert Craig.   **III. 5021**
Canada's national policy, 1883-1900; a study in Canadian-American relations. Princeton, N.J., Princeton University Press, 1964. xi, 436 p. illus., map. 21 cm. *1. Canada — Foreign relations — U.S. 2. U.S. — Foreign relations — Canada. I. T.*
E183.8.C2B78   327.73071   63-23401

Craig, Gerald M.   **III. 5022**
The United States and Canada [by] Gerald M. Craig. Cambridge, Harvard University Press, 1968. 376 p. col. map (on lining papers) 22 cm. (The American foreign policy library) *1. U.S. — Foreign relations — Canada. 2. Canada — Foreign relations — U.S. I. T. (S)*
E183.8.C2C8   327.71/073   67-30826

Keenleyside, Hugh Llewellyn, 1898-   **III. 5023**
Canada and the United States; some aspects of their historical relations. Rev. and enl. ed. prepared by Hugh Ll. Keenleyside and Gerald S. Brown. Introd. by W. P. M. Kennedy. New York, Knopf, 1952. xxvi, 406, xii p. map, diagrs. 22 cm. *1. Canada — Foreign relations — U.S. 2. U.S. — Foreign relations — Canada. I. Brown, Gerald Saxon, joint author. II. T.*
E183.8.C2K3 1952   327.730971   51-13225

Shippee, Lester Burrell, 1879-   **III. 5024**
Canadian-American relations, 1849-1874. New York, Russell & Russell [1970] xi, 514 p. map. 25 cm. (The relations of Canada and the United States) Reprint of the 1939 ed. *1. Canada — Foreign relations — United States. 2. United States — Foreign relations — Canada. I. T. (S:Carnegie Endowment for International Peace. Division of Economics and History. The relations of Canada and the United States)*
E183.8.C2S5 1970   327.73/071   72-102542

E183.8.C4   CHILE

Evans, Henry Clay, Jr.   **III. 5025**
Chile and its relations with the United States. Durham, N.C., Duke University Press, 1927. New York, Johnson Reprint Corp., 1971 [c1927] x, 243 p. 19 cm. (Reprints in government and political science) Original ed. issued in series: Duke University publications. Originally presented as the author's thesis, Columbia University. *1. Chile — Foreign relations — United States. 2. United States — Foreign relations — Chile. I. T.*
E183.8.C4E93 1971   327.73/083   71-165549

Pike, Fredrick B.   **III. 5026**
Chile and the United States, 1880-1962; the emergence of Chile's social crisis and the challenge to United States diplomacy. [Notre Dame, Ind.] University of Notre Dame Press, 1963. 466 p. 24 cm. (International studies of the Committee on International Relations, University of Notre Dame) *1. U.S. — Relations (general) with Chile. 2. Chile — Relations (general) with the U.S. I. T.*
E183.8.C4P5   983.061   63-9097

E183.8.C5   CHINA

Bueler, William M.   **III. 5027**
U.S. China policy and the problem of Taiwan, by William M. Bueler. Boulder, Colorado Associated University Press [1971] 143 p. 23 cm. *1. United States — Foreign relations — China. 2. China — Foreign relations — United*

States. 3. China — Foreign relations — 1949- — United States. I. T.
E183.8.C5B76   327.73/051   74-158666   ISBN:0870810138

Cohen, Warren I.   III. 5028
America's response to China; an interpretive history of Sino-American relations [by] Warren I. Cohen. New York, Wiley [1971] xiii, 242 p. maps. 22 cm. (America and the world) 1. U.S. — Foreign relations — China. 2. China — Foreign relations — U.S. I. T.
E183.8.C5C62   327.73/051   78-155117   ISBN:047116335X

Dulles, Foster Rhea, 1900-1970.   III. 5029
American policy toward Communist China, 1949-1969. Foreword by John K. Fairbank. New York, Crowell [1972] xiii, 273 p. illus. 25 cm. 1. United States — Foreign relations — China. 2. China — Foreign relations — 1949- — United States. I. T.
E183.8.C5D79 1972   327.73/052   70-184974
    ISBN:0690076126 0690076134 (lib. bdg.)

Dulles, Foster Rhea, 1900-   III. 5030
China and America; the story of their relations since 1784. Princeton, N.J., Princeton University Press, 1946. vii, 277 p. 21 cm. 1. U.S. — Foreign relations — China. 2. China — Foreign relations — U.S. 3. Eastern question (Far East) I. T.
E183.8.C5D8   A46-14

Fairbank, John King, 1907-   III. 5031
China: the people's middle kingdom and the U.S.A. [by] John K. Fairbank. Cambridge, Belknap Press of Harvard University Press, 1967. xi, 145 p. 22 cm. 1. China (People's Republic of China, 1949-   ) — Relations (general) with the U.S. 2. U.S. — Relations (general) with China (People's Republic of China, 1949-   ). I. T.
E183.8.C5F28   301.29/.51/073   67-17307

Feis, Herbert, 1893-   III. 5032
The China tangle; the American effort in China from Pearl Harbor to the Marshall mission. Princeton, Princeton University Press, 1953. x, 445 p. maps. 25 cm. 1. U.S. — Foreign relations — China. 2. China — Foreign relations — U.S. 3. U.S. — Foreign relations — 1933-1945. I. T.
E183.8.C5F4   327.730951   53-10142

Li, Tien-yi, 1915-   III. 5033
Woodrow Wilson's China policy, 1913-1917. [Kansas City, Mo.] University of Kansas City Press; [distributed by] Twayne Publishers, New York, 1952. 268 p. 23 cm. 1. U.S. — Foreign relations — China. 2. China — Foreign relations — U.S. 3. U.S. — Foreign relations — 1913-1921. I. T.
E183.8.C5L48   327.730951   53-5763

United States. Dept. of State.   III. 5034
United States relations with China, with special reference to the period 1944-1949. New York, Greenwood Press [1968] xli, 1054 p. fold. map. 24 cm. Reprint of the 1949 ed. 1. United States — Foreign relations — China. 2. China — Foreign relations — United States. I. T.
E183.8.C5U53 1968   327.73/051   68-55123

Varg, Paul A.   III. 5035
The making of a myth: the United States and China, 1879-1912, by Paul A. Varg. East Lansing, Michigan State University Press, 1968. 184 p. 25 cm. 1. United States — Foreign relations — China. 2. China — Foreign relations — United States. I. T.
E183.8.C5V3   327.51/073   68-20411

Young, Marilyn Blatt.   III. 5036
The rhetoric of empire; American China policy, 1895-1901. Cambridge, Mass., Harvard University Press, 1968 [i.e. 1969, c1968] viii, 302 p. 25 cm. (Harvard East Asian series, 36) "This book began as a doctoral dissertation at Harvard University." 1. United States — Foreign relations — China. 2. China — Foreign relations — United States. I. T. (S)
E183.8.C5Y63   327.51/073   68-54028

E183.8.C7 – .D
COLOMBIA. CUBA. DOMINICAN REPUBLIC

Bushnell, David, 1923-   III. 5037
Eduardo Santos and the good neighbor. 1938-1942. Gainesville, University of Florida Press, 1967. 128 p. 23 cm. (Latin American monographs, 2d ser., no. 4) 1. Santos, Eduardo, Pres. Colombia, 1888- 2. U.S. — Foreign relations — Colombia. 3. Colombia — Foreign relations — U.S. I. T. (S)
E183.8.C7B8   327.73/0861   67-65496

Parks, E. Taylor.   III. 5038
Colombia and the United States, 1765-1934, by E. Taylor Parks. New York, Greenwood Press, 1968 [c1935] xx, 554 p. illus., maps, ports. 24 cm. 1. United States — Foreign relations — Colombia. 2. Colombia — Foreign relations — United States. 3. Colombia — History. I. T.
E183.8.C7P37 1968   327.73/0861   68-9545

Bonsal, Philip Wilson, 1903-   III. 5039
Cuba, Castro, and the United States [by] Philip W. Bonsal. [Pittsburgh] University of Pittsburgh Press [1971] xii, 318 p. illus. 24 cm. 1. United States — Foreign relations — Cuba. 2. Cuba — Foreign relations — United States. 3. Castro, Fidel, 1927- I. T.
E183.8.C9B6   327.7291/073   72-151505   ISBN:0822932253

Healy, David F.   III. 5040
The United States in Cuba, 1898-1902: generals, politicians, and the search for policy. Madison, University of Wisconsin Press, 1963. 260 p. illus. 23 cm. 1. U.S. — Foreign relations — Cuba. 2. Cuba — Foreign relations — U.S. I. T.
E183.8.C9H4   327.7307291   63-13742

Smith, Robert Freeman, 1930-   III. 5041
The United States and Cuba: business and diplomacy, 1917-1960. New York, Bookman Associates [1961, c1960] 256 p. 23 cm. 1. United States — Foreign economic relations — Cuba. 2. Cuba — Foreign economic relations — United States. 3. United States — Foreign relations — Cuba. 4. Cuba — Foreign relations — United States. I. T.
E183.8.C9S6   327.7307291   60-53477

Smith, Robert Freeman, 1930-   III. 5042
What happened in Cuba? a documentary history. New York, Twayne Publishers [1963] 360 p. 21 cm. 1. U.S. — Foreign relations — Cuba. 2. Cuba — Foreign relations — U.S. 3. U.S. — Foreign relations — Sources. I. T.
E183.8.C9S62   327.7307291   62-19464

Lowenthal, Abraham F.   III. 5043
The Dominican intervention [by] Abraham F. Lowenthal. Cambridge, Mass., Harvard University Press, 1972. x, 246 p. 22 cm. 1. United States — Foreign relations — Dominican Republic. 2. Dominican Republic — Foreign relations — United States. I. T.
E183.8.D6L6   327.73/07293   79-183746   ISBN:0674214803

Slater, Jerome.   III. 5044
Intervention and negotiation; the United States and the Dominican revolution. Foreword by Hans J. Morgenthau. [1st ed.] New York, Harper & Row [1970] xviii, 254 p. col. map (on lining papers), ports. 22 cm. 1. United States — Foreign relations — Dominican Republic. 2. Dominican Republic — Foreign relations — United States. I. T.
E183.8.D6S55 1970   972/.93054   70-95985

Tansill, Charles Callan, 1890-   III. 5045
The United States and Santo Domingo, 1798-1873; a chapter in Caribbean diplomacy. Gloucester, Mass., P. Smith, 1967 [c1938] viii, 487 p. 21 cm. At head of title: The Walter Hines Page School of International Relations, the Johns Hopkins University. "Most of the chapters ... were given in the form of lectures ... in the Graduate School of the Johns Hopkins University." 1. U.S. — Foreign relations — Dominican Republic. 2. Dominican Republic — Foreign relations — U.S. I. Johns Hopkins University. Walter Hines Page School of International Relations. II. T.
E183.8.D6T3 1967   327.73/07293   67-4593

E183.8.F – .G
FRANCE. GERMANY

Blumenthal, Henry.   III. 5046
France and the United States; their diplomatic relation, 1789-1914. Chapel Hill, University of North Carolina Press [1970] xiv, 312 p. 21 cm. 1. United States — Foreign relations — France. 2. France — Foreign relations — United States. I. T.
E183.8.F8B54   327.44/073   73-80926   ISBN:0807811262

Haight, John McVickar, 1917-   III. 5047
American aid to France, 1938-1940. [1st ed.] New York, Atheneum, 1970. ix, 278 p. 22 cm. 1. United States — Foreign relations — France. 2. France — Foreign relations — United States. 3. United States — Foreign relations — 1933-1945. I. T.
E183.8.F8H17 1970   327.73/044   70-108828

Jones, Howard Mumford, 1892-   III. 5048
America and French culture, 1750-1848, by Howard Mumford Jones. Chapel Hill, University of North Carolina Press; London, H. Milford, Oxford University Press, 1927. xvi, 615 p. front. 24 cm. 1. U.S. — Civilization. 2. France — Civilization. 3. U.S. — Relations (general) with France. 4. France — Relations (general) with the U.S. I. T.
E183.8.F8J7   28-2551

McKay, Donald Cope.   III. 5049
The United States and France. Cambridge, Harvard University Press, 1951.

xvii, 334 p. maps. 20 cm. (The American foreign policy library) *1. U.S. — Foreign relations — France. 2. France — Foreign relations — U.S. 3. France. I. T. (S)*
E183.8.F8M3   327.7309   51-11375

Offner, Arnold A.   III. 5050
American appeasement; United States foreign policy and Germany, 1933-1938. Cambridge, Belknap Press of Harvard University Press, 1969. ix, 328 p. 24 cm. *1. United States — Foreign relations — Germany. 2. Germany — Foreign relations — United States. 3. United States — Foreign relations — 1933-1945. I. T.*
E183.8.G3O35   327.73/043   69-13767

E183.8.G7   GREAT BRITAIN

Thistlethwaite, Frank.   III. 5051
America and the Atlantic community: Anglo-American aspects, 1790-1850. New York, Harper & Row [1963, c1959] vi, 222 p. 21 cm. (Harper torchbooks. The Academy library) "TB 1107." First published in 1959 under title: The Anglo-American connection in the early nineteenth century. *1. U.S. — Relations (general) with Gt. Brit. 2. Gt. Brit. — Relations (general) with the U.S. I. T.*
E183.8.G7   327.73042   64-7406

Allen, Harry Cranbrook.   III. 5052
Great Britain and the United States; a history of Anglo-American relations, 1783-1952, by H. C. Allen. [Hamden, Conn.] Archon Books, 1969. 1028 p. maps. 23 cm. Reprint of the 1954 ed. *1. United States — Foreign relations — Great Britain. 2. Great Britain — Foreign relations — United States. I. T.*
E183.8.G7A47 1969   327.42/073   69-11550   ISBN:020800758X

Bourne, Kenneth.   III. 5053
Britain and the balance of power in North America, 1815-1908. Berkeley, University of California Press, 1967. xii, 439 p. maps. 23 cm. On spine: The balance of power in North America. *1. Great Britain — Foreign relations — United States. 2. United States — Foreign relations — Great Britain. I. The balance of power in North America. II. T.*
E183.8.G7B68 1967   327.42/073   67-26632

Brinton, Clarence Crane, 1898-1968.   III. 5054
The United States and Britain. Westport, Conn., Greenwood Press [1970, c1948] xiv, 312 p. 23 cm. (The American foreign policy library) *1. Great Britain — Foreign relations — United States. 2. United States — Foreign relations — Great Britain. 3. Great Britain — Civilization — 1945- I. T. (S)*
E183.8.G7B75 1970   327.42/073   75-97340   ISBN:0837129648

Burt, Alfred LeRoy, 1888-   III. 5055
The United States, Great Britain, and British North America from the Revolution to the establishment of peace after the War of 1812. New York, Russell & Russell, 1961 [c1940] vii, 448 p. maps (part fold.) 25 cm. (The relations of Canada and the United States) *1. U.S. — Foreign relations — Gt. Brit. 2. Gt. Brit. — Foreign relations — U.S. 3. U.S. — Relations (general) with Canada. 4. Canada — Relations (general) with the U.S. (S:Carnegie Endowment for International Peace. Division of Economics and History. The relations of Canada and the United States)*
E183.8.G7B9 1961   327.73042   61-13768

Campbell, Charles Soutter, 1911-   III. 5056
Anglo-American understanding, 1898-1903. Baltimore, Johns Hopkins Press [1957] vii, 385 p. map. 23 cm. *1. U.S. — Foreign relations — Gt. Brit. 2. Gt. Brit. — Foreign relations — U.S. I. T.*
E183.8.G7C28   327.730942   57-9518

Lillibridge, George D., 1921-   III. 5057
Beacon of freedom; the impact of American democracy upon Great Britain, 1830-1870. [Philadelphia] University of Pennsylvania Press, 1954 [c1955] xv, 159 p. 24 cm. *1. U.S. — Relations (general) with Great Britain. 2. Gt. Brit. — Relations (general) with the U.S. I. T.*
E183.8.G7L54   327.730942   54-11541

Neustadt, Richard E.   III. 5058
Alliance politics [by] Richard E. Neustadt. New York, Columbia University Press, 1970. xii, 167 p. 22 cm. A reworked version of the author's Radner Lectures, delivered at Columbia University in 1966. *1. United States — Foreign relations — 1945- 2. United States — Foreign relations — Great Britain. 3. Great Britain — Foreign relations — United States. I. T.*
E183.8.G7N47 1970   327.73/042   77-120855   ISBN:0231030665

Nicholas, Herbert George.   III. 5059
Britain and the U.S.A. Baltimore, Johns Hopkins Press, 1963. 191 p. 22 cm. (The Albert Shaw lectures on diplomatic history, 1961. Britain in the world today, 3) *1. U.S. — Foreign relations — Gt. Brit. 2. Gt. Brit. — Foreign relations — U.S. I. T.*
E183.8.G7N49   327.73042   63-10195

Perkins, Bradford, 1925-   III. 5060
The first rapprochement, England and the United States, 1795-1805. Philadelphia, University of Pennsylvania Press, 1955. xii, 257 p. ports., maps. 24 cm. *1. U.S. — Foreign relations — Gt. Brit. 2. Gt. Brit. — Foreign relations — U.S. 3. U.S. — Foreign relations — 1783-1815. I. T.*
E183.8.G7P4   327.73   55-9468

Perkins, Bradford, 1925-   III. 5061
The great rapprochement; England and the United States, 1895-1914. [1st ed.] New York, Atheneum, 1968. viii, 341 p. 25 cm. *1. United States — Foreign relations — Great Britain. 2. Great Britain — Foreign relations — United States. I. T.*
E183.8.G7P42 1968   327/.73/042   68-16870

Rippy, James Fred, 1892-   III. 5062
Rivalry of the United States and Great Britain over Latin America, 1808-1830. New York, Octagon Press, 1964 [c1929] xi, 322 p. maps. 21 cm. (The Albert Shaw lectures on diplomatic history, 1928) *1. U.S. — Foreign relations — Gt. Brit. 2. Gt. Brit. — Foreign relations — U.S. 3. U.S. — Foreign relations — Latin America. 4. Latin America — Politics — 1806-1830. 5. Gt. Brit. — Foreign relations — Latin America. I. T. (S)*
E183.8.G7R6 1964   327.73042   64-24839

Russett, Bruce M.   III. 5063
Community and contention; Britain and America in the twentieth century. Cambridge, M.I.T. Press, 1963. xii, 252 p. illus. 24 cm. "Originally ... [written] as a Ph.D. dissertation [Yale University]" *1. U.S. — Relations (general) with Great Britain. 2. Gt. Brit. — Relations (general) with the U.S. I. T.*
E183.8.G7R88 1963   327.73042   63-10453

E183.8.H   HAITI. HAWAII

Logan, Rayford Whittingham.   III. 5064
The diplomatic relations of the United States with Haiti, 1776-1891, by Rayford W. Logan. Chapel Hill, The University of North Carolina Press, 1941. xi, 516 p. 24 cm. *1. U.S. — Foreign relations — Haiti. 2. Haiti — Foreign relations — U.S. I. T.*
E183.8.H2L6   327.73097204   41-6260

Montague, Ludwell Lee, 1907-   III. 5065
Haiti and the United States, 1714-1938. With a foreword by J. Fred Rippy. New York, Russell & Russell, 1966 [c1940] xiv, 308 p. maps. 23 cm. (Duke University publications) Reprint of a thesis, Duke University, 1935. *1. Haiti — Foreign relations — U.S. 2. U.S. — Foreign relations — Haiti. I. T.*
E183.8.H2M6 1966   327.7294073   66-24732

Tate, Merze, 1905-   III. 5066
The United States and the Hawaiian Kingdom; a political history. New Haven, Yale University Press, 1965. ix, 374 p. maps. 24 cm. *1. U.S. — Foreign relations — Hawaii. 2. Hawaii — Foreign relations — U.S. 3. Hawaii — Politics and government. I. T.*
E183.8.H3T34   996.902   65-22342

E183.8.I   INDIA. ISRAEL. ITALY

Hess, Gary R.   III. 5067
America encounters India, 1941-1947 [by] Gary R. Hess. Baltimore, Johns Hopkins Press [c1971] xi, 211 p. 24 cm. *1. United States — Foreign relations — India. 2. India — Foreign relations — United States. I. T.*
E183.8.I4H4   327.73/054   72-163196   ISBN:0801812585

Safran, Nadav.   III. 5068
The United States and Israel. Cambridge, Mass., Harvard University Press, 1963. xvii, 341 p. maps (part col.) tables. 22 cm. (The American foreign policy library) *1. U.S. — Foreign relations — Israel. 2. Israel — Foreign relations — U.S. 3. Israel — Civilization. I. T. (S)*
E183.8.I7S2   327.7305694   63-17212

DeConde, Alexander.   III. 5069
Half bitter, half sweet; an excursion into Italian-American history. New York, Scribner [1971] vii, 466 p. 24 cm. *1. United States — Relations (general) with Italy. 2. Italy — Relations (general) with the United States. 3. Italians in the United States. I. T.*
E183.8.I8D4   301.29/73/045   75-123851   ISBN:0684123665

E183.8.J – K JAPAN. KOREA

Beers, Burton F. III. 5070
Vain endeavor: Robert Lansing's attempts to end the American-Japanese rivalry. Durham, N.C., Duke University Press, 1962. 207 p. 23 cm. (Duke historical publications) *1. Lansing, Robert, 1864-1928. 2. U.S. — Foreign relations — Japan. 3. Japan — Foreign relations — U.S. I. T.*
E183.8.J3B4   327.73052   61-16907

Harris, Townsend, 1804-1878. III. 5071
The complete journal of Townsend Harris first American consul and minister to Japan. Introd. and notes by Mario Emilia Cosenza. With a pref. by Douglas MacArthur, II. Rev. [i.e. 2d] ed. Rutland, Vt., C. E. Tuttle Co. [1959] xix, 616 p. plates, port., facsims. 23 cm. *1. U.S. — Foreign relations — Japan. 2. Japan — Foreign relations — U.S. 3. U.S. — Foreign relations — Thailand. 4. Thailand — Foreign relations — U.S. 5. Japan — Description and travel — 1801-1900. 6. Thailand — Description and travel.*
E183.8.J3H3 1959   327.73052   59-9397

Iriye, Akira. III. 5072
Pacific estrangement; Japanese and American expansion, 1897-1911. Cambridge, Mass., Harvard University Press, 1972. ix, 290 p. 25 cm. (Harvard studies in American-East Asian relations, 2) *1. United States — Foreign relations — Japan. 2. Japan — Foreign relations — United States. I. T. (S)*
E183.8.J3I74   327.52/073   72-79307   ISBN:0674650751

Kamikawa, Hikomatsu, 1889- ed. III. 5073
Japan-American diplomatic relations in the Meiji-Taisho era. Tokyo, Pan-Pacific Press, 1958. 458 p. ports., facsims. 22 cm. (Centenary Cultural Council series. [A history of Japanese-American cultural relations (1853-1926) v.3]) Translated and adapted by Kimura Michiko. *1. U.S. — Foreign relations — Japan. 2. Japan — Foreign relations — U.S. I. T. (S:Kaikoku Hyakunen Kinen Bunka Jigyōkai. A history of Japanese-American cultural relations, v.3)*
E183.8.J3K12   327.73052   59-65000

Neu, Charles E. III. 5074
An uncertain friendship: Theodore Roosevelt and Japan, 1906-1909 [by] Charles E. Neu. Cambridge, Mass., Harvard University Press, 1967. x, 347 p. 22 cm. *1. Roosevelt, Theodore, Pres. U.S., 1858-1919. 2. U.S. — Foreign relations — Japan. 3. Japan — Foreign relations — U.S. I. T.*
E183.8.J3N37   327.52/073   67-27091

Neumann, William Louis, 1915- III. 5075
America encounters Japan; from Perry to MacArthur. Baltimore, Johns Hopkins Press, 1963. viii, 353 p. 22 cm. (The Goucher College series) *1. U.S. — Relations (general) with Japan. 2. Japan — Relations (general) with the U.S. I. T.*
E183.8.J3N39   327.73052   63-17667

Packard, George R. III. 5076
Protest in Tokyo; the security treaty crisis of 1960, by George R. Packard, III. Princeton, N.J., Princeton University Press, 1966. xiv, 423 p. illus., ports. 21 cm. *1. U.S. — Foreign relations — Japan. 2. Japan — Foreign relations — U.S. 3. Japan — Politics and government — 1945- I. T.*
E183.8.J3P24   327.52073   65-17156

Rappaport, Armin. III. 5077
Henry L. Stimson and Japan, 1931-33. Chicago, University of Chicago Press [1963] viii, 238 p. 22 cm. *1. Stimson, Henry Lewis, 1867-1950. 2. U.S. — Foreign relations — Japan. 3. Japan — Foreign relations — U.S. 4. Japanese in Manchuria.*
E183.8.J3R3   327.73052   63-18847

Reischauer, Edwin Oldfather, 1910- III. 5078
The United States and Japan, by Edwin O. Reischauer. 3d ed. Cambridge, Harvard University Press, 1965. xxv, 396 p. maps (1 col. on lining paper) 22 cm. (The American foreign policy library) *1. United States — Foreign relations — Japan. 2. Japan — Foreign relations — United States. I. T. (S)*
E183.8.J3R4 1965   327.73052   64-8057

Schwantes, Robert S. III. 5079
Japanese and Americans; a century of cultural relations. [1st ed.] New York, Published for the Council on Foreign Relations by Harper, 1955. x, 380 p. 23 cm. *1. U.S. — Relations (general) with Japan. 2. Japan — Relations (general) with the U.S. I. T.*
E183.8.J3S35   327.730952   55-7220

United States-Japanese political relations: the critical issues affecting Asia's future. III. 5080
Washington, Center for Strategic Studies, Georgetown University, 1968. ix, 104 p. 22 cm. (Center for Strategic Studies, Georgetown University. Special report series, no. 7) Report of a study by a panel convened by the Center for Strategic Studies under the chairmanship of R. E. Ward, with a background paper by D. F. Anthony. *1. United States — Foreign relations — Japan. 2. Japan — Foreign relations — United States. (S:Georgetown University, Washington, D.C. Center for Strategic Studies. Special report series, no. 7)*
E183.8.J3U75   327.52/073   68-31062

Cho, Soon Sung, 1930- III. 5081
Korea in world politics, 1940-1950; an evaluation of American responsibility. Berkeley, University of California Press, 1967. x, 338 p. map. 23 cm. (Publications of the Center for Japanese and Korean Studies) *1. U.S. — Foreign relations — Korea. 2. Korea — Foreign relations — U.S. 3. Korea — History — 1948-1960. I. T. (S:California. University. Center for Japanese and Korean Studies. Publications)*
E183.8.K7C47 1967   327.519/073   67-14968

E183.8.M MEXICO. MOROCCO

Cronon, Edmund David. III. 5082
Josephus Daniels in Mexico. Madison, University of Wisconsin Press, 1960. xiii, 369 p. illus., ports., facsims. 23 cm. *1. Daniels, Josephus, 1862-1948. 2. Mexico — Foreign relations — U.S. 3. U.S. — Foreign relations — Mexico. 4. Mexico — Politics and government — 1910-1946.*
E183.8.M6C7   327.73072   60-5672

Haley, P. Edward. III. 5083
Revolution and intervention: the diplomacy of Taft and Wilson with Mexico, 1910-1917 [by] P. Edward Haley. Cambridge, M.I.T. Press [1970] 294 p. maps, ports. 24 cm. *1. Taft, William Howard, Pres. U.S., 1857-1930. 2. Wilson, Woodrow, Pres. U.S., 1856-1924. 3. United States — Foreign relations — Mexico. 4. Mexico — Foreign relations — United States. 5. Mexico — History — 1910-1946. I. T.*
E183.8.M6H3   327.72/073   72-107991   ISBN:0262080397

Hall, Luella J., 1890- III. 5084
The United States and Morocco, 1776-1956, by Luella J. Hall. Metuchen, N.J., Scarecrow Press, 1971. 1114 p. map. 22 cm. *1. United States — Foreign relations — Morocco. 2. Morocco — Foreign relations — United States. I. T.*
E183.8.M8H3   327.73/0449/49   71-142233   ISBN:0810803380

E183.8.P PERU. PRUSSIA. PUERTO RICO

Carey, James Charles. III. 5085
Peru and the United States, 1900-1962, by James C. Carey. [Notre Dame, Ind.] University of Notre Dame Press, 1964. xiii, 243 p. 24 cm. (International studies of the Committee on International Relations, University of Notre Dame) *1. U.S. — Foreign relations — Peru. 2. Peru — Foreign relations — U.S. I. T. (S:Notre Dame, Ind. University. Committee on International Relations. International studies)*
E183.8.P4C3   327.73085   64-23666

Adams, Henry Mason, 1907- III. 5086
Prussian-American relations, 1775-1871. [Cleveland] Press of Western Reserve University, 1960. 135 p. 24 cm. *1. U.S. — Relations (general) with Prussia. 2. Prussia — Relations (general) with the U.S. I. T.*
E183.8.P83A65   327.730431   60-12702

Mathews, Thomas G., 1925- III. 5087
Puerto Rican politics and the New Deal. Gainesville, University of Florida Press, 1960. 345 p. 24 cm. Issued in microfilm form, 1957, as thesis, Columbia University. *1. Puerto Rico — Politics and government — 1898-1952. 2. U.S. — Relations (general) with Puerto Rico. 3. Puerto Rico — Relations (general) with the U.S. I. The New Deal. II. T.*
E183.8.P9M3 1960   972.9505   60-15789

E183.8.R9 RUSSIA

Bailey, Thomas Andrew, 1902- III. 5088
America faces Russia; Russian-American relations from early times to our day. Ithaca, Cornell University Press, 1950. xi, 375 p. illus. 24 cm. *1. U.S. — Foreign relations — Russia. 2. Russia — Foreign relations — U.S. I. T.*
E183.8.R9B3   327.730947   50-10009

Bishop, Donald Gordon. III. 5089
The Roosevelt-Litvinov agreements; the American view [by] Donald G. Bishop. [1st ed. Syracuse, N.Y.] Syracuse University Press [1965] viii, 297 p. 24 cm. *1. Roosevelt, Franklin Delano, Pres. U.S. 1882-1945. 2. Litvinov,*

Maksim Maksimovich, 1876-1951. 3. U.S. — Foreign relations — Russia. 4. Russia — Foreign relations — U.S. I. T.
E183.8.R9B5   327.73047   65-15852

Browder, Robert Paul. III. 5090
The origins of Soviet-American diplomacy. Princeton, Princeton University Press, 1953. xi, 256 p. 23 cm. *1. U.S. — Foreign relations — Russia. 2. Russia — Foreign relations — U.S. 3. U.S. — Foreign relations — 1929-1933. I. T.*
E183.8.R9B7   327.730947   52-8762

Filene, Peter G. III. 5091
Americans and the Soviet experiment, 1917-1933 [by] Peter G. Filene. Cambridge, Mass., Harvard University Press, 1967. viii, 389 p. illus. 22 cm. *1. U.S. — Foreign relations — Russia. 2. Russia — Foreign relations — U.S. 3. Russia — History — Revolution, 1917-1921. 4. Russia — Foreign opinion, American. I. T.*
E183.8.R9F5   327.47073   67-11669

Kennan, George Frost, 1904- III. 5092
Soviet-American relations, 1917-1920. Princeton, Princeton University Press, 1956-   v. illus., ports., maps, facsims. 25 cm. *1. U.S. — Foreign relations — Russia. 2. Russia — Foreign relations — U.S. 3. Russia — History — Revolution, 1917-1921. I. T.*
E183.8.R9K4   327.730947   56-8382

Kennedy, Robert F., 1925-1968. III. 5093
Thirteen days; a memoir of the Cuban missile crisis. With introductions by Robert S. McNamara and Harold Macmillan. [1st ed.] New York, W. W. Norton [1969] 224 p. illus., facsim. (on lining papers), ports. 24 cm. "Documents": p. 163-218. *1. United States — Foreign relations — Russia. 2. Russia — Foreign relations — United States. 3. Military bases, Russian — Cuba. I. T.*
E183.8.R9K42   327.73/047   69-15949

LaFeber, Walter. III. 5094
America, Russia, and the cold war, 1945-1966. New York, Wiley [1967] xi, 295 p. maps. 22 cm. (America in crisis) *1. United States — Foreign relations — Russia. 2. Russia — Foreign relations — United States. 3. World politics — 1945- I. T. (S)*
E183.8.R9L26   327.47/073   67-29014

Rapoport, Anatol, 1911- III. 5095
The big two; Soviet-American perceptions of foreign policy. New York, Pegasus [1971] 249 p. 21 cm. (American involvement in the world) *1. U.S. — Foreign relations — Russia. 2. Russia — Foreign relations — U.S. I. T.*
E183.8.R9R23   327.47/073   72-124676

Ulam, Adam Bruno, 1922- III. 5096
The rivals: America and Russia since World War II [by] Adam B. Ulam. New York, Viking Press [1971] vi, 405 p. 25 cm. *1. U.S. — Foreign relations — Russia. 2. Russia — Foreign relations — U.S. I. T.*
E183.8.R9U4 1971   327.73/047   75-160204   ISBN:067059959X

Welch, William, 1917- III. 5097
American images of Soviet foreign policy; an inquiry into recent appraisals from the academic community. New Haven, Yale University Press, 1970. xiii, 316 p. 23 cm. *1. Russia — Foreign opinion, American. 2. Russia — Foreign relations — United States. 3. United States — Foreign relations — Russia. I. T.*
E183.8.R9W43   327.47/073   74-118739   ISBN:0300013604

Williams, William Appleman. III. 5098
American-Russian relations, 1781-1947. New York, Octagon Books, 1971 [c1952] 367 p. 24 cm. *1. U.S. — Foreign relations — United States. 2. United States — Foreign relations — Russia. I. T.*
E183.8.R9W63 1971   327.73/047   70-154671   ISBN:0374985812

Zabriskie, Edward Henry, 1892- III. 5099
American-Russian rivalry in the Far East, a study in diplomacy and power politics, 1895-1914, by Edward H. Zabriskie. Philadelphia, University of Pennsylvania Press; [etc.,etc.] 1946. vii, 226 p. map. 24 cm. Issued in part as thesis (PH.D.) Chicago university. *1. U.S. — Foreign relations — Russia. 2. Russia — Foreign relations — U.S. 3. Eastern question (Far East) I. T.*
E183.8.R9Z3   327.730947   46-1314

E183.8.S – .T   SPAIN. TURKEY

Griffin, Charles Carroll, 1902- III. 5100
The United States and the disruption of the Spanish Empire, 1810-1822; a study of the relations of the United States with Spain and with the rebel Spanish colonies. New York, Octagon Books, 1968 [c1937] 315 p. 23 cm. (Studies in history, economics, and public law, no. 429) *1. U.S. — Foreign relations — Spain. 2. Spain — Foreign relations — U.S. 3. South America — History — Wars of Independence, 1806-1830. 4. Washington, Treaty of, 1819. I. T. (S:Columbia studies in the social sciences, no. 429)*
E183.8.S7G7x (H31.C7 no. 429)   327.46/073   67-18765

Traina, Richard P. III. 5101
American diplomacy and the Spanish Civil War [by] Richard P. Traina. Bloomington, Indiana University Press [1968] xi, 301 p. 25 cm. (Indiana University international studies) *1. United States — Foreign relations — Spain. 2. Spain — Foreign relations — United States. 3. Spain — History — Civil War, 1936-1939 — Foreign participation — American. I. T. (S:Indiana. University. International studies)*
E183.8.S7T7   327.73/046   68-27356

Whitaker, Arthur Preston, 1895- III. 5102
Spain and defense of the West; ally and liability. [1st ed.] New York, Published for the Council on Foreign Relations by Harper, 1961. 408 p. illus. 22 cm. *1. U.S. — Foreign relations — Spain. 2. Spain — Foreign relations — U.S. 3. Spain — Foreign relations — 1939- 4. Spain — Politics and government — 1939- I. T.*
E183.8.S7W5   327.73046   61-6234

Thomas, Lewis Victor, 1914-1965. III. 5103
The United States and Turkey and Iran, by Lewis V. Thomas and Richard N. Frye. [Hamden, Conn.] Archon Books, 1971 [c1951] xii, 291 p. maps. 23 cm. *1. Turkey. 2. United States — Foreign relations — Turkey. 3. Turkey — Foreign relations — United States. 4. Iran. 5. United States — Foreign relations — Iran. 6. Iran — Foreign relations — United States. I. Frye, Richard Nelson, 1920- II. T.*
E183.8.T8T5 1971   327.73/055   75-147379   ISBN:0208009981

Trask, Roger R. III. 5104
The United States response to Turkish nationalism and reform, 1914-1939 [by] Roger R. Trask. Minneapolis, University of Minnesota Press [1971] 280 p. 25 cm. *1. United States — Foreign relations — Turkey. 2. Turkey — Foreign relations — United States. I. T.*
E183.8.T8T7 1971   327.561/073   74-153505   ISBN:0816606137

E183.8.V5   VIETNAM

Morgenthau, Hans Joachim, 1904- III. 5105
Vietnam and the United States [by] Hans J. Morgenthau. Washington, Public Affairs Press [1965] 112 p. map. 23 cm. *1. U.S. — Foreign relations — Vietnam. 2. Vietnam — Foreign relations — U.S. I. T.*
E183.8.V5M6   327.597073   65-28164

The Pentagon papers as published by the New York times. III. 5106
The Pentagon history was obtained by Neil Sheehan. Written by Neil Sheehan [and others] New York, Quadrangle Books [1971] xix, 810 p. illus. 24 cm. *1. United States — Foreign relations — Vietnam. 2. Vietnam — Foreign relations — United States. 3. Vietnam — Politics and government. 4. Vietnamese Conflict, 1961- I. Sheehan, Neil. II. New York times.*
E183.8.V5P4   959.7/0432   75-173846

The Pentagon papers; the Defense Department history of United States decisionmaking on Vietnam. III. 5107
The Senator Gravel ed. Boston, Beacon Press [1971-72] 5 v. 23 cm. Vol. 5: Critical essays, edited by N. Chomsky and H. Zinn, and an index to v. 1-4. *1. United States — Foreign relations — Vietnam. 2. Vietnam — Foreign relations — United States. 3. Vietnam — Politics and government. 4. Vietnamese Conflict, 1961- I. United States. Dept. of Defense.*
E183.8.V5P42   959.7/0432   75-178049
    ISBN:0807005266 0807005274 (pbk) (v. 14) 0807005223 0807005231 (pbk.) (v. 5)

Schlesinger, Arthur Meier, 1917- III. 5108
The bitter heritage: Vietnam and American democracy, 1941-1966 [by] Arthur M. Schlesinger, Jr. London, Deutsch, 1967. 127 p. 23 cm. *1. United States — Foreign relations — Vietnam. 2. Vietnam — Foreign relations — United States. 3. Vietnam — Politics and government — 1963- I. Vietnam and American democracy, 1941-1966. II. T.*
E183.8.V5S3 1967b   327.73/0597   68-86636

E183.9   Special Topics in Political History

Hyman, Harold Melvin, 1924- III. 5109
To try men's souls; loyalty tests in American history. Berkeley, University of California Press, 1959. 414 p. illus. 25 cm. *1. Loyalty oaths — United States. 2. Allegiance — United States. I. T.*
E183.9.H9   320.158   59-8761

Young, Alfred Fabian, 1925- comp. III. 5110
Dissent; explorations in the history of American radicalism, edited by Alfred F. Young. DeKalb, Northern Illinois University Press [1968] vi, 388 p. 24 cm. *1. United States — History — Addresses, essays, lectures. 2. Radicalism — United States — Addresses, essays, lectures. I. T.*
E183.9.Y6   322/.4/0973   68-57389   ISBN:0875800076

E184 – 185 Elements in the Population
E184.A1 GENERAL WORKS

Barron, Milton Leon, 1918- ed. III. 5111
American minorities; a textbook of readings in intergroup relations. [1st ed.] New York, Knopf, 1957. 518 p. 24 cm. *1. Minorities — U.S. 2. U.S. — Race question. I. T.*
E184.A1B25   325.73   57-5816

Fermi, Laura. III. 5112
Illustrious immigrants; the intellectual migration from Europe, 1930-41. Chicago, University of Chicago Press [1968] xi, 440 p. ports. 24 cm. *1. U.S. — Foreign population. 2. Intellectuals — Europe. 3. Intellectuals — U.S. 4. U.S. — Civilization — Foreign influences. I. T.*
E184.A1F47   917.3/03/917   67-25512

Gossett, Thomas F. III. 5113
Race; the history of an idea in America. Dallas, Southern Methodist University Press, 1963. ix, 512 p. 23 cm. *1. Race. 2. Minorities — United States. 3. United States — Race question.*
E184.A1G6   63-21187

Greeley, Andrew M., 1928- III. 5114
Why can't they be like us? America's white ethnic groups, by Andrew M. Greeley. [1st ed.] New York, E. P. Dutton, 1971. 223 p. 22 cm. Incorporates substantial portions of the author's Why can't they be like us? published in 1969 by the Institute of Human Relations Press of the American Jewish Committee. *1. Minorities — United States. 2. Ethnic attitudes. I. T.*
E184.A1G83 1971   301.45   72-148473   ISBN:0525233709

Handlin, Oscar, 1915- ed. III. 5115
Immigration as a factor in American history. Englewood Cliffs, N.J., Prentice-Hall, 1959. 206 p. 22 cm. *1. United States — Foreign population. 2. United States — Emigration and immigration. I. T.*
E184.A1H23   325.73   59-9516

Handlin, Oscar, 1915- III. 5116
Race and nationality in American life. [1st ed.] Boston, Little, Brown [1957] 300 p. 21 cm. *1. U.S. — Race question. 2. Minorities — U.S. I. T.*
E184.A1H25   325.73 (301.451)   57-5827

Handlin, Oscar, 1915- III. 5117
The uprooted; the epic story of the great migrations that made the American people. [1st ed.] Boston, Little, Brown, 1951. 310 p. 22 cm. "An Atlantic Monthly Press book." *1. U.S. — Foreign populations. 2. Acculturation. I. T.*
E184.A1H27   325.73   51-13013

Higham, John. III. 5118
Strangers in the land; patterns of American nativism, 1860-1925. Corrected and with a new pref. New York, Atheneum, 1963. 431 p. illus. 19 cm. (Atheneum paperbacks, 32) *1. United States — Foreign population. 2. Prejudices and antipathies. 3. United States — Emigration and immigration. 4. Nativism. I. T.*
E184.A1H5 1963   301.45   63-3476

McWilliams, Carey, 1905- III. 5119
Brothers under the skin. Rev. ed. Boston, Little, Brown, 1951. 364 p. 21 cm. *1. U.S. — Race question. 2. Race problems. 3. Minorities. I. T.*
E184.A1M19 1951   325.73   51-1031

Roche, John Pearson, 1923- III. 5120
The quest for the dream; the development of civil rights and human relations in modern America. New York, Macmillan [1963] xii, 308 p. 23 cm. *1. Minorities — U.S. 2. Civil rights — U.S. 3. U.S. — Social conditions. I. T.*
E184.A1R6   323.40973   63-15697

Rose, Arnold Marshall, 1918- ed. III. 5121
Race prejudice and discrimination: readings in intergroup relations in the United States. [1st ed.] New York, Knopf, 1951. xi, 605 p. 22 cm. *1. U.S. — Race question. 2. Minorities — U.S. I. T.*
E184.A1R7   325.73   51-11305

Warner, William Lloyd, 1898- III. 5122
The social systems of American ethnic groups, by W. Lloyd Warner and Leo Srole. New Haven, Yale University Press; London, H. Milford, Oxford University Press, 1945. xii, 318 p. tables, diagrs. 25 cm. (Yankee City series, vol.III) "Part of the material in this volume was written as a doctor's thesis by Dr. Leo Srole ... University of Chicago, 1940." — p. viii. "Published on the Richard Teller Crane, jr., memorial fund." *1. Minorities — U.S. 2. Acculturation. 3. U.S. — Foreign population. I. Srole, Leo, 1908- joint author. II. T.*
E184.A1W25   325.73   A45-3302

E184 ETHNIC GROUPS, A – Z
A – H

Capek, Thomas, 1861-1950. III. 5123
The Čechs (Bohemians) in America; a study of their national, cultural, political, social, economic, and religious life. New York, AMS Press [1969] xviii, 293 p. illus., maps, ports. 23 cm. Reprint of the 1920 ed. *1. Czechs in the Unites States. I. T.*
E184.B67C29 1969b   301.453/437/073   79-90095

Berthoff, Rowland Tappan, 1921- III. 5124
British immigrants in industrial America, 1790-1950. New York, Russell & Russell [1968, c1953] ix, 296 p. illus., maps. 22 cm. *1. British in the United States. 2. United States — Emigration and immigration. 3. Great Britain — Emigration and immigration. I. T.*
E184.B7B4 1968   325.2/42/0973   68-10901

O'Brien, David J. III. 5125
American Catholics and social reform; the New Deal years [by] David J. O'Brien. New York, Oxford University Press, 1968. xi, 287 p. 22 cm. *1. Catholics in the United States. 2. Church and social problems — Catholic Church. 3. United States — History — 1933-1945. I. T.*
E184.C3O2   301.45/282   68-8410

Barth, Gunther Paul. III. 5126
Bitter strength; a history of the Chinese in the United States. 1850-1870 [by] Gunther Barth. Cambridge, Harvard University Press, 1964. xi, 305 p. 22 cm. (A Publication of the Center for the Study of the History of Liberty in America, Harvard University) *1. Chinese in the U.S. I. T.* (S:Harvard University Center for the Study of the History of Liberty in America. Publication)
E184.C5B23   301.451   64-21785

Kung, Shien-woo, 1905- III. 5127
Chinese in American life: some aspects of their history, status, problems, and contributions by S. W. Kung. Seattle, University of Washington Press, 1962. xv, 352 p. tables. 24 cm. *1. Chinese in the U.S. I. T.*
E184.C5K8   325.2510973   62-9273

Wabeke, Bertus Harry, 1914- III. 5128
Dutch emigration to North America, 1624-1860, a short history by Bertus Harry Wabeke. New York city, The Netherlands Information Bureau, 1944. 160 p. illus., ports., maps (1 fold.) 24 cm. (Booklets of the Netherlands information bureau. No. 10) *1. Dutch in the U.S. 2. Netherlands — Emigration and immigration. 3. U.S. — Emigration and immigration.*
E184.D9W3   325.24920973   44-6534

Faust, Albert Bernhardt, 1870-1951. III. 5129
The German element in the United States. New York, Arno Press, 1969 [c1927] 2 v. illus., maps, ports. 23 cm. (The American immigration collection) *1. Germans in the United States. I. T.*
E184.G3F3 1969   973/.0974/3   69-18773

Saloutos, Theodore. III. 5130
The Greeks in the United States. Cambridge, Harvard University Press, 1964. xiv, 445 p. illus., ports. 25 cm. *1. Greeks in the U.S.*
E184.G7S29   64-13428

Lengyel, Emil, 1895- III. 5131
Americans from Hungary. [1st ed.] Philadelphia, J. B. Lippincott Co. [1948] 319 p. 22 cm. (The Peoples of America series) *1. Hungarians in the U.S. I. T.* (S)
E184.H95L4   325.243910973   48-5802

E184.I Irish. Italians

Brown, Thomas N., 1920- III. 5132
Irish-American nationalism, 1870-1890 [by] Thomas N. Brown. [1st ed.]

Philadelphia, Lippincott [1966] xvii, 206 p. 21 cm. (Critical periods of history) *1. Irish in the U.S. 2. Nationalism — Ireland. I. T.*
E184.I6B86   325.24150973   66-14695

Greeley, Andrew M., 1928-   **III. 5133**
That most distressful nation: the taming of the American Irish, by Andrew M. Greeley. Foreword by Daniel P. Moynihan. Chicago, Quadrangle Books, 1972. xxviii, 281 p. 22 cm. *1. Irish in the United States. I. T.*
E184.I6G73   301.45/19/162073   74-182501   ISBN:8812902567

Levine, Edward M., 1924-   **III. 5134**
The Irish and Irish politicians; a study of cultural and social alienation, by Edward M. Levine. Notre Dame [Ind.] University of Notre Dame Press [1966] ix, 241 p. 23 cm. *1. Irish in the U.S. — History. 2. Politics, Practical — Case studies. 3. Chicago — Politics and government. 4. Alienation (Social psychology) I. T.*
E184.I6L4   301.451916073   66-24921

Potter, George W.   **III. 5135**
To the golden door; the story of the Irish in Ireland and America. [1st ed.] Boston, Little, Brown [1960] 631 p. illus. 22 cm. *1. Irish in the U.S. 2. Ireland — Famine. 3. Ireland — Economic conditions. 4. Ireland — Emigration and immigration. I. T.*
E184.I6P6   325.24150973   60-5870

Shannon, William Vincent.   **III. 5136**
The American Irish, by William V. Shannon. [Rev. ed.] New York, Macmillan [1966] xiii, 484 p. illus., ports. 25 cm. *1. Irish in the U.S. — History. I. T.*
E184.I6S5 1966   301.4519162073   66-2047

Lopreato, Joseph.   **III. 5137**
Italian Americans. [1st ed.] New York, Random House [1970] xiv, 204 p. 21 cm. (Ethnic groups in comparative perspective) *1. Italians in the United States. I. T.*
E184.I8L78   301.453/45/073   71-105655

E184.J   Japanese. Jews

Caudill, William A.   **III. 5138**
Japanese-American personality and acculturation. Provincetown, Mass., Journal Press, 1952. 102 p. illus. 25 cm. (Genetic psychology monographs, v.45, 1st half) Abridgment of thesis — University of Chicago. *1. Japanese in the U.S. I. T. (S)*
E184.J3Cx (LB1101.G4 vol. 45, no. 1)   325.2520973   (301.451)   52-10648

Hosokawa, Bill.   **III. 5139**
Nisei: the quiet Americans. New York, W. Morrow, 1969. xvii, 522 p. illus., ports. 25 cm. *1. Japanese in the United States — History. I. T.*
E184.J3H6   301.453/52/073   73-88356

American Jewish year book.   **III. 5140**
v. [1]- ; 1899/1900- . New York, American Jewish Committee. v. illus. 19-22 cm. Issues for 1899/1900-1948/1949 called also 5660-5709. Title varies slightly. Edited 1899/1900-1905/06 by C. Adler (with H. Szold, 1904/05-1905/06) 1906/07-1907/08 by H. Szold; 1908/09- by the American Jewish Committee. Imprint varies: 1899/1900-1948/49, Philadelphia, Jewish Publication Society of America. Issues for 1900/01- include Report of the 12th- year of the Jewish Publication Society of America, 1899/1900- (Issued also separately in some years); issues for 1908/09- include Report of the American Jewish Committee for 1906/08- (issued also separately in some years) Indexes: Vols. 1-35, 1899/1900-1933/34, in v.36. Vols. 1-40, 1899/1900-1938/39, in v.40. Vols. 1-44, 1899/1900-1942/43, in v.45. Vols. 1-45, 1899/1900-1943/44, in v.46. Vols. 1-46, 1899/1900-1944/45, in v.47. Vols. 1-50, 1899/1900-1948/49, in v.50. *1. Jews in the United States — Yearbooks. I. Szold, Henrietta, 1860-1945, ed. II. Adler, Cyrus, 1863-1940, ed. III. American Jewish Committee.*
E184.J5A6   99-4040

Doroshkin, Milton, 1914-   **III. 5141**
Yiddish in America; social and cultural foundations. Rutherford, Fairleigh Dickinson University Press [1970, c1969] 281 p. illus., facsims., ports. 22 cm. *1. Jews in the United States — Political and social conditions. 2. Yiddish language in the United States. I. T.*
E184.J5D6 1970   301.451/924/073   72-78612   ISBN:838674534

Fuchs, Lawrence H.   **III. 5142**
The political behavior of American Jews. Glencoe, Ill., Free Press [1956] 220 p. 22 cm. *1. Jews in the U.S. 2. U.S. — Politics and government. 3. Political parties — U.S. I. T.*
E184.J5F8   296 (301.452)   56-6875

Handlin, Oscar, 1915-   **III. 5143**
Adventure in freedom; three hundred years of Jewish life in America. Port Washington, N.Y., Kennikat Press [1971, c1954] xii, 282 p. illus., ports. 23 cm. (Kennikat Press scholarly reprints. Series in American history and culture in the twentieth century) *1. Jews in the United States — History. I. T.*
E184.J5H29 1971   917.3/06/924   70-137970   ISBN:0804614288

Karp, Abraham J., comp.   **III. 5144**
The Jewish experience in America; selected studies from the publications of the American Jewish Historical Society. Edited with an introd. by Abraham J. Karp. Waltham, Mass., American Jewish Historical Society [1969] 5 v. illus., facsims., ports. 24 cm. *1. Jews in the United States — History — Collections. I. American Jewish Historical Society. II. T.*
E184.J5K17   973/.09/74924   72-77150

Rose, Peter Isaac, 1933- comp.   **III. 5145**
The ghetto and beyond; essays on Jewish life in America. Peter I. Rose, editor. New York, Random House [1969] viii, 504 p. 22 cm. *1. Jews in the United States — Collections. 2. Judaism — U.S. — Collections. 1. T.*
E184.J5R615   301.451/924/073   69-10778

Sklare, Marshall, 1921-   **III. 5146**
Jewish identity on the suburban frontier; a study of group survival in the open society [by] Marshall Sklare and Joseph Greenblum. New York, Basic Books [1967] xv, 362 p. 25 cm. (The Lakeville studies, v.1) *1. Jews in the U.S. 2. Suburban life. I. Greenblum, Joseph, joint author. II. T. (S)*
E184.J5S548   301.45/29/6073   67-17394

Sklare, Marshall, 1921- ed.   **III. 5147**
The Jews; social patterns of an American group. Glencoe, Ill., Free Press [1958] 669 p. 24 cm. *1. Jews in the U.S.*
E184.J5S55   296   57-9318

E184.M   Mexicans

Burma, John H., comp.   **III. 5148**
Mexican-Americans in the United States: a reader, by John H. Burma. [Cambridge, Mass.] Schenkman Pub. Co.; distributed by Canfield Press [1970] xviii, 487 p. 23 cm. *1. Mexicans in the United States. I. T.*
E184.M5B78   917.3/09/746   79-79678

Grebler, Leo.   **III. 5149**
The Mexican-American people, the Nation's second largest minority [by] Leo Grebler, Joan W. Moore [and] Ralph C. Guzman. With Jeffrey L. Berlant [and others] New York, Free Press [1970] xvii, 777 p., illus., forms, maps. 26 cm. *1. Mexicans in the United States. I. Moore, Joan W., joint author. II. Guzman, Ralph C., joint author. III. Berlant, Jeffrey L. IV. T.*
E184.M5G68   301.453/72/073   73-81931

Meier, Matt S.   **III. 5150**
The Chicanos; a history of Mexican Americans [by] Matt S. Meier and Feliciano Rivera. New York, Hill and Wang [1972] xviii, 302 p. maps. 21 cm. (American century series) *1. Mexican Americans — History. I. Rivera, Feliciano, joint author. II. T.*
E184.M5M45   301.45/1/6872073   72-187151
  ISBN:0809034166 0809013657 (pbk)

Steiner, Stanley.   **III. 5151**
La raza: the Mexican Americans [by] Stan Steiner. [1st ed.] New York, Harper [1970] xii, 418 p. plates, ports. 22 cm. *1. Mexicans in the United States. I. T.*
E184.M5S7   301.451/67/9073   77-83622

E184.N – .Z

Blegen, Theodore Christian, 1891-   **III. 5152**
Norwegian migration to America, 1825-1860 [by] Theodore C. Blegen. New York, Arno Press, 1969. xi, 413 p. illus., facsims., maps 24 cm. (The American immigration collection) A reprint of the 1931 ed. *1. Norwegians in the United States. 2. Norway — Emigration and immigration. I. T.*
E184.S2B62   301.453/481/073   69-18759

Benson, Adolph Burnett, 1881- ed.   **III. 5153**
Swedes in America, 1638-1938, edited by Adolph B. Benson and Naboth Hedin. Published for the Swedish American Tercentennial Association. New Haven, Yale University Press; London, H. Milford, Oxford University Press, 1938. xiv, 614 p. front., plates, ports. 25 cm. *1. Swedes in the U.S. 2. Swedes in the U.S. — Biography. I. Hedin, Naboth, 1884- joint ed. II. Swedish American Tercentenary Association. III. T.*
E184.S23B33   325.24850973   38-27493

Graham, Ian Charles Cargill, 1919-   **III. 5154**
Colonists from Scotland: emigration to North America, 1707-1783. Port Washington, N.Y., Kennikat Press [1972, c1956] x, 213 p. map. 23 cm. *1. Scotland — Emigration and immigration. 2. Scotch in the United States. I. T.*
E184.S3G7 1972   325.2/41/073   70-153216   ISBN:0804615268

Leyburn, James Graham. III. 5155
The Scotch-Irish: a social history. Chapel Hill, University of North Carolina Press [1962] xix, 377 p. maps. 24 cm. *1. Scotch-Irish in the U.S. 2. Scotland — Social conditions. 3. Scotch in Ireland. I. T.*
E184.S4L5   301.45   62-16063

Govorchin, Gerald Gilbert. III. 5156
Americans from Yugoslavia. Gainesville, University of Florida Press, 1961. xii, 352 p. illus., ports., map, tables. 24 cm. *1. Yugoslavs in the U.S. I. T.*
E184.Y7G6   325.24970973   61-11312

E185   Negroes

Aptheker, Herbert, 1915- ed. III. 5157
A documentary history of the Negro people in the United States. Pref. by W. E. B. Du Bois. [1st ed.] New York, Citadel Press [1951] xvi, 942 p. 22 cm. *1. Negroes — History — Sources. I. T.*
E185.A58   325.260973   51-14828

Broderick, Francis L., ed. III. 5158
Negro protest thought in the twentieth century. Edited by Francis L. Broderick and August Meier. Indianapolis, Bobbs-Merrill Co. [1966, c1965] xliii, 444 p. 21 cm. (The American heritage series) *1. Negroes — Civil rights — History — Sources. I. Meier, August, 1923- joint ed. II. T.*
E185.B87   301.45196073   65-23012

Cruse, Harold. III. 5159
Rebellion or revolution? New York, Morrow, 1968. 272 p. 22 cm. *1. Negroes — Addresses, essays, lectures. I. T.*
E185.C93   917.3/03/920917496   68-29609

Davis, John Preston, 1905- , ed. III. 5160
The American Negro reference book. Englewood Cliffs, N. J., Prentice-Hall [1966] xxii, 969 p. illus. 25 cm. *1. Negroes — History — Addresses, essays, lectures. I. T.*
E185.D25   301.45196073   65-12919

Drimmer, Melvin, comp. III. 5161
Black history; a reappraisal, edited with commentary by Melvin Drimmer. [1st ed.] Garden City, N.Y., Doubleday, 1968. xx, 553 p. 22 cm. Essays which present the Negro's role in American history, each prefaced by an analysis of the historical events surrounding the period it covers. *1. Negroes — History — Addresses, essays, lectures. I. T.*
E185.D7   909/.09/7496   67-19105

Ebony. III. 5162
The Negro handbook, compiled by the editors of Ebony. Chicago, Johnson Pub. Co., 1966. 535 p. 24 cm. *1. Negroes — Handbooks, manuals, etc. I. T.*
E185.E2   66-27472

Franklin, John Hope, 1915- III. 5163
From slavery to freedom; a history of Negro Americans. 3d ed. [rev. and enl.] New York, Knopf, 1967. xxii, 686, xliii p. illus., ports. 25 cm. *1. Negroes — History. 2. Slavery in the U.S. — History. I. T.*
E185.F825 1967   325.2/6/097   67-13102

Frazier, Edward Franklin, 1894- III. 5164
The Negro in the United States. Rev. ed. New York, Macmillan [1957] xxxiii, 796 p. maps, diagrs., tables. 22 cm. *1. Negroes. I. T.*
E185.F833 1957   325.260973   57-5224

Fredrickson, George M., 1934- III. 5165
The Black image in the white mind; the debate on Afro-American character and destiny, 1817-1914 [by] George M. Fredrickson. [1st ed.] New York, Harper & Row [1971] xiii, 343 p. 22 cm. *1. United States — Race question. 2. Negroes — History. 3. Prejudices and antipathies — United States. I. T.*
E185.F836   301.451/96/073   71-138721   ISBN:006011343X

Jordan, Winthrop D. III. 5166
White over black: American attitudes toward the Negro, 1550-1812 [by] Winthrop D. Jordan. Chapel Hill, Published for the Institute of Early American History and Culture at Williamsburg, Va., by the University of North Carolina Press [1968] xx, 651 p. map. 24 cm. *1. Negroes — History — To 1863. 2. Attitude (Psychology) I. Institute of Early American History and Culture, Williamsburg, Va. II. T.*
E185.J69   973/.0974/96   68-13295

Meier, August, 1923- III. 5167
From plantation to ghetto, by August Meier and Elliott Rudwick. Rev. ed. New York, Hill and Wang [1970] x, 340 p. map. 22 cm. (American century series) *1. Negroes — History. I. Rudwick, Elliott M., joint author. II. T.*
E185.M4 1970   973/.04/96073   71-106967   ISBN:0809047918

Meier, August, 1923- comp. III. 5168
The making of black America; essays in Negro life & history, edited by August Meier & Elliott Rudwick. [1st ed.] New York, Atheneum, 1969. xvi, 377, 507 p. 24 cm. (Studies in American Negro life) *1. Negroes — History. — Addresses, essays, lectures. I. Rudwick, Elliott M., joint comp. II. T.*
E185.M43   301.451/96/073   67-25486

Murray, Albert. III. 5169
The omni-Americans; new perspectives on Black experience and American culture. New York, Outerbridge & Dienstfrey; distributed by E. P. Dutton [1970] 227 p. 23 cm. *1. Negroes. I. T.*
E185.M9 1970   301.451/96/073   77-101313   ISBN:876900015

Ploski, Harry A.   , comp. III. 5170
The Negro almanac, compiled and edited by Harry A. Ploski and Roscoe C. Brown, Jr. [1st ed.] New York, Bellwether Pub. Co. [1967] xi, 1012p. illus. maps. ports. 25 cm. *1. Negroes. I. Brown, Roscoe Conkling, 1922-   , joint comp. II. T.*
E185.P55   66-29721

Redding, Jay Saunders, 1906- III. 5171
They came in chains; Americans from Africa. [1st ed.] Philadelphia, Lippincott [1950] 320 p. 22 cm. (The Peoples of America series) *1. Negroes — History. I. T. (S)*
E185.R4   325.260973   50-8476

Woodson, Carter Godwin, 1875-1950. III. 5172
The mind of the Negro as reflected in letters written during the crisis, 1800-1860. New York, Russell & Russell [1969] xxxii, 672 p. 25 cm. Reprint of the 1926 ed. *1. Negroes — History — To 1863. 2. Negroes — Moral and social conditions. 3. Slavery in the United States — Emancipation. I. T.*
E185.W8877 1969   917.35   69-14222

Woodson, Carter Godwin, 1875-1950. III. 5173
The Negro in our history, by Carter G. Woodson and Charles H. Wesley. 10th ed., further rev. and enl. Washington, Associated Publishers [1962] 833 p. illus. 22 cm. *1. Negroes — History. 2. Slavery in the U.S. I. Wesley, Charles Harris, 1891- joint author. II. T.*
E185.W89 1962   326.973   62-3979

E185.5 – 185.8   SOCIAL AND ECONOMIC CONDITIONS

Baruch, Ruth-Marion. III. 5174
The vanguard; a photographic essay on the Black Panthers, by Ruth-Marion Baruch and Pirkle Jones. With an introd. by William Worthy. Boston, Beacon Press [1970] 127 p. illus., ports. 26 cm. *1. Black Panther Party. I. Jones, Pirkle, joint author. II. T.*
E185.5.B3 1970   323.2   71-101317   ISBN:807005525

Du Bois, William Edward Burghardt 1868-1963. III. 5175
Darkwater; voices from within the veil. New York, Schocken Books [1969] viii, 276 p. 21 cm. Reprint of the 1920 ed. *1. Negroes. I. T.*
E185.5.D8 1969   910.03/174/96   69-19627

Du Bois, William Edward Burghardt, 1868-1963. III. 5176
The souls of black folk. With introductions by Nathan Hare and Alvin F. Poussaint. New York, New American Library [1969] 280 p. music. 18 cm. (A Signet classics) *1. Negroes. I. T.*
E185.5.D817 1969   301.451/96/073   71-82444

Du Bois, William Edward Burghardt, 1868-1963. III. 5177
W. E. B. Du Bois speaks; speeches and addresses. Edited by Philip S. Foner. New York, Pathfinder Press, 1970. 2 v. 23 cm. "A Merit book." *1. Negroes — Collected works. I. T.*
E185.5.D84   301.451/96/073   78-108719

Kellogg, Charles Flint. III. 5178
NAACP, a history of the National Association for the Advancement of Colored People. Baltimore, Johns Hopkins Press [1967-   v. illus., ports. 24 cm. *1. National Association for the Advancement of Colored People. I. T.*
E185.5.N276K4   301.45196073   66-28507

Ross, Barbara Joyce. III. 5179
J. E. Spingarn and the rise of the NAACP, 1911-1939 [by] B. Joyce Ross. [1st ed.] New York, Atheneum, 1972. xii, 305 p. 21 cm. (Atheneum [paperbacks] Studies in American Negro life, NL 32) Originally presented as the author's thesis, American University. *1. National Association for the Advancement of Colored People — History. 2. Spingarn, Joel Elias, 1875-1939. I. T.*
E185.5.N276R67 1972   301.45/19/6073062 (B)   78-139326

Parris, Guichard. III. 5180
Blacks in the city; a history of the National Urban League, by Guichard Parris and Lester Brooks. [1st ed.] Boston, Little, Brown [1971] xi, 534 p.

E185.61   **United States**   III. 5205

ports. 24 cm. *1. National Urban League. I. Brooks, Lester, joint author. II. T.*
E185.5.N33P3   301.451/96073/01732   76-161866

Bailey, Harry A., ed.   III. 5181
Negro politics in America, edited by Harry A. Bailey, Jr. Columbus, Ohio, C. E. Merrill Books [1967] vii, 455 p. illus., maps. 23 cm. *1. Negroes — Politics and suffrage — Addresses, essays, lectures. I. T.*
E185.6.B15   320.9/73   67-14375

Bontemps, Arna Wendell, 1902-   III. 5182
100 years of Negro freedom. New York, Dodd, Mead, 1961. 276 p. illus. 22 cm. *1. Negroes. 2. Negroes — Biography. I. T.*
E185.6.B74   325.2670973   61-11716

Dædalus.   III. 5183
The Negro American. Edited and with introductions by Talcott Parsons and Kenneth B. Clark, and with a foreword by Lyndon B. Johnson. Illustrated with a 32 page portfolio of photos. by Bruce Davidson, selected and introduced by Arthur D. Trottenberg. Boston, Houghton, Mifflin, 1966. xxix, 781 p. illus. 24 cm. (The Daedalus library [v. 7]) Most of the essays, some in slightly different form, appeared originally in the Fall 1965 and Winter 1966 issues of Daedalus. *1. Negroes — Addresses, essays, lectures. 2. Negroes — Civil rights — Addresses, essays, lectures. I. Parsons, Talcott, 1902- ed. II. Clark, Kenneth Bancroft, 1914- ed. III. T. (S)*
E185.6.D24   301.45196073   66-17174

Frazier, Edward Franklin, 1894-1962.   III. 5184
Negro youth at the crossways, their personality development in the Middle States. With an introd. by St. Clair Drake. Prepared for the American Youth Commission, American Council on Education. New York, Schocken Books [1967] xxxv, 299 p. maps. 21 cm. (Schocken paperbacks) *1. Negroes — Psychology. 2. Youth — Washington, D.C. 3. Youth — Louisville, Ky. 4. Personality. I. American Council on Education. American Youth Commission. II. T.*
E185.6.F74 1967   155.2/34/0917496   67-26987

Katz, William Loren.   III. 5185
Eyewitness; the Negro in American history. Rev. ed. New York, Pitman [1971] xx, 603 p. illus., ports. 26 cm. *1. Negroes — History — Sources. I. T.*
E185.6.K3 1971   917.3/06/96073   71-24129

Lewis, Hylan.   III. 5186
Blackways of Kent. Chapel Hill, University of North Carolina Press, 1955. xxiv, 337 p. diagrs., tables. 21 cm. (Field studies in the modern culture of the South) Based on thesis, University of Chicago. *1. Negroes — Southern States. I. T. (S)*
E185.6.L4   325.260975 (301.451)   55-62673

Meier, August, 1923-   III. 5187
Negro thought in America, 1880-1915; racial ideologies in the age of Booker T. Washington. Ann Arbor, University of Michigan Press [1963] x, 336 p. 24 cm. *1. Negroes — History — 1877-1964. 2. Washington, Booker Taliaferro, 1859?-1915. I. T.*
E185.6.M5   301.451   63-14008

Sternsher, Bernard, 1925- comp.   III. 5188
The Negro in depression and war; prelude to revolution, 1930-1945, edited with commentary by Bernard Sternsher. Chicago, Quadrangle Books [c1969] viii, 338 p. 22 cm. *1. Negroes — History — 1877-1964 — Addresses, essays, lectures. I. T.*
E185.6.S75 1969   301.451/96/073   76-84111

Washington, Booker Taliaferro, 1859?-1915.   III. 5189
The future of the American Negro. New York, Haskell House, 1968. x, 244 p. port. 23 cm. Reprint of the 1899 ed. *1. Negroes. I. T.*
E185.6.W313 1968   301.451/96/073   68-25002

Wolters, Raymond, 1938-   III. 5190
Negroes and the great depression; the problem of economic recovery. Westport, Conn., Greenwood Pub. Corp. [1970] xvii, 398 p. 22 cm. (Contributions in American history, no. 6) A revision of the author's thesis, University of California, Berkeley. *1. Negroes — History — 1877-1964. 2. Negroes — Economic conditions. I. T.*
E185.6.W85 1970   330.9/73   78-95510   ISBN:837123410

E185.61   Negro-White Relations
A – G

Baker, Ray Stannard, 1860-1946.   III. 5191
Following the color line; American Negro citizenship in the progressive era. Introd. and notes to the Torchbook ed. by Dewey W. Grantham, Jr. New York, Harper & Row [1964] xviii, 311, 8 p. illus., ports. 21 cm. (American perspectives. Harper torchbooks. The University library.) "TB 3053." Chapters 1-8, 10-14, with slight revisions, originally appeared in the American magazine, Apr. 1907-Sept. 1908. *1. Negroes. 2. United States — Race question. I. T.*
E185.61.B16 1964   301.451   64-2962

Baldwin, James, 1924-   III. 5192
The fire next time. New York, Dial Press, 1963. 120 p. 21 cm. *1. Negroes. 2. U.S. — Race question. 3. Mohammedans in the U.S. I. T.*
E185.61.B195   301.451   63-11713

Baldwin, James, 1924-   III. 5193
Nobody knows my name; more notes of a native son. New York, Dial Press, 1961. 241 p. 22 cm. *1. Negroes. 2. U.S. — Race question. I. T.*
E185.61.B197   301.451   61-11596

Baldwin, James, 1924-   III. 5194
Notes of a native son. New York, Dial Press, 1963 [c1955] 158 p. 21 cm. Essays. *1. Negroes. 2. United States — Race question. I. T.*
E185.61.B2 1963   64-115

Brink, William J.   III. 5195
The Negro revolution in America; what Negroes want, why and how they are fighting, whom they support, what whites think of them and their demands [by] William Brink [and] Louis Harris. New York, Simon and Schuster, 1964 [c1963] 249 p. tables. 21 cm. "Based on the nationwide survey by Newsweek magazine." *1. Negroes — History — 1877-1964. 2. United States — Race question. I. Harris, Louis, 1921- joint author. II. T.*
E185.61.B795   301.451   64-13340

Brisbane, Robert H.   III. 5196
The black vanguard; origins of the Negro social revolution, 1900-1960 [by] Robert H. Brisbane. Valley Forge [Pa.] Judson Press [1969, c1970] 285 p. 23 cm. *1. Negroes — History — 1877-1964. 2. Negroes — Civil rights — History. I. T.*
E185.61.B796   301.451/96/073   69-18900   ISBN:817004416

Burns, William Haywood.   III. 5197
The voices of Negro protest in America. With a foreword by John Hope Franklin. London, New York, Oxford University Press, 1963. 88 p. 19 cm. "Issued under the auspices of the Institute of Race Relations, London." *1. Negroes — Civil rights. 2. U.S. — Race question. I. T.*
E185.61.B96   323.40973   63-6378

Clark, Kenneth Bancroft, 1914-   III. 5198
The Negro protest: James Baldwin, Malcolm X, Martin Luther King talk with Kenneth B. Clark. Boston, Beacon Press [1963] 56 p. 21 cm. *1. Negroes. 2. U.S. — Race question. I. T.*
E185.61.C62   323.40973   63-21975

Coles, Robert.   III. 5199
Children of crisis; a study of courage and fear. [1st ed.] Boston, Little, Brown [1967] xiv, 401 p. illus. 22 cm. "An Atlantic monthly press book." *1. Negroes — Segregation. 2. Negro children. 3. Fear (Child psychology) I. T.*
E185.61.C66   301.451/96/073   67-14450

Draper, Theodore, 1912-   III. 5200
The rediscovery of Black nationalism. New York, Viking Press [1970] x, 211 p. 21 cm. *1. Negroes — Politics and suffrage. 2. United States — Race question. I. T.*
E185.61.D77 1970   323.1/19/6073   70-104163   ISBN:0670591149

Essien-Udom, Essien Udosen.   III. 5201
Black nationalism; a search for an identity in America. [Chicago] University of Chicago Press [1962] xiii, 367 p. illus., ports. 25 cm. *1. Mohammedans in the United States. 2. Negroes. 3. United States — Race question. I. T.*
E185.61.E75   297.0973   62-12632

Frazier, Edward Franklin, 1894-   III. 5202
Black bourgeoisie. Glencoe, Ill., Free Press [1957] 264 p. 22 cm. *1. Negroes. 2. U.S. — Race question. 3. Middle classes — U.S. I. T.*
E185.61.F833   325.260973   56-11964

Friedman, Leon, comp.   III. 5203
The civil rights reader; basic documents of the civil rights movement. Foreword by Martin Duberman. New York, Walker [1967] xxi, 348 p. 22 cm. *1. Civil rights — U.S. — History — Sources. 2. Negroes — Civil rights. I. T.*
E185.61.F857   323.4/0973   67-13235

E185.61   H – N

Handlin, Oscar, 1915-   III. 5204
Fire-bell in the night; the crisis in civil rights. [1st ed.] Boston, Little, Brown [1964] 110 p. 20 cm. *1. Negroes — Civil rights. I. T.*
E185.61.H23   323.40973   64-17728

Hernton, Calvin C.   III. 5205
White papers for white Americans [by] Calvin C. Hernton. [1st ed.] Garden

City, N.Y., Doubleday, 1966. 155 p. 22 cm. *1. U.S. — Race question. 2. Negroes — Psychology. I. T.*
E185.61.H53   301.45196073   66-12244

Institutional racism in America.　　　　　　　　　　　　**III. 5206**
Contributors: Owen Blank [and others] Edited by Louis L. Knowles and Kenneth Prewitt. With an appendix by Harold Baron. Englewood Cliffs, N.J., Prentice-Hall [1970, c1969] xii, 180 p. 22 cm. (A Spectrum book) Based on working papers prepared for a joint program sponsored by the Stanford chapter of the University Christian Movement and the Mid-Peninsula Christian Ministry of East Palo Alto, Calif. *1. Negroes — Civil rights. 2. Race discrimination — U.S. I. Blank, Owen. II. Knowles, Louis L., ed. III. Prewitt, Kenneth, ed.*
E185.61.I6   301.451/96/073   78-90975   ISBN:134677463

King, Martin Luther.　　　　　　　　　　　　　　　　**III. 5207**
Why we can't wait. [1st ed.] New York, Harper & Row [1964] xii, 178 p. illus., ports. 22 cm. *1. Negroes — Civil rights. I. T.*
E185.61.K54   301.451/96/073   64-19514

Ladd, Everett Carll.　　　　　　　　　　　　　　　　**III. 5208**
Negro political leadership in the South. Ithaca, N.Y., Cornell University Press [1966] ix, 348 p. fold. map. 23 cm. *1. Negroes — Politics and suffrage — Case studies. 2. Negroes — Winston-Salem, N.C. 3. Negroes — Greenville, S.C. 4. Community leadership — Case studies. I. T.*
E185.61.L22   320.975   66-11048

Lewis, Anthony, 1927-　　　　　　　　　　　　　　**III. 5209**
Portrait of a decade; the second American revolution [by] Anthony Lewis and the New York times. New York, Random House [1964] 322 p. illus. 25 cm. *1. Negroes — Civil rights. I. New York times. II. The second American revolution. III. T.*
E185.61.L52 1964   323.40973   64-14832

Lincoln, Charles Eric.　　　　　　　　　　　　　　　**III. 5210**
The Black Muslims in America. Foreword by Gordon Allport. Boston, Beacon Press [1961] 276 p. 21 cm. *1. Black Muslims.*
E185.61.L56   363.973   61-5881

Little, Malcolm, 1925-1965.　　　　　　　　　　　　**III. 5211**
By any means necessary; speeches, interviews, and a letter, by Malcolm X. Edited by George Breitman. New York, Pathfinder Press, 1970. viii, 184 p. ports. 22 cm. "A Merit book." *1. Negroes — Civil rights — Addresses, essays, lectures. 2. U.S. — Race question — Addresses, essays, lectures. I. Breitman, George, ed. II. T.*
E185.61.L577   74-108718

Logan, Rayford Whittingham, 1897-　　　　　　　　**III. 5212**
The betrayal of the Negro, from Rutherford B. Hayes to Woodrow Wilson, by Rayford W. Logan. New enl. ed. New York, Collier Books [1965] 447 p. 19 cm. "Originally published as The Negro in American life and thought: the nadir, 1877-1901." *1. Negroes — Civil rights. 2. Negroes — History — 1872-1964. I. T.*
E185.61.L64 1965   323.4   65-23835

Matthews, Donald R.　　　　　　　　　　　　　　　**III. 5213**
Negroes and the new southern politics [by] Donald R. Matthews [and] James W. Prothro. New York, Harcourt, Brace & World [1966] xvi, 551 p. illus. 24 cm. *1. Negroes — Politics and suffrage. 2. Suffrage — Southern States. 3. Southern States — Politics and government — 1865- 4. Negro students. I. Prothro, James Warren, 1922- joint author. II. T.*
E185.61.M38   323.1196073   66-28289

Muse, Benjamin.　　　　　　　　　　　　　　　　　**III. 5214**
Ten years of prelude: the story of integration since the Supreme Court's 1954 decision. New York, Viking Press [1964] ix, 308 p. 22 cm. *1. Negroes — Segregation. 2. Segregation in education. I. T.*
E185.61.M989   301.451   64-13298

Newby, Idus A.　　　　　　　　　　　　　　　　　**III. 5215**
Challenge to the Court; social scientists and the defense of segregation, 1954-1966 [by] I. A. Newby. Rev. ed. with commentaries by A. James Gregor [and others] Baton Rouge, Louisiana State University Press [1969] xii, 381 p. 24 cm. *1. Negroes — Segregation. 2. U.S. — Race question. I. Gregor, A. James. II. T.*
E185.61.N46 1969   301.451/96/073   69-17623   ISBN:807106283

Newby, Idus A.　　　　　　　　　　　　　　　　　**III. 5216**
Jim Crow's defense; anti-Negro thought in America, 1900-1930 [by] I. A. Newby. Baton Rouge, Louisiana State University Press, 1965. xv, 230 p. 24 cm. *1. Race discrimination — U.S. 2. U.S. — Race question. 3. Negro race. I. T.*
E185.61.N475   301.45196073   65-20297

E185.61   P – Z

Proctor, Samuel D.　　　　　　　　　　　　　　　　**III. 5217**
The young Negro in America, 1960-1980, by Samuel D. Proctor. New York, Association Press [1966] 160 p. 21 cm. *1. Negroes — Civil rights. 2. Negroes — History. I. T.*
E185.61.P76   301.4516073   66-15750

Record, Wilson, 1916-　　　　　　　　　　　　　　**III. 5218**
The Negro and the Communist Party. Chapel Hill, University of North Carolina Press [1951] x, 340 p. 21 cm. *1. Negroes. 2. Communism — U.S. — 1917- I. T.*
E185.61.R29   325.260973   51-10538

Reimers, David M.　　　　　　　　　　　　　　　　**III. 5219**
White Protestantism and the Negro [by] David M. Reimers. New York, Oxford University Press, 1965. ix, 236 p. 21 cm. *1. Negroes — Segregation. 2. Church and race problems — United States. 3. Protestant churches — United States. I. T.*
E185.61.R36   261.83   65-22800

Silberman, Charles E., 1925-　　　　　　　　　　　　**III. 5220**
Crisis in black and white. New York, Random House [1964] xii, 370 p. 22 cm. *1. Negroes. 2. United States — Race question. I. T.*
E185.61.S57   301.451   64-14843

Smith, Lillian Eugenia, 1897-　　　　　　　　　　　**III. 5221**
Killers of the dream. Rev. and enl. New York, Norton [1961] 253 p. 22 cm. *1. Negroes — Southern States. 2. Southern States — Social conditions. I. T.*
E185.61.S64 1961   917.5   61-8781

Stalvey, Lois Mark.　　　　　　　　　　　　　　　**III. 5222**
The education of a WASP. New York, Morrow, 1970. x, 327 p. 22 cm. *1. United States — Race question. 2. Discrimination — United States. I. T.*
E185.61.S77   301.45/0973   79-107363

Tumin, Melvin Marvin, 1919-　　　　　　　　　　　**III. 5223**
Desegregation: resistance and readiness, by Melvin M. Tumin, with the assistance of Warren Eason [and others] Princeton, N.J., Princeton University Press, 1958. xvii, 270 p. tables. 23 cm. *1. Negroes — Segregation. 2. Public opinion — North Carolina — Guilford Co. I. T.*
E185.61T88   325.26 (301.451)   58-13938

Warren, Robert Penn, 1905-　　　　　　　　　　　**III. 5224**
Segregation, the inner conflict in the South. New York, Random House [1956] 66 p. 21 cm. *1. Negroes — Segregation. 2. Negroes — Southern States.*
E185.61.W2   325.260975 (301.451)   56-11268

Waskow, Arthur I.　　　　　　　　　　　　　　　　**III. 5225**
From race riot to sit-in, 1919 and the 1960s; a study in the connections between conflict and violence, by Arthur I. Waskow. [1st ed.] Garden City, N.Y., Doubleday, 1966. xviii, 380 p. 22 cm. *1. Negroes — History — 1877-1964. 2. Riots — United States. 3. Passive resistance to government. I. T.*
E185.61.W24   301.1530973   66-11737

Woodward, Comer Vann, 1908-　　　　　　　　　　**III. 5226**
American counterpoint; slavery and racism in the North-South dialogue, by C. Vann Woodward. [1st ed.] Boston, Little, Brown [1971] 301 p. 22 cm. *1. United States — Race question — Addresses, essays, lectures. 2. Southern States — Social life and customs — Addresses, essays, lectures. I. T.*
E185.61.W85   301.451/96/073   76-143715

Woodward, Comer Vann, 1908-　　　　　　　　　　**III. 5227**
The strange career of Jim Crow [by] C. Vann Woodward. 2d rev. ed. New York, Oxford University Press, 1966. xiii, 205 p. 22 cm. *1. Negroes — Segregation. I. T.*
E185.61.W86 1966   301.45196073   66-12544

Young, Whitney M.　　　　　　　　　　　　　　　**III. 5228**
To be equal [by] Whitney M. Young, Jr. [1st ed.] New York, McGraw-Hill [1964] 254 p. 22 cm. *1. Negroes — Civil rights. 2. Negroes — Moral and social conditions. I. T.*
E185.61.Y73   323.41   64-23179

Zinn, Howard, 1922-　　　　　　　　　　　　　　　**III. 5229**
SNCC; the new abolitionists. [2d ed.] Boston, Beacon Press [1965] 286 p. 21 cm. *1. Student Nonviolent Coordinating Committee. 2. Negroes — Civil rights. 3. Civil rights — Southern States. I. T.*
E185.61.Z49 1965   323.406273   66-789

E185.615   1964 –

Boesel, David, comp.　　　　　　　　　　　　　　**III. 5230**
Cities under siege: an anatomy of the Ghetto riots, 1964-1968. Edited by David Boesel & Peter H. Rossi. New York, Basic Books [1971] xi, 436 p. 24 cm. *1. Riots — United States — Collections. 2. United States — Race question — Collections. I. Rossi, Peter Henry, 1921- joint comp. II. T.*
E185.615.B56   77-147019   ISBN:0465011357

Carmichael, Stokely.　　　　　　　　　　　　　　　**III. 5231**
Black power; the politics of liberation in America [by] Stokely Carmichael & Charles V. Hamilton. New York, Random House [1967] xii, 198 p. 22 cm. *1.*

Negroes — Civil rights. 2. Negroes — Politics and suffrage. I. Hamilton, Charles V., joint author. II. T.
E185.615.C32   323.40973   67-22656

King, Martin Luther. III. 5232
Where do we go from here: Chaos or community? [1st ed.] New York, Harper & Row [1967] 209 p. 22 cm. *1. Negroes — History — 1964- 2. Negroes — Civil rights. I. T. II. T:Chaos or community.*
E185.615.K5   301.451/96/073   67-17072

Lecky, Robert S. III. 5233
Black manifesto; religion, racism, and reparations, edited by Robert S. Lecky and H. Elliott Wright. New York, Sheed and Ward [1969] x, 182 p. 21 cm. (A Search book) *1. Negroes — Economic conditions. 2. Church and social problems — United States. I. Wright, H. Elliott, 1937- joint author. II. T.*
E185.615.L4   261.8/3   78-98090   ISBN:0836200802

Marx, Gary T. III. 5234
Protest and prejudice; a study of belief in the black community. [1st ed.] New York, Harper & Row [1967] xxviii, 228, 27 p. 24 cm. "Volume three in a series based on the University of California Five-year study of anti-Semitism in the United States, being conducted by the Survey Research Center...under a grant from the Antidefamation League of B'nai B'rith." *1. Negroes. 2. Ethnic attitudes. I. California. University. Survey Research Center. II. T.*
E185.615.M32   67-22531

Muse, Benjamin. III. 5235
The American Negro revolution; from nonviolence to black power, 1963-1967. Bloomington, Indiana University Press [1968] xii, 345 p. 22 cm. *1. Negroes — Civil rights. 2. Negroes — History — 1964- I. T.*
E185.615.M83   301.451/96/073   68-27350

Scott, Robert Lee, 1928- comp. III. 5236
The rhetoric of Black power [by] Robert L. Scott [and] Wayne Brockriede. New York, Harper & Row [1969] viii, 207 p. 21 cm. *1. Black power. 2. Negroes — Psychology. I. Brockriede, Wayne, joint comp. II. Black power. III. T.*
E185.615.S34   323.1/19/6073   69-12866

Verba, Sidney. III. 5237
Caste, race, and politics; a comparative study of India and the United States, by Sidney Verba, Bashiruddin Ahmed, and Anil Bhatt. Beverly Hills, Sage Publications [1971] 279 p. illus. 25 cm. *1. Negroes — Politics and suffrage. 2. Untouchables — Politics and suffrage. I. Ahmed, Bashiruddin, joint author. II. Bhatt, Anil, joint author. III. T.*
E185.615.V4   322.4   78-154207   ISBN:0803901186

E185.625 Psychological and Social Conditions

Hendin, Herbert. III. 5238
Black suicide. New York, Basic Books [1969] ix, 176 p. illus. 22 cm. *1. Negroes — Social conditions. 2. Negroes — Psychology. 3. Suicide — New York (City) I. T.*
E185.625.H4   364.15/22   72-92476

Kardiner, Abram, 1891- III. 5239
The mark of oppression; explorations in the personality of the American Negro [by] Abram Kardiner and Lionel Ovesey. With the assistance of William Goldfarb [and others] Cleveland, World Pub. Co. [1962, c1951] 396 p. illus. 21 cm. (Meridian Books, M141) *1. Negroes — Psychology. 2. Negroes — Moral and social conditions. I. Ovesey, Lionel, 1915-   , joint author. II. T.*
E185.625.K3 1962   325.2670973   62-19063

Pettigrew, Thomas F. III. 5240
A profile of the Negro American [by] Thomas F. Pettigrew. Princeton, N.J., Van Nostrand [1964] xiv, 250 p. illus. 21 cm. *1. Negroes — Psychology. 2. Negroes — Moral and social conditions. 3. United States — Race question. I. T.*
E185.625.P4   301.451   64-22340

E185.63 Negroes in the Armed Forces

Dalfiume, Richard M. III. 5241
Desegregation of the U.S. Armed Forces; fighting on two fronts, 1939-1953, by Richard M. Dalfiume. Columbia, University of Missouri Press [1969] viii, 252 p. 23 cm. *1. United States — Armed Forces — Negroes. 2. Negroes — Segregation. I. T.*
E185.63.D3   355.02/2   68-54897   ISBN:0826283187

E185.7 Religion

Cleage, Albert B. III. 5242
The black Messiah [by] Albert B. Cleage, Jr. New York, Sheed and Ward [1968] 278 p. 22 cm. *1. Negroes — Race identity. 2. Jesus Christ — Negro interpretations. I. T.*
E185.7.C59   200   68-9370

E185.8 – .82 Employment

Cayton, Horace Roscoe, 1903- III. 5243
Black workers and the new unions, by Horace R. Cayton and George S. Mitchell. College Park, Md., McGrath Pub. Co. [1969, c1939] xviii, 473 p. 24 cm. *1. Negroes — Employment. 2. Trade-unions — United States — Negro membership. I. Mitchell, George Sinclair, 1902-1962, joint author. II. T.*
E185.8.C39 1969   331.6/3/96073   69-17085

Cross, Theodore L., 1924- III. 5244
Black capitalism; strategy for business in the ghetto [by] Theodore L. Cross. [1st ed.] New York, Atheneum, 1969. xii, 274 p. 25 cm. *1. Negroes — Economic conditions. 2. Negroes as businessmen. 3. Economic assistance, Domestic — United States. I. T.*
E185.8.C9   658.42   72-80268

Ferman, Louis A., comp. III. 5245
Negroes and jobs; a book of readings. Edited by Louis A. Ferman, Joyce L. Kornbluh, and J. A. Miller. Foreword by A. Philip Randolph. Ann Arbor, University of Michigan Press [1968] xv, 591 p. 24 cm. *1. Negroes — Employment — Addresses, essays, lectures. I. Kornbluh, Joyce L., joint comp. II. Miller, Joe Alan, 1934- joint comp. III. T.*
E185.8.F45   331.6/3/96073   67-25340

Ginzberg, Eli, 1911- III. 5246
The Negro potential, by Eli Ginzberg assisted by James K. Anderson, Douglas W. Bray [and] Robert W. Smuts. New York, Columbia University Press, 1956. xvi, 144 p. tables. 23 cm. *1. Negroes — Employment. 2. Negroes — Education. I. T.*
E185.8.G58   325.260973   56-9606

Greene, Lorenzo Johnston, 1899- III. 5247
The Negro wage earner, by Lorenzo J. Greene and Carter G. Woodson. New York, Russell & Russell [1969] xiii, 388 p. 23 cm. Reprint of the 1930 ed. "This work is the first actual product of the three-year survey ... made by the Association for the Study of Negro Life and History." *1. Negroes — Employment. 2. Negroes — Social conditions — To 1964. I. Woodson, Carter Godwin, 1875-1950. II. Association for the Study of Negro Life and History, inc. III. T.*
E185.8.G79 1969   331.6/39/6073   69-17839

Jacobson, Julius. III. 5248
The Negro and the American labor movement, edited by Julius Jacobson. [1st ed.] Garden City, N.Y., Anchor Books, 1968. vi, 430 p. 18 cm. *1. Negroes — Employment. 2. Trade-unions — United States. 3. Discrimination in employment — United States. I. T.*
E185.8.J3   331.88   68-12042

Marshall, F. Ray. III. 5249
The Negro and organized labor [by] Ray Marshall. New York, Wiley [1965] ix, 327 p. 24 cm. *1. Negroes — Employment. 2. Discrimination in employment — United States. 3. Trade-unions — United States — Negro membership. I. T.*
E185.8.M25   331.63   65-15761

Negro employment in basic industry; a study of racial policies in six industries, III. 5250
by Herbert R. Northrup [and others] Philadelphia] Industrial Research Unit, Wharton School of Finance and Commerce, University of Pennsylvania [1970] xvii, 769 p. 24 cm. (Studies of Negro employment v. 1. Major industrial research unit studies, no. 46.) *1. Negroes — Employment. 2. Discrimination in employment — United States. I. Northrup, Herbert Roof, 1918- (S) (S:Pennsylvania. University. Wharton School of Finance and Commerce. Industrial Research Unit. Major industrial research unit studies, no. 46)*
E185.8.N43   331.6/3/96   79-128607   ISBN:0812276213

Northrup, Herbert Roof, 1918- III. 5251
Organized labor and the Negro [by] Herbert R. Northrup. Foreword by Sumner H. Slichter. [1st ed.] New York, Harper; New York, Kraus Reprint Co., 1971 [c1944] xviii, 312 p. 23 cm. *1. Negroes — Employment. 2. Trade-unions — United States — Negro membership. 3. Labor and laboring classes — United States. I. T.*
E185.8.N65 1971   331.88/0973   74-157520

Ross, Arthur Max, ed. III. 5252
Employment, race, and poverty. Edited by Arthur M. Ross and Herbert

III. 5253 United States **E185.8**

Hill. [1st ed. New York, Harcourt, Brace & World, 1967] ix, 598 p. 21 cm. One of a series of books from the four-year program of research and conferences on the subject of unemployment and the American economy supported by a Ford Foundation grant to the Institute of Industrial Relations at the Berkeley campus of the University of California. 1. *Negroes — Employment.* 2. *Discrimination in employment — U.S.* 3. *Poverty.* I. Hill, Herbert, 1924- joint ed. II. California. University. Institute of Industrial Relations. III. T.
E185.8.R6   331.1130973   65-23537

Wesley, Charles Harris, 1891- **III. 5253**
Negro labor in the United States, 1850-1925; a study in American economic history, by Charles H. Wesley. New York, Russell & Russell [1967, c1927] xiii, 343 p. map. 20 cm. 1. *Negroes — Employment.* I. T.
E185.8.W4 1967   331.6/3/96073   67-16001

Cruse, Harold. **III. 5254**
The crisis of the Negro intellectual. New York, Morrow, 1967. 594 p. 24 cm. 1. *Negroes — Intellectual life.* I. T.
E185.82.C74   917.3097496   67-25316

Edwards, Gilbert Franklin. **III. 5255**
The Negro professional class. With a foreword by Otis Dudley Duncan. Glencoe, Ill., Free Press [1959] 224 p. 22 cm. "A development of the author's doctoral dissertation at the University of Chicago." 1. *Negroes — Employment.* 2. *Professions — U.S.* I. T.
E185.82.E23   301.451   58-9399

E185.86 Social Conditions. Family Life

Bernard, Jessie Shirley, 1903- **III. 5256**
Marriage and family among Negroes [by] Jessie Bernard. Englewood Cliffs, N.J., Prentice-Hall [1966] xi, 160 p. illus. 21 cm. (A Spectrum book) 1. *Negroes — Moral and social conditions.* 2. *Marriage — United States.* 3. *Negro families.* I. T.
E185.86.B4   301.42   66-16338

Billingsley, Andrew. **III. 5257**
Black families in white America [by] Andrew Billingsley, with the assistance of Amy Tate Billingsley. Englewood Cliffs, N.J., Prentice-Hall [1968] v, 218 p. illus., map. 21 cm. (A Spectrum book) 1. *Negroes — Social conditions — 1964-* 2. *Family — United States.* I. T.
E185.86.B5   301.44/7/0973   68-54856

Cade, Toni, comp. **III. 5258**
The Black woman; an anthology. [New York] New American Library [1970] 256 p. 18 cm. (A Signet book) 1. *Women, Negro — Collections.* I. T.
E185.86.C28   301.41/2   70-121388

Carson, Josephine, 1919- **III. 5259**
Silent voices; the Southern Negro woman today. N[ew] Y[ork] Delacorte Press [1969] 273 p. 22 cm. 1. *Women, Negro.* 2. *Negroes — Southern States.* I. T.
E185.86.C3   301.41/2/0917496   69-17530

Davis, Allison, 1902- **III. 5260**
Children of bondage; the personality development of Negro youth in the urban South, by Allison Davis and John Dollard, prepared for the American Youth Commission. Washington, American Council on Education, 1940. xxviii, 299 [1] p., 1 l. diagrs. 23 1/2 cm. Illustration mounted on cover. 1. *Negroes — Moral and social conditions.* 2. *Personality.* 3. *Social psychology.* I. Dollard, John, 1900- joint author. II. American Council on Education. American Youth Commission. III. T.
E185.86.D38   325.260975   40-13685

Frazier, Edward Franklin, 1894-1962. **III. 5261**
The Negro family in the United States. Rev. and abridged ed. Foreword by Nathan Glazer. Chicago, University of Chicago Press [1966] xxii, 372 p. 21 cm. Revised and abridged edition first published in 1948. 1. *Negroes — Social conditions — To 1964.* 2. *Negro families.* I. T.
E185.86.F74 1966   301.45196073   66-13868

Ladner, Joyce A. **III. 5262**
Tomorrow's tomorrow: the Black woman [by] Joyce A. Ladner. [1st ed.] Garden City, N.Y., Doubleday, 1971. xxvi, 304 p. 22 cm. A revision of the author's thesis, Washington University. 1. *Women, Negro.* 2. *Negro families.* I. T.
E185.86.L34 1971   301.451/96/073   78-139038

Lerner, Gerda, 1920- comp. **III. 5263**
Black women in white America; a documentary history. [1st ed.] New York, Pantheon Books [1972] xxxvi, 630 p. 25 cm. 1. *Women, Negro — Collections.* I. T.
E185.86.L4   301.41/2/0973   77-173892   ISBN:0394475402

Life styles in the black ghetto **III. 5264**
[by] William McCord [and others. 1st ed.] New York, Norton [1969] 334 p. 22 cm. 1. *Negroes — Moral and social conditions — Case studies.* I. McCord, William Maxwell, 1930-
E185.86.L5   301.451/96/073   69-18479

Moore, William. **III. 5265**
The vertical ghetto; everyday life in an urban project. New York, Random House [1969] xix, 265 p. 21 cm. 1. *Negroes — Moral and social conditions.* 2. *Negroes — Housing.* 3. *Public housing — U.S.* I. T.
E185.86.M6   917.3   69-20029

Rainwater, Lee. **III. 5266**
Behind ghetto walls; Black families in a federal slum. Chicago, Aldine Pub. Co. [1970] xi, 446 p. 25 cm. 1. *Negroes — Social conditions — 1964-* 2. *Negroes — Social life and customs.* 3. *Negroes — St. Louis.* I. T.
E185.86.R29   301.45/23   77-113083   ISBN:202301133

Schechter, William. **III. 5267**
The history of Negro humor in America. New York, Fleet Press Corp. [1970] 214 p. illus., ports. 22 cm. 1. *Negroes — Social conditions.* 2. *Negro wit and humor.* 3. *Negroes — Psychology.* I. T.
E185.86.S29   917.3/09/7496   70-76028

Schulz, David A., 1933- **III. 5268**
Coming up black; patterns of ghetto socialization [by] David A. Schulz. Englewood Cliffs, N.J., Prentice-Hall [1969] xiv, 209 p. 21 cm. (A Spectrum book) 1. *Negro children — Case studies.* 2. *Negroes — Moral and social conditions — Case studies.* I. T.
E185.86.S3   301.43/1/0977866   69-15340

U.S. Dept. of Labor. Office of Policy Planning and Research. **III. 5269**
The Negro family, the case for national action. [Washington, For sale by the Superintendent of Documents, U.S. Govt. Print. Off.] 1965. 78 p. illus. 27 cm. Known as The Moynihan report. 1. *Negroes — Moral and social conditions.* 2. *Family — U.S.* I. Moynihan, Daniel Patrick. II. T.
E185.86.U52   L65-80

Rainwater, Lee. **III. 5270**
The Moynihan report and the politics of controversy; a Trans-action social science and public policy report [by] Lee Rainwater [and] William L. Yancey. Including the full text of The Negro family: the case for national action by Daniel Patrick Moynihan. Cambridge, Mass., M.I.T. Press [1967] xviii, 493 p. illus. 25 cm. 1. *U.S. Dept. of Labor. Office of Policy Planning and Research. The Negro family, the case for national action.* 2. *Negro families.* I. Yancey, William L., joint author. II. Moynihan, Daniel Patrick. III. T.
E185.86.U54R3   301.451/96/073   67-15238

Willie, Charles Vert, 1927- comp. **III. 5271**
The family life of Black people. Edited by Charles V. Willie. Columbus, Ohio, Merrill [1970] x, 341 p. 23 cm. (Merrill sociology series) 1. *Negro families.* I. T.
E185.86.W54   301.42   79-127082   ISBN:675092973

E185.89.A5 Anthropological Studies

Herskovits, Melville Jean, 1895- **III. 5272**
The American Negro; a study in racial crossing, by Melville J. Herskovits. New York, Knopf, 1928. xiv, 92 p. 20 cm. 1. *Negroes.* I. T.
E185.89.A5H5   28-4908

E185.89.H6 Housing

Clark, Henry, 1930- **III. 5273**
The church and residential desegregation; a case study of an open housing covenant campaign. New Haven, College & University Press [1965] 254 p. 21 cm. 1. *Negroes — Housing.* 2. *Discrimination in housing — U.S.* 3. *Church and race problems — U.S.* I. T.
E185.89.H6C55   261.83   64-20663

Laurenti, Luigi. **III. 5274**
Property values and race; studies in seven cities. Special research report to the Commission on Race and Housing [prepared under the direction of Davis McEntire] Berkeley, University of California Press, 1960. xix, 256 p. maps, diagrs., tables. 25 cm. 1. *Negroes — Housing.* 2. *Housing — U.S.* I. Commission on Race and Housing. II. T.
E185.89.H6L3   331.833   59-13464

President's Conference on Home Building and Home Ownership, Washington, D.C., 1931. **III. 5275**
Negro housing; report of the Committee on Negro Housing, Nannie H.

Burroughs, chairman. Prepared for the committee, by Charles S. Johnson. Edited by John M. Gries and James Ford. New York, Negro Universities Press [1969] xiv, 282 p. illus. 23 cm. Reprint of the 1932 ed. *1. Negroes — Housing. 2. Negroes — Moral and social conditions. I. Burroughs, Nannie Helen, 1879- II. Johnson, Charles Spurgeon, 1893-1956. III. Gries, John Matthew, 1877- ed. IV. Ford, James, 1884-1944, ed. V. T.*
E185.89.H6P7 1931c   301.5/4/0973   79-89053   ISBN:837119219

Taeuber, Karl E.   **III. 5276**
Negroes in cities; residential segregation and neighborhood change, by Karl E. Taeuber and Alma F. Taeuber. Chicago Aldine Pub. Co. [1965] xvii, 284 p. illus., maps. 24 cm. (Population Research and Training Center monographs) *1. Negroes — Housing. 2. Discrimination in housing — United States. 3. Housing — United States — Statistics. I. Taeuber, Alma F., joint author. II. T. (S:Chicago. University. Population Research and Training Center. Monographs)*
E185.89.H6T3   301.45196073   65-12459

E185.9 – .93 Special Regions. States

Litwack, Leon F   **III. 5277**
North of slavery; the Negro in the free States, 1790-1860. [Chicago] University of Chicago Press [1961] 318 p. 23 cm. *1. Negroes. 2. Freedmen in the United States. 3. Negroes — Segregation. I. T.*
E185.9.L5   326.973   61-10869

Woodson, Carter Godwin, 1875-1950.   **III. 5278**
A century of Negro migration. New York, Russell & Russell [1969] 221 p. maps. 20 cm. Reprint of the 1918 ed. *1. Negroes — History. 2. Migration, Internal — United States. I. Negro migration. II. T.*
E185.9.W89 1969   301.3/2   69-16770

Holloway, Harry, 1925-   **III. 5279**
The politics of the Southern Negro; from exclusion to big city organization. New York, Random House [c1969] x, 374 p. 22 cm. *1. Negroes — Politics and suffrage. 2. Southern States — Politics and government — 1951- I. T.*
E185.92.H6   323.1/196/075   69-10787

Kolchin, Peter.   **III. 5280**
First freedom; the responses of Alabama's Blacks to Emancipation and Reconstruction. Westport, Conn., Publishing Division, Greenwood Press [1972] xxi, 215 p. illus. 22 cm. (Contributions in American history, no. 20) *1. Negroes — Alabama. 2. Reconstruction — Alabama. I. T.*
E185.93.A3K64   301.45/19/60730761   72-816   ISBN:0837163854

Green, Constance (McLaughlin) 1897-   **III. 5281**
The secret city; a history of race relations in the Nation's Capital. Princeton, N.J., Princeton University Press, 1967. xv, 389 p. illus., ports. 23 cm. *1. Negroes — District of Columbia. 2. District of Columbia — Race question. I. T.*
E185.93.D6G7   301.451/96/0753   66-26585

Liebow, Elliot.   **III. 5282**
Tally's corner; a study of Negro streetcorner men. With a foreword by Hylan Lewis. [1st ed.] Boston, Little, Brown [1967] xvii, 260 p. 21 cm. Revision of thesis, Catholic University of America. *1. Negroes — Washington, D.C. 2. Negroes — Moral and social conditions. 3. Gangs. I. T.*
E185.93.D6L5 1967   301.451/96/0753   67-18106

Wharton, Vernon Lane, 1907-   **III. 5283**
The Negro in Mississippi, 1865-1890. Chapel Hill, Univ. of North Carolina Press, 1947. 298 p. 23 cm. (The James Sprunt studies in history and political science, v.28) *1. Negroes — Mississippi. I. T. (S)*
E185.93.M6Wx (F251.J28 vol. 28)   325.2609762   47-46626

Franklin, John Hope, 1915-   **III. 5284**
The free Negro in North Carolina, 1790-1860. New York, Russell & Russell [1969, c1943] x, 271 p. maps. 23 cm. *1. Freedmen in North Carolina. I. T.*
E185.93.N6F7 1969   301.451/96/0756   70-81492

Williamson, Joel.   **III. 5285**
After slavery; the Negro in South Carolina during Reconstruction, 1861-1877. Chapel Hill, University of North Carolina Press [1965] ix, 442 p. 24 cm. *1. Negroes — South Carolina. 2. Reconstruction — South Carolina. I. T.*
E185.93.S7W73   301.451   65-13671

Wynes, Charles E.   **III. 5286**
Race relations in Virginia, 1870-1902, by Charles E. Wynes. Totowa, N.J., Rowman and Littlefield, 1971 [c1961] ix, 164 p. 23 cm. *1. Virginia — Race question. 2. Negroes — Virginia. I. T.*
E185.93.V8W9 1971   323.1/19/60730755   75-32241
ISBN:0874710138

E185.96 Collective Biography

Bardolph, Richard, 1915-   **III. 5287**
The Negro vanguard. New York, Rinehart [1959] 388 p. 24 cm. *1. Negroes — Biography. 2. Negroes — History. I. T.*
E185.96.B28   325.2670973   59-6571

Boulware, Marcus H.   **III. 5288**
The oratory of Negro leaders, 1900-1968 [by] Marcus H. Boulware. Westport, Conn., Negro Universities Press [1969] xxii, 312 p. 22 cm. *1. Negro orators. 2. Negroes — History — 1877-1964. I. T.*
E185.96.B66   808.5/0922   72-90794   ISBN:837118492

Simmons, William J., 1849-   **III. 5289**
Men of mark; eminent, progressive, and rising. Chicago, Johnson Pub. Co., 1970 [c1887] xix, 829 p. ports. 24 cm. (Ebony classics) *1. Negroes — Biography. I. T.*
E185.96.S45 1970   920/.073   78-102983   ISBN:874850355

Who's who in colored America; a biographical dictionary of notable living persons of Negro descent in America. v.1- 1927-   **III. 5290**
New York, N.Y., Who's Who in Colored America Corp. [c1927- v. ports. 28 cm. Editor: 1927- J. J. Boris. *1. Negroes — Biography. I. Boris, Joseph J., 1888- ed.*
E185.96.W54   27-8470

E185.97 Individual Biography

(see also: E443 – 449)

Brown, Claude, 1937-   **III. 5291**
Manchild in the promised land. New York, Macmillan [1965] 415 p. 22 cm. Autobiographical. *1. Harlem, New York (City) — Social conditions. I. T.*
E185.97.B86A3   309.17471   65-16938

Brown, H. Rap, 1943-   **III. 5292**
Die, nigger, die! By H. Rap Brown. New York, Dial Press, 1969. 145 p. illus. 22 cm. *I. T.*
E185.97.B87A3   323.2/0924 (B)   77-76969

Cleaver, Eldridge, 1935-   **III. 5293**
Soul on ice. With an introd. by Maxwell Geismar. [1st ed.] New York, McGraw-Hill [1967, c1968] xv, 210 p. 22 cm. "A Ramparts book." *1. Negroes — Psychology. I. T.*
E185.97.C6   301.451/96/073 (B)   67-27277

DuBois, William Edward Burghardt, 1868-1963.   **III. 5294**
Dusk of dawn; an essay toward an autobiography of a race concept. New York, Schocken Books [1968] viii, 334 p. 21 cm. Reprint of the 1940 ed. *1. Negroes. 2. U.S. — Race question. I. T.*
E185.97.D73 1968   301.451/96/073   65-14825

DuBois, William Edward Burghardt, 1868-1963.   **III. 5295**
The autobiography of W. E. B. DuBois; a soliloquy on viewing my life from the last decade of its first century. [1st ed. New York] International Publishers [1968] 448 p. ports. 22 cm. *I. T.*
E185.97.D73A3   370/.924 (B)   68-14103

Broderick, Francis L.   **III. 5296**
W. E. B. Du Bois, Negro leader in a time of crisis. Stanford, Calif., Stanford University Press, 1959. 259 p. illus. 23 cm. *1. Du Bois, William Edward Burghardt, 1868-*
E185.97.D73B7   928.1   59-7422

Cronon, Edmund David.   **III. 5297**
Black Moses; the story of Marcus Garvey and the Universal Negro Improvement Association. Madison, University of Wisconsin Press, 1955. 278 p. illus. 23 cm. *1. Garvey, Marcus, 1887-1940. 2. Universal Negro Improvement Association. I. T.*
E185.97.G3C7   920.932526   54-6931

Johnson, James Weldon, 1871-1938.   **III. 5298**
Along this way; the autobiography of James Weldon Johnson. New York, Da Capo Press, 1973 [c1933] 418 p. illus. 23 cm. *I. T.*
E185.97.J692A3 1973   818/.5/209   72-8404   ISBN:0306705397

Lewis, David L.   **III. 5299**
King; a critical biography [by] David L. Lewis. New York, Praeger [1970] xii, 460 p. illus., ports. 22 cm. *1. King, Martin Luther. I. T.*
E185.97.K5L45 1970   323.4/0924 (B)   79-95678

Little, Malcolm, 1925-1965.   **III. 5300**
The autobiography of Malcolm X. With the assistance of Alex Haley. Introd. by M. S. Handler. Epilogue by Alex Haley. New York, Grove Press [1965] xvi, 455 p. illus., ports. 24 cm. *1. Black Muslims. I. Haley, Alex. II. T.*
E185.97.L5A3   301.451960730924   65-27331

Clarke, John Henrik, 1915- comp. III. 5301
Malcolm X; the man and his times. Edited, with an introd. and commentary, by John Henrik Clarke. Assisted by A. Peter Bailey and Earl Grant. [New York] Macmillan [1969] xxiv, 360 p. 22 cm. *1. Little, Malcolm, 1925-1965. I. Bailey, A. Peter, joint comp. II. Grant, Earl, joint comp. III. T.*
E185.97.L75C55 301.451/96/073 77-75902

Moody, Anne, 1940- III. 5302
Coming of age in Mississippi. New York, Dial Press, 1968. 348 p. 22 cm. Autobiographical. *I. T.*
E185.97.M65A3 917.62/25/0360924 (B) 68-55153

Anderson, Jervis. III. 5303
A. Philip Randolph; a biographical portrait. [1st ed.] New York, Harcourt Brace Jovanovich [1973] xiv, 398 p. illus. 25 cm. *1. Randolph, Asa Philip, 1889-*
E185.97.R27A82 323.4/092/4 (B) 73-159449 ISBN:0151078300

Terrell, Mary (Church) 1863- III. 5304
A colored woman in a white world, by Mary Church Terrell. Washington, D.C., Ransdell [c1940] 436 p. front. (port.) 24 cm. Autobiography. *I. T.*
E185.97.T47 920.7 40-34942

Fox, Stephen R. III. 5305
The guardian of Boston: William Monroe Trotter [by] Stephen R. Fox. [1st ed.] New York, Atheneum, 1970. ix, 307 p. 23 cm. (Studies in American Negro life) *1. Trotter, William Monroe, 1872-1934. 2. Negroes — History — 1877-1964. I. T.*
E185.97.T75F6 1970 323.1/19/6024 (B) 78-108522

Washington, Booker Taliaferro, 1859?-1915. III. 5306
Up from slavery; an autobiography, by Booker T. Washington ... New York, Doubleday, Page & co., 1909. xxiii p., 1 l., 330 p. front., plates, ports. 20 1/2 cm. *1. Tuskegee institute. I. T.*
E185.97.W314 20-16686

Harlan, Louis R. III. 5307
Booker T. Washington; the making of a Black leader, 1856-1901 [by] Louis R. Harlan. New York, Oxford University Press, 1972. xi, 379 p. illus. 24 cm. *1. Washington, Booker Taliaferro, 1859?-1915.*
E185.97.W4H37 378.1/11/0924 (B) 72-77499

White, Walter Francis, 1893-1955. III. 5308
A man called White. New York, Arno Press, 1969. viii, 382 p. port. 23 cm. (The American Negro, his history and literature) Reprint of the 1948 ed. *1. Negroes. I. T. (S)*
E185.97.W6A3 1969 323.4/0924 (B) 69-18561

E186–856 AMERICAN HISTORY, BY PERIOD
E186–199 Colonial History (1607–1775)

Force, Peter, 1790-1868, comp. III. 5309
Tracts and other papers relating principally to the origin, settlement, and progress of the colonies in North America, from the discovery of the country to the year 1776. Collected by Peter Force. New York, P. Smith, 1947. 4 v. fold. plan. 24 cm. "Reprinted under the auspices of the Out-of-Print Books Committee of the American Library Association." *1. U.S. — History — Colonial period — Sources. I. T.*
E187.Fx A48-44

Miller, John Chester, 1907- ed. III. 5310
The colonial image: origins of American culture, selected and edited with introd. and notes by John C. Miller. New York, G. Braziller, 1962. 500 p. 24 cm. *1. U.S. — History — Colonial period — Sources. 2. U.S. — Social life and customs — Colonial period. I. T.*
E187.O7M5 973.2 62-9930

Andrews, Charles McLean, 1863-1943. III. 5311
The colonial period of American history, by Charles M. Andrews. With a new foreword by Leonard W. Labaree. New Haven, Yale University Press [1964] 4 v. 21 cm. *1. U.S. — History — Colonial periodicals. 2. Gt. Brit. — Colonies — America. I. T.*
E188.A5745 973.2 64-54917

Andrews, Charles McLean, 1863-1943. III. 5312
Our earliest colonial settlements, their diversities of origin and later characteristics, by Charles M. Andrews. New York, New York University Press; London, H. Milford, Oxford University Press, 1933. vi, 179 p. 24 cm. (Anson G. Phelps lectureship on early American history. New York university) *1. Gt. Brit. — Colonies — America. 2. U.S. — History — Colonial period. 3. U.S. — Politics and government — Colonial period. I. T.*
E188.A575 973.2 33-28721

Boorstin, Daniel Joseph, 1914- III. 5313
The Americans; the colonial experience. New York, Random House [1958] 434 p. 24 cm. *1. U.S. — Civilization — History. 2. U.S. — History — Colonial period. 3. National characteristics, American. I. T.*
E188.B72 917.3 58-9884

Jernegan, Marcus Wilson, 1872-1949. III. 5314
Laboring and dependent classes in colonial America, 1607-1783. New York, Ungar [1960] 256 p. 25 cm. (American classics) *1. Labor and laboring classes — U.S. — Colonial period. 2. Public schools — U.S. 3. Public welfare — U.S. — Law. I. T.*
E188.J57 1960 973.2 60-13985

Labaree, Leonard Woods, 1897- III. 5315
Conservatism in early American history. New York, New York Univ. Press, 1948. xiii, 182 p. 24 cm. (New York University. Stokes Foundation. Anson G. Phelps lectureship on early American history) *1. U.S. — History — Colonial period. 2. U.S. — Civilization — History. I. T. (S)*
E188.L3 973.2 48-7475

Rowse, Alfred Leslie, 1903- III. 5316
The Elizabethans and America. New York, Harper [1959] 221 p. illus. 22 cm. *1. United States — History — Colonial period. 2. United States — Civilization — English influences. 3. Great Britain — History — Elizabeth, 1558-1603. 4. England — Civilization — History. I. T.*
E188.R885 973.2 59-10592

Savelle, Max, 1896- III. 5317
The origins of American diplomacy: the international history of Anglo-america, 1492-1763. With the assistance of Margaret Anne Fisher. New York, Macmillan [1967] xiii, 624 p. maps. 25 cm. (American diplomatic history series) *1. U.S. — Foreign relations — Colonial period. I. Fisher, Margaret Anne, joint author. II. T.*
E188.S3 327.73/04 67-20734

Tyler, Lyon Gardiner, 1853-1935. III. 5318
England in America, 1580-1652. New York, Greenwood Press [1969] xx, 355 p. maps, port. 23 cm. (The American nation: a history, v. 4) Reprint of the 1904 ed. *1. United States — History — Colonial period. I. T. (S:The American nation: a history (Gloucester, Mass.), v. 4)*
E188.T95 1969b 973.2 69-14127 ISBN:0837116341

Ver Steeg, Clarence Lester, 1922- III. 5319
The formative years, 1607-1763, by Clarence L. Ver Steeg. [1st ed.] New York, Hill and Wang [1964] 342 p. illus., maps. 22 cm. (The Making of America) *1. United States — History — Colonial period. I. T.*
E188.V49 973.2 64-14682

Wright, Louis Booker, 1899- III. 5320
The Atlantic Frontier; colonial American civilization, 1607-1763. Ithaca, N.Y., Cornell University Press [1959] xi, 354, xviii p. plates, maps. 22 cm. *1. U.S. — History — Colonial period. 2. U.S. — Civilization — History. I. T.*
E188.W8 1959 973.2 59-16888

E191–199 BY PERIOD

Bridenbaugh, Carl. III. 5321
Cities in the wilderness: the first century of urban life in America, 1625-1742. [2d ed.] New York, Knopf, 1955. xiv, 500 p. 25 cm. *1. United States — History — Colonial period. 2. United States — Social life and customs — Colonial period. 3. Cities and towns — United States. I. T.*
E191.B75 1955 323.352 (301.36*) 55-8593

Lovejoy, David Sherman, 1919- III. 5322
The glorious Revolution in America [by] David S. Lovejoy. [1st ed.] New York, Harper & Row [1972] xvi, 396 p. 25 cm. *1. United States — Colonial period. 2. Great Britain — History — Revolution of 1688. I. T.*
E191.L68 1972 973.3 71-156533 ISBN:006012721X

Osgood, Herbert Levi, 1855-1918. III. 5323
The American colonies in the seventeenth century, by Herbert L. Osgood. New York, Columbia University Press [c19 v. 23 cm. "Published 1904, reprinted 1930." *1. U.S. — Politics and government — Colonial period. 2. U.S. — History — Colonial period. I. T.*
E191.O83 973.2 30-26656

Pomfret, John Edwin, 1898- III. 5324
Founding the American colonies, 1583-1660, by John E. Pomfret with Floyd M. Shumway. [1st ed.] New York, Harper & Row [1970] xvii, 380 p. illus.,

maps, ports. 22 cm. (The New American Nation series) *1. United States — History — Colonial period.* I. Shumway, Floyd Mallory, joint author. II. T.
E191.P64 1970   973.2   68-15968

Adams, James Truslow, 1878- III. 5325
Provincial society, 1690-1763, by James Truslow Adams. New York, Macmillan, 1936. xvii, 374 p. plates, ports., facsim. 22 cm. (A History of American life, vol.III) Illustrated lining-papers. "Published November, 1927." *1. U.S. — Social life and customs — Colonial period. 2. U.S. — Civilization.* 1. T.
E195.A22x   (E169.1.H672 vol. 3)   917.3   37-20159

Anglo-American political relations, 1675-1775, III. 5326
edited by Alison Gilbert Olson and Richard Maxwell Brown. New Brunswick, N.J., Rutgers University Press [1970] x, 283 p. 24 cm. "Outgrowth of the Twentieth Conference on Early American History held ... Rutgers University on October 7-8, 1966." *1. U.S. — Politics and government — Colonial period. 2. Gt. Brit. — Colonies — Administration.* I. Olson, Alison Gilbert, ed. II. Brown, Richard Maxwell, ed.
E195.A55   325.3/1/0942   73-108758   ISBN:813506247

Jensen, Merrill. III. 5327
The founding of a nation; a history of the American Revolution, 1763-1776. New York, Oxford University Press, 1968. xiii, 735 p. 24 cm. *1. United States — History — Colonial period. 2. United States — History — Revolution — Causes.* I. T.
E195.J4   973.31/1   68-29720

Kammen, Michael G. III. 5328
A rope of sand; the colonial agents, British politics, and the American Revolution, by Michael G. Kammen. Ithaca, N.Y., Cornell University Press [1968] xviii, 349 p. illus., ports. 25 cm. *1. Colonial agents. 2. United States — Politics and government — Colonial period.* I. T.
E195.K28   325.3/42/0973   68-16383

Merritt, Richard L. III. 5329
Symbols of American community, 1735-1775, by Richard L. Merritt. New Haven, Yale University Press, 1966. xxii, 279 p. illus. 23 cm. (Yale studies in political science, 16) *1. U.S. — Politics and government — Colonial period. 2. Nationalism — U.S. 3. American newspapers.* I. T. (S)
E195.M4   320.1580973   66-12508

Osgood, Herbert Levi, 1855-1918. III. 5330
The American Colonies in the eighteenth century. Gloucester, Mass., P. Smith, 1958. 4 v. 21 cm. "The present volumes are a continuation of [the author's] The American Colonies in the seventeenth century." *1. U.S. — Politics and government — Colonial period. 2. U.S. — History — Colonial period. 3. Gt. Brit. — Colonies — America.* I. T.
E195.Ox   A59-5015

Peckham, Howard Henry, 1910- III. 5331
The colonial wars, 1689-1762. Chicago, University of Chicago Press [1964] ix, 239 p. illus., ports., maps. 21 cm. (The Chicago history of American civilization) *1. U.S. — History — Colonial period. 2. United States — History, Military — To 1900.* I. T. (S)
E195.P4   973.2   64-12606

Pole, Jack Richon. III. 5332
Foundations of American independence, 1763-1815 [by] J. R. Pole. Indianapolis, Bobbs-Merrill [1972] xix, 275 p. illus. 20 cm. (The History of American society) *1. United States — History — Colonial period. 2. United States — History — 1783-1815.* I. T. (S)
E195.P83   309.1/73   71-173983

Fregault, Guy. III. 5333
Canada: the war of the conquest. Translated by Margaret M. Cameron. Toronto, Oxford University Press, 1969. xii, 427 p. maps. 24 cm. Translation of La guerre de la conquête. *1. Canada — History — 1755-1763. 2. United States — History — French and Indian War, 1755-1763.* I. T.
E199.F8613   971.01/8   78-442956

Parkman, Francis, 1823-1893. III. 5334
Montcalm and Wolf. Introd. by Allan Nevins. New York, F. Ungar Pub. Co. [1965] 2 v. illus., maps (part fold.) ports. 22 cm. (His France and England in North America, v.8-9. American classics.) "Reprinted from the edition of 1884." *1. Wolfe, James, 1727-1759. 2. Montcalm-Gozon, Louis Joseph de, marquis de Saint Véran, 1712-1759. 3. U.S. — History — French and Indian War, 1755-1763.* I. T.
E199.P255x   973.26   66-1675

E201 – 298   American Revolution, 1775 – 1783

Bailyn, Bernard, ed. III. 5335
Pamphlets of the American Revolution, 1750-1776, edited by Bernard Bailyn, with the assistance of Jane N. Garrett. Cambridge, Belknap Press of Harvard University Press, 1965-   v.   facsims. 25 cm. (The John Harvard library) *1. United States — History — Revolution — Pamphlets.* I. T. (S)
E203.B3   973.3082   64-21784

Braeman, John. III. 5336
The road to independence; a documentary history of the causes of the American Revolution: 1763-1776. New York, Putnam [1963] 314 p. 23 cm. *1. U.S. — History — Revolution — Sources. 2. U.S. — History — Revolution — Causes.* I. T.
E203.B7   973.311   63-8217

Commager, Henry Steele, 1902- ed. III. 5337
The spirit of 'seventy-six; the story of the American Revolution as told by participants, edited by Henry Steele Commager and Richard B. Morris. New York, Harper & Row [1967] lii, 1348 p. illus., facsims., maps, ports. 25 cm. *1. United States — History — Revolution — Personal narratives. 2. United States — History — Revolution — Sources.* I. Morris, Richard Brandon, 1904- joint ed. II. T.
E203.C69 1967   973.3/08   67-11325

Morison, Samuel Eliot, 1887- ed. III. 5338
Sources and documents illustrating the American Revolution, 1764-1788, and the formation of the Federal Constitution. Selected and edited by Samuel Eliot Morison. 2d ed. New York, Oxford University Press, 1965. xlii, 380 p. 21 cm. (A Galaxy book, GB135) *1. United States — History — Revolution — Sources. 2. United States — History — Revolution — Causes. 3. United States. Constitution.* I. T.
E203.M86 1965   973.3   65-1330

Billias, George Athan, 1919- ed. III. 5339
George Washington's generals. New York, W. Morrow, 1964. xvii, 327 p. ports., maps. 22 cm. Essays. Includes bibliographical references. *1. U.S. Army — Biography. 2. U.S. — History — Revolution — Biography. 3. Generals — U.S.*
E206.B5   973.33   64-12038

Alden, John Richard, 1908- III. 5340
General Gage in America; being principally a history of his role in the American Revolution. New York, Greenwood Press [1969, c1948] xi, 313 p. map., ports. 23 cm. *1. Gage, Thomas, 1721-1787. 2. United States — History — Revolution — British forces.* I. T.
E207.G23A6 1969   973.33/0924 (B)   77-90459   ISBN:0837122643

Alden, John Richard, 1908- III. 5341
The American Revolution, 1775-1783. [1st ed.] New York, Harper [1954] 294 p. illus. 22 cm. (The New American nation series) *1. U.S. — History — Revolution.*
E208.A35   973.3   53-11826

Mackesy, Piers. III. 5342
The war for America, 1775-1783. Cambridge, Harvard University Press, 1964. xx, 565 p. illus., ports., maps (1 fold. col.) 23 cm. *1. U.S. — History — Revolution. 2. Gt. Brit. — History — 1760-1789.* I. T.
E208.M14   973.3   64-2777

Miller, John Chester, 1907- III. 5343
Triumph of freedom, 1775-1783. With maps by Van H. English. [1st ed.] Boston, Little, Brown, 1948. xviii, 718 p. maps. 25 cm. "An Atlantic Monthly Press book." *1. U.S. — History — Revolution.* I. T.
E208.M5 1948   973.3   48-6755

Morgan, Edmund Sears. III. 5344
The birth of the Republic, 1763-89. [Chicago] University of Chicago Press [1956] 176 p. 21 cm. (The Chicago history of American civilization) *1. U.S. — History — Revolution. 2. U.S. — History — Confederation, 1783-1789.* I. T.
E208.M85   973.3   56-11003

Morris, Richard Brandon, 1904- III. 5345
The American Revolution reconsidered [by] Richard B. Morris. [1st ed.] New York, Harper & Row [1967] xi, 178 p. 22 cm. *1. U.S. — History — Revolution — Causes. 2. U.S. — History — Revolution — Influences.* I. T.
E208.M872   973.31/1   67-13689

Robson, Eric, 1918-1954. III. 5346
The American Revolution in its political and military aspects, 1763-1783.

New York, Da Capo Press, 1972. ix, [1], 254 p. 22 cm. (The Era of the American Revolution) Reprint of the 1955 ed. *1. United States — History — Revolution. I. T.*
E208.R6 1972   973.3   74-171392   ISBN:030670417X

Smelser, Marshall.   III. 5347
The winning of independence. Chicago, Quadrangle Books, 1972. 427 p. 22 cm. (The Quadrangle bicentennial history of the American Revolution, 3) Bibliography: p. 409-413. *1. United States — History — Revolution. I. T. (S)*
E208.S64 1972   973.3   79-156334   ISBN:0812901894

Trevelyan, George Otto, Sir, bart., 1838-1928.   III. 5348
The American Revolution. Edited, arr., and with an introd. and notes by Richard B. Morris. New York, D. McKay Co. [1964] xxiii, 580 p. 22 cm. *1. United States — History — Revolution.*
E208.T836   973.3   63-19340

Van Alstyne, Richard Warner, 1900-   III. 5349
Empire and independence; the international history of the American Revolution [by] Richard W. Van Alstyne. New York, Wiley [1965] ix, 255 p. map. 22 cm. (America in crisis) *1. United States — History — Revolution. 2. Great Britain — Politics & government — 1760-1789. 3. Great Britain — Foreign relagions — 1760-1789. 4. Europe — Politics — 18th century. I. T. (S)*
E208.V25   973.31   65-27651

Van Tyne, Claude Halstead, 1869-1930.   III. 5350
The American revolution, 1776-1783. New York, Greenwood Press [1969] xix, 369 p. maps, port. 23 cm. (The American nation: a history, v. 9) Reprint of the 1905 ed. *1. United States — History — Revolution. I. T. (S:The American nation: a history (Gloucester, Mass.), v. 9)*
E208.V29 1969   973.3   69-14130   ISBN:0837117852

Wright, Esmond.   III. 5351
Fabric of freedom, 1763-1800. New York, Hill and Wang [1961] 298 p. illus. 22 cm. (The Making of America) *1. United States — History — Revolution. 2. United States — History — Constitutional period, 1789-1809. I. T.*
E208.W9   973.3   61-14479

Gipson, Lawrence Henry, 1880-   III. 5352
The coming of the Revolution, 1763-1775. [1st ed.] New York, Harper [1954] xiv, 287 p. illus., ports., maps. 22 cm. (The New American nation series) *1. U.S. — History — Revolution — Causes. I. T.*
E209.G5   973.311   54-8952

Jameson, John Franklin, 1859-1937.   III. 5353
The American revolution considered as a social movement, by J. Franklin Jameson. Princeton, Princeton University Press, 1926. 157 p. 20 cm. "Lectures delivered in November 1925 on the Louis Clark Vanuxem foundation." *1. U.S. — History — Revolution. 2. U.S. — Social conditions. I. T.*
E209.J33   26-10868

Wright, Esmond, ed.   III. 5354
Causes and consequences of the American Revolution. Chicago, Quadrangle Books, 1966. 316 p. 22 cm. *1. United States — History — Revolution — Addresses, sermons, etc. 2. United States — History — Revolution — Causes. 3. United States — History — Revolution — Influence. I. T.*
E209.W75   973.3   66-11876

E210 – 215 POLITICAL HISTORY

Abernethy, Thomas Perkins, 1890-   III. 5355
Western lands and the American Revolution. New York, Russell & Russell, 1959 [c1937] 410 p. illus. 24 cm. *1. Land tenure — U.S. — History. 2. U.S. — Public lands. 3. U.S. — History — Revolution — Causes. 4. Missippi Valley — History — To 1803. I. T.*
E210.A15 1959   973.311   59-63139

Adams, Randolph Greenfield, 1892-1951.   III. 5356
Political ideas of the American Revolution; Britannic-American contributions to the problem of imperial organization, 1765 to 1775. 3d ed., with commentary by Merrill Jensen. New York, Barnes & Noble [1958] 216 p. illus. 22 cm. *1. U.S. — History — Revolution — Causes. 2. Gt. Brit. — Colonies — America. I. T.*
E210.A22 1958   973.3   58-11659

Andrews, Charles McLean, 1863-1943.   III. 5357
The colonial background of the American Revolution; four essays in American colonial history. New Haven, Yale University Press [1961, c1958] 220 p. 21 cm. (A Yale paperbound, Y-44) *1. U.S. — History — Colonial period. 2. Gt. Brit. — Colonies — America. 3. U.S. — History — Revolution — Causes. I. T.*
E210.A55 1961   973.311   61-19714

Baldwin, Alice Mary, 1879-   III. 5358
The New England clergy and the American Revolution. New York, F. Ungar Pub. Co. [1958] xiii, 222 p. 23 cm. *1. U.S. — Politics and government — Revolution. 2. U.S. — Politics and government — Colonial period. 3. Clergy — U.S. I. Clergy and the American Revolution. II. T.*
E210.B18 1958   973.315   58-9335

Becker, Carl Lotus, 1873-1945.   III. 5359
The eve of the revolution; a chronicle of the breach with England, by Carl Becker. New Haven, Yale University Press; [etc., etc.] 1920. xiii, 267 p. port. 21 cm. (The chronicles of America series, v.11) Frontispiece accompanied by guard sheet with descriptive letter-press. "Graduates'edition." *1. U.S. — History — Revolution. 2. U.S. — Politics and government — Revolution. I. T.*
E210.B39x   A23-853

Davidson, Philip Grant, 1902-   III. 5360
Propaganda and the American revolution, 1763-1783 [by] Philip Davidson. Chapel Hill, The University of North Carolina Press, 1941. xvi, 460 p. pl., facsims. 24 cm. *1. U.S. — History — Revolution — Causes. 2. Propaganda, American. I. T.*
E210.D3   41-3098

Dunbar, Louise Burnham, 1894-   III. 5361
A study of "monarchical" tendencies in the United States from 1776 to 1801. New York, Johnson Reprint Corp., 1970. v, 164 p. 24 cm. (University of Illinois studies in the social sciences v. 10, no. 1. Reprints in government and political science.) Reprint of the 1922 ed., with a new pref. by the author. *1. Monarchy. 2. United States — Politics and government — Revolution. 3. United States — Politics and government — 1783-1809. I. T. (S:Illinois. University. Illinois studies in the social sciences, v. 10, no. 1)*
E210.D87 1970   301.15/43/3216   71-111389

Greene, Jack P., comp.   III. 5362
The reinterpretation of the American Revolution, 1763-1789, edited with an introd. by Jack P. Greene. New York, Harper & Row [1968] ix, 626 p. 21 cm. *1. United States — History — Revolution — Addresses, essays, lectures. I. T.*
E210.G7   973.3/08   68-23226

Higginbotham, Don.   III. 5363
The war of American independence; military attitudes, policies, and practice, 1763-1789. New York, Macmillan [1971] xvi, 509 p. maps. 24 cm. *1. United States — History — Revolution. I. T.*
E210.H63   973.3   74-132454

Knollenberg, Bernhard, 1892-   III. 5364
Origin of the American Revolution: 1759-1766. [Rev. ed.] New York, Collier Books [1961] 350 p. 18 cm. (Collier books, BS42) *1. United States — History — Revolution — Causes. I. T.*
E210.K65 1961   973.311   61-18563

McDonald, Forrest.   III. 5365
E pluribus unum: the formation of the American Republic, 1776-1790. Boston, Houghton Mifflin, 1965. xv, 326 p. 22 cm. *1. U.S. — History — Revolution. 2. U.S. — History — Confederation, 1783-1789. I. T.*
E210.M14   973.3   65-11322

Maier, Pauline, 1938-   III. 5366
From resistance to revolution; colonial radicals and the development of American opposition to Britain, 1765-1776. [1st ed.] New York, Knopf, 1972. *1. United States — History — Revolution — Causes. I. T.*
E210.M27   973.3   74-154904   ISBN:0394461908

Shy, John W.   III. 5367
Toward Lexington; the role of the British Army in the coming of the American Revolution, by John Shy. Princeton, N.J., Princeton University Press, 1965. x, 463 p. maps. 21 cm. *1. United States — History — Revolution — Causes. 2. Great Britain. Army — History. 3. United States — History, Military — To 1900. 4. Great Britain — Colonies — America — Defenses. I. T.*
E210.S5   973.3113   65-17160

Van Tyne, Claude Halstead, 1869-1930.   III. 5368
The causes of the war of independence, being the first volume of a history of the founding of the American republic, by Claude H. Van Tyne. Boston and New York, Houghton Mifflin, 1922. x, 499 p. 23 cm. *1. U.S. — History — Revolution — Causes. 2. Gt. Brit. — Colonies — North America. I. T.*
E210.V27 (E178.V28 vol. 1)   22-16374

Dickerson, Oliver Morton, 1875-   III. 5369
The navigation acts and the American Revolution. Philadelphia, University of Pennsylvania Press, 1951. xv, 344 p. 24 cm. *1. Navigation acts, 1649-1696. 2. U.S. — History — Revolution — Causes. 3. Gt. Brit. — Colonies — America — Commerce. I. T.*
E215.1.D53   973.3112   51-13206

Morgan, Edmund Sears.   III. 5370
The Stamp act crisis; prologue to revolution, by Edmund S. Morgan and Helen M. Morgan. Chapel Hill, Published for the Institute of Early American History and Culture at Williamsburg, Va. by the University of

North Carolina Press [1953] x, 310 p. 25 cm. *1. Stamp act, 1765. 2. U.S. — History — Revolution — Causes. I. Morgan, Helen M., joint author. II. Institute of Early American History and Culture, Williamsburg, Va.*
E215.2.M58   973.3111   53-10190

Empire and nation: Letters from a farmer in Pennsylvania, John   **III. 5371**
Dickinson. Letters from the Federal farmer, Richard Henry Lee.
With an introd. by Forrest McDonald. Englewood Cliffs, N.J., Prentice-Hall [1962] xvi, 173 p. 21 cm. (A Spectrum book; Classics in history series, S-CH-5) *1. U.S. Constitution. 2. U.S. Constitutional Convention, 1787. 3. U.S. — History — Revolution — Causes. 4. Gt. Brit. — Colonies — America — Financial questions. I. Dickinson, John, 1732-1808. Letters from a farmer in Pennsylvania to the inhabitants of the British Colonies. II. Lee, Richard Henry, 1732-1794. Observations leading to a fair examination of the system of government ... in a number of letters from the Federal farmer to the Republican.*
E215.5.E4   973.311   62-18084

E230 – 275 MILITARY AND DIPLOMATIC HISTORY

Peckham, Howard Henry, 1910-   **III. 5372**
The War for Independence, a military history. [Chicago] University of Chicago Press [1958] 226 p. 21 cm. (The Chicago history of American civilization) *1. U.S. — History — Revolution — Campaigns and battles. I. T.*
E230.P36   973.34   58-5685

Wallace, Willard Mosher, 1911-   **III. 5373**
Appeal to arms; a military history of the American Revolution. [1st ed.] New York, Harper [1951] viii, 308 p. illus., maps, facsims. 22 cm. *1. U.S. — History — Revolution — Campaigns and battles. I. T.*
E230.W3   973.33   51-348

Bemis, Samuel Flagg, 1891-   **III. 5374**
The diplomacy of the American Revolution. Bloomington, Indiana University Press [1957] xii, 293 p. 21 cm. (Midland books, MB6) *1. U.S. — Foreign relations — Revolution. 2. Europe — Politics — 18th cent. 3. Paris, Treaty of, 1783. I. T.*
E249.B44 1957   973.32   57-7873

Corwin, Edward Samuel, 1878-1963.   **III. 5375**
French policy and the American alliance of 1778. New York, B. Franklin [1970] ix, 430 p. 23 cm. (Burt Franklin research & source works series, 476. Selected essays in history, economics, & social science, 129.) Reprint of the 1916 ed. *1. United States — History — Revolution — French participation. 2. United States — Foreign relations — Revolution. 3. United States — Foreign relations — France. 4. France — Foreign relations — United States. I. T.*
E249.C83 1970   973.32/4   77-121599

Morris, Richard Brandon, 1904-   **III. 5376**
The peacemakers; the great powers and American independence, by Richard B. Morris. [1st ed.] New York, Harper & Row [1965] xviii, 572 p. illus., facsims., maps, ports. 25 cm. *1. Paris, Treaty of, 1783. 2. U.S. — Foreign relations — Revolution. 3. Europe — Politics — 18th cent. I. T.*
E249.M68   973.317   65-20435

Clark, Dora Mae.   **III. 5377**
British opinion and the American revolution, by Dora Mae Clark. New Haven, Yale University Press; London, H. Milford, Oxford University Press, 1930. viii, 308 p. diagr. 23 cm. (Yale historical publications. Miscellany, XX) "In its original form ... a doctoral dissertation at Yale university." — Pref. *1. Public opinion — Gt. Brit. 2. Gt. Brit. — Commerce — U.S. 3. U.S. — Commerce — Gt. Brit. 4. Gt. Brit. — Colonies — North America — Financial questions. 5. U.S. — History — Revolution — Causes. I. T.*
E249.3.C59   973.32   30-9714

Lutnick, Solomon.   **III. 5378**
The American Revolution and the British press, 1775-1783. Columbia, University of Missouri Press [1967] xi, 249 p. 24 cm. *1. United States — History — Revolution — Foreign public opinion. 2. Press — Great Britain. I. T.*
E249.3.L8   973.31/5/0701   67-15812

Lanctôt, Gustave, 1883-   **III. 5379**
Canada & the American Revolution, 1774-1783. Translated by Margaret M. Cameron. Cambridge, Harvard University Press, 1967. xiv, 321 p. illus., maps, ports. 24 cm. *1. Canada — History. — 1775-1783. 2. United States — History. — Revolution. I. T.*
E263.C2x   971.02   68-983

Oliver, Peter, 1713-1791.   **III. 5380**
Origin & progress of the American Rebellion; a Tory view. Edited by Douglass Adair & John A. Schutz. San Marino, Calif., Huntington Library, 1961. xxi, 173 p. port. 24 cm. (Huntington Library publications) Based on a copy of the original manuscript in the British Museum, no. 2671 in the Egerton manuscripts. *1. Massachusetts — History — Revolution. 2. U.S. — History — Revolution — Causes. 3. American loyalists. I. T. (S:Henry F. Huntington Library and Art Gallery, San Marino, Calif. Huntington Library publications)*
E263.M4O4   973.311   61-13687

Taylor, Robert Joseph, 1917-   **III. 5381**
Western Massachusetts in the Revolution. Providence, Brown University Press, 1954. viii, 227 p. map (on lining papers) 24 cm. (Brown University studies, v.17) *1. Massachusetts — History — Revolution. 2. Shays' Rebellion, 1786-1787. I. T. (S:Brown University. Brown University studies, v.17)*
E263.M4T19   973.3444   54-5644

Cary, John Henry, 1926-   **III. 5382**
Joseph Warren: physician, politician, patriot. Urbana, University of Illinois Press, 1961. ix, 260 p. port. 24 cm. *1. Warren, Joseph, 1741-1775.*
E263.M4W234   923.273   61-62763

Gruber, Ira D.   **III. 5383**
The Howe brothers and the American Revolution [by] Ira D. Gruber. [1st ed.] New York, Published for the Institute of Early American History and Culture at Williamsburg, Va. [by] Atheneum, 1972. ix, 396 p. maps. 25 cm. *1. United States — History — Revolution — British forces. 2. Howe, Richard Howe, Earl, 1726-1799. 3. Howe, William Howe, 5th Viscount, 1729-1814. I. T.*
E267.G86   973.3/3   71-183681

Quarles, Benjamin.   **III. 5384**
The Negro in the American Revolution. New York, Norton [1973, c1961] xiii, 231 p. front. 20 cm. (The Norton library) *1. United States — History — Revolution — Negroes. I. T.*
E269.N3Q3 1973   973.3/15/0396073   72-10364   ISBN:0393006743

Allen, Gardner Weld, 1856-   **III. 5385**
A naval history of the American Revolution. New York, Russell & Russell, 1962. 2 v. illus. 22 cm. *1. U.S. Navy — History — Revolution. 2. U.S. — History — Revolution — Naval operations.*
E271.A42 1962   973.35   61-17193

Scheer, George F.   **III. 5386**
Rebels and redcoats [by] George F. Scheer and Hugh F. Rankin. [1st ed.] Cleveland, World Pub. Co. [1957] 572 p. maps. 25 cm. *1. U.S. — History — Revolution — Personal narratives. I. Rankin, Hugh F., joint author. II. T.*
E275.S3   973.3   56-9263

E277 – 280 LOYALISTS. TRAITORS

Brown, Wallace, 1933-   **III. 5387**
The good Americans; the loyalists in the American Revolution. New York, Morrow, 1969. xi, 302 p. 22 cm. *1. American loyalists. I. T.*
E277.B8   973.31/4   69-11500

Brown, Wallace, 1933-   **III. 5388**
The king's friends; the composition and motives of the American loyalist claimants. Providence, Brown University Press, 1965. x, 411 p. maps. 22 cm. *1. American loyalists. 2. U.S. — History — Revolution — Claims. I. T.*
E277.B82   973.314   66-10179

Nelson, William H., 1923-   **III. 5389**
The American Tory. Oxford, Clarendon Press, 1961. 194 p. 21 cm. *1. American loyalists. I. T.*
E277.N48   973.314   62-8

Van Tyne, Claude Halstead, 1869-1930.   **III. 5390**
The loyalists in the American revolution, by Claude Halstead Van Tyne. New York, P. Smith, 1929. xii, 360 p. 20 cm. "Reprinted August, 1929." *1. American loyalists. I. T.*
E277.V242   30-4956

Wallace, Willard Mosher, 1911-   **III. 5391**
Traitorous hero; the life and fortunes of Benedict Arnold. [1st ed.] New York, Harper [1954] xiii, 394 p. ports., maps, facsims. 22 cm. *1. Arnold, Benedict, 1741-1801. I. T.*
E278.A7W26   923.573   54-6033

E301–453 Revolution to Civil War (1775/1783–1861)

Boorstin, Daniel Joseph, 1914-   III. 5392
The Americans: the national experience, by Daniel J. Boorstin. New York, Random House [1965] 517 p. 25 cm. Continuation of the author's The Americans: the colonial experience. *1. U.S. — Civilization — 1783-1865. 2. National characteristics, American. I. T.*
E301.B6   917.303   65-17440

Cunliffe, Marcus.   III. 5393
The Nation takes shape, 1789-1837. [Chicago] University of Chicago Press [1959] 222 p. illus. 21 cm. (The Chicago history of American civilization) *1. U.S. — History — 1783-1865. I. T.*
E301.C85   973.4   59-5770

Cunliffe, Marcus.   III. 5394
Soldiers & civilians; the martial spirit in America, 1775-1865. [1st ed.] Boston, Little, Brown [1968] 499 p. illus. 25 cm. *1. Militarism — United States. I. T.*
E301.C86   355.02/13/0973   68-22898

Darling, Arthur Burr, 1892-   III. 5395
Our rising empire, 1763-1803. [Hamden, Conn.] Archon Books [1972, c1940] 595 p. 24 cm. *1. United States — Politics and government — Colonial period. 2. United States — Politics and government — 1783-1865. 3. United States — Foreign relations. 4. United States — Territorial expansion. I. T.*
E301.D23 1972   327.73   72-183351   ISBN:0208003991

Goetzmann, William H.   III. 5396
When the eagle screamed; the romantic horizon in American diplomacy, 1800-1860 [by] William H. Goetzmann. New York, Wiley [1966] xvii, 138 p. maps. 22 cm. (America in crisis) *1. U.S. — Foreign relations — 1783-1865. 2. U.S. — Territorial expansion. 3. World politics. I. T. (S)*
E301.G6   327.73   66-26743

Krout, John Allen, 1896-   III. 5397
The completion of independence, 1790-1830, by John Allen Krout and Dixon Ryan Fox. New York, Macmillan, 1944. xxiii, 487 p. plates (part double) ports. 22 cm. (A History of American life, vol.V) "Critical essay on authorities": p. 430-463. *1. U.S. — History — 1783-1865. 2. U.S. — Civilization. I. Fox, Dixon Ryan, 1887- joint author. II. T.*
E301.K7 (E169.1.H67 vol. 5)   973.4   44-51219

Rossiter, Clinton Lawrence, 1917-1970.   III. 5398
The American quest, 1790-1860: an emerging nation in search of identity, unity, and modernity. [1st ed.] New York, Harcourt Brace Jovanovich [1971] xvi, 396 p. 22 cm. (The Founding of the American Republic) *1. United States — History — 1783-1865. I. T.*
E301.R68 1971   973.4   76-142095   ISBN:0151061106

E302 COLLECTED WORKS OF CONTEMPORARY STATESMEN

Adams, John, pres. U.S., 1735-1826.   III. 5399
The selected writings of John and John Quincy Adams, edited and with an introduction by Adrienne Koch and William Peden. 1st ed. New York, A. A. Knopf, 1946. xxxix (i.e. 41), 413, xxix p. 2 port. 22 cm. *I. Adams, John Quincy, pres. U.S., 1767-1848. II. Koch, Adrienne, 1912- ed. III. Peden, William Harwood, 1913- joint ed.*
E302.A28   308.2   46-6270

Franklin, Benjamin, 1706-1790.   III. 5400
Papers. Leonard W. Labaree, editor. Whitfield J. Bell, Jr., associate editor. Helen C. Boatfield and Helene H. Fineman, assistant editors. New Haven, Yale University Press, 1959- v. illus. (part fold., part col.), facsims., geneal. tables, ports. 23 cm. "Sponsored by the American Philosophical Society and Yale University." *I. Labaree, Leonard Woods, 1897- ed.*
E302.F82 1959   59-12697

Gallatin, Albert, 1761-1849.   III. 5401
Writings. Edited by Henry Adams. New York, Antiquarian Press, 1960. 3 v. tables. 25 cm. Each article in v.3 has special t.p. *1. U.S. — History — 1783-1865. 2. Finance, Public — U.S. 3. Currency question — U.S. I. Adams, Henry, 1838-1918, ed.*
E302.Gx   A62-8748

Hamilton, Alexander, 1757-1804.   III. 5402
Papers. Harold C. Syrett, editor; Jacob E. Cooke, associate editor. New York, Columbia University Press, 1961- v. illus., ports., maps. 24 cm. *1. U.S. — History — Revolution — Sources. 2. U.S. — History — Confederation, 1783-1789 — Sources. I. Cooke, Jacob E., ed. II. Syrett, Harold Coffin, 1913- ed. III. Cooke, Jacob E., ed.*
E302.H247   923.273   61-15593

Hamilton, Alexander, 1757-1804.   III. 5403
Alexander Hamilton and the founding of the Nation. Edited by Richard B. Morris. New York, Dial Press, 1957. xxi, 617 p. 25 cm. *I. Morris, Richard Brandon, 1904- ed.*
E302.H2573   923.273   56-12132

Jefferson, Thomas, pres. U.S., 1743-1826.   III. 5404
Thomas Jefferson and the national capital; containing notes and correspondence exchanged between Jefferson, Washington, L'Enfant, Ellicott, Hallet, Thornton, Latrobe, the commissioners, and others, relating to the founding, surveying, planning, designing, constructing, and administering of the city of Washington, 1783-1818. Preface by Harold L. Ickes. Edited by Saul K. Padover. Washington, U.S. Govt. Print. Off., 1946. xxxvi, 522 p. tables, plates, maps (part double) plans (part double) facsims. 25 cm. (U.S. National park service. Source book series, no. 4) *1. Cities and towns — Planning — Washington, D.C. 2. Washington, D.C. — History — Sources. I. Washington, George, pres. U.S., 1732-1799. II. L'Enfant, Pierre Charles, 1755-1825. III. Padover, Saul Kussiel, 1905- ed.*
E302.Jx (E160.U629 no. 4)   975.3   46-27758

Jefferson, Thomas, Pres. U.S., 1743-1826.   III. 5405
The complete Jefferson; containing his major writings, published and unpublished, except his letters. Assembled and arranged by Saul K. Padover. Freeport, N.Y., Books for Libraries Press [1969, c1943] xxix, 1322 p. illus., facsims., port. 23 cm. (Select bibliographies reprint series) *I. Padover, Saul Kussiel, 1905- ed. II. T.*
E302.J4564 1969   300/.8   78-80623   ISBN:836950275

Jefferson, Thomas, Pres. U.S., 1743-1826.   III. 5406
Papers. Julian P. Boyd, editor; Lyman H. Butterfield and [others] associate editors. Princeton, Princeton University Press, 1950- v. illus., ports., maps, facsims. 25 cm. Index, volumes 1- Compiled by Elizabeth J. Sherwood and Ida T. Hopper. Princeton, Princeton University Press, 1954- v. 24 cm. Vol.2 compiled by E. J. Sherwood. E302.J463 Index *I. Boyd, Julian Parks, 1903- ed.*
E302.J463   308.1   50-7486

Jefferson, Thomas, Pres. U.S., 1743-1826.   III. 5407
The Thomas Jefferson papers, by Frank Donovan. New York, Dodd, Mead [1963] ix, 304 p. ports., facsims. 22 cm. (The Papers of the Founding Fathers) *I. Donovan, Frank, 1906-*
E302.J4632   923.173   63-20410

Madison, James, Pres. U.S., 1751-1836.   III. 5408
The complete Madison; his basic writings. Edited and with an introd. by Saul K. Padover. New York, Harper. Millwood, N.Y., Kraus Reprint Co., 1973 [c1953] p. *1. Madison, James, Pres. U.S., 1751-1836. I. Padover, Saul Kussiel, 1905- ed. II. T.*
E302.M17 1973   321.8   73-12305   ISBN:0527603007

Madison, James, pres. U.S., 1751-1836.   III. 5409
The writings of James Madison, comprising his public papers and his private correspondence, including numerous letters and documents now for the first time printed. Ed. by Gaillard Hunt. New York [etc.] G. P. Putnam's Sons, 1900-10. 9 v. port., illus., 6 facsim. (part fold.) 24 cm. No. 124 of an edition of 750 copies. *1. U.S. — Politics and government — 1783-1865. I. Hunt, Gaillard, 1862-1924, ed.*
E302.M22   01-20807

Mason, George, 1725-1792.   III. 5410
The papers of George Mason, 1725-1792. Robert A. Rutland, editor. Chapel Hill, University of North Carolina Press, 1970. 3 v. (cxxvii, 1312 p.) illus., map, ports. 25 cm.
E302.M38 1970   973.2/0924   70-97016   ISBN:807811343

Padover, Saul Kussiel, 1905- ed.   III. 5411
The world of the Founding Fathers, their basic ideas on freedom and self-government. New York, T. Yoseloff [1960] 648 p. illus. 24 cm. *1. Statesmen, American. 2. Philosophy, American. I. T.*
E302.P3   973.3082   59-8901

E302.1 POLITICAL HISTORY

Adams, Henry, 1838-1918.   III. 5412
History of the United States of America during the administrations of Jefferson and Madison. Abridged and edited by Ernest Samuels. [Abridged ed.] Chicago, University of Chicago Press [1967] xx, 425 p. maps, port. 21

cm. (Classic American historians) "The selections ... are taken from the nine volumes of the 1921 edition." *1. U.S. — History — 1801-1809. 2. U.S. — History — 1809-1817. I. Samuels, Ernest, 1903- ed. II. T.*
E302.1.A253 1967   973.4   67-21380

Chambers, William Nisbet, 1916-   **III. 5413**
Political parties in a new Nation: the American experience, 1776-1809. New York, Oxford University Press, 1963. 231 p. 21 cm. *1. Political parties — U.S. 2. U.S. — Politics and government — Revolution. 3. U.S. — Politics and government — 1783-1809. I. T.*
E302.1.C45   329   63-12551

Clancy, Herbert John.   **III. 5414**
The Democratic Party: Jefferson to Jackson. Foreword by John W. McCormack. New York, Fordham University Press [1962] 240 p. port., maps, facsims. 24 cm. *1. Democratic Party. 2. U.S. — Politics and government — 1783-1865.*
E302.1.C55   329.3   61-17758

Greene, Evarts Boutell, 1870-   **III. 5415**
The revolutionary generation, 1763-1790. New York, Macmillan, 1943. xvii, 487 p. front., plates, ports., maps (1 double) facsims. (1 double) 22 cm. (A History of American life, vol.4) *1. U.S. — History — Colonial period. 2. U.S. — History — Revolution. 3. U.S. — History — Confederation, 1783-1789. 4. U.S. — Civilization. I. T.*
E302.1.G82 (E169.1.H67 vol.4)   973.27   43-16080

Lynd, Staughton.   **III. 5416**
Class conflict, slavery, and the United States Constitution; ten essays. Indianapolis, Bobbs-Merrill [1968, c1967] xiii, 288 p. geneal. table, maps. 22 cm. *1. U.S. — Politics and government — 1783-1809 — Addresses, essays, lectures. 2. U.S. — Politics and government — Revolution — Addresses, essays, lectures. I. T.*
E302.1.L9   973   67-21400

E302.6 BIOGRAPHY
A – G

Miller, John Chester, 1907-   **III. 5417**
Sam Adams; pioneer in propaganda. Stanford, Calif., Stanford University Press [1960, c1936] 437 p. illus. 24 cm. *1. Adams, Samuel, 1722-1803. 2. United States — History — Revolution.*
E302.6.A2M56 1960   923.273   60-7699

Schachner, Nathan.   **III. 5418**
Aaron Burr, a biography; with thirty-two illustrations from old prints. New York, Stokes, 1937. xii, 563 p. front., plates, ports., facsims. (1 fold.) 23 cm. *1. Burr, Aaron, 1756-1836.*
E302.6.B9S3   923.273   37-28643

Malone, Dumas, 1892-   **III. 5419**
The public life of Thomas Cooper, 1783-1839. Columbia, University of South Carolina Press, 1961. 434 p. illus. 23 cm. *1. Cooper, Thomas, 1759-1839. 2. U.S. — Politics and government — 1783-1865. I. T.*
E302.6.C7M2 1961   923.273   61-18084

Franklin, Benjamin, 1706-1790.   **III. 5420**
Autobiography, and other writings. Edited with an introd. and notes by Russel B. Nye. Boston, Houghton Mifflin [1958] xxiv, 197 p. illus. 21 cm. (Riverside editions, A32) *I. Nye, Russel Blaine, 1913- ed.*
E302.6.F7A2 1958   923.273   58-59440

Franklin, Benjamin, 1706-1790.   **III. 5421**
The autobiography of Benjamin Franklin, edited by Leonard W. Labaree [and others] New Haven, Yale University Press, 1964. 351 p. col. illus., facsim., col. port. 27 cm. *I. Labaree, Leonard Woods, 1897- ed.*
E302.6.F7A2 1964   923.273   64-12653

Aldridge, Alfred Owen, 1915-   **III. 5422**
Benjamin Franklin, philosopher & man. [1st ed.] Philadelphia, Lippincott [1965] xii, 438 p. port. 25 cm. *1. Franklin, Benjamin, 1706-1790.*
E302.6.F8A46   973.30924 (B)   65-20586

Aldridge, Alfred Owen, 1915-   **III. 5423**
Franklin and his French contemporaries. [New York] New York University Press, 1957. 260 p. 25 cm. *1. Franklin, Benjamin, 1706-1790. I. T.*
E302.6.F8A47   923.273   56-10778

Cohen, I. Bernard, 1914-   **III. 5424**
Benjamin Franklin: his contribution to the American tradition. [1st ed.] Indianapolis, Bobbs-Merrill [1953] 320 p. illus. 23 cm. (Makers of the American tradition series) *1. Franklin, Benjamin, 1706-1790.*
E302.6.F8C67   923.273   53-9874

Conner, Paul W.   **III. 5425**
Poor Richard's politicks; Benjamin Franklin and his new American order [by] Paul W. Conner. New York, Oxford University Press, 1965. xiv, 285 p. 22 cm. *1. Franklin, Benjamin, 1706-1790. I. T.*
E302.6.F8C72   320.50924   65-25056

Crane, Verner Winslow, 1889-   **III. 5426**
Benjamin Franklin and a rising people. [1st ed.] Boston, Little, Brown [1954] 219 p. 21 cm. (The Library of American biography) *1. Franklin, Benjamin, 1706-1790.*
E302.6.F8C77 1954   923.273   54-5136

Ketcham, Ralph Louis, 1927-   **III. 5427**
Benjamin Franklin [by] Ralph L. Ketcham. New York, Washington Square Press [1965] xiv, 226 p. 18 cm. (The Great American thinkers) *1. Franklin, Benjamin, 1706-1790.*
E302.6.F8K43   973.30924 (B)   65-5126

Van Doren, Carl Clinton, 1885-   **III. 5428**
Benjamin Franklin, by Carl Van Doren. New York, Viking Press, 1938 [i.e. 1939] xix, 845 p. ports. 24 cm. "Published in October, 1938 ... seventh printing, May 1939." *1. Franklin, Benjamin, 1706-1790.*
E302.6.F8V36   923.273   40-2537

Walters, Raymond, 1912-   **III. 5429**
Albert Gallatin: Jeffersonian financier and diplomat. New York, Macmillan, 1957. 461 p. 22 cm. *1. Gallatin, Albert, 1761-1849.*
E302.6.G16W3   923.273   57-8267

E302.6   H – Z

Hacker, Louis Morton, 1899-   **III. 5430**
Alexander Hamilton in the American tradition. New York, McGraw-Hill [1957] 273 p. 21 cm. *1. Hamilton, Alexander, 1757-1804.*
E302.6.H2H15   923.273   57-6393

Miller, John Chester, 1907-   **III. 5431**
Alexander Hamilton: portrait in paradox. [1st ed.] New York, Harper [1959] 659 p. illus. 25 cm. *1. Hamilton, Alexander, 1757-1804.*
E302.6.H2M58   923.273   59-10587

Mitchell, Broadus, 1892-   **III. 5432**
Alexander Hamilton. New York, Macmillan, 1957-62. 2 v. illus. 22 cm. *1. Hamilton, Alexander, 1757-1804.*
E302.6.H2M6   923.273   57-5506

Meade, Robert Douthat, 1903-   **III. 5433**
Patrick Henry: patriot in the making. [1st ed.] Philadelphia, Lippincott [1957-   v. illus. 24 cm. *1. Henry, Patrick, 1736-1799.*
E302.6.H5M4   923.273   57-9501

Ernst, Robert, 1915-   **III. 5434**
Rufus King, American federalist. Chapel Hill, Published for the Institute of Early American History and Culture at Williamsburg, Va., by University of North Carolina Press [1968] ix, 446 p. ports. 24 cm. *1. King, Rufus, 1755-1827. I. Institute of Early American History and Culture, Williamsburg, Va.*
E302.6.K5E7   973.4/0924 (B)   68-15747

Beveridge, Albert Jeremiah, 1862-1927.   **III. 5435**
The life of John Marshall, by Albert J. Beveridge. Boston and New York, Houghton Mifflin Company, 1919. 4 v. col. fronts., plates, ports, facsims. 23 cm. *1. Marshall, John, 1755-1835.*
E302.6.M4B582   923.473   33-29106

Rutland, Robert Allen, 1922-   **III. 5436**
George Mason, reluctant statesman. Foreword by Dumas Malone. Williamsburg, Va., Colonial Williamsburg; distributed by Holt, Rinehart and Winston, New York [1961] 123 p. illus. 21 cm. (Williamsburg in America series, 4) *1. Mason, George, 1725-1792.*
E302.6.M45Rx (F234.W7W7 vol. 4)   923.273   61-11480

Ver Steeg, Clarence Lester, 1922-   **III. 5437**
Robert Morris: revolutionary financier. With an analysis of his earlier career. Philadelphia, University of Pennsylvania Press, 1954. 276 p. 24 cm. Issued also in microfilm form as thesis, Columbia University. *1. Morris, Robert, 1734-1806.*
E302.6.M8V4 1954   923.273   54-7107

Zahniser, Marvin R.   **III. 5438**
Charles Cotesworth Pinckney, founding father, by Marvin R. Zahniser. Chapel Hill, Published for the Institute of Early American History and Culture, Williamsburg, Va., by the University of North Carolina Press [1967] ix, 295 p. port. 24 cm. *1. Pinckney, Charles Cotesworth, 1746-1825. I. Institute of Early American History and Culture, Williamsburg, Va. II. T.*
E302.6.P55Z3   973.4/0924 (B)   67-28010

Turner, Lynn W. III. 5439
William Plumer of New Hampshire, 1759-1850. Chapel Hill, Published for the Institute of Early American History and Culture, Williamsburg, Va., by University of North Carolina Press [1962] 366 p. illus. 24 cm. Based on thesis, Harvard University. *1. Plumer, William, 1759-1850.*
E302.6.P73T8   923.273   62-4988

Adams, Henry, 1838-1918. III. 5440
John Randolph. Boston, Houghton, Mifflin, 1899. [New York, AMS Press, 1972] 326 p. illus. 19 cm. (American statesmen, v. 16) *1. Randolph, John, 1773-1833. (S)*
E302.6.R2A2 1972   973.4/0924 (B)   70-128968   ISBN:0404508650

Rogers, George C. III. 5441
Evolution of a Federalist: William Loughton Smith of Charleston (1758-1812) Columbia, University of South Carolina Press, 1962. 439 p. illus. 24 cm. *1. Smith, William Loughton, 1758-1812. 2. U.S. — Politics and government — Constitutional period, 1789-1809.*
E302.6.S58R6   923.273   62-20559

Mudge, Eugene Tenbroeck. III. 5442
The social philosophy of John Taylor of Caroline; a study in Jeffersonian democracy [by] Eugene Tenbroeck Mudge. New York, Columbia University Press, 1939. xii, 227 p. 24 cm. (Columbia studies in American culture. no. 4) *1. Taylor, John, 1753-1824. 2. Political science. I. T.*
E302.6.T23M8   320.1   40-4266

Smith, Charles Page. III. 5443
James Wilson, founding father, 1742-1798. Chapel Hill, N.C., University of North Carolina Press for the Institute of Early American History and Culture [c1956] xii, 426 p. port. 24 cm. *1. Wilson, James, 1742-1798.*
E302.6.W64Sx   A56-2940

E303 – 440 BY PERIOD
E303 – 309 1775 – 1789
Confederation, 1783 – 1789

Burnett, Edmund Cody, 1864-1949. III. 5444
The Continental congress, by Edmund Cody Burnett. New York, Macmillan, 1941. xvii, 757 p. 25 cm. "First printing." *1. U.S. Continental congress. 2. U.S. — Politics and government — Revolution. I. T.*
E303.B93   973.312   41-20697

Farrand, Max, 1869-1945. III. 5445
The fathers of the Constitution; a chronicle of the establishment of the Union, by Max Farrand. New Haven, Yale University Press; [etc., etc., c1921] vii, 242 p. front. 17 cm. (The Chronicles of America series, Allen Johnson, editor. [v.13]) "Textbook edition." Appendix: The Declaration of independence. Articles of confederation. The Northwest territorial government. Constitution of the United States. *1. U.S. — History — Confederation, 1783-1789. 2. U.S. — Constitutional history. I. T.*
E303.F252   342.739   36-12581

Fiske, John, 1842-1901. III. 5446
The critical period of American history, 1783-1789, by John Fiske ... Boston and New York, Houghton, Mifflin, 1888. xviii, 368 p. 20 cm. *1. U.S. — History — Confederation, 1783-1789. I. T.*
E303.F54   01-670

Jensen, Merrill. III. 5447
The New Nation; a history of the United States during the Confederation, 1781-1789. [1st ed.] New York, Knopf, 1950. xvii, 433, xi p. 24 cm. *1. U.S. — History — Confederation, 1783-1789. I. T.*
E303.J45 1950   973.318   50-9344

Nevins, Allan, 1890- III. 5448
The American states during and after the revolution, 1775-1789, by Allan Nevins. New York, Macmillan, 1924. xviii, 728 p. 9 port. 22 cm. "The design of this volume is to present a conspectus of state history, as distinguished from national history." — Pref. *1. U.S. — Politics and government — Revolution. 2. U.S. — Politics and government — 1783-1789. 3. U.S. — History — Revolution. 4. U.S. — History — Confederation, 1783-1789. 5. State governments. I. T.*
E303.N52   24-23941

E310 – 337 Constitutional Period (1789 – 1809)

Bassett, John Spencer, 1867-1928. III. 5449
The Federalist system, 1789-1801. New York, Greenwood Press [1969] xviii, 327 p. maps, port. 23 cm. (The American nation: a history, v. 11) Reprint of the 1906 ed. *1. United States — History — Constitutional period, 1789-1809. I. T. (S:The American nation: a history (Gloucester, Mass.) v. 11)*
E310.B3 1969   973.4   69-13808   ISBN:0837120659

Charles, Joseph, 1906-1952. III. 5450
The origins of the American party system; three essays. Foreword by Frederick Merk. Williamsburg, Va., Institute of Early American History and Culture, 1956. 147 p. 25 cm. "A reprint from the William and Mary quarterly; a magazine of early American history, third series, volume XII, numbers 2, 3, and 4 (1955)" *1. U.S. — Politics and government — Constitutional period, 1789-1809. 2. Political parties — U.S. — History. I. T.*
E310.C5   973.4   57-1843

Link, Eugene Perry, 1908- III. 5451
Democratic-Republican societies, 1790-1800. New York, Octagon Books, 1965 [c1942] xii, 256 p. map. 24 cm. (Columbia studies in American culture, no. 9) *1. U.S. — History — Constitutional period, 1789-1809. 2. Political clubs. I. T. (S)*
E310.L6 1965   973.4   65-16776

Miller, John Chester, 1907- III. 5452
The Federalist era, 1789-1801. [1st ed.] New York, Harper [1960] 304 p. illus. 22 cm. (The New American nation series) *1. U.S. — History — Constitutional period, 1789-1809. I. T.*
E310.M5   973.4   60-15321

Schachner, Nathan, 1895- III. 5453
The Founding Fathers. New York, Putnam [1954] 630 p. 22 cm. *1. U.S. — History — Constitutional period, 1789-1809. I. T.*
E310.S4   973.4   54-5497

Stewart, Donald Henderson, 1911- III. 5454
The opposition press of the Federalist period [by] Donald H. Stewart. Albany, State University of New York Press [1969] xiii, 957 p. 24 cm. *1. United States — Politics and government — Constitutional period, 1789-1809. 2. American newspapers. 3. Journalism — Political aspects. I. T.*
E310.S8   329/.2   69-11319   ISBN:0873950429

Gilbert, Felix, 1905- III. 5455
To the Farewell address; ideas of early American foreign policy. Princeton, N.J., Princeton University Press, 1961. 173 p. 23 cm. *1. Washington, George, Pres. U.S. Farewell address. 2. U.S. — Foreign relations. I. T.*
E310.7.G5   327.73   61-7404

Varg, Paul A. III. 5456
Foreign policies of the founding fathers. [East Lansing] Michigan State University Press, 1963 [i.e. 1964, c1963] ix, 316 p. 22 cm. *1. U.S. — Foreign relations — Revolution. 2. U.S. — Foreign relations — 1783-1815. I. T.*
E310.7.V3   327.73   63-19117

E311 – 337 BY PRESIDENTIAL ADMINISTRATION

E311 – 320 Washington, 1789 – 1797

Bowers, Claude Gernade, 1879- III. 5457
Jefferson and Hamilton; the struggle for democracy in America, by Claude G. Bowers ... Boston and New York, Houghton Mifflin company, 1925. xvii p., 1 l., 531 p. front., plates, ports., facsim. 23 cm. On verso of t.-p.: Second impression, December 1925. *1. Jefferson, Thomas, pres. U.S., 1743-1826. 2. Hamilton, Alexander, 1757-1804. 3. U.S. — Politics and government — 1789-1797. 4. U.S. — Pol and government — 1797-1801. 5. Democracy. I. T.*
E311.B652   26-5588

De Conde, Alexander. III. 5458
Entangling alliance; politics & diplomacy under George Washington. Durham, N.C., Duke University Press, 1958. xiv, 536 p. 24 cm. *1. U.S. — Foreign relations — 1789-1797. 2. U.S. — Foreign relations — France. 3. France — Foreign relations — U.S. 4. U.S. — Politics and government — 1789-1797. I. T.*
E311.D4   327.73   58-8500

Cunliffe, Marcus. III. 5459
George Washington, man and monument. [1st ed.] Boston, Little, Brown [1958] 234 p. illus. 22 cm. *1. Washington, George, Pres. U.S., 1732-1799.*
E312.C88   923.173   58-7859

Freeman, Douglas Southall, 1886-1953. III. 5460
George Washington, a biography. New York, Scribner, 1948-[57] 7 v. ports., maps, facsims. 24 cm. *1. Washington, George, Pres. U.S., 1732-1799. I. Carroll, John Alexander. II. Ashworth, Mary Wells.*
E312.F82   923.173   48-8880

Flexner, James Thomas, 1908- III. 5461
George Washington: the forge of experience, 1732-1775. [1st ed.] Boston,

Little, Brown [1965] x, 390 p. illus., facsim., map (on lining papers) ports. 25 cm. ([His George Washington, v. 1]) *1. Washington, George, Pres. U.S., 1732-1799. I. T.*
E312.2.F6   973.20924   (B)   65-21361

Knollenberg, Bernhard, 1892-   **III. 5462**
Washington and the Revolution, a reappraisal; Gates, Conway, and the Continental Congress. [Hamden, Conn.] Archon Books, 1968 [c1940] xvi, 269 p. port. 22 cm. *1. Washington, George, Pres. U.S., 1732-1799. 2. United States — History — Revolution. I. T.*
E312.25.K64 1968   973.4/1   68-16331

Nettels, Curtis Putnam.   **III. 5463**
George Washington and American independence. [1st ed.] Boston, Little, Brown, 1951. 338 p. ports., maps. 22 cm. *1. Washington, George, Pres. U.S., 1732-1799. 2. U.S. — History — Revolution. I. T.*
E312.25.N4   923.173   51-6375

Flexner, James Thomas, 1908-   **III. 5464**
George Washington and the new nation, 1783-1793. [1st ed.] Boston, Little, Brown [1970] xi, 466 p. illus., facsims., fold. map, plan, ports. 25 cm. ([His George Washington, v. 3]) *1. Washington, George, Pres. U.S., 1732-1799. I. T.*
E312.29.F55   973.4/1/0924   78-117042

Flexner, James Thomas, 1908-   **III. 5465**
George Washington: anguish and farewell (1793-1799) [1st ed.] Boston, Little, Brown [1972] p. ([His George Washington, v. 4]) *1. Washington, George, Pres. U.S., 1732-1799. I. T.*
E312.29.F56   973.4/3/0924   (B)   72-6875   ISBN:0316286028

Sears, Louis Martin, 1885-   **III. 5466**
George Washington & the French Revolution. Detroit, Wayne State University Press, 1960. x, 378 p. 24 cm. *1. Washington, George, Pres. U.S., 1732-1799. 2. France — History — Revolution — Foreign public opinion.*
E312.29.S4   973.4   60-5773

Washington, George, Pres. U.S., 1732-1799.   **III. 5467**
The writings of George Washington from the original manuscript sources 1745-1799; prepared under the direction of the United States George Washington Bicentennial Commission and published by authority Congress. John C. Fitzpatrick, editor. Westport, Conn., Greenwood Press [1970] 39 v. illus., facsims., maps, plans, ports. 22 cm. Reprint of the 1931-1944 ed. "General index by David M. Matteson": v. 38-39. *1. United States — History. 2. United States — History — Revolution. 3. Washington family. I. Fitzpatrick, John Clement, 1876-1940. II. Matteson, David Maydole, 1871-1949. III. United States. George Washington Bicentennial Commission.*
E312.7 1970   973.2/6   68-31012   ISBN:0837131723

Washington, George, Pres. U.S., 1732-1799.   **III. 5468**
Basic writings of George Washington, ed., with an introd. and notes, by Saxe Commins. New York, Random House [1948] xvii, 697 p. 21 cm. *I. Commins, Saxe, ed.*
E312.72 1948   973.41   48-7853

Washington, George, Pres. U.S., 1732-1799.   **III. 5469**
The George Washington papers. Selected, edited and interpreted by Frank Donovan. New York, Dodd, Mead [1964] vii, 310 p. facsim., ports. 22 cm. (The Papers of the founding fathers) *I. Donovan, Frank Robert, 1906- ed. II. T.*
E312.72 1964   308.1   64-25772

Bemis, Samuel Flagg, 1891-   **III. 5470**
Pinckney's treaty; America's advantage from Europe's distress, 1783-1800. [Rev. ed.] New Haven, Yale University Press, 1960. 372 p. illus. 21 cm. *1. San Lorenzo treaty, 1795. 2. U.S. — Foreign relations — Spain. 3. Spain — Foreign relations — U.S. 4. Mississippi Valley — History — To 1803. I. T.*
E313.B44 1960   973.43   60-13681

Ritcheson, Charles R.   **III. 5471**
Aftermath of revolution; British policy toward the United States, 1783-1795 [by] Charles R. Ritcheson. Dallas, Southern Methodist University Press [1969] xiv, 505 p. 24 cm. *1. U.S. — Foreign relations — Gt. Brit. 2. Gt. Brit. — Foreign relations — U.S. 3. Jay's Treaty, 1794. I. T.*
E313.R5   327.42/073   77-86328

Bemis, Samuel Flagg, 1891-   **III. 5472**
Jay's treaty; a study in commerce and diplomacy. [2d ed.] New Haven, Yale University Press, 1962. xx, 526 p. maps. 21 cm. Appendix VI (p. [442]-488): A. Definitive treaty of peace and independence. — B. Jay's treaty (treaty of amity, commerce, and navigation) 1794. *1. Jay's treaty, 1794. 2. U.S. — Foreign relations — Gt. Brit. 3. Gt. Brit. — Foreign relations — U.S. I. U.S. Treaties, etc., 1789-1797 (Washington) II. Gt. Brit. Treaties, etc., 1760-1820 (George III)*
E314.B453 1962a   973.43   62-8233

Combs, Jerald A.   **III. 5473**
The Jay treaty; political battleground of the Founding Fathers [by] Jerald A. Combs. Berkeley, University of California Press, 1970. xi, 254 p. 24 cm. *1. Jay's treaty, 1794. 2. United States — Foreign relations — Great Britain. 3. Great Britain — Foreign relations — United States. I. T.*
E314.C6   327.73/042   70-84044   ISBN:0520015738

Baldwin, Leland Dewitt, 1897-   **III. 5474**
Whiskey rebels; the story of a frontier uprising by Leland D. Baldwin; decorations by Ward Hunter. [Pittsburgh] University of Pittsburgh Press, 1939. 326 p. illus. 24 cm. Map on lining-papers. "This book is one of a series relating western Pennsylvania history, written under the direction of the Western Pennsylvania historical survey sponsored jointly by the Buhl foundation, the Historical society of western Pennsylvania and the University of Pittsburgh." *1. Whiskey insurrection, 1794. I. Western Pennsylvania historical survey. II. T.*
E315.B25   973.43   39-11763

E321 – 330   Adams, 1797 – 1801

Dauer, Manning Julian, 1909-   **III. 5475**
The Adams Federalists. Baltimore, Johns Hopkins Press, 1953. xxiii, 381 p. maps. 24 cm. *1. Adams, John, Pres. U.S., 1735-1826. 2. Federal Party. 3. U.S. — Politics and government — 1797-1801. I. T.*
E321.D23   973.44   53-11171

Kurtz, Stephen G.   **III. 5476**
The Presidency of John Adams; the collapse of Federalism, 1795-1800. Philadelphia, University of Pennsylvania Press [1957] 448 p. illus. 22 cm. *1. Adams, John, Pres. U.S., 1735-1826. 2. U.S. — Politics and government — 1797-1801. I. T.*
E321.K8   973.44   57-7764

Adams, John, Pres. U.S., 1735-1826.   **III. 5477**
Diary and autobiography. L. H. Butterfield, editor, Leonard C. Faber and Wendell D. Garrett, assistant editors. Cambridge, Belknap Press of Harvard University Press, 1961. 4 v. illus., ports., maps, facsims. 26 cm. (His Papers. Series I: Diaries) *I. Butterfield, Lyman Henry, 1909- ed.*
E322.A3   923.173   60-5387

Adams, John, Pres. U.S., 1735-1826.   **III. 5478**
The Adams-Jefferson letters; the complete correspondence between Thomas Jefferson and Abigail and John Adams. Edited by Lester J. Cappon. Chapel Hill, Published for the Institute of Early American History and Culture at Williamsburg, Va., by the University of North Carolina Press [1959] 2 v. (li, 638 p.) illus., ports. 25 cm. *I. Adams, Abigail (Smith) 1744-1818. II. Jefferson, Thomas, Pres. U.S., 1743-1826. III. Cappon, Lester Jesse, 1900- ed. IV. T.*
E322.A516   923.173   59-16475

Adams, Charles Francis, 1807-1886.   **III. 5479**
The life of John Adams, begun by John Quincy Adams, completed by Charles Francis Adams. Rev. and corr. Philadelphia, Lippincott, 1871. St. Clair Shores, Mich., Scholarly Press, 1971. 2 v. 22 cm. *1. Adams, John, Pres. U.S., 1735-1826. I. Adams, John Quincy, Pres. U.S., 1767-1848.*
E322.A52 1971   973.4/4/0924   (B)   78-108455   ISBN:0403004705

Bowen, Catherine (Drinker) 1897-   **III. 5480**
John Adams and the American Revolution. [1st ed.] Boston, Little, Brown, 1950. xvii, 699 p. illus., ports., map (on lining paper) geneal. table. 22 cm. "An Atlantic Monthly Press book." *1. Adams, John, Pres. U.S., 1735-1826. 2. U.S. — History — Revolution.*
E322.B68   923.173   50-8182

Chinard, Gilbert, 1881-   **III. 5481**
Honest John Adams, by Gilbert Chinard. Boston, Little, Brown, 1933. xii, 359 p. plates, ports. 24 cm. *1. Adams, John, pres. U.S., 1735-1826. I. T.*
E322.C47   923.173   33-32200

Haraszti, Zoltán, 1892-   **III. 5482**
John Adams & the prophets of progress. Cambridge, Harvard University Press, 1952. viii, 362 p. port., facsims. 25 cm. *1. Adams, John, Pres. U.S., 1735-1826. 2. Political science — History.*
E322.H3   923.173   52-5030

Howe, John R.   **III. 5483**
The changing political thought of John Adams, by John R. Howe, Jr. Princeton, N.J., Princeton University Press, 1966. xv, 259 p. 22 cm. *1. Adams, John, Pres. U.S., 1735-1826. 2. United States — Politics & government — Revolution. 3. United States — Politics & government — 1783-1809. I. T.*
E322.H6   320.50924   66-10272

Smith, Page.   **III. 5484**
John Adams. [1st ed.] Garden City, N.Y., Doubleday, 1962. 2 v. (xx, 1170 p.) illus., ports., facsims. 25 cm. *1. Adams, John, Pres. U.S., 1735-1826.*
E322.S64   923.173   63-7188

Adams family. Archives.   **III. 5485**
Adams family correspondence. L. H. Butterfield, editor; Wendell D. Garrett, associate editor; Marjorie E. Sprague, assistant editor. Cambridge, Belknap Press of Harvard University Press, 1963-   v. illus., ports., maps,

III. 5486   **United States**   **E322.1**

charts, facsims. 26 cm. (The Adams papers, ser. 2) *I. Butterfield, Lyman Henry, ed. II. T. (S)*
E322.1.A27   929.2   63-14964

Adams, Abigail (Smith) 1744-1818.   **III. 5486**
New letters of Abigail Adams, 1788-1801; ed. with an introd. by Stewart Mitchell. Boston, Houghton Mifflin Co., 1947. xliii, 281 p. illus., ports., geneal. tables. 25 cm. Letters written to the author's sister, Mary Cranch, reprinted from the Proceedings of the American Antiquarian Society, v.55, p. [95]-232; [299]-444. *I. Cranch, Mary (Smith) 1741-1811. II. Mitchell, Stewart, 1892- ed.*
E322.1.A37   920.7   47-11763

De Conde, Alexander.   **III. 5487**
The quasi-war; the politics and diplomacy of the undeclared war with France 1797-1801. New York, Scribner [1966] xiv, 498 p. illus., map (on lining papers) ports. 24 cm. Sequel to Entangling alliance. *1. U.S. — History — War with France, 1798-1800. 2. U.S. — Foreign relations — France. 3. France — Foreign relations — U.S. 4. U.S. — Politics and government — 1797-1801. I. T.*
E323.D4   973.45   66-24492

Miller, John Chester, 1907-   **III. 5488**
Crisis in freedom: the Alien and Sedition acts. [1st ed.] Boston, Little, Brown, 1951. 253 p. 22 cm. "An Atlantic Monthly Press book." *1. Alien and Sedition laws, 1798. 2. U.S. — Politics and government — 1797-1801. I. T.*
E327.M5   973.4   51-14177

Smith, James Morton.   **III. 5489**
Freedom's fetters; the Alien and Sedition laws and American civil liberties. Ithaca, Cornell University Press [1956- v. 24 cm. (Cornell studies in civil liberty) *1. Alien and Sedition laws, 1798. I. T. (S:Cornell University. Cornell studies in civil liberty)*
E327.S59   973.44   56-2434

E331 – 337   Jefferson, 1801 – 1809

Bowers, Claude Gernade, 1879-1958.   **III. 5490**
Jefferson in power, the death struggle of the Federalists [by] Claude G. Bowers. Boston, Houghton Mifflin, 1936. xix, 538 p. plates, ports. 23 cm. "Books, manuscripts, public documents, contemporary pamphlets, and newspapers cited and consulted": p. [513]-516. *1. Jefferson, Thomas, pres. U.S., 1743-1826. 2. U.S. — Politics and government — 1801-1809. I. T.*
E331.B75   973.46   36-19161

Channing, Edward, 1856-1931.   **III. 5491**
The Jeffersonian system, 1801-1811. New York, Greenwood Press [1969] xii, 299 p. maps, port. 23 cm. Reprint of the 1906 ed. *1. United States — Politics and government — 1801-1815. 2. Jefferson, Thomas, Pres. U.S., 1743-1826. I. T.*
E331.C45 1969   973.4/6   69-13855

Fischer, David Hackett, 1935-   **III. 5492**
The revolution of American conservatism; the Federalist party in the era of Jeffersonian democracy. [1st ed.] New York, Harper & Row [1965] xx, 455 p. 25 cm. *1. Federal Party. 2. U.S. — Politics and government — 1801-1815. I. T.*
E331.F5   973.4   65-14680

Bowers, Claude Gernade, 1879-   **III. 5493**
The heritage of Jefferson [by] Claude G. Bowers, Earl Browder [and] Francis Franklin. New York, International publishers [1945] 48 p. 20 cm. "Addresses ... delivered at a Jefferson bicentennial commemoration meeting at Mecca temple, New York, on April 9, 1943." — p. [6] *1. Jefferson, Thomas, pres. U.S., 1743-1826. I. Browder, Earl Russell, 1891- II. Franklin, Francis. III. T.*
E332.B778   923.173   47-2437

Bowers, Claude Gernade, 1879-1958.   **III. 5494**
The young Jefferson, 1743-1789, by Claude G. Bowers. Boston, Houghton Mifflin, 1945. xxx, 544 p. front., plates, ports., facsim. 20 cm. *1. Jefferson, Thomas, pres. U.S., 1743-1826. I. T.*
E332.B78   923.173   45-2085

Chinard, Gilbert, 1881-   **III. 5495**
Thomas Jefferson, the apostle of Americanism. 2d ed., rev. [Ann Arbor] University of Michigan Press [1957, c1939] 548 p. 21 cm. (Ann Arbor paperbacks, AA13) *1. Jefferson, Thomas, Pres., U.S., 1743-1826.*
E332.C536 1957   923.173   57-4665

Jefferson, Thomas, pres. U.S., 1743-1826.   **III. 5496**
The life and selected writings of Thomas Jefferson, edited, and with an introduction, by Adrienne Koch & William Peden. New York, Modern Library [1944] xliv, 730 p. facsim. 19 cm. (The Modern library of the world's best books) *I. Koch, Adrienne, 1912- ed. II. Peden, William Harwood, 1913- joint ed.*
E332.J47   923.173   44-5049

Kimball, Marie (Goebel) 1889-   **III. 5497**
Jefferson, the road to glory, 1743 to 1776, by Marie Kimball. New York, Coward-McCann [1943] ix, 358 p. plates, ports., map, facsims. (1 double) 24 cm. Map on lining-papers. *1. Jefferson, Thomas, pres. U.S., 1743-1826.*
E332.K5   923.173   43-6215

Kimball, Marie (Goebel) 1889-   **III. 5498**
Jefferson, war and peace, 1776 to 1784. New York, Coward-McCann [1947] ix, 398 p. plate, ports. 24 cm. Map on lining-papers. *1. Jefferson, Thomas, Pres., U.S., 1743-1826.*
E332.K52   923.173   47-4981

Koch, Adrienne, 1912-   **III. 5499**
Jefferson and Madison; the great collaboration. [1st ed.] New York, Knopf, 1950. xv, 294, xiv p. 22 cm. *1. Jefferson, Thomas, Pres. U.S., 1743-1826. 2. Madison, James, Pres. U.S., 1751-1836. I. T.*
E332.K58 1950   973.46   50-6417

Koch, Adrienne, 1912-   **III. 5500**
The philosophy of Thomas Jefferson, by Adrienne Koch. New York, Columbia University Press, 1943. xiv, 208 p. 22 cm. Published also as Columbia studies in American culture, no. 14. "Woodbridge prize essay, 1942-43." Vita. *1. Jefferson, Thomas, pres. U.S., 1743-1826.*
E332.K6 1943a   923.173   A44-103

Malone, Dumas, 1892-   **III. 5501**
Jefferson and his time. [1st ed.] Boston, Little, Brown, 1948- v. illus., ports., maps. 23 cm. *1. Jefferson, Thomas, Pres. United States, 1743-1826. I. T.*
E332.M25   973.4/6/0924 (B)   48-5972

Peterson, Merrill D.   **III. 5502**
Thomas Jefferson and the new nation; a biography [by] Merrill D. Peterson. New York, Oxford University Press, 1970. ix, 1072 p. illus., ports. 24 cm. *1. Jefferson, Thomas, Pres. U.S., 1743-1826. I. T.*
E332.P45   973.4/6/0924 (B)   70-110394

Peterson, Merrill D.   **III. 5503**
The Jefferson image in the American mind. New York, Oxford University Press, 1960. 548 p. 21 cm. *1. Jefferson, Thomas, Pres. U.S., 1743-1826. I. T.*
E332.2.P4   923.173   60-6140

Kaplan, Lawrence S.   **III. 5504**
Jefferson and France; an essay on politics and political ideas, by Lawrence S. Kaplan. New Haven, Yale University Press, 1967. ix, 175 p. 23 cm. (Yale historical publications. The Wallace Notestein essays, 5) *1. Jefferson, Thomas, Pres. U.S., 1743-1826. 2. U.S. — Foreign relations — France. 3. France — Foreign relations — U.S. I. T. (S:The Wallace Notestein essays, 5)*
E332.45.K3   973.4/6   67-13441

Malone, Dumas, 1892-   **III. 5505**
Thomas Jefferson as political leader. Berkeley, University of California Press, 1963. viii, 75 p. 23 cm. (Jefferson memorial lectures) First presented in 1962 at the University of California, Berkeley. *1. Jefferson, Thomas, Pres. U.S., 1743-1826. 2. U.S. — Politics and government — 1797-1801. (S)*
E332.5.M3   923.173   63-14760

Abernethy, Thomas Perking, 1890-   **III. 5506**
The Burr conspiracy. New York, Oxford University Press, 1954. xi, 301 p. port., maps (on lining papers) 24 cm. *1. Burr Conspiracy, 1805-1807. 2. Burr, Aaron, 1756-1836.*
E334.A6   973.48   54-6907

Sears, Louis Martin, 1885-   **III. 5507**
Jefferson and the Embargo. New York, Octagon Books, 1966 [c1927] ix, 340 p. 24 cm. *1. Jefferson, Thomas, Pres., U.S. 1743-1826. 2. Embargo, 1807-1809. I. T.*
E336.5.S42 1966   973.4/8   66-28377

E337.5 – 400   Early 19th Century (1801/1809 – 1845)

Wise, Sydney F.   **III. 5508**
Canada views the United States nineteenth-century political attitudes, by S. F. Wise and Robert Craig Brown. With an introd. by Richard A. Preston and a commentary by David M. Potter. Seattle, University of Washington Press [1967] xi, 139 p. illus. 21 cm. *1. U.S. — Foreign opinion, Canadian. 2. Canada — Politics and government — 19th cent. I. Brown, Robert Craig. II. T.*
E337.5.W5   301.29/71/073   67-28046

E337.8 COLLECTED WORKS OF CONTEMPORARY STATESMEN

Adams, John Quincy, pres. U.S., 1767-1848.   **III. 5509**
Writings of John Quincy Adams, edited by Worthington Chauncey Ford.

New York, Macmillan, 1913-17. 7 v. fronts. (v.1-2, ports.) 23 cm. No more published. *1. Ford, Worthington Chauncey, 1858-1941, ed.*
E337.8.A21   13-2027

Calhoun, John Caldwell, 1782-1850.   III. 5510
Papers; edited by Robert L. Meriwether. Columbia, Published by the University of South Carolina Press for the South Caroliniana Society, 1959- v. port. 24 cm. *1. Meriwether, Robert Lee, 1890-1958, ed.*
E337.8.C148   973.4   59-10351

Clay, Henry, 1777-1852.   III. 5511
Papers. James F. Hopkins, editor; Mary W. M. Hargreaves, associate editor. [Lexington] University of Kentucky Press [c1959- v. illus., ports. 24 cm. Erratum slip inserted in v.1.
E337.8.C597   923.273   59-13605

Polk, James Knox, Pres. U.S., 1795-1849.   III. 5512
Correspondence of James K. Polk. Herbert Weaver, editor. Paul H. Bergeron associate editor. Nashville, Vanderbilt University Press, 1969- v. illus., maps, port. 25 cm. *I. Weaver, Herbert, ed. II. T.*
E337.8.P63   913.6/1   75-84005   ISBN:826511465

E338 GENERAL WORKS

Blau, Joseph Leon, 1909- ed.   III. 5513
Social theories of Jacksonian democracy; representative writings of the period 1825-1850. New York, Liberal Arts Press [1954] 383 p. 21 cm. (American heritage series, no.1) *1. U.S. — Politics and government — 1815-1861 — Sources. 2. U.S. — Economic conditions. 3. U.S. — Social conditions. I. Jacksonian democracy. II. T. (S)*
E338.B55 1954   973.56   55-169

Craven, Avery Odelle, 1886-   III. 5514
The coming of the Civil War. [2d ed. Chicago] University of Chicago Press [1957] 491 p. 24 cm. *1. U.S. — History — 1815-1861. 2. U.S. — History — Civil War — Causes. 3. Slavery in the U.S. I. T.*
E338.C92 1957   973.711   57-8572

Dangerfield, George, 1904-   III. 5515
The awakening of American nationalism, 1815-1828. [1st ed.] New York, Harper & Row [c1965] xiii, 331 p. illus., facsims., ports. 22 cm. (The New American Nation series) *1. U.S. — History — 1815-1861. 2. Nationalism — U.S. I. T.*
E338.D3   973.5   64-25112

Ekirch, Arthur Alphonse, 1915-   III. 5516
The idea of progress in America, 1815-1860. New York, P. Smith, 1951. 305 p. 21 cm. (Studies in history, economics, and public law, edited by the Faculty of Political Science of Columbia University, no. 511) Issued also as thesis, Columbia University. *1. U.S. — History — 1815-1861. 2. U.S. — Civilization. I. Progress in America, 1815-1860. (S:Columbia University. Faculty of Political Science. Studies in history, economics, and public law, no. 511)*
E338.E35 1944a (H31.C7 no. 511)   A52-9817

Garrison, George Pierce, 1853-1910.   III. 5517
Westward extension, 1841-1850. New York, Greenwood Press [1969, c1906] xiv, 366 p. maps, port. 23 cm. *1. United States — History — 1815-1861. 2. United States — Territorial expansion. I. T.*
E338.G35 1969   973.5/8   69-13904

Livermore, Shaw, 1926-   III. 5518
The twilight of federalism; the disintegration of the Federalist Party, 1815-1830, by Shaw Livermore, Jr. New York, Gordian Press, 1972 [c1962] ix, 292 p. 23 cm. Originally presented as the author's thesis, University of Wisconsin, 1959. *1. Federal Party. 2. United States — Politics and government — 1815-1861. I. T.*
E338.L5 1972   329/.1   73-150413   ISBN:0877521379

Meyers, Marvin.   III. 5519
The Jacksonian persuasion; politics and belief. Stanford, Stanford University Press, 1957. vi, 231 p. 24 cm. Issued also (in microfilm form) with variations, as thesis, Columbia University. *1. Jackson, Andrew, Pres. U.S., 1767-1845. 2. U.S. — Politics and government — 1815-1861. 3. U.S. — Civilization — 1785-1865. I. T.*
E338.M53   973.5   57-12515

Pessen, Edward, 1920-   III. 5520
Jacksonian America; society, personality, and politics. Homewood, Ill., Dorsey Press, 1969. xi, 408 p. 23 cm. (The Dorsey series in American history) *1. United States — History — 1815-1861. I. T.*
E338.P4   973   68-56870

Riegel, Robert Edgar, 1897-   III. 5521
Young America, 1830-1840. [1st ed.] Norman, University of Oklahoma Press [1949] xii, 435 p. illus., ports. 24 cm. *1. U.S. — History — 1815-1861. 2. U.S. — Social life and customs. I. T.*
E338.R5   973.56   49-50089

Risjord, Norman K.   III. 5522
The Old Republicans; southern conservatism in the age of Jefferson [by] Norman K. Risjord. New York, Columbia University Press, 1965. 340 p. 25 cm. *1. Democratic Party — History. 2. U.S. — Politics and government — 1783-1865. 3. Conservatism — Southern States. I. T.*
E338.R57   320.52   65-17642

Smelser, Marshall.   III. 5523
The Democratic Republic, 1801-1815. [1st ed.] New York, Harper & Row [1968] xiv, 369 p. illus., facsims., maps, ports. 22 cm. (The New American Nation series) *1. United States — History — 1801-1809. 2. United States — History — 1809-1817. I. T.*
E338.S57   973.4   68-28218

Turner, Frederick Jackson, 1861-1932.   III. 5524
The United States, 1830-1850; the Nation and its sections. With an introd. by Avery Craven. New York, Norton [1965 c1935] ix, 602 p. maps (1 fold.) 20 cm. (The Norton library, N308) The author's imcomplete manuscript was edited by M. H. Crissey, Max Farrand, and Avery Craven. "Chapter XIII 'Taylor administration and the compromise of 1850' ... was never written." *1. U.S. — History — 1815-1861. I. Craven, Avery Odelle, 1886- ed. II. T.*
E338.T92 1965   973.5   65-5736

Van Deusen, Glyndon Garlock, 1897-   III. 5525
The Jacksonian era, 1828-1848. [1st ed.] New York, Harper [1959] 291 p. illus. 22 cm. (The New American Nation series) *1. Jackson, Andrew, Pres. U.S., 1767-1845. 2. U.S. — Politics and government — 1815-1861. I. T.*
E338.V2   973.56   58-13810

Young, James Sterling.   III. 5526
The Washington community, 1800-1828. New York, Columbia University Press, 1966. xvi, 307 p. 24 cm. *1. U.S. — Politics and government — 1783-1865. 2. Statesmen, American. 3. Politics, Practical. 4. Washington, D.C. — Social life and customs. I. T.*
E338.Y6   975.302   66-14080

E340 BIOGRAPHY

Chambers, William Nisbet, 1916-   III. 5527
Old Bullion Benton, Senator from the new West: Thomas Hart Benton, 1782-1858. New York, Russell & Russell [1970, c1956] xv, 517 p. port. 23 cm. *1. Benton, Thomas Hart, 1782-1858. I. T.*
E340.B4C5 1970   973.5/0924 (B)   70-102476

Fladeland, Betty Lorraine, 1919-   III. 5528
James Gillespie Birney: slaveholder to abolitionist [by] Betty Fladeland. New York, Greenwood Press [1969, c1955] ix, 323 p. port. 23 cm. *1. Birney, James Gillespie, 1792-1857. 2. Slavery in the United States — Anti-slavery movements.*
E340.B6F55 1969   973.71140924 (B)   70-88985   ISBN:837123127

Capers, Gerald Mortimer.   III. 5529
John C. Calhoun, opportunist; a reappraisal. Gainesville, University of Florida Press, 1960. 275 p. illus. 24 cm. *1. Calhoun, John Caldwell, 1782-1850.*
E340.C15C25   923.273   60-15788

Coit, Margaret L.   III. 5529a
John C. Calhoun, American portrait. Boston, Houghton Mifflin, 1950. ix, 593 p. illus., ports. 23 cm. *1. Calhoun, John Caldwell, 1782-1850.*
E340.C15C63   923.273   50-5234

Wiltse, Charles Maurice, 1907-   III. 5530
John C. Calhoun, by Charles M. Wiltse. New York, Russell & Russell [1968, c1944-51] 3 v. illus., facsims., maps, ports. 24 cm. *1. Calhoun, John Caldwell, 1782-1850.*
E340.C15W5x   973.6/0924 (B)   68-11329

Woodford, Frank Bury, 1903-   III. 5531
Lewis Cass, the last Jeffersonian. New Brunswick, Rutgers University Press, 1950. ix, 380 p. port. 22 cm. *1. Cass, Lewis, 1782-1866.*
E340.C3W66   923.273   50-9741

Eaton, Clement, 1898-   III. 5532
Henry Clay and the art of American politics. [1st ed.] Boston, Little, Brown [1957] 209 p. 22 cm. (The Library of American biography) *1. Clay, Henry, 1777-1852.*
E340.C6E2   923.273   57-5825

Mayo, Bernard, 1902-   III. 5533
Henry Clay, spokesman of the new West. [Unaltered and unabridged ed. Hamden, Conn.] Archon Books, 1966, [c1937] 570 p. illus., ports. 23 cm. *1. Clay, Henry, 1777-1852.*
E340.C6M2 1966   973.40924   66-25184

Van Deusen, Glyndon Garlock, 1897-   III. 5534
The life of Henry Clay, by Glyndon G. Van Deusen. Boston, Little, Brown,

1937. xiii, 448 p. front., plates (1 double) ports., facsims. 24 cm. "First edition." *1. Clay, Henry, 1777-1852.*
E340.C6V3   923.273   37-24249

Kirwan, Albert Dennis. III. 5535
John J. Crittenden; the struggle for the Union. [Lexington] University of Kentucky Press [1962] 514 p. illus. 24 cm. *1. Crittenden, John Jordan, 1787-1863.*
E340.C9K5   ~~923.273~~   62-19380   973.7113 C869K

Morison, Samuel Eliot, 1887- III. 5536
Harrison Gray Otis, 1765-1848; the urbane Federalist. Boston, Houghton Mifflin, 1969. xxii, 561 p. illus., maps, ports. 24 cm. 1913 ed. published under title: The life and letters of Harrison Gray Otis. *1. Otis, Harrison Gray, 1765-1848. 2. Hartford Convention, 1814. I. T.*
E340.O8M8 1969   973.4/0924 (B)   68-26958

Rippy, James Fred, 1892- III. 5537
Joel R. Poinsett, versatile American, by J. Fred Rippy. Durham, N.C., Duke University Press, 1935. St. Clair Shores, Mich., Scholarly Press, 1970. xii, 257 p. illus., ports. 22 cm. *1. Poinsett, Joel Roberts, 1779-1851. I. T.*
E340.P77R5 1970   973.5/5/0924 (B)   75-131819   ISBN:403007062

Swisher, Carl Brent, 1897- III. 5538
Roger B. Taney. Hamden, Conn., Archon Books, 1961 [c1935] 608 p. illus. 25 cm. *1. Taney, Roger Brooke, 1777-1864.*
E340.T2S9 1961   923.473   61-4990

Webster, Daniel, 1782-1852. III. 5539
Speak for yourself, Daniel; a life of Webster in his own words. Edited and arr. by Walker Lewis. Boston, Houghton Mifflin, 1969. xix, 505 p. illus., facsims., ports. 22 cm. *I. Lewis, Walker, ed. II. T.*
E340.W4A13   973.5/0924 (B)   69-12574

Brown, Norman D. III. 5540
Daniel Webster and the politics of availability [by] Norman D. Brown. Athens, University of Georgia Press [1969] vii, 184 p. 24 cm. *1. Webster, Daniel, 1782-1852. 2. United States — Politics and government — 1815-1861. I. T.*
E340.W4B8   973.5/0924 (B)   68-54089   ISBN:0820302317

Current, Richard Nelson. III. 5541
Daniel Webster and the rise of national conservatism. [1st ed.] Boston, Little, Brown [1955] 215 p. 21 cm. (The Library of American biography) *1. Webster, Daniel, 1782-1852.*
E340.W4C87   923.273   55-7468

Fuess, Claude Moore, 1885-1963. III. 5542
Daniel Webster. New York, Da Capo Press, 1968 [c1930] 2 v. illus., facsims., ports. 24 cm. (The American scene. A Da Capo Press reprint edition.) *1. Webster, Daniel, 1782-1852.*
E340.W4F955 1968   973.5/0924 (B)   68-8722

E341 – 400 BY PRESIDENTIAL ADMINISTRATION

E341 – 370 Madison, 1809 – 1817

Babcock, Kendric Charles, 1864-1932. III. 5543
The rise of American nationality, 1811-1819. New York, Greenwood Press [1969] xvi, 339 p. port. 23 cm. (The American nation: a history [v. 13]) Reprint of the 1906 ed. "Critical essay on authorities": p. [309]-326. *1. United States — Politics and government — 1809-1817. 2. United States — Politics and government — 1817-1825. 3. United States — History — War of 1812. I. T. (S:The American nation: a history (Gloucester, Mass.) v. 13)*
E341.B3 1969b   320.9/73   69-13805   ISBN:0837113466

Brant, Irving, 1885- III. 5544
James Madison. Indianapolis, Bobbs-Merrill [1941-61] 6 v. plates, ports., facsims. 24 cm. Vols.1-4: 1st ed. *1. Madison, James, Pres. U.S., 1751-1836.*
E342.B7   923.173   41-19279

Burns, Edward McNall. III. 5545
James Madison, philosopher of the Constitution. New Brunswick, Rutgers University Press, 1938. x, 212 p. 21 cm. (Rutgers university studies in history. vol.I) *1. Madison, James, pres. U.S., 1751-1836. 2. U.S. — Constitutional history.*
E342.B87   ~~923.173~~   38-30407   973.51 M265b

Ketcham, Ralph Louis, 1927- III. 5546
James Madison; a biography, by Ralph Ketcham. New York, N.Y., Macmillan [1971] xiv, 753 p. map (on lining papers) plates, ports. 24 cm. *1. Madison, James, Pres. U.S., 1751-1836.*
E342.K46 1971   973.5/1/0924 (B)   79-85779

Coles, Harry Lewis, 1918- III. 5547
The War of 1812, by Harry L. Coles. Chicago, University of Chicago Press [1965] ix, 298 p. illus., maps, port. 21 cm. (The Chicago history of American civilization) *1. U.S. — History — War of 1812. I. T. (S)*
E354.C7   973.52   65-17283

Mahan, Alfred Thayer, 1840-1914. III. 5548
Sea power in its relations to the War of 1812. New York, Greenwood Press, 1968 [c1905] 2 v. illus., maps, ports. 22 cm. "The present work concludes the series of 'The influence of sea power upon history'". *1. United States — History — War of 1812. 2. United States — History — War of 1812 — Naval operations. 3. United States — Navy — History — War of 1812. 4. Sea-power. I. T.*
E354.M23   973.5/25   69-10129

White, Patrick Cecil Telfer. III. 5549
A nation on trial: America and the War of 1812 [by] Patrick C. T. White. New York, Wiley [1965] 177 p. illus., maps. 22 cm. (America in crisis) *1. United States — History — War of 1812. 2. United States — Foreign relations — 1801-1815. 3. Ghent, Treaty of, 1814. I. T. (S)*
E354.W5   973.521   65-27650

Brown, Roger Hamilton. III. 5550
The Republic in peril: 1812. New York, Columbia University Press, 1964. viii, 238 p. 25 cm. *1. U.S. — Politics and government — War of 1812. 2. U.S. — History — War of 1812 — Causes. I. T.*
E357.B88   973.52   64-12498

Horsman, Reginald. III. 5551
The causes of the War of 1812. Philadelphia, University of Pennsylvania Press [1962] 345 p. 22 cm. *1. U.S. — History — War of 1812 — Causes. I. T.*
E357.H72   973.521   61-15201

Perkins, Bradford, 1925- III. 5552
Prologue to war; England and the United States, 1805- 1812. Berkeley, University of California Press, 1961. x, 457 p. ports. 24 cm. Second vol. in a trilogy, the first of which is the author's The first rapprochement; and the third of which is his Castlereagh and Adams. *1. United States — History — War of 1812 — Causes. 2. United States — Foreign relations — Great Britain. 3. Great Britain — Foreign relations — United States. I. T.*
E357.P66   973.521   61-14018

Pratt, Julius William, 1888- III. 5553
Expansionists of 1812. New York, P. Smith, 1949 [c1925] 309 p. 21 cm. *1. U.S. — Territorial expansion. 2. U.S. — History — War of 1812 — Causes. 3. U.S. — Foreign relations — 1783-1865. 4. U.S. — Politics and government — 1783-1865. I. T.*
E357.P9 1949   49-9879

Taylor, George Rogers, 1895- ed. III. 5554
The War of 1812; past justifications and present interpretations. Boston, Heath [1963] 114 p. 24 cm. (His Problems in American civilization) *1. United States — History — War of 1812 — Causes.*
E357.T35   973.52   63-2848

Banner, James M., 1935- III. 5555
To the Hartford Convention: the Federalists and the origins of party politics in Massachusetts, 1789-1815 [by] James M. Banner, Jr. [1st ed.] New York, Knopf, 1970 [c1969] xiii , 378, xii, p. maps. 22 cm. *1. Hartford Convention, 1814. 2. Massachusetts — Politics and government. I. T.*
E357.7.B3   329/.009744   75-88753

Perkins, Bradford, 1925- III. 5556
Castlereagh and Adams; England and the United States, 1812-1823. Berkeley, University of California Press, 1964. viii, 364 p. ports. 24 cm. *1. U.S. — Foreign relations — War of 1812. 2. U.S. — Foreign relations — 1817-1825. 3. U.S. — Foreign relations — Gt. Brit. 4. Gt. Brit. — Foreign relations — U.S. I. T.*
E358.P4   327.73042   64-19696

Roosevelt, Theodore, pres. U.S., 1858-1919. III. 5557
The naval war of 1812; or, The history of the United States navy during the last war with Great Britain, to which is appended an account of the battle of New Orleans. [New library ed.] New York, Putnam [c1910] 2 v. in 1. fronts., illus. 21 cm. First published 1882. *1. U.S. — History — War of 1812 — Naval operations. 2. U.S. — Navy — History — War of 1812. 3. New Orleans, Battle of, 1815. I. T.*
E360.R86 1910   24-26459

E371 – 375 Monroe, 1817 – 1825

Dangerfield, George, 1904- III. 5558
The era of good feelings. [1st ed.] New York, Harcourt, Brace [1952] xiv, 525 p. maps. 25 cm. *1. Monroe doctrine. 2. U.S. — History — 1817-1825. 3. U.S. — History — 1825-1829. 4. Ghent, Treaty of, 1814. I. T.*
E371.D3   973.54   51-14815

Ammon, Harry.   **III. 5559**
James Monroe. the quest for national identity. [1st ed.] New York, McGraw-Hill [1971] xi, 706 p. 23 cm. *1. Monroe, James, Pres. U.S., 1758-1831. 2. U.S. — Politics and government — 1817-1825. I. T.*
E372.A65   973.5/4/0924   78-141294   ISBN:0070015821

Moore, Glover, 1911-   **III. 5560**
The Missouri controversy, 1819-1821. [Lexington] University of Kentucky Press [1953] viii, 383 p. ports., map, facsim. 24 cm. *1. Missouri compromise. 2. U.S. — Politics and government — 1817-1825. I. T.*
E373.M77   973.54   53-5518

E376 – 380   Adams, 1825 – 1829

Adams, John Quincy, Pres. U.S., 1767-1848.   **III. 5561**
Diary, 1794-1845; American diplomacy and political, social, and intellectual life from Washington to Polk. Edited by Allan Nevins. New York, Scribner, 1951. xxxv, 586 p. 25 cm. "A selection from 'The memoirs of John Quincy Adams, comprising portions of his diary from 1795 to 1848.' " *1. U.S. — History — 1783-1865. 2. U.S. — Politics and government — 1783-1865. 3. U.S. — Foreign relations — 1783-1865. I. Nevins, Allan, 1890- ed.*
E377.A213   923.173   51-10345

Bemis, Samuel Flagg, 1891-   **III. 5562**
John Quincy Adams and the foundations of American foreign policy. [1st ed.] New York, A. A. Knopf, 1949. xix, 588, xv p. ports., maps (part fold., part col.) 25 cm. *1. Adams, John Quincy, Pres. U.S., 1767-1848. 2. U.S. — Foreign relations — 1783-1865.*
E377.B45 1949   923.173   49-10664

Bemis, Samuel Flagg, 1891-   **III. 5563**
John Quincy Adams and the Union. [1st ed.] New York, Knopf, 1956. xix, 546 p. illus., ports. 25 cm. *1. Adams, John Quincy, Pres. U.S., 1767-1848.*
E377.B46   923.173   55-9271

Remini, Robert Vincent, 1921-   **III. 5564**
The election of Andrew Jackson. [1st ed.] Philadelphia, Lippincott [1963] 224 p. 21 cm. (Critical periods of history) *1. Jackson, Andrew, Pres. U.S., 1767-1845. 2. Presidents — U.S. — Election — 1828. 3. U.S. — Politics and government — 1825-1829. I. T.*
E380.R4   973.56   63-17677

E381 – 385   Jackson, 1829 – 1837

Bugg, James L., ed.   **III. 5565**
Jacksonian democracy: myth or reality? New York, Holt, Rinehart and Winston [1962] 122 p. 24 cm. (American problem studies) *1. Jackson, Andrew, Pres. U.S., 1767-1845. 2. U.S. — Politics and government — 1829-1837. I. T.*
E381.B89   973.56   62-19134

Cave, Alfred A.   **III. 5566**
Jacksonian democracy and the historians, by Alfred A. Cave. Gainsville, University of Florida Press, 1964. 86 p. 23 cm. (University of Florida monographs: social sciences, no. 22) Largely based on the author's doctoral dissertation. *1. U.S. — Politics and government — 1829-1837. 2. U.S. — History — 1815-1861 — Historiography. I. T. (S:Florida. University, Gainesville. University of Florida monographs. Social sciences, no. 22)*
E381.C2   973.56   64-63899

MacDonald, William, 1863-1938.   **III. 5567**
Jacksonian democracy, 1829-1837. New York, AMS Press [1971] xiv, 345 p. illus. 19 cm. (The American nation: a history, v. 15) Reprint of the 1906 ed. *1. United States — Politics and government — 1829-1837. I. T. (S:The American nation: a history from original sources by associated scholars, v. 15.)*
E381.M22 1971   320.9/73/056   74-169921   ISBN:0404041264

Schlesinger, Arthur Meier, 1917-   **III. 5568**
The age of Jackson, by Arthur M. Schlesinger, Jr. [1st ed.] Boston, Little, Brown and company, 1945. xiv, 577 p. 24 cm. "The outgrowth of a series of lectures entitled 'A reinterpretation of Jacksonian democracy' delivered at the Lowell institute in Boston in the fall of 1941" — Acknowledgments. *1. U.S. — Politics and government — 1829-1837. I. T.*
E381.S38   973.56   45-8340

James, Marquis, 1891-1955.   **III. 5569**
Andrew Jackson, the border captain. New York, Grosset & Dunlap [c1933] 461 p. 21 cm. (The Universal library, 47) *1. Jackson, Andrew, Pres. U.S., 1767-1845. 2. New Orleans, Battle of, 1815.*
E382.J26 1964   923.173   64-56683

James, Marquis, 1891-1955.   **III. 5570**
Andrew Jackson, portrait of a President. New York, Grosset & Dunlap [1961, c1937] 627 p. 21 cm. (The Universal library, UL94) *1. Jackson, Andrew, Pres. U.S., 1767-1845.*
E382.J273   923.173   61-2366

Syrett, Harold Coffin, 1913-   **III. 5571**
Andrew Jackson: his contribution to the American tradition [by] Harold C. Syrett. Westport, Conn., Greenwood Press [1971, c1953] 298 p. 23 cm. (Makers of the American tradition series) Includes letters, Presidential messages, and addresses of Jackson. *1. Jackson, Andrew, Pres. U.S., 1767-1845. I. Jackson, Andrew, Pres. U.S., 1767-1845. Andrew Jackson: his contribution to the American tradition. 1971. II. T.*
E382.S97 1971   973.56   75-138600   ISBN:0837158028

Ward, John William, 1922-   **III. 5572**
Andrew Jackson, symbol for an age. New York, Oxford University Press, 1955. xii, 274 p. plates, ports, facsim. 21 cm. Based on thesis, University of Minnesota. *1. Jackson, Andrew, Pres. U.S., 1767-1845. 2. U.S. — History — 1815-1861.*
E382.W24   973.56   55-8125

Gammon, Samuel Rhea, 1889-   **III. 5573**
The presidential campaign of 1832. Westport, Conn., Greenwood Press [1971] 180 p. 23 cm. Originally presented as the author's thesis, Johns Hopkins University, 1921. Reprint of the 1922 ed. which was published as series 40, no. 1 of Johns Hopkins University studies in historical and political science. *1. Presidents — United States — Election — 1832- 2. Political parties — United States. I. T.*
E383.G2 1971   320.9/73/056   79-114532   ISBN:0837148278

Bancroft, Frederic, 1860-1945.   **III. 5574**
Calhoun and the South Carolina nullification movement. Gloucester, Mass., P. Smith, 1966. vi, 199 p. 21 cm. Reprint of the 1928 ed. *1. Calhoun, John Caldwell, 1782-1850. 2. Nullification. 3. South Carolina — Politics and government — 1775-1865. 4. U.S. — Politics and government — 1815-1861. I. T.*
E384.3.B22 1966   973.5/61   67-2772

Boucher, Chauncey Samuel, 1886-1955.   **III. 5575**
The nullification controversy in South Carolina. New York, Greenwood Press [1968, c1916] xi, 399 p. maps. 23 cm. *1. Nullification. 2. South Carolina — Politics and government — 1775-1865. I. T.*
E384.3.B75 1968b   320.9/757   69-13834

Freehling, William W., 1935-   **III. 5576**
Prelude to Civil War: the nullification controversy in South Carolina, 1816-1836 [by] William W. Freehling. [1st ed.] New York, Harper & Row [1966] xiii, 395 p. maps. 22 cm. Based on the author's thesis, University of California at Berkeley. *1. Nullification. 2. South Carolina — Politics and government — 1775-1865. I. T.*
E384.3.F7   973.561   66-10629

Taylor, George Rogers, 1895- ed.   **III. 5577**
Jackson versus Biddle; the struggle over the second Bank of the United States. Boston, Heath [1949] 119 p. 24 cm. (Problems in American civilization; readings selected by the Dept. of American Studies, Amherst College, 3. Heath new history series.) *1. Jackson, Andrew, Pres. U.S., 1767-1845. 2. Biddle, Nicholas, 1786-1844. 3. Bank of the United States, 1816-1836. I. T.*
E384.7.T3   973.56   59-42020

E386 – 390   Van Buren, 1837 – 1841

Curtis, James C.   **III. 5578**
The fox at bay; Martin Van Buren and the Presidency, 1837-1841 [by] James C. Curtis. Lexington, University Press of Kentucky, 1970. xi, 233 p. 24 cm. *1. Van Buren, Martin, Pres. U.S. 1782-1862. 2. United States — Politics and government — 1837-1841. I. T.*
E386.C93   973.5/7/0924 (B)   72-111507   ISBN:0813112141

Sharp, James Roger, 1936-   **III. 5579**
The Jacksonians versus the banks; politics in the States after the panic of 1837. New York, Columbia University Press, 1970. xii, 392 p. illus., maps. 23 cm. *1. United States — Politics and government — 1815-1861. 2. Banks and banking — United States — History. I. T.*
E386.S5   332.1/0973   70-127783   ISBN:0231032609

Remini, Robert Vincent, 1921-   **III. 5580**
Martin Van Buren and the making of the Democratic Party. New York, Columbia University Press, 1959. viii, 271 p. 24 cm. *1. Van Buren, Martin, Pres. U.S., 1782-1862. 2. Democratic Party — History. I. T.*
E387.R4   329.3   58-13671

Gunderson, Robert Gray.   **III. 5581**
The log-cabin campaign. [Lexington] University of Kentucky Press [1957] 292 p. illus. 24 cm. *1. Presidents — U.S. — Election — 1840. I. T.*
E390.G85   973.57   57-11384

E396 – 400   Tyler, 1841 – 1845

Morgan, Robert J.   **III. 5582**
A Whig embattled; the Presidency under John Tyler. Lincoln, University of

III. 5583   **United States**   E396

Nebraska Press, 1954. xiii, 199 p. port. 24 cm. *1. Tyler, John, Pres. U.S., 1790-1862. 2. U.S. — Politics and government — 1841-1845. I. T.*
E396.M6   973.58   54-8442

Merk, Frederick, 1887-   III. 5583
Fruits of propaganda in the Tyler administration [by] Frederick Merk, with the collaboration of Lois Bannister Merk. Cambridge, Harvard University Press, 1971. x, 259 p. facsims., map (on lining paper) 24 cm. "Letter of Mr. Walker, of Mississippi, relative to the annexation of Texas": p. 221-252. *1. Tyler, John, Pres. U.S., 1790-1862. 2. Northeast boundary of the United States. 3. United States — Politics and government — 1841-1845. I. Walker, Robert James, 1801-1869. Letter of Mr. Walker, of Mississippi, relative to the annexation of Texas. 1971. II. T.*
E398.M55   973.5/8   79-135547   ISBN:0674326768

E401 – 415.2 War with Mexico, 1845 – 1848

Bill, Alfred Hoyt, 1879-   III. 5584
Rehearsal for conflict; the war with Mexico, 1846-1848. New York, Cooper Square, 1969 [c1947] xi, 342, x p. illus., ports. 23 cm. *1. United States — History — War with Mexico, 1845-1848. I. T.*
E404.B55 1969   973.6/2   79-105298   ISBN:081540316X

Singletary, Otis A.   III. 5585
The Mexican War. [Chicago] University of Chicago Press [1960] 181 p. illus. 21 cm. (The Chicago history of American civilization) *1. U.S. — History — War with Mexico, 1845-1848.*
E404.S5   973.62   60-7248

Smith, Justin Harvey, 1857-1930.   III. 5586
The war with Mexico. Gloucester, Mass., P. Smith, 1963 [c1919] 2 v. illus. 21 cm. *1. U.S. — History — War with Mexico, 1845-1848. I. T.*
E404.S66 1963   973.62   63-5089

Fuller, John Douglas Pitts, 1899-   III. 5587
The movement for the acquisition of all Mexico, 1846-1848, by John D. P. Fuller. New York, Da Capo Press, 1969 [c1936] 174 p. 24 cm. (The American scene; comments and commentators. A Da Capo Press reprint series.) *1. United States — History — War with Mexico, 1845-1848. 2. United States — Territorial expansion. I. T.*
E407.F85 1969   973.6/21   78-87545

E415.6 – 440.5 Middle 19th Century (1845/48 – 1861)

Berwanger, Eugene H.   III. 5588
The frontier against slavery; Western anti-Negro prejudice and the slavery extension controversy. Urbana, University of Illinois Press, 1967. viii, 176 p. 24 cm. *1. Slavery in the United States — Extension to the territories — History. I. T.*
E415.7.B45   973.7112   67-21850

Cole, Arthur Charles, 1886-   III. 5589
The irrepressible conflict, 1850-1865. New York, Macmillan, 1938. St. Clair Shores, Mich., Scholarly Press [1971?, c1934] xv, 468 p. illus. 22 cm. (A History of American life, v. 7) "Critical essay on authorities": p. 408-450. *1. United States — History — 1849-1877. 2. United States — History — Civil War — Causes. 3. United States — History — Civil War. I. T. (S)*
E415.7.C69 1971   973.6   71-144952   ISBN:0403009308

Craven, Avery Odelle, 1886-   III. 5590
Civil War in the making, 1815-1860. Baton Rouge, Louisiana State University Press [1959] 115 p. 21 cm. (The Walter Lynwood Fleming lectures in southern history) *1. United States — Politics and government — 1815-1861. 2. United States — History — Civil War — Causes. I. T.*
E415.7.C78   973.711   59-7943

Nevins, Allan, 1890-   III. 5591
The emergence of Lincoln. New York, Scribner, 1950. 2 v. illus., ports., maps. 24 cm. Sequel to Ordeal of the Union. *1. Lincoln, Abraham, Pres. U.S., 1809-1865. 2. U.S. — History — 1849-1877. 3. Slavery in the U.S. I. T.*
E415.7.N38   973.68   50-9920

Nevins, Allan, 1890-   III. 5592
Ordeal of the Union. New York, Scribner, 1947. 2 v. illus., ports., maps. 24 cm. *1. United States — History — 1849-1877. 2. United States — History — Civil War — Causes. 3. Slavery in the United States. I. T.*
E415.7.N4   973.6   47-11072

Nichols, Roy Franklin, 1896-   III. 5593
The stakes of power, 1845-1877. New York, Hill and Wang [1961] 246 p. illus. 22 cm. (The Making of America) *1. U.S. — History — 1849-1877. 2. U.S. — Politics and government — 1849-1877. I. T.*
E415.7.N5   973.6   61-7560

Rhodes, James Ford, 1848-1927.   III. 5594
History of the United States from the Compromise of 1850 to the McKinley-Bryan campaign of 1896. Port Washington, N.Y., Kennikat Press [1967, c1892-1919] 8 v. maps (part fold.), plans. 23 cm. *1. U.S. — History — 1849-1877. 2. U.S. — History — 1865-1898. I. T.*
E415.7.R485   973   67-27637

Simms, Henry Harrison, 1896-   III. 5595
A decade of sectional controversy, 1851-1861, by Henry H. Simms ... Chapel Hill, The University of North Carolina Press, 1942. xi, 284 p. 22 cm. *1. U.S. — Politics and government — 1849-1861. 2. U.S. — History — Civil war — Causes. 3. Slavery in the U.S. — Anti-slavery movements. I. T.*
E415.7.S6   973.66   42-51250

Smith, Elbert B.   III. 5596
The death of slavery; the United States, 1837-65, by Elbert B. Smith. Chicago, University of Chicago Press [1967] viii, 225 p. 21 cm. (The Chicago history of American civilization) *1. U.S. — History — 1815-1861. 2. U.S. — History — Civil War. I. T. (S)*
E415.7.S64   973.6   67-16779

E415.9 BIOGRAPHY

A – G

Chase, Salmon Portland, 1808-1873.   III. 5597
Inside Lincoln's Cabinet; the Civil War diaries of Salmon P. Chase, edited by David Donald. [1st ed.] New York, Longmans, Green, 1954. ix, 342 p. port. 24 cm. *1. U.S. — History — Civil War — Sources. I. T.*
E415.9.C4A3   973.71   54-7475

Belden, Thomas Graham.   III. 5598
So fell the angels, by Thomas Graham Belden and Marva Robins Belden. [1st ed.] Boston, Little, Brown [1956] 401 p. ports. 22 cm. *1. Chase, Salmon Portland, 1808-1873. 2. Sprague, Catherine Jane (Chase) 1840-1899. 3. Sprague, William, 1830-1915. I. Belden, Marva Robins, joint author. II. T.*
E415.9.C4B38   923.473   56-9066

Hart, Albert Bushnell, 1854-1943.   III. 5599
Salmon Portland Chase. New York, Greenwood Press [1969, c1899] ix, 465 p. 23 cm. *1. Chase, Salmon Portland, 1808-1873.*
E415.9.C4H28 1969   973.7/0924 (B)   69-13925

Fuess, Claude Moore, 1885-1963.   III. 5600
The life of Caleb Cushing. Hamden, Conn., Archon Books, 1965 [c1951] 2 v. illus., ports. 22 cm. *1. Cushing, Caleb, 1800-1879. I. T.*
E415.9.C98F9 1965   923.273   65-14189

Dana, Richard Henry, 1815-1882.   III. 5601
The journal. Edited by Robert F. Lucid. Cambridge, Belknap Press of Harvard University Press, 1968. 3 v. (xli, 1201 p.) illus., facsims., geneal. tables, ports. 25 cm. *I. Lucid, Robert Francis, ed.*
E415.9.D15A16   818/.3/03   68-14264

Shapiro, Samuel.   III. 5602
Richard Henry Dana, Jr., 1815-1882. [East Lansing] Michigan State University Press, 1961. xi, 251 p. 24 cm. *1. Dana, Richard Henry, 1815-1882.*
E415.9.D15S5   928.1   61-13704

King, Willard Leroy, 1893-   III. 5603
Lincoln's manager, David Davis. Cambridge, Harvard University Press, 1960. 383 p. illus. 24 cm. *1. Davis, David, 1815-1886. 2. Lincoln, Abraham, Pres. U.S., 1809-1865. 3. U.S. — Politics and government — 1849-1877. 4. Illinois — Social life and customs.*
E415.9.D25K5   923.473   60-13290

Douglas, Stephen Arnold, 1813-1861.   III. 5604
Letters. Edited by Robert W. Johannsen. Urbana, University of Illinois Press, 1961. xxxi, 558 p. illus., ports. 24 cm. *1. U.S. — Politics and government — 1815-1861. I. Johannsen, Robert Walter, 1925- ed.*
E415.9.D73A4   923.273   61-62768

Capers, Gerald Mortimer.   III. 5605
Stephen A. Douglas, defender of the Union. Edited by Oscar Handlin. [1st ed.] Boston, Little, Brown [1959] 239 p. 21 cm. (The Library of American biography) *1. Douglas, Stephen Arnold, 1813-1861.*
E415.9.D73C28   923.273   59-5277

Milton, George Fort, 1894-1955.   III. 5606
The eve of conflict; Stephen A. Douglas and the needless war. New York, Octagon Books, 1963 [c1934] 608 p. illus. 24 cm. *1. Douglas, Stephen Arnold,*

E422   **United States**   III. 5630

1813-1861. 2. U.S. — Politics and government — 1849-1861. 3. U.S. — Politics and government   Civil War. I. T.
E415.9.D73M5 1963   923.273   63-14346

Stewart, James Brewer.   **III. 5607**
Joshua R. Giddings and the tactics of radical politics. Cleveland, Press of Case Western Reserve University, 1970. xiv, 318 p. 24 cm. *1. Giddings, Joshua Reed, 1795-1864. 2. United States — Politics and government — 1815-1861. I. T.*
E415.9.G4S7   328.73/0924   77-84496   ISBN:082950169X

Isely, Jeter Allen.   **III. 5608**
Horace Greeley and the Republican Party, 1853-1861; a study of the New York tribune. New York, Octagon Books, 1965 [c1947] xiii, 368 p. illus., facsims., ports. 24 cm. *1. Greeley, Horace, 1811-1872. 2. Republican Party — History. 3. New York tribune. I. T.*
E415.9.G8I8 1965   973.7110924   65-25891

Van Deusen, Glyndon Garlock, 1897-   **III. 5609**
Horace Greeley, nineteenth-century crusader, by Glyndon G. Van Deusen. New York, Hill and Wang [1964, c1953] 444 p. illus., ports. 21 cm. (American century series, AC72) *1. Greeley, Horace, 1811-1872. I. T.*
E415.9.G8V3 1964   920.5   64-55560

E415.9   H – Z

Sewell, Richard H.   **III. 5610**
John P. Hale and the politics of abolition [by] Richard H. Sewell. Cambridge, Harvard University Press, 1965. viii, 290 p. port. 22 cm. *1. Hale, John Parker, 1806-1873. 2. Slavery in the U.S. — Anti-slavery movements. I. T.*
E415.9.H15S4 1965   923.273   65-13849

Hendrickson, James E.   **III. 5611**
Joe Lane of Oregon; machine politics and the sectional crisis, 1849-1861 [by] James E. Hendrickson. New Haven, Yale University Press, 1967. xiii, 274 p. facsim., ports. 21 cm. (Yale Western Americana series, 17) *1. Lane, Joseph, 1801-1881. 2. Oregon — Politics and government. 3. U.S. — Politics and government — 1849-1861. I. T. (S)*
E415.9.L2H4   328.73/0924   67-13436

Lowenthal, David.   **III. 5612**
George Perkins Marsh: versatile Vermonter. New York, Columbia University Press, 1958. 442 p. illus. 24 cm. *1. Marsh, George Perkins, 1801-1882.*
E415.9.M185L6   923.273   58-11679

Durden, Robert Franklin.   **III. 5613**
James Shepherd Pike: Republicanism and the American Negro, 1850-1882. Durham, N.C., Duke University Press, 1957. 249 p. illus. 24 cm. *1. Pike, James Shepherd, 1811-1882.*
E415.9.P53D8   923.273   57-6284

Van Deusen, Glyndon Garlock, 1897-   **III. 5614**
William Henry Seward [by] Glyndon G. Van Deusen. New York, Oxford University Press, 1967. xi, 666 p. illus., ports. 24 cm. *1. Seward, William Henry, 1801-1872.*
E415.9.S4V3   973.7/0924 (B)   67-28131

Current, Richard Nelson.   **III. 5615**
Old Thad Stevens, a story of ambition. Madison, University of Wisconsin Press, 1942. 344 p. front., illus. (map) plates, ports., facsim. 23 cm. *1. Stevens, Thaddeus, 1792-1868. I. T.*
E415.9.S84C8   43-52549

Strong, George Templeton, 1820-1875.   **III. 5616**
Diary; edited by Allan Nevins and Milton Halsey Thomas. New York, Macmillan, 1952. 4 v. illus., ports., facsims. 25 cm. *1. United States — Politics and government — 19th century. 2. New York (City) — Social life and customs. 3. United States — History — Civil War — Personal narratives.*
E415.9.S86A3   974.71   52-11147

Donald, David Herbert, 1920-   **III. 5617**
Charles Sumner and the coming of the Civil War. [1st ed.] New York, Knopf, 1960. 392 p. illus. 25 cm. *1. Sumner, Charles, 1811-1874.*
E415.9.S9D6   923.273   60-9144

Donald, David Herbert, 1920-   **III. 5618**
Charles Sumner and the rights of man, by David Donald. [1st ed.] New York, Knopf, 1970. xxiv, 595, xxxix p. illus., ports. 25 cm. *1. Sumner, Charles, 1811-1874. 2. United States — Politics and government — Civil War. 3. United States — Politics and government — 1865-1877. I. T.*
E415.9.S9D62 1970   973.7/0924   76-23393

Flick, Alexander Clarence, 1869-1942.   **III. 5619**
Samuel Jones Tilden; a study in political sagacity, by Alexander Clarence Flick, assisted by Gustav S. Lobrano. New York, Dodd, Mead, 1939. ix, 597 p. plates, ports. 24 cm. (American political leaders) *1. Tilden, Samuel Jones, 1814-1886. 2. U.S. — Politics and government — 1865-1900. I. Lobrano, Gustav Stubbs, joint author.*
E415.9.T5F5   923.273   39-31244

Trefousse, Hans Louis.   **III. 5620**
Benjamin Franklin Wade, radical Republican from Ohio. New York, Twayne Publishers [1963] 404 p. illus. 22 cm. *1. Wade, Benjamin Franklin, 1800-1878.*
E415.9.W16T7   923.273   63-11185

Shenton, James Patrick, 1925-   **III. 5621**
Robert John Walker, a politician from Jackson to Lincoln. New York, Columbia University Press, 1961. 288 p. illus. 24 cm. *1. Walker, Robert James, 1801-1869.*
E415.9.W2S5   923.273   61-11283

Van Deusen, Glyndon Garlock, 1897-   **III. 5622**
Thurlow Weed, wizard of the lobby, by Glyndon G. Van Deusen. New York, Da Capo Press, 1969 [c1947] xiv, 403 p. facsims., ports. 24 cm. (The American scene. A Da Capo Press reprint series.) *1. Weed, Thurlow, 1797-1882. I. T.*
E415.9.W39V3 1969   329/.00924 (B)   73-87698

E416 – E440   BY PRESIDENTIAL ADMINISTRATION

E416 – 420   Polk, 1845 – 1849

Merk, Frederick, 1887-   **III. 5623**
The Monroe doctrine and American expansionism, 1843-1849, by Frederick Merk with the collaboration of Lois Bannister Merk. [1st ed.] New York, Knopf, 1966. xii, 289, ix p. illus., map. 25 cm. *1. United States — Foreign relations — 1845-1849. 2. United States — Territorial expansion. 3. Monroe doctrine. I. T.*
E416.M4   973.61   66-19390

Morrison, Chaplain W.   **III. 5624**
Democratic politics and sectionalism; the Wilmot proviso controversy, by Chaplain W. Morrison. Chapel Hill, University of North Carolina Press [1967] viii, 244 p. 24 cm. *1. Democratic Party — History. 2. Wilmot proviso, 1846. 3. U.S. — Politics and government — 1845-1849. 4. Sectionalism (U.S.) I. The Wilmot proviso controversy. II. T.*
E416.M6   973.6/1   67-15101

Polk, James Knox, Pres. U.S., 1795-1849.   **III. 5625**
Polk; the diary of a president, 1845-1849, covering the Mexican War, the acquisition of Oregon, and the conquest of California and the Southwest, edited by Allan Nevins. London, New York, Longmans, Green, 1952. xxxiv, 412, [1] p. 24 cm. "A selection from 'The diary of James K. Polk during his Presidency, 1845-1849,' edited and annotated by Milo Milton Quaife." *1. U.S. — Politics and government — 1845-1849. 2. U.S. — History — War with Mexico, 1845-1848 — Sources. I. Nevins, Allan, 1890- ed.*
E416.P77 1952   923.173   52-8933

McCormac, Eugene Irving, 1872-1943.   **III. 5626**
James K. Polk; a political biography. New York, Russell & Russell, 1965. x, 746 p. port. 23 cm. Reissue of 1922 ed. *1. Polk, James Knox, Pres. U.S., 1795-1849.*
E417.M12 1965   923.173   64-66402

Sellers, Charles Grier.   **III. 5627**
James K. Polk, Jacksonian, 1795-1843. Princeton, N.J., Princeton University Press, 1957. v. illus. 25 cm. Vol. 2 has title: James K. Polk, continentalist, 1843-1846. *1. Polk, James Knox, Pres. U.S., 1795-1849.*
E417.S4   973.610924 (B)   57-5457

Rayback, Joseph G.   **III. 5628**
Free soil; the election of 1848 [by] Joseph G. Rayback. [Lexington] University Press of Kentucky [1971, c1970] ix, 326 p. col. maps (on lining papers) 24 cm. *1. U.S. — Politics and government — 1845-1849. 2. Wilmot proviso, 1846. 3. Slavery in the United States — Extension to the territories. I. T.*
E420.R24   329/.023/73061   79-111514   ISBN:0813112222

E421 – 423   Taylor, 1849 – 1850

Dyer, Brainerd, 1901-   **III. 5629**
Zachary Taylor. New York, Barnes & Noble [1967, c1946] viii, 455 p. illus., maps, ports. 22 cm. (Southern biography series) *1. Taylor, Zachary, Pres. U.S., 1784-1850. (S)*
E422.D995 1967   973.6/3/0924 (B)   67-16626

Hamilton, Holman.   **III. 5630**
Zachary Taylor. Hamden, Conn., Archon Books, 1966 [c1941-51] 2 v. illus.,

facsim., maps, ports. 23 cm. *1. Taylor, Zachary, Pres. U.S., 1784-1850.*
E422.H32   973.630924   66-25183

Hamilton, Holman.　　　　　　　　　　　　　　　　　　**III. 5631**
Prologue to conflict, the crisis and Compromise of 1850. [Lexington] University of Kentucky Press [1964] viii, 236 p. maps. 23 cm. *1. Compromise of 1850. 2. U.S. — Politics and government — 1849-1861. I. T.*
E423.H2   973.7113   64-13999

Smith, Theodore Clarke, 1870-　　　　　　　　　　　　**III. 5632**
Parties and slavery, 1850-1859, by Theodore Clarke Smith ... New York and London, Harper & Brothers, 1906. xvi, 341 p. front. (port.) maps (part double) 22 cm. (The American nation: a history v.18) Series title also at head of t.-p. "Critical essay on authorities": p. [305]-324. *1. U.S. — Politics and government — 1849-1861. 2. Slavery in the U.S.*
E423.S6x (E178.A54 vol. 18)   06-42362

E431 – 435   Pierce, 1853 – 1857

Malin, James Claude, 1893-　　　　　　　　　　　　　**III. 5633**
The Nebraska question, 1852-1854. Lawrence, Kan. [1953] 455 p. 22 cm. "This book, although designed to stand ... as a self-contained work, is, at the same time, an integral unit in the larger project of [the author's] Grassland historical studies." *1. Kansas-Nebraska bill. I. T.*
E433.M34   973.66   54-16070

Ray, Perley Orman, 1875-　　　　　　　　　　　　　　**III. 5634**
The repeal of the Missouri compromise, its origin and authorship, by P. Orman Ray. Boston, J. S. Canner, 1965. 315 p. 24 cm. First published in 1909. "Edition limited to 500 copies printed." *1. Missouri compromise. 2. U.S. — Politics and government — 1853-1857. 3. Kansas-Nebraska bill. I. T.*
E433.Rx   973.66   66-6229

Rawley, James A.　　　　　　　　　　　　　　　　　　**III. 5635**
Race & politics; "bleeding Kansas" and the coming of the Civil War, by James A. Rawley. [1st ed.] Philadelphia, Lippincott [1969] xvi, 304 p. map. 21 cm. (Critical periods of history) *1. United States — History — Civil War — Causes. 2. Kansas — Politics and government — 1854-1861. 3. United States — Race question. I. T.*
E433.R25   978.1/02   73-85110

E436 – 440   Buchanan, 1857 – 1861

Foner, Eric.　　　　　　　　　　　　　　　　　　　　**III. 5636**
Free soil, free labor, free men: the ideology of the Republican Party before the Civil War. New York, Oxford University Press, 1970. xii, 353 p. 24 cm. A revision of the author's thesis, Columbia University. *1. Republican Party. 2. United States — Politics and government — 1849-1861. 3. United States — History — Civil War — Causes. I. T.*
E436.F6 1970   329.6   70-97024

Nichols, Roy Franklin, 1896-　　　　　　　　　　　　**III. 5637**
The disruption of American democracy. New York, Macmillan Co., 1948. xviii, 612 p. illus., ports. 22 cm. *1. Democratic Party — History. 2. U.S. — Politics and government — 1857-1861. I. T.*
E436.N56   973.66   48-6344

Klein, Philip Shriver, 1909-　　　　　　　　　　　　**III. 5638**
President James Buchanan, a biography. University Park, Pennsylvania State University Press [1962] xviii, 506 p. illus., ports. 24 cm. *1. Buchanan, James, Pres. U.S., 1791-1868.*
E437.K53   923.173   62-12623

Crenshaw, Ollinger, 1904-　　　　　　　　　　　　　**III. 5639**
The slave states in the presidential election of 1860. Baltimore, Johns Hopkins Press, 1945. 332 p., 1 l. 23 cm. "Reprinted from the Johns Hopkins university studies in historical and political science, series LXIII, no. 3." Vita. *1. Presidents — U.S. — Election — 1860. 2. U.S. — Politics and government — 1857-1861. 3. Southern states — Politics and government — 1775-1865. I. T.*
E440.C88   973.68   A46-6218

Fite, Emerson David, 1874-1953.　　　　　　　　　　**III. 5640**
The presidential campaign of 1860. Port Washington, N.Y., Kennikat Press [1967, c1911] xiii, 356 p. 23 cm. *1. U.S. — Politics and government — 1857-1861. 2. Presidents — U.S. — Election — 1860. I. T.*
E440.F54 1967   329/.01/0973   67-27597

Luthin, Reinhard Henry, 1905-　　　　　　　　　　　**III. 5641**
The first Lincoln campaign, by Reinhard H. Luthin. Cambridge, Mass., Harvard University Press, 1944. viii, 328 p. 23 cm. Without thesis note. Another issue. Thesis note on cover. Vita on label mounted on p. 328. *1. Lincoln, Abraham, pres. U.S. — Political career before 1861. 2. Presidents — U.S. — Election — 1860. 3. U.S. — Politics and government — 1857-1861. I. T.*
E440.L85   973.7   A44-5189

Dumond, Dwight Lowell, 1895-　　　　　　　　　　　**III. 5642**
The secession movement, 1860-1861. New York, Octagon Books, 1963 [c1931] vi, 294 p. 21 cm. *1. Secession. 2. U.S. — Politics and government — 1857-1861. I. T.*
E440.5.D88 1963   973.713   63-20889

Dumond, Dwight Lowell, 1895- ed.　　　　　　　　　**III. 5643**
Southern editorials on secession. Gloucester, Mass., P. Smith, 1964 [c1931] xxxiii, 529 p. 21 cm. At head of title: The American Historical Association. *1. Secession. 2. U.S. — Politics and government — 1857-1861. I. American Historical Association. II. Editorials on secession. III. T.*
E440.5.D89 1964   973.713   64-3910

Gunderson, Robert Gray.　　　　　　　　　　　　　　**III. 5644**
Old gentlemen's convention; the Washington Peace Conference of 1861. Madison, University of Wisconsin Press, 1961. xiii, 168 p. illus., ports. 23 cm. *1. Washington, D.C. Peace Conference, 1861. 2. U.S. — Politics and government — 1857-1861. I. T.*
E440.5.G965   973.71   61-10690

Perkins, Howard Cecil, ed.　　　　　　　　　　　　　**III. 5645**
Northern editorials on secession, edited by Howard Cecil Perkins. New York, Appleton-Century [c1942] 2 v. 23 cm. At head of title: The American historical association. "Prepared and published under the direction of the American Historical Association from the income of the Albert J. Beveridge memorial fund." *1. U.S. — Politics and government — 1857-1861. 2. Secession. 3. U.S. — History — Civil war — Causes. I. American historical association. Albert J. Beveridge memorial fund. II. T.*
E440.5.P45   973.68   42-2297

Potter, David Morris.　　　　　　　　　　　　　　　　**III. 5646**
Lincoln and his party in the secession crisis, by David M. Potter. New Haven, Yale University Press; London, H. Milford, Oxford University Press, 1942. x, 408 p. 23 cm. (Yale historical publications. Studies, 13) "In an earlier form, this study was submitted as a doctoral dissertation at Yale [1940]" "Published under the direction of the Department of History from the income of the Frederick John Kingsbury memorial fund." *1. Lincoln, Abraham, pres. U.S., 1809-1865. 2. Republican party. 3. U.S. — Politics and government — 1857-1861. I. Yale university. Frederick John Kingsbury Memorial Fund. II. T.*
E440.5.P856   973.71   A42-4321

Stampp, Kenneth Milton.　　　　　　　　　　　　　　**III. 5647**
And the war came; the North and the secession crisis, 1860-1861. [Baton Rouge] Louisiana State University Press [1950] viii, 331 p. illus., ports. 24 cm. *1. U.S. — Politics and government — 1857-1861. 2. Secession. I. T.*
E440.5.S78   973.713   50-9835

Wooster, Ralph A.　　　　　　　　　　　　　　　　　**III. 5648**
The secession conventions of the South. Princeton, N.J., Princeton University Press, 1962. viii, 294 p. maps. 23 cm. *1. Secession. 2. U.S. — Politics and government — 1857-1861. I. T.*
E440.5.W9   973.713   62-7046

E441 – 453   SLAVERY. ANTI-SLAVERY MOVEMENTS

Davis, David Brion.　　　　　　　　　　　　　　　　　**III. 5649**
The slave power conspiracy and the paranoid style. Baton Rouge, Louisiana State University Press [1970, c1969] ix, 97 p. 23 cm. (The Walter Lynwood Fleming lectures in Southern history) *1. United States — Politics and government — 1815-1861. 2. Abolitionists. 3. Southern States — Politics and government — 1775-1865. I. T. (S:Louisiana. State University and Agricultural and Mechanical College. Walter Lynwood Fleming lectures in Southern history.)*
E441.D25   322/.4   79-96257   ISBN:0807109223

Donnan, Elizabeth, 1883-1955, ed.　　　　　　　　　**III. 5650**
Documents illustrative of the history of the slave trade to America. New York, Octagon Books, 1965. 4 v. fold map. 27 cm. *1. Slave trade — U.S. — History — Sources. 2. Slave trade — History — Sources. I. T.*
E441.D69   326.10973   65-15753

Drake, Thomas Edward, 1907-　　　　　　　　　　　　**III. 5651**
Quakers and slavery in America, by Thomas E. Drake. Gloucester, Mass., P. Smith, 1965 [c1950] viii, 245 p. 21 cm. *1. Slavery and the church — Friends, Society of. 2. Slavery in the U.S. — Anti-slavery movements. I. T.*
E441.D75 1965   326.973   65-3504

Du Bois, William Edward Burghardt, 1868-1963.　　　**III. 5652**
The suppression of the African slave-trade to the United States of America, 1638-1870. New York, Schocken Books [1969] xxxvi, 335 p. 21 cm. (Sourcebooks in Negro history) A reprint of the 1896 ed. with a new introd.

by A. Norman Klein, and the "Apologia" of the author, dated 1954. *1. Slave-trade — United States. I. T.*
E441.D81 1969   380.1/44/0973   69-20337

Duignan, Peter.   III. 5653
The United States and the African slave trade, 1619-1862, by Peter Duignan and Clarence Clendenen. [Stanford, Calif.] Hoover Institution on War, Revolution, and Peace, Stanford University, 1963. vii, 72 p. 23 cm. (Hoover Institution studies) *1. Slave trade — U.S. I. Clendenen, Clarence Clemens, joint author. II. T. (S)*
E441.D83   326.1   63-22310

Dumond, Dwight Lowell, 1895-   III. 5654
Antislavery; the crusade for freedom in America. Ann Arbor, University of Michigan Press [1961] x, 422 p. illus., ports, maps, facsims. 29 cm. *1. Slavery in the U.S. — Antislavery movements.*
E441.D84   326.973   61-5937
D891a

Jenkins, William Sumner, 1902-   III. 5655
Pro-slavery thought in the Old South. Gloucester, Mass., P. Smith, 1960 [c1935] 381 p. 21 cm. *1. Slavery — Justification. 2. Slavery in the U.S. 3. Slavery in the U.S. — Anti-slavery movements. I. T.*
E441.J46 1960   326.975   60-52213

Phillips, Ulrich Bonnell, 1877-1934.   III. 5656
American Negro slavery; a survey of the supply, employment and control of Negro labor as determined by the plantation regime. [1st paperback ed.] Baton Rouge, Louisiana State University Press [1966] xxi, 529 p. 22 cm. (Louisiana paperbacks, L9) *1. Slavery in the United States — Economic aspects. 2. Southern States — Economic conditions. 3. Slave labor. 4. Plantation life — Southern States. I. T.*
E441.P549 1966   301.45/22/0973   66-31730

Stampp, Kenneth Milton.   III. 5657
The peculiar institution; slavery in the ante-bellum South, by Kenneth M. Stampp. New York, Vintage Books [1964, c1956] xi, 435, xiii p. 19 cm. *1. Slavery in the United States — Economic aspects — Southern States. I. T.*
E441.S8 1956b   301.45/22/0975   77-18363

Starobin, Robert S.   III. 5658
Industrial slavery in the Old South [by] Robert S. Starobin. New York, Oxford University Press, 1970. xiii, 320 p. illus. 22 cm. *1. Slavery in the United States — Southern States. 2. Southern States — Economic conditions. I. T.*
E441.S83   301.45/22/0975   72-112894

Weinstein, Allen, comp.   III. 5659
American Negro slavery; a modern reader. Edited by Allen Weinstein and Frank Otto Gatell. New York, Oxford University Press, 1968. viii, 366 p. 21 cm. *1. Slavery in the United States. — History — Addresses, essays, lectures. I. Gatell, Frank Otto, joint comp. II. T.*
E441.W42 1968   326/.0973   68-18567

Bancroft, Frederic, 1860-1945.   III. 5660
Slave trading in the Old South. Introd. by Allan Nevins. New York, Ungar [1959] xiii, 415 p. illus., facsims. 24 cm. (American classics) *1. Slave-trade — U.S. I. T.*
E442.B21 1959   326.10975   59-10883

Genovese, Eugene D., 1930-   III. 5661
The political economy of slavery; studies in the economy & society of the slave South [by] Eugene D. Genovese. New York, Pantheon Books [1965] xiv, 304 p. 21 cm. *1. Slavery in the United States — Economic aspects — Southern States. 2. Southern States — Economic conditions. I. T.*
E442.G45   326   65-14583

E443 – 444 Slave Life. Biography

Beaumont de La Bonninière, Gustave Auguste de, 1802-1866.   III. 5662
Marie; or, Slavery in the United States: a novel of Jacksonian America. Translated from the French by Barbara Chapman. With an introd. by Alvis L. Tinnin. Stanford, Calif., Stanford University Press, 1958. 252 p. 24 cm. *1. Slavery in the U.S. — Condition of slaves. 2. U.S. — Social conditions. I. T.*
E443.B3713   326.973   58-11693

Blassingame, John W., 1940-   III. 5663
The slave community; plantation life in the antebellum South [by] John W. Blassingame. New York, Oxford University Press, 1972. xv, 262 p. illus. 23 cm. *1. Slavery in the United States — Southern States. 2. Plantation life — Southern States. I. T.*
E443.B55   917.3/06/96073075   72-77495

Elkins, Stanley M.   III. 5664
Slavery; a problem in American institutional and intellectual life [by] Stanley M. Elkins. 2d ed. Chicago, University of Chicago Press [1968] viii, 263 p. 21 cm. *1. Slavery in the United States. 2. Slavery in the United States — Condition of slaves. 3. Negroes — Social conditions — 1964- I. T.*
E443.E4 1968   326/.0973   68-7237

Lane, Ann J., 1932- comp.   III. 5665
The debate over Slavery; Stanley Elkins and his critics. Edited by Ann J. Lane. Urbana, University of Illinois Press [1971] vi, 378 p. 20 cm. (Illini books, IB-73) *1. Elkins, Stanley M. Slavery. 2. Slavery in the United States — Historiography. I. T.*
E443.E42L3   301.44/93   79-141518   ISBN:0252001575 (pbk.)

Postell, William Dosite, 1908-   III. 5666
The health of slaves on southern plantations. Baton Rouge, Louisiana State University Press [1951] xiii, 231 p. illus. 24 cm. (Louisiana State University studies. Social science series, no. 1) *1. Slavery in the U.S. — Condition of slaves. 2. Negroes — Health and hygiene. 3. Plantation life. I. T. (S)*
E443.P78   326.975   51-62974

Wade, Richard C.   III. 5667
Slavery in the cities; the South, 1820-1860 [by] Richard C. Wade. New York, Oxford University Press, 1964. x, 340 p. 22 cm. *1. Slavery in the United States — Southern States. 2. Cities and towns — Southern States. I. T.*
E443.W3   326.975   64-22366

Bibb, Henry, b. 1815.   III. 5668
Narrative of the life and adventures of Henry Bibb, an American slave. Written by himself. With an introd. by Lucius C. Matlack. 3d stereotype ed. New York, Negro Universities Press [1969] xiv, 204 p. illus., port. 23 cm. Reprint of the 1850 ed. *1. Slavery in the United States — Kentucky. I. T.*
E444.B58 1969b   301.45/22/0924 (B)   76-84686   ISBN:837112672

Federal writers' project.   III. 5669
Lay my burden down; a folk history of slavery, edited by B. A. Botkin. Chicago, Ill., University of Chicago press [1945] xxi, 285 p. front., plates. 24 cm. "A selective and integration of excerpts and complete narratives from the Slave narrative collection of the Federal writers' project." *1. Slavery in the U.S. — Condition of slaves. 2. Negroes — Biography. I. Botkin, Benjamin Albert, 1901- ed. II. T.*
E444.F26   326.973   A45-5576

Mullin, Gerald W.   III. 5670
Flight and rebellion; slave resistance in eighteenth-century Virginia [by] Gerald W. Mullin. New York, Oxford University Press, 1972. xii, 219 p. illus. 22 cm. *1. Slavery in the United States — Virginia. I. T.*
E445.V8M8   301.44/93/09755   73-173327   ISBN:0195015142

E446 – 448 History of Slavery to 1830

Adams, Alice Dana, 1864-   III. 5671
The neglected period of anti-slavery in America, 1808-1831. Gloucester, Mass., P. Smith, 1964 [c1908] xi, 307 p. 21 cm. (Radcliffe College monographs, no. 14) *1. Slavery in the U.S. — Anti-slavery movements. I. T. (S)*
E446.A21 1964   326.973   65-1236

Dillon, Merton Lynn, 1924-   III. 5672
Benjamin Lundy and the struggle for Negro freedom [by] Merton L. Dillon. Urbana, University of Illinois Press, 1966. vi, 285 p. port. 24 cm. *1. Lundy, Benjamin, 1789-1839. 2. Slavery in the United States — Anti-slavery movements. I. T.*
E446.D54   973.71140924 (B)   66-15473

Robinson, Donald L., 1936-   III. 5673
Slavery in the structure of American politics, 1765-1820 [by] Donald L. Robinson. [1st ed.] New York, Harcourt Brace Jovanovich [1970, c1971] xii, 564 p. 23 cm. (The Founding of the American Republic) *1. Slavery in the United States. 2. United States — Politics and government — Revolution. 3. United States — Politics and government — 1783-1865. I. T.*
E446.R63   326/.0973   78-117574   ISBN:0151829721

Zilversmit, Arthur.   III. 5674
The first emancipation; the abolition of slavery in the North. Chicago, University of Chicago Press [1967] x, 262 p. 23 cm. *1. Slavery in the United States — Anti-slavery movements. I. T.*
E446.Z5   301.45220973   67-15954

Apteker, Herbert, 1915-   III. 5675
American Negro slave revolts. New York, International Publishers [1963] 409 p. 21 cm. Issued also as thesis (PH.D.) Columbia University. *1. Slavery in the U.S. — Insurrections, etc. 2. Negroes — History — To 1863. I. T.*
E447.A67 1963   326.973   63-19661

Fox, Early Lee, 1890-   III. 5676
The American colonization society, 1817-1840, by Early Lee Fox. Baltimore,

Johns Hopkins, 1919. vii, 231 p. 25 cm. (Johns Hopkins university studies in historical and political science. ser. XXXVII, no. 3) Published also as thesis (PH.D.) Johns Hopkins university, 1917. *1. American colonization society. 2. Negroes — Colonization — Africa. 3. Slavery in the U.S. — Anti-slavery movements. 4. Abolitionists.*
E448.A5392 (HB.J6)   20-506

Staudenraus, P. J.   **III. 5677**
The African colonization movement, 1816-1865. New York, Columbia University Press, 1961. ix, 323 p. 25 cm. *1. Negroes — Colonization — Africa. I. American Colonization Society. II. T.*
E448.S78   326.4   61-8071

E449 – 453   1830 – 1863
E449 GENERAL WORKS, A – G

Barnes, Gilbert Hobbs.   **III. 5678**
The antislavery impulse, 1830-1844. With a new introd. by William G. McLoughlin. New York, Harcourt, Brace & World [1964] xxxv, 298 p. 21 cm. First published in 1933. *1. Slavery in the United States — Anti-slavery movements. I. T.*
E449.B264 1964   326.973   64-25327

Birney, James Gillespie, 1792-1857.   **III. 5679**
Letters of James Gillespie Birney, 1831-1857, edited by Dwight L. Dumond. New York, London, D. Appleton-Century [c1938] 2 v. ports., 2 facsim. 23 cm. At head of title: The American historical association. Paged continuously. "Prepared and published under the direction of the American historical association from the income of the Albert J. Beveridge memorial fund." "Published addresses, articles and monographs of James Gillespie Birney": vol. I, p. xxvii-xxviii. *1. Slavery in the U.S. — Controversial literature. I. Dumond, Dwight Lowell, 1895- ed. II. American historical association. Albert J. Beveridge memorial fund.*
E449.B6179   923.673   38-24538

Douglass, Frederick, 1817?-1895.   **III. 5680**
The life and writings of Frederick Douglass [by] Philip S. Foner. New York, International Publishers [1950-55] 4 v. ports. 22 cm. *1. Slavery in the U.S. — Anti-slavery movements. I. Foner, Philip Sheldon, 1910-*
E449.D736   923.673   50-7654

Douglass, Frederick, 1817?-1895.   **III. 5681**
Narrative of the life of Frederick Douglass, an American slave, written by himself. Edited by Benjamin Quarles. Cambridge, Mass., Belknap Press, 1960. xxvi, 163 p. port., map. 22 cm. (The John Harvard library) *1. Slavery in the United States — Maryland. (S)*
E449.D74905   326.92   59-11516

Quarles, Benjamin.   **III. 5682**
Frederick Douglass. With a new pref. by James M. McPherson. New York, Atheneum, 1968 [c1948] xvi, 378 p. illus., ports. 21 cm. (Studies in American Negro life. Atheneum NL4) *1. Douglass, Frederick, 1817?-1895.*
E449.D774 1968   973.8/0924 (B)   68-16416

Duberman, Martin B., ed.   **III. 5683**
The antislavery vanguard; new essays on the abolitionists, edited by Martin Duberman. Princeton, N.J., Princeton University Press, 1965. x, 508 p. 21 cm. Erratum slip inserted. *1. Abolitionists. 2. Slavery in the United States — Anti-slavery movements. I. T.*
E449.D84   973.7114   65-10824

Dumond, Dwight Lowell, 1895-   **III. 5684**
Antislavery origins of the Civil War in the United States. Foreword by Arthur Schlesinger, Jr. [Ann Arbor] University of Michigan Press [1959] 133 p. 21 cm. (Ann Arbor paperbacks, AA28) *1. Slavery in the U.S. — Anti-slavery movements. I. T.*
E449.D87 1959   326.973   59-16097

Filler, Louis, 1911-   **III. 5685**
The crusade against slavery, 1830-1860. [1st ed.] New York, Harper [1960] 318 p. illus 22 cm. (The New American nation series) *1. Slavery in the U.S. — Anti-slavery movements. I. T.*
E449.F49   326.973   60-13441

Fitzhugh, George, 1806-1881.   **III. 5686**
Cannibals all! or, Slaves without masters. Edited by C. Vann Woodward. Cambridge, Belknap Press of Harvard University Press, 1960. 264 p. 22 cm. (The John Harvard library) *1. Slavery in the U.S. — Controversial literature — 1857. 2. Slavery — Justification. 3. Labor and laboring classes. I. T.*
E449.F555 1960   326.973   60-5400

Merrill, Walter McIntosh.   **III. 5687**
Against wind and tide, a biography of Wm. Lloyd Garrison. Cambridge, Harvard University Press, 1963. xvi, 391 p. illus., ports. 24 cm. *1. Garrison, William Lloyd, 1805-1879. I. T.*
E449.G2557   923.673   63-10871

Nye, Russel Blaine, 1913-   **III. 5688**
William Lloyd Garrison and the humanitarian reformers. [1st ed.] Boston, Little, Brown [1955] 215 p. 21 cm. (The Library of American biography) *1. Garrison, William Lloyd, 1805-1879.*
E449.G2558   923.673   55-7470

Thomas, John L.   **III. 5689**
The liberator, William Lloyd Garrison, a biography. [1st ed.] Boston, Little, Brown [1963] 502 p. illus. 22 cm. *1. Garrison, William Lloyd, 1805-1879. I. T.*
E449.G26   923.673   63-8310

Lerner, Gerda, 1920-   **III. 5690**
The Grimké sisters from South Carolina; rebels against slavery. Illustrated with photos. Boston, Houghton Mifflin, 1967. xiv, 479 p. illus., facsims., ports. 22 cm. *1. Grimké, Angelina Emily, 1805-1879. 2. Grimké, Sarah Moore, 1792-1873. I. T.*
E449.G89   973.71140922   67-25218

E449 GENERAL WORKS, H – Z

Hart, Albert Bushnell, 1854-1943.   **III. 5691**
Slavery and abolition, 1831-1941. New York, Negro Universities Press [1968, c1906] xv, 360 p. maps, port. 23 cm. *1. Slavery in the United States. I. T.*
E449.H3 1968b   301.45/22/0973   68-55891

Helper, Hinton Rowan, 1829-1909.   **III. 5692**
The impending crisis of the South: how to meet it. Westport, Conn., Negro Universities Press [1970] 420 p. 23 cm. Reprint of the 1857 ed. *1. Slavery in the United States. 2. Slavery in the United States — Controversial literature — 1857. I. T.*
E449.H483 1970   301.44/93   73-107517   ISBN:0837137640

Howard, Warren S.   **III. 5693**
American slavers and the Federal law, 1837-1862. Berkeley, University of California Press, 1963. xii, 336 p. illus. 24 cm. *1. Slave-trade — U.S. I. T.*
E449.H8495   326.1   63-9800

Kraditor, Aileen S.   **III. 5694**
Means and ends in American abolitionism; Garrison and his critics on strategy and tactics, 1834-1850, by Aileen S. Kraditor. [New York] Pantheon Books [1969] xvi, 296 p. 22 cm. *1. Slavery in the United States — Anti-slavery movements. 2. Garrison, William Lloyd, 1805-1879. I. T.*
E449.K7   973.71/14   68-26046

Dillon, Merton Lynn, 1924-   **III. 5695**
Elijah P. Lovejoy, abolitionist editor. Urbana, University of Illinois Press, 1961. 190 p. 23 cm. *1. Lovejoy, Elijah Parish, 1802-1837.*
E449.L889D5   923.673   61-62765

McKitrick, Eric L., ed.   **III. 5696**
Slavery defended: the views of the Old South. Englewood Cliffs, N.J., Prentice-Hall [1963] 180 p. 21 cm. (A Spectrum book) *1. Slavery in the United States — Controversial literature. 2. Slavery in the United States — Southern States. I. T. (S)*
E449.M16   326.7   63-12270

Mathews, Donald G.   **III. 5697**
Slavery and Methodism; a chapter in American morality, 1780-1845, by Donald G. Mathews. Princeton, N.J., Princeton University Press, 1965. xi, 329 p. 21 cm. *1. Slavery and the church — Methodist Episcopal Church. I. T.*
E449.M428   261.8   65-17148

McPherson, James M.   **III. 5698**
The struggle for equality; abolitionists and the Negro in the Civil War and Reconstruction, by James M. McPherson. Princeton, N.J., Princeton University Press, 1964. ix, 474 p. illus. 25 cm. *1. Abolitionists. 2. Slavery in the U.S. — Emancipation. 3. Negroes — History. I. T.*
E449.M476   973.7   63-23411

Bartlett, Irving H.   **III. 5699**
Wendell Phillips, Brahmin radical. Boston, Beacon Press [1961] 438 p. 21 cm. *1. Phillips, Wendell, 1811-1884.*
E449.P5594   923.673   61-10570

Quarles, Benjamin.   **III. 5700**
Black abolitionists. New York, Oxford University Press [1969] x, 310 p. 22 cm. *1. Abolitionists. 2. Slavery in the United States — Anti-slavery movements. I. T.*
E449.Q17   69-17766

Richards, Leonard L.   **III. 5701**
Gentlemen of property and standing; anti-abolition mobs in Jacksonian America [by] Leonard L. Richards. New York, Oxford University Press, 1970. ix, 196 p. illus. 22 cm. *1. Slavery in the United States — Anti-slavery movements. 2. Mobs. I. T.*
E449.R5   322/.4   74-93862

Savage, William Sherman. III. 5702
The controversy over the distribution of abolition literature, 1830-1860, by W. Sherman Savage. [Washington, D.C.] The Association for the Study of Negro Life and History, 1938. xv, 141 p. 24 cm. *1. Slavery in the U.S. — Anti-slavery movements. 2. Slavery in the U.S. — Controversial literature. I. Association for the study of Negro life and history, inc. II. T.*
E449.S257   326.4   39-2080

Sorin, Gerald, 1940- III. 5703
Abolitionism: a new perspective. Foreword by James P. Shenton. New York, Praeger [1972] 187 p. 21 cm. (New perspectives in American history) *1. Slavery in the United States — Anti-slavery movements. 2. Abolitionists. I. T.*
E449.S697 1972   322.4/4/0973   79-143981

Stowe, Harriet Elizabeth (Beecher) 1811-1896. III. 5704
The key to Uncle Tom's cabin. New York, Arno Press, 1968. viii, 508 p. 22 cm. (The American Negro, his history and literature) Reprint of the 1854 ed. *1. Stowe, Harriet Elizabeth (Beecher) 1811-1896. Uncle Tom's cabin. 2. Slavery in the United States. — Condition of slaves. I. T. (S)*
E449.S89592 1968b   813/.3   69-19634

Wyatt-Brown, Bertram, 1932- III. 5705
Lewis Tappan and the evangelical war against slavery. Cleveland, Press of Case Western Reserve University, 1969. xxi, 376 p. port. 24 cm. *1. Tappan, Lewis, 1788-1873. 2. Slavery in the United States — Anti-slavery movements. I. T.*
E449.T18W9   326/.0924   68-19228   ISBN:829501460

Ten Broek, Jacobus. III. 5706
Equal under law [by] Jacobus ten Broek. New, enl. ed. New York, Collier Books [1965] 352 p. 18 cm. First ed. published in 1951 under title: The antislavery origins of the Fourteenth amendment. *1. Abolitionists. 2. United States. Constitution. 14th amendment. I. T.*
E449.T4 1965   342.7309   64-24351

Trefousse, Hans Louis. III. 5707
The radical Republicans; Lincoln's vanguard for racial justice [by] Hans L. Trefousse. [1st ed.] New York, Knopf, 1969 [c1968] xiv, 492, xviii p. illus., ports. 22 cm. *1. Slavery in the United States — Anti-slavery movements. 2. Republican Party. I. T.*
E449.T79   973.71   68-23937

Thomas, Benjamin Platt, 1902- III. 5708
Theodore Weld, crusader for freedom. New Brunswick, Rutgers University Press, 1950. xii, 307 p. port. 22 cm. *1. Weld, Theodore Dwight, 1803-1895. I. T.*
E449.W46   923.673   50-9667

E450 – 453   SPECIAL TOPICS

Gara, Larry. III. 5709
The liberty line; the legend of the Underground Railroad. Lexington, University of Kentucky Press [1961] ix, 201 p. 24 cm. *1. Underground railroad. 2. Slavery in the U.S. — Fugitive slaves. I. T.*
E450.G22   973.7115   61-6552

Oates, Stephen B. III. 5710
To purge this land with blood; a biography of John Brown [by] Stephen B. Oates. [1st ed.] New York, Harper & Row [1970] xii, 434 p. illus., maps, ports. 25 cm. *1. Brown, John, 1800-1859. I. T.*
E451.O17 1970   973.68/0924 (B)   77-95979

Villard, Oswald Garrison, 1872-1949. III. 5711
John Brown, 1800-1859; a biography fifty years after. Gloucester, Mass., P. Smith, 1965 [i.e. 1966, c1910] xiv, 738 p. facsims., map, plates, ports. 21 cm. *1. Brown, John, 1800-1859. I. T.*
E451.V72 1966   973.680924 (B)   66-2893

Franklin, John Hope, 1915- III. 5712
The Emancipation proclamation. [1st ed.] Garden City, N.Y., Doubleday, 1963. 181 p. illus. 22 cm. *1. Emancipation proclamation.*
E453.F8   973.714   63-8296

E456 – 665   Civil War Period (1861 – 1865)
E456 – 459   LINCOLN

Hendrick, Burton Jesse, 1870-1949. III. 5713
Lincoln's war cabinet. Garden City, N.Y., Dolphin Books [1961, c1946] 559 p. 18 cm. *1. Lincoln, Abraham, Pres. U.S., 1809-1865. 2. Cabinet officers — U.S. 3. U.S. — Politics and government — Civil War. I. T.*
E456.H4 1961   64-2815

Hesseltine, William Best, 1902- III. 5714
Lincoln's plan of reconstruction. Tuscaloosa, Ala., Confederate Pub. Co., 1960. 154 p. 22 cm. (Confederate centennial studies, no. 13) "Four hundred and fifty copies ... printed." *1. Lincoln, Abraham, Pres. U.S., 1809-1865. 2. U.S. — Politics and government — Civil War. 3. Reconstruction. (S)*
E456.H43   973.7   60-1606

Luthin, Reinhard Henry, 1905-1962. III. 5715
The real Abraham Lincoln; a complete one volume history of his life and times. Englewood Cliffs, N.J., Prentice-Hall [1960] 778 p. 24 cm. *1. Lincoln, Abraham, Pres. U.S., 1809-1865. I. T.*
E456.L8   923.173   60-13048

Stephenson, Nathaniel Wright, 1867-1935. III. 5716
Abraham Lincoln and the union; a chronicle of the embattled North, by Nathaniel W. Stephenson. New Haven, Yale University Press; [etc., etc.] 1921. xiii, 272 p. col. front. 18 cm. (The Chronicles of America series, [v.29]) "Textbook edition." *1. Lincoln, Abraham, pres. U.S., 1809-1865. 2. U.S. — History — Civil war. 3. U.S. — Politics and government — Civil war. 4. U.S. — Politics and government — 1849-1861. I. T.*
E456.S832 (E173.C vol. 29)   A23-820

E457 – 457.9   Biography of Lincoln

Angle, Paul McClelland, 1900- ed. III. 5717
The Lincoln reader, edited, with an introduction, by Paul M. Angle. New Brunswick, Rutgers University Press, 1947. xii, 564 p. plates, ports., facsims. 22 1/2 cm. "A biography written by sixty-five authors." — Foreword. *1. Lincoln, Abraham, pres. U.S., 1809-1865. I. T.*
E457.A58   923.173   47-30067

Charnwood, Godfrey Rathbone Benson, baron, 1864-1945. III. 5718
Abraham Lincoln, by Lord Charnwood. London, Constable, 1916. viii, 479 p. port., fold. map. 23 cm. (Makers of the nineteenth century.) On spine: 1st English ed. *1. Lincoln, Abraham, pres. U.S., 1809-1865. I. Williams, Basil, 1867- ed.*
E457.C475   16-20529

Current, Richard Nelson. III. 5719
The Lincoln nobody knows. New York, Hill and Wang [1963, c1958] vi, 314 p. 21 cm. (American century series) "AC59." *1. Lincoln, Abraham, Pres. U.S., 1809-1865. I. T.*
E457.C96 1963   63-6069

Quarles, Benjamin. III. 5720
Lincoln and the Negro. New York, Oxford University Press, 1962. 275 p. illus. 21 cm. *1. Lincoln, Abraham, Pres. U.S., 1809-1865. — Relations with Negroes. 2. Lincoln, Abraham, Pres. U.S., 1809-1865. — Views on slavery. I. T.*
E457.Q3   923.173   62-9829

Randall, James Garfield, 1881- III. 5721
Lincoln and the South [by] J. G. Randall. Baton Rouge, Louisiana State University Press, 1946. viii, 161 p. ports., facsims. 21 cm. (The Walter Lynwood Fleming lectures in southern history, Louisiana state university) *1. Lincoln, Abraham, pres. U.S., 1809-1865. 2. Southern states — Politics and government — 1775-1865. I. T.*
E457.R18   923.173   46-3035

Randall, James Garfield, 1881-1953. III. 5722
Lincoln, the President. New York, Dodd, Mead, 1945-55. 4 v. illus., ports., maps, facsims. 25 cm. (American political leaders) Vol.4 by J. G. Randall and R. N. Current. *1. Lincoln, Abraham, Pres. U.S., 1809-1865. I. T. (S)*
E457.R2   923.173   45-10041

Thomas, Benjamin Platt, 1902- III. 5723
Abraham Lincoln, a biography. [1st ed.] New York, Knopf, 1952. xiv, 548. xii p. illus., ports., maps. 22 cm. Another issue. 25cm. "Five hundred copies ... printed on all-rag paper with the Borzoi water-mark, each ... signed by the author ... under 500." E457.T427 1952a *1. Lincoln, Abraham, Pres. U.S., 1809-1865.*
E457.T427 1952   923.173   52-6425

Thomas, Benjamin Platt, 1902- III. 5724
Portrait for posterity: Lincoln and his biographers; illus. by Romaine Proctor. New Brunswick, Rutgers Univ. Press, 1947. xvii, 329 p. ports. 21 cm. *1. Lincoln, Abraham, Pres. U.S., 1809-1865. 2. Lincoln, Abraham, Pres. U.S. — Bibliography. I. T.*
E457.T43   923.173   47-30758

III. 5725 United States **E457.15**

Mitgang, Herbert, ed.   **III. 5725**
Lincoln as they saw him, edited and narrated by Herbert Mitgang. New York, Rinehart [1956] xv, 519 p. illus., ports. 24 cm. *1. Lincoln, Abraham, Pres. U.S., 1809-1865. 1. T.*
E457.15.M5   923.173   56-10181

Randall, Ruth (Painter)   **III. 5726**
Lincoln's sons. [1st ed.] Boston, Little, Brown [1955] 373 p. illus. 23 cm. Another issue. Heritage ed. "Autographed by the author for members of the Civil War Book Club." E457.25.R26 1955a *1. Lincoln, Abraham, Pres. U.S. — Family. 1. T.*
E457.25.R26   923.173   56-5046

Randall, Ruth (Painter)   **III. 5727**
Mary Lincoln; biography of a marriage. [1st ed.] Boston, Little, Brown [c1953] xiv, 555 p. illus., ports. 23 cm. *1. Lincoln, Mary (Todd) 1818-1882.*
E457.25.R3   920.7   52-12621

Sandburg, Carl, 1878-   **III. 5728**
Mary Lincoln, wife and widow; part I, by Carl Sandburg; part II, letters, documents & appendix, by Paul M. Angle. New York, Harcourt, [c1932] xii, 357 p. front., illus., plates, ports., facsims. 22 cm. "Acknowledgments and sources": p. v-viii. Second printing <first trade edition> November, 1932." *1. Lincoln, Mary (Todd) Mrs., 1818-1882. I. Angle, Paul McClelland, 1900-*
E457.25.S262   32-34498

Baringer, William Eldon, 1909-   **III. 5729**
Lincoln's rise to power. Boston, Little, Brown, 1937. St. Clair Shores, Mich., Scholarly Press, 1971. xi, 373 p. illus., facsim., ports. 22 cm. "First edition." *1. Lincoln, Abraham, Pres. U.S. — Political career before 1861. 2. Republic Party. National Convention. 2d, Chicago, 1860. I. T.*
E457.3.B24 1971   973.7/0924   75-144866   ISBN:0403008530

Beveridge, Albert Jeremiah, 1862-1927.   **III. 5730**
Abraham Lincoln, 1809-1858. Boston, Houghton Mifflin, 1928. St. Clair Shores, Mich., Scholarly Press, 1971. 2 v. illus., ports. 22 cm. *1. Lincoln, Abraham, Pres. U.S., 1809-1865.*
E457.3.B576 1971   973.7/0924 (B)   73-144879   ISBN:0403008654

Fehrenbacher, Don Edward, 1920-   **III. 5731**
Prelude to greatness; Lincoln in the 1850's. Stanford, Calif., Stanford University Press, 1962. 205 p. 23 cm. *1. Lincoln, Abraham, Pres. U.S., 1809-1865. I. T.*
E457.3.F4   923.173   62-8661

Sandburg, Carl, 1878-   **III. 5732**
Abraham Lincoln, the prairie years, by Carl Sandburg; with 105 illustrations from photographs, and many cartoons, sketches, maps, and letters ... New York, Harcourt, Brace [1927] 2 v. fronts., illus. (incl. maps) plates, ports., facsims. 24 cm. *1. Lincoln, Abraham, pres. U.S., 1809-1865.*
E457.3.S226   28-5762

Jaffa, Harry V.   **III. 5733**
Crisis of the house divided; an interpretation of the issues in the Lincoln-Douglas debates. [1st ed.] Garden City, N.Y., Doubleday, 1959. 451 p. 22 cm. *1. Lincoln, Abraham, Pres. U.S. — Political career before 1861. 2. Douglas, Stephen Arnold, 1813-1861. 3. Lincoln-Douglas debates, 1858. I. T.*
E457.4.J32   973.68   59-10671

Lincoln, Abraham, Pres. U.S., 1809-1865.   **III. 5734**
Created equal? The complete Lincoln-Douglas debates of 1858. Edited and with an introd. by Paul M. Angle. [Chicago] University of Chicago Press [1958] xxxiii, 421 p. ports., map (on lining papers) 24 cm. *1. U.S. — Politics and government — 1857-1861. I. Douglas, Stephen Arnold, 1813-1861. II. T.*
E457.4.L77   973.68   58-6885

Riddle, Donald Wayne, 1894-   **III. 5735**
Congressman Abraham Lincoln. Urbana, University of Illinois Press, 1957. vii, 280 p. 24 cm. *1. Lincoln, Abraham, Pres. U.S. — Political career before 1861. I. T.*
E457.4.R5   923.173   57-6956

Sandburg, Carl, 1878-1967.   **III. 5736**
Abraham Lincoln; the war years, by Carl Sandburg. With 414 half-tones of photographs and 249 cuts of cartoons, letters, documents ... New York, Harcourt, Brace [c1939] 4 v. illus., facsims., maps, plates, ports. 25 cm. *1. Lincoln, Abraham, pres. U.S., 1809-1865. 2. U.S. — History — Civil war.*
E457.4.S36   923.173   39-27998

Donald, David Herbert, 1920-   **III. 5737**
Lincoln reconsidered; essays on the Civil War era. [1st ed.] New York, Knopf, 1956. 200 p. 20 cm. Another issue. Documentary ed. "Autographed by the author for the members of the Civil War Book Club." E457.D69 1956a *1. Lincoln, Abraham, Pres. U.S. — Addresses, sermons, etc. 2. U.S. — History — Civil War — Addresses, sermons, etc. I. T.*
E457.8.D69   973.704   56-5785

E457.91 – .92 Lincoln's Writings

Lincoln, Abraham, Pres. U.S., 1809-1865.   **III. 5738**
Collected works. The Abraham Lincoln Association, Springfield, Illinois. Roy P. Basler, editor; Marion Dolores Pratt and Lloyd A. Dunlap, assistant editors. New Brunswick, N.J., Rutgers University Press, 1953-55. 9 v. ports., facsims. 24 cm. *I. Basler, Roy Prentice, 1906- ed. II. Abraham Lincoln Association, Springfield, Ill.*
E457.91 1953   308.1   53-6293

Lincoln, Abraham, Pres. U.S., 1809-1865.   **III. 5739**
Abraham Lincoln, his speeches and writings. Edited with critical and analytical notes by Roy P. Basler. Pref. by Carl Sandburg. Cleveland, World Pub. Co. [1946] xxx, 843 p. ports., facsim. (1 fold.) 24 cm. Issued also with the facsim. on lining papers. *I. Basler, Roy Prentice, 1906- ed.*
E457.92 1946a   308.1   53-28573

Mearns, David Chambers, 1899-   **III. 5740**
The Lincoln papers; the story of the collection, with selections to July 4, 1861; introd. by Carl Sandburg. [1st ed.] Garden City, N.Y., Doubleday, 1948. 2 v. (xvii, 681 p.) illus., ports. 22 cm. The selections consist chiefly of letters and memoranda to Abraham Lincoln from the Robert Todd Lincoln Collection in the Library of Congress. *1. Lincoln, Abraham, Pres. U.S., 1809-1865. 2. Lincoln, Robert Todd, 1843-1926. 3. Lincoln, Abraham, Pres. U.S., 1809-1865. 4. U.S. — History — Civil War — Sources. I. U.S. Library of Congress. II. T.*
E457.92 1948   973.7   48-9019

Lincoln, Abraham, Pres. U.S., 1809-1865.   **III. 5741**
The Lincoln encyclopedia; the spoken and written words of A. Lincoln arranged for ready reference; compiled and edited by Archer H. Shaw, with an introd. by David C. Mearns. New York, Macmillan, 1950. xii, 395 p. 26 cm. *I. Shaw, Archer Hayes, 1876- ed. II. T.*
E457.92 1950   308.1   50-5351

Lincoln, Abraham, Pres. U.S., 1809-1865.   **III. 5742**
The living Lincoln: the man, his mind, his times, and the war he fought, reconstructed from his own writings. Edited by Paul M. Angle and Earl Schenck Miers. New Brunswick, N.J., Rutgers University Press, 1955. viii, 673 p. 24 cm. *I. Angle, Paul McClelland, 1900- ed. II. Miers, Earl Schenck, 1910- ed. III. T.*
E457.92 1955   923.173   55-9955

Lincoln, Abraham, Pres. U.S., 1809-1865.   **III. 5743**
The collected poetry of Abraham Lincoln. Springfield, Ill., 1971. xv, 13 p. port. 21 cm. *I. T.*
E457.92 1971b   811/.3   76-142288

E458 – 459 POLITICAL HISTORY, 1861 – 1865

Catton, William Bruce, 1926-   **III. 5744**
Two roads to Sumter, by William and Bruce Catton. New York, McGraw-Hill [1963] 285 p. 22 cm. *1. United States — History — Civil War — Causes. 2. United States — Politics and government — 1849-1861. 3. Lincoln, Abraham, Pres. U.S., 1809-1865. 4. Davis, Jefferson, 1808-1889. I. Catton, Bruce, 1899- joint author. II. T.*
E458.C3   973.711   63-13930

Graebner, Norman A., ed.   **III. 5745**
Politics and the crisis of 1860 [by] William E. Baringer [and others] Urbana, University of Illinois Press, 1961. xii, 156 p. 21 cm. "Five essays ... presented originally at the Fourth Annual Civil War Conference at Gettysburg College in November 1960." *1. U.S. — History — Civil War — Causes. 2. Slavery in the U.S. 3. U.S. — Politics and government — 1857-1861. I. Baringer, William Eldon, 1909- II. T.*
E458.G7   973.711   61-14350

Nevins, Allan, 1890-   **III. 5746**
The statesmanship of the Civil War. New York, Macmillan, 1953. 82 p. 22 cm. (The Page-Barbour lectures, University of Virginia, 1951) *1. Lincoln, Abraham, Pres. U.S. — Personality. 2. U.S. — Politics and government — Civil War. I. T.*
E458.N45   973.71   53-12366

Zornow, William Frank.   **III. 5747**
Lincoln & the party divided. Westport, Conn., Greenwood Press [1972, c1954] xi, 264 p. illus. 22 cm. *1. Lincoln, Abraham, Pres. U.S., 1809-1865. 2. Presidents — United States — Election — 1864. I. T.*
E458.4.Z6 1972   973.7/1   73-152619   ISBN:0837160545

Hyman, Harold Melvin, 1924-   **III. 5748**
Era of the oath; Northern loyalty tests during the Civil War and reconstruction. Philadelphia, University of Pennsylvania Press, 1954. 229 p. illus. 24 cm. *1. Loyalty oaths — U.S. 2. U.S. — History — Civil War. 3. Reconstruction. I. T.*
E458.8.H9   973.78   54-7108

Klement, Frank L.   **III. 5749**
The Copperheads in the Middle West, by Frank L. Klement. Gloucester, Mass., P. Smith, 1972 [c1960] xiii, 341 p. illus. 21 cm. *1. Copperhead (Nickname) 2. Northwest, Old — History — Civil War. I. T.*
E458.8.K67 1972   973.7/18   72-191253

Belz, Herman.   **III. 5750**
Reconstructing the Union; theory and policy during the Civil War. Ithaca, N.Y., Published for the American Historical Association [by] Cornell University Press [1969] ix, 336 p. 24 cm. *1. United States — Politics and government — Civil War. 2. Reconstruction. I. American Historical Association. II. T.*
E459.B4   973.71   68-9747

Curry, Leonard P.   **III. 5751**
Blueprint for modern America; non-military legislation of the first Civil War Congress [by] Leonard P. Curry. Nashville, Vanderbilt University Press [1968] ix, 302 p. 24 cm. *1. United States — Politics and government — Civil War. 2. United States. 37th Congress, 1861-1863. 3. Legislation — United States — History. I. T.*
E459.C96   328.73/09/034   68-10827

Rozwenc, Edwin Charles, 1915- ed.   **III. 5752**
The causes of the American Civil War. Boston, Heath [1961] 233 p. 24 cm. (Problems in American civilization) *1. U.S. — History — Civil War — Causes. I. T.*
E459.R59   973.711   61-985

Williams, Thomas Harry, 1909-   **III. 5753**
Lincoln and the radicals [by] T. Harry Williams. [Madison] The University of Wisconsin Press [c1941] 413 p. illus., ports. 23 cm. *1. Lincoln, Abraham, pres. U.S., 1809-1865. 2. U.S. — Politics and government — Civil War. I. T.*
E459.W5   973.7   41-53088

E461 – 665   CIVIL WAR, 1861 – 1865

Dearing, Mary Rulkotter.   **III. 5754**
Veterans in politics; the story of the G. A. R. Baton Rouge, Louisiana State University Press [1952] x, 523 p. illus., ports. 24 cm. *1. Grand Army of the Republic. 2. U.S. — Politics and government. I. T.*
E462.1.A19D4   369.151   52-14879

Commager, Henry Steele, 1902- ed.   **III. 5755**
The Blue and the Gray; the story of the Civil War as told by participants. Indianapolis, Bobbs-Merrill [c1950] xxxviii, 1201 p. illus., maps. 24 cm. *1. U.S. — History — Civil War — Personal narratives. I. T.*
E464.C62   973.78   56-16536

Hesseltine, William Best, 1902- ed.   **III. 5756**
The tragic conflict; the Civil War and reconstruction. Selected and edited with introd. and notes by William B. Hesseltine. New York, G. Braziller, 1962. 528 p. 25 cm. (The American epochs series) *1. U.S. — History — Civil War — Sources. 2. Reconstruction. I. T.*
E464.H4   973.7   62-9693

E467 – 467.1   Biography

Hesseltine, William Best, 1902-1963.   **III. 5757**
Confederate leaders in the New South. Westport, Conn., Greenwood Press [1970, c1950] xi, 146 p. 23 cm. *1. Confederate States of America — Biography. 2. Southern States — History — 1865- I. T.*
E467.H58 1970   973.71/3   71-100230   ISBN:0837136865

Williams, Thomas Harry, 1909-   **III. 5758**
McClellan, Sherman, and Grant. New Brunswick, N.J., Rutgers University Press [1962] 113 p. illus. 20 cm. (The Brown and Haley lectures, 1962) *1. McClellan, George Brinton, 1826-1885. 2. Sherman, William Tecumseh, 1820-1891. 3. Grant, Ulysses Simpson, Pres. U.S., 1822-1885.*
E467.W5   923.573   62-21246

Duberman, Martin B.   **III. 5759**
Charles Francis Adams, 1807-1886, by Martin Duberman. Stanford, Calif., Stanford University Press [c1960] xvi, 525 p. illus., ports. 23 cm. *1. Adams, Charles Francis, 1807-1886.*
E467.1.A2D8 1968   973.7/0924 (B)   68-13742

Harrington, Fred Harvey, 1912-   **III. 5760**
Fighting politician, Major General N. P. Banks. Westport, Conn., Greenwood Press [1970, c1948] xi, 301 p. maps (on lining papers), port. 23 cm. At head of title: American Historical Association. *1. Banks, Nathaniel Prentice, 1816-1894. I. American Historical Association. II. T.*
E467.1.B23H28 1970   973.7/0924   73-100228   ISBN:837130077

Williams, Thomas Harry, 1909-   **III. 5761**
P. G. T. Beauregard; Napoleon in gray. Baton Rouge, Louisiana State University Press [1955, c1954] xiii, 345 p. illus., ports., maps. 23 cm. (Southern biography series) "Critical essay on authorities": p. 330-338. Another issue. Shiloh ed. "Autographed by the author for the members of the Civil War Book Club." E467.1.B38W5 1955a *1. Beauregard, Pierre Gustave Toutant, 1818-1893. (S)*
E467.1.B38W5   923.573   55-7362

Holzman, Robert S.   **III. 5762**
Stormy Ben Butler. New York, Macmillan, 1954. 297 p. illus. 22 cm. *1. Butler, Benjamin Franklin, 1818-1893. I. T.*
E467.1.B87H6   923.273   54-12163

Deloria, Vine.   **III. 5763**
Custer died for your sins; an Indian manifesto. By Vine Deloria, Jr. [New York] Macmillan [1969] 279 p. 22 cm. *1. Custer, George Armstrong, 1839-1876. I. T.*
E467.1.C99D37   970.1   69-20405

Dodd, William Edward, 1869-1940.   **III. 5764**
Jefferson Davis. New York, Russell & Russell, 1966. 396 p. port. 23 cm. First published in 1907. *1. Davis, Jefferson, 1808-1889.*
E467.1.D26D8 1966   973.7130924 (B)   65-17888

Strode, Hudson, 1893-   **III. 5765**
Jefferson Davis. [1st ed.] New York, Harcourt, Brace [1955-64] 3 v. ports. 25 cm. *1. Davis, Jefferson, 1808-1889.*
E467.1.D26S73   923.273   64-18295

Lewis, Charles Lee, 1886-   **III. 5766**
David Glasgow Farragut, by Charles Lee Lewis. Annapolis, United States Naval Institute [1941-43] 2 v. fronts., illus. (facsim.) plates, ports., map. 24 cm. Maps on lining-papers. *1. Farragut, David Glasgow, 1801-1870. I. United States naval institute, Annapolis.*
E467.1.F23L48   923.573   41-10196

Jarrell, Hampton McNeely, 1904-   **III. 5767**
Wade Hampton and the Negro; the road not taken. Columbia, University of South Carolina Press, 1949. xi, 209 p. port. 24 cm. *1. Hampton, Wade, 1818-1902. 2. South Carolina — Politics and government — 1865- 3. Negroes — South Carolina. I. T.*
E467.1.H19J3   923.273   50-5796

Henderson, George Francis Robert, 1854-1903.   **III. 5768**
Stonewall Jackson and the American Civil War. With an introd. by Viscount Wolseley and a pref. by Walter Bedell Smith. Authorized American ed. London, New York, Longmans, Green [1961] xxvi, 737 p. ports., maps (6 fold. in pocket) plans, tables. 23 cm. "Civil War centennial edition." *1. Jackson, Thomas Jonathan, 1824-1863. 2. U.S. — History — Civil War — Campaigns and battles. I. T.*
E467.1.J15H55 1961   923.573   61-324

Vandiver, Frank Everson, 1925-   **III. 5769**
Mighty Stonewall. New York, McGraw-Hill [1957] xi, 547 p. illus., ports., maps. 24 cm. *1. Jackson, Thomas Jonathan, 1824-1863. I. T.*
E467.1.J15V3   923.573   57-7247

Fishwick, Marshall William.   **III. 5770**
Lee after the war. New York, Dodd, Mead [1963] 242 p. illus. 22 cm. *1. Lee, Robert Edward, 1807-1870. I. T.*
E467.1.L4F5   923.573   63-10239

Freeman, Douglas Southall, 1886-1953.   **III. 5771**
R. E. Lee, a biography, by Douglas Southall Freeman. New York, London, Scribner, 1934-35. 4 v. illus., plates, ports., maps, facsims. 24 cm. *1. Lee, Robert Edward, 1807-1870.*
E467.1.L4F83   923.573   34-33660

Hassler, Warren W.   **III. 5772**
General George B. McClellan, shield of the Union. [1st ed.] Baton Rouge, Louisiana State University Press [1957] 350 p. illus. 24 cm. *1. McClellan, George Brinton, 1826-1885.*
E467.1.M2H4   923.573   57-7497

Nicolay, Helen, 1866-1954.   **III. 5773**
Lincoln's secretary; a biography of John G. Nicolay. Westport, Conn., Greenwood Press [1971, c1949] x, 363 p. illus. 23 cm. *1. Nicolay, John George, 1832-1901. I. T.*
E467.1.N5N5 1971   973.7/0924 (B)   70-138169   ISBN:0837156262

Athearn, Robert G.   III. 5774
William Tecumseh Sherman and the settlement of the West. [1st ed.] Norman, University of Oklahoma Press [1956] xix, 371 p. illus., ports., maps. 25 cm. 1. Sherman, William Tecumseh, 1820-1891. 2. The West — History. I. T.
E467.1.S55A8   923.573   56-11229

Lewis, Lloyd, 1891-1949.   III. 5775
Sherman, fighting prophet. Illustrated with reproductions of maps, engravings, and photos. With a new appraisal by Bruce Catton. New York, Harcourt, Brace [1958] xviii, 690 p. illus., ports., maps. 25 cm. 1. Sherman, William Tecumseh, 1820-1891.
E467.1.S55L48 1958   923.573   58-14960

Merrill, James M.   III. 5776
William Tecumseh Sherman, by James M. Merrill. Chicago, Rand McNally [1971] 445 p. illus., ports. 24 cm. 1. Sherman, William Tecumseh, 1820-1891.
E467.1.S55M4   355.3/31/0924 (B)   78-153112

Thomas, Benjamin Platt, 1902-1956.   III. 5777
Stanton; the life and times of Lincoln's Secretary of War [by] Benjamin P. Thomas and Harold M. Hyman. [1st ed.] New York, Knopf, 1962. xvii, 642, xii p. illus., ports., facsim. 25 cm. 1. Stanton, Edwin McMasters, 1814-1869. I. Hyman, Harold Melvin, 1924- joint author.
E467.1.S8T45   923.273   61-17829

Von Abele, Rudolph Radama, 1922-   III. 5778
Alexander H. Stephens, a biography, by Rudolph von Abele. Westport, Conn., Negro Universities Press [1971, c1946] xiii, 337, x p. ports. 23 cm. Originally presented as the author's thesis, Columbia, 1946. 1. Stephens, Alexander Hamilton, 1812-1883. I. T.
E467.1.S85V6 1971   973.7/13/0924 (B)   74-135614
ISBN:0837152011

McKinney, Francis F., 1891-   III. 5779
Education in violence; the life of George H. Thomas and the history of the Army of the Cumberland. Detroit, Wayne State University Press, 1961. 530 p. illus. 25 cm. 1. Thomas, George Henry, 1816-1870. 2. U.S. Army. Dept. of the Cumberland. 3. U.S. — History — Civil War — Regimental histories — Dept. of the Cumberland. I. T.
E467.1.T4M17   923.573   61-6040

E468 – 468.9 General Histories

Boatner, Mark Mayo, 1921-   III. 5780
The Civil War dictionary. Maps and diagrs. by Allen C. Northrop and Lowell L. Miller. New York, D. McKay Co. [1959] xvi, 974 p. illus., maps. 22 cm. 1. U.S. — History — Civil War — Dictionaries. I. T.
E468.B7   973.703   59-12267

Catton, Bruce, 1899-   III. 5782
America goes to war. [1st ed.] Middletown, Conn., Wesleyan University Press [1958] 126 p. illus. 21 cm. 1. U.S. — History — Civil War. I. T.
E468.C28   973.7   58-13602

Catton, Bruce, 1899-   III. 5783
The centennial history of the Civil War. E. B. Long, director of research. [1st ed.] Garden City, N.Y., Doubleday, 1961-65. 3 v. col. illus., col. maps. 25 cm. 1. U.S. — History — Civil War. I. The coming fury. II. Terrible swift sword. III. Never call retreat. IV. T.
E468.C29   973.7   61-12502

Catton, Bruce, 1899-   III. 5784
This hallowed ground; the story of the Union side of the Civil War. [1st ed.] Garden City, N.Y., Doubleday, 1956. ix, 437 p. maps. 25 cm. (Mainstream of America series) 1. U.S. — History — Civil War. I. T.
E468.C3   973.7   56-5960
C297

Donald, David Herbert, 1920- ed.   III. 5785
Why the North won the Civil War. Essays by Richard N. Current [and others. Baton Rouge] Louisiana State University Press [1960] 128 p. 23 cm. 1. Confederate States of America — History — Addresses, essays, lectures. 2. U.S. — History — Civil War — Addresses, essays, lectures. I. Current, Richard Nelson. II. T.
E468.D65   973.7   60-13170

Fuller, John Frederick Charles, 1878-   III. 5786
Grant & Lee, a study in personality and generalship. Bloomington, Indiana University Press, 1957. 323 p. illus. 21 cm. (Civil War centennial series) 1. Grant, Ulysses Simpson, Pres. U.S., 1822-1885. 2. Lee, Robert Edward, 1807-1870. 3. U.S. — History — Civil War. 4. U.S. — History — Civil War — Campaigns and battles. I. T.
E468.F96 1957   973.7   57-10723

Lonn, Ella, 1879-   III. 5787
Desertion during the civil war, by Ella Lonn. New York, London, Century Co. [c1928] vii, 251 p. fold. map. 23 cm. At head of title: The American historical association. "Published from a fund contributed to the American historical association by the Carnegie corporation of New York." 1. U.S. — History — Civil war. 2. Desertion, Military. I. American historical association. II. T.
E468.L86   29-770

McMaster, John Bach, 1852-1932.   III. 5788
Our house divided; a history of the people of the United States during Lincoln's administration. With an introd. by Philip Van Doren Stern. Greenwich, Conn., Fawcett Publications [1961] 639 p. illus. 19 cm. (Premier Civil War classics) "Originally published ... under the title A history of the people of the United States during Lincoln's administration." 1. U.S. — History — Civil War. I. T.
E468.M17 1961   973.7   61-1121

Nevins, Allan, 1890-   III. 5789
The War for the Union. New York, Scribner [1959-1971] 4 v. illus., ports., maps. 24 cm. (His The ordeal of the Union, v.5-8) 1. U.S. — History — Civil War. I. T.
E468.N43   973.7   59-3690

Randall, James Garfield, 1881-1953.   III. 5790
The Civil War and Reconstruction [by] J. G. Randall [and] David Donald. 2d ed. Boston, Heath [1961] 820 p. illus. 25 cm. 1. U.S. — History — Civil War. 2. Reconstruction. I. Donald, David Herbert, 1920- joint author. II. T.
E468.R26 1961   973.7   61-10357

Rhodes, James Ford, 1848-1927.   III. 5791
History of the Civil War, 1861-1865. Edited, with an introd., by E. B. Long. New York, Ungar [1961] 486 p. 25 cm. (American classics) 1. U.S. — History — Civil War.
E468.R47 1961   973.7   61-7087

Pressly, Thomas J.   III. 5792
Americans interpret their Civil War. With a new introd. by the author. New York, Collier Books [1962] 384 p. 18 cm. (Collier books, BS98) 1. U.S. — History — Civil War — Historiography. I. T.
E468.5.P7 1962   973.707   62-17572

Divided we fought; a pictorial history of the war, 1861-1865.   III. 5793
Picture editors: Hirst D. Milhollen and Milton Kaplan. Caption editors: Hirst D. Milhollen, Milton Kaplan, and Hulen Stuart. Author of the text and general editor: David Donald. New York, Macmillan [c1956] viii, 454 p. illus., ports. 29 cm. 1. U.S. — History — Civil War — Pictorial works. I. Milhollen, Hirst Dillon, 1906- ed. II. Kaplan, Milton, 1918- ed. III. Donald, David Herbert, 1920- ed.
E468.7.D5 1956   973.7084   56-58591

Gardner, Alexander, 1821-1882.   III. 5794
Photographic sketch book of the Civil War. New York, Dover Publications [1959] [8] p., reprint (2 v. 100 plates), [4] p. 23 x 28 cm. "An unabridged and unaltered republication of the first edition published in 1866 ... titled Gardner's photographic sketch book of the war." 1. U.S. — History — Civil War — Pictorial works. 2. Virginia — History — Civil War — Pictorial works. I. T.
E468.7.G19 1959   973.79   58-13933

Miller, Francis Trevelyan, 1877- ed.   III. 5795
The photographic history of the Civil War. Francis Trevelyan Miller, editor in chief; Robert S. Lanier, managing editor. With a new introd. by Henry Steele Commager. New York, T. Yoseloff [1957] 10 v. in 5. illus., ports., maps. 28 cm. Issued in a case. 1. U.S. — History — Civil War — Pictorial works. 2. U.S. — History — Civil War. I. Lanier, Robert Sampson, 1880- joint ed. II. T.
E468.7.M64 1957   973.7   57-2547

Fredrickson, George M., 1934-   III. 5796
The inner Civil War; northern intellectuals and the crisis of the Union [by] George M. Fredrickson. [1st ed.] New York, Harper & Row [1965] viii, 277 p. 22 cm. 1. U.S. — History — Civil War. 2. Intellectuals — U.S. I. T.
E468.9.F83   973.715   65-21013

E469 Diplomatic History

Adams, Ephraim Douglass, 1865-1930.   III. 5797
Great Britain and the American Civil War. New York, Russell & Russell [1958?] 2 v. in 1. illus. 22 cm. 1. U.S. — Foreign relations — 1861-1865. 2.

U.S. — History — Civil War — Foreign public opinion. 3. Gt. Brit. — Foreign relations — U.S. 4. U.S. — Foreign relations — Gt. Brit. I. T.
E469.A25   973.722   58-5369

Kirkland, Edward Chase, 1894- III. 5798
The peacemakers of 1864. New York, AMS Press [1969] 279 p. 23 cm. Reprint of the 1927 ed. 1. United States — History — Civil War — Peace. I. T.
E469.K57 1969   973.71/2   74-97888

Monaghan, James, 1891- III. 5799
Diplomat in carpet slippers: Abraham Lincoln deals with foreign affairs [by] Jay Monaghan. [Indianapolis] Charter Books; [distributed by the Macfadden-Bartell Corp., New York, 1962] 505 p. 21 cm. (American history library) "118." 1. Lincoln, Abraham, Pres. U.S., 1809-1865. 2. U.S. — Foreign relations — 1861-1865. I. T.
E469.Mx   973.72   64-9057

Winks, Robin W. III. 5800
Canada and the United States: the Civil War years. Baltimore, Johns Hopkins Press [1960] xviii, 430 p. 24 cm. "Originally submitted as a doctoral dissertation [Maple leaf and eagle: Canadian-American relations during the American Civil War] to the Department of History at the Johns Hopkins University, and subsequently revised and shortened." 1. U.S. — Foreign relations — 1861-1865. 2. U.S. — Foreign relations — Canada. 3. Canada — Foreign relations — U.S. I. T.
E469.W5   973.72   60-14699

Woldman, Albert A. III. 5801
Lincoln and the Russians. [1st ed.] Cleveland, World Pub. Co. [1952] 311 p. 22 cm. 1. Lincoln, Abraham, Pres. U.S., 1809-1865. 2. U.S. — Foreign relations — Russia. 3. Russia — Foreign relations — U.S. 4. U.S. — Foreign relations — 1861-1865. I. T.
E469.W6   327.730947   52-8436

E470 – 480 Military Operations. Finance

Cadwallader, Sylvanus, 1825 or 6- III. 5802
Three years with Grant, as recalled by war correspondent Sylvanus Cadwallader. Edited, and with an introd. and notes, by Benjamin P. Thomas. [1st ed.] New York, Knopf, 1955. xiv, 353, viii p. maps (1 fold.) 22 cm. Another issue. Wilderness ed. "Autographed by the editor for the members of the Civil War Book Club." E470.C14 1959a 1. Grant, Ulysses Simpson, Pres. U.S., 1822-1885. 2. U.S. — History — Civil War — Personal narratives. 3. War correspondents, American — Correspondence, reminiscences, etc. I. Thomas, Benjamin Platt, 1902-1956, ed. II. T.
E470.C14   973.781   55-9275

Williams, Kenneth Powers, 1887-1958. III. 5803
Lincoln finds a general; a military study of the Civil War. With maps by Clark Ray. New York, Macmillan, 1949-59. 5 v. ports., maps. 22 cm. 1. Lincoln, Abraham, Pres. U.S., 1809-1865. 2. U.S. — History — Civil War — Campaigns and battles. 3. Generals — U.S. I. T.
E470.W765   973.73   49-11530

Williams, Thomas Harry, 1909- III. 5804
Lincoln and his generals. [1st ed.] New York, Knopf, 1952. viii, 363, iv p. ports., map. 22 cm. 1. Lincoln, Abraham, Pres. U.S., 1809-1865. 2. Generals — U.S. 3. U.S. — History — Civil War — Campaigns and battles. I. T.
E470.W78   973.741   51-13211

Catton, Bruce, 1899- III. 5805
Glory Road; the bloody route from Fredericksburg to Gettysburg. [1st ed.] Garden City, N.Y., Doubleday, 1952. 416 p. maps. 22 cm. 1. U.S. — History — Civil War — Regimental histories — Army of the Potomac. 2. U.S. — History — Civil War — Campaigns and battles. I. T.
E470.2.C36   973.734   52-5538

Catton, Bruce, 1899- III. 5806
Mr. Lincoln's Army. Garden City, N.Y., Doubleday [1962] xii, 363 p. maps. 22 cm. (His The Army of the Potomac, v. 1) 1. United States — History — Civil War — Regimental histories — Army of the Potomac. 2. McClellan, George Brinton, 1826-1885. 3. United States — History — Civil War — Campaigns and battles. I. T.
E470.2.C37 1962   973.741   62-1068

Catton, Bruce, 1899- III. 5807
A stillness at Appomattox. [1st ed.] Garden City, N.Y., Doubleday, 1953. 438 p. illus. 22 cm. 1. U.S. — History — Civil War — Regimental histories — Army of the Potomac. 2. U.S. — History — Civil War — Campaigns and battles. I. T.
E470.2.C39   973.736   53-9982

Freeman, Douglas Southall, 1886-1953. III. 5808
Lee's lieutenants, a study in command, by Douglas Southall Freeman. New York, C. Scribner's Sons, 1942-44. 3 v. illus., ports., maps (part fold.) 24 cm. 1. Confederate states of America — Biography. 2. U.S. — History — Civil war — Campaigns and battles. 3. U.S. — History — Civil war — Biography. 4. U.S. — History — Civil war — Regimental histories — Army of northern Virginia. I. T.
E470.2.F7   973.73   42-24582

Hassler, Warren W. III. 5809
Commanders of the Army of the Potomac. Baton Rouge, Louisiana State University Press [1962] 281 p. illus. 24 cm. 1. U.S. — History — Civil War — Regimental histories — Army of the Potomac. 2. U.S. — History — Civil War — Biography. 3. Generals — U.S. I. T.
E470.2.H32   923.573   62-11738

Brownlee, Richard S. III. 5810
Gray ghosts of the Confederacy; guerrilla warfare in the West, 1861-1865. Baton Rouge, Louisiana State University Press [1958] 274 p. illus. 23 cm. 1. U.S. — History — Civil War — Guerrillas. 2. Crime and criminals — The West. 3. Missouri — History — Civil War. 4. Kansas — History — Civil War. I. T.
E470.45.B76   973.742   58-14213

Kerby, Robert Lee. III. 5811
Kirby Smith's Confederacy; the Trans-Mississippi South, 1863-1865, by Robert L. Kerby. New York, Columbia University Press, 1972. viii, 529 p. maps. 23 cm. 1. Southwest, Old — History — Civil War. 2. United States — History — Civil War — Campaigns and battles. 3. Kirby-Smith, Edmund, 1824-1893. I. T.
E470.9.K42   973.73   71-186387   ISBN:0231035853

Klingberg, Frank Wysor. III. 5812
The Southern Claims Commission. Berkeley, University of California Press, 1955. ix, 261 p. map, tables. 24 cm. (University of California publications in history, v.50) Based on thesis, University of California at Los Angeles. 1. U.S. Commissioners of Claims. 2. U.S. — History — Civil War — Claims. 3. U.S. — History — Civil War — Finance, commerce, confiscations, etc. I. T. (S:California. University. University of California publications in history, v.50)
E480.K58   (E173.C15 vol. 50)   A55-9444

E482 – 489 Confederate States of America

Chesnut, Mary Boykin (Miller) 1823-1886. III. 5813
A diary from Dixie, as written by Mary Boykin Chesnut, wife of James Chesnut, jr., United States senator from South Carolina, 1859-1861, and afterward an aide to Jefferson Davis and a brigadier-general in the Confederate Army; edited by Isabella D. Martin and Myrta Lockett Avary. New York, P. Smith [1929] xxii, 423 p. pl., port., facsims. 22 cm. "Reprinted, August, 1929." 1. Confederate States of America. 2. U.S. — History — Civil war — Personal narratives — Confederate side. I. Martin, Isabella D., ed. II. Avary, Myrta Lockett, joint ed. III. T.
E487.Cx   A30-1158

Coulter, Ellis Merton, 1890- III. 5814
The Confederate States of America, 1861-1865. [Baton Rouge] Louisiana State University Press, 1950. x, 644 p. illus., ports., fold. map. 25 cm. (A History of the South, v.7) 1. Confederate States of America — History. 2. U.S. — History — Civil War. (S)
E487.C83   973.713   50-6319

Davis, Jefferson, 1808-1889. III. 5815
The rise and fall of the Confederate Government. Foreword by Bell I. Wiley. New York, T. Yoseloff [1958] 2 v. illus., ports., maps. 24 cm. Issued in a case. 1. Confederate States of America — History. 2. U.S. — Politics and government — Civil War. 3. U.S. — History — Civil War. I. T.
E487.D263 1958   973.7   58-12480

Eaton, Clement, 1898- III. 5816
A history of the Southern Confederacy. New York, Macmillan, 1954. 351 p. 22 cm. 1. Confederate States of America — History. 2. U.S. — History — Civil War.
E487.E15   973.713   54-8772

Holmes, Sarah Katherine (Stone) 1841-1907. III. 5817
Brokenburn; the journal of Kate Stone, 1861-1868. Edited by John Q. Anderson. Baton Rouge, Louisiana State University Press [1955] 400 p. illus. 22 cm. 1. U.S. — History — Civil War — Personal narratives — Confederate side. I. Anderson, John Q., ed. II. T.
E487.H74   973.782   55-7363

Patrick, Rembert Wallace, 1909- III. 5818
Jefferson Davis and his cabinet [by] Rembert W. Patrick. Baton Rouge, Louisiana State University Press, 1944. x, 401 p. 24 cm. "Begun in 1936 as a

doctoral dissertation at ... the University of North Carolina." — Pref. *1. Davis, Jefferson, 1808-1889. 2. Confederate States of America — Politics and government. 3. Confederate States of America — Biography. 4. Cabinet officers — Confederate States of America.*
E487.P3   973.716   44-9637

Ramsdell, Charles William, 1877-1942.   III. 5819
Behind the lines in the Southern Confederacy. Edited with a foreword by Wendell H. Stephenson. New York, Greenwood Press [1969, c1944] xxi, 136 p. port. 23 cm. (The Walter Lynwood Fleming lectures in Southern history, Louisiana State University) *1. Confederate States of America — Social conditions. 2. Confederate States of America — Economic conditions. I. Stephenson, Wendell Holmes, 1899- ed. II. T. (S:Louisiana. State University and Agricultural and Mechanical College. Walter Lynwood Fleming lectures in Southern history)*
E487.R2 1969   973.71/3   73-88924   ISBN:83712218X

Roland, Charles Pierce, 1918-   III. 5820
The Confederacy. [Chicago] University of Chicago Press [1960] 218 p. illus. 21 cm. (The Chicago history of American civilization) *1. Confederate States of America — History. I. T. (S)*
E487.R7   973.713   60-12573

Tatum, Georgia Lee.   III. 5821
Disloyalty in the confederacy, by Georgia Lee Tatum. Chapel Hill, The University of North Carolina Press, 1934. xi, 176 p. 24 cm. "Prepared as a doctoral dissertation at Vanderbilt university [1933]" — Pref. *1. Confederate States of America — History. 2. Confederate States of America — Social conditions. 3. Public opinion — Confederate States of America. 4. U.S. — History — Civil war — Peace. I. T.*
E487.T176   975   34-22569

Owsley, Frank Lawrence, 1890-1956.   III. 5822
King Cotton diplomacy; foreign relations of the Confederate States of America. 2d ed., rev. by Harriet Chappell Owsley. [Chicago] University of Chicago Press [1959] xxiii, 614 p. tables. 23 cm. *1. Confederate States of America — Foreign relations. 2. Cotton trade. I. T.*
E488.O85 1959   973.721   58-11952

Massey, Mary Elizabeth.   III. 5823
Ersatz in the Confederacy. Columbia, University of South Carolina Press, 1952. xii, 233 p. illus. 24 cm. *1. Confederate States of America — Economic conditions. I. T.*
E489.M3   973.716   52-13204

E491 – 586   Armies

Bruce, Robert V.   III. 5824
Lincoln and the tools of war. Foreword by Benjamin P. Thomas. [1st ed.] Indianapolis, Bobbs-Merrill [1956] xi, 368 p. illus., ports. 23 cm. *1. Lincoln, Abraham, Pres. U.S. 1809-1865. 2. U.S. — History — Civil War — Supplies. 3. Ordnance. I. T.*
E491.B7   973.7   56-6779

Lord, Francis Alfred, 1911-   III. 5825
They fought for the Union. [1st ed.] Harrisburg, Pa., Stackpole Co. [1960] 375 p. illus., ports., map, facsims., tables. 29 cm. *1. United States — History — Civil War, 1861-1865. 2. United States. Army — History — Civil War, 1861-1865. 3. United States. Navy — History — Civil War, 1861-1865. 4. United States. Marine Corps — History — Civil War, 1861-1865. I. T.*
E491.L89   973.741   60-8813

Murdock, Eugene Converse.   III. 5826
One million men; the Civil War draft in the North [by] Eugene C. Murdock. Madison, State Historical Society of Wisconsin, 1971. xi, 366 p. illus. 24 cm. *1. United States. Army — Recruiting, enlistment, etc. — Civil War. 2. Military service, Compulsory — United States. I. T.*
E491.M97   973.7/1   72-168393   ISBN:0870201166

Shannon, Fred Albert, 1893-   III. 5827
The organization and administration of the Union Army, 1861-1865. Gloucester, Mass., P. Smith, 1965 [c1928] 2 v. illus., port. 21 cm. *1. U.S. Army — History — Civil War. 2. U.S. Army — Organization. I. Union Army, 1861-1865. II. T.*
E491.S52 1965   973.741   65-3210

Turner, George Edgar.   III. 5828
Victory rode the rails; the strategic place of the railroads in the Civil War. Maps by George Richard Turner. Westport, Conn., Greenwood Press [1972, c1953] 419 p. illus. 22 cm. *1. United States — History — Civil War — Transportation. 2. Railroads — United States — History. 3. Railroads — Confederate States of America. I. T.*
E491.T95 1972   973.78   73-184842   ISBN:0837163315

Weber, Thomas, 1916-   III. 5829
The Northern railroads in the Civil War, 1861-1865. Westport, Conn., Greenwood Press [1970, c1952] xii, 318 p. 23 cm. *1. United States — History — Civil War — Transportation. 2. Railroads — United States — History. I. T.*
E491.W4 1970   385/.0973   79-106725   ISBN:0837135494

Wiley, Bell Irvin, 1906-   III. 5830
The life of Billy Yank, the common soldier of the Union. [1st ed.] Indianapolis, Bobbs-Merrill [1952] 454 p. illus., ports. 24 cm. *1. U.S. Army — History — Civil War. 2. U.S. Army — Military life. 3. Soldiers — U.S. I. T.*
E491.W69   973.7411   52-5809

Higginson, Thomas Wentworth, 1823-1911.   III. 5831
Army life in a black regiment. With notes and a biographical introd. by John Hope Franklin. Foreword by E. Franklin Frazier. Boston, Beacon Press [1962] 300 p. 21 cm. *1. United States — History — Civil War — Regimental histories — United States — 33d Infantry (Colored) 2. United States. Army. 33d Infantry (Colored) 3. United States — History — Civil War — Personal narratives. I. T.*
E492.94 33d.H5 1962   973.7415   62-9217

Leech, Margaret, 1893-   III. 5832
Reveille in Washington, 1860-1865. Westport, Conn., Greenwood Press [1971, c1941] x, 483 p. illus. 24 cm. *1. Washington, D.C. — History — Civil War. I. T.*
E501.L4 1971   973.7/4/53   72-138121   ISBN:0837156971

Stampp, Kenneth Milton.   III. 5833
Indiana politics during the Civil War. Indianapolis, Indiana Historical Bureau, 1949. xiii, 300 p. 24 cm. (Indiana historical collections, v.31) *1. Indiana — Politics and government — Civil War. I. T. (S)*
E506.S73   977.2   49-45273

Castel, Albert E.   III. 5834
A frontier state at war: Kansas, 1861-1865. Ithaca, N.Y., Published for the American Historical Association [by] Cornell University Press [1958] 251 p. illus. 24 cm. Issued in microfilm form in 1955 as thesis, University of Chicago. *1. Kansas — History — Civil War. I. T.*
E508.C3 1958   978.103   58-4823

Coulter, Ellis Merton, 1890-   III. 5835
The civil war and readjustment in Kentucky, by Merton Coulter. Chapel Hill, University of North Carolina Press; [etc., etc.] 1926. viii, 468 p. illus., maps. 24 cm. *1. Kentucky — History — Civil war. 2. Reconstruction — Kentucky.*
E509.C83   26-12262

Curry, Richard Orr.   III. 5836
A house divided; a study of statehood politics and the Copperhead movement in West Virginia. [Pittsburgh] University of Pittsburgh Press [1964] 203 p. maps. 24 cm. *1. West Virginia — Politics and government. 2. West Virginia — History — Civil War. 3. Copperhead (Nickname) I. T.*
E536.C8   975.403   64-15358

Lonn, Ella, 1879-1962.   III. 5837
Foreigners in the Union Army and Navy. New York, Greenwood Press [1969, c1959] viii, 725 p. port. 23 cm. *1. United States — History — Civil War — Foreign participants. 2. United States. Army — History — Civil War. 3. United States. Navy — History — Civil War. 4. United States — History — Civil War — Biography. I. T.*
E540.F6L6 1969   973.7/41   74-90548   ISBN:0837122481

Cornish, Dudley Taylor.   III. 5838
The sable arm; Negro troops in the Union Army, 1861-1865. New York, W. W. Norton [1966] 337 p. 20 cm. (The Norton library, N334) *1. United States — History — Civil War — Negro troops. 2. Negroes as soldiers. I. Negro troops in the Union Army, 1861-1865. II. T.*
E540.N3C77 1966   973.7415   66-14074

Quarles, Benjamin.   III. 5839
The Negro in the Civil War. Boston, Little, Brown [1969] xvi, 379 p. 20 cm. *1. United States — History — Civil War — Negroes. I. T.*
E540.N3Q3 1969   973.71/5/30145196   71-11863

Black, Robert C., 1914-   III. 5840
The railroads of the Confederacy. Chapel Hill, University of North Carolina Press [1952] xiv, 360 p. illus., ports., maps (1 fold.) facsims. 25 cm. Without thesis statement. Subtitle, "a study in adversity," and thesis statement on labels mounted on t.p. *1. Confederate States of America. Army — Transportation. 2. U.S. — History — Civil War. — Transportation. 3. Railroads — Confederate States of America. I. T.*
E545.B55   973.7   52-3559

Vandiver, Frank Everson, 1925-   III. 5841
Rebel brass; the Confederate command system, by Frank E. Vandiver. Introd. by T. Harry Williams. New York, Greenwood Press [1969, c1956] xvii, 142 p. illus., ports. 23 cm. *1. Confederate States of America — History, Military. 2. Confederate States of America — Politics and government. I. T.*
E545.V3 1969   973.7/42   79-88963   ISBN:837123216

E591 – 600 Naval Operations

Anderson, Bern. III. 5842
By sea and by river; the naval history of the Civil War. [1st ed.] New York, Knopf, 1962. 303 p. illus. 22 cm. *1. U.S. — History — Civil War — Naval operations. 2. U.S. — History — Civil War — Campaigns and battles. I. T.*
E591.A54   973.757   62-15575

Jones, Virgil Carrington, 1906- III. 5843
The Civil War at sea. Foreword by E. M. Eller. [1st ed.] New York, Holt, Rinehart, Winston [1960-62) 3 v. illus. 22 cm. *1. U.S. — History — Civil War — Naval operations. I. T.*
E591.J6   973.75   60-14457

E601 – 609 Personal Narratives

De Forest, John William, 1826-1906. III. 5844
A volunteer's adventures; a Union captain's record of the Civil War. Edited, with notes, by James H. Croushore. With an introd. by Stanley T. Williams. [Hamden, Conn.] Archon Books, 1970 [c1946] xviii, 237 p. illus. 22 cm. *1. Connecticut Infantry. 12th Regt., 1861-1864. 2. U.S. — History — Civil War — Personal narratives. I. T.*
E601.D3 1970   973.78/1   70-120372

Holmes, Oliver Wendell, 1841-1935. III. 5845
Touched with fire; civil war letters and diary of Oliver Wendell Holmes, jr., 1861-1864, edited by Mark De Wolfe Howe. Cambridge, Mass., Harvard University Press, 1946. x p., 3 l., 3-158 p. front., illus. (incl. plans, facsims.) ports. 21 1/2 cm. *1. Massachusetts infantry. 20th regt., 1861-1865. 2. U.S. — History — Civil war — Personal narratives. I. Howe, Mark De Wolfe, 1906- ed. II. T.*
E601.H73   973.781   A47-364

Strong, George Templeton, 1820-1875. III. 5846
Diary of the Civil War, 1860-1865. Edited by Allan Nevins. New York, Macmillan, 1962. 664 p. illus. 25 cm. "Originally appeared as volume III of The diary of George Templeton Strong ... edited by Allan Nevins and Milton Halsey Thomas." *1. U.S. — History — Civil War — Personal narratives. I. T.*
E601.S888   973.7   62-4535

Wiley, Bell Irvin, 1906- III. 5847
The life of Johnny Reb, the common soldier of the Confederacy, by Bell Irvin Wiley. 1st ed. Indianapolis, New York, Bobbs-Merrill [1943] 444 p. plates, ports., facsims. 25 cm. *1. Confederate states of America. Army. 2. U.S. — History — Civil war — Personal narratives — Confederate side. I. T.*
E607.W5   973.784   43-3253

Andrews, J. Cutler, 1908- III. 5848
The North reports the Civil War. [Pittsburgh] University of Pittsburgh Press [1955] x, 813 p. illus., ports., maps (1 fold.) 24 cm. *1. U.S. — History — Civil War — Journalists. I. T.*
E609.A6   973.7   55-6873

Andrews, J. Cutler, 1908- III. 5849
The South reports the Civil War, by J. Cutler Andrews. Princeton, N.J., Princeton University Press, 1970. xiii, 611 p. illus., facsims., maps (1 fold.), ports. 25 cm. *1. United States — History — Civil War — Journalists. I. T.*
E609.A62   973.7   75-90942   ISBN:0691045976

Reynolds, Donald E., 1931- III. 5850
Editors make war; Southern newspapers in the secession crisis [by] Donald E. Reynolds. Nashville, Vanderbilt University Press [1970] xi, 304 p. 21 cm. *1. United States — History — Civil War — Journalists. 2. Secession. I. T.*
E609.R48   973.71/5/097   71-129050   ISBN:0826511643

Weisberger, Bernard A., 1922- III. 5851
Reporters for the Union. [1st ed.] Boston, Little, Brown [1953] xi, 316 p. illus. 22 cm. *1. U.S. — History — Civil War — Journalists. 2. Reporters and reporting. I. T.*
E609.W4   071 .3 52-12638
           w434

E611 – 655 Special Topics

Hesseltine, William Best, 1902- III. 5852
Civil war prisons; a study in war psychology [by] William Best Hesseltine. Columbus, The Ohio State University Press, 1930. xi, 290 p. 23 cm. *1. U.S. — History — Civil war — Prisoners and prisons. 2. U.S. — History — Civil war — Prisoners, Exchange of. I. T.*
E611.H45   30-19745

Steinmetz, Lee, ed. III. 5853
The poetry of the American Civil War. [East Lansing] Michigan State University Press [1960] xii, 264 p. 24 cm. *1. U.S. — History — Civil War — Poetry. 2. American poetry — 19th cent. I. T.*
E647.S85   811.3082   59-15220

Rawley, James A. III. 5854
Turning points of the Civil War [by] James A. Rawley. Lincoln, University of Nebraska Press [1966] ix, 230 p. map (on lining papers) 24 cm. *1. U.S. — History — Civil War — Addresses, sermons, etc. I. T.*
E649.R28   973.7   66-19266

Craven, Avery Odelle, 1886- III. 5855
The repressible conflict, 1830-1861, by Avery Craven. University, La., Louisiana State University Press, 1939. xi, 97 p. 21 cm. (The Walter Lynwood Fleming lectures in Southern history, Louisiana state university, 1938) *1. U.S. — History — Civil war — Causes. 2. U.S. — History — Civil war — Addresses, sermons, etc. I. T.*
E649.S89   973.711   39-10855

Botkin, Benjamin Albert, 1901- ed. III. 5856
A Civil War treasury of tales, legends, and folklore; illustrated by Warren Chappell. New York, Random House [1960] 625 p. illus. 25 cm. *1. U.S. — History — Civil War — Anecdotes. I. T.*
E655.B65   973.7088   60-5530

E660 – 738 Late 19th Century (1865 – 1900)

Garfield, James Abram, Pres. U.S., 1831-1881. III. 5857
The diary of James A. Garfield. Edited with an introd. by Harry James Brown [and] Frederick D. Williams. [East Lansing] Michigan State University, 1967-   v. illus., facsim., port. 25 cm. *I. Brown, Harry James, ed. II. Williams, Frederick D., ed. III. T.*
E660.G223   973.8/4/0924 (B)   67-12577

Grant, Ulysses Simpson, Pres. U.S., 1822-1885. III. 5858
The papers of Ulysses S. Grant. Edited by John Y. Simon. Carbondale, Southern Illinois University Press [1967-   v. illus., facsim., map, port. 26 cm. Prepared under the auspices of the Ulysses S. Grant Association. *I. Simon, John Y., ed.*
E660.G74   973.8/2/0924   67-10725

Morgan, Howard Wayne. III. 5859
From Hayes to McKinley; national party politics, 1877-1896 [by] H. Wayne Morgan. [1st ed.] Syracuse, N.Y., Syracuse University Press [1969] x, 618 p. illus., facsims., ports. 24 cm. *1. United States — Politics and government — 1865-1900. 2. Political parties — United States — History. I. T.*
E660.M6   329/.02/0973   69-17074

Bassett, John Spencer, 1867-1928. III. 5860
Makers of a new nation, by John Spencer Bassett. New Haven, Yale University Press; [etc., etc] 1928. 344 p. illus., ports., facsims., diagrs. 26 cm. (The pageant of America. [vol.IX]) "Independence edition." Lincoln and the imperiled Union. — Reconstructing the Union. — Readjustment under Grant. — Hayes and the spoilmen. — Political and economic reform under Cleveland. — New politics under Harrison. — Democratic revolt under Cleveland, 1893-97. — McKinley and the war with Spain. — Roosevelt and political reform. — Taft's efforts to obtain harmony. — Wilson and domestic issues. — World war politics and reconstruction. *1. U.S. — History — 1865- 2. U.S. — Politics and government — 1865- I. T.*
E661.B326x (E178.5.P vol. 9)   A29-34

Buck, Paul Herman, 1899- III. 5861
The road to reunion, 1865-1900, by Paul H. Buck. 1st ed. Boston, Little, Brown, 1937. xi, 320 p. 23 cm. *1. U.S. — History — 1865-1898. 2. U.S. — Politics and government — 1865-1898. 3. Reconstruction. I. T.*
E661.B84   973.8   37-4978
            B855

Destler, Chester McArthur, 1904- III. 5862
American radicalism, 1865-1901, essays and documents. New York, Octagon Books, 1963 [c1946] xii, 276 p. illus., facsims. 24 cm. (Connecticut College monograph no. 3) *1. U.S. — Politics and government — 1865-1900. 2. U.S. — Social conditions. 3. U.S. — Economic conditions. I. T.* (S:Connecticut College for Women, New London. Connecticut College monograph, no. 3)
E661.D45 1963   973.8   63-14344

Dobson, John M.   III. 5863
Politics in the gilded age; a new perspective on reform [by] John M. Dobson. Foreword by James P. Shenton. New York, Praeger Publishers [1972] 200 p. 21 cm. (New perspectives in American history) *1. United States — Politics and government — 1865-1900. 2. Civil service reform. 3. Political parties — United States. I. T.*
E661.D6   320.9/73/08   78-170467

Faulkner, Harold Underwood, 1890-   III. 5864
Politics, reform, and expansion, 1890-1900. [1st ed.] New York, Harper [1959] 312 p. illus. 22 cm. (The New American Nation series) *1. U.S. — History — 1865-1898. I. T.*
E661.F3   973.8   56-6022

Garraty, John Arthur, 1920-   III. 5865
The new commonwealth, 1877-1890, by John A. Garraty. New York, Harper & Row [1968] xv, 364 p. illus., ports. 20 cm. (The New American nation series. Harper torchbooks, TB1410.) *1. United States — History — 1865-1898. I. T.*
E661.G35x   973.8   72-367

Goldman, Eric Frederick, 1915-   III. 5866
Rendezvous with destiny; a history of modern American reform. [1st ed.] New York, Knopf, 1952. xiii, 503, xxxvii p. 22 cm. *1. U.S. — Politics and government — 1865- I. T.*
E661.G58   973.8   52-6418

Hirshson, Stanley P., 1928-   III. 5867
Farewell to the bloody shirt: northern Republicans & the southern Negro, 1877-1893. Introd. by David Donald. Bloomington, Indiana University Press [1962] 334 p. 21 cm. *1. U.S. — Politics and government — 1865-1900. 2. Southern States — Race question. 3. Negroes — Southern States. I. T.*
E661.H58   973.8   62-8975

Hollingsworth, Joseph Rogers, 1932-   III. 5868
The whirligig of politics; the democracy of Cleveland and Bryan. Chicago, University of Chicago Press [1963] xii, 263 p. illus., ports. 23 cm. *1. Cleveland, Grover, Pres. U.S., 1837-1908. 2. Bryan, William Jennings, 1860-1925. 3. Democratic Party. 4. U.S. — Politics and government. I. T.*
E661.H72   973.87   63-18846

Josephson, Matthew, 1899-   III. 5869
The politicos, 1865-1896, by Matthew Josephson. [1st ed.] New York, Harcourt, Brace [c1938] ix, 760 p. 24 cm. *1. U.S. — History — 1865-1898. 2. Statesmen, American. I. T.*
E661.J85   973.8   38-27301

May, Ernest R.   III. 5870
Imperial democracy; the emergence of America as a great power. [1st ed.] New York, Harcourt, Brace & World [1961] 318 p. 22 cm. *1. U.S. — Foreign relations — 1865-1898. 2. U.S. — Foreign relations — 1897-1901. 3. U.S. — Territorial expansion. I. T.*
E661.M34   973.8   61-13354

Shannon, Fred Albert, 1893-1963.   III. 5871
The centennial years, a political and economic history of America from the late 1870s to the early 1890s. Edited by Robert Huhn Jones. [1st ed.] Garden City, N.Y., Doubleday, 1967. xx, 362 p. illus., ports. 22 cm. *1. U.S. — Politics and government — 1865-1900. 2. U.S. — Economic conditions. I. Jones, Robert Huhn, 1927- ed. II. T.*
E661.S53   973.8   67-12857

Sparks, Edwin Erle, 1860-1924.   III. 5872
National development 1877-1885. New York, Harper. St. Clair Shores, Mich., Scholarly Press, 1970 [c1907] xiv, 378 p. maps. 22 cm. (The American nation: a history, v. 23) *1. United States — History — 1865-1898. I. T. (S:The American nation: a history (Gloucester, Mass.) v. 23)*
E661.S6 1970   973.8/3   70-145311   ISBN:0403012236

Sproat, John G.   III. 5873
The best men; liberal reformers in the gilded age, by John G. Sproat. New York, Oxford University Press, 1968. ix, 356 p. 22 cm. *1. United States — Politics and government — 1865-1900. I. Liberal reformers in the gilded age. II. T.*
E661.S65   320.9/73   68-8413

Wiebe, Robert H.   III. 5874
The search for order, 1877-1920, by Robert H. Wiebe. [1st ed.] New York, Hill and Wang [1967] xiv, 333 p. 22 cm. (The Making of America) *1. U.S. — Politics and government — 1865-1933. 2. U.S. — Social conditions — 1865-1918. 3. Middle classes — U.S. 4. Progressivism (U.S. politics) I. T.*
E661.W58   320.9/73   66-27609

E661.7   DIPLOMATIC HISTORY

Dulles, Foster Rhea, 1900-   III. 5875
Prelude to world power: American diplomatic history, 1860-1900. New York, Macmillan [1965] viii, 238 p. 22 cm. (History of American foreign policy series) *1. United States — Foreign relations — 1861-1865. 2. United States — Foreign relations — 1865-1898. 3. United States — Territorial expansion. I. T.*
E661.7.D8   327.73   65-11836

Grenville, John Ashley Soames.   III. 5876
Politics, strategy, and American diplomacy; studies in foreign policy, 1873-1917, by John A. S. Grenville, and George Berkeley Young. New Haven, Yale University Press, 1966. xviii, 352 p. 23 cm. *1. U.S. — Foreign relations — 1865- — Addresses, essays, lectures. I. Young, George Berkeley, 1913- joint author. II. T.*
E661.7.G7   327.73   66-12498

LaFeber, Walter.   III. 5877
The new empire; an interpretation of American expansion, 1860-1898. Ithaca, N.Y., Published for the American Historical Association [by] Cornell University Press [1963] xiii, 444 p. 24 cm. *1. U.S. — Territorial expansion. 2. U.S. — Foreign relations — 1865-1898. 3. Imperialism. I. T.*
E661.7.L2   973.8   63-20868

May, Ernest R.   III. 5878
American imperialism; a speculative essay [by] Ernest R. May. [1st ed.] New York, Atheneum, 1968. ix, 239 p. 22 cm. *1. United States — Foreign relations — 1865-1921. 2. United States — Territorial expansion. 3. Imperialism. I. T.*
E661.7.M3 1968   327.73   68-12544

Plesur, Milton.   III. 5879
America's outward thrust; approaches to foreign affairs, 1865-1890. DeKalb, Northern Illinois University Press [1971] vii, 276 p. 25 cm. *1. United States — Foreign relations — 1865-1898. 2. United States — Relations (general) with foreign countries. I. T.*
E661.7.P55   327.73   76-137882   ISBN:087580019X

E663 - 664   BIOGRAPHY

Merriam, Charles Edward, 1874-   III. 5880
Four American party leaders; Henry Ward Beecher foundation lectures, delivered at Amherst college by Charles Edward Merriam. New York, Macmillan, 1926. xvi, 104 p. ports. 20 cm. (Political parties and practical politics series) *1. Lincoln, Abraham, pres. U.S., 1809-1865. 2. Roosevelt, Theodore, pres. U.S., 1858-1919. 3. Wilson, Woodrow, pres. U.S., 1856-1924. 4. Bryan, William Jennings, 1860-1925. 5. Leadership. I. Amherst college. Henry Ward Beecher foundation. II. T.*
E663.M56   26-7892

E664   A - G

Adams, Charles Francis, 1835-1915.   III. 5881
Charles Francis Adams, 1835-1915; an autobiography; with a Memorial address delivered November 17, 1915, by Henry Cabot Lodge. Boston & New York, Houghton Mifflin, 1916. lx, 224 p. port 25 cm. *1. Lodge, Henry Cabot, 1850-1924.*
E664.A19A2   16-6471

Tansill, Charles Callan, 1890-   III. 5882
The foreign policy of Thomas F. Bayard, 1885-1897 [by] Charles Callan Tansill. New York, Fordham University Press, 1940. xxxix, 800 p. front. (port.) illus. (incl. map) 27 cm. *1. Bayard, Thomas Francis, 1828-1898. 2. U.S. — Foreign relations — 1865-1898. I. T.*
E664.B3T3   327.73   41-2416

Clapp, Margaret Antoinette, 1910-   III. 5883
Forgotten first citizen: John Bigelow, by Margaret Clapp. New York, Greenwood Press, 1968 [c1947] x, 390 p. port. 24 cm. *1. Bigelow, John, 1817-1911. I. T.*
E664.B55C5 1968   973.72/0924 ((B))   69-10075

Muzzey, David Saville, 1870-   III. 5884
James G. Blaine, a political idol of other days, by David Saville Muzzey. New York, Dodd, Mead, 1934. xi, 514 p. plates, ports., facsims. 24 cm. (American political leaders) *1. Blaine, James Gillespie, 1830-1893.*
E664.B6M8   923.273   34-32559

Brandeis, Louis Dembitz, 1856-1941.   III. 5885
Letters of Louis D. Brandeis. Edited by Melvin I. Urofsky and David W.

Levy. Albany, State University of New York Press, 1971- v. illus., ports. 22 cm. Vol. 3: 1st ed. *1. Brandeis, Louis Dembitz, 1856-1941.*
E664.B819A4 1971   347/.73/2634   73-129640
    ISBN:087395078X (v. 1)

Urofsky, Melvin I.   **III. 5886**
A mind of one piece; Brandeis and American reform, by Melvin I. Urofsky. New York, Scribner [1971] xiii, 210 p. 24 cm. *1. Brandeis, Louis Dembitz, 1856-1941. I. T.*
E664.B819U7   347/.7326/34 (B)   74-143945   ISBN:0684123681

Coletta, Paolo Enrico, 1916-   **III. 5887**
William Jennings Bryan, by Paolo E. Coletta. Lincoln, University of Nebraska Press, 1964-[69] 3 v. 24 cm. *1. Bryan, William Jennings, 1860-1925.*
E664.B87C55   973.91/0924 (B)   64-11352

Glad, Paul W., 1926-   **III. 5888**
The trumpet soundeth; William Jennings Bryan and his democracy, 1896-1912. [Lincoln] University of Nebraska Press, 1960. xii, 242 p. illus., ports. 24 cm. *1. Bryan, William Jennings, 1860-1925. I. T.*
E664.B87G55   923.273   60-12259

Bolles, Blair, 1911-   **III. 5889**
Tyrant from Illinois; Uncle Joe Cannon's experiment with personal power. [1st ed.] New York, Norton [1951] 248 p. port. 24 cm. *1. Cannon, Joseph Gurney, 1836-1926. I. T.*
E664.C22B6   923.273   51-1677

Barnes, James Anderson.   **III. 5890**
John G. Carlisle, financial statesman, by James A. Barnes. New York, Dodd, Mead, 1931. xiii, 552 p. front., plates, ports. 25 cm. (American political leaders) *1. Carlisle, John Griffin, 1835-1910. 2. Silver question. 3. U.S. — Politics and government — 1893-1897.*
E664.C27B2   923.273   31-32426

Clark, Champ, 1850-1921.   **III. 5891**
My quarter century of American politics. New York, Harper [c1920] 2 v. fronts., plates, ports. 22 cm. *1. U.S. — Politics and government — 1865- I. T.*
E664.C49C4   20-4643

Jordan, David M., 1935-   **III. 5892**
Roscoe Conkling of New York: voice in the Senate, by David M. Jordan. Ithaca [N.Y.] Cornell University Press [1971] xiii, 464 p. ports. 24 cm. *1. Conkling, Roscoe, 1829-1888. 2. United States — Politics and government — 1865-1900. I. T.*
E664.C75J6   328.73/0924 (B)   76-148021   ISBN:0801406250

Ridge, Martin.   **III. 5893**
Ignatius Donnelly; the portrait of a politician. [Chicago] University of Chicago Press [1962] 427 p. illus. 25 cm. *1. Donnelly, Ignatius, 1831-1901.*
E664.D68R5   928.1   62-19937

Nevins, Allan, 1890-   **III. 5894**
Hamilton Fish; the inner history of the Grant administration. With an introd. by John Bassett Moore. Rev. ed. New York, F. Ungar Pub. Co. [1957] xxi, 2 v. (932 p.) illus., ports., coat of arms. 24 cm. (American classics) *1. Fish, Hamilton, 1808-1893. 2. Grant, Ulysses Simpson, Pres. U.S., 1822-1885. 3. U.S. — Politics and government — 1869-1877. 4. U.S. — Foreign relations — 1869-1877.*
E664.F52N44   973.82   57-9967

Nixon, Raymond Blalock, 1903-   **III. 5895**
Henry W. Grady, spokesman of the New South, by Raymond B. Nixon. New York, Russell & Russell [1969, c1943] x, 360, xiv p. illus., ports. 23 cm. *1. Grady, Henry Woodfin, 1850-1889.*
E664.G73N5 1969   070.9/24 (B)   68-27076

E664.H – N

Croly, Herbert David, 1869-1930.   **III. 5896**
Marcus Alonzo Hanna, his life and work, by Herbert Croly. Hamden, Conn., Archon Books, 1965 [c1912] xiii, 495 p. facsims., plates, ports. 22 cm. *1. Hanna, Marcus Alonzo, 1837-1904.*
E664.H24C9 1965   923.273   65-15015

Hay, John, 1838-1905.   **III. 5897**
Lincoln and the Civil War in the diaries and letters of John Hay; selected and with an introd. by Tyler Dennett. Westport, Conn., Greenwood Press [1972, c1939] p. *1. Lincoln, Abraham, Pres. U.S., 1809-1865. 2. United States — History — Civil War. I. Dennett, Tyler, 1883-1949. II. T.*
E664.H41A44 1972   973.7/0924 (B)   79-135598   ISBN:0837151902

Dennett, Tyler, 1883-1949.   **III. 5898**
John Hay; from poetry to politics. Port Washington, N.Y., Kennikat Press [1963, c1961] 476 p. illus., ports., facism. 22 cm. *1. Hay, John, 1838-1905. 2. U.S. — Foreign relations — 1901-1909.*
E664.H41D3 1963   923.273   63-20589

Nevins, Allan, 1890-   **III. 5899**
Abram S. Hewitt: with some account of Peter Cooper, by Allan Nevins. New York, Harper, 1935. xiii, 623 p. front., illus., plates, ports., facsims. 23 cm. "First edition." *1. Hewitt, Abram Stevens, 1822-1903. 2. Cooper, Peter, 1791-1883. 3. Presidents — U.S. — Election — 1876. 4. New York (City) — Politics and government.*
E664.H523N4   926.7   35-30046

Welch, Richard E.   **III. 5900**
George Frisbie Hoar and the half-breed Republicans [by] Richard E. Welch, Jr. Cambridge, Harvard University Press, 1971. 364 p. illus., port. 25 cm. *1. Hoar, George Frisbie, 1826-1904. 2. Republican Party — History. I. T.*
E664.H65W4   329.6/00924 (B)   70-133214   ISBN:0674348761

Bowen, Catherine (Drinker) 1897-   **III. 5901**
Yankee from Olympus; Justice Holmes and his family [by] Catherine Drinker Bowen. Boston, Little, Brown, 1944. xvii, 475 p. illus. (facsim.) geneal. tables. ports. 22 cm. "An Atlantic monthly press book." "Published April 1944, reprinted April 1944 (three times)" *1. Holmes, Oliver Wendell, 1841-1935. I. T.*
E664.H773B6   923.473   44-3384

Younger, Edward, 1909-   **III. 5902**
John A. Kasson: politics and diplomacy from Lincoln to McKinley. Iowa City, State Historical Society of Iowa, 1955. 450 p. illus. 25 cm. *1. Kasson, John Adam, 1822-1910.*
E664.K18Y6   923.273   55-62663

Doan, Edward Newell, 1904-   **III. 5903**
The La Follettes and the Wisconsin idea. New York, Rinehart [1947] 311 p. port. 22 cm. *1. La Follette, Robert Marion, 1855-1925. 2. La Follette, Robert Marion, 1895- 3. U.S. — Politics and government — 20th cent. 4. Wisconsin — Politics and government — 1865- I. T.*
E664.L16D6   923.273   47-6998

La Follette, Belle (Case) 1859-1931.   **III. 5904**
Robert M. La Follette, June 14, 1855-June 18, 1925. Chapters I-XXVI by Belle Case La Follette and chapters XXVII-LXXII by Fola La Follette. New York, Macmillan, 1953. 2 v. (xx, 1305 p.) illus., ports., facisms. 22 cm. *1. La Follette, Robert Marion, 1855-1925. I. La Follette, Fola.*
E664.L16L13   923.273   53-13106

La Follette, Robert Marion, 1855-1925.   **III. 5905**
La Follettes autobiography; a personal narrative of political experiences. With a foreword by Allan Nevins. Madison, University of Wisconsin Press, 1960. 349 p. illus. 22 cm. *1. U.S. — Politics and government. 2. Wisconsin — Politics and government — 1848-1950. 3. Presidents — U.S. — Election — 1912.*
E664.L16L16 1960   923.273   60-50989

Maxwell, Robert S.   **III. 5906**
La Follette and the rise of the Progressives in Wisconsin [by] Robert S. Maxwell. New York, Russell & Russell [1973, c1956] viii, 271 p. illus. 23 cm. Reprint of the ed. published by the State Historical Society of Wisconsin, Madison. *1. La Follette, Robert Marion, 1855-1925. 2. Wisconsin — Politics and government — 1848-1950. 3. Progressivism (United States politics) I. T.*
E664.L16M3 1973   973.91/092/4 (B)   72-85000   ISBN:0846216965

Thelen, David Paul.   **III. 5907**
The early life of Robert M. La Follette, 1855-1884. Chicago, Loyola University Press, 1966. x, 147 p. port. 24 cm. "William P. Lyons master's essay award, 1965." *1. La Follette, Robert Marion, 1855-1925. I. T.*
E664.L16T5   977.5040924   66-11931

Garraty, John Arthur, 1920-   **III. 5908**
Henry Cabot Lodge, a biography. [1st ed.] New York, Knopf, 1953. xiii, 433, xvi p. ports. 25 cm. *1. Lodge, Henry Cabot, 1850-1924.*
E664.L7G3   923.273   53-6852

E664 P – Z

Pinchot, Gifford, 1865-1946.   **III. 5909**
Breaking new ground. Introd. by James Penick, Jr. Seattle, University of Washington Press [1972, c1947] (Americana library, AL-22) Autobiography. *1. Conservation of natural resources — United States. I. T.*
E664.P62A3 1972   333.7/5/0924 (B)   75-172901   ISBN:0295951818

McGeary, Martin Nelson, 1906-   **III. 5910**
Gifford Pinchot, forester-politician. Princeton, N.J., Princeton University Press, 1960. 481 p. illus. 25 cm. *1. Pinchot, Gifford, 1865-1946.*
E664.P62M2   926.349   60-12232

III. 5911   United States   E664

Robinson, William Alexander, 1884-   III. 5911
Thomas B. Reed, parliamentarian, by William A. Robinson. New York, Dodd, Mead, 1930. xii, 423 p. front., plates, ports. 24 cm. (On cover: American political leaders) *1. Reed, Thomas Brackett, 1839-1902.*
E664.R3R66   30-30931

Jessup, Philip Caryl, 1897-   III. 5912
Elihu Root, by Philip C. Jessup. [Unaltered and unabridged ed. Hamden, Conn.] Archon Books, 1964 [c1938] 2 v. illus., facsims., maps (part fold.) ports. 23 cm. *1. Root, Elihu, 1845-1937.*
E664.R7J5 1964   923.273   64-24716

Leopold, Richard William.   III. 5913
Elihu Root and the conservative tradition. [1st ed.] Boston, Little, Brown [1954] 222 p. 21 cm. (The Library of American biography) *1. Root, Elihu, 1845-1937. I. T.*
E664.R7L4   923.273   54-6870

Schurz, Carl, 1829-1906.   III. 5914
Autobiography; an abridgment in one volume by Wayne Andrews. With an introd. by Allan Nevins. New York, Scribner [1961] 331 p. 24 cm. "An abridgement ... of The reminiscences of Carl Schurz, originally published in three volumes, 1906-1908."
E664.S39A337   923.273   61-6900

Fuess, Claude Moore, 1855-1963.   III. 5915
Carl Schurz, reformer; 1829-1906. Port Washington, N.Y., Kennikat Press [1963] 421 p. illus., ports. 22 cm. *1. Schurz, Carl, 1829-1906.*
E664.S39F92 1963   923.273   63-20588

Simkins, Francis Butler, 1897-1966.   III. 5916
Pitchfork Ben Tillman, South Carolinian. Gloucester, Mass., P. Smith, 1964 [c1944] xii, 577 p. illus., facsim., ports. 21 cm. (Southern biography series) "Critical essay on authorities": p. [556]-566. *1. Tillman, Benjamin Ryan, 1847-1918. 2. South Carolina — Politics and government — 1865-1950. I. T. (S)*
E664.T57S5 1964   923.273   65-1581

Humes, Dollena Joy, 1921-   III. 5917
Oswald Garrison Villard, liberal of the 1920's. [Syracuse, N.Y.] Syracuse University Press, 1960. 276 p. illus. 21 cm. (Men and movements series) *1. Villard, Oswald Garrison, 1872-1949. 2. Liberalism. 3. U.S. — Politics and government — 20th cent.*
E664.V65H8   920.5   60-15159

Villard, Oswald Garrison, 1872-   III. 5918
Fighting years; memoirs of a liberal editor, by Oswald Garrison Villard. 1st ed. New York, Harcourt, Brace [c1939] 543 p. illus., facsim., plates, ports. 22 cm. *I. T.*
E664.V65V5   920.5   39-27286

Woodward, Comer Vann, 1908-   III. 5919
Tom Watson, agrarian rebel, by C. Vann Woodward. New York, Macmillan, 1938. xii, 518 p. pl., ports. 22 cm. "First printing." *1. Watson, Thomas Edward, 1856-1922. I. T.*
E664.W337W6   923.273   38-8354

E666 – 738   BY PRESIDENTIAL ADMINISTRATION

E666 – 670   Johnson, 1865 – 1869

Benedict, Michael Les.   III. 5920
The impeachment and trial of Andrew Johnson. [1st ed.] New York, Norton [1973] x, 212 p. 21 cm. (The Norton essays in American history) *1. Johnson, Andrew, Pres. U.S., 1808-1875 — Impeachment. I. T.*
E666.B46 1973   973.8/1/0924 (B)   72-10883
    ISBN:039305473X 0393094189 (pbk.)

Cox, LaWanda C. (Fenlason)   III. 5921
Politics, principle, and prejudice, 1865-1866; dilemma of Reconstruction America [by] LaWanda Cox and John H. Cox. [New York] Free Press of Glencoe [1963] 294 p. 22 cm. *1. U.S. — Politics and government — 1865-1869. 2. Reconstruction. 3. Negroes — Civil rights. I. Cox, John Henry, 1907- joint author. II. T.*
E666.C84   973.81   63-10647

Milton, George Fort, 1894-1955.   III. 5922
The age of hate; Andrew Johnson and the radicals. Hamden, Conn., Archon Books, 1965 [c1930] xi, 788 p. illus., facsims., ports. 22 cm. *1. Johnson, Andrew, Pres. U.S., 1808-1875. 2. U.S. — Politics and government — Civil War. 3. U.S. — Politics and government — 1865-1869. I. T.*
E667.M66 1965   923.173   65-14391

E668   Reconstruction, 1865 – 1877

Beale, Howard Kennedy, 1899-   III. 5923
The critical year; a study of Andrew Johnson and reconstruction. New York, F. Ungar Pub. Co. [1958] 454 p. illus. 22 cm. (American classics) *1. Johnson, Andrew, Pres. U.S., 1808-1875. 2. Reconstruction. 3. U.S. — Politics and government — 1865-1869. I. T.*
E668.B354 1958   973.81   58-9332

Bowers, Claude Gernade, 1879-1958.   III. 5924
The tragic era; the revolution after Lincoln, by Claude G. Bowers. Cambridge, Houghton Mifflin, 1929. xxii, 567 p. plates, facsim., ports. 23 cm. *1. Johnson, Andrew, pres. U.S., 1808-1875. 2. U.S. — Politics and government — 1865-1877. 3. Reconstruction. 4. Washington, D.C. — Social life and customs. I. T.*
E668.B779   29-17848

Brock, William Ranulf.   III. 5925
An American crisis: Congress and Reconstruction, 1865-1867. [New York] St Martin's Press [1963] xii, 312 p. 23 cm. *1. U.S. Congress — History. 2. Reconstruction. 3. U.S. — Politics and government — 1865-1869. I. T.*
E668.B85   973.8   63-11348

Craven, Avery Odelle, 1886-   III. 5926
Reconstruction: the ending of the Civil War [by] Avery Craven. New York, Holt, Rinehart and Winston [1969] vi, 330 p. 22 cm. *1. Reconstruction. 2. United States — Politics and government — 1865-1877. I. T.*
E668.C9   973.8   69-13424   ISBN:003073245X

Donald, David Herbert, 1920-   III. 5927
The politics of Reconstruction, 1863-1867 [by] David Donald. Baton Rouge, Louisiana State University Press [1965] xviii, 105 p. illus. 23 cm. (The Walter Lynwood Fleming lectures in Southern history) *1. Reconstruction. 2. United States — Politics and government — 1865-1869. 3. Republican Party — History. I. T. (S:Louisiana. State University and Agricultural and Mechanical College. Walter Lynwood Fleming lectures in Southern history.)*
E668.D67   973.81   65-24678

Dorris, Jonathan Truman, 1883-   III. 5928
Pardon and amnesty under Lincoln and Johnson; the restoration of the Confederates to their rights and privileges, 1861-1898. Introd. by J. G. Randall. Chapel Hill, University of North Carolina Press [1953] xxi, 459 p. 24 cm. *1. Pardon — U.S. 2. Amnesty — U.S. 3. Reconstruction. 4. Political crimes and offenses — Southern States. I. T.*
E668.D713   973.81   53-13363

Du Bois, William Edward Burghardt, 1868-   III. 5929
Black reconstruction; an essay toward a history of the part which black folk played in the attempt to reconstruct democracy in America, 1860-1880, by W. E. Burghardt Du Bois. New York, Harcourt [c1935] 746 p. 22 cm. "First edition." *1. Reconstruction. 2. Negroes. 3. Negroes — Politics and suffrage. 4. Negroes — Employment. 5. U.S. — Politics and government — 1865-1877. I. T.*
E668.D83   35-8545

Dunning, William Archibald, 1857-1922.   III. 5930
Essays on the civil war and reconstruction and related topics, by William Archibald Dunning. New York, P. Smith, 1931. ix, 397 p. 20 cm. "The final essay in the first edition has been omitted, and for it has been substituted the essay on 'The undoing of reconstruction,' which appeared in the Atlantic monthly in 1901." — Note, p. viii. *1. Reconstruction. 2. U.S. — Politics and government — 1865-1877. 3. U.S. — Constitutional history.*
E668.D926   31-26981

Dunning, William Archibald, 1857-1922.   III. 5931
Reconstruction, political & economic, 1865-1877. New York, Harper [1962, c1935] 378 p. illus. 21 cm. (Harper torchbooks, TB1073. The Academy library) "Originally published as volume 22 in the American Nation series." *1. Reconstruction.*
E668.D927 1962   973.8   62-5020

Fleming, Walter Lynwood, 1874-1932, ed.   III. 5932
Documentary history of Reconstruction; political, military, social, religious, education & industrial, 1865 to the present time. Gloucester, Mass., P. Smith, 1960 [c1935] 2 v. in 1. illus., facsims. 28 cm. (Micro-offset books) *1. Reconstruction. I. T. (S)*
E668.F58 1960   973.81082   60-52262

Franklin, John Hope, 1915-   III. 5933
Reconstruction: after the Civil War. [Chicago] University of Chicago Press [1961] 258 p. illus. 21 cm. (The Chicago history of American civilization) *1. Reconstruction.*
E668.F7   973.8   61-15931

McKitrick, Eric L.   III. 5934
Andrew Johnson and reconstruction. [Chicago] University of Chicago Press

272

[1960] ix, 533 p. 25 cm. *1. Johnson, Andrew, Pres. U.S., 1808-1875. 2. Reconstruction.*
E668.M156   973.81   60-5467

Radicalism, racism, and party realignment; the border states **III. 5935**
during Reconstruction.
Edited by Richard O. Curry. Baltimore, Johns Hopkins Press [1969] xxvi, 331 p. maps. 24 cm. *1. Reconstruction — Addresses, essays, lectures. 2. United States — Politics and government — 1865-1877 — Addresses, essays, lectures. I. Curry, Richard Orr, ed.*
E668.R15   973.8   72-90743   ISBN:0801810728

Rozwenc, Edwin Charles, 1915- ed.   **III. 5936**
Reconstruction in the South. Boston, Heath [1962] 109 p. 24 cm. (Problems in American civilization; readings selected by the Dept. of American Studies, Amherst College) *1. Reconstruction. 2. Southern States — History — 1865-1877. I. T.*
E668.R83   973.8   52-1818

Sefton, James E.   **III. 5937**
The United States Army and Reconstruction, 1865-1877, by James E. Sefton. Baton Rouge, Louisiana State University Press [1967] xx, 284 p. illus. 24 cm. *1. Reconstruction. 2. U.S. — History, Military — To 1900. I. T.*
E668.S46   973.8   67-21377

Singletary, Otis A.   **III. 5938**
Negro militia and reconstruction. Austin, University of Texas Press [1957] 181 p. illus. 22 cm. *1. Reconstruction — Negro troops. I. T.*
E668.S59   973.8   57-7559

Stampp, Kenneth Milton.   **III. 5939**
The era of reconstruction, 1865-1877, by Kenneth M. Stampp. [1st ed.] New York, Knopf, 1965. ix, 228, [1] p. 22 cm. *1. Reconstruction. I. T.*
E668.S79   973.81   64-13447

Trelease, Allen W.   **III. 5940**
White terror; the Ku Klux Klan conspiracy and Southern Reconstruction, by Allen W. Trelease. [1st ed.] New York, Harper & Row [1971] xlviii, 557 p. 25 cm. *1. Ku-Klux Klan. 2. Reconstruction. I. T.*
E668.T7 1971   973.8   79-123966

E670   Presidential Campaign of 1868

Coleman, Charles Hubert, 1900-   **III. 5941**
The election of 1868; the Democratic effort to regain control, by Charles H. Coleman. New York, 1933. 409 p. 23 cm. Vita. Published also as Studies in history, economics and public law, edited by the Faculty of political science of Columbia university, no. 392. *1. Democratic party. 2. Republican party. 3. Presidents — U.S. — Election — 1868. 4. U.S. — Politics and government — 1865-1869. 5. Reconstruction. I. T.*
E670.C72   324.73 (973.81)   33-30800

E671 – 680   Grant, 1869 – 1877

Grant, Ulysses Simpson, Pres. U.S., 1822-1885.   **III. 5942**
Personal memoirs. Edited with notes and an introd. by E. B. Long. New York, Grosset & Dunlap [1962, c1952] xxv, 608 p. maps. 21 cm. (Universal library, UL129) *1. U.S. — History — Civil War — Campaigns and battles. 2. U.S. — History — War with Mexico, 1845-1848 — Personal narratives.*
E672.Ax   923.173   Cd62-253

Catton, Bruce, 1899-   **III. 5943**
Grant moves south. With maps by Samuel H. Bryant. [1st ed.] Boston, Little, Brown [1960] x, 564 p. port., maps. 22 cm. A continuation of Lloyd Lewis' Captain Sam Grant. *1. Grant, Ulysses Simpson, Pres. U.S., 1822-1885. 2. United States — History — Civil War — Campaigns and battles. I. Lewis, Lloyd, 1891-1949. Captain Sam Grant. II. T.*
E672.C293   923.173   60-5860

Catton, Bruce, 1899-   **III. 5944**
Grant takes command, With maps by Samuel H. Bryant. [1st ed.] Boston, Little, Brown [1969] 556 p. maps, plans, port. 25 cm. *1. Grant, Ulysses Simpson, Pres., U.S., 1822-1885. 2. United States — History — Civil War — Campaigns and battles. I. T.*
E672.C295   973.73/0924   69-12632

Catton, Bruce, 1899-   **III. 5945**
U.S. Grant and the American military tradition. [1st ed.] Boston, Little, Brown [1954] x, 201 p. 22 cm. (The Library of American biography) *1. Grant, Ulysses Simpson, Pres. U.S., 1822-1885.*
E672.C3 1954   923.173   54-6860

Hesseltine, William Best, 1902-1963.   **III. 5946**
Ulysses S. Grant, politician. New York, F. Ungar Pub. Co. [1957, c1935] xiii, 480 p. plates, ports., facsim. 25 cm. (American classics) *1. Grant, Ulysses Simpson, Pres. U.S., 1822-1885. 2. United States — Politics and government — 1869-1877.*
E672.H46 1957   923.173   57-12323

E681 – 685   Hayes, 1877 – 1881

Woodward, Comer Vann, 1908-   **III. 5947**
Reunion and reaction; the compromise of 1877 and the end of reconstruction, by C. Vann Woodward. Boston, Little, Brown [1966] xii, 263 p. map. 20 cm. *1. United States — Politics and government — 1877-1881. 2. Reconstruction. I. T.*
E681.W83 1966   973.83   66-22490

Barnard, Harry, 1906-   **III. 5948**
Rutherford B. Hayes and his America. New York, Russell & Russell [1967, c1954] 606 p. illus., facsim., ports. 22 cm. *1. Hayes, Rutherford Birchard, Pres. U.S., 1822-1893. I. T.*
E682.B3 1967   973.8/3/0924   66-24667

Davison, Kenneth E.   **III. 5949**
The Presidency of Rutherford B. Hayes [by] Kenneth E. Davison. Westport, Conn., Greenwood Press, Pub. Division [1972] p. (Contributions in American studies, no. 3) *1. Hayes, Rutherford Birchard, Pres. U.S., 1822-1893. I. T.*
E682.D38   973.8/3/0924 (B)   79-176289   ISBN:0837162750

Eckenrode, Hamilton James, 1881-   **III. 5950**
Rutherford B. Hayes; statesman of reunion, assisted by Pocahontas Wilson Wight. Port Washington, N.Y., Kennikat Press [1963, c1957] 363 p. illus., ports., facsim. 22 cm. *1. Hayes, Rutherford Birchard, Pres. U.S., 1822-1893.*
E682.E19 1963   923.173   63-20590

Clancy, Herbert John.   **III. 5951**
The Presidential election of 1880. Chicago, Loyola University Press, 1958. 294 p. 24 cm. (Jesuit studies; contributions to the arts and sciences by members of the Society of Jesus) *1. Presidents — U.S. — Election — 1880. I. T.*
E685.C5   973.83   58-12311

E686 – 695   Garfield, 1881.
Arthur, 1881 – 1885

Pletcher, David M.   **III. 5952**
The awkward years; American foreign relations under Garfield and Arthur. Columbia, University of Missouri Press [c1962] 381 p. 25 cm. *1. U.S. — Foreign relations — 1881-1885. 2. U.S. — Politics and government — 1881-1885. I. T.*
E686.P5   973.84   62-15589

Smith, Theodore Clarke, 1870-   **III. 5953**
The life and letters of James Abram Garfield, by Theodore Clarke Smith. New Haven, Yale University Press, 1925. 2 v. fronts. (ports.) illus. (maps) 24 cm. Paged continuously. *1. Garfield, James Abram, pres. U.S., 1831-1881.*
E687.S66   25-19753

Howe, George Frederick.   **III. 5954**
Chester A. Arthur, a quarter-century of machine New York, F. Ungar Pub. Co. [1957, c1935] xi, 307 p. illus., ports. 24 cm. (American classics) *1. Arthur, Chester Alan, Pres. U.S., 1830-1886. 2. United States — Politics and government — 1881-1885.*
E692.H67 1957   923.173   57-12324

E696 – 700   Cleveland, 1885 – 1889

Ford, Henry Jones, 1851-1925.   **III. 5955**
The Cleveland era; a chronicle of the new order in politics, by Henry Jones Ford. New Haven, Yale University Press: [etc., etc.] 1921. ix, 232 p. col. port. 18 cm. (The chronicles of America series, v.44) "Roosevelt edition." *1. Cleveland, Grover, pres. U.S., 1837-1908. 2. U.S. — Politics and government — 1885-1889. 3. U.S. — Politics and government — 1893-1897. I. T.*
E696.F72 (E173.C56 vol. 44)   973.8   22-12189

Cleveland, Grover, pres. U.S., 1837-1908.   **III. 5956**
Letters of Grover Cleveland, 1850-1908; selected and edited by Allan Nevins. Boston and New York, Houghton Mifflin, 1933. xix, 640 p. port. 25 cm. *I. Nevins, Allan, 1890- ed. II. T.*
E697.C63   923.173   33-35003

Merrill, Horace Samuel.   **III. 5957**
Bourbon leader: Grover Cleveland and the Democratic Party. Edited by Oscar Handlin. [1st ed.] Boston, Little, Brown [1957] 224 p. 21 cm. (The Library of American biography) *1. Cleveland, Grover, Pres. U.S., 1837-1908. 2. U.S. — Politics and government — 1865-1900. I. T.*
E697.M4   973.85   57-12002

Nevins, Allan, 1890-   **III. 5958**
Grover Cleveland; a study in courage, by Allan Nevins. New York, Dodd, Mead, 1934. xiii, 832 p. plates, ports. 24 cm. (American political leaders) "Winner of the Pulitzer prize for American biography." "Published October 1932 ... Eighth printing, November, 1934." *1. Cleveland, Grover, pres. U.S., 1837-1908.*
E697.N468   923.173   38-4611

E701 – 705   Harrison, 1889 – 1893

Sievers, Harry Joseph, 1920-   **III. 5959**
Benjamin Harrison. Introd. by Hilton U. Brown. [2d ed., rev.] New York, University Publishers [c1960-   v. illus. 24 cm. *1. Harrison, Benjamin, Pres. U.S., 1833-1901.*
E702.S55   923.173   60-12711

E711 – 738   McKinley, 1897 – 1901

Leech, Margaret, 1893-   **III. 5960**
In the days of McKinley. [1st ed.] New York, Harper [1959] viii, 686 p. illus., ports., facsims. 25 cm. "Sources": p. 610-611. "Notes and references": p. 612-669. *1. McKinley, William, Pres. U.S., 1843-1901. I. T.*
E711.6.L4   923.173   59-6310

Morgan, Howard Wayne.   **III. 5961**
William McKinley and his America. [Syracuse, N.Y.] Syracuse University Press, 1963. xi, 595 p. illus., ports. 24 cm. *1. McKinley, William, Pres. U.S., 1843-1901. I. T.*
E711.6.M7   923.173   63-19723

Coolidge, Archibald Cary, 1866-1928.   **III. 5962**
The United States as a world power. New York, Macmillan, 1908. St. Clair Shores, Mich., Scholarly Press, 1971. vii, 385 p. 22 cm. *1. United States — Foreign relations. 2. United States — Territorial expansion. 3. Eastern question (Far East) I. T.*
E713.C765 1971   327.73   72-144955   ISBN:0403009073

Greene, Theodore P., 1920- ed.   **III. 5963**
American imperialism in 1898. Boston, Heath [1955] ix, 105 p. illus. 24 cm. (Problems in American civilization; readings selected by the Dept. of American Studies, Amherst College) *1. U.S. — Foreign relations — War of 1898. 2. U.S. — Colonial question. 3. Imperialism. I. T. (S)*
E713.G7   973.891   55-1630

Latané, John Holladay, 1869-1932.   **III. 5964**
America as a world power 1897-1907. New York, Harper. St. Clair Shores, Mich., Scholarly Press, 1970 [c1907] xvi, 350 p. maps. 22 cm. (The American nation: a history, v. 25) *1. United States — History — 1898- 2. United States — Territorial expansion. 3. United States — Colonial question. I. T. (S:The American nation: a history from original sources by associated scholars, v. 25)*
E713.L37   973.8/8   79-145131   ISBN:0403010640

Pratt, Julius William, 1888-   **III. 5965**
Expansionists of 1898; the acquisition of Hawaii and the Spanish islands. New York, P. Smith, 1951 [c1936] viii, 393 p. 21 cm. (The Albert Shaw lectures on diplomatic history, 1936) *1. United States — Territorial expansion. 2. United States — Foreign relations. 3. Hawaii — Annexation. I. T. (S)*
E713.P895 1936a   973.88   52-7706

Morgan, Howard Wayne.   **III. 5966**
America's road to empire; the war with Spain and overseas expansion [by] H. Wayne Morgan. New York, Wiley [1965] xii, 124 p. maps. 22 cm. (America in crisis) *1. U.S. — History — War of 1898. 2. U.S. — Territorial expansion. 3. Imperialism. I. T. (S)*
E715.M85   973.891   64-8714

Brown, Charles Henry, 1910-   **III. 5967**
The correspondents' war; journalists in the Spanish-American War [by] Charles H. Brown. New York, Scribner [1967] xi, 478 p. illus., maps. 24 cm. *1. United States — History — War of 1898 — Journalists. 2. United States — History — War of 1898 — Campaigns and battles. I. T.*
E717.B7   973.8/93   67-14167

E740   20th Century

Brock, Clifton.   **III. 5968**
Americans for Democratic Action: its role in national politics. Introd. by Max Lerner. Washington, Public Affairs Press [1962] 229 p. illus. 24 cm. *1. Americans for Democratic Action. 2. U.S. — Politics and government — 1945-*
E740.A632   973.92   61-15694

Allen, Frederick Lewis, 1890-   **III. 5969**
Only yesterday; an informal history of the nineteen-twenties, by Frederick Lewis Allen. New York, Harper, 1931. xiv, 370 p. illus. 23 cm. *1. U.S. — History — 20th cent. 2. U.S. — Social conditions. 3. U.S. — Economic conditions — 1918- I. T.*
E741.A64   973.91   31-28421

Allen, Frederick Lewis, 1890-   **III. 5970**
Since yesterday; the nineteen-thirties in America, September 3, 1929-September 3, 1939, by Frederick Lewis Allen. 1st ed. New York and London, Harper, 1940. xiv, 362 p. plates, ports, facsims. 23 cm. *1. U.S. — History — 20th cent. 2. U.S. — Social conditions. 3. U.S. — Economic conditions — 1918- I. T.*
E741.A66   973.916   40-27130

Barck, Oscar Theodore, 1902-   **III. 5971**
Since 1900; a history of the United States in our times. 4th ed. By Oscar Theodore Barck [and] Nelson Manfred Blake. New York, Macmillan [1965] x, 963 p. illus., maps. 24 cm. *1. U.S. — History — 20th cent. I. Blake, Nelson Manfred, 1908- joint author. II. T.*
E741.B34 1965   973.91   65-14074

Braeman, John, ed.   **III. 5972**
Change and continuity in twentieth-century America, edited by John Braeman, Robert H. Bremner [and] Everett Walters. [Columbus] Ohio State University Press [1965, c1964] x, 287 p. 22 cm. (Modern America, no. 1) *1. U.S. — History — 20th cent. — Addresses, essays, lectures. I. Bremner, Robert Hamlett, 1917- joint ed. II. Walters, Everett, 1915- joint ed. III. T. (S)*
E741.B68   973.9082   64-19380

Link, Arthur Stanley.   **III. 5973**
American epoch; a history of the United States since the 1890's, by Arthur S. Link. With the collaboration of William B. Catton and the assistance of William M. Leary, Jr. 3d ed. New York, Knopf [1967] xxii, 926, xliv p. illus., maps, ports. 25 cm. *1. U.S. — History — 20th cent. I. T.*
E741.L55 1967   973.91   67-12258

Mowry, George Edwin, 1909-   **III. 5974**
The urban nation, 1920-1960, by George E. Mowry. [1st ed.] New York, Hill and Wang [1965] x, 278 p. maps. 22 cm. (The Making of America) *1. United States — History — 20th century. 2. Urbanization — United States. I. T.*
E741.M7   973.9   65-17423

Regier, Cornelius C., 1884-   **III. 5975**
The era of the muckrakers, by C. C. Regier. Chapel Hill, The University of North Carolina Press, 1932. xi, 254 p. front. ports. 24 cm. Without thesis note. *1. U.S. — Politics and government — 20th cent. 2. Corruption (in politics) 3. Journalism — U.S. I. The muckrakers, The era of. II. T.*
E741.R34   973.91   32-30647

Rostow, Walt Whitman, 1916-   **III. 5976**
The United States in the world arena; an essay in recent history. New York, Harper [1960] xxii, 568 p. diagrs., tables. 24 cm. (Massachusetts Institute of Technology. Center for International Studies. American project series) *1. United States — History — 20th century. 2. United States — Foreign relations — 20th century. 3. World politics — 20th century. I. T. (S)*
E741.R67   327.73   60-7568

Slosson, Preston William, 1892-   **III. 5977**
The great crusade and after, 1914-1928. With an editorial foreword by Arthur M. Schlesinger and Dixon Ryan Fox. New York, Macmillan, 1930. xviii p., 1 l., 486 p. front., plates, facsims. 23 cm. *1. U.S. — History — 20th cent. 2. U.S. — Social conditions. 3. European war, 1914-1918 — U.S. I. T.*
E741.S63   973.91   30-22386

Snowman, Daniel.   **III. 5978**
America since 1920. [1st U.S. ed.] New York, Harper & Row [1969, c1968] 192 p. illus., map. 22 cm. ([A Twentieth-century nation series]) First published in 1968 under title: USA: the twenties to Vietnam. *1. United States — History — 20th century. 2. United States — Social conditions — 1933-1945. 3. United States — Social conditions — 1945- I. T.*
E741.S65 1969   973.9   68-28220

Strauss, Lewis L.   **III. 5979**
Men and decisions. [1st ed.] Garden City, N.Y., Doubleday, 1962. 468 p. illus. 24 cm. *1. U.S. — History — 20th cent. I. T.*
E741.S78   973.91   62-11304

Sullivan, Mark, 1874-1952.   **III. 5980**
Our times, 1900-1925. Introd. by Dewey W. Grantham. New York, Scribner [1971- c1926- v. illus., facsims., maps, ports. 24 cm. *1. United States — History — 20th century. 2. United States — Civilization — 20th century. 3. European War, 1914-1918 — United States. I. T.*
E741.S945   973.91   70-138308   ISBN:0684123541 (v. 1) varies

Mencken, Henry Louis, 1880-1956.   **III. 5981**
A carnival of buncombe. Edited by Malcolm Moos. Baltimore, Johns

Hopkins Press [1956] 370 p. 22 cm. *1. U.S. — Politics and government — 20th cent. I. T.*
E742.M4   973.91504   56-11658

E743   POLITICAL HISTORY

Barck, Oscar Theodore, 1902-   III. 5982
A history of the United States since 1945, by Oscar T. Barck, Jr. [New York, Dell Pub. Co., 1965] 480 p. 19 cm. (A Laurel edition) *1. U.S. — History — 1945- I. T.*
E743.B34   973.9   65-5953

Bates, James Leonard.   III. 5983
The origins of Teapot Dome; progressives, parties and petroleum, 1909-1921. [Urbana, University of Illinois Press, 1963] viii, 278 p. illus., ports. 24 cm. *1. Progressivism (U.S. politics) 2. Petroleum conservation. 3. Petroleum law and legislation — U.S. 4. Corruption (in politics) — U.S. I. T.*
E743.B36   353   63-17045

Chalmers, David Mark.   III. 5984
The social and political ideas of the muckrakers. [1st ed.] New York, Citadel Press [1964] 127 p. 21 cm. *1. Journalists, American — Biography. 2. Journalism — Social aspects. 3. Journalism — Political aspects. I. T.*
E743.C45   301.153   64-15960

Chamberlain, John, 1903-   III. 5985
Farewell to reform; the rise, life and decay of the progressive mind in America. Chicago, Quadrangle Books [1965, c1932] xi, 333 p. 21 cm. (Quadrangle paperbacks, QP19) *1. U.S. — Politics and government — 1901-1953. 2. Progressivism (U.S. politics) 3. Social problems in literature. I. T.*
E743.C46 1965   973.91   65-2646

Ellsworth, Ralph Eugene, 1907-   III. 5986
The American right wing; a report to the Fund for the Republic, by Ralph E. Ellsworth and Sarah M. Harris. Washington, Public Affairs Press [1962] 63 p. 23 cm. *1. Conservatism. 2. U.S. — Politics and government — 1945- I. Harris, Sarah M., joint author. II. T.*
E743.E37 1962   62-630

Fulbright, James William, 1905-   III. 5987
Fulbright of Arkansas: the public positions of a private thinker. Edited by Karl E. Meyer. With a pref. by Walter Lippmann. Washington, R. B. Luce [1963] 279 p. 21 cm. *1. U.S. — Politics and government — 20th cent. — Addresses, essays, lectures. 2. World politics — 1945- — Addresses, essays, lectures. I. T.*
E743.F8   327.73   63-9331

Graham, Otis L.   III. 5988
An encore for reform; the old progressives and the New Deal [by] Otis L. Graham, Jr. New York, Oxford University Press, 1967. viii, 256 p. 22 cm. *1. United States — Politics and government — 1901-1953. 2. Progressivism (U.S. politics) I. T.*
E743.G7   973.91   67-15126

Graham, Otis L.   III. 5989
The great campaigns: reform and war in America, 1900-1928 [by] Otis L. Graham, Jr. Englewood Cliffs, N.J., Prentice-Hall [1971] xiii, 386 p. illus., ports. 23 cm. (Prentice-Hall history of the American people series) *1. United States — Politics and government — 1901-1953. 2. European War, 1914-1918 — United States. 3. United States — Foreign relations — 1865-1921. I. T.*
E743.G72   973.91   79-135756   ISBN:0133635724

Henry, Laurin L.   III. 5990
Presidential transitions. Washington, Brookings Institution [1960] xviii, 755 p. 24 cm. *1. Presidents — U.S. — Transition periods. 2. U.S. — Politics and government — 20th cent. I. T.*
E743.H4   353.032   60-53252

Hofstadter, Richard, 1916-   III. 5991
The age of reform; from Bryan to F. D. R. [1st ed.] New York, Knopf, 1955. 328 p. 22 cm. *1. U.S. — Politics and government — 20th cent. 2. Progressivism (U.S. politics) I. T.*
E743.H63   973.91   54-7206

Hofstadter, Richard, 1916-   III. 5992
The paranoid style in American politics, and other essays. [1st ed.] New York, Knopf, 1965. xiv, 314 p. 22 cm. *1. United States — Politics and government. 2. Right and left (Political science) 3. United States — Territorial expansion. 4. Public opinion — United States. I. T.*
E743.H632   320.973   65-18758

Hoover, Herbert Clark, pres. U.S., 1874-   III. 5993
Addresses upon the American road, by Herbert Hoover. 1933-1938. New York, Scribner, 1938. viii, 390 p. 22 cm. *1. U.S. — Economic policy. 2. U.S. —* *Politics and government — 1933- 3. U.S. — Politics and government — Addresses, essays, lectures. I. T.*
E743.H65   973.917   38-29150

Johnson, Walter, 1915-   III. 5994
1600 Pennsylvania Avenue; Presidents and the people, 1929-1959. [1st ed.] Boston, Little, Brown [1960] 390 p. 22 cm. *1. Presidents — U.S. 2. U.S. — Politics and government — 1929- 3. U.S. — Foreign relations — 20th cent. I. T.*
E743.J6   973.91   60-6525

Josephson, Matthew, 1899-   III. 5995
The president makers; the culture of politics and leadership in an age of enlightenment, 1896-1919. With a new foreword by the author. New York, F. Ungar Pub. Co. [1964] xii, 584 p. 23 cm. (American classics) *1. U.S. — Politics and government — 1865-1933. 2. Statesmen, American. I. T.*
E743.J65 1964   973.9   64-8722

Krock, Arthur, 1886-   III. 5996
Memoirs; sixty years on the firing line. New York, Funk & Wagnalls [1968] xii, 508 p. 24 cm. *1. United States — Politics and government — 20th century. 2. Presidents — United States. I. T.*
E743.K7   973.9/0924   68-26106

Lora, Ronald.   III. 5997
Conservative minds in America. Chicago, Rand McNally [c1971] xiii, 274 p. 22 cm. (The Rand McNally series on the history of American thought and culture) *1. Conservatism — United States. 2. Conservatism. I. T.*
E743.L77   320.5/2/0973   78-170893

Lubell, Samuel.   III. 5998
The future of American politics. [1st ed.] New York, Harper [1952] 285 p. 22 cm. *1. U.S. — Politics and government — 1945- 2. U.S. — Social conditions. I. T.*
E743.L85   973.918 (973.92)   52-5462

Overstreet, Harry Allen, 1875-   III. 5999
The strange tactics of extremism [by] Harry and Bonaro Overstreet. [1st ed.] New York, Norton [1964] 315 p. 22 cm. *1. United States — Politics and government — 1945- 2. Anti-communist movements — United States. 3. Right and left (Political science) I. Overstreet, Bonaro (Wilkinson) 1902- joint author. II. T.*
E743.O9   301.153   64-13991

Roper, Elmo Burns, 1900-   III. 6000
You and your leaders, their actions and your reactions, 1936-1956. New York, Morrow [c1957] 288 p. 22 cm. *1. Public opinion — U.S. 2. U.S. — Politics and government — 1933-1953. 3. Statesmen, American. 4. Public opinion polls. I. T.*
E743.R67   973.917   58-6672

Wehle, Louis Brandeis, 1880-   III. 6001
Hidden threads of history, Wilson through Roosevelt; with an introd. by Allan Nevins. New York, Macmillan, 1953. 300 p. 22 cm. *1. Roosevelt, Franklin Delano, Pres. U.S., 1882-1945. 2. U.S. — Politics and government — 1913-1923. 3. U.S. — Politics and government — 1933-1945. 4. U.S. — Foreign relations — 20th cent. I. T.*
E743.W43   973.91   53-9519

Weinstein, James, 1926-   III. 6002
The corporate ideal in the liberal state, 1900-1918. Boston, Beacon Press [1968] xvii, 263 p. 24 cm. *1. United States — Politics and government — 20th century. 2. Progressivism (U.S. politics) 3. Business and politics — United States. I. T.*
E743.W44   320.9/73   68-12846

Wiebe, Robert H.   III. 6003
Businessmen and reform: a study of the progressive movement. Cambridge, Mass., Harvard University Press, 1962. 283 p. 22 cm. *1. Progressivism (U.S. politics) 2. Business and politics. I. T.*
E743.W59   323.3   62-18718

E743.5   "Un-American" Activities

Buckley, William Frank, 1925-   III. 6004
The committee and its critics; a calm review of the House Committee on Un-American Activities, by William F. Buckley, Jr. and the editors of National review. New York, Putnam [1962] 352 p. 22 cm. *1. U.S. Congress. House. Committee on Un-American Activities. I. National review (Washington, D.C.) II. T.*
E743.5.B82   328.36   62-7342

Carr, Robert Kenneth, 1908-   III. 6005
The House Committee on Un-American Activities, 1945-1950. Ithaca, Cornell University Press, 1952. xiii, 489 p. 24 cm. (Cornell studies in civil liberty) *1. U.S. Congress. House. Committee on Un-American Activities. 2.*

Communism — U.S. — 1917- (S:Cornell University. Cornell studies in civil liberty)
E743.5.C3   335   52-14423

Chambers, Whittaker. III. 6006
Witness. New York, Random House [1952] 808 p. 22 cm. Autobiographical. *1. Hiss, Alger. 2. Communism — U.S. — 1917-. I. T.*
E743.5.C47   351.74 (364.13)   52-5149

Davis, Elmer Holmes, 1890-1958. III. 6007
But we were born free. Westport, Conn., Greenwood Press [1971] 229 p. 23 cm. "Originally published 1954." *1. Communism — United States — 1917- — Addresses, essays, lectures. 2. United States — Politics and government — 1945-1953 — Addresses, essays, lectures. 3. United States — Civilization — Addresses, essays, lectures. I. T.*
E743.5.D33 1971   320.9/73   73-138585   ISBN:0837157846

Dies, Martin, 1901- III. 6008
Martin Dies' story. New York, Bookmailer [1963] 283 p. 22 cm. *1. U.S. Congress. House. Special Committee on un-American Activities (1938-1944) 2. Communism — U.S. — 1917- 3. Propaganda, Communist.*
E743.5.D52   328.36   63-14765

Hiss, Alger. III. 6009
In the court of public opinion. [1st ed.] New York, A. A. Knopf, 1957. 424 p. illus. 22 cm. *1. Chambers, Whittaker. 2. Communism — U.S. — 1917- I. T.*
E743.5.H54   351.74 (364.13)   57-7546

Cooke, Alistair, 1908- III. 6010
A generation on trial: U.S.A. v. Alger Hiss. [2d ed., enl.] New York, Knopf, 1952. 356 p. 22 cm. *1. Hiss, Alger. 2. Chambers, Whittaker. I. T.*
E743.5.H55C6 1952   351.74 (364.13)   52-4255

Latham, Earl. III. 6011
The communist controversy in Washington: from the New Deal to McCarthy. Cambridge, Harvard University Press, 1966. viii, 446 p. 25 cm. (Communism in American life) *1. Communism in the U.S. — 1917- 2. Internal security — U.S. 3. Subversive activities — U.S. I. T. (S)*
E743.5.L35   335.430973   66-14447   351.74 L346

Lattimore, Owen, 1900- III. 6012
Ordeal by slander. Westport, Conn., Greenwood Press [1971, c1950] viii, 236 p. 23 cm. *1. McCarthy, Joseph Raymond, 1908-1957. I. T.*
E743.5.L36 1971   973.91   72-138156   ISBN:0837156130

Murray, Robert K. III. 6013
Red scare; a study in national hysteria, 1919-1920. Minneapolis, University of Minnesota Press [c1955] 337 p. illus. 23 cm. *1. Communism — U.S. — 1917- 2. Subversive activities — U.S. 3. Hysteria (Social psychology) — Case studies. 4. U.S. — Economic conditions — 1918-1945. I. T.*
E743.5.M8   973.91   55-7034

Preston, William, 1924- III. 6014
Aliens and dissenters; Federal suppression of radicals, 1903-1933. Cambridge, Harvard University Press, 1963. 352 p. 22 cm. *1. Industrial Workers of the World. 2. Aliens — U.S. 3. Deportation — U.S. 4. Civil rights — U.S. I. T.*
E743.5.P7   323.67   63-10873

Shils, Edward Albert, 1911- III. 6015
The torment of secrecy; the background and consequences of American security policies. Glencoe, Ill., Free Press [c1956] 238 p. 22 cm. *1. Internal security — U.S. 2. Loyalty-security program, 1947- 3. Communism — U.S. — 1917- I. T.*
E743.5.S48   351.75 (364.13)   55-7333

Ogden, August Raymond. III. 6016
The Dies committee; a study of the special House committee for the investigation of un-American activities, 1938-1944, by August Raymond Ogden. Washington, D.C., Catholic University of America Press, 1945. vi, 318 p. 24 cm. "2nd, revised edition." "This study appeared originally as a dissertation submitted to the Faculty of the School of social science of the Catholic university of America ... for the degree of doctor of philosophy." — Pref. *1. Dies, Martin, 1901- 2. U.S. Congress. House. Special committee on un-American activities (1938-   ) 3. Propaganda. I. T.*
E743.5.U56O3 1945   335   A45-3189

Warren, Frank A. III. 6017
Liberals and communism; the "red decade" revisited, by Frank A. Warren, III. Bloomington, Indiana University Press [1966] ix, 276 p. 22 cm. *1. Intellectuals — U.S. 2. Liberalism — U.S. 3. Communism — U.S. — 1917- I. T.*
E743.5.W28   320.510973   66-12735

E744   DIPLOMATIC HISTORY
A – E

Acheson, Dean Gooderham, 1893-1971. III. 6018
Present at the creation; my years in the State Department [by] Dean Acheson. [1st ed.] New York, Norton [1969] xiv, 798 p. illus. 25 cm. *1. Acheson, Dean Gooderham, 1893-1971. 2. United States — Foreign relations — 1933-1945. 3. United States — Foreign relations — 1945-1953. I. T.*
E744.A2174   327.73   69-14692   ISBN:039307448X

Adler, Selig, 1909- III. 6019
The isolationist impulse: its twentieth-century reaction. London, New York, Abelard-Schuman [1957] 538 p. 22 cm. *1. U.S. — Foreign relations — 20th cent. 2. Public opinion — U.S. I. T.*
E744.A26   327.73   57-5629

Agar, Herbert, 1897- III. 6020
The price of power; America since 1945. [Chicago] University of Chicago Press [1957] 199 p. 21 cm. (The Chicago history of American civilization) *1. U.S. — Foreign relations — 1945- 2. U.S. — Politics and government — 1945- 3. World politics — 1945- I. T.*
E744.A3   327.73   57-8575   A915

Almond, Gabriel Abraham, 1911- III. 6021
The American people and foreign policy. New York, Praeger [1960] 269 p. 20 cm. (Praeger paperbacks, PPS-38. Books that matter.) *1. U.S. — Foreign relations — 1945-1953. 2. Public opinion — U.S. 3. National characteristics, American. I. T.*
E744.A47 1960a   327.73   61-3776

Anderson, George LaVerne, 1905- ed. III. 6022
Issues and conflicts; studies in twentieth century American diplomacy, edited by George L. Anderson. New York, Greenwood Press [1969, c1959] 374 p. 24 cm. *1. United States — Relations (general) with foreign countries. I. T.*
E744.A63 1969   327.73   69-13802

Barnet, Richard J. III. 6023
Roots of war [by] Richard J. Barnet. [1st ed.] New York, Atheneum, 1972. 350 p. 25 cm. *1. United States — Foreign relations — 20th century. 2. United States — Foreign relations administration. 3. United States — Foreign economic relations. 4. United States — Politics and government — 20th century. I. T.*
E744.B32   327.73   71-184725

Bowie, Robert Richardson, 1909- III. 6024
Shaping the future; foreign policy in an age of transition. New York, Columbia University Press, 1964. viii, 118 p. 21 cm. "Contains the Radner lectures ... [given by the author] at Columbia University in April, 1963." *1. U.S. — Foreign relations — 1945- 2. World politics — 1945- I. T.*
E744.B675   327   64-15740

Brown, Seyom. III. 6025
The faces of power; constancy and change in United States foreign policy from Truman to Johnson. New York, Columbia University Press, 1968. xii, 397 p. 23 cm. *1. United States — Foreign relations — 1945- I. T.*
E744.B78   327.73   68-11436

Carleton, William Graves. III. 6026
The revolution in American foreign policy, its global range [by] William G. Carleton. 2d ed. New York, Random House [1967] xii, 555 p. 21 cm. *1. U.S. — Foreign relations — 1945- 2. World politics — 1945- I. T.*
E744.C357 1967   327.73   67-20623

Cook, Thomas Ira, 1907- III. 6027
Power through purpose; the realism of idealism as a basis for foreign policy, by Thomas I. Cook and Malcolm Moos. Baltimore, Johns Hopkins Press [1954] 216 p. 23 cm. *1. U.S. — Foreign relations — 20th cent. 2. Communism. I. Moos, Malcolm Charles, 1916- joint author. II. T.*
E744.C762   327.73   54-11253

Cottrell, Leonard Slater, 1899- III. 6028
American opinion on world affairs in the atomic age, by Leonard S. Cottrell, Jr. & Sylvia Eberhart. With a foreword by Frederick Osborn. New York, Greenwood Press [1969, c1948] xxi, 152 p. 23 cm. "Based on a report prepared for the Committee on the Social and Economic Aspects of Atomic Energy of the Social Science Research Council." *1. Public opinion — United States. 2. United States — Foreign relations — 1945-1953. 3. Atomic bomb. I. Eberhart, Sylvia, joint author. II. Social Science Research Council. Committee on Social and Economic Aspects of Atomic Energy. Public reaction to the atomic bomb and world affairs. III. T.*
E744.C77 1969   327.73   69-13867

Davids, Jules. III. 6029
America and the world of our time; United States diplomacy in the

twentieth century. 3d ed. New York, Random House [1970] viii, 722 p. 25 cm. *1. United States — Foreign relations — 20th century. I. T.*
F744 D25 1970   327.73   76-97587

De Conde, Alexander, ed.   **III. 6030**
Isolation and security; ideas and interests in twentieth-century American foreign policy. The contributors: William R. Allen [and others] Durham, N.C., Duke University Press, 1957. xi, 204 p. 24 cm. *1. U.S. — Foreign relations — 20th cent. I. T.*
E744.D33   327.73   57-13022

Dulles, Foster Rhea, 1900-   **III. 6031**
America's rise to world power, 1898-1954. [1st ed.] New York, Harper [1955] 314 p. illus. 22 cm. (The New American nation series) *1. U.S. — Foreign relations — 20th cent. 2. World politics. I. T.*
E744.D8   327.73   55-6575

D888a

E744   F – M

Fulbright, James William, 1905-   **III. 6032**
The arrogance of power, by J. William Fulbright. New York, Random House [1967, c1966] xv, 264 p. 21 cm. Based on the Christian A. Herter lecture series, Johns Hopkins University, 1966. *1. U.S. — Foreign relations — 1945- — Addresses, essays, lectures. 2. World politics — 1945- — Addresses, essays, lectures. I. T.*
E744.F886   327.73   67-13859

Gaddis, John Lewis.   **III. 6033**
The United States and the origins of the cold war, 1941-1947. New York, Columbia University Press, 1972. ix, 396 p. 23 cm. (Contemporary American history series) *1. United States — Foreign relations — 1945- I. T.*
E744.G25   327.73   75-186388   ISBN:0231032897 0231083025 (pbk)

Goldwater, Barry Morris, 1909-   **III. 6034**
Why not victory? A fresh look at American foreign policy. [1st ed.] New York, McGraw-Hill [1962] 201 p. 22 cm. *1. U.S. — Foreign relations — 1945- 2. World politics — 1945- I. T.*
E744.G57   327.73   62-14674

Graebner, Norman A., ed.   **III. 6035**
An uncertain tradition; American Secretaries of State in the twentieth century. New York, McGraw-Hill, 1961. 341 p. 24 cm. (McGraw-Hill series in American history) *1. U.S. Dept. of State — Biography. 2. Cabinet officers — U.S. 3. U.S. — Foreign relations — 20th cent. I. T.*
E744.G7   353.1   61-8654

Heilbroner, Robert L.   **III. 6036**
The future as history; the historic currents of our time and the direction in which they are taking America. [1st ed.] New York, Harper [1960] 217 p. 22 cm. *1. United States — Relations (general) with foreign countries. 2. World politics — 1945- I. T.*
E744.H45   327.73   60-7527

Johnson, Walter, 1915-   **III. 6037**
The battle against isolation. New York, Da Capo Press, 1973 [c1944] xii, 269 p. illus. 22 cm. (Franklin D. Roosevelt and the era of the New Deal) Reprint of the ed. published by the University of Chicago. *1. United States — Foreign relations — 1933-1945. 2. World War, 1939-1945 — United States. I. T. (S)*
E744.J66 1973   327.73   72-2376   ISBN:0306704803

Kaplan, Lawrence S.   **III. 6038**
Recent American foreign policy; conflicting interpretations [by] Lawrence S. Kaplan. Homewood, Ill., Dorsey Press, 1968. xiii, 358 p. 23 cm. (The Dorsey series in American history) *1. United States — Foreign relations — 1945- — Addresses, essays, lectures. I. T.*
E744.K17   327.73/008   67-30244

Kennan, George Frost, 1904-   **III. 6039**
American diplomacy, 1900-1950. Chicago, University of Chicago Press [1951] ix, 154 p. 22 cm. (Charles R. Walgreen Foundation lectures) *1. U.S. — Foreign relations — 20th cent. 2. U.S. — Foreign relations — Russia. 3. Russia — Foreign rel — U.S. I. T. (S:Chicago. University. Charles R. Walgreen Foundation. Lectures)*
E744.K3 1951a   327.73   51-8841

Kolko, Joyce.   **III. 6040**
The limits of power: the world and United States foreign policy, 1945-1954 [by] Joyce and Gabriel Kolko. [1st ed.] New York, Harper & Row [c1972] xii, 820 p. 24 cm. *1. United States — Foreign relations — 1945-1953. I. Kolko, Gabriel, 1932- joint author. II. T.*
E744.K64 1972   327.73   70-156530   ISBN:0060124474

Kolko, Gabriel.   **III. 6041**
The politics of war; the world and United States foreign policy, 1943-1945. New York, Random House [c1968] x, 685 p. 25 cm. *1. United States — Foreign relations — 1933-1945. 2. World politics — 1933-1945. I. T.*
E744.K65   327.73   68-28560   Taylor

Langer, William Leonard, 1896-   **III. 6042**
The challenge to isolation; the world crisis of 1937-1940 and American foreign policy, by William L. Langer and S. Everett Gleason. Gloucester, Mass., Peter Smith, 1970 [c1952] 2 v. (xiii, 794 p.) 22 cm. *1. United States — Foreign relations — 1933-1945. 2. World War, 1939-1945 — United States. 3. World War, 1939-1945 — Diplomatic history. I. Gleason, Sarell Everett, 1905- joint author. II. T.*
E744.L3 1970   940.532/2/73   76-17008

Lerche, Charles O.   **III. 6043**
America in world affairs. New York, McGraw-Hill [1967] 118 p. 21 cm. (Foundations of American government and political science) *1. U.S. — Foreign relations. 2. World politics — 1945- I. International agencies. II. T. (S)*
E744.L488 1967   327.73   67-18391

May, Ernest R.   **III. 6044**
American intervention: 1917 and 1941. Washington, Service Center for Teachers of History [1960] 19 p. 23 cm. (Service Center for Teachers of History. Publication no. 30) *1. European War, 1914-1918 — U.S. 2. World War II, 1939-1945 — U.S. I. T.*
E744.M39   940.373   60-12444

Millis, Walter, 1899-   **III. 6045**
Arms and the state; civil-military elements in national policy, by Walter Millis, with Harvey C. Mansfield and Harold Stein. New York, Twentieth Century Fund, 1958. 436 p. 24 cm. "A volume in the Twentieth Century Fund's project on civil-military relations." *1. U.S. — Foreign relations — 20th cent. 2. Civil supremacy over the military — U.S. I. T.*
E744.M56   327.73   58-11837

Morgenthau, Hans Joachim, 1904-   **III. 6046**
In defense of the national interest; a critical examination of American foreign policy. [1st ed.] New York, Knopf, 1951. xii, 283, viii p. 22 cm. *1. U.S. — Foreign relations — 1945- I. T.*
E744.M68   327.73   51-11217

Morgenthau, Hans Joachim, 1904-   **III. 6047**
The purpose of American politics. [1st ed.] New York, Knopf, 1960. 359 p. 22 cm. *1. U.S. — Politics and government — 20th cent. 2. U.S. — History — Philosophy. I. T.*
E744.M69   973.91   60-16504

E744   N – Z

Nevins, Allan, 1890-   **III. 6048**
The New Deal and world affairs; a chronicle of international affairs, 1933-1945. New Haven, Yale University Press, 1950. ix, 332 p. ports. 21 cm. (The Chronicles of America series, v.56) *1. U.S. — Foreign relations — 1933-1945. 2. World politics. I. T. (S)*
E744.N487 (E173.C55 vol. 56)   327.73   50-8828

Nevins, Allan, 1890-   **III. 6049**
The United States in a chaotic world; a chronicle of international affairs, 1918-1933. New Haven, Yale University Press, 1950. ix, 252 p. front. 21 cm. (The Chronicles of American series, v.31) Benjamin Franklin ed. *1. U.S. — Foreign relations — 20th cent. 2. World politics. I. T. (S)*
E744.N493x (E173.C58 vol. 31)   327.73   52-4357

Niebuhr, Reinhold, 1892-1971.   **III. 6050**
The irony of American history. New York, Scribner, 1952. 174 p. 21 cm. *1. United States — Foreign relations — 1945-1953. 2. United States — History — Philosophy. 3. United States — Civilization. I. T.*
E744.N5   973   52-8724

Niebuhr, Reinhold, 1892-   **III. 6051**
The world crisis and American responsibility; nine essays. Collected and edited by Ernest W. Lefever. New York, Association Press [1958] 128 p. 16 cm. (A Reflection book) *1. U.S. — Relations (general) with foreign countries. 2. World politics — 1945- I. T.*
E744.N53   327.73   58-11534

Varg, Paul A.   **III. 6052**
Open door diplomat; the life of W. W. Rockhill. Urbana, University of Illinois Press, 1952. ix, 141 p. port. 26 cm. (Illinois studies in the social sciences, v.33, no. 4) *1. Rockhill, William Woodville, 1854-1914. 2. U.S. — Foreign relations — 20th cent. 3. Eastern question (Far East) I. T. (S:Illinois. University. Illinois studies in the social sciences, v.33, no. 4)*
E744.R68V3 (H31.I4 vol. 33, no. 4)   923.273   52-12402

Roosevelt, James, 1907- ed.   **III. 6053**
The liberal papers. Chicago, Quadrangle Books [1962] 354 p. 22 cm. *1. U.S.*

III. 6054   *United States*   E744

— *Foreign relations — 1945- — Addresses, essays, lectures.* 2. *U.S. — Defenses. I. T.*
E744.R79 1962a   327.73   62-4538

Skolnikoff, Eugene B.   **III. 6054**
Science, technology, and American foreign policy [by] Eugene B. Skolnikoff. Cambridge, M.I.T. Press [1967] xvi, 330 p. 22 cm. *1. U.S. — Foreign relations — 1945- 2. Science and state — U.S. 3. U.S. — Foreign relations administration. I. T.*
E744.S57   327.73   67-15239

Stillman, Edmund O.   **III. 6055**
The new politics; America and the end of the postwar world, by Edmund Stillman and William Pfaff. New York, Coward McCann [1961] 191 p. 22 cm. *1. U.S. — Foreign relations — 1945- 2. World politics — 1945- I. Pfaff, William, 1928- joint author. II. T.*
E744.S86   327.73   61-9177

Twentieth-century American foreign policy,   **III. 6056**
edited by John Braeman, Robert H. Bremner [and] David Brody. [Columbus] Ohio State University Press [1971] ix, 567 p. 22 cm. (Modern America, no. 3) *1. United States — Foreign relations — 20th century — Addresses, essays, lectures. I. Braeman, John, ed. II. Bremner, Robert Hamlett, 1917- ed. III. Brody, David, ed. (S)*
E744.T9   327.73   78-141495   ISBN:0814201512

The United States in world affairs; an account of American foreign   **III. 6057**
relations. 1931-
New York and London, Pub. for the Council on Foreign Relations by Harper, 1932-   v. illus. (maps) 23 cm. (Publications of the Council on foreign relations) Annual. Editors: 1931- Walter Lippmann and W. O. Scroggs. — 1934/35- W. H. Shepardson and W. O. Scroggs. *1. U.S. — Foreign relations. 2. U.S. — Economic policy. 3. World politics. 4. Economic conditions — 1918- I. Lippmann, Walter, 1889- ed. II. Scroggs, William Oscar, 1879- joint ed. III. Shepardson, Whitney Hart, 1890- ed. IV. Council on foreign relations, inc. V. T:American foreign relations.*
E744.U66   32-26065

Westerfield, H. Bradford, 1928-   **III. 6058**
The instruments of America's foreign policy. New York, Crowell [c1963] 538 p. 24 cm. *1. United States — Foreign relations — 1945- 2. United States — Military policy. 3. United States — Foreign economic relations. I. T.*
E744.W535   327.73   63-7119

Williams, William Appleman.   **III. 6059**
The tragedy of American diplomacy [by] William Appleman Williams. 2d rev. and enl. ed. [New York, Dell Pub. Co., 1972] v, 312 p. 21 cm. (A Delta book) *1. United States — Foreign relations — 20th century. I. T.*
E744.W56 1972   327/.2/0973   72-186145

Wolfers, Arnold, 1892- ed.   **III. 6060**
Alliance policy in the cold war. Baltimore, Johns Hopkins Press, 1959. ix, 314 p. col. map (on lining papers) 23 cm. *1. U.S. — Foreign relations — 1945- 2. World politics — 1945- 3. Alliances. I. T.*
E744.W58   327.73   59-10764

E744.5   CULTURAL RELATIONS

American Assembly.   **III. 6061**
Cultural affairs and foreign relations. [Rev.] Washington, Columbia Books, 1968. xi, 211 p. 21 cm. A revision and updating of the edition published in 1963 as background papers for the 22d American Assembly, Arden House, October, 1962. *1. United States — Relations (general) with foreign countries. 2. Cultural relations. I. T.*
E744.5.A8 1968   301.29/73   68-20455

Elder, Robert Ellsworth, 1915-   **III. 6062**
The foreign leader program: operations in the United States. Washington, Brookings Institution [1961] xii, 115 p. diagr. 23 cm. "A study made at the request of the Department of State [under an agreement with the Bureau of Educational and Cultural Affairs]" *1. Exchange of persons programs, American. 2. Visitors, Foreign — U.S. I. Brookings Institution, Washington, D.C. II. U.S. Bureau of Educational and Cultural Affairs. III. T.*
E744.5.E45   327.73   61-17961

Stephens, Oren.   **III. 6063**
Facts to a candid world; America's overseas information program. Stanford, Calif., Stanford University Press [1955] 164 p. 24 cm. (Stanford books in world politics) *1. U.S. — Relations (general) with foreign countries. 2. Propaganda, American. I. T.*
E744.5.S8   327.73   55-11261

Elder, Robert Ellsworth, 1915-   **III. 6064**
The information machine; the United States Information Agency and American foreign policy [by] Robert E. Elder. [1st ed. Syracuse, N.Y.] Syracuse University Press [1967] xvi, 356 p. 24 cm. *1. United States. Information Agency. I. T.*
E744.5.U6E4   327.73   68-14105

Whitton, John Boardman, 1892- ed.   **III. 6065**
Propaganda and the cold war; a Princeton University symposium. Washington, Public Affairs Press [1963] iv, 119 p. 24 cm. *1. Propaganda, American. 2. U.S. — Relations (general) with foreign countries. I. Princeton University. II. T.*
E744.5.W5   327.73   63-15329

E745   MILITARY HISTORY

Blumenson, Martin.   **III. 6066**
The Patton papers [by] Martin Blumenson. Illustrated with photos. and with maps by Samuel H. Bryant. Boston, Houghton Mifflin, 1972-   v. illus. 24 cm. *1. Patton, George Smith, 1885-1945. The Patton papers. 1972- II. T.*
E745.P3B55   355.3/31/0924 (B)   76-156490   ISBN:0395127068

Schwarz, Urs, 1905-   **III. 6067**
American strategy: a new perspective; the growth of politico-military thinking in the United States. Pref. by Henry a. Kissinger. [1st ed.] Garden City, N.Y., Doubleday, 1966. xiv, 178 p. 22 cm. *1. U.S. — Military policy. 2. U.S. — History, Military — 20th cent. 3. U.S. — Foreign relations — 20th cent. 4. Strategy. I. T.*
E745.S35   355.033573   66-15443

Tuchman, Barbara (Wertheim)   **III. 6068**
Stilwell and the American experience in China, 1911-45 [by] Barbara W. Tuchman. New York, Macmillan [1970] xv, 621 p. illus., maps, ports. 24 cm. *1. Stilwell, Joseph Warren, 1883-1946. 2. United States — Foreign relations — China. 3. China — Foreign relations — United States. 4. World War, 1939-1945 — China. I. T.*
E745.S68T8   951.04/2/0924 (B)   77-135647

E747   COLLECTIVE BIOGRAPHY

Lippmann, Walter, 1889-   **III. 6069**
Men of destiny. Introd. by Richard Lowitt. Drawings by Rollin Kirby. Seattle, University of Washington Press [1969, c1927] xxi, 244 p. illus. 23 cm. (Americana library) *1. United States — Biography — Addresses, essays, lectures. 2. United States — Politics and government — 1919-1933 — Addresses, essays, lectures. I. T.*
E747.L76 1969   320.9/73   71-9039

Luthin, Reinhard Henry, 1905-   **III. 6070**
American demagogues: twentieth century. With an introd. by Allan Nevins. Gloucester, Mass., P. Smith, 1959 [c1954] 368 p. 21 cm. *1. U.S. — Biography. 2. U.S. — Politics and government — 1901-1953. I. Demagogues. II. T.*
E747.L87 1959   973.91   60-51507

Moley, Raymond, 1886-   **III. 6071**
27 masters of politics, in a personal perspective. Westport, Conn., Greenwood Press [1972, c1949] xii, 276 p. illus. 22 cm. Original ed. issued in series: A Newsweek book. *1. United States — Biography. 2. United States — Politics and government — 1901-1953. I. T.*
E747.M7 1972   973.0992 (B)   79-163546   ISBN:0837162068

Salter, John Thomas, 1898- ed.   **III. 6072**
The American politician, edited by J. T. Salter. Chapel Hill, The University of North Carolina Press, 1938. xvi, 412 p. ports. 24 cm. *1. U.S. — Politics and government — 20th cent. 2. Politics, Practical. 3. U.S. — Biography. 4. Statesmen, American. I. T.*
E747.S29   923.273   38-36015

Tucker, Ray Thomas, 1893-   **III. 6073**
Sons of the wild jackass, by Ray Tucker and Frederick R. Barkley. Cartoons by R. G. List. Introd. by Robert S. Maxwell. Seattle, University of Washington Press [1970, c1932] xxviii, 398 p. illus. 23 cm. (Americana library 17) *1. Statesmen, American. 2. United States. Congress. Senate — Biography. I. Barkley, Frederick Reuben, 1892- joint author. II. T.*
E747.T94 1970   328.73/0922   78-125180

E748 INDIVIDUAL BIOGRAPHY
A – G

Baruch, Bernard Mannes, 1870-1965. III. 6074
Baruch. [1st ed.] New York, Holt [1957-60] 2 v. illus. 22 cm. Vol. 2 published by Holt, Rinehart and Winston.
E748.B32A3   923.273   57-11982

Coit, Margaret L. III. 6075
Mr. Baruch. Illustrated with photos. Boston, Houghton Mifflin, 1957. xiv, 784 p. illus., ports. 22 cm. *1. Baruch, Bernard Mannes, 1870- I. T.*
E748.B32C6   923.273   56-10289

Hyman, Sidney. III. 6076
The lives of William Benton. Chicago, University of Chicago Press [1969] xviii, 625 p. illus., ports. 24 cm. *1. Benton, William, 1900- I. T.*
E748.B337H9   030.924 (B)   72-88231   ISBN:226365484

Braeman, John. III. 6077
Albert J. Beveridge; American nationalist. Chicago, University of Chicago Press [1971] x, 370 p. 23 cm. *1. Beveridge, Albert Jeremiah, 1862-1927.*
E748.B48B7   973.91/0924 (B)   75-142041   ISBN:0226070603

Green, Adwin Wigfall, 1900- III. 6078
The man Bilbo. Baton Rouge, Louisiana State University Press, 1963. xiii, 150 p. illus., ports. 23 cm. *1. Bilbo, Theodore Gilmore, 1877-1947. I. T.*
E748.B5G7   923.273   63-16658

Bowles, Chester, 1901- III. 6079
Promises to keep; my years in public life, 1941-1969. [1st ed.] New York, Harper & Row [1971] xii, 657 p. illus., ports. 25 cm. *1. United States — Politics and government — 1933-1945. 2. Connecticut — Politics and government — 1951- 3. United States — Relations (general) with foreign countries. 4. United States — Foreign relations — India. 5. India — Foreign relations — United States. I. T.*
E748.B73A3   973.917/0924   76-123917

Byrnes, James Francis, 1879- III. 6080
All in one lifetime. [1st ed.] New York, Harper [1958] x, 432 p. illus., ports. 22 cm. *1. U.S. — Politics and government — 20th cent. 2. U.S. — Foreign relations — 20th cent. I. T.*
E748.B975A3   923.273   58-11390

Barnard, Harry, 1906- III. 6081
Independent man; the life of Senator James Couzens. New York, Scribner [1958] 376 p. illus. 24 cm. *1. Couzens, James, 1872-1936. I. T.*
E748.C87B3   923.273   58-7518

Creel, George, 1876- III. 6082
Rebel at large: recollections of fifty crowded years. New York, G. P. Putnam [1947] viii, 384 p. 22 cm. *I. T.*
E748.C937A3   923.273   47-11611

Farley, James Aloysius, 1888- III. 6083
Behind the ballots; the personal history of a politician [by] James A. Farley. Westport, Conn., Greenwood Press [1972] 392 p. port. 23 cm. Reprint of the 1938 ed. *1. United States — Politics and government — 1933-1945. 2. Politics, Practical. I. T.*
E748.F24A3 1972   320.9/73/0917 (B)   78-114521   ISBN:0837147387

Albion, Robert Greenhalgh, 1896- III. 6084
Forrestal and the Navy, by Robert Greenhalgh Albion and Robert Howe Connery. With the collaboration of Jennie Barnes Pope. Foreword by William T. R. Fox. New York, Columbia University Press, 1962. 359 p. illus. 24 cm. *1. Forrestal, James, 1892-1949. 2. U.S. Navy Dept. — History. I. Connery, Robert Howe, 1907- joint author. II. T.*
E748.F68A6   353.7   62-9974

Rogow, Arnold A. III. 6085
James Forrestal, a study of personality, politics, and policy. New York, Macmillan [c1963] xv, 397 p. ports. 21 cm. *1. Forrestal, James, 1892-1949.*
E748.F86R6   923.273   63-16126

Bell, Jack, 1904- III. 6086
Mr. Conservative: Barry Goldwater. [1st ed.] Garden City, N.Y., Doubleday, 1962. 312 p. 22 cm. *1. Goldwater, Barry Morris, 1909- I. T.*
E748.G64B4   923.273   62-11443

Rovere, Richard Halworth, 1915- III. 6087
The Goldwater caper [by] Richard H. Rovere. With cartoons by Bill Mauldin. [1st ed.] New York, Harcourt, Brace & World [1965] x, 182 p. illus. 21 cm. *1. Goldwater, Barry Morris, 1909- I. T.*
E748.G64R6 1965   329.01   65-16951

Grew, Joseph Clark, 1880- III. 6088
Turbulent era; a diplomatic record of forty years, 1904-1945. Edited by Walter Johnson, assisted by Nancy Harvison Hooker. Boston, Houghton Mifflin, 1952. 2 v. (xxvi, 1560 p.) illus., ports. 23 cm. *1. Diplomats — Correspondence, reminiscences, etc. 2. U.S. — Foreign relations — 20th cent. I. T.*
E748.G835A3   923.273   52-5262

Heinrichs, Waldo H. III. 6089
American ambassador; Joseph C. Grew and the development of the United States diplomatic tradition, by Waldo H. Heinrichs, Jr. [1st ed.] Boston, Little, Brown [1966] xii, 460 p. ports. 24 cm. *1. Grew, Joseph Clark, 1880-1965. 2. U.S. — Foreign relations — 20th cent. 3. U.S. — Foreign relations — Japan. 4. Japan — Foreign relations — U.S. 5. U.S. — Diplomatic and consular service. I. T.*
E748.G835H4   327.20924 (B)   66-21993

E748   H – L

Perkins, Dexter, 1889- III. 6090
Charles Evans Hughes and American democratic statesmanship. [1st ed.] Boston, Little, Brown [1956] xxiv, 200 p. 22 cm. (The Library of American biography) *1. Hughes, Charles Evans, 1862-1948. (S)*
E748.H88P4   923.473   56-6767

Wesser, Robert F. III. 6091
Charles Evans Hughes; politics and reform in New York, 1905-1910, by Robert F. Wesser. Ithaca, N.Y., Cornell University Press [1967] xvi, 366 p. illus., ports. 24 cm. *1. Hughes, Charles Evans, 1862-1948. 2. New York (State) — Politics and government — 1865-1950.*
E748.H88W4   974.7/04/0924   67-19029

Hull, Cordell, 1871-1955. III. 6092
The memoirs of Cordell Hull. New York, Macmillan Co., 1948. 2 v. (xii, 1804 p.) port. 22 cm. Prepared with the assistance of Andrew Berding. *I. Berding, Andrew Henry Thomas.*
E748.H93A3   923.273   48-6761

Ickes, Harold Le Claire, 1874-1952. III. 6093
The autobiography of a curmudgeon, by Harold L. Ickes. New York, Reynal & Hitchcock [1943] xi, 350 p. plates, ports., facsims. 22 cm. *1. U.S. — Politics and government — 20th cent. I. T.*
E748.I29A3   923.273   43-51100

Gorman, Joseph Bruce. III. 6094
Kefauver: a political biography. New York, Oxford University Press, 1971. viii, 434 p. ports. 22 cm. *1. Kefauver, Estes, 1903-1963. I. T.*
E748.K314G6   973.9/0924 (B)   77-159645   ISBN:0195014812

Kennan, George Frost, 1904- III. 6095
Memoirs [by] George F. Kennan. [1st ed.] Boston, Little, Brown [1967-72] 2 v. 24 cm. "An Atlantic Monthly Press book."
E748.K374A3   327/.73   67-23834

Burns, James MacGregor. III. 6096
John Kennedy: a political profile. [1st ed.] New York, Harcourt, Brace [1960] 309 p. illus. 21 cm. *1. Kennedy, John Fitzgerald, 1917-*
E748.K375B8   923.273   60-5440

La Guardia, Fiorello Henry, 1882-1947. III. 6097
The making of an insurgent, an autobiography, 1882-1919. Introductions by H. M. Christman and M. R. Werner. New York, Capricorn Books [1961] 222 p. 19 cm. (A Capricorn book, CAP54) *I. T.*
E748.L23A3 1961   923.273   61-4089

Mann, Arthur. III. 6098
La Guardia, a fighter against his times. [1st ed.] Philadelphia, Lippincott [1959-   v. illus. 22 cm. *1. La Guardia, Fiorello Henry, 1882-1947.*
E748.L23M3   923.273   59-13077

Mann, Arthur. III. 6099
La Guardia comes to power: 1933. [1st ed.] Philadelphia, Lippincott [1965] 199 p. maps. 22 cm. *1. La Guardia, Fiorello Henry, 1882-1947. 2. New York (City) — Politics and government — 1898-1961. 3. Politics, Practical — Case studies. I. T.*
E748.L23M32   320.974710924   65-24920

Zinn, Howard, 1922- III. 6100
La Guardia in Congress. Ithaca, N.Y., Published for the American Historical Association [by] Cornell University Press [1959] xi, 288 p. 24 cm. Issued also in microfilm form in 1958 as thesis, Columbia University. *1. La Guardia, Fiorello Henry, 1882-1947.*
E748.L23Z5 1959   923.273   59-65375

Blackorby, Edward C. III. 6101
Prairie rebel; the public life of William Lemke. Lincoln, University of Nebraska Press, 1963 [i.e. 1964, c1963] ix, 339 p. illus., maps. 24 cm. "A first

version of this study was a doctoral dissertation." *1. Lemke, William, 1878-1950. I. T.*
E748.L57B5   923.273   63-14690   973.917 L543b

Lilienthal, David Eli, 1899-   III. 6102
The journals of David E. Lilienthal. Introd. by Henry Steele Commager. [1st ed.] New York, Harper & Row [1964-   v.   illus., ports. 25 cm. *I. T.*
E748.L7A33   973.9/0924   64-18056

Williams, Thomas Harry, 1909-   III. 6103
Huey Long [by] T. Harry Williams. [1st ed.] New York, Knopf, 1969. xiv, 884, xxii p. illus., facsims., ports. 25 cm. *1. Long, Huey Pierce, 1893-1935.*
E748.L86W48 1969   976.3/06/0924   (B)   69-10692

Tarr, Joel Arthur.   III. 6104
A study in boss politics: William Lorimer of Chicago. Urbana, University of Illinois Press [1971] xi, 376 p. illus., facsim., map, ports. 24 cm. *1. Lorimer, William, 1861-1934. 2. Illinois — Politics and government — 1865-1950. I. T.*
E748.L892T3   328.73/0924   (B)   72-133945   ISBN:0252001397

E748   M – N

McAdoo, William Gibbs, 1863-1941.   III. 6105
Crowded years; the reminiscences of William G. McAdoo. Port Washington, N.Y., Kennikat Press [1971, c1931] x, 542 p. illus., maps, ports. 22 cm. (Kennikat Press scholarly reprints. Series in American history and culture in the twentieth century) *I. T.*
E748.M14M2 1971   973.91/3/0924   74-137974   ISBN:080461430X

Buckley, William Frank, 1925-   III. 6106
McCarthy and his enemies; the record and its meaning [by] Wm. F. Buckley, Jr. & L. Brent Bozell. Prologue by William Schlam. New Rochelle, N.Y., Arlington House [1970, c1954] xix, 425 p. 22 cm. *1. McCarthy, Joseph Raymond, 1908-1957. 2. Subversive activities — United States. 3. Communism — United States — 1917- I. Bozell, L. Brent, joint author. II. T.*
E748.M143B8 1970   973.918   70-18983   ISBN:0870001108

Griffith, Robert, 1940-   III. 6107
The politics of fear: Joseph R. McCarthy and the Senate. Lexington, Published for the Organization of American Historians [by] University Press of Kentucky, 1970. xi, 362 p. 23 cm. *1. McCarthy, Joseph Raymond, 1908-1957. I. Organization of American Historians. II. T.*
E748.M143G7   973.918/0924   73-119812   ISBN:0813112273

Rogin, Michael Paul.   III. 6108
The intellectuals and McCarthy: the radical specter [by] Michael Paul Rogin. Cambridge, M.I.T. Press [1967] xi, 366 p. illus., maps. 21 cm. *1. McCarthy, Joseph Raymond, 1909-1957. 2. Intellectuals — U.S. 3. Right and left (Political science) I. T.*
E748.M143R57   973.9/0924   67-16489

Rorty, James, 1890-   III. 6109
McCarthy and the Communists [by] James Rorty and Moshe Decter. Boston, Beacon Press [1954] viii, 163 p. 20 cm. *1. McCarthy, Joseph Raymond, 1909-1957. 2. Communism — U.S. — 1917- 3. Internal security — U.S. I. Decter, Moshe, joint author. II. T.*
E748.M143R6   923.273   54-11622

Marsh, Benjamin Clarke, 1877-1952.   III. 6110
Lobbyist for the people; a record of fifty years. Washington, Public Affairs Press [1953] 224 p. 21 cm. Autobiographical. *1. U.S. — Politics and government — 20th cent. 2. People's Lobby. I. T.*
E748.M34A3   923.273   53-10837

Martin, Joseph William, 1884-   III. 6111
My first fifty years in politics, as told to Robert J. Donovan. New York, McGraw-Hill [1960] 261 p. illus. 22 cm. *1. U.S. — Politics and government — 20th cent. I. Donovan, Robert J. II. T.*
E748.M375A3   923.273   60-15002   973.91 M364

Nicolson, Harold George, Hon., 1886-   III. 6112
Dwight Morrow, by Harold Nicolson. 1st ed. New York, Harcourt, Brace [c1935] xvi, 409 p. ports., facsim. 22 cm. *1. Morrow, Dwight Whitney, 1873-1931.*
E748.M75N5   923.273   35-18404

Nixon, Richard Milhous, 1913-   III. 6113
Six crises. [1st ed.] Garden City, N.Y., Doubleday, 1962. 460 p. 24 cm. *1. United States — History — 1945- I. T.*
E748.N5A3   973.92   62-8074

Norris, George William, 1861-1944.   III. 6114
Fighting liberal, the autobiography of George W. Norris. New York, Macmillan, 1945. xiv, 419 p. illus., map, ports. 22 cm. *I. T.*
E748.N65A3   923.273   45-3790

Lowitt, Richard, 1922-   III. 6115
George W. Norris; the persistence of a progressive, 1913-1933. Urbana, University of Illinois Press [1971] xv, 590 p. illus. 24 cm. *1. Norris, George William, 1861-1944.*
E748.N65L62   328.73/0924   (B)   76-147923   ISBN:0252001761

Cole, Wayne S.   III. 6116
Senator Gerald P. Nye and American foreign relations. Minneapolis, University of Minnesota Press [1962] 293 p. illus. 24 cm. *1. Nye, Gerald Prentice, 1892- 2. U.S. — Foreign relations — 1933-1945. 3. U.S. — Neutrality. I. T.*
E748.N9C6 1962   327.73   62-21813

E748   P – S

Coben, Stanley.   III. 6117
A. Mitchell Palmer: politician. New York, Da Capo Press, 1972 [c1963] xii, 351 p. 23 cm. (Civil liberties in American history) *1. Palmer, Alexander Mitchell, 1872-1936. (S)*
E748.P24C6 1972   973.91/3/0924   (B)   79-180787   ISBN:0306702088

Pepper, George Wharton, 1867-   III. 6118
Philadelphia lawyer, an autobiography by George Wharton Pepper. 1st ed. Philadelphia and New York, J. B. Lippincott [1944] 407 p. illus., plates, ports. 22 cm. *I. T.*
E748.P46A3   923.473   44-9713

Israel, Fred L.   III. 6119
Nevada's Key Pittman. Lincoln, University of Nebraska Press [1963] 210 p. illus. 24 cm. *1. Pittman, Key, 1872-1940.*
E748.P6I8   923.273   63-8118

Richberg, Donald Randall, 1881-   III. 6120
My hero; the indiscreet memoirs of an eventful but an heroic life. New York, Putnam [1954] 367 p. illus. 22 cm. *I. T.*
E748.R38A3 1954   923.273   54-10504

Roper, Daniel Calhoun, 1867-   III. 6121
Fifty years of public life [by] Daniel C. Roper, in collaboration with Frank H. Lovette. Durham, N.C., Duke University Press, 1941. x, 422 p. front. (port.) 24 cm. (Duke university publications) *1. U.S. — Politics and government — 20th cent. I. Lovette, Frank Henry.*
E748.R7A3   923.273   41-26547

Handlin, Oscar, 1915-   III. 6122
Al Smith and his America. [1st ed.] Boston, Little, Brown [1958] 207 p. 21 cm. (The Library of American biography) *1. Smith, Alfred Emanuel, 1873-1944. I. T.*
E748.S63H16   923.273   57-6446

Josephson, Matthew, 1899-   III. 6123
Al Smith: hero of the cities; a political portrait drawing on the papers of Frances Perkins [by] Matthew and Hannah Josephson. Boston, Houghton Mifflin, 1969. xx, 505 p. ports. 22 cm. *1. Smith, Alfred Emanuel, 1873-1944. I. Josephson, Hannah (Geffen) joint author. II. Perkins, Frances, 1882-1965.*
E748.S63J6   973.91/5/0924   (B)   73-79391

Smith, Alfred Emanuel, 1873-1944.   III. 6124
Up to now; an autobiography, by Alfred E. Smith. New York, Viking Press, 1929. 434 p. plates, ports., facsims. 25 cm. *1. New York (State) — Politics and government — 1865- I. T.*
E748.S63S6   29-21291

Smith, Frank Ellis, 1918-   III. 6125
Congressman from Mississippi [by] Frank E. Smith. New York, Pantheon Books [1964] ix, 338 p. 22 cm. *I. T.*
E748.S656A3   923.273   64-18350

Stevenson, Adlai Ewing, 1900-1965.   III. 6126
The papers of Adlai E. Stevenson. Walter Johnson, editor. Carol Evans, assistant editor. [1st ed.] Boston, Little, Brown [1972-   v. illus. 24 cm. *1. Stevenson, Adlai Ewing, 1900-1965.*
E748.S84A25 1972   973.9/092/4 (B)   73-175478
    ISBN:0316467510 (v. 2)

Brown, Stuart Gerry, 1912-   III. 6127
Conscience in politics; Adlai E. Stevenson in the 1950's. [Syracuse, N.Y.] Syracuse University Press, 1961. 313 p. illus. 21 cm. (Men and movements series) *1. Stevenson, Adlai Ewing, 1900-1965. 2. U.S. — Politics and government — 1953-1961. I. T. (S:Men and movements (Syracuse))*
E748.S84B72   923.273   61-17124

Current, Richard Nelson.   III. 6128
Secretary Stimson, a study in statecraft. New Brunswick, Rutgers University Press, 1954. 272 p. 22 cm. *1. Stimson, Henry Lewis, 1867-1950. I. T.*
E748.S883C8   923.273   54-6835

Morison, Elting Elmore. III. 6129
Turmoil and tradition; a study of the life and times of Henry L. Stimson. Boston, Houghton Mifflin, 1960. 686 p. illus. 22 cm. *1. Stimson, Henry Lewis, 1867-1950. I. T.*
E748.S883M6   923.273   60-10132

E748   T – Z

Patterson, James T. III. 6130
Mr. Republican; a biography of Robert A. Taft [by] James T. Patterson. Boston, Houghton Mifflin, 1972. xvi, 749 p. illus. 24 cm. *1. Taft, Robert Alphonso, 1889-1953. I. T.*
E748.T2P37   328.73/092/4 (B)   72-516   ISBN:0395139384

Blum, John Morton, 1921- III. 6131
Joe Tumulty and the Wilson era, by John M. Blum. With a new pref. [Hamden, Conn.] Archon Books, 1969 [c1951] xiii, 337 p. group port. 21 cm. "Notes and bibliography": p. 271-324. *1. Tumulty, Joseph Patrick, 1879-1954. 2. Wilson, Woodrow, Pres. U.S., 1856-1924. 3. United States — Politics and government — 1913-1921. I. T.*
E748.T84B6 1969   973.91/3/0924 (B)   69-15787   ISBN:0208007369

Holmes, William F. III. 6132
The White Chief: James Kimble Vardaman, by William F. Holmes. Baton Rouge, Louisiana State University Press [1970] xiii, 418 p. port. 24 cm. (Southern biography series) *1. Vardaman, James Kimble, 1861-1930. I. T. (S)*
E748.V24H6   976.2/06/0924 (B)   70-108201   ISBN:807109312

Huthmacher, J. Joseph. III. 6133
Senator Robert F. Wagner and the rise of urban liberalism [by] J. Joseph Huthmacher. [1st ed.] New York, Atheneum, 1968. xi, 362 p. ports. 25 cm. *1. Wagner, Robert Ferdinand, 1877-1953. I. T.*
E748.W2H8 1968   973.91/0924 (B)   68-16869

Lord, Russell, 1895-1964. III. 6134
The Wallaces of Iowa. New York, Da Capo Press, 1972 [c1947] xiii, 615 p. illus. 23 cm. (Franklin D. Roosevelt and the era of the New Deal) *1. Wallace, Henry Agard, 1888-1965. 2. Wallace, Henry Cantwell, 1866-1924. 3. Wallace, Henry, 1836-1916. I. T. (S)*
E748.W23L6 1972   973/.0099   76-167843   ISBN:0306703254

Markowitz, Norman D. III. 6135
The rise and fall of the people's century: Henry A. Wallace and American liberalism, 1941-1948 [by] Norman D. Markowitz. New York, Free Press [1973] xi, 369 p. illus. 22 cm. *1. Wallace, Henry Agard, 1888-1965. 2. United States — Politics and government — 1933-1945. 3. United States — Politics and government — 1945- I. T.*
E748.W23M37   973.917/092/4 (B)   72-86508

Schapsmeier, Edward L. III. 6136
Henry A. Wallace of Iowa: the agrarian years, 1910-1940 [by] Edward L. and Frederick H. Schapsmeier. [1st ed.] Ames, Iowa State University Press [1968] xiii, 327 p. ports. 24 cm. *1. Wallace, Henry Agard, 1888-1965. 2. Agriculture — Economic aspects — United States. 3. Agriculture and state — United States. I. Schapsmeier, Frederick H., joint author. II. T.*
E748.W23S3   973.917/0924 (B)   68-9690   ISBN:0813817412

O'Keane, Josephine. III. 6137
Thomas J. Walsh, a Senator from Montana. Francestown, N.H., M. Jones Co. [1955] 284 p. port. 23 cm. *1. Walsh, Thomas James, 1859-1933. I. T.*
E748.W25O38   923.273   55-3800

Wheeler, Burton Kendall, 1882- III. 6138
Yankee from the West; the candid, turbulent life story of the Yankee-born U.S. Senator from Montana [by] Burton K. Wheeler with Paul F. Healy. [1st ed.] Garden City, N.Y., Doubleday, 1962. 436 p. illus. 22 cm. *I. Healy, Paul F. II. T.*
E748.W5A3   923.273   62-15909

Barnard, Ellsworth, 1907- III. 6139
Wendell Willkie, fighter for freedom. Marquette, Northern Michigan University Press [1966] xi, 611 p. ports. 24 cm. *1. Willkie, Wendell Lewis, 1892-1944.*
E748.W7B3   973.9170924 (B)   66-19668

Johnson, Donald Bruce, 1921- III. 6140
The Republican Party and Wendell Willkie. Urbana, University of Illinois Press, 1960. ix, 354 p. 23 cm. (Illinois studies in the social sciences, v.46) *1. Willkie, Wendell Lewis, 1892-1944. 2. Republican Party. I. T. (S:Illinois. University. Illinois studies in the social sciences, v.46)*
E748.W7J6 (H31.I4 vol. 46)   923.373   60-5352

Rovere, Richard Halworth, 1915- III. 6141
The American establishment and other reports, opinions, and speculations.
[1st ed.] New York, Harcourt, Brace & World [1962] 308 p. 21 cm. *1. United States — Politics and government — 20th century. I. T.*
E753.R68   973.92   62-9438

R769

E756 – 856   BY PRESIDENTIAL ADMINISTRATION

E756 – 760   Roosevelt, 1901 – 1909

Hill, Howard Copeland, 1878-1940. III. 6142
Roosevelt and the Caribbean. New York, Russell & Russell, 1965 [c1927] xi, 232 p. map. 23 cm. *1. Roosevelt, Theodore, Pres. U.S., 1858-1919. 2. U.S. — Foreign relations — 1901-1909. 3. U.S. — Foreign relations — Latin America. 4. Latin America — Foreign relations — U.S. 5. Panama — History — Revolution, 1903. 6. Venezuela — History — Anglo-German blockade, 1902. I. T.*
E756.H65 1965   327.7308   65-17900

Mowry, George Edwin, 1909- III. 6143
The era of Theodore Roosevelt, 1900-1912. [1st ed.] New York, Harper [1958] 330 p. illus. 22 cm. (The New American Nation series) *1. Roosevelt, Theodore, Pres. U.S., 1858-1919. 2. U.S. — Politics and government — 1901-1909. 3. U.S. — Politics and government — 1909-1913. I. T.*
E756.M85   973.911   58-8835

Phillips, David Graham, 1867-1911. III. 6144
The treason of the Senate. Stanford, Calif., Academic Reprints [195-] 100 p. illus. 24 cm. A reprint of 9 articles and an editorial foreword which appeared in Cosmopolitan between Mar. and Nov. 1906. *1. U.S. Congress. Senate. 2. U.S. — Politics and government — 1901-1909. 3. Corruption (in politics) — U.S. I. T.*
E756.P45   973.911   53-3930

Beale, Howard Kennedy, 1899- III. 6145
Theodore Roosevelt and the rise of America to world power. Baltimore, Johns Hopkins Press, 1956. 600 p. 23 cm. (The Albert Shaw lectures on diplomatic history, 1953) *1. Roosevelt, Theodore, Pres. U.S., 1858-1919. 2. U.S. — Foreign relations 1901-1909.*
E757.B4   973.911   56-10255

Blum, John Morton, 1921- III. 6146
The Republican Roosevelt. Cambridge, Harvard University Press, 1954. 170 p. 22 cm. *1. Roosevelt, Theodore, Pres. U.S., 1858-1919. 2. U.S. — Politics and government — 1901-1909. I. T.*
E757.B65   823.173   54-5182

Chessman, G. Wallace. III. 6147
Theodore Roosevelt and the politics of power [by] G. Wallace Chessman. Edited by Oscar Handlin. Boston, Little, Brown [1969] viii, 214 p. 21 cm. (The Library of American biography) "A note on the sources": p. [200]-204. *1. Roosevelt, Theodore, Pres. U.S., 1858-1919. I. T. (S)*
E757.C55   973.91/1/0924 (B)   68-20501

Gardner, Joseph Lawrence, 1933- III. 6148
Departing glory; Theodore Roosevelt as ex-President [by] Joseph L. Gardner. New York, Scribner [1973] xv, 432 p. illus. 24 cm. *1. Roosevelt, Theodore, Pres. U.S., 1858-1919. I. T.*
E757.G29   973.91/1/0924 (B)   72-11116   ISBN:0684133008

Harbaugh, William Henry, 1920- III. 6149
Power and responsibility; the life and times of Theodore Roosevelt. New York, Farrar, Straus and Cudahy [1961] 568 p. illus. 22 cm. *1. Roosevelt, Theodore, Pres. U.S., 1858-1919. I. T.*
E757.H28   973.911   61-10128

Pringle, Henry Fowles, 1897- III. 6150
Theodore Roosevelt, a biography. [Rev.] New York, Harcourt, Brace [c1956] 435 p. 19 cm. (A Harvest book, 15) *1. Roosevelt, Theodore, Pres. U.S., 1858-1919.*
E757.P967   923.173   56-13739

Roosevelt, Theodore, Pres. U.S., 1858-1919. III. 6151
Autobiography. Condensed from the original ed., supplemented by letters, speeches, and other writings, and edited with an introd. by Wayne Andrews. Centennial ed. New York, Scribner [1958] xi, 372 p. 22 cm.
E757.R794   923.173   58-11634

Roosevelt, Theodore, Pres. U.S., 1858-1919. III. 6152
Letters, selected and edited by Elting E. Morison; John M. Blum, associate editor, John J. Buckley, copy editor. Cambridge, Harvard University Press, 1951-54. 8 v. illus., ports. 25 cm. Vols.3-4: Hope W. Wigglesworth, assistant editor; Sylvia Rice, copy editor. Vols.5-8: Alfred D. Chandler, Jr., assistant editor; Sylvia Rice, copy editor.
E757.R7958   923.173   51-10037

Roosevelt, Theodore, pres. U.S., 1858-1919. III. 6153
Selections from the correspondence of Theodore Roosevelt and Henry Cabot Lodge, 1884-1918. New York, Scribner, 1925. 2 v. fronts. (ports.) 25 cm. *1. Lodge, Henry Cabot, 1850-1924.*
E757.R799   25-8869

Wagenknecht, Edward Charles, 1900- III. 6154
The seven worlds of Theodore Roosevelt. [1st ed.] New York, Longmans, Green, 1958. xvii, 325 p. port. 22 cm. *1. Roosevelt, Theodore, Pres. U.S., 1858-1919. I. T.*
E757.W14   923.173   58-12762

E761 – 765   Taft, 1909 – 1913

Coletta, Paolo Enrico, 1916- III. 6155
The Presidency of William Howard Taft, by Paolo E. Coletta. Lawrence, University Press of Kansas [1973] ix, 306 p. 24 cm. (American Presidency series) *1. United States — Politics and government — 1909-1913. 2. Taft, William Howard, Pres. U.S., 1857-1930. I. T. (S)*
E761.C64   973.91/2/0924 (B)   72-92564   ISBN:0700600965

Hechler, Kenneth William, 1914- III. 6156
Insurgency; personalities and politics of the Taft era, by Kenneth W. Hechler. New York, AMS Press [1970, c1940] 252 p. 23 cm. (Studies in history, economic, and public law, no. 470) Series also appears as: Columbia Unversity studies in the social sciences, 470. *1. United States — Politics and government — 1909-1913. 2. Republican Party. I. T. (S:Columbia studies in the social sciences, 470)*
E761.H462 1970   320.9/73/0912   72-127442   ISBN:0404514707

Holt, Laurence James. III. 6157
Congressional insurgents and the party system, 1909-1916 [by] James Holt. Cambridge, Mass., Harvard University Press, 1967. viii, 188 p. 21 cm. (Harvard historical monographs, 60) *1. Republican Party — History. 2. U.S. — Politics and government — 1909-1913. 3. U.S. — Politics and government — 1913-1921. I. T. (S)*
E761.H6   329/.00973   67-22866

Scholes, Walter Vinton, 1916- III. 6158
The foreign policies of the Taft administration, by Walter V. Scholes and Marie V. Scholes. Columbia, University of Missouri Press [c1970] 259 p. port. 25 cm. *1. United States — Foreign relations — 1909-1913. 2. Taft, William Howard, Pres. U.S., 1857-1930. I. Scholes, Marie V., joint author. II. T.*
E761.S3   327.73   70-122310   ISBN:082620094X

Pringle, Henry Fowles, 1897-1958. III. 6159
The life and times of William Howard Taft, a biography. [Unaltered and unabridged ed.] Hamden, Conn., Archon Books, 1964 [c1939] 2 v. (xii, 1106 p.) illus., ports., facsims. 23 cm. *1. Taft, William Howard, Pres. U.S., 1857-1930. I. T.*
E762.P75 1964   923.173   64-13175

Wilson, Woodrow, Pres. U.S., 1856-1924. III. 6160
A crossroads of freedom, the 1912 campaign speeches. Edited by John Wells Davidson; with a pref. by Charles Seymour. New Haven, Published for the Woodrow Wilson Foundation [by] Yale University Press, 1956. xviii, 570 p. illus., ports., facsims. 25 cm. *1. U.S. — Politics and government — 1909-1913 — Addresses, essays, lectures. 2. Campaign literature, 1912 — Democratic. I. Davidson, John Wells, ed. II. T.*
E765.W5   973.912   56-11796

E766 – 783   Wilson, 1913 – 1921

Buehrig, Edward Henry, 1910- ed. III. 6161
Wilson's foreign policy in perspective. Bloomington, Indiana University Press, 1957. 176 p. 21 cm. *1. Wilson, Woodrow, Pres. U.S., 1856-1924. 2. U.S. — Foreign relations — 1913-1921. I. T.*
E766.B92   327.73   57-10721

Buehrig, Edward Henry, 1910- III. 6162
Woodrow Wilson and the balance of power [by] Edward H. Buehrig. Gloucester, Mass., P. Smith, 1968 [c1955] x, 325 p. 21 cm. *1. United States — Foreign relations — 1913-1921. 2. Wilson, Woodrow, Pres. U.S., 1856-1924. I. T.*
E766.B95 1968   327.73   73-753

Daniels, Josephus, 1862-1948. III. 6163
The cabinet diaries of Josephus Daniels, 1913-1921. Edited by E. David Cronon. Lincoln, University of Nebraska Press [1963] x, 648 p. illus., ports., facsim. 24 cm. "Diaries for 1914 and 1916 are lacking." *1. U.S. Navy — History — Sources. 2. U.S. — Politics and government — 1913-1921. 3. Cabinet officers — U.S. I. Cronon, Edmund David, ed. II. T.*
E766.D29 1963   973.913   62-7874

Daniels, Josephus, 1862-1948. III. 6164
The Wilson era; years of peace, 1910-1917, by Josephus Daniels. Chapel Hill, University of North Carolina Press, 1944. xvi, 615 p. illus., ports. (part double) fold. facsims. 25 cm. *1. Wilson, Woodrow, pres. U.S., 1856-1924. 2. U.S. — Politics and government — 1913-1921. I. T.*
E766.D3   973.913   44-40206

Daniels, Josephus, 1862-1948. III. 6165
The Wilson era; years of war and after, 1917-1923, by Josephus Daniels. Chapel Hill, University of North Carolina Press, 1946. xviii, 654 p. illus., plates, ports., maps, facsims. 25 cm. *1. Wilson, Woodrow, pres. U.S., 1856-1924. 2. League of nations. 3. European war, 1914-1918 — U.S. 4. U.S. — Politics and government — 1913-1921. I. T.*
E766.D33   973.913   46-25158

House, Edward Mandell, 1858-1938. III. 6166
The intimate papers of Colonel House. Arr. as a narrative by Charles Seymour. Boston, Houghton Mifflin. St. Clair Shores, Mich., Scholarly Press [1971, c1926-28] 4 v. illus. 22 cm. *1. Wilson, Woodrow, Pres. U.S., 1856-1924. 2. European War, 1914-1918. 3. United States — Politics and government — 1913-1921. 4. League of Nations. 5. Versailles, Treaty of, June 28, 1919 (Germany) I. Seymour, Charles, 1885-1963, ed. II. T.*
E766.H8523   973.91/3/0924 (B)   71-145093   ISBN:0403010314

Houston, David Franklin, 1866-1940. III. 6167
Eight years with Wilson's Cabinet, 1913 to 1920; with a personal estimate of the President. Garden City, N.Y., Doubleday, Page, 1926. St. Clair Shores, Mich., Scholarly Press, 1970. 2 v. ports. 22 cm. *1. United States — Politics and government — 1913-1921. 2. Wilson, Woodrow, Pres. U.S., 1856-1924. I. T.*
E766.H86 1970   973.91/3/0924   79-145095   ISBN:0403007682

Link, Arthur Stanley. III. 6168
Woodrow Wilson and the progressive era, 1910-1917. [1st ed.] New York, Harper, [c1954] xvii, 331 p. illus., ports., maps. 22 cm. (The New American nation series) *1. Wilson, Woodrow, Pres. U.S., 1856-1924. 2. U.S. — Politics and government — 1913-1921.*
E766.L5   973.913   53-11849

Lippmann, Walter, 1889- III. 6169
Early writings. Introd. and annotations by Arthur Schlesinger, Jr. New York, Liveright [1970] xii, 356 p. 22 cm. *1. United States — Politics and government — 1913-1921 — Addresses, essays, lectures. 2. United States — Civilization — 20th century — Addresses, essays, lectures.*
E766.L57   917.3/03/91308   70-114385   ISBN:0871405032

Seymour, Charles, 1885- III. 6170
Woodrow Wilson and the world war; a chronicle of our own times, by Charles Seymour. New Haven, Yale University Press; [etc., etc.] 1921. ix, 382 p. front., ports. 21 cm. (The chronicles of America series, Allen Johnson, editor ... v.48) "Abraham Lincoln edition." *1. Wilson, Woodrow, pres. U.S., 1856-1924. 2. U.S. — Politics and government — 1913-1921. 3. European war, 1914-1918 — U.S. I. T.*
E766.S5   (E173.C55 vol. 48)   21-14812

E767   Biography of Wilson

Baker, Ray Stannard, 1870-1946. III. 6171
Woodrow Wilson; life and letters. [1st ed.] New York, Greenwood Press, 1968 [c1927] 8 v. facsims., ports. 24 cm. *1. Wilson, Woodrow, Pres. U.S., 1856-1924.*
E767.B16 1968   973.8/0924 (B)   68-8332

Blum, John Morton, 1921- III. 6172
Woodrow Wilson and the politics of morality. [1st ed.] Boston, Little, Brown [1956] 215 p. 21 cm. (The Library of American biography) *1. Wilson, Woodrow, Pres. U.S., 1856-1924.*
E767.B64   923.173   56-10643

Bragdon, Henry Wilkinson. III. 6173
Woodrow Wilson: the academic years. Cambridge, Mass., Belknap Press of Harvard University Press, 1967. xiii, 519 p. illus. ports. 24 cm. *1. Wilson, Woodrow, Pres. U.S., 1856-1924. I. T.*
E767.B75   973.8/0924   67-27081

Diamond, William, 1917- III. 6174
The economic thought of Woodrow Wilson, by William Diamond. Baltimore, Johns Hopkins Press, 1943. 210 p. 24 cm. (The Johns Hopkins university studies in historical and political science ... Ser. LXI, no. 4) *1. Wilson, Woodrow, pres. U.S., 1856-1924. 2. U.S. — Economic policy.*
E767.D5   (H31.J6 ser. 61, no. 4)   923.173 (308.2)   44-5332

Dodd, William Edward, 1869- III. 6175
Woodrow Wilson and his work, by William E. Dodd. New and rev. ed. New York, P. Smith, 1932. xiv, 454 p. front. (port.) illus. (maps) 22 cm. *1. Wilson, Woodrow, pres. U.S., 1856-1924. 2. U.S. — Politics and government — 1913-1921.*
E767.D637   923.173   32-18923

Garraty, John Arthur, 1920- III. 6176
Woodrow Wilson; a great life in brief. [1st ed.] New York, Knopf, 1956. 206 p. 19 cm. (Great lives in brief; a new series of biographies) *1. Wilson, Woodrow, Pres. U.S., 1856-1924.*
E767.G26   923.173   56-5802

George, Alexander L. III. 6177
Woodrow Wilson and Colonel House; a personality study [by] Alexander L. George and Juliette L. George. New York, J. Day Co. [1956] 362 p. illus. 22 cm. *1. Wilson, Woodrow, Pres. U.S., 1856-1924. 2. House, Edward Mandell, 1858-1938. I. George, Juliette L., joint author.*
E767.G4   923.173   56-13372

Hoover, Herbert Clark, Pres. U.S., 1874-1964. III. 6178
The ordeal of Woodrow Wilson. [1st ed.] New York, McGraw-Hill [1958] xiii, 318 p. illus., ports. 24 cm. *1. Wilson, Woodrow, Pres. U.S., 1856-1924. 2. U.S. — Foreign relations — 1913-1921. I. T.*
E767.H78   973.913   58-9257

Link, Arthur Stanley. III. 6179
Wilson. Princeton, Princeton University Press, 1947-   v. illus., plates, ports. 24 cm. *1. Wilson, Woodrow, Pres. U.S., 1856-1924. I. T.*
E767.L65   923.173   47-3554

Notter, Harley. III. 6180
The origins of the foreign policy of Woodrow Wilson. New York, Russell & Russell, 1965 [c1937] vi, 695 p. 23 cm. *1. Wilson, Woodrow, Pres. U.S., 1856-1924. 2. U.S. — Foreign relations — 1913-1921. I. T.*
E767.N67 1965   327.73   65-17916

Tumulty, Joseph Patrick, 1879-1954. III. 6181
Woodrow Wilson as I know him. New York, AMS Press [1970] xvi, 553 p. facsims., port. 24 cm. Reprint of the 1921 ed. *1. Wilson, Woodrow, Pres. U.S., 1856-1924. I. T.*
E767.T9 1970   973.91/3/0924   71-127912   ISBN:0404065279

Walworth, Arthur Clarence, 1903- III. 6182
Woodrow Wilson [by] Arthur Walworth. 2d ed., rev. Boston, Houghton Mifflin Co., 1965. xiv, 436, 439 p. port. 24 cm. *1. Wilson, Woodrow, Pres. U.S., 1856-1924.*
E767.W34 1965   923.173   64-21740

E768 – 780   Period of World War I

Cohen, Warren I. III. 6183
The American revisionists; the lessons of intervention in World War I [by] Warren I. Cohen. Chicago, University of Chicago Press [1967] xv, 252 p. 22 cm. *1. U.S. — Foreign relations — 1913-1921. 2. European War, 1914-1918 — U.S. I. Revisionists. II. T.*
E768.C6   327.73   66-20594

The Immigrants' influence on Wilson's peace policies. III. 6184
Edited by Joseph P. O'Grady. [Lexington] University of Kentucky Press, 1967. x, 329 p. 23 cm. Developed from a lecture series at La Salle College, Philadelphia. *1. U.S. — Foreign relations — 1913-1921 — Addresses, essays, lectures. 2. U.S. — Foreign population — Addresses, essays, lectures. I. O'Grady, Joseph P., ed. II. La Salle College, Philadelphia.*
E768.I4   327.73   67-23776

Smith, Daniel Malloy, 1922- III. 6185
Robert Lansing and American neutrality, 1914-1917, by Daniel M. Smith. New York, Da Capo Press, 1972. iv, 241 p. illus. 23 cm. (The American scene: comments and commentators) Reprint of the 1958 ed., which was issued as v. 59 of University of California publications in history. *1. Lansing, Robert, 1864-1928. 2. United States — Neutrality. 3. United States — Foreign relations — 1913-1921. I. T. (S:California. University. University of California publications in history, v. 59.)*
E768.L32S58 1972   327/.2/0924 (B)   79-126610   ISBN:0306700573

Levin, Norman Gordon. III. 6186
Woodrow Wilson and world politics; America's response to war and revolution [by] N. Gordon Levin. London, New York, Oxford University Press [1970, c1968] xii, 340 p. 21 cm. (A Galaxy Book, 309) *1. United States — Foreign relations — 1913-1921. 2. Wilson, Woodrow, Pres. U.S., 1856-1924. I. T.*
E768.L62 1970   327.73   70-463170

Smith, Daniel Malloy, 1922- III. 6187
The great departure; the United States and World War I, 1914-1920 [by] Daniel M. Smith. New York, J. Wiley [1965] xiii, 221 p. maps. 22 cm. (America in crisis) *1. United States — Foreign relations — 1913-1921. 2. European War, 1914-1918 — United States. I. T. (S)*
E768.S62   940.373   65-19813

Livermore, Seward W. III. 6188
Politics is adjourned; Woodrow Wilson and the War Congress, 1916-1918 [by] Seward W. Livermore. [1st ed.] Middletown, Conn., Wesleyan University Press [1966] 324 p. 22 cm. *1. United States — Politics and government — 1913-1921. 2. Wilson, Woodrow, Pres. U.S., 1856-1924. I. T.*
E780.L5   973.913   66-14666

Peterson, Horace Cornelius, 1902-1952. III. 6189
Opponents of war, 1917-1918 [by] H. C. Peterson and Gilbert C. Fite. Madison, University of Wisconsin Press, 1957. xiii, 399 p. illus., ports. 24 cm. *1. European War, 1914-1918 — U.S. 2. U.S. — History — 1913-1921. 3. Pacifism. 4. Conscientious objectors — U.S. I. Fite, Gilbert Courtland, 1918- joint author. II. T.*
E780.P4   973.913   57-5239

E784   1919 – 1933

Ellis, Lewis Ethan, 1898- III. 6190
Republican foreign policy, 1921-1933, by L. Ethan Ellis. New Brunswick, N.J., Rutgers University Press [1968]. ix, 404 p. illus., ports. 25 cm. *1. United States — Foreign relations — 1921-1923. 2. United States — Foreign relations — 1923-1929. 3. United States — Foreign relations — 1929-1933. I. T.*
E784.E4   327.73   68-20886

Faulkner, Harold Underwood, 1890- III. 6191
From Versailles to the New Deal; a chronicle of the Harding-Coolidge-Hoover era. New Haven, Yale University Press, 1950. ix, 388 p. front. 18 cm. (The Chronicles of America series, v.51) On cover: Roosevelt ed. *1. U.S. — History — 1919-1933. I. T. (S)*
E784.F38 1950a (E173.C56 vol. 51)   973.91   53-272

Hicks, John Donald, 1890- III. 6192
Republican ascendancy, 1921-1933. [1st ed.] New York, Harper [1960] 318 p. illus. 22 cm. (The New American nation series) *1. United States — History — 1919-1933. I. T.*
E784.H5   973.914   60-7528

E785 – 786   Harding, 1921 – 1923

Noggle, Burl. III. 6193
Teapot Dome: oil and politics in the 1920's. [Baton Rouge] Louisiana State University Press [1962] 234 p. illus. 24 cm. *1. U.S. — Politics and government — 1921-1923. 2. Presidents — U.S. — Election — 1924. 3. Corruption (in politics) — U.S. 4. Petroleum — U.S. I. T.*
E785.N6   973.914   62-15031

Vinson, John Chalmers. III. 6194
The parchment peace; the United States Senate and the Washington Conference, 1921-1922. Athens, University of Georgia Press [1955] xi, 259 p. group port. 25 cm. *1. Washington, D.C. Conference on the Limitation of Armament, 1921-1922. 2. U.S. Congress. Senate. 3. U.S. — Foreign relations — 1921-1923. I. T.*
E785.V58   327.73   55-6913

Murray, Robert K. III. 6195
The Harding era; Warren G. Harding and his administration, by Robert K. Murray. Minneapolis, University of Minnesota Press [1969] ix, 626 p. illus., ports. 25 cm. *1. Harding, Warren Gamaliel, Pres. U.S., 1865-1923. I. T.*
E786.M8 1969   973.91/4/0924   74-91797

Murray, Robert K. III. 6196
The politics of normalcy: governmental theory and practice in the Harding-Coolidge era [by] Robert K. Murray. [1st ed.] New York, Norton [c1973] xii, 162 p. 21 cm. (The Norton essays in American history) *1. Harding, Warren Gamaliel, Pres. U.S., 1865-1923. 2. Coolidge, Calvin, Pres. U.S., 1872-1933. 3. United States — Politics and government — 1921-1923. I. T.*
E786.M83   973.91/4/0924   72-8354
    ISBN:0393054748   0393094227 (pbk)

Sinclair, Andrew. III. 6197
The available man; the life behind the masks of Warren Gamaliel Harding. New York, Macmillan [1965] viii, 344 p. illus., ports. 22 cm. *1. Harding, Warren Gamaliel, Pres. U.S., 1865-1923. I. T.*
E786.S5   923.173   65-14332

E791 – 796   Coolidge, 1923 – 1929

Ellis, Lewis Ethan, 1898- III. 6198
Frank B. Kellogg and American foreign relations, 1925-1929. New Brunswick, N.J., Rutgers University Press [1961] 303 p. 22 cm. *1. Kellogg, Frank Billings, 1856-1937. 2. U.S. — Foreign relations — 1923-1929.*
E791.E5   327.73   61-10260

Fuess, Claude Moore, 1885- III. 6199
Calvin Coolidge, the man from Vermont, by Claude M. Fuess. 1st ed. Boston, Little, Brown, 1940. xii, 522 p. plates, ports., facsims. 25 cm. *1. Coolidge, Calvin, pres. U.S., 1872-1933. I. T.*
E792.F85   923.173   40-27145

McCoy, Donald R.   **III. 6200**
Calvin Coolidge; the quiet President [by] Donald R. McCoy. New York, Macmillan [1967] viii, 472 p. 21 cm. *1. Coolidge, Calvin, Pres. U.S., 1872-1933.*
E792.M117   973.9150924   (B)   67-11629

White, William Allen, 1868-   **III. 6201**
A Puritan in Babylon, the story of Calvin Coolidge, by William Allen White. New York, Macmillan, 1938. xvi, 460 p. front. (port.) 24 cm. "First printing." *1. Coolidge, Calvin, pres. U.S., 1872-1933. I. T.*
E792.W577   923.173   38-34760

MacKay, Kenneth Campbell, 1911-   **III. 6202**
The progressive movement of 1924. New York, Octagon Books, 1966 [c1947] 298 p. maps. 24 cm. (Studies in history, economics, and public law, no. 527) Issued also as thesis, Columbia University. *1. Progressive Party (Founded 1912) 2. U.S. — Politics and government — 1923-1929. I. T. (S:Columbia studies in the social sciences, no. 527)*
E795.M3x (H31.C7 no. 527 1966)   329.8   66-18046

Moore, Edmund Arthur, 1903-   **III. 6203**
A Catholic runs for President; the campaign of 1928. New York, Ronald Press Co. [1956] 220 p. illus. 21 cm. *1. Smith, Alfred Emanuel, 1873-1944. 2. Presidents — U.S. — Election — 1928. 3. Catholic Church in the U.S. 4. Church and state in the U.S. I. T.*
E796.M6   329.01   56-10167

Smith, Alfred Emanuel, 1873-1944.   **III. 6204**
Campaign addresses of Governor Alfred E. Smith, Democratic candidate for President, 1928. New York, AMS Press [1970] 322 p. illus., ports. 23 cm. Reprint of the 1929 ed. *1. Campaign literature, 1928 — Democratic. I. T.*
E796.S64 1970   329/.01   70-126683   ISBN:0404061176

E801 – 805 Hoover, 1929 – 1933

Myers, William Starr, 1877-1956.   **III. 6205**
The Hoover administration; a documented narrative, by William Starr Myers and Walter H. Newton. New York, Charles Scribner's Sons, 1936. St. Clair Shores, Mich., Scholarly Press, 1971. viii, 553 p. port. 22 cm. *1. United States — Politics and government — 1929-1933. I. Hoover, Herbert Clark, Pres. U.S., 1874-1964. II. Newton, Walter Hughes, 1880-1941, joint author. III. T.*
E801.M94 1971   973.91/6/0924   79-145202   ISBN:0403011264

Romasco, Albert U.   **III. 6206**
The poverty of abundance; Hoover, the Nation, the depression [by] Albert U. Romasco. New York, Oxford University Press, 1965. x, 282 p. 22 cm. *1. United States — Politics and government — 1929-1933. 2. Depressions — 1929 — United States. 3. Hoover, Herbert Clark, Pres. U.S., 1874-1964. I. Hoover, the Nation, the depression. II. T.*
E801.R6   973.916   65-26565

Schwarz, Jordan A., 1937-   **III. 6207**
The interregnum of despair: Hoover, Congress, and the depression [by] Jordan A. Schwarz. Urbana, University of Illinois Press [1970] ix, 281 p. 24 cm. *1. Hoover, Herbert Clark, Pres. U.S., 1874-1964. 2. U.S. — Politics and government — 1929-1933. I. T.*
E801.S3   973.91/6   78-113768   ISBN:252001125

Sternsher, Bernard, 1925- comp.   **III. 6208**
Hitting home; the Great Depression in town and country. Chicago, Quadrangle Books, 1970. x, 291 p. illus., map. 22 cm. *1. United States — Economic conditions — 1918-1945. 2. United States — Social conditions — 1918-1932. I. T.*
E801.S7   330.9/73   72-124511

Warren, Harris Gaylord, 1906-   **III. 6209**
Herbert Hoover and the great depression. New York, Oxford University Press, 1959. 372 p. 22 cm. *1. Hoover, Herbert Clark, Pres. U.S., 1874-1965. 2. U.S. — Politics and government — 1929-1933. 3. Depressions — 1929 — U.S.*
E801.W28   973.916   59-5663

Hoover, Herbert Clark, Pres. U.S., 1874-1964.   **III. 6210**
Memoirs. New York, Macmillan, 1951-1952. 3 v. illus., ports. 25 cm.
E802.H7   923.173   51-13301

Peel, Roy Victor, 1896-   **III. 6211**
The 1932 campaign, an analysis, by Roy V. Peel and Thomas C. Donnelly. New York, Farrar & Rinehart [c1935] viii, 242 p. 20 cm. *1. Presidents — U.S. — Election — 1932. 2. U.S. — Politics and government — 1929-1933. 3. Politics, Practical. I. Donnelly, Thomas Claude, 1905- joint author. II. T.*
E805.P44   973.916   35-7208

Tugwell, Rexford Guy, 1891-   **III. 6212**
The Brains Trust, by R. G. Tugwell. New York, Viking Press [1968] xxxii, 538 p. 23 cm. *1. Presidents — United States — Election — 1932. 2. Roosevelt, Franklin Delano, Pres. U.S., 1882-1945. I. T.*
E805.T8   329.023   68-16079

E806 – 812 Roosevelt, 1933 – 1945

E806 General Works A – M

Barnes, Harry Elmer, 1889-1968, ed.   **III. 6213**
Perpetual war for perpetual peace; a critical examination of the foreign policy of Franklin Delano Roosevelt and its aftermath. Edited by Harry Elmer Barnes, with the collaboration of William Henry Chamberlin [and others] New York, Greenwood Press [1969, c1953] xiii, 679 p. map. 23 cm. *1. United States — Foreign relations — 1933-1945. 2. Roosevelt, Franklin Delano, Pres. U.S., 1882-1945. 3. Pearl Harbor, Attack on, 1941. I. T.*
E806.B33 1969   327.73   70-90468   ISBN:0837121442

Beard, Charles Austin, 1874-1948.   **III. 6214**
American foreign policy in the making, 1932-1940; a study in responsibilities. [Hamden, Conn.] Archon Books, 1968 [c1946] 336 p. 22 cm. Sequel: President Roosevelt and the coming of the war, 1941. *1. United States — Foreign relations — 1933-1945. 2. United States — Foreign relations — 20th century. 3. United States — Neutrality. I. T.*
E806.B42 1968   327.73   68-8011   ISBN:0208006109

Beard, Charles Austin, 1874-1948.   **III. 6215**
President Roosevelt and the coming of the war, 1941; a study in appearances and realities. [Hamden, Conn.] Archon Books, 1968 [c1948] vi, 614 p. 22 cm. Sequel to American foreign policy in the making, 1932-1940. *1. United States — Foreign relations — 1933-1945. 2. World War, 1939-1945 — United States. 3. Roosevelt, Franklin Delano, Pres. U.S., 1882-1945. I. T.*
E806.B434 1968   327.73   68-8012   ISBN:0208002650

Brogan, Denis William, 1900-   **III. 6216**
The era of Franklin D. Roosevelt; a chronicle of the New Deal and global war. New Haven, Yale University Press, 1950. ix, 382 p. front. 18 cm. (The Chronicles of America series, v.52) On cover: Roosevelt ed. *1. Roosevelt, Franklin Delano, Pres. U.S., 1882-1945. 2. U.S. — History — 1933-1945. I. T. (S)*
E806.B78 1950a (E173.C56 vol. 52)   973.917   53-53

Conkin, Paul Keith.   **III. 6217**
The New Deal [by] Paul K. Conkin. New York, Crowell [1967] vii, 118 p. 21 cm. (Crowell American history series. Crowell publications in history.) "A note on New Deal historiography": p. 107-112. *1. Roosevelt, Franklin Delano, Pres. U.S., 1882-1945. 2. U.S. — Politics and government — 1933-1945. 3. U.S. — Social policy. I. T.*
E806.C6   973.917   67-14297

Divine, Robert A.   **III. 6218**
The illusion of neutrality. [Chicago] University of Chicago Press [1962] xi, 370 p. 23 cm. *1. U.S. — Foreign relations — 1933-1945. 2. U.S. — Neutrality. I. T.*
E806.D58   327.73   62-10993

Divine, Robert A.   **III. 6219**
Second chance; the triumph of internationalism in America during World War II [by] Robert A. Divine. [1st ed.] New York, Atheneum, 1967. ix, 371 p. 25 cm. *1. U.S. — Foreign relations — 1933-1945. 2. International organization. I. T.*
E806.D59   327.73   67-14101

Drummond, Donald Francis, 1917-   **III. 6220**
The passing of American neutrality, 1937-1941 [by] Donald F. Drummond. New York, Greenwood Press, 1968 [c1955] vi, 409 p. 24 cm. A revision of the author's thesis, University of Michigan. *1. United States — Foreign relations — 1933-1945. 2. United States — Neutrality. I. T.*
E806.D7 1968   327.73   68-54416

Einaudi, Mario, 1904-   **III. 6221**
The Roosevelt revolution. [1st ed.] New York, Harcourt, Brace [1959] 372 p. 22 cm. *1. Roosevelt, Franklin Delano, Pres. U.S., 1882-1945. 2. U.S. — Politics and government — 1933-1945. I. T.*
E806.E5   973.917   59-7535

Ekirch, Arthur Alphonse, 1915-   **III. 6222**
Ideologies and Utopias; the impact of the new deal on American thought, by Arthur A. Ekirch, Jr. Chicago, Quadrangle Books, 1969. ix, 307 p. 22 cm. *1. Roosevelt, Franklin Delano, Pres. U.S., 1882-1945. 2. United States — Politics and government — 1933-1945. I. T.*
E806.E53   973.917   79-78307

Farley, James Aloysius, 1888-   **III. 6223**
Jim Farley's story; the Roosevelt years. New York, Whittlesey House [1948] x, 338 p. ports., facsim. 24 cm. *1. Roosevelt, Franklin Delano, Pres. U.S., 1882-1945. 2. U.S. — Politics and government — 1933-1945.*
E806.F255   973.917   48-946

Ickes, Harold Le Claire, 1874-1952.   **III. 6224**
The secret diary of Harold L. Ickes. New York, Simon and Schuster [1953- v. 23 cm. *1. U.S. — Politics and government — 1933-1953. I. T.*
E806.I2   973.917   53-9701

Keller, Morton, ed.   III. 6225
The New Deal, what was it? New York, Holt, Rinehart and Winston [1963] 122 p. 24 cm. (American problem studies) *1. U.S. — Politics and government — 1933-1945. I. T.*
E806.K4   973.917082   63-8816

Leuchtenburg, William Edward, 1922-   III. 6226
Franklin D. Roosevelt and the New Deal, 1932-1940. [1st ed.] New York, Harper & Row [1963] 393 p. illus. 22 cm. (The New American Nation series) *1. U.S. — Hist — 1933-1945. I. T.*
E806.L475   973.917   63-12053

Lingeman, Richard R.   III. 6227
Don't you know there's a war on? The American home front, 1941-1945 [by] Richard R. Lingeman. New York, Putnam [1970] 400 p. 24 cm. *1. U.S. — Social life and customs — 1918-1945. I. T.*
E806.L568 1970   917.3/03/917   79-127721

Moley, Raymond, 1886-   III. 6228
After seven years. New York, Da Capo Press, 1972 [c1939] xii, 446 p. illus. 22 cm. (Franklin D. Roosevelt and the era of the New Deal) *1. United States — Politics and government — 1933-1945. I. T. (S)*
E806.M67 1972   973.917   71-168390   ISBN:0306703270

Moley, Raymond, 1886-   III. 6229
The first New Deal [by] Raymond Moley, with the assistance of Elliot A. Rosen. Foreword by Frank Freidel. [1st ed.] New York, Harcourt, Brace & World [1966] xxiii, 577 p. 24 cm. *1. U.S. — Politics and government — 1933-1945. 2. U.S. — Economic policy. I. T.*
E806.M68   973.917   66-22282

E806   General Works N – Z

[Notter, Harley]   III. 6230
Postwar foreign policy preparation, 1939-1945. Washington, 1949. ix, 726 p. maps (1 fold.) 24 cm. ([U.S.] Dept. of State. Publication 3580. General foreign policy series, 15) Errata slip inserted. *1. U.S. — Foreign relations — 1933-1945. 2. U.S. — Foreign relations — 1945- I. U.S. Dept. of State. Office of Public Affairs. II. T. (S:U.S. Dept. of State. Publication 3580.) (S:U.S. Dept. of State. General foreign policy series, 15)*
E806.Nx   Sd50-55

Patterson, James T.   III. 6231
Congressional conservatism and the New Deal; the growth of the conservative coalition in Congress, 1933-1939, by James T. Patterson. [Lexington] For the Organization of American Historians [by] University of Kentucky Press, 1967. ix, 369 p. illus., ports. 23 cm. *1. U.S. — Politics and government — 1933-1945. 2. U.S. — Social policy. 3. Conservatism — U.S. I. Organization of American Historians. II. T.*
E806.P365   353/.03/72   67-17845

Perkins, Dexter, 1889-   III. 6232
The new age of Franklin Roosevelt, 1932-45. [Chicago] University of Chicago Press [1957] 193 p. 21 cm. (The Chicago history of American civilization) *1. Roosevelt, Franklin Delano, Pres. U.S., 1882-1945. 2. U.S. — History — 1933-1945. I. T.*
E806.P465   973.917   56-11263

Perrett, Geoffrey.   III. 6233
Days of sadness, years of triumph; the American people, 1939-1945. New York, Coward, McCann & Geoghegan [1973] 512 p. 24 cm. *1. United States — History — 1933-1945. 2. World War, 1939-1945 — United States. I. T.*
E806.P466 1973   309.1/73/0917   72-87594   ISBN:0698104889

Rauch, Basil, 1908-   III. 6234
The history of the new deal, 1933-1938, by Basil Rauch. New York, Creative Age Press [1944] xi, 368 p. 21 cm. *1. U.S. — Politics and government — 1933- I. T.*
E806.R3   973.917   44-8426

Robinson, Edgar Eugene, 1887-   III. 6235
The Roosevelt leadership, 1933-1945. [1st ed.] Philadelphia, Lippincott [c1955] 491 p. 22 cm. *1. Roosevelt, Franklin Delano, Pres. U.S., 1882-1945. 2. U.S. — History — 1933-1945. I. T.*
E806.R722   973.917   54-10698

Roosevelt, Franklin Delano, Pres. U.S., 1882-1945.   III. 6236
Complete presidential press conferences of Franklin D. Roosevelt. Introd. by Jonathan Daniels. New York, Da Capo Press, 1972-   v. front. 26 cm. *1. United States — Politics and government — 1933-1945. 2. Presidents — United States — Press conferences.*
E806.R7424 1972   973.917   78-155953   ISBN:030677500X

Roosevelt, Franklin Delano, Pres. U.S., 1882-1945.   III. 6237
Franklin D. Roosevelt and foreign affairs. Edited by Edgar B. Nixon. Cambridge, Belknap Press of Harvard University Press, 1969-   v. ports. 26 cm. *1. United States — Foreign relations — 1933-1945. I. Nixon, Edgar Burkhardt, 1902- ed. II. T.*
E806.R7427   327.73   68-25617

Rose, Lisle Abbott, 1904-   III. 6238
After Yalta [by] Lisle A. Rose. New York, Scribner [1973] vi, 216 p. 21 cm. *1. United States — Foreign relations — 1933-1945. 2. United States — Foreign relations — 1945-1953. 3. United States — Foreign relations — Russia. 4. Russia — Foreign relations — United States. I. T.*
E806.R83 1973   327.73   72-7866   ISBN:0684131897

Schlesinger, Arthur Meier, 1917-   III. 6239
The age of Roosevelt. Boston, Houghton Mifflin, 1957-1960. 3 v. 22 cm. *1. Roosevelt, Franklin Delano, Pres. U.S., 1882-1945. 2. U.S. — History — 1919-1933. 3. U.S. — History — 1933-1945. I. T.*
E806.S34   973.917   56-10293

Tansill, Charles Callan, 1890-   III. 6240
Back door to war; the Roosevelt foreign policy, 1933-1941. [1st ed.] Chicago, H. Regnery Co. [1952] xxi, 690 p. 24 cm. *1. U.S. — Foreign relations — 1933-1945. 2. World politics. I. T.*
E806.T3   327.73   52-9622

Terkel, Louis.   III. 6241
Hard times; an oral history of the great depression [by] Studs Terkel. New York, Pantheon Books [1970] xiii, 462 p. 25 cm. *1. United States — Economic conditions — 1918-1945 — Addresses, essays, lectures. 2. United States — Social conditions — 1933-1945 — Addresses, essays, lectures. I. T.*
E806.T45   309.1/73   69-20195

Wecter, Dixon, 1906-   III. 6242
The age of the great depression, 1929-1941. New York, Macmillan, 1948. xiv, 434 p. illus., ports. 22 cm. (A History of American life, v.13) *1. U.S. — Civilization. 2. U.S. — Social conditions. 3. U.S. — Economic conditions — 1918- 4. U.S. — Politics and government — 1933-1945. I. T. (S)*
E806.W43 1948a (E169.1.H67 vol. 13)   973.917   48-10172

Westerfield, H. Bradford, 1928-   III. 6243
Foreign policy and party politics: Pearl Harbor to Korea [by] H. Bradford Westerfield. New York, Octagon Books, 1972 [c1955] x, 448 p. illus. 24 cm. *1. United States — Foreign relations — 1933-1945. 2. United States — Foreign relations — 1945-1953. 3. Political parties — United States. I. T.*
E806.W455 1972   327.73   70-159236   ISBN:0374983631

Wolfskill, George, 1921-   III. 6244
All but the people; Franklin D. Roosevelt and his critics, 1933-39 [by] George Wolfskill & John A. Hudson. [New York] Macmillan [1969] xii, 386 p. illus. 24 cm. *1. Roosevelt, Franklin Delano, Pres. U.S., 1882-1945. 2. United States — Politics and government — 1933-1945. 3. Public opinion — United States. I. Hudson, John A., joint author. II. T.*
E806.W67   320.9/73   69-10191

Young, Roland Arnold, 1910-   III. 6245
Congressional politics in the Second World War, by Roland Young. New York, Da Capo Press, 1972 [c1956] 281 p. illus. 22 cm. (Franklin D. Roosevelt and the era of the New Deal) *1. United States — Politics and government — 1933-1945. 2. World War, 1939-1945 — United States. 3. United States. Congress — History. I. T. (S)*
E806.Y69 1972   320.9/73/0917   70-38757   ISBN:0306704420

E807   Biography of Roosevelt

Bellush, Bernard, 1917-   III. 6246
Franklin D. Roosevelt as Governor of New York. New York, AMS Press [1968] xiii, 338 p. 22 cm. (Columbia studies in the social sciences, no. 585) Reprint of the 1955 ed. *1. Roosevelt, Franklin Delano, Pres. U.S., 1882-1945. 2. New York (State) — Politics and government — 1865-1950. I. T. (S)*
E807.B4x (H31.C7 no. 585 1968)   973.917/0924   (B)   68-54257

Burns, James MacGregor.   III. 6247
Roosevelt: the lion and the fox. [1st ed.] New York, Harcourt, Brace [1956] 553 p. illus. 23 cm. *1. Roosevelt, Franklin Delano, Pres. U.S., 1882-1945. 2. U.S. — Politics and government — 1933-1945.*
E807.B835   923.173   56-7920

Burns, James MacGregor.   III. 6248
Roosevelt: the soldier of freedom. [1st ed.] New York, Harcourt Brace Jovanovich [1970] xiv, 722 p. illus., ports. 22 cm. *1. Roosevelt, Franklin Delano, Pres. U.S., 1882-1945. 2. World War, 1939-1945 — U.S. I. T.*
E807.B836   940.532/2/730924   71-95877   ISBN:0151788715

Davis, Kenneth Sydney, 1912-   III. 6249
FDR: the beckoning of destiny, 1882-1928; a history, by Kenneth S. Davis. New York, Putnam [1972] 936 p. 25 cm. *1. Roosevelt, Franklin Delano, Pres. U.S., 1882-1945. I. T.*
E807.D36 1972   973.917/092/4   (B)   72-79519   ISBN:0399109986

Divine, Robert A.   **III. 6250**
Roosevelt and World War II, by Robert A. Divine. Baltimore, Johns Hopkins Press [1969] x, 107 p. illus. 22 cm. (The Albert Shaw lectures in diplomatic history, 1968) *1. Roosevelt, Franklin Delano, Pres. U.S., 1882-1945. 2. United States — Foreign relations — 1933-1945 — Addresses, essays, lectures. I. T. (S:The Albert Shaw lectures on diplomatic history, 1968)*
E807.D57   940.532/2/730924   69-13655

Freidel, Frank Burt.   **III. 6251**
Franklin D. Roosevelt. [1st ed.] Boston, Little, Brown [1952-   v. ports. 23 cm. *1. Roosevelt, Franklin Delano, Pres. U.S., 1882-1945.*
E807.F74   923.173   52-5521

Fusfeld, Daniel Roland, 1922-   **III. 6252**
The economic thought of Franklin D. Roosevelt and the origins of the New Deal, by Daniel R. Fusfeld. New York, AMS Press [1970] 337 p. 23 cm. (Columbia studies in the social sciences, no. 586) Reprint of the 1956 ed. *1. Roosevelt, Franklin Delano, Pres. U.S., 1882-1945. 2. United States — Economic policy — To 1933. I. T. (S)*
E807.F8 1970   330.973   71-120205   ISBN:040451581X

Gosnell, Harold Foote, 1896-   **III. 6253**
Champion campaigner: Franklin D. Roosevelt. New York, Macmillan, 1952. 235 p. illus. 22 cm. *1. Roosevelt, Franklin Delano, Pres. U.S., 1882-1945. 2. Elections — U.S. I. T.*
E807.G68   923.173   52-4277

Gunther, John, 1901-   **III. 6254**
Roosevelt in retrospect, a profile in history. [1st ed.] New York, Harper [1950] xii, 410 p. 22 cm. *1. Roosevelt, Franklin Delano, Pres. U.S., 1882-1945. I. T.*
E807.G85   923.173   50-8078

Halasz, Nicholas, 1895-   **III. 6255**
Roosevelt through foreign eyes. Princeton, N.J., Van Nostrand [1961] 340 p. 24 cm. *1. Roosevelt, Franklin Delano, Pres. U.S., 1882-1945. I. T.*
E807.H3   973.917   61-16106

Hassett, William D., 1880-   **III. 6256**
Off the record with F. D. R., 1942-1945. With an introd. by Jonathan Daniels. New Brunswick, N.J., Rutgers University Press, 1958. 366 p. illus. 25 cm. *1. Roosevelt, Franklin Delano, Pres. U.S., 1882-1945. I. T.*
E807.H34   923.173   58-10832

Rollins, Alfred Brooks, 1921-   **III. 6257**
Roosevelt and Howe. [1st ed.] New York, Knopf, 1962. 479 p. illus. 22 cm. *1. Roosevelt, Franklin Delano, Pres. U.S., 1882-1945. 2. Howe, Louis McHenry, 1871-1936.*
E807.R627   923.173   62-15578

Roosevelt, Elliott, 1910-   **III. 6258**
As he saw it, with a foreword by Eleanor Roosevelt. New York, Duell, Sloan and Pearce [1946] xviii, 270 p. 22 cm. *1. Roosevelt, Franklin Delano, Pres. U.S., 1882-1945. 2. World War, 1939-1945 — Congresses, conferences, etc. I. T.*
E807.R64   973.917   46-7078

Roosevelt, Franklin Delano, Pres. U.S., 1882-1945.   **III. 6259**
Selected speeches, messages, press conferences, and letters. Edited with an introd. by Basil Rauch. New York, Rinehart [1957] 391 p. 19 cm. (Rinehart editions, 83)
E807.R6483   923.173   56-12049

Roosevelt, Franklin Delano, Pres. U.S., 1882-1945.   **III. 6260**
F. D. R.: his personal letters. Foreword by Eleanor Roosevelt; edited by Elliott Roosevelt. [1st ed.] New York, Duell, Sloan and Pearce [1947-50] 4 v. illus., ports., facsims., geneal. table. 22 cm. Vol.2 edited by Elliott Roosevelt, assisted by James N. Rosenau; v.3-4 edited by Elliott Roosevelt, assisted by Joseph P. Lash. *I. Roosevelt, Elliott, 1910- ed. II. T.*
E807.R649   923.173   47-11935

Roosevelt, James, 1907-   **III. 6261**
Affectionately, F.D.R.; a son's story of a lonely man, by James Roosevelt and Sidney Shalett. [1st ed.] New York, Harcourt, Brace [1959] 394 p. illus. 23 cm. *1. Roosevelt, Franklin Delano, Pres. U.S., 1882-1945. 2. Roosevelt family. I. Shalett, Sidney, joint author. II. T.*
E807.R657   923.173   59-10248

Rosenman, Samuel Irving, 1896-   **III. 6262**
Working with Roosevelt, by Samuel I. Rosenman. New York, Da Capo Press, 1972 [c1952] xiv, 560 p. illus. 22 cm. (Franklin D. Roosevelt and the era of the New Deal) *1. Roosevelt, Franklin Delano, Pres. U.S., 1882-1945. 2. Authorship — Collaboration. I. T. (S)*
E807.R73 1972   973.917   75-168391   ISBN:0306703289

Sherwood, Robert Emmet, 1896-   **III. 6263**
Roosevelt and Hopkins, an intimate history. Rev. ed. New York, Harper [1950] xix, 1002 p. illus., ports., map. 22 cm. *1. Roosevelt, Franklin Delano, Pres. U.S., 1882-1945. 2. Hopkins, Harry Lloyd, 1890-1946. 3. U.S. — Politics and government — 1933-1945. I. T.*
E807.S45 1950   973.917   50-6867

Tugwell, Rexford Guy, 1891-   **III. 6264**
The democratic Roosevelt; a bibliography of Franklin D. Roosevelt. [1st ed.] Garden City, N.Y., Doubleday, 1957. 712 p. illus. ports. 25 cm. *1. Roosevelt, Franklin Delano, Pres. U.S., 1882-1945. I. T.*
E807.T76   923.173   57-7290

Tugwell, Rexford Guy, 1891-   **III. 6265**
In search of Roosevelt [by] Rexford G. Tugwell. Cambridge, Harvard University Press, 1972. ix, 313 p. 24 cm. *1. Roosevelt, Franklin Delano, Pres. U.S., 1882-1945. I. T.*
E807.T765   973.917/092/4   72-76559

E807.1 Biography of Eleanor Roosevelt

Roosevelt, Eleanor (Roosevelt) 1884-1962.   **III. 6266**
Autobiography. [1st ed.] New York, Harper [1961] 454 p. illus. 25 cm.
E807.1.R35   920.7   61-12222

Roosevelt, Eleanor (Roosevelt) 1884-1962.   **III. 6267**
This I remember. [1st ed.] New York, Harper [1949] x, 387 p. illus., ports. 24 cm. *1. Roosevelt, Franklin Delano, Pres. U.S., 1882-1945. I. T.*
E807.1.R428   923.173   49-48262

Lash, Joseph P., 1909-   **III. 6268**
Eleanor and Franklin; the story of their relationship, based on Eleanor Roosevelt's private papers [by] Joseph P. Lash. Foreword by Arthur M. Schlesinger, Jr. Introd. by Franklin D. Roosevelt, Jr. New York, Norton [1971] xviii, 765 p. illus., geneal. table (on lining papers), ports. 24 cm. *1. Roosevelt, Eleanor (Roosevelt) 1884-1962. 2. Roosevelt, Franklin Delano, Pres. U.S., 1882-1945. I. T.*
E807.1.R572   973.917/0924 (B)   72-152667   ISBN:0393074595

Lash, Joseph P., 1909-   **III. 6269**
Eleanor: the years alone [by] Joseph P. Lash. Foreword by Franklin D. Roosevelt, Jr. New York, Norton [1972] 368 p. 24 cm. Continues the biography of Mrs. Roosevelt which began in the author's Eleanor and Franklin. *1. Roosevelt, Eleanor (Roosevelt) 1884-1962. I. T.*
E807.1.R574   973.917/092/4 (B)   72-2674   ISBN:0393073610

E813 – 816 Truman, 1945 – 1953

Alperovitz, Gar.   **III. 6270**
Atomic diplomacy: Hiroshima and Potsdam; the use of the atomic bomb and the American confrontation with Soviet power. New York, Simon and Schuster [1965] 317 p. 25 cm. *1. United States — Foreign relations — 1945-1953. 2. United States — Foreign relations — Russia. 3. Russia — Foreign relations — United States. I. Hiroshima and Potsdam.*
E813.A75   327.73047   65-15029

Bernstein, Barton J., ed.   **III. 6271**
The Truman administration; a documentary history, edited by Barton J. Bernstein and Allan J. Matusow. [1st ed.] New York, Harper & Row [1966] viii, 518 p. illus., ports. 22 cm. *1. United States — Politics and government — 1933-1953 — Sources. 2. United States — Foreign relations — 1945-1953 — Sources. 3. Truman, Harry S., Pres. U.S., 1884- I. Matusow, Allen J., joint ed. II. T.*
E813.B45   973.918   66-13938

Cohen, Bernard Cecil, 1926-   **III. 6272**
The political process and foreign policy; the making of the Japanese peace settlement. Princeton, Princeton University Press, 1957. x, 293 p. 25 cm. "Part of a continuing inquiry ... on the part of the Center of International Studies." *1. U.S. — Foreign relations — 1945- 2. World War, 1939-1945 — Japan. I. Princeton University. Center of International Studies. II. T.*
E813.C62   327.73   57-8665

Freeland, Richard M., 1941-   **III. 6273**
The Truman Doctrine and the origins of McCarthyism; foreign policy, domestic politics, and internal security, 1946-1948 [by] Richard M. Freeland. [1st ed.] New York, Knopf, 1972 [c1971] xii, 419, xii p. 22 cm. *1. United States — Politics and government — 1945-1953. 2. Internal security — United States. 3. United States — Foreign relations — 1945-1953. 4. Communism — United States — 1917- I. T.*
E813.F74 1971   327.73   71-142958   ISBN:0394465970

Gardner, Lloyd C., 1934-   **III. 6274**
Architects of illusion; men and ideas in American foreign policy, 1941-1949, by Lloyd C. Gardner. Chicago, Quadrangle Books, 1970. xi, 365 p. 22 cm. *1. United States — Foreign relations — 1933-1945. 2. United States — Foreign relations — 1945-1953. I. T.*
E813.G27   327.73   69-20163

Goldman, Eric Frederick, 1915-   III. 6275
The crucial decade: America, 1945-1955. [1st ed.] New York, Knopf, 1956. 298 p. 22 cm. *1. U.S. — History — 1945- I. T.*
E813.G6   973.918   55-9285

Harper, Alan D.   III. 6276
The politics of loyalty; the White House and the Communist issue, 1946-1952 [by] Alan D. Harper. Westport, Conn., Greenwood Pub. Corp. [1969] xii, 318 p. 22 cm. (Contributions in American history, no. 2) *1. United States — Politics and government — 1945-1953. 2. Communism — United States — 1917- 3. Loyalty-security program, 1947- I. T.*
E813.H366   323   73-95509   ISBN:0837123437

Hartmann, Susan M.   III. 6277
Truman and the 80th Congress [by] Susan M. Hartmann. Columbia, University of Missouri Press, 1971. viii, 241 p. 23 cm. *1. Truman, Harry S., Pres. U.S., 1884- 2. United States. 80th Congress, 1947-1948. 3. United States — Politics and government — 1945-1953. I. T.*
E813.H39   973.918   78-149008   ISBN:0826201059

Jones, Joseph Marion, 1908-   III. 6278
The fifteen weeks (February 21-June 5, 1947) New York, Viking Press, 1955. 296 p. 22 cm. *1. U.S. — Foreign relations — 1945- 2. World politics — 1945- I. T.*
E813.J6   327.73   55-8923

Lee, R. Alton.   III. 6279
Truman and Taft-Hartley; a question of mandate [by] R. Alton Lee. Lexington, University of Kentucky Press, 1966. viii, 254 p. 23 cm. *1. Truman, Harry S., Pres. U.S., 1884- 2. U.S. — Laws, statutes, etc. — Labor management relations act, 1947. I. T.*
E813.L4   973.918   66-26689

Phillips, Cabell B. H.   III. 6280
The Truman Presidency; the history of a triumphant succession [by] Cabell Phillips. New York, Macmillan [1966] xiii, 463 p. 24 cm. *1. United States — Politics and government — 1945-1953. 2. Truman, Harry S., Pres. U.S., 1884- I. T.*
E813.P5 1966   973.918   66-16709

Politics and policies of the Truman Administration.   III. 6281
Edited with an introd. by Barton J. Bernstein. Chicago, Quadrangle Books, 1970. 330 p. 22 cm. *1. United States — Politics and government — 1945-1953 — Addresses, essays, lectures. 2. United States — Foreign relations — 1945-1953 — Addresses, essays, lectures. 3. Truman, Harry S., Pres. U.S., 1884- — Addresses, essays, lectures. I. Bernstein, Barton J., ed.*
E813.P6 1970   973.918   70-78302

Theoharis, Athan G.   III. 6282
Seeds of repression; Harry S. Truman and the origins of McCarthyism, by Athan Theoharis. Chicago, Quadrangle Books, 1971. xi, 238 p. 22 cm. *1. United States — Foreign relations — 1945-1953. 2. United States — Politics and government — 1945-1953. 3. McCarthy, Joseph Raymond, 1908-1957. 4. Internal security — United States. I. T.*
E813.T48   973.918   71-116089   ISBN:081290169X

Truman, Harry S., Pres. U.S., 1884-   III. 6283
The Truman administration, its principles and practice, edited by Louis W. Koenig. New York, New York University Press, 1956. xii, 394 p. 25 cm. *1. U.S. — Politics and government — 1945- I. Koenig, Louis William, 1916- ed. II. T.*
E813.T68   973.918   56-7425

Vandenberg, Arthur Hendrick, 1884-1951.   III. 6284
The private papers of Senator Vandenberg, edited by Arthur H. Vandenberg, Jr., with the collaboration of Joe Alex Morris. Boston, Houghton Mifflin, 1952. xxii, 599 p. illus., ports. 23 cm. *1. U.S. — Politics and government — 1945- — Sources. 2. U.S. — Foreign relations — 1945- — Sources. I. Vandenberg, Arthur Hendrick, ed. II. Morris, Joe Alex, 1904- ed. III. T.*
E813.V3   973.917   52-5248

Daniels, Jonathan, 1902-   III. 6285
The man of Independence. Port Washington, N.Y., Kennikat Press [1971, c1950] 384 p. 22 cm. (Kennikat Press scholarly reprints. Series in American history and culture in the twentieth century) *1. Truman, Harry S., Pres. U.S., 1884- I. T.*
E814.D3 1971   973.918/0924 (B)   75-137969   ISBN:80461427X

Truman, Harry S., Pres. U.S., 1884-1972.   III. 6286
Memoirs. [Kansas City ed.] Garden City, N.Y., Doubleday, 1955-56. 2 v. map (on lining paper, v.1) 22 cm. *1. U.S. — Politics and government — 1945- — Sources. I. Year of decisions.*
E814.T76   973.917   55-4830

Ross, Irwin.   III. 6287
The loneliest campaign; the Truman victory of 1948. [New York] New American Library [1968] viii, 304 p. illus., ports. 22 cm. *1. Presidents — United States — Election — 1948. 2. Truman, Harry S., Pres. U.S., 1884- I. T.*
E815.R6   329/.023   68-18257

Schmidt, Karl M., 1917-   III. 6288
Henry A. Wallace, quixotic crusade 1948. [Syracuse] Syracuse University Press, 1960. 362 p. illus. 21 cm. (Men and movements series) *1. Wallace, Henri Agard, 1888- 2. Progressive Party (Founded 1948) 3. Presidents — U.S. — Election — 1948.*
E815.S35   329.8   60-16440

Eulau, Heinz, 1915-   III. 6289
Class and party in the Eisenhower years; class roles and perspectives in the 1952 and 1956 elections. [New York] Fress Press of Glencoe [1962] 162 p. 22 cm. *1. Presidents — U.S. — Election — 1952. 2. Presidents — U.S. — Election — 1956. 3. Voting — U.S. — Case studies. 4. Class distinction — U.S. I. T.*
E816.E78   973.921   62-15358

E835 – 837   Eisenhower, 1953 – 1961

Adams, Sherman, 1899-   III. 6290
Firsthand report; the story of the Eisenhower administration. [1st ed.] New York, Harper [1961] 481 p. illus. 22 cm. *1. Eisenhower, Dwight David, Pres. U.S., 1890- 2. U.S. — Politics and government — 1953-1961. 3. U.S. — Foreign relations — 1953-1961.*
E835.A3   973.921   61-6191

Bell, Daniel, ed.   III. 6291
The new American right. New York, Criterion Books [1955] xii, 239 p. 22 cm. *1. U.S. — Politics and government — 1953- 2. Conservatism. I. T.*
E835.B4   973.9104   55-11024

Benson, Ezra Taft.   III. 6292
Cross fire; the eight years with Eisenhower. [1st ed.] Garden City, N.Y., Doubleday, 1962. 627 p. illus. 24 cm. *1. U.S. — Politics and government — 1953-1961. 2. Agriculture and state — U.S. I. T.*
E835.B43   973.921   62-11368

Branyan, Robert L., comp.   III. 6293
The Eisenhower administration, 1953-1961; a documentary history [by] Robert L. Branyan [and] Lawrence H. Larsen. [1st ed.] New York, Random House [1971] 2 v. (1414 p.) 25 cm. *1. Eisenhower, Dwight David, Pres. U.S., 1890-1969. 2. United States — Politics and government — 1953-1961 — Sources. I. Larsen, Lawrence Harold, 1931- joint comp. II. T.*
E835.B685   973.921/.0924 (B)   71-164935   ISBN:0394472411

Donovan, Robert J.   III. 6294
Eisenhower: the inside story. [1st ed.] New York, Harper [1956] xviii, 423 p. ports. 22 cm. "About one fourth of the material ... was first published in the New York herald tribune under the title: Eisenhower in the White House." *1. Eisenhower, Dwight David, Pres. U.S., 1890- 2. U.S. — Politics and government — 1953- 3. U.S. — Foreign relations — 1945-*
E835.D6   973.92   56-9653

Finer, Herman, 1898-   III. 6295
Dulles over Suez: the theory and practice of his diplomacy. Chicago, Quadrangle Books [1964] xix, 538 p. ports., maps (on lining papers) 25 cm. *1. Dulles, John Foster, 1888-1959. 2. U.S. — Foreign relations — 1953-1961. 3. Egypt — History — Intervention, 1956. I. T.*
E835.D85F5   973.921   64-10924

Guhin, Michael A., 1940-   III. 6296
John Foster Dulles: a statesman and his times [by] Michael A. Guhin. New York, Columbia University Press, 1972. p. *1. Dulles, John Foster, 1888-1959.*
E835.D85G8   973.921/092/4 (B)   72-5873   ISBN:0231036647

Hughes, Emmet John, 1920-   III. 6297
The ordeal of power; a political memoir of the Eisenhower years. [1st ed.] New York, Atheneum, 1963. 372 p. 22 cm. *1. Eisenhower, Dwight David, Pres. U.S., 1890- 2. U.S. — Politics and government — 1953-1961. I. T.*
E835.H8 1963   973.921   63-12783

Humphrey, George Magoffin, 1890-   III. 6298
The basic papers of George M. Humphrey as Secretary of the Treasury, 1953-1957. Edited by Nathaniel R. Howard. Cleveland, Western Reserve Historical Society [1965] xxix, 644 p. illus., ports. 25 cm. (Western Reserve Historical Society. Publication no. 119) *1. Finance, Public — U.S. 2. U.S. — Politics and government — 1953-1961. 3. U.S. — Foreign economic relations. (S:Western Reserve Historical Society, Cleveland. Publication no. 119)*
E835.H85 (F486.W58 no. 119)   353.007208   65-17514

Kennan, George Frost, 1904-   III. 6299
Realities of American foreign policy [by] George F. Kennan. New York, Norton [1966] ix, 119 p. 20 cm. (The Norton library, N320) First published in 1954. *1. United States — Foreign relations — 1953-1961. 2. World politics — 1945- I. T.*
E835.K4 1966   327.73   66-15309

Kissinger, Henry Alfred.   III. 6300
The necessity for choice; prospects of American foreign policy. [1st ed.] New York, Harper [1961] 370 p. 22 cm. *1. U.S. — Foreign relations — 1953- 2. U.S. — Military policy. 3. World politics — 1955- I. T.*
E835.K5   327.73   61-6187

Larson, Arthur.   III. 6301
A Republican looks at his party. [1st ed.] New York, Harper [1956] 210 p. 22 cm. *1. Republican Party. 2. U.S. — Politics and government — 1953- I. T.*
E835.L3   329.6   56-9671

Lubell, Samuel.   III. 6302
Revolt of the moderates. [1st ed.] New York, Harper [1956] 308 p. illus. 22 cm. *1. U.S. — Politics and government — 1953- I. T.*
E835.L8   973.92   56-6118

Parmet, Herbert S.   III. 6303
Eisenhower and the American crusades [by] Herbert S. Parmet. New York, Macmillan [1972] xi, 660 p. illus. 24 cm. *1. Eisenhower, Dwight David, Pres. United States, 1890-1969. 2. United States — Politics and government — 1953-1961. I. T.*
E835.P3 1972   973.921/092/4   73-189680

Pusey, Merlo John, 1902-   III. 6304
Eisenhower, the President. New York, Macmillan, 1956. 300 p. 22 cm. *1. Eisenhower, Dwight David, Pres. U.S. 1890- 2. U.S. — Politics and government — 1953- 3. U.S. — Foreign relations — 1945-*
E835.P8   973.92   56-8365

Rovere, Richard Halworth, 1915-   III. 6305
The Eisenhower years; affairs of state. New York, Farrar, Straus and Cudahy [1956] 390 p. 22 cm. *1. U.S. — Politics and government — 1953- 2. U.S. — Foreign relations — 1945- I. Affairs of state. II. T.*
E835.R6   973.92   56-6153

Stevenson, Adlai Ewing, 1900-1965.   III. 6306
What I think. [1st ed.] New York, Harper [c1956] 240 p. 22 cm. "Selected speeches and articles written ... since the Presidential campaign of 1952." *1. U.S. — Politics and government — 1953- — Addresses, essays, lectures. 2. World politics, 1945- — Addresses, essays, lectures. I. T.*
E835.S78   973.92   55-11788

Wechsler, James Arthur, 1915-   III. 6307
Reflections of an angry middle-aged editor. New York, Random House [1960] 245 p. 21 cm. *1. U.S. — Politics and government — 1953- 2. Public opinion — U.S. I. T.*
E835.W4   973.921   60-7683

Ambrose, Stephen E.   III. 6308
The Supreme Commander; the war years of General Dwight D. Eisenhower [by] Stephen E. Ambrose. [1st ed.] Garden City, N.Y., Doubleday, 1970. ix, 732 p. col. maps, port. 24 cm. *1. Eisenhower, Dwight David, Pres. U.S., 1890-1969. 2. World War, 1939-1945 — Campaigns. I. T.*
E836.A83   940.54 (B)   77-111141

Childs, Marquis William, 1903-   III. 6309
Eisenhower: captive hero; a critical study of the general and the President. [1st ed.] New York, Harcourt, Brace [1958] 310 p. illus. 21 cm. *1. Eisenhower, Dwight David, Pres. U.S., 1890-*
E836.C5   923.173   58-10905

Larson, Arthur.   III. 6310
Eisenhower: the President nobody knew. New York, Scribner [1968] xii, 210 p. illus., ports. 22 cm. *1. Eisenhower, Dwight David, Pres. U.S., 1890- I. T.*
E836.L3   973.921/0924   68-27778

E838   Later 20th Century (1961 –

Brzezinski, Zbigniew K., 1928-   III. 6311
Between two ages; America's role in the technetronic era [by] Zbigniew Brzezinski. New York, Viking Press [1970] xvii, 334 p. 23 cm. "Prepared under the auspices of the Research Institute on Communist Affairs, Columbia University." *1. United States — Civilization — 1970- 2. International relations. I. Columbia University. Research Institute on Communist Affairs. II. T.*
E839.B7 1970   301.2/4   76-104162   ISBN:0670160415

O'Neill, William L.   III. 6312
Coming apart; an informal history of America in the 1960's [by] William L. O'Neill. Chicago, Quadrangle Books, 1971. ix, 442, xxvi p. illus., ports. 24 cm. *1. United States — History — 1945- 2. United States — Politics and government — 1945- I. T.*
E839.O5 1971   973.921   79-152098   ISBN:0812901908

Thomson, Charles Alexander Holmes, 1913-   III. 6313
The 1956 Presidential campaign, by Charles A. H. Thomson [and] Frances M. Shattuck. Washington, Brookings Institution [1960] xv, 382 p. tables. 24 cm. *1. Presidents — U.S. — Election — 1956. I. Shattuck, Frances M., joint author. II. Presidential campaign. III. T.*
E839.T48   329.01   60-12085

Lubell, Samuel.   III. 6314
The hidden crisis in American politics. [1st ed.] New York, Norton [1970] 306 p. 22 cm. *1. United States — Politics and government — 1945- I. T.*
E839.5.L8 1970   320.9/73   69-17630   ISBN:0393053709

Peirce, Neal R.   III. 6315
The megastates of America; people, politics, and power in the ten great States [by] Neal R. Peirce. [1st ed.] New York, Norton [1972] 745 p. 24 cm. *1. United States — Politics and government — 1945- 2. State governments. 3. United States — Economic conditions — 1961- 4. United States — Social conditions — 1960- I. T.*
E839.5.P35   917.3/03/92   70-163375   ISBN:0393054586

David, Paul Theodore, 1906- ed.   III. 6316
The Presidential election and transition, 1960-1961; Brookings lectures and additional papers [by] Paul T. David [and others] Washington, Brookings Institution [1961] ix, 353 p. 22 cm. *1. Presidents — U.S. — Election — 1960. 2. Presidents — U.S. — Transition periods. I. T.*
E840.D38   973.921   61-18112

Morgenthau, Hans Joachim, 1904-   III. 6317
A new foreign policy for the United States [by] Hans J. Morgenthau. New York, Published for the Council on Foreign Relations by F. A. Praeger [1969] xii, 252 p. 22 cm. *1. United States — Foreign relations — 1945- I. Council of Foreign Relations. II. T.*
E840.M593   327.73   68-28475

No more Vietnams? The war and the future of American foreign policy.   III. 6318
Contributors: Eqbal Ahmad [and others] Edited by Richard M. Pfeffer. [1st ed.] New York, Published for the Adlai Stevenson Institute of International Affairs by Harper & Row [1968] x, 299 p. 22 cm. *1. United States — Foreign relations — 1963-1969. 2. Vietnamese Conflict, 1961- — United States. I. Ahmad, Eqbal. II. Pfeffer, Richard M., ed. III. Adlai Stevenson Institute of International Affairs.*
E840.N6   327.73   68-58302

White, Theodore Harold, 1915-   III. 6319
The making of the President, 1960. [1st ed.] New York, Atheneum Publishers, 1961. 400 p. 25 cm. *1. Presidents — U.S. — Election — 1960. I. T.*
E840.W5   973.921   61-9259

Chisholm, Shirley, 1924-   III. 6320
Unbought and unbossed. Boston, Houghton Mifflin, 1970. xii, 177 p. 22 cm. *1. U.S. — Politics and government — 1969- I. T.*
E840.8.C48A3   328.73/0924   79-120834

E841 – 843   Kennedy, 1961 – 1963

Mailer, Norman.   III. 6321
The presidential papers. New York, Putnam [1963] 310 p. 22 cm. *1. Kennedy, John Fitzgerald, Pres. U.S., 1917-1963. 2. U.S. — Politics and government — 1961- — Addresses, essays, lectures. I. T.*
E841.M25   818.54   63-20753

Salinger, Pierre.   III. 6322
With Kennedy. [1st ed.] Garden City, N.Y., Doubleday, 1966. xvi, 391 p. ports. 24 cm. *1. United States — History — 1945- 2. Kennedy, John Fitzgerald, Pres. U.S., 1917-1963. I. T.*
E841.S2   973.9220924   66-17423

Schlesinger, Arthur Meier, 1917-   III. 6323
A thousand days; John F. Kennedy in the White House [by] Arthur M. Schlesinger, Jr. Boston, Houghton Mifflin, 1965. xiv, 1087 p. 22 cm. *1. Kennedy, John Fitzgerald, Pres. U.S., 1917-1963. 2. U.S. — Politics and government — 1961-1963. I. T.*
E841.S3   973.922   65-20218

Sorensen, Theodore C.   III. 6324
Kennedy [by] Theodore C. Sorensen. [1st ed.] New York, Harper & Row [1965] viii, 783 p. port. 25 cm. *1. Kennedy, John Fitzgerald, Pres. U.S., 1917-1963. 2. U.S. — History — 1945- I. T.*
E841.S6   973.922   65-14660

Manchester, William Raymond, 1922-   III. 6325
Portrait of a President; John F. Kennedy in profile [by] William Manchester. Rev. ed., with a new introd. and epilogue. Boston, Little, Brown [1967] xxii,

266 p. 21 cm. *1. Kennedy, John Fitzgerald, Pres. U.S., 1917-1963. I. T.*
E842.M3 1967   973.922/0924   67-12910

Wicker, Tom. III. 6326
JFK and LBJ; the influence of personality upon politics. New York, Morrow, 1968. 297 p. 22 cm. *1. Kennedy, John Fitzgerald, Pres. U.S., 1917-1963. 2. Johnson, Lyndon Baines, Pres. U.S., 1908- I. T.*
E842.W54 1968   353/.03/0922   68-21130

U.S. President's Commission on the Assassination of President III. 6327
Kennedy.
Report of the Warren Commission on the Assassination of President Kennedy. Introd. by Harrison E. Salisbury. With additional material prepared by the New York Times exclusively for this edition. [1st ed.] New York, McGraw-Hill Book Co. [1964] xl, 726 p. illus., ports. 22 cm. *1. Kennedy, John Fitzgerald, Pres. U.S., 1917-1963 — Assassination. I. T.*
E842.9.A55 1964b   364.152   64-24803

Epstein, Edward Jay, 1935- III. 6328
Inquest; the Warren Commission and the establishment of truth. Introd. by Richard H. Rovere. New York, Viking Press [1966] xix, 224 p. illus., map. 22 cm. *1. United States. Warren Commission. Report of the President's Commission on the Assassination of President John F. Kennedy. 2. Kennedy, John Fitzgerald, Pres. U.S. 1917-1963 — Assassination. I. T.*
E842.9.E6   364.15/24   66-21197

E846 – 848   Johnson, 1963 – 1969

Free, Lloyd A. III. 6329
The political beliefs of Americans; a study of public opinion, by Lloyd A. Free and Hadley Cantril. New Brunswick, N.J., Rutgers University Press [1967] xiv, 239 p. 22 cm. *1. U.S. — Politics and government — 1963- 2. Political psychology. 3. Public opinion — U.S. I. Cantril, Hadley, 1906- joint author. II. T.*
E846.F7   329/.05   67-28415

Johnson, Lyndon Baines, Pres. U.S. 1908- III. 6330
The vantage point; perspectives of the Presidency, 1963-1969. [1st ed.] New York, Holt, Rinehart and Winston [1971] x, 636 p. illus. 25 cm. *1. United States — Politics and government — 1963-1969. I. T.*
E846.J58   973.923   74-102146   ISBN:0030844924

Evans, Rowland, 1921- III. 6331
Lyndon B. Johnson; the exercise of power; a political biography, by Rowland Evans & Robert Novak. [New York] New American Library [1966] viii, 597 p. 24 cm. *1. Johnson, Lyndon Baines, Pres. U.S., 1908- 2. United States — Politics and government — 1933-1945. 3. United States — Politics and government — 1945- I. Novak, Robert D., joint author.*
E847.E9   973.9230924   66-26040

E850 – 851   Presidential Campaigns of 1964, 1968

Cummings, Milton C., ed. III. 6332
The national election of 1964 [by] Paul Tillett [and others] Edited by Milton C. Cummings, Jr. Washington, Brookings Institution [1966] xi, 295 p. 22 cm. *1. Presidents — U.S. — Election — 1964. 2. Elections — U.S. I. Tillett, Paul. II. T.*
E850.C8   973.923   66-23335

White, Theodore Harold, 1915- III. 6333
The making of the President, 1964 [by] Theodore H. White. [1st ed.] New York, Atheneum Publishers, 1965. xi, 431 p. 25 cm. *1. Presidents — U.S. — Election — 1964. 2. U.S. — Politics and government — 1963- I. T.*
E850.W5   973.923   65-18328

McCarthy, Eugene J., 1916- III. 6334
The year of the people [by] Eugene J. McCarthy. [1st ed.] Garden City, N.Y., Doubleday, 1969. viii, 323 p. 22 cm. *1. Presidents — United States — Election — 1968. I. T.*
E851.M28   329/.023/0973   71-93229

McGinniss, Joe. III. 6335
The selling of the President, 1968. New York, Trident Press [1969] 253 p. 22 cm. *1. Presidents — United States — Election — 1968. 2. Nixon, Richard Milhous, 1913- 3. Television in politics. I. T.*
E851.M3   329/.023/0973   77-92157   ISBN:0671270435

White, Theodore Harold, 1915- III. 6336
The making of the President, 1968 [by] Theodore H. White. [1st ed.] New York, Atheneum Publishers, 1969. xii, 459 p. maps (on lining papers) 25 cm. *1. Presidents — U.S. — Election — 1968. I. T.*
E851.W5   329/.023/0973   78-81935

E855 – 856   Nixon, 1969 –

Brandon, Henry, 1916- III. 6337
The retreat of American power. [1st ed.] Garden City, N.Y., Doubleday, 1973. xiii, 368 p. 22 cm. *1. United States — Foreign relations — 1969- 2. Nixon, Richard Milhous, 1913- 3. Kissinger, Henry Alfred. I. T.*
E855.B67   327.73   72-90969   ISBN:0385016557

Evans, Rowland, 1921- III. 6338
Nixon in the White House: the frustration of power [by] Rowland Evans, Jr., & Robert D. Novak. [1st ed.] New York, Random House [1971] viii, 431 p. 25 cm. *1. Nixon, Richard Milhous, 1913- 2. United States — Politics and government — 1969- I. Novak, Robert D., joint author. II. T.*
E855.E9   973.924/0924 (B)   75-140702   ISBN:0394462734

Macrae, Norman, 1923- III. 6339
The neurotic trillionaire; a survey of Mr. Nixon's America. New York, Harcourt, Brace & World [1970] xii, 112 p. 20 cm. "First appeared as a special supplement to the London economist on May 10, 1969." *1. United States — Economic conditions — 1961- 2. United States — Social conditions — 1960- I. T.*
E855.M3   309.1/73   72-117929   ISBN:0155657216

Ungar, Sanford J. III. 6340
The papers & the papers; an account of the legal and political battle over the Pentagon papers, by Sanford J. Ungar. [1st ed.] New York, Dutton, 1972. 319 p. 25 cm. *1. The Pentagon papers. 2. United States — Politics and government — 1969- 3. United States — Politics and government — 1963-1969. 4. Liberty of the press — United States. I. T.*
E855.U5 1972   323.44/5/0973   77-190699   ISBN:0525174559

Wills, Garry, 1934- III. 6341
Nixon Agonistes; the crisis of the self-made man. Boston, Houghton Mifflin, 1970. xiv, 617 p. 22 cm. *1. Nixon, Richard Milhous, 1913- 2. United States — Politics and government — 1945- I. T.*
E856.W53   973.924/0924   72-80426

F1 – 970   U.S. LOCAL HISTORY
F1 – 105 New England

Federal Writers' Project. III. 6342
Here's New England! A guide to vacationland, written and compiled by members of the Federal Writers' Project of the Works Progress Administration in the New England States. Boston, Houghton Mifflin, 1939. St. Clair Shores, Mich., Somerset Publishers, 1973. 122 p. illus. 22 cm. Original ed. issued in series: American guide series. *1. New England — Description and travel — Guide-books. I. T. (S:American guide series.)*
F2.3.F42 1973   917.4/04/4   72-84521   ISBN:040302207X

Bacon, Martha Sherman, 1917- III. 6343
Puritan promenade, by Martha Bacon. Boston, Houghton Mifflin, 1964. 160 p. ports. 22 cm. *1. Women in New England — Biography. I. T.*
F3.B3   920.7   64-24642

Shipton, Clifford Kenyon, 1902- III. 6344
New England life in the 18th century; representative biographies from Sibley's Harvard graduates. Cambridge, Belknap Press of Harvard University Press, 1963. xxvii, 626 p. ports., maps (on lining papers) 24 cm. A selection of biographies from the volumes written by Shipton. *1. Harvard University — Biography. 2. New England — Biography. I. Sibley's Harvard graduates. II. T.*
F3.S5   920.073   63-9562

Warren, Austin, 1899- III. 6345
New England saints. Ann Arbor, University of Michigan Press [1956] 192 p. 22 cm. *1. New England — Biography. 2. Religious thought — New England. 3. American literature — New England — History and criticism. 4. New England — Intellectual life. I. T.*
F3.W3   917.4   56-9721

Who's who in New England; a biographical dictionary of leading III. 6346
living men and women of the states of Maine, New Hampshire, Vermont, Massachusetts, Rhode Island and Connecticut.
[1st]- ed. Chicago, Marquis [1909]- v. 24 cm. Editor: 1909- , A. N. Marquis. *1. New England — Biography. I. Marquis, Albert Nelson, ed.*
F3.W61   09-9799

Adams, James Truslow, 1878-1949. III. 6347
The history of New England. New York, Cooper Square Publishers, 1968- v. illus., facsims., maps, ports. 24 cm. "Originally published 1923." 1. New England — History. I. T.
F4.A243   974   68-19139

Rosenberry, Lois (Kimball) Mathews, 1873- III. 6348
The expansion of New England; the spread of New England settlement and institutions to the Mississippi River, 1620-1865. New York, Russell & Russell, 1962 [c1936] xiv, 303 p. maps. 22 cm. 1. New England — History. 2. New Englanders in the Northeastern States. I. T.
F4.R81 1962   974   61-13781

Solomon, Barbara Miller. III. 6349
Ancestors and immigrants, a changing New England tradition. Cambridge, Harvard University Press, 1956. ix, 276 p. 22 cm. "An outgrowth of a doctoral thesis, entitled 'New England pride and prejudice: a study in the origins of immigration restriction.'" 1. Immigration Restriction League, Boston. 2. New Englanders. 3. New England — Race question. I. T.
F4.S67   325.73   56-10163

Adams, James Truslow, 1878- III. 6350
Revolutionary New England, 1691-1776, by James Truslow Adams. Boston, Atlantic Monthly Press [c1923] xiv, 469 p. front., illus. (facsims.) plates, ports. 23 cm. Forms v.2 of the author's series "The history of New England", although title of series does not appear on t.-p. nor half-title. cf. Pref. 1. New England — History — Colonial period. 2. New England — History — Revolution. 3. New England — History — Revolution — Causes. I. T.
F7.A223   23-15926

Andrews, Charles McLean, 1863-1943. III. 6351
The fathers of New England; a chronicle of the Puritan commonwealth, by Charles M. Andrews. New Haven, Yale University Press; [etc., etc.] 1921. ix, 210 p. col. front., fold. map. 18 cm. (The Chronicles of America series, v.6) "Roosevelt edition." 1. New England — History — Colonial period. I. T.
F7.A57 (E173.C56 vol. 6)   22-12128

Foster, Stephen, 1942- III. 6352
Their solitary way, the Puritan social ethic in the first century of settlement in New England. New Haven, Yale University Press, 1971. xxii, 214 p. 23 cm. (Yale historical publications. Miscellany, 94) Revision of the author's thesis, Yale, 1966. 1. Puritans — New England. 2. Social ethics. I. T. (S)
F7.F76 1971   917.4/03   76-151573   ISBN:0300014082

Miller, Perry, 1905- III. 6353
The New England mind: from colony to province. Cambridge, Harvard University Press, 1953. xi, 513 p. front. 25 cm. "Sequel to The New England mind: the seventeenth century." 1. New England — Intellectual life. 2. New England — History — Colonial period. 3. Puritans. 4. American literature — New England. 5. New England theology. I. T.
F7.M54   917.4   53-5072

Miller, Perry, 1905- III. 6354
The New England mind: the seventeenth century. Cambridge, Harvard University Press, 1954. xi, 528 p. 24 cm. 1. Puritans. 2. Religious literature, American. 3. American literature — Colonial period — History and criticism. 4. American literature — New England. I. T.
F7.M56 1954   917.4   54-7507

Morgan, Edmund Sears. III. 6355
The Puritan family; religion & domestic relations in seventeenth-century New England [by] Edmund S. Morgan. New ed., rev. and enl. New York, Harper & Row [1966] x, 196 p. 21 cm. (Harper torchbooks. The Academy library, TB1227L) 1. New England — Social life and customs. 2. Puritans — New England. I. T.
F7.M8 1966   309.174   65-25695

Morison, Samuel Eliot, 1887- III. 6356
The intellectual life of colonial New England. [2d ed.] New York, New York University Press, 1956. 288 p. 21 cm. First published in 1936 under title: The Puritan pronaos. 1. New England — Intellectual life. 2. Education — New England — History. 3. Libraries — New England. 4. American literature — Colonial period — History and criticism. 5. Puritans. I. T.
F7.M82 1956   917.4   56-8487

Vaughan, Alden T., 1929- III. 6357
New England frontier; Puritans and Indians, 1620-1675 [by] Alden T. Vaughan. [1st ed.] Boston, Little, Brown [1965] xvii, 430 p. illus., facsim., map. ports. 22 cm. 1. New England — History — Colonial period. 2. Indians of North America — New England. 3. Indians, Treatment of — New England. I. T.
F7.V3   974.02   65-20736

Adams, James Truslow, 1878-1949. III. 6358
New England in the republic, 1776-1850, by James Truslow Adams. Boston, Little, Brown, 1926. xiv, 438 p. illus.,facsims., plates, ports. 23 cm. Forms v.3 of the author's series "The history of New England," although title of series does not appear on t.-p. nor half-title. cf. Pref. 1. New England — History. 2. New England — History — Revolution.
F8.A23   26-9006

F16 – 60   MAINE. NEW HAMPSHIRE. VERMONT

Federal writers' project. Maine. III. 6359
Maine, a guide 'down east,' written by workers of the Federal writers' project of the Works progress administration for the state of Maine, sponsored by the Maine development commission. Boston, Houghton Mifflin, 1937. xxvi, 476 p. plates, maps (1 fold. in pocket) 21 cm. (American guide series) The plates are in eight groups, each preceded by half-title not included in paging. 1. Maine. 2. Maine — Description and travel — Guide-books.
F25.F44   38-30

Squires, James Duane, 1904- III. 6360
The Granite State of the United States; a history of New Hampshire from 1623 to the present. New York, American Historical Co. [1956] 4 v. illus., ports. 28 cm. Vols.3-4: Family and personal history. 1. New Hampshire — History. 2. New Hampshire — Biography. I. T.
F34.S68   974.2   56-2076

Daniell, Jere R. III. 6361
Experiment in republicanism; New Hampshire politics and the American Revolution, 1741-1794 [by] Jere R. Daniell. Cambridge, Mass., Harvard University Press, 1970. xiv, 261 p. illus., facsims., map, ports. 25 cm. 1. New Hampshire — Politics and government — Colonial period. 2. New Hampshire — Politics and government — 1775-1865. I. T.
F37.D26   320.9/742   75-122219   ISBN:0674278062

Cole, Donald B. III. 6362
Jacksonian democracy in New Hampshire, 1800-1851 [by] Donald B. Cole. Cambridge, Mass., Harvard University Press, 1970. xi, 283 p. 3 maps, 2 ports. 22 cm. 1. New Hampshire — Politics and government — 1775-1865. 2. Hill, Isaac, 1788-1851. 3. Woodbury, Levi, 1789-1851. I. T.
F38.C6 1970   320.9/742/03   79-127878   ISBN:0674469909

Federal Writers' Project. New Hampshire. III. 6363
New Hampshire, a guide to the granite state. Boston, Houghton Mifflin. St. Clair Shores, Mich., Somerset Publishers, 1973 [c1938] p. Original ed. issued in series: American guide series. 1. New Hampshire. 2. New Hampshire — Description and travel — Guide-books. I. T. (S:American guide series.)
F39.F43 1973   917.42/04/4   72-84490   ISBN:0403021790

Federal Writers' Project. Vermont. III. 6364
Vermont; a guide to the Green Mountain State. Boston, Houghton Mifflin, 1937. St. Clair Shores, Mich., Somerset Publishers, 1973. xxi, 392 p. illus., 1 fold. map. 22 cm. "Sponsored by the Vermont State Planning Board." Original ed. issued in series: American guide series. 1. Vermont — Description and travel — Guide-books. I. Vermont. Development Commission. (S:American guide series.)
F47.3.F42 1973   917.43/04/4   72-84511   ISBN:0403021944

Fisher, Dorothea Frances (Canfield) 1879- III. 6365
Vermont tradition; the biography of an outlook on life. [1st ed.] Boston, Little, Brown [1953] 488 p. 22 cm. 1. Vermont — History. 2. Vermont — Social life and customs. I. T.
F49.F57   917.43   53-10226

Williamson, Chilton, 1916- III. 6366
Vermont in quandary, 1763-1825. Montpelier, Vermont Historical Society, 1949. xiv, 318 p. ports. maps. 23 cm. (Growth of Vermont, v.4) Issued also as thesis, Columbia Univ. 1. Vermont — History. I. T. (S)
F52.W69   974.3   49-2275

F61 – 75   MASSACHUSETTS

Litt, Edgar. III. 6367
The political cultures of Massachusetts. Cambridge, Mass., M.I.T. Press [1965] xiv, 224 p. 21 cm. 1. Massachusetts — Politics and government. I. T.
F64.L58   320.9744   65-26663

Adams, Brooks, 1848-1927. III. 6368
The emancipation of Massachusetts; the dream and the reality. With a new introd. by Perry Miller. Boston, Houghton Mifflin, 1962. 534 p. 21 cm. (Sentry edition, 19) 1. Massachusetts — History — Colonial period. 2. Massachusetts — Church history. 3. Puritans. 4. History — Philosophy. I. T.
F67.A22 1962   974.402   62-6030

Brown, Robert Eldon, 1907-   III. 6369
Middle-class democracy and the Revolution in Massachusetts, 1691-1780, by Robert E. Brown. New York, Russell & Russell [1968, c1955] ix, 458 p. 24 cm. 1. *Massachusetts — Politics and government — Colonial period.* 2. *Massachusetts — Politics and government — Revolution.* 3. *Democracy.* I. T.
F67.B86 1968   974.4   68-10906

Battis, Emery John, 1915-   III. 6370
Saints and sectaries; Anne Hutchinson and the Antinomian controversy in the Massachusetts Bay Colony. Chapel Hill, Published for the Institute of Early American History and Culture at Williamsburg, Va., by the University of North Carolina Press [1962] xv, 379 p. port., maps. 24 cm. 1. *Hutchinson, Anne (Marbury) 1590?-1643.* 2. *Antinomianism.* I. Institute of Early American History and culture, Williamsburg, Va. II. T.
F67.H907   922   63-8

Hutchinson, Thomas, 1711-1780.   III. 6371
The history of the colony and province of Massachusetts-bay, by Thomas Hutchinson. Edited from the author's own copies of volumes I and II and his manuscript of volume III, with a memoir and additional notes, by Lawrence Shaw Mayo. Cambridge, Mass., Harvard University Press, 1936. 3 v. 25 cm. With reproductions of original title-pages of vols.I and II, 2d ed., London. 1765-68. "The text of the appendix has been carried over bodily ... from the edition of 1828. It does not appear in the author's manuscript, for it was compiled by his grandson, the Reverend John Hutchinson, the first editor of volume III." — Editor's pref. to vol.III. 1. *Massachusetts — History — Colonial period.* I. Mayo, Lawrence Shaw, 1888- ed. II. Hutchinson, John, 1793-1865, comp.
F67.H985   974.4   36-12398

Morison, Samuel Eliot, 1887-   III. 6372
Builders of the bay colony, by Samuel Eliot Morison. Boston and New York, Houghton Mifflin, 1930. xiv, 365 p. front., plates, ports., map, facsims. 23 cm. Published also under title: Massachusettensis de conditoribus. Contains biographies of Richard Hakluyt, John Smith, Thomas Morton, John White, John Winthorp, Thomas Shepard, John Hull, Henry Dunster, Nathaniel Ward, Robert Child, John Winthrop, jr., John Eliot and Anne Bradstreet. 1. *Massachusetts — History — Colonial period.* 2. *Massachusetts — Biography.* 3. *Puritans.* I. Massachusettensis de conditoribus. II. T.
F67.Mx   A30-1055

Mather, Cotton, 1663-1728.   III. 6373
Diary of Cotton Mather. New York, F. Ungar Pub. Co. [1957?] 2 v. fold. map. 25 cm. (American classics) 1. *Massachusetts — History — Colonial period — Sources.*
F67.M4213   974.4   57-8651   285.9 M421d1

Murdock, Kenneth Ballard, 1895-   III. 6374
Increase Mather, the foremost American Puritan. New York, Russell & Russell, 1966 [c1953] xv, 442 p. illus., facsims., maps, ports. 22 cm. 1. *Mather, Increase, 1639-1723.* I. T.
F67.M477 1966   974.4/02/0924   66-24736

Middlekauff, Robert.   III. 6375
The Mathers; three generations of Puritan intellectuals, 1596-1728. New York, Oxford University Press, 1971. xii, 440 p. 24 cm. 1. *Mather, Richard, 1596-1669.* 2. *Mather, Increase, 1639-1723.* 3. *Mather, Cotton, 1663-1728.* 4. *Puritans — Massachusetts.* I. T.
F67.M4865   285/.9/0922   79-140912   ISBN:0195013050

Chamberlain, Nathan Henry, 1830 (ca.)-1901.   III. 6376
Samuel Sewall and the world he lived in. Boston, De Wolfe, Fiske, 1897. xv, 319 p. plates, ports. 20 cm. Based on the Diary of Samuel Sewall. 1. *Sewall, Samuel, 1652-1730.* 2. *Massachusetts — History — Colonial period.* 3. *Massachusetts — Social life and customs — Colonial period.* I. T.
F67.S52   923.473   03-4904

Winslow, Ola Elizabeth.   III. 6377
Samuel Sewall of Boston. New York, Macmillan [c1964] vii, 235 p. illus., port., facsims. 22 cm. 1. *Sewall, Samuel, 1652-1730.*
F67.S547   923.473   63-16140

Wertenbaker, Thomas Jefferson, 1879-1966.   III. 6378
The Puritan oligarchy; the founding of American civilization. New York, Scribner [1970] xiv, 359 p. illus., ports. 21 cm. Reprint of the 1947 ed. 1. *Massachusetts — History — Colonial period.* 2. *Massachusetts — Civilization.* 3. *Church and state in Massachusetts.* 4. *Puritans — Massachusetts.* I. T.
F67.W4 1970   917.44/03/2   71-100352

Dunn, Richard S.   III. 6379
Puritans and Yankees; the Winthrop dynasty of New England, 1630-1717. Princeton, N.J., Princeton University Press, 1962. xi, 379 p. ports., map. 25 cm. 1. *Winthrop family.* 2. *New England — History — Colonial period.* I. T.
F67.W7957   974.402   62-7400

Morgan, Edmund Sears.   III. 6380
The Puritan dilemma; the story of John Winthrop. Edited by Oscar Handlin. [1st ed.] Boston, Little, Brown [1958] 224 p. 21 cm. (The Library of American biography) 1. *Winthrop, John, 1588-1649.* I. T.
F67.W798   923.273   58-6029

Bradford, William, 1588-1657.   III. 6381
Of Plymouth Plantation, 1620-1647; the complete text, with notes and an introd. by Samuel Eliot Morison. New ed. New York, Knopf, 1952. xliii, 448, xv p. maps. 25 cm. First ed. published in 1856 under title: History of Plymouth Plantation. 1. *Massachusetts — History — Colonial period (New Plymouth)* 2. *Pilgrim Fathers.* I. Morison, Samuel Eliot, 1887- ed. II. T.
F68.B8073   974.4   51-13222

Langdon, George D.   III. 6382
Pilgrim colony; a history of New Plymouth, 1620-1691, by George D. Langdon, Jr. New Haven, Yale University Press, 1966. xi, 257 p. map (on lining papers) 24 cm. (Yale publications in American studies, 12) 1. *Massachusetts — History — Colonial period (New Plymouth)* I. T. (S)
F68.L25   974.402   66-21526

Brauer, Kinley J.   III. 6383
Cotton versus conscience; Massachusetts Whig politics and southwestern expansion, 1843-1848 [by] Kinley J. Brauer. Lexington, University of Kentucky Press [1967] vi, 272 p. 23 cm. 1. *Whig Party. Massachusetts.* 2. *Massachusetts — Politics and government — 1775-1865.* 3. *Slavery in the U.S. — Anti-slavery movements.* 4. *U.S. — Territorial expansion.* I. T.
F69.B83   329/.4/09744   66-26692

Hall, Van Beck.   III. 6384
Politics without parties: Massachusetts, 1780-1791. [Pittsburgh] University of Pittsburgh Press [1972] xvii, 375 p. 24 cm. 1. *Massachusetts — Politics and government — 1775-1865.* I. T.
F69.H3   320.9/744/03   78-158186   ISBN:0822932342

Abrams, Richard M.   III. 6385
Conservatism in a progressive era; Massachusetts politics, 1900-1912 [by] Richard M. Abrams. Cambridge, Harvard University Press, 1964. xiv, 327 p. 22 cm. 1. *Massachusetts — Politics and government — 1865-1950.* 2. *Conservatism — Massachusetts.* I. T.
F70.A18   974.404   64-21236

Blodgett, Geoffrey.   III. 6386
The gentle reformers: Massachusetts Democrats in the Cleveland era. Cambridge, Harvard University Press, 1966. xiii, 342 p. 22 cm. 1. *Democratic Party. Massachusetts.* 2. *Massachusetts — Politics and government — 1865-1950.* I. T.
F70.B6 1966   320.9744   66-13178

Federal Writers' Project. Massachusetts.   III. 6387
Massachusetts; a guide to its places and people, written and compiled by the Federal Writers' Project of the Works Progress Administration for the State of Massachusetts. Boston, Houghton Mifflin; St. Clair Shores, Mich., Somerset Publishers, 1972. p. Reprint of the 1937 ed., issued in series: American guide series. 1. *Massachusetts — Description and travel — Guide-books.* (S:American guide series.)
F70.F295 1972   917.44/04/4   72-84481   ISBN:0403021502

Huthmacher, J. Joseph.   III. 6388
Massachusetts people and politics, 1919-1933. Cambridge, Belknap Press of Harvard University Press, 1959. 328 p. illus. 22 cm. 1. *Massachusetts — Politics and government — 1865-* 2. *Massachusetts — Population.* 3. *Political parties — Massachusetts.* I. T.
F70.H8   342.744   59-9276

F72 – 74   Regions. Cities

Birdsall, Richard Davenport.   III. 6389
Berkshire County: a cultural history. New Haven, Yale University Press, 1959. 401 p. illus. 22 cm. 1. *Berkshire Co., Mass. — Intellectual life.* 2. *Berkshire Co., Mass. — History.*
F72.B5B72   917.441   59-6792

Thoreau, Henry David, 1817-1862.   III. 6390
Cape Cod; arranged with notes by Dudley C. Lunt. Introd. by Henry Beston. Illustrated by Henry Bugbee Kane. [1st ed.] New York, Norton [1951] 360 p. illus., map (on lining papers) 22 cm. 1. *Cape Cod — Description and travel.*
F72.C3T434   917.449   51-10937

Thoreau, Henry David, 1817-1862.   III. 6391
Guide to Cape Cod; based on Cape Cod, by Henry David Thoreau. Edited and illustrated by Alexander B. Adams. With a biographical sketch of Thoreau by Ralph Waldo Emerson. New York, Devin-Adair Co. [1962] x, 148 p. illus., map (on lining papers) 24 cm. 1. *Cape Cod — Description and travel.* I. Adams, Alexander B., ed.
F72.C3T437   917.449   62-20031

Tourtellot, Arthur Bernon. III. 6392
The Charles, by Arthur Bernon Tourtellot, illustrated by Ernest J. Donnelly. New York, Toronto, Farrar & Rinehart [c1941] x, 356 p. illus. 21 cm. (The rivers of America, ed. by S. V. Bénet and Carl Carmer) Illustrated lining-papers. *1. Charles river, Mass. 2. Massachusetts — History.*
F72.C46T7   974.44   41-52052

Thoreau, Henry David, 1817-1862. III. 6393
A week on the Concord and Merrimack Rivers. Edited with introd. and notes by Walter Harding. New York, Holt, Rinehart & Winston [1963] xxiii, 340 p. 19 cm. (Rinehart editions) *1. Concord River — Description and travel. 2. Merrimack River — Description and travel. I. T.*
F72.M7T5 1963   818.3   63-7886

Whitehill, Walter Muir, 1905- III. 6394
Boston; a topographical history. 2d ed., enl. Cambridge, Mass., Belknap Press of Harvard University Press, 1968. xl, 299 p. illus., maps. 25 cm. *1. Boston — History. 2. Boston — Description.*
F73.3.W57 1968   974.4/61   69-13769

Amory, Cleveland. III. 6395
The Proper Bostonians. [1st ed.] New York, E. P. Dutton, 1947. 381 p. port., map (on lining-paper) 23 cm. (American society series, v.1) *1. Boston — Social life and customs. I. T. (S:Society in America series)*
F73.37.A5   917.4461   47-11061

Brown, Richard D. III. 6396
Revolutionary politics in Massachusetts; the Boston Committee of Correspondence and the towns, 1772-1774 [by] Richard D. Brown. Cambridge, Harvard University Press, 1970. xiv, 282 p. illus., facsim., maps, ports. 24 cm. *1. Boston. Committee of Correspondence. 2. Massachusetts — Politics and government — Colonial period. 3. Boston — Politics and government — Colonial period. I. T.*
F73.4.B89   320.9/744   71-119072   ISBN:0674767810

Rutman, Darrett Bruce. III. 6397
Winthrop's Boston; portrait of a puritan town, 1630-1649, by Darrett B. Rutman. New York, Norton [1972, c1965] x, 324 p. 20 cm. (The Norton library, N627) *1. Boston — History — Colonial period. 2. Winthrop, John, 1588-1649. I. T.*
F73.4.R8 1972   974.4/61/02   70-39159   ISBN:0393006271

Warden, Gerard B. III. 6398
Boston, 1689-1776, by G. B. Warden. [1st ed.] Boston, Little, Brown [1970] 404 p. illus., maps, ports. 24 cm. *1. Boston — History — Colonial period. I. T.*
F73.4.W37   974.4/61/02   70-100577

Howe, Helen Huntington, 1905- III. 6399
The gentle Americans, 1864-1960; biography of a breed [by] Helen Howe. [1st ed.] New York, Harper & Row [1965] xix, 458 p. illus., ports. 22 cm. *1. Boston — Intellectual life. 2. Howe, Mark Antony De Wolfe, 1864-1960. 3. Authors — Correspondence, reminiscences, etc. I. T.*
F73.5.H84   818.520924 (B)   65-20431

Handlin, Oscar, 1915- III. 6400
Boston's immigrants [1790-1880]; a study in acculturation. Rev. and enl. ed. Cambridge, Mass., Belknap Press of Harvard University Press, 1959. 382 p. illus. 22 cm. "Originally published in 1941 as volume L of the Harvard historical studies." *1. Boston — Foreign population. 2. Boston — Social conditions. 3. Irish in Boston. I. T.*
F73.9.A1H3 1959   325.7446   59-7653

Greven, Philip J. III. 6401
Four generations: population, land, and family in colonial Andover, Massachusetts [by] Philip J. Greven, Jr. Ithaca, N.Y., Cornell University Press, 1970. xvi, 329 p. illus., fold. map. 23 cm. *1. Andover, Mass. — Social life and customs. I. T.*
F74.A6G7   301.42/09744/5   76-87018   ISBN:801405394

Lockridge, Kenneth A. III. 6402
A New England town: the first hundred years, Dedham, Massachusetts, 1636-1736 [by] Kenneth A. Lockridge. [1st ed.] New York, Norton [1970] xv, 208 p. maps. 21 cm. (The Norton essays in American history) *1. Dedham, Mass. — History — Colonial period. 2. New England — Civilization. I. T.*
F74.D3L83 1970   320.9/744/7   69-14703

Cole, Donald B. III. 6403
Immigrant city: Lawrence, Massachusetts, 1845-1921. Chapel Hill, University of North Carolina Press [1963] ix, 248 p. illus., maps. 24 cm. "Originally ... a doctoral dissertation at Harvard ... but since then ... completely revised." *1. Lawrence, Mass. — Foreign population. I. T.*
F74.L4C6   974.45   63-3915

Frisch, Michael H. III. 6404
Town into city; Springfield, Massachusetts, and the meaning of community, 1840-1880 [by] Michael H. Frisch. Cambridge, Mass., Harvard University Press, 1972. ix, 301 p. illus. 24 cm. (Harvard studies in urban history) Originated from the author's thesis, Princeton. *1. Springfield, Mass. — History. I. T. (S)*
F74.S8F7 1972   301.36/3/0974426   72-178075   ISBN:0674898206

Powell, Sumner Chilton, 1924- III. 6405
Puritan village; the formation of a New England town. [1st ed.] Middletown, Conn., Wesleyan University Press [1963] xx, 215 p. plates, maps, tables. 29 cm. *1. Sudbury, Mass. — Politics and government. 2. Sudbury, Mass. — History — Colonial period. 3. Municipal government — Gt. Brit. I. T.*
F74.S94P74   974.44   63-8862

F76 – 105 RHODE ISLAND. CONNECTICUT

Federal writers' project. Rhode Island. III. 6406
Rhode Island, a guide to the smallest state, written by workers of the Federal writers' project of the Works progress administration for the state of Rhode Island. Boston, Houghton Mifflin, 1937. xxvi, 500 p. plates, ports., maps (1 fold., in pocket) 21 cm. (American guide series) Map on lining-paper. *1. Rhode Island. 2. Rhode Island — Description and travel — Guide books.*
F79.F38   917.45   37-28463

Lovejoy, David Sherman, 1919- III. 6407
Rhode Island politics and the American Revolution, 1760-1776. Providence, Brown University Press, 1958. 256 p. fold. map. 24 cm. (Brown University studies, v.23) *1. Rhode Island — Politics and government — Colonial period. 2. U.S. — History — Revolution — Causes. I. T. (S:Brown University. Brown University studies, v.23)*
F82.L68   974.502   58-10478

Miller, Perry, 1905- III. 6408
Roger Williams: his contribution to the American tradition. [1st ed.] Indianapolis, Bobbs-Merrill [1953] 273 p. 23 cm. (Makers of the American tradition series) *1. Williams, Roger, 1604?-1683.*
F82.W788   923.273   53-8874

Morgan, Edmund Sears. III. 6409
Roger Williams; the church and the state [by] Edmund S. Morgan. [1st ed.] New York, Harcourt, Brace & World [1967] 170 p. 21 cm. *1. Williams, Roger, 1604?-1683. 2. Church and state.*
F82.W789   322.1   67-25999

Winslow, Ola Elizabeth. III. 6410
Master Roger Williams, a biography. New York, Octagon Books, 1973 [c1957] xi, 328 p. illus. 23 cm. Original ed. published by Macmillan, New York. *1. Williams, Roger, 1604?-1683.*
F82.W855 1973   974.5/02/0924 (B)   73-8608   ISBN:0374986827

Thompson, Mack, 1921- III. 6411
Moses Brown, reluctant reformer. Chapel Hill, Published for the Institute of Early American History and Culture at Williamsburg, Virginia by the University of North Carolina Press [1962] 316 p. illus. 22 cm. *1. Brown, Moses, 1738-1836.*
F83.B875   923.273   62-52443

Coleman, Peter J. III. 6412
The transformation of Rhode Island, 1790-1860. Providence, Brown University Press, 1963. xiv, 314 p. maps, tables. 24 cm. *1. Rhode Island — History — 1775-1865. 2. Rhode Island — Economic conditions. I. T.*
F83.C6   975.503   63-14420

Goldstein, Sidney, 1927- III. 6413
Jewish Americans: three generations in a Jewish community [by] Sidney Goldstein [and] Calvin Goldscheider. Englewood Cliffs, N.J., Prentice-Hall [1968] xvii, 274 p. illus., forms, map. 24 cm. (Ethnic groups in American life series) *1. Jews in Providence — Political and social conditions. I. Goldscheider, Calvin, joint author. II. T.*
F89.P9G64   301.451/924/07452   68-24185

Bushman, Richard L. III. 6414
From Puritan to Yankee; character and the social order in Connecticut, 1690-1765 [by] Richard L. Bushman. Cambridge, Harvard University Press, 1967. xiv, 343 p. illus., maps. 22 cm. (A publication of the Center for the Study of the History of Liberty in America, Harvard University) *1. Connecticut — History — Colonial period. 2. Connecticut — Social conditions. I. T. (S:Harvard University. Center for the Study of the History of Liberty in America. Publication)*
F97.B89   917.46/03/2   67-17304

Zeichner, Oscar, 1916- III. 6415
Connecticut's years of controversy, 1750-1776. [Hamden, Conn.] Archon Books, 1970 [c1949] xiv, 404 p. illus., maps, ports. 24 cm. *1. Connecticut — History — Colonial period. I. T.*
F97.Z4 1970   974.6/02   78-122398   ISBN:208009884

Calder, Isabel MacBeath. III. 6416
The New Haven colony. [Hamden, Conn.] Archon Books, 1970 [c1962] vi, 301 p. port. 22 cm. 1. Connecticut — History — Colonial period. 2. New Haven — History — Colonial period. I. T.
F98.C26 1970   974.6/02   71-95022   ISBN:208008635

Purcell, Richard Joseph, 1887-1950. III. 6417
Connecticut in transition: 1775-1818. New ed., with a foreword by S. Hugh Brockunier. Middletown, Conn., Wesleyan University Press [1963] xvii, 305 p. maps. 25 cm. Rev. and shortened version of the author's thesis, Yale University, first published in 1918. 1. Connecticut — History — 1775-1865. 2. Connecticut — Politics and government — 1775-1865. 3. Connecticut — Church history. I. T.
F99.P98 1963   974.603   63-11058

Federal writers' project. Connecticut. III. 6418
Connecticut; a guide to its roads, lore, and people, written by workers of the Federal writers' project of the Works progress administration for the state of Connecticut; sponsored by Wilbur L. Cross. Boston, Houghton Mifflin, 1938. xxxiii, 593 p. plates, maps (1 fold., in pocket) diagr. 21 cm. (American guide series) Map on lining-paper. The plates are in eight groups, each preceded by half-title not included in paging. 1. Connecticut. 2. Connecticut — Description and travel — Guide-books. 3. Connecticut — Historic houses, etc. 4. Automobiles — Road guides — Connecticut.
F100.F45   917.46   38-27339

F106 – 205 Atlantic States
F116 – 130 NEW YORK

Brown, Ralph Hall, 1898- III. 6419
Mirror for Americans; likeness of the eastern seaboard, 1810, by Ralph H. Brown. New York, American geographical society, 1943. xxxii p., 3 l., [5]-312 p. front., illus. (incl. ports., maps) 26 x 20 cm. (American geographical society. Special publication no.27) An account of the period told as if written by Thomas Pownall Keystone, a fictitious character, presenting, as a composite observer, the contemporary scene. 1. Atlantic states — Description and travel. I. T. (S)
F106.B9   917.4   43-9759

Federal Writers' Project. III. 6420
U.S. one: Maine to Florida, compiled and written by the Federal Writers' Project of the Works Progress Administration. New York, Modern Age Books. St. Clair Shores, Mich., Somerset Publishers, 1972 [c1938] xxvii, 344 p. illus., fold map. 22 cm. "Sponsored by the U.S. No. 1 Highway Association." Original ed. issued in series: American guide series. 1. Atlantic States — Description and travel — Guide-books. 2. Automobiles — Road guides — Atlantic States. 3. United States Highway 1. I. T. (S:American Guide series.)
F106.F45 1972   917.4   72-84519   ISBN:0403022088

James, Henry, 1843-1916. III. 6421
The American scene. Introd. and notes by Leon Edel. Bloomington, Indiana University Press [1968] xxiv, 486 p. 21 cm. 1. Atlantic States — Description and travel. 2. United States — Description and travel — 1900-1920. 3. United States — Social life and customs — 1865-1918. I. Edel, Leon, 1907- ed. II. T.
F106.J273 1968   917.4   68-14605

Myers, Albert Cook, 1874- ed. III. 6422
Narratives of early Pennsylvania, West New Jersey and Delaware, 1630-1707. New York, Scribner, 1912. xiv, 476 p. fold. map, fold. plan, facsim. 23 cm. (Original narratives of early American history.) Series title also at head of t.-p. 1. Delaware river — History. 2. New Sweden — History — Sources. 3. Pennsylvania — History — Colonial period — Sources. 4. Delaware — History — Colonial period — Sources. 5. New Jersey — History — Colonial period — Sources. I. T.
F106.M98   12-4611

Wertenbaker, Thomas Jefferson, 1879- III. 6423
The founding of American civilization: the Middle Colonies. New York, Cooper Square Publishers, 1963 [c1938] xiii, 364 p. illus. 24 cm. 1. Middle States — Civilization. I. The Middle Colonies. II. T.
F106.W52   917.4   63-17541

Alexander, De Alva Stanwood, 1846-1925. III. 6424
Four famous New Yorkers; the political careers of Cleveland, Platt, Hill and Roosevelt; forming volume four of "The political history of the state of New York" 1882-1905. New York, Holt, 1923. xvii, 488 p. 23 cm. 1. Cleveland, Grover, pres. U.S., 1837-1908. 2. Platt, Thomas Collier, 1833-1910. 3. Hill, David Bennett, 1843-1910. 4. Roosevelt, Theodore, pres. U.S., 1858-1919. 5. New York (State) — Politics and government — 1865- I. T.
F119.A371   23-9922

Ellis, David Maldwyn. III. 6425
A history of New York State [by] David M. Ellis [and others. Rev. ed.] Published in co-operation with the New York State Historical Association. Ithaca, N.Y., Cornell University Press [1967] xx, 732 p. illus. 24 cm. First published in 1957 under title: A short history of New York State. 1. New York (State) — History. I. T.
F119.E46 1967   917.47/03   67-20587

New York State Historical Association. III. 6426
History of the State of New York. [Edited by Alexander C. Flick, State historian] Port Washington, N.Y., I. J. Friedman, 1962 [c1961] 10 v. in 5. illus., ports., maps (1 fold. in pocket, v.3) 24 cm. (Empire State historical publication 18) 1. New York (State) — History. I. Flick, Alexander Clarence, 1869-1942, ed. II. T. (S)
F119.N65 1962   974.7   62-20154

Bonomi, Patricia U. III. 6427
A factious people; politics and society in colonial New York [by] Patricia U. Bonomi. New York, Columbia University Press, 1971. xiii, 342 p. 23 cm. 1. New York (State) — History — Colonial period. 2. New York (State) — Politics and government — Colonial period. I. T.
F122.B65   917.47/03/2   74-156803   ISBN:0231035098

Fox, Dixon Ryan, 1887-1945. III. 6428
Yankees and Yorkers [by] Dixon Ryan Fox. New York, University Press; London, H. Milford, Oxford University Press, 1940. x, 237 p. fold. map. 24 cm. (Anson G. Phelps lectureship on early American history, New York university) Illustrated t.-p. 1. New York (State) — History — Colonial period. 2. New York (State) — Boundaries — Connecticut. 3. New York (State) — Boundaries — Massachusetts. 4. New York (State) — Boundaries — Vermont. 5. Connecticut — Boundaries — New York (State) 6. Massachusetts — Boundaries — New York (State) 7. Vermont — Boundaries — New York (State) 8. New England — Civilization. I. T.
F122.F78   974   40-13441

Reich, Jerome R. III. 6429
Leisler's Rebellion; a study of democracy in New York, 1664-1720. [Chicago] University of Chicago Press [1953] ix, 194 p. 24 cm. 1. New York (State) — History — Colonial period. I. Leisler, Jacob, d. 1691. II. T.
F122.R3   974.7   53-10910

Irving, Washington, 1783-1859. III. 6430
Knickerbocker's History of New York; edited by Anne Carroll Moore; with pictorial pleasantries by James Daugherty. New York, F. Ungar Pub. Co. [1959, c1956] xi, 427 p. illus. 23 cm. 1. New York (State) — History — Colonial period. I. T.
F122.1.I835 1959   974.702   59-11666

Jameson, John Franklin, 1859- ed. III. 6431
Narratives of New Netherland, 1609-1664; ed. by J. Franklin Jameson with three maps and a facsimile. New York, Scribner, 1909. xx, 478 p. 3 maps (incl. front.) facsim. 23 cm. (Original narratives of early American history ...) Series title also at head of t.-p. 1. New York (State) — History — Colonial period — Sources.
F122.1.J31 (E187.O7.J3)   09-24463

Benson, Lee. III. 6432
The concept of Jacksonian democracy; New York as a test case. Princeton, N.J., Princeton University Press, 1961. xi, 351 p. 25 cm. 1. New York (State) — Politics and Government — 1775-1865. 2. Political parties — New York (State) I. T. II. T:Jacksonian democracy.
F123.B49   974.703   61-6286

Fox, Dixon Ryan, 1887-1945. III. 6433
The decline of the aristocracy in the politics of New York, 1801-1840. Edited by Robert V. Remini. New York, Harper & Row [1965] xxxv, 460 p. maps., ports. 21 cm. (American perspectives. Harper torchbooks. University library, TB3064.) "Originally published in 1919." 1. New York (State) — Politics and government — 1775-1865. 2. New York (State) — History — 1775-1865. I. T.
F123.F79 1965   974.703   65-1393

Miller, Douglas T. III. 6434
Jacksonian aristocracy; class and democracy in New York, 1830-1860 [by] Douglas T. Miller. New York, Oxford University Press, 1967. xiii, 228 p. 22 cm. 1. New York (State) — Social life and customs. 2. Upper classes — New York (State) 3. Labor and laboring classes — New York (State) I. T.
F123.M6   917.47/03/3   67-15130

Chessman, G. Wallace. III. 6435
Governor Theodore Roosevelt; the Albany apprenticeship, 1898-1900, by G. Wallace Chessman. Cambridge, Harvard University Press, 1965. ix, 335 p. port. 22 cm. Based on thesis, Harvard University. 1. Roosevelt, Theodore, Pres. U.S., 1858-1919. 2. New York,(State) — Politics and government — 1865-1950. I. T.
F124.C46   974.704   65-13838

Gosnell, Harold Foote, 1896- III. 6436
Boss Platt and his New York machine; a study of the political leadership of

Thomas C. Platt, Theodore Roosevelt, and others, by Harold F. Gosnell with an introduction by Charles E. Merriam. Chicago, The University of Chicago Press [c1924] xxiv, 370 p. plates, ports. 21 cm. *1. Platt, Thomas Collier, 1833-1910. 2. Roosevelt, Theodore, pres. U.S., 1858-1919. 3. New York (State) — Politics and government — 1865- I. T.*
F124.G68   24-2633

Nevins, Allan, 1890-   **III. 6437**
Herbert H. Lehman and his era. New York, Scribner [1963] 456 p. illus. 24 cm. *1. Lehman, Herbert Henry, 1878- 2. New York (State) — Politics and government — 1865-1950.*
F124.L532   923.273   63-8464

Moscow, Warren.   **III. 6438**
Politics in the Empire State. [1st ed.] New York, A. A. Knopf, 1948. 238, x p. map. 22 cm. *1. New York (State) — Politics and government — 1865- I. T.*
F124.M88   974.7   48-7919

Writers' Program. New York.   **III. 6439**
New York; a guide to the Empire State. Compiled by workers of the Writers' Program of the Work Projects Administration in the State of New York. New York, Oxford University Press; St. Clair Shores, Mich., Somerset Publishers, 1972. p. Reprint of the 1940 ed., sponsored by the New York State Historical Association, and issued in series: American guide series. *1. New York (State) — Description and travel — Guide-books. I. New York State Historical Association. (S:American guide series.)*
F124.W89 1972   917.47/04/4   72-84496   ISBN:0403021510

Thompson, John Henry, 1919- ed.   **III. 6440**
Geography of New York State. John H. Thompson, editor. [1st ed. New York] Syracuse University Press [1966] 543 p. illus., maps (part fold.) 27 cm. *1. New York (State) — Description and travel — 1951-*
F125.T5   330.9747   66-14602

F128   New York City

Botkin, Benjamin Albert, 1901- ed.   **III. 6441**
New York City folklore: legends, tall tales, anecdotes, stories, sagas, heroes and characters, customs, traditions, and sayings; edited, with an introd. New York, Random House [1956] 492 p. illus. 22 cm. *1. New York (City) — History — Anecdotes. 2. New York (City) — Social life and customs. 3. American literature (Selections: Extracts, etc.) I. T.*
F128.B6   917.471   56-8815

Federal Writers' Project. New York (City).   **III. 6442**
New York City guide. [Rev. ed.] New York, Random House [c1939] St. Clair Shores, Mich., Somerset Publishers, 1972. xx, 680 p. illus. 22 cm. (American guide series) "Companion volume to New York panorama." *1. New York (City) — Description — Guide-books. I. T. (S)*
F128.18.F37 1972   917.47/1/044   76-145011   ISBN:0403007917

Still, Bayrd.   **III. 6443**
Mirror for Gotham: New York as seen by contemporaries from Dutch days to the present. New York, University Press, 1956. 417 p. illus. 25 cm. *1. New York (City) — Description. 2. New York (City) — History. 3. New York (City) in literature. I. T.*
F128.3.S85   974.71   56-11979

Whitman, Walt, 1819-1892.   **III. 6444**
Walt Whitman's New York; from Manhattan to Montauk. Edited by Henry M. Christman. New York, Macmillan [1963] xiv, 188 p. illus., port. 22 cm. "On June 8, 1861, the Brooklyn standard published the first of an unsigned series of [the author's] ... articles to which the newspaper gave title of 'Brooklyniana.' It is these articles that appear in this book." — p. x. *1. New York (City) — History — Addresses, essays, lectures. 2. Brooklyn — History — Addresses, essays, lectures. 3. Long Island — History, Local.*
F128.3.W5   974.72   63-14529

Mayer, Grace M.   **III. 6445**
Once upon a city; New York from 1890 to 1910 as photographed by Byron and described by Grace M. Mayer. With a foreword by Edward Steichen. New York, Macmillan, 1958. xii, 511 p. illus., ports. 29 cm. "The photographs reproduced ... are from the Bryon Collection, Museum of the City of New York." *1. New York (City) — Description — Views. 2. New York (City) — History. 3. New York (City) — Social life and customs. I. Byron, Percy C. II. New York. Museum of the City of New York. Byron Collection. III. T.*
F128.37.M3   917.471   57-10777

Abbott, Wilbur Cortez, 1869-1947.   **III. 6446**
New York in the American Revolution. Illus. selected by Victor H. Paltsits. Port Washington, N.Y., I. J. Friedman, 1962. xii, 302 p. illus., map (on lining papers) facsims. 23 cm. *1. New York (City) — History — Revolution. I. T.*
F128.44.A13 1962   974.71   62-13523

Foner, Philip Sheldon, 1910-   **III. 6447**
Business & slavery: the New York merchants & the irrepressible conflict [by] Philip S. Foner. New York, Russell & Russell [1968] ix, 356 p. 25 cm. *1. New York (City) — History — Civil War. 2. New York (City) — Commerce — History. 3. Slavery in the U.S. — Anti-slavery movements. 4. United States — Politics and government — 1849-1861. I. T.*
F128.44.F67 1968   320.97471   68-15122

Pomerantz, Sidney Irving, 1909-   **III. 6448**
New York, an American city, 1783-1803; a study of urban life, by Sidney I. Pomerantz, PH.D. New York, Columbia University Press; London, P. S. King, 1938. 531 p. illus. double map. 23 cm. (Studies in history, economics and public law, ed. by the Faculty of political science of Columbia university. no. 442) Issued also as thesis (PH.D.) Columbia university. *1. New York (City) — History. I. T.*
F128.44.P752   974.71   39-1229

Wertenbaker, Thomas Jefferson, 1879-   **III. 6449**
Father Knickerbocker rebels: New York City during the Revolution. New York, C. Scribner's Sons, 1948. xv, 308 p. illus., ports., maps 25 cm. *1. New York (City) — History — Revolution. I. T.*
F128.44.W4   974.71   48-11329

Callow, Alexander B.   **III. 6450**
The Tweed Ring [by] Alexander B. Callow, Jr. New York, Oxford University Press, 1966. xi, 351 p. illus. 22 cm. *1. Tweed Ring. 2. Corruption (in politics) — New York (City)*
F128.47.C25   974.7104   66-24440

Mandelbaum, Seymour J.   **III. 6451**
Boss Tweed's New York [by] Seymour J. Mandelbaum. [New York, J. Wiley, 1965] ix, 196 p. illus., map. 22 cm. (New dimensions in history: historical cities) *1. Tweed, William Marcy, 1823-1878. 2. New York (City) — Politics and government — To 1898. 3. Tweed ring. I. T. (S)*
F128.47.M28   320.97471   65-16417

Weiss, Nancy Joan.   **III. 6452**
Charles Francis Murphy, 1858-1924; respectability and responsibility in Tammany politics. Northampton, Mass., Smith College, 1968. x, 139 p. illus., map, port. 24 cm. (The Edwin H. Land prize essays) *1. Murphy, Charles Francis, 1858-1924. 2. Tammany Hall. I. Respectability and responsibility in Tammany politics. (S)*
F128.47.W45   974.71/04/0924 (B)   67-21037

Flynn, Edward Joseph, 1891-   **III. 6453**
You're the boss. [Autobiography] New York, Viking Press, 1947. x, 244 p. 22 cm. *I. T.*
F128.5.F6   923.273   47-30772

Garrett, Charles, 1925-   **III. 6454**
The La Guardia years, machine and reform politics in New York City. New Brunswick, N.J., Rutgers University Press [1961] 423 p. illus. 24 cm. *1. New York (City) — Politics and government — 1898-1951. 2. La Guardia, Fiorello Henry, 1882-1947. I. T.*
F128.5.G25   974.71   61-10262

Nevins, Allan, 1890- ed.   **III. 6455**
The greater city: New York, 1898-1948, ed. by Allan Nevins and John A. Krout. New York, Columbia Univ. Press, 1948. vii, 260 p. illus., ports. 21 cm. *1. New York (City) — History — 1898- I. Krout, John Allen, 1896- joint ed. II. T.*
F128.5.N4   974.71   48-8678

Goodman, Walter.   **III. 6456**
A percentage of the take. New York, Farrar, Straus and Giroux [1971] xiii, 225 p. illus., ports. 23 cm. *1. New York (City) — Politics and government — 1951- 2. Corruption (in politics) — New York (City) I. T.*
F128.52.G66   352.07471   72-137751   ISBN:374230749

Davidson, Bruce, 1933-   **III. 6457**
East 100th Street. Cambridge, Mass., Harvard University Press, 1970. [129] p. (chiefly illus.) 32 cm. *1. New York (City) — Streets — 100th Street. 2. Harlem, New York (City) — Description — Views. I. T.*
F128.67.O5D3   917.471   76-120714   ISBN:0674224353

The Village voice.   **III. 6458**
The Village voice reader; a mixed bag from the Greenwich Village newspaper, edited by Daniel Wolf and Edwin Fancher. With line drawings by Muriel Jacobs [and others. 1st ed.] Garden City, N.Y., Doubleday, 1962. 349 p. illus. 22 cm. *1. Greenwich Village, New York (City) 2. Bohemianism. 3. American literature — 20th cent. I. Wolf, Daniel, ed. II. Fancher, Edwin, ed.*
F128.68.G8V52   817.54082   61-12596

Ware, Caroline Farrar, 1899-   **III. 6459**
Greenwich Village, 1920-1930; a comment on American civilization in the post-war years. Boston, Houghton Mifflin, 1935. xii, 496 p. maps (1 fold.) diagrs. 23 cm. "Prepared under the auspices of Columbia university council for research in the social sciences in collaboration with Greenwich house." *1.*

Greenwich Village, New York (City) 2. New York (City) — Social conditions.
F128.68.G8W25   309.17471   35-6370

Clarke, John Henrik, 1915- ed. **III. 6460**
Harlem, a community in transition. [1st ed.] New York, Citadel Press [c1964] 223 p. illus., ports. 21 cm. "Much of the material in this book is from the Summer 1963 (Volume III, no. 3) issue of Freedomways." 1. Harlem, New York (City) 2. Negroes — New York (City)
F128.68.H3C55   917.471   64-21891

F128.9 FOREIGN POPULATION. MINORITIES

Ernst, Robert, 1915- **III. 6461**
Immigrant life in New York City, 1825-1863. New York, King's Crown Press, 1949. xvi, 331 p. 24 cm. 1. New York (City) — Foreign population. 2. U.S. — Emigration and immigration. I. T.
F128.9.A1E7 1949   325.7471   49-9759

Glazer, Nathan. **III. 6462**
Beyond the melting pot; the Negroes, Puerto Ricans, Jews, Italians, and Irish of New York City, by Nathan Glazer and Daniel Patrick Moynihan. 2d ed. Cambridge, M.I.T. Press [1970] xcviii, 363 p. map (on lining papers) 22 cm. (Publications of the Joint Center for Urban Studies) 1. New York (City) — Foreign population. 2. Minorities — New York (City) I. Moynihan, Daniel Patrick, joint author. II. T. (S:Joint Center for Urban Studies. Publications)
F128.9.A1G55 1970   301.451   78-118346   ISBN:262070391

Gold, Michael, 1894- **III. 6463**
Jews without money, by Michael Gold; woodcuts by Howard Simon. New York, Liveright [c1930] 309 p. plates. 22 cm. Illustrated lining-papers. Autobiography. "Some sections of this book have appeared in the American mercury, the Menorah journal, and the New masses." 1. Jews — Social life and customs. 2. Jews in New York (City) I. T.
F128.9.J5G61   30-5614

Rischin, Moses, 1925- **III. 6464**
The promised city; New York's Jews, 1870-1914. Cambridge, Harvard University Press, 1962. 342 p. illus. 22 cm. 1. Jews in New York (City) I. T.
F128.9.J5R5   301.452   62-11402

Clark, Kenneth Bancroft, 1914- **III. 6465**
Dark ghetto; dilemmas of social power, by Kenneth B. Clark. Foreword by Gunnar Myrdal. [1st ed.] New York, Harper & Row [1965] xxix, 251 p. illus. 22 cm. 1. Negroes — New York (City) 2. Negroes — Segregation. 3. Harlem, New York (City) — Social conditions. I. T.
F128.9.N3C65   301.451   64-7834

Osofsky, Gilbert, 1935- **III. 6466**
Harlem; the making of a ghetto; Negro New York, 1890-1930. [1st ed.] New York, Harper & Row [1966] xi, 259 p. illus., facsims., ports. 22 cm. 1. Negroes — New York (City) 2. Harlem, New York (City) — History. I. T.
F128.9.N3O73   301.34   66-10913

Lewis, Oscar, 1914- **III. 6467**
A study of slum culture; backgrounds for La vida. With the assistance of Douglas Butterworth. New York, Random House [1968] xiv, 240 p. 21 cm. 1. Puerto Ricans in New York (City) 2. New York (City) — Poor. 3. San Juan, P.R. — Poor. I. T.
F128.9.P8L38   301.451/6/07471   68-11969

Lewis, Oscar, 1914- **III. 6468**
La vida; a Puerto Rican family in the culture of poverty—San Juan and New York. New York, Random House [1966] lix, 669 p. 25 cm. 1. Puerto Ricans in New York (City) 2. New York (City) — Poor. 3. San Juan, P.R. — Poor. I. T.
F128.9.P8L4   301.451607471   66-11983

Padilla, Elena, 1923- **III. 6469**
Up from Puerto Rico. New York, Columbia University Press, 1958. 317 p. illus. 23 cm. 1. Puerto Ricans in New York (City) I. T.
F128.9.P8P3   325.27295097471   58-7171

Rand, Christopher. **III. 6470**
The Puerto Ricans. New York, Oxford University Press, 1958. 178 p. 21 cm. 1. Puerto Ricans in New York (City) 2. Puerto Rico. I. T.
F128.9.P8R3   327.729509747   58-10733

Thomas, Piri, 1928- **III. 6471**
Down these mean streets. [1st ed.] New York, Knopf, 1967. xiii, 333 p. 22 cm. Autobiographical. 1. Puerto Ricans in New York (City) — Personal narratives. I. T.
F128.9.P8T5   301.451/67/97471   66-19402

F129 Other Cities

McKelvey, Blake, 1903- **III. 6472**
Rochester: an emerging metropolis, 1925-1961. Rochester, N.Y., Christopher Press, 1961. 404 p. illus. 24 cm. (Rochester Public Library. Kate Gleason Fund publications. Publication 4) 1. Rochester, N.Y. — History.
F129.R7M228   974.789   61-18763

Palmer, Dave Richard, 1934- **III. 6473**
The river and the rock; the history of Fortress West Point, 1775-1783. New York, Greenwood Pub. Corp. [1969] xii, 395 p. illus., maps (part col.), plans, ports. 32 cm. (The West Point military library) 1. West Point, N.Y. — History. I. T.
F129.W7P17   973.33   77-79061   ISBN:837114977

F131 – 145   NEW JERSEY

MacCracken, Henry Noble, 1880- **III. 6474**
Prologue to independence; the trials of James Alexander, American, 1715-1756. New York, J. H. Heineman [1964] vii, 187 p. 24 cm. 1. Alexander, James, 1691-1756. 2. New Jersey — Politics and government — Colonial period. 3. New York (State) — Politics and government — Colonial period. I. T.
F137.M23   974.9   64-20213

Pomfret, John Edwin, 1898- **III. 6475**
The Province of East New Jersey, 1609-1702, the rebelious proprietary. Princeton, N.J., Princeton, University Press, 1962. x, 407 p. map. 25 cm. (The Princeton history of New Jersey series) 1. New Jersey — History — Colonial period. I. T. (S)
F137.P73   974.91   62-7045

Pomfret, John Edwin, 1898- **III. 6476**
The Province of West New Jersey, 1609-1702; a history of the origins of an American colony. Princeton, Princeton University Press, 1956. xii, 298 p. map. 25 cm. (The Princeton history of New Jersey series) 1. New Jersey — History — Colonial period. I. T. (S)
F137.P74   974.9   55-6700

Federal Writers' Project. New Jersey. **III. 6477**
New Jersey; a guide to its present and past. New York, Hastings House, 1946 [c1939] xxxii, 735 p. illus., maps (part fold. (1 col. in pocket)) 21 cm. (American guide series) 1. New Jersey — Description and travel — Guide-books. 2. Automobiles — Road guides — New Jersey. (S)
F139.F45 1946   917.49   58-35882

McKean, Dayton David, 1904- **III. 6478**
The boss; the Hague machine in action. New York, Russell & Russell [1967, c1940] xvii, 284 p. port. 23 cm. 1. Hague, Frank, 1876- 2. Jersey City — Politics and government. 3. Politics, Practical. I. T.
F144.J5H3 1967   66-24726

F146 – 160   PENNSYLVANIA

Buck, Solon Justus, 1884- **III. 6479**
The planting of civilization in western Pennsylvania. By Solon J. Buck and Elizabeth Hawthorn Buck. Illustrated from the drawings of Clarence McWilliams & from photographs, contemporary pictures, & maps. [Pittsburgh] University of Pittsburgh Press, 1939. xiv, 565 p. illus., plates, ports., maps, plans, facsims. 24 cm. Illustrated t.-p. "This book is one of a series relating western Pennsylvania history, written under the direction of the Western Pennsylvania historical survey sponsored by the Buhl foundation, the Historical society of western Pennsylvania and the University of Pittsburgh." 1. Pennsylvania — History — Colonial period. 2. Pennsylvania. I. Buck, Elizabeth (Hawthorn) joint author. II. Western Pennsylvania historical survey. III. T.
F149.B83   974.8   39-25307

Bronner, Edwin B., 1920- **III. 6480**
William Penn's holy experiment; the founding of Pennsylvania, 1681-1701. New York, Temple University Publications; distributed by Columbia University Press, 1962. 306 p. illus. 24 cm. 1. Penn, William, 1644-1718. 2. Friends, Society of. Pennsylvania. 3. Pennsylvania — History — Colonial period.
F152.B84   974.802   62-14819

Hanna, William S. **III. 6481**
Benjamin Franklin and Pennsylvania politics [by] William S. Hanna. Stanford, Calif., Stanford University Press, 1964. x, 239 p. 23 cm. 1. Franklin,

Ill. 6482
Benjamin, 1706-1790. 2. Pennsylvania — Politics and government — Colonial period. I. T.
F152.H37   974.802   64-14557

Hawke, David. **Ill. 6482**
In the midst of a revolution. Philadelphia, University of Pennsylvania Press [1961] 235 p. 22 cm. *1. Pennsylvania — Politics and government — Colonial period. 2. U.S. — History — Revolution — Causes. I. T.*
F152.H4   974.802   60-7078

Hutson, James H. **Ill. 6483**
Pennsylvania politics, 1746-1770; the movement for royal government and its consequences, by James H. Hutson. Princeton, N.J., Princeton University Press, 1972. viii, 264 p. 23 cm. *1. Pennsylvania — Politics and government — Colonial period. I. T.*
F152.H86   320.9/748/02   74-173756   ISBN:0691046115

Tolles, Frederick Barnes, 1915- **Ill. 6484**
James Logan and the culture of provincial America. [1st ed.] Boston, Little, Brown [1957] 228 p. 21 cm. (The Library of American biography) *1. Logan, James, 1674-1751. 2. Pennsylvania — History — Colonial period.*
F152.L85   923.273   57-6439

Nash, Gary B. **Ill. 6485**
Quakers and politics; Pennsylvania, 1681-1726, by Gary B. Nash. Princeton, N.J., Princeton University Press, 1968. xii, 362 p. 23 cm. *1. Pennsylvania — History. 2. Friends, Society of. Pennsylvania — History. I. T.*
F152.N25   974.8/02   68-29386

Rothermund, Dietmar. **Ill. 6486**
The layman's progress; religious and political experience in colonial Pennsylvania, 1740-1770. Philadelphia, University of Pennsylvania Press [1962, c1961] xvi, 202 p. 22 cm. *1. Pennsylvania — Politics and government — Colonial period. 2. Pennsylvania — Religion. 3. Church and state in Pennsylvania. I. T.*
F152.R84   974.802   61-6883

Volwiler, Albert Tangeman. **Ill. 6487**
George Croghan and the westward movement, 1741-1782, by Albert T. Volwiler Cleveland, Clark, 1926. 370 p. front., maps (1 double) facsim. 25 cm. (Early western journals, no. III) Published in part in the Pennsylvania magazine of history and biography, 1922-23. Published also as thesis (PH.D.) University of Pennsylvania, 1926. *1. Croghan, George, d. 1782. 2. Frontier and pioneer life — Ohio valley. 3. Indians of North America — Ohio valley. 4. Pennsylvania — History — Colonial period. 5. Indians of North America — Commerce.*
F152.V942   26-7285

Bradley, Erwin Stanley. **Ill. 6488**
The triumph of militant Republicanism; a study of Pennsylvania and presidential politics, 1860-1872. Philadelphia, University of Pennsylvania Press [1964] 467 p. ports. 22 cm. *1. Republican Party. Pennsylvania. 2. Pennsylvania — Politics and government — Civil War. 3. Pennsylvania — Politics and government — 1865-1950. I. T.*
F153.B8   974.803   63-15007

Crèvecœur, Michel Guillaume St. Jean de, called Saint John de **Ill. 6489**
Crèvecœur, 1735-1813.
Eighteenth-century travels in Pennsylvania & New York. Translated & edited by Percy G. Adams. [Lexington] University of Kentucky Press [1961] xliv, 172 p. illus., ports. 24 cm. "Translation of selections from Jean de Crèvecoeur's Voyage dans la haute Pensylvanie et dans l'état de New York." *1. Pennsylvania — Description and travel. 2. New York (State) — Description and travel. 3. U.S. — Description and travel — 1783-1848. 4. Indians of North America — Legends. I. Adams, Percy G., ed. and tr. II. T.*
F153.C923   917.48   61-15625

Snyder, Charles McCool. **Ill. 6490**
The Jacksonian heritage; Pennsylvania politics, 1833-1848. Harrisburg, Pennsylvania Historical and Museum Commission, 1958. x, 256 p. ports., map. 24 cm. *1. Pennsylvania — Politics and government — 1775-1865. 2. U.S. — Politics and government — 1815-1861. I. T.*
F153.S69   974.803   A59-9122

Writers' Program. Pennsylvania. **Ill. 6491**
Pennsylvania; a guide to the Keystone State. Compiled by workers of the Writers' Program of the Work Projects Administration in the State of Pennsylvania. New York, Oxford University Press. St. Clair Shores, Mich., Somerset Publishers, 1973 [c1940] p. Original ed. issued in series: American guide series. *1. Pennsylvania — Description and travel — Guide-books. 2. Pennsylvania. (S:American guide series.)*
F154.W94 1973   971.48/04/4   72-84502   ISBN:0403021871

Baltzell, Edward Digby, 1915- **Ill. 6492**
Philadelphia gentlemen; the making of a national upper class. Glencoe, Ill., Free Press [1958] 440 p. illus. 22 cm. *1. Philadelphia — Social life and customs. 2. Class distinction — Case studies. I. T.*
F158.3.B3   917.4811   57-12630

Warner, Sam Bass, 1928- **Ill. 6493**
The private city; Philadelphia in three periods of its growth [by] Sam Bass Warner, Jr. Philadelphia, University of Pennsylvania Press [1968] xii, 236 p. illus., maps. 24 cm. *1. Philadelphia — History. I. T.*
F158.3.W18   974.8/11   68-21557

Bridenbaugh, Carl. **Ill. 6494**
Rebels and gentlemen; Philadelphia in the age of Franklin, by Carl and Jessica Bridenbaugh. New York, Reynal & Hitchcock [1942] xvii, 393 p. plates, ports., 2 maps 22 cm. *1. Philadelphia — History — Colonial period. 2. Philadelphia — Social life and customs. I. Bridenbaugh, Jessica, joint author. II. T.*
F158.4.B6   974.811   42-22812

Baldwin, Leland Dewitt, 1897- **Ill. 6495**
Pittsburgh: the story of a city, 1750-1865, by Leland D. Baldwin. Illus. by Ward Hunter. [Pittsburgh] University of Pittsburgh Press [1970, c1937] xi, 341 p. illus., maps. 21 cm. (Pitt paperback, 56) "This book is one of a series relating to Western Pennsylvania history written under the direction of the Western Pennsylvania Historical Survey sponsored jointly by the Buhl Foundation, the Historical Society of Western Pennsylvania, and the University of Pittsburgh." *1. Pittsburgh — History. I. Western Pennsylvania Historical Survey. II. Buhl Foundation. III. T.*
F159.P6B2 1970   917.48/86/034   73-104172   ISBN:822952165

F161 – 205 DELAWARE. MARYLAND. DISTRICT OF COLUMBIA

Federal Writers' Project. Delaware. **Ill. 6496**
Delaware, a guide to the first State. Compiled and written by the Federal Writers' Project of the Works Progress Administration for the State of Delaware. New and rev. ed. by Jeannette Eckman; edited by Henry G. Alsberg. New York, Hastings House [1955] xxvi, 562 p. illus., ports., maps. 21 cm. (American guide series) *1. Delaware. 2. Delaware — Description and travel — Guide-books. (S)*
F164.F45 1955   917.51   55-14794

Munroe, John A., 1914- **Ill. 6497**
Federalist Delaware, 1775-1815. New Brunswick, N.J., Rutgers University Press, 1954. xiv, 286 p. fold. map. 24 cm. (University of Delaware monograph series, no. 6) *1. Delaware — History. I. T. (S:Delaware. University, Newark. University of Delaware monograph series, no. 6)*
F168.M8   975.1   54-11929

Barker, Charles Albro, 1904- **Ill. 6498**
The background of the Revolution in Maryland. [Hamden, Conn.] Archon Books, 1967 [c1940] x, 419 p. 22 cm. (Yale historical publications. Miscellany, 38) Based on thesis, Yale University. *1. Maryland — History — Colonial period. 2. Maryland — History — Revolution. I. T. (S)*
F184.B25 1967   975.2/02   67-19512

Land, Aubrey C. **Ill. 6499**
The Dulanys of Maryland; a biographical study of Daniel Dulany, the Elder (1685-1753) and Daniel Dulany, the Younger (1722-1797) by Aubrey C. Land. Baltimore, Johns Hopkins Press [1968, c1955] xiv, 390 p. 24 cm. "Originally published by the Maryland Historical Society." *1. Dulany, Daniel, 1685-1753. 2. Dulany, Daniel, 1722-1797. I. T.*
F184.D8L3 1968   975.2/02/0922   68-28873

Steiner, Bernard Christian, 1867-1926. **Ill. 6500**
Maryland under the commonwealth; a chronicle of the years 1649-1658, by Bernard C. Steiner. Baltimore, Johns Hopkins, 1911. vii, 178 p. 25 cm. (Johns Hopkins university studies in historical and political science ... Series XXIX, no. 1) Appendix. A summary of the proceedings of the Provincial courts, 1649 to 1658, chronologically arranged: p. 117-178. *1. Maryland — Politics and government — Colonial period.*
F184.S813 (H31.J6 ser. 29, no. 1)   11-16268

Crowl, Philip Axtell, 1914- **Ill. 6501**
Maryland during and after the revolution; a political and economic study, ... Baltimore, Johns Hopkins, 1943. 185 p., 1 l. incl. front. (map) 24 cm. "Reprinted from the Johns Hopkins university studies in historical and political science, LXI, no. 1." Vita. *1. Maryland — History — Revolution. 2. Maryland — Politics and government — 1775-1865.*
F185.C7   975.2   A43-2184

Green, Constance (McLaughlin) 1897- **Ill. 6502**
Washington. Princeton, N.J., Princeton University Press, 1962-63. 2 v. illus. 25 cm. *1. Washington, D.C. — History.*
F194.G7   917.53   62-7402

Daniels, Roger. III. 6503
The Bonus March; an episode of the great depression. Westport, Conn., Greenwood Pub. Co. [1971] xiii, 370 p. illus. 22 cm. (Contributions in American history, no. 14) 1. Bonus Expeditionary Force, 1932. I. T.
F199.D18   973.91/6   75-133497   ISBN:0837151740

F206 – 220   Southern States: General

Brown, William Garrott, 1868-1913. III. 6504
The lower South in American history. New York, Greenwood Press [1969] xi, 271 p. 23 cm. Reprint of the 1902 ed. 1. Southern States — History. 2. Ku-Klux Klan. 3. Confederate States of America — Politics and government. 4. Yancey, William Lowndes, 1814-1863. 5. Hobson, Richmond Pearson, 1870-1937. I. T.
F206.B88 1969   975   69-13843

Page, Thomas Nelson, 1853-1922. III. 6505
The Old South; essays social and political; the novels, stories, sketches, and poems of Thomas Nelson Page. New York, Negro Universities Press [1969, c1906] vii, 369 p. illus., port. 23 cm. "Originally published in 1892." 1. Southern States. 2. Virginia — Social life and customs. I. T.
F206.P13 1969   917.5/03   69-14026   ISBN:837119774

Link, Arthur Stanley, ed. III. 6506
Writing southern history; essays in historiography in honor of Fletcher M. Green, edited by Arthur S. Link & Rembert W. Patrick. [Baton Rouge] Louisiana State University Press [1966, c1965] x, 502 p. port. 25 cm. 1. Green, Fletcher Melvin, 1895- 2. Southern States — History — Historiography — Addresses, essays, lectures. I. Green, Fletcher Melvin, 1895- II. Patrick, Rembert Wallace, 1909- joint ed. III. T.
F208.2.L5   975.07   65-23761

Stephenson, Wendell Holmes, 1899-1970. III. 6507
The South lives in history; southern historians and their legacy. New York, Greenwood Press [1969, c1955] xiii, 163 p. 23 cm. 1. Southern States — Historiography. 2. Dodd, William Edward, 1869-1940. 3. Fleming, Walter Lynwood, 1874-1932. 4. Phillips, Ulrich Bonnell, 1877-1934. I. T.
F208.2.S8 1969   975/.07/2   79-88947   ISBN:0837122198

Bertelson, David. III. 6508
The lazy South. New York, Oxford University Press, 1967. ix, 284 p. 22 cm. 1. Southern States — Social life and customs. 2. Work — Psychological aspects. 3. Laziness. I. T.
F209.B42   917.5/03   67-10854

Cash, Wilbur Joseph, 1900-1941. III. 6509
The mind of the South. Garden City, N.Y., Doubleday, 1954 [c1941] 444 p. 19 cm. (Doubleday anchor book, A27) 1. Southern States — Civilization. 2. Southern States — Social conditions. I. T.
F209.C3 1954   975   54-3719

Dabney, Virginius, 1901- III. 6510
Liberalism in the South. New York, AMS Press [1970] xix, 456 p. 23 cm. Reprint of the 1932 ed. 1. Liberalism — Southern States. 2. Southern States — Social conditions. 3. Southern States — Politics and government. I. T.
F209.D16 1970   309.1/75   77-128983   ISBN:0404001467

Fenton, John H. III. 6511
Politics in the Border States; a study of the patterns of political organization, and political change, common to the Border States: Maryland, West Virginia, Kentucky, and Missouri. New Orleans, Hauser Press [1957] vi, 230 p. maps, diagrs., tables. 24 cm. (Galleon books) 1. Maryland — Politics and government. 2. West Virginia — Politics and government. 3. Kentucky — Politics and government. 4. Missouri — Politics and government. I. T.
F209.F4   975   58-16327

Gaston, Paul M., 1928- III. 6512
The new South creed; a study in southern mythmaking [by] Paul M. Gaston. [1st ed.] New York, Knopf, 1970. viii, 298, vi p. 22 cm. 1. Southern States — Civilization. 2. Southern States — Race question. I. T.
F209.G3   917.5/03   70-98640

Hesseltine, William Best, 1902- III. 6513
The South in American history, by William B. Hesseltine and David L. Smiley. 2d ed. Englwood Cliffs, N.J., Prentice-Hall, 1960. 630 p. illus. 24 cm. First published in 1936 under title: A history of the South, 1607-1936. 1. Southern States — History. I. Smiley, David L., joint author. II. T.
F209.H48 1960   975   60-6880

Nicholls, William Hord, 1914- III. 6514
Southern tradition and regional progress. Chapel Hill, University of North Carolina Press [1960] 202 p. 24 cm. 1. Southern States — Civilization. 2. Southern States — Race question. 3. Public opinion — Southern States. I. T.
F209.N5   917.5   60-10535

North Carolina. University. III. 6515
Essays in southern history presented to Joseph Gregoire de Roulhac Hamilton, PH.D., LL.D., by his former students at the University of North Carolina. Edited by Fletcher Melvin Green. Chapel Hill, University of North Carolina Press, 1949. vii, 156 p. 24 cm. (The James Sprunt studies in history and political science, v.31) 1. Hamilton, Joseph Grégoire de Roulhac, 1878- 2. Southern States — History — Addresses, essays, lectures. I. Green, Fletcher Melvin, 1895- ed. II. T. (S)
F209.N67   (F251.J28 vol. 31)   975.004   49-47271

Phillips, Ulrich Bonnell, 1877-1934. III. 6516
Life and labor in the old South. Boston, Little, Brown, 1929. xix, 375 p. front., illus., maps (1 fold.) diagr. 23 cm. 1. Southern states — Social conditions. 2. Southern states — Economic conditions. 3. Slavery in the U.S. I. T.
F209.P56   29-11204

Sellers, Charles Grier, ed. III. 6517
The southerner as American. [By] John Hope Franklin [and others] Chapel Hill, University of North Carolina Press [1960] 216 p. 24 cm. 1. National characteristics, American. 2. Southern States — Civilization. 3. Southern States — History — Historiography. 4. Southern States — Race question. I. T.
F209.S44   917.5   60-4104

Simkins, Francis Butler, 1897-1966. III. 6518
The everlasting South. [Baton Rouge] Louisiana State University Press [1963] xv, 103 p. front. 22 cm. Five essays. 1. Southern States — Civilization. I. T.
F209.S488   917.5   63-20407

Simkins, Francis Butler, 1897-1966. III. 6519
A history of the South. 3d ed. New York, Knopf, 1963. xiii, 675, xxiv p. illus., ports. 24 cm. First ed. published in 1947 under title: The South, old and new; a history; 1820-1947. 1. Southern States — History.
F209.S5 1963   975   63-16714

Taylor, William Robert, 1922- III. 6520
Cavalier and Yankee; the Old South and American national character. New York, G. Braziller, 1961. 384 p. 22 cm. 1. Southern States — History — 1775-1865 — Philosophy. 2. National characteristics, American. I. T.
F209.T3 1961   975   61-15493

Thorp, Willard, 1899- ed. III. 6521
A southern reader. [1st ed.] New York, Knopf, 1955. 760 p. illus. 25 cm. 1. Southern States — Civilization. 2. American literature — Southern States. I. T.
F209.T48   917.5   53-9473

Nixon, Herman Clarence, 1886- III. 6522
Lower Piedmont country, by Herman C. Nixon. Freeport, N.Y., Books for Libraries Press [1971, c1946] xxiii, 244 p. 23 cm. (Essay index reprint series) 1. Southern States. 2. Appalachian Mountains, Southern. I. T.
F210.N5 1971   917.5/03   78-142685   ISBN:0836920643

F212 – 214   EARLY TO 1865

Bridenbaugh, Carl. III. 6523
Myths and realities; societies of the colonial South. Baton Rouge, Louisiana State University Press [1952] x, 208 p. 23 cm. (The Walter Lynwood Fleming lectures in southern history, Louisiana State University) 1. Southern States — Social life and customs — Colonial period. 2. Southern States — Intellectual life. I. T. (S:Louisiana. State University and Agricultural and Mechanical College. Walter Lynwood Fleming lectures in southern history)
F212.B75   917.5   52-13024

Craven, Wesley Frank, 1905- III. 6524
The southern colonies in the seventeenth century, 1607-1689. [Baton Rouge] Louisiana State Univ. Press, 1949. xv, 451 p. illus., maps, facsims. 24 cm. (A History of the South, v.1) 1. Southern States — History — Colonial period. I. T. (S)
F212.C7   975   49-3595

Alden, John Richard, 1908- III. 6525
John Stuart and the Southern colonial frontier; a study of Indian relations, war, trade, and land problems in the Southern wilderness, 1754-1775. New York, Gordian Press, 1966 [c1944] xiv, 384 p. maps. 24 cm. (University of Michigan publications. History and political science, v.15) 1. Stuart, John, 1718-1779. 2. Southern States — History — Colonial period. 3. Indians of North America — Southern States. 4. Indians of North America — Government relations — To 1789. (S:Michigan, University. University of Michigan publications. History and political science, v.15)
F212.S7A6 1966   970.5   66-29459

Wertenbaker, Thomas Jefferson, 1879- III. 6526
The Old South; the founding of American civilization. New York, Cooper Square Publishers, 1963 [c1942] xiv, 364 p. illus., facsims., plans. 24 cm. *1. Southern States — Civilization. 2. Southern States — History — Colonial period. I. The founding of American civilization. II. T.*
F212.W5 1963   917.5   63-17542

Abernethy, Thomas Perkins, 1890- III. 6527
The South in the new nation, 1789-1819. [Baton Rouge] Louisiana State University Press, 1961. xvi, 529 p. maps. 25 cm. (A History of the South, v.4) *1. Southern States — History — 1775-1865. I. T. (S)*
F213.A2   975   61-15488

Alden, John Richard, 1908- III. 6528
The first South. Baton Rouge, Louisiana State University Press [1961] 144 p. 21 cm. (The Walter Lynwood Fleming lectures in southern history) *1. Southern States — History — Revolution. 2. Sectionalism (U.S.) 3. U.S. — Constitutional history. I. T.*
F213.A39   973.345   61-10831

Alden, John Richard, 1908- III. 6529
The South in the Revolution, 1763-1789. [Baton Rouge] Louisiana State University Press, 1957. xv, 442 p. illus., ports., maps. 24 cm. (A History of the South, v.3) "Critical essay on authorities": p. 401-426. *1. Southern States — History — Revolution. I. T. (S)*
F213.A4   975   57-12096

Carpenter, Jesse Thomas. III. 6530
The South as a conscious minority, 1789-1861; a study in political thought. Gloucester, Mass., P. Smith, 1963 [c1930] 315 p. 21 cm. "Originally prepared as a doctoral dissertation at Harvard University." *1. Confederate States of America. Constitution. 2. Southern States — Politics and government — 1775-1865. 3. U.S. — Constitutional history. 4. Proportional representation. I. Mrs. Simon Baruch University Prize of the United Daughters of the Confederacy. II. T.*
F213.C29 1963   320.975   63-3098

Craven, Avery Odelle, 1886- III. 6531
The growth of Southern nationalism, 1848-1861. [Baton Rouge] Louisiana State University Press [and] the Littlefield Fund for Southern History of the University of Texas [Austin] 1953. xi, 433 p. illus., group port. 24 cm. (A History of the South, v.6) *1. Sectionalism (U.S.) 2. Southern States — Politics and government — 1775-1865. I. T. (S)*
F213.C75   975   53-11470

Dodd, William Edward, 1869-1940. III. 6532
The cotton kingdom; a chronicle of the old South, by William E. Dodd. New York, Yale University Press; [etc., etc.] 1921. ix, 161 p. col. front., fold. map. 18 cm. (The Chronicles of America series, [v.27]) "Textbook edition." *1. Southern states. I. T.*
F213.D6x (E173.C vol. 27)   A23-818

Eaton, Clement, 1898- III. 6533
The growth of Southern civilization, 1790-1860. [1st ed.] New York, Harper [1961] xvii, 357 p. illus., ports. 22 cm. (The New American Nation series) *1. Southern States — Civilization. 2. Southern States — History — 1775-1865. I. T.*
F213.E18   975   61-12219

Eaton, Clement, 1898- III. 6534
A history of the Old South. 2d ed. New York, Macmillan [1966] xiv, 562 p. illus., maps, ports. 24 cm. *1. Southern States — History — Colonial period. 2. Southern States — History — 1775-1865. I. T.*
F213.E2 1966   975.03   66-10399

Eaton, Clement, 1898- III. 6535
The mind of the Old South. Rev. ed. [Baton Rouge] Louisiana State University Press [1967] xi, 348 p. ports. 23 cm. *1. Southern States — Civilization. 2. Southern States — Biography. 3. National characteristics, American. I. T.*
F213.E22 1967   917.5/04/3   67-11684

Franklin, John Hope, 1915- III. 6536
The militant South, 1800-1861. Cambridge, Belknap Press of Harvard University Press, 1956. 317 p. 22 cm. *1. Southern States — History — 1775-1865. 2. Militarism. I. T.*
F213.F75   975   56-10160

Olmstead, Frederick Law, 1822-1903. III. 6537
The Cotton Kingdom; a traveller's observations on cotton and slavery in the American slave States. Based upon three former volumes of journeys and investigations by the same author. Edited, with an introd., by Arthur M. Schlesinger. New York, Knopf, 1953. lxiii, 626, xvi p. facsim. 25 cm. *1. Southern States — Description and travel. 2. Southern States — Economic conditions. 3. Slavery in the United States — Personal narratives. 4. Cotton growing — Southern States. I. T.*
F213.O53 1953   917.5   52-12193

Osterweis, Rollin Gustav, 1907- III. 6538
Romanticism and nationalism in the Old South, by Rollin G. Osterweis. Gloucester, Mass., P. Smith, 1964 [c1949] x, 275 p. illus. 21 cm. (Yale historical publications. Miscellany, 49) *1. Southern States — Civilization. 2. Romanticism — Southern States. I. T. (S)*
F213.O8 1964   917.5   64-55417

Owsley, Frank Lawrence, 1890- III. 6539
Plain folk of the Old South. [Baton Rouge] Louisiana State University Press, 1949. xxi, 235 p. maps, tables. 22 cm. (The Walter Lynwood Fleming lectures in Southern history, Louisiana State University) *1. Southern States — Social life and customs. 2. Southern States — History — 1775-1865. I. T. (S:Louisiana. State University and Agricultural and Mechanical College. Walter Lynwood Fleming lectures in Southern history)*
F213.O94   917.5   49-11743

Phillips, Ulrich Bonnell, 1877-1934. III. 6540
The course of the South to secession, an interpretation. Edited by E. Merton Coulter. [1st ed.] New York, Hill and Wang [1964, c1939] xi, 176 p. 21 cm. (American century series) "AC 70." *1. Southern States — History — 1775-1865. 2. Secession. I. T.*
F213.P65 1964   975   64-24835

Rose, Lisle Abbott, 1904- III. 6541
Prologue to democracy; the Federalists in the South, 1789-1800 [by] Lisle A. Rose. Lexington, University of Kentucky Press, 1968. xvii, 326 p. 23 cm. *1. Federal Party. Southern States. 2. Southern States — Politics and government — 1775-1865. I. T.*
F213.R83   329/.1/009033   67-29342

Sydnor, Charles Sackett, 1898- III. 6542
The development of Southern sectionalism, 1819-1848. [Baton Rouge] Louisiana State Univ. Press, 1948. xii, 400 p. illus., ports., maps. 25 cm. (A History of the South, v.5) *1. Southern States — History — 1775-1865. 2. Sectionalism (U.S.) I. T. (S)*
F213.S92   975   48-7627

Potter, David Morris. III. 6543
The South and the sectional conflict [by] David M. Potter. Baton Rouge, Louisiana State University Press, 1968. xi, 321 p. 23 cm. Essays. *1. Southern States — History — Addresses, essays, lectures. 2. United States — History — Civil War — Historiography. I. T.*
F214.P6   975   68-8941

Wiley, Bell Irvin, 1906- III. 6544
The plain people of the Confederacy [by] Bell Irvin Wiley. Baton Rouge, La., Louisiana State University Press, 1943. ix, 104 p. pl., ports. 21 cm. (The Walter Lynwood Fleming lectures in Southern history, Louisiana state university, 1943) *1. Confederate States of America — Social life and customs. 2. Confederate States of America — Army. I. T.*
F214.W56   973.716   44-40038

F215 – 216   1865 –

Dykeman, Wilma. III. 6545
Seeds of Southern change: the life of Will Alexander [by] Wilma Dykeman and James Stokely. [Chicago] University of Chicago Press [1962] 343 p. illus. 23 cm. *1. Alexander, Will Winton, 1884-1956. 2. Southern States — Social conditions. 3. Southern States — Race question. I. Stokely, James, joint author. II. T.*
F215.A55D9   920   62-13923

Clark, Thomas Dionysius, 1903- III. 6546
Pills, petticoats, and plows; the Southern country store. Norman, University of Oklahoma Press [1964, c1944] xiv, 306 p. illus. 21 cm. *1. Southern States — Social life and customs — 1865- 2. Retail trade — Southern States. 3. Country life — Southern States. I. T.*
F215.C6 1964   917.5   64-11333

Clark, Thomas Dionysius, 1903- III. 6547
The South since Appomattox; a century of regional change [by] Thomas D. Clark and Albert D. Kirwan. New York, Oxford University Press, 1967. vii, 438 p. illus., maps, ports. 24 cm. *1. Southern States — History — 1865- I. Kirwan, Albert Dennis, joint author. II. T.*
F215.C62   975.04   66-22259

Daniels, Jonathan, 1902- III. 6548
A southerner discovers the South. New introd. by the author. New York, Da Capo Press, 1970. xix, 346 p. map. 24 cm. (A Da Capo Press reprint series. The American scene) Originally published in 1938. *1. Southern States. 2. Southern States — Social conditions. I. T.*
F215.D257   917.5   68-16228   ISBN:306710110

De Santis, Vincent P. III. 6549
Republicans face the Southern question: the new departure years,

1877-1897. Baltimore, Johns Hopkins Press, 1959. 275 p. maps. 23 cm. (The Johns Hopkins University studies in historical and political science, ser. 77, no 1) 1. Republican Party. 2. Southern States — Politics and government — 1865- 3. Political parties — Southern States. I. T. (S:Johns Hopkins University. Studies in historical and political science, ser. 77, no. 1)
F215.D345   (H31.J6 ser. 77, no. 1)   329.6   59-10767

Dollard, John, 1900-   **III. 6550**
Caste and class in a southern town. 3d ed. Garden City, N.Y., Doubleday, 1957 [c1949] xii, 466 p. 18 cm. (Doubleday anchor books, A95) 1. Southern States — Social conditions. 2. Southern States — Civilization. 3. Negroes — Southern States. 4. Negroes — Moral and social conditions. I. T.
F215.D65 1957   309.175   57-505

Ezell, John Samuel.   **III. 6551**
The South since 1865. New York, Macmillan [1963] 511 p. illus. 24 cm. 1. Southern States — History — 1865- 2. Southern States — Civilization. I. T.
F215.E94   975   63-13126

Federal Writers' Project.   **III. 6552**
These are our lives, as told by the people and written by members of the Federal Writers' Project of the Works Progress Administration in North Carolina, Tennessee, and Georgia. Chapel Hill, University of North Carolina Press, 1939. St. Clair Shores, Mich., Somerset Publishers, 1972. xx, 421 p. 22 cm. 1. Southern States — Social conditions — Case studies. I. T.
F215.F4 1972   309.1/75   73-145013   ISBN:040300778X

I'll take my stand; the South and the agrarian tradition,   **III. 6553**
by twelve southerners. New York, P. Smith, 1951. xx, 359 p. 21 cm. 1. Southern States. 2. Southern States — Social conditions. 3. Southern States — Economic conditions. 4. Twelve southerners.
F215.Ix   A53-9817

Key, Valdimer Orlando, 1908-1963.   **III. 6554**
Southern politics in State and Nation [by] V. O. Key, Jr., with the assistance of Alexander Heard. [1st ed.] New York, A. A. Knopf, 1949. xxvi, 675, xiv p. illus., ports., maps. 25 cm. 1. Southern States — Politics and government — 1865- I. T.
F215.K45 1949   975   49-10825

Kirby, Jack Temple.   **III. 6555**
Darkness at the dawning; race and reform in the progressive South. Philadelphia, Lippincott [1972] vii, 210 p. 22 cm. (Critical periods of history) 1. Progressivism (United States politics) 2. Southern States — Race question. I. T.
F215.K57   322.4/4/0975   77-161416
ISBN:0397472633 0397472099 (pbk)

McGill, Ralph Emerson, 1898-   **III. 6556**
The South and the southerner. [1st ed.] Boston, Little, Brown [1963] 307 p. 22 cm. 1. Southern States — Civilization. 2. Southern States — Race question. I. T.
F215.M16 1963   917.5   63-8314

Odum, Howard Washington, 1884-   **III. 6557**
An American epoch; southern portraiture in the national picture, by Howard W. Odum. New York, H. Holt [c1930] xi, 379 p. 22 cm. Maps on lining-papers. 1. Southern states — Civilization. 2. Southern states — Social conditions. I. T.
F215.O27   917.5   30-27845

Odum, Howard Washington, 1884-   **III. 6558**
Southern regions of the United States, by Howard W. Odum for the Southern regional committee of the Social Science Research Council. Chapel Hill, University of North Carolina Press, 1936. xi, 664 p. illus. 26 cm. 1. Southern states — Social conditions. 2. Southern states — Civilization. 3. Regionalism — Southern states. I. Social science research council. Southern regional committee. II. T.
F215.O28   309.175   36-10075

Potter, David Morris.   **III. 6559**
The South and the concurrent majority [by] David M. Potter. Edited by Don E. Fehrenbacher and Carl N. Degler. Baton Rouge, Louisiana State University Press [1972] viii, 89 p. 23 cm. (The Walter Lynwood Fleming lectures in southern history) 1. Southern States — Politics and government — 1865-1950. 2. United States — Politics and government — 1865-1950. 3. United States — Politics and government — 1901-1953. (S:Louisiana. State University and Agricultural and Mechanical College. Walter Lynwood Fleming lectures in southern history.)
F215.P66   320.9/75/04   72-84123

Tindall, George Brown.   **III. 6560**
The disruption of the solid South. New York, Norton [1972] xiv, 98 p. 20 cm. (The Norton library, N663) 1. Southern States — Politics and government. I. T.
F215.T58   320.9/75   72-4629   ISBN:0393006638

Tindall, George Brown.   **III. 6561**
The emergence of the new South, 1913-1945. [Baton Rouge] Louisiana State University Press, 1967. xv, 807 p. illus., ports. 24 cm. (A History of the South, v.10) 1. Southern States — History. I. T. (S)
F215.T59   975   67-24551

Woodward, Comer Vann, 1908-   **III. 6562**
Origins of the new South, 1877-1913. [Baton Rouge] Louisiana State University Press, 1951. xi, 542 p. illus. 24 cm. (A History of the South, v. 9) 1. Southern States — History — 1865- 2. Southern States — Social conditions. I. T. (S)
F215.W85   975   51-14582

Sherrill, Robert.   **III. 6563**
Gothic politics in the Deep South; stars of the new Confederacy. New York, Grossman Publishers, 1968. 335 p. 24 cm. 1. Southern States — Politics & government — 1951- I. T.
F216.2.S48   320.9/75   67-21236

Sindler, Allan P., ed.   **III. 6564**
Change in the contemporary South. Durham, N.C., Duke University Press, 1963. x, 247 p. diagrs., tables. 24 cm. A revision of papers presented at a conference on "the impact of political and legal change in the postwar South" sponsored by the Dept. of Political Science, Duke University, July 12-14, 1962. 1. Southern States — Civilization. 2. Southern States — Politics and government — 1865- I. Duke University, Durham, N.C. II. T.
F216.2.S5   917.5   63-21317

F221 – 295   South Atlantic States

F221 – 235   VIRGINIA

Fishwick, Marshall William.   **III. 6565**
Virginia: a new look at the Old Dominion. [1st ed.] New York, Harper [1959] 305 p. illus. 22 cm. (A Regions of America book) 1. Virginia — History. I. A new look at the Old Dominion.
F226.F49   975.5   58-6148

Simkins, Francis Butler, 1897-1966.   **III. 6566**
Virginia: history, government, geography [by] Francis Butler Simkins, Spotswood Hunnicutt [and] Sidman P. Poole. New York, Scribner [1957] 599 p. illus. 24 cm. 1. Virginia — History.
F226.S5   975.5   57-3576

Abernethy, Thomas Perkins, 1890-   **III. 6567**
Three Virginia frontiers [by] Thomas Perkins Abernethy. University, La., Louisiana State University Press, 1940. xiii, 96 p. 21 cm. (The Walter Lynwood Fleming lectures in southern history, Louisiana state university, 1940) 1. Virginia — History — Colonial period. 2. Kentucky — History. 3. Frontier and pioneer life — Virginia. 4. Frontier and pioneer life — Kentucky. I. T.
F229.A25   975.5   41-3353

Beverley, Robert, ca. 1673-ca. 1722.   **III. 6568**
The history and present state of Virginia; ed., with an introd., by Louis B. Wright. Chapel Hill, Pub. for the Institute of Early American History and Culture at Williamsburg, Va., by the Univ. of North Carolina Press, 1947. xxxv, 366 p. illus. 25 cm. Reproduction of the Huntington Library copy of the original edition (London, 1705) Cf. p. xxxiv. 1. Virginia — History — Colonial period. 2. Virginia. 3. Indians of North America — Virginia. I. Wright, Louis Booker, 1899- ed. II. Institute of Early American History and Culture, Williamsburg, Va.
F229.B593   975.5   47-30522

Bruce, Philip Alexander, 1856-1933.   **III. 6569**
Economic history of Virginia in the seventeenth century; an inquiry into the material condition of the people, based upon original and contemporaneous records. New York, Johnson Reprint Corp. [1966] 2 v. 23 cm. Title page includes original imprint: New York, Macmillan, 1896. 1. Virginia — History — Colonial Period. 2. Virginia — Economic conditions. I. T.
F229.B882 1966   330.9755   67-7008

Byrd, William, 1674-1744.   **III. 6570**
Histories of the dividing line betwixt Virginia and North Carolina. With introd. and notes by William K. Boyd, and a new introd. by Percy G. Adams. New York, Dover Publications [1967] xxxix, 340 p. facsims., maps (1 fold.), port. 22 cm. (Dover Americana) Contains the author's "The history of the dividing line betwixt Virginia and North Carolina" and "The secret history of the line," which is another version of the same subject matter, printed on opposite pagings. "An unabridged republication of the work first

III. 6571   United States   **F229**

published by the North Carolina Historical Commission in 1929 .. [with] a new introduction." *1. Virginia — Boundaries — North Carolina. 2. North Carolina — Boundaries — Virginia. 3. Virginia — Description and travel. 4. North Carolina — Description and travel. I. Boyd, William Kenneth, 1879-1938, ed. II. T.*
F229.B968 1967   917.55   67-24220

Byrd, William, 1674-1744.   **III. 6571**
The London diary, 1717-1721, and other writings. Edited by Louis B. Wright and Marion Tinling. New York, Oxford University Press, 1958. vi, 647 p. illus., port. 24 cm. "The diary ... is transcribed from a shorthand notebook (Mss 5:1B 9964:1) in the library of the Virginia Historical Society." *1. London — Social life and customs. 2. Virginia — Social life and customs. I. Wright, Louis Booker, 1899- ed. II. Tinling, Marion Rose (Goble) 1904- ed. III. T.*
F229.B9685   923.273   57-10389

Byrd, William, 1674-1744.   **III. 6572**
The secret diary of William Byrd of Westover, 1709-1712, edited by Louis B. Wright and Marion Tinling. Richmond, Va., The Dietz Press, 1941. xxviii, 622 p. 2 facsim. 24 cm. Title vignette (coat of arms) A transcription from the original shorthand of the first part of Byrd's diary now in the Henry E. Huntington library. Parts covering the period from December 13, 1717, to May 19, 1721, and from August 10, 1739, to August 31, 1741, are located in the Virginia historical society and the University of North Carolina library respectively. cf. Introd. *1. Virginia — Social life and customs. I. Wright, Louis Booker, 1899- ed. II. Tinling, Marion Rose (Goble) 1904 joint ed. III. T.*
F229.B9715   923.273   41-21807

Byrd, William, 1674-1744.   **III. 6573**
Another Secret diary of William Byrd of Westover, 1739-1741, with letters & literary exercises, 1696-1726. Edited by Maude H. Woodfin, translated and collated by Marion Tinling. Richmond, Va., The Dietz Press, 1942. xiv, 490 p. front., facsims. 24 cm. Reproduced at the Henry E. Huntington library from shorthand and holograph manuscripts owned by the University of North Carolina. *1. Virginia — Social life and customs. I. Woodfin, Maude Howlett, ed. II. Tinling, Marion Rose (Goble) 1904- III. Secret diary of William Byrd of Westover.*
F229.B9717   923.273   43-1881

Beatty, Richmond Croom, 1905-1961.   **III. 6574**
William Byrd of Westover. With a new pref. and bibliography by M. Thomas Inge. [Hamden, Conn.] Archon Books, 1970 [c1932] xxxix, 243 p. illus., ports. 21 cm. *1. Byrd, William, 1674-1744. I. T.*
F229.B972 1970   975.5/02/0924   70-122393   ISBN:208009442

Morton, Louis.   **III. 6575**
Robert Carter of Nomini hall, a Virginia tobacco planter of the eighteenth century, by Louis Morton. Williamsburg, Va., Colonial Williamsburg, incorporated, 1941. xi, 332 p. illus., tables., plates, ports. 24 cm. ([Williamsburg restoration historical studies, no. 2) *1. Carter, Robert, 1728-1804. I. T.*
F229.C34M6   926.3   41-19439

Craven, Wesley Frank, 1905-   **III. 6576**
Dissolution of the Virginia Company; the failure of a colonial experiment. Gloucester, Mass., P. Smith, 1964 [c1932] vi, 350 p. 21 cm. *1. Virginia Company of London. 2. Virginia — History — Colonial period. I. T.*
F229.C895 1964   975.501   65-1398

Morton, Richard Lee, 1889-   **III. 6577**
Colonial Virginia. Chapel Hill, Published for the Virginia Historical Society by the University of North Carolina Press, 1960. 2 v. (xiv, 883 p.) illus., ports., maps, facsims. 25 cm. *1. Virginia — History — Colonial period. I. T.*
F229.M75   975.502   60-51846

Tyler, Lyon Gardiner, 1853-1935, ed.   **III. 6578**
Narratives of early Virginia, 1606-1625; ed. by Lyon Gardiner Tyler, with a map and two facsimiles. New York, Scribner, 1907. xv, 478 p. fold. map, 2 facsims. (1 fold.) 23 cm. (Original narratives of early American history ...) Series title also at head of t.-p. *1. Virginia — History — Colonial period — Sources.*
F229.T994   07-33220

Washburn, Wilcomb E.   **III. 6579**
The Governor and the rebel; a history of Bacon's Rebellion in Virginia. Chapel Hill, Published for the Institute of Early American History and Culture at Williamsburg by the University of North Carolina Press [1957] xv, 248 p. port., maps, facsim. 25 cm. *1. Bacon's Rebellion, 1676. I. Institute of Early American History and Culture, Williamsburg, Va. II. T.*
F229.W28   975.5   58-97

Wertenbaker, Thomas Jefferson, 1879-   **III. 6580**
Patrician and plebian in Virginia; or, The origin and development of the social classes of the Old Dominion. New York, Russell & Russell, 1959. 239 p. 22 cm. *1. Virginia — Social life and customs. 2. Virginia — History — Colonial period. I. T.*
F229.W49 1959   975.502   59-11227

Wertenbaker, Thomas Jefferson, 1879-1966.   **III. 6581**
The planters of colonial Virginia. New York, Russell & Russell, 1959. 260 p. 22 cm. *1. Virginia — History — Colonial period. 2. Virginia — Economic conditions. 3. Slavery in the U.S. — Virginia. I. T.*
F229.W493 1959   975.502   59-11228

Wertenbaker, Thomas Jefferson, 1879-   **III. 6582**
The shaping of colonial Virginia. New York, Russell & Russell [1958] vii, 239, 260, v, 271 p. maps. 22 cm. Consists of three works previously published separately. *1. Virginia — History — Colonial period. 2. Virginia — Social life and customs — Colonial period. I. T:The planters of colonial Virginia. II. T:Virginia under the Stuarts, 1607-1688. III. T. IV. T:Patrician and plebeian in Virginia.*
F229.W495   975.5   58-5370

Wertenbaker, Thomas Jefferson, 1879-   **III. 6583**
Virginia under the Stuarts, 1607-1688. New York, Russell & Russell, 1959. 271 p. 22 cm. *1. Virginia — History — Colonial period. I. T.*
F229.W5 1959   975.502   59-11229

Wright, Louis Booker, 1899-   **III. 6584**
The first gentlemen of Virginia; intellectual qualities of the early colonial ruling class, by Louis B. Wright. San Marino, Calif., The Huntington Library, 1940. xi, 373 p. 25 cm. *1. Virginia — Social life and customs — Colonial period. 2. Virginia — Intellectual life. 3. Virginia — Biography. I. T.*
F229.W965   975.5   40-8029

F230 – 231   1775 –

Davis, Richard Beale.   **III. 6585**
Intellectual life in Jefferson's Virginia, 1790-1830. Chapel Hill, University of North Carolina Press [1964] x, 507 p. illus., ports. 24 cm. *1. Virginia — Intellectual life. 2. American literature — Virginia. I. T.*
F230.D3   917.55   64-13548

Jefferson, Thomas, Pres. U.S., 1743-1826.   **III. 6586**
Notes on the State of Virginia; edited with an introd. and notes by William Peden. Chapel Hill, Published for the Institute of Early American History and Culture, Williamsburg, Va., by the University of North Carolina Press, 1955 [c1954] xxv, 315 p. maps (1 fold.) 24 cm. Includes a reproduction of the t.p. of the 1787 ed., with imprint: London, Printed for J. Stockdale. *1. Virginia. I. Peden, William Harwood, 1913- ed.*
F230.J5102 1955   917.55   55-14659

Mays, David John, 1896-   **III. 6587**
Edmund Pendleton, 1721-1803; a biography. Cambridge, Harvard University Press, 1952. 2 v. illus., ports., maps. 25 cm. *1. Pendleton, Edmund, 1721-1803. 2. Virginia — Politics and government — Colonial period. 3. Virginia — Politics and government — 1775-1865.*
F230.P425   923.273   52-5036

Craven, Avery Odelle, 1886-   **III. 6588**
Edmund Ruffin, southerner; a study in secession, by Avery Craven. New York, D. Appleton, 1932. ix, 283 p. front., plates, ports., facsims. 23 cm. *1. Ruffin, Edmund, 1794-1865. 2. Southern states — Politics and government — 1775-1865. 3. Secession.*
F230.R94   923.273   32-8631

Shanks, Henry Thomas.   **III. 6589**
The secession movement in Virginia, 1847-1861, by Henry T. Shanks. [1st AMS ed.] New York, AMS Press [1971] xi, 296 p. maps. 24 cm. Reprint of the 1934 ed. *1. Virginia — Politics and government — 1775-1865. 2. Secession. I. T.*
F230.S56 1971   973.71/3   77-155611   ISBN:0404002110

Sydnor, Charles Sackett, 1898-   **III. 6590**
Gentlemen freeholders; political practices in Washington's Virginia. Chapel Hill, Published for the Institute of Early American History and Culture at Williamsburg, Va., by the University of North Carolina Press [1952] x, 180 p. 22 cm. *1. Virginia — Politics and government — Colonial period. 2. Virginia — Politics and government — 1775-1865. I. Institute of Early American History and Culture, Williamsburg, Va. II. T.*
F230.S9   975.5   52-3497

Maddex, Jack P., 1941-   **III. 6591**
The Virginia conservatives, 1867-1879; a study in Reconstruction politics, by Jack P. Maddex, Jr. Chapel Hill, University of North Carolina Press [1970] xx, 328 p. maps (on lining papers) 24 cm. *1. Virginia — Politics and government — 1865-1950. 2. Reconstruction — Virginia. I. T.*
F231.M2   320.9/755   76-109465   ISBN:807811408

Moger, Allen Wesley, 1905-   **III. 6592**
Virginia: Bourbonism to Byrd, 1870-1925 [by] Allen W. Moger. Charlottesville, University Press of Virginia [1968] ix, 397 p. illus., maps, ports. 26 cm. *1. Virginia — History. I. T.*
F231.M66   975.5   68-8538

Pearson, Charles Chilton. III. 6593
The readjuster movement in Virginia. Gloucester, Mass., P. Smith, 1969 [c1917] viii, 191 p. maps. 22 cm. (Yale historical publications. Miscellany, 4) *1. Virginia — Politics and government — 1865-1950. 2. Debts, Public — Virginia. 3. Reconstruction — Virginia. I. T. (S)*
F231.P36 1969   320.9/755   75-7804

Pulley, Raymond H. III. 6594
Old Virginia restored; an interpretation of the progressive impulse, 1870-1930 [by] Raymond H. Pulley. Charlottesville, University Press of Virginia [1968] x, 207 p. ports. 24 cm. *1. Virginia — Politics and government — 1865-1950. I. T.*
F231.P94   320/.09755   68-8539

Writers' program. Virginia. III. 6595
Virginia; a guide to the Old Dominion, compiled by workers of the Writers' program of the Work projects administration in the state of Virginia. Sponsored by James H. Price, governor of Virginia. New York, Oxford University Press [1946] xxix, 710 (i.e. 726) p. illus., plates, maps (2 on 1 fold. l., in pocket) 21 cm. (American guide series) "First published in May 1940 ... Third printing, with corrections, 1946." *1. Virginia. 2. Virginia — Description and travel — Guide-books.*
F231.W88 1946   917.55   46-5684

Gottmann, Jean. III. 6596
Virginia in our century. Charlottesville, University Press of Virginia [1969] xii, 656 p. illus., maps. 25 cm. 1955 ed. published under title: Virginia at mid-century. *1. Virginia — Description and travel — 1951- I. T.*
F231.2.G6 1969   917.55   68-8541

Wilkinson, J. Harvie, 1944- III. 6597
Harry Byrd and the changing face of Virginia politics, 1945-1966 [by] J. Harvie Wilkinson III. Charlottesville, University Press of Virginia [1968] xvi, 403 p. illus., maps, ports. 25 cm. *1. Virginia — Politics and government — 1951- 2. Byrd, Harry Flood, 1887-1966. I. T.*
F231.2.W5   320.9/755   68-22731

F232 – 234   Regions. Cities

Bridenbaugh, Carl. III. 6598
Seat of empire; the political role of eighteenth-century Williamsburg. New ed. Williamsburg, Va., Colonial Williamsburg; distributed by Holt, New York [1958] 85 p. illus. 21 cm. (Williamsburg in American series, 1) *1. Williamsburg, Va. — History. 2. Virginia — Politics and government — Colonial period. I. T.*
F234.W7W7 vol. 1a   975.5425   58-13522

Morgan, Edmund Sears. III. 6599
Virginians at home; family life in the eighteenth century. Williamsburg, Va., Colonial Williamsburg [1952] 99 p. illus. 21 cm. (Williamsburg in America series, 2) *1. Virginia — Social life and customs — Colonial period. I. T.*
F234.W7W7x (P234.W7W7 vol. 2)   917.55   52-14250

F236 – 250   WEST VIRGINIA

Ambler, Charles Henry, 1876- III. 6600
West Virginia, the Mountain State [by] Charles H. Ambler [and] Festus P. Summers. 2d ed. Englewood Cliffs, N.J., Prentice-Hall, 1958. 584 p. illus. 24 cm. *1. West Virginia — History. I. Summers, Festus Paul, 1895- joint author.*
F241.A523 1958   975.4   57-12033

Writers' Program. West Virginia. III. 6601
West Virginia, a guide to the Mountain State. Compiled by workers of the Writers' Program of the Work Projects Administration in the State of West Virginia. New York, Oxford University Press. St. Clair Shores, Mich., Somerset Publishers, 1973 [c1941] p. Original ed. issued in series: American guide series. *1. West Virginia. 2. West Virginia — Description and travel — Guide-books. I. T. (S:American guide series.)*
F241.W85 1973   917.54/04/4   72-84516   ISBN:0403021979

F251 – 265   NORTH CAROLINA. SOUTH CAROLINA

Hawks, Francis Lister, 1798-1866. III. 6602
History of North Carolina. Fayetteville, N.C., E. J. Hale, 1857-58. [Spartanburg, S.C., Reprint Co., 1961] 2 v. illus., port., maps. 23 cm. (North Carolina heritage series, no. 2-3) *1. North Carolina — History — Colonial period. 2. Raleigh's Roanoke colonies, 1584-1590. (S)*
F251.N87 no. 2-3   975.601   61-3775

Lefler, Hugh Talmage, 1901- III. 6603
North Carolina, the history of a Southern State, by Hugh Talmage Lefler and Albert Ray Newsome. Rev. ed. Chapel Hill, University of North Carolina Press [1963] xii, 756 p. maps. 25 cm. *1. North Carolina — History. I. Newsome, Albert Ray, 1894-1951, joint author.*
F254.L39 1963   975.6   63-3932

Federal Writers' Project. North Carolina. III. 6604
The North Carolina guide; edited by Blackwell P. Robinson. Chapel Hill, University of North Carolina Press [1955] xxi, 649 p. illus., maps. 21 cm. *1. North Carolina. 2. North Carolina — Description and travel — Guide-books. I. Robinson, Blackwell P., ed.*
F259.F44 1955   917.56   55-2216

Hamilton, Joseph Grégoire de Roulhac, 1878- III. 6605
Reconstruction in North Carolina, by J. G. de Roulhac Hamilton. Gloucester, Mass., P. Smith, 1964 [c1914] x, 683 p. 21 cm. (Studies in history, economics and public law, v.58, no. 141) *1. Reconstruction — North Carolina. 2. North Carolina — Politics and government — 1865-1950. (S:Columbia studies in the social sciences, no. 141)*
F259.H23   975.604   65-2575

Ramsay, David, 1749-1815. III. 6606
History of South Carolina: from its first settlement in 1670 to the year 1808. Newberry, S.C., W. J. Duffie, 1858. [Spartanburg, S.C., Reprint Co., 1959-60] 2 v. 23 cm. (South Carolina heritage series, 3-4) *1. South Carolina — History. (S)*
F266.S53 no. 3-4   975.702   61-24234

Wallace, David Duncan, 1874-1951. III. 6607
South Carolina, a short history, 1520-1948. Chapel Hill, University of North Carolina Press, 1951. xi, 753 p. maps, diagrs. 25 cm. "The present volume represents a reduction of ... [the author's] three-volume History of South Carolina published in 1934." *1. South Carolina — History. I. T.*
F269.W26   975.7   51-13847

Writers' program. South Carolina. III. 6608
South Carolina; a guide to the Palmetto state, compiled by workers of the Writers' program of the Work projects administration in the state of South Carolina. Sponsored by Burnet R. Maybank, governor of South Carolina. New York, Oxford University Press [1941] xxvii, 514 p. illus., plates, port., maps (1 fold. in pocket) 21 cm. (American guide series) Map on lining-paper. The plates are in eight groups, each preceded by half-title not included in paging. "First published in February 1941." *1. South Carolina — Description and travel — Guide-books.*
F269.W7   917.57   41-52304

Brown, Richard Maxwell. III. 6609
The South Caroline Regulators. Cambridge, Belknap Press of Harvard University Press, 1963. xi, 230 p. maps. 24 cm. (A publication of the Center for the Study of the History of Liberty in America, Harvard University) *1. Vigilance committee — South Carolina. 2. South Carolina — History — Colonial period. 3. Crime and criminals — South Carolina. I. T. (S:Harvard University. Center for the Study of the History of Liberty in America. Publication)*
F272.B75   974.102   63-7589

Crane, Verner Winslow, 1889- III. 6610
The southern frontier, 1670-1732. [Ann Arbor] University of Michigan Press [1956, c1929] 359 p. 21 cm. (Ann Arbor books, AA4) *1. Southern States — History — Colonial period. 2. South Carolina — History — Colonial period. 3. Gt. Brit. — Colonies — America. 4. Indians of North America — Commerce. I. T.*
F272.Cx   975   57-1007

Sirmans, Marion Eugene, 1934-1965. III. 6611
Colonial South Carolina: a political history, 1663-1763, by M. Eugene Sirmans. Foreword by Wesley Frank Craven. Chapel Hill, Published for the Institute of Early American History and Culture at Williamsburg, Va., by the University of North Carolina Press [1966] xiii, 394 p. map (on lining papers) 24 cm. *1. South Carolina — Politics and government — Colonial period. I. Institute of Early American History and Culture, Williamsburg, Va. II. T.*
F272.S5   975.702   66-25363

Woodmason, Charles, ca. 1720-ca. 1776. III. 6612
The Carolina Backcountry on the eve of the Revolution; the Journal and other writings of Charles Woodmason, Anglican itinerant, edited with an introd. by Richard J. Hooker. Chapel Hill, Published for the Institute of Early American History and Culture at Williamsburg, Va. by the University of North Carolina Press, 1953. xxxix, 305 p. map (on lining papers) 21 cm. *1. Frontier and pioneer life — South Carolina. 2. South Carolina — History — Colonial period — Sources. 3. Church of England in South Carolina — Sermons. 4. Sermons, American. I. Hooker, Richard James, 1913- ed. II. T.*
F272.W77   975.7   53-13218

Channing, Steven A.   III. 6613
Crisis of fear: secession in South Carolina [by] Steven A. Channing. New York, Simon and Schuster [1970] 315 p. map, ports. 22 cm. *1. South Carolina — Politics and government — 1775-1865. 2. Secession. 3. South Carolina — History — Civil War. I. T.*
F273.C45   973.71/3   72-116503   ISBN:671205161

White, Laura Amanda.   III. 6614
Robert Barnwell Rhett, father of secession, by Laura B. White. Gloucester, Mass., P. Smith, 1965, [c1931] ix, 264 p. illus., geneal. table, fold. map, ports. 21 cm. At head of title: The American Historical Association. *1. Rhett, Robert Barnwell, 1800-1876. 2. South Carolina — Politics and government — 1775-1865. 3. Secession. I. American Historical Association.*
F273.R52 1965   973.7130924   66-824

Lander, Ernest McPherson.   III. 6615
A history of South Carolina, 1865-1960. 2d ed. Columbia, University of South Carolina Press [1970] xxiv, 260 p. maps. 23 cm. *1. South Carolina — History. I. T.*
F274.L32 1970   917.57/03/4   70-119333   ISBN:872491692

Pike, James Shepherd, 1811-1882.   III. 6616
The prostrate state; South Carolina under Negro government; introduction by Henry Steele Commager. New York, Loring & Mussey [c1935] xxiv, 279 p. front. 22 cm. At head of title: James S. Pike. The text is a reprint of the edition of 1874. *1. South Carolina — Politics and government — 1865- 2. Reconstruction — South Carolina. I. Commager, Henry Steele, 1902- II. T.*
F274.P632   975.7   35-5094

Simkins, Francis Butler, 1897-1966.   III. 6617
South Carolina during Reconstruction by Francis Butler Simkins [and] Robert Hilliard Woody. Gloucester, Mass., P. Smith, 1966 [c1932] xiv, 590 p. illus., fold. map, ports. 21 cm. Reprint of a thesis. Duke University, 1930. *1. Reconstruction — South Carolina. 2. South Carolina — Politics and government — 1865-1950. 3. South Carolina — Economic conditions. 4. South Carolina — Social conditions. I. Woody, Robert Hilliard, 1903- joint author. II. T.*
F274.S57 1966   917.57034   66-31306

Simkins, Francis Butler, 1897-1966.   III. 6618
The Tillman movement in South Carolina. Gloucester, Mass., P. Smith, 1964 [c1926] ix, 274 p. illus., maps, ports. 22 cm. *1. Tillman, Benjamin Ryan, 1847-1918. 2. South Carolina — Politics and government — 1865-1950. I. T.*
F274.S583   975.704   65-1328

Rose, Willie Lee Nichols, 1927-   III. 6619
Rehearsal for Reconstruction; the Port Royal experiment [by] Willie Lee Rose. With an introd. by C. Vann Woodward. Indianapolis, Bobbs-Merrill [1964] xviii, 442 p. illus., fold. map, ports. 24 cm. *1. Negroes — Sea Islands, S.C. 2. Port Royal (S.C.) Expedition, 1861. 3. Sea Islands, S.C. — History. I. T.*
F277.B3R6   975.7995   64-16720

Bowes, Frederick Patten, 1902-   III. 6620
The culture of early Charleston, by Frederick P. Bowes. Chapel Hill, The University of North Carolina Press, 1942. ix, 156 p. front. 22 cm. Revision of thesis (PH.D.) — Princeton university, 1941. *1. Charleston, S.C. — Intellectual life.*
F279.C4B6   917.57911   A43-857

F281 – 295   GEORGIA

Coulter, Ellis Merton, 1890-   III. 6621
Georgia, a short history. Rev. and enl. ed. Chapel Hill, University of North Carolina Press [1960] 537 p. illus. 24 cm. First published in 1933 under title: A short history of Georgia. *1. Georgia — History.*
F286.C78 1960   975.8   60-16233

Abbot, William Wright, 1922-   III. 6622
The royal governors of Georgia, 1754-1775. Chapel Hill, Published for the Institute of Early American History and Culture at Williamsburg by the University of North Carolina Press [1959] 198 p. illus. 24 cm. *1. Georgia — Politics and government — Colonial period. 2. Georgia — Governors. I. T.*
F289.A58   975.802   59-9568

Ettinger, Amos Aschbach.   III. 6623
James Edward Oglethorpe, imperial idealist. Oxford, The Clarendon Press, 1936. xi, 348 p. front., plates, ports., fold. map. 23 cm. *1. Oglethorpe, James Edward, 1696-1785. 2. Georgia — History — Colonial period.*
F289.O33   36-8115

Saye, Albert Berry.   III. 6624
New viewpoints in Georgia history. Athens, The University of Georgia Press, 1943. vii, 256 p. 22 cm. *1. Georgia — History. I. T.*
F289.S25   975.8   44-2061

Coleman, Kenneth.   III. 6625
The American Revolution in Georgia, 1763-1789. Athens, University of Georgia Press [c1958] viii, 352 p. maps. 25 cm. *1. Georgia — History — Colonial period. 2. Georgia — History — 1775-1865. I. T.*
F290.C55   975.802   58-59848

Kemble, Frances Anne, 1809-1893.   III. 6626
Journal of a residence on a Georgian plantation in 1838-1839. Edited, with an introd., by John A. Scott. New York, Knopf, 1961. lxx, 415, viii p. port., maps, facsim. 22 cm. *1. Georgia — Social life and customs. 2. Slavery in the U.S. — Georgia. I. Scott, John Anthony, 1916- ed. II. T.*
F290.K332 1961   975.803   60-53234

Myers, Robert Manson, 1921-   III. 6627
The children of pride; a true story of Georgia and the Civil War. Edited by Robert Manson Myers. New Haven, Yale University Press, 1972. xxv, 1845 p. maps (on lining papers) 26 cm. "Who's who": p. [1449] - 1738. "[Selected] from the voluminous family papers of the Rev. Dr. Charles Colcock Jones (1804-1863), of Liberty County, Georgia." *1. Georgia — History — Civil War — Sources. 2. United States — Biography. I. Jones, Charles Colcock, 1804-1863. II. T.*
F290.M9   917.58/03/3   79-99835   ISBN:0300012144

Phillips, Ulrich Bonnell, 1877-1934.   III. 6628
Georgia and state rights. [Yellow Springs, Ohio] Antioch Press [1968] xiv, 224 p. maps. 24 cm. Reprint of the 1902 ed., with an introd. by Louis Filler. *1. Georgia — Politics and government — 1775-1865. 2. State rights. I. T.*
F290.P56 1968   320.9/758   67-30578

Shryock, Richard Harrison, 1893-   III. 6629
Georgia and the Union in 1850, by Richard Harrison Shryock. Durham, N.C., Duke University Press [c1926] viii, 406 p. 8 maps (1 fold.) 24 cm. (Duke university publications) Issued also as thesis (PH.D.) University of Pennsylvania. *1. Georgia — History. I. T.*
F290.S55   27-584

Writers' Program. Georgia.   III. 6630
Atlanta, a city of the modern South, compiled by workers of the Writers' program of the Work Projects Administration in the state of Georgia. Sponsored by the Board of Education of the City of Atlanta. New York, Smith & Durrell [1942] xxvi, 266 p. plates, fold. map. 21 cm. (American guide series) *1. Atlanta. 2. Atlanta — Description — Guide-books.*
F294.A8W8   917.58   42-15374

F296 – 395   Gulf States
F301 – 350 FLORIDA. ALABAMA. MISSISSIPPI

Cox, Isaac Joslin, 1873-   III. 6631
The West Florida controversy, 1798-1813; a study in American diplomacy. Gloucester, Mass., P. Smith, 1967 [c1918] xii, 699 p. maps (1 fold.) 21 cm. (The Albert Shaw lectures on diplomatic history, 1912) *1. West Florida — History. 2. U.S. — Foreign relations — 1783-1815. I. T. (S)*
F301.C87 1967   976/.03   67-8906

Brooks, Philip Coolidge, 1906-   III. 6632
Diplomacy and the borderlands; the Adams-Onís treaty of 1819, by Philip Coolidge Brooks. Berkeley, Calif., University of California Press, 1939. x, 262 p. 2 port. (incl. front.) fold. maps, facsim. 24 cm. (University of California publications in history, vol.XXIV) *1. Washington, Treaty of, 1819. 2. Florida — History — Colonial period to 1821. 3. U.S. — Foreign relations — Spain. 4. Spain — Foreign relations — U.S. I. T.*
F314.B87 (E173.C15 vol. 24)   973.54   A40-130

Thompson, Arthur William.   III. 6633
Jacksonian democracy on the Florida frontier. Gainesville, University of Florida Press, 1961. 88 p. 23 cm. (University of Florida monographs. Social sciences, no. 9) *1. Jackson, Andrew, Pres. U.S., 1767-1845. 2. Florida — Politics and government — 1821-1865. I. T.*
F315.T45   975.904   61-63107

Federal writers' project. Florida.   III. 6634
Florida; a guide to the southern-most state, compiled and written by the Federal writers' project of the Work projects administration for the state of Florida; sponsored by state of Florida Department of Public instruction. New York, Oxford University Press, 1939. xxvi, 600 p. illus., maps (1 fold. in pocket) plates. 21 cm. (American guide series) "First published in November 1939." Map on lining-papers. *1. Florida. 2. Florida — Description and travel — Guide-books.*
F316.F44   917.59   39-29497

Fagen, Richard R. III. 6635
Cubans in exile; disaffection and the revolution, by Richard R. Fagen, Richard A. Brody [and] Thomas J. O'Leary. Stanford, Calif., Stanford University Press, 1968. xii, 161 p. 23 cm. *1. Cubans in Miami, Florida. 2. Refugees, Cuban. 3. Cuba — History — 1959- I. Brody, Richard A., joint author. II. O'Leary, Thomas J., joint author. III. T.*
F319.M6F3   301.453/7291/0759381   68-26777

Agee, James, 1909-1955. III. 6636
Let us now praise famous men; three tenant families [by] James Agee [and] Walker Evans. Boston, Houghton Mifflin [1960] xxii, 471 p. illus. 22 cm. *1. Alabama — Social conditions. I. Evans, Walker, 1903- joint author. II. Three tenant families. III. T.*
F326.A17 1960   917.61   60-4027

Fleming, Walter Lynwood, 1874-1932. III. 6637
Civil War and reconstruction in Alabama. New York, P. Smith, 1949 [c1905] xxiii, 815 p. illus., ports., maps. 27 cm. (Micro-offset books) Pages 4-807 reproduced 4 to a page. *1. Reconstruction — Alabama. 2. Alabama — History — Civil War. (S)*
F326.F71 1949   976.1   49-50357

Hackney, Sheldon. III. 6638
Populism to progressivism in Alabama. Princeton, N.J., Princeton University Press, 1969. xv, 390 p. maps. 23 cm. *1. Alabama — Politics and government — 1865-1950. I. T.*
F326.H14   320.9/761   68-56311

Rogers, William Warren. III. 6639
The one-galllused rebellion; agrarianism in Alabama, 1865-1896. Baton Rouge, Louisiana State University Press [1970] x, 354 p. 24 cm. *1. Alabama — Politics and government — 1865-1950. 2. People's Party of the United States. Alabama. I. T.*
F326.R85   322/.44   74-108202   ISBN:0807109355

Writers' Program. Alabama. III. 6640
Alabama; a guide to the Deep South. Compiled by workers of the Writers' Program of the Works [sic] Projects Administration in the State of Alabama. Sponsored by the Alabama State Planning Commission. New York, Hastings House [1949, c1941] xxii, 442 p. illus., maps (part fold., in pocket) 21 cm. (American guide series) *1. Alabama. 2. Alabama — Description and travel — Guide-books. (S)*
F326.W7 1949   917.61   52-3711

Baldwin, Joseph Glover, 1815-1864. III. 6641
The flush times of Alabama and Mississippi; a series of sketches. Introd. by William A. Owens. New York, Sagamore Press, 1957. 244 p. 21 cm. (American century series, S-5) *1. Alabama — Social life and customs. 2. Mississippi — Social life and customs. 3. Law — Anecdotes, facetiae, satire, etc. I. T.*
F327.B19   917.61   57-9757

Ranck, James Byrne. III. 6642
Albert Gallatin Brown, radical Southern nationalist. New York, D. Appleton-Century [c1937] xiv, 320 p. maps, port. 23 cm. At head of title: The American Historical Association. *1. Brown, Albert Gallatin, 1813-1880. 2. Mississippi — Politics and government. 3. Slavery in the U.S. I. American historical association.*
F341.B88   923.273   37-15024

Federal Writers' Project. Mississippi. III. 6643
Mississippi; a guide to the Magnolia State, comp. and written by the Federal Writers' Project of the Works Progress Administration. New York, Hastings House [1949] xxiv, 545 p. illus., maps. 21 cm. (American guide series) "Sponsored by the Mississippi Agricultural and Industrial Board." *1. Mississippi. 2. Mississippi — Description and travel. 3. Automobiles — Road guides — Mississippi. (S)*
F341.F45 1949   917.62   49-5823

Harris, William Charles, 1933- III. 6644
Presidential Reconstruction in Mississippi [by] William C. Harris. Baton Rouge, Louisiana State University [1967] x, 279 p. illus., maps, ports. 24 cm. *1. Reconstruction — Mississippi. I. T.*
F341.H3   917.62/03/6   67-24418

Kirwan, Albert Dennis. III. 6645
Revolt of the rednecks; Mississippi politics: 1876-1925, by Albert D. Kirwan. Gloucester, Mass., P. Smith, 1964 [c1951] x, 328 p. illus., maps, ports. 21 cm. *1. Mississippi — Politics and government — 1865- I. T.*
F341.K5 1964   976.206   64-56715

Silver, James Wesley, 1907- III. 6646
Mississippi: the closed society [by] James W. Silver. [1st ed.] New York, Harcourt, Brace & World [1964] xxii, 250 p. facsim., map. 21 cm. *1. Mississippi — Race question. 2. Mississippi — Politics and government. I. T.*
F345.S5   301.451   64-19939

Dain, Martin J. III. 6647
Faulkner's county: Yoknapatawpha, by Martin J. Dain. New York, Random House [1964] 159 p. illus., facsims., ports. 30 cm. *1. Lafayette Co., Miss. — Description — Views. 2. Faulkner, William, 1897-1962. I. T.*
F347.L2D3 1964   917.6283   64-17484

Walker, Peter Franklin. III. 6648
Vicksburg; a people at war, 1860-1865. Chapel Hill, University of North Carolina Press [1960] xvi, 235 p. illus., map. 24 cm. *1. Vicksburg, Miss. — History. I. T.*
F349.V6W3   973.746229   59-65497

F351 – 355 MISSISSIPPI VALLEY. MIDDLE WEST

Baldwin, Leland Dewitt, 1897- III. 6649
The keelboat age on western waters [by] Leland D. Baldwin; with chapter decorations by Harvey B. Cushman. [Pittsburgh] University of Pittsburgh Press, 1941. xiv, 268 p. illus., plates, maps, facsims. 24 cm. Map on lining-papers. "This monograph in its original form was submitted to ... the University of Michigan ... for the degree of doctor of philosophy [1932]" — Pref. "This book is one of a series from the Western Pennsylvania historical survey sponsored jointly by the Buhl foundation, the Historical society of western Pennsylvania, and the University of Pittsburgh." *1. Mississippi river — History. 2. Ohio river — History. 3. Transportation — Mississippi valley. 4. Boats and boating. I. Western Pennsylvania historical survey. II. T.*
F351.B18   977   41-10342

Dondore, Dorothy Anne, 1894-1946. III. 6650
The prairie and the making of middle America: four centuries of description. New York, Antiquarian Press, 1961. xiii, 472 p. illus., facsims. 21 cm. *1. Mississippi Valley — Description and travel. 2. American literature — History and criticism. I. T.*
F351.Dx   A64-5982

Roosevelt, Theodore, pres. U.S., 1858-1919. III. 6651
The winning of the West, by Theodore Roosevelt New York, The Current Literature Publishing Company, 1905. 6 v. fronts. 19 cm. *1. Mississippi valley — History. 2. Ohio valley — History. 3. Northwest, Old — History. 4. Louisiana — History. 5. Kentucky — History. 6. Tennessee — History. I. T.*
F351.R8x   A13-1434

Alvord, Clarence Walworth, 1868-1928. III. 6652
The Mississippi Valley in British politics; a study of the trade, land speculation, and experiments in imperialism culminating in the American Revolution. New York, Russell & Russell, 1959. 2 v. illus. 25 cm. *1. Mississippi Valley — History — To 1803. 2. Gt. Brit. — Colonies — America. I. T.*
F352.A47 1959   977   59-6233

Caldwell, Norman Ward, 1905- III. 6653
The French in the Mississippi Valley, 1740-1750, by Norman Ward Caldwell. Urbana, University of Illinois Press, 1941. 113 p. illus. (map) 27 cm. (Illinois studies in the social sciences, vol.XXVI, no. 3) *1. Mississippi valley — History. 2. French in the Mississippi valley. 3. France — Colonies — North America. I. T.*
F352.Cx (H31.I4 vol. 26, no. 3)   977   41-46101

Hennepin, Louis, 17th cent. III. 6654
Father Louis Hennepin's Description of Louisiana, newly discovered to the southwest of New France by order of the king; translated from the original edition by Marion E. Cross, with an introduction by Grace Lee Nute. [Minneapolis] Pub. for the Minnesota society of the Colonial dames of America, The University of Minnesota Press, 1938. xvii, 190 p. front. (port.) illus. (maps) facsim. 22 cm. Includes reproduction of t.-p. of the original edition, 1683. *1. Louisiana — Description and travel. 2. New France — Discovery and exploration. 3. Mississippi river — Discovery and exploration. 4. Mississippi valley — History — To 1803. 5. Indians of North America — Mississippi valley. I. Cross, Marion E., tr. II. National society of the colonial dames of America. Minnesota.*
F352.H564   917.7   38-38693

Ogg, Frederic Austin, 1878-1951. III. 6655
The opening of the Mississippi; a struggle for supremacy in the American interior. New York, Greenwood Press [1969] xi, 670 p. maps. 23 cm. Reprint of the 1904 ed. *1. Mississippi River — Discovery and exploration. 2. Mississippi Valley — History. I. T.*
F352.O34 1969c   977/.01   69-14017

Whitaker, Arthur Preston, 1895- III. 6656
The Mississippi question, 1795-1803; a study in trade, politics, and diplomacy, by Arthur Preston Whitaker New York, Appleton-Century [c1934] ix, 342 p. fold. map. 23 cm. At head of title: The American historical association. *1. Mississippi valley — History — To 1803. 2. Louisiana — History — Colonial period. I. American historical association. II. T.*
F352.W56   34-13409

III. 6657   *United States*   **F352**

Winsor, Justin, 1831-1897.   **III. 6657**
The westward movement; the Colonies and the Republic west of the Alleghanies, 1763-1798, with full cartographical illustrations from contemporary sources. New York, B. Franklin [1968] viii, 595 p. illus., maps, ports. 23 cm. (American classics in history & social science, 59. Burt Franklin research & source works series, 307.) "Originally published: 1897." *1. Mississippi Valley — History — To 1803. I. T.*
F352.W78 1968   977/.01   68-56583

Clemens, Samuel Langhorne, 1835-1910.   **III. 6658**
Life on the Mississippi, by Mark Twain (Samuel L. Clemens) With an introd. by Dixon Wecter. New York, Harper [1950] xvi, 526 p. 21 cm. (Harper's modern classics) *1. Mississippi River — Description and travel. 2. Mississippi Valley — Social life and customs. I. T.*
F353.C6456 1950   917.7 (817.44)   50-6261

Atherton, Lewis Eldon.   **III. 6659**
Main Street on the middle border. Bloomington, Indiana University Press, 1954. xix, 423 p. illus. 24 cm. *1. Middle West — Social life and customs. 2. City and town life. 3. Villages — Middle West. I. T.*
F354.A8   917.7   54-7970

Garland, John Henry, 1914- ed.   **III. 6660**
The North American Midwest, a regional geography. New York, Wiley [1955] viii, 252 p. maps, charts, diagrs. 27 cm. *1. Middle West — Description and travel. I. T.*
F354.G3   917.7   55-9845

Jensen, Richard J.   **III. 6661**
The winning of the Midwest: social and political conflict, 1888-1896 [by] Richard Jensen. Chicago, University of Chicago Press [1971] xvii, 357 p. 23 cm. *1. Middle West — Politics and government. I. T.*
F354.J4   309.1/77/03   71-149802   ISBN:0226398250

Kleppner, Paul.   **III. 6662**
The cross of culture; a social analysis of midwestern politics, 1850-1900. [2d ed.] New York, Free Press [1970] x, 402 p. 22 cm. *1. Middle West — Politics and government. 2. United States — Politics and government — 19th century. I. T.*
F354.K55   320.9/77   72-83365

Merrill, Horace Samuel.   **III. 6663**
Bourbon democracy of the Middle West, 1865-1896. Seattle, University of Washington Press [1967] xiv, 300 p. illus., ports. 23 cm. (Americana library, 2) Unabridged text of the 1953 ed., with a new introd. by the author. *1. Middle West — Politics and government. 2. United States — Politics and government. — 1865-1900. I. T.*
F354.M45 1967   329.3/0977   68-1509

F366 – 380   LOUISIANA

Howard, Perry H.   **III. 6664**
Political tendencies in Louisiana [by] Perry H. Howard. Rev. and expanded ed. Baton Rouge, Louisiana State University Press [1971] xxxvi, 476 p. maps. 24 cm. 1957 ed. published under title: Political tendencies in Louisiana, 1812-1952. *1. Louisiana — Politics and government. I. T.*
F369.H85 1971   320.9/763   74-123205   ISBN:0807109444

Giraud, Marcel, 1900-   **III. 6665**
Histoire de la Louisiane française. [1. éd.] Paris, Presses universitaires de France, 1953-   v. maps (part fold.) 23 cm. *1. Louisiana — History — Colonial period.*
F372.G5   976.3   54-23338

Shugg, Roger Wallace.   **III. 6666**
Origins of class struggle in Louisiana; a social history of white farmers and laborers during slavery and after, 1840-1875, by Roger W. Shugg. [Baton Rouge] Louisiana State University Press [1968] xiv, 372 p. 22 cm. (Louisiana paperbacks, L-36) *1. Louisiana — Social conditions. 2. Slavery in the United States — Economic aspects — Louisiana. 3. Plantations — Louisiana. I. T.*
F374.S58 1968   301.44/09763   74-1055   309.1763 S492

Kane, Harnett Thomas, 1910-   **III. 6667**
Louisiana hayride; The American rehearsal for dictatorship, 1928-1940, by Harnett T. Kane. New York, Morrow, 1941. viii, 471 p. plates, ports. 22 cm. *1. Long, Huey Pierce, 1893-1935. 2. Louisiana — Politics and government — 1865- I. T.*
F375.K16   41-7143

Sindler, Allan P.   **III. 6668**
Huey Long's Louisiana: State politics, 1920-1952. Baltimore, Johns Hopkins Press, 1956. xv, 316 p. maps, tables. 23 cm. *1. Long, Huey Pierce, 1893-1935. 2. Louisiana — Politics and government.*
F375.L846   976.3   56-11664

Writers' Program. Louisiana.   **III. 6669**
Louisiana; a guide to the state, compiled by workers of the Writers' Program of the Work Projects Administration in the state of Louisiana sponsored by the Louisiana Library Commission at Baton Rouge. New York, Hastings House, 1941. xxx, 746 p. illus., maps. plates. 21 cm. (American guide series) Maps on lining-papers. *1. Louisiana — Description and travel — Guide-books.*
F375.W8   917.63   41-52389

Liebling, Abbott Joseph, 1904-1963.   **III. 6670**
The Earl of Louisiana [by] A. J. Liebling. Baton Rouge, Louisiana State University Press [1970] 252 p. 23 cm. Portions originally appeared in the New Yorker. *1. Long, Earl Kemp, 1895-1960. 2. Louisiana — Politics and government — 1865-1950. I. T.*
F376.L6L5 1970   976.3/06/0924 (B)   76-130664   ISBN:0807105376

Federal Writers' Project. New Orleans.   **III. 6671**
New Orleans city guide. Rev. by Robert Tallant. Boston, Houghton Mifflin, 1952. lx, 416 p. illus., ports., map (on lining paper) 21 cm. (American guide series) *1. New Orleans. 2. New Orleans — Description — Guide-books.* (S)
F379.N5F34 1952   917.6335   52-14722

Soulé, Leon Cyprian.   **III. 6672**
The Know Nothing Party in New Orleans: a reappraisal. [Baton Rouge] Louisiana Historical Association [1962, c1961] 128 p. illus. 23 cm. *1. American Party. New Orleans. 2. New Orleans — Politics and government.*
F379.N5S7   329.509763355   61-18381

Jackson, Joy J.   **III. 6673**
New Orleans in the gilded age; politics and urban progress, 1880-1896 [by] Joy J. Jackson. [Baton Rouge] Published by Louisiana State University Press for the Louisiana Historical Association [1969] xi, 355 p. illus. 23 cm. *1. New Orleans — History. I. Louisiana Historical Association. II. T.*
F379.N557J3   309.1/763/355   70-89828   ISBN:80710910X

F381 – 395   TEXAS

Meinig, Donald William, 1924-   **III. 6674**
Imperial Texas; an interpretive essay in cultural geography, by D. W. Meinig. Introd. by Lorrin Kennamer. Austin, University of Texas Press [1969] 145 p. illus., maps. 25 cm. *1. Texas — Description and travel. 2. Texas — Population. I. T.*
F386.M35   301.29/764   69-18807   ISBN:292783817

Richardson, Rupert Norval, 1891-   **III. 6675**
Texas, the Lone Star State [by] Rupert Norval Richardson, Ernest Wallace [and] Adrian N. Anderson. 3d ed. Englewood Cliffs, N.J., Prentice-Hall [1970] xi, 448 p. illus., maps (part col.), ports. 24 cm. *1. Texas — History. I. Wallace, Ernest, joint author. II. Anderson, Adrian N., joint author. III. T.*
F386.R52 1970   976.4   70-92380   ISBN:139124365

Dobie, James Frank, 1888-   **III. 6676**
The flavor of Texas, by J. Frank Dobie, with illustrations by Alexander Hogue. Dallas, Dealey and Lowe, 1936. 287 p. illus. 23 cm. *1. Texas — Social life and customs. 2. Frontier and pioneer life — Texas. 3. Texas — History — Anecdotes. I. T.*
F387.D63   917.64   37-13369   D659

Barker, Eugene Campbell, 1874-1956.   **III. 6677**
The life of Stephen F. Austin, founder of Texas, 1793-1836; a chapter of the Westward movement by the Anglo-American people. New introd. by Seymour V. Connor. New York, Da Capo Press, 1968. ix, xv, 551 p. maps, ports. 24 cm. (The American scene. A Da Capo Press reprint edition.) "An unabridged republication of the first edition published ... in 1925." *1. Austin, Stephen Fuller, 1793-1836. 2. Texas — History — to 1846. I. T.*
F389.A936 1968   976.4/03/0924 (B)   68-27723

Bolton, Herbert Eugene, 1870-1953.   **III. 6678**
Texas in the middle eighteenth century; studies in Spanish colonial history and administration. New York, Russell & Russell, 1962. 501 p. illus. 23 cm. *1. Texas — History — To 1846. 2. Spain — Colonies — Administration. 3. Spain — Colonies — North America.*
F389.B75 1962   976.4   62-15151

Morfi, Juan Agustín, d. 1783.   **III. 6679**
History of Texas, 1673-1779, ... translated, with biographical introduction and annotations, by Carlos Eduardo Castañeda ... Albuquerque, The Quivira Society, 1935. 2 v. IV pl. (incl. front., facsims.) fold map. 26 cm. (Quivira society. Publications. vol.VI) Paged continuously. "Five hundred copies printed." *1. Texas — History — To 1846. 2. Indians of North America — Texas. 3. Indians of North America — Missions. 4. Missions — Texas. I. Castañeda, Carlos Eduardo, 1896- tr.*
F389.M72 (F786.Q8 vol. 6)   976.4   36-4006

Adams, Ephraim Douglass, 1865-1930.   **III. 6680**
British interests and activities in Texas, 1838-1846. Gloucester, Mass., P.

Smith, 1963 [c1910] viii, 13-267 p. 21 cm. (The Albert Shaw lectures on diplomatic history, 1909) 1. Texas — History — Republic, 1836-1846. 2. Texas — Annexation to the U.S. 3. Gt. Brit. — Foreign relations — Texas. 4. Texas — Foreign relations — Gt. Brit. 5. California — History — To 1846. I. T. (S)
F390.A208 1963   976.404   64-3505

Binkley, William Campbell, 1889-   III. 6681
The Texas Revolution. Baton Rouge, Louisiana State University Press [1952] viii, 131 p. 21 cm. (The Walter Lynwood Fleming lectures in southern history, Louisiana State University) 1. Texas — History — Revolution, 1835-1836. I. T. (S:Louisiana. State University and Agricultural and Mechanical College. Walter Lynwood Fleming lectures in southern history)
F390.B588   976.4   52-11548

Hogan, William Ransom, 1908-   III. 6682
The Texas republic; a social and economic history, by William Ransom Hogan. Norman, University of Oklahoma Press [1946] xiii, 338 p. illus., maps, plates, ports., facsims. 22 cm. 1. Texas — History — Republic, 1836-1846. 2. Texas — Social conditions. I. T.
F390.H6   976.4   46-8214

Houston, Samuel, 1793-1863.   III. 6683
The autobiography of Sam Houston, edited by Donald Day & Harry Herbert Ullom. [1st ed.] Norman, University of Oklahoma Press [1954] xviii, 298 p. illus., ports., maps. 25 cm. 1. Texas — History — Sources. I. Day, Donald, 1899- ed. II. Ullom, Harry Herbert, ed. III. T.
F390.H8474   923.273   54-10051

James, Marquis, 1891-1955.   III. 6684
The raven; a biography of Sam Houston. Dunwoody, Ga., N. S. Berg [1968, c1929] 489 p. illus., maps, ports. 23 cm. 1. Houston, Samuel, 1793-1863. I. T.
F390.H8494   976/.03/0924 (B)   68-2545

Merk, Frederick, 1887-   III. 6685
Slavery and the annexation of Texas. With the collaboration of Lois Bannister Merk. [1st ed.] New York, Knopf, 1972. xiii, 290, x p. 25 cm. 1. Texas — History — Republic, 1836-1846. 2. United States — Politics and government — 1841-1845. 3. United States — Politics and government — 1845-1849. I. T.
F390.M55   976.4/04   72-2229   ISBN:0394481046

Nance, Joseph Milton.   III. 6686
After San Jacinto; the Texas-Mexican frontier, 1836-1841. Austin, University of Texas Press [1963] xiv, 642 p. illus., ports., 4 fold. maps. 24 cm. 1. Texas — History — Republic, 1836-1846. 2. Texas — Foreign relations — Mexico. 3. Mexico — Foreign relations — Texas. I. T.
F390.N3   976.404   62-9789

Smith, Justin Harvey, 1857-1930.   III. 6687
The annexation of Texas. [1st AMS ed.] New York, AMS Press [1971] ix, 496 p. 23 cm. Reprint of the 1911 ed. 1. Texas — Annexation to the United States. I. T.
F390.S647 1971   976.4/04   77-175984   ISBN:0404061257

McKay, Seth Shepard, 1888-   III. 6688
Texas and the Fair Deal, 1945-1952. San Antonio, Naylor Co. [1954] 437 p. 22 cm. 1. Texas — Politics and government — 1865- I. T.
F391.M133   976.4   54-12959

McKay, Seth Shepard, 1888-   III. 6689
W. Lee O'Daniel and Texas politics, 1938-1942. [Lubbock, Texas Technological College Research Funds, 1944] 628 p. 24 cm. 1. O'Daniel, Wilbert Lee, 1890- 2. Texas — Politics and government — 1865- I. Texas technological college, Lubbock.
F391.O395   923.273   46-656

Olmsted, Frederick Law, 1822-1903.   III. 6690
A journey through Texas; or, A saddle-trip on the southwestern frontier, with a statistical appendix. New York, B. Franklin [1969] xxxiv, 516 p. 19 cm. (Burt Franklin research & source works series, 348. American classics in history & social science, 78) Reprint of the 1860 ed. 1. Texas — Description and travel. 2. Slavery in the United States — Texas. I. A saddle-trip on the southwestern frontier. II. T.
F391.O512 1969   917.64/04/5   69-18606

Webb, Walter Prescott, 1888-1963.   III. 6691
The Texas Rangers; a century of frontier defense. Illustrated with drawings by Lonnie Rees and with photos. Foreword by Lyndon B. Johnson. [2d ed.] Austin, University of Texas Press [1965] xx, 583 p. illus., facsims., ports. 24 cm. 1. Texas Rangers. 2. Frontier and pioneer life — Texas. 3. Texas — History.
F391.W43 1965   976.4   65-23166

Wheeler, Kenneth W.   III. 6692
To wear a city's crown; the beginnings of urban growth in Texas, 1836-1865 [by] Kenneth W. Wheeler. Cambridge, Mass., Harvard University Press, 1968. 222 p. illus., map, ports. 22 cm. 1. Cities and towns — Texas. 2. Texas — History. I. T.
F391.W57   917.64/03/4091732   68-28698

Writers' Program. Texas.   III. 6693
Texas; a guide to the Lone Star State. Harry Hansen, editor. New rev. ed. New York, Hastings House [1969] xxxiv, 717 p. illus., maps, ports. 22 cm. (American guide series) "Originally compiled by the Federal Writers' Program of the Work Projects Administration in the State of Texas." 1. Texas. 2. Texas — Description and travel. — Guide-books. 3. Automobiles — Road guides — Texas. I. Hansen, Harry, 1884- ed. (S)
F391.W95 1969   917.64/04/6   68-31690   ISBN:803870558

Horgan, Paul, 1903-   III. 6694
Great river: the Rio Grande in North American history. New York, Holt, Rinehart and Winston [c1954] 2 v. in 1. illus. 22 cm. 1. Rio Grande. 2. Rio Grande Valley — History. I. T.
F392.R5H65 1954a   976.44   60-14369

F396 – 475   Old Southwest. Lower Mississippi Valley

Dick, Everett, Newfon, 1898-   III. 6695
The Dixie frontier, a social history of the southern frontier from the first transmontane beginnings to the Civil War. [1st ed.] New York, A. A. Knopf, 1948. xix, 374, xxv p. illus. 22 cm. 1. Southwest, Old — History. 2. Frontier and pioneer life — Southwest, Old. I. T.
F396.D5   975   48-5379

New Spain and the Anglo-American west;   III. 6696
historical contributions presented to Herbert Eugene Bolton. [Los Angeles, Priv. Print., 1932] 2 v. front. (port.) 27 cm. "A documentary collection ... Volume I has been edited by Professors Charles W. Hackett ... George P. Hammond ... and J. Lloyd Mecham ... volume II by Professors William C. Binkley ... Cardinal Goodwin ... and J. Fred Rippy." — Pref. 1. Bolton, Herbert Eugene, 1870- 2. Southwest, Old — History — Sources. 3. Southwest, New — History — Sources. 4. Mexico — History — Spanish colony, 1540-1810.— Sources. 5. Spain — Colonies — North America. 6. The West — History — Sources. 7. U.S. — Territorial expansion. 8. Frontier and pioneer life — The West. I. Hackett, Charles Wilson, 1888- II. Hammond, George Peter, 1896- joint ed. III. Mecham, John Lloyd, 1893- joint ed. IV. Binkley, William Campbell, 1889- joint ed. V. Goodwin, Cardinal Leonidas, 1880- joint ed. VI. Rippy, James Fred, 1892- joint ed. VII. Ross, Mary, comp. VIII. The Anglo-American west, New Spain and.
F396.N58   978.004   33-3181

Whitaker, Arthur Preston, 1895-   III. 6697
The Spanish-American frontier, 1783-1795; the westward movement and the Spanish retreat in the Mississippi Valley. With an introd. by Samuel Eliot Morison. Lincoln, University of Nebraska Press [1969, c1927] viii, 255 p. maps. 21 cm. "A Bison book." 1. Southwest, Old — History. 2. Mississippi Valley — History. 3. Spain — Colonies — North America. I. T.
F396.W57 1969   976/.02   75-2465

F406 – 420   ARKANSAS

Fletcher, John Gould, 1886-   III. 6698
Arkansas. Chapel Hill, Univ. of North Carolina Press, 1947. x, 421 p. 24 cm. Map on lining-papers. 1. Arkansas — History.
F411.F5   976.7   47-30331

Writers' Program. Arkansas.   III. 6699
Arkansas; a guide to the state, compiled by workers of the Writers' Program of the Work Projects Administration in the state of Arkansas. Sponsored by C. G. Hall, secretary of state, Arkansas. New York, Hastings House, 1941. xxvii, 447 p. illus. (incl. maps) plates. 21 cm. (American guide series) Maps on lining-papers. The plates are in eight groups, each preceded by half-title not included in paging. "First published in 1941." 1. Arkansas. 2. Arkansas — Description and travel — Guide-books.
F411.W8   917.67   41-52931

Wilson, Charles Morrow, 1905-   III. 6700
Backwoods America; with illustrations by Bayard Wootten. Chapel Hill, The University of North Carolina Press [c1934] 209 p. front., plates. 23 cm. 1. Ozark mountains. 2. Mountain whites (Southern states) 3. Arkansas — Social

life and customs. 4. Missouri — Social life and customs. 5. Folk-lore — Ozark mountains. I. T.
F417.O9W5   917.67   35-27064

F431 – 445 TENNESSEE

Abernethy, Thomas Perkins, 1890-   III. 6701
From frontier to plantation in Tennessee; a study in frontier democracy. University, Ala., University of Alabama Press [1967] xi, 392 p. illus., maps. 21 cm. (Southern historical publications, no. 12) Reprint of the 1932 ed. *1. Tennessee — History. 2. Tennessee — Politics and government — To 1865. I. T. (S)*
F436.A17 1967   976.8/03   67-9183

Alexander, Thomas Benjamin, 1918-   III. 6702
Political reconstruction in Tennessee, by Thomas B. Alexander. New York, Russell & Russell [1968, c1950] 292 p. 23 cm. *1. Tennessee — Politics and government — 1865-1950. 2. Reconstruction — Tennessee. I. T.*
F436.A38 1968   976.8/05   68-25026

Crockett, David, 1786-1836.   III. 6703
The autobiography of David Crockett, with an introduction by Hamlin Garland. New York, Scribner [c1923] 328 p. 18 cm. (The modern student's library. American division.) Includes "Col. Crockett's exploits and adventures in Texas," a pseudoautobiography generally ascribed to Richard Penn Smith. *I. Smith, Richard Penn, 1799-1854. Col. Crockett's exploits and adventures in Texas. II. T.*
F436.C89   923.973   23-10909

Shackford, James Atkins.   III. 6704
David Crockett, the man and the legend. Edited by John B. Shackford. Chapel Hill, University of North Carolina Press [1956] xiv, 338 p. port., map (on lining papers) 24 cm. *1. Crockett, David, 1786-1836.*
F436.C9594   923.973   56-13913

Federal Writers' Project. Tennessee.   III. 6705
Tennessee; a guide to the State, comp. and written by the Federal Writers' Project of the Work Projects Administration for the State of Tennessee. New York, Hastings House [1949] xxiv, 558 p. illus., maps. 21 cm. (American guide series) "Sponsored by Department of Conservation, Division of Information." *1. Tennessee. 2. Tennessee — Description and travel — Guide-books. 3. Automobiles — Road guides — Tennessee. (S)*
F436.F45 1949   917.68   49-5822

Patton, James Welch, 1900-   III. 6706
Unionism and reconstruction in Tennessee, 1860-1869. Gloucester, Mass., P. Smith, 1966 [c1934] xii, 267 p. illus., port. 21 cm. *1. Brownlow, William Gannaway, 1805-1877. 2. Tennessee — History — Civil War. 3. Reconstruction — Tennessee. I. T.*
F436.P32 1966   976.804   66-8976

Arnow, Harriette Louisa (Simpson) 1908-   III. 6707
Seedtime on the Cumberland. New York, Macmillan, 1960. 449 p. illus. 24 cm. *1. Frontier and pioneer life — Tennessee. 2. Frontier and pioneer life — Kentucky. 3. Cumberland River. I. T.*
F442.2.A7   976.85   60-7414

Proudfoot, Merrill.   III. 6708
Diary of a sit-in. Foreword by Frank P. Graham. Chapel Hill, University of North Carolina Press [1962] 204 p. 21 cm. *1. Segregation — Knoxville, Tenn. 2. Negroes — Knoxville, Tenn. 3. Knoxville, Tenn. — Restaurants, lunch rooms, etc. I. T.*
F444.K7P95   301.45   62-16049

Capers, Gerald Mortimer, jr.   III. 6709
The biography of a river town; Memphis: its heroic age, by Gerald M. Capers, jr. Chapel Hill, The University of North Carolina Press, 1939. x, 292 p. illus., maps, plates, diagrs. 23 cm. This study was begun in the Graduate school of Yale university ... and was submitted to that university in 1936 ... for the degree of doctor of philosophy." — Foreword. *1. Memphis — History. I. T.*
F444.M5C3   976.8   39-27481

Miller, William D.   III. 6710
Mr. Crump of Memphis [by] William D. Miller. Baton Rouge, Louisiana State University Press, 1964. xiii, 373 p. illus., ports. 24 cm. (Southern biography series) "Critical essay on authorities": p. 353-359. *1. Crump, Edward Hull, 1874-1954. 2. Memphis — Politics and government. I. T. (S)*
F444.M5M66   923.273   64-21594

F446 – 460 KENTUCKY

Clark, Thomas Dionysius, 1903-   III. 6711
Kentucky, land of contrast, by Thomas D. Clark. [1st ed.] New York, Harper & Row [1968] xii, 304 p. maps (part col.) 22 cm. (A Regions of America book) *1. Kentucky — History. I. T.*
F451.C645   917.69/03   67-28804

Watlington, Patricia.   III. 6712
The Partisan spirit; Kentucky politics, 1779-1792. [1st ed.] New York, Atheneum, 1972. viii, 276 p. 22 cm. "Published for the Institute of Early American History and Culture at Williamsburg, Virginia." *1. Kentucky — Politics and government — To 1792. I. Institute of Early American History and Culture, Williamsburg, Va. II. T.*
F454.W3 1972   976.9/02   76-181463

Davenport, Francis Garvin, 1905-   III. 6713
Ante-bellum Kentucky, a social history, 1800-1860, by F. Garvin Davenport ... Oxford, O., The Mississippi Valley Press, 1943. xviii p., 1 l., 238 p. front. 24 cm. (Annals of America, v.5) *1. Kentucky — History. 2. Kentucky — Social life and customs. I. T.*
F455.D36   976.9   43-17548

Federal Writers' Project. Kentucky.   III. 6714
Kentucky; a guide to the Bluegrass State, compiled and written by the Federal Writers' Project of the Work Projects Administration for the State of Kentucky. Sponsored by the University of Kentucky. [Rev. ed.] New York, Hastings House [1954] xxix, 492 p. illus., maps. 22 cm. (American guide series) *1. Kentucky. 2. Kentucky — Description and travel — Guide-books. (S)*
F456.F44 1954   917.69   54-1591

F461 – 475 MISSOURI

A History of Missouri.   III. 6715
[William E. Parrish, general editor: the Missouri sesquicentennial ed. Columbia] University of Missouri Press [1971-   v. 25 cm. "Essay on sources": v. 1, p. 207-229. *1. Missouri — History. I. Parrish, William Earl, 1931- ed. II. Foley, William E., 1938- III. McCandless, Perry, 1917-*
F466.H58   977.8   76-155844   ISBN:0826201083 (v. 1)

McReynolds, Edwin C.   III. 6716
Missouri; a history of the Crossroads State. [1st ed.] Norman, University of Oklahoma Press [1962] xiv, 483 p. illus., ports., maps. 25 cm. *1. Missouri — History.*
F466.M2   977.8   62-18052

Mitchell, Franklin D.   III. 6717
Embattled democracy; Missouri democratic politics, 1919-1932 [by] Franklin D. Mitchell. Columbia, University of Missouri Press [1968] 219 p. 22 cm. (University of Missouri studies, v. 47) *1. Missouri — Politics and government — 1865-1950. I. T. (S:Missouri. University. The University of Missouri studies, v. 47)*
F466.M69   320.9/778   68-11347

Writers' Program. Missouri.   III. 6718
Missouri, a guide to the "Show Me" State, compiled by workers of the Writers' Program of the Work Projects Administration in the State of Missouri. New York, Duell, Sloan and Pearce. St. Clair Shores, Mich., Somerset Publishers, 1973 [c1941] 652 p. illus. 22 cm. Original ed. issued in series: American guide series. *1. Missouri. 2. Missouri — Description and travel — Guide-books. (S:American guide series.)*
F466.W85 1973   917.78/04/4   72-84486   ISBN:0403021758

Sauer, Carl Ortwin, 1889-   III. 6719
The geography of the Ozark highland of Missouri, by Carol O. Sauer. Chicago, Pub. for the Geographical Society of Chicago by the University of Chicago Press [1920] xviii, 245 p. illus., maps, plates, diagrs. 25 cm. (The Geographic Society of Chicago. Bulletin no. 7) Issued also as thesis University of Chicago. *1. Ozark mountains. I. T.*
F472.O9S2   20-2277

F476 – 485 Old Northwest. Northwest Territory

Bond, Beverley Waugh, 1881-   III. 6720
The civilization of the Old Northwest; a study of political, social, and

economic development, 1788-1812, by Beverley W. Bond, Jr. New York, Macmillan, 1934. St. Clair Shores, Mich., Scholarly Press, 1970. ix, 543 p. 22 cm. *1. Northwest, Old — Politics and government. 2. Northwest, Old — Economic conditions. 3. Northwest, Old — Social life and customs. I. T.*
F479.B69 1970b   309.1/77/02   77-144888   ISBN:0403008735

Caruso, John Anthony.   **III. 6721**
The Great Lakes frontier; an epic of the Old Northwest. Maps by Francis J. Mitchell. [1st ed.] Indianapolis, Bobbs-Merrill [1961] 432 p. maps. 24 cm. *1. Northwest, Old — History. I. T.*
F479.C3   977   60-12631

Ogg, Frederic Austin, 1878-   **III. 6722**
The Old Northwest; a chronicle of the Ohio valley and beyond, by Frederic Austin Ogg. New Haven, Yale University Press; [etc., etc.] 1921. ix, 220 p. col. front., fold. map. 18 cm. (The Chronicles of America series, v.19) "Roosevelt edition." *1. Northwest, Old — History. 2. Ohio valley — History.*
F479.O35   (E173.C56 vol. 19)   22-12141

Kellogg, Louise Phelps, ed.   **III. 6723**
Early narratives of the Northwest, 1634-1699, ed. by Louise Phelps Kellogg with a facsimile and two maps. New York, Scribner, 1917. xiv, 382 p. 2 fold. maps, facsim. 23 cm. (Original narrative of early American history) *1. America — Discovery and exploration — French. 2. Northwest, Old — Discovery and exploration. I. T.*
F482.K29   17-6235

Wainwright, Nicholas B.   **III. 6724**
George Croghan, wilderness diplomat. Chapel Hill, Published for the Institute of Early American History and Culture, at Williamsburg by the University of North Carolina Press [1959] 334 p. illus. 24 cm. *1. Croghan, George, d. 1782.*
F483.C76W3   923.273   59-2353

Sosin, Jack M.   **III. 6725**
Whitehall and the wilderness; the Middle West in British colonial policy, 1760-1775. Lincoln, University of Nebraska Press, 1961. xi, 307 p. maps. 24 cm. *1. Northwest, Old — History. 2. Gt. Brit. — Colonies — America. 3. Indians of North America — Government relations — To 1789. I. T.*
F483.S6   977   61-10152

Buley, Roscoe Carlyle.   **III. 6726**
The Old Northwest; pioneer period, 1815-1840. Bloomington, Indiana University Press, 1951 [c1950] 2 v. illus., ports., maps. 25 cm. *1. Northwest, Old — History.*
F484.3.B94 1951   977   52-6466

Hubbart, Henry Clyde, 1882-   **III. 6727**
The older Middle West, 1840-1880; its social, economic, and political life, and sectional tendencies before, during, and after the Civil War. New York, Russell & Russell, 1963 [c1936] 305 p. illus. 23 cm. At head of title: The American Historical Association. *1. Northwest, Old — History. 2. Northwest, Old — Social life and customs. I. American Historical Association. II. Middle West. III. T.*
F484.3.H885 1963   977   63-8364

Kohlmeier, Albert Ludwig.   **III. 6728**
The Old Northwest as the keystone of the arch of American federal union; a study in commerce and politics, by A. L. Kohlmeier. Bloomington, Ind., The Principia Press, 1938. v, 257 p. 24 cm. *1. Northwest, Old — History. 2. U.S. — History — 1815-1861. 3. U.S. — Commerce — History. 4. U.S. — Politics and government — 1815-1861. I. T.*
F484.3.K798   38-22330

Power, Richard Lyle, 1896-   **III. 6729**
Planting Corn Belt culture; the impress of the upland southerner and Yankee in the Old Northwest. Indianapolis, Indiana Historical Society, 1953. xvi, 196 p. illus., maps. 24 cm. (Indiana Historical Society. Publications, v.17) *1. Northwest, Old — Civilization. I. T. (S)*
F484.3.P6 (F521.I41 vol. 17)   977   54-618

Schoolcraft, Henry Rowe, 1793-1864.   **III. 6730**
Travels through the northwestern regions of the United States. Ann Arbor [Mich] University Microfilms [1966] xiv, 419 p. map, plates. 22 cm. (March of America facsimile series, no. 66) Original t.p. reads: Narrative journal of travels through the northwestern regions of the United States; extending from Detroit through the great chain of American lakes, to the sources of the Mississippi River. Performed as a member of the expedition under Governor Cass. In the year 1820. By Henry R. Schoolcraft ... With a map and eight copper plate engravings, Printed and published by E. & E. Hosford ... [1821] Added t.p. engraved. *1. Northwest, Old — Description and travel. 2. Great Lakes — Description and travel. 3. Mississippi River — Description and travel. I. T. (S)*
F484.3.S37 1821a   917.704   66-26336

F486 – 520   OHIO. OHIO VALLEY

Roseboom, Eugene Holloway, 1892-   **III. 6731**
A history of Ohio, by Eugene H. Roseboom and Francis P. Weisenburger. Edited and illustrated by James H. Rodabaugh. [Rev.] Columbus, Ohio State Archaeological and Historical Society, 1954 [c1953] xiii, 417 p. illus., ports., maps, facsims. 29 cm. *1. Ohio — History. I. Weisenburger, Francis Phelps, 1900- joint author.*
F491.R76 1954   977.1   56-1597

Wittke, Carl Frederick, 1892- ed.   **III. 6732**
The history of the state of Ohio, edited by Carl Wittke. Published under the auspices of the Ohio state archaeological and historical society. Publication committee: Harlow Lindley, chairman, Carl Wittke, William T. Utter. [Columbus, O., 1941-44] 6 v. illus., ports., facsims., maps (1 fold.) diagrs. (1 double) 24 cm. Each volume has also special t.-p. *1. Ohio — History. I. Bond, Beverley Waugh, 1881- II. Utter, William Thomas, 1895- III. Weisenburger, Francis Phelps, 1900- IV. Roseboom, Eugene Holloway, 1892- V. Jordan, Philip Dillon, 1903- VI. Lindley, Harlow, 1875- VII. Ohio state archaeological and historical society.*
F491.W78   977.1   41-7471

Bonadio, Felice A.   **III. 6733**
North of Reconstruction: Ohio politics, 1865-1870, by Felice A. Bonadio. New York, New York University Press, 1970. xi, 204 p. 24 cm. *1. Ohio — Politics and government — 1865-1950. 2. Reconstruction. I. T.*
F496.B6   320.9/771   72-92520   ISBN:0814700527

Johnson, Tom Loftin, 1854-1911.   **III. 6734**
My story. Edited by Elizabeth J. Hauser. Introd. by Melvin G. Holli. Seattle, University of Washington Press [1970, c1911] lvi, 326 p. illus., ports. 23 cm. (Americana library, 18) *1. Ohio — Politics and government — 1865-1950. 2. Cleveland — Politics and government. I. T.*
F496.J69 1970   977.1/32/040924 (B)   71-125181

Warner, Hoyt Landon.   **III. 6735**
Progressivism in Ohio, 1897-1917. [Columbus] Ohio State University Press for the Ohio Historical Society [1964] xiii, 556 p. 24 cm. A completely revised and rewritten version of the author's doctoral dissertation, Ohio's crusade for reform, 1897-1917, Harvard, 1950. *1. Ohio — Politics and government — 1865-1950. 2. Progressivism (U.S. politics) I. T.*
F496.W3   977.104   64-19164

Writers' Program. Ohio.   **III. 6736**
The Ohio guide, compiled by workers of the Writers' Program of the Work Projects Administration in the State of Ohio. Sponsored by the Ohio State Archaeological and Historical Society. New York, Oxford University Press. St. Clair Shores, Mich., Somerset Publishers, 1973. p. Reprint of the 1940 ed., issued in series: American guide series. *1. Ohio. 2. Ohio — Description and travel — Guide-books. I. T. (S:American guide series.)*
F496.W96 1973   917.71/04/4   72-84499   ISBN:0403021847

Barnhart, John Donald, 1895-   **III. 6737**
Valley of democracy: the frontier versus the plantation in the Ohio Valley, 1775-1818. Bloomington, Indiana University Press, 1953. x, 338 p. fold. map. 25 cm. *1. Ohio Valley — Politics and government. 2. Ohio Valley — Economic conditions. I. T.*
F517.B3   977   53-10020

James, Alfred Procter, 1886-   **III. 6738**
The Ohio Company, its inner history. [Pittsburgh] University of Pittsburgh Press [1959] xxiv, 375 p. 24 cm. *1. Ohio Company (1747-1779)*
F517.J3   977   58-7176

Wade, Richard C.   **III. 6739**
The urban frontier; the rise of western cities, 1790-1830. Cambridge, Harvard University Press, 1959. 362 p. 21 cm. (Harvard historical monographs, 41) *1. Cities and towns — Ohio Valley. 2. City and town life. I. T. (S)*
F518.W15   977   59-9285

F521 – 535   INDIANA

Thornbrough, Emma Lou.   **III. 6740**
Indiana in the Civil War era, 1850-1880. Indianapolis, Indiana Historical Bureau, 1965. xii, 758 p. illus., facsims., ports. 24 cm. (The History of Indiana, v.3) *1. Indiana — History. I. T. (S)*
F526.Hx (F526.H55 vol. 3)   66-63323

Phillips, Clifton Jackson.   **III. 6741**
Indiana in transition; the emergence of an industrial commonwealth, 1880-1920, by Clifton J. Phillips. Indianapolis, Indiana Historical Bureau,

III. 6742   **United States**   **F526**

1968. xiv, 674 p. illus., ports, maps. 24 cm. (The history of Indiana, v. 4) *1. Indiana — History. I. T.* (S)
F526.H55 vol. 4   917.72/03/4   71-15507

Writers' Program. Indiana.   **III. 6742**
Indiana, a guide to the Hoosier state, compiled by workers of the Writers' Program of the Work Projects Administration in the state of Indiana. Sponsored by the Department of public relations of Indiana State Teachers College. New York, Oxford University Press [1945] xxvi, 548 (i.e. 564) p. illus., plates, ports., maps (3 on fold. 1. in pocket] 21 cm. (American guide series) "First published in September 1941. Second printing, with corrections, 1945." *1. Indiana. 2. Indiana — Description and travel — Guide-books.*
F526.W93   917.72   46-5683

F536 – 550   ILLINOIS

Federal Writer's Project. Illinois.   **III. 6743**
Illinois; a descriptive and historical guide, compiled and written by the Federal Writer's Project of the Work Projects Administration for the State of Illinois. St. Clair Shores, Mich., Somerset Publishers, 1973. xxii, 687 p. illus. 22 cm. Original ed. issued in series: American guide series. "Sponsored by Henry Horner, governor." *1. Illinois — Description and travel — Guide-books. 2. Illinois — History. I. T.* (S:American guide series.)
F539.3.F4 1973   917.73/04   72-145010   ISBN:0403012929

Illinois. Centennial commission.   **III. 6744**
The centennial history of Illinois. Springfield, Centennial Commission, 1918-1920. 5 v. 23 cm. (Illinois centennial publications) Edited by C. W. Alvord. *1. Illinois — History. I. Alvord, Clarence Walworth, 1868-1928, ed.*
F541.Ix

Pease, Theodore Calvin, 1887-1948.   **III. 6745**
The story of Illinois. 3d ed., rev. by Marguerita Jenison Pease. Chicago, University of Chicago Press [1965] xvi, 331 p. illus., maps, ports. 21 cm. *1. Illinois — History. I. T.*
F541.P36 1965   977.3   65-17299

Altgeld, John Peter, 1847-1902.   **III. 6746**
The mind and spirit of John Peter Altgeld: selected writings and addresses. Edited by Henry M. Christman. Urbana, University of Illinois Press, 1960. 183 p. 24 cm. *1. Illinois — Politics and government — Addresses, essays, lectures. I. Christman, Henry M., ed.*
F546.A45   977.304   60-5349

Barnard, Harry, 1906-   **III. 6747**
Eagle forgotten; the life of John Peter Altgeld. New York, Duell, Sloan and Pearce [1948] 484 p. 21 cm. *1. Altgeld, John Peter, 1847-1902. I. T.*
F546.A45x   ~~923.273~~   A50-9082   977.3
                                         A1796

F548   Chicago

Mayer, Harold Melvin, 1916-   **III. 6748**
Chicago: growth of a metropolis [by] Harold M. Mayer and Richard C. Wade. With the assistance of Glen E. Holt. Cartography by Gerald F. Pyle. Chicago, University of Chicago Press [1969] ix, 510 p. illus., facsims., maps, plans, ports. 25 cm. *1. Chicago — History — Pictorial works. I. Wade, Richard C., joint author. II. T.*
F548.3.M37   917.73/11/03   68-54054   ISBN:226512738

Pierce, Bessie Louise, 1890-   **III. 6749**
A history of Chicago. 1st ed. New York, London, A. A. Knopf, 1937- v. illus., plates, maps, diagrs. 25 cm. At head of title: By Bessie Louise Pierce. *1. Chicago — History. I. T.*
F548.3.P54   977.31   37-8801

Gottfried, Alex.   **III. 6750**
Boss Cermak of Chicago; a study of political leadership. Seattle, University of Washington Press, 1962. 459 p. illus. 24 cm. *1. Cermak, Anton Joseph, 1873-1933. 2. Chicago — Politics and government. I. T.*
F548.5.C38   923.273   61-15063

Ginger, Ray.   **III. 6751**
Altgeld's America; the Lincoln ideal versus changing realities. Chicago, Quadrangle Books [1965, c1958] 376 p. 21 cm. (Quadrangle paperbacks, QP21) *1. Altgeld, John Peter, 1847-1902. 2. Chicago — History. I. T.*
F548.5.G45 1965   66-5630

Liebling, Abbott Joseph, 1904-   **III. 6752**
Chicago, the second city. Drawings by Steinberg. [1st ed.] New York, Knopf, 1952. 143 p. illus. 21 cm. *1. Chicago — Description.*
F548.5.L5   917.7311   52-8506

Merriam, Charles Edward, 1874-1953.   **III. 6753**
Chicago: a more intimate view of urban politics. New York, Arno Press, 1970 [c1929] 305 p. 23 cm. (The Rise of urban America) *1. Chicago — Politics and government — To 1950. 2. Chicago — Social conditions.* (S)
F548.5.M56 1970   309.1/773/11   71-112579   ISBN:0405024673

Zorbaugh, Harvey Warren, 1896-   **III. 6754**
Gold coast and slum: a sociological study of Chicago's Near North side, by Harvey Warren Zorbaugh. Chicago, Ill., University of Chicago Press [c1929] xv, 287 p. maps, diagrs. 20 cm. (The University of Chicago sociological series) *1. Chicago — Social conditions. 2. Chicago — Description — 1875-1950. I. T.*
F548.5.Z89   309.177311   29-12607

Walker, Daniel.   **III. 6755**
Rights in conflict; the violent confrontation of demonstrators and police in the parks and streets of Chicago during the week of the Democratic National Convention of 1968. A report submitted by Daniel Walker, director of the Chicago Study Team, to the National Commission on the Causes and Prevention of Violence. [Chicago, 1968] xiii, 88, 233 p. illus. 28 cm. Commonly known as the Walker report. Cover title. *1. Chicago — Riot, Aug. 1968. 2. Chicago — Police. 3. Democratic Party. National Convention, Chicago, 1968. I. Walker report on the violent confrontation of demonstrators and police in the parks and streets of Chicago. II. United States. National Commission on the Causes and Prevention of Violence. III. T.*
F548.52.W3   977.3/11/04   68-67375

Nelli, Humbert S., 1930-   **III. 6756**
Italians in Chicago, 1880-1930; a study in ethnic mobility [by] Humbert S. Nelli. New York, Oxford University Press, 1970. xx, 300 p. illus., maps. 22 cm. (The Urban life in America series) *1. Italians in Chicago. I. T.*
F548.9.I8N4   301.453/45/077311   76-123610

Drake, St. Clair.   **III. 6757**
Black metropolis; a study of Negro life in a northern city [by] St. Clair Drake and Horace R. Cayton. Rev. and enl. ed. New York, Harcourt, Brace & World [1970] 2 v. (lxx, 814 p.) illus., maps. 21 cm. (A Harbinger book, H 078-H 079) *1. Negroes — Chicago. 2. Negroes — Social conditions — To 1964. 3. Negroes — Economic conditions — Chicago. I. Cayton, Horace Roscoe, 1903- joint author. II. T.*
F548.9.N3D68 1970   ~~301.451/96/077311~~   73-12271   325.26
                                                         D769

Duncan, Otis Dudley.   **III. 6758**
The Negro population of Chicago; a study of residential succession [by] Otis Dudley Duncan and Beverly Duncan. [Chicago] University of Chicago Press [1957] xxiv, 367 p. maps (part fold.) diagrs., tables. 24 cm. (Monograph series of the Chicago Community Inventory of the University of Chicago) *1. Negroes — Chicago. 2. Negroes — Housing. I. Duncan, Beverly, joint author. II. T.*
F548.9.N3D8   325.260973   57-5271

Gosnell, Harold Foote, 1896-   **III. 6759**
Negro politicians; the rise of Negro politics in Chicago, by Harold F. Gosnell. With an introduction by Robert E. Park. Chicago, University of Chicago Press [1935] xxxi, 404 p. illus. (ports., maps) 24 cm. (Social science studies, directed by the Social science research committee of the University of Chicago. no. XXXII) *1. Negroes — Chicago. 2. Negroes — Politics and suffrage. 3. Chicago — Politics and government. I. T.*
F548.9.N3G67   325.26097731   35-15258

Spear, Allan H.   **III. 6760**
Black Chicago; the making of a Negro ghetto, 1890-1920 [by] Allan H. Spear. Chicago, University of Chicago Press [1967] xvii, 254 p. illus., col. maps, ports. 23 cm. *1. Negroes — Chicago — History. I. T.*
F548.9.N3S65   301.451/96/077311   67-21381

Tuttle, William M., 1937-   **III. 6761**
Race riot; Chicago in the Red Summer of 1919 [by] William M. Tuttle, Jr. [1st ed.] New York, Atheneum, 1970. ix, 305 p. illus., maps. 22 cm. (Studies in American Negro life) *1. Chicago — Riot, 1919. 2. Negroes — Chicago. I. T.*
F548.9.N3T8   977.3/11/04   71-130983

F549   East St. Louis

Rudwick, Elliott M.   **III. 6762**
Race riot at East St. Louis, July 2, 1917 [by] Elliott M. Rudwick. Foreword by Oscar Handlin. Carbondale, Southern Illinois University Press [1964] xvii, 300 p. illus., maps. 22 cm. *1. East St. Louis, Ill. — Riot, July, 1917. 2. Negroes — East St. Louis, Ill. I. T.*
F549.E2R8   301.451   64-13634

F561 – 575 MICHIGAN

Bald, Frederick Clever, 1897-   III. 6763
Michigan in four centuries. Line drawings by William Thomas Woodward. Rev. and enl. ed. New York, Harper [1961] 528 p. illus. 22 cm. *1. Michigan — History. I. T.*
F566.B2 1961   977.4   61-17179

Russell, Nelson Vance, 1895-   III. 6764
The British régime in Michigan and the Old Northwest, 1760-1796, by Nelson Vance Russell. Northfield, Minn., Carleton College [c1939] xi, 302 p. 23 cm. *1. Michigan — History. 2. Northwest, Old — History. I. T.*
F566.R87   977.4   40-6569

Writers' Program. Michigan.   III. 6765
Michigan, a guide to the Wolverine State. Compiled by workers of the Writers' Program of the Work Projects Administration in the State of Michigan. New York, Oxford University Press. St. Clair Shores, Mich., Somerset Publishers, 1973 [c1941] p. Original ed. issued in series: American guide series. *1. Michigan. 2. Michigan — Description and travel — Guide-books. I. T. (S:American guide series.)*
F566.W9 1973   917.74/04/4   72-84482   ISBN:0403021723

Kornhauser, Arthur William, 1896-   III. 6766
Detroit as the people see it; a survey of attitudes in an industrial city. Detroit, Wayne University Press, 1952 [i.e. 1953] xi, 221 p. map, diagrs., tables. 24 cm. A summary was published in 1952 under title: Attitudes of Detroit people toward Detroit. *1. Detroit. 2. Social surveys — Detroit. I. T.*
F574.D4K6   977.434   53-1343

Lee, Alfred McClung, 1906-   III. 6767
Race riot, by Alfred McClung Lee and Norman Daymond Humphrey. New York, Dryden Press, 1943. xi, 143 p. illus. (maps) diagr. 21 cm. *1. Negroes — Detroit. 2. U.S. — Race question. I. Humphrey, Norman Daymond, joint author. II. T.*
F574.D4L4   325.260774   43-17460

F576 – 590 WISCONSIN

Gara, Larry.   III. 6768
A short history of Wisconsin. Madison, State Historical Society of Wisconsin [1962] 287 p. illus. 22 cm. *1. Wisconsin — History.*
F581.G33   977.5   62-5389

Kellogg, Louise Phelps, d. 1942.   III. 6769
The French régime in Wisconsin and the Northwest. New York, Cooper Square Publishers, 1968. 474 p. illus., maps. 24 cm. (Publications of the State Historical Society of Wisconsin) Reprint of the 1925 ed. *1. Wisconsin — History — To 1848. 2. Northwest, Old — History — To 1775. 3. America — Discovery and exploration — French. 4. French in Wisconsin. I. T. (S:Wisconsin. State Historical Society. Publications)*
F584.K27 1968   977.5/01   68-31296

Margulies, Herbert F.   III. 6770
The decline of the progressive movement in Wisconsin, 1890-1920 [by] Herbert F. Margulies. Madison, State Historical Society of Wisconsin, 1968. ix, 310 p. 23 cm. *1. Wisconsin — Politics and government — 1848-1950. 2. Progressivism (U.S. politics) I. Wisconsin. State Historical Society. II. T.*
F586.M35   320.5/09775   68-63073

Thelen, David Paul.   III. 6771
The new citizenship; origins of progressivism in Wisconsin, 1885-1900 [by] David P. Thelen. [Columbia] University of Missouri Press [1972] 340 p. 25 cm. *1. Wisconsin — Politics and government — 1848-1950. 2. United States — Politics and government — 1865-1900. 3. Progressivism (U.S. politics) I. T.*
F586.T47   320.9/775/03   79-158075   ISBN:0826201113

Writers' Program. Wisconsin.   III. 6772
Wisconsin, a guide to the Badger State. Compiled by workers of the Writers' Program of the Work Projects Administration in the State of Wisconsin. New York, Duell, Sloan and Pearce. St. Clair Shores, Mich., Somerset Publishers, 1973 [c1941] 651 p. illus. 22 cm. Original ed. issued in series: American guide series. *1. Wisconsin — Description and travel — Guide-books. I. T. (S:American guide series.)*
F586.W97 1973   917.75/04/4   72-84517   ISBN:0403021987

Still, Bayrd.   III. 6773
Milwaukee, the history of a city. Madison, State Historical Society of Wisconsin, 1948. xvi, 638 p. illus., ports., maps. 25 cm. *1. Milwaukee — History.*
F589.M6S8   977.595   49-7868

F591 – 598 The West: General

Billington, Ray Allen, 1903-   III. 6774
The Far Western frontier, 1830-1860. [1st ed.] New York, Harper [1956] 324 p. illus. 22 cm. (The New American nation series) *1. The West — History. 2. Frontier and pioneer life — The West. 3. U.S. — Territorial expansion. I. T.*
F591.B55   978   56-9665

Conference on the History of Western America. 2d, Denver, 1962.   III. 6775
The American West, an appraisal; papers. Edited by Robert G. Ferris. Editorial advisers: LeRoy R. Hafen, Allen D. Breck [and] Robert M. Utley. Introd. by Ray A. Billington. Pref. by James Taylor Forrest. Santa Fe, Museum of New Mexico Press [c1963] viii, 287 p. 24 cm. *1. The West — History — Addresses, essays, lectures. 2. The West — History — Congresses. I. Ferris, Robert G., ed. II. T.*
F591.C75 1962   978.0082   63-22144

Dick, Everett Newfon, 1898-   III. 6776
The sod-house frontier, 1854-1890; a social history of the northern plains from the creation of Kansas & Nebraska to the admission of the Dakotas, by Everett Dick. New York, Appleton-Century, 1937. xviii, 550 p. front., plates, port. 23 cm. Maps on lining-papers. *1. The West — History. 2. Frontier and pioneer life — The West. I. T.*
F591.D54   37-19335

Gard, Wayne, 1899-   III. 6777
Frontier justice. [1st ed.] Norman, Univ. of Oklahoma Press, 1949. xi, 324 p. illus., ports., map. 22 cm. *1. The West — History. 2. Crime and criminals — The West. 3. Vigilance committees. I. T.*
F591.G215   978   49-10511

Goetzmann, William H.   III. 6778
Exploration and empire; the explorer and the scientist in the winning of the American West, by William H. Goetzmann. [1st ed.] New York, Knopf, 1966. xxii, 656, xviii p. illus., maps. 24 cm. *1. The West — Discovery and exploration. I. T.*
F591.G62   917.8   65-11123

Greever, William S.   III. 6780
The Bonanza West; the story of the Western mining rushes, 1848-1900. [1st ed.] Norman, University of Oklahoma Press [1963] 430 p. illus. 24 cm. *1. Mines and mineral resources — The West. 2. Frontier and pioneer life — The West. 3. Klondike gold fields. I. T.*
F591.G79   978   63-8991

Hafen, Le Roy Reuben, 1893-   III. 6781
Western America; the exploration, settlement, and development of the region beyond the Mississippi, by Le Roy R. Hafen and Carl Coke Rister. 2d ed. New York, Prentice-Hall, 1950. xviii, 695 p. illus., maps (part col.) 24 cm. (Prentice-Hall history series) *1. The West — History. 2. The West — Discovery and exploration. I. Rister, Carl Coke, 1889- joint author. II. T.*
F591.H2 1950   978   50-8267

Hinc, Robert V., 1921-   III. 6782
The American West; an interpretive history [by] Robert V. Hine. Boston, Little, Brown [1973] x, 371 p. illus. 23 cm. *1. The West — History. I. T.*
F591.H663   917.8/03   72-9004

Jonas, Frank H.   III. 6783
Politics in the American West. Edited by Frank H. Jonas. Salt Lake City, University of Utah Press [1969] 544 p. illus., maps. 26 cm. *1. The West — Politics and government. I. T.*
F591.J619   320.9/78   69-19308

Kraenzel, Carl Frederick, 1906-   III. 6784
The Great Plains in transition. [1st ed.] Norman, University of Oklahoma Press [1955] xiv, 428 p. illus., maps (1 fold. col.) diagrs., tables. 25 cm. *1. Great Plains. 2. Anthropo-geography — Great Plains.*
F591.K7   978   55-9628

Malin, James Claude, 1893-   III. 6785
The grassland of North America; prolegomena to its history, with addenda and postscript, by James C. Malin. Gloucester, Mass., P. Smith, 1967. viii, 490 p. 21 cm. *1. Anthropo-geography — The West. 2. Physical geography — The West. I. T.*
F591.M3 1967   917.8   67-4595

Paul, Rodman Wilson, 1912- III. 6786
Mining frontiers of the Far West, 1848-1880. New York, Holt, Rinehart and Winston [1963] 236 p. illus. 24 cm. (Histories of the American frontier) *1. Mines and mineral resources — The West. 2. Frontier and pioneer life — The West. I. T.*
F591.P3   978   63-8818

Paxson, Frederic Logan, 1877- III. 6787
When the West is gone, by Frederic L. Paxson. New York, P. Smith, 1941. 137 p. 20 cm. (Brown University, the Colver Lectures, 1929) "Copyright, 1930" *1. The West — History. 2. U.S. — Territorial expansion. 3. U.S. — Politics and government. 4. U.S. — Civilization. I. T.*
F591.P35 1941   978   41-24443

Riegel, Robert Edgar, 1897- III. 6788
America moves west [by] Robert E. Riegel [and] Robert G. Athearn. 5th ed. New York, Holt, Rinehart and Winston [1971] xiii, 599 p. illus., maps, ports. 25 cm. *1. The West — History. 2. Mississippi Valley — History. I. Athearn, Robert G., joint author. II. T.*
F591.R53 1971   978   72-113832   ISBN:0030843162

Root, Frank Albert, 1837-1926. III. 6789
The overland stage to California; personal reminiscences and authentic history of the great overland stage line and pony express from the Missouri River to the Pacific Ocean, by Frank A. Root and William Elsey Connelley. Glorieta, N.M., Rio Grande Press [1970, c1901] xvii, 645 p. illus., 2 fold. maps, ports. 29 cm. (A Rio Grande classic) Includes a new index and an additional map. *1. Overland journeys to the Pacific. 2. The West — Description and travel. I. Connelley, William Elsey, 1855-1930, joint author. II. T.*
F591.R68 1970   383/.143/0978   77-117484   ISBN:0873800494

Smith, Henry Nash. III. 6790
Virgin land; the American West as symbol and myth. Cambridge, Harvard University Press [1971, c1950] xviii, 305 p. illus. 21 cm. (A Harvard paperback, HP 21) *1. The West. 2. The West in literature. 3. American literature — 19th century — History and criticism. I. T.*
F591.S65 1971   917.8/03/2   75-30212   ISBN:0674939557

Webb, Walter Prescott, 1888-1963. III. 6791
The Great Plains. New York, Grosset & Dunlap [1957, c1931] 525 p. illus. 21 cm. (Grosset's universal library, UL-29) *1. Great Plains — History. 2. Mississippi Valley — History. I. T.*
F591.W35x   978   57-4356

Shannon, Fred Albert, 1893- III. 6792
An appraisal of Walter Prescott Webb's The great plains: a study in institutions and environment, by Fred A. Shannon, with comments by Walter Prescott Webb, a panel discussion, and a commentary by Read Bain. New York, Social Science Research Council [1940] xi, 254 p. 23 cm. (Critiques of research in the social sciences: III. Social science research council. Bulletin 46, 1940.) *1. Webb, Walter Prescott, 1888- The great plains. I. Bain, Read. II. T.*
F591.W36S5   978   41-10896

F592 – 595   BY PERIOD

Alter, J. Cecil, 1879- III. 6793
Jim Bridger. [New and rev. ed.] Norman, University of Oklahoma Press [1962] xi, 358 p. illus., port., maps. 25 cm. First published in 1925 under title: James Bridger, trapper, frontiersman, scout and guide. *1. Bridger, James, 1804-1881. 2. Frontier and pioneer life — The West.*
F592.B85 1962   923.973   62-16478

Estergreen, M. Morgan. III. 6794
Kit Carson, a portrait in courage. [1st ed.] Norman, University of Oklahoma Press [1962] 320 p. illus. 24 cm. *1. Carson, Christopher, 1809-1868.*
F592.C365   923.973   62-11274

Cleland, Robert Glass, 1885- III. 6795
This reckless breed of men; the trappers and fur traders of the Southwest. [1st ed.] New York, Knopf, 1950. xv, 361, xx p. illus., maps. 22 cm. *1. Fur trade — The West. 2. The West — History. 3. Southwest, New — History. I. T.*
F592.C62 1950   979   50-6356

Cline, Gloria Griffen. III. 6796
Exploring the Great Basin. [1st ed.] Norman, University of Oklahoma Press [1963] 254 p. illus. 24 cm. (The American exploration and travel series [39]) *1. Great Basin — Description and travel. 2. U.S. — Exploring expeditions. 3. Fur trade — The West. I. T.*
F592.C635   917.9   63-8988

De Voto, Bernard Augustine, 1897-1955. III. 6797
Across the wide Missouri; illus. with paintings by Alfred Jacob Miller, Charles Bodmer and George Catlin. With an account of the discovery of the Miller collection by Mae Reed Porter. Boston, Houghton Mifflin Co., 1947.

xxvii, 483 p. plates (part col.) maps (on lining-papers) 25 cm. *1. Fur trade — The West. 2. The West — History. I. Miller, Alfred Jacob, 1810-1874, illus. II. T.*
F592.D36 1947a   978   48-3175

De Voto, Bernard Augustine, 1897- III. 6798
The year of decision, 1846. Boston, Houghton Mifflin, 1950 [c1943] xv, 538 p. maps. 22 cm. *1. The West — History. 2. U.S. — History — 1815-1861. 3. U.S. — History — War with Mexico, 1845-1848. I. T.*
F592.D38 1950   978   50-11676

Parkman, Francis, 1823-1893. III. 6799
The Oregon Trail; sketches of prairie and Rocky-Mountain life. With biographical illus. and pictures of the setting of the book, together with an introd. by Harry Sinclair Drago. New York, Dodd, Mead [1964] xi, 337 p. illus., ports. 23 cm. First published in 1849 under title: The California and Oregon Trail. *1. The West — Description and travel. 2. Indians of North America — The West. 3. Frontier and pioneer life — The West. 4. Oregon Trail.*
F592.P284 1964   64-14819

Hollon, William Eugene, 1913- III. 6800
The lost pathfinder, Zebulon Montgomery Pike. [1st ed.] Norman, University of Oklahoma Press, 1949. xv, 240 p. illus., ports., map, facsim. 24 cm. (American exploration and travel [12]) *1. Pike, Zebulon Montgomery, 1779-1813. I. T. (S:The American exploration and travel series, 12)*
F592.P657   923.573   49-5390

Ruxton, George Frederick Augustus, 1820-1848. III. 6801
Life in the Far West; edited by Le Roy R. Hafen, with a foreword by Mae Reed Porter. [1st ed.] Norman, University of Oklahoma Press [1951] xviii, 252 p. illus. 24 cm. (American exploration and travel [14]) *1. The West — Description and travel. 2. Frontier and pioneer life — The West. 3. Hunting — The West. I. T. (S:The American exploration and travel series [14])*
F592.R983   917.8   51-1678

Turner, Frederick Jackson, 1861-1932. III. 6802
Rise of the new West, 1819-1829. Gloucester, Mass., P. Smith, 1961 [c1906] xviii, 366 p. port., maps (part fold. col.) 21 cm. (The American nation: a history, v.14) *1. The West — History. 2. Mississippi Valley — History — 1803-1865. 3. Oregon — History — To 1859. 4. U.S. — Politics and government — 1815-1861. (S:The American nation: a history (Gloucester, Mass.) v.14)*
F592.T87x (E178.A555 vol. 14)   978.102   61-43184

Cutright, Paul Russell, 1897- III. 6803
Lewis and Clark, pioneering naturalists. Urbana, University of Illinois Press, 1969. xiii, 506 p. illus., facsims., ports. 23 cm. *1. Lewis and Clark Expedition. 2. Natural history — Great Plains. 3. Natural history — Northwest, Pacific. I. T.*
F592.4 1969   917.8   69-11043   ISBN:252784227

Lewis, Meriwether, 1774-1809. III. 6804
Original journals of the Lewis and Clark Expedition, 1804-1806; printed from the original manuscripts in the library of the American Philosophical Society and by direction of its Committee on Historical Documents, together with manuscript material of Lewis and Clark from other sources, including note-books, letters, maps, etc., and the journals of Charles Floyd and Joseph Whitehouse, now for the first time published in full and exactly as written. Edited with introd., notes, and index, by Reuben Gold Thwaites. New York, Antiquarian Press, 1959. 8 v. illus. (part fold.) ports., maps (part fold.) facsims. 24 cm. Vol.8 has title: Atlas accompanying the original journals of the Lewis and Clark Expedition, 1804-1806, being facsimile reproductions of maps, chiefly by William Clark ... Now for the first time published, from the original manuscripts, together with a modern map of route ... *1. Lewis and Clark Expedition. 2. The West — Description and travel. 3. Missouri River. 4. Columbia River. I. Clark, William, 1770-1838, joint author. II. Thwaites, Reuben Gold, 1853-1913, ed.*
F592.4x   A62-8749

Bakeless, John Edwin, 1894- III. 6805
Lewis & Clark, partners in discovery. New York, W. Morrow, 1947. xii, 498 p. illus., ports., maps (1 fold. col.) 22 cm. *1. Lewis, Meriwether, 1774-1809. 2. Clark, William, 1770-1838. 3. Lewis and Clark Expedition. I. T.*
F592.7.B3   917.8   47-12243

Jackson, Donald Dean, 1919- ed. III. 6806
Letters of the Lewis and Clark Expedition, with related documents, 1783-1854. Urbana, University of Illinois Press [1962] xxi, 728 p. illus., ports., maps, facsims. 24 cm. *1. Lewis and Clark Expedition. 2. The West — History — Sources.*
F592.7.J14   917.8   62-7119

310

F594 – 595 1860 –

Athearn, Robert G. **III. 6807**
Westward the Briton. New York, Scribner, 1953. 208 p. illus. 25 cm. *1. The West — Description and travel. 2. Travellers, English. 3. National characteristics, American. I. T.*
F594.A85   917.8   53-11215

Bartlett, Richard A. **III. 6808**
Great surveys of the American West. [1st ed.] Norman, University of Oklahoma Press [1962] xxiii, 408 p. illus., ports., maps. 25 cm. (The American exploration and travel series [38]) *1. The West — Surveys. 2. The West — Discovery and exploration. 3. U.S. — Exploring expeditions. I. T. (S)*
F594.B28   557.8   62-16475

Pomeroy, Earl Spencer, 1915- **III. 6809**
In search of the golden West; the tourist in western America. [1st ed.] New York, Knopf, 1957. 233 p. illus. 22 cm. *1. The West — Description and travel. 2. Tourist trade — The West. I. T.*
F595.P78   917.8   57-5658

F596 – 597 FRONTIER AND PIONEER LIFE

Atherton, Lewis Eldon. **III. 6810**
The cattle kings. Bloomington, Indiana University Press [1961] 308 p. illus. 25 cm. *1. Cattle trade — The West. 2. Ranch life — The West. 3. The West — Biography. I. T.*
F596.A8   917.8   61-13722

Dale, Edward Everett, 1879- **III. 6811**
Cow country. Norman, University of Oklahoma Press, 1942. ix, 265 p. illus. 21 cm. A collection of essays which have been published in various periodicals during the past quarter of a century. cf. Pref. "First edition." *1. Frontier and pioneer life — The West. 2. Cowboys. 3. Cattle trade — The West. I. T.*
F596.D25   42-15483

Dale, Edward Everett, 1879- **III. 6812**
Frontier ways; sketches of life in the old West. Illus. by Malcolm Thurgood. Austin, University of Texas Press [c1959] 265 p. illus. 24 cm. *1. Frontier and pioneer life — The West. 2. Cowboys. 3. Ranch life. I. T.*
F596.D26   917.8   59-9423

Frantz, Joe Bertram, 1917- **III. 6813**
The American cowboy: the myth & the reality [by] Joe B. Frantz and Julian Ernest Choate, Jr. [1st ed.] Norman, University of Oklahoma Press [1955] 232 p. illus. 22 cm. *1. Cowboys. 2. Frontier and pioneer life — The West. 3. Cowboys in literature. I. Choate, Julian Ernest, 1916- joint author. II. T.*
F596.F75   978   55-9629

Gard, Wayne, 1899- **III. 6814**
The Chisholm Trail; with drawings by Nick Eggenhofer. [1st ed.] Norman, University of Oklahoma Press [1954] xi, 296 p. illus., ports., maps. 25 cm. *1. Chisholm Trail. 2. Cattle trade — The West.*
F596.G3   917.64   54-6204

Ross, Nancy Wilson, 1905- **III. 6815**
Westward the women. Freeport, N.Y., Books for Libraries Press [1970, c1944] 199 p. 23 cm. (Essay index reprint series) *1. Women in the West. 2. Frontier and pioneer life — The West. I. T.*
F596.R82 1970   978   76-117832   ISBN:836918460

Sonnischen, Charles Leland, 1901- **III. 6816**
Cowboys and cattle kings; life on the range today. [1st ed.] Norman, University of Oklahoma Press [1950] xviii, 316 p. illus., ports. 24 cm. *1. Cowboys. 2. Ranch life. 3. Cattle trade — The West. I. T.*
F596.S72   978   50-14081

Westermeier, Clifford Peter, 1910- ed. **III. 6817**
Trailing the cowboy, his life and lore as told by frontier journalists. Caldwell, Idaho, Caxton Printers, 1955. 414 p. illus. 22 cm. *1. Cowboys. I. T.*
F596.W5   917.8   55-6757

Prucha, Francis Paul. **III. 6818**
Broadax and bayonet; the role of the United States Army in the development of the Northwest, 1815-1860. [Madison] State Historical Society of Wisconsin [c1953] xii, 263 p. illus., ports., map (on lining papers) 24 cm. *1. U.S. Army — History. 2. Northwestern States — History. 3. Frontier and pioneer life — Northwestern States. I. T.*
F597.P7   977   53-6511

Sharp, Paul Frederick, 1918- **III. 6819**
Whoop-Up country; the Canadian-American West, 1865-1885. Minneapolis, University of Minnesota Press [1955] 347 p. illus. 23 cm. *1. Frontier and pioneer life — Northwestern States. 2. Frontier and pioneer life — Northwest, Canadian. 3. U.S. — Relations (general) with Canada. 4. Canada — Relations (general) with the U.S. I. T.*
F597.S35   978   55-11710

F598 MISSOURI VALLEY

Baumhoff, Richard G., 1899- **III. 6820**
The dammed Missouri Valley, one sixth of our Nation. [1st ed.] New York, Knopf, 1951. 291 p. illus. 22 cm. *1. Missouri Valley. I. T.*
F598.B3   333.91   51-11082

Briggs, Harold Edward, 1896- **III. 6821**
Frontiers of the Northwest; a history of the upper Missouri valley, by Harold E. Briggs. New York, London, D. Appleton-Century, 1940. xiv, 629 p. illus., maps, plates, 4 port. on 1 pl. 23 cm. Map on lining-papers. *1. Northwestern states — History. 2. Frontier and pioneer life — Northwestern states. 3. Missouri valley — History. I. T.*
F598.B84   978   40-12572

F601 – 705 Northwestern States
F601 – 630 MINNESOTA. IOWA

Blegen, Theodore Christian, 1891- **III. 6822**
Minnesota history; a guide to reading and study, by Theodore C. Blegen and Theodore L. Nydahl. Minneapolis, University of Minnesota Press [1960] 223 p. maps. 24 cm. A revision of the author's Minnesota, its history and its people, published in 1937. *1. Minnesota — History — Outlines, syllabi, etc. 2. Minnesota — History — Bibliography. I. Nydahl, Theodore L., joint author.*
F606.B672 1960   977.6002   60-14287

Chrislock, Carl Henry. **III. 6823**
The progressive era in Minnesota, 1899-1918, by Carl H. Chrislock. St. Paul, Minnesota Historical Society, 1971. xiii, 242 p. illus. 24 cm. (Minnesota Historical Society. Public Affairs Center. Publications) *1. Minnesota — Politics and government — 1858-1950. 2. Progressivism (U.S. politics) I. T. (S)*
F606.C477   320.9/776/05   79-178677   ISBN:0873410674

Federal Writers' Project. Minnesota. **III. 6824**
Minnesota, a State guide. Sponsored by the Executive Council, State of Minnesota. [Rev. ed.] New York, Hastings House [1954] xxx, 545 p. illus., maps. 21 cm. (American guide series) *1. Minnesota. 2. Minnesota — Description and travel — Guide-books. (S)*
F606.F44 1954   917.76   54-589

Shannon, James P. **III. 6825**
Catholic colonization on the western frontier. New Haven, Yale University Press, 1957. xiii, 302 p. illus., maps, facsims. 25 cm. (Yale publications in American studies, 1) *1. Ireland, John, Abp., 1838-1918. 2. Catholics in Minnesota. 3. Agricultural colonies — Minnesota. 4. Frontier and pioneer life — Minnesota. I. T. (S)*
F615.C3S45   977.6   57-6876

Federal Writers' Project. Iowa. **III. 6826**
Iowa, a guide to the Hawkeye State. New York, Hastings House [1949] xxviii, 583 p. illus., port., maps. 21 cm. (American guide series) "Sponsored by the State Historical Society of Iowa to commemorate the centenary of the organization of Iowa Territory." *1. Iowa — Description and travel — Guide-books. 2. Iowa. (S)*
F621.F45 1949   917.77   49-5480

F631 – 660 NORTH DAKOTA. SOUTH DAKOTA

Federal Writers' Project. North Dakota. **III. 6827**
North Dakota, a guide to the northern prairie state. [2d ed.] New York, Oxford University Press, 1950. xix, 352 p. illus., ports., maps. 21 cm. (American guide series) "Sponsored by the State Historical Society of North

Dakota." *1. North Dakota. 2. North Dakota — Description and travel — Guide-books. (S)*
F636.F45 1950   917.84   50-9076

Robinson, Elwyn B.　　　　　　　　　　　　　　　　III. 6828
History of North Dakota, by Elwyn B. Robinson. Line drawings by Jack Brodie. Lincoln, University of Nebraska Press, 1966. xi, 599 p. illus., maps, ports. 24 cm. *1. North Dakota — History. I. T.*
F636.R6   978.4   66-10877

Schell, Herbert Samuel, 1899-　　　　　　　　　　III. 6829
History of South Dakota, by Herbert S. Schell. Line drawings by Jack Brodie. [2d ed., rev.] Lincoln, University of Nebraska Press, 1968. xiii, 444 p. illus., maps (on lining papers), ports. 24 cm. *1. South Dakota — History. I. T.*
F651.S29 1968   978.3   68-6401

Lamar, Howard Roberts.　　　　　　　　　　　　　III. 6830
Dakota Territory, 1861-1889; a study of frontier politics. New Haven, Yale University Press, 1956. x, 304 p. ports., maps, facsim. 25 cm. (Yale historical publications. Miscellany 64) "Originally prepared as a doctoral dissertation at Yale University." *1. Dakota — Politics and government. I. T. (S)*
F655.L25   978.3   56-10098

Federal Writers' Project. South Dakota.　　　　　III. 6831
South Dakota, a guide to the State. 2d ed. completely revised by M. Lisle Reese. New York, Hastings House [1952] xxvii, 421 p. illus., maps. 21 cm. (American guide series) "Sponsored by the State of South Dakota." "Both an enlargement and sequel to ... South Dakota guide which was published in 1938." *1. South Dakota. 2. South Dakota — Description and travel — Guide-books. (S)*
F656.F45 1952   917.83   52-7601

F661 – 690　NEBRASKA. KANSAS

Federal Writers' Project. Nebraska.　　　　　　　III. 6832
Nebraska, a guide to the Cornhusker State. Sponsored by the Nebraska State Historical Society. New York, Hastings House [1947] xxiii, 424 p. illus., maps (1 fold. in pocket) 21 cm. (American guide series) *1. Nebraska — Description and travel — Guide-books. 2. Automobiles — Road guides. I. T. (S)*
F666.F46 1947   917.82   48-1227

Olson, James C.　　　　　　　　　　　　　　　　III. 6833
History of Nebraska, by James C. Olson. Line drawings by Franz Altschuler. Additional line drawings by Jack Brodie. [2d ed.] Lincoln, University of Nebraska Press, 1966. xii, 387 p. illus., maps, ports. 24 cm. *1. Nebraska — History. I. T.*
F666.O48 1966   978.2   67-8965

Sandoz, Mari, 1896-1966.　　　　　　　　　　　　III. 6834
Old Jules. 20th anniversary ed. New York, Hastings House [1955, c1935] 424 p. illus. 22 cm. *1. Sandoz, Jules Ami, 1857?-1928. 2. Frontier and pioneer life — Nebraska. I. T.*
F666.Sx   923.973   55-7948

Rich, Everett, ed.　　　　　　　　　　　　　　　III. 6835
The heritage of Kansas, selected commentaries on past times. Lawrence, University of Kansas Press, 1960. 359 p. 24 cm. *1. Kansas — History — Addresses, essays, lectures. 2. Frontier and pioneer life — Kansas.*
F681.R5   978.10082   60-9210

Zornow, William Frank.　　　　　　　　　　　　III. 6836
Kansas; a history of the Jayhawk State. [1st ed.] Norman, University of Oklahoma Press [1957] 417 p. illus. 25 cm. *1. Kansas — History.*
F681.Z6   978.1   57-7334

Malin, James Claude, 1893-　　　　　　　　　　III. 6837
John Brown and the legend of fifty-six by James C. Malin. New York, Haskell House, 1971. 2 v. (xii, 794 p.) facsims., maps. 24 cm. *1. Brown, John, 1800-1859. 2. Kansas — History — 1854-1861.*
F685.B877M3 1971   973.6/8/0924   70-117588   ISBN:0838310214

Johnson, Samuel A.　　　　　　　　　　　　　　III. 6838
The battle cry of freedom; the New England Emigrant Aid Company in the Kansas crusade. Lawrence, University of Kansas Press, 1954. 357 p. illus.,ports., maps. 24 cm. *1. New England Emigrant Aid Company, Boston. 2. Kansas — History — 1854-1861. I. T.*
F685.J75   978.1   54-11612

Federal Writers' Project. Kansas.　　　　　　　　III. 6839
Kansas; a guide to the Sunflower State, comp. and written by the Federal Writers' Project of the Work Projects Administration for the State of Kansas. New York, Hastings House [1949] xviii, 538 p. illus., maps. 21 cm. (American guide series) "Sponsored by State Department of Education." *1. Kansas. 2. Kansas — Description and travel — Guide-books. 3. Automobiles — Road guides — Kansas. (S)*
F686.F45 1949   917.81   49-5821

McCoy, Donald R.　　　　　　　　　　　　　　　III. 6840
Landon of Kansas [by] Donald R. McCoy. Lincoln, University of Nebraska Press [1966] x, 607 p. illus., ports. 24 cm. *1. Landon, Alfred Mossman, 1887- I. T.*
F686.L26   329.6/00924   65-16190

F691 – 705　OKLAHOMA

Dale, Edward Everett, 1879-　　　　　　　　　　III. 6841
History of Oklahoma, by Edward Everett Dale and Morris L. Wardell. New York, Prentice-Hall, 1948. x, 572 p. illus., maps (1 fold. col.) 21 cm. *1. Oklahoma — History. I. Wardell, Morris L., 1889- joint author.*
F694.D128   976.6   48-7592

McReynolds, Edwin C.　　　　　　　　　　　　　III. 6842
Oklahoma; the story of its past and present, by Edwin C. McReynolds, Alice Marriott [and] Estelle Faulconer. Rev. ed. Norman, University of Oklahoma Press [1971] xx, 499 p. illus. 24 cm. *1. Oklahoma — History. I. Marriott, Alice Lee, 1910- joint author. II. Faulconer, Estelle, joint author. III. T.*
F694.M17 1971   976.6   79-32120   ISBN:0806905097

Ruth, Kent, ed.　　　　　　　　　　　　　　　　III. 6843
Oklahoma; a guide to the Sooner State, compiled by Kent Ruth and the staff of the University of Oklahoma Press, with articles by leading authorities, and photographic sections arranged by J. Eldon Peek. [Rev. ed.] Norman, University of Oklahoma Press [1957] xxxv, 532 p. illus., ports., maps (1 fold.) 21 cm. First ed. compiled in 1941 by the Writers' Program of the Work Projects Administration in the State of Oklahoma. *1. Oklahoma. 2. Oklahoma — Description and travel — Guide-books. I. Oklahoma. University. Press. II. Writers' Program. Oklahoma. Oklahoma; a guide to the Sooner State.*
F694.R8   917.66   57-7333

Rister, Carl Coke, 1889-　　　　　　　　　　　　III. 6844
Land hunger: David L. Payne and the Oklahoma boomers, by Carl Coke Rister. Norman, University of Oklahoma Press, 1942. xiii, 245 p. front., illus., maps, plates, ports., facsims. 24 cm. *1. Payne, David Lewis, 1836-1884. 2. Oklahoma — History. I. T.*
F697.P35   976.6   43-1028

Debo, Angie, 1890-　　　　　　　　　　　　　　III. 6845
Oklahoma, foot-loose and fancy-free. [1st ed.] Norman, University of Oklahoma Press, 1949. xi, 258 p. illus., ports., map. 23 cm. *1. Oklahoma — Description and travel.*
F700.D4   917.66   49-48798

Bryant, Keith L.　　　　　　　　　　　　　　　　III. 6846
Alfalfa Bill Murray, by Keith L. Bryant, Jr. [1st ed.] Norman, University of Oklahoma Press [1968] xiii, 287 p. illus., maps, ports. 24 cm. *1. Murray, William Henry, 1869-1956. I. T.*
F700.M697   976.6/05/924 (B)   68-10299

F721　Rocky Mountain States

Peirce, Neal R.　　　　　　　　　　　　　　　　III. 6847
The Mountain States of America: people, politics, and power in the eight Rocky Mountain States [by] Neal R. Peirce. [1st ed.] New York, Norton [1972] 317 p. illus. 24 cm. *1. Rocky Mountain region. I. T.*
F721.P45 1972   917.8/03/3   72-437   ISBN:0393052559

F726 – 755　MONTANA. IDAHO

Federal Writers' Project. Montana.　　　　　　　III. 6848
Montana, a State guide book. New York, Hastings House [1949] xxiii, 430 p. illus., port., maps. 21 cm. (American guide series) "Sponsored by Department of Agriculture, Labor and Industry, State of Montana." *1. Montana. 2. Montana — Description and travel — Guide-books. 3. Automobiles — Road guides — Montana. (S)*
F731.F44 1949   917.86   49-5522

Hamilton, James McLellan. III. 6849
From wilderness to statehood; a history of Montana, 1805-1900. Foreword by A. L. Strand; edited by Merrill G. Burlingame. Pen sketches by Betty G. Ryan. Portland, Or., Binfords & Mort [1957] 620 p. illus. 25 cm. *1. Montana — History. I. T.*
F731.H28   978.6   57-9233

Howard Joseph Kinsey, 1906-1951. III. 6850
Montana: high, wide, and handsome. Pref. by A. B. Guthrie, Jr. Drawings by Peter Hurd. New illustrated ed. New Haven, Yale University Press, 1959. 347 p. illus. 24 cm. *1. Montana — History. I. T.*
F731.H86 1959   978.6   59-9606

Toole, Kenneth Ross, 1920- III. 6851
Twentieth-century Montana: a State of extremes, by K. Ross Toole. [1st ed.] Norman, University of Oklahoma Press [1972] xix, 307 p. illus. 21 cm. *1. Montana — History. I. T.*
F731.T66   978.6/03   75-177348   ISBN:0806109920

Writers' Program. Montana. III. 6852
Copper camp; stories of the world's greatest mining town, Butte, Montana, compiled by workers of the Writers' Program of the Work Projects Administration in the state of Montana. New York, Hastings House [1943] x, 308 p. illus., plates, ports. 21 cm. "First published in 1943." *1. Butte, Mont. — History. I. T.*
F739.B8W7   978.6   43-12488

Donaldson, Thomas Corwin, 1843-1898. III. 6853
Idaho of yesterday. Introd. by Thomas B. Donaldson. Westport, Conn., Greenwood Press [1970, c1941] 406 p. illus., facsims., ports. 23 cm. *1. Idaho — History. 2. Frontier and pioneer life — Idaho. I. T.*
F746.D6 1970   979.6   70-104218   ISBN:837133351

Federal Writers' Project. Idaho. III. 6854
Idaho, a guide in word and picture. [2d ed. rev.] New York, Oxford University Press, 1950. xiv, 300 p. illus., map (on lining paper) 21 cm. (American guide series) "Sponsored by the Secretary of State of Idaho." *1. Idaho. 2. Idaho — Description and travel — Guide-books. I. T. (S)*
F746.F453   917.96   50-13175

Malone, Michael P. III. 6855
C. Ben Ross and the New deal in Idaho, by Michael P. Malone. Seattle, University of Washington Press [1970] xxiii, 191 p. ports. 22 cm. *1. Ross, Charles Benjamin. 2. Idaho — Politics and government. I. T.*
F746.M3   320.9/796   (B)   69-14207   ISBN:295950689

F756 – 785 WYOMING. COLORADO

Gould, Lewis L. III. 6856
Wyoming; a political history, 1868-1896, by Lewis L. Gould. New Haven, Yale University Press, 1968. xiii, 298 p. map (on lining papers), port. 23 cm. (Yale Western Americana series, 20) *1. Wyoming — Politics and government. I. T. (S)*
F761.G6   320.9/787   68-27754

Larson, Taft Alfred, 1910- III. 6857
History of Wyoming, by T. A. Larson. Line drawings by Jack Brodie. Lincoln, University of Nebraska Press, 1965. xi, 619 p. illus., maps, ports. 24 cm. *1. Wyoming — History. I. T.*
F761.L3   978.7   65-15277

Writers' program. Wyoming. III. 6858
Wyoming; a guide to its history, highways, and people, compiled by workers of the Writers' program of the Work projects administration in the state of Wyoming. Sponsored by Dr. Lester C. Hunt, secretary of state. New York, Oxford University Press [c1941] xxvii, 490 p. illus., plates, ports, maps (4 on fold. l., in pocket) 21 cm. (American guide-series) Map on lining-paper. The plates are in eight groups, each preceded by half-title not included in paging. "First published in April 1941." *1. Wyoming. 2. Wyoming — Description and travel — Guide-books. I. T.*
F761.W58   917.87   41-52444

Writers' Program. Colorado. III. 6859
Colorado; a guide to the highest State. Compiled by workers of the Writers' Program of the Work Projects Administration in the State of Colorado. New York, Hastings House. St. Clair Shores, Mich., Somerset Publishers, 1973. xxxiii, 511 p. illus. 22 cm. Reprint of the 1948 ed. issued in series: American guide series. *1. Colorado — Description and travel — Guide-books. I. T. (S:American guide series.)*
F774.3.W74 1973   917.88/04/3   72-84463   ISBN:0403021588

Hafen, Le Roy Reuben, 1893- III. 6860
Colorado; the story of a western commonwealth, by LeRoy R. Hafen. New York, AMS Press [1970] 328 p. illus., maps, ports. 23 cm. Reprint of the 1933 ed. *1. Colorado — History. I. T.*
F776.H13 1970   978.8   78-100528   ISBN:0404006043

Henderson, Junius, 1865-1937. III. 6861
Colorado: short studies of its past and present, by Junius Henderson [and others] New York, AMS Press [1969] x, 202 p. 23 cm. Reprint of the 1927 ed. *1. Colorado — History.*
F776.H5 1969   978.8   73-100508

Ubbelohde, Carl. III. 6862
A Colorado history. Boulder, Colo., Pruett Press [c1965] x, 339 p. illus., col. map. 24 cm. *1. Colorado — History. I. T.*
F776.U195   978.8   65-27239

F786 – 850 New Southwest. Colorado River

Bender, Averam Burton, 1891- III. 6863
The march of empire; frontier defense in the Southwest, 1848-1860. Lawrence, University of Kansas Press, 1952. 323 p. illus., map. 24 cm. *1. Southwest, New — History, Military. 2. Frontier and pioneer life — U.S. 3. Southwest, New — Defenses. I. T.*
F786.B45   979   52-10553

Dobie, James Frank, 1888- III. 6864
Coronado's children; tales of lost mines and buried treasures of the Southwest. Illustrated by Ben Carlton Mead. New York, Grosset & Dunlap [1961, c1930] 367 p. illus. 24 cm. *1. Southwest, New. 2. Legends — Southwest, New. 3. Mines and mineral resources — Southwest, New. I. Lost mines and buried treasures of the Southwest. II. Buried treasures of the Southwest. III. T.*
F786.Dx   978   Cd62-206

Faulk, Odie B. III. 6865
Land of many frontiers; a history of the American Southwest [by] Odie B. Faulk. New York, Oxford University Press, 1968. x, 358 p. maps. 22 cm. *1. Southwest, New — History. I. T.*
F786.F337   979.1   68-29719

Garber, Paul Neff, 1899- III. 6866
The Gadsden treaty. Gloucester, Mass., P. Smith, 1959 [c1923] 222 p. illus. 21 cm. Reprint of thesis — University of Pennsylvania. *1. Gadsden treaty, 1853. 2. U.S. — Boundaries — Mexico. 3. Mexico — Boundaries — U.S. 4. U.S. — Foreign relations — Mexico. 5. Mexico — Foreign relations — U.S.*
F786.Gx   973.66   A63-5116

Hollon, William Eugene, 1913- III. 6867
The Southwest: old and new. [1st ed.] New York, Knopf, 1961. xiv, 486, [1], xviii p. illus., ports., maps. 25 cm. *1. Southwest, New — History. I. T.*
F786.H6   979   61-9232

Lamar, Howard Roberts. III. 6868
The far Southwest, 1846-1912; a territorial history. New Haven, Yale University Press, 1966. xii, 560 p. illus., fold. map, ports. 25 cm. (Yale Western Americana series, 12) *1. Southwest, New — History. I. T. (S)*
F786.L27   979.104   66-12505

McWilliams, Carey, 1905- III. 6869
North from Mexico; the Spanish-speaking people of the United States. With an introd. to the Greenwood reprint ed. by the author. New York, Greenwood Press, 1968 [c1948] 324 p. map. 23 cm. *1. Southwest, New — History. 2. Mexican Americans. I. T.*
F786.M215 1968   301.453/72/0791   68-28595

Robertson, Frank Chester, 1890- III. 6870
Boom towns of the Great Basin [by] Frank C. Robertson and Beth Kay Harris. Denver, Sage Books [1962] 331 p. illus. 23 cm. *1. Great Basin — History. I. Harris, Beth Kay, joint author. II. T.*
F786.R66   979.2   62-12399

Powell, John Wesley, 1834-1902. III. 6871
The exploration of the Colorado River. Abridged from the 1st ed. of 1875. With an introd. by Wallace Stegner. [Chicago] University of Chicago Press [1957] 137 p. illus. 23 cm. "Based on the [Smithsonian Institution] text ... which appeared under the full title: Exploration of the Colorado River of the West and its tributaries." *1. Colorado River. 2. U.S. — Exploring expeditions. I. Smithsonian Institution. Exploration of the Colorado River of the West and its tributaries. II. T.*
F788.P886   917.8811   57-6988

Moore, Joan W.   **III. 6872**
Mexican Americans [by] Joan W. Moore with Alfredo Cuéllar. Englewood, Cliffs, N.J., Prentice-Hall [1970] xii, 172 p. illus. 24 cm. (Ethnic groups in American life series) *1. Mexicans in the New Southwest. I. Cuéllar, Alfredo B., joint author. II. T.*
F790.M5M6   917.91/0975/6   77-113844   ISBN:135794900

F791 – 820   NEW MEXICO. ARIZONA

Scholes, France Vinton, 1897-   **III. 6873**
Troublous times in New Mexico, 1659-1670, by France V. Scholes. Albuquerque, University of New Mexico Press [1942] vii, 276 p. 23 cm. (Historical society of New Mexico. Publications in history, vol.11. January,1942.) "First printed in the New Mexico historical review, volume XII (numbers 2, 4, 1937), volume XIII (number 1, 1938), volume XV (numbers 3-4, 1940), and volume XVI (numbers 1-3, 1941) ... Certain corrections and minor changes have been made in this reprinting." — Pref. *1. New Mexico — History. I. T.*
F791.N45x   978.9 (978.90062)   42-36827

Writers' Program. New Mexico.   **III. 6874**
New Mexico; a guide to the colorful State. Compiled by workers of the Writers' Program of the Work Projects Administration in the State of New Mexico. New and completely rev. ed. by Joseph Miller; edited by Henry G. Alsberg. New York, Hastings House, 1962. xxxii, 472 p. illus., maps. 21 cm. (American guide series) *1. New Mexico — Description and travel — Guide-books. I. Miller, Joseph, 1899- ed. (S)*
F794.3.W7 1962   917.89   62-53065

Bancroft, Hubert Howe, 1832-1918.   **III. 6875**
History of Arizona and New Mexico, 1530-1888. New Mexico foreword by Clinton P. Anderson. Arizona foreword by Barry Goldwater. A facsim. of the 1889 ed. published coincident to the 50th anniversary of New Mexico & Arizona statehood. Albuquerque, Horn & Wallace, 1962. 19 p., facsim.: xxxviii, 829 p. maps. 24 cm. According to W. A. Morris in the Quarterly of the Oregon Historical Society, v.4, p. 311 and 333, this work was written by H. L. Oak. Published in 1888 as v.12 of Bancroft's History of the Pacific States of North America, under title: Arizona and New Mexico. *1. Arizona — History. 2. New Mexico — History. I. Oak, Henry Lebbeus, 1844-1905.*
F796.B192   979   62-13296

Twitchell, Ralph Emerson, 1859-1925.   **III. 6876**
The leading facts of New Mexican history. Albuquerque, Horn & Wallace, 1963. 2 v. illus., ports., maps (part fold.) facsims. 25 cm. Reproduction of the first 2 of the 5 volumes published 1911-17. *1. New Mexico — History. I. T.*
F796.T97 1963   978.9   63-20440

Bolton, Herbert Eugene, 1870-1953, ed.   **III. 6877**
Spanish exploration in the Southwest, 1542-1706, ed. by Herbert Eugene Bolton with three maps. New York, Scribner, 1916. xii, 487 p. 3 fold. maps 23 cm. (Original narratives of early American history) *1. America — Discovery and exploration — Spanish. 2. Southwest, New — Discovery and exploration. I. T.*
F799.B69   16-6066

Hammond, George Peter, 1896- ed. and tr.   **III. 6878**
Don Juan de Oñate, colonizer of New Mexico, 1595-1628 [by] George P. Hammond [and] Agapito Rey [Albuquerque] University of New Mexico Press, 1953. 2 v. (xvi, 1187 p.) fronts., fold. map. 28 cm. (Coronado Cuarto Centennial publications, 1540-1940, v.5, 6) A translation of documentary sources chiefly from the Archives of the Indies in Seville. *1. Oñate, Juan de, fl. 1595-1622. 2. New Mexico — History — Sources. I. Rey, Agapito, 1892- joint ed. and tr. (S)*
F799.H3   978.9   53-12919

Bolton, Herbert Eugene, 1870-1953.   **III. 6879**
Rim of Christendom; a biography of Eusebio Francisco Kino, Pacific coast pioneer. New York, Russell & Russell, 1960 [c1936] xiv, 644 p. illus., fold. maps, facsims. 25 cm. *1. Kino, Eusebio Francisco, 1644-1711. I. T.*
F799.K59 1960   922.273   60-10705

Sauer, Carl Ortwin, 1889-   **III. 6880**
The road of Cibola, by Carl Sauer. Berkeley, Calif., University of California Press, 1932. 58 p. fold. map. 28 cm. (Ibero-americana: 3) "Appendix of unpublished (early seventeenth century) documentary materials on the explorations into the Northwest": p. 51-58. *1. Cibola. 2. Southwest, New — Discovery and exploration. I. T.*
F799.S27 (F1401.I22 vol. 3)   A32-1971

Gregg, Josiah, 1806-1850.   **III. 6881**
Commerce of the prairies. Introd. by Archibald Hanna. [1st ed.] Philadelphia, Lippincott [1962] 2 v. (351 p.) illus., map, facsim. 21 cm. (Keystone Western Americana series, KB52-53) "The 1844 edition, unabridged." *1. Southwest, New. 2. New Mexico. 3. Mexico — Description and travel. 4. Santa Fe Trail. 5. Indians of North America — The West. I. T.*
F800.G844   979   62-11339

Larson, Robert W., 1927-   **III. 6882**
New Mexico's quest for statehood, 1846-1912 [by] Robert W. Larson. [1st ed. Albuquerque] University of New Mexico Press [1968] viii, 405 p. 25 cm. *1. New Mexico — Politics and government — 1848-1950. I. T.*
F801.L32   320.9/78.9   68-23022

Vogt, Evon Zartmann, 1918- ed.   **III. 6883**
People of Rimrock; a study of values in five cultures. Edited by Evon Z. Vogt and Ethel M. Albert. Cambridge, Mass., Harvard University Press, 1966. xiv, 342 p. illus., maps. 25 cm. A publication from the Comparative study of values in five cultures project of the Laboratory of Social Relations, Harvard University. *1. Rimrock, N.M. — Social life and customs. I. Albert, Ethel M., joint ed. II. Harvard University. Laboratory of Social Relations. III. T.*
F804.R5V6   917.8983035   66-23469

Horgan, Paul, 1903-   **III. 6884**
The centuries of Santa Fe. [1st ed.] New York, Dutton, 1956. 363 p. illus. 22 cm. *1. Santa Fe, N.M. I. T.*
F804.S2H68   978.9   56-8318

González, Nancie L. Solien, 1929-   **III. 6885**
The Spanish-Americans of New Mexico; a heritage of pride [by] Nancie L. González. [Rev. and enl. ed.] Albuquerque, University of New Mexico Press [1969] xv, 246 p. illus., map. 21 cm. *1. Mexican Americans — New Mexico. I. T.*
F805.M5G6 1969   917.89/0974/6   75-89517   ISBN:826301541

Writers' Program. Arizona.   **III. 6886**
Arizona, the Grand Canyon State; a State guide. Completely rev. by Joseph Miller; edited by Henry G. Alsberg and Harry Hansen. [4th completely rev. ed.] New York, Hastings House [1966] xxvi, 532 p. illus., maps, ports. 21 cm. (American guide series) First published in 1940 under title: Arizona; a State guide. "Originally compiled by the Federal Writers' Project of the Works Progress Administration in the State of Arizona." *1. Arizona — Description and travel — Guide-books. I. Miller, Joseph, 1899- ed. II. T. (S)*
F809.3.W7 1966   917.91045   66-20364

F821 – 850   UTAH. NEVADA

Writers' Program. Utah.   **III. 6887**
Utah; a guide to the State. Compiled by workers of the Writers' Program of the Work Projects Administration for the State of Utah. New York, Hastings House, 1941. St. Clair Shores, Mich., Somerset Publishers, 1972. xxvi, 595 p. illus. 22 cm. "Sponsored by the Utah State Institute of Fine Arts; co-sponsored by the Salt Lake County Commission." Original ed. issued in series: American guide series. *1. Utah — Description and travel — Guide-books. (S:American guide series.)*
F824.3.W74 1972   917.92/04/3   72-84510   ISBN:0403021936

Burton, Richard Francis, Sir, 1821-1890.   **III. 6888**
The city of the saints, and across the Rocky Mountains to California. New York, Harper, 1862. [New York, AMS Press, 1971] xii, 574 p. illus. 22 cm. *1. Utah — Description and travel. 2. Mormons and Mormonism. 3. Salt Lake City. 4. Overland journeys to the Pacific. I. T.*
F826.B97 1971   917.92/25   72-134390   ISBN:0404084338

Burton, Richard Francis, Sir, 1821-1890.   **III. 6889**
The look of the West, 1860; across the plains to California. Foreword by Robert G. Athearn. Lincoln, University of Nebraska Press [1963] xviii, 333 p. illus., maps. 21 cm. (A Bison book) "BB148." Previously published as chapters of the author's larger work. The City of the Saints and across the Rocky Mountains to California. *1. Utah — Description and travel. 2. Mormons and Mormonism. 3. Salt Lake City. 4. Overland journeys to the Pacific. I. T.*
F826.B974   917.92   63-17030

Furniss, Norman F.   **III. 6890**
The Mormon conflict, 1850-1859. New Haven, Yale University Press, 1960. viii, 311 p. illus., ports., map. 25 cm. (Yale historical publications. Miscellany, 72) *1. Mormons and Mormonism in Utah. 2. Utah Expedition, 1857-1858. I. T. (S)*
F826.F85   979.202   60-7824

Larson, Gustive Olof, 1897-   **III. 6891**
Prelude to the kingdom; Mormon desert conquest, a chapter in American cooperative experience. Francestown, N.H., M. Jones Co. [1947] 321, [6] p. illus. 22 cm. *1. Mormons and Mormonism. 2. Utah — History. I. T.*
F826.L3   979.2   48-762

Stegner, Wallace Earle, 1909-   **III. 6892**
Mormon country, by Wallace Stegner. New York, Duell, Sloan & Pearce [1942] x, 362 p. 23 cm. (American folkways, ed. by Erskine Caldwell) Map on lining-papers. "First printing." *1. Utah — History. 2. Mormons and Mormonism. I. T.*
F826.S75   979.2   42-22811

Morgan, Dale Lowell, 1914-   **III. 6893**
The Great Salt Lake [by] Dale L. Morgan. 1st ed. Indianapolis, New York, Bobbs-Merrill [1947] 432 p. illus., maps, plates. 22 cm. (The American lake series.) *1. Great Salt Lake. 2. Utah — History.*
F832.G7M6   979.2   47-2728

Writer's Program. Utah.   **III. 6894**
Provo, pioneer Mormon city, compiled by the workers of the Writers' Program of the Work Projects Administration for the state of Utah. Sponsored by the Utah State Institute of Fine Arts. Co-sponsored by the Provo City Commission, the Provo Board of Education, Brigham Young University, and Provo Chamber of Commerce. Portland, Or., Binfords & Mort [c1942] 223 p. plates. 21 cm. (American guide series) *1. Provo, Utah — History. 2. Provo, Utah — Description.*
F834.P8W7   979.2   43-1606

Lillard, Richard Gordon, 1909-   **III. 6895**
Desert challenge, an interpretation of Nevada, by Richard G. Lillard. 1st ed. New York, A. A. Knopf, 1942. viii, 388 p., ix p. plates, maps (1 fold.) 25 cm. Part of thesis (PH.D.) — University of Iowa, 1943. Without thesis note. *1. Nevada — Description and travel. 2. Nevada — History. I. T.*
F841.L5   979.3   42-20630

Ostrander, Gilman Marston, 1923-   **III. 6896**
Nevada, the great rotten borough, 1859-1964 [by] Gilman M. Ostrander. [1st ed.] New York, Knopf, 1966. xii, 247, [1], viii p. 22 cm. *1. Nevada — Politics and government. I. T.*
F841.O8   979.3   66-10747

Writers' Program. Nevada.   **III. 6897**
Nevada; a guide to the Silver state; compiled by workers of the Writers' Program of the Work Projects Administration in the state of Nevada. Sponsored by Dr. Jeanne Elizabeth Wier, Nevada State Historical Society, inc. Portland, Or., Binfords & Mort [1940] xviii, 315 p. plates, maps (1 fold. in pocket) 21 cm. (American guide series) *1. Nevada. 2. Nevada — Description and travel — Guide-books.*
F841.W77   917.93   41-71

F851 – 951 Pacific States

Bancroft, Hubert Howe, 1832-1918.   **III. 6898**
The works of Hubert Howe Bancroft. San Francisco, A. L. Bancroft, 1883-90. [New York] Arno Press [196-?] 39 v. illus., maps. 23 cm. On spine: Bancroft's works. Vol. 2-8, 12, 14, 16-17, 19-26, 29-32, 34-39 have imprint: San Francisco, History Co. *1. Pacific States — History. 2. Mexico — History. 3. Central America — History. 4. British Columbia — History. 5. Indians of North America. 6. The West — History. I. Bancroft's works.*
F851.B216   67-29422

Fuller, George Washington, 1876-1940.   **III. 6899**
A history of the Pacific Northwest, by George W. Fuller. New York, A. A. Knopf, 1931. xvi, 383 p. plates, ports., maps (1 fold.) 25 cm. *1. Northwest, Pacific — History.*
F851.F96   979   31-26862

Peirce, Neal R.   **III. 6900**
The Pacific States of America; people, politics, and power in the five Pacific Basin States [by] Neal R. Peirce. [1st ed.] New York, W. W. Norton [1972] 387 p. maps. 24 cm. *1. Pacific States. 2. Alaska. 3. Hawaii. I. T.*
F851.P43 1972   917.9/03   72-2333   ISBN:0393052729

Pomeroy, Earl Spencer, 1915-   **III. 6901**
The Pacific slope; a history of California, Oregon, Washington, Idaho, Utah, and Nevada, by Earl Pomeroy. [1st ed.] New York, Knopf, 1965. xii, 403, [1], xvi p. illus., fold. maps. 25 cm. *1. Northwest, Pacific — History. 2. Southwest, New — History. I. T.*
F851.P57   979.5   65-11128

Simpson, George, Sir, 1792?-1860.   **III. 6902**
Fur trade and empire; George Simpson's journal entitled Remarks connected with the fur trade in the course of a voyage from York Factory to Fort George and back to York Factory 1824-25, with related documents. Edited with a new introd. by Frederick Merk. Rev. ed. Cambridge, Mass., Belknap Press of Harvard University Press, 1968. lxii, 370 p. fold. map. 24 cm. *1. Fur trade — Northwest, Canadian. 2. Hudson's Bay Company. 3. Northwest, Canadian — Description and travel — 1821-1867. I. Merk, Frederick, 1887- ed. II. T.*
F851.S67 1968   917.12   68-15646

Cook, Warren L.   **III. 6903**
Flood tide of empire; Spain and the Pacific Northwest, 1543-1819, by Warren L. Cook. New Haven, Yale University Press, 1973. xiv, 620 p. illus., 2 fold. maps (in pocket) 26 cm. (Yale Western Americana series, 24) *1. Northwest coast of North America — Discovery and exploration. 2. Northwest, Pacific — History. 3. Spain — Exploring expeditions. I. T. (S)*
F851.5.C83   979.5/01   72-75187   ISBN:0300015771

Johannsen, Robert Walter, 1925-   **III. 6904**
Frontier politics and the sectional conflict; the Pacific Northwest on the eve of the Civil War. Seattle, University of Washington Press [c1955] xiii, 240 p. ports., maps. 23 cm. *1. Northwest, Pacific — Politics and government. 2. U.S. — Politics and government — 1857-1861.*
F852.J65   979.5   55-11915

Johansen, Dorothy O.   **III. 6905**
Empire of the Columbia: a history of the Pacific Northwest, by Dorothy O. Johansen and Charles M. Gates. 2d ed. New York, Harper & Row [1967] xiii, 654 p. illus., maps. 24 cm. *1. Northwest, Pacific — History. I. Gates, Charles Marvin. II. T.*
F852.J67 1967   979.5   67-12548

Warren, Sidney, 1916-   **III. 6906**
Farthest frontier; the Pacific Northwest. Port Washington, N.Y., Kennikat Press [1970, c1949] ix, 375 p. 22 cm. *1. Northwest, Pacific — History. I. T.*
F852.W28 1970   979.5   79-110332   ISBN:804608768

Winther, Oscar Osburn, 1903-   **III. 6907**
The Great Northwest; a history. 2d ed., rev. and enl. New York, Knopf, 1950. xviii, 491, xxx p. illus., ports., maps. 22 cm. (Western Americana) *1. Northwest, Pacific — History. I. T.*
F852.W65 1950   979.5   50-12482

Meinig, Donald William, 1924-   **III. 6908**
The Great Columbia Plain; a historical geography, 1805-1910, by D. W. Meinig. Seattle, University of Washington Press [1968] xxi, 576 p. illus., maps. (part fold.) 25 cm. (The Emil and Kathleen Sick lecture-book series in western history and biography) *1. Columbia River Valley. I. T. (S)*
F853.M4   979.7   68-11044

F856 – 870 CALIFORNIA

Lewis, Oscar, 1893-   **III. 6909**
The big four; the story of Huntington, Stanford, Hopkins, and Crocker, and of the building of the Central Pacific. 1st ed. By Oscar Lewis. New York, London, A. A. Knopf, 1938. xii, 418, vi p. plates, ports., facsims. 24 cm. "Part of this book appeared in the Atlantic monthly under the title, Men against mountains." *1. Huntington, Colis Potter, 1821-1900. 2. Stanford, Leland, 1824-1893. 3. Hopkins, Mark, 1813-1878. 4. Crocker, Charles, 1822-1888. 5. Central Pacific railroad. I. T.*
F860.L44   923.373   38-18366

Caughey, John Walton, 1902-   **III. 6910**
California; a remarkable State's life history [by] John W. Caughey. 3d ed. Englewood Cliffs, N.J., Prentice-Hall [1970] xxiv, 674 p. illus., maps, ports. 25 cm. (Prentice-Hall history series) *1. California — History.*
F861.C34 1970   917.94/03   73-118334   ISBN:013112482X

Cleland, Robert Glass, 1885-   **III. 6911**
From wilderness to empire; a history of California. A combined and rev. ed. of From wilderness to empire, 1542-1900 & California in our time, 1900-1940. Edited and brought down to date by Glenn S. Dumke. [1st ed.] New York, Knopf, 1959. 445 p. illus. 22 cm. *1. California — History. I. T.*
F861.C598   979.4   59-8037

Hunt, Rockwell Dennis, 1868-   **III. 6912**
California in the making; essays and papers in California history. Introd. by Malcolm R. Eiselen. Caldwell, Idaho, Caxton Printers, 1953. 325 p. 22 cm. *1. California — History — Addresses, essays, lectures. I. T.*
F861.H933   979.4004   53-10248

McWilliams, Carey, 1905-   **III. 6913**
California: the great exception. Westport, Conn., Greenwood Press [1971, c1949] xiii, 377 p. 23 cm. *1. California. I. T.*
F861.M25 1971   917.94/03   75-138398   ISBN:0837159261

Rolle, Andrew F.   **III. 6914**
California; a history [by] Andrew F. Rolle. 2d ed. New York, Crowell [1969] xxiii, 739 p. illus., maps, ports. 25 cm. *1. California — History.*
F861.R78 1969   979.4   69-13261

Bolton, Herbert Eugene, 1870-1953. III. 6915
Anza's California expeditions. New York, Russell & Russell, 1966 [c1930] 5 v. illus., facsims., maps (part fold.) ports. 23 cm. Vols.2-5 translated from original Spanish manuscripts. *1. Anza, Juan Bautista de, 1735-1788. 2. California — Description and travel. 3. San Francisco — History. I. Diaz, Juan. II. Garcés, Francisco Tomas Hermenegildo, 1738-1781. III. Palóu, Francisco, 1723-1789. IV. Font, Pedro. V. Eixarch, Thomas. VI. Moraga, José Joaquín, 1741-1785. VII. California expeditions. VIII. T.*
F864.B68 1966 979.4 66-11364

Bolton, Herbert Eugene, 1870-1953. III. 6916
An outpost of empire. New York, Russell & Russell, 1965 [i.e. 1966, c1930] xxi, 529 p. illus., maps (part fold.) port. 23 cm. Published in 1930 as v.1 of the author's Anza's California expeditions. *1. Anza, Juan Bautista de, 1735-1788. 2. San Francisco — History. 3. California — Description and travel. I. T.*
F864.B683 1966 979.402 66-11365

Chapman, Charles Edward, 1880- III. 6917
The founding of Spanish California, the northwestward expansion of New Spain, 1687-1783. New York, Macmillan, 1916. xxxii, 485 p. front. (port.) maps, double facsim. 23 cm. Issued also as thesis (PH.D.) University of California, 1915. *1. California — History — To 1846.*
F864.C46 16-14582

Chapman, Charles Edward, 1880-1941. III. 6918
A history of California: the Spanish period. New York, Macmillan, 1921. St. Clair Shores, Mich., Scholarly Press [1971] x, 527 p. illus. 20 cm. *1. California — History — To 1846. I. T.*
F864.C465 1971 979.4 74-144942 ISBN:0403009264

Clavijero, Francisco Javier, 1731-1787. III. 6919
The history of Lower California. Translated from the Italian by Sra E. Lake. Edited by A. A. Gray. Riverside, Calif., Manessier Pub. Co. [1971, c1937] liii, 413 p. illus. 24 cm. *1. California — History — To 1846. 2. Baja California — History. I. T.*
F864.C615 1971 917.94 79-150156

Crespi, Juan. III. 6920
Fray Juan Crespi, missionary explorer on the Pacific coast, 1769-1774, by Herbert Eugene Bolton. Berkeley, University of California Press, 1927. lxiv, 402 p. front., plates, maps, facsim. 23 cm. "Crespi's diaries are printed here as the primary part of this book. They have never before been assembled in one volume or published as a separate work. They were scattered through the tomes of Palóu's New California, and are here reprinted from my English edition of that treatise (Berkeley, 1926), with the addition of several important hitherto unpublished documents, a special introduction, and editorial notes." — Pref. *1. Portola's expedition, 1769-1770. 2. Pacific coast — Discovery and exploration. 3. Missions — California. 4. Franciscans in California. I. Bolton, Herbert Eugene, 1870- ed.*
F864.C92 28-6102

Dunne, Peter Masten, 1889- III. 6921
Black Robes in Lower California. Berkeley, University of California Press, 1952. x, 540 p. illus., ports., fold. map. 23 cm. *1. Jesuits in Lower California. 2. Missions — California, Lower. 3. Indians of North America — California, Lower. I. T.*
F864.D9 972.2 52-14415

Larkin, Thomas Oliver, 1802-1858. III. 6922
First and last consul: Thomas Oliver Larkin and the Americanization of California; a selection of letters edited by John A. Hawgood. San Marino, Calif., Huntington Library, 1962. xxxviii, 123 p. port. 25 cm. (Huntington Library publications) *1. California — History — To 1846 — Sources. 2. California — History — 1846-1850 — Sources. I. Hawgood, John Arkas, 1905- ed. II. T. (S:Henry E. Huntington Library and Art Gallery, San Marino, Calif. Huntington Library publications)*
F864.L29 979.403 62-17797

Englebert, Omer, 1893- III. 6923
The last of the conquistadors, Junípero Serra, 1713-1784. Translated from the French by Katherine Woods. [1st ed.] New York, Harcourt, Brace [1956] 368 p. illus. 25 cm. *1. Serra, Junípero, 1713-1784. I. T.*
F864.S442 922.2 56-7917

Winther, Oscar Osburn, 1903- III. 6924
Via western express & stagecoach, by Oscar Osburn Winther. Stanford University, Calif., Stanford University Press [1945] xi, 158 p. illus. (incl. ports., facsims.) 27 cm. Maps on lining-papers. "Decorative illustrations by Arthur Lites." *1. California — History. 2. Express service — California. 3. Coaching — California. I. T.*
F864.W83 979.4 A46-262

F865 – 866 1848 –

Bingham, Edwin R., ed. III. 6925
California gold; selected source materials for college research papers. Boston, Heath [1959] 117 p. 24 cm. *1. California — Gold discoveries. 2. California — History — 1846-1850 — Sources. I. T.*
F865.B57 979.404 59-2058

Caughey, John Walton, 1902- III. 6926
Gold is the cornerstone; with vignettes by W. R. Cameron. Berkeley, Univ. of Calif. Press, 1948. xvi, 321 p. illus. 23 cm. (Chronicles of California) *1. California — Gold discoveries. 2. Gold mines and mining — California. I. T. (S)*
F865.C33 979.4 48-10984

Gillis, William Robert, 1840-1929. III. 6927
Gold rush days with Mark Twain. With an introd. by Cyril Clemens. Illustrated with woodcuts by H. Glintenkamp. New York, Albert & Charles Boni, 1930. St. Clair Shores, Mich., Scholarly Press, 1970. xiv, 264 p. illus. 22 cm. *1. California — Gold discoveries. 2. Clemens, Samuel Langhorne, 1835-1910. I. T.*
F865.G48 1970 917.94/03/40924 (B) 77-131719 ISBN:403006066

Kemble, John Haskell, 1912- III. 6928
The Panama route, 1848-1869, by John H. Kemble. New York, Da Capo Press, 1972. viii, 316 p. illus. 22 cm. (University of California publications in history, v. 29. The American scene: comments and commentators) Reprint of the 1943 ed. Based on the author's thesis, University of California, 1937. *1. Voyages to the Pacific Coast. 2. Pacific Mail Steamship Company. 3. United States Mail Steamship Company. 4. Postal service — United States. I. T. (S:California. University. University of California publication in history, v. 29.)*
F865.K32 1972 917.9 79-139195 ISBN:0306700832

Paul, Rodman Wilson. III. 6929
California gold; the beginning of mining in the far West. Cambridge, Harvard Univ. Press, 1947. xvi, 380 p. illus., maps. 23 cm. *1. California — Gold discoveries. 2. Gold mines and mining — California. 3. Frontier and pioneer life — California. I. T.*
F865.P25 979.4 47-5141

Dana, Julian, 1907- III. 6930
Sutter of California; a biography by Julian Dana. New York, Macmillan, 1936. xi, 423 p. plates, ports., map. 22 cm. Maps on lining-papers. First published 1934. "Reissued, January 1936; March 1936." "Descendants": p. 411-413. *1. Sutter, John Augustus, 1803-1880. I. T.*
F865.S9483 923.873 37-3007

Taylor, Bayard, 1825-1878. III. 6931
Eldorado; or, Adventures in the path of empire: comprising a voyage to California, via Panama; life in San Francisco and Monterey; pictures of the gold region, and experiences of Mexican travel. With illus. by the author. Glorieta, N.M., Rio Grande Press [1967] 2 v. in 1. illus. 23 cm. (A Rio Grande classic) *1. California — Gold discoveries. 2. California — Description and travel — 1848-1869. 3. Voyages to the Pacific coast. 4. Mexico — Description and travel. I. T.*
F865.T23 1967 917.94/04/4 67-26678

Mowry, George Edwin, 1909- III. 6932
The California progressives. Berkeley, University of California Press, 1951. xi, 349 p. illus., ports. 23 cm. (Chronicles of California) *1. California — Politics and government. 2. Progressivism (U.S. politics) I. T. (S)*
F866.M89 979.4 51-63048

Olin, Spencer C. III. 6933
California's prodigal sons; Hiram Johnson and the Progressives, 1911-1917, by Spencer C. Olin, Jr. Berkeley, University of California Press, 1968. ix, 253 p. ports. 23 cm. *1. California — Politics and government — 1850-1950. 2. Progressivism (U.S. politics) 3. Johnson, Hiram Warren, 1866-1945. I. T.*
F866.O47 979.4/05 68-11968

Burke, Robert Eugene, 1921- III. 6934
Olson's new deal for California. Berkeley, University of California Press, 1953. 279 p. group port. 25 cm. "Based upon the author's doctoral dissertation, 'The Olson regime in California.' " *1. Olson, Culbert Levy, 1876-2. California — Politics and government. I. T.*
F866.O5B8 979.4 53-11244

Durrenberger, Robert W. III. 6935
Sources of information about California. Northridge, Calif., Roberts Pub. Co. [1961] 126 p. 22 cm. *1. Information services — California. I. T.*
F866.2.D8 917.94 61-16255

Federal Writers' Project. California. III. 6936
California, a guide to the Golden State. Sponsored by Mabel R. Gillis, California State librarian. [Rev. ed.] New York, Hastings House [1955, c1954] xxxi, 716 p. illus., maps. 21 cm. (American guide series) *1. California. 2. California — Description and travel — Guide-books. 3. Automobiles — Road guides — California. (S)*
F866.2.F4 1954 917.94 55-4472

F867–868 Regions.

Cleland, Robert Glass, 1885-   **III. 6937**
The cattle on a thousand hills; Southern California, 1850-1880. [2d ed.] San Marino, Huntington Library, 1951. xvi, 365 p. illus., ports., maps. 24 cm. (Huntington Library publications) *1. California, Southern — History. I. T. (S:Henry E. Huntington Library and Art Gallery, San Marino, Calif. Huntington Library publications)*
F867.C6 1951   979.49   51-14546

Jaeger, Edmund Carroll, 1887-   **III. 6938**
The California deserts [by] Edmund C. Jaeger. 4th ed. Stanford, Calif., Stanford University Press, 1965. x, 208 p. illus., maps. 23 cm. *1. Deserts — California, Southern. I. T.*
F867.J232 1965   917.9490954   65-26823

Stewart, George Rippey, 1895-   **III. 6939**
Ordeal by hunger; the story of the Donner Party. New ed., with a suppl. and 3 accounts by survivors. Boston, Houghton Mifflin, 1960. 394 p. illus. 22 cm. *1. Donner Party. I. T.*
F868.N5S7 1960   978   60-9361

Vance, James E.   **III. 6940**
Geography and urban evolution in the San Francisco Bay area by James E. Vance, Jr. Berkeley, Institute of Governmental Studies, University of California, 1964. 89 p. maps. 24 cm. (The Franklin K. Lane project) *1. San Francisco Bay region. I. T. (S:The 1963 Franklin K. Lane project)*
F868.S156V3   917.946   65-63287

Lewis, Oscar, 1893-   **III. 6941**
High Sierra country. [1st ed.] New York, Duell, Sloan and Pearce [1955] ix, 291 p. map (on lining papers) 22 cm. (American folkways) *1. Sierra Nevada Mountains. I. T. (S)*
F868.S5L64   917.94   55-9834

Muir, John, 1838-1914.   **III. 6942**
My first summer in the Sierra. With illus. from drawings made by the author in 1869, and front. from a photo. by Herbert W. Gleason. Dunwoody, Ga., N. S. Berg, 1972 [c1911] 353 p. illus. 24 cm. On cover: "John Muir, Earth-planet universe." *1. Sierra Nevada Mountains. I. T.*
F868.S5M9 1972   917.94/4/044   72-185700   ISBN:0910220344

Muir, John, 1838-1914.   **III. 6943**
Yosemite and the Sierra Nevada; photos. by Ansel Adams. Selections from the works of John Muir, ed. by Charlotte E. Mauk. Boston, Houghton Mifflin, 1948. xix, 132 p. 64 plates. 26 cm. *1. Yosemite Valley. 2. Sierra Nevada Mountains. I. Mauk, Charlotte E., ed. II. Adams, Ansel Easton, 1902- illus. III. T.*
F868.Y6M915   917.9447   49-7030

F869 Cities

Cohen, Jerry.   **III. 6944**
Burn, baby, burn! The Los Angeles race riot, August, 1965, by Jerry Cohen and William S. Murphy. Introd. by Robert Kirsch. [1st ed.] New York, Dutton, 1966. 318 p. illus., ports. 22 cm. *1. Los Angeles — Riots, 1965. 2. Negroes — Los Angeles. I. Murphy, William Sarsfield, joint author. II. T.*
F869.L8C6   323.1196079494   66-21295

Fogelson, Robert M.   **III. 6945**
The fragmented metropolis: Los Angeles, 1850-1930, by Robert M. Fogelson. Cambridge, Harvard University Press, 1967. xv, 362 p. illus., maps, plans, ports. 25 cm. (A publication of the Joint Center for Urban Studies of the Massachusetts Institute of Technology and Harvard University) *1. Los Angeles — History. I. T. (S:Joint Center for Urban Studies. Publications)*
F869.L8F6   917.94/93/034   67-20876

Writers' Program. California.   **III. 6946**
Los Angeles; a guide to the city and its environs, compiled by workers of the Writers' Program of the Work Projects Administration in Southern California. Completely revised. 2d ed. New York, Hastings House [1951] liv, 441 p. illus., maps. 21 cm. (American guide series) "Sponsored by the Los Angeles County Board of Supervisors." *1. Los Angeles — Description — Guide-books. (S)*
F869.L8W85 1951   917.9494   51-11827

Caen, Herbert Eugene, 1916-   **III. 6947**
Only in San Francisco. [1st ed.] Garden City, N.Y., Doubleday, 1960. 286 p. 22 cm. *1. San Francisco — Description. I. T.*
F869.S3C127   917.9461   60-15169

Clemens, Samuel Langhorne, 1835-1910.   **III. 6948**
Mark Twain's San Francisco. Edited by Bernard Taper. [1st ed.] New York, McGraw-Hill [1963] xxvi, 263 p. illus., port. 26 cm. Selections from his contributions to newspapers and journals, 1863-1866. *1. San Francisco — Social life and customs. I. Taper, Bernard, ed.*
F869.S3C57   917.9461   63-19737

Lewis, Oscar, 1893- ed.   **III. 6949**
This was San Francisco, being first-hand accounts of the evolution of one of America's favorite cities. [1st ed.] New York, D. McKay Co. [1962] 291 p. illus. 24 cm. *1. San Francisco — History. 2. San Francisco — Description. I. T.*
F869.S3L613   917.9461   61-18348

Older, Fremont, 1856-   **III. 6950**
My own story, by Fremont Older. New York, Macmillan, 1926. xx, 340 p. 23 cm. "New edition, revised." *1. San Francisco — Politics and government.*
F869.S3O43   26-19123

Writers' Program. California.   **III. 6951**
San Francisco, the bay and its cities; comp. by workers of the Writers' Program of the Work Projects Administration in northern California. Sponsored by the City and County of San Francisco. [Rev. 2d ed.] New York, Hastings House, 1947. xvii, 531 p. plates, maps. 21 cm. (American guide series) *1. San Francisco — Description — Guide-books. 2. San Francisco Bay Region. (S)*
F869.S3W95 1947   917.9461   47-11536

Writers' Program. California.   **III. 6952**
Santa Barbara; a guide to the Channel City and its environs, compiled and written by the Southern California Writers' Project of the Work Projects Administration ... Sponsored by Santa Barbara State College. New York, Hastings House, 1941. xviii, 206 p. illus., plates. 21 cm. (American guide series) *1. Santa Barbara Co., California — Description and travel — Guide-books. 2. Santa Barbara, Calif. — Description.*
F869.S45W86   917.9491   41-46110

F870 Japanese Population

Daniels, Roger.   **III. 6953**
The politics of prejudice, the anti-Japanese movement in California, and the struggle for Japanese exclusion. Berkeley, University of California Press, 1962. ix, 165 p. 24 cm. (University of California publications in history, v.71) *1. Japanese in California. 2. Race discrimination — California. I. T. (S:California. University. University of California publications in history, v.71)*
F870.J3D17 (E173.C15 vol. 71)   323.1   62-63248

F871–885 OREGON

Corning, Howard McKinley, 1896- ed.   **III. 6954**
Dictionary of Oregon history, compiled from the research files of the former Oregon Writers' Project with much added material. Portland, Binfords & Mort [c1956] 281 p. facsim. 27 cm. (A Peter Binford Foundation book) *1. Oregon — History — Dictionaries. I. T.*
F874.C6   979.5003   57-1975

Federal Writers' Project.   **III. 6955**
The Oregon trail; the Missouri River to the Pacific Ocean. Compiled and written by the Federal Writers' Project of the Works Progress Administration. New York, Hastings House. St. Clair Shores, Mich., Scholarly Press [1972? c1939] xii, 244 p. illus. 21 cm. (American guide series) "Sponsored by Oregon Trail Memorial Association, inc." *1. Oregon Trail. 2. The West — Description and travel — Guide-books. (S)*
F874.3.F4 1972   917.8/04   70-145012   ISBN:0403012902

Merk, Frederick, 1887-   **III. 6956**
Albert Gallatin and the Oregon problem; a study in Anglo-American diplomacy. Cambridge, Harvard University Press, 1950. xi, 97 p. 21 cm. (Harvard historical monographs, 23) *1. Gallatin, Albert, 1761-1849. 2. Oregon question. (S)*
F880.G18M4   327.730942   50-10277

Irving, Washington, 1783-1859.   **III. 6957**
Astoria. Illus. by Harold Cramer Smith. Portland, Or., Binfords & Mort [1951] xxx, 467 p. illus., maps (on lining papers) 24 cm. *I. T.*
F880.I7x   A52-9339

Merk, Frederick, 1887-   **III. 6958**
The Oregon question; essays in Anglo-American diplomacy and politics. Cambridge, Belknap Press of Harvard University Press, 1967. xiv, 427 p. map. 25 cm. *1. Oregon question. 2. Northwest boundary of the U.S. 3. U.S. — Foreign relations — Gt. Brit. 4. Gt. Brit. — Foreign relations — U.S.*
F880.M537   327.73/042   67-14345

Skinner, Constance Lindsay, d. 1939. III. 6959
Adventurers of Oregon; a chronicle of the fur trade, by Constance L. Skinner. New Haven, Yale University Press; [etc., etc.] 1921. ix, 290 p. col. front., fold. map. 18 cm. (The chronicles of America series, v.22) "Roosevelt edition." *1. Oregon — History — To 1859. 2. Fur trade — Oregon. 3. Fur trade — North America. I. T.*
F880.S62 (E173.C56 vol. 22)   22-12144

Writers' Program. Oregon. III. 6960
Oregon, end of the trail. Rev. ed. with added material by Howard McKinley Corning. Portland, Binfords & Mort [1951, c1940] xxxii, 549 p. illus. 22 cm. (American guide series) Map on lining paper. *1. Oregon. 2. Oregon — Description and travel — Guide-books. I. Corning, Howard McKinley, 1896- (S)*
F881.W76 1951   917.95   52-11474

F886 – 900   WASHINGTON

Avery, Mary Williamson, 1907- III. 6961
History and government of the State of Washington. Seattle, University of Washington Press, 1961. 583 p. illus. 23 cm. Part 2 previously published separately under title: Government of the State of Washington. *1. Washington (State) — History. 2. Washington (State) — Politics and government.*
F891.A8   979.7   61-8211

Writers' Program. Washington. III. 6962
The new Washington; a guide to the Evergreen State. Rev. ed. with added material, by Howard McKinley Corning. Portland, Or., Binfords & Mort [1950, c1941] xxx, 687 p. illus., maps. 21 cm. (American guide series) First ed. published in 1941 under title: Washington, a guide to the Evergreen State. *1. Washington (State) 2. Washington (State) — Description and travel — Guide-books. I. Corning, Howard McKinley, 1896- II. T. (S)*
F891.W9 1950   917.97   51-3893

Ogden, Daniel M. III. 6963
Washington politics, by Daniel M. Ogden, Jr., and Hugh A. Bone. [Prepared under the auspices of the Citizenship Clearing House. New York] New York University Press, 1960. 77 p. illus. 22 cm. *1. Washington (State) — Politics and government. I. Bone, Hugh Alvin, 1909- joint author. II. T.*
F895.O35   329.09797   60-14317

F901 – 951   ALASKA

Bancroft, Hubert Howe, 1832-1918. III. 6964
History of Alaska, 1730-1885; with a new introd. by Ernest Gruening. New York, Antiquarian Press, 1959. xxxviii, 755 p. maps (part fold.) 24 cm. *1. Alaska — History.*
F904.Bx   A62-8742

Brooks, Alfred Hulse, 1871-1924. III. 6965
Blazing Alaska's trails; edited by Burton L. Fryxell, with foreword by John C. Reed. [College, Alaska] Published jointly by the University of Alaska and the Arctic Institute of North America [Washington] 1953. xxi, 528 p. illus., port., maps. 24 cm. *1. Alaska. I. T.*
F904.B83   917.98   53-4121

Gruening, Ernest Henry, 1887- III. 6966
The State of Alaska [by] Ernest Gruening. New York, Random House [c1968] 661 p. illus., maps. 24 cm. *1. Alaska — History. I. T.*
F904.G7 1968   979.8   65-11285

Hulley, Clarence Charles, 1907- III. 6967
Alaska, past and present. [Rev.] Portland, Or., Binfords & Mort, 1958 [c1953] 422 p. illus. 23 cm. First published in 1953 under title: Alaska, 1741-1953. *1. Alaska — History.*
F904.H8 1958   979.8   57-9285

Nichols, Jeannette (Paddock) 1890- III. 6968
Alaska, a history of its administration, exploitation, and industrial development during its first half century under the rule of the United States. New York, Russell & Russell, 1963. 456 p. illus. 23 cm. Originally issued in 1924 as thesis, Columbia University. *1. Alaska — History — 1867-1959. 2. Alaska — Politics and government — 1867-1959. 3. American newspapers — Alaska — Bibliography.*
F904.N61 1963   979.803   63-12567

Chevigny, Hector, 1904- III. 6969
Lord of Alaska; Baranov and the Russian adventure. Portland, Or., Binfords & Mort, 1951 [c1942] 320 p. map (on lining papers) 22 cm. *1. Baranov, Aleksandr Andreevich, 1745-1819. 2. Alaska — History. I. T.*
F907.B2 1951   923.873   51-4156

Farrar, Victor J. III. 6970
The purchase of Alaska. Washington, Roberts, 1935. 118 p. 22 cm. "The present monograph is an elaboration of my smaller work of the same title (Washington, 1934)" — Foreword. *1. Alaska — Annexation. I. T.*
F907.F282   35-13621

James, James Alton, 1864-1962. III. 6971
The first scientific exploration of Russian America and the purchase of Alaska, by James Alton James. Evanston and Chicago, Northwestern University, 1942. xii, 276 p. plates, ports., double map. 24 cm. (Northwestern university studies in the social sciences, no. 4) *1. Kennicott, Robert, 1835-1866. 2. Bannister, Henry Martyn, 1844-1920. 3. Alaska — Description and travel. 4. U.S. — Exploring expeditions. I. T.*
F907.J3   979.8   42-50931

Federal writers' project. III. 6972
A guide to Alaska, last American frontier, by Merle Colby, Federal writers' project ... New York, The Macmillan company, 1945. lxv, 427 p. illus., plates, maps (part fold., 1 in pocket) 21 cm. (American guide series) Maps on lining-papers. The plates are in eight groups, each preceded by half-title not included in paging. *1. Alaska. 2. Alaska — Description and travel — Guide-books. I. Colby, Merle Estes, 1902- II. T.*
F909.F45   917.98   39-27616

Marshall, Robert, 1901-1939. III. 6973
Arctic wilderness. Edited, with an introd., by George Marshall; foreword by A. Starker Leopold. Berkeley, University of California Press, 1956. 171 p. illus. 24 cm. *1. Alaska — Description and trav. I. T.*
F909.M373   917.98   56-6774

Oswalt, Wendell H. III. 6974
Napaskiak; an Alaskan Eskimo community. Illustrated by the author. Tucson, University of Arizona Press, 1963. xii, 178 p. illus., maps. 24 cm. Based on thesis, University of Arizona. *1. Napaskiak, Alaska.*
F914.N3O7   309.17984   63-11978

Berton, Pierre, 1920- III. 6975
The Klondike fever; the life and death of the last great gold rush. New York, Knopf, 1959. 457 p. illus. 22 cm. *1. Klondike gold fields. I. T.*
F931.B49   971.21   58-9666

(Hawaii: see DU620 – 629)

F970   ISLAND POSSESSIONS

Coulter, John Wesley, 1893- III. 6976
The Pacific dependencies of the United States. New York, Macmillan, 1957. 388 p. illus. 22 cm. *1. U.S. — Insular possessions. 2. Micronesia. I. T.*
F970.C6   996   57-9543

Pratt, Julius William, 1888- III. 6977
America's colonial experiment; how the United States gained, governed, and in part gave away a colonial empire, by Julius W. Pratt. Gloucester, Mass., P. Smith, 1964 [c1950] xi, 460 p. maps 21 cm. *1. U.S. — Insular possessions. 2. Imperialism. I. T.*
F970.P7 1964   325.373   64-56504

F1001 – 1140 Canada

F1001 – 1006 REFERENCE WORKS

Canadian annual review. III. 6978
[Toronto] University of Toronto Press, 1960- v. 25 cm. English and French. Editor: 1960- J. T. Saywell. *1. Canada. I. Saywell, John T., ed.*
F1001.C215   971.064   61-3380

Talman, James John, 1904- ed. III. 6979
Basic documents in Canadian history. Princeton, N.J., Van Nostrand [1959] 189 p. 19 cm. (An Anvil original no. 40) *1. Canada — History — Sources. I. T.*
F1003.T3   971.   9-9760

Bissell, Claude Thomas, 1916- ed. III. 6980
Our living tradition: seven Canadians. [Toronto] Published in association with Carleton University by University of Toronto Press [c1957] x, 149 p. 22 cm. "Given as public lectures at Carleton University." *1. Canada — Biography. I. T.*
F1005.B586   920.071   A58-526

Dictionary of Canadian biography. III. 6981
v.1- ; 1000/1700- . Toronto, University of Toronto Press [1966- v. 26 cm. *1. Canada — Biography.*
F1005.D49   920.07103   66-31909

The Macmillan dictionary of Canadian biography, III. 6982
by W. Stewart Wallace. 3d ed., rev. and enl. London, Macmillan; New York, St. Martin's, 1963. 822 p. 25 cm. "Canadians...who died before 1961." Previous editions published under title: The Dictionary of Canadian biography. *1. Canada — Biography. I. Wallace, William Stewart, 1884- , ed.*
F1005.D5 1963   920.071   64-10158

Encyclopedia Canadiana. III. 6983
[Editor-in-chief: John E. Robbins] Ottawa, Canadiana Co. [c1960] 10 v. illus. (part col.) ports., maps (part col.) 27 cm. *1. Canada — Dictionaries and encyclopedias. I. T:Canadiana.*
F1006.E625   917.1   60-50632

F1013 – 1021 DESCRIPTION. CIVILIZATION

Berton, Pierre, 1920- III. 6984
The mysterious north. [1st ed.] New York, Knopf, 1956. 345 p. illus. 22 cm. "[Personal] narrative of several trips made into various parts of the Canadian north ... since the war." *1. Canada — Description and travel. I. T.*
F1015.B49   917.1   55-9272

Hutchison, Bruce, 1901- III. 6985
The unknown country, Canada and her people, by Bruce Hutchison. New York, Coward-McCann, [c1942] x, 386 p. plates. 22 cm. Map on lining-papers. *1. Canada — Description and travel. 2. National characteristics, Canadian. I. T.*
F1015.M96   917.1   42-3124

Notman, William. III. 6986
Portrait of a period; a collection of Notman photographs, 1856-1915, edited by J. Russell Harper and Stanley Triggs, with an introduction by Edgar Andrew Collard. Montreal, McGill University Press, 1967. lv. illus. 35 cm. *1. Canada — Description and travel — Views. I. Harper, J. Russell, ed. II. Triggs, Stanley, ed. III. T.*
F1015.N6   779/.9/9171   67-29772

Taylor, Thomas Griffith, 1880- III. 6987
Canada; a study of cool continental environments and their effect on British and French settlement. [2d ed., rev.] London, Methuen; New York, Dutton [1950] xv, 526 p. illus., maps. 23 cm. (Methuen's advanced geographies) *1. Canada — Description and travel. 2. Anthropo-geography — Canada. 3. Canada — Industries.*
F1015.T24 1950   917.1   50-12863

Canadian Association of Geographers. III. 6988
Canada: a geographical interpretation. Prepared under the auspices of the Canadian Association of Geographers and edited by John Warkentin. Toronto, London [etc.] Methuen, 1968. xvi, 608 p. illus. (part col.), maps (part col.), port. 25 cm. Part of illustrative matter in pocket. Updated French ed. published under title: Le Canada: une interprétation géographique. *1. Canada — Description and travel — 1951- I. Warkentin, John, 1928- ed. II. T.*
F1016.C28   917.1   68-82888

Irving, Robert McCardle, 1930- comp. III. 6989
Readings in Canadian geography, edited by Robert M. Irving. Toronto, Montreal, Holt, Rinehart and Winston of Canada [c1968] viii, 398 p. illus., maps. 24 cm. *1. Canada — Description and travel — 1951- I. T.*
F1016.I7   72-491230

Putnam, Donald Fulton, 1903- III. 6990
Canadian regions; a geography of Canada. [7th ed.] Editor: Donald F. Putnam. Toronto, J. M. Dent (Canada) [1965] ix, 601 p. illus. 25 cm. Contributors: Donald F. Putnam, Benoit Brouillette, Donald P. Kerr, J. Lewis Robinson. *1. Canada — Description and travel — 1951- I. T.*
F1016.P8 1965   67-95396

Bailey, Alfred Goldsworthy. III. 6991
The conflict of European and Eastern Algonkian cultures 1504-1700: a study in Canadian civilization. [2. ed. Toronto] University of Toronto Press [1969] xxiii, 218 p. 26 cm. *1. Canada — Civilization. 2. Indians of North America — Canada. 3. Algonquian Indians. 4. French-Canadians. I. T.*
F1021.B25 1969   917.1/03/1   78-434310   ISBN:802015069

Lower, Arthur Reginald Marsden, 1889- III. 6992
Canadians in the making; a social history of Canada. Toronto, Longmans, Green, 1958. 475 p. illus. 24 cm. *1. Canada — Civilization — History. 2. National characteristics, Canadian. I. T.*
F1021.L67   917.1   59-818

F1024 – 1140   HISTORY

Winks, Robin W. III. 6993
Recent trends and new literature in Canadian history. Washington, Service Center for Teachers of History [1959] 56 p. 23 cm. (Service Center for Teachers of History. Publication no. 19) *1. Canada — History — Historiography. 2. Canada — History — Bibliography. I. T.*
F1024.W5   971.007   59-8080

Brebner, John Bartlet, 1895-1957. III. 6994
Canada, a modern history, by J. Bartlet Brebner. New ed., rev. and enl. by Donald C. Masters. Ann Arbor, University of Michigan Press [1970] xvii, 570, xviii p. maps. 25 cm. (The University of Michigan history of the modern world) *1. Canada — History. I. Masters, Donald Campbell, 1908- (S:Michigan. University. The University of Michigan history of the modern world)*
F1026.B84 1970   971   72-107983   ISBN:472070916

Brown, George Williams, 1894-1963. III. 6995
Canada in the making. Westport, Conn., Greenwood Press [1970, c1953] vii, 151 p. 23 cm. *1. Canada — History — Addresses, essays, lectures. I. T.*
F1026.B8743 1970   917.1/03   72-100217   ISBN:837130328

Careless, James Maurice Stockford, 1919-   III. 6996
Canada, a story of challenge, by J. M. S. Careless. [Rev. and enl. ed.] New York, St Martin's Press [1964, c1963] xiii, 444 p. illus., maps. 20 cm. *1. Canada — History. I. T.*
F1026.C33 1964   971   64-20638

Clark, Samuel Delbert, 1910-   III. 6997
Movements of political protest in Canada, 1640-1840. Toronto, University of Toronto Press, 1959. 518 p. 24 cm. (Social Credit in Alberta, 9) *1. Canada — Politics and government — To 1763. 2. Canada — Politics and government — 1763-1867. I. T.*
F1026.C6   971.01   60-29

Creighton, Donald Grant.   III. 6998
The empire of the St. Lawrence. Boston, Houghton Mifflin, 1958. 441 p. illus. 24 cm. First published in 1937 under title: The commercial empire of the St. Lawrence, 1760-1850. *1. Canada — History. 2. Canada — Commerce. 3. St. Lawrence River — Commerce. 4. Canada — Relations (general) with the U.S. 5. U.S. — Relations (general) with Canada. I. T.*
F1026.C74 1958   971.4   59-587

Creighton, Donald Grant.   III. 6999
A history of Canada, Dominion of the North. Rev. and enl. ed. Boston, Houghton Mifflin, 1958. 619 p. illus. 22 cm. First ed. published in 1944 under title: Dominion of the North. *1. Canada — History.*
F1026.C75 1958   971   58-5741

Creighton, Donald Grant.   III. 7000
The story of Canada, by Donald Creighton. [Rev. ed.] Toronto, Macmillan of Canada [1971] 319 p. maps. 23 cm. *1. Canada — History. I. T.*
F1026.C76 1971   971   72-178573

Lanctôt, Gustave, 1883-   III. 7001
A history of Canada. Translated by Josephine Hambleton. Cambridge, Harvard University Press, 1963- v. illus. 24 cm. *1. Canada — History.*
F1026.L263   971   63-2859

McInnis, Edgar, 1899-   III. 7002
Canada; a political and social history. 3d ed. Toronto, Holt, Rinehart and Winston of Canada [1969] xxii, 761 p. illus., maps, ports. 24 cm. *1. Canada — History.*
F1026.M15 1969   971   73-453745

Martin, Chester Bailey, 1882-   III. 7003
Foundations of Canadian nationhood. Toronto, University of Toronto Press, 1955. xx, 554 p. illus., maps. 24 cm. *1. Canada — History. I. T.*
F1026.M3x   A56-4047

Morton, William Lewis, 1908-   III. 7004
The kingdom of Canada, a general history from earliest times [by] W. L. Morton. [Toronto] McClelland and Stewart [1963] 556 p. maps. 24 cm. *I. T.*
F1026.M74 1963   65-73815

Reid, J. H. Stewart, 1909-   III. 7005
A source-book of Canadian history; selected documents and personal papers [by] J. H. Stewart Reid, Kenneth McNaught [and] Harry S. Crowe. Toronto, Longmans, Green [c1959] 472 p. 26 cm. *1. Canada — History — Sources.*
F1026.R44   971.0082   60-2438

Underhill, Frank Hawkings, 1889-   III. 7006
In search of Canadian liberalism. Toronto, Macmillan Co. of Canada, 1960 [i.e. 1961] xiv, 282 p. 23 cm. "Articles written ... over the last thirty years." *1. Canada — Politics and government — Addresses, essays, lectures. 2. Liberalism. I. T.*
F1026.U5   971.06   A61-237

F1027 Nationalism. French Canadians

Armstrong, Elizabeth Howard, 1898-   III. 7007
The crisis of Quebec, 1914-18, by Elizabeth H. Armstrong. New York, Columbia University Press, 1937. xii, 270 p. 24 cm. Issued also as thesis (PH. D.) Columbia university. *1. French-Canadians. 2. European war, 1914-1918 — Quebec (Province) 3. European war, 1914-1918 — Canada. 4. Canada — Nationality. I. T.*
F1027.A74   971.4   37-22241

Le Canada français d'aujourd'hui; études rassemblées par la Société royale du Canada.   III. 7008
Léopold Lamontagne, éd. [Toronto] Publié pour le compte de la société par University of Toronto Press et les Presses de l'Université Laval [1970] viii, 161 p. 24 cm. (Société royale du Canada. Collection Studia varia, 14) *1. French-Canadians. 2. Quebec (Province) — Civilization. I. Lamontagne, Léopold, ed. II. Royal Society of Canada. (S:Royal Society of Canada. Studia varia series, 14)*
F1027.C233   78-489431

Chaput, Marcel, 1918-   III. 7009
Why I am a separatist. Translated by Robert A. Taylor. Toronto, Ryerson Press [1962] 101 p. 21 cm. (An encounter book, 3) *1. French-Canadians. 2. Nationalism — Quebec (Province) I. T.*
F1027.C443   63-4553

Cook, Ramsay.   III. 7010
Canada and the French-Canadian question. Toronto, Macmillan of Canada, 1966. 219 p. 22 cm. Nine essays, most of which were previously published in various periodicals. *1. Canada — English-French relations. 2. Quebec (Province) — History — Autonomy and independence movements. I. T.*
F1027.C76   301.29/71   67-79220

Monet, Jacques.   III. 7011
The last cannon shot; a study of French-Canadian nationalism 1837-1850. [Toronto] University of Toronto Press [c1969] x, 422 p. 24 cm. *1. Canada — English-French relations — History. 2. Canada — Politics and government — 19th century. 3. French-Canadians. I. T.*
F1027.M66   320.9/71   70-455781   ISBN:802052118

Park, Julian, 1888- ed.   III. 7012
The culture of contemporary Canada. Ithaca, N.Y., Cornell University Press [1957] 404 p. illus. 24 cm. *1. Canada — Intellectual life. I. T.*
F1027.P32   917.1   57-4016

Quinn, Herbert Furlong, 1910-   III. 7013
The Union nationale; a study in Quebec nationalism. [Toronto] University of Toronto Press [1963] ix, 249 p. tables. 24 cm. Based on thesis, Columbia University. *1. Union nationale (Canada) 2. Quebec (Province) — Politics and government. 3. Nationalism — Quebec (Province)*
F1027.Q86   329.971   63-5826

Rioux, Marcel, ed.   III. 7014
French-Canadian society, edited, and with an introd., by Marcel Rioux and Yves Martin. [Toronto] McClelland and Stewart [c1964- v. 19 cm. (The Carleton library, no. 18-) *1. French-Canadians. 2. French in Canada. 3. Quebec (Province) — Civilization. I. Martin, Yves, 1929- joint ed. II. T.*
F1027.R53   309.1714   66-265

Vallières, Pierre.   III. 7015
White niggers of America. Translated by Joan Pinkham. Toronto, McClelland and Stewart [c1971] 278 p. 22 cm. Translation of Nègres blancs d'Amérique: autobiographie précoce d'un terroriste québécois. *1. French-Canadians. 2. Quebec (Province) — History — Autonomy and independence movements. 3. Quebec (Province) — Social conditions. I. T.*
F1027.V313 1971b   322.4/2/0924 (B)   72-180519   ISBN:0771086709

Wade, Mason, 1913- ed.   III. 7016
Canadian dualism; studies of French-English relations. [Toronto] University of Toronto Press [1960] xxv, 427 p. diagrs., tables. 24 cm. "Edited ... for a committee of the Social Science Research Council of Canada under the chairmanship of Jean-C. Falardeau." Added t.p. in French. Prefatory matter in French and English. Articles in English or French. *1. Nationalism — Canada. 2. French-Canadians. 3. French in Canada. 4. Canada — Civilization — Addresses, essays, lectures. I. Social Science Research Council of Canada. Committee on Biculturalism. II. La dualité canadienne. III. T.*
F1027.W14   917.1   A61-3019

Wade, Mason, 1913-   III. 7017
The French-Canadian outlook; a brief account of the unknown North Americans, by Mason Wade. New York, Viking Press, 1946. 192 p. 20 cm. Erratum slip inserted. *1. French-Canadians. 2. Canada — History.*
F1027.W15   971.4   46-25235

Wade, Mason, 1913-   III. 7018
The French Canadians; 1760-1967. Revised edition. Toronto, London, Macmillan; New York, St. Martin's Press, 1968. 2 v. illus. 23 cm. *1. French-Canadians. 2. Canada — History. I. T.*
F1027.W165   917.14/03   68-16861

F1029 Diplomatic History

Canada in world affairs. [1935/39]-   III. 7019
Toronto, Oxford University Press. v. 23 cm. Some vols. have also distinctive titles: 1935/39, The pre-war years. — 1939/41, Two years of war. —

1944/46, From Normandy to Paris. — 1946/49, From UN to NATO. "Published under the auspices of the Canadian Institute of International Affairs." Vols. for 1935/39, 1944/46 by F. H. Soward (with J. F. Parkinson, N. A. M. MacKenzie, and T. W. L. MacDermot, 1935/39) — 1939/41 by R. M. Dawson. — 1941/44 by C. C. Lingard and R. G. Trotter. — 1946/49 by R. A. Spencer. — 1949/50 by W. E. C. Harrison. — 1951/53 by B. S. Kierstead. — 1953/55 by D. C. Masters. — 1955/57 by J. Eayrs. *1. Canada — Foreign relations. I. Soward, Frederic Hubert, 1899- II. Dawson, Robert MacGregor, 1895- III. Lingard, Charles Cecil, 1901- IV. Spencer, Robert A. V. Harrison, William Eric Craven. VI. Kierstead, Burton Seely, 1907- VII. Masters, Donald Campbell, 1908- VIII. Eayrs, James.*
F1029.C3   56-2289

Duke University, Durham, N.C. Commonwealth-Studies Center.   **III. 7020**
The growth of Canadian policies in external affairs [by] Hugh L. Keenleyside [and others] Durham, Duke University Press, 1960. x, 174 p. 24 cm. (Its Publication no. 14) Lectures, with one exception, given as part of the 1959 program of the center's Summer Seminar and Research Group. *1. Canada — Foreign relations. I. Keenleyside, Hugh Llewellyn, 1898- II. T.* (S)
F1029.D8   327.71   60-13605

Glazebrook, George Parkin de Twenebroker.   **III. 7021**
A history of Canadian external relations. Toronto, New York, Oxford University Press, 1950. vii, 449 p. 23 cm. "Issued under the auspices of the Canadian Institute of International Affairs." "Part I is a re-printing of the author's Canadian external relations; an historical study to 1914." — Dust jacket. *1. Canada — Foreign relations. 2. Canada — History. I. T.*
F1029.G55 1950   327.71   50-4723

Morton, William Lewis, 1908-   **III. 7022**
The Canadian identity [by] W. L. Morton. 2d ed. [Madison] University of Wisconsin Press [1972] xi, 162 p. map. 22 cm. *1. Canada — Foreign relations — 1945- — Addresses, essays, lectures. 2. Canada — History — Addresses, essays, lectures. I. T.*
F1029.M6 1972b   327.71   72-194373
ISBN:0299061302 0299061345 (pbk)

F1030 – 1034 History, by Period
F1030 NEW FRANCE (1603 – 1763)

Eccles, William John.   **III. 7023**
Canada under Louis XIV, 1663-1701 [by] W. J. Eccles. [Toronto] McClelland and Stewart; New York, Oxford University Press, 1964. xii, 275 p. illus., facsims., maps, ports. 24 cm. (The Canadian centenary series) *1. Canada — History — To 1763 (New France) I. T.* (S)
F1030.E3   971.016   64-56760

Eccles, William John.   **III. 7024**
The Canadian frontier, 1534-1760 [by] W. J. Eccles. New York, Holt, Rinehart and Winston [1969] xv, 234 p. illus., maps, ports. 24 cm. (Histories of the American frontier) *1. Canada — History — To 1763 (New France) I. T.*
F1030.E312   971.01   70-81783   ISBN:030818346

Eccles, William John.   **III. 7025**
Frontenac, the courtier governor. Toronto, McClelland and Stewart [1959] 406 p. illus. 24 cm. *1. Frontenac, Louis de Buade, comte de, 1620-1668. 2. Canada — History — To 1763 (New France) I. T.*
F1030.F9276   971.01   59-31011

Parkman, Francis, 1823-1893.   **III. 7026**
Francis Parkman's works. New library ed. [Boston, Little, Brown, and Company, 1902-03] 12 v. fronts., plates, ports., maps. 21 cm. Half-title. Each volume has special t.-p. Vols. 1-9 have subtitle: France and England in North America. Pt. 1-7. *1. Canada — History. 2. U.S. — History — Colonial periodicals. 3. New France — Discovery and exploration. 4. America — Discovery and exploration — French.*
F1030.P24 1902   04-19149

Parkman, Francis, 1823-1893.   **III. 7027**
The Parkman reader; from the works of Francis Parkman. Selected and edited with an introd. and notes by Samuel Eliot Morison. [1st ed.] Boston, Little, Brown [1955] xv, 533 p. port., maps (1 fold.) 22 cm. "Selections from ... France and England in North America." *1. Canada — History — To 1763 (New France) 2. U.S. — History — Colonial periodicals. I. T.*
F1030.P246   971.01   55-6535

Parkman, Francis, 1823-1893.   **III. 7028**
Count Frontenac and New France under Louis XIV. With a prefatory note by Oscar Handlin. Boston, Beacon Press [1966] xiv, 463 p. map. 21 cm. (Beacon paperback, BP222) "A reprint of the 1880 ed." *1. Frontenac, Louis de Buade, comte de, 1620-1698. 2. Canada — History — To 1763 (New France) I. T.*
F1030.P267 1966   971.01   66-1981

Savelle, Max, 1896-   **III. 7029**
The diplomatic history of the Canadian boundary, 1749-1763. New York, Russell & Russell [1968, c1940] xiv, 172 p. maps. 25 cm. *1. Canada — Boundary. 2. Canada — History — To 1763 (New France) 3. Great Britain — Foreign relations — France. 4. France — Foreign relations — Great Britain. 5. Great Britain — Foreign relations — Spain. 6. Spain — Foreign relations — Great Britain. 7. Great Britain — Colonies — America. 8. France — Colonies — America. 9. Spain — Colonies — America. I. T.*
F1030.S28 1968   327.71/073 Sa94   68-27084

Wrong, George McKinnon, 1860-1948.   **III. 7030**
The rise and fall of New France. New York, Octagon Books, 1970 [c1928] 2 v. (xiii, 925 p.) maps. 23 cm. *1. Canada — History — To 1763 (New France) I. T.*
F1030.W952 1970   971.01   75-120683

Bishop, Morris, 1893-   **III. 7031**
Champlain, the life of fortitude. [1st ed.] New York, Knopf, 1948. 364, vii p. illus., maps (1 fold.) 22 cm. *1. Champlain, Samuel de, 1567-1635. 2. Canada — History — To 1763 (New France)*
F1030.1.B6   923.971   48-8873

Champlain, Samuel de, 1567-1635.   **III. 7032**
Voyages of Samuel de Champlain, 1604-1618; ed. by W. L. Grant with a map and two plans. New York, C. Scribner's Sons, 1907. viii, 377 p. map, plans. 23 cm. (Original narratives of early American history ...) Series title also at head of t.-p. "This volume presents the texts of the Voyages of 1613 and the Voyages et descouvertures of 1619, as given in the excellent translation by Dr. Charles Pomery Otis, in the second and third volumes of the late Dr. Edmund F. Slafter's Voyages of Samuel de Champlain, published in three volumes by the Prince society." — Note. *1. New France — Discovery and exploration. 2. America — Discovery and exploration — French. 3. Indians of North America — Canada. I. Grant, William Lawson, 1872- ed.*
F1030.1.C494   07-22899

Morison, Samuel Eliot, 1887-   **III. 7033**
Samuel de Champlain, Father of New France. [1st ed.] Boston, Little, Brown [1972] xix, 299 p. illus. 25 cm. "An Atlantic Monthly Press book." *1. Champlain, Samuel de, 1567-1635. 2. New France — Discovery and exploration. 3. America — Discovery and exploration — French. 4. Indians of North America — Canada.*
F1030.1.M6   971.01/13/0924   71-186963

Parkman, Francis, 1823-1893.   **III. 7034**
The discovery of the great West: La Salle. Edited by William R. Taylor. New York, Rinehart [1956] 354 p. illus. 21 cm. *1. La Salle, Robert Cavelier, sieur de, 1643-1687. 2. New France — Discovery and exploration. 3. Mississippi River — Discovery and exploration. I. T.*
F1030.5.P225 1956a   977   56-59238

Kennedy, John Hopkins.   **III. 7035**
Jesuit and savage in new France, by J. H. Kennedy. [Hamden, Conn.] Archon Books, 1971 [c1950] 206 p. map. 22 cm. *1. Jesuits in Canada. 2. Canada — History — To 1763 (New France) 3. Indians of North America — Canada. I. T.*
F1030.7.K44 1971   971.01   70-131377   ISBN:0208010467

Jesuits. Letters from missions (North America)   **III. 7036**
The Jesuit relations and allied documents; travels and explorations of the Jesuit missionaries in North America, 1610-1791. With an introd. by Reuben Gold Thwaites. Selected and edited by Edna Kenton. Pref. by George N. Shuster. New York, Vanguard Press [1954] liv, 527 p. illus., maps. 23 cm. *1. Jesuits in North America. 2. New France — Discovery and exploration. 3. Indians of North America — Canada. 4. Indians of North America — Missions. I. Kenton, Edna, 1876- ed. II. T.*
F1030.7.Z8965   971.011   54-11519

Stanley, George Francis Gilman.   **III. 7037**
New France: the last phase, 1744-1760 [by] George F. G. Stanley. [Toronto] McClelland and Stewart [1968] xvi, 320 p. illus., maps. 23 1/2 cm. (The Canadian centenary series, 5) *1. Canada — History — To 1763 (New France) I. T.* (S)
F1030.9.S7   971.01/8   68-143124

F1031 – 1032 1763 – 1867

Wilson, George Earl, 1891-   **III. 7038**
The life of Robert Baldwin, a study in the struggle for responsible government, by George E. Wilson. Toronto, Ryerson Press [1933] vii, 312 p. 21 cm. "First undertaken as the thesis necessary for ... the degree of doctor

Canada

Careless, James Maurice Stockford, 1919-   III. 7039
Brown of the Globe. Toronto, Macmillan, 1959 [i.e. 1960]-1963. 2 v. illus. 26 cm. *1. Brown, George, 1818-1880. 2. Canada — Politics and government — 1841-1867.*
F1032.B87   923.271   60-30

Burt, Alfred LeRoy, 1888-   III. 7040
The old province of Quebec. New York, Russell & Russell [1970, c1933] xiii, 551 p. illus., maps, plans, ports. 25 cm. *1. Canada — History — 1763-1791. 2. Quebec (Province) — History. I. T.*
F1032.B94 1970   971.02   70-83856

Careless, James Maurice Stockford, 1919-   III. 7041
Colonists & Canadiens, 1760-1867; edited by J. M. S. Careless. Toronto, Macmillan of Canada, 1971. ix, 278 p. 22 cm. *1. Canada — History — 1763-1867 — Addresses, essays, lectures. I. T.*
F1032.C277   971.02   70-155261

Careless, James Maurice Stockford, 1919-   III. 7042
The union of the Canadas; the growth of Canadian Institutions, 1841-1857 [by] J. M. S. Careless. Toronto, McClelland and Stewart [1967] 256 p. illus., facsims., maps, ports. 24 cm. (The Canadian centenary series [10]) *1. Canada — History — 1841-1867. I. T. (S)*
F1032.C28   971.04   68-70117

Confederation; essays   III. 7043
by D. G. Creighton [and others] Introd. by Ramsay Cook. [Toronto] University of Toronto Press [1967] xiii, 118 p. 23 cm. (Canadian historical readings, 3) *1. Canada — History — 1841-1867 — Addresses, essays, lectures. I. Creighton, Donald Grant. (S)*
F1032.C75   971.04   67-113270

Corey, Albert Bickmore.   III. 7044
The crisis of 1830-1842 in Canadian-American relations, by Albert B. Corey. New York, Russell & Russell [1970] xi, 203 p. maps. 25 cm. (Relations of Canada and the United States) "First published in 1941." *1. United States — Foreign relations — Canada. 2. Canada — Foreign relations — United States. 3. Canada — History — Rebellion, 1837-1838. 4. United States — History — 1815-1861. 5. Northeast boundary of the United States. 6. Hunter's Lodges (Secret societies) I. T. (S:Carnegie Endowment for International Peace. Division of Economics and History. The relations of Canada and the United States)*
F1032.C77 1970   327.71/073   77-102483

Coupland, Reginald, 1884-   III. 7045
The Quebec act; a study in statesmanship, by R. Coupland. Oxford, Clarendon Press, 1925. 224 p. 23 cm. *1. Quebec act, 1774. 2. Canada — Politics and government — 1763-1791.*
F1032.C85   26-3120

Creighton, Donald Grant.   III. 7046
The road to confederation; the emergence of Canada, 1863-1867 [by] Donald Creighton. [1st American ed.] Boston, Houghton Mifflin, 1965 [c1964] 489 p. illus., maps, ports. 23 cm. *1. Canada — Politics and government — 1841-1867. I. T.*
F1032.C9 1965   971.04   65-15162

Durham, John George Lambton, 1st earl of, 1792-1840.   III. 7047
Lord Durham's report; an abridgement of Report on the affairs of British North America, by Lord Durham. Edited and with an introd. by G. M. Craig. [Toronto] McClelland and Stewart [1963] 179 p. 19 cm. (Carleton library no. 1) *1. Canada — History — Rebellion, 1837-1838. 2. Canada — Politics and government — 1791-1841. I. Craig, Gerald M., ed. II. T.*
F1032.D966   971.03/8   67-6368

Skelton, Oscar Douglas, 1878-   III. 7048
The life and times of Sir Alexander Tilloch Galt, by Oscar Douglas Skelton. Toronto, Oxford University Press, 1920. 586 p. front., plates, ports., maps, facsim. 25 cm. *1. Galt, Alexander Tilloch, Sir, 1817-1893. 2. Canada — Politics and government — 1841-1867. 3. Canada — Politics and government — 1867- I. T.*
F1032.G2   21-8655

Guillet, Edwin Clarence, 1898-   III. 7049
The lives and times of the patriots; an account of the Rebellion in Upper Canada, 1837-1838, and of the patriot agitation in the United States, 1837-1842 [by] Edwin C. Guillet. [Toronto] University of Toronto Press [1968] xiv, 304 p. illus., maps, ports. 24 cm. (Canadian university paperbooks, 81) First published Toronto, T. Nelson, 1938. *1. Canada — History — Rebellion, 1837-1838. 2. United States — History — 1815-1861. 3. Hunters' Lodges (Secret societies) I. T.*
F1032.G89 1968   971.03/8   68-115557

Phelan, Josephine.   III. 7050
The ardent exile; the life and times of Thos. Darcy McGee. Toronto, Macmillan of Canada, 1951. 317 p. illus. 22 cm. *1. McGee, Thomas D'Arcy, 1825-1868. 2. Canada — Politics and government — 1841-1867. I. T.*
F1032.M123   923.271   52-19494

Kilbourn, William.   III. 7051
The Firebrand: William Lyon Mackenzie and the rebellion in Upper Canada. Wood engravings by Rosemary Kilbourn. Toronto, Clarke, Irwin, 1956. 283 p. illus. 24 cm. *1. Mackenzie, William Lyon, 1795-1861. 2. Canada — History — Rebellion, 1837-1838. I. T.*
F1032.M148   971.038   57-249

Morton, William Lewis, 1908-   III. 7052
The critical years; the union of British North America, 1857-1873 [by] W. L. Morton. [Toronto] McClelland and Stewart; New York, Oxford University Press, 1964. 322 p. illus., maps, ports. 24 cm. (The Canadian centenary series) *1. Canada — History — 1841-1867. 2. Canada — History — 1867-1914. I. T. (S)*
F1032.M88   971.04   65-3125

Neatby, Hilda Marion, 1904-   III. 7053
Quebec: the revolutionary age, 1760-1791 [by] Hilda Neatby. [Toronto] McClelland and Stewart [c1966] xii, 300 p. illus., maps, ports. 24 cm. (The Canadian centenary series, 6) *1. Quebec (Province) — History. 2. Canada — History — To 1763 (New France) 3. Canada — History — 1763-1791. I. T. (S)*
F1032.N34   971.4/02   67-81811

Stacey, Charles Perry, 1906-   III. 7054
Canada and the British Army, 1846-1871; a study in the practice of responsible government. Rev. ed. [Toronto] Published in association with the Royal Commonwealth Society by University of Toronto Press [1963] xiv, 293 p. illus. 23 cm. *1. Canada. Army. 2. Canada — History — 1763-1867. 3. Canada — Defenses. I. T.*
F1032.S78 1963   971.04   64-7285

Waite, Peter B.   III. 7055
The life and times of confederation, 1864-1867; politics, newspapers, and the union of British North America. [Toronto] University of Toronto Press [c1962] 379 p. 24 cm. *1. Canada — Politics and government — 1841-1867. I. T.*
F1032.W16   971.04   63-796

Whitelaw, William Menzies, 1890-   III. 7056
The Maritimes and Canada before confederation, by William Menzies Whitelaw. With a foreword by the Right Honourable Sir Robert Laird Borden. Toronto, Oxford University Press, 1934. x, 328 p. front., illus. (maps) 24 cm. Maps on lining-papers. *1. Canada — Politics and government — 1841-1867. 2. Maritime provinces, Canada. I. T.*
F1032.W437   971.04   34-25363

F1033   1867 – 1914

Berger, Carl.   III. 7057
The sense of power; studies in the ideas of Canadian imperialism, 1867-1914. [Toronto] University of Toronto Press [1970] 277 p. 24 cm. A revision of the author's thesis, University of Toronto. *1. Canada — Politics and government — 1867-1914. 2. Nationalism — Canada. 3. National characteristics, Canadian. I. T.*
F1033.B49 1970   320.1/58/0971   79-470040   ISBN:802016693

Borden, Robert Laird, Sir, 1854-1937.   III. 7058
Robert Laird Borden: his memoirs; edited and with a preface by Henry Borden, with an introduction by Arthur Meighen. Toronto, Macmillan of Canada, 1938. 2 v. fronts., plates, ports. 23 cm. Paged continuously. *1. Canada — Politics and government — 1867- 2. European war, 1914-1918 — Canada. I. Borden, Henry, 1901- ed.*
F1033.B76   923.271   39-4233

The Canadian who's who ... A handbook of Canadian biography of living characters. v.1- 1910-   III. 7059
Toronto, Can., Trans-Canada Press; [etc., etc.] c1910- v. 20 cm. "With which is incorporated 'Canadian men and women of the time'." Vol.1 lacks subtitle. Editors: 1936/37- Sir C. G. D. Roberts, A. L. Tunnell. *1. Canada — Biography. I. Roberts, Charles George Douglas, Sir, 1860-1943, ed. II. Tunnell, Arthur Leonard, ed.*
F1033.C23   920.071   10-17752

Creighton, Donald Grant.   III. 7060
Canada's first century, 1867-1967. New York, St. Martin's Press [1970] 372 p. illus., ports. 24 cm. *1. Canada — History — 1867- I. T.*
F1033.C83   971   75-125604

Cook, Ramsay.   III. 7061
The politics of John W. Dafoe and the Free press. [Toronto] University of Toronto Press [1963] xii, 305 p. illus. 24 cm. *1. Dafoe, John Wesley,*

1866-1944. 2. Canada — Politics and government — 1867-1914. 3. Canada — Politics and government — 1914- I. T.
F1033.D2C6   64-1761

Dawson, Robert MacGregor, 1895- III. 7062
William Lyon Mackenzie King, a political biography. [Toronto] University of Toronto Press [1958-   v. illus. 24 cm. *1. King, William Lyon Mackenzie, 1874-1950.*
F1033.K53D3   923.271   59-347

Ferns, Henry Stanley, 1913- III. 7063
The age of Mackenzie King; the rise of the leader, by H. S. Ferns and B. Ostry. London, Heinemann [1955] xii, 356 p. plates, ports., map. 22 cm. *1. King, William Lyon Mackenzie, 1874-1950. 2. Canada — History — 1914- I. Ostry, Bernard, 1927- joint author. II. T.*
F1033.K53F4   971.065   A56-2307

Hutchison, Bruce, 1901- III. 7064
The incredible Canadian; a candid portrait of Mackenzie King: his works, his times, and his nation. [1st American ed.] New York, Longmans, Green, 1953. 454 p. illus. 22 cm. *1. King, William Lyon Mackenzie, 1874-1950. 2. Canada — History — 1914- I. T.*
F1033.K53H8 1953   923.271   53-299

McGregor, Fred A. III. 7065
The fall & rise of Mackenzie King, 1911-1919. Toronto, Macmillan of Canada, 1962 [i.e. 1963] 358 p. 24 cm. *1. King, William Lyon Mackenzie, 1874-1950. I. T.*
F1033.K53M2 1963   923.271   63-3079

Pickersgill, J. W., 1905- III. 7066
The Mackenzie King record. [Toronto] University of Toronto Press [1960-   v. illus. 24 cm. Continues the record begun in William Lyon Mackenzie King, a political biography by R. M. Dawson. *1. King, William Lyon Mackenzie, 1874-1950. 2. Canada — Politics and government — 1914- 3. Canada — Foreign relations. I. T.*
F1033.K53P5   923.271   60-51004

Dafoe, John Wesley, 1866- III. 7067
Laurier, a study in Canadian politics, by J. W. Dafoe. Toronto, T. Allen [c1922] 182 p. 20 cm. "... Originally published in ... the Monthly book review of the Manitoba free press." *1. Laurier, Wilfrid, Sir, 1841-1919. 2. Canada — Politics and government — 1867-*
F1033.L3595   23-10112

Schull, Joseph. III. 7068
Laurier: the first Canadian. New York, St. Martin's Press, 1965 [i.e. 1966] 658 p. illus., ports. 23 cm. *1. Laurier, Wilfrid, Sir, 1841-1919.*
F1033.L377   354.71030924 (B)   65-26119

Skelton, Oscar Douglas, 1878-1941. III. 7069
Life and letters of Sir Wilfrid Laurier, by Oscar Douglas Skelton; illustrated with photographs. New York, Century, 1922. 2 v. fronts., plates, ports. 23 cm. *1. Laurier, Wilfrid, Sir, 1841-1919. 2. Canada — Politics and government — 1867-*
F1033.L386   21-21755

Creighton, Donald Grant. III. 7070
John A. Macdonald. Boston, Houghton Mifflin, 1953-   2 v. illus., ports., maps (on lining papers) 23 cm. *1. Macdonald, John Alexander, Sir, 1815-1891. 2. Canada — Politics and government — 1841-1867.*
F1033.M125C72   923.271   52-13914

Penlington, Norman. III. 7071
Canada and imperialism, 1896-1899. [Toronto] University of Toronto Press [1965] xiv, 288 p. 24 cm. *1. Canada — History — 1867-1914. 2. Canada — Foreign relations — U.S. 3. U.S. — Foreign relations — Canada. 4. Imperial federation. I. T.*
F1033.P4   971.05   65-1619

Siegfried, André, 1875- III. 7072
Canada, by André Siegfried; translated from the French by H. H. Hemming & Doris Hemming. [1st American ed.] New York, Harcourt, Brace [c1937] 341 p. illus. (maps) 21 cm. Maps on lining-papers. *1. Canada — Population. 2. Canada — Economic conditions — 1918- 3. Canada — Politics and government — 1867- I. Hemming, Henry Harold, 1893- tr. II. Hemming, Doris, 1891- joint tr.*
F1033.S562   917.1   37-27316

Smith, Goldwin Albert. III. 7073
The Treaty of Washington, 1871; a study in imperial history, by Goldwin Smith. New York, Russell & Russell [1971, c1941] xiii, 134 p. 23 cm. *1. Washington, Treaty of, 1871. 2. Canada — Politics and government — 1867-1914. 3. United States — Foreign relations — Great Britain. 4. Great Britain — Foreign relations — United States. 5. United States — Foreign relations — Canada. 6. Canada — Foreign relations — United States. I. T.*
F1033.S67 1971   971.05   70-139940

Saunders, Edward Manning, 1829-1916, ed. III. 7074
The life and letters of the Rt. Hon. Sir Charles Tupper, ed. by E. M. Saunders, with an introduction by the Rt. Hon. Sir R. L. Borden. Eight photogravure plates. London, New York [etc.] Cassell, 1916. 2 v. 8 port. (incl. fronts.) 24 cm. *1. Tupper, Charles, Sir, bart., 1821-1915. 2. Canada — Politics and government — 1867-1914.*
F1033.T9   17-6541

Waite, Peter B. III. 7075
Canada 1874-1896: arduous destiny [by] Peter B. Waite. Toronto, McClelland and Stewart [1971] xii, 340 p. illus., maps., ports. 24 cm. (Canadian centenary series, 13) *1. Canada — History — 1867-1914. I. T. (S)*
F1033.W15   971.05   76-597589   ISBN:0771088000

F1034   1914 –

Allen, Ralph, 1913- III. 7076
Ordeal by fire; Canada, 1910-1945. [1st ed.] Garden City, N.Y., Doubleday, 1961. ix, 492 p. maps. 22 cm. (The Canadian history series, v.5) *1. Canada — History — 1914- I. T. (S:Canadian history series, v.5)*
F1034.A6   971.06   61-12490

Newman, Peter Charles. III. 7077
Renegade in power: the Diefenbaker years [by] Peter C. Newman. Indianapolis, Bobbs-Merrill [1964, c1963] xvi, 414 p. 23 cm. *1. Diefenbaker, John George. 2. Canada — Politics and government — 1914- I. T.*
F1034.D5N4   971.064   64-4761

Eayrs, James George, 1926- III. 7078
In defence of Canada [by] James Eayrs. [Toronto] University of Toronto Press [1965-   v. illus., ports. 24 cm. (Studies in the structure of power: decision making in Canada, 1, 3) *1. Canada — Armed Forces. 2. Canada — History, Military. 3. Canada — Foreign relations. I. T. (S)*
F1034.E17   327.71   66-3834

Graham, Roger. III. 7079
Arthur Meighen, a biography. Toronto, Clarke, Irwin, 1960-65. 3 v. illus., ports. 24 cm. *1. Meighen, Arthur, 1874-1960.*
F1034.M45G7   971.060924 (B)   60-52261

Morton, William Lewis, 1908- III. 7080
The Progressive Party in Canada, by W. L. Morton. [Reprinted with corrections. Toronto] University of Toronto Press [1967, c1950] xiii, 331 p. 24 cm. (Social credit in Alberta; its background and development, 1) *1. Progressive Party (Canada) 2. Progressivism (Canadian politics) (S)*
F1034.M6 1967   329.9/71   67-2778

Riddell, Walter Alexander, 1881- ed. III. 7081
Documents on Canadian foreign policy, 1917-1939. Toronto, Oxford University Press, 1962. liii, 806 p. 24 cm. *1. Canada — History — 1914- Sources. 2. Canada — Foreign relations.*
F1034.R55   327.71   62-5019

McNaught, Kenneth William Kirkpatrick, 1918- III. 7082
A prophet in politics; a biography of J. S. Woodsworth. [Toronto] University of Toronto Press [1959] 339 p. illus. 24 cm. *1. Woodsworth, James Shaver, 1874-1942. I. T.*
F1034.W6M23   923.271   59-4879

Fraser, Blair, 1909- III. 7083
The search for identity: Canada, 1945-1967. [1st ed.] Garden City, N.Y., Doubleday, 1967. viii, 325 p. map (on lining papers) 22 cm. (The Canadian history series, v.6) *1. Canada — Politics and government — 1945- I. T. (S)*
F1034.2.F7   320.9/71   67-23823

Schwartz, Mildred A. III. 7084
Public opinion and Canadian identity [by] Mildred A. Schwartz. Foreword by Seymour Martin Lipset. Berkeley, University of California Press, 1967. xvii, 263 p. illus. 24 cm. *1. Nationalism — Canada. 2. Canada — Politics and government — 1945- 3. Canada — Foreign relations. 4. Public opinion — Canada. I. T.*
F1034.2.S3 1967   320.9/71   67-17693

Thomson, Dale C. III. 7085
Louis St. Laurent, Canadian [by] Dale C. Thomson. New York, St. Martin's Press, 1968 [c1967] x, 564 p. illus., ports. 23 cm. *1. St. Laurent, Louis Stephen, 1882-*
F1034.3.S2T48   971.06/3/0924 (B)   68-11107

F1035 Negroes in Canada

Winks, Robin W. III. 7086
The Blacks in Canada; a history, by Robin W. Winks. Montreal, McGill-Queen's University Press; New Haven, Yale University Press, 1971. xvii, 546 p. maps. 24 cm. *1. Negroes in Canada — History. I. T.*
F1035.N3W5   971/.04/96   79-118740   ISBN:0300013612

F1035.8 – 1140 REGIONS. PROVINCES
F1035.8 – 1049 Maritime Provinces

Kerr, Wilfred Brenton, 1896-1950. III. 7087
The Maritime Provinces of British North America and the American Revolution. New York, Russell & Russell [1970] 172 p. 21 cm. Reprint of the 1941 ed. *1. Maritime Provinces, Can. — History. 2. Canada — History — 1763-1791. 3. United States — History — Revolution — Foreign public opinion. I. T.*
F1035.8.K4 1970   971   73-83849

MacNutt, William Stewart, 1908- III. 7088
The Atlantic Provinces: the emergence of colonial society, 1712-1857 [by] W. S. MacNutt. [Toronto] McClelland and Stewart [c1965] xii, 305 p. illus., maps, ports. 24 cm. (The Canadian centenary series, 9) *1. Maritime Provinces, Can. — History. 2. Newfoundland — History. I. T. (S)*
F1035.8.M2   971.5   66-77421

Brebner, John Bartlet, 1895-1957. III. 7089
The neutral Yankees of Nova Scotia; a marginal colony during the revolutionary years. New York, Russell & Russell [1970, c1937] xv, 388 p. fold. map. 25 cm. *1. Nova Scotia — History. 2. New Englanders in Nova Scotia. I. T.*
F1038.B815 1970   971.6/02   72-102471

Brebner, John Bartlet, 1895-1957. III. 7090
New England's outpost; Acadia before the conquest of Canada. Hamden, Conn., Archon Books, 1965 [c1927] 291 p. map. 22 cm. *1. Nova Scotia — History — To 1763. 2. Acadia. I. T.*
F1038.B822 1965   971.6   65-16895

MacNutt, William Stewart, 1908- III. 7091
New Brunswick, a history: 1784-1867. Toronto, Macmillan of Canada, 1963. xv, 496 p. illus., ports., maps. 24 cm. *1. New Brunswick — History.*
F1043.M29   971.5   63-6068

Clark, Andrew Hill, 1911- III. 7092
Three centuries and the island; a historical geography of settlement and agriculture in Prince Edward Island, Canada. [Toronto] University of Toronto Press [1959] xiii, 287 p. illus., maps. 26 cm. *1. Prince Edward Island — Historical geography. 2. Agriculture — Prince Edward Island. I. T.*
F1047.C57   911.717   59-2157

Harvey, Daniel Cobb, 1886- III. 7093
The French régime in Prince Edward Island, by D. C. Harvey. New York, AMS Press [1970] xi, 265 p. map. 23 cm. "Reprinted from the edition of 1926." *1. Prince Edward Island — History. 2. French in Prince Edward Island. I. T.*
F1048.H34 1970   971.7   72-113193   ISBN:404031536

F1050 – 1059 Quebec. Ontario

Dumont, Fernand, 1927- ed. III. 7094
Situation de la recherche sur le Canada français; premier colloque de la revue Recherches sociographiques du Département de sociologie et d'anthropologie de l'Université Laval. Ouvrage réalisé sous la direction de Fernand Dumont et Yves Martin. Québec, Presses de l'Université Laval, 1962 [c1963] 296 p. 27 cm. *1. Quebec (Province) — History — Study and teaching. 2. Quebec (Province) — Bibliography. 3. French-Canadians. I. Martin, Yves, 1929- joint ed. II. Recherches sociographiques. III. Quebec (City) Université Laval. Département de sociologie et d'anthropologie. IV. T.*
F1052.D85   64-149

Thoreau, Henry David, 1817-1862. III. 7095
A Yankee in Canada, with anti-slavery and reform papers. 12th ed. New York, Haskell House, 1969. 286 p. 23 cm. Reprint of the 1892 ed. *1. Quebec (Province) — Description and travel. 2. Slavery in the United States — Controversial literature — 1844-1860. 3. Brown, John, 1800-1859. I. T.*
F1052.T48 1969   081   68-25271   ISBN:838302483

Manning, Helen (Taft) 1891- III. 7096
The revolt of French Canada, 1800-1835; a chapter of the history of the British Commonwealth. [New York] St Martins Press, 1962. 426 p. illus. 23 cm. *1. Nationalism — Quebec (Province) 2. Canada — Politics and government — 1791-1841. 3. Gt. Brit. — Colonies — America. I. T.*
F1053.M2   971.03   62-1899

Hughes, Everett Cherrington, 1897- III. 7097
French Canada in transition, by Everett Cherrington Hughes. Chicago, University of Chicago Press [1943] ix, 227 p. front., illus. (maps) diagrs. 24 cm. *1. Quebec (Province) — Social conditions. 2. French-Canadians. I. T.*
F1053.5.H8   971.4   A43-2759

Miller, Horace Mitchell, 1912- III. 7098
St. Denis, a French-Canadian parish. [Chicago] University of Chicago Press [1963, c1939] xix, 299 p. illus., maps. 21 cm. *1. St. Denis, Que. (Kamouraska Co.) — Social life and customs. 2. French-Canadians. I. T.*
F1054.S224M5 1963   917.1475   63-13068

Craig, Gerald M. III. 7099
Upper Canada; the formative years, 1784-1841. [Toronto] McClelland and Stewart; New York, Oxford University Press, 1963. xiv, 315 p. illus., ports., maps, facsims. 24 cm. (The Canadian centenary series, 7) *1. Ontario — History. (S)*
F1058.C68   971.3   64-2294

Guillet, Edwin Clarence, 1898- III. 7100
Early life in Upper Canada, by Edwin C. Guillet. With 302 illus. selected and arr. by the author. [Toronto] University of Toronto Press, 1963 [c1933] xliii, 782 p. illus., facsims., maps, ports. 23 cm. *1. Ontario — History. 2. Frontier and pioneer life — Ontario. I. T.*
F1058.G87 1963   64-4393

Landon, Fred, 1880- III. 7101
Western Ontario and the American frontier. New York, Russell & Russell [1970] xxiii, 295 p. maps. 25 cm. (The Relations of Canada and the United States) "First published in 1941." *1. Canada — Relations (general) with the United States. 2. United States — Relations (general) with Canada. 3. Ontario — History. I. T. (S:Carnegie Endowment for International Peace. Division of Economics and History. The relations of Canada and the United States.)*
F1058.L3 1970   301.29/713/073   78-102514

Hamil, Frederick Coyne, 1903- III. 7102
The valley of the lower Thames, 1640 to 1850. [Toronto] University of Toronto Press, 1951. xi, 390 p. plates, maps (1 fold.) 24 cm. *1. Kent Co., Ont. — History. 2. Chatham, Ont. — History. I. T.*
F1059.K3H3   971.333   53-17557

F1060 – 1110 Canadian Northwest

Campbell, Marjorie Elliott (Wilkins) 1901- III. 7103
The North West Company. New York, St Martin's Press, 1957. 295 p. illus. 23 cm. *1. Northwest Company of Canada.*
F1060.C18   971.2   57-59416

Innis, Harold Adams, 1894-1952. III. 7104
The fur trade in Canada; an introduction to Canadian economic history. Rev. ed. [Toronto] University of Toronto Press, 1956. xi, 463 p. 24 cm. *1. Fur trade — Canada. 2. Canada — Economic conditions. 3. Northwest, Canadian — History. 4. Canada — History — To 1763 (New France)*
F1060.I58 1956   338.1791   57-2937

Morton, Arthur Silver, 1870- III. 7105
A history of the Canadian West to 1870-71; being a history of Rupert's land

(The Hudson's bay company's territory) and of the North-west territory (including the Pacific slope) by Arthur S. Morton. London, New York [etc.] Nelson [1939] xiv, 987 p. 12 maps (part fold.) 24 cm. Errata slip inserted. *1. Hudson's bay company. 2. Northwest, Canadian — History. 3. Northwest, Pacific — History.*
F1060.M76   971.2   39-22430

Wallace, William Stewart, 1884- ed.   III. 7106
Documents relating to the North West Company [edited with introd., notes, and appendices, by W. Stewart Wallace] New York, Greenwood Press, 1968. xv, 527 p. illus., ports. 24 cm. (Champlain Society publication, 22) Title on spine: The North West Company. Reprint of the 1934 ed. Appendices (p. 425-513): — A. A biographical dictionary of the Nor'westers. — B. A select bibliography relating to the history of the North West Company. *1. Northwest Company of Canada. 2. Fur trade — Canada. 3. Northwest, Canadian — Biography. I. T. (S:Champlain Society, Toronto. Publications, 22)*
F1060.W19 1968   338.7/63/911   68-28610

Crouse, Nellis Maynard, 1884-   III. 7107
La Verendrye, fur trader and explorer [by] Nellis M. Crouse. Port Washington, N.Y., Kennikat Press [1972, c1956] ix, 247 p. illus., maps (part fold.) 23 cm. *1. La Verendrye, Pierre Gaultier de Varennes, sieur de, 1685-1749. 2. New France — Discovery and exploration. I. T.*
F1060.7.L3914 1972   970/.03/0924 (B)   79-153210   ISBN:0804615209

Mackenzie, Alexander, Sir, 1763-1820.   III. 7108
First man West; Alexander Mackenzie's journal of his voyage to the Pacific coast of Canada in 1793. Edited by Walter Sheppe. Berkeley, University of California Press, 1962. ix, 366 p. port., maps (part fold.) 24 cm. First edition published in 1801 under title: Voyages from Montreal. *1. Northwest Canadian — Description and travel. 2. Indians of North America — Canada. I. Sheppe, Walter, ed. II. T.*
F1060.7.M1774   917.12   62-15084

Masson, Louis François Redrigue, 1833-1903.   III. 7109
Les bourgeois de la Compagnie du Nord-Ouest; récits de voyages, lettres et rapports inédits relatifs au Nord-Ouest canadien. Pub. avec une esquisse historique et des annotations par L. R. Masson. Québec, Impr. générale A. Coté, 1889-90. 2 v. fold. map. 23 cm. *1. Northwest company. 2. Northwest, Canadian — Description and travel. I. T.*
F1060.7.M42   01-24515

Radisson, Pierre Esprit, 1620?-1710.   III. 7110
Voyages of Peter Esprit Radisson, being an account of his travels and experiences among the North American Indians, from 1652 to 1684. Transcribed from original manuscripts in the Bodleian Library and the British Museum. With historical illus. and an introd. by Gideon D. Scull. New York, B. Franklin [1971?] vi, 385 p. 23 cm. (Burt Franklin research and source works series, 131. American classics in history and social science, 2) Reprint of the 1885 ed., which was issued as v. 16 of the Publications of the Prince Society. *1. New France — Discovery and exploration. 2. Northwest, Canadian — History. 3. Hudson's Bay Company. 4. Indians of North America — Canada. 5. Iroquois Indians. I. T. (S:Prince Society, Boston. Publications, v. 16.)*
F1060.7.R12 1971   917.1/04/16   72-184164

Galbraith, John S.   III. 7111
The Hudson's Bay Company as an imperial factor, 1821-1869. Berkeley, University of California Press, 1957. viii, 500 p. maps (1 fold. in pocket) 24 cm. *1. Hudson's Bay Company.*
F1060.8.G3   971.2   57-12392

Spry, Irene Mary (Biss)   III. 7112
The Palliser expedition; an account of John Palliser's British North American expedition, 1857-1860. Toronto, Macmillan of Canada, 1963 [i.e. 1964] vii, 310 p. illus., ports., maps. 23 cm. *1. Palliser, John, 1807-1887. 2. Northwest, Canadian — Description and travel. 3. Canada — Exploring expeditions. I. T.*
F1060.8.P2S6   971.2   64-933

Mackintosh, William Archibald, 1895-   III. 7113
Prairie settlement, the geographical setting, by W. A. Mackintosh. Toronto, Macmillan, 1934. xv, 242 p. illus., plates, maps, diagrs. 26 cm. (Canadian frontiers of settlement, ed. by W. A. Mackintosh and W. L. Joerg. vol.I) The prairie provinces: Manitoba, Saskatchewan, and Alberta. *1. Canada — Description and travel. 2. Agriculture — Canada. 3. Canada — Economic conditions — 1918- 4. Canada — Emigration and immigration. 5. Manitoba. 6. Saskatchewan. 7. Alberta. I. T.*
F1060.9.M28 (F1060.C23 vol. 1)   917.12   34-23504

Stanley, George Francis Gilman.   III. 7114
Louis Riel [by] George F. G. Stanley. Toronto, Ryerson Press [c1963] 433 p. maps, ports. 25 cm. *1. Riel, Louis David, 1844-1885.*
F1060.9.R5S8   64-4396

Stanley, George Francis Gilman.   III. 7115
The birth of western Canada; a history of the Riel Rebellions. Maps by C. C. J. Bond. [Toronto] University of Toronto Press [1961, c1960] 475 p. illus. 22 cm. *1. Northwest, Canadian — History. 2. Red River Rebellion, 1869-1870. 3. Riel Rebellion, 1885. I. T.*
F1060.9.S79 1961   971.051   61-1393

F1061   INDIVIDUAL PROVINCES

Morton, William Lewis, 1908-   III. 7116
Manitoba, a history [by] W. L. Morton. [2d ed. Toronto] University of Toronto Press [1967] xii, 547 p. illus., 7 maps. 24 cm. *1. Manitoba — History. I. T.*
F1063.M88 1967   971.27   67-4598

Pritchett, John Perry, 1902-   III. 7117
The Red River Valley, 1811-1849; a regional study. New York, Russell & Russell [1970, c1942] xvii, 295 p. map. 25 cm. (The Relations of Canada and the United States) *1. Red River Valley (Red River of the North) — History. 2. Red River Settlement. 3. Selkirk, Thomas Douglas, 5th Earl of, 1771-1820. (S:Carnegie Endowment for International Peace. Division of Economics and History. The relations of Canada and the United States)*
F1064.R3P7 1970   971.27/4   75-102532

Howard, Joseph Kinsey, 1906-1951.   III. 7118
Strange empire, a narrative of the Northwest. New York, Morrow, 1952. xii, 601 p. maps. 22 cm. *1. Riel, Louis David, 1844-1885. 2. Red River Rebellion, 1869-1870. 3. Riel Rebellion, 1885. 4. Indians of North America — Mixed bloods. 5. Canada — Boundaries — U.S. 6. U.S. — Boundaries — Canada. I. T.*
F1069.9.H7   971.051   52-9705

Bennett, John William, 1915-   III. 7119
Northern plainsmen; adaptive strategy and agrarian life [by] John W. Bennett. Foreword by Walter R. Goldschmidt. Chicago, Aldine Pub. Co. [1969] xvi, 352 p. illus. 22 cm. *1. Saskatchewan — Civilization. 2. Agriculture — Saskatchewan. I. T.*
F1071.B45   301.29/7124   76-75043

Campbell, Marjorie Elliott (Wilkins) 1901-   III. 7120
The Saskatchewan; illustrated by Illingworth H. Kerr. New York, Rinehart [1950] 400 p. illus., map. 21 cm. (Rivers of America) *1. Saskatchewan River. 2. Northwest, Canadian — History. (S)*
F1076.C18   971.23   50-6401

Ormsby, Margaret Anchoretta, 1909-   III. 7121
British Columbia, a history. [Toronto] Macmillans in Canada, 1958. 558 p. illus. 25 cm. *1. British Columbia — History.*
F1088.O7   971.1   59-23058

Hutchison, Bruce, 1901-   III. 7122
The Fraser; illustrated by Richard Bennett. New York, Rinehart [1950] 368 p. illus., map. 21 cm. (Rivers of America) *1. Fraser River, British Columbia. (S)*
F1089.F7H8   971.1   50-10549

F1121 – 1139   Newfoundland. Labrador

MacKay, Robert Alexander, 1894- ed.   III. 7123
Newfoundland; economic, diplomatic, and strategic studies, edited by R. A. MacKay, with a foreword by Sir Campbell Stuart. Toronto, Oxford University Press, 1946. xiv, 577 p. illus. (maps) diagrs. 24 cm. Issued under the auspices of the Royal institute of international affairs. *1. Newfoundland — Economic conditions. 2. Newfoundland — Politics and government. 3. Newfoundland — History. 4. Fisheries — Newfoundland.*
F1122.M17   971.8   46-5095

Kerr, James Lennox, 1899-   III. 7124
Wilfred Grenfell, his life and work. With a foreword by Lord Grenfell of Kilvey. London, Harrap [1959] 272 p. illus. 22 cm. *1. Grenfell, Wilfred Thomason, Sir, 1865-1940.*
F1137.G7K4 1959   926.1   60-38934

F1201 – 3799 Latin America

F1201 – 1392 MEXICO

Cline, Howard Francis.   **III. 7125**
Mexico; revolution to evolution, 1940-1960. London, New York, Oxford University Press, 1962. xiv, 375 p. maps, tables. 21 cm. 1. Mexico — History — 1910-1946. 2. Mexico — History — 1946- 3. Mexico — Civilization.
F1208.C55   972.081   62-4941

Leonard, Irving Albert, 1896-   **III. 7126**
Baroque times in old Mexico; seventeenth-century persons, places, and practices. Ann Arbor, University of Michigan Press [1959] xi, 260 p. illus., ports., map. 24 cm. 1. Mexico — Social life and customs. 2. Mexico — History — Spanish colony, 1540-1810. I. T.
F1210.L4   917.2   59-9734

Paz, Octavio, 1914-   **III. 7127**
The labyrinth of solitude; life and thought in Mexico. Translated by Lysander Kemp. New York, Grove Press [1962, c1961] 212 p. 21 cm. Essays. 1. Mexico — Civilization. 2. National characteristics, Mexican. I. T.
F1210.P313   917.2   61-11777

Ramos, Samuel.   **III. 7128**
Profile of man and culture in Mexico. Translated by Peter G. Earle. Introd. by Thomas B. Irving. [Austin] University of Texas Press [1962] 198 p. 22 cm. (The Texas Pan-American series) 1. Mexico — Civilization. 2. Mexico — Intellectual life. 3. National characteristics, Mexican. I. T.
F1210.R353   917.2   62-9792

Wolf, Eric Robert, 1923-   **III. 7129**
Sons of the shaking earth. [Chicago] University of Chicago Press [1959] 302 p. illus. 21 cm. 1. Mexico — Civilization. 2. Guatemala — Civilization. 3. Indians of Mexico. 4. Indians of Central America — Guatemala. I. T.
F1210.W6   917.2   59-12290

Gage, Thomas, 1603?-1656.   **III. 7130**
Travels in the new world. Edited and with an introd. by J. Eric S. Thompson. [New ed.] Norman, University of Oklahoma Press [1958] li, 379 p. illus., port., maps. 24 cm. First published in 1648 under title: The English-American, his travail by sea and land; or, A new survey of the West-India's. 1. Catholic Church — Missions. 2. Mexico — Description and travel. 3. Central America — Description and travel. 4. Missions — Latin America. I. Thompson, John Eric Sidney, 1898- ed. II. T.
F1211.G13 1958   917.2   58-6856

Humboldt, Alexander, Freiherr von, 1769-1859.   **III. 7131**
Political essay on the kingdom of New Spain. With physical sections and maps founded on astronomical observations and trigonometrical and barometrical measurements. Translated from the original French by John Black. London, Printed for Longman, Hurst, Rees, Orme, and Brown, 1811. New York, AMS Press, 1966, [i.e. 1970] 4 v. illus., fold. maps. 23 cm. Translation of Essai politique sur le royaume de la Nouvelle-Espagne. 1. Mexico — Description and travel. 2. Mexico — Economic conditions. I. T.
F1211.H924   917.2/03/2   71-16283

Calderón de la Barca, Frances Erskine (Inglis) 1804-1882.   **III. 7132**
Life in Mexico during a residence of two years in that country, by Madame Calderon de la Barca. London, Dent; New York, Dutton [1913] xxxviii, 542 p. 17 cm. (Everyman's library. Travel and topography. [no. 664]) Introduction by Henry Baerlein. Preface signed: William H. Prescott. Glossary of Spanish or Mexican words: p. xxxvii-xxxviii. 1. Mexico — Description and travel. 2. Mexico — Social life and customs. I. Baerlein, Henry Philip Bernard, 1875- ed. II. T.
F1213.C145   917.2   A14-1168

Tylor, Edward Burnett, Sir, 1832-1917.   **III. 7133**
Anahuac: or, Mexico and the Mexicans, ancient and modern. New York, Bergman Publishers [1970] xi, 344 p. illus., map. 24 cm. Reprint of the 1861 ed. 1. Mexico — Description and travel. 2. Mexico — Antiquities. I. T.
F1213.T98 1970   917.2/03/6   66-29078

Flandrau, Charles Macomb, 1871-1938.   **III. 7134**
Viva Mexico! New York, Harper [1951?] 218 p. 23 cm. 1. Mexico — Description and travel. I. T.
F1215.F583   917.2   51-11911

Verissimo, Erico, 1905-   **III. 7135**
Mexico. Translated from the Portuguese by Linton Barrett. New York, Orion Press [1960] 341 p. illus. 22 cm. Translation of México; história duma viagem. 1. Mexico — Description and travel — 1951-
F1216.V413   917.2   60-13621

F1219 – 1221 Antiquities. Indians

Beals, Ralph Leon, 1901-   **III. 7136**
The comparative ethnology of northern Mexico before 1750, by Ralph L. Beals. Berkeley, Calif., University of California Press, 1932. vi, [93]-225 p. maps (1 fold.) tables. 28 cm. (Ibero-Americana: 2) 1. Ethnology — Mexico. 2. Indians of Mexico. I. T.
F1219.B4x   A32-1113

Bernal, Ignacio.   **III. 7137**
The Olmec world. Translated by Doris Heydon and Fernando Horcasitas. Berkeley, University of California Press, 1969. xiv, 273 p. illus., maps. 29 cm. 1. Olmecs. 2. Indians of Mexico — Culture. 3. Vera Cruz, Mexico (State) — Antiquities. I. T.
F1219.B51713   970.3   68-13351

Coe, Michael D.   **III. 7138**
America's first civilization, by Michael D. Coe. Consultant: Richard B. Woodbury. [New York] American Heritage; distribution by Van Nostrand [Princeton, N.J., 1968] 159 p. illus. (part col.), col. maps, ports. 27 cm. (The Smithsonian library) 1. Olmecs. I. T.
F1219.C7569   970.3   68-55791

Coe, Michael D.   **III. 7139**
Mexico. New York, Praeger [1962] 244 p. illus. 21 cm. (Ancient peoples and places, v.29) 1. Mexico — History — To 1519. 2. Mexico — Antiquities. 3. Indians of Mexico — Culture.
F1219.C757   972.01   62-16846

Linné, Sigvald, 1899-   **III. 7140**
Mexican highland cultures; archaeological researches at Teotihuacan, Calpulalpan and Chalchicomula in 1934/35, by S. Linné. [Stockholm, 1942] 223 p. illus. (maps, plans) 6 pl. (part col.; fold. plan) 30 cm. (The Ethnographical museum of Sweden, Stockholm (Statens etnografiska museum) New series. Publication no. 7) Translated from the Swedish manuscript into English by Mr. Magnus Leijer. cf. Introd. "The Humanistic foundation of Sweden (Humanistiska fonden) has defrayed the printing costs." 1. Mexico — Antiquities. 2. Teotihuacán, Mexico. 3. Calpulalpan, Mexico (District) 4. Chalchicomula, Mexico (District) I. Leijer, Magnus, tr. II. T.
F1219.L6   913.72   46-3496

Motolinia, Toribio, d. 1568.   **III. 7141**
History of the Indians of New Spain. Translated and edited by Elizabeth Andros Foster. [Berkeley, Calif.] Cortés Society, 1950. x, 294 p. illus. 27 cm. (Documents and narratives concerning the discovery & conquest of Latin America, new ser., no. 4) 1. Indians of Mexico. 2. Franciscans in Mexico. (S)
F1219.M922 (F1411.D63 n. s., no. 4)   970.4   50-2863

Peterson, Frederick A.   **III. 7142**
Ancient Mexico; an introduction to the pre-Hispanic cultures. Maps and drawings by José Luis Franco. New York, Putnam [1959] 313 p. illus. 25 cm. 1. Indians of Mexico — Culture. 2. Mexico — History — To 1519. 3. Mexico — Antiquities. I. T.
F1219.P42   970.42   58-5697

Sahagún, Bernardino de, d. 1590.   **III. 7143**
General history of the things of New Spain; Florentine codex, translated from the Aztec into English, with notes and illustrations, by Arthur J. O. Anderson [and] Charles E. Dibble. Santa Fe, N.M., School of American

Research, 1950- v. illus. 29 cm. (Monographs of the School of American Research, no. 14, pt,) English and Aztec. "Temporary foreword": 2 p. inserted. *1. Indians of Mexico — Antiquities. 2. Aztecs. 3. Mexico — History — Conquest, 1519-1540. 4. Natural history — Mexico. 5. Calendar, Mexican. 6. Aztec language — Texts. I. T:Florentine codex. (S:Santa Fe, N.M. School of American Research. Monographs, no. 14)*
F1219.S1319   972.014   51-2409

Soustelle, Jacques, 1912-   III. 7144
The daily life of the Aztecs, on the eve of the Spanish conquest. Translated from the French by Patrick O'Brian. New York, Macmillan, 1962 [c1961] 319 p. illus. 23 cm. (Daily life series) *1. Aztecs. 2. Indians of Mexico — Social life and customs. I. T.*
F1219.S723 1962   972.014   62-53354

Spores, Ronald.   III. 7145
The Mixtec kings and their people. [1st ed.] Norman, University of Oklahoma Press [1967] xvii, 269 p. illus., facsims., maps. 23 cm. (The Civilization of the American Indian series, 85) *1. Mixtex Indians — History. I. T. (S)*
F1219.S768   970.3   66-22717

Vaillant, George Clapp, 1901-1945.   III. 7146
Aztecs of Mexico: origin, rise, and fall of the Aztec Nation. Rev. by Suzannah B. Vaillant. Garden City, N.Y., Doubleday, 1962. xxii, 312 p. illus., maps, tables. 24 cm. *1. Aztecs. 2. Mexico — History — To 1519. I. T.*
F1219.V13 1962   972.014   62-10466

Weaver, Muriel Porter.   III. 7147
The Aztecs, Maya, and their predecessors; archaeology of Mesoamerica. New York, Seminar Press [1972] xvi, 347 p. illus. 29 cm. (Studies in archeology) *1. Mexico — Antiquities. 2. Guatemala — Antiquities. 3. Indians, Aztec. 4. Indians, Maya. I. T.*
F1219.Wx

Zurita, Alonso de, b. 1511 or 12.   III. 7148
Life and labor in ancient Mexico; the brief and summary relation of the Lords of New Spain. Translated, and with an introd. by Benjamin Keen. New Brunswick, N.J., Rutgers University Press [1963] 328 p. illus., maps. 22 cm. Translation of Breve y sumaria relación de los señores de la Nueva España. *1. Indians of Mexico. 2. Mexico — Antiquities. 3. Mexico — History — Spanish colony, 1540-1810. I. T.*
F1219.Z943   972.02   63-15521

F1219.1   SPECIAL LOCALITIES, A – Z

Aschmann, Homer, 1920-   III. 7149
The Central Desert of Baja California; demography and ecology. Riverside, Calif., Manessier Pub. Co. [1967] xx, 315 p. illus., maps (1 fold. col.) 24 cm. *1. Indians of Mexico — Baja California. 2. Indians of Mexico — Missions. I. T.*
F1219.1.B3A7 1967   970.422   66-29636

Bernal, Ignacio.   III. 7150
Mexico before Cortez; art, history, legend. Translated by Willis Barnstone. [1st ed.] Garden City, N.Y., Doubleday, 1963. 135 p. illus. 19 cm. (A Dolphin original) "C422." Translation of Tenochtitlán en una isla. *1. Indians of Mexico — Mexico, Valley of. 2. Mexico, Valley of — Antiquities. 3. Mexico — History — To 1519. I. T.*
F1219.1.M53B43   972.01   63-13078

Gibson, Charles, 1920-   III. 7151
The Aztecs under Spanish rule; a history of the Indians of the Valley of Mexico, 1519-1810. Stanford, Calif., Stanford University Press, 1964. xii, 657 p. illus. (1 col.) maps. 24 cm. *1. Indians of Mexico — Mexico, Valley of. 2. Mexico — History — To 1810. 3. Spain — Colonies — America — Administration. I. T.*
F1219.1.M53G5   972.02   64-12071

Madsen, William.   III. 7152
The Virgin's children; life in an Aztec village today. New York, Greenwood Press [1969, c1960] xv, 248 p. illus. 24 cm. *1. Aztecs — Social life and customs. 2. San Francisco Tecospa, Mexico. I. T.*
F1219.1.S2M3 1969   970.3   74-88900   ISBN:0837120985

F1219.3   SPECIAL TOPICS, A – Z

Marquina, Ignacio.   III. 7153
Arquitectura prehispánica. México, Instituto Nacional de Antropología e Historia, Secretaría de Educación Pública, 1951. xix, 970 p. illus. (part col.) maps, plans. 32 cm. (Memorias del Instituto Nacional de Antropología e Historia, 1) *1. Mexico — Antiquities. 2. Architecture — Mexico. 3. Indians of Mexico — Architecture. I. T. (S:Mexico. Instituto Nacional de Antropología e Historia. Memorias, 1)*
F1219.3.A6M37   A52-8534

Covarrubias, Miguel, 1904-1957.   III. 7154
Indian art of Mexico and Central America. Color plates and line drawings by the author. [1st ed.] New York, Knopf, 1957. xvi, 360, xvii p. illus., plates (part col.) maps. 28 cm. *1. Indians of Mexico — Art. 2. Indians of Central America — Art. 3. Mexico — Antiquities. 4. Central America — Antiquities. I. T.*
F1219.3.A7C58   970.65717   57-59203

Covarrubias, Miguel, 1904-1957.   III. 7155
Mezcala, ancient Mexican sculpture. With notes by William Spratling and a pref. by André Emmerich. New York, André Emmerich Gallery [1956] 36 p. illus., map. 23 cm. *1. Indians of Mexico — Art. 2. Sculpture — Guerrero, Mexico (State) 3. Guerrero, Mexico (State) — Antiquities. I. T.*
F1219.3.A7C6   913.72 (972.01)   57-1714

Dockstader, Frederick J.   III. 7156
Indian art in Middle America [by] Frederick J. Dockstader. Photography by Carmelo Guadagno. Greenwich, Conn., New York Graphic Society [1964] 221 p. 249 illus. (part col.) maps. 29 cm. *1. Indians of Mexico — Art. 2. Mexico — Antiquities. 3. Indians of Central America — Art. 4. Central America — Antiquities. 5. Indians of the West Indies — Art. 6. West Indies — Antiquities. I. T.*
F1219.3.A7D6   970.67   64-21815

Groth-Kimball, Irmgard.   III. 7157
The art of ancient Mexico. 109 photos. by Irmgard Groth-Kimball; text and notes by Franz Feuchtwanger. London, New York, Thames and Hudson [1954] 125 p. illus., map. 32 cm. *1. Indians of Mexico — Art. 2. Mexico — Antiquities. 3. Art — Mexico. I. Feuchtwanger, Franz. II. T.*
F1219.3.A7G713   913.72 (972.01)   54-4625

Toscano, Salvador, 1912-1949.   III. 7158
Arte precolombino de México y de la América Central. Prólogo del doctor Miguel León-Portilla. Edición de Beatriz de la Fuente. [3. ed.] México, Universidad Nacional Autónoma de México, Instituto de Investigaciones Estéticas, 1970. 286 p. illus. (part col.) 29 cm. *1. Indians of Mexico — Art. 2. Indians of Central America — Art. 3. Mexico — Antiquities. 4. Central America — Antiquities. I. Fuente, Beatrize de la. II. Mexico (City) Universidad Nacional. Instituto de Investigaciones Estéticas. III. T.*
F1219.3.A7T6 1970   70-26940

León-Portilla, Miguel.   III. 7159
Aztec thought and culture; a study of the ancient Nahuatl mind. Translated from the Spanish by Jack Emory Davis. [1st ed.] Norman, University of Oklahoma Press [1963] 241 p. illus. 24 cm. (The Civilization of the American Indian series, 67) A translation and adaptation of the author's La filosofía náhuatl. *1. Nahuas. 2. Indians of Mexico — Philosophy. I. T.*
F1219.3.P5L43   972.014   63-11019

Caso, Alfonso, 1896-   III. 7160
The Aztecs; people of the sun. Illustrated by Miguel Covarrubias; translated by Lowell Dunham. [1st ed.] Norman, University of Oklahoma Press [1958] xvii, 125 p. col. illus., 16 plates. 28 cm. (The Civilization of the American Indian series, 50) Translation of El pueblo del sol. *1. Aztecs. 2. Indians of Mexico — Religion and mythology. (S)*
F1219.3.R38C313   972.014   58-11603

F1221   TRIBES, A – Z

Foster, George McClelland, 1913-   III. 7161
A primitive Mexican economy. New York, J. J. Augustin [1942] vii, 115 p. illus. (map, plans) IV pl. 25 cm. (Monographs of the American Ethnological Society, v) "Centennial anniversary publication, the American Ethnological Society, 1842-1942." *1. Popoloca Indians. 2. Indians of Mexico — Economic conditions. I. T.*
F1221.P6F7 (E51.A556 vol. 5)   970.3   43-3896

Pennington, Campbell W.   III. 7162
The Tarahumar of Mexico: their environment and material culture. Salt Lake City, University of Utah Press [1963] 267 p. illus., 4 fold. maps (in pocket) 24 cm. *1. Tarahumare Indians. 2. Indians of Mexico — Implements. 3. Anthropo-geography — Mexico — Chihuahua (State) I. T.*
F1221.T25P4   970.3   64-1645

Beals, Ralph Leon, 1901-   III. 7163
Cherán: a Sierra Tarascan village, by Ralph L. Beals. Prepared in cooperation with the U.S. Dept. of State as a project of the Interdepartmental Committee on Cultural and Scientific Cooperation. Westport, Conn., Greenwood Press [1970] x, 225 p. illus., maps, plans. 29 cm.

(Smithsonian Institution. Institute of Social Anthropology. Publication no. 2) Reprint of the 1946 ed. *1. Cherán, Mexico. 2. Tarasco Indians. I. United States. Interdepartmental Committee on Scientific and Cultural Cooperation. (S)*
F1221.T3B4 1970   980.3   69-13812   ISBN:0837131669

Foster, George McClelland, 1913-   III. 7164
Empire's children; the people of Tzintzuntzan, by George M. Foster, assisted by Gabriel Ospina. Westport, Conn., Greenwood Press [1973] v, 297 p. illus. 29 cm. "Prepared in cooperation with the United States Department of State as a project of the Interdepartmental Committee on Scientific and Cultural Cooperation." Reprint of the 1948 ed., which was issued as Publication no. 6 of Smithsonian Institution Institute of Social Anthropology. *1. Tzintzuntzan, Mexico. 2. Tarascan Indians. I. T. (S:Smithsonian Institution. Institute of Social Anthropology. Publication no. 6.)*
F1221.T3F67 1973   970.4/2/3   73-118760   ISBN:0837150779

Zantwijk, Rudolf A. M. van.   III. 7165
Servants of the saints. The social and cultural identity of a Tarascan community in Mexico. [By] R. A. M. van Zantwijk. Assen, Van Gorcum & Comp., 1967. xiv, 304 p. fold. map, fold. table. 16 p. of photos. 23 1/2 cm. (Samenlevingen buiten Europa, Non-European societies, 7) Issued also as thesis, University of Amsterdam. Summary in Spanish. *1. Ihuatzio — Social life and customs. 2. Tarasco Indians — Social life and customs. I. T. (S:Samenlevingen buiten Europa, 7)*
F1221.T3Z3 1967   970.3   68-73532

Cancian, Frank.   III. 7166
Economics and prestige in a Maya community; the religious cargo system in Zinacantán. Stanford, Calif., Stanford University Press, 1965. xv, 238 p. illus., maps, ports. 23 cm. Revision of thesis, Harvard University. Based on work of the Harvard Chiapas project. *1. Tzotzil Indians. 2. Zinacantán, Mexico — Social conditions. 3. Prestige. I. T.*
F1221.T9C3   970.3   65-18976

Leslie, Charles M., 1923-   III. 7167
Now we are civilized; a study of the world view of the Zapotec Indians of Mitla, Oaxaca. Detroit, Wayne State University Press, 1960. xi, 108 p. illus., group port., map (on lining paper) 24 cm. *1. Zapotec Indians. 2. Mitla, Mexico (Oaxaca) — Social life and customs. I. T.*
F1221.Z3L4   970.3   60-7651

F1223 – 1235   History

Cline, Howard Francis.   III. 7168
The United States and Mexico. Rev. ed., enl. Cambridge, Harvard University Press, 1963. 484 p. maps (1 fold.) 20 cm. (The American foreign policy library) *1. Mexico — History. 2. U.S. — Relations (general) with Mexico. 3. Mexico — Relations (general) with the U.S. I. T. (S)*
F1226.C6 1963a   972.08   63-25301

Parkes, Henry Bamford, 1904-   III. 7169
A history of Mexico. 3d ed., rev. and enl. Boston, Houghton Mifflin, 1960. 458 p. illus. 22 cm. *1. Mexico — History.*
F1226.P27 1960   972   60-9360

Simpson, Lesley Byrd, 1891-   III. 7170
Many Mexicos. 4th ed. rev. Berkeley, University of California Press, 1966. xiii, 389 p. illus., maps (part fold.) 24 cm. *1. Mexico — History. 2. Mexico — Civilization. I. T.*
F1226.S63 1966   972   66-19101

F1230   1519 – 1535

Braden, Charles Samuel, 1887-   III. 7171
Religious aspects of the conquest of Mexico, by Charles S. Braden. Durham, N.C., Duke University Press, 1930. xv, 344 p. plates. 24 cm. (Duke university publications) Without thesis note. *1. Cortés, Hernando, 1485-1547. 2. Mexico — History — Conquest, 1519-1540. 3. Indians of Mexico — Missions. 4. Catholic church in Mexico. 5. Indians of Mexico — Religion and mythology. 6. Mexico — Church history. I. T.*
F1230.B79   30-31135

Cortés, Hernando, 1485-1547.   III. 7172
Five letters, 1519-1526. Translated by J. Bayard Morris, with an introd. New York, W. W. Norton [1962] xlvii, 388 p. 20 cm. (The Norton library, N180) *1. Mexico — History — Conquest, 1519-1540. I. Morris, John Bayard, ed. and tr.*
F1230.C8522 1962   972.02   62-51066

Gómara, Francisco López de, 1510-1560?   III. 7173
Cortés: the life of the conqueror by his secretary. Translated and edited by Lesley Byrd Simpson. Berkeley, University of California Press, 1964. xxvi, 425 p. illus., map (on lining papers) 24 cm. Translation of Istoria de la conquista de Mexico, the 2d part of the author's Historia general de las Indias. *1. Cortés, Hernando, 1485-1547. 2. Mexico — History — Conquest, 1519-1540. I. Simpson, Lesley Byrd, 1891- ed. and tr.*
F1230.C9216   923.572   64-13474

Madariaga, Salvador de, 1886-   III. 7174
Hernán Cortés, conqueror of Mexico. Coral Gables, Fla., University of Miami Press [1967, c1942] ix, 554 p. port., maps. 24 cm. *1. Cortes, Hernando, 1485-1547. 2. Mexico — History — Conquest, 1519-1540.*
F1230.C927 1967   972/.02/0924 (B)   67-28274

Díaz del Castillo, Bernal, 1496-1584.   III. 7175
The discovery and conquest of Mexico, 1517-1521. Edited from the only exact copy of the original MS. (and published in Mexico) by Genaro García. Translated with an introd. and notes by A. P. Maudslay. Introd. to the American ed. by Irving A. Leonard. [New York] Farrar, Straus, and Cudahy [c1956] xxxi, 478 p. illus., port., maps. 24 cm. Translation of Historia verdadera de la conquista de la Nueva España. *1. Mexico — History — Conquest, 1519-1540. I. T.*
F1230.D5442 1956   972.02   56-5758

Fuentes, Patricia de, ed. and tr.   III. 7176
The conquistadors; first-person accounts of the conquest of Mexico. Pref. by Howard F. Cline. New York, Orion Press [1963] xxii, 250 p. illus., ports., maps, plan. 23 cm. *1. Mexico — History — Conquest, 1519-1540. 2. America — Early accounts to 1600. I. T.*
F1230.F9   972.01   63-9525

León Portilla, Miguel, ed.   III. 7177
The broken spears; the Aztec account of the conquest of Mexico. English translation by Lysander Kemp. Illus., adapted from original codices paintings, by Alberto Beltran. Boston, Beacon Press [1962] xxxi, 168 p. illus., map. 24 cm. Translation of Visión de los vencidos which was translated from Náhuatl by Angel Maria Garibay K. *1. Mexico — History — Conquest, 1519-1540 — Sources. 2. Aztec literature — Translations into English. 3. English literature — Translations from Aztec. I. Kemp, Lysander, 1920- tr. II. T.*
F1230.L383   972.02   62-7247

Gardiner, Clinton Harvey.   III. 7178
Martín López, conquistador citizen of Mexico. Lexington, University of Kentucky Press, 1958. 193 p. 24 cm. *1. López, Martín. 2. Mexico — History — Conquest, 1519-1540.*
F1230.L84G3   923.972   58-6599

Padden, R. C.   III. 7179
The hummingbird and the hawk; conquest and sovereignty in the valley of Mexico, 1503-1541, by R. C. Padden. [Columbus] Ohio State University Press [1967] xvi, 319 p. illus., facsim., maps. 23 cm. *1. Mexico — History — Conquest, 1519-1540. 2. Mexico — History — To 1519. I. T.*
F1230.P3   972/.02   67-12912

Prescott, William Hickling, 1796-1859.   III. 7180
The conquest of Mexico ... [by] W. H. Prescott. London, Dent; New York, Dutton [1931-33] 2 v. double map. 18 cm. (Everyman's library. History. [no. 397-398]) First published in this edition, 1909. "Introduction by Thomas Seccombe." *1. Cortés, Hernando, 1485-1547. 2. Mexico — History — Conquest, 1519-1540.*
F1230.P9692x (AC1.E8 no. 397-398)   972.02   36-37452

F1230.3 – 2239   History. Ethnography

F1231 – 1232   1535 – 1849

Aiton, Arthur Scott, 1894-1955.   III. 7181
Antonio de Mendoza, first viceroy of New Spain. New York, Russell & Russell [1967] xii, 240 p. illus., map, port. 23 cm. Reprint of the 1927 ed. *1. Mendoza, Antonio de, conde de Tendilla, 1491-1552. 2. Mexico — History — Conquest, 1519-1540. 3. Mexico — History — Spanish colony, 1540-1810.*
F1231.A37 1967   972/02/0924   66-24664

Benítez, Fernando, 1911- III. 7182
The century after Cortés. Translated by Joan MacLean. Chicago, University of Chicago Press [1965] 296 p. illus. 25 cm. Translation of Los primeros Mexicanos: la vida criolla en el siglo XVI. *1. Mexico — Social life and customs. 2. Mexcio — History — Spanish colony, 1540-1810. I. T.*
F1231.B4513   917.2032   65-25121

Bobb, Bernard E. III. 7183
The viceregency of Antonio María Bucareli in New Spain, 1771-1779. Austin, University of Texas Press [1962] 313 p. illus. 24 cm. (The Texas Pan-American series) *1. Bucareli y Ursúa, Antonio Maria, Viceroy of Mexico, 1717-1779. 2. Mexico — Politics and government — 1540-1810. 3. Spain — Colonies — America — Administration. I. T.*
F1231.B6   972.02   62-9785

Priestley, Herbert Ingram, 1875-1944. III. 7184
José de Gálvez, visitor-general of New Spain (1765-1771) by Herbert Ingram Priestley. Berkeley, University of California Press, 1916. xiv, 449 p. front. (port.) pl., maps (2 fold.) plan. 25 cm. (University of California publications in history. vol.V) Appendix: Instruction to José de Gálvez (404-417 p.) *1. Gálvez, José de, marqués de Sonora, 1720-1787. 2. Mexico — History — Spanish colony, 1540-1810. 3. Spain — Colonies — Administration.*
F1231.G2 (E173.C15 vol. 5)   A16-1488

Powell, Philip Wayne. III. 7185
Soldiers, Indians & silver; the northward advance of New Spain, 1550-1600. Berkeley, University of California Press, 1952. ix, 317 p. maps. 24 cm. *1. Mexico — History — Spanish Colony, 1540-1810. 2. Mexico — Politics and government — 1540-1810. 3. Chichimecs. I. T.*
F1231.P6   972.02   52-62534

Callcott, Wilfrid Hardy, 1895- III. 7186
Liberalism in Mexico, 1857-1929. Hamden, Conn., Archon Books, 1965 [c1959] xi, 410 p. illus. 22 cm. "Reprinted ... 1965, with a new introduction." *1. Mexico — Politics and government. 2. Mexico — Social conditions. 3. Liberalism — Mexico. I. T.*
F1231.5.C27 1965   972.08   65-19595

Callcott, Wilfrid Hardy, 1895- III. 7187
Church and state in Mexico, 1822-1857. New York, Octagon Books, 1965 [c1926] 357 p. 24 cm. *1. Mexico. Constitution. 2. Church and state in Mexico. 3. Mexico — Politics and government — 1821-1861.*
F1232.C142 1965   972.04   65-16767

Hamill, Hugh M. III. 7188
The Hidalgo revolt; prelude to Mexican independence [by] Hugh M. Hamill, Jr. Gainesville, University of Florida Press, 1966. xi, 284 p. facsims., ports. 25 cm. *1. Hidalgo y Costilla, Miguel, 1753-1811. 2. Mexico — History — Wars of Independence, 1810-1821. I. T.*
F1232.H6243   972.030924   66-23070

Robertson, William Spence, 1872- III. 7189
Iturbide of Mexico. New York, Greenwood Press, 1968 [c1952] ix, 361 p. illus., coat of arms, map, ports. 24 cm. (Duke Univeristy publications) *1. Iturbide, Agustín de, Emperor of Mexico, 1783-1824. 2. Mexico — History — Wars of Independence, 1810-1821. 3. Mexico — History — 1821-1861.*
F1232.I925 1968   972/.03/0924 (B)   68-23321

Rives, George Lockhart, 1849-1917. III. 7190
The United States and Mexico, 1821-1848 a history of the relations between the two countries from the independence of Mexico to the close of the war with the United States, by George Lockhart Rives. New York, Scribner, 1913. 2 v. maps (2 fold.) plans (1 double) 24 cm. *1. Mexico — History — 1821-1861. 2. U.S. — History — War with Mexico, 1845-1848. 3. Mexico — Foreign relations — U.S. 4. U.S. — Foreign relations — Mexico. I. T.*
F1232.R62   13-20399

Callcott, Wilfrid Hardy, 1895- III. 7191
Santa Anna; the story of an enigma who once was Mexico. Hamden, Conn., Archon Books, 1964 [c1963] xiv, 381 p. illus., ports. 22 cm. *1. Santa Anna, Antonio López de, Pres. Mexico, 1794?-1876. 2. Mexico — History — 1821-1861.*
F1232.S2312 1964   923.172   64-13173

F1233   1849/1861 – 1910

Hanna, Alfred Jackson, 1893- III. 7192
Napoleon III and Mexico; American triumph over monarchy, by Alfred Jackson Hanna and Kathryn Abbey Hanna. Chapel Hill, University of North Carolina Press [1971] xxii, 350 p. illus. 24 cm. *1. Mexico — History — European Intervention, 1861-1867. 2. Mexico — Foreign relations — 1861-1867. 3. United States — Foreign relations — 1861-1865. I. Hanna, Kathryn Trimmer (Abbey) 1895- joint author. II. T.*
F1233.H2   972/.07   72-156761   ISBN:0807811718

Roeder, Ralph, 1890- III. 7193
Juarez and his Mexico; a biographical history. New York, Greenwood Press, 1968 [c1947] 2 v. (763 p.) ports. 24 cm. *1. Juárez, Benito Pablo, Pres. Mexico, 1806-1872. 2. Mexico — History — European intervention, 1861-1867. I. T.*
F1233.J949 1968   972/.07/0924 (B)   68-23322

Blasio, José Luis, 1842-1923. III. 7194
Maximiliano íntimo, el Emperador Macimiliano y su corte; memorias de un secretario particular. México, Editora Nacional, 1956. 478 p. illus. 17 cm. (Colección económica, libros de bolsillo buenos, bonitos, baratos, v.73) *1. Maximilian, Emperor of Mexico, 1832-1867. 2. Mexico — History — European intervention, 1861-1867.*
F1233.M452 1956   57-37161

Corti, Egon caesar, conte, 1886-1953. III. 7195
Maximilain and Charlotte of Mexico [by] Egon Caesar. Count Corti, translated from the German by Catherine Alison Phillips. New York, & London, Knopf, 1928. 2 v. plates, ports., double map, facsims. (part fold.) 25 cm. Paged continuously. "Originally published as Maximilian und Charlotte von Mexico ... 1924 by Amalthea-verlag, Vienna." *1. Maximilian, emperor of Mexico, 1832-1867. 2. Charlotte, consort of Maximilian, emperor of Mexico, 1840-1927. 3. Mexico — History — European intervention, 1861-1867. I. Phillips, Catherine Alison, 1884-*
F1233.M4542   28-9888

Scholes, Walter Vinton, 1916- III. 7196
Mexican politics during the Juárez regime, 1855-1872 [by] Walter V. Scholes. Columbia, University of Missouri Press [1969] 190 p. port. 22 cm. (University of Missouri studies, v. 30) *1. Mexico — Politics and government. 2. Juárez, Benito Pablo, Pres. Mexico, 1806-1872. I. T. (S:Missouri. University. The University of Missouri studies, v. 30)*
F1233.S37 1969   972/.06   73-629894   ISBN:082620581X

Cosío Villegas, Daniel, 1900- III. 7197
Historia moderna de México. México, Editorial Hermes [1955-   v. illus., maps (part fold.) 23 cm. (Historia) *1. Mexico — History — 1867-1910. 2. Mexico — Foreign relations. I. Calderón, Francisco R. II. González y González, Luis. III. González Navarro, Moisés. IV. T.*
F1233.5.C6   55-40220

Beals, Carleton, 1893- III. 7198
Porfirio Diaz, dictator of Mexico. Westport, Conn., Greenwood Press [1971, c1959] 463 p. illus., map, ports. 24 cm. *1. Diaz, Porfirio, Pres. Mexico, 1830-1915.*
F1233.5.D53B4 1971   972.08/1/0924 (B)   72-135241
ISBN:0837151597

F1234   1910 –

Brandenburg, Frank Ralph, 1926- III. 7199
The making of modern Mexico [by] Frank Brandenburg. Introd. by Frank Tannenbaum. Englewood Cliffs, N.J., Prentice-Hall [1964] xv, 379 p. map. 24 cm. *1. Mexico — History — 1910-1946. 2. Mexico — History — 1946- I. T.*
F1234.B815   972.082   63-16743

Calvert, Peter. III. 7200
The Mexican Revolution, 1910-1914: the diplomacy of Anglo-American conflict. Cambridge, London, Cambridge U.P., 1968. x, 331 p. maps. 22 cm. (Cambridge Latin American studies, 3) *1. Mexico — History — 1910-1946. 2. United States — Foreign relations — 1909-1913. 3. Great Britain — Foreign relations — 1910-1936. I. T. (S)*
F1234.C2125   972.08   68-12056   ISBN:0521044235

Cumberland, Charles Curtis. III. 7201
Mexican Revolution, genesis under Madero. New York, Greenwood Press [1969, c1952] ix, 298 p. illus., map, ports. 23 cm. *1. Mexico — History — 1910-1946. 2. Madero, Francisco Indalecio, Pres. Mexico, 1873-1913. I. T.*
F1234.C975 1969   972.08/1   71-90495   ISBN:837121264

Guzmán, Martín Luis, 1887- III. 7202
The eagle and the serpent. Translated from the Spanish by Harriet de Onís. With an introd. by Federico de Onís. Garden City, N.Y., Dolphin Books [1965] xiv, 386 p. 18 cm. *1. Mexico — History — 1910-1946. I. Villa, Francisco, 1877-1923. II. De Onís, Harriet, 1899- tr. III. T.*
F1234.G9745 1965   972.081   65-13087

Meyer, Michael C. III. 7203
Huerta; a political portrait, by Michael C. Meyer. Lincoln, University of Nebraska Press [1972] xvi, 272 p. 24 cm. *1. Huerta, Victoriano, Pres. Mexico, 1854-1916. I. T.*
F1234.H87M48   972.08/1/0924 (B)   70-162343   ISBN:0803208022

Lieuwen, Edwin, 1923- III. 7204
Mexican militarism; the political rise and fall of the revolutionary army, 1910-1940. [Albuquerque, University of New Mexico Press [1968] xiii, 194 p.

illus., map. 25 cm. *1. Mexico — History — 1910-1946. 2. Civil supremacy over the military — Mexico. 3. Mexico — Armed Forces — Political activity. I. T.*
F1234.L69   972.08/2   68-19738

Ross, Stanley Robert, 1921-   III. 7205
Francisco I. Madero, apostle of Mexican democracy, by Stanley R. Ross. New York, AMS Press [1970, c1955] xii, 378 p. maps, port. 23 cm. Originally presented as author's thesis, Columbia University, 1955, under title: Mexican apostle; the life of Francisco I. Madero. *1. Madero, Francisco Indalecio, Pres. Mexico, 1873-1913. 2. Díaz, Porfirio, Pres. Mexico, 1830-1915. 3. Mexico — Politics and government — 1910-1946.*
F1234.M244 1970   972.08/1/0924   79-122591   ISBN:404054099

Meyer, Michael C.   III. 7206
Mexican rebel; Pascual Orozco and the Mexican Revolution, 1910-1915, by Michael C. Meyer. Lincoln, University of Nebraska Press [1967] x, 172 p. illus., ports. 24 cm. *1. Orozco, Pascual. I. T.*
F1234.O73M4   972.08/1/0924 (B)   67-10667

Quirk, Robert E.   III. 7207
The Mexican revolution, 1914-1915; the Convention of Aguascalientes. Bloomington, Indiana University Press [1960] 325 p. maps (on lining papers) 22 cm. *1. Mexico. Soberana Convención Revolucionaria, 1914-1915. 2. Mexico — History — 1910-1946. I. T.*
F1234.Q63   972.081   60-8914

Tannenbaum, Frank, 1893-   III. 7208
Mexico, the struggle for peace and bread. [1st ed.] New York, Knopf, 1950. xiv, 293, xi p. fold. map. 22 cm. *1. Mexico — Politics and government — 1919- 2. Mexico — Social conditions. 3. Mexico — Economic conditions — 1918- 4. Mexico — Foreign relations — 1910- I. T.*
F1234.T13   972.082   50-5736

Tannenbaum, Frank, 1893-1969.   III. 7209
Peace by revolution; an interpretation of Mexico Drawings by Miguel Covarrubias. Freeport, N.Y., Books for Libraries Press [1971, c1933] 316 p. illus. 23 cm. *1. Mexico — History — 1910-1946. 2. Mexico — History — 1810- 3. Mexico — Social conditions. I. T.*
F1234.T14 1971   917.2/03   72-169776   ISBN:0836959965

Womack, John, 1937-   III. 7210
Zapata and the Mexican Revolution. [1st ed.] New York, Knopf, 1969, [c1968] xi, 435, xxi p. illus., ports. 25 cm. *1. Mexico — History — 1910-1946. 2. Zapata, Emiliano, 1879-1919. I. T.*
F1234.W8   972.08/1/0924 (B)   68-23947

F1241 – 1391   Regions. Cities

Blaisdell, Lowell L.   III. 7211
The desert revolution: Baja California, 1911. Madison, University of Wisconsin Press, 1962. xiii, 268 p. illus., ports. 23 cm. *1. Flores Magón, Ricardo, 1873-1922. 2. Baja California — History. 3. Mexico — History — 1910-1946. I. T.*
F1246.B55   972.2   62-9258

Sauer, Carl Ortwin, 1889-   III. 7212
Colima of New Spain in the sixteenth century. Berkeley, Univ. of California Press, 1948. vii, 104 p. illus., plates, fold. map. 24 cm. (Ibero-Americana, 29) *1. Colima, Mexico (State)*
F1271.S3x   A48-6711

Stanislawski, Dan.   III. 7213
The anatomy of eleven towns in Michoacán. Austin, University of Texas Press, 1950. 77 p. illus., maps, plans. 26 cm. (Latin-American studies, 10) *1. Cities and towns — Mexico — Michoacan. 2. Michoacan, Mexico — Description and travel. I. T. (S:Texas. University. Institute of Latin-American Studies. Latin-American studies, 10)*
F1306.S8x (F1401.T45 no. 10)   917.23   A50-9535

Gibson, Charles, 1920-   III. 7214
Tlaxcala in the sixteenth century. Stanford, Calif., Stanford University Press [1967, c1952] xvi, 300 p. illus., geneal. tables, map, plan. 24 cm. *1. Tlaxcala, Mexico (State) — History. 2. Tlascalan Indians. 3. Spain — Colonies — Administration. I. T.*
F1366.G4 1967   972/.4   67-27516

Landa, Diego de, 1524-1579.   III. 7215
Landa's Relación de las cosas de Yucatan, a translation, edited with notes by Alfred M. Tozzer. Cambridge, Mass., The Museum, 1941. xiii, 394 p., 1 l. port., illus., 3 maps on 1 l. 27 cm. (Papers of the Peabody museum of American archaeology and ethnology, Harvard university, vol. XVIII) Based on the English text made by C. P. Bowditch but compared with the original manuscript, and many corrections and emendations made, principally by Eleanor B. Adams, aided by the author. cf. Introd. *1. Yucatan — History. 2. Mayas — Antiquities. I. Tozzer, Alfred Marston, 1877- ed. II. Bowditch, Charles Pickering, 1842-1921, tr. III. Herrera y Tordesillas, Antonio de, 1559-1625. Historia general de los hechos de los castellanos ... IV. López Medel, Tomás. Relación. V. Chi, Gaspar Antonio, ca. 1531-ca. 1610. Relación. VI. Cervantes de Salazar, Francisco, ca. 1514-ca. 1575. Crónica de Nueva España. VII. T.*
F1376.L248   (E51.H337 vol.18)   972.6   41-15387

Cervantes de Salazar, Francisco, ca. 1514-ca. 1575.   III. 7216
Life in the imperial and loyal city of Mexico in New Spain, and the Royal and Pontifical University of Mexico, as described in the dialogues for the study of the Latin language prepared by Francisco Cervantes de Salazar for use in his classes and printed in 1554 by Juan Pablos. Now published in facsim. with a translation by Minnie Lee Barrett Shepard and an introd. and notes by Carlos Eduardo Castañeda. Westport, Conn., Greenwood Press [1970, c1953] vii, 113, [132] p. 23 cm. Half title: The dialogues of Cervantes de Salazar. The facsimile (in Latin) is of leaves 228-[294] of a Cervantes de Salazar volume in the University of Texas' Latin American Collection. The original t.p. for that part reads: Francisci Ceruantis Salazar Toletāi Ad Ludouici Viuis Valentini exercitationem aliquot dialogi. 1554. Leaf 289 is wanting here as in the University of Texas copy. *1. Mexico (City) — Description. 2. Mexico (City). Universidad. 3. Games — Spain. I. Shepard, Minnie Lee Barrett, 1886- tr. II. Castañeda, Carlos Eduardo, 1896-1958, ed. III. The dialogues of Cervantes de Salazar. IV. T.*
F1386.C4 1970   917.25   79-100224   ISBN:837130336

Lewis, Oscar, 1914-   III. 7217
Life in a Mexican village: Tepoztlán restudied; with drawings by Alberto Beltrán. Urbana, University of Illinois Press, 1951. xxvii, 512 p. illus., maps. 27 cm. *1. Tepoztlán, Mexico. 2. Ethnology — Mexico. 3. Mexico — Social life and customs. I. T.*
F1391.T3L4   917.24   51-11683

Redfield, Robert, 1897-   III. 7218
Tepoztlan, a Mexican village; a study of folk life, by Robert Redfield. Chicago, University of Chicago Press [c1930] xi, 247 p. illus., double map, music, plates. 21 cm. (The University of Chicago publications in anthropology. Ethnological series) *1. Tepoztlán, Mexico. 2. Ethnology — Mexico. 3. Mexico — Social life and customs.*
F1391.T3R31   917.24   30-15556

F1392   Negroes in Mexico

Aguirre Beltrán, Gonzalo.   III. 7219
La población negra de México, 1519-1810; estudio etnohistórico. Portada por Juan Alberto Barragán. México, D. F., Ediciones Fuente cultural [1946] 3 p. l., ix-x p., 2 l., 3-347 p., 3 l. maps, diagr. 23 cm. "Primera edición." *1. Negroes in Mexico. 2. Slavery in Mexico. I. T.*
F1392.N4A3   325.260972   47-15862

F1401 – F1419 LATIN AMERICA: GENERAL
F1401 – 1407 Reference Works. Organization of American States

The South American handbook; a year book and guide to the countries and resources of South and Central America, Mexico, and Cuba.   III. 7220
[1st- annual ed.; London, 1924- v. illus., maps. 19 cm. "Founded upon 'The Anglo-South American handbook.'" Subtitle varies. Editor: 1924- J. A. Hunter.- H. Davis. Published by Trade and Travel Publications (called 1924- South American Publications) *1. Latin America. 2. Latin America — Statistics — Yearbooks. I. Hunter, J. A., ed. II. Davies, Howell, ed.*
F1401.S71   25-514

Manger, Willian, 1899-   III. 7221
Pan America in crisis; the future of the OAS. With an introd. by Alberto Lleras Camargo and a foreword by Hector David Castro. Washington, Public Affairs Press [1961] 104 p. 24 cm. *1. Organization of American States. 2. Pan-Americanism. I. T.*
F1402.M3   341.187   61-15691

Thomas, Ann (Van Wynen) III. 7222
The Organization of American States [by] Ann Van Wynen Thomas [and] A. J. Thomas, Jr. Dallas, Southern Methodist University Press, 1963. xii, 530 p. 24 cm. "A Law Institute of the Americas study." 1. Organization of American States. I. Thomas, Aaron Joshua, 1918- joint author.
F1402.T4x   341.187   63-9754

Alexander, Robert Jackson, 1918- III. 7223
Prophets of the revolution, profiles of Latin American leaders. New York, Macmillan, 1962. 322 p. 22 cm. 1. Latin America — Biography. 2. Latin America — Politics.
F1407.A38   923.28   62-7363

Davis, Harold Eugene, 1902- III. 7224
Latin American leaders, by Harold E. Davis. New York, Cooper Square Publishers, 1968 [c1949] 170 p. 24 cm. (Library of Latin American history and culture) With a new preface by the author. 1. Latin America — Biography. I. T.
F1407.D29 1968   920.08   68-56189

F1408 – 1409.3 General Works. Description

Arciniegas, Germán, 1900- III. 7225
The state of Latin America; translated from the Spanish by Harriet de Onís. [1st ed.] New York, Knopf, 1952. 416 p. illus. 22 cm. 1. Latin America. 2. Latin America — Politics. I. T.
F1408.A735   980   51-13220

James, Preston Everett, 1899- III. 7226
Latin America, by Preston E. James. Maps by Eileen W. James. 4th ed. New York, Odyssey Press [1969] xx, 947 p. illus., maps (part col.) 24 cm. 1. Latin America.
F1408.J28 1969   918   69-10222

Martin, Michael Rheta, 1917- III. 7227
Encyclopedia of Latin-American history [by] Michael Rheta Martin [and] Gabriel H. Lovett. Consulting editor: Fritz L. Hoffman. Rev. ed. by L. Robert Hughes. Indianapolis, Bobbs-Merrill [1968] vi, 348 p. 24 cm. 1. Latin America — Dictionaries and encyclopedias. I. Lovett, Gabriel H., joint author. II. Hughes, L. Robert, joint author. III. T.
F1408.M36 1968   980/.003   66-28231

Nehemkis, Peter Raymond. III. 7228
Latin America: myth and reality. [1st ed.] New York, Knopf, 1964. xii, 286, xiv p. 22 cm. 1. Latin America — Politics. 2. Latin America — Economic conditions. 3. Alliance for progress. I. T.
F1408.N4 1964   309.18   64-21995

Véliz, Claudio. III. 7229
Latin America and the Caribbean; a handbook, edited by Claudio Véliz. New York, Praeger [1968] xxiv, 840 p. illus., maps. 24 cm. (Handbooks to the modern world) 1. Latin America. I. T.
F1408.V43   918/.03   68-14143

West, Robert Cooper, 1913- III. 7230
Middle America; its lands and peoples [by] Robert C. West [and] John P. Augelli. Englewood Cliffs, N.J., Prentice-Hall [1966] 482 p. illus., maps. 26 cm. 1. West Indies. 2. Mexico. 3. Central America. I. Augelli, John P., joint author. II. T.
F1408.W44   917.2   66-14748

Cosío Villegas, Daniel, 1900- III. 7231
Change in Latin America: the Mexican and Cuban revolutions. Lincoln, University of Nebraska, 1961. 54 p. 21 cm. (Montgomery lectureship on contemporary civilization, 1960) 1. America — Politics. 2. Latin America — Economic conditions. I. T.
F1408.25.C6   61-63835

Arciniegas, Germán, 1900- III. 7232
Latin America: a cultural history. Translated from the Spanish by Joan MacLean. [1st American ed.] New York, Knopf, 1967 [c1966] xxvii, 594 p. illus., maps. 22 cm. Translation of El continente de siete colores. 1. Latin America — Civilization — History. I. T.
F1408.3.A663   918/.03   66-11342

Considine, John Joseph, 1897- III. 7233
New horizons in Latin America. Illustrated with photo. Freeport, N.Y., Books for Libraries Press [1970, c1958] xvi, 379 p. illus., map. 23 cm. (Essay index reprint series) 1. Latin America — Civilization. 2. Latin America — Religion. I. T.
F1408.3.C674 1970   918/.03   74-93330   ISBN:836915615

Crawford, William Rex, 1898- III. 7234
A century of Latin-American thought. Rev. ed. Cambridge, Mass., Harvard University Press, 1961. 322 p. 22 cm. 1. Latin America — Intellectual life. 2. Latin America — Civilization. 3. Philosophers, Latin American. I. T.
F1408.3.C7 1961   918   61-13749

Foster, George McClelland, 1913- III. 7235
Culture and conquest: America's Spanish heritage. New York, Wenner-Gren Foundation for Anthropological Research, 1960. ix, 272 p. illus., map, plans. 26 cm. (Viking Fund publications in anthropology, no. 27) 1. Latin America — Civilization — Spanish influences. 2. Spain — Civilization. 3. Acculturation. I. T. (S)
F1408.3.F6   918   60-1351

Henríquez Ureña, Pedro, 1884-1946. III. 7236
A concise history of Latin American culture. Translated and with a supplementary chapter by Gilbert Chase. New York, Praeger [1966] ix, 214 p. 21 cm. Translation of Historia de la cultura en la América Hispánica. 1. Latin America — Civilization. I. Chase, Gilbert, 1906- ed. and tr. II. T.
F1408.3.H4513   918.03   65-18079

Picón-Salas, Mariano, 1901- III. 7237
A cultural history of Spanish America, from conquest to independence. Translated by Irving A. Leonard. Berkeley, University of California Press, 1962. 192 p. 22 cm. Translation of De la conquista a la independencia. 1. Latin America — Civilization.
F1408.3.P5213 1962   918   62-15381

Schurz, William Lyttle, 1886- III. 7238
This New World: the civilization of Latin America. Illus. by Carl Folke Sahlin. [1st ed.] New York, Dutton, 1954. 429 p. illus. 22 cm. 1. Latin America — Civilization. I. T.
F1408.3.S4   918   54-5043

Whitaker, Arthur Preston, 1895- ed. III. 7239
Latin America and the enlightenment; essays by Arthur P. Whitaker [and others] Introd. by Federico de Onís. 2d ed. Ithaca, N.Y., Great Seal Books [1961] 156 p. 19 cm. 1. Enlightenment. 2. Latin America — Intellectual life. 3. Brazil — Intellectual life. I. T.
F1408.3.W5 1961   918.1   61-16668

Platt, Robert Swanton, 1891- III. 7240
Latin America, countrysides and united regions, by Robert S. Platt. 1st ed. New York, McGraw-Hill, 1942. x, 564 p. illus., tables, diagrs. 24 cm. (McGraw-Hill series in geography) 1. Latin America — Description and travel.
F1409.P55   918   43-74

Schmid, Peter, 1916- III. 7241
Beggars on golden stools; report on Latin America. Translated from the German by Mervyn Savill. New York, Praeger [1956] 327 p. illus. 23 cm. 1. Latin America — Description and travel — 1951- I. T.
F1409.2.S3   918   55-8112

F1409.6 – 1414 History

Latin America in transition; problems in training and research. III. 7242
Edited by Stanley R. Ross. Albany, State University of New York Press [1970] xxxi, 150 p. 24 cm. Papers originally presented at a conference held at the State University of New York at Stony Brook, March 22-23, 1968. 1. Latin American studies — Addresses, essays, lectures. 2. Research — Latin America. I. Ross, Stanley Robert, 1921- ed. II. New York (State). State University at Stony Brook.
F1409.9.L37   918/.03   71-112607   ISBN:873950682

Seminar on Latin American Studies in the United States, III. 7243
Stanford, Calif., 1963.
Social science research on Latin America; report and papers. Edited by Charles Wagley. New York, Columbia University Press, 1964. xiv, 338 p. 23 cm. Sponsored by the Joint Committee on Latin American Studies of the Social Science Research Council and the American Council of Learned Societies. 1. Latin America — Civilization — Study and teaching. 2. Area studies. I. Wagley, Charles, 1913- ed. II. SSRC-ACLS Joint Committee on Latin American Studies. III. T.
F1409.9.S4 1963c   309.18   65-11971

Bernstein, Harry, 1909- III. 7244
Modern and contemporary Latin America. New York, Russell & Russell,

1965 [c1962] x, 717 p. illus., maps, ports. 23 cm. *1. Latin America — History. I. T.*
F1410.B52 1965   980   65-18142

Chapman, Charles Edward, 1880-1941. III. 7245
Colonial Hispanic America: a history. New York, Hafner Pub. Co., 1971 [c1933] xvii, 405 p. maps, ports. 22 cm. "Facsimile of 1937 edition." *1. Latin America — History — To 1830. 2. Spain — Colonies — America. 3. Portugal — Colonies — America. I. T.*
F1410.C433 1937a   980/.01   72-152257

Diffie, Bailey Wallys, 1902- III. 7246
Latin-American civilization, colonial period, by Bailey W. Diffie, with the assistance of Justine Whitfield Diffie. New York, Octagon Books, 1967. lxxxvi, 812 p. illus., facsim., maps, ports. 24 cm. *1. Latin America — Civilization. 2. Latin America — History — To 1830. I. Diffie, Justine Whitfield, 1902- II. T.*
F1410.D5 1967   918/.03/1   67-18760

Dozer, Donald Marquand. III. 7247
Latin America, an interpretive history. New York, McGraw-Hill, 1962. 618 p. illus. 24 cm. *1. Latin America — History.*
F1410.D69   980   62-10206

Fisher, Lillian Estelle, 1891- III. 7248
Viceregal administration in the Spanish-American colonies. New York, Russell & Russell [1967] x, 397 p. 23 cm. (University of California publications in history, v.15) Reissue of the 1926 ed. of the author's thesis, University of California, 1924. *1. Spain — Colonies — America — Administration. I. T. (S:California. University. University of California publications in history, v.15)*
F1410.F53x (E173.C15 vol. 15 1967)   325.3/1/0946   66-27069

Humphreys, Robert Arthur, 1907- III. 7249
The evolution of modern Latin America, by Robin A. Humphreys. Oxford, Clarendon Press, 1946. 4 p. l., 196 p. illus., maps, 19 cm. *1. Latin America — History. I. T.*
F1410.Hx   A46-4766

Hamill, Hugh M., ed. III. 7250
Dictatorship in Spanish America, edited with an introd. by Hugh M. Hamill, Jr. [1st ed.] New York, Knopf, 1965. x, 242 p. 19 cm. (Borzoi books on Latin America) *1. Latin America — Politics. 2. Dictators. I. T.*
F1410.H24   321.64098   64-23731

Haring, Clarence Henry, 1885- III. 7251
The Spanish empire in America [by] C. H. Haring. New York, Oxford University Press, 1947. viii, 388 p. 25 cm. Map on lining-papers. "This book has its inception in a series of twelve lectures delivered in the spring of 1934 at the Instituto hispano-cubano of the University of Seville in Spain." — Foreword. *1. Latin America — History — To 1830. 2. Spain — Colonies — America. 3. Spain — Colonies — Administration. I. T.*
F1410.H25   980   47-1142

Herring, Hubert Clinton, 1889- III. 7252
A history of Latin America, from the beginnings to the present, by Hubert Herring with the assistance of Helen Baldwin Herring. 3d ed. [rev., enl.] New York, Knopf [1968] xxii, 1002, xxv p. maps. 24 cm. *1. Latin America — History. I. Herring, Helen Baldwin, joint author. II. T.*
F1410.H47 1968   980   67-25977

Johnson, John J., 1912- III. 7253
The military and society in Latin America. Stanford, Calif., Stanford University Press, 1964. x, 308 p. 23 cm. *1. Latin America — Armed Forces. 2. Armed Forces — Political activity. 3. Sociology, Military. I. T.*
F1410.J7   980   64-12073

Kirkpatrick, Frederick Alexander, 1861- III. 7254
Latin America, a brief history, by F. A. Kirkpatrick. Cambridge [Eng.] University Press, 1938. xi, 456 p. illus. 23 cm. (Cambridge historical series) *1. Latin America — History. I. T.*
F1410.K57   980   38-37532

Lambert, Jacques. III. 7255
Latin America: Social structure and political institutions. Translated by Helen Katel. Berkeley, University of California Press, 1967. viii, 413 p. 23 cm. *1. Latin America — Politics. 2. Latin America — Social conditions. I. T.*
F1410.L2713   320.9/8   67-29784

Madariaga, Salvador de, 1886- III. 7256
The fall of the Spanish American empire. New, rev. ed. New York, Collier Books [1963] 414 p. 18 cm. "BS176v." A companion to The rise of the Spanish American empire. *1. Latin America — Hist — To 1830. 2. Spain — Colonies — America. I. T.*
F1410.M23 1963   980   63-9893

Madariaga, Salvador de, 1886- III. 7257
The rise of the Spanish American empire. New York, Macmillan Co., 1947. xix, 408 p. illus., port., maps (on lining-papers) 22 cm. "This study ... is divided into two equal parts of which this book, 'The rise' is part one ... Part two, 'The fall,' will follow." *1. Latin America — History — To 1830. 2. Spain — Colonies — America. I. T.*
F1410.M25 1947a   980   47-12400

Needler, Martin C. III. 7258
Latin American politics in perspective [by] Martin Needler. [Rev. ed.] Princeton, N.J., Van Nostrand [1967] v, 191 p. 21 cm. (New perspectives in political science, 3) *1. Latin America — Politics. I. T.*
F1410.N4 1967   980   68-2125

Ots Capdequi, José María. III. 7259
Instituciones sociales de la América española en el período colonial, por José Ma. Ots. La Plata, República Argentina [Buenos Aires, Imprenta López] 1934. vii, 269 p. 23 cm. (Biblioteca humanidades t. XV) *1. Spain — Colonies — America. 2. Latin America — Social conditions. 3. Indians. I. T.*
F1410.O77   918   35-13313

Parry, John Horace. III. 7260
The Spanish seaborne empire, by J. H. Parry. [1st American ed.] New York, Knopf, 1966. 416 p. illus., facsim., maps. 22 cm. (The History of human society) *1. Spain — Colonies — America. 2. Latin America — History — To 1830. I. T.*
F1410.P3 1966   325.346098   66-10754

Rippy, James Fred, 1892- III. 7261
Latin America; a modern history, by J. Fred Rippy. New ed., rev. and enl. Ann Arbor, University of Michigan Press [1968] xiv, 594, xxii p. illus., map. 25 cm. (The University of Michigan history of the modern world) *1. Latin America — History. I. T. (S:Michigan. University. The University of Michigan history of the modern world)*
F1410.R454 1968   980   68-29268

Schäfer, Ernst, 1872-1946. III. 7262
El Consejo Real y Supremo de las Indias; su historia, organización y labor administrativa hasta la terminación de la casa de Austria. [Traducción castellana hecha por el autor] Sevilla, Imp. M. Carmona, 1935-   v. plates, plan, facsim. 25 cm. Vol.1: Universidad de Sevilla. Publicaciones del Centro de Estudios de Historia de América; v.2: Publicaciones de la Escuela de Estudios Hispano-Americanos de Sevilla, 28 (no. general) Serie 2: Monografías no. 10. *1. Spain. Consejo de las Indias. 2. Spain. Casa de Contratación da las Indias. 3. Spain — Colonies — America. 4. Spain — Colonies — Administration. 5. Latin America — History — To 1830. (S:Seville. Universidad. Centro de Estudios de Historia de América. Publicaciones) (S:Seville. Universidad. Escuela de Estudios Hispano-Americanos. Publicaciones, 28.) (S:Seville. Universidad. Escuela de Estudios Hispano-Americanos. Publicaciones. Ser. 2: Monografías, no. 10)*
F1410.S36   980 (325.346)   36-19485

Silvert, Kalman H. III. 7263
The conflict society: reaction and revolution in Latin America [by] Kalman H. Silvert. Rev. ed. New York, American Universities Field Staff [1966] xiv, 289 p. 24 cm. *1. Latin America — Politics. 2. Latin America — Social conditions — 1945- I. T.*
F1410.S6 1966   320.98   66-20311

Whitaker, Arthur Preston, 1895- III. 7264
Nationalism in Latin America, past and present. Gainesville, University of Florida Press, 1962. 91 p. 21 cm. *1. Nationalism — Latin America. I. T.*
F1410.W5   980   62-17696

Zavala, Silvio Arturo, 1909- III. 7265
La filosofía política en la conquista de América. [1. ed.] México, Fondo de Cultura Económica [1947] 163 p. 22 cm. (Colección Tierra firme, 27) *1. Spain — Colonies — America. 2. Spain — Colonies — Administration. 3. Indians, Treatment of — Latin America. I. T. (S:Colección Tierra firme, México, 27.)*
F1410.Z29   980.5   48-947

F1411 – 1414 BY PERIOD

Casas, Bartolomé de las, Bp. of Chiapa, 1474-1566. III. 7266
History of the Indies. Translated and edited by Andrée Collard. New York, Harper & Row [1971] xxvi, 302 p. 21 cm. (European perspectives. Harper torchbooks, TB 1540) Translation of Historia de las Indias, with some omissions. *1. America — Discovery and exploration — Spanish. 2. Colombo, Cristoforo. 3. Indians, Treatment of — Latin America. 4. Spain — Colonies — America. I. T.*
F1411.C4275 1971   973.1/6   74-146797   ISBN:0061315400

Descola, Jean. III. 7267
The conquistadors. Translated by Malcolm Barnes. New York, A. M. Kelley, 1970 [c1957] vi, 404 p. illus., maps, ports. 22 cm. (Viking reprint editions) *1. America — Discovery and exploration — Spanish. 2. Latin America — History — To 1600. I. T.*
F1411.D453 1970   973.1/6   72-122060

Hanke, Lewis. III. 7268
Aristotle and the American Indians; a study in race prejudice in the modern world. Bloomington, Indiana University Press [1970, c1959] x, 164 p. illus., ports. 20 cm. (A Midland book, MB132) *1. Indians, Treatment of. 2. Casas, Bartolomé de las, Bp. of Chiapa, 1474-1566. 3. Sepúlveda, Juan Ginés de, 1490-1573. 4. Aristoteles — Influence. I. T.*
F1411.H33 1970   301.451/97   79-108206   ISBN:253201322

Hanke, Lewis. III. 7269
The Spanish struggle for justice in the conquest of America. Philadelphia, University of Pennsylvania Press, 1949. xi, 217 p. ports., maps (on lining-papers) facsims. 23 cm. At head of title: American Historical Association. *1. Spain — Colonies — America. 2. Indians, Treatment of — Latin America. 3. Latin America — History — To 1830. I. T.*
F1411.H37   970.5   49-3817

Kirkpatrick, Frederick Alexander, 1861-1953. III. 7270
The Spanish conquistadores, by F. A. Kirpatrick. 2d ed. New York, Barnes & Noble [1967] xiii, 366 p. maps. 23 cm. (The Pioneer histories) Reprint of the 1946 ed. *1. Latin America — History — To 1600. 2. America — Discovery and exploration — Spanish. I. T.*
F1411.K57 1967   980/.01   67-6852

Leonard, Irving Albert, 1896- III. 7271
Books of the brave, being an account of books and of men in the Spanish conquest and settlement of the sixteenth century New World [by] Irving A. Leonard. New York, Gordian Press, 1964. xiii, 381 p. illus. 24 cm. "Originally published 1949. Reprinted 1964." *1. Latin America — History — To 1600. 2. America — Discovery and exploration — Spanish. 3. Latin America — Intellectual life. 4. Book industries and trade — Latin America. 5. Spanish literature — Classical period, 1500-1700 — History and criticism. I. T.*
F1411.L57 1964   980.01   64-8177

Simpson, Lesley Byrd, 1891- III. 7272
The encomienda in New Spain; the beginning of Spanish Mexico. [Rev. and enl. ed.] Berkeley, University of California Press, 1950. xv, 257 p. map, facsim. 21 cm. *1. Encomiendas (Latin America) 2. Mexico — History — Spanish colony, 1540-1810. I. T.*
F1411.S62 1950   972.02   50-63487

George Washington University, Washington, D.C. Seminar Conference on Hispanic American Affairs. III. 7273
Colonial Hispanic America. Edited by A. Curtis Wilgus. New York, Russell & Russell, 1963 [c1936] ix, 690 p. maps. 23 cm. (Studies in Hispanic American affairs, v.4) Lectures delivered at the Fourth Annual Seminar Conference on Hispanic American Affairs, July 1 to August 9, 1935. *1. Latin America — History — To 1830. 2. Brazil — History — To 1821. 3. Spain — Colonies — America. 4. Latin America — History — Historiography. 5. Brazil — History — Historiography. I. Wilgus, Alva Curtis, 1897- ed. II. T. (S)*
F1412.G46 1963   980   63-8374

Robertson, William Spence, 1872- III. 7274
Rise of the Spanish-American Republics, as told in the lives of their liberators. New York, Free Press [1965, c1946] 348 p. 21 cm. (A Free Press paperback) *1. South America — Biography. 2. Mexico — Biography. 3. South America — History — Wars of Independence, 1806-1830 4. Mexico — History — Wars of Independence, 1810-1821. I. T.*
F1412.R65 1965   923.28   65-1916

Macdonald, Austin Faulks, 1898- III. 7275
Latin American politics and government. 2d ed. New York, Crowell, 1954. 712 p. illus. 22 cm. *1. Latin America — Politics. I. T.*
F1413.M15 1954   980   54-7577

Berle, Adolf Augustus, 1895- III. 7276
Latin America: diplomacy and reality. [1st ed.] New York, Published for the Council on Foreign Relations by Harper & Row [1962] 144 p. 22 cm. (Policy books) *1. Latin America — Civilization. 2. Communism — Latin America. 3. Latin America — Relations (general) with the U.S. 4. U.S. — Relations (general) with Latin America.*
F1414.B49   327.7308   62-16826

Lieuwen, Edwin, 1923- III. 7277
Generals vs. presidents; neomilitarism in Latin America. New York, Praeger [1964] vi, 160 p. 22 cm. *1. Latin America — Politics — 1948- 2. Civil supremacy over the military — Latin America. 3. Militarism — Latin America. 4. United States — Foreign relations — Latin America. I. T.*
F1414.L5   320.98   64-22492

Pike, Fredrick B. III. 7278
Hispanismo, 1898-1936; Spanish conservatives and liberals and their relations with Spanish America [by] Fredrick B. Pike. Notre Dame, University of Notre Dame Press [1971] xx, 486 p. 24 cm. (International studies of the Committee on International Relations, University of Notre Dame) *1. Pan-Hispanism. I. T. (S:Notre Dame, Ind. University. Committee on International Relations. International studies.)*
F1414.P54   320.5/4   75-159272

Whitaker, Arthur Preston, 1895- III. 7279
Nationalism in contemporary Latin America [by] Arthur P. Whitaker and David C. Jordan. New York, Free Press [1966] ix, 229 p. 22 cm. (Studies in contemporary Latin America) *1. Nationalism — Latin America. I. Jordan, David C., joint author. II. T. (S)*
F1414.W5   320.98   66-12891

Haya de la Torre, Víctor Raúl, 1895- III. 7280
Treinta años de aprismo. [1. ed.] México, Fondo de Cultura Económica [1956] 247 p. 22 cm. (Fondo de Cultura Económica. Sección de obras de política) *1. Partido Aprista Peruano. 2. Imperialism. 3. Latin America — Politics — 1948- I. T.*
F1414.2.H36 1956   57-18358

Maier, Joseph, 1911- ed. III. 7281
Politics of change in Latin America, edited by Joseph Maier [and] Richard W. Weatherhead. New York, F. A. Praeger [1964] x, 258 p. 22 cm. *1. Latin America — Politics — 1948- — Addresses, essays, lectures. 2. Latin America — Social conditions — 1945- — Addresses, essays, lectures. I. Weatherhead, Richard W., joint ed. II. T.*
F1414.2.M25   320   64-13382

F1415 – 1418   Diplomatic History

Robertson, William Spence, 1872- III. 7282
France and Latin-American independence. New York, Octagon Books, 1967 [c1939] xv, 626 p. 3 maps. 22 cm. (The Albert Shaw lectures on diplomatic history, 1939) *1. Latin America — Foreign relations — France. 2. France — Foreign relations — Latin America. 3. Latin America — History — Wars of Independence, 1806-1830. I. T. (S)*
F1416.F7R6 1967   980/.02   67-18782

Kaufmann, William W. III. 7283
British policy and the independence of Latin America. 1804-1828, by William W. Kaufmann. [Hamden, Conn.] Archon Books, 1967 [c1951] viii, 238 p. 23 cm. *1. Gt. Brit. — Foreign relations — 1800-1837. 2. Gt. Brit. — Foreign relations — Latin America. 3. Latin America — Foreign relations — Gt. Brit. 4. Latin America — History — Wars of Independence, 1806-1830. I. T.*
F1416.G7K3 1967   327.42   67-19547

Webster, Charles Kingsley, Sir, 1886-1961, ed. III. 7284
Britain and the independence of Latin America, 1812-1830; select documents from the Foreign Office Archives. Edited by C. K. Webster. New York, Octagon Books, 1970. 2 v. 24 cm. Reprint of the 1938 ed. *1. Great Britain — Foreign relations — Latin America. 2. Latin America — Foreign relations — Great Britain. 3. Latin America — History — Wars of Independence, 1806-1830 — Sources. I. Great Britain. Foreign Office. II. T.*
F1416.G7W4 1970   980/.02   79-96194

F1418   RELATIONS WITH THE UNITED STATES
A – L

American Assembly. III. 7285
The United States and Latin America. [Edited by Herbert L. Matthews] 2d ed. Englewood Cliffs, N.J., Prentice-Hall [1963] 179 p. illus. 21 cm. (A Spectrum book) Essays. *1. Latin America — Civilization. 2. Latin America — Relations (general) with the U.S. 3. U.S. — Relations (general) with Latin America. I. Matthews, Herbert Lionel, 1900- ed. II. T.*
F1418.A549 1963   327.7308   63-8966

Bemis, Samuel Flagg, 1891- III. 7286
The Latin American policy of the United States, an historical interpretation by Samuel Flagg Bemis. 1st ed. New York, Harcourt, Brace [1943] xiv, 470 p. illus., maps, diagrs. 24 cm. Institute of international studies, Yale university. *1. U.S. — Foreign relations — Latin America. 2. Latin America — Foreign relations — U.S. I. Yale university. Institute of international studies. II. T.*
F1418.B4   327.73098   43-51167

Bernstein, Harry, 1909- III. 7287
Making an inter-American mind. Gainesville, University of Florida Press, 1961. 190 p. 24 cm. *1. U.S. — Relations (general) with Latin America. 2. Latin America — Relations (general) with the U.S. 3. America — Intellectual life. I. T.*
F1418.B484   327.7308   61-11110

Bernstein, Harry, 1909-   **III. 7288**
Origins of inter-American interest, 1700-1812. New York, Russell & Russell, 1965 [i.e. 1966, c1945] ix, 125 p. 23 cm. *1. U.S. — Relations (general) with Latin America. 2. Latin America — Relations (general) with the U.S. I. T.*
F1418.B486 1966   301.297308   66-13164

Burr, Robert N., ed. and tr.   **III. 7289**
Documents on inter-American cooperation, by Robert N. Burr and Roland D. Hussey. Philadelphia, University of Pennsylvania Press, 1955. 2 v. 23 cm. (University of Pennsylvania. Dept. of History. Translations and reprints from the original sources of history, 4th ser.) *1. Pan-Americanism. 2. America — Politics — Sources.* I. Hussey, Roland Denis, joint ed. and tr. II. T. III. T:Inter-American cooperation. (S:Pennsylvania. University. Dept. of History. Translations and reprints from the original sources of history, 4th ser.)
F1418.B928   (D101.P4 ser. 4 vol. 1-2)   341.187   55-9972

Callcott, Wilfrid Hardy, 1895-   **III. 7290**
The Caribbean policy of the United States, 1890-1920. New York, Octagon Books, 1966 [c1942] xiv, 524 p. 21 cm. (The Albert Shaw lectures on diplomatic history, 1942) *1. Caribbean area. 2. U.S. — Foreign relations — Latin America. 3. Latin America — Foreign relations — U.S. I. T. (S)*
F1418.C22 1966   327.73/08   66-28374

Colloquium on Latin America, Washington, D.C., 1961.   **III. 7291**
The Alliance for progress: a critical appraisal; [papers] Edited by William Manger. Washington, Public Affairs Press [1963] 131 p. 24 cm. "Georgetown University, through its Summer School and its Latin American Studies Program, invited a group of distinguished authorities from the United States and Latin America, along with representatives of interested national and international organizations to participate." *1. Alliance for progress. 2. Pan-Americanism. 3. U.S. — Relations (general) with Latin America. 4. Latin America — Relations (general) with the U.S.* I. Manger, William, 1899- ed. II. Georgetown University, Washington, D.C.
F1418.C667 1961   327.7308   63-14682

Council on Foreign Relations.   **III. 7292**
Social change in Latin America today, its implications for United States policy. [By] Richard N. Adams [and others] Introd. by Lyman Bryson. [1st ed.] New York, Published for the Council on Foreign Relations by Harper [c1960] xiv, 353 p. 22 cm. *1. U.S. — Relations (general) with Latin America. 2. Latin America — Relations (general) with the U.S. 3. Latin America — Social conditions. 4. Latin America — Politics — 1948-* I. Adams, Richard N. II. T.
F1418.C85 1960   327.7308   60-13715

De Onís, José.   **III. 7293**
The United States as seen by Spanish American writers, 1776-1890. New York, Hispanic Institute in the United States, 1952. viii, 226 p. 26 cm. *1. U.S. — Relations (general) with Latin America. 2. Latin America — Relations (general) with the U.S. 3. United States in literature. 4. Latin American literature — History and criticism.* I. T.
F1418.D45   917.3   52-2725

Duggan, Laurence, 1905-1948.   **III. 7294**
The Americas; the search for hemisphere security. Foreword by Herschel Brickell. New York, Holt [1949] ix, 242 p. map. 21 cm. "Synopsis of Inter-American conferences, 1826-1948": p. 219-230. *1. Pan-Americanism. 2. U.S. — Relations (general) with Latin America. 3. Latin America — Relations (general) with the U.S. I. T.*
F1418.D8   341.187   49-48265

Gantenbein, James Watson, 1900- ed.   **III. 7295**
The evolution of our Latin-American policy, a documentary record. New York, Columbia University Press, 1950. xxvii, 979 p. 24 cm. *1. U.S. — Foreign relations — Latin America. 2. Latin America — Foreign relations — U.S. I. T.*
F1418.G2   327.73098   49-50406

Lieuwen, Edwin, 1923-   **III. 7296**
Arms and politics in Latin America. Rev. [i.e. 2d] ed. New York, Published for the Council on Foreign Relations by Praeger, 1961. 335 p. 22 cm. *1. Civil supremacy over the military — Latin America. 2. Latin America — Politics. 3. United States — Foreign relations — Latin America. 4. United States — Military policy. I. T.*
F1418.L53 1961   355.098   61-18248

F1418   M – Z

Manning, William Ray, 1871-1942, ed.   **III. 7297**
Diplomatic correspondence of the United States concerning the independence of the Latin-American nations; selected and arranged by William R. Manning. New York, Oxford University Press, 1925. 3 v. 26 cm. (Publication of the Carnegie endowment for international peace, Division of international law) *1. U.S. — Foreign relations — Latin America. 2. Latin America — Foreign relations — U.S. 3. Latin America — History — Wars of independence, 1806-1830* Sources. I. U.S. Dept. of state. II. T.
F1418.M27   25-19089

Mecham, John Lloyd, 1893-   **III. 7298**
A survey of United States-Latin American relations [by] J. Lloyd Mecham. Boston, Houghton Mifflin [1965] viii, 487 p. maps. 25 cm. *1. U.S. — Relations (general) with Latin America. 2. Latin America — Relations (general) with the U.S. I. T. II. T:United States-Latin American relations.*
F1418.M373   327.7308   65-9049

Mecham, John Lloyd, 1893-   **III. 7299**
The United States and inter-American security, 1889-1960. Austin, University of Texas Press [1961] xii, 514 p. map, diagrs. 24 cm. "Published for the Institute of Latin American Studies, the University of Texas." *1. Organization of American States. 2. U.S. — Relations (general) with Latin America. 3. Latin America — Politics. 4. Security, International.* I. Texas. University. Institute of Latin American Studies. II. T.
F1418.M374   327.7308   61-10426

Morrison, DeLesseps Story, 1912-1964.   **III. 7300**
Latin American mission; an adventure in hemisphere diplomacy. Edited, and with an introd., by Gerold Frank. New York, Simon and Schuster [1965] 288 p. 22 cm. Autobiographical. *1. U.S. — Foreign relations — Latin America. 2. Latin America — Politics — 1948- 3. U.S. — Foreign relations — 1961-1963.* I. Frank, Gerold, 1907- ed. II. T.
F1418.M85   327.7308   65-11977

Munro, Dana Gardner, 1892-   **III. 7301**
Intervention and dollar diplomacy in the Caribbean, 1900-1921. Princeton, N.J., Princeton University Press, 1964. ix, 553 p. map (on lining papers) 24 cm. *1. U.S. — Foreign relations — Latin America. 2. Latin America — Politics — 1830-1948. 3. Intervention (International law) I. T.*
F1418.M92   327.7308   63-18647

Palmer, Thomas Waverly, 1920-1957.   **III. 7302**
Search for a Latin American policy. Gainesville, University of Florida Press, 1957. 217 p. 24 cm. *1. U.S. — Foreign relations — Latin America. 2. Latin America — Politics — 1948- I. T.*
F1418.P1863   327.73098   57-12883

Plaza Lasso, Galo, Pres. Ecuador, 1906-   **III. 7303**
Problems of democracy in Latin America. Chapel Hill, University of North Carolina Press [1955] 88 p. 21 cm. (The Weil lectures on American citizenship) *1. U.S. — Relations(general) with Latin America. 2. Latin America — Relations (general) with the U.S. 3. Ecuador — Politics and government. 4. Latin America — Politics — 1948- I. T.*
F1418.P63   327.73098   55-3248

Rippy, James Fred, 1892-   **III. 7304**
Globe and hemisphere; Latin America's place in the postwar foreign relations of the United States, by J. Fred Rippy. Westport, Conn., Greenwood Press [1972, c1958] p. Original ed. issued as no. 1 of the Foundation for Foreign Affairs series. *1. United States — Relations (general) with Latin America. 2. Latin America — Relations (general) with the United States. I. T. (S:Foundation for Foreign Affairs series, no. 1.)*
F1418.R54 1972   327.73/08   72-606   ISBN:0837157188

Ugarte, Manuel, 1878-1951.   **III. 7305**
The destiny of a continent. Edited, with an introd. and bibliography, by J. Fred Rippey. Translated from the Spanish by Catherine A. Phillips. New York, AMS Press [1970] xxi, 296 p. 22 cm. Reprint of the 1925 translation of El destino de un continente. *1. Latin America — Politics — 1830-1948. 2. Latin America — Relations (general) with the United States. 3. United States — Relations (general) with Latin America.* I. Rippey, James Fred, 1892- ed. II. T.
F1418.U2713 1970   301.29/73/08   71-111476   ISBN:040406700X

Whitaker, Arthur Preston, 1895-   **III. 7306**
The United States and the independence of Latin America, 1800-1830. New York, Russell & Russell, 1962 [c1941] 632 p. 22 cm. (The Albert Shaw lectures on diplomatic history, 1938) *1. Monroe doctrine. 2. U.S. — Foreign relations — Latin America. 3. Latin America — Politics — 1806-1830. 4. Latin America — Wars of Independence, 1806-1830. I. T.*
F1418.W6 1962   327.7308   61-13785

Whitaker, Arthur Preston, 1895-   **III. 7307**
The Western Hemisphere idea: its rise and decline. Ithaca [N.Y.] Cornell University Press [1954] 194 p. 23 cm. *1. Pan-Americanism. 2. America — Politics. I. T.*
F1418.W62   341.187   54-13291

Wood, Bryce, 1909-   **III. 7308**
The making of the good neighbor policy. New York, Columbia University Press, 1961. x, 438 p. 24 cm. *1. United States — Foreign relations — Latin America. 2. Latin America — Foreign relations — United States. I. T.*
F1418.W683   327.7308   61-15470

F1419 Ethnography

Harris, Marvin, 1927-   III. 7309
Patterns of race in the Americas. New York, Walker [1964] v. 154 p. illus. (part col.) col. maps. 22 cm. (The Walker summit library, no. 1) *1. Latin America — Race question. 2. Ethnology — Latin America. I. T.*
F1419.A1H3   301.451   64-23054

F1421 – 1577 CENTRAL AMERICA: GENERAL

Munro, Dana Gardner, 1892-   III. 7310
The five republics of Central America: their political and economic development and their relations with the United States, by Dana G. Munro. Edited by David Kinley. New York, Russell & Russell [1967] xvi, 332 p. map. 23 cm. Reprint of the 1918 ed. *1. Central America — Politics. 2. Central America — Economic conditions. 3. Central America — Foreign relations — U.S. 4. U.S. — Foreign relations — Central America. I. T.*
F1428.M95 1967   309.1/728   66-27128

Parker, Franklin Dallas, 1918-   III. 7311
The Central American Republics. London, New York, Oxford University Press, 1964. x, 348 p. 2 fold. maps. 21 cm. "Issued under the auspices of the Royal Institute of International Affairs." *1. Central America. I. Royal Institute of International Affairs. II. T.*
F1428.P3   917.28   64-2479

Huxley, Aldous Leonard, 1894-1963.   III. 7312
Beyond the Mexique Bay. New York, Vintage Books, 1960 [c1934] 262 p. illus. 19 cm. (A Vintage book K-104) *1. Central America — Description and travel. 2. Guatemala — Description and travel. I. T.*
F1432.H89 1960   917.28   60-2942

Stephens, John Lloyd, 1805-1852.   III. 7313
Incidents of travel in Central America, Chaipas, & Yucatan. Edited with an introd. & notes. by Richard L. Predmore. New Brunswick, Rutgers University Press, 1949. 2 v. illus., port., map (on lining-papers) 23 cm. *1. Central America — Description and travel. 2. Yucatan — Description and travel. 3. Chiapas, Mexico — Description and travel. 4. Central America — Antiquities. 5. Mayas — Antiquities.*
F1432.S883   917.28   49-9589

F1434 – 1435.3 Antiquities. Indians

Baudez, Claude F.   III. 7314
Central America [by] Claude F. Baudez; translated from the French by James Hogarth. London, Barrie & Jenkins, 1970. 255 p. illus. (some col.), maps (on lining papers) 24 cm. (Ancient civilizations) On spine: The ancient civilization of Central America. Translation of Amérique centrale. *1. Indians of Central America — Antiquities. I. The ancient civilization of Central America. II. T. (S)*
F1434.B313   970.4/28   70-577189   ISBN:0214652165

Handbook of Middle American Indians.   III. 7315
Robert Wauchope, general editor. Austin, University of Texas Press [1964- v. illus., maps, plans. 28 cm. *1. Indians of Central America. 2. Indians of Mexico. I. Wauchope, Robert, 1909- ed.*
F1434.H3   970.4/2   64-10316   ISBN:0292700148(v.9)

Stone, Doris (Zemurray) 1909-   III. 7316
Pre-Columbian man finds Central America; the archaeological bridge [by] Doris Stone. Cambridge, Mass., Peabody Museum Press [1972] xvii, 231 p. illus. 24 cm. *1. Indians of Central America — Antiquities. 2. Central America — Antiquities. I. T.*
F1434.S87   970.4/28   72-80168   ISBN:0873657764

Tax, Sol, 1907-   III. 7317
Heritage of conquest; the ethnology of Middle America, by Sol Tax and members of the Viking Fund seminar on Middle American Ethnology [held in New York City, Aug. 28 through Sept. 3, 1949] Glencoe, Ill., Free Press [1952] 312 p. maps. 22 cm. *1. Ethnology — Central America. 2. Ethnology — Mexico. 3. Acculturation. I. Wenner-Gren Foundation for Anthropological Research, New York. II. T.*
F1434.T3   572.972   51-13787

Coe, Michael D.   III. 7318
The Maya [by] Michael D. Coe. New York, Praeger [1966] 252 p. illus., maps, plans. 21 cm. (Ancient peoples and places, v.52) *1. Mayas — Antiquities. I. T.*
F1435.C72 1966a   970.3   66-25117

Morley, Sylvanus Griswold, 1883-1948.   III. 7319
The ancient Maya. Rev. by George W. Brainerd. 3d ed. Stanford, Calif., Stanford University Press [1956] x, 494 p. illus., maps, diagrs., tables. 24 cm. *1. Mayas — Antiquities. 2. Mayas. 3. Mayas — Bibliography. I. T.*
F1435.M75 1956   972.015   56-5580

Thompson, John Eric Sidney, 1898-   III. 7320
The rise and fall of Maya civilization, by J. Eric S. Thompson. 2d ed. enl. Norman, University of Oklahoma Press [1966] xv, 328 p. illus., maps. 24 cm. (The Civilization of the American Indian series [39]) *1. Mayas — Antiquities. I. T.*
F1435.T497 1966   970.3   66-16530

Redfield, Robert, 1897-   III. 7321
Chan Kom, a Maya village, by Robert Redfield and Alfonso Villa R. [Washington] Carnegie Institution of Washington, 1934. viii, 387 p. illus. (incl. maps, diagrs., music) 16 pl. 31 x 23 cm. (Carnegie institution of Washington. Publication no. 448) *1. Chan Kom, Mexico. 2. Mayas — Social life and customs. 3. Mayas — Religion and mythology. 4. Maya language — Texts. I. Villa Rojas, Alfonso, joint author.*
F1435.1.C47R3   917.26   34-32750

Redfield, Robert, 1897-   III. 7322
A village that chose progress; Chan Kom revisited. Chicago] University of Chicago Press [1950] xiv, 187 p. maps. 22 cm. (The University of Chicago publications in anthropology. Social anthropological series) *1. Chan Kom, Mexico. 2. Mayas — Social life and customs. 3. Mayas — Religion and mythology. I. T. (S:Chicago. University. University of Chicago publications in anthropology. Social anthropological series.)*
F1435.1.C47R32   917.26   50-5750

F1435.3 – 1439 History

Proskouriakoff, Tatiana Avenirovna, 1909-   III. 7323
An album of Maya architecture. [New ed.] Norman, University of Oklahoma Press [1963] xxi, 142 p. illus., map. 23 x 30 cm. *1. Architecture, Maya. 2. Mayas — Antiquities. I. T.*
F1435.3.A6P7 1963   972.015   63-17166

Spinden, Herbert Joseph, 1879-   III. 7324
Maya art and civilization. Rev. and enl. with added illus. [Indian Hills, Colo.] Falcon's Wing Press [1957] xliii, 432 p. illus. (part col.) maps. 27 cm. First published in 1913 under title: A study of Maya art. *1. Mayas — Antiquities. 2. Art, Maya. I. T.*
F1435.3.A7S75 1957   972.015   56-5124

Ireland, Gordon, 1880-1950.   III. 7325
Boundaries, possessions, and conflicts in Central and North America and the Caribbean. New York, Octagon Books, 1971 [c1941] xiii, 432 p. maps. 27 cm. Companion volume to the author's Boundaries, possessions, and conflicts in South America, published in 1938. *1. Central America — Boundaries. 2. North America — Boundaries. 3. America — Politics. 4. West Indies — History. I. T.*
F1438.I7 1971   341.42   76-159196   ISBN:0374941157

Karnes, Thomas L.   III. 7326
The failure of union; Central America, 1824-1960. Chapel Hill, University of North Carolina Press [1961] 277 p. illus. 23 cm. *1. Central America — Politics. I. T.*
F1438.K26   972.804   61-3459

Chamberlain, Robert Stoner, 1903-   III. 7327
Francisco Morazán, champion of Central American federation. Coral Gables, University of Miami Press, 1950. 58 p. 23 cm. (University of Miami Hispanic-American Studies, no. 9) *1. Morazán, Francisco, Pres. Central America, 1792-1842. (S:Miami, University of, Coral Gables, Fla. University of Miami Hispanic-American studies, no. 9)*
F1438.Mx (F1401.M53 no. 9)   972.8   50-2550

Rodríguez, Mario, 1922-   III. 7328
A Palmerstonian diplomat in Central America: Frederick Chatfield, Esq. Tucson, University of Arizona Press, 1964. 385 p. maps, port. 24 cm. *1. Chatfield, Frederick, 1801-1872. 2. Gt. Brit. — Foreign relations — Central America. 3. Central America — Politics. I. T.*
F1438.R684   327.420728   64-17260

F1441 – 1457   British Honduras

Waddell, David Alan Gilmour, 1927-   III. 7329
British Honduras, a historical and contemporary survey. Issued under the auspices of the Royal Institute of International Affairs. London, New York, Oxford University Press, 1961. 151 p. illus. 21 cm. *1. British Honduras.*
F1443.W3   917.282   61-19406

Humphreys, Robert Arthur, 1907-   III. 7330
The diplomatic history of British Honduras, 1638-1901. London, New York, Oxford University Press, 1961. 196 p. 23 cm. *1. British Honduras question. I. T.*
F1449.B7H8   972.8203   61-4088

F1461 – 1477   Guatemala

Dombrowski, John.   III. 7331
Area handbook for Guatemala. Co-authors: John Dombrowski [and others] Washington; For sale by the Supt. of Docs., U.S. Govt. Print. Off., 1970. xiv, 361 p. 3 maps. 24 cm. "DA pam 550-78." "Prepared by Foreign Area Studies (FAS) of the American University." *1. Guatemala. I. American University, Washington, D.C. Foreign Area Studies. II. T.*
F1463.D65   917.281/03   79-607286

Whetten, Nathan Laselle, 1900-   III. 7332
Guatemala, the land and the people. New Haven, Yale University Press, 1961. xvi, 399 p. illus., maps, diagrs. 25 cm. (Caribbean series, 4) *1. Guatemala — Rural conditions. 2. Guatemala — Social conditions. 3. Guatemala — Civilization. (S)*
F1463.5.W5   309.17281   61-7189

Fergusson, Erna, 1888-   III. 7333
Guatemala, by Erna Fergusson. [1st ed.] New York, Knopf, 1937. x, 320, vii p. plates, port., fold. map. 22 cm. *1. Guatemala — Description and travel. 2. Guatemala — Social life and customs. 3. Mayas.*
F1464.F47   917.281   37-27187

Coe, Michael D.   III. 7334
La Victoria, an early site on the Pacific coast of Guatemala. Cambridge, Mass., Peabody Museum, 1961. xiv, 163 p. illus., maps (part fold.) profiles. 27 cm. (Papers of the Peabody Museum of Archaeology and Ethnology, Harvard University, v.53) *1. Guatemala — Antiquities. 2. Indians of Central America — Guatemala. (S:Harvard University. Peabody Museum of Archaeology and Ethnology. Papers, v.53)*
F1465.Cx (E51.H337 vol.53)   970.4281   61-19491

Popol vuh.   III. 7335
Popol vuh; the sacred book of the ancient Quiché Maya. English version by Delia Goetz and Sylvanus G. Morley from the Spanish translation by Adrián Recinos. [1st ed.] Norman, University of Oklahoma Press [1950] xix, 267 p. map, facsims. 24 cm. (The Civilization of the American Indian [29]) *1. Quichés — Religion and mythology. 2. Guatemala — Antiquities. I. Recinos, Adrián, 1886- tr. (S:The Civilization of the American Indian series [29])*
F1465.P8385 1950   913.7281   50-6643

Bunzel, Ruth Leah, 1898-   III. 7336
Chichicastenango, a Guatemalan village. Seattle, University of Washington Press [1959] xxvi, 438 p. plans. 23 cm. (Publications of the American Ethnological Society, 22) *1. Chichicastenango, Guatemala. 2. Indians of Central America — Guatemala. 3. Quichés. (S:American Ethnological Society. Publications, v.22)*
F1465.1.Q5B8x (PM101)   917.281   A63-5160

Tax, Sol, 1907-   III. 7337
Penny capitalism; a Guatemalan Indian economy. New York, Octagon Books, 1972. x, 230 p. illus. 28 cm. Reprint of the 1953 ed., which was issued as no. 16 of Smithsonian Institution. Institute of Social Anthropology. Publication. *1. Panajachel, Guatemala — Economic conditions. 2. Indians of Central America — Guatemala — Economic conditions. 3. Agriculture — Economic aspects — Guatemala — Panajachel. I. T. (S:Smithsonian Institution. Institute of Social Anthropology. Publication no. 16.)*
F1465.3.E2T3 1972   330.9/7281   78-159254   ISBN:0374977852

Jones, Chester Lloyd, 1881-1941.   III. 7338
Guatemala, past and present. New York, Russell & Russell, 1966 [c1940] xii, 420 p. illus., map. 23 cm. *1. Guatemala — History. 2. Guatemala — Economic conditions. 3. Guatemala — Social conditions. I. T.*
F1466.J67 1966   917.281   66-24713

U.S. Dept. of State.   III. 7339
Intervention of international communism in Guatemala. [Washington, U.S. Govt. Print. Off., 1954] iii, 96 p. 24 cm. (Its Publication 5556. Inter-American series, 48) *1. Partido Guatemalteco del Trabajo. 2. Guatemala — Politics and government — 1945- 3. Communism — Guatemala. I. T. (S:U.S. Dept. of State. Publication 5556.) (S:U.S. Dept. of State. Inter-American series, 48)*
F1466.5.U52 (F1401.U65 no. 48)   54-60604

F1481 – 1537   Salvador. Honduras. Nicaragua

Blutstein, Howard I.   III. 7340
Area handbook for El Salvador. Co-authors: Howard I. Blutstein [and others]. Washington; For sale by the Supt. of Docs., U.S. Govt. Print. Off.] 1971. xii, 259 p. maps. 24 cm. "DA pam 550-150." "One of a series of handbooks prepared by Foreign Area Studies (FAS) of the American University." *1. Salvador. I. American University, Washington, D.C. Foreign Area Studies. II. T.*
F1483.B55   309.1/7284/05   78-609951

Osborne, Lilly de Jongh.   III. 7341
Four keys to El Salvador. New York, Funk & Wagnalls [1956] 221 p. illus. 22 cm. *1. Salvador — Description and travel — 1951- 2. Salvador — Civilization. I. T.*
F1484.2.O8   917.284   56-10708

Blutstein, Howard I.   III. 7342
Area handbook for Honduras. Co-authors: Howard I. Blutstein and others. Washington; For sale by the Supt. of Docs., U.S. Govt. Print. Off.] 1971. xiv, 225 p. maps. 24 cm. "DA pam 550-151." "One of a series of handbooks prepared by Foreign Area Studies (FAS) of the American University." *1. Honduras. I. American University, Washington, D.C. Foreign Area Studies. II. T.*
F1503.B55   309.1/7283/05   72-610126

Chamberlain, Robert Stoner, 1903-   III. 7343
The conquest and colonization of Honduras, 1502-1550 [by] Robert S. Chamberlain. New York, Octagon Books, 1966. v, 264 p. illus., maps. (1 fold.) 26 cm. Reprint of the 1953 ed., which was issued as Carnegie Institution of Washington. Publication no. 598. *1. Honduras — History — To 1838. I. T.*
F1506.C53 1966   972.83   66-28383

Ryan, John Morris.   III. 7344
Area handbook for Nicaragua. Co-authors: John Morris Ryan [and others] Prepared for the American University by Johnson Research Associates. [Washington; For sale by the Supt. of Docs., U.S. Govt. Print. Off.] 1970. xvi, 393 p. illus. 25 cm. "DA pam 550-88." "One of a series of handbooks prepared under the auspices of Foreign Area Studies (FAS) of the American University." *1. Nicaragua. I. Johnson Research Associates. II. American University, Washington, D.C. Foreign Area Studies. III. T.*
F1523.R9   917.285/03/5   79-608283

F1541 – 1577   Costa Rica. Panama

Blutstein, Howard I.   III. 7345
Area handbook for Costa Rica. Co-authors: Howard I. Blutstein [and others] [Washington; For sale by the Supt. of Docs., U.S. Govt. Print. Off.] 1970. xiv, 323 p. illus., maps. 24 cm. "DA pam 550-90." "One of a series of handbooks prepared by Foreign Area Studies (FAS) of the American

F1787.5 / III. 7367

University." *1. Costa Rica. I. American University, Washington, D.C. Foreign Area Studies. II. T.*
F1543.B66   917.286/03/5   79-608713

Jones, Chester Lloyd, 1881-1941.   III. 7346
Costa Rica and civilization in the Caribbean. New York, Russell & Russell [1967] ix, 172, 3 p. map. 23 cm. (University of Wisconsin studies in the social sciences and history, no. 23) Reprint of the 1935 ed. *1. Costa Rica. 2. Costa Rica — Economic conditions. 3. Latin America — Civilization. I. T. (S:Wisconsin. University. University of Wisconsin studies: Social sciences and history, no. 23)*
F1543.J66 1967   917.286   66-24712

Biesanz, John Berry, 1913-   III. 7347
Costa Rican life, by John and Mavis Biesanz. New York, Columbia University Press, 1944. x, 272 p. illus. (map) plates. 21 cm. *1. Costa Rica — Social life and customs. I. Biesanz, Mavis (Hiltunen) joint author. II. T.*
F1544.B5   917.286   A44-5796

American University, Washington, D.C. Foreign Areas Studies Division.   III. 7348
Area handbook for Panama. [Prepared by Lyman H. Legters and others. Washington] Headquarters, Dept. of the Army, 1962; reprint: 1965. xi, 488 p. maps. 24 cm. At head of title: U.S. Army. Cover title. "Department of the Army pamphlet no. 550-46." *1. Panama. I. Legters, Lyman Howard, 1928- II. U.S. Army. III. T.*
F1563.A63 1965   70-31713

Biesanz, John Berry, 1913-   III. 7349
The people of Panama, by John and Mavis Biesanz. New York, Columbia University Press, 1955. 418 p. illus. 23 cm. *1. Panama — Civilization. I. Biesanz, Mavis (Hiltunen) joint author. II. T.*
F1563.8.B5   918.62   55-8276   986.2 B478

Wafer, Lionel, 1660?-1705?   III. 7350
A new voyage and description of the Isthmus of America. Edited by George Parker Winship. New York, B. Franklin [1970] 212 p. illus., maps. 23 cm. (Literature of discovery, exploration & geography series, 5. Burt Franklin research & source works series, 459) Reprint of the 1903 ed. *1. Panama — Description and travel. 2. Indians of Central America — Panama. 3. Natural history — Panama. I. Winship, George Parker, 1871-1952, ed. II. T.*
F1564.W153   918.62/03/2   79-114820

Ealy, Lawrence O., 1915-   III. 7351
The Republic of Panama in world affairs, 1903-1950, by Lawrence O. Ealy. Westport, Conn., Greenwood Press [1970, c1951] xi, 207 p. 23 cm. *1. Panama — Foreign relations. I. T.*
F1566.5.E2 1970   327.862   76-97343   ISBN:0837128064

F1601 – 2151   WEST INDIES: GENERAL

Newton, Arthur Percival, 1873-1942.   III. 7352
The European nations in the West Indies, 1493-1688. New York, Barnes & Noble [1967] xviii, 356 p. maps (part fold.) 23 cm. (The Pioneer histories) Reprint of the 1933 ed. *1. West Indies — History. 2. Buccaneers. I. T. (S:The Pioneer histories (New York))*
F1621.N46 1967   972.902   67-826

Pares, Richard, 1902-1958.   III. 7353
War and trade in the West Indies, 1739-1763. [London] F. Cass [1963] xi, 631 p. fold. map. 22 cm. Imprint covered by label: New York, Barnes & Noble. First published 1936. *1. West Indies — History. 2. West Indies — Commerce. 3. Anglo-Spanish War, 1739-1748. 4. Anglo-French War, 1755-1763. I. T.*
F1621.P32 1963   64-59

Parry, John Horace.   III. 7354
A short history of the West Indies [by] J. H. Parry and P. M. Sherlock. 3d ed. London, Macmillan; New York, St. Martin's, 1971. xiii, 337 p., 14 plates. illus., map (on lining papers) 23 cm. *1. West Indies — History. I. Sherlock, Philip Manderson, Sir, joint author. II. T.*
F1621.P33 1971   972.9   73-145588   ISBN:0333074572

Waddell, David Alan Glimur, 1927-   III. 7355
The West Indies & the Guianas [by] D. A. G. Waddell. Englewood Cliffs, N.J., Prentice-Hall [1967] x, 149 p. map. 21 cm. (A Spectrum book: The Modern nations in historical perspective) *1. West Indies — History. 2. Guiana — History. I. T.*
F1621.W27   972.9   67-18702

Williams, Eric Eustace, 1911-   III. 7356
From Columbus to Castro: the history of the Caribbean, 1492-1969 [by] Eric Williams. [1st U.S. ed.] New York, Harper & Row [1971, c1970] 576 p. illus., facsims., map (on lining papers), ports. 23 cm. *1. West Indies — History. I. T.*
F1621.W68 1970b   972.9   75-138773   ISBN:0060146680

The United States and the Caribbean.   III. 7357
[Edited by Tad Szulc] Englewood Cliffs, N.J., Prentice-Hall [1971] vii, 212 p. map. 22 cm. (A Spectrum book) At head of title: The American Assembly, Columbia University. Intended as background reading for the 38th American Assembly, Arden House, October 1970. *1. West Indies — Politics. I. Szulc, Tad, ed. II. American Assembly.*
F1623.U53   309.1/729   79-140265   ISBN:013938555X

Craton, Michael.   III. 7358
A history of the Bahamas. London, Collins, 1962. 320 p. illus. 22 cm. *1. Bahamas — History.*
F1656.C7   972.96   63-4124

F1751 – 1849   Cuba

Blutstein, Howard I.   III. 7359
Area handbook for Cuba. Co-authors: Howard I. Blutstein [and others. Washington; For sale by the Supt. of Docs., U.S. Govt. Print. Off.] 1971. xii, 505 p. map. 24 cm. "DA PAM 550-152." "One of a series of handbooks prepared by Foreign Area Studies (FAS) of the American University." *1. Cuba. I. American University, Washington, D.C. Foreign Area Studies. II. T.*
F1758.B55   309.1/7291/064   75-610124

Smith, Robert Freeman, 1930- ed.   III. 7360
Background to revolution; the development of modern Cuba. [1st ed.] New York, Knopf [c1966] xi, 224 p. 19 cm. (Borzoi books on Latin America) *1. Cuba — History — Addresses, essays, lectures. I. T.*
F1776.S6   972.9106   65-17485

Lizaso, Félix, 1891-   III. 7361
Martí, martyr of Cuban independence; translated by Esther Elise Shuler. [Albuquerque] University of New Mexico Press [1953] vii, 260 p. mounted port. 24 cm. Translation of Martí, místico del deber. *1. Martí, José, 1853-1895.*
F1783.M38L492   928.6   53-12559

Mañach, Jorge, 1898-   III. 7362
Martí: apostle of freedom; translated from the Spanish by Coley Taylor. With a pref. By Gabriela Mistral. New York, Devin-Adair, 1950. xvi, 363 p. illus., ports., map. 22 cm. *1. Martí, José, 1853-1895. 2. Cuba — History — 1878-1895.*
F1783.M38M2413   928.6   50-7768

Chapman, Charles Edward, 1880-1941.   III. 7363
A history of the Cuban Republic; a study in Hispanic American politics. New York, Octagon Books, 1969 [c1927] xii, 685 p. map (on lining paper) 24 cm. *1. Cuba — History — 1895- I. T.*
F1787.C45 1969   972.91/06   75-96177

Fitzgibbon, Russell Humke, 1902-   III. 7364
Cuba and the United States, 1900-1935. New York, Russell & Russell, 1964. xi, 311 p. map. 23 cm. *1. Cuba — Politics and government — 1895- 2. U.S. — Foreign relations — Cuba. 3. Cuba — Foreign relations — U.S. 4. Cuba — Economic conditions.*
F1787.F56 1964   972.91062   64-16466

Millett, Allan Reed.   III. 7365
The politics of intervention; the military occupation of Cuba, 1906-1909. [Columbus, Ohio State University Press [1968] x, 306 p. 22 cm. "A publication of the Mershon Center for Education in National Security." *1. Cuba — History — American occupation, 1906-1909. I. Ohio. State University, Columbus. Mershon Center for Education in National Security. II. T.*
F1787.M63   972.91/062   68-10270

Guevara, Ernesto, 1920-   III. 7366
Reminiscences of the Cuban Revolutionary War [by] Ernesto Che Guevara. Translated by Victoria Ortiz. New York, M[onthly] R[eview] Press; distributed by Grove Press [1968] 287 p. illus., map (on lining papers), ports. 22 cm. Revised and much enlarged translation of Pasajes de la Guerra Revolucionaria. *1. Cuba — History — 1933-1959. 2. Cuba — History, Military. I. T.*
F1787.5.G8313   972.91/06   68-13655

Calderío, Francisco, 1908-   III. 7367
The Cuban revolution; report to the Eight[h] National Congress of the

Popular Socialist Party of Cuba, by Blas Roca [pseud.] New York, New Century Publishers, 1961. 127 p. 20 cm. *1. Partido Socialista Popular (Cuba) 2. Cuba — Politics and government — 1933-1959. 3. Cuba — Politics and government — 1959–*
F1788.C23   972.91063   61-2735

Castro, Fidel, 1927- III. 7368
Revolutionary struggle, 1947-1958. Edited and with an introd. by Rolando E. Bonachea and Nelson P. Valdés. Cambridge, MIT Press [1972] xx, 471 p. illus. 24 cm. (Selected works of Fidel Castro, v. 1) *1. Cuba — History — 1933-1959 — Addresses, essays, lectures. 2. Cuba — History — 1959- — Addresses, essays, lectures. 3. Communism — Cuba — Addresses, essays, lectures. I. Bonachea, Rolando E., ed. II. Valdés, Nelson P., ed. III. T.*
F1788.C2713 1972   972.91/064/0924 (B)   74-103892
ISBN:0262020653 0262520273 (pbk)

Castro, Fidel, 1927- III. 7369
History will absolve me. Translation from the Spanish of a defense plea by Fidel Castro. [New York, L. Stuart, 1961] 79 p. 23 cm. *1. Cuba — Politics and government — 1933-1959. I. T.*
F1788.C27753 1961   972.91063   61-11365

Draper, Theodore, 1912- III. 7370
Castroism, theory and practice. New York, F. A. Praeger [1965] xiii, 263 p. 22 cm. *1. Castro, Fidel, 1927- 2. Cuba — History — 1959- 3. Cuba — History — 1933-1959. 4. Communism — Cuba. I. T.*
F1788.D68   972.91064   65-18072

Draper, Theodore, 1912- III. 7371
Castro's revolution, myths and realities. New York, Praeger [1962] 211 p. 22 cm. (Books that matter) *1. Castro, Fidel, 1927- 2. Cuba — Politics and government — 1959- 3. Cuba — History — Invasion, 1961. 4. Communism — Cuba.*
F1788.D69   972.91064   62-13305

Huberman, Leo, 1903- III. 7372
Cuba: anatomy of a revolution [by] Leo Huberman [and] Paul M. Sweezy. 2d ed., with new material added. New York, Monthly Review Press, 1961[c1960] 208 p. illus. 22 cm. *1. Castro, Fidel, 1927- 2. Cuba — History — 1933-1959. 3. Cuba — Social conditions. I. Sweezy, Paul Marlor, 1910- joint author.*
F1788.H8 1961   972.91063   61-3092

Lockwood, Lee. III. 7373
Castro's Cuba, Cuba's Fidel; an American journalist's inside look at today's Cuba in text and picture. New York, Macmillan [1967] 288 p. illus., ports. 28 cm. *1. Cuba — History — 1959- 2. Cuba — Social conditions. 3. Castro, Fidel, 1927- I. Cuba's Fidel. II. T.*
F1788.L57   972.91/064   67-11885

Meyer, Karl Ernest. III. 7374
The Cuban Invasion; the chronicle of a disaster, by Karl E. Meyer and Tad Szulc. New York, Praeger [1962] 160 p. 21 cm. (Books that matter) *1. Cuba — History — Invasion, April, 1961. I. Szulc, Tad, joint author. II. T.*
F1788.M45   972.91064   62-15262

Miller, Warren. III. 7375
90 miles from home; the face of Cuba today. [1st ed.] Boston, Little, Brown [1961] 279 p. 21 cm. *1. Cuba — Description and travel. 2. Cuba — Politics and government — 1959- 3. Cuba — Social life and customs. I. T.*
F1788.M48   917.291   61-12645

Pflaum, Irving Peter, 1906- III. 7376
Tragic island; how communism came to Cuba. Englewood Cliffs, N.J., Prentice-Hall [1961] 196 p. illus. 22 cm. *1. Castro, Fidel, 1927- 2. Cuba — History — 1959- 3. Communism — Cuba. I. T.*
F1788.P48   972.91063   61-16757

Phillips, Ruby Hart. III. 7377
Cuba, island of paradox. New York, McDowell, Obolensky [1959] 434 p. illus. 25 cm. *1. Cuba — Politics and government — 1933-*
F1788.P5   972.91063   59-12433

Thomas, Hugh, 1931- III. 7378
Cuba; the pursuit of freedom. [1st U.S. ed.] New York, Harper & Row [1971] xxiv, 1696 p. illus., maps, ports. 24 cm. *1. Cuba — History. I. Pursuit of freedom. II. T.*
F1788.T47 1971   972/.91   79-162565   ISBN:0060142596

F1861 – 1941   Jamaica. Haiti. Dominican Republic

Semmel, Bernard. III. 7379
Jamaican blood and Victorian conscience; the Governor Eyre controversy. [1st American ed.] Boston, Houghton Mifflin, 1963[c1962] 188 p. 23 cm. (Studies in society) First published in London in 1962 under title: The Governor Eyre controversy. *1. Eyre, Edward John, 1815-1901. 2. Jamaica — History — Insurrection, 1865. I. T. (S)*
F1886.E96 1963   972.9204   63-13685

Rouse, Irving, 1913- III. 7380
Prehistory in Haiti; a study in method. [New Haven] Reprinted by Human Relations Area Files Press, 1964. 202 p. illus., maps, plates. 25 cm. (Yale University publications in anthropology, no. 21) First published in 1939. *1. Haiti — Antiquities. 2. Fort Liberté, Haiti. 3. Indians of the West Indies — Haiti — Antiquities. I. T. (S:Yale University. Dept. of Anthropology. Yale University publications in anthropology, no. 21)*
F1909.R6x (GN2.Y3 no. 21 1964)   64-21834

Davis, Harold Palmer, 1878- III. 7381
Black democracy; the story of Haiti, by H. P. Davis. With a pref. by Alec Waugh. Rev. ed. New York, Biblo and Tannen, 1967. xiii, 360 p. illus., maps (part fold.), port. 21 cm. *1. Haiti — History. 2. Haiti — Foreign relations — U.S. 3. U.S. — Foreign relations — Haiti. I. T.*
F1921.D263 1967   972.94   66-30792

Leyburn, James Graham. III. 7382
The Haitian people, by James G. Leyburn. With a new introd. by Sidney W. Mintz. [Rev. ed.] New Haven, Yale University Press, 1966. xlviii, 342 p. fold. map. 21 cm. (Caribbean series, 9) *1. Haiti. 2. Haiti — Social life and customs. 3. National characteristics, Haitian. I. T. (S)*
F1921.L6 1966   972.94   66-9411

James, Cyril Lionel Robert, 1901- III. 7383
The Black Jacobins; Toussaint L'Ouverture and the San Domingo Revolution. 2d ed., rev. New York, Vintage Books [1963] xi, 426 p. map. 19 cm. "V242." *1. Toussaint Louverture, François Dominique, 1743-1803. 2. Haiti — History — Revolution, 1791-1804. I. T.*
F1923.T85 1963   972.9403   63-15043

Korngold, Ralph, 1886- III. 7384
Citizen Toussaint, by Ralph Korngold. [1st ed.] Boston, Little, Brown, 1944. xvii, 358 p. col. front. (port.) 23 cm. Map on lining-papers. *1. Toussaint Louverture, Pierre Dominique, 1746?-1803. 2. Haiti — History — Revolution, 1791-1804. I. T.*
F1923.T855   923.27294   44-7566

Schmidt, Hans, 1938- III. 7385
The United States occupation of Haiti, 1915-1934. New Brunswick, N.J., Rutgers University Press [1971] x, 303 p. illus., ports., map. 24 cm. *1. Haiti — History — American occupation, 1915-1934. I. T.*
F1927.S35   972.94/05   70-152721   ISBN:0813506905

Roberts, Thomas Duval, 1903- III. 7386
Area handbook for the Dominican Republic, Co-authors: T. D. Roberts, Susan G. Callaway [and others] Washington, For sale by the Supt. of Docs., U.S. Govt. Print. Off., 1966. xii, 446 p. maps. 23 cm. "DA pam no. 550-54." "Prepared by Foreign Area Studies (FAS) of the American University." *1. Dominican Republic. I. American University, Washington, D.C. Foreign Area Studies. II. Callaway, Susan G. III. T.*
F1934.R58   67-61872

Welles, Sumner, 1892- III. 7387
Naboth's vineyard; the Dominican Republic, 1844-1924. New foreword by Germán Arciniegas. Mamaroneck, N.Y., P. P. Appel, 1966. 2 v. (1058 p.) illus., fold. maps, ports. 24 cm. *1. Dominican Republic — History — 1844-1930. 2. Dominican Republic — Foreign relations — U.S. 3. U.S. — Foreign relations — Dominican Republic. I. T.*
F1938.4.W4 1966   972.93   66-31307

Galíndez Suárez, Jesús, 1915- III. 7388
La era de Trujillo; un estudio casuístico de dictadura hispanoamericana. Santiago, Editorial del Pacífico [1956] 452 p. 19 cm. "Constituye ... la tesis que el autor presentó para postular al doctorado de filosofía en la Universidad de Columbia, New York." *1. Trujillo Molina, Rafael Leonidas, Pres. Dominican Republic, 1891- 2. Trujillo Molina, Hector Bienvenido, Pres. Dominican Republic, 1908- 3. Dominican Republic — Politics and government — 1930- I. T.*
F1938.5.G3   57-45317

Szulc, Tad. III. 7389
Dominican diary. New York, Delacorte Press [1965] xii, 306 p. illus., map (on lining papers) ports. 22 cm. *1. Dominican Republic — History — 1961- 2. U.S. — Foreign relations — Dominican Republic. 3. Dominican Republic — Foreign relations — U.S. I. T.*
F1938.55.S95   972.93054   65-26188

F1951 – 1983   Puerto Rico

Lewis, Gordon K. III. 7390
Puerto Rico; freedom and power in the Caribbean. New York [Monthly Review Press] 1963. xii, 626 p. 24 cm. *1. Puerto Rico. I. T:Freedom and power in the Caribbean.*
F1958.L4   917.295   63-20065

Picó, Rafael. III. 7391
The geographic regions of Puerto Rico. Río Piedras, University of Puerto Rico Press, 1950. xiii, 256 p. illus., maps. 24 cm. Based on thesis — Clark University. *1. Puerto Rico. I. T.*
F1958.P5   330.97295   51-26021

Morales Carrión, Arturo. III. 7392
Puerto Rico and the non Hispanic Caribbean; a study in the decline of Spanish exclusivism. Rio Piedras, P.R., University of Puerto Rico Press, 1952. viii, 160 p. 24 cm. Thesis — Columbia University. *1. Puerto Rico — History. 2. West Indies — History. 3. Spain — Commercial policy. I. T.*
F1973.M67   972.9503   52-4021

Goodsell, Charles T. III. 7393
Administration of a revolution; executive reform in Puerto Rico under Governor Tugwell, 1941-1946 [by] Charles T. Goodsell. Cambridge, Harvard University Press, 1965. xv, 254 p. illus., ports. 22 cm. (Harvard political studies) *1. Tugwell, Rexford Guy, 1891- 2. Puerto Rico — Politics and government — 1898-1952. I. T. (S)*
F1975.G57   354.729503   65-16684

Tugwell, Rexford Guy, 1891- III. 7394
The stricken land; the story of Puerto Rico. New York, Greenwood Press, 1968 [c1946] xxxi, 704 p. map. 22 cm. *1. Puerto Rico — Politics and government — 1898-1952. 2. Puerto Rico — Economic conditions. I. T.*
F1975.T8 1968   309.1/7295   68-23335

F2001 – 2151   Other Islands

Herskovits, Melville Jean, 1895-1963. III. 7395
Trinidad village [by] Melville J. Herskovits and Frances S. Herskovits. New York, Octagon Books, 1964 [c1947] viii, 351, xxv p. plan, plates. 24 cm. Includes music for the Sankey version of the hymn, Jesus, lover of my soul. *1. Toco, Trinidad. 2. Negroes in Trinidad. I. Herskovits, Frances (Shapiro) 1897- joint author. II. T.*
F2121.H4 1964   917.2983   64-24843

Klass, Morton, 1927- III. 7396
East Indians in Trinidad; a study of cultural persistence. New York, Columbia University Press, 1961. 265 p. illus. 22 cm. Issued in 1959 in microfilm form, as thesis, Columbia University, under title: Cultural persistence in a Trinidad East Indian community. *1. East Indians in Trinidad.*
F2121.K6 1961   301.3   61-7945

Burn, William Laurence. III. 7397
The British West Indies. London, New York, Hutchinson House, 1951. 196 p. map (on lining paper) 19 cm. (Hutchinson's university library: British Empire history) *1. West Indies, British — History.*
F2131.Bx   A51-9815

Bridenbaugh, Carl. III. 7398
No peace beyond the line; the English in the Caribbean, 1624-1690 [by] Carl and Roberta Bridenbaugh. New York, Oxford University Press, 1972. xxii, 440 p. illus. 24 cm. (The Beginnings of the American people, 2) *1. West Indies, British — History. 2. West Indies — History — 17th century. I. Bridenbaugh, Roberta, joint author. II. T.*
F2131.B84   917.29/03/3   70-182421

Lowenthal, David. III. 7399
The West Indies Federation; perspectives on a new nation. New York, Columbia University Press, 1961. 142 p. illus. 21 cm. (American Geographical Society. Research series, no. 23) *1. West Indies (Federation)*
F2131.L8   972.97   61-7176

Tansill, Charles Callan, 1890- III. 7400
The purchase of the Danish West Indies. New York, Greenwood Press, 1968 [c1932] 548 p. 20 cm. *1. Virgin Islands of the United States — Sale to the United States. 2. United States — Foreign relations — Denmark. 3. Denmark — Foreign relations — United States. I. T.*
F2136.T18 1968   972.97/22   68-23332

F2161 – 2175   Caribbean Sea

Exquemelin, Alexandre Olivier. III. 7401
The buccaneers of America. Translated from the Dutch by Alexis Brown, with an introd. by Jack Beeching. Baltimore, Penguin Books [1969] 232 p. maps. 18 cm. (The Penguin classics, L212) Translation of De Americaenesche zee-roovers. *1. Buccaneers. 2. Pirates. 3. Spanish Main. 4. West Indies — History. I. T.*
F2161.E8433 1969   917.29/03/3   73-7683

Sauer, Carl Ortwin, 1889- III. 7402
The early Spanish Main. Berkeley, University of California Press, 1966. xii, 306 p. illus., maps. 27 cm. *1. Spanish Main. 2. America — Discovery and exploration — Spanish. 3. Indians of the West Indies. I. T.*
F2161.S25   972.902   66-15004

Jones, Chester Lloyd, 1881-1941. III. 7403
The Caribbean since 1900. New York, Russell & Russell [1970] xi, 511 p. map. 23 cm. Reprint of the 1936 ed. *1. Caribbean area — Foreign relations — United States. 2. United States — Foreign relations — Caribbean area. I. T.*
F2171.J66 1970   327/.09728   72-77674

Arciniegas, Germán, 1900- III. 7404
Caribbean, sea of the new world [by] Germán Arciniegas, translated from the Spanish by Harriet de Onís. [1st American ed.] New York, Knopf, 1946. xi, 464, xiv p. plates, ports., fold. map. 22 cm. Translation of El mar del nuevo mundo. *1. Spanish main. 2. Caribbean sea. 3. West Indies — History. I. De Onís, Harriet, 1899- tr.*
F2175.A7   972.9   46-3862

Conference on the Caribbean, University of Florida. III. 7405
Papers delivered at the conference. 1st- 1950- [Gainesville, University of Florida Press] v. illus. 25 cm. Annual. Vols. for 1950- issued as the Caribbean conference series. Vols. for 1950-62 as a Publication of the School of Inter-American Studies; 1963- as a Publication of the Center for Latin American Studies. Sponsored 1950-62 by the School of Inter-American Studies, University of Florida; 1963- by the university's Center for Latin American Studies. Each vol. has also a distinctive title. Editor: 1950- A. C. Wilgus. *1. Caribbean area — Congresses. I. Wilgus, Alva Curtis, 1897- ed. II. Florida. University, Gainesville. School of Inter-American Studies. III. Florida. University, Gainesville. Center for Latin American Studies.*
F2175.C55   972.9   51-12532

Proudfoot, Mary (Macdonald) III. 7406
Britain and the United States in the Caribbean; a comparative study in methods of development. With an introd. by Margery Perham. London, Faber & Faber [1954] xxi, 434 p. fold. map, tables. 23 cm. (Colonial and comparative studies) *1. Caribbean area. 2. Gt. Brit. — Colonies — Administration. 3. U.S. — Insular possessions. I. T. (S)*
F2175.P7 1954a   972.9   54-14449

F2201 – 2239   SOUTH AMERICA: GENERAL

Gunther, John, 1901- III. 7407
Inside South America. [1st ed.] New York, Harper & Row [c1967] xvi, 610 p. maps. 22 cm. *1. South America. I. T.*
F2208.G94   320.98   66-10630

Royal Institute of International Affairs. III. 7408
The republics of South America, a report by a study group of members of the Royal Institute of International Affairs. London, New York [etc.] Oxford

University Press, 1937. x, 374 p. maps (part fold.) 25 cm. *1. South America. 2. American republics. I. T.*
F2208.R78   918   38-5086

Clark, Sydney Aylmer, 1890-   III. 7409
All the best in South America, west coast: Panama, Colombia, Ecuador, Peru, Bolivia, Chile [by] Sydney Clark. New York, Dodd, Mead [1966] x, 271 p. illus., maps. 18 cm. First published in 1941 under title: The west coast of South America. *1. South America — Description and travel — Guide-books. 2. Pacific coast — Description and travel — Guide-books. I. T.*
F2213.C5 1966   918.043   66-13264

Humboldt, Alexander, Freiherr von, 1769-1859.   III. 7410
Personal narrative of travels to the equinoctial regions of America, during the years 1799-1804, by Alexander von Humboldt and Aimé Bonpland. Written in French by Alexander von Humboldt. Translated and edited by Thomasina Ross. New York, B. Blom, 1971. 3 v. 21 cm. (Bohn's scientific library) Abridged translation of Voyage aux régions équinoxiales du nouveau continent, which forms pt. 1 of Voyage de Humboldt et Bonpland. Reprint of the 1852-53 ed. *1. South America — Description and travel. 2. Natural history — South America. 3. Scientific expeditions. I. Bonpland, Aimé Jacques Alexandre Goujaud, called, 1773-1858. II. Ross, Thomasina, ed. (S)*
F2216.H928   918   69-13241

Whitaker, Arthur Preston, 1895-   III. 7411
The United States and South America, the northern republics. Cambridge, Harvard University Press, 1948. xix, 280 p. maps. 20 cm. (The American foreign policy library) *1. Bolivia. 2. Peru. 3. Ecuador. 4. Colombia. 5. Venezuela. 6. U.S. — Foreign relations — South America. 7. South America — Foreign relations — U.S. I. T. (S)*
F2216.W45   980   48-6353

F2221 – 2230.2 Description. Indians

Hanson, Earl Parker, 1899-   III. 7412
South from the Spanish main; South America seen through the eyes of its discoverers, edited, annotated and introduced by Earl Parker Hanson. [New York] Delacorte Press [1967] xv, 463 p. maps. 24 cm. (The Great explorers series) *1. South America — Description and travel. 2. America — Discovery and exploration. 3. Explorers. I. T.*
F2221.H3   980   67-19789

Ulloa, Antonio de, 1716-1795.   III. 7413
A voyage to South America [by] Jorge Juan and Antonio de Ulloa. The John Adams translation, abridged. Introd. by Irving A. Leonard. New York, Knopf, 1964. ix, 245 p. 19 cm. (Borzoi books on Latin America "LA-5.") A translation of Ulloa's Relación histórica del viage a la America Meridional ... Madrid, 1748. The account of the scientific work of the expedition, written by Jorge Juan y Santacilia, was published separately, Madrid, 1748, under title: "Observaciones astronomicas, y phisicas hechas ... en los reynos del Perù ..." It is not included in this translation. *1. South America — Description and travel. 2. South America — Social life and customs. 3. Scientific expeditions. I. Juan y Santacilia, Jorge, 1713-1773. II. Adams, John, of Waltham Abbey. III. T.*
F2221.U43   918   64-13454

Von Hagen, Victor Wolfgang, 1908-   III. 7414
South America called them; explorations of the great naturalists: Charles-Marie de la Condamine, Alexander von Humboldt, Charles Darwin, Richard Spruce. London, Hale [1949] xiv, 401 p. plates, ports., maps. 22 cm. *1. La Condamine, Charles Marie de, 1701-1774. 2. Humboldt, Alexander, Freiherr von, 1769-1859. 3. Darwin, Charles Robert, 1809-1882. 4. Spruce, Richard, 1817-1893. 5. South America — Description and travel. I. T.*
F2221.V8 1949   918   50-13441

Bryce, James Bryce, viscount, 1838-1922.   III. 7415
South America, observations and impressions, by James Bryce. New ed., cor. and rev. New York, Macmillan, 1917. xxiv, 611 p. maps. 22 cm. *1. South America. 2. South America — Description and travel.*
F2223.B91 1917   23-16192

Jones, Tom Bard, 1909-   III. 7416
South America rediscovered, by Tom B. Jones. New York, Greenwood Press, 1968 [c1949] ix, 285 p. illus., maps (part fold.) 23 cm. *1. South America — Description and travel. 2. Travelers — South America. I. T.*
F2223.J67 1968   918   69-10111

Clark, Sydney Aylmer, 1890-   III. 7417
All the best in South America, east coast: Venezuela, Surinam, Brazil, Paraguay, Uruguay, Argentina [by] Sydney Clark. New York, Dodd, Mead [1966] x, 264 p. illus., map (on lining papers) 18 cm. (A Sydney Clark travel book) First published 1940 under title: The East coast of South America. *1. South America — Description and travel — 1951- I. T.*
F2224.C55 1966   918.043   66-13263

Steward, Julian Haynes, 1902-   III. 7418
Native peoples of South America [by] Julian H. Steward [and] Louis G. Faron. New York, McGraw-Hill, 1959. xi, 481 p. illus., maps. 24 cm. *1. Indians of South America. I. Faron, Louis C., 1923- joint author. II. T.*
F2229.S77   980.1   58-10010

Bennett, Wendell Clark, 1905-1953.   III. 7419
Ancient arts of the Andes. With an introd. by René d'Harnoncourt. The Museum of Modern Art, New York, in collaboration with the California Palace of the Legion of Honor, San Francisco [and] the Minneapolis Institute of Arts. [New York, Museum of Modern Art, 1954] 186 p. 209 illus. (part col.) maps. 27 cm. *1. Indians of South America — Art. 2. Indians of South America — Antiquities. 3. Indians of Central America — Art. 4. Indians of Central America — Antiquities. I. New York. Museum of Modern Art. II. T.*
F2230.1.A7B4   980.65715 (980.1)   54-6135

Wood, Bryce, 1909-   III. 7420
The United States and Latin America wars, 1932-1942. New York, Columbia University Press, 1966. x, 519 p. 4 fold. maps. 24 cm. *1. U.S. — Foreign relations — South America. 2. South America — Foreign relations — U.S. 3. South America — History — 20th cent. I. T.*
F2231.5.W6   327.7308   65-25493

Belaúnde, Victor Andrés, 1883-1966.   III. 7421
Bolivar and the political thought of the Spanish American Revolution. New York, Octagon Books, 1967 [c1938] xxiv, 451 p. 21 cm. (The Albert Shaw lectures on diplomatic history, 1930) *1. Bolivar, Simon, 1783-1830. 2. Latin America — History — Wars of Independence, 1806-1830. 3. Latin America — Politics — 1806-1830. I. T. (S)*
F2235.B673 1967   980/.02   67-18750

Hasbrouck, Alfred, 1879-1948.   III. 7422
Foreign legionaries in the liberation of Spanish South America. New York, Octagon Books, 1969 [c1928] 470 p. map. 24 cm. *1. South America — History — Wars of Independence, 1806-1830 — Foreign participation. I. T.*
F2235.H34 1969   980/.02   73-75995

O'Leary, Daniel Florencio, 1800-1854.   III. 7423
Bolívar and the war of independence. Translated and edited by Robert F. McNerney, Jr. Austin, University of Texas Press [1970] xvi, 386 p. illus., maps, ports. 24 cm. (The Texas pan-American series) Abridged translation of Memorias del General Daniel Florencio O'Leary, v. 27-28: Narración. *1. South America — History — Wars of Independence, 1806-1830. 2. Venezuela — History — War of Independence, 1810-1823. 3. Bolívar, Simón, 1783-1830. I. T.*
F2235.O4   980.02/0924   70-137997   ISBN:292700474

Bolívar, Simón, 1783-1830.   III. 7424
Selected writings; compiled by Vicente Lecuna, edited by Harold A. Bierck, Jr., translation by Lewis Bertrand. Published by Banco de Venezuela. New York, Colonial Press, 1951. 2 v. (lii, 822 p.) illus., ports., maps. 25 cm. *1. Latin America — History — Wars of Independence, 1806-1830 — Sources.*
F2235.3.A13   980   51-3913

Bolívar, Simón, 1783-1830.   III. 7425
The liberator Simón Bolívar; man and image. Edited with an introd. by David Bushnell. New York, Knopf [1970] xxxiv, 218 p. map, port. 20 cm. (Borzoi books on Latin America.) *I. Bushnell, David, 1923- comp.*
F2235.3.A156   980.02/0924 (B)   74-88158

Madariaga, Salvador de, 1886-   III. 7426
Bolívar. Coral Gables, Fla., University of Miami Press [1967, c1952] xix, 711 p. illus., maps (on lining papers), ports. 24 cm. *1. Bolívar, Simón, 1783-1830.*
F2235.3.M163 1967   67-28273

Masur, Gerhard, 1901-   III. 7427
Simon Bolivar. [Rev. ed.] Albuquerque, University of New Mexico Press [1969] xiv, 572 p. maps. 25 cm. *1. Bolívar, Simón, 1783-1830.*
F2235.3.M39 1969   980/.02/0924 (B)   68-56230   ISBN:826301312

Parra-Pérez, Caracciolo, 1888-   III. 7428
Bolívar; a contribution to the study of his political ideas, by C. Parra-Pérez. Translated by N. Andrew N. Cleven. Paris, Editions Excelsior, 1928. 198 p. port. 24 cm. *1. Bolívar, Simón, 1783-1830. 2. South America — History — Wars of independence, 1806-1830. I. Cleven, Nels Andrew Nelson, 1874- tr.*
F2235.3.P254   923.28   31-2002

Rojas, Ricardo, 1882-1957.   III. 7429
San Martín, knight of the Andes. Translated by Herschel Brickell and Carlos Videla. Introd. and notes by Herschel Brickell. New York, Cooper Square Publishers, 1967 [c1945] xiii, 370 p. port. 24 cm. (Library of Latin-American history and culture) Translation of El santo de la espada. *1. San Martín, José de, 1778-1850.*
F2235.4.R852 1967   980/.02/0924 (B)   66-30783

George Washington university, Washington, D.C. Seminar conference on Hispanic American affairs. III. 7430
South American dictators during the first century of independence, edited by A. Curtis Wilgus, PH.D. Washington, D.C., The George Washington University Press, 1937. viii, 502 p. 24 cm. (Studies in Hispanic American affairs. vol. V, 1936) "A symposium embracing lectures given before the fifth Seminar conference on Hispanic American affairs held during the summer session of 1936 at the George Washington university." — Pref. 1. South America — History — 1830- 2. South America — Politics — 1830- 3. Dictators. I. Wilgus, Alva Curtis, 1897- ed. II. T.
F2236.G46   980   37-33136

Humphreys, Robert Arthur, 1907- III. 7431
The evolution of modern Latin America [by] Robin A. Humphreys. [1st American ed.] New York, Oxford University Press, 1946. 176 p. front., illus. (maps) 21 cm. "Originally took the form of lectures given at Cambridge in the spring of 1945." — Pref. 1. Latin America — History — 1930- 2. Latin America — Politics. 3. Latin America — Foreign relations. I. T.
F2236.H8   980   46-8003

Normano, João Frederico, 1890- III. 7432
The Japanese in South America; an introductory survey with special reference to Peru, by J. F. Normano and Antonello Gerbi ... Issued in cooperation with the Latin American economic institute. New York, International secretariat, Institute of Pacific relations, 1943. 135 p. illus. (facsim.) 20 1/2 cm. (I.P.R. International research series) "A supplement to ... Trans-Pacific relations of Latin America, by Anita Bradley." — Pref. 1. Japanese in South America. 2. Japanese in Peru. I. Gerbi, Antonello, 1904- II. Bradley, Anita. Trans-Pacific relations of Latin America. III. Latin American economic institute.
F2239.J3N6 1943a   325.252098   44-1879

F2251 – 3799 INDIVIDUAL COUNTRIES
F2251 – 2299 Colombia

Galbraith, W. O. III. 7433
Colombia: a general survey [by] W. O. Galbraith. 2nd ed. London, New York [etc.] issued under the auspices of the Royal Institute of International Affairs by Oxford U.P., 1966. xii, 177 p. maps, tables. 21 cm. 1. Colombia. I. Royal Institute of International Affairs.
F2258.G3 1966   918.61   67-72179

Weil, Thomas E. III. 7434
Area handbook for Colombia. Co-authors: Thomas E. Weil [and others] [Washington; For sale by the Supt. of Docs., U.S. Govt. Print. Off.] 1970. xiv, 595 p. illus. 24 cm. "DA Pam 550-26." "One of a series of handbooks prepared under the auspices of Foreign Area Studies (FAS) of the American University." Issued in 1964 by the American University Foreign Areas Studies Division as Dept. of the Army pamphlet 550-26. 1. Colombia. I. American University, Washington, D.C. Foreign Area Studies. II. American University, Washington, D.C. Foreign Areas Studies Division. Area handbook for Colombia. III. T.
F2258.W43   918.61/03/63   70-608487

Gordon, Burton Le Roy, 1920- III. 7435
Human geography and ecology in the Sinú Country of Colombia. Berkeley, University of California Press, 1957. viii, 136 p. illus., maps. 24 cm. (Ibero-Americana, 39) Issued also as thesis, University of California. 1. Sinú Valley. 2. Indians of South America — Colombia — Sinú Valley. I. T. (S)
F2269.G6 (F1401.I22 no. 39)   980.4   A58-9064

Reichel-Dolmatoff, Gerardo. III. 7436
Colombia [by] G. Reichel-Dolmatoff. New York, Praeger [1965] 231 p. illus., maps, plates. 21 cm. (Ancient peoples and places, 44) 1. Colombia — Antiquities. 2. Indians of South America — Colombia — Antiquities. I. T.
F2269.R4   980.461   65-23078

Reichel-Dolmatoff, Gerardo. III. 7437
San Agustín: a culture of Colombia. New York, Praeger [1972] 163 p. illus. 26 cm. (Art and civilization of Indian America) 1. San Agustín culture, Colombia. I. T.
F2269.R423   918.61/5   70-143979

Henao, Jesús María, 1870- III. 7438
History of Colombia, by Jesús María Henao and Gerardo Arrubla. Translated and edited by J. Fred Rippy. New York, Greenwood Press [1969, c1938] xii, 578 p. 23 cm. 1. Colombia — History. I. Arrubla, Gerardo, 1873-1946, joint author. II. Rippy, James Fred, 1892- ed. III. T.
F2271.H4963 1969   986.1   76-90527   ISBN:837122945

Bushnell, David, 1923- III. 7439
The Santander regime in Gran Colombia. Westport, Conn., Greenwood Press [1970, c1954] ix, 381 p. map. 23 cm. Based on the author's thesis, Harvard. 1. Colombia — History — 1822-1832. 2. Santander, Francisco de Paula, Pres. New Granada, 1792-1840. I. T.
F2275.B8 1970   986.1/04   78-100248   ISBN:0837129818

Fluharty, Vernon Lee. III. 7440
Dance of the millions; military rule and the social revolution in Colombia, 1930-1956. [Pittsburgh] University of Pittsburgh Press [1957] 336 p. illus., maps. 24 cm. 1. Colombia — Politics and government — 1930-1946. 2. Colombia — Politics and government — 1946- 3. Colombia — Social conditions. I. T.
F2277.F58   986.1   57-7360

Martz, John D. III. 7441
Colombia; a contemporary political survey. Chapel Hill, University of North Carolina Press [c1962] 384 p. illus. 24 cm. 1. Colombia — Politics and government — 1946-
F2278.M3   986.1063   62-12

Parsons, James Jerome, 1915- III. 7442
Antioqueño colonization in Western Colombia, by James J. Parsons. [2d] rev. ed. Berkeley, University of California Press, 1968. vi, 233 p. illus., maps (1 fold. in pocket) 23 cm. (University of California publications in Ibero-Americana, v. 32) 1. Antioquia, Colombia (Dept.) 2. Caldas, Colombia (Dept.) 3. Cauca Valley. I. T. (S:Ibero-Americana, v. 32)
F2281.A6P3x (F1401.I22 no. 32 1968)   918.61   68-58002

F2301 – 2349 Venezuela

Lieuwen, Edwin, 1923- III. 7443
Venezuela. Issued under the auspices of the Royal Institute of International Affairs. London, New York, Oxford University Press, 1961. 193 p. illus. 21 cm. 1. Venezuela.
F2308.L54   918.7   61-66619

Weil, Thomas E. III. 7444
Area handbook for Venezuela. Co-authors: Thomas E. Weil [and others]. Washington; For sale by the Supt. of Docs., U.S. Govt. Print. Off.] 1971. xiv, 525 p. maps. 25 cm. "DA Pam 550-71." Revision of 1964 ed. by American University, Foreign Areas Studies Division. "One of a series of handbooks prepared by Foreign Area Studies (FAS) of the American University." 1. Venezuela. I. American University, Washington, D.C. Foreign Areas Studies Division. Area handbook for Venezuela. II. American University, Washington, D.C. Foreign Area Studies. III. T.
F2308.W4 1971   309.1/87/063   74-611208

Rouse, Irving, 1913- III. 7445
Venezuelan archaeology, by Irving Rouse and José M. Cruxent. New Haven, Yale University Press, 1963. xiii, 179 p. illus. 22 cm. (Caribbean series, 6) 1. Venezuela — Antiquities. 2. Indians of South America — Venezuela. I. Cruxent, José María, joint author. II. T. (S)
F2319.R78   980.47   63-13972

Marsland, William David. III. 7446
Venezuela through its history [by] William D. and Amy L. Marsland. New York, Crowell [1954] 277 p. illus. 22 cm. 1. Venezuela — History. I. Marsland, Amy Louise, joint author. II. T.
F2321.M3   987   54-6333

Robertson, William Spence, 1872- III. 7447
The life of Miranda. New York, Cooper Square Publishers, 1969. 2 v. illus., maps, ports. 24 cm. (Library of Latin American history and culture) Reprint of the 1929 ed. I. Miranda, Francisco de, 1750-1816. II. T.
F2323.M6R62 1969   987/.04/0924 (B)   77-79203   ISBN:815402910

Alexander, Robert Jackson, 1918- III. 7448
The Venezuelan Democratic Revolution; a profile of the regime of Rómulo Betancourt. New Brunswick, N.J., Rutgers University Press [1964] xiii, 345 p. illus., map. 25 cm. 1. Betancourt, Rómulo, Pres. Venezuela, 1908- 2. Venezuela — Politics and government — 1935- I. T.
F2326.A7   987.063   64-19176

F2361 – 2471 Guyana

Johnson Research Associates. III. 7449
Area handbook for Guyana. [Co-authors: William B. Mitchell and others. Prepared for the American University. Washington, For sale by the Supt. of Docs., U.S. Govt. Print. Off.] 1969. xiv, 378 p. maps. 25 cm. Cover title. "DA pam no. 550-82." 1. Guyana. I. Mitchell, William Burton. II. American University, Washington, D.C. III. T.
F2368.J6   918.8/1   79-606159

Smith, Raymond Thomas, 1925- III. 7450
British Guiana. London, New York, Oxford University Press, 1962. vi, 218 p. fold. col. map. 21 cm. "Issued under the auspices of the Royal Institute of International Affairs." 1. British Guiana.
F2368.S6 1962   988.1   62-4677

Farabee, William Curtis, 1865-1925. III. 7451
The central Arawaks, by William Curtis Farabee. Philadelphia, The University museum, 1918. 288 p. illus., XXXVI pl., double map. 27 cm. (University of Pennsylvania. The University museum. Anthropological publications. vol. IX) A study of the Arawaks of northern Brazil and southern British Guiana. "The language of the central Arawaks": p. [183]-286. 1. Arawak Indians. 2. Arawakan languages. I. T.
F2380.1.A6F2 (GN2.P5 vol. IX)   19-15262

Farabee, William Curtis, 1865-1925. III. 7452
The central Caribs, by William Curtis Farabee. Philadelphia, The University museum, 1924. 299 p. col. front., illus., XL pl. fold. map. 28 cm. (University of Pennsylvania. The University museum. Anthropological publications. vol. X) A study of the Carib Indians of southern British Guiana and northern Brazil. Includes vocabularies of various Cariban languages. 1. Carib Indians. 2. Cariban languages. I. T.
F2380.1.C2F2 (GN2.P5 vol. X)   25-3954

F2501 – 2659 Brazil

Vanderbilt University, Nashville. Institute for Brazilian Studies. III. 7453
Four papers presented in the Institute for Brazilian Studies, Vanderbilt University, by Charles Wagley [and others] Nashville, Vanderbilt University Press, 1951. 138 p. illus., map. 24 cm. 1. James, William, 1842-1910. 2. Amazon Valley — Social conditions. 3. Brazil — Industries. 4. Agriculture — Brazil — Parahyba do Sul Valley. I. Wagley, Charles, 1913- II. T.
F2501.V3 1951b   981.004   51-5423

Camacho, Jorge Abel, 1908- III. 7454
Brazil; an interim assessment, by J. A. Camacho. 2d ed. Westport, Conn., Greenwood Press [1972] viii, 126 p. 22 cm. Reprint of the 1952 ed. 1. Brazil.
F2508.C18 1972   918.1   78-138144   ISBN:0837156017

Schurz, William Lytle, 1886- III. 7455
Brazil, the infinite country. [1st ed.] New York, Dutton [1961] 346 p. 22 cm. 1. Brazil.
F2508.S39   918.1   61-5038

Smith, Thomas Lynn, 1903- III. 7456
Brazil: people and institutions. [Rev. ed.] Baton Rouge, Louisiana State University Press, 1963. xx, 667 p. illus., maps, diagrs., tables. 25 cm. 1. Brazil.
F2508.S6 1963   918.1   63-13239

Smith, Thomas Lynn, 1903- ed. III. 7457
Brazil, portrait of half a continent. Edited by T. Lynn Smith and Alexander Marchant. Westport, Conn., Greenwood Press [1972, c1951] viii, 466 p. illus. 23 cm. Original ed. issued in series: The Dryden Press sociology publications. 1. Brazil. I. Marchant, Alexander Nelson De Armond, 1912- joint ed. II. T.
F2508.S62 1972   918.1   73-138183   ISBN:0837156408

Weil, Thomas E. III. 7458
Area handbook for Brazil. Co-authors: Thomas E. Weil [and others]. Washington; For sale by the Supt. of Docs., U.S. Govt. Print. Off.] 1971. xviii, 645 p. maps. 24 cm. "DA pam no. 550-20." "One of a series of handbooks prepared by Foreign Area Studies (FAS) of the American University." Issued in 1964 by Foreign Areas Studies Division of American University. 1. Brazil. I. American University, Washington, D.C. Foreign Area Studies. II. American University, Washington, D.C. Foreign Areas Studies Division. Area handbook for Brazil. III. T.
F2508.W44   918.1/03/6   73-608516

Azevedo, Fernando de, 1894- III. 7459
Brazilian culture; an introduction to the study of culture in Brazil. Translated by William Rex Crawford. New York, Hafner Pub. Co., 1971 [c1950] xxix, 562 p. illus., facsims., maps, ports. 27 cm. Translation of A culture brasileira. 1. Brazil — Civilization. 2. Brazil — Intellectual life. 3. Education — Brazil. I. T.
F2510.A933 1950a   918.1/03   76-151829

Baklanoff, Eric N., ed. III. 7460
New perspectives of Brazil, edited by Eric N. Baklanoff. [Nashville] Vanderbilt University Press [1966] xvi, 328 p. illus., maps. 24 cm. 1. Brazil — Civilization — Addresses, essays, lectures. I. T.
F2510.B23   309.181   66-10327

Freyre, Gilberto, 1900- III. 7461
New world in the Tropics; the culture of modern Brazil. [1st ed.] New York, Knopf, 1959. 285 p. 22 cm. "Expanded and completely rewritten version of [the author's] Brazil: an interpretation." 1. Brazil — Civilization. I. T.
F2510.F7519   918.1   59-5488

Freyre, Gilberto, 1900- III. 7462
The masters and the slaves (Casa-grande & senzala) A study in the development of Brazilian civilization; translated from the Portuguese by Samuel Putnam. 2d English-language ed., rev. New York, Knopf, 1956. lxxi, 537, xliv p. plans. 25 cm. 1. Brazil — Social conditions. 2. Slavery in Brazil. 3. Negroes in Brazil. 4. Indians of South America — Brazil. I. T.
F2510.F7522 1956   918.1   56-5787

Freyre, Gilberto, 1900- III. 7463
Order and progress; Brazil from monarchy to republic. Edited and translated from the Portuguese by Rod W. Horton. [1st American ed.] New York, Knopf, 1970. 1, 422, xxxiv p. illus., maps. 25 cm. In ... the English-language version of Ordem e progresso, cuts and condensations were made in the original text." 1. Brazil — Civilization. 2. Brazil — Social conditions. I. T.
F2510.F754163 1970   918.1/03/5   69-10713

Freyre, Gilberto, 1900- III. 7464
The mansions and the shanties (Sobrados e mucambos); the making of modern Brazil. Translated from the Portuguese and edited by Harriet de Onís. With an introd. by Frank Tannenbaum. [1st American ed.] New York, Knopf, 1963. 431 p. illus. 25 cm. 1. Brazil — Civilization. 2. Brazil — Social conditions. 3. Brazil — Race question. I. T.
F2510.F7563   918.1   62-15561

Graham, Richard. III. 7465
Britain and the onset of modernization in Brazil 1850-1914. London, Cambridge U.P., 1968. xvi, 385 p. 6 plates, 6 illus., 3 maps. 22 cm. (Cambridge Latin American studies, no. 4) 1. Brazil — Civilization — British influences. I. T. (S)
F2510.G7   301.29/81/042   68-21393   ISBN:521-07078-3

Moog, Clodomir Vianna, 1906- III. 7466
Bandeirantes and pioneers. Translated from the Portuguese by L. L. Barrett. New York, G. Braziller [1964] 316 p. 25 cm. 1. Brazil — Civilization. 2. U.S. — Civilization. I. T.
F2510.M583   301.37   62-19926

Wagley, Charles, 1913- III. 7467
An introduction to Brazil. Rev. ed. New York, Columbia University Press, 1971. xv, 341 p. illus., maps. 22 cm. 1. Brazil — Civilization. 2. Brazil — Social conditions. I. T.
F2510.W26 1971   918.1/03/6   71-146267   ISBN:0231035438

Wagley, Charles, 1913- ed. III. 7468
Race and class in rural Brazil. Photos. by Pierre Verger. [Paris] UNESCO [c1952] 160 p. illus., map. 22 cm. At head of title: Race and society. 1. Brazil — Race question. 2. Class distinction. I. T.
F2510.W27   918.1   53-502

F2519 – 2520.1 INDIANS

Lathrap, Donald Ward, 1927- III. 7469
The upper Amazon [by] Donald W. Lathrap. New York, Praeger Publishers [1970] 256 p. illus., maps. 21 cm. (Ancient peoples and places, v.70) 1. Indians of South America — Amazon Valley. I. T.
F2519.1.A6L3 1970   301.29/801   79-100031

Murphy, Robert Francis, 1924- III. 7470
Headhunter's heritage; social and economic change among the Mundurucú

Indians. Berkeley, University of California Press, 1960. 202 p. illus. 22 cm. *1. Mundurucu Indians. I. T.*
F2520.1.M8M8   980.3   59-15691

Murphy, Robert Francis, 1924-   **III. 7471**
Mundurucú religion. Berkeley, University of California Press, 1958. iv, 146 p. illus., maps. 26 cm. (University of California publications in American archaeology and ethnology, v.49, no. 1) *1. Mundurucu Indians — Religion and mythology. 2. Mundurucu Indians — Rites and ceremonies. I. T.* (S:California. University. University of California publications in American archaeology and ethnology, v.49, no. 1)
F2520.1.M8M8x (E51.C15 vol. 49, no. 1)   299.8   A58-9992

Wagley, Charles, 1913-   **III. 7472**
The Tenetehara Indians of Brazil; a culture in transition [by] Charles Wagley and Eduardo Galvão. New York, AMS Press [1969] xv, 200 p. illus., map. 24 cm. (Columbia University contributions to anthropology, no. 35) Reprint of the 1949 ed. *1. Tenetehara Indians. I. Galvão, Eduardo Eneas, joint author. II. T.* (S:Columbia University. Columbia University contributions to anthropology, no. 35)
F2520.1.T4W3 1969   970.3   79-82359

Nimuendaju, Curt.   **III. 7473**
The eastern Timbira, by Curt Nimuendajú. Translated and edited by Robert H. Lowie. Berkeley, University of California Press, 1946. x, 357 p. illus., plates, diagrs. maps. (2 fold.) 27 cm. (University of California publications in American archaeology and ethnology, vol.XLI.) *1. Timbira Indians. I. Lowie, Robert Harry, 1883- ed. and tr. II. T.*
F2520.1.T5N5 (E51.C15 vol. 41)   980.3   A46-1638

Nimuendajú, Curt.   **III. 7474**
The Tukuna. Edited by Robert H. Lowie. Translated by William D. Hohenthal. Berkeley, University of California Press, 1952. x, 209 p. illus., maps. 27 cm. (University of California publications in American archaeology and ethnology, v.45) *1. Tucuna Indians. 2. Tucuna Indians — Legends.* (S:California. University. University of California publications in American archaeology and ethnology, v.45)
F2520.1.T925N55 (E51.C15 vol. 45)   980.3 (980.1)   A52-9441

Huxley, Francis.   **III. 7475**
Affable savages; an anthropologist among the Urubu Indians of Brazil. New York, Viking Press, 1957 [c1956] 285 p. illus. 22 cm. *1. Urubu Indians. 2. Maranhão, Brazil (State) — Description and travel. I. T.*
F2520.1.U7H8 1957   980.3   57-5307

F2520.3 – 2538   HISTORY

Burns, E. Bradford, ed.   **III. 7476**
A documentary history of Brazil, edited, with an introd., by E. Bradford Burns. [1st ed.] New York, Knopf, 1966. xii, 398 p. 19 cm. (Borzoi books on Latin America) *1. Brazil — History — Sources. I. T.*
F2521.B88   981.008   65-17482

Calogeras, João Pandia, 1870-1934.   **III. 7477**
A history of Brazil. Translated and edited by Percy Alvin Martin. New York, Russell & Russell, 1963 [c1939] 374 p. 25 cm. (The Inter-American historical series) Translation of Formação historica do Brasil. *1. Brazil — History.*
F2521.C273 1963   981   63-8360

Hill, Lawrence Francis, ed.   **III. 7478**
Brazil; chapters by Manoel Cardozo [and others] Berkeley, Univ. of California Press, 1947. xxi, 394 p. illus., ports., map. 23 cm. (The United Nations series) *1. Brazil — History. 2. Brazil — Civilization. 3. Brazil — Foreign relations.* (S)
F2521.H5   981   47-12016

Oliveira Lima, Manuel de, 1867-1928.   **III. 7479**
The evolution of Brazil compared with that of Spanish and Anglo-Saxon America, by Manoel de Oliveira Lima. Ed. with introduction and notes by Percy Alvin Martin. Stanford University, Cal., The University, 1914. 159 p. 26 cm. (Leland Stanford Junior University publications. University ser.) "The six lectures included in the present volume were delivered at Leland Stanford Junior University in the autumn of 1912." — Introd. *1. Brazil — History. 2. Latin America — History. 3. North America — History. I. Martin, Percy Alvin, ed. II. T.* (S:Stanford University. Leland Stanford University publication. University series.)
F2521.O47   14-19868

Poppino, Rollie E.   **III. 7480**
Brazil: the land and people [by] Rollie E. Poppino. Illus. by Carybé and Poty. New York, Oxford University Press, 1968. 370 p. illus., maps. 22 cm. (Latin American histories) "A selective guide to the literature on Brazil": p. 326-355. *1. Brazil — History. I. T.*
F2521.P58   981   68-17608

Marchant, Alexander Nelson De Armond, 1912-   **III. 7481**
From barter to slavery; the economic relations of Portuguese and Indians in the settlement of Brazil, 1500-1580, by Alexander Marchant Baltimore, The John Hopkins press, 1942. 160 p.,1 l. front. (map) 23 cm. "Reprinted from the Johns Hopkins university studies in historical and political science, series LX, no. 1." Vita. *1. Brazil — History — 1500-1548. 2. Brazil — History — 1549-1762. 3. Portuguese in Brazil. 4. Indians of South America — Brazil. I. T.*
F2524.M23 1942a   981   A42-4570

Southey, Robert, 1774-1843.   **III. 7482**
History of Brazil. New York, Greenwood Press [1969] 3 v. fold. map. 24 cm. Reprint of the 1817-22 ed. *1. Brazil — History — To 1821. 2. Paraguay — History — To 1811. 3. Uruguay — History — To 1810. I. T.*
F2524.S73   981   68-31004   ISBN:837114047 v. 1 (varies)

Boxer, Charles Ralph, 1904-   **III. 7483**
The golden age of Brazil, 1695-1750; growing pains of a colonial society. Berkeley, Published in coöperation with the Sociedade de Estudos Históricos Dom Pedro Segundo, Rio de Janeiro, by the University of California Press, 1962. xiii, 443 p. illus., ports., maps. 24 cm. *1. Brazil — History — 1549-1762. I. T.*
F2528.B6 1962   981.03   62-11583

Boxer, Charles Ralph, 1904-   **III. 7484**
Salvador de Sá and the struggle for Brazil and Angola, 1602-1686. [London] University of London, 1952. xvi, 444 p. illus., ports., maps. 23 cm. *1. Correia de Sá e Benavídes, Salvador, 1594-1688. 2. Brazil — History — 1549-1762. 3. Angola — History.*
F2528.C67B6   981.03   54-194

Boxer, Charles Ralph, 1904-   **III. 7485**
The Dutch in Brazil, 1624-1654. Oxford, Clarendon Press, 1957. xiii, 327 p. port., maps. 23 cm. *1. Brazil — History — Dutch Conquest, 1624-1654. I. T.*
F2532.B7   981.03   57-1712

Alden, Dauril.   **III. 7486**
Royal government in colonial Brazil; with special reference to the administration of the Marquis of Lavradio, viceroy, 1769-1779. Berkeley, University of California Press, 1968. xxvii, 545 p. illus., facsims., maps, port. 25 cm. *1. Almeida Soares Portugal Alarcão Eca e Melo, Luis d', marquez de Lavradio, 1727-1790. 2. Brazil — History — 1763-1821. I. T.*
F2534.A7   981/.03/0924   68-26064

Haring, Clarence Henry, 1885-   **III. 7487**
Empire in Brazil; a New World experiment with monarchy. Cambridge, Harvard University Press, 1958. 182 p. fold. map. 22 cm. *1. Brazil — History — 1822-1889. I. T.*
F2536.H3   981.04   58-7250

Marchant, Anyda, 1911-   **III. 7488**
Viscount Mauá and the empire of Brazil; a biography of Irineu Evangelista de Sousa, 1813-1889. Berkeley, University of California Press, 1965. xx, 291 p. port. 23 cm. *1. Maua, Irineo Evangelista de Souza, visconde de, 1813-1889. 2. Brazil — History — 1822-1889. 3. Brazil — Economic conditions. I. T.*
F2536.M2675 1965   380.0924 (B)   65-10773

Williams, Mary Wilhelmine, 1878-1944.   **III. 7489**
Dom Pedro, the Magnanimous, second Emperor of Brazil. New York, Octagon Books, 1966 [c1937] xi, 414 p. illus., fold. map, ports. 24 cm. *1. Pedro II, Emperor of Brazil, 1825-1891. 2. Brazil — History — 1822-1889. I. T.*
F2536.P388 1966   981.040924 (B)   66-18031

F2537 – 2538   Republic, 1889 –

Bello, José Maria, 1880-   **III. 7490**
A history of modern Brazil, 1889-1964. Translated from the Portuguese by James L. Taylor. With a new concluding chapter by Rollie E. Poppino. Stanford [Calif.] Stanford University Press, 1966. xix, 362 p. maps. 24 cm. Translation of História da República. *1. Brazil — History — 1889- I. T.*
F2537.B4413   981.05   65-21494

Cunha, Euclydes da, 1866-1909.   **III. 7491**
Rebellion in the backlands (Os sertões) Translated by Samuel Putnam. [Chicago] University of Chicago Press [1957, c1944] 532 p. 21 cm. (Phoenix books, P22) *1. Brazil — History — Conselheiro, Insurrection, 1897. I. T.*
F2537.C9752x   981.05   57-4329

Hahner, June Edith, 1940-   **III. 7492**
Civilian-military relations in Brazil, 1889-1898, by June E. Hahner. [1st ed.] Columbia, University of South Carolina Press [1969] xiii, 232 p. 22 cm. *1. Brazil — Politics and government — 1889-1930. 2. Civilian supremacy over the military — Brazil. I. T.*
F2537.H34   981/.05   74-625583   ISBN:872491463

Loewenstein, Karl, 1891-   III. 7493
Brazil under Vargas, by Karl Loewenstein. [1st ed.] New York, Macmillan, 1942. xix, 381 p. front. (map) 21 cm. *1. Vargas, Getulio, pres. Brazil, 1883- 2. Brazil — Politics and government — 1930- I. T.*
F2538.L6   981   42-22052

Skidmore, Thomas E.   III. 7494
Politics in Brazil, 1930-1964; an experiment in democracy [by] Thomas E. Skidmore. New York, Oxford University Press, 1967. xviii, 446 p. map. 22 cm. *1. Brazil — Politics and government — 1930-1954. 2. Brazil — Politics and government — 1954- I. T.*
F2538.S56   320.9/81   67-20406

De Kadt, Emanuel Jehuda.   III. 7495
Catholic radicals in Brazil, by Emanuel de Kadt. London, New York, Oxford U.P., 1970. xii, 304 p. 23 cm. Issued under the auspices of the Royal Institute of International Affairs. Based on author's thesis, University of London. *1. Movimento de Educação de Base. 2. Brazil — Politics and government — 1954- 3. Catholics in Brazil. I. Royal Institute of International Affairs. II. T.*
F2538.2.D45   322/.44/0981   72-20402   ISBN:0192149849

Page, Joseph A.   III. 7496
The revolution that never was; Northeast Brazil, 1955-1964 [by] Joseph A. Page. New York, Grossman, 1972. xi, 273 p. map (on lining papers) 24 cm. *1. Brazil, Northeast — Politics and government. 2. Brazil, Northeast — Economic conditions. 3. Brazil — Politics and government — 1954- I. T.*
F2538.2.P26   322.4/2   71-106293   ISBN:0670597066

Schneider, Ronald M.   III. 7497
The political system of Brazil; emergence of a "modernizing" authoritarian regime, 1964-1970 [by] Ronald M. Schneider. New York, Columbia University Press, 1971. xviii, 431 p. 24 cm. *1. Brazil — History — Revolution, 1964. 2. Brazil — Politics and government — 1954- I. T.*
F2538.2.S37   320.9/81/06   75-154860   ISBN:0231035063

F2540 – 2651 REGIONS. CITIES

Wagley, Charles, 1913-   III. 7498
Amazon town; a study of man in the tropics. With a new epilogue by the author. Illus. by João José Rescála. New York, Knopf, 1964. xi, 315 p. illus., map. 19 cm. (Borzoi books on Latin America) "LA-4." *1. Amazonas, Brazil — Description and travel. 2. Amazonas, Brazil — Social life and customs. 3. Anthropo-geography — Brazil — Amazonas. I. T.*
F2546.W16 1964   64-12068

Wallace, Alfred Russel, 1823-1913.   III. 7499
A narrative of travels on the Amazon and Rio Negro, with an account of the native tribes, and observations on the climate, geology, and natural history of the Amazon Valley. With a biographical introd. by the editor. New York, Greenwood Press [1969] xiv, 363 p. illus. 23 cm. Reprint of the 1895 ed. *1. Amazon Valley — Description and travel. 2. Natural history — Amazon Valley. 3. Indians of South America — Amazon Valley. I. T.*
F2546.W18 1969b   918/.11/044   68-55226   ISBN:0837116414

Costa, Luiz Edmundo da, 1878-   III. 7500
Rio in the time of the viceroys; O Rio de Janeiro no tempo dos vice-reis, by Luis Edmundo; introduction by Hugh Gibson; translated from the Portuguese, with epilogue, by Dorothea H. Momsen. [Rio de Janeiro, Printed by J. R. de Oliveira] 1936. 353 p. incl. illus., plates. 19 cm. *1. Rio de Janeiro — History. 2. Rio de Janeiro — Social life and customs. I. Momsen, Dorothea (Harnecker) tr. II. T.*
F2646.C874   918.1   38-24547

Pierson, Donald, 1900-   III. 7501
Cruz das Almas, a Brazilian village, by Donald Pierson, with the assistance of Levi Cruz [and others] Westport, Conn., Greenwood Press [for sale by the Supt. of Docs. U.S. Govt. Print. Off., Washington, 1973] x, 226 p. illus. 29 cm. "Prepared in cooperation with the United States Department of State as a project of the Interdepartmental Committee on Scientific and Cultural Cooperation." Reprint of the 1951 ed., which was issued as Publication no. 12 of Smithsonian Institution Institute of Social Anthropology. *1. Cruz das Almas, Brazil. 2. Brazil — Social life and customs. 3. Sociology, Rural. I. T. (S:Smithsonian Institution. Institute of Social Anthropology. Publication no. 12.)*
F2651.C72P53 1973   918.1/4   75-118766   ISBN:0837150833

Harris, Marvin, 1927-   III. 7502
Town and country in Brazil. [1st AMS ed.] New York, AMS Press [1969] x, 302 p. illus. 23 cm. Reprint of the 1956 ed., which was issued as no. 37 of Columbia University contributions to anthropology. *1. Minas Velhas, Brazil. 2. Cities and towns — Brazil — Case studies. I. T. (S:Columbia University. Columbia University contributions to anthropology, no. 37.)*
F2651.M5H3 1969   301.29/81/4   78-82364

Hutchinson, Harry William, 1922-   III. 7503
Village and plantation life in northeastern Brazil. Seattle, University of Washington Press, 1957. ix, 199 p. illus., maps. 23 cm. At head of title: American Ethnological Society ... A monograph from the Research and Training Program for the Study of Man in the Tropics. *1. Monte Recôncavo, Brazil. 2. Plantation life. I. T.*
F2651.M57H8   918.14   57-8753

Morse, Richard McGee, 1922-   III. 7504
From community to metropolis; a biography of São Paulo, Brazil. Gainesville, University of Florida Press, 1958. xxiii, 341 p. plates, maps. 24 cm. *1. São Paulo, Brazil (City) — History. I. T.*
F2651.S2M6   981.6   58-11098

Stein, Stanley J.   III. 7505
Vassouras, a Brazilian coffee county, 1850-1900. Cambridge, Harvard University Press, 1957. xv, 316 p. illus., maps. 22 cm. (Harvard historical studies, v.69) Based on the author's thesis, Harvard University, which has title: Vassouras, a plantation society, 1850-1900. *1. Plantation life. 2. Vassouras, Brazil — Social life and customs. 3. Coffee — Brazil — Vassouras. 4. Coffee trade — Vassouras, Brazil. I. T. (S)*
F2651.V3S7   A57-8627

F2659 NEGROES IN BRAZIL

Degler, Carl N.   III. 7506
Neither Black nor white; slavery and race relations in Brazil and the United States [by] Carl N. Degler. New York, Macmillan [1971] xvi, 302 p. 21 cm. *1. Negroes in Brazil. 2. Negroes — Social conditions. 3. Slavery in Brazil. 4. Slavery in the United States. I. T.*
F2659.N4D42   301.451/96   73-130946

Fernandes, Florestan.   III. 7507
The Negro in Brazilian society. Translated by Jacqueline D. Skiles, A. Brunel, and Arthur Rothwell. Edited by Phyllis B. Eveleth. New York, Columbia University Press, 1969. xxv, 489 p. 23 cm. Translation of A integração do negro na sociedade de classes. *1. Negroes in Brazil. 2. Brazil — Race question. I. T.*
F2659.N4F413   301.451/96/081   78-76247

Pierson, Donald, 1900-   III. 7508
Negroes in Brazil; a study of race contact at Bahia. Foreword by Herman R. Lantz. Carbondale, Southern Illinois University Press [1967] lxxxiii, 420 p. illus., map. 22 cm. (Perspectives in sociology) Originated as thesis, University of Chicago. *1. Negroes in Salvador, Brazil. 2. Salvador, Brazil — Social conditions. 3. Brazil — Race question. I. T. (S)*
F2659.N4P5 1967   301.451/96/0814   66-15058

F2661 – 2799 Paraguay. Uruguay

Pendle, George.   III. 7509
Paraguay: a riverside nation. 3rd ed. London, New York [etc.] issued under the auspices of the Royal Institute of International Affairs [by] Oxford U.P., 1967. ix, 96 p. maps, tables. 21 cm. *1. Paraguay. I. Royal Institute of International Affairs.*
F2668.P4 1967   918.92/03   67-76622

Weil, Thomas E.   III. 7510
Area handbook for Paraguay. Co-authors, Thomas E. Weil [and others. Washington; For sale by the Supt. of Docs., U.S. Govt. Print. Off.] 1972. xiv, 316 p. map. 24 cm. "DA pam 550-156." "This volume is one of a series of handbooks prepared by Foreign Area Studies (FAS) of the American University." *1. Paraguay. I. American University, Washington, D.C. Foreign Area Studies. II. T.*
F2668.W4   309.1/892/07   72-181509

Warren, Harris Gaylord, 1906-   III. 7511
Paraguay, an informal history. Norman, University of Oklahoma Press, 1949. xii, 393 p. illus., ports., maps. 24 cm. *1. Paraguay — History.*
F2681.W3   989.2   49-8903

Fitzgibbon, Russell Humke, 1902-   III. 7512
Uruguay; portrait of a democracy. New Brunswick, N.J., Rutgers University Press, 1954. 301 p. illus. 22 cm. *1. Uruguay — Civilization.*
F2708.F5   918.1 (918.95)   54-6837

Pendle, George. **III. 7513**
Uruguay. 3d ed. London, New York, Oxford University Press, 1963. 127 p. illus. 21 cm. "Issued under the auspices of the Royal Institute of International Affairs." First ed. published in 1952 under title: Uruguay, South America's first welfare state. *1. Uruguay — Civilization. 2. Uruguay — Economic conditions — 1918-*
F2710.P4 1963   989.506   63-3986

Street, John. **III. 7514**
Artigas and the emancipation of Uruguay. Cambridge [Eng.] University Press, 1959. 406 p. illus. 23 cm. *1. Artigas, José Gervasio, 1764-1850. 2. Uruguay — History — 1810-1830.*
F2725.A7S75   989.504   59-65015

Vanger, Milton I. **III. 7515**
José Batlle y Ordoñez of Uruguay; the creator of his times, 1902-1907. Cambridge, Harvard University Press, 1963. viii, 320 p. illus., ports., maps. 24 cm. *1. Batlle y Ordóñez, José, Pres. Uruguay, 1856-1929.*
F2728.B357   989.506   62-19225

F2801 – 3021   Argentina

Munson, Frederick P. **III. 7516**
Area handbook for Argentina. Co-authors: Frederick P. Munson [and others] Washington, For sale by the Supt. of Docs., U.S. Govt. Print. Off., 1969. xiv, 446 p. map. 24 cm. "DA pam 550-73." "This volume is one of a series of handbooks prepared by Foreign Area Studies (FAS) of the American University." *1. Argentine Republic. I. American University, Washington, D.C. Foreign Area Studies. II. T.*
F2808.M98   918.1   78-605289

Scobie, James R., 1929- **III. 7517**
Argentina: a city and a nation [by] James R. Scobie. 2d ed. New York, Oxford University Press, 1971. 323 p. illus. 22 cm. (Latin American histories) *1. Argentine Republic — History. I. T.*
F2808.S42 1971   982   78-166005

Nichols, Madaline Wallis, 1898- **III. 7518**
The gaucho, cattle hunter, cavalryman, ideal of romance, by Madaline Wallis Nichols. Durham, N.C., Duke University Press, 1942. ix, 152 p. 23 cm. (Inter-American bibliographical and library association. Publications. Ser. I. v.7) *1. Gauchos.*
F2809.N5x   918.2   A44-4633

Denis, Pierre. **III. 7519**
The Argentine republic, its development and progress, by Pierre Denis. Translated by Joseph McCabe. London, T. F. Unwin [1922] 296 p. 7 maps, 24 pl. 23 cm. *1. Argentine republic — Economic conditions — 1918- 2. Argentine republic — Description and travel. 3. Agriculture — Argentine republic. I. McCabe, Joseph, 1867- tr. II. T.*
F2815.D392   918.2   22-26968

Ibarra Grasso, Dick Edgar. **III. 7520**
Argentina indígena & prehistoria americana. Buenos Aires, Tip. Editora Argentina, 1967. 685 p. illus. (part col.), facsims., maps. 29 cm. *1. Argentine Republic — Antiquities. 2. Indians of South America — Argentine Republic. I. T.*
F2821.I2   980.4/2   67-105566

Haring, Clarence Henry, 1885- **III. 7521**
Argentina and the United States, by Clarence H. Haring. Boston, World Peace Foundation, 1941. 77 p. front. (map) 20 cm. (America looks ahead, a pamphlet series: no. 5) *1. Argentine Republic — Politics and government. 2. Argentine Republic — Economic conditions. 3. Argentine Republic — Foreign relations — U.S. 4. U.S. — Foreign relations — Argentine Republic. I. World Peace Foundation, Boston. II. T.*
F2831.H3   982   41-25917

Levene, Ricardo, 1885-1959. **III. 7522**
A history of Argentina, by Ricardo Levene. Translated and edited by William Spence Robertson. Chapel Hill, The University of North Carolina press, 1937. xii p., 2 l., 565 p. front., plates, ports., fold. maps, coat of arms. 24 cm. (The Inter-American historical series) "An English version of the eleventh edition of Levene's Lecciones de historia argentina." — Pref. by the translator and editor. *1. Argentine republic — History. I. Robertson, William Spence, 1872- ed. and tr. (S)*
F2831.L653   982   37-34878

Whitaker, Arthur Preston, 1895- **III. 7523**
The United States and Argentina. Cambridge, Harvard University Press, 1954. 272 p. illus. 20 cm. (The American foreign policy library) *1. Argentine Republic — History. 2. Argentine Republic — Foreign relations — U.S. 3. U.S. — Foreign relations — Argentine Republic.*
F2831.W5   327.820973   55-5541

Cady, John Frank, 1901- **III. 7524**
Foreign intervention in the Rio de la Plata, 1838-50; a study of French, British, and American policy in relation to the Dictator Juan Manuel Rosas, by John F. Cady. New York, AMS Press [1969, c1929] xiv, 296 p. map. 23 cm. "First AMS edition." *1. Argentine Republic — Foreign relations. I. T.*
F2833.C26 1969   327.82   71-100817

Ferns, Henry Stanley, 1913- **III. 7525**
Britain and Argentina in the nineteenth century. Oxford, Clarendon Press, 1960. x, 517 p. maps, tables. 23 cm. *1. Argentine Republic — Foreign relations — Gt. Brit. 2. Gt. Brit. — Foreign relations — Argentine Republic. I. T.*
F2833.5.G7F4   982.03   60-50761

F2834 – 2849   HISTORY, BY PERIOD

George Washington University, Washington, D.C. Seminar Conference on Hispanic American Affairs. **III. 7526**
Argentina, Brazil and Chile since independence. Argentina, by J. Fred Rippy. Brazil, by Percy Alvin Martin. Chile, by Isaac Joslin Cox. Edited by A. Curtis Wilgus. New York, Russell & Russell, 1963 [c1935] ix, 481 p. 23 cm. (Studies in Hispanic American affairs, v.3, 1934) Lectures delivered at the Third Annual Seminar Conference on Hispanic American Affairs, July 2 to August 10, 1934. *1. Argentine Republic — History — 1810- 2. Brazil — History — 1822- 3. Chile — History — 1810- I. Rippy, James Fred, 1892- II. Wilgus, Alva Curtis, 1897- ed. III. T. (S)*
F2843.G46 1963   982   63-8373

Davis, Thomas Brabson. **III. 7527**
Carlos de Alvear, man of revolution; the diplomatic career of Argentina's first Minister to the United States, by Thomas B. Davis, Jr. New York, Greenwood Press [1968, c1955] vii, 305 p. port. 24 cm. *1. Alvear, Carlos Maria de, 1789-1852. 2. United States — Foreign relations — Argentine Republic. 3. Argentine Republic — Foreign relations — United States.*
F2846.A4815D3 1968   327/.2/0924 (B)   69-13878

Greenup, Ruth (Robinson) **III. 7528**
Revolution before breakfast; Argentina, 1941-1946, by Ruth and Leonard Greenup. Chapel Hill, Univ. of North Carolina Press, 1947. xiii, 266 p. plates. 24 cm. *1. Argentine Republic — Description and travel. 2. Argentine Republic — Politics and government — 1943- I. Greenup, Leonard, joint author. II. T.*
F2846.G8   918.2   47-30421

Rennie, Ysabel (Fisk) 1918- **III. 7529**
The Argentine Republic, by Ysabel F. Rennie. [1st ed.] New York, Macmillan, 1945. xvii, 431 p. plates. 22 cm. Map on lining-paper. *1. Argentine Republic — History — 1817-*
F2846.R394   982   45-2874

Sarmiento, Domingo Faustino, Pres. Argentine Republic, 1811-1888. **III. 7530**
A Sarmiento anthology. Translated from the Spanish by Stuart Edgar Grummon. Edited, with introd. and notes, by Allison Williams Bunkley. Port Washington, N.Y., Kennikat Press [1972, c1948] 336 p. port. 23 cm. *I. T.*
F2846.S2185 1972   982.05/0924 (B)   73-159104   ISBN:0804616477

Sarmiento, Domingo Faustino, Pres. Argentine Republic, 1811-1888. **III. 7531**
Life in the Argentine Republic in the days of the tyrants; or, Civilization and barbarism. From the Spanish. With a biographical sketch of the author by Mrs. Horace Mann. 1st American from the 3d Spanish ed. New York, Hafner Pub. Co. [1960] 400 p. illus. 21 cm. (The Hafner library of classics, no. 21) Translation of Civilización i barbarie. *1. Quiroga, Juan Facundo, 1790-1835. 2. Aldao, José Félix, d. 1845. 3. Argentine Republic — History — 1817-1860. 4. Argentine Republic — Description and travel.*
F2846.S2472 1960   982.03   60-11057

Bunkley, Allison Williams. **III. 7532**
The life of Sarmiento. New York, Greenwood Press [1969, c1952] xv, 566 p. illus., facsim., geneal. table, ports. 23 cm. *1. Sarmiento, Domingo Faustino, Pres. Argentine Republic, 1811-1888. I. T.*
F2846.S26B84 1969   982/.05/0924 (B)   77-90475   ISBN:837123925

McGann, Thomas Francis, 1920- **III. 7533**
Argentina, the United States, and the Inter-American system 1880-1914. Cambridge, Harvard University Press, 1957. viii, 332 p. 22 cm. (Harvard historical studies, v.70) *1. Argentine Republic — History — 1860-1910. 2. Argentine Republic — History — 1910- 3. Argentine Republic — Relations*

(general) with the U.S. 4. U.S. — Relations (general) with the Argentine Republic. I. T. (S)
F2847.Mx   A57-8626

Perón, Eva (Duarte) 1919-1952. III. 7534
My mission in life; translated from the original by Ethel Cherry. New York, Vantage [c1953] 216 p. illus. 23 cm. Translation of La razón de mi vida. *1. Perón, Juan Domingo, Pres. Argentine Republic, 1895- 2. Argentine Republic — Social conditions. I. T.*
F2849.P313   920.7   53-11625

Whitaker, Arthur Preston, 1895- III. 7535
Argentine upheaval; Perón's fall and the new regime. New York, Praeger [1956] x, 179 p. 22 cm. (The Foreign Policy Research Institute series, no. 1) *1. Perón, Juan Domingo, Pres. Argentine Republic, 1895- 2. Argentine Republic — Politics and government — 1943- 3. Argentine Republic — Foreign relations. I. T. (S)*
F2849.W5   982.06   55-12175

F2850 – 3011   REGIONS

Falkner, Thomas, 1707-1784. III. 7536
A description of Patagonia and the adjoining parts of South America. With an introduction and notes, by Arthur E. S. Neumann. Chicago, Armann & Armann, 1935. viii p., facsim. (2 p. l., iv, 168 p. 2 fold. maps) 28 cm. "A full-size facsimile of the original edition [Hereford, 1774] complete from title-page to 'The end,' and including the map in two parts." — Introd. *1. Patagonia — Description and travel. 2. Indians of South America — Patagonia. 3. Falkland islands. 4. Moluche language. I. Neumann, Arthur Edward Schreiber, ed.*
F2936.F185   918.2   36-766

Hudson, William Henry, 1841-1922. III. 7537
Idle days in Patagonia. [1st AMS ed.] New York, AMS Press [1968] ix, 237 p. facsim. 23 cm. (The Collected works of W. H. Hudson) Reprint of the 1923 ed. *1. Patagonia — Description and travel. 2. Natural history — Patagonia. I. T.*
F2936.H88 1968   918.2/7   72-181458

F3051 – 3285   Chile

Butland, Gilbert J. III. 7538
Chile; an outline of its geography, economics, and politics. 3d ed. London, New York, Royal Institute of International Affairs [1956] 128 p. illus. 21 cm. *1. Chile.*
F3058.B89 1956   918.2   56-14779

Callcott, Maria (Dundas) Graham, lady, 1785-1842. III. 7539
Diario de su residencia en Chile (1822) y de su viaje al Brasil (1823). San Martin.—Cochrane.—O' Higgins. Prólogo de Don Juan Concha. Madrid, Editorial-América [1916] 451 p. 23 cm. (Biblioteca Ayacucho [x]) At head of title: María Graham. "Prólogo del traductor" signed: José Valenzuela D. The English original was pub. with title: "Journal of a residence in Chile, during the year 1822. And a voyage from Chile to Brazil in 1823" London, 1824. The present translation does not include the appendix of the original. *1. Chile — Description and travel. 2. Chile — History — War of independence, 1810-1824. I. Valenzuela D., José, tr. II. T.*
F3063.C162   16-25455

Clissold, Stephen. III. 7540
Chilean scrap-book. London, Cresset Press, 1952. 315 p. illus. 22 cm. *1. Chile — Description and travel. I. T.*
F3063.C6 1952a   918.3   53-533
C 619

Donoso, Ricardo, 1896- III. 7541
Las ideas políticas en Chile. [1. ed.] México, Fondo de Cultura Económica [1946] 526 p. 23 cm. (Colección Tierra firme, 23) *1. Chile — Politics and government. I. T. (S:Colección Tierra firme. Mexico. 23)*
F3081.D68   983   47-5390

Encina, Francisco Antonio, 1874- III. 7542
Historia de Chile desde la prehistoria hasta 1891. Santiago, Chile, Editorial Nascimento, 1940-   v. port. 23 cm. At head of title: Francisco A. Encina. *1. Chile — History.*
F3081.E63   42-3496

Galdames, Luis, 1881- III. 7543
A history of Chile. Translated and edited by Isaac Joslin Cox. New York, Russell & Russell, 1964 [c1941] xii, 565 p. illus., ports., maps. 23 cm. Translation of Estudio de la historia de Chile. *1. Chile — History.*
F3081.G168 1964   983   64-16467

Collier, Simon Daniel White. III. 7544
Ideas and politics of Chilean independence 1808-1833, by Simon Collier. London, Cambridge U.P., 1967. xviii, 396 p. 22 1/2 cm. (Cambridge Latin American studies, no. 1) *1. Chile — Politics and government — 1810-1824. 2. Chile — Politics and government — 1824-1920. I. T. (S)*
F3094.C7   320.9/83   67-15395

Clissold, Stephen. III. 7545
Bernardo O'Higgins and the independence of Chile. New York, Praeger [1969] 254 p. maps, ports. 23 cm. *1. O'Higgins, Bernardo, Supreme Director of Chile, 1778-1842. 2. O'Higgins, Ambrosio, marqués de Osorno, 1720-1801. 3. Chile — History — War of Independence, 1810-1824. I. T.*
F3094.O35517 1969   983/.04/0924 (B)   69-11332

Eyzaguirre, Jaime. III. 7546
O'Higgins. [Santiago de Chile] Zig-zag [1946] 477 p. 21 cm. (Colección Biografías) *1. O'Higgins, Bernardo, supreme director of Chile, 1778-1842. 2. Chile — History — 1810-*
F3094.O3555   923.183   A47-931

Bulnes, Gonzalo, 1851-1936. III. 7547
Guerra del Pacífico. Santiago de Chile, Editorial del Pacífico [1955] v. fold. map. 26 cm. "Don Gonzálo Bulnes y la Guerra del Pacífico, por Francisco A. Encina": v.1, p. 7-31. *1. War of the Pacific, 1879-1884. I. T.*
F3097.B932   56-22711

Stevenson, John Reese. III. 7548
The Chilean Popular Front. Westport, Conn., Greenwood Press [1970, c1942] xi, 155 p. 23 cm. *1. Chile — Politics and government — 1920- 2. Frente Popular (Chile) I. T.*
F3099.S85 1970   320.9/83   70-100254   ISBN:837129877

Bowman, Isaiah, 1878-1950. III. 7549
Desert trails of Atacama, by Isaiah Bowman. New York, American Geographical Society, 1924. v, 362 p. illus., double plates, maps. 26 cm. (American Geographical Society. Special publication no. 5) *1. Atacama desert. 2. Atacama, Chile. 3. Physical geography — Chile. 4. Chile — Description and travel. I. T.*
F3131.B78   24-2631

F3169   EASTER ISLAND

Métraux, Alfred, 1902- III. 7550
Easter Island; a stone-age civilization of the Pacific. Translated from the French by Michael Bullock. New York, Oxford University Press, 1957. 249 p. illus. 21 cm. *1. Easter Island.*
F3169.M443   997.2   57-13826
996.18
m567

Norwegian Archaeological Expedition to Easter Island and the East Pacific. III. 7551
Reports. With contributions by Thor Heyerdahl [and] Edwin N. Ferdon, Jr., editors [and others]. Stockholm, Forum Pub. House]; distributed in U.S.A. by Rand McNally, Chicago, 1961-65. 2 v. illus., facsims., maps (part fold.), plates (part col.) 29 cm. (Monographs of the School of American Research and the Museum of New Mexico, no. 24, pt. 1) Vol.2 issued as no. 24, pt. 2 of Monographs of the School of American Research and the Kon-Tiki Museum. *1. Easter Island — Antiquities. 2. Polynesia — Antiquities. 3. Excavations (Archaeology) — Polynesia. I. Heyerdahl, Thor, ed. II. Ferdon, Edwin N., 1913- ed. (S:Santa Fe, N.M. School of American Research. Monographs, no. 24, pts. 1-2)*
F3169.N6   913.9618   62-4648

F3301 – 3359   Bolivia

Leonard, Olen Earl, 1909- III. 7552
Bolivia; land, people, and institutions. Washington, Scarecrow Press, 1952. 297 p. illus. 23 cm. *1. Bolivia.*
F3308.L4   918.4   52-14169

Osborne, Harold, 1905- III. 7553
Bolivia, a land divided. 3d ed. London, New York, Oxford University Press, 1964. xii, 181 p. maps, diagrs., tables. 21 cm. "Issued under the auspices of the Royal Institute of International Affairs." *1. Bolivia.*
F3308.O8 1964   918.4   64-1698

Arnade, Charles W.   **III. 7554**
The emergence of the Republic of Bolivia [by] Charles W. Arnade. New York, Russell & Russell [1970, c1957] xi, 269 p. maps. 23 cm. *1. Bolivia — History — Wars of Independence, 1809-1825. I. T.*
F3323.A695 1970   984/.041   70-102468

Klein, Herbert S.   **III. 7555**
Parties and political change in Bolivia, 1880-1952, by Herbert S. Klein. London, Cambridge U.P., 1969. xvi, 451 p. map. 23 cm. (Cambridge Latin American studies, 5) *1. Bolivia — History — 1879-1938. 2. Bolivia — History — 1938- I. T. (S)*
F3325.K4   320.9/84   77-85722   ISBN:521076145

Ostria Gutiérrez, Alberto, 1897-   **III. 7556**
The tragedy of Bolivia; a people crucified. [Translation by Eithne Golden] New York, Devin-Adair Co. [1958] 224 p. 20 cm. "First published in Spanish in Chile as Un pueblo en la cruz." *1. Bolivia — Politics and government — 1879- I. T.*
F3325.O793   984.05   58-12624

Alexander, Robert Jackson, 1918-   **III. 7557**
The Bolivian national revolution. New Brunswick, N.J., Rutgers University Press, 1958. xviii, 302 p. illus., ports., map. 22 cm. *1. Bolivia — History — Revolution, 1952. 2. Bolivia — Politics and government — 1938- I. T.*
F3326.A6   984.05   58-10827

James, Daniel, comp.   **III. 7558**
The complete Bolivian diaries of Ché Guervara, and other captured documents. Edited and with an introd. by Daniel James. New York, Stein and Day [1968] 330 p. illus., facsims., maps, ports. 21 cm. *1. Bolivia — History — 1938- 2. Guerrillas — Bolivia. 3. Subversive activities — Bolivia. I. Guevara, Ernesto, 1928-1967. II. T.*
F3326.J3   984/.05/0922   68-55642

Malloy, James M.   **III. 7559**
Bolivia: the uncompleted revolution [by] James M. Malloy. [Pittsburgh] University of Pittsburgh Press [1970] x, 396 p. map. 24 cm. *1. Bolivia — History — Revolution, 1952. 2. Bolivia — Politics and government — 1938- I. T.*
F3326.M25   984/.05   77-101486   ISBN:822932032

Hanke, Lewis.   **III. 7560**
The imperial city of Potosí; an unwritten chapter in the history of Spanish America. The Hague, Nijhoff, 1956. 60 p. illus. 25 cm. *1. Potosí, Bolivia. 2. Potosí, Bolivia — History — Historiography. I. T.*
F3351.P85H29   984.1   57-522

F3401 – 3619 Peru

Mariátegui, José Carlos, 1894-1930.   **III. 7561**
Seven interpretive essays on Peruvian reality. Translated by Marjory Urquidi. Introd. by Jorge Basadre. Austin, University of Texas Press [1971] xxxvi, 301 p. 23 cm. (Texas pan-American series) Translation of 7 [i.e. Siete] ensayos de interpretación de la realidad peruana. *1. Peru — Addresses, essays, lectures. I. T.*
F3408.M3313   918/.5/03   73-156346   ISBN:0292701152

Palma, Ricardo, 1833-1919.   **III. 7562**
Tradiciones peruanas. Editadas con sus fuentes originales y un estudio preliminar por Alberto Tauro. Lima, Universidad Nacional Mayor de San Marcos; [Distribuidora Inca, 1969] 138 p. 25 cm. *1. Legends — Peru. 2. Peru — History. I. Tauro, Alberto, 1914- ed. II. T.*
F3409.P1734 1969   70-460549

Karen, Ruth.   **III. 7563**
The seven worlds of Peru. New York, Funk & Wagnalls [1969] vii, 238 p. illus. 22 cm. *1. Peru — Description and travel — Guide-books. I. T.*
F3409.5.K3   918.5/03   68-21642

Valcárcel, Luis Eduardo, 1891-   **III. 7564**
Ruta cultural del Perú. México, Fondo de Cultura Económica [1945] 279 p. 23 cm. (Colección Tierra firme, 7) At head of title: Luis E. Valcárcel. "Primera edición, 1945." *1. Peru — Civilization. 2. Indians of South America — Peru — Culture. I. T.*
F3410.V3   918.5   A46-2755

Tschopik, Harry, 1915-1956.   **III. 7565**
Highland communities of central Peru; a regional survey. Westport, Conn., Greenwood Press [1973] viii, 56 p. illus. 29 cm. Reprint of the 1947 ed., which was issued as Publication no. 5 of the Smithsonian Institution, Institute of Social Anthropology. *1. Peru — Description and travel. 2. Cities and towns — Peru. 3. Indians of South America — Peru. I. T. (S:Smithsonian Institution. Institute of Social Anthropology. Publication no. 5.)*
F3423.187 1973   918.5/2/0463   79-118759   ISBN:0837150760

F3429 – 3430.1 ANTIQUITIES. INDIANS

Baudin, Louis, 1887-   **III. 7566**
A socialist empire; the Incas of Peru. Translated from the French by Katherine Woods; edited by Arthur Goddard. Princeton, N.J., Van Nostrand [1961] xxii, 442 p. illus., maps (part fold.) 24 cm. (The William Volker Fund series in the humane studies) Translation of L'empire socialiste des Inka. *1. Incas. 2. Indians of South America — Peru. I. T. (S)*
F3429.B353   985.01   51-3532

Bennett, Wendell Clark, 1905- comp.   **III. 7567**
A reappraisal of Peruvian archaeology. Menasha, Wis., Published jointly by the Society for American Archaeology and the Institute of Andean Research, 1948. ix, 128 p. illus., maps. 26 cm. (Memoirs of the Society for American Archaeology, no. 4) Includes papers and comments submitted to a conference entitled "A reappraisal of Peruvian archaeology," held in New York, July 17-19, 1947, under the auspices of the Viking Fund and the Institute of Andean Research. "Supplement to American antiquity, volume XIII, number 4, part 2, April 1948." *1. Peru — Antiquities. I. Institute of Andean Research. II. American antiquity. Supplement. III. T. (S:Society for American Archaeology. Memoirs, no. 4)*
F3429.B4x (E51.S7 no. 4)   913.85 (985.01)   54-2038

Bennett, Wendell Clark, 1905-   **III. 7568**
Andean culture history, by Wendell C. Bennett and Junius B. Bird. New York, 1949. 319 p. illus., maps. 21 cm. *1. Peru — History — To 1548. 2. Peru — Antiquities. 3. Incas. 4. Indians of South America — Antiquities. I. Bird, Junius Bouton, 1907- II. T. (S:American Museum of Natural History [New York] Handbook series, no. 15)*
F3429.B475   985   49-2638

Brundage, Burr Cartwright, 1912-   **III. 7569**
Empire of the Inca. With a foreword by Arnold J. Toynbee. [1st ed.] Norman, University of Oklahoma Press [1963] 396 p. illus. 24 cm. (The Civilization of the American Indian series) *1. Incas. 2. Peru — History — To 1548. I. T.*
F3429.B84   985.01   63-18070

Bushnell, Geoffrey Hext Sutherland.   **III. 7570**
Peru. Rev. ed. New York, Praeger [1963, c1956] 216 p. illus., map 21 cm. (Ancient peoples and places) *1. Peru — Antiquities. 2. Peru — History — To 1548. I. T.*
F3429.B87 1963   985.01   63-15849

Obras completas del Inca Garcilaso de la Vega.   **III. 7571**
Edición y estudio preliminar del P. Carmelo Sáenz de Santa María. Madrid, Ediciones Atlas, 1960. 4 v. 26 cm. (Biblioteca de autores españoles desde la formación del lenguaje hasta nuestros días (continuación) v.132-135) *1. Garcilaso de la Vega, el Inca, 1539-1616. 2. Peru — History — To 1548. 3. Incas. I. Leo Hebraeus, d. 1535. Diálogos de amor. II. Sarmiento de Gamboa, Pedro, 1532?-1608? Historia indica. III. Sáenz de Santa María, Carmelo, ed. (S:Biblioteca de autores españoles, t.132-135)*
F3429.G3x (PQ6171.A2B6 t. 132-135)   62-35806

Lanning, Edward P.   **III. 7572**
Peru before the Incas [by] Edward P. Lanning. Englewood Cliffs, N.J., Prentice-Hall [1967] 216 p. illus., maps. 21 cm. (A Spectrum book) *1. Peru — Antiquities. 2. Indians of South America — Peru — Antiquities. I. T.*
F3429.L18   980.4/5   67-28395

Markham, Clements Robert, Sir, 1830-1916.   **III. 7573**
The Incas of Peru. New York, AMS Press [1969] xvi, 443 p. illus., map. 23 cm. "Reprinted from the edition of 1910, London." *1. Peru — Antiquities. 2. Incas. I. T.*
F3429.M34 1969   980.3   79-84877

Mason, John Alden, 1885-1967.   **III. 7574**
The ancient civilizations of Peru. [Rev. ed. Harmondsworth, Eng.] Penguin Books [1968] xvi, 335 p. illus., map. 19 cm. (Pelican books, A395) *1. Peru — Antiquities. 2. Indians of South America — Peru — Antiquities. 3. Incas. I. T.*
F3429.M36 1968   75-490842

Means, Philip Ainsworth, 1892-1944.   **III. 7575**
Ancient civilizations of the Andes. New York, Gordian Press, 1964. xviii, 586 p. illus. (1 col.) maps, plans. 24 cm. "Originally published 1931. Reprinted 1964." *1. Peru — Antiquities. 2. Andes — Antiquities. 3. Incas. 4. Indians of South America — Andes. 5. Peru — History — To 1548. I. T.*
F3429.M53 1964   980.1   64-8175

Willey, Gordon Randolph, 1913- III. 7576
Early Ancón and Early Supe culture, Chavín horizon sites of the Central Peruvian coast, by Gordon R. Willey and John M. Corbett. With special sections by Lila M. O'Neale and others. New York, Columbia University Press, 1954. xix, 180 p. illus., 31 plates, maps. 27 cm. (Columbia studies in archeology and ethnology, v.3) Number 3e of the Publications of the Institute of Andean Research. *1. Ancón, Peru — Antiquities. 2. Supe, Peru — Antiquities. I. Corbett, John Maxwell, 1913- joint author. II. Institute of Andean Research. III. T. (S)*
F3429.W66   913.85   (985.2)   54-11221

Rowe, John Howland, 1918- III. 7577
Chavin art, an inquiry into its form and meaning. New York, Museum of Primitive Art, distributed by University Publishers, 1962. 23 p. illus., map. 28 cm. *1. Art — Chavin, Peru. 2. Chavin, Peru — Antiquities. 3. Indians of South America — Peru. 4. Indians of South American — Art. I. T.*
F3429.1.C48R6   709.85   62-4940

Bingham, Hiram, 1875- III. 7578
Lost city of the Incas, the story of Machu Picchu and its builders. [1st ed.] New York, Duell, Sloan and Pearce [1948] xviii, 263 p. illus., map (on lining-paper) 24 cm. *1. Machu Picchu, Peru. 2. Incas. 3. Peru — Antiquities. I. T.*
F3429.1.M3P617   985   48-9227

Kubler, George, 1912- III. 7579
The Indian caste of Peru, 1795-1940; a population study based upon tax records and census reports. Westport, Conn., Greenwood Press [1973] 71 p. illus. 29 cm. Reprint of the 1952 ed., which was issued as publication no. 14 of Smithsonian Institution, Institute of Social Anthropology. *1. Indians of South America — Peru. 2. Peru — Population. I. T. (S:Smithsonian Institution. Institute of Social Anthropology. Publication no. 14.)*
F3430.K82 1973   312/.93   78-119552   ISBN:083715085X

Von Hagen, Victor Wolfgang, 1908- III. 7580
The desert kingdoms of Peru [by] Victor W. von Hagen. Greenwich, Conn., New York Graphic Society Publishers [1965, c1964] 190 p. illus. (part col.) maps. 24 cm. *1. Chimu Indians. 2. Mochica Indians. 3. Peru — Antiquities. I. T.*
F3430.1.C46V6 1965   980.3   65-10432

F3430.3 – 3619   HISTORY

Markham, Clements Robert, Sir, 1830-1916. III. 7581
A history of Peru. New York, Greenwood Press, 1968 [c1892] xviii, 556 p. illus., maps (part fold.), ports. 22 cm. (Latin-American republics) *1. Peru — History. I. T. (S)*
F3431.M34 1968   985   68-8069

Pike, Fredrick B. III. 7582
The modern history of Peru [by] Fredrick B. Pike. London, Weidenfeld & Nicolson [1967]. xix, 386 p. 12 plates (incl. ports.), maps. 22 1/2 cm. (Latin America series) *1. Peru — History. I. T.*
F3431.P52 1967b   985   67-101020

Cieza de León, Pedro de, 1518-1560. III. 7583
The Incas. Translated by Harriet de Onis. Edited, with an introd., by Victor Wolfgang von Hagen. [1st ed.] Norman, University of Oklahoma Press [1959] lxxx, 397 p. plates (part col.) fold. maps (1 col.) facsims. 24 cm. (The Civilization of the American Indian series, v. 53) Translated from Chrónica del Perú. *1. Peru — Description and travel. 2. Peru — History — To 1548. 3. Incas. 4. America — Early accounts to 1600. I. De Onis, Harriet, 1890- tr. II. Von Hagen, Victor Wolfgang, 1908- ed. (S)*
F3442.C5826   59-7955

Garcilaso de la Vega, el Inca, 1539-1616. III. 7584
Royal commentaries of the Incas, and general history of Peru. Translated with an introd. by Harold V. Livermore. Foreword by Arnold J. Toynbee. Austin, University of Texas Press [1966] 2 v. maps. 24 cm. (The Texas Pan-American series) Translation of Commentarios reales, pt. 1 of which was first published in 1609 under title: Primera parte de los Commentarios reales, and pt. 2 of which was first published in 1617 under title: Historia general del Perú. *1. Incas. 2. Peru — History — to 1548. 3. Indians of South America — Peru. 4. Peru — History — 1548-1820. I. Livermore, Harold Victor, 1914- ed. and tr. II. T.*
F3442.G1823 1966   985.2   65-13518

Hemming, John, 1935- III. 7585
The conquest of the Incas. [1st American ed.] New York, Harcourt, Brace, Jovanovich [1970] 641 p. illus., facsim., geneal. tables, maps, plates, ports. 24 cm. *1. Incas. 2. Peru — History — Conquest, 1522-1548. I. T.*
F3442.H47   985/.02   74-117573   ISBN:151225605

Pizarro, Pedro, 16th cent. III. 7586
Relation of the discovery and conquest of the kingdoms of Peru. Translated into English and annotated by Philip Ainsworth Means. Boston, Milford House [1972] p. Translation of Relación del descubrimiento y conquista de los reinos del Perú. Reprint of the 1921 ed., which was issued as no. 4 of Documents and narratives concerning the discovery and conquest of Latin America. *1. Peru — History — Conquest, 1522-1548. I. T. (S:Documents and narratives concerning the discovery and conquest of Latin America, no. 4.)*
F3442.P78 1972   985/.02   73-133345   ISBN:0878210830

Prescott, William Hickling, 1796-1859. III. 7587
History of the conquest of Peru. Introd. by Samuel Eliot Morison. Illus. by Everett Gee Jackson. New York, Heritage Press [1957] lii, 504 p. col. illus., col. map. 24 cm. "Authorities and notes": P. xxxix-xl. *1. Peru — History — Conquest, 1522-1548. 2. Incas.*
F3442.P933   985.02   57-3308

Fisher, Lillian Estelle, 1891- III. 7588
The last Inca revolt, 1780-1783. [1st ed.] Norman, University of Oklahoma Press [1966] xiii, 426 p. illus., maps. 23 cm. (The Civilization of the American Indian series) *1. Peru — History — Insurrection of Tupac-Amaru, 1780-1781. 2. Indians of South America — Wars. 3. Incas. I. T. (S)*
F3444.F55   985.03   65-11237

Lohmann Villena, Guillermo. III. 7589
El corregidor de indios en el Perú bajo los Austrias. Madrid, Ediciones Cultura Hispánica, 1957. 627 p. 23 cm. *1. Peru — Politics and government — 1548-1820. 2. Indians of South America — Peru. 3. Spain — Colonies — America — Administration. I. T.*
F3444.L84   57-4816

Means, Philip Ainsworth, 1892-1944. III. 7590
Fall of the Inca empire and the Spanish rule in Peru, 1530-1780. New York, Gordian Press, 1964. xii, 351 p. illus., maps (1 fold.) 24 cm. "Originally published 1931, reprinted 1964." Continues the author's Ancient civilizations of the Andes. *1. Peru — History — Conquest, 1522-1548. 2. Peru — History — 1548-1820. 3. Incas. 4. Spain — Colonies — America — Administration. 5. Peru — Antiquities. I. T. II. T:The Spanish rules in Peru: 1530-1780.*
F3444.M43 1964   985.02   64-8176

Zimmerman, Arthur Franklin, 1892- III. 7591
Francisco de Toledo; fifth viceroy of Peru, 1569-1581. New York, Greenwood Press [1968, c1938] 307 p. maps. 24 cm. Based on the author's thesis, University of Illinois. *1. Toledo, Francisco de, 1515-1582. 2. Peru — History — 1548-1820.*
F3444.T66   985/.03/0924   69-10177

Whitaker, Arthur Preston, 1895- III. 7592
The Huancavelica mercury mine; a contribution to the history of the Bourbon renaissance in the Spanish Empire. Westport, Conn., Greenwood Press [1971, c1941] xiii, 150 p. 23 cm. Original ed. issued as no. 16 of Harvard historical monographs. *1. Mercury mines and mining — Peru — Huancavelica (City) 2. Huancavelica, Peru (City) 3. Ulloa, Antonio de, 1716-1795. I. T. (S:Harvard historical monographs, no. 16.)*
F3611.H8W5 1971   338.2/7/45409852   70-136090   ISBN:0837152402

Gillin, John Philip, 1907- III. 7593
Moche, a Peruvian coastal community. Washington, U.S. Govt. Print. Off. [1947] vii, 166 p. illus. 26 cm. (Smithsonian Institution. Institute of Social Anthropology. Publication no. 3) *1. Moche, Peru. 2. Ethnology — Peru. I. T. (S)*
F3611.M6x (E51.S7 no. 3)   918.5   47-30434

Stewart, Watt, 1892- III. 7594
Chinese bondage in Peru; a history of the Chinese coolie in Peru, 1849-1874. Durham, Duke University Press, 1951. x, 247 p. illus., port., map. 23 cm. (Duke University publications) *1. Chinese in Peru. I. T.*
F3619.C5S8   325.2510985   51-10928

F3701 – 3799   Ecuador

Linke, Lilo. III. 7595
Ecuador, country of contrasts. 3d ed. Issued under the auspices of the Royal Institute of International Affairs. London, New York, Oxford University Press, 1960. 193 p. illus. 22 cm. *1. Ecuador.*
F3708.L5 1960   918.66   60-4406

Meggers, Betty Jane. III. 7596
Ecuador [by] Betty J. Meggers. New York, Praeger [1966] 220 p. illus. 22 cm. (Ancient peoples and places, v.49) *1. Ecuador — Antiquities. 2. Indians of South America — Ecuador — Antiquities. I. T.*
F3721.M4   980.4   66-18341

Parsons, Elsie Worthington (Clews) 1875-1941. III. 7597
Peguche, canton of Otavalo, province of Imbabura, Ecuador; a study of Andean Indians, by Elsie Clews Parsons. Chicago, University of Chicago Press [1945] viii, 225 p. illus. (incl. music) XL pl. (incl. front. (port.)) on 21 l. 24 cm. (The University of Chicago publications in anthropology. Ethnological series) *1. Indians of South America — Ecuador — Imbabura (Province) 2. Indians of South America — Social life and customs. I. T.*
F3721.1.I3P3   980.4   A45-4599

Phelan, John Leddy, 1924- III. 7598
The kingdom of Quito in the seventeenth century; bureaucratic politics in the Spanish Empire. Madison, University of Wisconsin Press, 1967. xvi, 432 p. maps. 25 cm. *1. Morga, Antonio de, 1559-1636. 2. Quito. Real Audiencia. 3. Ecuador — Politics and government — To 1814. 4. Spain — Colonies — America — Administration. I. T.*
F3733.P48   918.66/03/2   67-25940

Whymper, Edward, 1840-1911. III. 7599
Travels amongst the great Andes of the equator, by Edward Whymper. New York, Scribner, 1892. xxiv, 456 p. illus., maps (part fold.) fold. plan. 24 cm. *1. Andes — Description and travel. 2. Ecuador — Description and travel. 3. Mountains — Ecuador.*
F3741.A6W6   918.6   01-21680

Whitten, Norman E. III. 7600
Class, kinship, and power in an Ecuadorian town; the Negroes of San Lorenzo [by] Norman E. Whitten, Jr. Stanford, Calif., Stanford University Press, 1965. viii, 238 p. illus., maps. 24 cm. Based on thesis, University of North Carolina. *1. Negroes in San Lorenzo, Ecuador (Esmeraldas) I. T.*
F3799.N4W5   301.44098663   65-18979

Z
1035
B72
1975
V.3

Casshuart Bros.
Book Bindery
West Spfld., Mass.